An Introduction to the History of Psychology

Second Edition

B. R. Hergenhahn
Hamline University

BROOKS/COLE PUBLISHING COMPANY
Pacific Grove, California
A Division of Wadsworth, Inc.

Psychology Editor: Kenneth King
Editorial Assistant: Cynthia Campbell
Production Editor: Janelle Rohr, Bookman Productions
Print Buyer: Randy Hurst
Designer: Cecilia Brunazzi
Copy Editor: Betty Duncan
Cover: Andrew H. Ogus
Signing Representative: Tom Tucker
Compositor: TCSystems, Inc.

I(T)P ™ The trademark ITP is used under license.

This book is printed on acid-free paper that meets Environmental Protection Agency standards for recycled paper.

5 6 7 8 9 10

Library of Congress Cataloging-in-Publication Data

Hergenhahn, B. R., 1934—
    An introduction to the history of psychology / B.R. Hergenhahn. — 2nd ed.
      p. cm.
    Includes bibliographical references and indexes.
    ISBN 0-534-16812-4
    1. Psychology—History. I. Title.
BF81.H39 1992
150′.9—dc20   91-17035
                            CIP

CONTENTS

CHAPTER 5

Empiricism, Sensationalism, and Positivism 104

CHAPTER 6

Rationalism 159

CHAPTER 7

Romanticism and Existentialism 188

CHAPTER 14

Gestalt Psychology 397

CHAPTER 15

Early Diagnosis, Explanation, and Treatment of Mental Illness 427

CHAPTER 18

Contemporary Psychology   531

PREFACE

Like the first edition of *An Introduction to the History of Psychology*, the primary purpose of the second edition is to provide introductory students with a comprehensive overview of the history of psychology. Observations made by adopters, students, and reviewers, and the fact that there has been a virtual explosion of information on the history of psychology, have necessitated an essential rewriting of the first edition. To aid students seeking information beyond the text, "Suggestions for Further Reading" was added to each chapter. Other major changes made in this edition include the following:

• Chapter 2: Sections on early Greek religion and medicine were added, and coverage of Aristotle's philosophy was expanded.

• Chapter 4: A section on Ptolemaic astronomy was added, and the coverage of Copernicus, Kepler, and Galileo was expanded.

• Chapter 5: The material on Hobbes, Locke, Berkeley, Hume, Hartley, James Mill, John Stuart Mill, Bain, La Mettrie, and Condillac was greatly expanded, and Mach's version of positivism was added.

• Chapter 6: The material on Kant was substantially expanded.

• Chapter 7: The material on Schopenhauer, Nietzsche, and Kierkegaard was greatly expanded.

• Chapter 8: Coverage of Fechner's life and work was expanded, and a section on the work of Ewald Hering was added.

• Chapter 9: The sections on Wundt's voluntarism and Husserl's pure phenomenology were expanded, and the important dif-

ferences between Wundt's voluntarism and Titchener's structuralism were clarified.

• Chapter 10: Spearman's concept of general intelligence (g) was added.

• Chapter 11: James's analysis of voluntary behavior was added, Dewey's criticism of the analysis of behavior in terms of reflexes was added, and the coverage of Hall's recapitulation theory was revised.

• Chapter 12: The coverage of Pavlov was revised and expanded.

• Chapter 13: The sections on logical positivism, Tolman, Hull, and Skinner were revised and expanded.

• Chapter 15: Sections were added on the early diagnosis, explanation, and treatment of mental illness; on Witmer's pioneering clinical work; and on the tension existing between the psychological and medical models of mental illness.

• Chapter 16: Sections were added on Freud's involvement with cocaine, his involvement in the infamous case of Emma Eckstein, and his 1909 trip to the United States, and on Karen Horney's version of psychoanalysis.

• Chapter 18: The work of Jean Piaget was removed from the chapter on Gestalt psychology in the first edition and was added to this chapter as an example of early modern cognitive psychology. Sections were added on the historical influences in contemporary psychology, the controversy concerning the training of clinical psychologists, the genetic influences on intelligence and personality, the return of faculty psychology, the return of the mind–body problem, artificial intelligence, and psychology's two cultures.

I would like to express my appreciation to the following individuals who reviewed the first edition of this text and made many important suggestions for improvement: James Antes, University of North Dakota; John Nygaard, California State University, Long Beach; Michael J. Scavio, California State University, Fullerton; Paul Sheldon, Villanova University; and Ben Williams, University of California, San Diego. I would like to especially thank Leonard Zusne, Professor Emeritus of the University of Tulsa (now living in Vancouver, Washington). Dr. Zusne first voluntarily reviewed the first edition of the present text and then was the official reviewer of the revised manuscript. In both cases, he removed errors, redundancies, irrelevancies, and ambiguities and suggested the addition of pertinent material. Although the recommendations of the reviewers greatly improve the present edition, I alone am responsible for any shortcomings that remain.

I would also like to express my deep gratitude to Linda Samson who typed several drafts of this edition, typed all correspondence related to the manuscript, obtained a large number of articles and books from various libraries around Minneapolis-St. Paul, proofread the page proofs, wrote and typed the name index, and typed the subject index and instructor's manual. Linda works with quiet, pleasant efficiency.

Once again I wish to express my appreciation to members of the Hamline University psychology department for covering for me as my time and energy are spent on writing projects such as this one. Matt Olson, R. Kim Guenther, Chuck LaBounty, and Dorothee Dietrich have been very understanding and supportive.

Anyone who has written a college text knows how vitally important the production editor and copyeditor are. I was most fortunate to have Janelle Rohr as my production editor and Betty Duncan as my copyeditor. Both of these individuals combined professional competence with kindness, sensitivity, and humor. It was a genuine pleasure working with Janelle and Betty; I hope our paths cross again someday.

Last, but certainly not least, I would like to express my continuing appreciation to Neil R. Bartlett who instilled in me, as a graduate student at the University of Arizona, an interest in the history of psychology that has never wavered.

B. R. HERGENHAHN
Hamline University
St. Paul, Minnesota

CHAPTER 1

Introduction

The way in which psychology has been defined has changed as the focus of psychology has changed. At various times in history, psychology has been defined as the study of the psyche or mind, of the spirit, of consciousness, and more recently as the study of, or the science of, behavior. Perhaps, then, we can arrive at an acceptable definition of modern psychology by observing what psychologists are currently focusing on.

- Some psychologists are seeking the biological correlates of mental events such as sensation, perception, or ideation.
- Some concentrate on understanding the principles that govern learning and memory.
- Some seek to understand humans by studying nonhuman animals.
- Some study unconscious motivation.
- Some seek to improve industrial-organizational productivity, educational practices, or child-rearing practices by utilizing psychological principles.
- Some attempt to explain human behavior in terms of evolutionary theory.
- Some attempt to account for individual differences among people in such areas as personality, intelligence, and creativity.
- Some are primarily interested in perfecting therapeutic tools that can be used to help mentally disturbed individuals.
- Some focus on the information-processing techniques that people use in adjusting to the environment or in problem solving.
- Still others study how humans change as a function of the maturational process.

These are just a few of the activities that engage contemporary psychologists.

Clearly, no single definition of psychology can take into consideration the wide variety of activities engaged in by the more than 70,000 members and affiliates of the American Psychological Association, not to mention the many other psychologists around the world. It seems best to say simply that psychology is defined by the professional activities of psychologists. These activities are characterized by a rich diversity of methods, topics of interest, and assumptions about human nature. A primary purpose of this book is to examine the origins of modern psychology and to show that most of the concerns of today's psychologists are manifestations of themes that have been part of psychology for hundreds or, in some cases, thousands of years.

PROBLEMS IN WRITING A HISTORY OF PSYCHOLOGY

Where to Start

Literally, *psychology* means the study of the psyche or mind, and this study is as old as the human species. The ancients, for example, attempted to account for dreams, mental illness, emotions, and fantasies. Was this psychology? Or did psychology commence when explanations of human cognitive experience, such as those proposed by the early Greeks, became more systematic? Plato and Aristotle, for example, created elaborate theories that attempted to account for such processes as memory, perception, and learning. Is this the point at which psychology started? Or did psychology come into existence when it became a separate science in the 19th century? It is common these days to begin a history of psychology at the point where psychology became a separate science. This latter approach is unsatisfactory for two reasons: (1) It ignores the vast philosophical heritage that molded psychology into the type of science that it eventually became, and (2) it omits important aspects of psychology that are outside the realm of science. Although it is true that since the mid-19th century psychology has, to a large extent, embraced the scientific method, there have been highly influential psychologists who did not feel compelled to follow the dictates of the scientific method. Their work cannot be ignored.

Our coverage of the history of psychology will not go back to the conceptions of the ancients, although we believe that such conceptions are within the domain of psychology. Space does not permit such a comprehensive history. Rather, we will start with the major Greek philosophers because their explanations of human behavior and thought processes are the ones that philosophers and psychologists have been reacting to ever since.

What to Include

Typically, in determining what to include in a history of anything, one generally traces those people, ideas, and events that led to what is important now. We, too, will take this approach by looking at the way psychology is today and then attempting to show how it became that way. Using the present state of psychology as a guide in writing its history involves at least one major danger. Stocking (1965) calls such an approach to history **presentism**. Presentism is contrasted with what Stocking calls **historicism**, or the study of the past for its own sake without attempting to show the relationship between the past and present. Presentism implies that the present state of a discipline represents its highest state of development and that earlier events led directly to this state. In this view, the latest is the best. Although we are using present psychology as our guide as to what to include in psychology's

history, we do not believe that current psychology is necessarily the best psychology. The field is simply too diverse to make such a judgment. At present, psychology is exploring many topics, methods, and assumptions. Which of these explorations will survive for inclusion in future history books is impossible to say. Our use of psychology's present as a frame of reference therefore does not rest on the assumptions that psychology's past necessarily evolved into its present or that current psychology represents the best psychology.

Although contemporary psychology provides a guide for deciding what individuals, ideas, and events to include in our history of psychology, there remains the question of how much detail to include. If, for example, one attempted to trace all causes of an idea, one would be engaged in an almost unending search. In fact, after attempting to trace the origins of an idea or concept in psychology, one is left with the impression that nothing is ever entirely new. Seldom, if ever, is a single individual solely responsible for an idea or a concept. Rather, individuals are influenced by other individuals, who in turn were influenced by other individuals, and so on. A history of almost anything, then, can be viewed as an unending stream of interrelated events. The "great" individuals are typically those who synthesize existing nebulous ideas into a clear, forceful viewpoint. Attempting to fully document the origins of an important idea or concept in a history book would involve so many details that the book would become too long and boring. The usual solution is to omit large amounts of information, thus making any history selective. Typically, only those individuals who did the most to develop or popularize an idea are covered. For example, Charles Darwin is generally associated with evolutionary theory when, in fact, evolutionary theory existed in one form or another for thousands of years. Darwin documented and reported evidence supporting evolutionary theory in a way that made the theory's validity hard to ignore. Thus, although Darwin was not the first to formulate evolutionary theory, he did much to substantiate and popularize it, and we therefore associate it with his name. The same is true for Freud and the notion of unconscious motivation.

In this book, we will focus on those individuals who either did the *most* to develop an idea or, for whatever reason, have become closely associated with an idea. This does not do justice to many important individuals who could be mentioned and to other individuals who are lost to antiquity or who were not loud or lucid enough to demand historical recognition.

Choice of Approach

Once the material to be included in a history of psychology has been chosen, the choice of approach remains. One could emphasize the influence of such nonpsychological factors as developments in other sciences, political climate, technological advancement, and economic conditions. Together, these and other factors create a **Zeitgeist**, or a spirit of the times, which many historians consider vital to the understanding of any historical development. Or one could take the **great-person approach** by emphasizing the works of individuals such as Plato, Aristotle, Descartes, Darwin, or Freud. Or one could take the **historical development approach** by showing how various individuals or events contributed to changes in an idea or concepts through the years. For example, one could focus on how the idea of mental illness has changed throughout history.

In his approach to the history of psychology, E. G. Boring (1886–1968) stressed the importance of the Zeitgeist in determining whether, or to what extent, an idea or viewpoint will be accepted. Clearly, ideas do not occur in a vacuum. A new idea, to be accepted or even considered, must be compatible with existing ideas. In other words, a new idea will be tolerated only if it arises within an environment that can assimilate it. An idea or viewpoint that arises before people are prepared for it will not be understood well enough to be critically evaluated. The important point here is that validity is not the only criterion by which ideas are judged; psychological and

sociological factors are at least as important. New ideas are always judged within the context of existing ideas. If new ideas are close enough to existing ideas, they will at least be understood; whether they are accepted, rejected, or ignored is another matter.

Our approach will use the Zeitgeist, the great individuals, and the historical development approaches to writing history. We will attempt to show that sometimes the spirit of the times seems to produce great individuals and sometimes great individuals influence the spirit of the times. We will also show how great individuals and the general climate of the times can both help change an idea or a concept. In other words, we will take an **eclectic approach** in that we will use whatever approach seems best able to illuminate an aspect of the history of psychology.

WHY STUDY THE HISTORY OF PSYCHOLOGY?

Perspective

As we have seen, ideas are seldom, if ever, born full-blown. Rather, they typically develop over a long period of time. Seeing ideas in their historical perspective allows the student to more fully appreciate the subject matter of modern psychology. However, seeing the problems and questions currently dealt with in psychology as manifestations of centuries-old problems and questions is humbling and sometimes frustrating. After all, if psychology's problems have been worked on for centuries, should they not be solved by now? Conversely, knowing that one's current studies have been shared and contributed to by some of the greatest minds in human history is exciting.

Deeper Understanding

With greater perspective comes deeper understanding. With a knowledge of history, the student need not take on faith the importance of the subject matter of modern psychology. A student with a historical awareness knows where psychology's subject matter came from and why it is considered important. Just as one gains a greater understanding of a person's current behavior by learning more about that person's past experiences, so does one gain a greater understanding of current psychology by studying its historical origins. Boring made this point in relation to experimental psychologists:

> The experimental psychologist . . . needs historical sophistication within his own sphere of expertness. Without such knowledge he sees the present in distorted perspective, he mistakes old facts and old views for new, and he remains unable to evaluate the significance of new movements and methods. In this matter I can hardly state my faith too strongly. A psychological sophistication that contains no component of historical orientation seems to me to be no sophistication at all. (1957, p. ix)

Recognition of Fads and Fashions

While studying the history of psychology, one is often struck by the realization that a viewpoint does not always fade away because it is wrong; rather, some viewpoints disappear simply because they become unpopular. What is popular in psychology varies with the Zeitgeist. For example, when psychology first emerged as a science, the emphasis was on "pure" science—that is, on the gaining of knowledge without any concern for its usefulness. Later, when Darwin's theory became popular, psychology shifted its attention to human processes that were related to survival or that allowed humans to live more effective lives. Today, one major emphasis in psychology is on cognitive processes and that emphasis is due, in part, to recent advances in computer technology.

In her presidential address to the International Society for Cell Biology, entitled "Fashion in Cell Biology," Fell pointed out that not recognizing that fashions recur in science may lead to wasted time and energy:

> In science, as in the world of dress, fashions recur. There is one form of recurrence that is wholly regrettable, and which is one of the un-fortunate consequences of the vast expansion of research and the monstrous and unwieldy literature that it now produces. I will mention a small example of the sort of thing I have in mind. In the 1920's some of my colleagues did a rather extensive series of experiments which they duly published. A few years ago, an account of an almost identical research with the same results appeared in one of the journals, but with no mention of the earlier study. One of my colleagues wrote and pointed this out to the author, who replied that he never quoted any literature prior to 1946. (1960, p. 1625f.)

With such examples of how research topics move in and out of vogue in science, we see again that "factuality" is not the only variable determining whether an idea is accepted. Studying the emotional and societal factors related to the accumulation of knowledge allows the student to place currently accepted knowledge into a more realistic perspective. Such a perspective allows the student to realize that what body of knowledge is accepted as important or as "true" is at least partially subjective and arbitrary. As Zeitgeists change, so does what is considered fashionable in science, and psychology has not been immune to this process.

Avoiding Repetition of Mistakes

George Santayana once said, "Those who do not know history are doomed to repeat it." Such repetition would be bad enough if it involved only successes because so much time and energy would be wasted. It is especially unfortunate, however, if mistakes are repeated. As we will see in this text, psychology has had its share of mistakes and dead ends. One mistake was believing that the faculties of the mind could be strengthened with exercise, just as one would strengthen his or her biceps. One dead end may have been the entire school of structuralism, whose members attempted to study the elements of thought by using the introspective method. It is generally thought that the efforts of the structuralists, although extremely popular at the time, were sterile and unproductive. Yet it was important for psychology that such an effort was made, for we learned that such an approach led to little that was useful. This, and other important lessons, would be lost if the errors of the past were repeated because of a lack of historical information.

A Source of Valuable Ideas

By studying history, one may discover ideas that were developed at an earlier time but, for whatever reason, remained dormant. The history of science claims several examples of an idea taking hold only after it was rediscovered long after it had originally been proposed. This fact fits nicely into the Zeitgeist interpretation of history, suggesting that some conditions are better suited for the acceptance of an idea than others. The notions of evolution, unconscious motivation, and conditioned responses had been proposed and reproposed several times before they were offered in an atmosphere that allowed their critical evaluation. No doubt, many potentially fruitful ideas in psychology's history are still waiting to be tried again under new, perhaps more receptive, circumstances.

Curiosity

Instead of asking the question Why study the history of psychology? it might make more sense to ask Why not? Many people study U.S. history because they are interested in the United States, and younger members of a family often delight in hearing stories about the early days of the family's elder members. In other words, wanting to know as much as possible about a topic or person of interest, including a topic's or a person's history, is natural. Psychology is not an exception.

Studying the history of psychology allows the student to place modern psychology in historical perspective, understand modern psychology more thoroughly, recognize that what is popular in psychology is often determined by societal or emotional factors, see past mistakes so that they are not repeated, discover potentially useful ideas, and satisfy one's curiosity about something deemed important.

WHAT IS SCIENCE?

At various times in history, influential individuals (e.g., Galileo and Kant) have claimed that psychology could never be a **science** because of its concern with subjective experience. Many natural scientists still believe this, and some psychologists would not argue with them. How one writes a history of psychology will be influenced by whether psychology can be considered a science. To answer the question of whether psychology is a science, however, we must first attempt to define science. Science came into existence as a way of answering questions about nature by examining nature directly, rather than by depending on church dogma, past authorities, superstition, or abstract thought processes alone. From science's inception, its ultimate authority has been **empirical observation** (i.e., the direct observation of nature), but there is more to science than simply observing nature. To be useful, observations must be organized or categorized in some ways, and the ways in which they are similar to or different from other observations must be noted. After noting similarities and differences among observations, many scientists take the additional step of attempting to explain what they have observed. Science, then, is often characterized as having two major components: (1) empirical observation and (2) theory. According to Hull, these two aspects of science can be seen in the earliest efforts of humans to understand their world:

> Men are ever engaged in the dual activity of making observations and then seeking explanations of the resulting revelations. All normal men in all times have observed the rising and setting of the sun and the several phases of the moon. The more thoughtful among them have then proceeded to ask the question, "Why? Why does the moon wax and wane? Why does the sun rise and set, and where does it go when it sets?" Here we have the two essential elements of modern science: The making of observations constitutes the empirical or factual component, and the systematic attempt to explain these facts constitutes the theoretical component. As science has developed, specialization, or division of labor, has occurred; some men

have devoted their time mainly to the making of observations, while a smaller number have occupied themselves with the problems of explanation. (1943, p. 1)

The two major components of science can also be seen in the definition of science offered by Stevens: "Science seeks to generate confirmable propositions by fitting a formal system of symbols (language, mathematics, logic) to empirical observation" (1951, p. 22).

Combination of Rationalism and Empiricism

What makes science such a powerful tool is that it combines two ancient methods of attaining knowledge: **rationalism** and **empiricism**. The rationalist believes that mental operations or principles must be employed before knowledge can be attained. For example, the rationalist says that the validity or invalidity of certain propositions can be determined by carefully applying the rules of logic. The empiricist maintains that the source of all knowledge is sensory observation. True knowledge therefore can only be derived from or validated by sensory experience. After centuries of inquiry, it was discovered that by themselves rationalism and empiricism had limited usefulness. Science combined the two positions and knowledge has been accumulating at an exponential rate ever since.

The rational aspect of science keeps it from being a way of collecting an endless array of disconnected empirical facts. Because the scientist must somehow make sense out of what he or she observes, theories are formulated. A **scientific theory** has two main functions: (1) It organizes empirical observations, and (2) it acts as a guide for future observations. The latter function of a scientific theory generates what Stevens refers to as confirmable propositions. In other words, a theory suggests propositions that are tested experimentally. If the propositions generated by a theory are confirmed through experimentation, the theory gains strength; if the propositions are not confirmed by experimentation, the theory loses strength. If the theory generates too many erroneous propositions, it must be either revised or abandoned. Thus, scientific theories must be testable. That is, they must generate hypotheses that can be validated or invalidated empirically. In science, then, the direct observation of nature is important, but such observation is often guided by theory, making **controlled observation** an important aspect of science. Controlled observation means essentially the same thing as experimentation, and most experimentation in science is guided by theory.

The Search for Laws

Another feature of science is that it seeks to discover lawful relationships. A **scientific law** can be defined as a consistently observed relationship between two or more classes of empirical events. For example, when X occurs, Y also tends to occur. Science, then, uses theories to find and explain lawful, empirical events. By stressing lawfulness, science is proclaiming an interest in the general case rather than the particular case. Traditionally, science is not interested in private or unique events but in general laws that can be publicly observed and verified. That is, a scientific law is general and, because it describes a relationship between empirical events, it is amenable to **public observation**.

There are two general classes of scientific laws. One class is **correlational laws**, which describe how classes of events vary together in some systematic way. For example, scores on intelligence tests tend to correlate positively with scores on creativity tests. With such information, only prediction is possible. That is, if one knew a person's score on an intelligence test, one could predict his or her score on a creativity test and vice versa. A more powerful class of laws is **causal laws**, which specify how events are causally related. For example, if one knew the causes of a disease, one could predict *and* control that disease—preventing the causes of a disease from occurring prevents the disease from occurring. Thus, correlational laws allow prediction, but causal laws allow prediction and control. For this reason, causal laws are more powerful than correlational laws and thus are generally considered more desirable. A major goal of science is to discover the causes of natural phenomena. Specifying the causes of natural events, however, is highly complex and usually requires substantial experimental research. It cannot be assumed, for example, that contiguity proves causation. If rain follows a rain dance, it cannot be assumed that the dance necessarily caused the rain. Also complicating matters is that events seldom, if ever, have a single cause; rather, they have multiple causes. Questions such as What caused the Second World War? and What causes schizophrenia? are still far from answered. Even simpler questions such as Why did John quit his job? or Why did Mary marry John? are, in reality, enormously complex.

The Assumption of Determinism

Because a main goal of science is to discover lawful relationships, science assumes that what is being investigated is lawful. For example, the chemist assumes that chemical reactions are lawful, and the physicist assumes that the physical world is lawful. The assumption that what is being studied can be understood in terms of causal laws is called **determinism**. The determinist assumes that everything that occurs is a function of a finite number of causes and that, if these causes were known, an event could be predicted with complete accuracy. However, knowing *all* causes of an event is not necessary; the determinist simply assumes that they exist and that as more causes are known predictions become more accurate. For example, almost everyone would agree that the weather is a function of a finite number of variables such as sunspots, high-altitude jet streams, and barometric pressure; yet weather forecasts are always probabilistic because many of these variables change constantly and others are simply unknown. The *assumption* underlying weather prediction, however, is determinism. *All sciences assume determinism.*

REVISIONS IN THE TRADITIONAL VIEW OF SCIENCE

The traditional view is that science involves empirical observation, theory formulation, theory testing, theory revision, prediction, control, the search for lawful relationships, and the assumption of determinism. Some prominent philosophers of science, however, take issue with at least some aspects of the traditional view of science. Among them are Karl Popper and Thomas Kuhn.

Karl Popper

Karl Popper disagrees with the traditional description of science in two fundamental ways. First, he disagrees that scientific activity starts with empirical observation. According to Popper, the older view of science implies that scientists wander around making observations and then attempt to explain what they have observed. Popper shows the problem with such a view:

> Twenty-five years ago I tried to bring home [this] point to a group of physics students in Vienna by beginning a lecture with the following instructions: "Take pencil and paper: carefully observe, and write down what you have observed!" They asked, of course, *what* I wanted them to observe. Clearly the instruction, "observe!" is absurd . . . observation is always selective. It needs a chosen object, a definite task, an interest, a point of view, a problem. (1963, p. 46)

So for Popper, scientific activity starts with a problem, and the problem determines what observations scientists will make. The next step is to propose solutions to the problem, and attempts are then made to find fault with the proposed solutions. Popper sees scientific method as involving three stages: problems, theories (proposed solutions), and criticism.

Principle of falsifiability. What distinguishes a scientific theory from a nonscientific theory, according to Popper, is the **principle of falsifiability**. A scientific theory must be refutable. Contrary to what many believe, if any conceivable observation agrees with a theory, the theory is weak, not strong. Popper spends a great deal of time criticizing the theories of Freud and Adler for this reason. Without exception, everything a person does can be seen as supportive of either of these theories. Popper contrasts such theories with that of Einstein, which predicts what should or should not happen if the theory is correct. Thus, Einstein's theory, unlike the theories of Freud and Adler, was refutable and therefore scientific. According to Popper, the fact that no observation can be specified that would falsify astrology makes astrology unscientific. Here is how Popper summarizes his views on scientific theory:

(1) It is easy to obtain confirmations, or verifications, for nearly every theory—if we look for confirmations.

(2) Confirmations should count only if they are the result of risky predictions; that is to say, if, unenlightened by the theory in question, we should have expected an event which was incompatible with the theory—an event which would have refuted the theory.

(3) Every "good" scientific theory is a prohibition: it forbids certain things to happen. The more a theory forbids, the better it is.

(4) A theory which is not refutable by any conceivable event is non-scientific. Irrefutability is not a virtue of a theory (as people often think) but a vice.

(5) Every genuine test of a theory is an attempt to falsify it, or to refute it. Testability is falsifiability; but there are degrees of testability: some theories are more testable, more exposed to refutation, than others; they take, as it were, greater risks.

(6) Confirming evidence should not count except when it is the result of a genuine test of the theory; and this means that it can be presented as a serious but unsuccessful attempt to falsify the theory.

(7) Some genuinely testable theories, when found to be false, are still upheld by their admirers—for example, by introducing *ad hoc* some auxiliary assumption, or by re-interpreting the theory *ad hoc* in such a way that it escapes

refutation. Such a procedure is always possible, but it rescues the theory from refutation only at the price of destroying, or at least lowering, its scientific status. (1963, pp. 36–37)

Thus, for Popper, for a theory to be scientific, it must make **risky predictions**—predictions that run a real risk of being incorrect. Theories that do not make risky predictions or that explain phenomena after they have already occurred are, according to Popper, not scientific. A major problem with many psychological theories (such as Freud's and Adler's) is that they engage in **postdiction** (explaining phenomena after they have already occurred) rather than in prediction. Because for these theories no risky *pre*dictions are being made, they are in no danger of being falsified and are therefore unscientific.

In Popper's view, *all* scientific theories will eventually be found to be false and will be replaced by more adequate theories; it is always just a matter of time. For this reason, the highest status of a scientific theory, according to Popper, is that it is *not yet disconfirmed*. Popperian science is an unending search for better and better solutions to problems or explanations of phenomena. Brett nicely captured the preceding point:

We tend to think of science as a "body of knowledge" which began to be accumulated when men hit upon "scientific method." This is a superstition. It is more in keeping with the history of thought to describe science as the myths about the world which have not yet been found to be wrong. (1965, p. 37)

Does this mean Popper believes that nonscientific theories are useless? Absolutely not! He says,

Historically speaking all—or very nearly all—scientific theories originate from myths, and . . . a myth may contain important anticipations of scientific theories. . . . I thus [feel] that if a theory is found to be non-scientific, or "metaphysical" . . . it is not thereby found to be unimportant, or insignificant, or "meaningless," or "nonsensical." (1963, p. 38)

Popper uses falsification as a means of distinguishing between a scientific and a nonscientific theory but not between a useful and useless theory. Many theories in psychology fail Popper's test of falsifiability because either they are stated in such general terms that they are confirmed by almost any observation or they engage in postdiction rather than prediction. Such theories lack scientific rigor but are often still found to be useful. Freud's theory is an example.

Thomas Kuhn

Until recently it was widely believed that the scientific method guaranteed objectivity and that science produced information in a steady, progressive way. It was assumed that within any science there were knowable "truths" and that following scientific procedures allowed a science to systematically approximate those truths. Thomas Kuhn (1973) has changed that conception of science by showing science to be a highly subjective enterprise.

Paradigms and normal science. According to Kuhn, in the physical sciences one viewpoint is commonly shared by most members of a science. In physics or chemistry, for example, most researchers share a common set of assumptions or beliefs about their subject matter. Kuhn refers to such a widely accepted viewpoint as a **paradigm**. For those scientists accepting a paradigm, it becomes *the* way of looking at and analyzing the subject matter of their science. Once a paradigm is accepted, the activities of those accepting it become a matter of exploring the implications of that paradigm. Kuhn refers to such activities as **normal science**. Normal science provides what Kuhn calls a "mopping-up" operation for a paradigm. While following a paradigm, scientists explore in depth the problems defined by the paradigm and utilize the techniques suggested by the paradigm while exploring those problems. Kuhn likens normal science to **puzzle solving**. Like puzzles, the problems of normal science have an assured solution, and there are "rules that limit both the nature of acceptable solutions and the steps by which they are to be obtained" (Kuhn, 1973, p. 38). Kuhn sees neither normal science nor puzzle solving as involving much creativity: "Perhaps the most striking feature of . . . normal research problems . . . is how little they aim to produce major novelties, conceptual or phenomenal" (1973, p. 35). Although a paradigm restricts the range of phenomena scientists examine, it does guarantee that certain phenomena are studied thoroughly:

> By focusing attention upon a small range of relatively esoteric problems, the paradigm forces scientists to investigate some part of nature in a detail and depth that would otherwise be unimaginable. . . . During the period when the paradigm is successful, the profession will have solved problems that its members could scarcely have imagined and would never have undertaken without commitment to the paradigm. And at least part of that achievement always proves to be permanent. (Kuhn, 1973, pp. 24–25)

That is the positive side of having research guided by a paradigm, but there is also a negative side. Although normal science allows for the thorough analysis of the phenomena on which a paradigm focuses, it blinds scientists to other phenomena and perhaps better explanations for what they are studying:

> Mopping-up operations are what engage most scientists throughout their careers. They constitute what I am here calling normal science. Closely examined, whether historically or in the contemporary laboratory, that enterprise seems an attempt to force nature into the preformed and relatively inflexible box that the paradigm supplied. No part of the aim of normal science is to call forth new sorts of phenomena; indeed, those that will not fit the box are often not seen at all. Nor do scientists normally aim to invent new theories, and they are often intolerant of those invented by others. Instead, normal-scientific research is directed to the articulation of those phenomena and theories that the paradigm already supplies. (Kuhn, 1973, p. 24)

A paradigm, then, determines what constitutes a research problem *and* how the solution to that problem is sought. In other words, a paradigm guides all of the researcher's activities. More important, however, is that researchers become emotionally involved in their paradigm; it becomes part of their lives and is therefore very difficult to give up.

How sciences change. How do scientific paradigms change? According to Kuhn, not very easily. First, there must be persistent observations that a currently accepted paradigm cannot explain; these are called **anomalies**. Usually a single scientist or a small group of scientists will propose an alternative viewpoint, one that will account for most of the phenomena that the prevailing paradigm accounts for and will also explain the anomalies. Kuhn indicates that there is typically great resistance to the new paradigm and that converts to it are won over very slowly. Eventually, however, the new paradigm wins out and displaces the old one. According to Kuhn, this describes what happened when Einstein challenged the Newtonian conception of the universe. Now the Einsteinian paradigm is generating its own normal science and will continue to do so until it is overthrown by another paradigm.

Kuhn portrays science as a method of inquiry that combines the objective scientific method and the emotional makeup of the scientist. Science progresses, according to Kuhn, because scientists are forced to change their *belief systems*; and belief systems are very difficult to change, whether for a group of scientists or for anyone else.

The stages of scientific development. According to Kuhn, the development of a paradigm that comes to dominate a science occurs over a long period of time. Prior to the development of a paradigm, a science typically goes through a **preparadigmatic stage** during which a number of competing viewpoints exist. During this period, which Kuhn refers to as prescientific, a discipline is characterized by a number of rival camps or schools, a situation contrary to unification and which results in essentially random fact gathering. Such circumstances continue to exist until one school succeeds in defeating its competitors and becomes a paradigm. At this point, the discipline becomes a science, and a period of normal science begins. The normal science generated by the paradigm continues until the paradigm is displaced by a new one,

which, in turn, will generate its own normal science. Kuhn sees sciences as passing through three distinct stages: the preparadigmatic stage during which rival camps or schools compete for dominance of the field, the **paradigmatic stage** during which the puzzle-solving activity called normal science occurs, and the **revolutionary stage** during which an existing paradigm is displaced by another paradigm.

Paradigms and psychology. What has all of this to do with psychology? Psychology has been described as a preparadigmatic discipline (Staats, 1981) because it does not have one widely accepted paradigm but several competing schools or camps that exist simultaneously. For example, in psychology today we see camps that can be labeled behavioristic, functionalistic, cognitive, neurophysiological, psychoanalytic, and humanistic. Some see this preparadigmatic situation as negative and insist that psychology is ready to synthesize all of its diverse elements into one unified paradigm:

> Our science [psychology] is presently characterized by separatism, a feature that has a pervasive effect and that constitutes an obstacle to scientific progress. The concept of separatism describes our science as split into unorganized bits and pieces, along many dimensions. Divisions exist on the basis of theory, method, and the types of findings that are accepted, as well as on the basis of student training, organizational bodies such as divisions, journals and individual strivings. Our field is constructed of small islands of knowledge organized in ways that make no connection with the many other existing islands of knowledge. (Staats, 1981, p. 239)

According to Staats, psychology is ready to become a paradigmatic science and should do so:

> A unified theory of large scope might be enormously advantageous to psychology and . . . we must begin generally to allocate a part of our resources to the development of a unified science. . . . My view is that our science requires development of the methodology for the creation of such theory, as well as development of methods and standards of evaluation of theories

in terms of their unity and comprehensiveness. (1981, pp. 239–240)

Other psychologists do not agree that psychology is a preparadigmatic discipline. They say that psychology is a science that has several coexisting paradigms (e.g., Koch, 1981; Royce, 1975; Rychlak, 1975). The latter psychologists view the coexistence of several paradigms in psychology as healthy and productive and perhaps inevitable because psychology studies humans. It is assumed in this text that psychology is a multiparadigmatic science rather than a discipline at the preparadigmatic stage of development.

Popper Versus Kuhn

A major source of disagreement between Kuhn and Popper concerns Kuhn's concept of normal science. As we have seen, Kuhn says that once a paradigm has been accepted, most scientists busy themselves with research projects dictated by the paradigm—that is, doing normal science.

For Popper, what Kuhn calls normal science is not science at all. Scientific problems are not like puzzles because there are neither restrictions on what counts as a solution nor on what procedures can be followed in solving a problem. According to Popper, scientific problem solving is a highly imaginative, creative activity. Such activity is nothing like the puzzle solving described by Kuhn. Furthermore, for Kuhn, paradigms develop, are accepted, and are overthrown for psychological or sociological reasons. In Popperian science, such factors are foreign; problems exist, and proposed solutions either pass the rigorous attempts to refute them or they do not. Thus, Kuhn's analysis of science stresses convention and subjective factors, and Popper's analysis stresses logic and creativity. D. N. Robinson suggests that the views of both Kuhn and Popper may be correct: "In a conciliatory spirit, we might suggest that the major disagreement between Kuhn and Popper vanishes when we picture Kuhn as describing what science has been historically, and Popper asserting what it ought to be" (1986, p. 24).

Even with the revisions suggested by Popper and Kuhn, many of the traditional aspects of science remain. Empirical observation is still considered the ultimate authority, lawful relationships are still sought, theories are still formulated and tested, and determinism is still assumed.

IS PSYCHOLOGY A SCIENCE?

Is psychology a science? The scientific method has been used with great success in psychology. Experimental psychologists have demonstrated lawful relationships between classes of environmental events (stimuli) and classes of behavior, and they have devised rigorous, refutable theories to account for those relationships. The theories of Hull and Tolman are examples, and there are many others. Other psychologists work hand-in-hand with chemists and neurologists who are attempting to determine the biochemical correlates of memory and other cognitive processes. Other psychologists are working with evolutionary biologists and geneticists in an effort to understand evolutionary origins of human social behavior. In fact, we can safely say that scientifically oriented psychologists have provided a great deal of useful information in every major area of psychology—for example, learning, perception, memory, personality, intelligence, motivation, and psychotherapy.

Determinism, Indeterminism, and Nondeterminism

Determinism. Scientifically oriented psychologists are willing to assume determinism while studying humans. Although all determinists believe that all behavior is caused, there are different types of determinism. **Biological determinism** emphasizes the importance of physiological conditions or genetic predispositions in the explanation of behavior. For example, the sociobiologists claim that the master motive for human behavior (as well as that of nonhuman animals) is to perpetuate one's genes into the next generation. Much human behavior, say the sociobiologists, is derived from this genetically determined motive. **Environmental determinism** stresses the importance of environmental stimuli as determinants of behavior. The following comments nicely illustrate the type of determinism that places the cause of human behavior in the environment:

> Behavior theory emphasizes that environmental events play the key role in determining human behavior. The source of action lies not inside the person, but in the environment. By developing a full understanding of how environmental events influence behavior, we will arrive at a complete understanding of behavior. It is this feature of behavior theory—its emphasis on environmental events as the determinants of human action—which most clearly sets it apart from other approaches to human nature. . . . If behavior theory succeeds, our customary inclination to hold people responsible for their actions, and look inside them to their wishes, desires, goals, intentions, and so on, for explanations of their actions, will be replaced by an entirely different orientation . . . one in which responsibility for action is sought in environmental events. (Schwartz & Lacey, 1982, p. 13)

Sociocultural determinism assumes that it is the rules, regulations, customs, and beliefs characterizing a culture or society that cause human behavior. For example, Erikson refers to culture as "a version of human existence." To a large extent, what is considered desirable, undesirable, normal, and abnormal are culturally determined; thus, culture acts as a powerful determinant of behavior.

Other determinists claim that behavior is caused by the interaction of biological, environmental, and sociocultural influences. In any case, the determinist believes that behavior is caused by antecedent events and sets as his or her job the discovery of those events. It is assumed that, as more causes are discovered, human behavior will become more predictable and controllable. In fact, the prediction and control of behavior is usually recognized as an acceptable criterion for demonstrating that the causes of behavior have been discovered.

Although determinists assume that behavior is caused, they generally agree that it is virtually impossible to know *all* causes of behavior. There are at least two reasons for this. First, behavior typically has many causes. As Freud said, much behavior is *overdetermined*. That is, seldom, if ever, is behavior caused by a single event or even a few events. Rather, a multitude of interacting events typically causes behavior. For example, to predict whether a person will accept a specific job offer, one must answer such questions as

- How does the person perceive the job?
- What are alternative jobs?
- What types of experiences has the person had with similar jobs?
- What is the compensation being offered?
- What is the person's financial situation?
- Does the job require a change in location?

Second, some causes of behavior may be fortuitous. For example, a reluctant decision to attend a social event may result in a meeting with one's future spouse. Jung (see Progoff, 1973) referred to such meaningful coincidences as **synchronicity** and believed they played a major role in most people's lives. Bandura agrees with Jung on the importance of synchronicity by saying, "Chance encounters play a prominent role in shaping the course of human lives" (1982, p. 748). Bandura gives the following example:

> It is not uncommon for college students to decide to sample a given subject matter only to leave enrollment in a particular course to the vagaries of time allocation and course scheduling. Through this semifortuitous process some meet inspiring teachers who have a decisive influence on their choice of careers. (1982, p. 748)

Fortuitous circumstances do not violate a deterministic analysis of behavior; they simply make it more complicated. By definition, fortuitous circumstances are not predictable relative to one's life, but when they occur they are causally related to one's behavior:

> Fortuity of influence does not mean that behavior is undetermined. Unforeseeability of de-

terminants and determination of actions by whatever events happen to occur are separate matters. Fortuitous influences may be unforeseen, but having occurred, they enter as evident factors in causal chains in the same way as prearranged ones do. (Bandura, 1982, p. 749)

The point of the preceding examples is that the causation of human behavior is seldom simple and the determinists realize this. The determinists maintain that it is the complexity of the causation of human behavior that explains why predictions concerning human behavior must be probabilistic. Still, the determinists believe that as our knowledge of the causes of behavior increases, so will the accuracy of our predictions concerning that behavior.

What biological, environmental, and sociocultural determinism all have in common is that the determinants of behavior they emphasize are directly measurable. Genes, environmental stimuli, and cultural customs are all accessible and quantifiable and thus represent forms of **physical determinism**. However, some scientific psychologists emphasize the importance of cognitive and emotional experience in their explanation of human behavior. For them the most important determinants of human behavior are subjective and include a person's beliefs, emotions, perceptions, ideas, values, and goals. These psychologists emphasize **psychical determinism** rather than physical determinism. Among the psychologists assuming psychical determinism are those who stress the importance of mental events of which we are conscious and those, like Freud, who stress the importance of mental events of which we are not conscious.

Scientific psychologists, besides accepting some type of determinism, also seek general laws, develop theories, and use empirical observation as their ultimate authority in judging the validity of those theories. Psychology, as it is practiced by these psychologists, is definitely scientific, but not all psychologists agree with their assumptions and methods.

Indeterminism. First, some psychologists believe that human behavior is determined but

that the causes of behavior cannot be accurately measured. With this belief, these psychologists are accepting Heisenberg's **uncertainty principle**. The German physicist Werner Karl Heisenberg (1901–1976) found that the very act of observing an electron influences its activity and casts doubt on the validity of the observation. Heisenberg concluded that nothing can ever be known with certainty in science. When translated into psychology, this principle says that, although human behavior is indeed determined, we can never learn at least some causes of behavior because in attempting to observe them we change them. In this way, the experimental setting itself may act as a confounding variable in the search for the causes of human behavior. Psychologists accepting this viewpoint believe that there are specific causes of behavior but that they cannot be accurately known. Such a position is called **indeterminism**. Another example of indeterminacy is Immanuel Kant's (1724–1804) conclusion that a science of psychology is impossible because the mind could not be objectively employed to study itself. MacLeod summarized Kant's position:

Kant challenged the very basis of a science of psychology. If psychology is the study of "the mind," and if every observation and every deduction is an operation of a mind which silently imposes its own categories on that which is being observed, then how can a mind turn in upon itself and observe its own operations when it is forced by its very nature to observe in terms of its own categories? *Is there any sense in turning up the light to see what the darkness looks like?* [Italics added.] (1975, p. 146)

Nondeterminism. Some psychologists completely reject science as a way of studying humans. These psychologists, usually working within either a humanistic or an existential paradigm, believe that the most important causes of behavior are found in one's self, ego, or psyche and are self-generated. For this group, behavior is freely chosen rather than determined by physical or psychical causes. This belief in free will is contrary to the assumption of determinism, and therefore the endeavors of these psychologists are nonscientific. Such a position is known as **nondeterminism**. For the nondeterminists, because the individual freely chooses courses of action, he or she alone is responsible for them. The concept of personal responsibility is but one of the many points of disagreement between the determinist and the nondeterminist.

Whether or not we consider psychology a science depends on which aspect of psychology we focus. One highly respected psychologist and philosopher of science answers the question Is psychology a science? in a way that stresses psychology's nonscientific nature:

> I have been addressing this question for 40 years and, over the past 20, have been stable in my view that psychology is not a single or coherent discipline but rather a collection of studies of varied cast, some few of which may qualify as science, while most do not. (Koch, 1981, p. 268)

Psychology should not be judged too harshly because some of its aspects are not scientific or even antiscientific. Science, as we now know it, is relatively new, whereas the subject matter of most, if not all, sciences is very old. What is now studied scientifically was once, as Popper has noted, studied philosophically or theologically. First came the nebulous categories that were debated for centuries in a nonscientific way. This debate readied various categories of inquiry for the "fine tuning" that science provides.

In psychology today, there is inquiry on all levels. Some concepts have a long philosophical heritage and are ready to be treated scientifically; other concepts are still in their early stages of development and are not ready for scientific treatment; and still other concepts, by their very nature, may never be amenable to scientific inquiry. All these levels and types of inquiry appear necessary for the growth of psychology, and all sustain each other. Also, many subjective factors play an important role in the development of science, bringing scientific and nonscientific inquiry closer together. Indeed, a new field of interest called the psychology of science has opened up (see, e.g., Maslow, 1966).

PERSISTENT QUESTIONS IN PSYCHOLOGY

Many questions that psychology is now attempting to answer are the same questions it has been trying to answer from its inception. In many cases, only the methods for dealing with these persistent questions have changed. In this section, we review psychology's persistent questions and, in so doing, preview much of what will be covered in the remainder of this text.

What Is the Nature of Human Nature?

A theory of human nature attempts to specify what is universally true about humans. That is, it attempts to specify what all humans come equipped with at birth. One question of interest here is how much of our animal heritage remains in human nature? For example, are we inherently aggressive? Yes, say the Freudians. Is human nature basically good and nonviolent? Yes, say members of the humanistic camp, such as Rogers and Maslow. Or is our nature neither good nor bad but neutral, as the behaviorists such as Watson and Skinner claim? The behaviorists maintain that experience makes a person good or bad or whatever the person is. Do humans possess a free will? Yes, say the existential psychologists; no, say the scientifically oriented psychologists. Associated with each of psychology's paradigms is an assumption about the nature of human nature, and each assumption has a long history. Throughout this text, we will sample these conceptions about human nature and the methodologies they generate.

How Are the Mind and the Body Related?

The question of whether there is a mind and, if so, how it is related to the body is as old as psychology itself. Every psychologist must address this question either explicitly or implicitly. Through the years, almost every conceivable position has been taken on the mind–body relationship. Some psychologists attempt to explain everything in physical terms; for them, even so-called mental events are ultimately explained by the laws of physics or chemistry. These individuals are called **materialists** because they believe that matter is the only reality and therefore everything in the universe, including the behavior of organisms, must be explained in terms of matter. They are also called **monists** because they attempt to explain everything in terms of one type of reality (i.e., matter). Other psychologists take the other extreme and claim that everything is mental, saying that even the so-called physical world is a creation of the human mind. These individuals are called **idealists**, and they too are monists because they attempt to explain everything in terms of human consciousness or perception. Many psychologists, however, accept the existence of both physical and mental events and assume that the two are governed by different principles. Such a position is called dualism. The **dualist** believes that there are physical events and mental events. Once it is assumed that both a physical and a mental realm exist, the question becomes how the two are related. For the monist, of course, there is no mind–body problem.

Types of dualisms. One form of dualism, called **interactionism**, claims that the mind and body interact. That is, the mind influences the body, and the body influences the mind. According to this interactionistic conception, the mind is capable of initiating behavior. This was the position taken by Descartes and is the one taken by most members of the humanistic-existential camp. The psychoanalysts from Freud to the present are also interactionists. For them, many bodily ailments are *psychogenic*, that is, caused by mental events such as conflict, anxiety, or frustration.

Another form of dualism claims that bodily experiences cause mental events but that mental events cannot cause behavior. This position is called **epiphenomenalism** because it claims that mental events are by-products (epiphenomena) of bodily experience and as such have no causal relationship to behavior. Another dualist position is that an environmental experience causes both mental events and bodily responses *simultaneously* and that the two are totally independent of each other. This position is referred to as **psychophysical parallelism**.

According to another dualistic position, called **double aspectism**, a person cannot be divided into a mind and a body but is a unity that simultaneously experiences events physiologically and mentally. Just as "heads" and "tails" are two aspects of a coin, mental events and physiological events are two aspects of a person. Mind and body do not interact, nor can they ever be separated. They are simply two aspects of each experience we have as humans. Other dualists maintain that there is a **pre-established harmony** between bodily and mental events. That is, the two types of events are different and separate but are coordinated by some external agent—for example, God. Finally, in the 17th century, Nicholas Malebranche (1638–1715) suggested that when a desire occurs in the mind God causes the body to act. Similarly, when something happens to the body, God causes the corresponding mental experience. Malebranche's position on the mind–body relationship is called **occasionalism**.

All of the above positions on the mind–body problem are represented in psychology's history, and we will therefore encounter them throughout this text. Figure 1.1 shows Chisholm's whimsical summary of the proposed mind–body relationships.

Nativism Versus Empiricism

To what extent are human attributes such as intelligence inherited and to what extent are they determined by experience? The **nativist** emphasizes the role of inheritance in his or her explanation of the origins of various human attributes, whereas the empiricist emphasizes the role of experience. Those who consider some

FIGURE 1.1 Chisholm's depictions of various mind–body relationships. The bird drawn with the broken line represents the mind, and the bird drawn with the unbroken line represents the body. (Redrawn from Taylor, 1963, p. 130.) Used by permission of Roderick M. Chisholm.

aspect of human behavior instinctive or who take a stand on human nature as being good, bad, gregarious, and so on are also nativists. The empiricists, on the other hand, claim that humans are the way they are largely because of their experiences. Obviously, this question is still unresolved. The nativism–empiricism controversy is closely related to the question concerning the nature of human nature. For example, those who claim that humans are aggressive by nature are saying that humans are innately predisposed to be aggressive.

Most, if not all, psychologists now concede that human behavior is influenced by both experience and inheritance; what differentiates nativists from empiricists is the emphasis they place on either inheritance or experience.

Freedom Versus Determinism

Do humans possess a free will? If so, a science of human behavior is not possible because, as we have seen, science assumes determinism. That is, if human behavior varies as a function of a person's will, it is not subject to scientific investigation. Though existential and humanistic psychologists take this position, most psychologists accept a deterministic model while studying humans. But to say that human behavior is determined is not the same as saying that a physical event is determined. Even when a psychologist accepts that human behavior is determined, the question Determined by what? remains. As we have seen, the physical determinist looks for causes of behavior in stimulation from the environment, sensory apparatus, brain mechanisms, genes, the biochemistry of the body, or a combination of these, as well as in other physical events.

Another group of psychologists, however, looks for the major causes of behavior in one's subjective experience. For these psychologists, a person's beliefs, perceptions, values, attitudes, or expectations are the primary causes of behavior:

> Self-generated activities lie at the very heart of causal processes. . . . The capacity to exercise control over one's own thought processes, motivation, and action is a distinctively human characteristic. Because judgments and actions are partly self-determined, people can effect change in themselves and their situations through their own efforts. . . . A major function of thought is to enable people to predict the occurrence of events and to create the means for exercising control over those that affect their daily lives. (Bandura, 1989, pp. 1175–1176)

Unlike physical events, mental events can be manipulated at will into any number of configurations resulting in creative ideas and behavior: "Through their capacity to manipulate symbols and to engage in reflective thought people can generate novel ideas and innovative actions that transcend their past experiences" (Bandura, 1989, p. 1182).

Psychical determinism has problems associated with it that physical determinism does not. Because cognitive determinants are private and impossible to measure directly, it seems to these psychologists that a person's behavior is not determined by the same types of things that the physical determinist assumes it is. Rather, it appears that much behavior is under the control of a person's subjective reality and is therefore self-regulated. That is, a person ponders the array of cognitive material available, *selects* from it, and then acts accordingly. Whether or not **self-regulated behavior** is "free"—that is, not determined—depends on one's definition of freedom. The psychical determinist argues that those emphasizing subjective reality merely shift the causes of behavior from physical reality to

subjective reality and that behavior is therefore still determined. Also, the determinist maintains that these subjective experiences are caused by the various experiences a person has had and are therefore themselves subject to scientific scrutiny. The psychical determinist assumes that as more is learned about a person's beliefs, values, attitudes, expectations, and so on, his or her behavior will appear more lawful and more predictable. Thus, according to the psychical determinist, behavior can be self-regulated and still not be free: "Self-generated influences operate deterministically on behavior the same way as external sources of influence do" (Bandura, 1989, p. 1182).

For most, but not all, contemporary psychologists, the argument is over whether the causes of human behavior are physical or psychical rather than whether human behavior is determined or free. Once it is assumed, however, that the causes of behavior are mental rather than physical, the task of the psychologist attempting to explore the causes of human behavior becomes much more complex. It is a task unlike that in any other science.

Mechanism Versus Vitalism

Another persistent question in psychology's history is whether human behavior is completely explicable in terms of mechanical laws. According to **mechanism**, the behavior of all organisms, including humans, can be explained in the same way that the behavior of any machine can be explained—that is, in terms of its parts and the laws governing those parts. To the mechanist, explaining human behavior is like explaining the behavior of a clock except that humans are more complex. According to **vitalism**, life can never be completely reduced to material things and mechanical laws. Living things contain a vital force that does not exist in inanimate objects. In ancient times, this force was referred to as soul, spirit, or breath of life, and it was its departure from the body that caused death.

The mechanism–vitalism debate has been

prominently featured in psychology's history, and we will encounter it in various forms throughout this text.

Rationalism Versus Irrationalism

Rationalistic explanations of human behavior usually emphasize the importance of logical, systematic, and intelligent thought processes. Perhaps for this reason, most of the great contributions to mathematics have been made by philosophers in the rationalistic tradition (e.g., Descartes and Leibniz). Rationalists tend to search for the abstract principles that govern events in the empirical world. Most of the early Greek philosophers were rationalists, and some of them went so far as to equate wisdom with virtue. When one knows the truth, said Socrates, one acts in accordance with it. Thus, wise humans are good humans. The greatest passion, to the Greeks, was the passion to know. There are other passions, of course, but they should be rationally controlled. Western philosophy and psychology has, to a large extent, perpetuated the glorification of the intellect at the expense of emotional experience.

It was not always agreed, however, that the intellect is the best guide for human thought and behavior. At various times in history, human emotionality has been appreciated more than the human intellect. This was the case during the early Christian era, during the Renaissance, and at various other times under the influence of existential-humanistic philosophy and psychology. All these viewpoints stress human feeling over human rationality and are therefore referred to as irrational.

Any explanation of human behavior that stresses unconscious determinants is also irrational. The psychoanalytic theories of Freud and Jung, for example, exemplify **irrationalism** because they claim that the true causes of behavior are unconscious and therefore cannot be pondered rationally.

The tension between conceptions of humans that stress intellect (reason) and those that stress the emotions or the unconscious mind (spirit) has appeared throughout psychology's history and still manifests itself in contemporary psychology.

How Are Humans Related to Nonhuman Animals?

The major question here is whether humans are qualitatively or quantitatively different from other animals. If the difference is quantitative (one of degree), then at least something can be learned about humans by studying other animals. The school of behaviorism relies heavily on animal research and maintains that the same principles govern the behavior of both "lower" organisms and humans. Therefore, the results of animal research can be readily generalized to the human level. Representing the other extreme are the humanists and the existentialists who believe that humans are unique in the animal kingdom and that nothing important about humans can be learned by studying nonhuman animals. Humans, they say, are the only animals that freely choose their courses of action and are therefore morally responsible for that action. It makes sense therefore to judge human behavior as "good" or "bad." Similar judgments of animal behavior are meaningless. Without the ability to reason and to choose, there can be no guilt. Most psychologists can be placed somewhere between the two extremes, saying that some things can be learned about humans by studying other animals and some things cannot.

What Is the Origin of Human Knowledge?

The study of knowledge is called **epistemology**. The epistemologist asks such questions as What can we know, what are the limits of knowledge, and how is knowledge attained? Psychology has always been involved in epistemology because one of its major concerns has been determining how humans gain information about themselves and their world. The empiricist insists that all knowledge is derived from sensory experience, which is somehow registered and stored in the brain. The rationalist agrees that sensory information is often, if not always, an important first step in attaining knowledge but argues that the mind must then actively transform this information in some way before knowledge is attained. Many nativists would say that some knowledge is innate. Plato and Descartes, for example, believed that many ideas were a natural part of the mind.

In answering epistemological questions, the empiricists postulate a **passive mind** that represents physical experiences as mental images, recollections, and associations. In other words, the passive mind is seen as reflecting cognitively what is occurring, or what has occurred, in the physical world. Physical experiences that occur consistently in some particular pattern will be represented cognitively in that pattern and will tend to be recalled in that pattern. The rationalists, however, postulate an **active mind** that *transforms* the data from experience in some important way. Whereas a passive mind is seen as representing physical reality, the active mind is seen as a mechanism by which physical reality is organized, pondered, understood, or valued. For the rationalist, the mind adds something to our mental experience that is not found in our physical experience.

For the empiricist then, knowledge consists of the accurate description of physical reality as it is revealed by sensory experience and recorded in the mind. For the rationalist, knowledge consists of concepts and principles that can be attained only by a pondering, active mind. For some nativists, at least some knowledge is inherited as a natural component of the mind. The empiricist, rationalist, and nativist positions, and various combinations of them, have always been part of psychology; in one form or another, they are still with us today. In this text, we will see how these three major philosophical positions have manifested themselves in various ways throughout psychology's history.

Objective Versus Subjective Reality

The difference between what is "really" present physically (physical or objective reality) and what we actually experience mentally (subjective or phenomenal reality) has been an issue at least since the early Greeks. Some accept **naive realism**, saying that what we experience mentally is exactly the same as what is present physically. Many others, however, say that at least something is lost in the translation from physical to phenomenal experience. A discrepancy between the two types of experience can exist if the sense receptors can only respond partially to what is physically present—for example, to only certain sounds or colors. A discrepancy can also exist if information is lost or distorted as it is being transmitted from the sense receptors to the brain. Also, the brain itself can transform sensory information, thus creating a discrepancy between physical and phenomenal reality. The important question here is, Given the fact that there is a physical world and a psychological world, how are the two related? A related question is, Given the fact that all we can ever experience directly is our own subjective reality, how can we come to know anything about the physical world?

The Problem of the Self

Our physical experiences are highly diverse, and yet we experience unity among them. Also, we grow older, gain and lose weight, change locations, exist in different times, and yet with all of this and more, our life's experiences have continuity. We perceive ourself as the same person from moment to moment, from day to day, and from year to year even though little about us remains the same. The question is, What accounts for the unity and continuity of our experience? Through the centuries, entities such as a soul, a mind, or a self have been proposed. In more recent times, the self has been the most popular proposed organizer of experience.

Often the self has been viewed as having a separate existence of its own, as is implied by the statement "I said to myself." Besides organizing one's experiences and providing a sense of continuity over time, the self has often been endowed with other attributes such as being the instigator and evaluator of action. As we will see, to postulate a self with autonomous powers creates a number of problems that psychology has struggled with through the years and is still struggling with. Clearly, whether an autono-

mous self or mind is proposed as the organizer of experience or the instigator of behavior, one is confronted with the mind–body problem.

As we will see throughout this text, the positions that psychologists have taken on the preceding issues have represented a wide variety of assumptions, interests, and methodologies, and this continues to be the case in contemporary psychology.

SUMMARY

Psychology is best defined in terms of the activities of psychologists, and those activities have changed through the centuries. Although psychology goes back at least to the dawn of civilization, our version of the history of psychology begins with the early Greeks. Our approach to writing this text exemplifies presentism because current psychology is used as a guide in determining what to cover historically. In presenting the history of psychology, this text combines coverage of great individuals, persistent ideas, the spirit of the times, and contributions from other fields. Such a combined approach is referred to as eclectic. By studying the history of psychology, a student gains perspective and a deeper understanding of modern psychology. Also, he or she will learn that sometimes sociocultural conditions determine what is emphasized in psychology. Finally, by studying the history of psychology, previous mistakes can be avoided, potentially important ideas can be discovered, and the natural curiosity about something thought to be important can be satisfied.

Traditionally, science was viewed as starting with empirical observation and then proceeding to the development of theory. Theories were then evaluated in terms of their ability to generate predictions that were either supported by experimental outcome or not. Theories that generated predictions that were confirmed became stronger, and those making erroneous predictions were revised or abandoned. By linking empirical observation and theory, science combined the philosophical schools of empiricism and rationalism. Science assumes determinism and seeks general laws. Popper disagrees with the traditional view of science, saying that scientific activity does not start with empirical observation but with a problem of some type that guides the scientist's empirical observations. Furthermore, Popper maintains that if a scientific theory is consistently confirmed, it is more likely a

bad theory than a good one. A good theory must make risky predictions that if not confirmed refute the theory. To be classified as a scientific theory, a theory must specify in advance the observations that if made would refute it. What distinguishes a scientific theory from a nonscientific theory is the principle of falsifiability. A scientific theory must run the risk of being incorrect, and it must specify the conditions under which it would be. Kuhn also disagrees with the traditional view of science. Kuhn's analysis of science stresses sociological and psychological factors. At any given time, scientists accept a general framework within which they perform their research, a framework Kuhn calls a paradigm. A paradigm determines what constitutes research problems and how those problems are solved. Which paradigm is accepted by a group of scientists is determined as much by subjective factors as by objective factors. For Popper, scientific activity is guided by problems; whereas for Kuhn, scientific activity is guided by a paradigm that scientists believe to be true. For Popper, science involves creative problem solving; for Kuhn, it involves puzzle solving. According to Kuhn, scientific progress occurs in three stages: the preparadigmatic, the paradigmatic, and the revolutionary.

Some aspects of psychology are scientific, and some are not. Psychologists who are willing to assume physical or psychical determinism while studying humans are more likely to have a scientific orientation than those who are unwilling to make that assumption. Nondeterminists assume that human behavior is freely chosen and therefore not amenable to scientific analysis. The indeterminist believes that human behavior is determined but that the determinants of behavior cannot always be known with certainty. Psychology need not apologize for its nonscientific aspects because those aspects have often made significant contributions to the understanding of humans. Often the concepts developed by nonscientific psychologists are later fine-tuned by psychologists using the scientific method. Many of the questions that have persisted throughout psychology's history were summarized. They include the following: What is the nature of human nature? How are the mind and body related? To what extent are human attributes determined by heredity (nativism) as opposed to experience (empiricism)? To what extent are humans free, and to what extent is their behavior determined by knowable causes? Can human behavior be completely understood in terms of mechanistic principles, or must some additional vitalistic principle be postulated? To what extent is human behavior rational as opposed to irrational? How are humans related to other animals? What are the origins of human knowledge? What is the difference between what exists physically and what is experienced mentally, and how is this difference known and accounted for? How has the concept of self been used throughout psychology's history to account for one's continuity of experience over time, and what are the problems associated with the concept of self?

DISCUSSION QUESTIONS

1. Discuss the choices that must be made before writing a history of psychology.

2. What is gained by studying the history of psychology?

3. Summarize the major characteristics of science.

4. Discuss why psychology can be described as both a science and a nonscience. Include in your answer the characteristics of science that some psychologists are not willing to accept while studying humans.

5. In what ways does Popper's view of science differ from the traditional view?

6. Why does Popper consider Freud's theory to be nonscientific?

7. Summarize Kuhn's views on how sciences change. Include in your answer the definitions of the terms *preparadigmatic discipline, paradigm, normal science,* and *scientific revolution.*

8. Should psychology aspire to become a single-paradigm discipline? Defend your answer.

9. Is psychology a science? Defend your answer.

10. Define the terms *physical determinism, psychical determinism, indeterminism,* and *nondeterminism.*

11. What does a theory of human nature attempt to accomplish?

12. Summarize the various proposed answers to the mind–body problem. Include in your answer definitions of the terms *monism, dualism, materialism, idealism, interactionism, psychophysical parallelism, epiphenomenalism, pre established harmony, double aspectism,* and *occasionalism.*

13. Discuss the nativist and empiricist explanations of the origin of human attributes.

14. Is human behavior free or determined? Defend your answer. Include in your answer a discussion of self-regulated behavior.

15. First describe the positions of mechanism and vitalism and then indicate which of the two positions you accept and why.

16. Discuss rationalism and irrationalism as they apply to explanations of human behavior.

17. What can be learned about humans by studying other animals?

18. Describe how each of the following would explain how we gain knowledge: the empiricist, the rationalist, and the nativist.

19. Discuss the problems involved in discovering and explaining discrepancies that may exist between what is physically before us and what we experience subjectively.

20. For what reasons has a concept of self been employed by psychologists? What problems does this concept solve, and what problems does it create?

SUGGESTIONS FOR FURTHER READING

Benjamin, Jr., L. T. (Ed.). (1988). *A history of psychology: Original sources and contemporary research.* New York: McGraw-Hill.
   This excellent collection of articles is pertinent to the study of the history of psychology. The book includes a few current articles on issues involved in writing and understanding the history of psychology and many extracts from pertinent, primary-source materials. (Available in paperback.)

Kuhn, T. S. (1973). *The structure of scientific revolutions* (2nd ed.). Chicago: University of Chicago Press.

This highly influential book shows the importance of subjective factors in science. Kuhn discusses the research activities of preparadigmatic disciplines, the concept of paradigm, normal science, and paradigmatic science as puzzle solving. It is very readable, interesting, and a must for anyone majoring in the physical or the social sciences. (Available in paperback.)

Maslow, A. H. (1966). *The psychology of science: A reconnaissance.* New York: Harper & Row.

As a humanist, Maslow explains why, in his opinion, mechanistic science (the type of science that uses physics as its model) cannot be used to understand humans. Such science has as its goal the prediction and control of events. According to Maslow, a different type of science must be used to study humans, a science that studies those things most important and unique to humans. Unlike the traditional sciences that are based on the assumptions of determinism, materialism, and mechanism, humanistic science assumes that humans are free, naturally good, and important. (Available in paperback.)

Robinson, D. N. (1982). *Toward a science of human nature: Essays on the psychologies of Mill, Hegel, Wundt, and James.* New York: Columbia University Press.

Robinson discusses the theories of human nature proposed by the individuals listed in the title of this book. Although all these individuals will be covered in subsequent chapters of the present text, Robinson goes into each of their theories in much greater depth. (Available in paperback.)

Robinson, D. N. (1985). *Philosophy of psychology.* New York: Columbia University Press.

This is a relatively difficult account of how psychology and philosophy are inseparable. Chapters include "The Armchair and the Laboratory"; "Determinism, 'Hard' and 'Soft'"; "Reductionism: Models, Metaphors and Similes"; "Explanations"; and "Ethics and Psychological Inquiry." (Available in paperback.)

Stanovich, K. E. (1989). *How to think straight about psychology* (2nd ed.). Glenview, IL: Scott, Foresman.

This book is an excellent introduction to the science of psychology. In an informative yet entertaining manner, many misunderstandings of psychology are corrected. Also, a number of concepts from the philosophy of science are elaborated—for example, falsification and causation. (Available in paperback.)

Stevenson, L. (Ed.). (1981). *The study of human nature.* New York: Oxford University Press.

Stevenson presents an interesting sampling of primary source material reflecting religious, philosophical, and scientific conceptions of human nature. (Available in paperback.)

Stevenson, L. (1987). *Seven theories of human nature* (2nd ed.). New York: Oxford University Press.

This is an excellent, brief presentation of the theories of human nature held by Christianity, Freud, Lorenz, Marx, Sartre, Skinner, and Plato. Stevenson also offers a critical evaluation of each theory. (Available in paperback.)

GLOSSARY

Active mind A mind that transforms, interprets, understands, or values physical experience. The rationalists assume an active mind.

Anomalies Persistent observations that cannot be explained by an existing paradigm. Anomalies eventually cause one paradigm to displace another.

Biological determinism The type of determinism that stresses the biochemical, genetic, physiological, or anatomical causes of behavior.

Causal laws Laws describing causal relationships. Such laws specify the conditions that are necessary and sufficient to produce a certain event. Knowledge of causal laws allows both the prediction and control of events.

Controlled observation Experimentation designed to test the predictions of a scientific theory.

Correlational laws Laws that specify the systematic relationships among classes of empirical events. Unlike causal laws, the events described by correlational laws do not need to be causally related. One can note, for example, that as average daily temperature rises so does the crime rate without knowing (or even caring) if the two events are causally related.

Determinism The belief that everything that occurs does so because of known or knowable causes, and that if these causes were known in advance, an event could be predicted with complete accuracy. Also, if the causes of an event were known, the event could be prevented by preventing its causes. Thus, the knowledge of an event's causes allows the prediction and control of the event.

Double aspectism The belief that bodily and mental events are inseparable. They are two aspects of every experience.

Dualist Anyone who believes that there are two aspects to humans, one physical and one mental.

Eclectic approach Taking the best from a variety of viewpoints. The approach to the history of psychology taken in this text is eclectic because it combines coverage of great individuals, the development of ideas and concepts, the spirit of the times, and contributions from other disciplines.

Empirical observation The direct observation of that which is being studied in order to understand it.

Empiricism The belief that the basis of all knowledge is experience.

Environmental determinism The type of determinism that stresses causes of behavior that are external to the organism.

Epiphenomenalism The contention that bodily experiences cause mental events but that mental events do not, in turn, cause bodily activity.

Epistemology The study of the nature of knowledge.

Great-person approach The approach to history that concentrates on the most prominent contributors to the topic or field under consideration.

Historical development approach The approach to history that concentrates on an element of a field or discipline and describes how the understanding or approach to studying that element has changed over time. An example is a description of how mental illness has been defined and studied throughout history.

Historicism The study of the past for its own sake, without attempting to show how the past is related to the present, as is the case with presentism.

Idealist Anyone who believes that ultimate reality consists of ideas or perceptions and is therefore not physical.

Indeterminism The contention that even though determinism is true, attempting to measure the causes of something influences those causes, making it impossible to know them with certainty. This contention is also called Heisenberg's uncertainty principle.

Interactionism A proposed answer to the mind–body problem maintaining that bodily experiences influence the mind and that the mind influences the body.

Irrationalism Any explanation of human behavior stressing determinants that are not under rational control—for example, explanations that emphasize the importance of emotions or unconscious mechanisms.

Materialist Anyone who believes that everything in the universe is material (physical), including those things that others refer to as mental.

Mechanism The belief that the behavior of organisms, including humans, can be explained entirely in terms of mechanical laws.

Monist Anyone who believes that there is only one reality. Materialists are monists because they believe that everything is reducible to material substance. Idealists are also monists because they believe that everything, including the "material" world, is the result of human consciousness and is therefore mental.

Naive realism The belief that what one experiences mentally is the same as what is present physically.

Nativist Anyone who believes that important human attributes such as intelligence are inherited.

Nondeterminism The belief that human thought or behavior is freely chosen by the individual and is therefore not caused by antecedent physical or mental events.

Normal science According to Kuhn, the research activities performed by scientists as they explore the implications of a paradigm.

Occasionalism The belief that the relationship between the mind and body is mediated by God.

Paradigm A viewpoint shared by many scientists while exploring the subject matter of their science. A paradigm determines what constitutes legitimate problems and the methodology used in solving those problems.

Paradigmatic stage According to Kuhn, the stage in the development of a science during which scientific activity is guided by a paradigm. That is, it is during this stage that normal science occurs. (*See also* **Normal science**.)

Passive mind A mind that simply reflects cognitively one's experiences with the physical world. The empiricists tend to assume a passive mind.

Physical determinism The type of determinism that stresses material causes of behavior.

Postdiction An attempt to account for something after it has occurred. Postdiction is contrasted with prediction, which attempts to specify the conditions under which an event that has not yet occurred will occur.

Pre-established harmony The belief that bodily events and mental events are separate but correlated because both were designed to run identical courses.

Preparadigmatic stage According to Kuhn, the first stage in the development of a science. This stage is characterized by warring factions vying to define the subject matter and methodology of a discipline.

Presentism Use of the current state of a discipline as a guide in writing the discipline's history.

Principle of falsifiability Popper's contention that for a theory to be considered scientific it must specify the observations that if made would refute the theory. To be considered scientific, a theory must make risky predictions. (*See also* **Risky prediction**.)

Psychical determinism The type of determinism that stresses mental causes of behavior.

Psychophysical parallelism The contention that experiencing something in the physical world causes bodily and mental activity simultaneously and that the two types of activities are independent of each other.

Public observation The stipulation that scientific laws must be available for any interested person to observe. Science is interested in general, empirical relationships that are publicly verifiable.

Puzzle solving According to Kuhn, normal science is like puzzle solving in that the problems worked on are specified by a paradigm, the problems have guaranteed solutions, and certain rules must be followed in arriving at those solutions.

Rationalism The philosophical belief that knowledge can be attained only by engaging in some type of systematic mental activity.

Revolutionary stage According to Kuhn, the stage of scientific development during which an existing paradigm is displaced by a new one. Once the displacement is complete, the new paradigm generates normal science and continues doing so until it too is eventually displaced by a new paradigm.

Risky prediction According to Popper, a prediction derived from a scientific theory that runs a real chance of showing the theory to be false. For example, if a meteorological theory predicts that it will rain at a specific place at a specific time, then it must do so or the theory will be shown to be incorrect.

Science Traditionally, the systematic attempt to rationally categorize or explain empirical observations. Recently, Popper has described science as a way of rigorously testing proposed solutions to problems, and Kuhn has emphasized the importance of paradigms that guide the research activities of scientists.

Scientific law A consistently observed relationship between classes of empirical events.

Scientific theory Traditionally, a proposed explanation of a number of empirical observations; according to Popper, a proposed solution to a problem.

Self-regulated behavior Behavior that varies as a function of one's own subjective experience rather than as a function of the physical environment.

Sociocultural determinism The type of determinism that stresses cultural or societal rules, customs, regulations, or expectations as the causes of behavior.

Synchronicity Jung's term for meaningful coincidence. The term refers to fortuitous experiences that change the course of a person's life.

Uncertainty principle See **Indeterminism**.

Vitalism The belief that life cannot be explained in terms of inanimate processes. For the vitalist, life requires a force that is more than the material objects or inanimate processes in which it manifests itself. For there to be life, there must be a vital force present.

Zeitgeist The spirit of the times.

CHAPTER 2

The Early Greek Philosophers

THE WORLD OF PRECIVILIZED HUMANS

Imagine living about 15,000 years ago. What would your life be like? It seems safe to say that in your lifetime you would experience most of the following: lightning, thunder, rainbows, the phases of the moon, death, birth, illness, dreams (including nightmares), meteors, eclipses of the sun or moon, and perhaps one or more earthquakes, tornadoes, or volcanic eruptions. Because these events would touch your life directly, it seems natural that you would want to account for them in some way, but how? Many of these events—for example, lightning—cannot be explained by the average citizens of civilized countries even today; but we have faith that scientists can explain such events, and we are comforted and less fearful. However, as an early human, you would have no such scientific knowledge on which to draw, and therefore you would be on your own. We mentioned in the last chapter that thoughtful humans have always made empirical observations and then attempted to explain those observations. Although observation and explanation became key components of science, the explanations early humans offered were anything but scientific.

Animism and Anthropomorphism

The earliest attempts to explain natural events involved a projection of human attributes onto nature, which was seen as alive with human emotions. For example, the sky or earth could be-

come angry or could be tranquil, just as a human could. Looking at all of nature as though it were alive is called **animism**, and the projection of human attributes onto nature is called **anthropomorphism**; both were involved in early attempts to make sense out of life (Cornford, 1957; Murray, 1955). The early human made no distinctions between animate (living) and inanimate objects or between material and immaterial things.

Another approach to explanation assumed that a ghost or spirit dwelt in everything, including humans, and that these spirits were as real as anything else. The events in nature and human conduct were both explained as the whims of the spirits that resided in everything. The word *spirit* is derived from the Latin word for "breath" (Hulin, 1934, p. 7). Breath (later spirit, soul, psyche, or ghost) is what gives things life, and when it leaves a thing, death results. This spirit can sometimes leave the body and return, as was assumed to be the case in dreaming. Also, because one can dream of or think of a person after his or her biological death, it was assumed that the person must still exist, for it was believed that if something could be thought of it must exist. With this logic, anything the mind could conjure up was assumed to be real; therefore, imagination and dreams provided an array of demons, spirits, monsters, and later, gods, who lurked behind all natural events.

Magic

Because an array of spirits with human qualities was believed to exist, attempting to communicate with the spirits and otherwise influence them seemed a natural impulse. If, for example, a spirit was providing too much or too little rain, humans made attempts to persuade the spirit to modify its influence. Similarly, a sick person was thought to be possessed by an evil spirit, which had to be coaxed to leave the body or be driven out. Elaborate methods, called **magic**, evolved that were designed to influence the spirits. People believed that appropriate words, ceremonies, or human actions could influence the spirits.

As rudimentary as these beliefs were, they at least gave early humans the feeling that they had some control over their fate. These magical practices were pervasive in ancient Egypt and Babylonia:

> Like the Egyptian, and even more so, the Babylonian lived in a world that was haunted by evil spirits. They were everywhere, in the dark corners of the house, in the attic, in ruins, and on waste lands; they roamed the streets of the city at night, hid behind rocks and trees on the open land ready to attack you when you passed by; they rode howling with the storm wind. There was not a place where you could feel safe. Yet, it would be a great mistake to assume that the life of the Babylonian was one of perpetual terror, far from it. If you led a righteous life, worshipping the gods, keeping the ghosts of your ancestors in the Underworld by feeding them with regular offerings, if you respected taboos and possessed the necessary amulets and charms, there was no reason why you should be afraid of spirits. They were kept in check and had no power over you, although it happened here and there that they attacked a man without apparent reason. (Sigerist, 1951, p. 442)

Humans have always needed to understand, predict, and control nature. Animism, anthropomorphism, magic, religion, philosophy, and science can all be seen as efforts to satisfy those needs.

EARLY GREEK RELIGION

In the fifth and sixth centuries B.C., the explanations of things offered by the Greeks were still predominately religious in nature. There were two major theologies to choose from: the Olympian and the Dionysiac-Orphic. **Olympian religion** consisted of a belief in the Olympian gods as described in the Homeric poems. The gods depicted typically showed little concern with the anxieties of ordinary humans. Instead, they tended to be irascible, amoral, and little concerned with the immortality of humans. Within Olympian religion, it was believed that the "breath-soul" (psyche) did survive death but it did so without any of the memories or personality traits of the person whose body it had occupied. Such a belief concerning life after death encouraged living one's life in the fullest, most enjoyable way. The Olympian gods also personified orderliness and rationality and valued intelligence. In short, the Olympian gods tended to have the same characteristics and beliefs as the members of the Greek upper class; it hardly seems surprising that the Greek nobility favored the Olympian religion.

The major alternative to Olympian religion was **Dionysiac-Orphic religion**. The wealthy Greek upper class was made possible, to a large extent, by a large class of peasants, laborers, and slaves whose lives were characterized by economic and political uncertainty. To these relatively poor, uneducated individuals, the Dionysiac-Orphic religion was most appealing. The Dionysiac-Orphic religion was based on the legend of Dionysus, the god of vegetation, and his disciple Orpheus. Central to Dionysiac-Orphic religion was the belief in the **transmigration of the soul**. One version of this belief was that during its divine existence, during which time it dwelled among the gods, the soul had committed a sin; the punishment for which was being locked into a physical body, which acted as its prison. Until the soul was redeemed, it continued a "circle of births" whereby it may find itself first inhabiting a plant, then an animal, and then a human, then a plant again, and so on. What was longed for by the soul is its liberation from this transmigration and a return to its divine, pure, transcendent life among the gods. The rites that were practiced in hopes of freeing the soul from its "prison" (the body) included fasting, special diets, dramatic ceremonies, and various taboos.

Later in history, the Orphic idea that the soul seeks to escape its contaminated, earthly existence and enter into a more heavenly state following death gained enormous popularity and indeed was an integral part of our Judeo-Christian heritage.

Dionysiac-Orphic religion may have given rise to the origins of philosophical notions that have troubled psychology ever since:

> For what we think of as the typical Greek view that the true and happy life is life here on earth—the view, to be sure, of favored classes and of heroic and prosperous times—was substituted for the view that life on earth is really death. Thus in these "poor men's religions" the notion of a soul, the bearer of all the mental faculties, degraded by its temporary association with the unclean and contemptible body but separable from that body and immortal, was launched upon the stream of philosophical tradition to be developed by Pythagoras and Plato into those abstractions which ever since have been the bane of psychological science. (Esper, 1964, p. 34)

In their efforts to make sense out of themselves and their world, the early Greeks had Olympian and Dionysiac-Orphic religion from which to choose. Then, as now, which types of explanations individuals found congenial was as much a matter of temperament and circumstances as it was a matter of rational deliberation:

> In accounting for the . . . systems of the first philosophers, who had nothing but theology behind them, the two main causes are to be found in two opposed schemes of religious representation [Olympian and Dionysiac-Orphic], and in the temperament of the individual philosophers, which made one or other of those schemes the more congenial to them. (Cornford, 1957, p. 138)

As we will see next, many of the first Greek philosophers leaned toward the relative rationality of Olympian religion. A few highly influential philosophers, however, embraced the mysticism of Dionysiac-Orphic religion; Pythagoras and Plato are two prominent examples.

THE FIRST PHILOSOPHERS

Magic, superstition, and mysticism, in one form or another, dominated attempts to understand nature for most of early history. It was therefore a monumental step in human thought when *natural* explanations were offered instead of supernatural ones. Such explanations, although understandably simple, were first offered by the early Greeks. Philosophy began when natural explanations replaced supernatural ones. The first philosophers were called cosmologists because they sought to explain the origin, the structure, and the processes governing the cosmos (universe). However, the Greek word *kosmos* did not only refer to the totality of things but also suggested an elegant, ordered universe. The aesthetic aspect of the meaning of the term *kosmos* is reflected in the English word *cosmetic*. Thus, to the early Greek cosmologists, the universe was ordered and pleasant to contemplate. The assumption of orderliness was extremely important because an orderly universe is, at least in principle, an explicable universe.

Thales

As noted in chapter 1, no idea is born full-blown within a single individual. **Thales** (ca. 625–545 B.C.), often referred to as the first philosopher, had a rich, intellectual heritage. He traveled to Egypt and Babylonia, both of which enjoyed advanced civilizations that no doubt influenced him. For example, the Egyptians had known for centuries the knowledge of geometry that Thales demonstrated. In Egypt and Babylonia, however, knowledge was either practical (geometry was used to lay out the fields for farming) or was used primarily in a religious context (anatomy and physiology were used to prepare the dead for their journey into the next world). Thales was important because he *emphasized* natural explanations and *minimized* supernatural ones. That is, in his **cosmology**, Thales said that things in the universe consist of natural substances and are governed by natural principles; they do not reflect the whims of the gods. The universe is therefore knowable and within the realm of human understanding.

Thales searched for that *one* substance or element from which everything else is derived. The Greeks called such a primary element or substance a **physis**, and those who sought it were **physicists**. Physicists to this day are searching for the "stuff" from which everything is made. Thales concluded that the physis was water because many things seem to be a form of water. Life depends on water, water exists in many forms (e.g., ice, steam, hail, snow, clouds, fog, and dew), and some water is found in everything. This conclusion that water is the primary substance had considerable merit:

> The most important of Thales' views is his statement that the world is made of water. This is neither so far fetched as at first glance it might appear, nor yet a pure figment of imagination cut off from observation. Hydrogen, the stuff that generates water, has been held in our time to be the chemical element from which all other elements can be synthesized. The view that all matter is one is quite a reputable scientific hypothesis. As for observation, the proximity of the sea makes it more than plausible that one should notice that the sun evaporates water, that mists rise from the surface to form clouds, which dissolve again in the form of rain. The earth in this view is a form of concentrated water. The details might thus be fanciful enough, but it is still a handsome feat to have discovered that a substance remains the same in different states of aggregation. (Russell, 1959, pp. 16–17)

Besides this achievement, Thales also predicted eclipses, developed methods of navigation based on the stars and planets, and applied geometric principles to the measurement of such things as the heights of buildings. He is even said to have cornered the market on olive oil by predicting weather patterns. Such practical accomplishments brought great fame to Thales and respectability to philosophy. Thales showed that a knowledge of nature, which minimized supernaturalism, could provide power

over the environment, something humans had been seeking since the dawn of history.

Perhaps the most important thing about Thales, however, was the fact that he offered his ideas as speculations and he welcomed criticism. With his invitation for others to criticize and improve on his teachings, Thales started the *critical tradition* that was to characterize early Greek philosophy: "I like to think that Thales was the first teacher who said to his students: 'This is how I see things—how I believe that things are. Try to improve upon my teaching'" (Popper, 1958, p. 29). We will have more to say about the importance of this critical tradition later in this chapter.

Anaximander

Anaximander (ca. 610–540 B.C.), who studied with Thales, argued that even water was a compound of more basic material. (Notice that Anaximander took the advice of his teacher and criticized him.) According to Anaximander, the physis was something that had the capability of becoming anything. This something he called the "boundless" or the "indefinite." Anaximander also proposed a rudimentary theory of evolution. From a mixture of hot water and earth, there arose fish. Because human infants cannot survive without a long period of protection, the first human infants grew inside of these fish until puberty at which time the carrier fish burst and humans emerged that were developed enough to survive on their own. Anaximander urged us not to eat fish because they are, in a sense, our mothers and fathers. We can see how the physical environment can influence one's philosophizing. Both Thales and Anaximander lived near the shores of the Mediterranean Sea, and its influence on their philosophies is obvious.

Heraclitus

Impressed by the fact that everything in nature seemed to be in a constant state of flux, or change, **Heraclitus** (ca. 540–480 B.C.) assumed fire to be the physis because in the presence of fire everything is transformed into something else. To Heraclitus, the overwhelming fact about the world was that nothing ever "is"; rather, everything is "**becoming**." Nothing is either hot or cold but is becoming hotter or colder; nothing is fast or slow but is becoming faster or slower. Heraclitus's position is summarized in his famous statement: "No man steps into the same river twice." Heraclitus meant that the river becomes something other than what it was when it was first stepped into.

Heraclitus believed that all things existed somewhere between polar opposites—for example, night-day, life-death, winter-summer, up-down, heat-cold, sleeping-waking. For him, one end of the pole defined the other, and the two poles were inseparable. For example, only through injustice can justice be known, and only through health can illness be known. In other words, as Hegel would say many centuries later, "Everything carries within itself its own negation."

Heraclitus raised an epistemological question that has persisted to this day: How can something be known if it is constantly changing? If something is different at two points in time, and therefore not really the same object, how can it be known with certainty? Does not knowledge require permanence? It was at this point in history that the senses became a questionable means of acquiring knowledge because they could only provide information about a constantly changing world. In answer to the question What can be known with certainty? empirical events could not be included because they were in a constant state of flux. Those seeking something unchangeable, and thus knowable, had two choices. They could choose something that was real but undetectable by the senses, as the atomists and the Pythagorean mathematicians did (discussed later), or they could choose something mental (e.g., ideas or the soul) as the Platonists and the Christians did. Both groups believed that anything experienced through the senses was too unreliable to be known. Even today, the goal of science is to discover general

laws that are abstractions *derived* from sensory experience. Scientific laws as abstractions are thought to be flawless; when manifested in the empirical world, however, they are only probabilistic.

Heraclitus's philosophy clearly described the major problem inherent in various brands of empiricism. That is, the physical world is in a constant state of flux, and even if our sense receptors could accurately detect physical objects and events, we would only be aware of objects and events that change from moment to moment. It is for this reason that empiricists are said to be concerned with the process of becoming rather than with being. **Being** implies permanence and thus at least the possibility of certain knowledge, whereas a knowledge of empirical events (because they are becoming) can be only probabilistic at best. Throughout psychology's history, those claiming that there are certain permanent and therefore knowable things about the universe or about humans have tended to be rationalists. Those saying that everything in the universe, including humans, is constantly changing and thus incapable of being known with certainty have tended to be empiricists.

Parmenides

Taking a view exactly the opposite of Heraclitus's, **Parmenides** (fl. ca. 515 B.C.) believed that all change was an illusion. There is only one reality; it is finite, uniform, motionless, and fixed and can be understood only through reason. Thus, for Parmenides, knowledge is attained only through rational thought because sensory experience provides only illusion. Parmenides supported his position with logic. Like the earliest humans, he believed that being able to speak or think of something implied its existence because we cannot think of something that does not exist. The following is a summary of Parmenides' argument:

When you think, you think of something; when you use a name, it must be of something. Therefore both thought and language require objects outside themselves, and since you can think of a thing or speak of it at one time as well as another, whatever can be thought or spoken of must exist at all times. Consequently there can be no change, since change consists in things coming into being and ceasing to be. (Russell, 1945, p. 49)

Zeno of Elea (ca. 495–430 B.C.), a disciple of Parmenides, used logical arguments to show that motion was an illusion. He said that for an object to go from point A to point B, it must first go half the distance between A and B. Then it must go half the remaining distance, then half of that distance, and so on. Because there is an infinite number of points between any two points, the process can never stop. Also, the object must pass through an infinite number of points in a finite amount of time, and this is impossible. Therefore, it is logically impossible for the object ever to reach point B. The fact that it seems to do so is a weakness of the senses. This reasoning, usually known as **Zeno's paradox**, is often expressed in the following form: If one runner in a race is allowed to leave slightly before a second runner, the second runner can never overtake the first runner no matter how slow the first runner or how swift the second.

We have in Parmenides and in Zeno examples of how far unabated reason can take a person. They concluded that either logic, mathematics, and reason were correct or the information provided by the senses was; and they opted for logic, mathematics, and reason. The same mistake has been made many times in history. Other misconceptions can result from relying exclusively on sensory data. It was not until science emerged in the 16th century that **rationalism** and **empiricism** were wed, and sensory information provided that which was reasoned about. Science therefore minimized the extremes of both rationalism and empiricism.

Pythagoras

Largely through his influence on Plato, **Pythagoras** (ca. 580–500 B.C.) has had a significant influence on Western thought. Pythagoras postulated that the basic explanation for everything

in the universe was found in numbers and in numerical relationships. He noted that the square of the hypotenuse of a right-angle triangle is exactly equal to the sum of the squares of its other two sides. Although this came to be called the Pythagorean theorem, it had probably been known to the Babylonians. Pythagoras also observed that a harmonious blending of tone results when one string on a lyre is exactly twice as long as another. This observation that strings of a lyre must bear certain relationships with one another to produce pleasant, harmonious sounds was, perhaps, psychology's first psychophysical law. Indeed, physical events (relationships between strings on musical instruments) were demonstrated to be systematically related to psychological events (perceived pleasantness of sounds). In fact, the Pythagoreans expressed this psychophysical relationship in mathematical terms.

Just as pleasant music results from the harmonious blending of certain tones, so too does health depend on the harmonious blending of bodily elements. Illness was thought by the Pythagoreans to result from a disruption of the body's equilibrium, and medical treatment consisted of attempts to restore that equilibrium. We will see later that the Pythagorean approach to medicine was to be extremely influential. Pythagoras took these and several other observations and created a school of thought that glorified mathematics. He and his followers applied mathematical principles to almost every aspect of human existence, creating "a great muddle of religious mysticism, music, mathematics, medicine, and cosmology" (Esper, 1964, p. 52).

According to the Pythagoreans, numbers and numerical relationships, although abstract, were nonetheless real and exerted an influence on the empirical world. The world of numbers existed independently of the empirical world and could be known in its pure form only through reason. When conceptualized the Pythagorean theorem is exactly correct and applies to all right-angle triangles that ever were or ever will be. As long as the theorem is applied rationally to imagined triangles, it is flawless; when applied to actual triangles, however, the results are not absolutely correct because there are no perfect triangles in the empirical world. In fact, according to the Pythagoreans, *nothing* is perfect in the empirical world. Perfection is found only in the abstract mathematical world that lies beyond the senses and therefore can be embraced only by reason.

The Pythagoreans assumed a dualistic universe: one part abstract, permanent, and intellectually knowable (like that proposed by Parmenides) and the other empirical, changing, and known through the senses (like that proposed by Heraclitus). Sensory experience, then, cannot provide knowledge. In fact, such experience interferes with the attainment of knowledge and should be avoided. This viewpoint grew into outright contempt for sensory experiences and for bodily pleasures, and the Pythagoreans launched a crusade against vice, lawlessness, and bodily excess of any type. Members of this school imposed on themselves long periods of silence to enhance clear, rational thought. Moreover, they attempted to cleanse their minds by imposing certain taboos (e.g., against eating flesh) and by hard physical and mental exercise.

The Pythagoreans believed that the universe was characterized by a mathematical harmony and that everything in nature was interrelated. Following this viewpoint, they encouraged women to join their organization (it was *very* unusual for Greeks to look upon women as equal to men in any area), argued for the humane treatment of slaves, and, as mentioned, developed medical practices based on the assumption that health resulted from the harmonious workings of the body and illness resulted from some type of imbalance or discord.

The belief that experiences of the flesh are inferior to those of the mind—a belief that plays such an important role in Plato's theory and is even more important in early Christian theology—can be traced directly to the Pythagoreans. Eventually, Plato became a member of their organization. He based his Academy on Pythagorean concepts, and a sign above the entrance read "Let no one without an understanding of mathematics enter here."

Pythagoras postulated two worlds, one physical and one abstract, the two interacting with one another. Of the two, the abstract was considered the better. Pythagoras also postulated a dualism in humans, claiming that, besides the flesh of the body, we have reasoning powers that allow us to attain an understanding of the abstract world. Furthermore, reasoning is a function of the soul, which the Pythagoreans believed to be immortal. Pythagoras's philosophy provides one of the first clear-cut mind–body dualisms in the history of Western thought.

We see many elements in common between Dionysiac-Orphic religion and Pythagorean philosophy. Both viewed the body as a prison from which the soul should escape or, at the very least, the soul should minimize the lusts of the vile body that houses it by engaging in the rational contemplation of unchanging truths. Both accepted the notion of the transmigration of souls, and both believed that only purification could stop the "circle of births." The notion of transmigration fostered in the Pythagoreans a spirit of kinship with all living things. It is for this reason that they accepted women into their organizations, argued for the humane treatment of slaves, and were opposed to the maltreatment of animals. It is said of Pythagoras that "when he passed a puppy that was being whipped . . . he took pity on it and made this remark: 'Stop, do not beat it; for it is the soul of a dear friend' " (Barnes, 1987, p. 82). It was for the same reason that the Pythagoreans were vegetarians.

We will see later in this chapter that Plato borrowed much from the Pythagoreans and it was through Platonic philosophy that elements of the Dionysiac-Orphic religion became part of the heritage of Western civilization.

Empedocles

Empedocles (ca. 495–435 B.C.) was a disciple of Pythagoras. Indeed, he claimed his soul had been migrating for quite a while: "For already have I once been a boy and a girl and a bush and a bird and a silent fish in the sea" (Barnes, 1987, p. 196). Instead of one physis, Empedocles suggested four elements from which everything in the world is made: earth, fire, air, and water. Humans, too, consist of these four elements, with earth forming the solid part of the body, water accounting for the liquids in the body, air providing the breath of life, and fire providing our reasoning ability.

Besides the four elements, Empedocles postulated two causal powers of the universe: love and strife. Love is a force that attracts and mixes the elements. Strife is a force that separates the elements. Operating together, these two forces create an unending cosmic cycle consisting of four recurring phases. In phase one, love dominates, and there is a perfect mixture of the four elements ("one-from-many"). In phase two, strife disrupts the perfect mixture by progressively separating them. In phase three, strife has managed to completely separate the elements ("many-from-one"). In phase four, love again becomes increasingly dominant, and the elements are gradually recombined. As this cycle recurs, new worlds come into existence and then are destroyed. A world consisting of things we would recognize could only exist during the second and fourth phases of the cycle, when a mixture of the elements can exist. Along with the four elements, humans also possess the forces of love and strife, and these forces wax and wane within us just as they do in other material bodies. When love dominates, we have an urge to establish a union with the world and with other people; when strife dominates, we seek separation. Clearly, the ingredients are here for the types of intrapersonal and extrapersonal conflicts described by Freud and others much later in human history.

For Empedocles, the four elements and the forces of love and strife have always existed. In fact, all that can ever be must be a mixture of the elements and the two forces. Nothing beyond these mixtures is possible. He said, "From what does not exist nothing can come into being, and for what exists to be destroyed is impossible and unaccomplishable" (Barnes, 1987, p. 173). This comes very close to the modern law of conservation of energy, which states that energy can take different forms but cannot be created or destroyed.

Empedocles also offered a theory of evolution that was more complex than the one sug-

gested by Anaximander. In one of the phases mentioned above, when there is a mixture of love and strife, all types of things are created, some of them very bizarre. Animals did not form all at once but part by part; and the same was true of humans: "Here many neckless heads sprang up . . . naked arms strayed about, devoid of shoulders, and eyes wandered alone, begging for foreheads" (Barnes, 1987, p. 180). As these various body parts roamed around, they were combined in a random fashion: "Many grew double-headed, double-chested—man-faced oxen arose, and again ox-headed men—creatures mixed partly from male partly from female form" (Barnes, 1987, p. 181). Elsewhere, Empedocles described what happens when the four elements are acted on by love and strife: "As they mingle, innumerable types of mortal things pour forth, fitted with every sort of shape, a wonder to see" (Barnes, 1987, p. 170). Most random pairings resulted in creatures incapable of surviving, and they eventually perished. Some chance unions produced viable creatures, however, and they survived—humans among them. What we have here is an early version of natural selection by the survival of the fittest (Esper, 1964, p. 97).

Empedocles was also the first philosopher to offer a theory of perception. He assumed that each of the four elements was found in the blood. Objects in the outside environment throw off tiny copies of themselves called "emanations," or **eidola** (singular *eidolon*), which enter the blood through the pores of the body. Because like attracts like, the eidola will combine with elements that are like them. The fusion of external elements with internal elements results in perception. Empedocles believed that the matching of eidola with their corresponding internal elements occurred in the heart.

Because Empedocles was the first to attempt to describe how we form images of the world through a process similar to sensory perception, he is sometimes referred to as the first empirical philosopher. His view was that we perceive objects by internalizing copies of them.

To the Pythagorean notion that health reflected a bodily equilibrium, Empedocles added the four elements. Health occurs when the four elements of the body are in proper balance; illness results when they are not. Shortly we will see that the medical theories of Pythagoras and Empedocles were to be highly influential on later thinkers.

Democritus

Democritus (ca. 460–370 b.c.) was the last of the early Greek cosmologists; later philosophers were more concerned with human nature than with the nature of the physical universe. Democritus said that all things are made of tiny, indivisible parts called atoms. The differences among things are explained by the shape, size, number, location, and arrangement of atoms. Atoms themselves were believed to be unalterable, but they could have different arrangements; so although the actual atoms do not change, the objects of which they are made can change. Humans, too, are bundles of atoms, and the soul or mind is made up of smooth, highly mobile fire atoms that provide our mental experiences. For Democritus, therefore, animate, inanimate, and cognitive events were reduced to atomic activity. Because the behavior of atoms was thought to be lawful, Democritus's view was deterministic. It also exemplified physical monism (materialism) because everything was explained in terms of the arrangement of atoms and there was no separate life force; that is, he denied vitalism. Democritus's view also showed **elementism** because no matter how complex something was, Democritus believed it could be explained in terms of atoms and their activity. Finally, Democritus's philosophy exemplified **reductionism** because he attempted to explain objects and events on one level (observable phenomena) in terms of events on another level (atoms and their activities). Reductionism is contrasted with elementism in that the former involves two different domains of explanation, whereas the latter attempts to understand a complex phenomenon by separating it into its simpler, component parts. Attempting to explain human behavior in terms of biochemical processes would exemplify reductionism, as would attempting to explain

biochemical processes in terms of physics. Attempting to understand human thought processes by isolating and studying one process at a time or attempting to understand complex human behavior by isolating specific habits or stimulus–response associations would exemplify elementism. Democritus was both a reductionist and an elementist.

Democritus agreed with Empedocles that perceptions and sensations arise when atoms emanate from the surfaces of objects, but he said that eidola enter the body through one of five sensory systems and are transmitted to the brain. Upon entering the brain, the emanations sent by an object cause the highly mobile fire atoms to form a copy of them. This match between eidola and atoms in the brain causes perception. Democritus stressed that eidola are not the object itself and that the match between the eidola and the atoms in the brain may not be exact. Therefore, there may be differences between the physical object and the perception of it. As was noted in chapter 1, one of the most persistent problems in psychology has been determining what is gained or lost as objects in the environment are experienced through the senses.

Democritus placed thinking in the brain, emotion in the heart, and appetite in the liver. He discussed five senses: vision, hearing, smell, touch, and taste; and he suggested four primary colors: black, red, white, and green from which all colors were derived. Because he believed that all bodily atoms scattered at death, he also believed that there was no life after death. His was the first completely naturalistic view of the universe, devoid of any supernatural considerations. Although his view contained no gods or spirits to guide human action, Democritus did not condone a life of hedonism (pleasure seeking). He preached moderation, as did his disciple Epicurus, 100 years later.

EARLY GREEK MEDICINE

In the *Odyssey*, Homer described medical practitioners as roaming around selling their services to anyone needing them. The successful practitioners gained a reputation that preceded them; a few became viewed as godlike, and after their deaths, temples were erected in their honor. At these temples, priests practiced medicine in accordance with the teachings of the deceased, famous practitioners. The priests kept such teachings secret and carefully guarded. This **temple medicine** became very popular, and many wonderful cures were claimed. In fact, insofar as the ailments treated were psychosomatic, it is entirely possible that temple medicine was often effective because such medicine was typically accompanied by an abundance of ritual and ceremony. For example, patients would need to wait before being seen by a priest, drink "sacred" water, wear special robes, and sleep in a sanctuary. During the period of sleep, a high point in treatment, the patient (it was claimed) often had a dream in which a priest or god would directly cure the patient or tell him or her what to do in order to be cured. Thus, any healing that took place was essentially faith healing, and medical practices were magical.

Alcmaeon

Among the first to move away from temple medicine and toward more rational, naturalistic medicine was **Alcmaeon** (ca. 500 B.C.). Alcmaeon (perhaps a Pythagorean) equated health with a balance of such qualities as warm and cold, moist and dry, and bitter and sweet. If one or more qualities dominates a person's system, sickness results. According to Alcmaeon, it is the job of the physician to help the patient regain a lost equilibrium, thereby regaining health. For example, a fever represented excess heat, and the treatment involved cooling the patient; excessive dryness was treated with moisture; and so forth. Diagnosis involved discovering the source of the disturbance of equilibrium, and treatment involved a procedure that would restore equilibrium. This view of health as a balance, or a harmony, was to have a profound influence on medicine, including the present time.

Besides promoting naturalistic medicine, Alcmaeon was important for other reasons. He

was among the first (if not the first) to dissect human bodies. Among the important things he learned from these dissections was that the brain was connected to the sense organs. For example, he dissected the eye and traced the optic nerve to the brain. Unlike later thinkers such as Empedocles and Aristotle, who placed mental functions in the heart, Alcmaeon concluded that sensation, perception, memory, thinking, and understanding occurred in the brain. Alcmaeon's feats were truly remarkable, considering when they occurred. He did much to rid medicine of superstition and magic, and he used physiological information to reach conclusions concerning psychological functioning. As a physician interested in psychological issues, Alcmaeon started an illustrious tradition later followed by such individuals as Helmholtz, Freud, Wundt, and James.

Hippocrates

Hippocrates (ca. 460–377 B.C.) was born on the Greek island of Cos into a family of priests and physicians. He was educated at a famous school in Cos and received medical training from his father and other medical practitioners. By the time Hippocrates moved to Athens, he had acquired remarkable proficiency in the diagnosis, prognosis, and treatment of disease. He kept detailed records that gave precise accounts of mumps, epilepsy, hysteria, arthritis, and tuberculosis, to name only a few. From his training and observations, Hippocrates concluded that all disorders (both mental and physical) were caused by natural factors such as inherited susceptibility to disease, organic injury, and an imbalance of bodily fluids. Hippocrates is often referred to as the father of medicine, but this is only correct if we view him as "a culmination rather than a beginning" (Brett, 1965, p. 54). Several important physicians before Hippocrates (e.g., Alcmaeon and Empedocles) had challenged medical practices based on superstition and magic. However, Hippocrates' great accomplishment was that he took the development of naturalistic medicine to new heights.

Hippocrates forcefully attacked the vestiges

of supernatural medicine that still existed in his day. For example, epilepsy was called the "sacred disease," suggesting possession by an evil spirit. Hippocrates disagreed, saying that all illness had natural and not supernatural causes. He agreed with Empedocles that everything was made from four elements—earth, air, fire, and water—and that humans, too, were made up of these elements. In addition, however, Hippocrates associated the four elements with four humors in the body. He associated earth with black bile, air with yellow bile, fire with blood, and water with phlegm. Individuals for whom the humors were properly balanced were healthy; an imbalance among the humors resulted in illness.

Hippocrates strongly believed that the body had the ability to heal itself and that it was the physician's job to facilitate this natural healing ability. Thus, the "cures" recommended by Hippocrates included rest, proper diet, exercise, fresh air, massage, and baths. According to Hippocrates, the *worst* thing a physician could do would be to interfere with the body's natural healing power. Treating the total, unique patient, and not a disease, was also emphasized. The Hippocratic approach to treatment emphasized an understanding physician and a trusting, hopeful patient. Hippocrates also advised physicians not to charge a fee if a patient was in financial difficulty:

> Sometimes give your services for nothing, calling to mind a previous benefaction or present satisfaction. And if there be an opportunity of serving one who is a stranger in financial straits, give full assistance to all such. For where there is love of man, there is also love of the art. For some patients, though conscious that their condition is perilous, recover their health simply through their contentment with the goodness of the physician. (W. H. S. Jones, 1923, Vol. 1, p. 319)

Hippocrates agreed with Alcmaeon that the brain is responsible for our intellectual abilities. Hippocrates added that it is also the brain that causes many of our emotional problems:

> Men ought to know that from the brain, and from the brain only arise our pleasures, joys, laughter and jests, as well as our sorrows, pains, griefs and tears. Through it, in particular, we think, see, hear, and distinguish the ugly from the beautiful, the bad from the good, the pleasant from the unpleasant. . . . It is the same thing which makes us mad or delirious, inspires us with dread and fear, whether by night or by day, brings sleeplessness, inopportune mistakes, aimless anxieties, absent-mindedness, and acts that are contrary to habit. These things that we suffer all come from the brain, when it is not healthy, but becomes abnormally hot, cold, moist, or dry, or suffers any other unnatural affection to which it is not accustomed. (W. H. S. Jones. 1923, Vol. 2, p. 175)

We will have more to say about Hippocrates when we review the treatment of the mentally ill in chapter 15.

About 500 years after Hippocrates, **Galen** (A.D. 130–200) associated the four humors of the body with four temperaments. If one of the humors dominated, the person would display the characteristics associated with that humor (see Table 2.1).

Galen's extension of Hippocrates' views created the first rudimentary theory of personality, as well as a way of diagnosing illness that was to dominate medicine for about the next 14 centuries.

THE RELATIVITY OF TRUTH

The step from supernatural explanations of things to natural ones was enormous, but perhaps too many philosophers took it. Various philosophers found the basic element (physis) to be water, fire, numbers, the atom, and the boundless, and some philosophers found more than one basic element. Some said that things are constantly changing, others that nothing changes, and still others that some things change and some do not. Furthermore, most of these philosophers and their disciples were outstanding orators who presented and defended their views forcefully and with convincing logic. Where does this leave the individual seeking the truth? Such an individual is much like the modern college student who goes to one class and is convinced of something (e.g., psychology is a

TABLE 2.1 Galen's extension of Hippocrates' theory of humors.

Humor	Temperament	Characteristic
Phlegm	Phlegmatic	Sluggish, unemotional
Blood	Sanguine	Cheerful
Yellow bile	Choleric	Quick-tempered, fiery
Black bile	Melancholic	Sad

science), only to go to another class to be convinced of the opposite (psychology is not a science). Which is true? In response to the confusion, one group of philosophers concluded that there was not just one truth but many. In fact, they believed that anything is true if you can convince someone that it is true. In a sense, they maintained that believing something makes it true. These philosophers were called Sophists. The **Sophists** were professional teachers of rhetoric and logic who believed that effective communication determined whether an idea was accepted, rather than the idea's validity. Truth was considered relative, and therefore no single truth was thought to exist. This belief marked a major shift in philosophy. The question was no longer What is the universe made of? but What can humans know and how can they know it? In other words, there was a shift toward epistemological questions.

Protagoras

Protagoras (ca. 485–415 B.C.), the best-known Sophist, summarized the Sophists' position with his famous statement: "Man is the measure of all things: Of that which is that it is, and that which is not that it is not" (Brett, 1965, p. 63). This statement is pregnant with meaning. First, truth depends on the perceiver rather than on physical reality. Second, because perceptions vary with the previous experiences of the perceiver, they will vary from person to person. Third, what is considered to be true will be, in part, culturally determined because one's culture influences one's experiences. Fourth, to understand why a person believes as he or she does,

one must understand the person. According to Protagoras, therefore, each of the preceding philosophers was presenting his subjective viewpoint rather than the objective "truth" about physical reality. Paraphrasing Heraclitus's famous statement, Protagoras said, "Man never steps into the same river *once*" because the river is different for each individual *to begin with*.

With Protagoras, the focus of philosophical inquiry shifted from the physical world to human concerns. We now had a theory of *becoming* that was different from the one offered by Heraclitus. *Man* is the measure of all things, and therefore there is no permanent truth or code of ethics or anything else.

Gorgias

Gorgias (ca. 485–380 B.C.) was a Sophist whose position was even more extreme than Protagoras's. Protagoras concluded that, because each person's experience furnishes him or her with what seems to be true, "all things are equally true." Gorgias, however, regarded the fact that knowledge is subjective and relative as proof that "all things are equally false." Furthermore, because the individual can only know his or her private perceptions, there can be no objective basis for determining truth. Gorgias's position, as well as Protagoras's, exemplified **nihilism** because it stated that there can be no objective way of determining knowledge or truth. The Sophist position also exemplifies **solipsism** because the self can be aware of nothing except its own experiences and mental states. Thus, Gorgias reached his three celebrated conclusions: Nothing (except individual perceptions) exists; if anything external to the individual did exist, it could never be known; and if anything could be known, it could not be communicated to another person. According to Gorgias, for communication between two individuals to be possible, the conditions within the mind of the listener would have to be made the same as the conditions of the mind of the speaker, and this can never be. Similarly, to know an object external to the mind, it and the mind would have to be the same. Therefore, both knowing something outside the mind and communication of knowledge from one mind to another are impossible.

The Sophists clearly and convincingly described the gulf that exists between the physical world and the perceiving person. Later in history, this gulf would be described in terms of primary qualities of objects (those qualities that have the power to produce sensations corresponding to actual characteristics of physical things) and secondary qualities of objects (those qualities that produce sensations not corresponding to any attributes of physical things). The Sophists also raised the thorny question as to what one human consciousness can know about another human consciousness. No satisfactory answer has ever been provided.

Xenophanes

Even before the Sophists, **Xenophanes** (ca. 560–478 B.C.) had attacked religion as a human invention. He noted that the Olympian gods acted suspiciously like humans; they lie, steal, philander, and even murder: "Homer . . . attributed to the gods all the things which among men are shameful and blameworthy—theft and adultery and mutual deception" (Barnes, 1987, p. 95). He also noted that dark-skinned people had dark-skinned gods and light-skinned people had light-skinned gods. Xenophanes went so far as to say that if animals could describe their gods, they would have the characteristics of the animals describing them:

> Mortals think that the gods are born, and have clothes and speech and shape like their own. . . . But if cows and horses or lions had

hands [and] could draw with their hands and make the things men can make, then horses would draw the forms of gods like horses, cows like cows, and they would make their bodies similar in shape to those which each had themselves. (Barnes, 1987, p. 95)

With regard to religion, Xenophanes can be seen as an early Sophist. Not only do humans create whatever "truth" exists, but they also create whatever religion exists. Moral codes, then, are not divinely inspired; they are human inventions.

The relativist nature of truth, which the Sophists suggested, was distasteful to many who wanted "truth" to be more than the projection of one's subjective reality onto the world. Among those most concerned was Socrates, who both agreed and disagreed with the Sophists.

Socrates

Socrates (469–399 B.C.) agreed with the Sophists that individual experience is important (witness his famous expressions "Know thyself" and "An unexamined life is not worth living"), but he disagreed with the Sophists' contention that no truth exists beyond personal opinion. In his search for truth, Socrates used a method sometimes called **inductive definition**, which started with an examination of instances of such concepts as beauty, love, justice, or truth and then moved on to such questions as What is it that *all* instances of beauty have in common? In other words, Socrates asked what it is that makes something beautiful, just, or true. In this way, he sought to discover general principles from examining isolated examples. It was thought that these general principles, or concepts, transcend their individual manifestations and are therefore stable and knowable. What Socrates sought was the **essence** of such things as beauty, justice, and truth. The essence of something is its basic nature, its identifying, enduring characteristics. To truly know something, according to Socrates, is to understand its essence. It is not enough to identify something as beautiful; one must know *why* it is beautiful. One must know what *all* in-

Socrates

he was accused of disrespect for the city gods and of corrupting the youth of Athens. He was tried, convicted, and sentenced to death. The wisdom of Socrates, however, was perpetuated and greatly elaborated by his famous student Plato. Plato requires more attention than other philosophers because his theory created a theme that runs throughout the history of psychology and continues to exert an influence on modern psychology.

PLATO

The writings of **Plato** (ca. 427–347 B.C.) can be divided into two periods. During the first period, Plato was essentially reporting the thoughts and methods of his teacher Socrates. When Socrates was executed, however, Plato went into self-imposed exile in southern Italy, where he came under the influence of the Pythagoreans. After he returned to Athens, he founded his own school, the Academy, and his subsequent writings combined the Socratic method with mystical Pythagorean philosophy. Like Socrates, Plato wished to find something permanent that could be the object of knowledge, but his search for permanence carried him far beyond the essences for which Socrates had settled.

stances of beauty have in common; one must know the essence of beauty.

For Socrates, the understanding of essences constituted knowledge, and the goal of life was to gain knowledge. When one's conduct is guided by knowledge, it is necessarily moral. For example, if one knows what justice is, one acts justly. For Socrates, knowledge and morality were intimately related; knowledge is virtue, and improper conduct results from ignorance. Unlike most of the earlier philosophers, Socrates was concerned mainly with what it means to be human and the problems related to human existence. It is because of these concerns that Socrates is sometimes referred to as the first existential philosopher.

In 399 B.C., when Socrates was 70 years old,

The Theory of Forms or Ideas

As we have seen, the Pythagoreans believed that although numbers and numerical relationships were abstractions (i.e., they could not be experienced through the senses), they were nonetheless real and could exert an influence on the empirical world. The result of the influence, however, was believed to be inferior to the abstraction that caused the influence. As already mentioned, the Pythagorean theorem is absolutely true when applied to abstract (imagined) triangles but is never completely true when applied to a triangle that exists in the empirical world (e.g., one that is drawn on paper). This is because, in the empirical world, the lines making up the right angle will never be exactly even.

Plato took an additional step. According to his **theory of forms**, everything in the empirical world was a manifestation of a pure form (idea) that existed in the abstract. Thus, chairs, chariots, rocks, cats, dogs, and even people were inferior manifestations of pure **forms**. For example, the thousands of cats that one encounters are but inferior copies of an abstract idea or form of "catness" that exists in pure form in the abstract. This is true for every object for which we have a name. What we experience through the senses results from the interaction of the pure form with matter; and because matter is constantly changing and is experienced through the senses, the result of the interaction must be less perfect than the pure idea before that idea interacts with matter. Plato replaced the essence that Socrates sought with the concept of form as the aspect of reality that was permanent and therefore knowable. That is, Socrates accepted the fact that a thorough definition specified an object's or a concept's essence; whereas for Plato, an object's or a concept's essence was equated with its form. For Plato, essence (form) had an existence separate from its individual manifestations. Socrates and Plato did agree, however, that knowledge could be attained only through reason.

The Analogy of the Divided Line

What, then, becomes of those who attempt to gain knowledge by examining the empirical world via sensory experience? According to Plato, they are doomed to ignorance or, at best, opinion. The only true knowledge involves grasping the forms themselves, and this can be done only by rational thought. Plato summarized this viewpoint with his famous **analogy of the divided line**, which is illustrated in Figure 2.1.

Imagining is seen as the lowest form of understanding because it is based on images—for example, a portrait of a person, which is once removed from the person. Reflections in the water are also images because they are a step removed from the objects reflected. We are

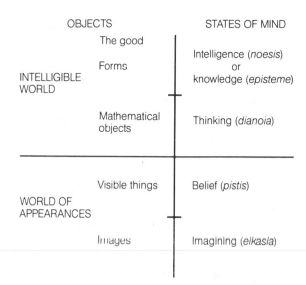

FIGURE 2.1 Plato's analogy of the divided line. (From Cornford's translation of Plato's *Republic*, 1968, p. 222.)

slightly better off confronting the objects themselves rather than their images, but the best we can do even when confronting objects directly is to form beliefs about them. Beliefs, however, do not constitute knowledge. Still better is the contemplation of mathematical relationships, but mathematical knowledge is still not the highest type because it often depends on events in the empirical world and many of its relationships exist only by definition. That is, mathematical relationships are assumed to be true, but these assumptions could conceivably be false. To think about mathematics in the abstract, however, is better than dealing with images or empirical objects. The highest form of thinking involves embracing the forms themselves, and true intelligence or knowledge results *only* from an understanding of the abstract forms. The "good" or the "form of the good" constitutes the highest form of wisdom because it encompasses all other forms and shows their interrelatedness. The form of the good is like the sun, in that it illuminates all other forms and makes them knowable. It is the highest truth. Later, in Christian theology, the form of the good is equated with God.

The Allegory of the Cave

In the **allegory of the cave** (see Cornford, 1968), Plato described fictitious prisoners who have lived their entire lives in the depths of a cave. The prisoners are chained so they can see only forward. Behind them is a road over which individuals pass, carrying a variety of objects. Behind the road a fire is blazing, causing a projection of shadows of the travelers and the objects onto the wall in front of the prisoners. For the prisoners, the projected shadows constitute reality. Plato then described what might happen if one of the prisoners were to escape his bondage and leave the cave. Turning toward the fire would cause his eyes to ache, and he might decide to return to his world of shadows. If not, he would eventually adjust to the flames and see the individuals and objects of which he had previously seen only shadows. Plato now asks us to suppose that the prisoner continues his journey and leaves the cave. Once in the "upper world," the prisoner would be blinded by sunlight. Only after a period of adjustment could he see things in this "upper world" and recognize that they were more real than the shadows that he had experienced in the cave. Finally, Plato asks us to imagine what might happen to the escaped prisoner if he went back into the cave to enlighten his fellow prisoners. Still partially blinded by such an illuminating experience, the prisoner would find it difficult to readjust to the previous life of shadows. He would make mistakes in describing the shadows and in predicting which objects would follow which. This would be evidence enough for his fellow prisoners that no good could come from leaving the world of shadows. In fact, anyone who attempted to lead the prisoners out of the shadowy world of the cave would be killed.

The bound prisoners represent humans who confuse the shadowy world of sense experience with reality. The prisoner who escapes represents the individual whose actions are governed by reason instead of sensory impressions. The escaped prisoner sees the real objects (forms) responsible for the shadows in the cave (sensory information) and thus embraces true knowledge. After such an enlightening experience, an effort is often made to steer others away from ignorance and toward wisdom. The plight of Socrates is evidence of what can happen to the individual attempting to free others from the chains of ignorance.

The Reminiscence Theory of Knowledge

How does one come to know the forms if they cannot be known through sensory experience? The answer to this question involves the most mystical aspect of Plato's theory. Plato's answer was influenced by the Pythagorean notion of the immortality of the soul. According to the Pythagoreans, the highest form of thought was reason, which was a function of the immortal soul. Plato expanded this idea and said that before the soul was implanted in the body, it dwelled among the forms. After the soul entered the body, sensory information began to contaminate this knowledge. The only way to arrive at true knowledge is to ignore sensory experience and focus one's thoughts on the contents of the mind. According to Plato's **reminiscence theory of knowledge,** all knowledge is innate and can be attained only through **introspection,** which is the searching of one's inner experiences. At most, sensory experience can only remind one of what was already known. Therefore, for Plato, all knowledge comes from reminiscence, from remembering the experiences the soul had before entering the body. We see, then, that Plato was a **nativist** as well as a rationalist because he stressed mental operations as a means of arriving at the truth (rationalism) and he stressed that the truth ultimately arrived at was inborn (nativism). He was also an **idealist** because he believed that ultimate reality consisted of ideas or forms.

The Nature of the Soul

Plato not only believed that the soul had a rational component that was immortal but also that it had two other components: the courageous (sometimes translated as emotional or spirited) and the appetitive. The courageous and appetitive aspects of the soul were part of the body and thus mortal. With his concept of the three-part soul, Plato postulated a situation in which humans were almost always in a state of conflict, a situation not unlike the one Freud described many centuries later. According to Plato, the body has appetites (needs such as hunger, thirst, and sex) that must be met and that play a major motivational role in everyday life. Humans also have varied emotions such as fear, love, and rage. However, if true knowledge is to be attained, the person must suppress the needs of the body and concentrate on rational pursuits, such as introspection. Because bodily needs do not go away, the person must spend considerable energy keeping them under control—but they must be controlled. It is the job of the rational component of the soul to postpone or inhibit immediate gratifications when it is to a person's long-term benefit to do so. The person whose rational soul dominates is not impulsive. His or her life is dominated by moral principles and future goals, not the immediate satisfaction of biological or emotional needs. The supreme goal in life, according to Plato, should be to free the soul as much as possible from the adulterations of the flesh. In this he agreed with the Pythagoreans.

Plato realized that not everyone was capable of intense rational thought; he believed that in some individuals the appetitive aspect of the soul would dominate, in others the courageous (emotional) aspect of the soul would dominate, and in still others the rational aspect would dominate. In his *Republic,* he created a utopian society in which the three types of individuals would have special functions. Those in whom the appetitive aspect dominated would be workers and slaves, those in whom courage (emotion) dominated would be soldiers, and those in whom reason dominated would be philosopher-kings. In Plato's scheme, an inverse relationship exists between concern with bodily experiences and one's status in society. In Book V of the *Republic,* Plato forcibly stated his belief that societies have little chance of survival unless they are led by individuals with the wisdom of philosophers:

> Until philosophers are kings, or the kings and princes of this world have the spirit and power of philosophy, and political greatness and wisdom meet in one, and those of commoner natures who pursue either to the exclusion of the other are compelled to stand aside, cities will never have rest from their evils . . . then only will this our state have a possibility of life and behold the light of day. (Jowett, 1908, p. 473)

We see that Plato was a nativist not only where knowledge was concerned but also where character or intelligence was concerned. He felt that education was of limited value for children of low aptitude. To a large extent then, whether one was destined to be a slave, a guardian, or a philosopher-king was a matter of inheritance.

Plato's Legacy

Because science depends on empirical observation, Plato's theory did little to promote science and much to inhibit it. Plato created a dualism that divided the human into a body, which was material and imperfect, and a mind (soul), which contained pure knowledge. Furthermore, the rational soul was immortal. Had philosophy remained unencumbered by theological concerns, perhaps Plato's theory would have been challenged by subsequent philosophers and gradually displaced by more tempered philosophic views. Aristotle, in fact, went a long way in modifying Plato's position, but the challenge was aborted. The mysticism of early Christianity was combined with Platonic philosophy, creating unchallengeable religious dogma. When Aristotle's writings were rediscovered centuries later, they were also carefully modified and assimilated into church dogma. It was not until the Renaissance that Platonism (and Aristotelianism) was finally questioned openly and largely discarded.

ARISTOTLE

Aristotle (384–322 B.C.) was born in the obscure Macedonian city of Stagira located between the Black Sea and the Aegean Sea. His father Nico-

THE BETTMANN ARCHIVE

Aristotle

machus was court physician to King Amyntas III of Macedonia. In keeping with Greek tradition, it is assumed that Aristotle's father instructed his son in medicine. In 367 B.C., Aristotle journeyed to Athens and soon established himself as one of Plato's most brilliant students; he was 17 years old at the time, and Plato was 60. When Plato died in 347 B.C., Aristotle moved to Asia Minor where he engaged in biological and zoological field work. In 343 B.C., Aristotle began tutoring King Philip's son, the future Alexander the Great, and continued to do so for four years. After a few more journeys, Aristotle returned to Athens where, at the age of 48, he founded his own school called the *Lyceum*. Because the Lyceum had many teachers, regular lectures, a substantial library, and large natural science collections, it is considered the world's first university (Esper, 1964, p. 128). Aristotle fled Athens when Alexander the Great died in 323 B.C. and died a year later in Challis.

Aristotle was the first philosopher to exten-

sively treat many topics that were later to become part of psychology. In his vast writings, he covered memory, sensation, sleep, dreams, geriatrics, and learning. He also began his book *De Anima* ("On the Soul") with what is considered to be the first history of psychology. Taken alone, Aristotle's contributions to psychology were truly impressive. It must be realized, however, that with the possible exception of mathematics, he made contributions to every branch of knowledge. The influence of his thoughts on such philosophical and scientific topics as logic, metaphysics, physics, biology, ethics, politics, rhetoric, and poetics have lasted. It is often said that Aristotle was the last human to know everything that was knowable during his lifetime.

The Basic Difference Between Plato and Aristotle

Both Plato and Aristotle were primarily interested in essences or truths that went beyond the mere appearance of things, but their methods for discovering those essences were distinctly different. For Plato, essences corresponded to the forms that existed *independent* of nature and that could only be arrived at by ignoring sensory experience and turning one's thoughts inward (i.e., by introspection). For Aristotle, essences existed but could only become known by studying nature. He believed that if enough individual manifestations of a principle or phenomenon were investigated, eventually one could infer the essence that they exemplified.

Aristotle's philosophy shows the difficulty that is often encountered when attempting to clearly separate the philosophies of rationalism and empiricism. As was noted in chapter 1, the rationalist claims that logical, mental operations must be used to gain knowledge, and the empiricist emphasizes the importance of sensory information in gaining knowledge. Aristotle embraced both rationalism and empiricism. He believed that the mind must be employed before knowledge can be attained (rationalism) but that it was the information furnished by the senses (empiricism) that was the object of rational thought. Aristotle's position is not unique, however. Throughout history most rationalists have recognized and accepted the importance of sensory experience, and most empiricists have postulated one or more mental operations that are presumed to act on sensory information. In other words, finding a *pure* rationalist or empiricist is very difficult, and a philosopher is usually categorized as one or the other depending on whether he or she emphasizes mental operations or sensory experience. With this in mind, we can say that Aristotle was more of a rationalist than he was an empiricist.

The general principles that were thought by Plato and Aristotle (and other philosophers) to be real and knowable have been referred to in different ways through the years—for example, as first principles, essences, or universals. In each case, it was assumed that something basic existed that could not be discovered by only studying individual instances or manifestations of the abstract principle involved. Some type of rational activity was needed to find the principle (essence) underlying individual cases. The search for first principles, essences, or universals characterized most early philosophy and, in a sense, continues in modern science as the search for laws governing nature.

For Plato, first principles were arrived at by pure thought; for Aristotle, they were attained by examining nature directly. For Plato, all knowledge existed independently of nature; for Aristotle, nature and knowledge were inseparable. In Aristotle's view, therefore, the body was not a hindrance in the search for knowledge, as it was for Plato and the Pythagoreans. Also, Aristotle disagreed with Plato on the importance of mathematics. For Aristotle, mathematics was essentially useless, his emphasis being on the careful examination of nature by observation and classification. Here we see again the empirical component of Aristotle's philosophy. In Aristotle's Lyceum, an incredibly large number of observations of physical and biological phenomena were made. Categories into which the observations fit were then determined. Through this method of observation, definition, and classification, Aristotle compiled what has been called an encyclopedia of nature. He was interested in studying the things in the empirical world and learning their functions.

Because Aristotle sought to explain several psychological phenomena in biological terms, he can be considered the first physiological psychologist:

> When we study the philosophers before Aristotle, we can uncover, here and there, a psychological orientation that is materialist in tone . . . however, no predecessor could possibly or plausibly lay claim to the title of an early physiological psychologist, and this is precisely the title we may assign to Aristotle. He was the first authority to delineate a domain specifically embracing the subject matter of psychology and, within that domain, to restrict his explanations to principles of a biological sort. That the entire body of Aristotelian philosophy does not fit into a materialist mold is clear. But on the narrower issues of learning, memory, sleep and dreams, routine perceptions, animal behavior, emotion, and motivation, Aristotle's approach is naturalistic, physiological, and empirical. (D. N. Robinson, 1986, pp. 81–82)

Plato's philosophy followed in the Pythagorean, mathematical tradition and Aristotle's in the Hippocratic biological tradition. The views of Plato and Aristotle concerning the sources of knowledge set the stage for epistemological inquiry that has lasted. Almost every philosopher, and most psychologists, can be evaluated in terms of their agreement or disagreement with the views of Plato or Aristotle.

Causation and Teleology

To truly understand anything, according to Aristotle, we must know four things about it. That is, everything has four causes:

1. **Material cause** is the matter of an object. For example, a statue is made of marble.

2. **Formal cause** is the particular form, or pattern, of an object. For example, a piece of marble takes on the form of Venus.

3. **Efficient cause** is the force that transforms the matter into a certain form—for example, the energy of the sculptor.

4. **Final cause** is the purpose for which an object exists. In the case of a statue, the purpose may be to bring pleasure to those who view it.

Aristotle's philosophy exemplified **teleology** because, for him, everything in nature exists for a purpose. By purpose, however, Aristotle did not mean conscious intention. Rather, he meant that everything in nature had a function built into it. This built-in purpose, or function, is called **entelechy**. Entelechy keeps an object moving or developing in its prescribed direction until its full potential is reached. For example, the eye exists to provide vision, and it continues developing until it does so. The final cause of living things is part of their nature; it exists as a potentiality from the organism's very inception. An acorn has the potential to become an oak tree, but it cannot become a frog or an olive tree. In other words, the purpose, or entelechy, of an acorn is to become an oak tree. Nature is characterized by the change and motion that occurs as objects are slowly transformed from their potentialities to their actualities—that is, as objects move toward their final causes or purposes, such as when an acorn becomes an oak tree. The final cause, or purpose, of something was also seen by Aristotle as its essence.

According to Aristotle, all natural things, both animate and inanimate, have a purpose built into them. In addition, however, nature itself has a grand design or purpose. Although Aristotle believed that the categories of things in nature remain fixed, thus denying evolution, he spoke of a grand hierarchy among all things. The *scala naturae* refers to the fact that nature is arranged in a hierarchy ranging from neutral matter to the **unmoved mover**, which is pure actuality and is the cause of everything in nature. For Aristotle, the unmoved mover is what gives all natural objects their purposes. In his *scala naturae*, the closer to the unmoved mover something was, the more perfect it was. Among animals, humans were closest to the unmoved mover, with all other animals at various distances behind us. Although Aristotle did not accept evolution, his *scala naturae* does create a phylogenetic scale of sorts, making it possible to study "lower" animals in order to understand humans. Such information will always be of limited value, however, because for Aristotle, humans were unique among the animals. Again, Aristotle's position was thoroughly teleological: All objects in nature have a purpose, and nature itself has a purpose.

The Hierarchy of Souls

For Aristotle, as for most Greek philosophers, a soul was that which gives life; therefore, all living things possess a soul. According to Aristotle, there were three types of souls, and a living thing's potential (purpose) was determined by what type of a soul it possessed:

1. A **vegetative** (or nutritive) **soul** is possessed by plants. It allows only growth, the assimilation of food, and reproduction.

2. A **sensitive soul** is possessed by animals but not plants. Besides the above functions, organisms that possess a sensitive soul sense and respond to the environment, experience pleasure and pain, and have a memory.

3. A **rational soul** is possessed only by humans. It provides all the functions of the other two souls but also allows thinking or rational thought.

Sensation

Aristotle said that information about the environment is provided by the five senses: sight, hearing, taste, touch, and smell. Unlike earlier philosophers, (e.g., Empedocles and Democritus), Aristotle did not believe objects sent off tiny copies of themselves (eidola). Rather, he felt that perception was explained by the motion of objects that stimulate one of the senses. The movement of environmental objects created movements through different media, and each of the five senses was maximally sensitive to movements in a certain medium. For example, seeing resulted from the movement of light caused by an object, hearing and smelling resulted from the movement of air, and taste and touching from movement of the flesh. In this way, Aristotle explained how we could actually sense environmental objects without those objects sending off physical copies of themselves. Unlike Plato, Aristotle believed we could trust our senses to yield an accurate representation of the environment.

Common Sense, Passive Reason, and Active Reason

As important as sensory information was to Aristotle, it was only the first step in acquiring knowledge. In other words, *sensory experience was a necessary but not a sufficient element in the attainment of knowledge.* In the first place, each sensory system provides isolated information about the environment that by itself is not very useful. For example, seeing a baby tossing and turning provides a clue as to its condition, hearing it cry provides another clue, smelling it may give a clue as to why it is so uncomfortable, and touching may reveal that it has a fever. It is the combined information from all the senses that allows for the most effective interactions with the environment.

Aristotle postulated a **common sense** as the mechanism that coordinated the information from all the senses. The common sense, like all other mental functions, was assumed to be located in the heart. The job of common sense was to synthesize sensory experience, thereby making it more meaningful. However, sensory information, even after it was synthesized by common sense, could provide information only about particular instances of things. **Passive reason** involved the utilization of synthesized experience for getting along effectively in everyday life, but it did not result in an understanding of essences, or first principles. The abstraction of first principles from one's many experiences could be accomplished only by **active reason**, which was considered the highest form of thinking. Aristotle therefore delineated levels of knowing or understanding much like Plato's divided line. These levels are as follows:

- **Active reason:** The abstraction of principles, or essences, from synthesized experience
- **Passive reason:** Utilization of synthesized experience
- **Common sense:** Synthesized experience
- **Sensory information:** Isolated experiences

An example of how these levels of understanding are related might be to experience electricity through the senses of sight (seeing an electrical discharge), pain (being shocked), and hearing (hearing the electrical discharge). These experiences would correspond to the level of sense reception. The common sense would indicate that all these experiences had a common source—electricity. Passive reason would indicate how electricity could be used in a variety of practical ways, whereas active reason would seek the laws governing electricity and an understanding of its essence. What started as a set of empirical experiences ends as a search for the principles that can explain those experiences.

The active reason part of the soul provides humans with their highest purpose. That is, it provides their entelechy. Just as the ultimate goal of an acorn is to become an oak tree, the ultimate goal of humans is to engage in active reason. Aristotle also believed that acting in accordance with one's nature caused pleasure and that acting otherwise brought pain. In the case of humans, engaging in active reason was the source of greatest pleasure. On this matter, Aristotle was essentially in agreement with Socrates and Plato. Also, because Aristotle postulated an inner potential in humans that may or may not be reached, his theory represents psychology's first self-actualization theory. The self-actualization theories of Jung, Maslow, and Rogers reflect Aristotle's thoughts on the human entelechy.

With his concept of active reason, Aristotle inserted a mystical or supernatural component into an otherwise naturalistic theory. The active reason part of the soul was considered immortal, but when it left the body upon death, it carried no recollections with it. It was considered a mechanism for pure thought and was believed to be identical for all humans. It was not judged in accordance with the moral character of its prior possessor, and there was no union or reunion with God. The active reason part of the soul went neither to heaven nor hell. Later, however, the Christianized version of the Aristotelian soul was to be characterized by all these things.

Another mystical component in Aristotle's theory was his notion of the unmoved mover. For Aristotle, everything in nature had a purpose that was programmed into it. This purpose, or entelechy, explained why a thing was like it was and why it did what it did. But if everything in nature has a purpose, what causes that purpose? As we have seen, Aristotle postulated an unmoved mover, or that which caused everything else but was not caused by anything itself. For Aristotle, the unmoved mover set nature in motion and did little else; it was a logical necessity, not a deity. Along with Aristotle's notion of the immortal aspect of the soul, the Christians also found his unmoved mover very much to their liking.

Memory and Recall

In keeping with the empirical aspect of his philosophy, Aristotle explained memory and recall as the results of sense perception. This contrasts with Plato's explanation, which was essentially nativistic. **Remembering**, for Aristotle, was a spontaneous recollection of something that had been previously experienced. For example, you see a person and remember that you saw that person before and perhaps engaged in a certain conversation. **Recall**, however, involves an active mental search for a past experience. It was in conjunction with recall that Aristotle postulated his now famous **laws of association**. The most basic law of association is the **law of contiguity**, which states that when we think of something, we will also tend to think of things that were experienced along with it. The **law of frequency** states that the more times something is experienced, the easier it will be to recall. The **law of similarity** states that when we think of

something, we will tend to think of things similar to it. The **law of contrast** states that when we think of something, we will also tend to think of things that are its opposite. Aristotle's laws of association were to become the basis of learning theory for more than 2,000 years. In fact, the concept of mental association is still at the heart of most theories of learning. The belief that one or more laws of association can be used to explain the origins of ideas, the phenomena of memory, or how complex ideas are formed from simple ones came to be called **associationism**. Thus, Aristotle had great influence on modern psychology:

> A moment's recollection . . . shows that Aristotle's doctrines are at the heart of contemporary thought in epistemology and the psychology of learning. The centrality of associationism as the mechanism of the mind is so well known as to require only the observation that *not one single learning theory* propounded in this century *has failed to base its account on associative principles.* (Weimer, 1973, p. 18)

Recall from chapter 1 that no historically important idea is produced by a single person. Even Aristotle, one of the great thinkers of all time, extended or modified the thoughts of previous philosophers, and many philosophers shared his search for universals (essences). Even the laws of association, usually attributed to Aristotle, can be clearly seen in the following passage from Plato's *Phaedo*:

> And yet what is the feeling of lovers when they recognize a lyre, or a garment, or anything else which the beloved has been in the habit of using? Do not they, from knowing the lyre, form in the mind's eye an image of the youth to whom the lyre belongs? And this is recollection. In like manner anyone who sees Simmias may remember Cebes; and there are endless examples of the same thing . . . and recollection is most commonly a process of recovering that which has already been forgotten through time and inattention . . . so much is clear—that when we perceive something, either by the help of sight, or hearing, or some other sense, from that perception we are able to obtain a notion of some other thing like or unlike which is associated with it but has been forgotten. (Jowett, 1942, pp. 105–108)

Imagination and Dreaming

We have seen that Aristotle's philosophy had both rational and empirical components. For example, his account of memory and recall was empirical. We see that component again in his explanation of **imagination** and **dreaming**. According to Aristotle, when sensations occur, they create images that long outlast the stimulation that caused them. The retention of these images is what constitutes memory. These images also create the important link between sensation and rational thought because it is the images provided by experience that are pondered by the passive and active intellects. Imagination, then, is explained as the lingering effects of sensory experience.

Dreaming, too, was explained by Aristotle in terms of the images of past experience. During sleep the images of past experience may be stimulated by events inside or outside the body. The reasons that our residual impressions (images) may seem odd during a dream include the following: During sleep the images are not organized by reason. While awake our images are coordinated with or controlled by ongoing sensory stimulation, which interacts with the images of previous experience; during sleep this does not occur.

Concerning a dream's ability to provide information about future events, Aristotle was extremely skeptical. Most often we dream about activities we have recently engaged in, but it is possible that a course of action is dreamed about so vividly that it will suggest an actual course of action in the dreamer's life. However, according to Aristotle, most cases of apparent prophecy by dreams are to be taken as mere coincidences:

> [Just as] mentioning a particular person is neither token nor cause of this person's presenting himself, so, in the parallel instance, the dream is, to him who has seen it, neither token nor cause of its fulfillment, but a mere coincidence. Hence the fact that many dreams have no "fulfillment," for coincidences do not occur according to any universal or general law. . . . For the principle which is expressed in the gambler's maxim: "If you make many throws your luck must change,"

holds good [for dreams] also. (Barnes, 1984, Vol. 1, p. 737)

Motivation

Happiness, for Aristotle, was doing what is natural because doing so fulfills one's purpose. For humans, our purpose is to think rationally and therefore doing so brings the greatest happiness. However, humans are also biological organisms characterized by the functions of nutrition, sensation, reproduction, and movement. That is, although humans are distinct from other animals (because of our reasoning ability), we do share many of their motives. Like other animals, much human behavior is motivated by appetites. Action is always directed at the satisfaction of an appetite. That is, behavior is motivated by such internal states as hunger, sexual arousal, thirst, or the desire for bodily comfort. Because the existence of an appetite causes discomfort, it stimulates activity that will eliminate it. If the activity is successful, the animal or person experiences pleasure. Much human behavior, then, like all animal behavior, is hedonistic; its purpose is to bring pleasure or to avoid pain.

Unlike other animals, however, we can use our rational powers to inhibit our appetites. Furthermore, our greatest happiness does not come from satisfying our biological needs. Rather, it comes from exercising our rational powers to their fullest. Given the fact that humans have both appetites and rational powers, conflict often arises between the immediate satisfaction of our appetites and more remote rational goals. Even the best of humans, however, are capable of acting hedonistically rather than rationally: "For desire is a wild beast, and passion perverts the minds of rulers, even when they are the best of men" (Barnes, 1984, vol. 2, p. 2042). According to Aristotle, the lives of many humans are governed by nothing more than the pleasure and pain that comes from the satisfaction and frustration of appetites. These people are indistinguishable from animals. Appetites and reason are part of every human, but his or her character is revealed by which of the two dominates.

The Emotions and Selective Perception

In general, the emotions, in Aristotelian philosophy, had the function of amplifying any existing tendency. For example, people might run more quickly if they were frightened than if they were merely jogging for exercise. Also, the emotions provide a motive for acting—for example, people might be inclined to fight if they are angry. However, the emotions may also influence how people perceive things; that is, they may cause *selective perception*. Aristotle gave the following examples:

> We are easily deceived respecting the operations of sense-perception when we are excited by emotion, and different persons according to their different emotions; for example, the coward when excited by fear and the amorous person by amorous desire; so that with but little resemblance to go upon, the former thinks he sees his foes approaching, the latter that he sees the object of his desire; and the more deeply one is under the influence of the emotion, the less similarity is required to give rise to these impressions. Thus, too, in fits of anger, and also in all states of appetite, all men become easily deceived, and more so the more their emotions are excited. (Barnes, 1984, Vol. 1, p. 732)

Aristotle made several mistakes. For example, he assigned thinking and common sense to the heart and claimed that the main function of the brain was to cool the blood. He also believed that the number of species of living things in the world was fixed and thereby denied evolution. But compared to his many positive contributions, his mistakes are minor. Although many of his observations were incorrect, he did observe almost everything, and in doing so, he brought Greek philosophy to new heights.

THE IMPORTANCE OF EARLY GREEK PHILOSOPHY

To realize the importance of the early Greek philosophers, remembering Popper's philosophy of science is important. As we saw in chapter

1, Popperian science consists of specifying a problem, proposing solutions to the problem, and attempting to refute the proposed solutions. What survives in such a process is a solution to a problem that, at the moment, cannot be refuted. Again, the highest status that a proposed solution to a problem can ever attain is *not yet disconfirmed*. The assumption in Popper's view of science is that all scientific "facts" and "theories" will eventually be found to be false.

What has this to do with the importance of early Greek philosophy? In Popper's view, science began when humans first began to question the stories that they were told about themselves and the world. According to Brett, "The Greek cosmologists were important because they broke loose from the accepted religious traditions and produced what they considered to be better stories about the origin and stuff of the world. They speculated" (1965, p. 38). Not only did the Greek philosophers speculate, but they also respected the speculations of others. With the exception of the Pythagoreans, who created a secretive cult designed to perpetuate dogma, the Greek philosophers engaged in open, critical discussion of each other's ideas. For Popper, this willingness to engage in critical discussion was the beginning of an extremely important tradition:

> Here is a unique phenomenon, and it is closely connected with the astonishing freedom and creativeness of Greek philosophy. How can we explain this phenomenon? *What we have to explain is the rise of a tradition.* It is a tradition that allows or encourages critical discussions between various schools and, more surprisingly still, within one and the same school. For nowhere outside the Pythagorean school do we find a school devoted to the preservation of a doctrine. Instead we find changes, new ideas, modifications, and outright criticism of the master. (1958, p. 27)

As we have seen, Popper attributes the founding of this new tradition of freedom to Thales, who not only could tolerate criticism but also encouraged it. According to Popper, this was a "momentous innovation" because it broke with the dogmatic tradition that permitted only one true doctrine and permitted a plurality of doctrines all attempting to approach the truth via critical discussion. Coupled with this tradition of free, critical discussion is the realization that our inquiries are never final but always tentative and capable of improvement. Popper says of this tradition,

> It . . . leads, almost by necessity, to the realization that our attempts to see and to find the truth are not final, but open to improvement; that our knowledge, our doctrine, is conjectural; that it consists of guesses, of hypotheses, rather than of final and certain truths; and that criticism and critical discussion are our only means of getting nearer to the truth. It thus leads to the tradition of bold conjectures and of free criticism, the tradition which created the rational or

scientific attitude, and with it our Western civilization. (1958, p. 29)

Aristotle died in 322 B.C. at the age of 62. His death marked the end of the Golden Age of Greece, which had started about 300 years earlier with the philosophy of Thales. Most, if not all, of the philosophical concepts that have been pursued ever since this Golden Age were produced during this period. After Aristotle's death, philosophers began either to rely on the teaching of past authorities or they turned their attention to questions concerning models for human conduct. It was not until the Renaissance, many centuries after Aristotle's death, that the critical tradition of the early Greek philosophers was rediscovered and revived.

SUMMARY

Primitive humans looked upon everything in nature as if it were alive; there was no distinction between the animate and the inanimate—this was called animism. Moreover, there was a tendency to project human feelings and emotion onto nature, and this was called anthropomorphism. A spirit or ghost was thought to reside in everything, giving it life. The course of natural events was explained in terms of the whims and wishes of these resident spirits. The dwelling of a spirit in humans explained such things as dreams and illness, and the spirit's permanent departure resulted in death; although when the body died, the spirit was thought to continue living. An array of magical practices evolved that were designed to influence various spirits. These practices gave humans the feeling that they had some control over nature. Early Greek religion was of two main types: Olympian, which consisted of a number of gods whose activities were very much like those of upper-class Greeks, and Dionysiac-Orphic, which preached that the soul was a prisoner of the body and that it longed to be released so that it could once again dwell among the gods. Whereas Olympian religion was the favorite of the wealthier Greeks, Dionysiac-Orphic religion was favored by the lower classes.

The first philosophers emphasized natural explanations instead of supernatural ones. They sought a primary element, called the physis, from which everything was made. For Thales, the physis was water; for Anaximander, it was the boundless; for Heraclitus, it was fire; for Parmenides, it was the "one" or "changelessness"; for Pythagoras, it was numbers; for Democritus, it was the atom; and for Hippocrates and Empedocles, there were four primary elements: water, earth, fire, and air. The earliest Greek philosophers were called cosmologists because they sought to explain the origin, structure, and processes of the universe (cosmos). Besides the four elements, Empedocles postulated the forces of love, which tends to bring the elements together, and strife, which tends to separate them. When the mixture of elements and forces is just right, parts of animals and humans form and combine into almost all possible arrangements. Only a limited number of the random arrangements were capable of survival, and humans were among them.

The debate between Heraclitus, who believed everything was constantly changing, and Parmenides, who believed nothing ever changed, raised a number of epistemological questions such as What, if anything, is permanent enough to be known with certainty? and If sensory experience provides information only about a continually changing world, how can it be a source of knowledge? These and related questions have persisted to the present.

Most of the first philosophers were monists because they made no distinction between the mind and the body; whatever element or elements they arrived at were supposed to account for everything. In Pythagoras, however, we have a full-fledged dualism between the mind and the body and between the physical and the abstract. Numbers were abstractions but were real, and they could be known only by rational thought, not by sensory experience. Sensory experience could only inhibit attainment of abstract knowledge and was to be avoided. The mind, or soul, was thought to be immortal. The mind–body dualism that the Pythagoreans emphasized has remained part of philosophy, psychology, and natural science.

Early Greek medicine was temple medicine based on superstition and magical practices. Through the efforts of such individuals as Alcmaeon and Hippocrates, medical practice became objective and naturalistic. Displacing such beliefs as illness being due to the possession of spirits was the belief that health resulted from a balance among bodily elements or processes and illness from an imbalance.

The Sophists concluded that there were many equally valid philosophical positions. "Truth" was believed to be a function of a person's education, personal experiences, culture, and beliefs, and whether this "truth" was accepted by others depended on one's communicative skills. Socrates agreed with the Sophists that truth was subjective, but he also believed that a careful examination of one's subjective experiences would reveal certain concepts or principles that were stable and knowable and which, when known, would generate proper conduct.

Plato, influenced by the Pythagoreans, took Socrates' belief an additional step by saying that principles, ideas, or concepts had an independent existence, just as the Pythagorean number did. For Plato, ideas or forms were the ultimate reality, and they could be known only by reason. Sensory experience leads only to ignorance—or at best, opinion—and should be avoided. The soul, before becoming implanted in the body, dwells in pure and complete knowledge, which can be remembered if one turns one's thoughts inward and away from the empirical world. For Plato, knowledge results from remembering what the soul experienced prior to its implantation in the body. This is called the reminiscence theory of knowledge. Plato believed that the rational powers of the mind (rationalism) should be turned inward (introspection) to rediscover ideas that had been present at birth (nativism).

Aristotle was also interested in principles instead of isolated facts, but unlike Plato he felt that the way to find principles was to examine nature. Instead of urging the avoidance of sensory experience, he claimed that it was the source of all knowledge. Aristotle's brand of rationalism relied heavily on empiricism because he believed that principles are derived from the careful scrutiny of sensory observations. He believed that all things contained an entelechy, or purpose. An acorn, for example, has the potential to become an oak tree, and its purpose is to do so. There were three categories of living things: those possessing a vegetative soul, those possessing a sensitive soul, and those possessing a rational soul. Humans alone possess a rational soul, which has two functions: passive reason and active reason. Passive reason ponders information from the five senses and from the common sense, whereas the common sense synthesizes sensory information. Active reason is used to isolate enduring principles (essences) that manifest themselves in sensory experience. Aristotle considered active reason immortal. He also postulated an unmoved mover that was the entelechy for all of nature; it caused everything else but was not itself caused by anything. Aristotle believed that nature was organized on a grand scale ranging from formless matter to plants, to animals, to humans, and finally to the unmoved mover. Because humans have much in common with other animals, we can learn about ourselves by studying them.

Aristotle distinguished between memory, which was spontaneous, and recall, which was the active search for a recollection of a past experience. It was with regard to recall that Aristotle postulated his laws of association—the laws of contiguity, frequency, similarity, and contrast. Aristotle explained imagination and dreaming as the pondering of images that linger after sensory experience has ceased. Contrary to what almost everyone else at the time believed, Aristotle believed that dreams do not foretell the future and if they appear to do so it is because of coincidence. Humans are motivated by their very nature to engage their rational powers in an effort to attain knowledge. In addition, however, we have appetites not unlike those of other animals. The presence of an appetite stimulates behavior that will satisfy it. When an appetite is satisfied, the person or animal experiences pleasure; when it is not satisfied, pain is experienced. Human rationality can and should be used to control appetites and emotions, but both sometimes overwhelm even the best of humans. Emotions amplify ongoing thoughts and behavior and sometimes cause people to selectively perceive or misperceive events in the environment. Although Aristotle made several mistakes, his accomplishments far exceed his failures.

Early Greek philosophy was significant because it replaced supernatural explanations with naturalistic ones and because it encouraged the open criticism and evaluation of ideas.

DISCUSSION QUESTIONS

1. Describe some of the events that may have concerned primitive humans and discuss how they accounted for and attempted to control those events.

2. Summarize the major differences between Olympian and Dionysiac-Orphic religion.

3. What distinguishes the attempts of the first philosophers to understand nature from the attempts of those who preceded them?

4. What did the cosmologists attempt to do?

5. Why were the first philosophers called physicists? List the physes arrived at by Thales, Anaximander, Heraclitus, Parmenides, Pythagoras, Empedocles, and Democritus.

6. Summarize Empedocles' view of the universe

7. Summarize Empedocles' view of how species of animals, including humans, came into existence.

8. What epistemological question did Heraclitus's philosophy raise?

9. Give examples of how logic was used to defend Parmenides' belief that change and motion were illusions.

10. Differentiate between elementism and reductionism and give an example of each.

11. What were the major differences between temple medicine and the type of medicine practiced by Alcmaeon and Hippocrates?

12. How did the Sophists differ from the philosophers who preceded them? What was their attitude toward knowledge? In what way did Socrates agree with the Sophists, and in what way did he disagree?

13. What observations did Xenophanes make about religion?

14. What, for Socrates, was the goal of philosophical inquiry? What method did he use in pursuing that goal?

15. Describe Plato's theory of forms or ideas.

16. In Plato's philosophy, what was the analogy of the divided line?

17. Summarize Plato's cave allegory. What points was Plato making with this allegory?

18. Discuss Plato's reminiscence theory of knowledge.

19. Compare Aristotle's attitude toward sensory experience with that of Plato.

20. Provide evidence that Aristotle's philosophy had both rational and empirical components.

21. According to Aristotle, what were the four causes of things?

22. Discuss Aristotle's concept of entelechy.

23. Discuss Aristotle's concept of *scala naturae* and indicate how that concept justifies a comparative psychology.

24. Discuss the relationship among sensory experience, common sense, passive reason, and active reason.

25. Summarize Aristotle's views on imagination and dreaming.

26. Discuss Aristotle's views on motivation.

27. Discuss Aristotle's views on emotions.

28. In Aristotle's philosophy, what was the function of the unmoved mover?

29. Describe the laws of association that Aristotle proposed.

30. Summarize the reasons Greek philosophy was important to the development of Western civilization.

SUGGESTIONS FOR FURTHER READING

Barnes, J. (1982). *The presocratic philosophers*. London: Routledge/Kegan Paul.

Barnes covers the contributions of such philosophers as Thales, Anaximander, Heraclitus, Xenophanes, Pythagoras, Parmenides, Protagoras, Empedocles, Gorgias, and Democritus in much greater detail than in his shorter 1987 book described below. (Available in paperback.)

Barnes, J. (1987). *Early Greek philosophy*. New York: Viking Press/Penguin Books.

This is an excellent sampling of the remaining fragments of the works of the pre-Socratic Greek philosophers and discussion of the meaning of those fragments. Many of the philosophers mentioned in your textbook are discussed in greater detail—for example, Thales, Anaximander, Pythagoras, Alcmaeon, Heraclitus, Parmenides, Empedocles, and Democritus. (Available in paperback.)

Bowra, C. M. (1957). *The Greek experience*. New York: New American Library.

This is an authoritative discussion of not only Greek philosophy but also of Greek sculpture, painting, poetry, drama, law, politics, religion, and mythology. The book is generously illustrated with pictures of

Greek architecture, sculpture, painting, and coinage. (Available in paperback.)

Clagett, M. (1963). *Greek science in antiquity*. New York: Macmillan.

This book traces Greek medicine, biology, mathematics, physics, and astronomy from their primitive origins through their assimilation into the Roman Empire. Many line drawings illustrate scientific concepts. (Available in paperback.)

Hathorn, R. Y. (1977). *Greek mythology*. Beirut, Lebanon: American University of Beirut.

This is a detailed and fascinating account of the gods and myths that characterized Olympian, Dionysian, and other religions and mythologies of the Greek world prior to and during the time of the first philoso-

phers. By reading this book, one can easily see the beliefs on which later philosophies and religions were built.

Robinson, D. N. (1989). *Aristotle's psychology*. New York: Columbia University Press.

Robinson does a remarkable job of abstracting from Aristotle's many works those that apply especially to psychology. He discusses Aristotle's thoughts on ethology, psychobiology, perception, learning, memory, emotion, motivation, rationality, volition, the self, and morality. This book is a little difficult for the beginning student but well worth the effort. (Available only in hardback, but the book is only 144 pages long.)

GLOSSARY

Active reason According to Aristotle, the faculty of the soul that searches for the essences or abstract principles that manifest themselves in the empirical world. Aristotle thought that the active reason part of the soul was immortal.

Alcmaeon (ca. 500 B.C.) One of the first Greek physicians to move away from the magic and superstition of temple medicine and toward a naturalistic understanding and treatment of illness.

Allegory of the cave Plato's description of individuals who live their lives in accordance with the shadows of reality provided by sensory experience instead of in accordance with the true reality beyond sensory experience.

Analogy of the divided line Plato's illustration of his contention that there is a hierarchy of understanding. The lowest type of understanding is based on images of empirical objects. Next highest is an understanding of empirical objects themselves, which results only in opinion; next is an understanding of abstract mathematical principles; next is an understanding of the forms; the highest understanding (true knowledge) is an understanding of the form of the good and includes a knowledge of all forms and their organization.

Anaximander (ca. 610–540 B.C.) Suggested the "infinite" or "boundless" as the physis and formulated a rudimentary theory of evolution.

Animism The belief that everything in nature is alive.

Anthropomorphism The projection of human attributes onto nonhuman things.

Aristotle (384–322 B.C.) Believed sensory experience to be the basis of all knowledge, although the five senses and the common sense provided only the information from which knowledge could be derived. Aristotle also believed that everything in nature had within it an entelechy (purpose) that determined its potential. Active reason, which was considered the immortal part of the human soul, provided humans with their greatest potential, and therefore fully actualized humans engage in active reason. Because everything was

thought to have a cause, Aristotle postulated an unmoved mover that caused everything in the world but was not itself caused.

Associationism The philosophical belief that mental phenomena, such as learning, remembering, and imagining, can be explained in terms of the laws of association.

Becoming According to Heraclitus, the state of everything in the universe. Nothing is static and unchanging; rather, everything in the universe is dynamic, that is, becoming something other than what it was.

Being Something that is unchanging and thus, in principle, is capable of being known with certainty. Being implies stability and certainty; becoming implies instability and uncertainty.

Common sense According to Aristotle, the faculty located in the heart that synthesizes the information provided by the five senses.

Cosmology The study of the origin, structure, and the processes governing the universe.

Democritus (ca. 460–370 B.C.) Offered atoms as the physis. Everything in nature, including humans, was explained in terms of atoms and their activities. His was the first completely naturalistic view of the world and of humans. There was no mind–body distinction and no immortal soul. Democritus also refined Empedocles' theory of perception. According to Democritus, eidola from environmental objects enter the body through one or more of the five sensory systems and are transmitted to the brain, where the highly mobile fire atoms form copies of them. This match between eidola and the fire atoms results in perception. Democritus's philosophy was materialistic, deterministic, elementistic, and reductionistic.

Dionysiac-Orphic religion Religion whose major belief was that the soul becomes a prisoner of the body because of some transgression committed by the soul. The soul continues on a circle of transmigrations until it has been purged of sin, at which time it can escape its earthly existence and return to its pure, divine existence among the gods. A number of magical practices were thought useful in releasing the soul from its bodily tomb.

Dreaming According to Aristotle, the experience of images retained from waking experience. Dreams are often bizarre because the images experienced during sleep are neither organized by our rational powers nor supported by ongoing sensory experience. That dreams sometimes correspond to future events was, for Aristotle, mere coincidence.

Efficient cause According to Aristotle, the force that transforms a thing.

Eidolon (plural, **eidola**) A tiny replication that some early Greek philosophers thought emanated from the surfaces of things in the environment, allowing the things to be perceived.

Elementism The belief that complex processes can be understood by studying the elements of which they consist.

Empedocles (ca. 495–435 B.C.) Postulated earth, fire, air, and water as the four basic elements from which everything is made and two forces, love and strife, that alternately synthesize and separate those elements. He was also the first philosopher to suggest a theory of perception, and he offered a theory of evolution that emphasized a rudimentary form of natural selection.

Empiricism The belief that knowledge is based on that which can be directly experienced.

Entelechy According to Aristotle, the purpose for which a thing exists and which remains a potential until actualized. Active reason, for example, is the human entelechy, but it exists only as a potential in many humans.

Essence Those indispensable characteristics of a thing that gives it its unique identity.

Final cause According to Aristotle, the purpose for which a thing exists.

Formal cause According to Aristotle, the form of a thing.

Forms According to Plato, the pure, abstract realities that are unchanging and timeless and therefore knowable. Such forms create imperfect manifestations of themselves when they interact with matter. It is these imperfect manifestations of the forms that are the objects of our sense impressions. (*See also* **Theory of forms**.)

Galen (A.D. 130–200) Associated each of Hippocrates' four humors with a temperament, thus creating a rudimentary theory of personality.

Gorgias (ca. 485–380 B.C.) A Sophist who believed that the only reality that a person can experience is his or her subjective reality and that this reality can never be communicated to another individual.

Heraclitus (ca. 540–480 B.C.) Suggested fire as the physis because in its presence nothing remained the same. He viewed the world as in a constant state of flux and thereby raised the question as to what could be known with certainty.

Hippocrates (ca. 460–377 B.C.) Considered the father of modern medicine because he assumed that disease had natural causes, not supernatural ones. Health prevails when the four humors of the body are in balance, disease when there is an imbalance. The phy-

sician's task was to facilitate the body's natural tendency to heal itself.

Idealist One who believes that the ultimate reality consists of ideas. Plato was an idealist.

Imagination According to Aristotle, the pondering of the images retained from past experiences.

Inductive definition The technique used by Socrates that examined many individual examples of a concept to discover what they all had in common.

Introspection The careful examination of one's subjective experiences.

Law of contiguity A thought of something will tend to cause thoughts of things that are usually experienced along with it.

Law of contrast A thought of something will tend to cause thoughts of opposite things.

Law of frequency The more often something is experienced, the easier it will be to recall it.

Law of similarity A thought of something will tend to cause thoughts of similar things.

Laws of association Those laws thought responsible for holding mental events together and thus making them meaningful. For Aristotle, the laws of association consisted of the laws of contiguity, frequency, contrast, and similarity.

Magic Various ceremonies and rituals that are designed to influence spirits.

Material cause According to Aristotle, what a thing is made of.

Nativist One who believes that an important human attribute is innate and therefore not derived from experience.

Nihilism The belief that there is no certain truth, and even if there were, it could not be communicated from one person to another. The Sophists were nihilists.

Olympian religion The religion based on a belief in the Olympian gods as they were described in the Homeric poems. Olympian religion was favored by the privileged classes, whereas peasants, laborers, and slaves favored the more mystical Dionysiac-Orphic religion. (*See also* **Dionysiac-Orphic religion**.)

Parmenides (fl. ca. 515 B.C.) Believed that the world was solid, fixed, and motionless and therefore that all apparent change or motion was an illusion.

Passive reason According to Aristotle, the practical utilization of the information provided by the common sense.

Physicist A person who searches for or postulates a physis.

Physis A primary substance or element from which everything is thought to be derived.

Plato (ca. 427–347 B.C.) First a disciple of Socrates, came under the influence of the Pythagoreans, and postulated the existence of an abstract world of forms or ideas that, when manifested in matter, make up the objects in the empirical world. The only true knowledge is that of the forms, a knowledge that can be gained only by reflecting on the innate contents of the soul. Sensory experience interferes with the attainment of knowledge and should be avoided.

Protagoras (ca. 485–415 B.C.) A Sophist who taught that "man is the measure of all things." In other words, what is considered true varies with a person's personal experiences; therefore, there is no objective truth, only individual versions of what is true.

Pythagoras (ca. 580–500 B.C.) Believed that an abstract world consisting of numbers and numerical relationships exerted an influence on the physical world. He created a dualistic view of humans by saying that in addition to our body we have a mind (soul), which through reasoning could understand the abstract world of numbers. Furthermore, he believed the human soul to be immortal. Pythagoras's philosophy had a major influence on Plato and, through Christianity, on the entire Western world.

Rationalism The belief that knowledge is attained by mentally embracing some abstract principle or concept.

Rational soul According to Aristotle, the soul possessed only by humans. It incorporates the functions of the vegetative and sensitive souls and allows thinking about events in the empirical world (passive reason) and the abstraction of the principles that characterize events in the empirical world (active reason).

Recall For Aristotle, the active mental search for past experiences.

Reductionism The attempt to explain objects or events in one domain by using terminology, concepts, laws, or principles from another domain. Explaining observable phenomena (domain$_1$) in terms of atomic theory (domain$_2$) would be an example; explaining human behavior and cognition (domain$_1$) in terms of biochemical principles (domain$_2$) would be another. In a sense, it can be said that events in domain$_1$ are *reduced* to events in domain$_2$.

Remembering For Aristotle, the passive recollection of past experiences.

Reminiscence theory of knowledge Plato's belief that knowledge is attained by remembering the experiences the soul had when it dwelt among the forms before entering the body.

Scala naturae Aristotle's description of nature as being arranged in a hierarchy from formless matter to the unmoved mover. In this grand design, the only thing higher than humans was the unmoved mover.

Sensitive soul According to Aristotle, the soul possessed by animals. It allows the functions provided by the vegetative soul and provides the ability to interact with the environment and to retain the information gained from that interaction.

Socrates (469–399 B.C.) Disagreed with the Sophists' contention that there is no objective truth but only subjective opinion. Socrates believed that by examining a number of individual manifestations of a principle or concept, the general principle or concept itself could be defined clearly and precisely. These general definitions were stable and knowable and, when known, generated moral behavior.

Solipsism The belief that a person's subjective reality is the only reality that exists and can be known.

Sophists A group of philosopher-teachers who believed that "truth" was what people thought it to be. To convince others that something is "true," one needs effective communication skills, and it was those skills that the Sophists taught.

Teleology The belief that nature is purposive. Aristotle's philosophy was teleological.

Temple medicine The type of medicine practiced by priests in early Greek temples that was characterized by superstition and magic. Individuals such as Alcmaeon and Hippocrates severely criticized temple medicine and were instrumental in displacing such practices with naturalistic medicine—that is, medicine that sought natural causes of disorders rather than supernatural causes.

Thales (ca. 625–545 B.C.) Often called the first philosopher because he emphasized natural instead of supernatural explanations of things. By encouraging the critical evaluation of his ideas and those of others, he is thought to have started the Golden Age of Greek philosophy. He believed water to be the primary element from which everything else was derived.

Theory of forms Plato's contention that ultimate reality consists of abstract ideas or forms that correspond to all objects in the empirical world. Knowledge of these abstractions is innate and can be attained only through introspection.

Transmigration of the soul The Dionysiac-Orphic belief that because of some transgression the soul is compelled to dwell in one earthly prison after another until it is purified. The transmigration may find the soul at various times in plants, animals, and humans as it seeks redemption.

Unmoved mover According to Aristotle, that which gave nature its purpose, or final cause, but was itself uncaused. In Aristotle's philosophy, the unmoved mover was a logical necessity.

Vegetative soul The soul possessed by plants. It allows only growth, the intake of nutrition, and reproduction.

Xenophanes (ca. 560–478 B.C.) Believed people created gods in their own image. He noted that dark-skinned people created dark-skinned gods and light-skinned people created light-skinned gods. He speculated that the gods created by nonhuman animals would have animal characteristics.

Zeno's paradox The assertion that in order for an object to pass from point A to point B, it must first traverse half the distance between those two points, and then half of the remaining distance, and so forth. Because this process must occur an infinite number of times, Zeno concluded that an object could logically never reach point B.

CHAPTER 3

After Aristotle:
A Search for the Good Life

After Sparta defeated Athens in the Peloponnesian War (431–404 B.C.) the Greek city-states began to collapse, and the Greek people became increasingly demoralized. In this postwar atmosphere, Socrates, Plato, and Aristotle flourished, but a gulf was beginning to develop between philosophy and the psychological needs of the people. Shortly after Aristotle's death (322 B.C.), the Romans invaded Greek territory, making an already unstable situation even more uncertain. In this time of great personal strife, complex and abstract philosophies were of little comfort. A more worldly philosophy was needed, a philosophy that addressed the problems of everyday living. The major questions were no longer What is the nature of physical reality? or What and how can humans know? but rather How is it best to live? or What is the nature of the good life? or What is worth believing in? In response to the latter questions emerged the philosophies of the Skeptics, Cynics, Epicureans, Stoics, and, finally, the Christians.

SKEPTICISM AND CYNICISM

Both Skepticism and Cynicism were critical of other philosophies, contending that they were either completely false or irrelevant to human needs. As a solution, Skepticism promoted a suspension of belief in anything, and Cynicism promoted a retreat from society.

Skepticism

Pyrrho (ca. 365–275 B.C.) founded the school of **Skepticism** based on a mistrust of any so-called essences or universal truths. As we have seen, many Greek philosophers (Pythagoras, Plato, and Aristotle) were skeptical concerning the ability of sensory information to provide knowledge. It was believed that such information should either be avoided in one's quest for knowledge or used only as a starting point. Pyrrho extended Skepticism to moral and rational concerns. For him, no rational grounds existed for preferring one course of action over another. Rather than agonizing over such matters, he taught that one should merely conform to the customs of whatever country one was inhabiting:

> A modern disciple [of Skepticism] would go to church on Sundays and perform the correct genuflexions, but without any of the religious beliefs that are supposed to inspire these actions. Ancient Sceptics went through the whole pagan ritual, and were even sometimes priests; their Scepticism assured them that this behaviour could not be proved wrong, and their common sense . . . assured them that it was convenient. (Russell, 1945, p. 233)

It should be pointed out that the philosophy of Skepticism was not one only of *doubt*. The Skeptic was not saying, "At this moment I don't know, but someday I might" or "I think I know, but I'm not sure." The Skeptics held "that no one at all could know anything at all; and with commendable consistency they proceeded to deny that they themselves knew even that distressing fact" (Barnes, 1982, p. 136).

No matter what one believed, it could turn out to be false, and therefore one could avoid the frustration of being wrong by simply not believing in anything. There is a kinship between the Skeptics and the earlier Sophists such as Protagoras, who said all things are equally true, and Gorgias, who said all things are equally false. Both the Skeptic and the Sophist advised people to suspend belief but to act pragmatically.

Cynicism

Antisthenes (ca. 445–365 B.C.) completely lost faith in philosophy and renounced his comfortable upper-class life. He believed that society, with its emphasis on material goods, status, and employment, was a distortion of nature and should be avoided. Questioning the value of art, mathematics, and learning, Antisthenes preached a back-to-nature philosophy that involved a life free from wants and passions and from the many conventions of society. He thought that true happiness depended on self-sufficiency. It was the quest for the simple, independent, natural life that characterized **Cynicism**. The following is an account of the type of life that Antisthenes lived after he renounced his aristocratic life:

> He would have nothing but simple goodness. He associated with working men, and dressed as one of them. He took to open-air preaching, in a style that the uneducated could understand. All refined philosophy he held to be worthless; what could be known, could be known by the plain man. He believed in the "return to nature," and carried this belief very far. There was to be no government, no private property, no marriage, no established religion. His followers, if not he himself, condemned slavery. . . . He despised luxury and all pursuit of artificial pleasures of the senses. (Russell, 1945, pp. 230–231)

The considerable fame of Antisthenes was even exceeded by his disciple **Diogenes** (ca. 412–323 B.C.), the son of a disreputable money-changer who had been sent to prison for defacing money. Diogenes decided to outdo his father by defacing the "currency" of the world. Conventional labels such as *king*, *general*, *honor*, *wisdom*, and *happiness* were social currencies that needed to be exposed, that is, defaced. In his personal life, Diogenes rejected conventional religion, manners, housing, food, and fashion. He lived by begging and proclaimed his brotherhood with not only all humans but also animals. It is said that Alexander the Great once visited him and asked if he could do him any favor; "Only to stand out of my light" was his answer (Russell, 1945, p. 231). Diogenes lived an extremely primitive life and was given the nickname "Cynic," which means doglike. Originally, the Cynic was one who retreated from society and lived close to nature.

Diogenes equated virtue with liberation from the desire for material things, for such things are precarious and transitory. Only the contentment that comes from resignation is secure and therefore worth pursuing. Clearly, the Cynic philosophy was most appealing to people who experienced disappointment in the world and therefore sought a retreat from it. For such individuals, subjective values were more important than material goods. As we will see next, much of Cynicism survived in Stoicism; the Stoic, however, did not feel the need to reject the amenities of civilization. The Cynics not only encouraged social disengagement, but they also attacked society for being characterized by hypocrisy, greed, envy, and hate. Happiness results only when an individual acts naturally; nothing natural, said the Cynics, can be bad. Living in accordance with social conventions, making sacrifices for others, patriotism, and devotion to a common cause are just plain foolish. Besides individualism, Cynics typically advocated free love and viewed themselves as citizens of the world rather than of any particular country.

EPICUREANISM AND STOICISM

Epicureanism and **Stoicism** were responses to the claim of the Skeptics and Cynics that philosophy had nothing useful to say about everyday life. Both were philosophies that spoke directly to the moral conduct of humans, and both were based on experience in the empirical world.

Epicureanism

Epicurus (ca. 341–270 B.C.) based his philosophy on Democritus's atomism but rejected his determinism. According to Epicurus, the atoms making up humans never lose their ability to move freely; hence, he postulated free will. Epicurus agreed with Democritus that there was no afterlife because the soul was made up of freely moving atoms that scattered upon death. Atoms were never created or destroyed; they were only rearranged. It followed that the atoms comprising an individual would become part of another configuration following the individual's death. However, it was assumed that nothing was retained or transferred from one configuration to another. In this way, Epicurus freed humans from one of their major concerns: What is life like after death, and how should one prepare for it? The good life must be attained in this world, for there is no other. In general, Epicurus believed that postulating supernatural influences in nature was a source of terror for most people and that the idea of immortality destroyed the only hope most people had for finally escaping pain. Epicurus did believe in the Olympian gods, but he felt that they did not concern themselves with the world or with human affairs. The Epicureans preferred naturalistic explanations to supernatural ones, and they strongly protested against magic, astrology, and divination. It was this disbelief in supernatural influences that led Epicurus's passionate disciple Lucretius (ca. 99–55 B.C.) to pridefully refer to him as "destroyer of religion."

Epicurus and his followers lived simple lives. For example, their food and drink consisted mainly of bread and water, which was all right with Epicurus: "I am thrilled with pleasure in the body when I live on bread and water, and I spit on luxurious pleasures, not for their own sake, but because of the inconveniences that follow them" (Russell, 1945, p. 242). Intense pleasure was to be avoided because it was often followed by pain (e.g., indigestion following eating or drinking too much) or because such uncommon pleasure would make common experiences

Epicurus

less pleasant. Thus, the type of hedonism prescribed by Epicurus emphasized the pleasure that results from having one's basic needs satisfied. In this sense, the good life for the Epicurean consisted more of the absence of pain than the presence of pleasure—at least, intense pleasure. Epicurus urged his followers to avoid power and fame because such things make others envious and they may become enemies. Wise individuals attempt to live their lives unnoticed. Insofar as the Epicureans have been characterized as fun-seeking hedonists, that characterization is inaccurate. Concerning sexual intercourse, Epicurus said, "[It] has never done a man good and he is lucky if it has not harmed him" (Russell, 1945, p. 245). For Epicurus, the highest form of social pleasure was friendship.

We see then, that according to Epicurus, the goal of life was individual happiness, but his notion of happiness was not a simple **hedonism** (i.e., seeking pleasure and avoiding pain). He was more interested in a person's long-term happiness, which could be attained only by avoiding extremes. Extreme pleasures are short-lived and ultimately result in pain or frustration; thus, humans should strive for the tranquility that comes from a balance between the lack and an excess of something. Therefore, humans cannot simply follow their impulses to attain the good life; reason and choice must be exercised in order to provide a balanced life, which in turn provides the greatest amount of pleasure over the longest period of time. For Epicurus, the good life was free, simple, rational, and moderate.

Epicureanism survived with diminishing influence for 600 years following the death of Epicurus. As people became increasingly oppressed by the miseries of life, however, they looked to philosophy and religion for greater comfort than was provided by Cynicism, Skepticism, and Epicureanism. The philosophers and theologians responded by becoming increasingly mystical. By the time Christianity emerged, it was believed that the best life was the one beyond the grave, thus completely reversing the Epicurean position.

Stoicism

Because **Zeno of Citium** (ca. 333–262 B.C.) taught in a school that had a *stoa poikile*, a covered hallway of many colors, his philosophy came to be known as Stoicism (Russell, 1959, p. 110). Zeno believed that the world was ruled by a divine plan and that everything in nature, including humans, was there for a reason. The Stoics believed that to live in accordance with nature was the ultimate virtue. The most important derivative of this "divine plan" theory was the belief that whatever happens, happens for a reason; that there are no accidents; and that it must simply be accepted as part of the plan. The good life involved accepting one's fate with indifference, even if suffering was involved. Indeed, courage in the face of suffering or danger was considered most admirable. You must die, but you need not die groaning; you must be imprisoned, but you need not whine; you must suffer exile, but you can do so with a smile, courage, and at peace. Your body can be chained, but not your will. In short, a Stoic is a person who may be sick, in pain, in peril, dying, in exile, or disgraced but is still happy: "Every man is an actor in a play, in which God has assigned the parts; it is our duty to perform our part worthily, whatever it may be" (Russell, 1945, p. 264).

The Stoics did not highly value material possessions because they could be lost or taken away. Virtue alone was important. All people were expected to accept their stations in life and perform their duties without question. The joy in life came in knowing that one was participating in a master plan, even if that plan was incomprehensible to the individual. The only personal freedom was in choosing whether to act in accordance with nature's plan. When the individual's will was compatible with natural law, the individual was virtuous. When it was not, the individual was immoral. The Stoics did not solve the problem of how the human will can be free in a completely determined universe. The same problem re-emerges within Christianity because an all-knowing, all-powerful God is postulated along with the human ability to choose between good and evil. In fact, both the Stoics and the Christians had trouble explaining the existence of both evil and sinners. If everything in the universe was planned by a beneficent providence, what accounts for evil, the ability to choose evil, and those humans who do so?

In the Roman Empire, Stoicism won out over Epicureanism perhaps because Stoicism was compatible with the Roman emphasis on law and order. The widespread appeal of Stoicism can be seen in the fact that it was embraced by Seneca (ca. 3 B.C.–A.D. 65), a philosopher; Epictetus (ca. A.D. 55–100), a slave; and Marcus Aurelius (A.D. 121–180), an emperor. As long as the Roman government provided minimal happiness and safety, Stoicism remained the accepted philosophy, but then the Roman Empire began to fail. There was government corruption, crop failures, economic problems, and barbarian invasions, which could not be stopped. The people sought a new definition of the good life, one that would provide comfort and hope in perilous times. It was time to look toward the heavens for help. Before turning to the Christian alternative, however, we must look briefly at another philosophy that became part of Christian thought.

NEOPLATONISM

Besides Stoicism and Epicureanism, there appeared in Rome renewed interest in Plato's philosophy. **Neoplatonism**, however, stressed the most mystical aspects of Plato's philosophy and minimized its rational aspects. The following two examples of Neoplatonist philosophers should make it easy to see why, when the Christian theologians sought a philosophical basis for their religion, Neoplatonism was very appealing.

One brand of Neoplatonism combined Platonic philosophy with Hebrew religion and in so doing created two things lacking in the prevailing religions and philosophies—a concern with individual immortality and human passion:

> In spite of the lofty aspirations of Plato and the equally lofty resignation of the Stoic, the literature of the West lacked something [and] no Greek could have named the deficiency . . . it required a temper of a different make; it required a people whose God was jealous and whose faith was a flaming fire; in a word, the Greek had thought about himself until he was indifferent to all things and desperately sceptical; the Hebrew had still the fire of passion and the impetuosity of faith; with these he made life interesting and fused in one molten mass the attractive elements of every known doctrine. The result was pre-eminently unintelligible, but it was inspired. The strength of the new influence lay exactly in that strange fervour which must have seemed to the Greek a form of madness. (Brett, 1965, p. 171)

We see this blending of Platonism and Hebrew religion for the first time in the philosophy of Philo.

Philo

Nicknamed the "Jewish Plato," **Philo** (ca. 25 B.C.–A.D. 50) took as the starting point of his philosophy the Biblical account of the creation of man. From that account, we learn that the human body was created from the earth but that the human soul was part of God himself: "Then the Lord God formed man of dust from the ground, and breathed into his nostrils the breath of life; and man became a living being" (Genesis 2:7). Thus, humans have a dual nature: The body is lowly and despicable, and the soul is a fragment of the Divine Being or, at least, a ray of Divine Light. The life of an individual human can develop in one of two directions: downward, away from the inner light and toward the experiences of the flesh, or upward, away from experiences of the flesh and toward the inner light. Philo, like the Pythagoreans and Plato before him, condemned sensory experience because it could not provide knowledge. To this, however, Philo added the belief that sensory experience should be condemned because such experience interferes with a direct understanding of and communication with God.

According to Philo, all knowledge comes from God. To receive God's wisdom, however, the soul (mind) must be purified. That is, the mind must be made free of all sensory distractions. Real knowledge can only be attained when a purified, passive mind acts as a recipient of Divine Illumination. Humans by themselves know nothing, nor can they ever know anything. God alone has knowledge, and he alone can impart that knowledge.

We see then that Philo agreed with Pythagoras and Plato that knowledge cannot be attained via sensory experience. Indeed, for all three philosophers, sensory experience inhibits the attainment of knowledge. Unlike Pythagoras and Plato, however, Philo did not believe that introspecting on the contents of the soul would reveal knowledge. For Philo, knowledge came from a direct, personal relationship with God. Philo described his own experience of receiving the word of God:

> Sometimes when I come to my work empty, I have suddenly become full, ideas being in an invisible manner showered upon me and implanted in me from on high; so that through the influence of Divine Inspiration I have become greatly excited, and have known neither the place in which I was nor those who were present, nor myself, nor what I was saying, nor what I was writing; for then I have been conscious of a richness of interpretation and enjoyment of light, a most penetrating sight, a most manifest energy in all that was to be done, having such an effect on my mind as the clearest ocular demonstration would have on the eyes. (Brett, 1965, p. 178)

This statement represented a new view of knowledge, one that would have been foreign to the Greeks. Rather than knowledge being sought rationally, it was revealed by God but only to souls that were prepared to receive it—that is, to souls that through intense meditation had purged themselves of all influences of the flesh. Again, humans can know only that which God provides. Besides meditation, the soul can receive knowledge from God in dreams and trances because, during both, the mind is divorced from matters of the world. Thus, to the Pythagorean-Platonic mistrust and dislike of sensory information and the glorification of rationality, Philo added the belief that the soul (mind) is the breath of God within humans and is the means by which God makes himself and his wisdom known to man.

Regarding the philosophy of Philo and all the philosophies and religions following his that emphasized the importance of intense, inner experience, Brett made the following important observation:

> Psychology is lived as well as described; personal experiences go to make its history; to the mind that will strive and believe new worlds may be opened up, and if we find little enough in these writers on the senses or attention or such subjects, they are a mine of information on the life of the spirit. . . . A history of psychology is a history of two distinct things: first, the observation made by men upon one another; secondly, the observations which now and again the more powerful minds are able to make upon themselves. For many a long century after Philo we shall have to record the progress of psychology in both senses. It would be unwise to begin with any prejudices against those subjective data which are incapable of proof; they may seem at last to be the axioms of all psychology. (1965, p. 171)

It would pay to keep Brett's comments, regarding the importance of subjective data, in mind while reading the remainder of this chapter, if not for the remainder of the book.

Plotinus

Plotinus (204–270), like Philo, found refuge from a world of woe in the spiritual world: "He was in harmony with all the most serious men of his age. To all of them, Christians and pagans alike, the world of practical affairs seemed to offer no hope, and only the Other World seemed worthy of allegiance" (Russell, 1945, p. 284).

Plotinus arranged all things into a hierarchy, at the top of which was the One, or God. The One was supreme and unknowable. Next in the hierarchy was the Spirit, which was the image of the One. It was the Spirit that was part of every human soul, and it was by reflecting on it that we could come close to knowing the One. The third and lowest member of the hierarchy was the Soul. Although the Soul was inferior to the One and to the Spirit, it was the cause of all things that existed in the physical world. From the One emanated the Spirit, and from the Spirit emanated the Soul, and from the Soul emanated nature. When the Soul entered something material, like a body, it attempted to create a copy of the Spirit, which was a copy of the One. Because the One was reflected in Spirit, the Spirit was reflected in the Soul, and the Soul created the physical world, the unknowable One was very much a part of nature. Although Plotinus was generally in agreement with Plato's philosophy, he did not share Plato's low opinion of sensory experience. Rather, he felt that the sensible world was beautiful, and he gave art, music, and attractive humans as examples. It was not that the sensible world was evil, but it was simply less perfect than the spiritual world.

Even though Plotinus's philosophy was more congenial to sensory information than was Platonism, Plotinus still concluded that the physical world was an inferior copy of the divine realm. He also followed Plato in believing that when the soul entered the body it merged with something inferior to itself and thus the truth that it contained was obscured. We must aspire to learn about the world beyond the physical world, the abstract world from which the physical world was derived. It is only in the world beyond the physical world that things are eternal, immutable, and in a state of bliss.

The step from Neoplatonism to early Christianity was not a large or difficult one. To the Christian, the Other World of the Neoplatonists became the Kingdom of God to be enjoyed after death. There was to be an important and unfortunate revision in Plotinus's philosophy, however: "[T]here is in the mysticism of Plotinus nothing morose or hostile to beauty. But he is the last religious teacher, for many centuries, of whom this can be said" (Russell, 1945, p. 292).

Like Plato and all other Neoplatonists, Plotinus saw the body as the soul's prison. Through intense meditation, the soul could be released from the body and dwell among the eternal and the changeless. Plotinus believed that all humans were capable of such transcendental experiences and encouraged them to have them because no other experience was more important or satisfying. To the Stoic's definition of the good life as quiet acceptance of one's fate and the Epicurean's seeking of pleasure, we can now add a third suggestion—the turning away from the empirical world in order to enter a union with those eternal things that dwell beyond the world of flesh. Plotinus's theory was not itself Christian, but it strongly influenced subsequent Christian thought.

There are five classical doctrines of human nature (MacLeod, 1975):

1. The relativistic doctrine of the Sophists, which claimed that human nature was a function of one's experiences

2. The materialistic doctrine of the atomists, which claimed that everything in nature, including humans, was made of atoms and that everything both mental and physical could be explained by the movement and arrangement of atoms

3. The idealistic doctrine of the Pythagoreans and Plato, which claimed that the ultimate reality consisted of abstractions such as numbers, forms, or ideas

4. The teleological doctrine of Aristotle, which claimed that everything in nature, including humans, had a purpose built into it

5. The religious doctrine, which emphasized the immortal soul and the word of God above all else

It is to the religious doctrine of human nature that we turn next.

EMPHASIS ON SPIRIT

The Roman period lasted from about 30 B.C. to about A.D. 300. At the height of its influence, the Roman Empire included the entire Western world, from the Near East to the British Isles. The imperial expansion of the Roman Empire, and then its collapse, brought a number of influences to bear on Roman culture. One such influence came from the religions of India and Persia. Indian **Vedantism**, for example, taught that perfection could be approximated by entering into semiecstatic trances. Another example is **Zoroastrianism**, which taught that individuals are caught in an eternal struggle between wisdom and correctness on the one hand and ignorance and evil on the other. All good things were thought to derive from the brilliant, divine sun, and all bad things from darkness. Another influence came from Greek culture. Generally, the

Romans recognized the importance of Greek scholarship and sought to preserve and disseminate it. Although both Stoicism and Epicureanism became Roman philosophies, they originated in Greek philosophy; this was also true of Neoplatonism. Another major influence on Roman thought was the Hebrew religion. The Hebrews believed in one Supreme God who, unlike the rather indifferent Olympian and Roman gods, was concerned with the conduct of individual humans. The Hebrews also had a strict moral code, and if an individual's conduct was in accordance with this code, God rewarded the person; if it was not, God punished the person. Thus, individuals were responsible for their transgressions. It was from this mixture of many influences that Christianity emerged. The city of Alexandria, Egypt, provided the setting where the Eastern religions, the Hebrew tradition, and Greek philosophy all combined to form early Christian thought.

Jesus

Of course, the Christian religion centered around **Jesus** (4 B.C.–A.D. 30) who taught, among other things, that knowledge of good and evil is revealed by God and that, once revealed, such knowledge should guide human conduct. But Jesus himself was not a philosopher; he was a simple man with limited goals:

> Jesus himself had no speculative interest, his concern being primarily with the religious development of the individual. In his attitude to the learned he typified the practical man of simple faith and intuitive insight who trusts experience rather than a book and his heart rather than his head. He knew intuitively what to expect from people and the influences which shape their development of character. A brilliant diagnostician and curer of souls, he had little interest in formalizing or systematizing his assumptions. (Brett, 1965, pp. 143–144)

None of the philosophers who formalized Jesus' teachings ever met him. How much of Jesus' original intent survived the various attempts to formalize his ideas is still a matter of speculation. In any case, those who claimed that Jesus was the Son of God were called Christians. But before it was to become a dominant force in the Western world, Christianity needed a philosophical basis, and this was provided to a large extent by Plato's philosophy. The early Christian church is best thought of as a blending of the Judeo-Christian tradition with Platonism or, more accurately, with Neoplatonism. This blending occurred gradually and reached its peak with Augustine (discussed later). As the blending of the Judeo-Christian tradition and the Platonic philosophy proceeded, there was a major shift in emphasis from the rational (emphasized by Greek philosophy) to the spiritual (emphasized in the Judeo-Christian tradition).

St. Paul

The many influences converging on early Christianity are nicely illustrated in the work of **St. Paul** (ca. 10–64), the first to claim and preach that Jesus of Nazareth was the Messiah. While on the road to Damascus, Paul had a vision that told him Jesus was the Messiah foretold by Hebrew prophets. Upon this vision, Saul of Tarsus was converted to Paul, Jesus became the Christ, and Christianity was born. Paul was a Roman citizen whose education involved both Hebrew religion and Greek philosophy. From the Hebrew tradition, he learned that there was one God who created the universe and who shapes the destiny of humans. God is omniscient (knows everything), omnipresent (is everywhere), and omnipotent (has unlimited power). Humans fell from a state of grace in the Garden of Eden, and they have been seeking atonement ever since for this Original Sin. To these Hebrew beliefs, Paul added the belief that God had sacrificed his Son to atone for our shared transgression—that is, Original Sin. This sacrifice made a personal reunion with God possible. In a sense, each individual was now able to start life with a clean slate: "For as in Adam all die so also in Christ shall all be made alive" (I Corinthians 15:22). Acceptance of Christ, as the Savior, was the only means of redemption.

In his training in Greek philosophy, St. Paul

was especially influenced by Plato. Paul took Plato's notion that true knowledge can be attained only by escaping from the influence of sensory information and transformed it into a battle between the soul, which contains the spark of God, and the desires of the flesh. But then he did something that most Greek philosophers would have found abhorrent: He placed faith above reason. Faith alone can provide personal salvation. The good life is no longer defined in terms of rationality but in terms of one's willingness to surrender one's existence to God's will. God is the cause of everything, knows everything, and has a plan for everything. By believing—by having faith—one affiliates himself or herself with God and receives his grace. By living a life in accordance with God's will, one is granted the privilege of spending eternity in God's grace when one's mortal coil is shed. For many, given their earthly conditions, this seemed like a small price to pay for eternal bliss.

Paul's efforts left major questions for future theologians to answer. Given the fact that God is all-knowing and all-powerful, is there any room for human free will? And given the importance of faith for salvation, what is the function or value of human reason? The questions can be stated in slightly different terms: Given the fact that everything is determined by God's will, why did God apparently give humans the ability to choose? And if we are incapable of understanding God's plan—and, indeed, if it is not necessary for us to do so—why do we possess reasoning powers? There was also a third question: Given the fact that God is perfect and loving, what accounts for the evil in the world? Following St. Paul, theologians were to agonize over these and related questions for many centuries.

The human was now clearly divided into three parts: the body, the mind, and the spirit. As with the Pythagoreans, Plato, and the Neoplatonists, the body was our major source of difficulty. The spirit was the spark of God within us and was the most highly valued aspect of human nature. Through our spirit, we were capable of becoming close to God, and the spirit was viewed as immortal. The mind, the rational part of humans, was seen as caught between the body and the spirit—sometimes serving the body, which is bad, and at other times serving the spirit, which is good. St. Paul described the situation nicely:

> We know that the law is spiritual; but I am carnal. . . . I do not understand my own actions. For I do not do what I want, but I do the very thing I hate. Now if I do what I do not want, I agree the law is good. So then it is no longer I that do it, but sin which dwells within me. For I know that nothing good dwells within me, that is, in my flesh. I can will what is right, but I cannot do it. For I do not do the good I want, but the evil I do not want is what I do. Now if I do what I do not want, it is no longer I that do it, but sin which dwells within me. (Romans 7:14–20)

Humans, then, are caught in an eternal struggle between sinful, bodily urges and God's law. The law can be understood and accepted, and a desire can exist to act in accordance with it, but often the passions of the body conflict with the law and they win the struggle. To know what is moral does not guarantee moral behavior. This perpetual struggle results from the fact that humans are animals who possess a spark of God. We are partly animalistic and partly divine; conflict is the necessary consequence. For Paul, all physical pleasure was sinful, but most sinful of all was sexual pleasure. This state of conflict involving the good, the bad, and the rational is very much like the one described by Freud many centuries later.

The early Christians left unanswered the question of how one comes to know God. Is God to be known through the Scriptures, through revelation, or through reason, or is God's existence to be taken entirely on faith? It is this question that St. Augustine addressed, as well as the question concerning the function of the human will.

St. Augustine

The 300 years following the death of Jesus were marked by the gradual decline of the Roman Empire and an increased acceptance of Christianity. During this time, Christianity was mainly

St. Augustine

religion into a powerful Christian worldview that would dominate Western life and thought until the 13th century. The authoritative, theological works of Augustine mark the beginning of the Middle Ages, also called the medieval period of history.

Augustine concentrated almost exclusively on human spirituality. About the physical world, one needs to know only that God created it. Augustine shared with the Pythagoreans, Plato, the Neoplatonists, and the earlier Christians a contempt for the flesh. When thoughts are focused on God, there is little need for worldly things. Arrival at true knowledge requires the passage from an awareness of the body, to sense perception, to an internal knowledge of the forms (universal ideas), and, finally, to an awareness of God, the author of the forms. For Augustine, as for the earlier Christians, ultimate knowledge consisted of knowing God. The human was seen as a dualistic being consisting of a body not unlike that possessed by animals and a spirit that was close to or part of God. The war between the two aspects of human nature, already present in Platonic philosophy, became the Christian struggle between heaven and hell—that is, between God and Satan.

The will. God speaks to each individual through his or her soul, *but the individual need not listen.* According to Augustine, individuals are free to choose between the way of the flesh (Satan), which is sinful, and the way of God, which leads to everlasting life in heaven. The human ability to choose explains why evil is present in the world: Evil exists because people choose it.

The insertion of free will into Christian theology made several things possible. With freedom comes responsibility. If an individual chooses correctly (i.e., to live in accordance with God's will), he or she will be rewarded by God's grace. If one chooses incorrectly, one is denied an afterlife in heaven; but more immediately, if the person chooses incorrectly, he or she feels guilty. According to Augustine, people have an **internal sense** that helps them evaluate their experiences by providing an awareness of truth, error,

the type described by St. Paul. That is, it was a combination of Hebrew religion and Neoplatonism. Salvation was attained by living a simple, pure life and recognizing the poverty of material things. A confession of sin and ignorance paved the way for eternal salvation through God's grace.

In 313 Emperor Constantine established Christianity as the official religion of the Roman Empire, and a debate ensued within the church concerning the status of non-Christian beliefs. On one side was St. Jerome (345–420) who argued that non-Christian philosophy should be condemned as pagan and heretical. On the other side was St. Ambrose (340–400) who argued that the elements of other philosophies that are compatible with Christianity should be accepted by the church. St. Ambrose's position was victorious, and its greatest spokesman was **St. Augustine** (354–430). It was Augustine who combined Stoicism, Neoplatonism, and Hebrew personal obligation, and moral right. Deviation from this internal sense causes the feeling of guilt. In fact, one need not actually act contrary to this internal sense to feel guilty but only *intend* to do so. Just thinking about doing something sinful will cause as much guilt as actually *doing* something sinful. All this results in behavior being controlled internally rather than externally. That is, instead of behavior being controlled by externally administered rewards and punishments, it is controlled by personal feelings of virtue or guilt.

Augustine's *Confessions.* Augustine was instrumental in shifting the locus of control of human behavior from the outside to the inside. For him, the acceptance of free will made personal responsibility meaningful. Because individuals were personally responsible for their actions, it was possible to praise or blame them, and people could feel good or bad about *themselves* depending on what choices they made. If one periodically chose evil over good, however, one need not feel guilty forever. By disclosing the actual or intended sin (e.g., by confession), one was forgiven and again could pursue the pure, Christian life. In fact, Augustine's *Confessions* (written about 400) describes a long series of his own sins ranging from stealing for the sake of stealing to the sins of the flesh. The latter involved having at least two mistresses, one of whom bore him a child. When Augustine's mother decided it was time for him to marry, he was forced to abandon his mistress, an event that caused Augustine great anguish:

> My concubine being torn from my side as a hindrance to my marriage, my heart which clave unto her was torn and wounded and bleeding. [She left] vowing unto Thee never to know any other man, leaving with me my son by her. (Pusey, 1961, p. 94)

Augustine's marriage had to be delayed for two years because his bride-to-be was so young; however, he took another mistress in the meantime. Augustine was beginning to realize that he was a "wretched young man," and he prayed to God, "Give me chastity and continency, only not

yet." His explanation to God for such a prayer was, "I feared lest Thou shouldest hear me too soon, and soon cure me of the disease of [lust], which I wished to have satisfied, rather than extinguished" (Pusey, 1961, p. 125). It was not until he was 32 that Augustine abandoned his lusty ways and converted to Christianity. Following his conversion, Augustine was consumed by the passion to know God, and the rest of his life was lived to that end.

The Christian alternative had wide appeal. To people suffering hunger, plague, and war, a religion that focused on a more perfect, nonphysical world was comforting. To slaves and others with low status, a feeling of justice came from knowing that all humans were created in God's image and were finally judged by the same criteria. The poor were consoled by learning that material wealth was irrelevant to living the good life. Criminals did not need to remain criminals; they could be forgiven and given the opportunity for salvation, just like anyone else. All humans were part of a brotherhood; our origins were the same, as was our ultimate goal. Eternal life with God in heaven was available to everyone; to attain it, all one needed to do was live a Christian life.

Knowing God. For Augustine, one did not need to wait for the death of the body to know God; knowledge of God was attainable within an individual's lifetime. Before arriving at this conclusion, Augustine needed something about human experience of which he could be certain. He searched for something that could not be doubted and finally concluded that the fact that he doubted could not be doubted. In Book 20, Chapter 10, of *On the Trinity*, Augustine said,

> Who ever doubts that he himself lives, and remembers, and understands, and wills and thinks, and knows, and judges? Seeing that even if he doubts, he lives; if he doubts, he remembers why he doubts; if he doubts, he understands that he doubts; if he doubts, he wishes to be certain; if he doubts, he thinks; if he doubts, he knows that he does not know; if he doubts, he judges that he ought not to assert rashly. Whosoever therefore doubts about anything else,

ought not to doubt of all these things; which if they were not, he would not be able to doubt of anything. (Hadden, 1912, pp. 133–134)

Thus, Augustine established the validity of inner, subjective experience. (As we will see in chapter 3, Descartes used the same technique to arrive at his famous conclusion, "I think, therefore I am.") The internal sense, not outer (sensory) experience, could be trusted. For Augustine then, a second way of knowing God (the first being the Scriptures) was **introspection**, or the examination of one's inner experiences. We see here the influence of Plato, who also believed that truth must be attained through introspection. Augustinian introspection, however, became a means of achieving a personal communion with God. According to St. Augustine, the feeling of love that one experiences when one is contemplating God creates an ecstasy unsurpassed among human emotions. Such a feeling is the primary goal of human existence; anything that is compatible with achieving such a state of ecstasy is good, whereas anything that distracts from its achievement is bad. Faith and a personal, emotional union with God were, for Augustine, the most important ingredients of human existence. Reason, which had been supreme for the Greeks, became inferior not only to faith but also to human emotion. Reason remained in an inferior position for almost 1,000 years, during which time the writings of Augustine prevailed and provided the cornerstone of church dogma. Augustine had demonstrated that the human mind could know itself without confronting the empirical world. Because the Holy Spirit dwelled in this realm of pure thought, intense, highly emotional introspection was encouraged. Such introspection carried the individual farther away from the empirical world.

THE DARK AGES

Some historians mark the beginning of that portion of the Middle Ages, known as the Dark Ages, with the fall of Rome to the Goths in 410,

others mark it with the death of Augustine in 430, and still others with Emperor Justinian's closing of the Academy in Athens in 529. In any case, it is about this time in history when Greek and Roman books were lost or destroyed; little or no progress was made in science, philosophy, or literature; uniform Roman law collapsed and was replaced by a variety of local customs; and villages armed themselves against attack from both their neighbors and invaders from afar. During all of this uncertainty, or perhaps because of it, the Christian church became increasingly powerful. From about 400–1000, Europe was dominated by mysticism, superstition, and anti-intellectualism; Europe was truly dark.

During the Dark Ages, because church dogma was no longer challengeable, it wielded tremendous power. The questions with which the church grappled concerned inconsistencies within church doctrine. The question of what was true had already been answered, and there was no need to look elsewhere. People were either believers or heretics, and heretics were dealt with harshly. The church owned vast properties, the Pope could make or break kings, and priests controlled the behavior, feelings, and thoughts of the citizens. The eight crusades (1095–1291) against the Muslims showed the power of Christianity to organize its followers to stop the Islamic influence that had been spreading so rapidly throughout Europe.

It was during these "holy wars" that the writings of Aristotle were rediscovered. Many centuries earlier, mainly because of the conquests of Alexander the Great, the Greek influence had been spread over a large area in which Greek philosophy, science, and art came to flourish. In fact, many believe that the Greeks overextended themselves and were thus unable to control their empire. When the Romans began to invade this empire, Greek scholars fled into territories later conquered by the Arabs. These scholars carried with them many Greek works of art and philosophy, among them the works of Aristotle. Aristotle's works were preserved in the great Islamic mosques and were used to develop Arabic philosophy, religion, mathematics, and medicine.

Under the influence of Islam, the Arabs moved west; under the influence of Christianity, the European armies moved east. The clash between the two resulted in the bloody holy wars, but it also brought the West back into contact with Aristotle's philosophy. At first, church authorities welcomed Aristotle's writings; then, after more careful analysis, the works were banned. It was clear that in order for Aristotle's thoughts to be "accepted" they needed to be Christianized.

Long before Aristotle's writings were rediscovered by the West, however, the Arabs were benefiting greatly from them. In fact, more than 200 years before the West attempted to Christianize Aristotle's philosophy, several Arab philosophers busied themselves attempting to make it compatible with Islam.

THE ARABIC INFLUENCE

Although the years between about 400–1000 are often referred to as the Dark Ages, they are only dark with reference to the Western world. During this time, Islam was a powerful force in the world. Mahomet was born in Mecca in 570, and in middle age, he received a revelation from God instructing him to preach. He called his religion Islam, which means surrender to God, and his followers were called Muslims (or Moslems). His teachings are contained in the Koran. Islam spread with incredible speed. Within 30 years of Mahomet's death in 632, the Muslims had conquered Arabia, Syria, Egypt, Persia, Sicily, and Spain. Within 100 years after the prophet's death, the Muslim Empire extended over an area larger than that of the Roman Empire at its peak (R. I. Watson, 1978, p. 106). This expansion brought the Muslims into contact with ancient works long lost to the Western world. Arab philosophers translated, studied, and expanded on the ancient wisdom of Greece and Rome, and the writings of Aristotle were of special interest. By utilizing this wisdom, the Arabs made great strides in medicine, science, and mathematics, subjects that were of greatest

Avicenna

interest during the expansion of the Islamic Empire because of their practical value. When conditions stabilized, however, there was greater interest in making the ancient wisdom compatible with Islam. Although these efforts focused mainly on Aristotle's philosophy, Neoplatonism was also very influential. The Arabic translations of the Greek and Roman philosophers, and the questions that were raised in attempting to make this ancient wisdom compatible with Islam, were used many years later when the Christians attempted the same thing; and in a surprising number of ways, the two efforts were similar.

Avicenna

There were many outstanding Arabic philosophers, but we will briefly mention only two. **Avicenna** (980–1037) wrote books on many topics including medicine, mathematics, logic, metaphysics, Muslim theology, astronomy, politics, and linguistics. His book on medicine, *The*

Canon, was used in European universities for more than five centuries (S. Smith, 1983). In most of his work, he borrowed heavily from Aristotle, but he made modifications in Aristotle's philosophy that persisted for hundreds of years.

In his analysis of human thinking, Avicenna started with the five external senses—vision, hearing, touch, taste, and smell. Then he postulated seven "interior senses," which were arranged in a hierarchy. First is the common sense, which synthesizes the information provided by the external senses. Second is retentive imagination, the ability to remember the synthesized information from the common sense. The third and fourth are compositive animal imagination and compositive human imagination. Compositive imagination allows both humans and animals to learn what to approach or avoid in the environment. For animals, this is a strictly associative process. Those objects or events associated with pain are subsequently avoided, and those associated with pleasure are subsequently approached. Human compositive imagination, however, allows the creative combination of information from the common sense and from the retentive imagination. For example, humans can imagine a unicorn without ever having experienced one; nonhuman animals do not possess this ability. Fifth is the estimative power, the innate ability to make judgments about environmental objects. Lambs may have an innate fear of wolves, and humans may have an innate fear of spiders and snakes, or there may be a natural tendency to approach the things conducive to survival. Sixth is the ability to remember the outcomes of all the information processing that occurs lower in the hierarchy, and seventh is the ability to use that information.

Although Aristotle postulated only three internal senses (common sense, imagination, and memory) and Avicenna seven, Avicenna was essentially an Aristotelian. His major departure from Aristotle's philosophy concerns the active intellect. For Aristotle, the active intellect was used in understanding the universal principles that could not be gained by simply observing empirical events. For Avicenna, the active intellect took on supernatural qualities; it was the aspect of humans that allowed them to understand the cosmic plan and to enter into a relationship with God. For Avicenna, an understanding of God represented the highest level of intellectual functioning. Avicenna's work had great significance for subsequent philosophical development in the West:

> Had it not been for Avicenna and his colleagues in the Islamic world of the eleventh century, the philosophical achievements of twelfth- and thirteenth-century Europe—achievements based so sturdily upon Aristotelianism—are nearly unimaginable. (D. N. Robinson, 1986, p. 145)

Averroës

Averroës (1126–1198) disagreed with Avicenna that human intelligence is arranged in a hierarchy with only the highest level enabling humans to have contact with God. According to Averroës, all human experiences reflect God's influence. In almost everything else, Averroës agreed with Avicenna, and he too was basically an Aristotelian. Averroës's writings are mainly commentaries on Aristotle's philosophy, with special emphasis on Aristotle's work on the senses, memory, sleep and waking, and dreams. Also, following Aristotle, Averroës said that the soul dies with the body. Only the active intellect survives death, and because the active intellect is the same for everyone, nothing personal survives death. This was, of course, contrary to Christian thought, and Averroës's interpretation of Aristotle was labeled "Averroism" and was severely attacked by later Christian philosophers.

It was almost time for the Western world to assimilate Aristotelianism into its religious beliefs, but an intermediate step needed to be taken. Human reasoning powers, which had been minimized in St. Augustine's philosophy but were so important in Aristotle's philosophy, had to be made respectable again. Reason and faith had to be made compatible. We will mention only two of the philosophers who took on this important task.

RECONCILIATION OF FAITH AND REASON

St. Anselm

In *Faith Seeking Understanding*, **St. Anselm** (ca. 1033–1109) argued that perception and reason can and should supplement Christian faith. Although St. Anselm was basically an Augustinian, this acceptance of reason as a means of understanding God represented a major departure from Christian tradition, which had emphasized faith. St. Anselm exemplified how reason could be used within the Christian faith with his famous **ontological argument for the existence of God**. This is a complex argument, but essentially it says that if we can think of something, something must be causing the thought. That is, when we think of things, there must be real things corresponding to those thoughts. St. Anselm beckoned us to continue thinking of a being until we could think of none better or greater a being "than which nothing greater can be conceived." This perfect being that we have conjured up is God, and because we can think of him, he exists. St. Anselm was one of the first Christian theologians to attempt to use logic to support religious belief.

Peter Lombard

Also an Augustinian, **Peter Lombard** (ca. 1095–1160) argued even more forcefully for the place of reason within Christianity than did St. Anselm. Perhaps even more important, Lombard insisted that God could be known by studying his works. There is no need to escape from the empirical world to understand God; one can learn about God by studying the empirical world. Thus, for Lombard, there were three ways to learn about God: faith, reason, and the study of God's works (the empirical world). Philosophers such as St. Anselm and Lombard helped create a receptive atmosphere for the works of Aristotle, which were about to have a major and long-lasting impact on Western philosophy.

SCHOLASTICISM

The holy wars had brought the Western world into contact with the works of Aristotle. The question now was what to do with those works. The reaction of the church to the recovered works from antiquity occurred in three stages. At first the works were welcomed, but when the inconsistencies with church dogma were realized, the works were condemned as pagan. Finally, efforts were made to modify the works, especially those of Aristotle, and in modified form, they were incorporated into church dogma. Some of the keenest minds in the history of Western thought took on the monumental task of synthesizing Aristotle's philosophy and Christian theology and showing what implications that synthesis had for living one's life. This synthesis came to be called **Scholasticism**.

Peter Abelard

Peter Abelard (1079–1142) marks the shift toward Aristotle as *the* philosopher in Western philosophy. Besides translating Aristotle's writings, Abelard introduced a method of study that was to characterize the Scholastic period. In his book *Sic et Non (Yes and No)* Abelard elaborated his **dialectic method**. In this book, he listed some 158 theological questions that were answered in contradictory ways by Scripture and by various Christian theologians. Abelard believed that examining arguments and counter-arguments was a good way of clarifying issues and of arriving at valid conclusions. His goal was not to contradict church dogma but to overcome inconsistencies in the statements made by theologians through the years. Using his yes-and-no method, he pitted conflicting authorities against one another; but through it all, the authority of the Bible prevailed. The dialectic method was controversial because it sometimes seemed to question the validity of religious assumptions. Abelard was not overly concerned about this, however, because he believed that God existed and therefore all methods of inquiry should prove that fact. The believer, then, has nothing to fear from logic, reason, or even the direct study of nature.

Realism versus nominalism. During Abelard's time, there was great debate over whether universals existed—that is, whether there really are essences such as "catness," "humanness," or "sweetness" independent of individual instances of such things. One side said yes, such essences do exist in pure form and individual members of such classes differ only by accident. Those claiming that universals and essences had a real, independent existence were called realists. The other side said that what we call universals are nothing more than verbal labels allowing the grouping of objects or events that resemble one another. To these nominalists, what others call universals are nothing more than convenient verbal labels that summarize similar experiences. The debate was profound because both the philosophies of Plato and Aristotle accepted **realism. Nominalism** was much more in accordance with empirical philosophy than it was with rationalism.

At this time in history, the cathedral of Notre Dame in Paris was the most famous school in Christendom, and William of Champeaux was its most famous teacher. His lecture hall was typically filled with students from all over Europe, and "the excitement produced by his brilliant discourses sometimes ran so high that the civil authorities were obliged to interfere in the interests of good order" (Luddy, 1947, p. 3). At the age of 20, Abelard decided to debate William on the matter of realism versus nominalism. William was a devout and informed realist, but using his considerable skills in rhetoric and logic, Abelard skillfully exposed the fallacies in William's position. The main thrust of Abelard's argument was that we should not confuse words with things. The conclusions reached when logic is applied to words do not necessarily generalize to the physical world. When applied to the debate concerning universals, this meant that just because we use words to describe and understand universals, and even use words to logically deduce their existence, it does not *necessarily* fol-

low that they actually exist. Abelard argued that logic and physics were two different disciplines, and he wanted to keep them sharply separate. Abelard accused William of confusing the two disciplines, and in the process, committing the fallacy of believing that if you can think of something, there must necessarily be something real that corresponds to the thought. At first, William was full of admiration for Abelard as a promising young student, but he became increasingly annoyed: "The upshot of the matter was that the world's most famous professor felt obliged to modify his doctrine under pressure from this . . . stripling of twenty" (Luddy, 1947, p. 4). Having conquered William, Abelard decided to study theology with the famous Anselm, and Abelard was not impressed by him either:

> A few lectures gave him enough of the Doctor of Doctors [Anselm], whom . . . he found eloquent enough, but utterly devoid of sense and reason. He compares the unfortunate professor to a barren fig-tree, abounding in leaves, but bare of fruit; and to a greenwood fire that blinds us with smoke instead of giving us light. (Luddy, 1947, p. 5)

Abelard decided to open his own school, and as a teacher he displayed "a most amazing originality, vivacity and versatility." Soon Abelard, or "Master Peter" as his students called him, was so famous as a teacher that the classrooms of the older professors were essentially empty:

> His eloquence, wit and power of luminous exposition, his magnificent voice, noble bearing, and beauty of face and figure, his boldness in criticising the most venerable authorities and attempting a natural solution of the mysteries of faith: all combined to make him beyond comparison the most popular teacher of his age. (Luddy, 1947, pp. 6–7)

Anselm suffered greatly from his clash with Abelard and died soon afterward.

Abelard's relationship with Heloise. And so continued Abelard's fame and glory until, at the age of 42, he met Heloise, a girl of 17. As a canon of the Notre Dame Cathedral, Abelard's fame and influence as a teacher brought him wealth and distinction, which pleased his friends but angered his enemies such as his old teacher William of Champeaux. With his success came leisure time, and said Abelard, "Just at the time I excelled all the world in philosophy, I relaxed the reins of libido, which I had previously grasped most continently" (Robertson, 1972, pp. 39–40). Heloise was the bright and beautiful niece of a canon of Notre Dame Cathedral, named Fulbert. By his own admission, when Abelard first saw Heloise, he set out to seduce her. Heloise's uncle, who loved her dearly, was very much interested in continuing her education, and being aware of Abelard's considerable skill as a scholar and teacher, he struck a deal with Abelard. The uncle offered Abelard room and board in his (and Heloise's) home, if Abelard would agree to tutor his niece. Abelard was astonished at the canon's naiveté: "No less dumbfounded indeed than if he had entrusted a tender lamb to a hungry wolf" (Robertson, 1972, p. 43). Abelard described what happened next:

> Under the pretence of lessons we abandoned ourselves to our love undisturbed, and . . . when we had opened our books, more words of love appeared than of reading; kisses were more numerous than sentences. More often hands found their way to her bosom than to the books; . . . we left no phase of love untried in our passion, and if love-making could find the unusual, we tried this also. And the less experience we had in these joys, the greater was our burning ardour in abandoning ourselves to them, and the less did we feel fatigue. (Grane, 1970, p. 49)

The "tutoring" went on for several months before the uncle found out what was really happening and threw Abelard out of the house. When Heloise announced her pregnancy, Abelard took her to his sister's home where she eventually gave birth to their son. Although he offered to marry Heloise, she at first refused because she believed that marriage would damage his chances of advancement within the church. Instead, she preferred to remain his mistress. The situation became so complicated, however, that marriage became necessary and

they were married in Paris. For various reasons, Abelard wanted to keep the marriage a secret, and Heloise's uncle wanted it known for fear of Heloise's reputation. Finally, Abelard could stand the strain no longer, and he dressed Heloise in a nun's habit and took her to a convent, where she could appear to be a nun without actually taking vows. Here Abelard would secretly visit his loved one from time to time.

Believing that Abelard had forced Heloise to become a nun to cover his own sins, her uncle's wrath became uncontrollable. Abelard described the action taken by the uncle and some of his aides:

> One night when I was asleep in a private chamber of my lodgings they bribed a servant of mine to let them enter, and they punished me with that most savage and shameful revenge that filled all the world with astonishment. That is, they cut off those parts of my body with which I had done the deed they deplored. (Robertson, 1972, p. 55)

Abelard became a monk, Heloise became a nun, and their future intercourse was limited to romantic and spicy love letters.

After recovering from his ordeal, Abelard resumed his studies and his teaching using the dialectic method. This controversial method and his abrasive manner again led to trouble with church authorities. In 1140 he was ordered to stop teaching and writing by Pope Innocent II, and within a few years he died a lonely and bitter man.

St. Albertus Magnus

St. Albertus Magnus (ca. 1193–1280) was one of the first Western philosophers to make a comprehensive review of Aristotle's works, as well as of the interpretations of Aristotle's works by Islamic scholars. This was no mean feat, considering that the church still regarded Aristotle as a heretic. Magnus presented Aristotle's views on sensation, intelligence, and memory to the church scholars and attempted to show how human rational powers could be used to achieve

St. Thomas Aquinas

St. Thomas Aquinas

St. Thomas Aquinas (1225–1274) was a large, introspective person, whom his fellow students referred to as the "dumb ox." He came from a distinguished, aristocratic family, and his father had considerable influence at the Benedictine Abbey of Monte Cassino, which was only a few miles from their castle home. It was assumed that following his training for the priesthood, Thomas would return to Monte Cassino where the family's influence would help him become abbot. Instead, Thomas joined the Dominican order and became a begging friar. With this decision, Thomas turned his back on family wealth and power and reduced his chances of advancement within the church hierarchy. His father had already died, but his mother was so angered by Thomas's choice that she and a group of relatives kidnapped and imprisoned him in their family castle for about a year. Strangely enough, the imprisonment did not anger him. If fact, he spent the time attempting to convert his family members. Thomas did become angry, however, when his brothers tested his willingness to remain chaste by slipping a seductive prostitute into his prison quarters. Thomas drove her from the room with a hot iron from the fire. He was more upset that his brothers believed that something so mundane would tempt him than he was by the temptation itself. In 1245 Thomas was set free by his family, and he returned to the Dominicans. As a student, Aquinas was prodigious. There was a rule at the University of Paris that a doctorate in theology could not be earned until after one's 34th birthday. An exception was made in Aquinas's case, however, and the degree was given to him at the age of 31. He was then appointed to one of the two Dominican chairs at the University of Paris.

Aquinas did as much as anyone to synthesize Aristotle's philosophical works and the Christian tradition. This was a major feat, but it had an important negative aspect. Once Aristotle's ideas were assimilated into church dogma, they were no longer challengeable. In fact, Aristotle's

salvation. Following Aristotle, Magnus performed detailed observations of nature, and he himself made significant contributions to botany. He was among the first since the Greeks to attempt to learn about nature by making careful, empirical observations. But as instrumental as Abelard and Magnus were in bringing Aristotle's philosophy into the Christian tradition, the greatest Scholastic of all was St. Thomas Aquinas.

writings became almost as sacred as the Bible. This was unfortunate because much of what Aristotle had said later turned out to be false. With Aristotle, as earlier with Plato, the church emphasized those ideas that were most compatible with its theology. Ideas that were not compatible were either changed or ignored. Although this "Christianization" was easier to perform with Plato's philosophy than with Aristotle's, Aristotle has said several things that, with minor shifts and embellishments, could be construed as supporting church doctrine—for example, his thoughts on the immortality of active reason, on the *scala naturae* (the hierarchical design of nature), and on the unmoved mover.

The reconciliation of faith and reason. The Aristotelian emphasis on reason was so great that it could not be ignored. After all, the huge body of information Aristotle had generated was a product of empirical observation guided by reason. This emphasis on reason placed the church in a difficult position because from its inception it had emphasized revelation, faith, and spiritual experience and minimized empirical observation and rationality. It turned out that Aquinas's greatest task (and achievement) was the reconciliation of faith and reason, which he accomplished by arguing effectively that *reason and faith are not incompatible*. For Aquinas, as for the other Scholastics, all paths led to the same truth—God and his glory. Thus, God could now be known through revelation, through Scripture, through examination of inner experience, or through logic, reason, and the examination of nature.

Although sensory information was again accepted as an accurate source of knowledge, Aquinas, following Aristotle, said that the senses could provide information only about particulars, not about universals, which reason must abstract from sensory information. Reason and faith cannot conflict because both lead to the same ultimate reality, God. The philosopher uses logical proof and demonstration to verify God's existence, whereas the Christian theologian takes the existence of God on faith. Both

arrived at the same truth but by different means. Aquinas spent considerable time discussing the differences between humans and "lower" animals. The biggest difference he recognized was that nonhuman animals do not possess rational souls and therefore salvation is not available to them.

Aquinas's synthesis of Aristotelian and Christian thought was bitterly argued within the church. Earlier in this chapter we saw that the conservative members of the early Christian church (e.g., St. Jerome and St. Ambrose) argued that non-Christian philosophers should be condemned and ignored. Augustine argued, however, that insofar as possible non-Christian philosophy should be assimilated into church dogma. Augustine won the debate. Now, some 900 years later, we have a similar debate over the works of Aristotle. One of the most influential voices of conservatism was **St. Bonaventure** (1221–1274), who condemned the works of Aristotle. Bonaventure, following Augustine, believed that one comes to know God through introspection, not through reasoning or by studying nature. Aquinas's position prevailed, however, and was finally accepted as official church doctrine and, with some modifications, remains the cornerstone of Catholicism to this day. The view represented by Bonaventure lives on in Protestantism, where Scripture is valued more highly than reason and a personal relationship with God is valued more highly than ritual and church prescriptions.

Aquinas's influence. Aquinas's work eventually had several effects: It divided reason and faith, making it possible to study them separately; it made the study of nature respectable; and it showed the world that argument over church dogma was possible. Although Aquinas's goal was to strengthen the position of the church by admitting reason as a means of understanding God, his work had the opposite effect. Several philosophers following Aquinas argued that faith and reason could be studied separately, without considering its theological implications. Philosophy without religious overtones was becoming a possibility—a possibility that had not existed for well over 1,000 years.

Aquinas, at least partially, shifted attention away from the heavens and back to earth, although his emphasis was still on the heavens. This shift had to occur before the Renaissance could take place. The Renaissance was still in the future, however, and the church still controlled most human activities.

Limitations of Scholastic Philosophy

It is one thing to examine nature and try to arrive at the principles that seem to govern it, as most Greek philosophers did; it is another thing to assume that something is true and then attempt to make nature conform to that truth. The Christian theologians attempted to do the latter. During the time from Augustine to, and including, Aquinas, scholarship consisted of demonstrating the validity of church dogma. New information was accepted only if it could be shown to be compatible with church dogma; if this was not possible, the information was rejected. The "truth" had been found, and there was no need to search elsewhere.

Although the Scholastics were outstanding scholars and hair-splitting logicians, they offered little of value to either philosophy or psychology. They were much more interested in maintaining the status quo than in revealing any new information. Certainly, there was little concern with physical nature, except for those aspects that could be used to prove God's existence or to show something about God's nature. As with the major Greek philosophers who preceded them, the Scholastics searched for the universal truths or principles that were beyond the world of appearance. For the Pythagoreans, it was numerical relationships; for Plato, it was the pure forms, or ideas; for Aristotle, it was the entelechy, which gave a class of things its essence; and for the Scholastics, it was God. All assumed that there was a higher truth beyond the one that could be experienced through the senses. For all, a knowledge of universals, prin-

ciples, essences, or abstractions was the only true knowledge.

As was mentioned earlier, once Aquinas separated faith and reason, it was only a matter of time before there would be those wishing to exercise reason while remaining unencumbered by faith. William of Occam was one who took this step. In so doing, he challenged the whole idea of universals, essences, or first principles, thus dealing a severe blow to Scholasticism.

WILLIAM OF OCCAM: A TURNING POINT

William of Occam (sometimes spelled *Ockham*, ca. 1290–1350), a British-born Franciscan monk, accepted Aquinas's division of faith and reason and pursued the latter. Occam believed that in explaining things, no unnecessary assumptions should be made—in other words, that explanations should always be kept as parsimonious (simple) as possible. This belief that extraneous assumptions should be "shaved" from explanations or arguments came to be known as **Occam's razor**.

Occam applied his "razor" to the debate concerning the existence of universals. As we have seen, some scholars believed that universal ideas or principles existed and that individual empirical experiences were only manifestations of those universals. Again, those believing in the independent existence of universals were called realists. Conversely, scholars believing that so-called universals were nothing more than verbal labels used to describe groups of experiences that had something in common were called nominalists. Because Occam saw the assumption that universals had an independent existence as unnecessary, he sided with the nominalists, arguing forcefully that so-called universals were nothing more than verbal labels. For example, because all cats have certain features in common, it is convenient to label all objects with those features as cats. The same thing is true for dogs, trees, books, or any other class of objects or experiences. According to Occam, the fact that experiences have features in common allows us to use general labels to describe those experiences; but the use of such labels does not mean that there is a pure idea, essence, or form that exists beyond our experiences. Occam believed we could trust our senses to tell us what the world was really like, that we could know the world *directly* without needing to worry about what lurked beyond our experience.

Occam changed the question concerning the nature of knowledge from a metaphysical problem to a psychological problem. He was not concerned with a transcendent reality that could be understood only by abstract reasoning or intense introspection. For him, the question was how the mind classifies experience, and his answer was that we habitually respond to similar objects in a similar way. We apply the term *female* to a person because that person has enough in common with others we have called female.

Previously, we saw that Abelard's position on the realism-versus-nominalism debate was one of skepticism. He believed that one could not reach conclusions about the world by simply manipulating words. That is, Abelard believed that the existence of essences could not be proven or disproven logically. Occam's position was that the assumption that essences exist was unnecessary. We can simply assume that nature is as we experience it.

In his empiricism, Occam went beyond Aristotle. Aristotle believed that sensory experience was the basis of knowledge but that reason needed to be applied in order to extract from individual experiences knowledge of universals and essences. For Occam, sensory experience provided information about the world—*period*. Occam's philosophy marks the end of Scholasticism. Despite the church's efforts to silence them, Occam's views were widely taught and can be viewed as the beginning of modern empirical philosophy. Indeed, we see in Occam a strong hint of the coming Renaissance. Despite his radical empiricism, Occam was still a Franciscan monk, and he believed in God. He did say, however, that God's existence could never be confirmed by studying nature because there was

nothing in nature that directly proved his existence. God's existence, then, must be accepted on faith.

THE SPIRIT OF THE TIMES BEFORE THE RENAISSANCE

During the 14th and 15th centuries, philosophy still served religion, as did everyone and everything else. There were two classes of people, believers and nonbelievers. The latter, if they could not be converted, were physically punished, imprisoned, or killed, and they were considered either stupid or possessed by the devil. There was no in-between. If the God contemplated through introspection was real, so must other objects of thought be real, such as demons and monsters. Astrology was extremely popular, and magic was practiced almost everywhere. Superstition was not only confined to the peasant but also characterized kings, scholars, and clergy.

All bodily experiences were seen as sinful, but sex became the worst sin of all. Attitudes toward sex and toward women went hand in hand. The early Christians perpetuated the negative attitude toward women that the Greeks and Romans had demonstrated. Plato, for example, believed that women and the lower animals were degenerated forms of men (Esper, 1964, p. 80). Similarly, Aristotle felt that a man was superior to a woman and therefore should rule his house, his children, and his wife as a king rules his kingdom and his subjects (Esper, 1964, p. 192). There were three types of women: those who were promiscuous and therefore sinful; mothers, who did their duty by having children; and virgins, who were glorified. When men gave in to sexual desire, it was thought to be the woman's fault, and even mothers were not entirely free from ridicule.

Clearly, this was not a time of open inquiry. To use Kuhn's (1973) terminology, inquiry was characterized by a single paradigm: the Christian conception of humans and the world. Although Kuhn was mainly concerned with science, his notion of paradigms can also be applied to other fields of inquiry. As with other paradigms, the Christian paradigm determined what was acceptable as a problem and what counted as a solution. Philosophers were engaged in "normal philosophy," which, like normal science, is concerned only with exploring the implications of the accepted paradigm. Little creativity is involved in either normal science or normal philosophy. Kuhn tells us that for there to be a paradigm shift, anomalies must arise within the accepted paradigm; that is, consistent observations that cannot be explained must oc-

cur. As the anomalies persist, a new paradigm gradually gains recruits and eventually overthrows the old paradigm. The process is long, difficult, and often traumatic for the early dissenters from the old paradigm. In the period before the Renaissance, anomalies were appearing everywhere in Christian doctrine, and it was clear that church authority was on the decline. For centuries there had been little philosophical, scientific, or theological growth. For progress to occur, the authority of the church had to be broken, and the cracks were beginning to appear almost everywhere.

SUMMARY

After Aristotle's death, philosophers began to concern themselves with principles of human conduct and asked the question What constitutes the good life? Pyrrho preached Skepticism. To him, nothing could be known with certainty, so why believe anything? The Skeptic did not commit himself or herself to any particular belief. Antisthenes and Diogenes advocated a back-to-nature approach to life because they viewed society as a distortion of nature that should be rejected. A simple life, close to nature and free of wants and passions, was best. The position of Antisthenes and Diogenes was later called Cynicism. Epicurus said the good life involved seeking the greatest amount of pleasure over the longest period of time. Such pleasure did not come from having too little or too much but from a life of moderation. Zeno of Citium, the founder of Stoicism, claimed that the good life involved living in harmony with nature, which was designed in accordance with a divine plan. Because everything happens for a reason, one should accept whatever happens with courage and indifference. The Stoics believed material possessions to be unimportant, and they emphasized virtue (the acceptance of one's fate).

Clearly, the preceding moral philosophers were often contradictory, and they lacked a firm philosophical base. This problem was "solved" when philosophers switched their attention from ethics to religion. In Alexandria there was a mixture of Greek philosophy, Hebrew traditions, and Eastern religions. Philo, a Neoplatonist, combined the Hebrew tradition with Plato's philosophy and created a system that glorified the spirit and condemned the flesh. Plotinus, another Neoplatonist, believed

that from the "One" (God) emanates the Spirit, from the Spirit emanates the Soul, and from the Soul emanates the physical world. The Soul then reflects the Spirit and God. Like all the Neoplatonists, Plotinus taught that it is only by pondering the contents of the Soul that one can embrace eternal, immutable truth. St. Paul claimed Jesus to be the Son of God and thereby established the Christian religion.

St. Augustine said that humans can know God through intense introspection. The ecstasy that comes from cognitively embracing God was considered the highest human emotion and could only be achieved by avoiding or minimizing experiences of the flesh. By postulating human free will, Augustine accomplished several things: He explained evil as the result of humans choosing evil over good; humans became responsible for their own destiny; and personal guilt became an important means of controlling behavior. Augustine claimed that an internal sense reveals to each person how he or she should act as a Christian. Acting contrary to this internal sense, or even intending to act contrary to it, causes guilt.

During the Dark Ages, Arabic culture flourished and expanded throughout Europe. Arab scholars translated the works of the Greek and Roman philosophers and used this wisdom to make great advances in medicine, science, and mathematics. Avicenna and Averroës concentrated mainly on the works of Aristotle, translating and expanding them and attempting to make them compatible with Islam.

Before the Western world could embrace Aristotle's philosophy, human reasoning powers had to be made respectable. St. Anselm and Lombard were instrumental in showing that reason and faith were compatible, whereas Abelard and St. Albertus Magnus were among the first Western philosopher-theologians to embrace the work of Aristotle. Those who attempted to synthesize Aristotle's philosophy with the Christian religion were called Scholastics. The greatest Scholastic was St. Thomas Aquinas, and the major outcome of his work was the acceptance of both reason and faith as ways of knowing God. Before Aquinas, faith alone had been emphasized. The acceptance of reason as a means of knowing God made the examination of nature, the use of logical argument, and even debate within the church itself respectable. It is widely believed that Aquinas inadvertently created an atmosphere that led ultimately to the decline of church authority and therefore to the Renaissance.

Within the church, there was a debate between the realists and the nominalists. The realists believed in the existence of universals, of which individual, empirical events were only manifestations.

The nominalists believed that so-called universals were nothing more than verbal labels applied to classes of experience. William of Occam sided with the nominalists by explaining universals as simply verbal labels. Occam took this position because it required the fewest assumptions. Occam's razor is the belief that of two or more adequate explanations, the one requiring the fewest assumptions should be chosen.

In the heyday of early Christianity, a largely negative social climate prevailed. There was widespread superstition and fear, persecution of nonbelievers, discrimination against women, and harsh treatment of the mentally ill. Any action or thought not in accordance with church dogma was a sin. A minimum amount of sexual activity was tolerated so that humans could reproduce; anything beyond that was considered a hideous sin. The church had absolute power, and any dissension was dealt with harshly. Clearly, the spirit of the times was not conducive to open, objective inquiry.

DISCUSSION QUESTIONS

1. Briefly state what constituted the good life according to Skepticism, Cynicism, Epicureanism, and Stoicism.

2. What five doctrines of human nature did MacLeod suggest? Briefly summarize each.

3. Describe the factors that contributed to the development of early Christian theology.

4. What characterized St. Paul's version of Christianity?

5. Summarize the philosophy of Neoplatonism.

6. Discuss the importance of free will in Augustine's philosophy.

7. How did Augustine change the locus of control of human behavior from forces outside the person to forces inside the person?

8. Of what did Augustine feel humans could be certain, and how did he arrive at his conclusion? How, according to Augustine, could humans experience God, and what type of emotion resulted from this experience?

9. In what way were the Dark Ages dark? Explain.

10. What was the importance of Avicenna's and Averroës's philosophies to Western thought?

11. How did the works of St. Anselm and Lombard prepare the Western world for the acceptance of Aristotle's philosophy?

12. What was St. Anselm's ontological argument for the existence of God?

13. What was the significance of the work of Abelard and Magnus?

14. Summarize the debate between the realists and the nominalists. What was Abelard's position in this debate?

15. How, according to Aquinas, can humans know God? What are some of the implications of Aquinas's position?

16. What was Scholasticism? Give an example of what the Scholastics did.

17. Why does William of Occam represent an important turning point in the history of psychology?

18. Was William of Occam a realist or a nominalist? Explain.

19. What is Occam's razor?

SUGGESTIONS FOR FURTHER READING

Grane, L. (1970). *Peter Abelard: Philosophy and Christianity in the Middle Ages* (F. Crowley & C. Crowley, Trans.). New York: Harcourt, Brace & World.

This small book places Abelard's life in historical perspective. Grane describes the 12th century as a Renaissance that saw the revival of Greek philosophy and Roman law. During these exciting times, Abelard was one of the most exciting figures.

Oates, W. J. (Ed.). (1940). *The Stoic and Epicurean philosophers*. New York: Random House.

An old but still highly informative source of Epicurean and Stoic philosophy, the book contains translations of the surviving works of Epicurus, Epictetus, Lucretius, and Marcus Aurelius.

Pusey, E. B. (Trans.). (1961). *The confessions of St. Augustine*. New York: Macmillan.

In the first 10 chapters of this classic book, Augustine vividly and candidly describes his licentious youth and early manhood. He describes his mother's efforts to save him from self-destruction and, at the age of 32, his conversion to Christianity. The last 3 chapters outline Augustine's interpretation of the Biblical account of creation and of the mystery of the Trinity. (Available in paperback.)

Russell, B. (1945). *A history of Western philosophy*. New York: Simon & Schuster.

This is one of the most readable histories of philosophy available. It not only expands on Cynicism, Skepticism, Epicureanism, Stoicism, Neoplatonism, and Christianity but on most of the other philosophies found in the present text as well. (Available in paperback.)

Worthington, M. (1960). *The immortal lovers: Heloise and Abelard*. Garden City, NY: Doubleday.

This book is a well-written account of the relationship between Abelard and Heloise. The author describes in detail the historical context within which the relationship took place and includes many quotations from Abelard's autobiography and from the love letters between Abelard and Heloise.

GLOSSARY

Abelard, Peter (1079–1142) One of the first Western philosopher-theologians to emphasize the works of Aristotle.

Antisthenes (ca. 445–365 B.C.) Founder of Cynicism.

Averroës (1126–1198) An Arabic scholar who attempted to make Aristotelian philosophy compatible with the Muslim religion.

Avicenna (980–1037) An Arabic scholar who translated and modified Aristotelian philosophy and attempted to make it compatible with Islam.

Cynicism The belief that the best life is one lived close to nature and away from the rules and regulations of society.

Dialectic method The technique used by Abelard in seeking truth. Questions are raised and several possible answers to those questions are explored. The technique is similar to Popper's approach to science, where possible solutions to a problem are proposed and then critically examined.

Diogenes (ca. 412–323 B.C.) Like his mentor Antisthenes, advocated retreating from society and living a simple life close to nature.

Epicureanism The belief that the best life is one of long-term pleasure resulting from moderation.

Epicurus (ca. 341–270 B.C.) Founder of Epicureanism.

Hedonism The belief that the good life consists of seeking pleasure and avoiding pain.

Internal sense The internal knowledge of moral right that individuals use in evaluating their behavior and thoughts. Postulated by St. Augustine.

Introspection The examination of one's subjective experiences.

Jesus (4 B.C.–A.D. 30) A simple, sensitive man whom St. Paul and others claimed was the Messiah. Those who believe Jesus to be the Son of God are called Christians.

Lombard, Peter (ca. 1095–1160) Insisted that God could be known through faith, reason, or the study of his work in nature.

Neoplatonism Philosophy that emphasized the most mystical aspects of Plato's philosophy. Transcendental experiences were considered the most significant type of human experience.

Nominalism The belief that so-called universals are nothing more than verbal labels or mental habits that are used to denote classes of experience.

Occam's razor The belief that of several, equally effective alternative explanations, the one that makes the fewest assumptions should be accepted.

Ontological argument for the existence of God St. Anselm's contention that if we can think of something, it must be real. Because we can think of a perfect being (God), that perfect being must exist.

Philo (ca. 25 B.C.–A.D. 50) A Neoplatonist who combined Hebrew theology with Plato's philosophy. Philo differentiated between the lower self (the body) and a spiritual self, which is made in God's image. The body is the source of all evil; therefore, for the spiritual self to develop fully, one should avoid or minimize sensory experience.

Plotinus (204–270) A Neoplatonist who emphasized the importance of embracing the soul through introspection. These subjective experiences were more important and informative than physical experiences.

Pyrrho (ca. 365–275 B.C.) Founder of Skepticism.

Realism The belief that abstract universals exist and that empirical events are only manifestations of those universals.

St. Albertus Magnus (ca. 1193–1280) Made a comprehensive review of Aristotle's work. Following Aristotle's suggestion, he also made careful, direct observations of nature.

St. Anselm (ca. 1033–1109) Argued that sense perception and rational powers should supplement faith. (*See also* **Ontological argument for the existence of God**.)

St. Augustine (354–430) After having demonstrated the validity of inner, subjective experience, said that one can know God through introspection as well as through the revealed truth of the Scriptures. Augustine also wrote extensively on human free will.

St. Bonaventure (1221–1274) A contemporary of St. Thomas Aquinas, argued that Christianity should remain Augustinian and should reject any effort to assimilate Aristotelian philosophy into church dogma.

St. Paul (ca. 10–64) Founded the Christian church by claiming that Jesus was the Son of God. Paul placed the soul or spirit in the highest position among the human faculties, the body in the lowest, and the mind in a position somewhere between these two.

St. Thomas Aquinas (1225–1274) Epitomized Scholasticism. He sought to "Christianize" the works of Aristotle and to show that both faith and reason lead to the truth of God's existence.

Scholasticism The synthesis of Aristotelian philosophy with Christian teachings.

Skepticism The belief that all beliefs can be proved false; thus, to avoid the frustration of being wrong, it is best to believe nothing.

Stoicism The belief that one should live according to nature's plan and accept one's fate with indifference or, in the case of extreme hardship, with courage.

Vedantism The Indian religion that emphasized the importance of semiecstatic trances.

William of Occam (ca. 1290–1350) Denied the contention of the realists that what we experience are but manifestations of abstract principles. Instead, he sided with the nominalists who said that so-called abstract principles, or universals, were nothing more than verbal labels that we use to describe classes of experiences. For Occam, reality is what we experience directly; there is no need to assume a "higher" reality beyond our senses.

Zeno of Citium (ca. 333–262 B.C.) Founder of Stoicism.

Zoroastrianism The Persian religion that equated truth and wisdom with the brilliance of the sun and ignorance and evil with darkness.

CHAPTER 4

The Beginnings of Modern Science, Philosophy, and Psychology

The **Renaissance** is generally dated from approximately 1450–1600, although many historians would date its beginning much earlier. Renaissance means "rebirth," and during this period, the tendency was to go back to the more open-minded method of inquiry that had characterized early Greek philosophy. It was a time when Europe gradually switched from being God-centered to being human-centered. If God existed, he existed in nature; therefore, to study nature was to study God. Also, because God had given humans the ability to create works of art, why not exercise that ability to the fullest? The new view was that there was more to humans than their souls; they had reliable sensory systems, so why not use them? They had reasoning powers, so why not exercise them? And they had the capacity for enjoyment, so why not enjoy? After all, God, in his infinite wisdom, must have given humans these attributes for a reason. Attention was diverted from the heavens, where the Pythagoreans, Platonists, and early Christians had focused it, to humans living in the world. Nowhere is this spirit of the times better illustrated than in the work of the Renaissance humanists.

RENAISSANCE HUMANISM

Major Themes

The term *humanism*, as it applies to the Renaissance, does not mean *humanitarianism*. That is, it does not refer to a deep concern about the welfare of humans. Nor does it refer to *humaneness*—that is, treating one's fellow humans with respect, sensitivity, and dignity. As it applies to

the Renaissance, **humanism** denotes an intense interest in human beings, as if we were discovering ourselves for the first time. Interest was focused on a wide range of human activities. How do we think, behave, and feel? Of what are we capable? These and related questions are reflected in the four major themes that characterized Renaissance humanism:

1. *Individualism.* There was great concern with human potential and achievement. The belief in the power of the individual to make a positive difference in the world created a spirit of optimism.

2. *Personal religion.* Although all Renaissance humanists were devout Christians, they wanted religion to be more personal and less formal and ritualistic. They argued for a religion that could be personally experienced rather than one that the church hierarchy imposed on the people.

3. *Intense interest in the past.* The Renaissance humanists became enamored with the past. The works of the early Greek and Roman poets, philosophers, and politicians were of special interest. Renaissance scholars wanted to read what the ancients had really said, instead of someone's interpretation. They sought to assign correct authorship to old manuscripts because the authorship of several manuscripts had been assigned incorrectly, and they attempted to expose forgeries. These activities exposed Renaissance scholars to a wide range of viewpoints from the past, and many of these views found considerable support among the humanists. For example, much that was previously unknown

of Plato's philosophy was discovered, resulting in a wave of interest in Plato. In 1462 **Marsilio Ficino** (1433–1499) founded a Platonic academy in Florence. He sought to do for Plato's philosophy what the Scholastics had done for Aristotle's. Among the humanists, almost every early Greek and Roman philosophy had its adherents, but Plato was especially influential. Even some extremely old Eastern religions were rediscovered, stimulating great interest in the occult.

4. *Anti-Aristotelianism.* Many of the humanists believed that the church had gone too far in its embracing of Aristotle's philosophy. It had reached the point where Aristotle's philosophy was as authoritative as the Bible. Passages from Aristotle commonly settled theological disputes. To the humanists, this was ridiculous because Aristotle had been only human, and like any human, he was capable of error. To the regret of the humanists, Aristotle's philosophy, along with Christian theology, had been used to create a set of rules, regulations, and beliefs that one had to accept in order to be a Christian. Accepting church dogma became more important than one's personal relationship with God; therefore, the humanists attacked church dogma harshly. Although there were many interesting Renaissance humanists, space permits only a brief review of a few of them.

Francesco Petrarch

So influential was **Francesco Petrarch** (1304–1374) that many historians argue that his writings mark the beginning of the Renaissance. Clearly, all the themes discussed above are found in Petrarch's work. Above all else, Petrarch was concerned with freeing the human spirit from the confines of medieval traditions, and the main target of his attack was Scholasticism. He felt that the classics should be studied as the works of humans and not be interpreted or embellished by others. He had a low opinion of those who used the classics to support their

own beliefs, saying of these interpreters, "Like those who have no notion of architecture, they make it their profession to whitewash walls." An obvious example of this type of interpreter was the Scholastic.

Like most Renaissance humanists, Petrarch urged a return to a personal religion like that described by St. Augustine—a religion based on the Bible, personal faith, and personal feelings. He felt that Scholasticism, in its attempt to make religion compatible with Aristotelian rationalism, had made it too intellectual. Petrarch also argued that a person's life in this world is at least as important as life after death. God wanted humans to use their vast capabilities, not inhibit them, Petrarch argued. By actualizing the potential God has given to us, we can change the world for the better. By focusing on human potential, Petrarch helped stimulate the explosion of artistic and literary endeavors that characterized the Renaissance.

Petrarch did not create anything new philosophically, but his challenge of religious and philosophical authority helped pave the way for individuals such as Copernicus, Kepler, and Galileo. In other words, Petrarch's skepticism toward all forms of dogma helped pave the way for modern science.

Giovanni Pico

Giovanni Pico (1463–1494) argued that God had granted humans a unique position in the universe. Angels are perfect and thus have no need to change, whereas animals are bound by their instincts and cannot change. Humans alone, being between angels and animals, are capable of change. We can choose to live sensual, instinctive lives, thereby becoming brutish, or to exercise our rationality and intelligence, thereby becoming more angelic and godlike.

Our freedom not only allows us to choose from a variety of lifestyles, but it also permits us to embrace almost any viewpoint. Pico insisted that all philosophies had common elements; for example, they reflected human rationality and individuality. He argued further that, if properly understood, the major philosophical viewpoints (e.g., those of Plato and Aristotle) were essentially in agreement. All viewpoints therefore should be studied objectively with the aim of discovering what they have in common. Pico urged that all philosophical perspectives be studied and assimilated into the Christian worldview. Clearly, Pico sought peace among philosophical and religious rivals. All human works, he said, should be respected. Had Pico's plea for individuals with different viewpoints to understand each other been heeded, perhaps the Inquisition could have been averted. This was not to be, however, and only the fact that Pico died so young spared him the sight of his books being burned.

Martin Luther

Martin Luther (1483–1546), an Augustinian priest and Biblical scholar, was extremely upset with what Christianity had become in his day. His view of Christianity, like those of the other humanists, was much more in accordance with St. Paul's and St. Augustine's views than with St. Thomas Aquinas's. All that one needed to know about humans or the world could be found in the New Testament. Humans are born in sin, and only a renunciation of the flesh prepares the soul to be saved by God's grace. Human intentions were inspired either by God or by Satan; the former resulted in doing God's work, the latter in sin. People should not be able to escape the consequences of sin through penance or absolution; if they have sinned, they should suffer the consequences, which could be eternal damnation. In the spirit of Augustinian theology, Luther insisted on an intensely personal religion in which each person is answerable only to God, a religion that de-emphasized ritual and church hierarchy.

Traditionally, the **Reformation** is said to have begun in 1517 when Luther nailed his Ninety-Five Theses (challenges to church dogma and hierarchy) to the door of Wittenberg Cathedral. Besides the issues already mentioned, Luther was especially opposed to the Catholic church's

sale of indulgences, which allowed sinners to reduce the retribution for their sins by paying a fee to church officials. God alone, he preached, determined what was sinful and how sinfulness was to be treated. In Luther's eyes, the church had drifted far from the teachings of Jesus and the Bible. Jesus had preached the glory of the simple life, devoid of luxury and privilege, but the church had come to value these things and to engage in too many formal rituals. For Luther, a major reason for the downfall of Catholicism was its assimilation of Aristotle's philosophy; Luther had harsh words for Aristotle:

> What are the universities . . . but . . . schools of Greek fashion and heathenish manners full of dissolute living, where very little is taught of the Holy Scriptures and of the Christian faith, and the blind heathen teacher, Aristotle, rules even further than Christ. Now, my advice would be that the books of Aristotle, the "Physics," the "Metaphysics," "Of the Soul," "Ethics," which have hitherto been considered the best, be altogether abolished. . . . My heart is grieved to see how many of the best Christians this accursed, proud, knavish heathen has fooled and led astray with his false words. God sent him as a plague for our sins. (Blucher, 1946, p. 630)

When Luther was excommunicated in 1520, the protest that he represented grew into a new religious movement, **Protestantism**, and Luther was its leader. The new religion denied the authority of the Pope and insisted that every individual had the right to interpret the Bible for himself or herself. To facilitate the latter, Luther translated the Bible into the German vernacular. The Catholic church's response to the criticisms of Luther and others was to make Aquinas's Christianized version of Aristotle's philosophy official church dogma that all Christians were expected to follow. The dispute over which version of Christianity was correct soon divided Europe into two warring factions.

Early Protestantism had at least two negative aspects. First, as a religion, it was grim, austere, harsh, and unforgiving. In terms of individual happiness, imagining its adherents being any better off than those embracing Catholicism is difficult. Second, Protestantism insisted that one accept the existence of God on faith alone; attempting to understand him through reason or empirical observations was foolish and was to be avoided. Thus, if one believes that the acceptance of reason and the observation of nature as ways of knowing God exemplified progress, then Protestantism exemplified regression. On the positive side, however, Protestantism was a liberating influence in the sense that it challenged the authority of the Pope and of Aristotle; replacing them was the belief that individual feelings can provide the only truth that one needs in living one's life.

Desiderius Erasmus

Like Pico, **Desiderius Erasmus** (1466–1536) was opposed to a fanatical belief in anything. Erasmus was fond of pointing out mistakes in the classics, claiming that anything created by humans could not be perfect. He exposed exorcism and alchemy as nonsense, attacking these and other forms of superstition and begging people to take their lessons from the simple life of Jesus instead of from the pomp and circumstance of the organized church. He believed that war was caused by fanaticism and was nothing more than homicide, and he was especially disturbed by bishops who became rich and famous because of war. Eclectic and practical, Erasmus was a keen observer of the world and its problems. During the Reformation, he could not side with either the Catholics or the Protestants and was condemned by both.

There were many other Renaissance humanists. Some manifested the power of the individual in art (Leonardo da Vinci, 1452–1519), some in politics (Niccolò Machiavelli, 1469–1527), some in education (Juan Luis Vives, 1492–1540), and some in literature (William Shakespeare, 1564–1616). The emphasis was always the same—the individual. Now to be judged by their work instead of their words, people were seen as having the power to change things for the better rather than simply accepting the world as it was or hoping that it would become better. Although the Renaissance humanists

added nothing new in philosophy or psychology, the belief that individuals could act upon the world to improve it was conducive to the development of science. During the Renaissance, art, literature, and architecture benefited, but the age of science was still in the future.

To say the least, the Renaissance was a paradoxical time. On the one hand, there was an explosion of interest in human potential, coupled with great human achievements. In this respect, the Renaissance resembled classical Greece and Rome. On the other hand, it was a time of persecution, superstition, witch hunting and burning, fear, torture, and exorcism. Although astrologers and alchemists were generally highly regarded and popular, abnormal individuals were treated with extreme harshness. Wars destroyed much of France and Germany, the Black Death cut Europe's population nearly in half, there were major famines, and syphilis was epidemic. Yet despite all this, there was almost unparalleled creativity. The Renaissance displayed the best and worst of humanity—the stuff from which modern philosophy, psychology, and science emerged.

FURTHER CHALLENGES TO CHURCH AUTHORITY

The Renaissance and the breakdown of church authority went hand in hand. Church dogma consisted of fixed truths such as there being exactly seven heavenly bodies in the solar system, the earth being the center of the solar system, humans being created in God's image, and the earth being flat. Gradually, these "truths" were challenged and each successful challenge focused suspicion on other "truths." Once begun, the questioning increased rapidly, and the church tried desperately to discourage these challenges to its authority. Church scholars attempted to show that contradictions were only apparent. Failing in this, they attempted to impose censorship, but it was too late; the challenging spirit was too widespread. The decline in the church's authority was directly related to the rise of a new spirit of inquiry that took as its ultimate authority empirical observation instead of the Scriptures, faith, or revelation. Gradually, church dogma was replaced by the very thing it had opposed the most—the direct observation of nature without the intervention of theological considerations. But the transition, although steady, was slow and painful. Many Renaissance scholars were caught between theology and science, either because of personal beliefs or because of fear of retaliation by the church. They reported their observations with extreme caution; in some cases, they requested that their observations be reported only after their deaths.

There is no single reason for this reawakening of the spirit of objective inquiry; several factors are believed responsible. One was Aquinas's acceptance of reason and the examination of nature as ways of knowing God. Once sanctioned by the church, the human capacity to reason was focused everywhere, including on church dogma. Another factor was the work of the humanists, which recaptured the spirit of open inquiry reflected in the classics. The humanists also stressed the human potential to act upon the world and change it for the better. In addition, the following events are considered factors in the acceptance of the objective study of nature because they weakened the authority of the church:

- The explorations of Marco Polo (ca. 1254– 1324)

- Invention of the printing press by Johann Gutenberg (ca. 1400–1468)

- Discovery of America (1492)

- Luther's challenge to Catholicism (1517)

- Circumnavigation of the globe by Magellan (ca. 1480–1521)

These and other events expanded the known world. The discovery that the earth was round and filled with strange peoples with strange customs created many problems for the church. For example, a long debate occurred concerning whether "savages" found in America had rational souls (it was decided that they did). The printing press made the widespread, accurate, and rapid exchange of ideas possible. And as we have seen, Luther's challenge to Catholicism resulted in the development of the Protestant movement, which argued against centralized church authority and for increased individualism within the Christian religion.

As influential as the above events were, however, the work of a few astronomer-physicists was most detrimental to church dogma and most influential in creating a new way of examining nature's secrets. That new way was called science.

PTOLEMY, COPERNICUS, KEPLER, AND GALILEO

Ptolemy

In the 2nd century A.D., **Ptolemy**, a Graeco-Egyptian, summarized in his *Mathematical Syntaxis* the mathematical and observational astronomy of his time and that of antiquity. The **Ptolemaic system** included the beliefs that the heavenly bodies, including the earth, were spherical in shape, and the sun, moon, and planets travel around the earth in orbits that are circular and uniform. Although this system reflected the views of most astronomers, including those of Aristotle, there were exceptions. A notable exception was **Aristarchus of Samos** (ca. 310–230 B.C.), the brilliant astronomer at the Museum at Alexandria. Aristarchus believed that the earth rotated on its own axis and that the earth and the other planets revolved around the sun. In other words, Aristarchus arrived at the basic assumptions of the Copernican system, almost 2,000 years before Copernicus. Despite a few such dissenters, the view of the universe reflected in the Ptolemaic system prevailed until the 17th century. The Ptolemaic system was resilient for at least three reasons:

1. It accorded well with the testimony of the senses (i.e., the earth does appear to be the fixed center of the solar system).

2. It allowed astronomical predictions as accurate as could be expected without the aid of modern measuring instruments.

3. Later, it was congenial to Christian theology because it gave humans a central place in the universe and thus was in agreement with the Biblical account of creation.

In medieval theology, the teachings of Ptolemy, like those of Aristotle, became part of official church dogma and were therefore unchallengeable. The worldview based on the Ptolemaic system became deeply entrenched in philosophy, theology, science, and everyday life.

Nicolaus Copernicus

It was not until a devout Roman Catholic priest named **Nicolaus Copernicus** (1473–1543) published his book *De Revolutionibus Orbium Coelestium* that the Ptolemaic system was seriously challenged. In his book, Copernicus argued successfully that, rather than the sun revolving around the earth (the **geocentric theory**), the earth revolved around the sun (the **heliocentric theory**). Copernicus was well aware that his observation directly opposed church dogma and therefore arranged for his work to be published only after his death. Probably more important than the observation itself was that it questioned the place of humankind in the universe. Were we favored by God and therefore placed in the center of the universe? If not, why not? If the church was wrong about this vital fact, was it wrong about other things? Were there other solar systems that contained life? If so, how were they related to ours, and which did God favor? **Giordano Bruno** (1548–1600), besides accepting Copernicus's heliocentric theory, speculated that there were other life-containing solar systems, and he was burned at the stake for his speculations. Bruno's fate helps explain the caution exhibited by scientists and philosophers during these times.

Copernicus was aware that Aristarchus had proposed a theory very similar to his many centuries before and took some comfort in knowing

Nicolaus Copernicus

THE BETTMANN ARCHIVE

this. Nonetheless, he realized that the heliocentric theory was nothing short of revolutionary, and he was justifiably worried. Furthermore, Copernicus knew that despite the theological and philosophical turmoil caused by his theory, *nothing in terms of scientific accuracy was gained by it.* That is, the astrological predictions made by his theory were no more accurate than the ones made by the Ptolemaic system. Also, all known celestial phenomena could be accounted for by the Ptolemaic system; there were no major mysteries that needed explanation. The *only* justification for accepting Copernicus's heliocentric theory was that it cast the known astrological facts into a simpler, more harmonious mathematical order.

In the Ptolemaic system, making a number of complex assumptions concerning the paths of the planets around the earth was necessary. Once these assumptions were made, however, predictions concerning the paths of the planets and eclipses of the sun and moon could be made with considerable accuracy. What Copernicus's system did was to reduce the number of assumptions that needed to be made in order to make those same predictions. As we have seen, a strong resurgence of interest in Platonic philosophy arose in the 15th and 16th centuries, and the Pythagorean aspect of Platonism was stressed during this revival. Working in favor of accepting the Copernican viewpoint was the Pythagorean-Platonic view that the universe operated according to mathematical principles and that those principles are always the simplest and most harmonious possible. It is no accident that the first to accept Copernicus's theory were, like himself, mathematicians who embraced the Pythagorean-Platonic viewpoint. To those embracing nonmathematical Aristotelian philosophy, the idea of contradicting observation in favor of mathematical simplicity was ridiculous.

We have in the Ptolemaic-Copernican debate the first, to use Kuhn's (1973) terminology, scientific revolution. The Ptolemaic system represented the accepted scientific paradigm of the day. Like any paradigm, it defined problems and specified solutions and provided those accepting it with a worldview. The Copernican paradigm focused on different problems, different methods of solution, and a distinctly different worldview. Because to follow Copernicus was to reject the prevailing view of the universe, the opposition to his view was widespread and harsh. The clash between these two paradigms created one of the most violent, intellectual controversies in human history.

Converts to Copernicus's heliocentric theory came slowly. Among the first was Johannes Kepler, a Pythagorean-Platonic mathematician.

Johannes Kepler

As a Protestant, **Johannes Kepler** (1571–1630) was in no danger from the Inquisition, although Luther had condemned the heliocentric theory as a flagrant contradiction of Biblical teachings. Kepler appeared to have two reasons why he risked embracing Copernican theory. First, he, like Copernicus, was a Platonist seeking the simple mathematical harmony that described the

universe. Second, Kepler was a sun worshiper and, as such, was attracted to the greater dignity given the sun in the Copernican system. Throughout his life, when he gave his reasons for accepting Copernican theory, the enhanced position given the sun by that theory was always cited, and it was usually cited first. In keeping with his Pythagorean-Platonic philosophy, Kepler believed that *true* reality was the mathematical harmony that existed beyond the world of appearance. The sensory world, the world of appearances, was an inferior reflection of the certain, unchanging mathematical world. As far as his sun worship is concerned, we will let Kepler speak for himself:

> In the first place, lest perchance a blind man might deny it to you, of all the bodies in the universe the most excellent is the sun, whose whole essence is nothing else than the purest light, than which there is no greater star; which singly and alone is the producer, conserver, and warmer of all things; it is a fountain of light, rich in fruitful heat, most fair, limpid, and pure to the sight, the source of vision, portrayer of all colours, though himself empty of colour, called king of the planets for his motion, heart of the world for his power, its eye for his beauty, and which alone we should judge worthy of the Most High God, should he be pleased with a material domicile and choose a place in which to dwell with the blessed angels. . . . No part of the world, and no star, accounts itself worthy of such a great honour; hence by the highest right we return to the sun, who alone appears, by virtue of his dignity and power . . . worthy to become the home of God himself. (Burtt, 1932, p. 59)

Armed with a mixture of Platonic philosophy, mysticism, and Copernican theory, Kepler not only made a living as an astrologer (he believed the heavenly bodies affected human destiny) but also made significant contributions to astronomy. He worked out and proved many of the mathematical details of the Copernican system, thereby winning its further acceptance. Through mathematical deduction and observation, he found that the paths of the planets around the sun were elliptical rather than circular (as Copernicus had believed). He observed that the velocities of the planets vary inversely with their distance from the sun, thus anticipating Newton's concept of gravitation. Finally, he demonstrated that all the different planetary motions could be described by a single mathematical statement. Perhaps Kepler's most important contribution to science, however, was his insistence that all mathematical deductions be verified by empirical observation.

Kepler also studied vision directly and found that environmental objects project an inverted image onto the retina. This observation contrasted with earlier theories that explained vision as the result of the projection of exact copies of objects directly into the sense receptors. Kepler also questioned our ability to perceive things correctly when the image projected onto the retina is upside down, but he left that problem for others to solve.

Galileo

Galileo (1564–1642) was a brilliant mathematician who, at the young age of 25, was appointed professor of mathematics at the University of Pisa. He, like Copernicus and Kepler, viewed the universe as a perfect machine whose working could be understood only in mathematical terms:

> Philosophy is written in that great book which ever lies before our eyes—I mean the universe—but we cannot understand it if we do not first learn the language and grasp the symbols in which it is written. This book is written in the mathematical language, and the symbols are triangles, circles, and other geometric figures, without whose help it is impossible to comprehend a single word of it; without which one wanders in vain through a dark labyrinth. (Burtt, 1932, p. 75)

Also, like Copernicus and Kepler, Galileo saw his task as explaining the true mathematical reality that existed beyond the world of appearances. Armed with these Pythagorean-Platonic beliefs, Galileo set out to correct a number of misconceptions about the world and about heavenly bodies. He challenged Aristotle's contention that heavy objects fall faster than lighter

ones because of their inherent tendency to do so by *demonstrating* that both fall at the same rate. He accepted the Copernican heliocentric theory and wrote a book in which he demolished all arguments against it. In 1609 he made a telescope with which he discovered the mountains of the moon, sunspots, and the fact that the Milky Way is made up of many stars not visible to the naked eye. He also discovered four moons of Jupiter, and this meant that there were at least 11 bodies in the solar system instead of 7 as was claimed by the church. Most people refused to look through Galileo's telescope because they felt to do so was an act of heresy. Galileo shared one such experience with his friend Kepler.

> Oh, my dear Kepler, how I wish that we could have one hearty laugh together! Here at Padua is the principal professor of philosophy, whom I have repeatedly and urgently requested to look at the moon and planets through my glass, which he pertinaciously refuses to do. Why are you not here? What shouts of laughter we should have at this glorious folly! And to hear the professor of philosophy at Pisa labouring before the Grand Duke with logical arguments, as if with magical incantations, to charm the new planets out of the sky. (Burtt, 1932, p. 77)

With his studies of the dynamics of projectiles, Galileo demonstrated that the motions of all bodies under all circumstances are governed by a single set of mathematical laws. His studies showed that notions of "animation" were unnecessary in explaining physical events. That is, because behavior of objects and events can be explained in terms of external forces, there is no need to postulate "natural places," "passions," "ends," "essences," or any other inherent properties.

In his attitude toward experimentation, we again see Galileo's Pythagorean-Platonic beliefs. For Galileo, discovering a physical law was like discovering a Platonic form. Observation suggests that a lawful relationship may exist, and an experiment is performed to either confirm or disconfirm the possibility. Once a law is discovered, however, further experimentation is not necessary; mathematical deduction is used to precisely describe all possible manifestations of the law. Besides being useful in verifying the existence of laws, Galileo felt that experiments could also function as demonstrations that help convince those skeptical about the existence of certain laws. Galileo, then, relied much more on mathematical deduction than he did on experimentation. On the question of realism versus nominalism, he was clearly on the side of realism. Actual laws (forms) existed, and those laws acted on the physical world. Like a true Platonist, Galileo said that the senses can only provide a hint about the nature of reality. The ultimate explanation of reality must be in terms of the rational order of things; that is, the ultimate explanation must be mathematical.

Objective and subjective reality. Galileo made a sharp distinction between objective and subjective reality. Objective reality exists independent of anyone's perception of it, and its attributes are what later in history were called **primary qualities**. Primary qualities include quantity, shape, size, position, and motion or stationarity. Primary qualities are absolute, objective, immutable, and capable of precise mathematical description. Besides the primary qualities (which constitute physical reality), another type of reality is created by the sensing organism; this reality consists of what later were called **secondary qualities**. Secondary qualities (which constitute subjective reality) are purely psychological experiences and have no counterparts in the physical world. Examples of secondary qualities include the experiences of color, sound, temperature, smell, and taste. According to Galileo, secondary qualities are relative, subjective, and fluctuating. Of primary qualities (like Plato's forms), we can have true knowledge; of secondary qualities, there is only opinion and illusion.

Although secondary qualities may seem as real as primary qualities, they are not. Primary qualities are real, but secondary qualities are merely names we use to describe our subjective (psychological) experiences:

> Hence I think that these tastes, odours, colours, etc., on the side of the object in which they seem

to exist, are nothing else than mere names, but hold their residence solely in the sensitive body; so that if the animal were removed, every such quality would be abolished and annihilated. Nevertheless, as soon as we have imposed names on them . . . we induce ourselves to believe that they also exist just as truly and really as the [primary qualities]. (Burtt, 1932, p. 85)

In studying the physical world, secondary qualities are, at best, irrelevant. If one physical object hits another, the color, smell, or taste of the objects is irrelevant in determining their subsequent paths. For Galileo, it was physical reality, not subjective reality, that could be and should be studied scientifically.

The impossibility of a science of conscious experience. Because so much of our conscious experience consists of secondary qualities and because such qualities can never be described and understood mathematically, Galileo believed that consciousness could never be studied by the objective methods of science. Galileo's position marked a major philosophical shift concerning man's place in the world. Almost without exception, all philosophers and theologians prior to Galileo gave humans a prominent position in the world. If there were good things and bad things in the world and if there were changing and unchanging things in the world, those things also existed in humans. Humans were viewed as a microcosm that reflected the vast macrocosm: "Till the time of Galileo it had always been taken for granted that man and nature were both integral parts of a larger whole, in which man's place was the more fundamental" (Burtt, 1932, p. 89). With Galileo, this view of humans changed. Those experiences that are most human—our pleasures; our disappointments; our passions; our ambitions; our visual, auditory, and olfactory experiences—were now considered inferior to the real world outside of human experience.

At best, humans can come to know the world of astronomy and the world of resting and moving terrestrial objects. However, this knowledge can never be attained by sensory experience alone. It can only be attained by rationally grasping the mathematical laws that exist beyond sensory experience. For the first time in history, we have a view of human conscious experience as secondary, unreal, and totally dependent on the senses, which are deceitful. What is real, important, and dignified was the world outside of man: "Man begins to appear for the first time in the history of thought as an irrelevant spectator and insignificant effect of the great mathematical system which is the substance of reality" (Burtt, 1932, p. 90).

Thus, Galileo excluded from science much of what is now included in psychology, and many modern natural scientists refuse to accept psychology as a science for the same reason that Galileo did not accept it. There have been many efforts to quantify cognitive experience since the time of Galileo, and insofar as these efforts have been successful, Galileo's conclusions about the measurement of secondary qualities were incorrect. How successful these efforts have been, however, has been and is widely disputed.

As we have seen, Aristotle was Galileo's prime target. Using empirical observation and mathematical reasoning, Galileo discredited one Aristotelian "truth" after another—thus attacking the very core of church dogma. At the age of 70, crippled by rheumatism and almost blind, Galileo was brought before the Inquisition and made to recant his scientific conclusions. For the several years that he lived afterward, he is said to have felt severe guilt for having denied what he truly believed. Only recently did the Catholic church admit wrongdoing in the condemnation of Galileo and his views.

With the work of Copernicus, Kepler, and Galileo, the old materialistic view of Democritus was resurrected. The universe appeared to consist of matter whose motion was determined by forces external to it. God had become minimally important in the scheme of things, and now even the place of man was seriously questioned. Are humans part of the natural world? If so, they should be explicable in terms of natural science. Or is there something special about humans that sets them apart from the natural world? If so,

Isaac Newton

how are humans special, and what special laws govern human behavior? The new science favored the view of humans as natural phenomena. Newton's epic-making accomplishments furthered the materialistic view of the universe and encouraged the generalization of that view to humans. Soon the universe and everything in it would be viewed as materialistic and machine-like, including humans.

ISAAC NEWTON

Isaac Newton (1642–1727) was born the year that Galileo died. Like Galileo, Newton conceived of the universe as a complex, lawful machine created by God. Guided by these conceptions, Newton developed differential and integral calculus (Leibniz made the same discovery independently), developed the universal law of gravitation, and did pioneer work in optics. Newton created a conception of the universe that was to prevail in physics and astronomy for more than two centuries, until Einstein revised it. His methods of verification, like those of Galileo, included observation, mathematical deduction, and experimentation. In Newton, who was deeply religious, we have a complete reversal of the earlier faith-oriented way of knowing God: Because God made the universe, studying it objectively was a way of understanding God. In this he agreed with most of the Scholastics and with Copernicus and Kepler.

Although Newton believed in God as the creator of the universe, Newton's work greatly diminished God's influence. God created the universe and set it in motion, but that exhausted his functions. After Newton, it was but a short step to removing God altogether. Similarly, it was only a matter of time before humans, too, would be viewed and analyzed as just another machine that operated in accordance with Newtonian principles.

Perhaps Newton's most significant contribution was his universal law of gravitation. This law synthesized a number of previous findings such as Kepler's observation that planetary motion is elliptical and Galileo's measurements of the acceleration of falling bodies. According to the law of gravitation, *all* objects in the universe attract each other. The amount of attraction is directly proportional to the product of the masses of the bodies and inversely proportional to the square of the distance between them. This single law was able to explain the motion of all physical bodies everywhere in the universe. Although the universe was a machine that God had created, it operated according to principles that humans could discover, and Newton found that these principles could be expressed precisely in mathematical terms—thus his conclusion that "God was a mathematician."

Principles of Newtonian Science

The powerful and highly influential principles of Newtonian science can be summarized as follows:

1. Although God is the creator of the world, he does not actively intervene in the events of the world. It is therefore inappropriate to invoke his will as an explanation of any particular thing or event in the material world.

2. The material world is governed by natural laws, and there are no exceptions to these laws.

3. There is no place for purpose in natural law, and therefore Aristotle's final causes must be rejected. In other words, natural events can never be explained by postulating properties inherent in them. Bodies fall, for example, not because of an inherent tendency to fall, as Aristotle had assumed, but because of various forces acting on them. In other words, as a Newtonian scientist, one must not invoke teleological explanations.

4. Occam's razor is to be accepted. Explanations must always be as simple as possible. In Book III of his *The Mathematical Principles of Natural Philosophy* (1687/1964), Newton gives this advice: "We are to admit no more causes of natural things than such as are both true and sufficient to explain their appearances." This is the principle that caused Copernicus, and many of his fellow mathematicians, to reject the geocentric system in favor of the heliocentric system. Because with God, the simplest is always the best, so too should it be with mathematicians and scientists.

Newton's conception of the universe could not have been simpler. Everything that happens can be explained in terms of (a) space, consisting of points; (b) time, consisting of moments; (c) matter, existing in space and possessing mass; and (d) force, that which provides change in the motion of matter. Newton and his followers believed that the entire physical universe could be explained in terms of these four constructs. In fact, an explanation of any natural event meant restating it mathematically in terms of space, time, matter, and force.

5. Natural laws are absolute, but at any given time our understanding is imperfect. Therefore, scientists often need to settle for proba-

bilities rather than certainty. This is because of human ignorance, not because of any flexibility in natural laws.

6. Classification is not explanation. To note that chasing cats seems to be a characteristic of dogs does not explain *why* dogs tend to chase cats. To understand why anything acts as it does, it is necessary to know the physical attributes of the object being acted on (e.g., its mass) and the nature of the forces acting on it. Again, no purpose of any type can be attributed to either the object or to the forces acting on it.

The success of Copernicus, Kepler, Galileo, and Newton with empirical observation and mathematical deduction stimulated scholars in all fields and launched a spirit of curiosity and experimentation that has lasted. Similarly, the success that resulted from viewing the universe as a machine was to have profound implications for psychology. Science had become a proven way of unlocking nature's secrets, and it was embraced with intense enthusiasm. In many ways, science was becoming the new religion:

> For centuries the Church had been impressing on man the limitations of his own wisdom. The mind of God is unfathomable. God works in a mysterious way his wonders to perform. Man must be content with partial understanding; the rest he must simply believe. For a Galileo or a Newton such a restriction of human curiosity was unacceptable. The scientist was willing to concede that some things may be ultimately unintelligible except on the basis of faith; but as he stubbornly continued to observe, measure and experiment, he discovered that more and more of the puzzles of nature were becoming clear. He was actually explaining in natural terms phenomena that had hitherto been unintelligible. Small wonder, then, that the new science began to generate a faith that ultimately science would displace theology. There is little evidence that in the sixteenth and seventeenth centuries such a faith was more than a dim hope. Nevertheless the seeds had been sown; scientists were uncovering more and more of the secrets of nature; and more and more explanations were now being given "without benefit of clergy." (MacLeod, 1975, p. 105)

Francis Bacon

NATIONAL LIBRARY OF MEDICINE

FRANCIS BACON

It has become traditional to list **Francis Bacon** (1561–1626) as the main spokesman for the new science in its revolt against past authorities, especially Aristotle. His sharp wit and brilliant style of writing have tempted some to speculate that he was the true author of the Shakespearean plays. He was a contemporary of Galileo, almost 100 years younger than Copernicus, and 35 years older than Descartes (whom we will consider next). Bacon was a radical empiricist who believed that nature could only be understood by studying it directly and objectively. Accounts of how nature *should be* based on Scripture, faith, or any philosophical or theological authority will only hamper one's efforts to learn how the world actually functions. Bacon authored the following satirical story, which clearly demonstrates his own positivistic approach and his disdain for authority:

> In the year of our Lord 1432, there arose a grievous quarrel among the brethren over the number of teeth in the mouth of a horse. For 13 days the disputation raged without ceasing. All the ancient books and chronicles were fetched

out, and a wonderful and ponderous erudition, such as was never before heard of in this region, was made manifest. At the beginning of the 14th day, a youthful friar of goodly bearing asked his learned superiors for permission to add a word, and straightway, to the wonderment of the disputants, whose deep wisdom he sore vexed, he beseeched them to unbend in a manner coarse and unheard-of, and to look in the open mouth of a horse and find answer to their questionings. At this, their dignity being grievously hurt, they waxed exceedingly wroth and joining in a mighty uproar, they flew upon him and smote him hip and thigh, and cast him out forthwith. For, said they, surely Satan hath tempted this bold neophyte to declare unholy and unheard-of ways of finding truth contrary to all the teachings of the fathers. After many days of grievous strife the dove of peace sat on the assembly, and they as one man, declaring the problem to be an ever-lasting mystery because of a grievous dearth of historical and theological evidence thereof, so ordered the same writ down. (Baars, 1986, p. 19)

Baconian Science

Although Bacon and Galileo were contemporaries, their approaches to science were very different. Galileo sought general principles (laws) that could be expressed mathematically and from which deductions could be made, an approach that actually required very little experimentation. For Galileo, discovering the laws that governed the physical world was important. Once such laws had been isolated and expressed mathematically, a large number of manifestations of those laws could be deduced (**deduction** involves predicting a particular event from a general principle); Bacon, on the other hand, demanded science based on **induction**. According to Bacon, science should include no theories, no hypotheses, no mathematics, and no deductions but should involve only the facts of observation. He felt that anyone doing research with preconceived notions would tend to see nature in light of those preconceptions. In other words, Bacon felt that accepting a theory was likely to bias one's observations, and he offered Aristotle as an example of a biased researcher. Bacon said that because Aristotle had assumed that the ob-

jects in nature were governed by final causes, his research confirmed the existence of final causes: "[Bacon] declared that when we assume 'final causes' and apply them to science, we are carrying into nature what exists only in our imagination. Instead of understanding *things*, we dispute about *words*, which each man interprets to suit himself" (Esper, 1964, p. 290).

Bacon distrusted rationalism because of its emphasis on words, and he distrusted mathematics because of its emphasis on symbols: Bacon said "words are but the images of matter . . . to fall in love with them is [like falling] in love with a picture" (1605/1878). Bacon trusted only the direct observation and recording of nature. With his radical empiricism, Bacon made it clear that the ultimate authority in science was to be empirical observation. No authority, no theory, no words, no mathematical formulation, no belief, and no fantasy could displace empirical observation as the basis of factual knowledge. Later in history, Bacon's approach to science would be called **positivism**.

But Bacon did not avoid classifying empirical observations. He believed that after many observations, generalizations could be made, and similarities and differences among observations noted. These generalizations could be used to describe classes of events or experiences. In Baconian science, one proceeds from observation to generalization (induction); in Galilean science, one proceeds from a general law to the prediction of specific, empirical events (deduction). Bacon did not deny the importance of the rational powers of the mind, but he believed that those powers should be used to understand the facts of nature rather than the figments of the human imagination.

Bacon (1620/1960) summarized the four sources of error that he felt could creep into scientific investigation in his famous "idols":

- The **idols of the cave** are personal biases that arise from a person's genetic endowment, experiences, education, and feelings. Any of these things can influence how an individual perceives and interprets the world.

• The **idols of the tribe** are biases due to human nature. All humans have in common the abilities to imagine, to will, and to hope, and these human attributes can and usually do distort perceptions. For example, it is common for people to see events as they would like them to be rather than how they really are. Thus, to be human is to have the tendency to perceive selectively.

• The **idols of the marketplace** are biases that result from being overly influenced by the meaning assigned to words. Verbal labels and descriptions can influence one's understanding of the world and distort one's observations of it. Bacon believed that many philosophical disputes were over the definition of words rather than over the nature of reality.

• The **idols of the theater** are biases that result from the blind allegiance to any viewpoint whether it be philosophical or theological.

Science Should Provide Useful Information

Bacon also thought that science could and should change the world for the better. Science would furnish the knowledge that would improve technology, and improved technology would improve the world. As evidence for the power of technical knowledge, Bacon offered the inventions of printing, gunpowder, and the magnetic compass:

> These three [inventions] have changed the whole face and state of things throughout the world; the first in literature, the second in warfare, the third in navigation; whence have followed innumerable changes insomuch that no empire, no sect, no star seems to have exerted greater power and influence in human affairs than these mechanical discoveries. (Bacon, 1620/1960, p. 118).

Although Bacon believed that science should always be judged by its practical consequences, he also believed that "nature to be commanded must be obeyed." Thus, for Bacon, understand-ing nature precedes any attempt to command it. By understanding nature, Bacon meant knowing how things are causally related; once these relationships are known, their practical implications could be explored. Bacon, then, proposed two different types of experiments: *experimenta lucifera* (experiments of light) designed to discover causal relationships and *experimenta fructifera* (experiments of fruit) designed to explore how the laws of nature might be utilized. Whether it involved experiments of light or fruit, Bacon's approach to science was inductive; in both cases, one needed to guard against the idols. Experiments will only yield nature's secrets and provide practical information if they are performed correctly; for Bacon, this meant in an *unbiased manner*.

By insisting that scientists purge their minds of their biases, Bacon was ahead of his time. He was observing that scientists are human too, and like anyone else, their preconceptions can influence their observations. Kuhn (1973) points out the same thing with his concept of paradigm; currently, it is generally agreed that the observations of all scientists (or anyone else) are "theory-laden." That is, one's theory influences what one observes and how one interprets what one observes.

History has shown that Bacon's inductive approach to science was largely ignored and that the deductive approach of Galileo and Newton was highly influential. Contrary to what Bacon believed, it was the case that productive science required bold theory and hypothesis testing. It is not bad to have hunches or even beliefs about how things are; what *is* bad is not modifying those hunches or beliefs if the data require it. One renowned philosopher of science notes that important scientific discoveries never come from induction, as Bacon had believed: "Bold ideas, unjustified anticipations, and speculative thought, are our only means for interpreting nature: . . . our only instrument for grasping her . . . [the] experiment is planned action in which every step is guided by theory" (Popper, 1968, p. 280).

Most scientists since the time of Bacon have

René Descartes

rejected his extreme reliance on the method of induction, but not all. In psychology, Skinner and his followers have adopted Bacon's atheoretical philosophy. In 1950 Skinner wrote an article entitled "Are Theories of Learning Necessary?" and his answer was no. In 1956 Skinner described his approach to experimentation. The approach involved trying one thing and then another, pursuing those things that showed promise, and abandoning those that did not. In the Skinnerian approach to research, there is no theory, no hypotheses, no mathematical analysis, and (supposedly) no preconceptions. Also in the Baconian spirit, the Skinnerians believe that the main goal of science should be to improve the human condition.

Bacon is a pivotal figure because of his extreme skepticism concerning all sources of knowledge except the direct examination of nature. He urged that nature itself be the only authority in settling epistemological questions. We see in Bacon an insistence that observations be made without any philosophical, theological, or personal preconceptions. Skepticism concerning information from the past also characterized the first great philosopher of the new age, René Descartes, to whom we turn next.

RENÉ DESCARTES

Born of wealthy parents in La Haye, France, **René Descartes** (1596–1650) was truly a Renaissance man; at one time or another, he was a soldier, mathematician, philosopher, scientist, and psychologist. In addition, he was a man of the world who enjoyed gambling, dancing, and adventure. But he was also an intensely private person who preferred solitude and avoided emotional attachments with people. At a time when his fame had begun to grow, he moved to Holland; while he was there, he moved 24 times without leaving a forwarding address so that he would not be bothered.

Descartes's mother died shortly after he was born. Because his father, a wealthy lawyer, practiced law some distance from the home, Descartes was reared mainly by his grandmother, a nurse, and an older brother and sister. As one might expect, Descartes was a very bright child. He was enrolled in a Jesuit school at La Fléche when he was 10 years old; he graduated when he was 16. While at La Fléche, he, like other students at the time, studied the writings of Plato, Aristotle, and the early Christian philosophers. At that time, education consisted of logically demonstrating the validity of revealed truths (Scholasticism). As a student, Descartes was especially fond of mathematics, and by the time he was 21, he knew essentially everything there was to be known on the subject.

After his graduation from La Fléche, Descartes roamed freely and sampled many of life's pleasures, finally taking up residence in St. Germain, a suburb of Paris. It was here that Descartes observed a group of mechanical statues, which the queen's fountaineers had constructed for her amusement. The statues contained a system of water pipes that, when activated by a person stepping on a hidden floor-plate, caused a series of complex movements and sounds. As we will see shortly, this idea of complex movement being caused by a substance flowing through pipes was to have a profound influence on Descartes's later philosophy.

Descartes's Search for Philosophical Truth

About the time Descartes moved to St. Germain, he experienced an intellectual crisis. It occurred to him that everything he had ever learned was useless, especially philosophy. He noted that philosophers had been seeking truth for centuries but had been unable to agree among themselves about anything; he concluded that nothing in philosophy was beyond doubt. This realization thrust Descartes into deep depression. He decided that he would be better off learning things for himself instead of from the "experts": "I resolved to seek no other knowledge than that which I might find within myself, or perhaps in the great book of nature" (1637/1956, p. 6).

Descartes's method of self-exploration was almost immediately productive. Usually, Descartes explored his many new ideas during intense meditation while lying in bed; during one of these meditations, one of his greatest insights occurred. Descartes invented analytic geometry after watching a fly in his room. He noted that he could precisely describe the fly's position at any given instance with just three numbers: the fly's perpendicular distances from two walls and from the ceiling. Generalizing from this observation, Descartes showed how geometry and algebra could be integrated, making it possible to represent astronomical phenomena such as planetary orbits with numbers. More generally, Descartes had discovered an exact correspondence between the realm of numbers and the realm of physics. However complicated, all natural events were now describable in mathematical terms. Like Copernicus, Kepler, and Galileo before him and Newton after him, Descartes reached the conclusion that ultimate knowledge is always mathematical knowledge. With the invention of analytic geometry, precisely describing and measuring essentially all known physical phenomena was now possible. In this way, Descartes further substantiated the Pythagorean-Platonic conception of the universe that had been accepted by Copernicus, Kepler, and Galileo and that was about to be elaborated further by Newton.

Next, Descartes sought other areas of human knowledge that could be understood with the same certainty as analytic geometry. Stimulated by his success in mathematics, he summarized his four rules for attaining certainty in any area:

The first rule was never to accept anything as true unless I recognized it to be evidently as such: that is, carefully to avoid all precipitation and prejudgment, and to include nothing in my conclusions unless it presented itself so clearly and distinctly to my mind that there was no reason or occasion to doubt it.

The second was to divide each of the difficulties which I encountered into as many parts as possible, and as might be required for an easier solution.

The third was to think in an orderly fashion, beginning with the things which were simplest and easiest to understand, and gradually and by degrees reaching toward a more complex knowledge, even treating, as though ordered, materials which were not necessarily so.

The last was always to make enumerations so complete, and reviews so general, that I would be certain that nothing was omitted. (1637/1956, p. 12)

Thus began Descartes's search for philosophical truth. He resigned himself to doubt everything that could be doubted and to use whatever was certain just as one would use axioms in mathematics. That is, that which was certain could be used to deduce other certainties. After a painful search, Descartes concluded that the only thing of which he could be certain was the fact that he was doubting, but doubting was thinking and thinking necessitated a thinker. Thus, he arrived at his celebrated conclusion *Cogito, ergo sum* (I think, therefore I am). In this way, Descartes established the certainty of his own thought processes, a certainty that, for him, made the introspective search for knowledge valid.

Innate Ideas

Descartes further analyzed the content of his thought and found that some ideas were experienced with such clarity and distinctiveness that they needed to be accepted as true, and yet they had no counterparts in his personal experience. Descartes thought that such ideas were **innate**— that is, they were natural components of the mind. For example, he observed that even though he was imperfect, he still entertained ideas that were perfect. Because something perfect could not come from something imperfect, Descartes concluded that he could not have been the author of such ideas: "The only hypothesis left was that this idea was put in my mind by a nature that was really more perfect than I was, which had all the perfections that I could imagine, and which was, in a word, God" (1637/1956, p. 22). Among the innate ideas, Descartes included those of unity, infinity, perfection, the axioms of geometry, and God.

Because God exists and is perfect and will not deceive humans, we can trust the information provided by our senses. However, even sensory information must be clear and distinct before it can be accepted as valid. *Clear* means that the information is represented clearly in consciousness, and *distinct* means that the conscious experience cannot be doubted or divided for further analysis. Descartes gave the example of seeing a stick partially submerged in water and concluding that it is bent. Seeing the apparently bent stick provides a clear, cognitive experience, but further analysis, such as removing the stick from the water, would show that the experience was an illusion. Thus, Descartes concluded that rational processes were valid and that knowledge of the physical world gained through the senses could be accepted because God would not deceive us but that even sensory information had to be analyzed rationally in order to determine its validity.

Descartes's method, then, consisted of intuition and deduction. **Intuition** is the process by which an unbiased and attentive mind arrives at a clear and distinct idea, an idea whose validity cannot be doubted. Once such an idea is discovered, one can deduce from it many other valid ideas. An example would be first arriving at the idea that God exists and then deducing that we

can trust our sensory information because God would not deceive us. It is important to note that Descartes's method restored the dignity to purely subjective experience, which had been lost because of Galileo's philosophy. In fact, Descartes found that he could doubt the existence of everything physical (including his own body) but he could not doubt the existence of himself as a thinking being. The first principles of Descartes's philosophy were cognitive in nature and were arrived at by intuition. There is also no mathematical concept any more certain than *Cogito, ergo sum*; this being so, we can turn our attention inward to the mind (self, soul, ego) and examine such subjective experiences as thinking, willing, perceiving, feeling, and imagining. Thus, although Descartes was a rationalist (he stressed the importance of logical thought processes) and a nativist (he stressed the importance of innate ideas), he was also a **phenomenologist**. That is, he introspectively studied the nature of intact, conscious experience. Descartes's method of intuition and deduction was believed to be as valid when directed toward the world of inner experience as it is when directed toward the physical world.

Although Descartes's philosophy was anchored in rational and phenomenological processes, he had an entirely mechanistic conception of the physical world, of all animal behavior, and of much human behavior. In his view, animals responded to the world in a way that could be explained in terms of physical principles. To understand these principles, we must recall Descartes's observation of the statues in St. Germain.

The Reflex

Descartes took the statues at St. Germain as his model in explaining all animal behavior and much human behavior (i.e., Descartes explained both the behavior of the statues and the behavior of animals in terms of mechanical principles). The sense receptors of the body were like the pressure plates, which started the water flowing through the tubes and activated the statues.

Descartes thought of the nerves as hollow tubes containing "delicate threads" that connected the sense receptors to the brain. These threads were connected to the cavities or ventricles of the brain, which were filled with **animal spirits**. The concept of animal spirits was popular among the early Greeks (e.g., Aristotle) and was perpetuated by the highly influential physician Galen (ca. 130–200). These philosophers and physicians believed that the presence of animal spirits distinguished the living from the nonliving. Descartes described animal spirits as a gentle wind or a subtle flame. The delicate threads in the nerves were ordinarily taut, but when an external event stimulated a sense organ, the threads were tightened further and opened a "pore" or "conduit" in the corresponding brain area; the pore then released animal spirits into the nerves. When the animal spirits flowed to the appropriate muscles, they caused the muscles to expand and thus cause behavior. Descartes gave as an example a person's foot coming near a flame. The heat causes a pull on the threads connected to cavities of the brain containing animal spirits. The pull opens one or more of these cavities, allowing animal spirits to travel down small, hollow tubes (nerves) to the foot muscles, which in turn expand and withdraw the foot from the flame. This was the first description of what was later called a reflex. That is, an environmental event (heat) automatically causes a response (foot withdrawal) because of the way the organism is constructed (nerves, muscles, and animal spirits).

By saying that both animal and human interactions with the environment were reflexive, Descartes made it legitimate to study nonhuman animals to learn more about the functioning of the human body. He did a great deal of dissecting and concluded from his research that not only could interactions with the environment be explained through mechanical principles but also so could digestion, respiration, nourishment and growth of the body, circulation of the blood, and even sleeping and dreaming. In 1628 the British physiologist William Harvey (1578–1657) had demonstrated that the heart was a large pump that forced blood into the arteries, then into the veins, then into the lungs, and then back into the arteries. In other words, Harvey discovered that the heart caused the circulation of blood and that the heart's function could be explained using the same mechanical and hydraulic principles that apply to inorganic systems. Descartes took Harvey's discovery as further evidence that many (if not all) bodily functions are mechanical in nature.

Even in Descartes's lifetime, evidence showed that his analysis of reflexive behavior was incorrect. There was fairly conclusive evidence that nerves were not hollow; there was growing evidence that there were two distinctly different types of nerves, sensory nerves carrying information from the sense receptors to the brain and motor nerves carrying information from the brain to the muscles; it had been commonly observed that several animals continued to move and react to certain types of stimulation even after they were decapitated; and it was common knowledge that animals could acquire new responses. Although all these observations posed problems for Descartes's analysis of reflexive behavior, he never modified his position. Before long, however, others would make the necessary corrections in Cartesian theory (*Cartesian* or *Cartesianism* are terms used when referring to some aspect of Descartes's philosophy or methodology).

Descartes's Explanation of Sleep and Dreams

Descartes's explanation of sleep begins by noting that while organisms are awake the cavities of the brain are so filled with animal spirits that the brain tissue engulfing a cavity expands, slightly increasing the tautness of the delicate threads and thus making them maximally responsive to sensory stimulation. Through the day, the amount of animal spirits in the brain cavities diminishes, and the tissue surrounding them becomes lax, whereupon the delicate threads become slack. Under these conditions, the organism is not very responsive to the environment, and we say it is asleep. There are random flows of animal spirits in the cavities, and every now and then isolated cavities will be filled, their connecting threads becoming tight. This causes the random, disconnected experiences we refer to as dreams.

The Mind–Body Interaction

As mentioned, Descartes believed that all animal behavior and internal processes could be explained mechanically, as well as much human behavior and many internal processes. There was, however, an important difference between humans and other animals. Only humans possessed a mind that provided consciousness, free choice, and rationality. Furthermore, the mind was nonphysical and the body physical—that is, the body occupied space but the mind did not. In the process of arriving at the first principle of his philosophy—his "I think, therefore I am" observation, Descartes felt that he had discovered the fact that the mind was nonmaterial. Descartes described what he next deduced from this first principle:

> I then examined closely what I was, and saw that I could imagine that I had no body, and that there was no world nor any place that I occupied, but that I could not imagine for a moment that I did not exist. On the contrary, from the very fact that I doubted the truth of other things, it followed very evidently and very certainly that I existed. On the other hand, if I had . . . ceased to think while all the rest of what I had ever imagined remained true, I would have had no reason to believe that I existed; therefore I concluded that I was a substance whose whole essence or nature was only to think, and which, to exist, has no need of space nor of any material thing. Thus it follows that this ego, this soul, by which I am what I am, is entirely distinct from the body and is easier to know than the latter, and that even if the body were not, the soul would not cease to be all that it now is. (1637/1956, p. 21)

By saying that the nonphysical mind could influence the physical body, Descartes confronted the ancient mind–body problem head-

on. What had been implicit in many philosophies from the time of Pythagoras was explicit in Descartes's philosophy. He clearly stated that humans possessed a body that operated according to physical principles and a mind that did not and that the two interacted (influenced one another). So, on the mind–body problem, Descartes was a **dualist**, and the type of dualism that he subscribed to was **interactionism** (sometimes referred to as *Cartesian dualism*). The question, of course, is how this interaction occurs.

Because the mind was thought of as nonphysical, it could not be located anywhere. Descartes felt that the mind permeated the entire body. That the mind is not housed in the body as a captain is housed in a ship is demonstrated by the fact that our sensory experiences embellish our cognitive experiences, with color for example, and by the fact that we consciously feel bodily states such as hunger, thirst, and pain. None of these experiences or feelings would be possible if the mind was not closely related to the body. Still, Descartes sought a place where the mind exerted its influence on the body. He sought a structure in the brain because the brain stored the animal spirits. Also, the structure had to be unitary because our conscious experience, although often resulting from stimulation coming from the two eyes or two ears, is unitary. Finally, the structure had to be uniquely human because humans alone possess a mind. Descartes chose the *pineal gland* because it was surrounded by animal spirits (what we now call cerebrospinal fluid), it was not duplicated like other brain structures, and (he erroneously believed) it was found only in the human brain. It was through the pineal gland that the mind willed the body to act or inhibited action. When the mind willed something to happen, it stimulated the pineal gland, which in turn stimulated appropriate brain areas, causing animal spirits to flow to various muscles and thus bringing about the willed behavior.

Because the mind is free, it can inhibit or modify the reflexive behavior that the environment would elicit mechanically. Emotions are related to the amount of animal spirits involved in a response; the more animal spirits, the stronger the emotion. Emotions are experienced consciously as *passions* such as love, wonder, hate, desire, joy, anger, or sadness. According to Descartes, the will can and should control the passions so that virtuous conduct results. If, for example, anger is experienced and angry behavior is appropriate, the mind will allow or even facilitate such behavior. If, however, such behavior is seen as inappropriate, the mind will attempt to inhibit it. In the case of an intense passion, the will may be unable to prevent the reflexive behavior, and the person will act irrationally.

Descartes was well aware of the difficulties in explaining how a nonphysical mind could interact with a physical body. After several attempts to explain this interaction, he finally decided that it could not be explained logically. Rather, he supported his argument for separate but interacting mind–body entities with common sense. Everyone, he said, has both bodily and conscious experiences and senses the fact that the two influence one another. Thus, the supreme, rational philosopher supported one of his most basic conceptions by appealing to everyday experience (Tibbetts, 1975).

Descartes's Contributions to Psychology

Descartes attempted a completely mechanistic explanation of many bodily functions and of much behavior. His mechanistic analysis of reflexive behavior can be looked on as the beginning of both stimulus–response and behavioristic psychology. He focused attention on the brain as an important mediator of behavior, and he specified the mind–body relationship with such clarity that it could be supported or refuted by others. Reactions to his notion of innate ideas were so intense that they launched new philosophical and psychological positions (e.g., modern empiricism and modern sensationalism). By actually investigating the bodies of animals to learn more about their functioning, and thus about the functioning of human bodies, he gave birth to both modern physiological and comparative psychology. By making purely subjective experience respectable again, Descartes paved the way for the scientific study of consciousness. His work on conflict did not focus on sinful-versus-moral behavior but on animal-versus-human, rational behavior; he was interested in the type of conflict that Freud later studied. Finally, because of his use of introspection to find clear and distinct ideas, Descartes can be looked on as an early phenomenologist. The phenomenologist studies intact, meaningful, conscious experience without dissecting it in any way.

After Descartes, some philosophers elaborated the mechanical side of his theory by saying that humans were *nothing but* machines and that the concept of mind was unnecessary. Others stressed the cognitive side of his philosophy, saying that consciousness was the most important aspect of humans. In any case, what followed Descartes was, in one way or another, a reaction to him; for that reason, he is often considered the father of modern philosophy in general and of modern psychology in particular.

Controversy concerning Descartes's religious beliefs clearly reflects the transitional period in which he lived. If one accepts at face value what Descartes said, he undoubtfully believed in the existence of God and accepted the authority of the church. Descartes even withdrew his acceptance of Galileo's scientific observations when he learned that Catholic church officials opposed them. From all this, one might assume that Descartes was a devout believer. However,

The opposite hypothesis, that Descartes was essentially atheistic, may be argued with greater plausibility than the first assumption. According to this hypothesis, Descartes was a pure naturalist caught in a social situation where nonconformity meant persecution and even death. He had no taste for martyrdom, and consequently disguised those of his views which might get him into trouble, and embellished the remainder with a show of piety that must be understood, quite literally, as life insurance. (Descartes, 1637/1956, p. xviii)

Descartes's Fate

Despite efforts to appease the church, Descartes's books were placed on the Catholic index of banned books because it was felt that they led to atheism. As a result, Descartes slowed his writing and instead communicated personally with small groups or individuals who sought his knowledge. One such individual was Queen Christina of Sweden, who in 1650 invited Descartes to be her philosopher-in-residence and he accepted. Unfortunately, the queen insisted on being tutored at five o'clock each morning, and one day Descartes had to travel to the palace before sunrise during a severe Swedish winter. After only six months in Sweden, Descartes caught pneumonia and died. Descartes was first buried in Sweden in a cemetery for distinguished foreigners, but there is more to this unfortunate story:

Sixteen years later, his body was exhumed, as it had been decided by various friends and disciples that it would be more fitting for his bodily remains to rest in France; perhaps they did not respect as seriously as he might have wished, Descartes' belief in the possibility of a disembodied spirit and the existence of mental processes in the absence of any brain. The French ambassador to Sweden took charge and first cut off Descartes' right forefinger as a personal souvenir. It was then found that the special copper coffin provided for transporting the body was too short. So the neck was severed and skull removed to be shipped separately. The coffin returned safely to Paris and Descartes' headless body was reburied with great pomp. The skull had a more sordid fate: it was stolen by an army captain, passed from one Swedish collector to another, and took 150 years to reach Paris, where it was awkwardly shelved in the Academie des Sciences and has apparently remained there ever since. (Boakes, 1984, p. 88)

SUMMARY

Renaissance humanism had four major themes: a belief in the potential of the individual, an insistence that religion be more personal and less institutionalized, an intense interest in the classics, and a negative attitude toward Aristotle's philosophy. The humanists did much to break the authority of the organized church and of Aristotle's philosophy; this had to happen before a scientific attitude could develop. Although the Renaissance was a troubled time, it was a time of great curiosity and creativity. As the power of the church deteriorated, inquiry became increasingly objective because findings no longer needed to fit church dogma. Prior to Copernicus, the Ptolemaic system, which claimed that the earth was the stationary center of the solar system, was essentially universally accepted. Copernicus demonstrated that the earth was not the center of the solar system; Kepler found that the paths of the planets were not circular but elliptical. Galileo found, among other things, that all material bodies fall at the same rate; and using a telescope, he discovered four of Jupiter's moons. Galileo concluded that the universe was lawful and that the results of experiments could be summarized mathematically. He also concluded that a science of psychology was impossible because of the subjective nature of human thought processes.

Newton viewed the universe as a complex, lawful, knowable machine that had been created and set in motion by God. Newton's science was highly theoretical and stressed deduction. Newton's success in explaining much of the physical universe in terms of a few basic laws had a profound influence on science, philosophy, and, eventually, psychology. In fact, Newtonian science was so successful that people began to believe science had the potential to answer all questions. In a sense, science was becoming the new religion.

Bacon wanted science to be completely untainted by past mistakes and therefore urged that scientific investigations be inductive and devoid of theories, hypotheses, and mathematical formulations. Bacon also wanted science to be aimed at the solution of human problems. He described four sources of error that can creep into scientific investigation: the idols of the cave, or biases resulting from personal experience; the idols of the tribe, or cultural prejudice; the idols of the marketplace, or biases due to the traditional meanings of words; and the idols of the theater, or blind acceptance of authority or tradition.

Like Bacon, Descartes wanted a method of inquiry that would yield knowledge about which one could be certain. Descartes doubted everything except for the fact that he doubted and thus concluded that introspection was a valid method for seeking truth. Descartes also decided that sensory information could be trusted because God had created our sensory apparatus and would not deceive us. Taking his inspiration from mechanical statues that he had observed, Descartes concluded that all animal behavior and much human behavior was mechanical. He likened sense receptors to pressure plates that, when stimulated, pulled on tiny strings in the nerves. When pulled, the strings opened pores in the brain that allowed animal spirits to move down the nerves into the muscles, causing them to expand. The expanding muscles, in turn, caused behavior. Descartes saw the mind and body as separate but interacting; that is, the body can influence the mind, and the mind can influence the body. Descartes's version of dualism is called interactionism. Descartes also believed that the mind contained several innate ideas and that emotional behavior, experienced consciously as a passion, was determined by the amount of animal spirits involved in the behavior. Descartes brought much attention to the mind–body relationship, caused great controversy over innate ideas, introspectively studied the phenomena of the mind, stimulated animal research (and thus physiological and comparative psychology), and was the first to describe the reflex, a concept that was to become extremely important in psychology.

The philosophers and scientists of the 16th and 17th centuries that we have reviewed in this chapter were transitional figures. In their lives, we see a mixture of religious subjectivity and the need to be completely objective. These thinkers were not antireligion; they were antidogma. Most of them felt that their work was revealing God's secrets. What made them different from those who had preceded them was their refusal to allow past beliefs or methods to influence their inquiries; and, in fact, their investigations were motivated by apparent errors in previously accepted dogma.

DISCUSSION QUESTIONS

1. Describe the four themes that characterized Renaissance humanism and give an example of each.

2. Why is the Renaissance referred to as a paradoxical period?

3. Describe the Ptolemaic astronomical system and explain why that system was embraced by Christian theologians.

4. On what basis did Copernicus argue that his heliocentric theory should replace Ptolemy's geocentric theory?

5. On what philosophical conception of the universe was the work of Copernicus, Kepler, and Galileo based? Explain.

6. Summarize the theological implications of Copernicus's heliocentric theory.

7. In what way(s) can the clash between the Ptolemaic and Copernican systems be likened to a Kuhnian scientific revolution?

8. Discuss the implications for psychology of Galileo's distinction between primary and secondary qualities.

9. What was Newton's conception of science?

10. Summarize Bacon's view of science.

11. Describe the idols of the cave, marketplace, theater, and tribe.

12. Distinguish between Bacon's experiments of light and experiments of fruit and describe how the two are related.

13. Summarize Descartes's view of the mind–body relationship.

14. Of what was it that Descartes thought he could be certain? Once this certainty was arrived at, how did Descartes use it in further developing his philosophy?

15. Describe the importance of intuition and deduction in Descartes's philosophy.

16. Why is it appropriate to refer to Descartes as a phenomenologist?

17. How did Descartes reach the conclusion that the mind is nonmaterial and has an existence independent of the body?

18. What were Descartes's contributions to psychology?

19. In general, what attitude toward religion did the individuals covered in this chapter have?

SUGGESTIONS FOR FURTHER READING

Bacon, F. (1960). *Bacon: The new organon.* (F. H. Anderson, Ed.). New York: Macmillan. (Original work published 1620.)

In this, his most famous work, Bacon offers his doctrine of the idols and argues that there had been little advance in scientific knowledge because scientific activity had been guided (or misguided) by metaphysical abstractions—that is, science had been deductive. To improve the situation, Bacon calls for a completely inductive approach to science where the starting point of scientific activity is always the direct observation of nature. Bacon did not deny the importance of the rational powers of the mind, but he felt strongly that those powers should be directed toward the understanding of natural events rather than imagined ones.

Burtt, E. A. (1932). *The metaphysical foundations of modern science.* Garden City, NY: Doubleday.

Although quite old, this book does an excellent job of explaining how science was conceived of and advanced by various individuals such as Copernicus, Kepler, Galileo, Descartes, and Newton. (Available in paperback.)

Descartes, R. (1956). *Discourse on method.* (L. J. Lafleur, Ed. and Trans.). Indianapolis: Bobbs-Merrill. (Original work published 1637.)

In this small book, Descartes describes how he arrived at his famous method of seeking truth and discusses the implications of that method for morality, theology, and science. (Available in paperback.)

McMahon, C. E. (1975). Harvey on the soul: A unique episode in the history of psychophysiological thought. *Journal of the History of the Behavioral Sciences, 11,* 276–283.

McMahon discusses Harvey's contention that the characteristics of blood determine the mind–body relationship, not animal spirits (as Descartes contended).

Tibbetts, P. (1975). An historical note on Descartes' psychophysical dualism. *Journal of the History of the Behavioral Sciences, 9,* 162–165.

Tibbetts reviews the correspondence in which Descartes attempted to convince a doubtful Princess Elizabeth that a nonmaterial mind could interact with a material body. Descartes finally conceded that the nature of this interaction could not be explained philosophically or logically. Instead, he concluded that there is a mind and a body and that they interact can only be sensed in the course of everyday life.

GLOSSARY

Animal spirits The substance Descartes, and others, thought was located in the cavities of the brain. When this substance moved, via the nerves, from the brain to the muscles, the muscles swelled, and behavior was instigated.

Aristarchus of Samos (ca. 310–230 B.C.) Sometimes called the "Copernicus of antiquity," speculated that the planets, including the earth, rotated around the sun and that the earth rotates on its own axis, and he did so almost 2,000 years before Copernicus.

Bacon, Francis (1561–1626) Urged an inductive, practical science that was free from the misconceptions of the past and from any theoretical considerations.

Bruno, Giordano (1548–1600) Accepted Copernicus's heliocentric theory and suggested that many solar systems may contain life. For his beliefs, he was burned at the stake.

Copernicus, Nicolaus (1473–1543) Argued that the earth rotated around the sun and therefore the earth was not the center of the solar system as the church had maintained.

Deduction The method of reasoning by which conclusions must follow from certain assumptions, principles, or concepts. If there are five people in a room, for example, one can deduce that there are also four; or if it is assumed that everything in nature exists for a purpose, then one can conclude that humans, too,

exist for a purpose. Deductive reasoning proceeds from the general to the particular.

Descartes, René (1596–1650) Believed that much human behavior can be explained in mechanical terms, that the mind and the body are separate but interacting entities, and that the mind contains innate ideas. With Descartes began comparative-physiological psychology, stimulus–response psychology, phenomenology, and a debate over whether innate ideas exist. Descartes also focused attention on the nature of the relationship between the mind and the body.

Dualist One who believes that a person consists of two separate entities: a mind, which accounts for one's mental experiences and rationality, and a body, which functions according to the same biological and mechanical principles as do the bodies of nonhuman animals.

Erasmus, Desiderius (1466–1536) A Renaissance humanist who opposed fanaticism, religious ritual, and superstition.

Ficino, Marsilio (1433–1499) Founded a Platonic academy in 1462 and sought to do for Plato's philosophy what the Scholastics had done for Aristotle's.

Galileo (1564–1642) Showed several of Aristotle's "truths" to be false and, by using a telescope, extended the known number of bodies in the solar system to 11. Galileo argued that science could deal only with objective reality and that because human perceptions were subjective, they were outside the realm of science.

Geocentric theory The theory, proposed by Ptolemy, that the sun and planets rotate around the earth.

Heliocentric theory The theory, proposed by Copernicus, that the planets, including the earth, rotate around the sun.

Humanism A viewpoint that existed during the Renaissance. It emphasized four themes: individualism, a personal relationship with God, interest in classical wisdom, and a negative attitude toward Aristotle's philosophy.

Idols of the cave Bacon's term for personal biases that result from one's personal characteristics or experiences.

Idols of the marketplace Bacon's term for error that results when one accepts the traditional meanings of the words used to describe things.

Idols of the theater Bacon's term for the inhibition of objective inquiry that results when one accepts dogma, tradition, or authority.

Idols of the tribe Bacon's term for biases that result from humans' natural tendency to view the world selectively.

Induction The method of reasoning that moves from the particular to the general. After a large number of individual instances are observed, a theme or principle common to all of them might be inferred. Deductive reasoning starts with some assumption, whereas inductive reasoning does not. Inductive reasoning proceeds from the particular to the general.

Innate ideas Ideas, like perfection and the axioms of geometry, that Descartes believed could not be derived from one's own experience. Such ideas, according to Descartes, were placed in the mind by God.

Interactionism The version of dualism that accepts the separate existence of a mind and a body and claims that they interact.

Intuition In Descartes's philosophy, the introspective process by which clear and distinct ideas are discovered.

Kepler, Johannes (1571–1630) By observation and mathematical deduction, determined the elliptical paths of the planets around the sun. Kepler also did pioneer work in optics.

Luther, Martin (1483–1546) Was especially disturbed by corruption within the church and by the church's emphasis on ritual. He believed that a major reason for the church's downfall was its embracing of Aristotle's philosophy, and he urged a return to the personal religion that Augustine had described. His attack of the established church contributed to the Reformation, which divided Europe into two warring camps.

Newton, Isaac (1642–1727) Extended the work of Galileo by showing that the motion of all objects in the universe could be explained by his law of gravitation. Although Newton believed in God, he believed that God's will could not be evoked as an explanation of any physical phenomenon. Newton viewed the universe as a complex machine that God had created, set in motion, and then abandoned.

Petrarch, Francesco (1304–1374) A Renaissance humanist referred to by many historians as the father of the Renaissance. He attacked Scholasticism as stifling the human spirit and urged that the classics be studied not for their religious implications but because they were the works of unique human beings. He insisted that God had given humans their vast potential so that it could be utilized. Petrarch's views about human potential helped stimulate the many artistic and literary achievements that characterized the Renaissance.

Phenomenologist One who introspectively studies the nature of conscious experience. Descartes was a phenomenologist.

Pico, Giovanni (1463–1494) Maintained that humans, unlike angels and animals, were capable of changing themselves and the world. He felt that all philosophical positions should be respected and the common elements among them sought.

Positivism The belief that only those objects or events that can be experienced directly should be the object of scientific inquiry. The positivist actively avoids metaphysical speculations.

Primary qualities Attributes of physical objects. For example, size, shape, number, position, and stationarity or movement.

Protestantism The religious movement that denied the authority of the Pope and of Aristotle. It argued against church hierarchy and ritual and instead wanted a simple, deeply personal, and introspective religion like that described by Paul and Augustine.

Ptolemaic system A conception of the solar system that has the earth as its center. During the Middle Ages, the Ptolemaic system was widely accepted because it (1) agreed with everyday experience; (2) was able to predict and account for all astronomical phenomena known at the time; (3) gave humans a central place in the universe; and (4) agreed with the Biblical account of creation.

Ptolemy (fl. second century A.D.) The Graeco-Egyptian astronomer whose synthesis of earlier and contemporary astronomical works came to be called the Ptolemaic system. (See also **Ptolemaic system**.)

Reformation The attempt of Luther and others to reform the Christian church by making it more Augustinian in character. This effort resulted in the division of western European Christianity into Protestantism and Roman Catholicism.

Renaissance The period from about 1450 to about 1600 when there was a rebirth of the open, objective inquiry that had characterized the early Greek philosophers.

Secondary qualities Those apparent attributes of physical objects that, in fact, exist only in the mind of the perceiver—for example, the experiences of color, sound, odor, hot, cold, and taste. Without a perceiver, these phenomena would cease to exist.

CHAPTER 5

Empiricism, Sensationalism, and Positivism

Descartes was so influential that most of the philosophies that developed after him were reactions to some aspect of his philosophy. The major reactions were concentrated in several regions of Europe. The British and the French philosophers denied Descartes's contention that some ideas are innate, saying instead that all ideas are derived from experience. These philosophers attempted to explain the functioning of the mind as Newton had explained the functioning of the universe. That is, they sought a few principles, or laws, that could account for all human cognitive experience.

The German philosophers, instead of denying the existence of a mind, made an active mind central to their conception of human nature. In general, they postulated a mind that could discover and understand the abstract principles that constitute ultimate reality. Instead of postulating a mind that simply recorded and stored sensory experiences, they saw the mind as actively transforming sensory information, thereby giving that information meaning it otherwise would not have. For these German rationalists, knowing the operations of this active mind was vital in determining how humans confronted and understood their world.

Scattered throughout Europe, the romantic philosophers rebelled against the views of the empiricists and rationalists. According to the romantics, both of these philosophies concentrated on one aspect of humans and neglected others. The romantics urged a focus on the total human, a focus that included two aspects the other philosophies either minimized or neglected: human feelings and the uniqueness of each individual.

After Descartes, and to a large extent because of him, the ancient philosophies of empiricism, rationalism, and romanticism were presented more clearly and in greater detail than they had ever been before. It was from the modern manifestations of these philosophies that psychology as we know it today emerged. In this chapter, we focus on British and French empiricism. We will review German rationalism in chapter 6 and romanticism in chapter 7.

BRITISH EMPIRICISM

An empiricist is anyone who believes that knowledge is derived from experience. The importance of experience is usually stressed instead of innate ideas, which are supposed to emerge independently of experience. **Empiricism**, then, is a philosophy that stresses the importance of experience in the attainment of knowledge. The term *experience*, in the definition of empiricism, complicates matters because there are many types of experience. There are "inner" experiences such as dreams, imaginings, fantasies, and a variety of emotions. Also, when one thinks logically, such as during mathematical deduction, one is having vivid, mental (inner) experiences. It has become general practice, however, to exclude inner experience from a definition of empiricism and to refer exclusively to *sensory experience*. However, even after focusing on sensory experience in the definition of empiricism, there is still a problem because it is implied that any philosopher who claims sensory experience to be important in attaining knowledge can be labeled an empiricist. If this were true, even

Descartes could be called an empiricist because, for him, many ideas came from sensory experience. Thus, acknowledging the importance of sensory experience *alone* does not qualify one as an empiricist.

Before discussing what *does* qualify one as an empiricist, one additional source of confusion surrounding the term *empiricism* must be mentioned. In psychology, empiricism is often contrasted with mentalism; this is a mistake, however, because most modern empiricists were also mentalistic. In fact, their main research tool was introspection, and their main goal was to explain mental phenomena (e.g., ideas). What then is an empiricist? In this text, we will use the following definition of empiricism:

> Empiricism . . . is the epistemology that asserts that *the evidence of sense constitutes the primary data of all knowledge; that knowledge cannot exist unless this evidence has first been gathered; and that all subsequent intellectual processes must use this evidence and only this evidence in framing valid propositions about the real world.* (D. N. Robinson, 1986, p. 205)

Highlighting a number of terms in Robinson's definition is important. First, it asserts that sensory experience constitutes the *primary* data of all knowledge; it does not say that such experience alone constitutes knowledge. Second, it asserts that knowledge cannot exist until sensory evidence has *first* been gathered; so for the empiricist, attaining knowledge *begins with* sensory experience. Third, *all subsequent intellectual processes* must focus only on sensory experience in formulating propositions about the world. Thus, it is not the recognition of mental processes that distinguishes the empiricist from the rationalist; rather, it is on what those thought processes are focused. Again, most epistemological approaches use sensory experience as part of their explanation of the origins of knowledge; for the empiricist, however, sensory experience is of supreme importance.

Thomas Hobbes

Although he followed in the tradition of William of Occam and Francis Bacon, **Thomas Hobbes**

Thomas Hobbes

(1588–1679) is often referred to as the founder of British empiricism. Hobbes was educated at Oxford and was friends with both Galileo and Descartes. He also served as Bacon's secretary for a short time. Hobbes was born in Malmesbury, Wiltshire, England. He often joked that he and fear were born twins because his mother attributed his premature birth to her learning of the approach of the Spanish armada. A wealthy uncle provided Hobbes with an Oxford education, but Hobbes claimed that he learned little of value from that education. Hobbes noted that Oxford had a strong Puritan tradition but also had an abundance of "drunkenness, wantonness, gaming, and other such vices" (Peters, 1962, p. 7). Hobbes lived a long, productive, and influential life. He played tennis until the age of 70, and at 84 he wrote his own autobiography. At 86 he published a translation of the *Iliad* and *Odyssey* just for something to do. Prior to his death, he amused himself by having his friends prepare epitaphs for him. Hobbes achieved great fame in his lifetime: "Indeed, like Bernard Shaw, by the time of his death he had become almost an English institution" (Peters, 1962, p. 16).

Humans as machines. Hobbes did not become serious about psychology and philosophy until the age of 40, when he came across a copy of Euclid's *Elements*. This book convinced him that humans could be understood using the techniques of geometry. That is, starting with a few undeniable premises, a number of undeniable conclusions could be drawn. The question was what premises to begin with, and the answer came from Galileo. After visiting Galileo in 1635, Hobbes became convinced that the universe consisted only of matter and motion and that both could be understood in terms of mechanistic principles. Why, asked Hobbes, could not humans too be viewed as machines consisting of nothing but matter and motion? Galileo was able to explain the motion of physical objects in terms of the external forces acting on them— that is, without appealing to inner states or essences. Are not humans part of nature, wondered Hobbes, and if so, cannot their behavior also be explained as matter in motion? This became the self-evident truth that Hobbes needed to apply the deductive method of geometry: *Humans were machines*. Humans were viewed as machines functioning within a larger machine (the universe): "For seeing life is but motion of limbs. . . . For what is the *heart* but a *spring*; and the *nerves* but so many *strings*; and the *joints* but so many *wheels*, giving motion to the whole body" (Hobbes, 1651/1962, p. 19).

It is interesting to note that although Hobbes was a close friend of Bacon, and had himself a considerable reputation, Hobbes was never asked to join the prestigious British Royal Society (founded in 1663). The reason was that the society was dominated by Baconians, and Hobbes had nothing but contempt for Bacon's inductive method. He accused the Baconians of spending too much time on gadgets and experiments and of preferring their eyes, ears, and fingertips to their brains. Instead, Hobbes chose the deductive method of Galileo and Descartes. With Hobbes, we have the first serious attempt to apply the ideas and techniques of Galileo to the study of humans.

Government protects humans from their own destructive instincts. Hobbes's primary interest was politics. He was thoroughly convinced that the best form of government was an absolute monarchy. He believed that humans were innately aggressive, selfish, and greedy; therefore, democracy was dangerous because it gives too much latitude to these negative, natural tendencies. Only when people and the church are subservient to a monarch, he felt, could there be law and order. Without such regulation, human life would be "solitary, poor, nasty, brutish, and short" (Hobbes, 1651/1962, p. 11). It is, according to Hobbes, fear of death that motivates humans to create social order. In other words, civilization is created as a matter of self-defense; each of us must be discouraged from committing crimes against the other. Unless interfered with, humans would selfishly seek power over others so as to guarantee the satisfaction of their own personal needs. The monarch was seen by Hobbes as the final arbitrator in all matters of law, morals, and religion, and the freedom of a person consisted only in those activities not forbidden by law. The laws are determined and enforced by the monarch. Hobbes offended all types of Christians by saying that the church should be subservient to the state and that all human actions could be explained mechanically and therefore free-will was an illusion. Hobbes's most famous work, *Leviathan* (1651), was mainly a political treatise, an attempt to explain and justify rule by an absolute monarch. Hobbes began *Leviathan* with his views on psychology because it was his belief that to govern effectively a monarch needed to have an understanding of human nature.

Hobbes's empiricism. Although Hobbes rejected Bacon's inductive method in favor of the deductive method, he did agree with Bacon on the importance of sensory experience:

The [origin of all thoughts] is that which we can *sense*, for there is no conception in a man's mind, which hath not at first, totally, or by parts, been begotten upon the organs of sense. The rest are derived from that original. (Hobbes, 1651/1962, p. 21)

Thus, although Hobbes accepted Descartes's deductive method, he rejected his concept of innate ideas. For Hobbes, all ideas came from experience or, more specifically, from *sensory experience*.

Hobbes's materialism. Following in the tradition of Democritus, Hobbes believed that everything that exists consists of matter. Hobbes's materialism is clearly evident in the following quotation:

[The universe] is corporeal, that is to say, body; and hath the dimensions of magnitude, namely, length, breadth, and depth: Also every part of body, is likewise body, and hath the like dimensions; and consequently every part of the universe is body, and that which is not body, is no part of the universe: And because the universe is all, that which is no part of it, is *nothing*; and consequently *nowhere*. (1651/1962, p. 483)

Because all that exists is matter and motion, to postulate a nonmaterial mind, as Descartes had done, was to Hobbes absurd. All so-called mental phenomena could be explained by the sense experiences that result when the motion of external bodies stimulates the sense receptors, thereby causing internal motion. What others refer to as "mind," for Hobbes, was nothing more than the sum total of a person's thinking activities—that is, a series of motions within the individual. Concerning the mind–body problem, Hobbes was a **physical monist**; that is, he denied the existence of a nonmaterial mind. Hobbes believed that anything that existed must be physical and therefore could be explained in terms of the laws of physics. Unlike the type of mind Descartes postulated, the mind that Hobbes postulated was physical and therefore subject to the laws of nature.

Explanation of psychological phenomena. *Attention* was explained by the fact that as long as sense organs retain the motion caused by certain external objects, they cannot respond to others. *Imagination* was explained by the fact that sense impressions decay over time. Hobbes said, "*Imagination* therefore is nothing but decaying sense; and is found in men, and many other living creatures, as well sleeping as waking" (1651/1962, p. 23). When a sense impression has decayed for a considerable amount of time, it is called *memory*; "so . . . imagination and memory are but one thing which for divers considerations hath divers names" (1651/1962, p. 24). Memory can be simple or compounded:

Much memory, or memory of many things, is called *experience*. Again, imagination being only of those things which have been formerly perceived by sense, either all at once, or by parts at several times, the former, which is the imagining the whole object as it was presented to the sense is *simple* imagination, as when one imagineth a man, or horse, which he hath seen before. The other is *compounded*; as when, from the sight of a man at one time, and of a horse at another, we conceive in our mind a Centaur. So when a man compoundeth the image of his own person with the image of the actions of another man, as when a man imagines himself a Hercules or an Alexander, which happenth often to them that are much taken with reading of romances, it is a compound imagination, and properly but a fiction of the mind. (Hobbes, 1651/1962, p. 24)

Dreams too have a sensory origin: "The imaginations of them that sleep are those we call *dreams*. And these also, as all other imaginations, have been before, either totally or by parcels, in the sense" (Hobbes, 1651/1962, p. 25). The reason that dreams are typically so vivid is because during sleep there are no new sensory impressions to compete with the imagination.

Explanation of motivation. Hobbes argued that external objects not only produce sense impressions but also influence the vital functions of the body. Those incoming impressions that facilitate vital functions are experienced as pleasurable, and the person seeks to preserve them or to seek them out. Conversely, sense impressions incompatible with the vital functions are experienced as painful, and the person seeks to terminate or avoid them. Human behavior, then, is motivated by *appetite* (the seeking or maintaining of pleasurable experiences) and *aversion* (the avoidance or termination of painful experiences). In other words, Hobbes accepted a hedonistic theory of motivation. According to Hobbes, we use the terms *love* and *hate* to describe our appetites (desires) and aversions:

> That which men desire, they are also said to *love*: And to *hate* those things for which they have aversion. So that desire and love are the same thing; save that by desire, we always signify the absence of the object; by love, most commonly the presence of the same. So also by aversion, we signify the absence; and by hate, the presence of the object. (1651/1962, p. 48)

Denial of free will. In Hobbes's deterministic view of human behavior, there was no place for *free will*. People may *feel* that they are "choosing" because at any given moment one may be confronted with a number of appetites and aversions, and therefore there may be conflicting tendencies to act. Hobbes referred to the recognition of such conflicting tendencies as "deliberation" and to the behavioral tendency that survives that deliberation as *will*: "In *deliberation*, the last appetite, or aversion, immediately adhering to the action, or to the omission thereof, is that we call the *will*. . . . [A]nd beasts that have *deliberation* must necessarily also have *will* (1651/1962, p. 54). In other words, will was defined as the action tendency that prevails when a number of such tendencies exist simultaneously. What appears to be choice is nothing more than a verbal label we use to describe the attractions and aversions we experience while interacting with the environment.

Complex thought processes. So far we have discussed sense impressions and the images and memories derived from them and the general, hedonistic tendency to seek pleasure and avoid pain. Now we discuss how Hobbes explained more complex "thought processes" within his materialistic, mechanistic philosophy. For example, Hobbes attempted to explain "trains of thought," by which he meant the tendency of one thought to follow another in some coherent

manner. The question was how such a phenomenon occurs, and Hobbes answered as follows:

> All fancies are motions within us, relics of those made in the sense: And those motions that immediately succeeded one another in the sense, continue also together after sense: Insofar as the former coming again to take place, and be predominant, the latter followeth, by coherence of the matter moved, in such manner, as water upon a plane table is drawn which way any one part of it is guided by the finger. But because in sense, to one and the same thing perceived, sometimes one thing, sometimes another succeedeth, it comes to pass in time, that in the imagining of anything, there is no certainty what we shall imagine next; only this is certain, it shall be something that succeeded the same before, at one time or another. (1651/1962, p. 28)

Thus, in explaining the cohesion of thoughts, Hobbes reintroduced the law of contiguity that was first proposed by Plato and Aristotle. That is, events that are experienced together are remembered together and are subsequently thought of together. All the British empiricists who followed Hobbes accepted the concept of association as their explanation as to why mental events are experienced or remembered in a particular order.

To summarize Hobbes's position, we can say that he was a *materialist* because he believed that all that existed was physical; he was a *mechanist* because he believed that the universe and everything in it (including humans) were machines; he was a *determinist* because he believed that all activity (including human behavior) is caused by forces acting on physical objects; he was an *empiricist* because he believed that all knowledge was derived from sensory experience; and he was a *hedonist* because he believed that human behavior (as well as the behavior of nonhuman animals) was motivated by the seeking of pleasure and the avoidance of pain. Although, as we will see, not all the empiricists that followed Hobbes were as materialistic or mechanistic as he was, they all joined him in denying the existence of innate ideas. To find someone holding views similar to Hobbes's, one would have to go back to the atomic theory of Democritus.

John Locke

John Locke (1632–1704) was born on August 29 at Wrington in Somerset, England, six years after the death of Francis Bacon. His father was a Puritan, a small landowner, and an attorney. Locke was a 17-year-old student at Westminster School when on January 30, 1649, King Charles I was executed as a traitor to his country. The execution, which Locke may have witnessed, took place in the courtyard of Whitehall Palace, which was close to Locke's school. Locke was born 10 years before the outbreak of civil war, and he lived through this great rebellion that was so important to English history. It was at least partially due to the *Zeitgeist*, then, that Locke, as well as several of his fellow students, were to develop a lifelong interest in politics. Indeed, Locke was to become one of the most influential political philosophers in post-Renaissance Europe.

In 1652 Locke obtained a scholarship from Oxford University where he obtained his bachelor's degree in 1656 and his master's degree in 1658. His first publication was a poem that he wrote, as an undergraduate, as a tribute to Oliver Cromwell. Locke remained at Oxford for 30 years, having academic appointments in Greek, rhetoric, and moral philosophy. He also studied medicine and empirical philosophy, and on his third attempt, he finally attained his doctorate in medicine in 1674. It was through his medical and empirical studies that Locke met Robert Boyle (1627–1691), who was to have a major influence on him. Boyle was one of the founders of the Royal Society and one of the founders of modern chemistry. Locke became Boyle's friend, student, and research assistant. From Boyle, Locke learned that physical objects were composed of "minute corpuscles" that have just a few intrinsic qualities. These corpuscles can be experienced in many numbers and arrangements. Some arrangements result in the experience of primary qualities and some in the experience of secondary qualities. We will see shortly that Boyle's "corpuscular hypothesis" strongly influenced Locke's philosophy. Locke

John Locke

became a member of the Royal Society and as a member performed some studies and demonstrations in chemistry and meteorology. Newton was only 10 years old when Locke arrived at Oxford, but in 1689 the two men met and Locke referred to him as the "incomparable Mr. Newton." Locke corresponded with Newton for the rest of his life, primarily on theological matters (both were deeply religious men).

Among Locke's lesser known publications were his editing of Boyle's *General History of the Air*; an edition of Aesop's *Fables*, which was designed to help children to learn Latin; and a book on money and interest rates (Gregory, 1987). His most famous work, however, and the one most important to psychology was *An Essay Concerning Human Understanding* (1690). Locke worked on the *Essay* for 17 years, and it was finally published when Locke was almost 60 years old. Although the *Essay* was originally published in 1690, Locke revised it several times, and it eventually went into five editions. The fifth edition appeared posthumously in 1706, and it is on this final edition that most of what follows is based. Locke had published very little before the *Essay*, but afterward he published prolifically on such topics as education, government, economics, and Christianity. Voltaire (1694–1778) greatly admired Locke and compared him favorably to Newton. Voltaire did much to create a positive impression of Locke on the continent, especially in France.

Although Hobbes was clearly an empiricist, it was Locke who influenced most of the subsequent British empiricists. For example, most of the British empiricists followed Locke in accepting a mind–body dualism; that is, they rejected Hobbes's physical monism. Whereas Hobbes equated mental images with the motions in the brain that were caused by external motions acting on the sense receptors, Locke was content to say that *somehow* sensory stimulation caused ideas. Early in the *Essay*, Locke washed his hands of the question as to how something physical could cause something mental—it just did.

> I shall not at present meddle with the physical consideration of the mind; or trouble myself to examine wherein its essence consists; or by what motions of our spirits or alterations of our bodies we come to have any *sensation* by our organs, or any *ideas* in our understandings; and whether those ideas do in their formation, any or all of them, depend on matter or no. (1706/1974, p. 63)

Opposition to innate ideas. Locke's *Essay* was, in part, a protest against Descartes's philosophy. It was not Descartes's dualism that Locke attacked, however; it was his notion of **innate ideas**. Despite Hobbes's efforts, the notion of innate ideas was still very popular in Locke's time. Especially influential was the belief that God had instilled in humans innate ideas of morality. Because it was mainly clergymen who accepted the innateness of morality, by attacking the existence of innate ideas, Locke was attacking the church. Locke observed that if the mind contained innate ideas, then all humans should have those

ideas, and clearly they do not. Humans, he said, are not born with any innate ideas whether they be moral, theological, logical, or mathematical.

Where, then, do all the ideas that humans have come from? Locke's famous answer was as follows:

> Let us then suppose the mind to be, as we say, white paper, void of all characters, without any ideas; how comes it to be furnished? Whence comes it by that vast store which the busy and boundless fancy of man has painted on it with an almost endless variety? Whence has it all the materials of reason and knowledge? To this I answer, in one word, from *experience*. In that all our knowledge is founded, and from that it ultimately derives itself. Our observation employed either about external sensible objects, or about the internal operations of our minds perceived and reflected on by ourselves, is that which supplies our understandings with all the materials of thinking. These two are the fountains of knowledge, from whence all the ideas we have, or can naturally have, do spring. (1706/1974, pp. 89–90)

Sensation and reflection. For Locke, an **idea** was simply a mental image that could be employed while thinking: "Whatsoever the mind perceives in itself, or is the immediate object of perception, thought, or understanding, that I call idea" (1706/1974, pp. 111–112). As examples of ideas, Locke gave those expressed by the words "*whiteness, hardness, sweetness, thinking, motion, man, elephant, army,* and *drunkenness*" (1706/1974, p. 89). For Locke, all ideas come from either **sensation** or **reflection**. That is, ideas result either by direct sensory stimulation or by reflection on the remnants of prior sensory stimulation. Reflection, the second fountain of knowledge referred to in the above quotation, is the mind's ability to reflect on itself. Locke had this to say about reflection:

> This source of ideas, every man has wholly in himself; and though it be not sense, as having nothing to do with external objects, yet it is very like it, and might properly enough be called internal sense. But as I call the other sensation, so I call this *reflection*, the ideas it affords being such only, as the mind gets by reflecting on its own operations within itself. (1706/1974, p. 90)

Thus, the source of all ideas is sensation, but the ideas obtained by sensation can be acted on and rearranged by the operations of the mind, thereby giving rise to new ideas. The operations that the mind can bring to bear on the ideas furnished by sensation include "perception, thinking, doubting, believing, reasoning, knowing, and willing" (Locke, 1706/1974, p. 90). Locke is often said to have postulated a passive mind that simply received and stored ideas caused by sensory stimulation. This was true, however, only of sensations. Once the ideas furnished by sensation are in the mind, they can be actively transformed in an almost endless variety of other ideas by the mental operations involved in reflection.

It is important to note that it is Locke's insistence that *all* knowledge is ultimately derived from sensory experience that allows him to be properly labeled an empiricist. However, although the *content* of the mind is derived from sensory stimulation, the operations of the mind are not. The operations of the mind are part of human nature; that is, they are innate. Thus, Locke's philosophy, although labeled empirical, is partially nativistic. Locke opposed the notion of specific innate ideas but not innate operations (faculties) of the mind. Simple ideas concerning the physical world come from sensation (e.g., whiteness, bitterness, motion), and simple ideas concerning our minds come from reflection (e.g., perceiving, willing, reasoning, remembering).

Simple and complex ideas. **Simple ideas,** whether from sensation or reflection, constitute the atoms (corpuscles) of experience because they cannot be divided or analyzed further into other ideas. **Complex ideas,** however, are composites of simple ideas and therefore can be analyzed into their component parts (simple ideas). When the operations of the mind are applied to simple ideas through reflection, complex ideas are formed. That is, through such operations as comparing, remembering, discriminating, combining and enlarging, abstracting, and reasoning, simple ideas are combined into complex ones. Locke explained:

> Simple ideas, the materials of all our knowledge, are suggested and furnished to the mind only by . . . sensation and reflection. When the understanding is once stored with these simple ideas, it has the power to repeat, compare, and unite them, even to an almost infinite variety, and so can make at pleasure new complex ideas. But it is not in the power of the most exalted wit or enlarged understanding, by any quickness or variety of thought, to *invent* or *frame* one new simple idea in the mind, not taken in by the ways before mentioned: nor can any force of the understanding *destroy* those that are there. I would have anyone try to fancy any taste which had never affected his palate, or frame the idea of a scent he had never smelt: and when he can do this, I will also conclude that a blind man hath ideas of colours, and a deaf man true distinct notions of sounds. (1706/1974, pp. 99–100)

The mind, then, can neither create nor destroy ideas, but it can arrange existing ideas in an almost infinite number of configurations.

Emotions. Locke maintained that the feelings of pleasure or pain accompany both simple and complex ideas. The other passions (emotions)—like love, desire, joy, hatred, sorrow, anger, fear, despair, envy, shame, and hope—he felt were all derived from the two basic feelings of pleasure and pain. Things that cause pleasure are good, and things that cause pain are evil:

> Things then are good or evil only in reference to pleasure or pain. That we call *good* which is apt to cause or increase pleasure, or diminish pain in us . . . and, on the contrary, we name that *evil* which is apt to produce or increase any pain, or diminish any pleasure in us. . . . By *pleasure* and *pain* I must be understood to mean of body or mind, as they are commonly distinguished, though in truth they be only different constitutions of the mind, sometimes occasioned by disorder in the body, sometimes by thoughts of the mind. (Locke, 1706/1974, pp. 159–160)

For Locke, the "greatest good" was the freedom to think pleasurable thoughts. Like Hobbes, his theory of human motivation was hedonistic because it maintained that humans are motivated by the search for pleasure and the avoidance of pain. For Locke then, the information that the senses provided was the stuff the mind thought about and had emotional reactions toward.

Primary and secondary qualities. The distinction between primary and secondary qualities is the distinction that several early Greeks, and later Galileo, made between what is physically present and what is experienced psychologically. However, it was Locke's friend and teacher Robert Boyle who introduced the terms **primary qualities** and **secondary qualities**, and Locke borrowed the terms from him (Locke, 1706/1974). Unfortunately, primary and secondary qualities have been defined in two distinctively different ways through the centuries. One way has been to define primary qualities as attributes of physical reality and secondary qualities as attributes of subjective or psychological reality. That is, primary qualities refer to actual attributes of physical objects or events, but secondary qualities refer to psychological experiences that have no counterparts in the physical world. We followed this approach in our discussion of Galileo in chapter 4. Boyle and Locke took a different approach. For them, both primary and secondary qualities referred to characteristics of the physical world; what distinguished between them was the type of psychological experience they caused. Following Boyle, Locke referred to any aspect of a physical object that had the power to produce an idea, a **quality**. Primary qualities have the power to create in us ideas that correspond to actual physical attributes of physical objects—for example, the ideas of solidity, extension, shape, motion or rest, and quantity. With primary qualities, there is a match between what is physically present and what is experienced psychologically. The secondary qualities of objects also have the power to produce ideas, but the ideas that they produce do not correspond to anything in the physical world. The ideas produced by secondary qualities include those of color, sound, temperature, and taste.

Both primary and secondary qualities produce ideas. With primary qualities, the physical stimulation is substantial enough to cause an idea that matches the physical attribute that caused it. With secondary qualities, however, it is only fractions (minute particles) of physical bodies that stimulate us. This fractional stimulation emanates from the physical body stimulating us, but our sensory apparatus is not refined enough to note the physical nature of such stimulation. Instead, we experience something psychologically that is not present (as such) physically:

I think, it is easy to draw this observation, that the ideas of primary qualities of bodies, are resemblances of them, and their patterns do really exist in the bodies themselves, but the ideas, produced in us by these secondary qualities, have no resemblance of them at all. There is nothing like our ideas, existing in the bodies themselves. They are, in the bodies we denominate from them, only a power to produce those sensations in us; and what is sweet, blue, or warm in idea is but the certain bulk, figure, and motion of the insensible parts, in the bodies themselves, which we call so. (Locke, 1706/1974, p. 114)

Locke gave an example:

Blood, to the naked eye, appears all red; but by a good microscope, wherein its lesser parts appear, shows only some few globules of red, swimming in a pellucid liquor, and how these red globules would appear, if glasses could be found that yet could magnify them a thousand or ten thousand times more, is uncertain. (1706/1974, p. 191)

The difference between the ideas caused by primary and secondary qualities then comes down to a matter of the acuteness of the senses.

With his **paradox of the basins**, Locke dramatically demonstrated the nature of ideas caused by secondary qualities. One might ask, Is temperature a characteristic of the physical world? In other words, Is it not safe to assume that objects in the physical world are hot or cold or somewhere in between? Looked at in this way, temperature would be a primary quality. Locke beckoned his readers to take three water basins:

one containing cold water (basin A), one containing hot water (basin B), and the other containing warm water (basin C). If a person places one hand in basin A and the other in basin B, one hand will feel hot and the other cold, supporting the contention that hot and cold are properties of the water (i.e., that temperature is a primary quality). Next, Locke instructs the reader to place both hands in basin C, which contains the warm water. To the hand that was previously in basin A (cold water), the water in basin C will feel hot; to the hand that was previously in basin B (hot water), the water will feel cold, even though the temperature of the water in basin C is physically the same for both hands. Thus, Locke demonstrated that the experience of hot and cold depended on the experiencing person, and temperature therefore reflected secondary qualities:

> The same water, at the same time, may produce the idea of cold by one hand and of heat by the other, whereas it is impossible that the same water, if those ideas were really in it, should at the same time be both hot and cold. (1706/1974, p. 117)

For Locke, the important point was that some of our psychological experiences reflected the physical world as it actually was (those experiences caused by primary qualities) and some did not (those experiences caused by secondary qualities). He did not say, as Galileo had, that subjective reality was inferior to physical reality. For Locke, subjective reality could be studied as objectively as physical reality, and he set out to do just that.

Association of ideas. Associationism is "a psychological theory which takes association to be the fundamental principle of mental life, in terms of which even the higher thought processes are to be explained" (Drever, 1968, p. 11). According to this definition, it is possible to reject associationism and still accept the fact that associative learning does occur. Such was the case with Locke. In fact, Locke's discussion of association came as an afterthought, and a short chapter entitled "Association of Ideas" did not appear until the fourth edition of *Essay*; even then, association was used to explain only *errors* in reasoning.

As we have seen, Locke believed that most knowledge is attained by actively reflecting on the ideas in the mind. By comparing, combining, relating, and otherwise thinking about ideas, our understanding of the world, morality, and ourselves is attained. Where, then, does association enter into Locke's deliberations? Locke used association to explain the *faulty beliefs* that can result from accidents of time or circumstance. Locke called the beliefs that resulted from associative learning "a degree of madness" (1706/1974, p. 250) because they were in opposition to reason. Besides ideas that are clustered in the mind because of some logical connection among them, some ideas are naturally associated, such as when the odor of baking bread causes one to have the idea of bread. These are safe and sure types of associations because they are determined by natural relationships. The types of associations that constitute "a degree of madness" are learned by chance, custom, or mistake. These associations lead to errors in understanding, whereas natural associations cannot. Here is how Locke distinguished between natural and unnatural associations:

> Some of our ideas have a *natural* correspondence and connexion one with another; it is the office and excellency of our reason to trace these, and hold them together in that union and correspondence which is founded in their peculiar beings. Besides this there is another connexion of ideas wholly owing to *chance* or *custom*; ideas that in themselves are not at all kin come to be so united in some men's minds that it is very hard to separate them; they always keep in company, and the one no sooner at any time comes into the understanding but its associate appears with it; and if they are more than two which are thus united, the whole gang, always inseparable, show themselves together. (1706/1974, pp. 250–251)

Locke believed that ideas that succeeded each other because of natural or rational reasons represented true knowledge but that ideas that became associated fortuitously, because of their contiguity, could result in unreasonable beliefs. Locke gave several examples:

> A grown person surfeiting [overindulging] with honey no sooner hears the name of it, but his fancy immediately carries sickness and qualms to his stomach, and he cannot bear the very idea of it; other ideas of dislike, and sickness, and vomiting presently accompany it, and he is disturbed; but he knows from whence to date this weakness, and can tell how he got this indisposition. Had this happened to him by an over-dose of honey when a child, all the same effects would have followed; but the cause would have been mistaken, and the antipathy counted natural. . . . The ideas of goblins and sprites [*sic*] have really no more to do with darkness than light; yet let but a foolish maid inculcate these often on the mind of a child, and raise them there together, possibly he shall never be able to separate them again so long as he lives, but darkness shall ever afterwards bring with it those frightful ideas, and they shall be so joined that he can no more bear the one than the other. . . . A friend of mine knew one perfectly cured of madness by a very harsh and offensive operation. The gentleman who was thus recovered with great sense of gratitude and acknowledgment owned the cure all his life after as the greatest obligation he could have received; but, whatever gratitude and reason suggested to him, he could never bear the sight of the operator; that image brought back with it the idea of that agony which he suffered from his hands, which was too mighty and intolerable for him to endure.
>
> Many children, imputing the pain they endured at school to their books they were corrected for, so join those ideas together that a book becomes their aversion, and they are never reconciled to the study and use of them all their lives after; and thus reading becomes a torment to them, which otherwise possibly they might have made the great pleasure of their lives. (1706/1974, pp. 252–254)

Following Drever's (1968) definition of associationism as an attempt to reduce all mental activity to associative principles, Locke's philosophy certainly did not exemplify associationism. His theory of the mind was essentially complete before he added his comments on the association of ideas. He seemed to overlook the fact that natural relationships are learned by association, just as unnatural ones are. As we have already

seen, this was not true of Hobbes, and as we will see, it was not true of the British empiricists who followed Locke.

Government by the people and for the people. Locke attacked not only the notion of innate ideas but also the notion of innate moral principles. He believed that much dogma was built on the assumption of one innate moral truth or another and that people should seek the truth for themselves rather than having it imposed on them. For this and other reasons, empiricism was considered to be a radical movement that sought to replace religion based on revelation with natural law. Very influential politically, Locke challenged the divine right of kings and proposed a government by and for the people. His political philosophy was accepted enthusiastically by the 19th-century utilitarians; and it was influential in the drafting of America's Declaration of Independence.

George Berkeley

George Berkeley (1685–1753) was born on March 12 in Kilkenny, Ireland. He first attended Kilkenny College; in 1700 at the age of 15, he entered the University of Dublin where he earned his bachelor's degree in 1704, at the age of 20, and his master's degree in 1707, at the age of 22. He received ordination as a deacon of the Anglican church at the age of 24. Also, when he was 24, he published *An Essay Towards a New Theory of Vision* (1709), and a year later he published, perhaps his most important work, *A Treatise Concerning the Principles of Human Knowledge* (1710). His third major work, *Three Dialogues Between Hylas and Philonous* was published during his first trip to England in 1713. Berkeley's fame was firmly established by the three books before he was 30 years old. He continued on at the University of Dublin and lectured in divinity and Greek philosophy until 1724, when he became involved in the founding of a new college in Bermuda intended for both native and white colonial Americans. In 1728 he sailed to Newport, Rhode Island, where he waited for funding for his project. The hoped-for government grants were not forthcoming, however, and Berkeley returned to London. Berkeley's home in Whitehall (near Newport) still stands as a museum containing artifacts of his visit to colonial America. Although Berkeley never traveled west of New England, the city of Berkeley, California, and the University of California campus there bear his name. For the last 18 years of his life, Berkeley was an Anglican bishop of Cloyne in County Cork, Ireland. He died suddenly on January 14, 1753, at Oxford, where he had been helping his son enroll as an undergraduate.

Opposition to materialism. Berkeley observed that the downfall of Scholasticism, caused by attacks on Aristotle's philosophy, had resulted in widespread religious skepticism, if not actual atheism. He also noted that the new philosophy of *materialism* was further deteriorating the foundations of religious belief. While at the University of Dublin, Berkeley studied the works of such individuals as Descartes, Hobbes, Locke, and Newton, and he held these individuals responsible for the dissemination of materialistic philosophy. The worldview created by the materialistic philosophy, Berkeley felt, was that all matter is atomic or corpuscular in nature and that all physical events could be explained in terms of mechanical laws. The world becomes nothing but matter in motion, and the motion of moving objects is explained by natural laws, which are expressible in mathematical terms. Berkeley correctly perceived that materialistic philosophy was pushing God further and further out of the picture, and therefore it was dangerous, if not potentially fatal, to both religion and morality. Berkeley therefore decided to attack materialism at its very foundation, its assumption that *matter* exists:

> For, as we have shewn the doctrine of Matter of Corporeal Substance to have been the main pillar and support of Scepticism, so likewise upon the same foundation have been raised all the impious schemes of Atheism and Irreligion. . . . How great a friend *material substance* has been to Atheists in all ages were needless to

George Berkeley

relate. All their monstrous systems have so visible and necessary a dependence on it, that when this cornerstone is once removed, the whole fabric cannot choose but fall to the ground. (Armstrong, 1965, p. 99)

To be is to be perceived. Berkeley's solution to the problem was bold and sweeping; he attempted to demonstrate that matter does not exist and all claims made by materialistic philosophy must therefore be false. In Berkeley's denial of matter, he both agreed and disagreed with Locke. He agreed with Locke that human knowledge is based *only* on ideas. In fact, in the following quotation we see a great deal of similarity between Berkeley's philosophy and that of Locke. That is, both believed that ideas are the objects of human knowledge and that a mind exists that acts on those ideas:

> It is evident to any one who takes a survey of the *objects of human knowledge*, that they are either *ideas* actually imprinted on the senses; or else such as are perceived by attending to the passions and operations of the mind; or lastly, *ideas* formed by help of memory and imagination—either compounding, dividing, or barely representing those originally perceived in the aforesaid ways. . . . But, besides all that endless variety of ideas or objects of knowledge, there is

likewise Something which knows or perceives them; and exercises divers operations, as willing, imagining, remembering, about them. This perceiving, active being is what I call *mind, spirit, soul,* or *myself.* By which words I do not denote any one of my ideas, but a thing entirely distinct from them, wherein they exist, or, which is the same thing, whereby they are perceived; for the existence of an idea consists in being perceived. (Armstrong, 1965, pp. 61–62)

However, Berkeley strongly disagreed with Locke's contention that a physical world caused our ideas. Even if there were such a world, Berkeley said, we could never know it directly. All things come into existence when they are perceived, and therefore reality consists of our perceptions and nothing more:

It is indeed an opinion strangely prevailing amongst men, that houses, mountains, rivers, and in a word all sensible objects, have an existence, natural or real, distinct from their being perceived by the understanding. But, with how great an assurance and acquiescence soever this Principle may be entertained in the world, yet whoever shall find in his heart to call it in question may, if I mistake not, perceive it to involve a manifest contradiction. For, what are the forementioned objects but the things we perceive by sense? and what do we perceive besides our own ideas or sensations? and is it not plainly repugnant that any one of these, or any combination of them, should exist unperceived? (Armstrong, 1965, p. 62)

Berkeley then reduced matter, and everything else, to the realm of perception:

Some truths there are so near and obvious to the mind that a man need only open his eyes to see them. Such I take this important one to be, viz. that all the choir of heaven and furniture of the earth, in a word all those bodies which compose the mighty frame of the world, have not any subsistence without a mind; that their *being* is to be perceived or known; that consequently so long as they are not actually perceived by me, or do not exist in my mind, or that of any other created spirit, they must either have no existence at all, or else subsist in the mind of some Eternal Spirit: it being perfectly unintelligible, and involving all the absurdity of abstraction, to attribute to any single part of them an existence independent of a spirit. To be convinced of

which, the reader need only reflect, and try to separate in his own thoughts the *being* of a sensible thing from its *being perceived.* (Armstrong, 1965, p. 63)

Only secondary qualities exist. In his discussion of primary and secondary qualities, Berkeley referred to the former as the supposed attributes of physical things and to the latter as ideas or perceptions. Having made this distinction, he then rejected the existence of primary qualities. For him, only secondary qualities (perceptions) existed. This, of course, follows from his contention that "to be is to be perceived." Berkeley argued that materialism could be rejected because there was no physical world:

Some there are who make a distinction betwixt *primary* and *secondary* qualities. By the former they mean extension, figure, motion, rest, solidity or impenetrability, and number; by the latter they denote all other sensible qualities, as colours, sounds, tastes, and so forth. The ideas we have of these last they acknowledge not to be the resemblances of anything existing without the mind, or unperceived; but they will have our ideas of the *primary qualities* to be patterns or images of things which exist without the mind, in an unthinking substance which they call Matter. By Matter, therefore, we are to understand an inert, senseless substance, in which extension, figure, and motion do actually subsist. But it is evident, from what we have already shewn, that extension, figure and motion are only ideas existing in the mind, and that an idea can be like nothing but another idea; and that consequently neither they nor their archetypes can exist in an unperceiving substance. Hence, it is plain that the very notion of what is called *Matter* or *corporeal substance,* involves a contradiction in it. (Armstrong, 1965, p. 64)

Berkeley did not deny the existence of external reality. Of course, Berkeley's contention that everything that exists is a perception raises several questions. For example, if reality is only a matter of perception, does reality cease to exist when one is not perceiving it? And, on what basis can it be assumed that the reality one person perceives is the same reality that others perceive? First, it must be realized that Berkeley did not deny the existence of external reality. What he did deny was that external reality consisted of inert matter, as the materialists maintained:

> I do not argue against the existence of any one thing that we can apprehend, either by sense or reflection. That the things I see with my eyes and touch with my hands do exist, really exist, I make not the least question. The only thing whose existence we deny is that which *philosophers* call Matter or corporeal substance. (Armstrong, 1965, p. 74)

And elsewhere Berkeley said,

> Ideas imprinted on the senses are *real* things, or do really exist: this we do not deny; but we deny they *can* subsist without the minds which perceive them, or that they are resemblances of any archetypes existing without the mind; since the very being of a sensation or idea consists in being perceived, and an idea can be like nothing but an idea. Again, the things perceived by sense may be termed *external*, with regard to their origin; in that they are not generated from within by the mind itself, but imprinted by a Spirit distinct from that which perceives them. Sensible objects may likewise be said to be "without the mind" in another sense, namely when they exist in some other mind. Thus, when I shut my eyes, the things I saw may still exist; but it must be in another mind. (Armstrong, 1965, p. 98)

What creates external reality is God's perception. It is the fact that external reality is God's perception that makes it stable over time and the same for everyone. The so-called laws of nature are ideas in God's mind. On rare occasions, God may "change his mind and thus vary the 'laws of nature,'" thus creating "miracles," but most of the time his perceptions remain the same:

> It may indeed on some occasions be necessary that the Author of nature display His overruling power in producing some appearance out of the ordinary series of things. Such exceptions from the general rules of nature are proper to surprise and awe men into an acknowledgment of the Divine Being; but then they are to be used but seldom, otherwise there is a plain reason why they should fail of that effect. Besides, God seems to choose the convincing our reason of His attributes by the works of nature, which discover so much harmony and contrivance in their make, and are such plain indications of wisdom and beneficence in their Author, rather than to astonish us into a belief of His Being by anomalous and surprising events. (Armstrong, 1965, p. 87)

What we experience through our senses, then, are the ideas in God's mind; with experience, the ideas in our minds come to resemble those in God's mind, in which case it is said that we are accurately perceiving external reality. "To be is to be perceived," and God perceives the physical world, thus giving it existence; we perceive God's perceptions, thus giving those perceptions life in our minds as ideas. If secondary qualities are understood as ideas whose existence depends on a perceiver, then all reality consists of secondary qualities.

Principle of association. According to Berkeley, each sense modality furnishes a different and separate type of information (idea) about an object. It is only through experience that we learn that certain ideas are always associated with a specific object:

> By sight I have the ideas of light and colours, with their several degrees and variations. By touch I perceive hard and soft, heat and cold, motion and resistance; and of all these more and less either as to quantity or degree. Smelling furnishes me with odours; the palate with tastes; and hearing conveys sounds to the mind in all their variety of tone and composition.
>
> And as several of these are observed to accompany each other, they come to be marked by one name, and so to be reputed as one *thing.* Thus, for example, a certain colour, taste, smell, figure and consistence having been observed to go together, are accounted one distinct thing, signified by the name apple; other collections of ideas constitute a stone, a tree, a book, and the like sensible things; which as they are pleasing or disagreeable excite the passions of love, hatred, joy, grief, and so forth. (Armstrong, 1965, p. 61)

Thus, the objects that we name are aggregates of sensations that typically accompany each other. Like Locke, Berkeley accepted the law of contiguity as his associative principle. Unlike Locke, however, he did not use the law to explain only fortuitous or arbitrary associations. For Berkeley, *all* sensations that are consistently experienced together become associated. In fact, for Berkeley, objects were aggregates of sensations and nothing more:

> I see this cherry, I feel it, I taste it: and I am sure *nothing* cannot be seen, or felt, or tasted: it is therefore *real*. Take away the sensations of softness, moisture, redness, tartness, and you take away the cherry, since it is not a being distinct from sensations. A cherry, I say, is nothing but a congeries of sensible impressions, or ideas perceived by various senses: which ideas are united into one thing (or have one name given them) by the mind, because they are observed to attend each other. Thus, when the palate is affected with such a particular taste, the sight is affected with a red colour, the touch with roundness, softness, [etc.]. Hence, when I see, and feel, and taste, in sundry certain manners I am sure the cherry exists, or is real; its reality being in my opinion nothing abstracted from those sensations. But if by the word *cherry* you mean an unknown nature, distinct from all those sensible qualities, and by its *existence* something distinct from its being perceived; then, indeed, I own, neither you nor I, nor any one else, can be sure it exists. (Armstrong, 1965, p. 211)

Berkeley's theory of distance perception. Berkeley agreed with Locke that if a person who was born blind was later able to see, he or she would not be able to distinguish a cube from a triangle. Such discrimination requires the association of visual and tactile experiences. Berkeley went further by saying that such a person would also be incapable of perceiving distance. The reason is the same. For the distance of an object to be judged properly, many sensations must be associated. For example, when viewing an object, the person receives tactile stimulation while walking to it. After several such experiences from the same and from different distances, the visual characteristics of an object alone suggest its distance. That is, when the object is small, it suggests great distance, and when large, it suggests a short distance. Thus, the cues for distance are learned through the process of association. Also, stimulation from other sense modalities become cues for distance for the same reason. Berkeley gave an example:

> Sitting in my study I hear a coach drive along the street; I look through the casement and see it; I walk out and enter into it. Thus, common speech would incline one to think I heard, saw, and touched the same thing, to wit, the coach. It is nevertheless certain the ideas intromitted by each sense are widely different, and distinct from each other; but, having been observed constantly to go together, they are spoken of as one and the same thing. By the variation of the noise, I perceive the different distances of the coach, and that it approaches before I look out. Thus, by the ear I perceive distance just after the same manner as I do by the eye. (Armstrong, 1965, pp. 302–303)

With his empirical theory of distance perception, Berkeley was refuting the theory held by Descartes and others that distance perception was based on the geometry of optics. According to the latter theory, a triangle is formed with the distance between the two eyes as its base and the object fixated on as its apex. A distant object forms a long, narrow triangle, and a nearby object forms a short, broad triangle. Also, the apex angle of the triangle will vary directly with the distance of the object attended to; the greater the distance, the greater the apex angle and vice versa. The convergence and divergence of the eyes are important to this theory but only because it is such movement of the eyes that creates the geometry of distance perception.

According to Berkeley, the problem with the theory of distance perception based on "natural geometry" is that people simply do not perceive distance in that way:

> But those lines and angles, by means whereof some men pretend to explain the perception of distance, are themselves not at all perceived; nor are they in truth ever thought of by those unskillful in optics. I appeal to any one's experience, whether, upon sight of an object, he computes its distance by the bigness of the angle made by the meeting of the two optic axes? or whether he ever thinks of the greater or lesser divergency of the rays which arrive from any point to his pupil? nay, whether it be not perfectly impossible for him to perceive by sense the various angles wherewith the rays, according to their greater or lesser divergence, do fall on the eye? Every one is himself the best judge of what he perceives, and what not. In vain shall

any man tell me, that I perceive certain lines and angles, which introduce into my mind the various ideas of distance, so long as I myself am conscious of no such thing. (Armstrong, 1965, p. 287)

The convergence and divergence of the eyes were extremely important in Berkeley's analysis but not because of the visual angles that such movement created. Rather, they were important because the sensations caused by the convergence and divergence of the eyes became associated with other sensations that became cues for distance:

And, *first*, it is certain by experience, that when we look at a near object with both eyes, according as it approaches or recedes from us, we alter the disposition of our eyes, by lessening or widening the interval between the pupils. This disposition or turn of the eyes is attended with a sensation, which seems to me to be that which in this case brings the idea of greater or lesser distance into the mind.

Not that there is any natural or necessary connexion between the sensation we perceive by the turn of the eyes and greater or lesser distance. But—because the mind has, by constant experience, found the different sensations corresponding to the different dispositions of the eyes to be attended each with a different degree of distance in the object—there has grown an habitual or customary connexion between those two sorts of ideas; so that the mind no sooner perceives the sensation arising from the different turn it gives the eyes, in order to bring the pupils nearer or farther asunder, but it withal perceives the different idea of distance which was wont to be connected with that sensation. Just as, upon hearing a certain sound, the idea is immediately suggested to the understanding which custom had united with it. (Armstrong, 1965, p. 288)

The analysis of the perception of magnitude (size) is the same as for distance perception. In fact, the meaning that any word has is determined by the sensations that typically accompany that word. We have already seen this in the case of "apple" and "cherry." Berkeley gave other examples:

As we see distance so we see magnitude. And we see both in the same way that we see shame or

David Hume

THE BETTMANN ARCHIVE

anger, in the looks of a man. Those passions are themselves invisible; they are nevertheless let in by the eye along with colours and alterations of countenance which are the immediate object of vision, and which signify them for no other reason than barely because they have been observed to accompany them. Without which experience we should no more have taken blushing for a sign of shame than of gladness. (Armstrong, 1965, p. 309)

Berkeley's empirical account of perception and meaning was a milestone in psychology's history because it showed how complex perceptions could be understood as compounds of elementary sensations such as sight, hearing, and touch.

David Hume

Born on April 26 in Edinburgh, Scotland, **David Hume** (1711–1776) was educated at the University of Edinburgh, where he studied law and commerce but left without a degree. Given relative freedom by an inheritance, Hume moved to

La Flèche in France, where Descartes had studied as a young man. It was at La Flèche that Hume, before the age of 28, wrote his most famous work, *Treatise of Human Nature, Being an Attempt to Introduce the Experimental Method of Reasoning into Moral Subjects,* the first volume of which was published in 1739 and the second volume in 1740. About his *Treatise,* Hume said that "it fell dead-born from the press, without reaching such distinction as even to excite a murmur among the zealots" (Flew, 1962, p. 305). In 1742 Hume published his *Philosophical Essays,* which was well received. Hume was always convinced that his *Treatise* was poorly received because of its manner of presentation rather than its content, and in 1748 he published an abbreviated version of the *Treatise* entitled *An Enquiry Concerning Human Understanding.* Much of what follows is based on the posthumous 1777 edition of the *Enquiry.*

Unlike many of the other philosophers of his time, Hume was never a university professor. He was nominated for an academic position twice but the opposition of the Scottish clergy denied him the posts. Hume was skeptical of most religious beliefs, and friction with the church was a constant theme in his life. Toward the end of his life, Hume left the manuscript for his *Dialogues Concerning Natural Religion* with his friend and famous economist Adam Smith, with the understanding that Smith would arrange for its publication. When Hume died in 1776, however, Smith, perhaps fearing reprisal against himself, advised against the publication of the book, and it did not appear until 1779 and then without a publisher's name (Steinberg, 1977).

Hume's goal. According to Hume, "It is evident, that all the sciences have a relation, greater or less, to human nature; and that, however wide any of them may seem to run from it, they still return back by one passage or another" (Flew, 1962, p. 172). Under the heading of science, Hume included such topics as mathematics, natural philosophy (physical science), religion, logic, morals, criticism, and politics. In other words, all important matters reflect human nature, and understanding that nature is therefore essential:

> There is no question of importance, whose decision is not comprised in the science of man; and there is none, which can be decided with any certainty, before we become acquainted with that science. In pretending, therefore, to explain the principles of human nature, we in effect propose a complete system of the sciences, built on a foundation almost entirely new, and the only one upon which they can stand with any security. (Flew, 1962, p. 173)

In developing his science of man, Hume followed in the empirical tradition of Occam, Bacon, Hobbes, Locke, and Berkeley: "As the science of man is the only solid foundation for the other sciences, so, the only solid foundation we can give to this science itself must be laid on experience and observation" (Flew, 1962, p. 173).

Hume, however, was very impressed by the achievements of Newtonian science, and he wanted to do for "moral philosophy" what Newton had done for "natural philosophy":

> Hume believed that he could bring about a reform in moral philosophy comparable to the Newtonian revolution in physics by following the very method of inquiry that Newton had followed. He aspired to be the Newton of the moral sciences. His achievement would in fact surpass Newton's, the science of man is not only the indispensable foundation of natural philosophy, but is also of "greater importance" and "much superior in utility." (E. F. Miller, 1971, p. 156)

In Hume's day, "moral philosophy" referred roughly to what we now call the social sciences, and "natural philosophy" referred to what we now call the physical sciences.

Besides being an empirical science, the science of man would also be an "experimental" science. Because experiments were so useful in the physical sciences, they would also be used in the science of man. However, Hume did not employ experiments in his science of man the same way that they were employed by physical scientists. For the physical scientists, an experiment involved the purposive manipulation of some environmental variable and noting the effect of that manipulation on another variable. Both variables were observable and measurable. As we will see, the major determinants of behavior in Hume's system were cognitive and not directly observable. For Hume, the term *experience* meant *cognitive* experience. What, then, could the term *experiment* mean to Hume? By experiment, Hume meant careful observation of how experiences are related and how experience is related to behavior. Hume noted that his experimental science of human nature would be different from the physical sciences, but different did not mean inferior. In fact, his science might even be superior to the other sciences:

> Moral philosophy has, indeed, this peculiar disadvantage, which is not found in natural [philosophy], that in collecting its experiments, it cannot make them purposely, with premeditation, and after such a manner as to satisfy itself concerning every particular difficulty which may arise. When I am at a loss to know the effects of one body upon another in any situation, I need only put them in that situation, and observe what results from it. But should I endeavour to clear up after the same manner any doubt in moral philosophy, by placing myself in the same case with that which I consider, it is evident this reflection and premeditation would so disturb the operation of my natural principles, as must render it impossible to form any just conclusion from the phenomenon. We must, therefore, glean up our experiments in this science from a cautious observation of human life, and take them as they appear in the common course of the world, by men's behaviour in company, in affairs, and in their pleasures. Where experiments of this kind are judiciously collected and compared, we may hope to establish on them a science which will not be inferior in certainty, and will be much superior in utility, to any other of human comprehension. (Flew, 1962, p. 175)

Hume's goal, then, was to combine the empirical philosophy of his predecessors with the principles of Newtonian science and, in the process, create a science of human nature. It is ironic that with all of Hume's admiration for Newton, Hume tended to use the Baconian inductive method more so than the Newtonian deductive method. The major thrust of Hume's approach was to make careful observations and then to carefully generalize from those observations. Hume occasionally did formulate a hypothesis and test it against experience, but his emphasis was clearly on induction rather than deduction.

Impressions and ideas. Like the empiricists that preceded him, Hume believed that the contents of the mind came only from experience. Also, like his predecessors, he believed that experience (perception) could be stimulated by either internal or external events. Hume agreed with Berkeley that we never experience the physical directly, we can only have perceptions of it:

> It is a question of fact, whether the perceptions of the senses be produced by external objects, resembling them: How shall this question be determined? By experience surely, as all other questions of a like nature. But here experience is, and must be entirely silent. The mind has never any thing present to it but the perceptions, and cannot possibly reach any experience of their connexion with objects. The supposition of such a connexion is, therefore, without any foundation in reasoning. (Steinberg, 1977, p. 105)

Hume distinguished between **impressions,** which were strong, vivid perceptions, and ideas, which were relatively weak perceptions:

> All the perceptions of the human mind resolve themselves into two distinct kinds, which I shall call *impressions* and *ideas*. The difference betwixt these consists in the degrees of force and liveliness, with which they strike upon the mind, and make their way into our thought or consciousness. Those perceptions which enter with most force and violence, we may name *impressions;* and, under this name, I comprehend all our sensations, passions, and emotions, as they make their first appearance in the soul. By *ideas,* I mean the faint images of these in thinking and reasoning. (Flew, 1962, p. 176)

Simple and complex ideas and the imagination. Hume went on to make the same distinction that

Locke made between simple ideas and complex ideas:

> There is another division of our perceptions, which it will be convenient to observe, and which extends itself both to our impressions and ideas. This division is into *simple* and *complex*. Simple perceptions, or impressions and ideas, are such as admit of no distinction nor separation. The complex are the contrary to these, and may be distinguished into parts. Though a particular colour, taste, and smell, are qualities all united together in this apple, it is easy to perceive they are not the same, but are at least distinguishable from each other. (Flew, 1962, p. 177)

Although all simple ideas were once impressions, not all complex ideas necessarily correspond to complex impressions. Once ideas exist in the mind, they can be rearranged in an almost infinite number of ways by the **imagination:**

> Nothing is more free than the imagination of man; and though it cannot exceed that original stock of ideas, furnished by the internal and external senses, it has unlimited power of mixing, compounding, separating, and dividing these ideas, in all the varieties of fiction and vision. It can feign a train of events, with all the appearance of reality, ascribe to them a particular time and place, conceive them as existent, and paint them out to itself with every circumstance, that belongs to any historical fact, which it believes with the greatest certainty. Wherein, therefore, consists the difference between such a fiction and belief? It lies not merely in any peculiar idea, which is annexed to such a conception as commands our assent, and which is wanting to every known fiction. For as the mind has authority over all its ideas, it could voluntarily annex this particular idea to any fiction, and consequently be able to believe whatever it pleases; contrary to what we find by daily experience. We can, in our conception, join the head of a man to the body of a horse; but it is not in our power to believe, that such an animal has ever really existed. (Steinberg, 1977, p. 31)

It is interesting to note that, for Hume, the only difference between fact and fiction is the different feelings that an experience produces. Ideas that have been consistently experienced together create the *belief* that one will follow the other. Such beliefs, for us, constitute reality.

Ideas simply explored by the imagination do not have a history of concordance, and therefore they do not elicit a strong belief that one belongs to the other (like a blue banana). What distinguishes fact from fantasy, then, is the degree of belief that one idea belongs with another, and such belief is determined only by experience.

Again, the contents of the mind come only from experience, but once in the mind, ideas can be rearranged at will. Therefore, we can ponder thoughts that do not necessarily correspond to reality. Hume gave the idea of God as an example: "The idea of God, as meaning an infinitely intelligent, wise, and good Being, arises from reflecting on the operations of our own mind, and augmenting, without limit, those qualities of goodness and wisdom" (Steinberg, 1977, p. 11).

To understand Hume, it is important to remember that all human knowledge is based on simple impressions. Hume stated this fact in the form of a general proposition: *That all our simple ideas in their first appearance, are derived from simple impressions, which are correspondent to them, and which they exactly represent* (Flew, 1962, p. 178).

The association of ideas. If ideas were combined only by the imagination, they would be "loose and unconnected," and chance alone would join them together. Also, the associations among ideas would be different for each person because there would be no reason for them to be similar. Hume, however, observed that this was not the case. Rather, a great deal of similarity exists among the associations of all humans, and this similarity must be explained.

Hume considered his account of the association of ideas as one of his greatest achievements: "If anything can entitle the author to so glorious a name as that of an 'inventor,' it is the use he makes of the principle of the association of ideas, which enters into most of his philosophy" (Flew, 1962, p. 302). Hume seems to have overlooked the fact that the laws of association go back at least as far as Plato and Aristotle and were employed by Hobbes, to a lesser extent by Locke, and extensively by Berkeley. It is true, however, that Hume depended on the principles of association to the point where his philosophy can be said to exemplify *associationism*. For Hume, the laws of association do not cement ideas together so that their association becomes immutable. As we have already seen, the imagination can reform the ideas in the mind into almost any configuration. Rather, Hume saw the laws of association as a "gentle force," which created certain associations as opposed to others:

> Were ideas entirely loose and unconnected, chance alone wou'd join them; and 'tis impossible the same simple ideas should fall regularly into complex ones (as they commonly do) without some bond of union among them, some associating quality, by which one idea naturally introduces another. This uniting principle among ideas is not to be consider'd as an inseparable connexion; for that has been already excluded from the imagination: Nor yet are we to conclude, that without it the mind cannot join two ideas; for nothing is more free than that faculty: but we are only to regard it as a gentle force, which commonly prevails, and is the cause why, among other things, languages so nearly correspond to each other; nature in a manner pointing out to every one those simple ideas, which are most proper to be united into a complex one. The qualities, from which this association arises, and by which the mind is after this manner convey'd from one idea to another, are three, *viz.* RESEMBLANCE, CONTIGUITY in time or place, and CAUSE and EFFECT. (Mossner, 1969, p. 58)

Our thoughts, then, are at least influenced by three laws of association. The **law of resemblance** states that our thoughts run easily from one idea to other similar ideas, such as when thinking of one friend stimulates the recollection of other friends. The **law of contiguity** states that when one thinks of an object there is a tendency to recall other objects that were experienced at the same time and place as the object being pondered, such as when remembering a gift will stimulate thoughts of the gift-giver. The **law of cause and effect** states that when we think of an outcome (effect) we tend to also think of the events that typically precede that outcome, such as when we see lightning and consequently

think of thunder. According to Hume, "There is no relation which produces a stronger connexion in the fancy, and makes one idea more readily recall another, than the relation of cause and effect betwixt their objects" (Mossner, 1969, pp. 58–59). Because Hume considered cause and effect to be the most important law of association, we examine it in more detail.

Analysis of causation. From the time of Aristotle, through Scholasticism, and to the science of Hume's day, it was believed that certain causes by their very nature produced certain effects. To make the statement A causes B was to state something of the essences of A and B; that is, there was assumed to be a logical relation between the two events so that knowing A would allow for the prediction of B. This prediction could be made from knowing the essences of A and B and independent of having observed the two events together. Hume completely disagreed with this analysis of causation. For him, we can never know that two events occur together unless we have experienced them occurring together. In fact, for Hume, a causal relationship is a consistently observed relationship and nothing more. There is no way to predict what experiences will follow from other experiences. Causation, then, is not a logical necessity, it is a psychological experience:

> I shall venture to affirm, as a general proposition, which admits of no exception, that the knowledge of this [causal] relation is not, in any instance, attained by reasoning *a priori*; but arises entirely from experience, when we find, that any particular objects are constantly conjoined with each other. Let an object be presented to a man of ever so strong natural reason and abilities; if that object be entirely new to him, he will not be able, by the most accurate examination of its sensible qualities, to discover any of its causes or effects. ADAM, though his rational faculties be supposed, at the very first, entirely perfect, could not have inferred from the fluidity, and transparency of water, that it would suffocate him, or from the light and warmth of fire, that it would consume him. . . . This proposition, *that causes and effects are discoverable, not by reason, but by experience,* will readily

be admitted with regard to such objects, as we remember to have once been altogether unknown to us; since we must be conscious of the utter inability, which we then lay under, of foretelling, what would arise from them. Present two smooth pieces of marble to a man, who has no tincture of natural philosophy; he will never discover, that they will adhere together, in such a manner as to require great force to separate them in a direct line, while they make so small a resistance to a lateral pressure. (Steinberg, 1977, p. 17)

According to Hume, all matters of fact are forms of cause-and-effect relationships, and therefore they can only be learned from experience:

If you were to ask a man, why he believes any matter of fact, which is absent; for instance, that his friend is in the country, or in FRANCE; he would give you a reason; and this reason would be some other fact; as a letter received from him, or the knowledge of his former resolutions and promises. A man, finding a watch or any other machine in a desert island, would conclude, that there had once been men in that island. All our reasonings concerning fact are of the same nature. And here it is constantly supposed, that there is a connexion between the present fact and that which is inferred from it. Were there nothing to bind them together, the inference would be entirely precarious. The hearing of an articulate voice and rational discourse in the dark assures us of the presence of some person: Why? because these are the effects of the human make and fabric, and closely connected with it. (Steinberg, 1977, pp. 16–17)

It was not Hume's intention to deny the existence of causal relationships and thereby undermine science, which searches for them. Rather, Hume attempted to specify what is meant by a causal relationship and how beliefs in such relationships developed. Hume described the observations that need to be made in order to conclude that two events are causally related:

1. The cause and effect must be contiguous in space and time.
2. The cause must be prior to the effect.
3. There must be a constant union betwixt the cause and effect. It is chiefly this quality that constitutes the relation.
4. The same cause always produces the same effect, and the same effect never arises but from the same cause. (Flew, 1962, p. 216)

Thus, it is on the basis of consistent observations that causal inferences are drawn. Predictions based on such observations assume that what happened in the past will continue to happen in the future, but *there is no guarantee of that being the case.* What we operate with is the *belief* that relationships observed in the past will continue to exist in the future and such a belief is accepted on faith alone. Also, even if all conditions listed above are met, one could still be incorrect in drawing a causal inference, such as when one concludes that the sunset causes the sunrise because one always precedes the other and one never occurs without the other first occurring. According to Hume then, it is not rationality that allows us to live effective lives, it is cumulative experience, or what Hume called custom:

Custom, then, is the great guide of human life. It is that principle alone, which renders our experience useful to us, and makes us expect, for the future, a similar train of events with those which have appeared in the past. Without the influence of custom, we should be entirely ignorant of every matter of fact, beyond what is immediately present to the memory and senses. We should never know how to adjust means to ends, or to employ our natural powers in the production of any effect. There would be an end at once of all action, as well as of the chief part of speculation. (Steinberg, 1977, p. 29)

Analysis of the mind and the self. As was mentioned in chapter 1, a persistent problem throughout psychology's history has been to account for the unity of experience. Although we are confronted with a myriad of changing situations, our experience maintains a continuity over time and across conditions. The entities that have been postulated most often to explain the unity of experience are a mind or a self. It was a significant event in psychology's history, then, when Hume claimed that there is neither a mind nor a self.

All beliefs, according to Hume, result from recurring experiences and are explained by the laws of association. All metaphysical entities such as God, soul, and matter are products of the imagination as are the so-called laws of nature. Hume extended his skepticism to include the concept of mind that was so important to many philosophers including Descartes, Locke, and Berkeley. According to Hume, the "mind" is no more than the perceptions that we are having at any given moment: "We may observe, that what we call a *mind,* is nothing but a heap or collection of different perceptions, united together by certain relations, and suppos'd, tho' falsely, to be endow'd with a perfect simplicity and identity" (Mossner, 1969, p. 257).

Just as there is no mind independent of perceptions, there is also no self independent of perceptions:

There are some philosophers who imagine we are every moment intimately conscious of what we call our *self*; that we feel its existence and its continuance in existence; and are certain, beyond the evidence of a demonstration, both of its perfect identity and simplicity. . . . But self or person is not any one impression, but that to which our several impressions and ideas are supposed to have a reference. If any impression gives rise to the idea of self, that impression must continue invariably the same, through the whole course of our lives; since self is supposed to exist after that manner. But there is no impression constant and invariable. Pain and pleasure, grief and joy, passions and sensations succeed each other, and never all exist at the same time. It cannot therefore be from any of these impressions, or from any other, that the idea of self is derived; and consequently there is no such idea. . . . For my part, when I enter most intimately into what I call *myself*, I always stumble on some particular perception or other, of heat or cold, light or shade, love or hatred, pain or pleasure. I never can catch *myself* at any time without a perception, and never can observe anything but the perception. When my perceptions are removed for any time, as by sound sleep, so long am I insensible of *myself*, and may truly be said not to exist. And were all my perceptions removed by death, and could I neither think, nor feel, nor see, nor love, nor hate, after the dissolution of my body, I should be entirely annihilated. (Flew, 1962, pp. 258–259)

The passions (emotions) as the ultimate determinants of behavior. Hume pointed out that throughout human history humans have had the same passions and these passions have motivated similar behaviors:

It is universally acknowledged, that there is a great uniformity among the actions of men, in all nations and ages, and that human nature remains still the same, in its principles and operations. The same motives always produce the same actions: The same events follow from the same causes. Ambition, avarice, self-love, vanity, friendship, generosity, public spirit; these passions, mixed in various degrees, and distributed through society, have been, from the beginning of the world, and still are, the source of all the actions and enterprises, which have ever been observed among mankind. (Steinberg, 1977, p. 55)

Hume noted that even though all humans possess the same passions, they do not do so in the same degree and, because different individuals possess different patterns of passions, they will respond differently to situations. The pattern of passions that a person possesses determines his or her *character,* and it is character that determines behavior. It is a person's character that allows for his or her consistent interactions with people:

The characters, which are peculiar to each individual, have a uniformity in their influence; otherwise our acquaintance with the persons and our observation of their conduct, could never teach us their dispositions, or serve to direct our behaviour with regard to them. (Steinberg, 1977, p. 57)

Thus, different experiences cause different characters, and different characters cause different behaviors:

We must not, however, expect, that this uniformity of human actions should be carried to such a length, as that all men, in the same circumstances, will always act precisely in the same manner, without making any allowance for the diversity of characters, prejudices, and opinions. . . . We learn thence the great force of custom and education, which mould the human mind from its infancy, and form it into a fixed and established character. (Steinberg, 1977, pp. 56–57)

It is through individual experience that certain impressions and ideas become associated with certain emotions. It is the passions elicited by these impressions and ideas, however, that will determine one's behavior. This is another application of the laws of association, only in this case the associations are between various experiences and the passions (emotions) and between passions and behavior. In general, we can say that individuals will seek experiences associated with pleasure and avoid experiences associated with pain.

The fact that human behavior is at times inconsistent does not mean that it is free any more than the weather being sometimes unpredictable means that the weather is free:

> The internal principles and motives may operate in a uniform manner, notwithstanding these seeming irregularities; in the same manner as the winds, rain, clouds, and other variations of the weather are supposed to be governed by steady principles; though not easily discoverable by human sagacity and enquiry. (Steinberg, 1977, p. 58)

Humans learn how to act in different circumstances the same way that nonhuman animals do, that is, through the experience of reward and punishment. In both cases, reasoning ability has nothing to do with it:

> This is . . . evident from the effects of discipline and education on animals, who, by the proper application of rewards and punishments, may be taught any course of action, the most contrary to their natural instincts and propensities. Is it not experience, which renders a dog apprehensive of pain, when you menace him, or lift up the whip to beat him? Is it not even experience, which makes him answer to his name, and infer, from such an arbitrary sound, that you mean him rather than any of his fellows, when you pronounce it in a certain manner, and with a certain tone and accent? . . . Animals, therefore, are not guided in these inferences by reasoning: Neither are children: Neither are the generality of mankind, in their ordinary actions and conclusions:

> Neither are philosophers themselves, who, in all the active parts of life, are, in the main, the same with the vulgar, and are governed by the same maxims. (Steinberg, 1977, pp. 70–71)

It is not ideas or impressions that cause behavior but the passions associated with those ideas or impressions. It is for this reason that Hume said,

> We speak not strictly and philosophically when we talk of the combat of passion and of reason. Reason is, and ought only to be the slave of the passions, and can never pretend to any other office than to serve and obey them. (Mossner, 1969, p. 462)

Hume's influence. Hume vastly increased the importance of what we now call psychology. In fact, he reduced philosophy, religion, and science to psychology. Everything that humans know is learned from experience. All beliefs are simply expectations that events that have been correlated in the past will remain correlated in the future. Such beliefs are not rationally determined, nor can they be rationally defended. They result from experience, and we can only have faith that what we learned from experience will be applicable to the future. According to Hume then, humans can be certain of nothing. It is for this reason that Hume is sometimes referred to as the supreme Skeptic.

Hume accepted only two types of knowledge: demonstrative and empirical. *Demonstrative knowledge* relates ideas to ideas such as in mathematics. Such knowledge is true only by accepted definitions and does not necessarily say anything about facts or objects outside the mind. Demonstrative knowledge is entirely abstract and entirely the product of the imagination. This is not to say that demonstrative knowledge is useless because the relations gleaned in arithmetic, algebra, and geometry are of this type and they represent clear and precise thinking. Such knowledge, however, is based entirely on deduction from one idea to another; therefore, it does not necessarily say anything about empirical events. Conversely, *empirical knowledge* is based on experience, and it alone can furnish knowledge that can effectively guide our conduct in the world. According to Hume, for knowledge to be useful, it must be either demonstrative or empirical; if it is neither, it is not real knowledge and therefore is useless:

> When we run over libraries, persuaded of these principles, what havoc must we make? If we take in our hand any volume; of divinity or school metaphysics, for instance; let us ask, *Does it contain any abstract reasoning concerning quantity or number?* No. *Does it contain any experimental reasoning concerning matter of fact and existence?* No. Commit it then to the flames: For it can contain nothing but sophistry and illusion. (Steinberg, 1977, p. 114)

Hume's insistence that all propositions must be either demonstrably or empirically true places him clearly in the positivistic tradition of Bacon. We have more to say about positivism later in this chapter.

David Hartley

David Hartley (1705–1757), the son of a clergyman, had completed his training as a minister at the University of Cambridge before an interest in biology caused him to seek a career as a physician. Hartley remained deeply religious all his life, believing that understanding natural phenomena increased one's faith in God. It took several years for Hartley to write his long and difficult *Observations on Man, His Frame, His Duty, and His Expectations* (1749). This ponderous book is divided into two parts; the first part (concerning the human frame) contains his contributions to psychology, and the second (concerning the duty and expectations of humans) is almost totally theological. The following statement contained in the preface of Hartley's book reveals his theological concerns:

> I do most firmly believe, upon the authority of the Scriptures, that the future punishment of the wicked will be exceedingly great both in Degree and Duration. . . . And were I able to urge any thing upon a profane careless world, which might convince them of the infinite haz-

David Hartley

ard to which they expose themselves, I would not fail to do it. (Hartley, 1749/1834, p. vii)

Hartley's goal. Although Hartley's *Observations* (1749) appeared several years after Hume's *Treatise on Human Nature* (1739–1740), Hartley had been working on his book for many years and appears not to have been influenced by Hume. His two major influences were Locke and Newton. Hartley accepted Newton's contention that nerves are solid (not hollow as Descartes had believed) and that sensory experience caused vibrations in the nerves. These vibrations were called *impressions*. The impressions reach the brain and cause vibrations in the "infinitesimal, medullary particles," which cause *sensations*. Newton had also observed that vibrations in the brain show a certain inertia; that is, they continue vibrating after the impressions causing them cease. This, according to Newton, was why we see a whirling piece of coal as a circle of light. Hartley expanded on Newton's observations:

> When a person has had a candle, a window, or any other lucid and well-defined object, before his eyes for a considerable time, he may perceive a very clear and precise image thereof to be left in the *sensorium*, fancy, or mind (for these I consider as equivalent expressions . . .) for some time after he has closed his eyes. (1749/1834, pp. 6–7)

For Hartley, it was the lingering vibrations in the brain following a sensation that constituted ideas. Ideas, then, were faint replications of sensations.

Hartley's goal was to synthesize Newton's conception of nerve transmission by vibration with previous versions of empiricism, especially Locke's.

Hartley's explanation of association. Hartley correctly indicated that the idea of association was not new with him:

> The influence of association over our ideas, opinions, and affections, is so great and obvious, as scarcely to have escaped the notice of any writer who has treated of these, though the word *association*, in the particular sense here affixed to it, was first brought into use by Mr. Locke. But all that has been delivered by the ancients and moderns, concerning the power of habit, custom, example, education, authority, party prejudice, the manner of learning the manual and liberal arts, [etc.] goes upon this doctrine as its foundation, and may be considered as the detail of it, in various circumstances. (1749/1834, pp. 41–42)

As we have seen, Hartley believed that sense impressions produced vibrations in the nerves, which traveled to the brain causing similar vibrations in the "medullary substance" of the brain. The brain vibrations caused by sense impressions give rise to sensations. After sense impressions cease, there remains in the brain diminutive vibrations that Hartley called **vibratiuncles.** It is the vibratiuncles that correspond to ideas. Ideas, then, are weaker copies of sensations. Vibratiuncles are like the brain vibrations associated with sensations in every way except they

(the vibratiuncles) are weaker. So much for how sense impressions cause ideas; now the question is How do ideas become associated?

> *Any Sensations* A, B, C, [etc.] *by being associated with one another a sufficient Number of Times, get such a Power over the corresponding Ideas* a, b, c, [etc.] *that any one of the Sensations* A, *when impressed alone, shall be able to excite in the Mind,* b, c, [etc.] *the Ideas of the rest.* (Hartley, 1749/1834, p. 41)

Hartley's notion that experiences consistently occurring together are recorded in the brain as an interrelated package and that experiencing one element in the package will make one conscious of the entire package is remarkably modern. For example, contrast the above quotation from Hartley with the following statement by the modern physiological psychologist Donald Hebb (1904–1985) (the cell assemblies referred to in the following quotation refer to groups of cells in the brain):

> Cell-assemblies that are active at the same time become interconnected. Common events in the child's environment establish assemblies, and then when these events occur together the assemblies become connected (because they are active together). When the baby hears footsteps, let us say, an assembly is excited; while this is still active he sees a face and feels hands picking him up, which excites other assemblies—so that "footsteps assembly" becomes connected with the "face assembly" and the "being-picked-up assembly." After this has happened, when the baby hears footsteps only, all three assemblies are excited; the baby then has something like a perception of a mother's face and the contact of her hands before she has come in sight—but since the sensory stimulations have not yet taken place, this is ideation or imagery, not perception. (Hebb, 1972, p. 67)

Thus, sensations occurring consistently together cause ideas that consistently occur together. Hartley noted that sensations can occur consistently together in two ways; they can occur *simultaneously* or *successively*:

> Thus the sight of part of a large building suggests the idea of the rest instantaneously; and the sound of words which begin a familiar sentence, brings the remaining part to our

memories in order, the association of the parts being synchronous [simultaneous] in the first case, and successive in the last. (1749/1834, p. 42)

As evidence for successive associations, Hartley noted that associative ideas always occur in the direction of the experiences that caused them:

It is to be observed, that, in successive associations, the power of raising the ideas is only exerted according to the order in which the association is made. Thus, if the impressions A, B, C, be always made in the order of the alphabet, B impressed alone will not raise *a,* but *c* only. Agreeably to which it is easy to repeat familiar sentences in the order in which they always occur, but impossible to do it readily in an inverted one. The reason of this is, that the compound idea, *c, b, a,* corresponds to the compound sensation C, B, A; and therefore requires the impression of C, B, A, in the same manner as *a, b, c,* does that of A, B, C. (1749/1834, p. 42)

Although Hartley distinguished between simultaneous and successive associations, both are examples of the *law of contiguity.* Successive experiences follow each other closely in time, and simultaneous events occur at the same time; both exemplify a type of contiguity. As with most accounts of association then, the law of contiguity was at the heart of Hartley's. What made Hartley's account of association significantly different from previous accounts was his attempt to correlate all mental activity with neurophysiological activity.

Simple and complex ideas. Unlike Locke, who believed that complex ideas are formed from simple ideas via reflection, Hartley believed that all complex ideas are formed automatically by the process of association. For Hartley, there were no active mind processes involved at all. Simple ideas that are associated by contiguity form complex ideas. Similarly, complex ideas that are associated by contiguity become associated into "decomplex" ideas. As simple ideas combine into complex ideas and complex ideas combine to form "decomplex" ideas, remembering the individual sensations that make up such

ideas may be difficult. However, for Hartley, all ideas, no matter how complex, are made up of sensations. Furthermore, association is the *only* process responsible for converting simple ideas into complex ones.

The laws of association applied to behavior. Hartley attempted to show that so-called voluntary behavior developed from involuntary, or reflexive, behavior. He used the laws of association to explain how involuntary behavior gradually became voluntary and then became almost involuntary (automatic) again. Involuntary behavior occurs automatically (reflexively) in response to sensory stimulation, voluntary behavior occurs in response to one's ideas or to stimuli not originally associated with the behavior, and voluntary behavior itself can become so habitual that it too becomes automatic, not unlike involuntary behavior. The basic assumption in Hartley's explanation is that all behavior is at first involuntary and gradually becomes voluntary through the process of association. In the following example, we can see that Hartley's explanation of the development of voluntary behavior comes very close to what was later called a conditioned reflex:

The fingers of young children bend upon almost every impression which is made upon the palm of the hand, thus performing the action of grasping, in the original automatic manner. After a sufficient repetition of the motory vibrations which concur in this action, their vibratiuncles are generated, and associated strongly with other vibrations or vibratiuncles, the most commmon of which, I suppose, are those excited by the sight of a favourite plaything which the child uses to grasp, and hold in his hand. He ought, therefore, according to the doctrine of association, to perform and repeat the action of grasping, upon having such a plaything presented to his sight. But it is a known fact, that children do this. By pursuing the same method of reasoning, we may see how, after a sufficient repetition of the proper associations, the sound of the words *grasp, take hold,* [etc.] the sight of the nurse's hand in a state of contraction, the idea of a hand, and particularly of the child's own hand, in that state, and innumerable other associated circumstances, *i.e.* sensations, ideas, and motions, will put the child upon grasping, till, at last, that idea, or state of mind which we may call the will to grasp, is generated, and sufficiently associated with the action to produce it instantaneously. It is therefore perfectly voluntary in this case; and, by the innumerable repetitions of it in this perfectly voluntary state, it comes, at last, to obtain a sufficient connection with so many diminutive sensations, ideas, and motions, as to follow them in the same manner as originally automatic actions do the corresponding sensations, and consequently to be automatic secondarily. And, in the same manner, may all the actions performed with the hands be explained, all those that are very familiar in life passing from the original automatic state through the several degrees of voluntariness till they become perfectly voluntary, and then repassing through the same degrees in an inverted order, till they become secondarily automatic on many occasions, though still perfectly voluntary on some, *viz.* whensoever an express act of the will is exerted. (1749/1834, pp. 66–67)

Thus, behavior is first involuntary, and then it becomes increasingly voluntary as, through the process of association, more and more stimuli become capable of eliciting the behavior. Finally, when performing the voluntary action becomes habitual, it is said to be "secondarily automatic." Hartley's effort to explain the relationship between ideas and behavior was rare among philosophers of his time and practically unheard of before his time. We see in Hartley's explanation much that would later become part of modern learning theory.

The importance of emotion. In general, Hartley believed that excessive vibrations caused the experience of pain and mild or moderate vibrations caused the experience of pleasure. Again, association plays a prominent role in Hartley's analysis. Through experience certain objects, events, and people become associated with pain and others with pleasure. We learn to love and desire those things that give us pleasure, hope for them when they are absent, and experience joy when they are present. Similarly, we learn to hate and avoid those things that give us pain, fear their eventuality, and experience grief when they are present. It was Hartley's disciple

Joseph Priestley (1733–1804), the famous chemist and codiscoverer of oxygen, who saw the implications of Hartley's analysis of emotions for education:

Till the mind has been affected with a sense of pleasure or pain, all objects are alike indifferent to it; but some, in consequence of being always accompanied with a perception of pleasure, become pleasing to us while others, in consequence of being accompanied with a sense of pain, become displeasing; and to effect this nothing can be requisite but the association of agreeable sensations and ideas with the one, and of disagreeable ones with the other. Admitting, therefore, the doctrine of association or that two ideas often occurring together will afterwards introduce one another, we have all that is requisite to the formation of all our passions or affections, or of some things being the objects of love and others of hatred to us. (Sahakian, 1975, p. 48)

Priestley also wrote *Hartley's Theory of the Human Mind, on the Principle of the Association of Ideas* (1775), which did much to promote the popularity of Hartley's ideas.

Hartley's influence. Hartley took the speculations concerning neurophysiology of his time and used them in his analysis of association. His effort was the first major attempt to explain the neurophysiology of thought and behavior since Descartes. The neurophysiological mechanisms that Hartley postulated were largely fictitious, but as more became known about neural transmission and brain mechanisms, the more accurate information replaced the older fictions. Thus, Hartley started the search for the biological correlates of mental events that has continued to the present.

Earlier in this chapter, associationism was defined as any psychological theory that has association as its fundamental principle (Drever, 1968). Using this definition, neither Hobbes's nor Locke's philosophies qualify. Hume probably qualified, but "Hartley . . . was the first man to whom the term associationist can be applied without qualification" (Drever, 1968, p. 14). Hartley's brand of associationism became highly influential and was the authoritative account for about 80 years, or until the time of James Mill.

James Mill

James Mill (1773–1836), a Scotsman, was educated for the ministry at the University of Edinburgh. In 1802 he moved to London to start a literary career, becoming editor of the *Literary Journal* and writing for various periodicals. With the publication of perhaps his greatest literary achievement, *History of British India*, which he began writing in 1806 and finished in 1818, Mill entered a successful career with the East India Company. Mill's most significant contribution to psychology was *Analysis of the Phenomena of the Human Mind*, which originally appeared in 1829 and was revised under the editorship of his son John Stuart Mill in 1869. We will use the 1869 edition of *Analysis* as our primary source in our summary of Mill's ideas. Mill's *Analysis* is regarded as the most complete summary of associationism ever offered. As we will see, Mill's analysis of association was influenced by Hume and especially Hartley. In the 1869 revision of his father's book, John Stuart Mill said of his father,

> At an early period of Mr. Mill's philosophical life Hartley's work had taken a strong hold on his mind; and in the maturity of his powers he formed and executed the purpose of following up Hartley's leading thought, and completing what that thinker had begun. (J. S. Mill, 1869/1967, p. xvii)

Utilitarianism and associationism. In 1808 James Mill met **Jeremy Bentham** (1748–1832), and the two became close, lifelong friends. Bentham was the major spokesman for the British political movement called **utilitarianism.** Bentham rejected all metaphysical and theological arguments for government, morality, and social institutions and instead took the ancient concept of **hedonism** (from the Greek word *hedone,* meaning "pleasure") and made it the cornerstone of his political and ethical theory:

> Nature has placed mankind under the governance of two sovereign masters, *pain* and *plea-*

sure. It is for them alone to point out what we ought to do, as well as to determine what we shall do. On the one hand the standard of right and wrong, on the other the chain of causes and effects, are fastened to their throne. They govern us in all we do, in all we say, in all we think: every effort we can make to throw off their subjection will serve but to demonstrate and confirm it. (Bentham, 1781/1988, p. 1)

Thus, Bentham defined human happiness entirely in terms of the ability to obtain pleasure and avoid pain. Similarly, the best government was defined as one that brought the greatest amount of happiness to the greatest number of people. Although utilitarianism was implicit in the philosophies of a number of the earlier British empiricists, it was Bentham who applied hedonism to society as a whole. Bentham's efforts were highly influential and resulted in a number of reforms in legal and social institutions. In psychology, Bentham's "pleasure principle" not only showed up later in Freudian theory but also in a number of learning theories—for example, in the reinforcement theories of Thorndike and Skinner.

James Mill was one of Bentham's most enthusiastic disciples, and we will see shortly how utilitarianism entered Mill's version of associationism. Mill is best known, however, for his Newtonian, mechanistic, and elementistic view of the mind.

James Mill's analysis of association. Following Hartley, Mill attempted to show that the mind consisted of only sensations and ideas held together by contiguity:

> Thought succeeds thought; idea follows idea, incessantly. If our senses are awake, we are continually receiving sensations, of the eye, the ear, the touch, and so forth; but not sensations alone. After sensations, ideas are perpetually excited of sensations formerly received; after those ideas, other ideas: and during the whole of our lives, a series of those two states of consciousness, called sensations, and ideas, is constantly going on. I see a horse: that is a sensation. Immediately I think of his master: that is an idea. The idea of his master makes me think of his office; he is a minister of state: that is

another idea. The idea of a minister of state makes me think of public affairs; and I am led into a train of political ideas; when I am summoned to dinner. This is a new sensation, followed by the idea of dinner, and of the company with whom I am to partake it. The sight of the company and of the food are other sensations; these suggest ideas without end; other sensations perpetually intervene, suggesting other ideas: and so the process goes on. (J. S. Mill, 1869/1967, pp. 70–71)

Also following Hartley, Mill said that complex ideas are composed of simple ideas. However, when ideas are continuously experienced together, the association among them becomes so strong that they appear in consciousness as one idea:

The word gold, for example, or the word iron, appears to express as simple an idea, as the word colour, or the word sound. Yet it is immediately seen, that the idea of each of those metals is made up of the separate ideas of several sensations; colour, hardness, extension, weight. Those ideas, however, present themselves in such intimate union, that they are constantly spoken of as one, not many. We say, our idea of iron, our idea of gold; and it is only with an effort that reflecting men perform the decomposition. . . . It is to this great law of association, that we trace the formation of our ideas of what we call external objects; that is, the ideas of a certain number of sensations, received together so frequently that they coalesce as it were, and are spoken of under the idea of unity. Hence, what we call the idea of a tree, the idea of a stone, the idea of a horse, the idea of a man. (J. S. Mill, 1869/1967, pp. 91–93)

In fact, all things to which we refer as external objects are clusters of sensations that have been consistently experienced together. In other words, they are complex ideas and, as such, are reducible to simple ideas.

Mill explicitly pointed out what was more implicit in the other "Newtonians of the mind" like Locke, Berkeley, Hume, and Hartley. That is, no matter how complex an idea becomes, it can always be reduced to the simple ideas of which it is constructed. Simple ideas can be added to other simple ideas making a complex idea; complex ideas can be added to complex ideas, making a still more complex idea; and so forth. Still,

at the base of all mental experience are sensations and the ideas that they initiate. In the famous quotation that follows, Mill used Hartley's term *duplex idea*, by which is meant an idea that is formed from the association of two or more complex ideas:

Brick is one complex idea, mortar is another complex idea; these ideas, with ideas of position and quantity, compose my idea of a wall. My idea of a plank is a complex idea, my idea of a rafter is a complex idea, my idea of a nail is a complex idea. These, united with the same ideas of position and quantity, compose my duplex idea of a floor. In the same manner my complex idea of glass, and wood, and others, compose my duplex idea of a window; and these duplex ideas, united together, compose my idea of a house, which is made up of various duplex ideas. How many complex, or duplex ideas, are all united in the idea of furniture? How many more in the idea of merchandize? How many more in the idea called Every Thing? (J. S. Mill, 1869/1967, pp. 115–116)

Still following Hartley, Mill contended that contiguity can occur in two ways: *synchronically* (simultaneously) and *successively*. He gave the following example of simultaneous contiguity: "I have smelt a rose, and looked at, and handled a rose, synchronically; accordingly the name rose suggests to me all those ideas synchronically; and this combination of those simple ideas is called my idea of the rose" (J. S. Mill, 1869/1967, p. 79). About successive contiguity, he said,

Of this important case of association, or of the successive order of our ideas, many remarkable instances might be adduced. Of these none seems better adapted to the learner than the repetition of any passage, or words; the Lord's Prayer, for example, committed to memory. In learning the passage, we repeat it; that is, we pronounce the words, in successive order, from the beginning to the end. The order of the sensations is successive. When we proceed to repeat the passage, the ideas of the words also rise in succession, the preceding always suggesting the succeeding, and no other. *Our* suggests *Father, Father* suggests *which, which* suggests *art*; and so on, to the end. How remarkably this is the case, any one may convince himself, by trying to repeat backwards, even a passage with which he is as familiar as the Lord's Prayer. The case is the same with numbers. A man can go on with the numbers in the progressive order, one, two, three, [etc.] scarcely thinking of his act; and though it is possible for him to repeat them backward, because he is accustomed to subtraction of numbers, he cannot do so without an effort. (J. S. Mill, 1869/1967, pp. 80–81)

The determinants of the strength of associations. Mill believed that two factors caused variation in strengths of associations: *vividness* and *frequency*. That is, sensations or ideas that are more vivid form stronger associations than those that are less vivid; and sensations and ideas that are paired frequently form stronger associations than those paired less frequently.

As far as vividness is concerned, Mill said that (1) sensations are more vivid than ideas, and therefore the associations between sensations are stronger than those between ideas; (2) sensations and ideas that are associated with pleasure or pain are more vivid and therefore form stronger associations than sensations and ideas not related to pleasure or pain; and (3) recent ideas are more vivid and therefore form stronger associations than more remote ideas.

Mill referred to frequency or repetition as "the most remarkable and important cause of the strength of our associations" (J. S. Mill, 1869/1967, p. 87). For Mill, frequency of association explained language development:

Every child learns the language which is spoken by those around him. He also learns it by degrees. He learns first the names of the most familiar objects; and among familiar objects, the names of those which he most frequently has occasion to name; himself, his nurse, his food, his playthings.
A sound heard once in conjunction with another sensation; the word mamma, for example, with the sight of a woman, would produce no greater effect on the child, than the conjunction of any other sensation, which once exists and is gone for ever. But if the word mamma is frequently pronounced, in conjunction with the sight of a particular woman, the sound will by degrees become associated with the sight; and as the pronouncing of the name will call up the idea of the woman, so the sight of the woman will call up the idea of the name. (J. S. Mill, 1869/1967, p. 88)

Similarly, Mill explained many of the experiences associated with arithmetic in terms of the strength of associations based on frequency of occurrence:

In few cases is the strength of association, derived from repetition, more worthy of attention, than in performing arithmetic. All men, whose practice is not great, find the addition of a long column of numbers, tedious, and the accuracy of the operation, by no means certain. Till a man has had considerable practice, there are few acts of the mind more toilsome. The reason is, that the names of the numbers, which correspond to the different steps, do not readily occur; that is, are not strongly associated with the names which precede them. Thus, 7 added to 5, make 12, but the antecedent, 7 added to 5, is not strongly associated with the consequent 12, in the mind of the learner, and he has to wait and search till the name occurs. Thus, again, 12 and 7 make 19; 19 and 8 make 27, and so on to any amount; but if the practice of the performer has been small, the association in each instance is imperfect, and the process irksome and slow. Practice, however; that is, frequency of repetition; makes the association between each of these antecedents and its proper consequent so perfect, that no sooner is the one conceived than the other is conceived, and an expert arithmetician can tell the amount of a long column of figures, with a rapidity, which seems almost miraculous to the man whose faculty of numeration is of the ordinary standard. (J. S. Mill, 1869/1967, pp. 89–90)

In general then, vivid sensations and ideas form stronger associations than nonvivid ones, and the more often sensations or ideas are experienced together, the stronger will be their association.

James Mill's influence. Mill's *Analysis* is regarded as the most complete summary of associationism ever offered. As we have seen, he attempted to show that the mind consisted of only sensations and ideas held together by contiguity. He insisted that any mental experience could be reduced to the simple ideas that made it up. Thus, he gave us a conception of the mind based on Newtonian physics. For Newton, the universe could be understood as consisting of material elements held together by physical forces and behaving in a predictable manner. For Mill, the mind consisted of mental elements held together by the laws of association; therefore, mental experience was as predictable as physical events.

James Mill added nothing new to associationism. His professed goal was to provide evidence for associationism that was lacking in Hartley's account. This he did, and in so doing, he carried associationism to its logical conclusion; many believe, however, that Mill's detailed elaboration of associationism exposed it as an absurdity. In any case, the mind as viewed by Mill (and by Hartley) was completely passive; that is, it had no creative abilities. Association was the only process that organized ideas, and it did so automatically. This conception of the mind, sometimes referred to as "mental physics" or "mental mechanics," essentially ended with James Mill. In fact, as we see next, James Mill's son John Stuart Mill was among the first to revise the purely mechanistic, elementistic view of his father.

John Stuart Mill

James Mill's interest in psychology was only secondary. He was a social reformer and, like Hobbes, he believed social, political, and educational change is facilitated by an understanding of human nature. He believed that Benthamism, coupled with associationism, justified a radical, libertarian political philosophy. James Mill and his followers were quite successful in bringing about substantial social change. He also tried his theory of human nature on a smaller, more personal scale by using it as a guide in rearing his son **John Stuart Mill** (1806–1873). James Mill's attempt at using associative principles in raising his son must have been at least partially successful because John Stuart had learned Greek by the time he was 3 years old, Latin and algebra by age 8, and logic by age 12.

J. S. Mill's most famous work was *A System of Logic, Ratiocinative and Inductive, Being a Connected View of the Principles of Evidence, and the Methods of Scientific Investigation* (1843). This book was an immediate success, went through eight editions in Mill's own lifetime, and remained a best-seller throughout the 19th century. Mill's book was considered must reading for any late-19th-century scientist. In our summary of Mill's work, we will use the eighth edition of his *System of Logic* that appeared in 1893. In *Examination of Sir William Hamilton's Philosophy* (1865), he responded to criticisms of his philosophy and elaborated and defended the views of human nature that he had presented in his *System of Logic*. In 1869 he published a new edition of his father's *Analysis*, adding numerous footnotes of his own that extended and clarified his father's views on associationistic psychology and sometimes criticizing his father's views.

J. S. Mill did as much as anyone at the time to facilitate the development of psychology as a science. This he did by describing the methodology that should be used by all sciences and showing in great detail how that methodology could be used in a science of human nature. In fact, he felt that the lawfulness of human thought, feeling, and action was entirely conducive to scientific inquiry.

Mental chemistry versus mental physics. In most important respects, J. S. Mill accepted his father's brand of associationism. J. S. Mill believed that (1) every sensation leaves in the mind an idea that resembles the sensation but is weaker in intensity (J. S. Mill called ideas secondary mental states, sensations being primary); (2) similar ideas tend to excite one another (James Mill had reduced the law of similarity to the law of frequency, but J. S. Mill accepted it as a separate law); (3) when sensations or ideas are frequently experienced together, either simultaneously or successively, they become associated (law of contiguity); (4) more vivid sensations or ideas form stronger associations than do less vivid ones; and (5) strength of association varies with frequency of occurrence. With only the minor exception of the law of similarity, this list summarizes James Mill's notion of "mental physics" or "mental mechanics," a view that J. S. Mill accepted to a large extent.

John Stuart took issue with his father on one important issue, however. Instead of agreeing that complex ideas are *always* aggregates of simple ideas, he proposed a type of **mental chemistry**. He was impressed by the fact that often chemicals would combine and produce something entirely different from the elements that made them up, such as when hydrogen and oxygen combine to produce water. Also, Newton had shown that when all the colors of the spectrum were combined, white light was produced. J. S. Mill believed that the same kind of thing sometimes happened in the mind. That is, it was possible for elementary ideas to fuse and to produce an idea that was different from the elements that made it up. Mill described mental chemistry as follows:

> The laws of the phenomena of the mind are sometimes analogous to mechanical, but sometimes also to chemical laws. When many impressions or ideas are operating in the mind together, there sometimes takes place a process of a similar kind to chemical combination. When impressions have been so often experienced in conjunction, that each of them calls up readily and instantaneously the ideas of the whole group, those ideas sometimes melt and coalesce into one another, and appear not as several ideas but one, in the same manner as when the seven prismatic colors are presented to the eye in rapid succession, the sensation produced is that of white. But in this last case it is correct to say that the seven colors when they rapidly follow one another *generate* white; so it appears to me that the Complex Idea, formed by the blending together of several simpler ones, should, when it really appears simple, (that is, when the separate elements are not consciously distinguishable in it) be said to *result from*, or be *generated by*, the simple ideas, not to *consist* of them. . . . These . . . are cases of mental chemistry: in which it is proper to say that the simple ideas generate, rather than that they compose, the complex ones. (1893, p. 558)

J. S. Mill's contention that an entirely new idea, one not reducible to simple ideas or sensations, could emerge from contiguous experiences, emancipated associationistic psychology from the rigid confines of mental mechanics. However, if one is seeking an active, autono-

John Stuart Mill

THE BETTMANN ARCHIVE

mous mind, one must look elsewhere. When a new idea does emerge from the synthesis of contiguous ideas or sensations, it does so automatically. Just as the proper combination of hydrogen and oxygen cannot help but become water, a person experiencing the rapid, successive presentation of the primary colors cannot help but experience white. Certainly, the observation that sometimes a phenomenon akin to mental chemistry occurred did nothing to dampen Mill's enthusiasm over the development of a science of human nature (psychology).

Toward a science of human nature. Others before him (e.g., Locke, Hume, and Hartley) had as their goal the creation of a mental science on par with the natural sciences. It was J. S. Mill, however, speaking from the vantage point of perhaps the most respected philosopher of science of his day, who contributed most to the development of psychology as a science.

J. S. Mill began his analysis by attacking the common belief that human thoughts, feelings, and actions are not subject to scientific investigation in the same way that physical nature is. He stressed the point that any system governed by laws is subject to scientific scrutiny and this is true even if those laws are not presently understood. Mill gave the example of meteorology. He indicated that no one would disagree that meteorological phenomena are governed by natural laws, and yet such phenomena cannot be predicted with certainty, only probabilistically. Even though a number of the basic laws governing weather are known (e.g., those governing heat, electricity, vaporization, and elastic fluids), a number are still unknown. Also, observing how all causes of weather interact to cause a meteorological phenomenon at any given time is extremely difficult, if not impossible. Thus, meteorology is a science because its phenomena are governed by natural laws, but it is an inexact science because knowledge of those laws is incomplete and measurement of particular manifestations of those laws is difficult. Sciences, then, can range from those whose laws are known and the manifestations of those laws easily and precisely measured to those whose laws are only partially understood and the manifestations of those laws measured only with great difficulty. In the latter category, Mill placed sciences whose **primary laws** are known, and *if no other causes intervene*, their phenomena can be observed, measured, and predicted precisely. However, **secondary laws** often interact with primary laws, making precise understanding and prediction impossible. Because the primary laws are still operating, the overall, principal effects will still be observable, but the secondary laws create variations and modifications that cause predictions to be probabilistic rather than certain. Mill gave the example of tidology:

> It is thus, for example, with the theory of the tides. No one doubts that Tidology . . . is really a science. As much of the phenomena as depends on the attraction of the sun and moon is

completely understood, and may, in any, even unknown, part of the earth's surface, be foretold with certainty; and the far greater part of the phenomena depends on those causes. But circumstances of a local or casual nature, such as the configuration of the bottom of the ocean, the degree of confinement from shores, the direction of the wind, etc., influence, in many or in all places, the height and time of the tide; and a portion of these circumstances being either not accurately knowable, not precisely measurable, or not capable of being certainly foreseen, the tide in known places commonly varies from the calculated result of general principles by some difference that we can not explain, and in unknown ones may vary from it by a difference that we are not able to foresee or conjecture. Nevertheless, not only is it certain that these variations depend on causes, and follow their causes by laws of unerring uniformity; not only, therefore, is tidology a science, like meteorology, but it is, what hitherto at least meteorology is not, a science largely available in practice. General laws may be laid down respecting those laws, and the result will in the main, though often not with complete accuracy, correspond to the predictions. (1893, p. 553)

Thus, meteorology and tidology are sciences, but they are not *exact* sciences. An inexact science, however, might become an exact science; astronomy is an example. Astronomy became an exact science when the laws governing the motions of astronomical bodies became sufficiently understood to allow prediction of not only the general courses of such bodies but also apparent aberrations:

> It has become an exact science, because its phenomena have been brought under laws comprehending the whole of the causes by which the phenomena are influenced, whether in a great or only in a trifling degree, whether in all or only in some cases, and assigning to each of those causes the share of effect which really belongs to it. (J. S. Mill, 1893, p. 553)

It is the inability of a science to deal with secondary causation that makes it inexact:

> In the theory of the tides the only laws as yet accurately ascertained are those of the causes which affect the phenomenon in all cases, and in a considerable degree; while others which affect it in some cases only, or, if in all, only in a slight

degree, have not been sufficiently ascertained and studied to enable us to lay down their laws; still less to deduce the completed law of the phenomenon, by compounding the effects of the greater with those of the minor causes. Tidology, therefore, is not yet an exact science; not from any inherent incapacity of being so, but from the difficulty of ascertaining with complete precision the real derivative uniformities. (J. S. Mill, 1893, p. 553)

Mill viewed the science of human nature (psychology) as roughly in the same position as tidology or astronomy before secondary causation was understood. The thoughts, feelings, and actions of individuals cannot be predicted with great accuracy because we cannot foresee the circumstances in which individuals will be placed. This in no way means that human thoughts, feelings, and actions are not caused; it means that the primary causes of thoughts, feelings, and actions interact with a large number of secondary causes, making accurate prediction extremely difficult. Humans, of course, are much more complicated than tides:

> The impressions and actions of human beings are not solely the result of their present circumstances, but the joint result of those circumstances and of the characters of the individuals; and the agencies which determine human character are so numerous and diversified (nothing which has happened to the person throughout life being without its portion of influence), that in the aggregate they are never in any two cases exactly similar. Hence, even if our science of human nature were theoretically perfect, that is, if we could calculate any character as we can calculate the orbit of any planet, *from given data*; still, as the data are never all given, nor ever precisely alike in different cases, we could neither make positive predictions, nor lay down universal propositions. (J. S. Mill, 1893, p. 554)

However, the difficulty is understanding and predicting the *details* of human behavior and thought, not predicting its more global features. Just as with the tides, human behavior is governed by a few primary laws, and that fact allows for the understanding and prediction of general human behavior, feeling, and thought. In many cases, such a general understanding is all that is necessary:

Inasmuch, however, as many of those effects which it is of most importance to render amenable to human foresight and control are determined, like the tides, in an incomparably greater degree by general causes, than by all partial causes taken together; depending in the main on those circumstances and qualities which are common to all mankind, or at least to large bodies of them, and only in a small degree on the idiosyncrasies of organization or the peculiar history of individuals; it is evidently possible with regard to all such effects, to make predictions which will *almost* always be verified, and general propositions which are almost always true. And whenever it is sufficient to know how the great majority of the human race, or of some nation or class of persons, will think, feel, and act, these propositions are equivalent to universal ones. For the purposes of political and social science this *is* sufficient. As we formerly remarked, an approximate generalization is, in social inquiries, for most practical purposes equivalent to an exact one; that which is only probable when asserted of individual human beings indiscriminately selected, being certain when affirmed of the character and collective conduct of masses. (J. S. Mill, 1893, p. 554)

What the science of human nature has then is a set of primary laws that apply to all humans and that can be used to predict general tendencies in human thought, feeling, and action. What the science of human behavior does *not* have is a knowledge of how its primary laws interact with secondary laws (individual characters and circumstances) to result in specific thoughts, feelings, and actions. Mill believed that it would just be a matter of time before "corollaries" would be deduced from the primary (universal) laws of human nature, which would allow for more refined understanding and prediction of human thought, feeling, and action. What are these primary (universal) laws of human nature on which a more exact science of human nature will be deduced? They are the laws of the mind by which sensations cause ideas and by which ideas become associated. In other words, they are the laws established by the British empiricists, in general, but more specifically by Hume, Hartley, and James Mill. What J. S. Mill added was the notion of mental chemistry.

J. S. Mill's proposed science of ethology. In chapter 5, Book VI, of his *Logic*, Mill argued for the development of a "science of the formation of character," and he called this science **ethology**. It should be noted that Mill's proposed science of ethology bore little resemblance to modern ethology, which studies animal behavior in the animal's natural habitat and then attempts to explain that behavior in evolutionary terms. As Mill saw it, ethology would be derived from a more basic science of human nature. That is, first the science of human nature (psychology) would discover the universal laws according to which all human minds operate, and then ethology would explain how individual minds or characters form under specific circumstances. The science of human nature would furnish the primary mental laws, and ethology would furnish the secondary laws. Putting the matter another way, we can say that the science of human nature provides information concerning what all humans have in common (human nature), and ethology explains individual personalities (individual differences).

What Mill was seeking, then, was the information necessary to convert psychology from an inexact science, like tidology or early astronomy, into an exact science. In other words, he wanted to explain more than general tendencies; he also wanted to explain the subtleties of individual behavior in specific circumstances.

It is interesting that Mill did little more than outline his ideas for ethology. He never personally attempted to develop such a science himself, and although most other sections of his *Logic* were substantially revised during its many editions, the section on ethology was never developed further or substantially modified. According to Leary (1982), Mill's attempt to develop a science of ethology failed because the science of human nature from which it was to be deduced was itself inadequate. Mill's theory of human nature was excessively intellectual. That is, it stressed how ideas become associated. It is difficult to imagine how something like character (personality), which to a large extent is emotional, could be deduced from a philosophy stressing the association of ideas. Mill's science of ethology was to sink or swim on the basis of the adequacy of his theory of human nature, and sink it did. It did not sink completely, however. Ethology re-emerged in France as the study of individual character. The French approach placed greater emphasis on emotional factors than Mill and his followers had, and their approach was somewhat more successful. Leary (1982) tracks the French efforts to study character and the influence of those efforts on later psychology.

Alexander Bain

Born in Aberdeen, Scotland, **Alexander Bain** (1818–1903) was a precocious child whose father was a weaver; from an early age, Bain himself had to work at the loom to earn money for his education. He was fortunate to be living in perhaps the only country (Scotland) where, at the time, any student showing intellectual promise was provided a university education. He attended Marischal College, which in 1858 became the University of Aberdeen. Following graduation Bain moved to London where he worked as a free-lance journalist. While in London, Bain joined a lively intellectual circle, which included John Stuart Mill, and the two became close, lifelong friends. The year before J. S. Mill published his famous *Logic* (1843), Bain assisted him with the revision of the manuscript. Bain also helped J. S. Mill with the annotation of the 1869 edition of James Mill's *Analysis* and wrote the biography of James Mill.

While in London, Bain tried repeatedly to obtain a university appointment but without success. He finally distinguished himself, however, with the publication of his two classic texts in psychology: *The Senses and the Intellect* (1855) and *Emotions and the Will* (1859). These were to be a two-volume work published together, but the publisher delayed publishing the second volume (*Emotions*) for four years because the first volume sold so poorly. In any case, in 1860, with his reputation established, at the age of 42 he finally obtained an academic post at the University of

Aberdeen. He returned to his alma mater as professor of logic and rhetoric; he remained there, in this and a variety of honorary positions, for the remainder of his long, productive life.

Bain is often referred to as the first full-fledged psychologist. His books *The Senses* and *Emotions* are considered the first systematic textbooks on psychology. These books underwent three revisions each and were standard texts in psychology on both sides of the Atlantic for nearly 50 years. Until William James's *Principles of Psychology* (1890), Bain's two volumes provided many with their first experience with psychology. Besides writing the first textbooks in psychology, Bain was also the first to write a book exclusively dedicated to the relationship between the mind and the body (*Mind and Body*, 1873); and in 1876 he founded *Mind*, which is generally considered the first journal devoted exclusively to psychological issues.

Bain's goal. In 1851 Bain wrote John Stuart Mill and described the progress that he (Bain) had been making on his text on psychology:

Alexander Bain

> I have just finished rough drafting the first division . . . which includes the Sensations, Appetites, and Instincts. All through this portion I keep up a constant reference to the material structure of the parts concerned, it being my purpose to exhaust in this division the physiological basis of mental phenomena. . . . And although I neither can, nor at the present, desire to carry Anatomical explanation into the Intellect, I think that the state of the previous part of the subject will enable Intellect and Emotion to be treated to great advantage and in a manner altogether different from anything that has hitherto appeared. There is nothing I wish more than so to unite psychology and physiology that physiologists may be made to appreciate the true ends and drift of their researches into the nervous system. (Young, 1970, pp. 102–103)

Bain's goal, then, was to describe the physiological correlates of mental and behavioral phenomena. In preparation for writing *The Senses*, Bain made it a point to digest the most current information on neurology, anatomy, and physi-

ology. He then attempted to show how these biological processes were related to psychological processes. His text was modern in the sense that it started with a chapter on neurology, a practice most introductory psychology textbooks have followed ever since.

After Bain, the major effort in psychology was to explore the relationships between physiological and psychological processes, an effort that continues to this day. Bain was the first to attempt to relate real physiological processes to psychological phenomena. Hartley had earlier attempted to do this, but his physiological principles were largely imaginary.

The mind–body relationship. On the mind–body issue, Bain accepted the position of **psychophysical parallelism**, the contention that every sensory input causes both a physical (biological) and a mental reaction but that the two do not interact:

NATIONAL LIBRARY OF MEDICINE

We have every reason for believing that there is, in company with all our mental processes, *an unbroken material succession*. From the ingress of a sensation, to the outgoing responses in action, the mental succession is not for an instant dissevered from a physical succession. A new prospect bursts upon the view; there is a mental result of sensation, emotion, thought—terminating in outward displays of speech or gesture. Parallel to this mental series is the physical series of facts, the successive agitation of the physical organs, called the eye, nerves, muscles, [etc.]. While we go the round of the mental circle of sensation, emotion, and thought, there is an unbroken physical circle of effects. It would be incompatible with everything we know of the cerebral action, to suppose that the physical chain ends abruptly in a physical void, occupied by an immaterial substance; which immaterial substance, after working alone, imparts its results to the other edge of the physical break, and determines the active response—two shores of the material with an intervening ocean of the immaterial. There is, in fact, no rupture of nervous continuity. The only tenable supposition is, that mental and physical proceed together, as undivided twins. When, therefore, we speak of a mental cause, a mental agency, we have always a *two-sided cause*; the effect produced is not the effect of mind alone, but of mind in company with body. (Bain, 1873/1875, pp. 130–131)

Laws of association. For Bain, the mind had three components: feeling, volition, and intellect. The intellect was explained by the laws of association. Like the other British empiricists, Bain stressed the law of contiguity as the basic associative principle. According to Bain, the law of contiguity applied to sensations, ideas, actions, and feelings:

Actions, sensations, and states of feeling, occurring together or in close succession, tend to grow together, or cohere, in such a way that, when any one of them is afterwards presented to the mind, the others are apt to be brought up in idea. (Bain, 1855/1894, p. 341)

Again, as was common among the British empiricists, Bain supplemented the law of contiguity with the law of frequency:

As a general rule, Repetition is necessary in order to render coherent in the mind a train or aggregate of images, as, for example, the successive aspects of a panorama, with a sufficient degree of force to make one suggest the others at an after period. (Bain, 1855/1894, p. 341)

What was unusual about Bain's presentations of the laws of contiguity and frequency was his suggestion that both laws had their effects because of neurological changes, or what we would now call changes in the synapses between neurons: "For every act of memory, every exercise of bodily aptitude, every habit, recollection, train of ideas, there is a specific grouping, or co-ordination, of sensation and movements, by virtue of specific growth in the cell junctions" (Bain, 1873/1875, p. 91).

Like John Stuart Mill, Bain also accepted the law of similarity as one of his associative principles. Whereas the law of contiguity associates events that are experienced at the same time or in close succession, the law of similarity explains why events separated in time can come to be associated. That is, the experience of an event elicits memories of similar events even if those similar events were experienced under widely different times and circumstances. Bain pointed out that although the laws of contiguity and similarity are different, in order for repetition to strengthen an association, the two laws must operate together:

Thus, if I am disciplining myself in the act of drawing a round figure with my hand, any one present effort must recall the state of the muscular and nervous action, or the precise bent acquired at the end of the previous effort, while that effort had to reinstate the condition at the end of the one preceding, and so on. It is only in this way that repetition can be of any avail in confirming a physical habit, or in forming an intellectual aggregate. But this reinstatement of a former condition by a present act of the same kind, is really and truly a case of the operation of the associating principle of similarity, or of like recalling like; and we here plainly see, that without such recall, the adhesion of contiguous things would be impossible. Hence it would appear, that all through the exposition of Contiguity, the principle of Similarity has been tacitly assumed; we have everywhere taken for granted, that a present occurrence of any object to the view, recalls the total impression made by all the previous occurrences, and adds its own effect to the total. (Bain, 1855/1894, p. 487)

To the traditional laws of association, Bain added two of his own: the law of compound association and the law of constructive association. The **law of compound association** states that associations are seldom links between one idea and another. Rather, an idea is usually associated with several other ideas either through contiguity or similarity. When this is true, we have a compound association. With such associations, it is sometimes the case that experiencing one, or perhaps even a few elements in the compound, will not be enough to elicit the associated idea. However, if the idea is associated with many elements and several of those elements are present, the associated idea will be recalled. Bain thought that this law suggested a way to improve memory and recall: "Past actions, sensations, thoughts, or emotions, are recalled more easily, when associated either through contiguity or through similarity, with *more than one* present object or impression" (1855/1894, p. 578).

With his **law of constructive association**, Bain inserted a creative element into associationism in much the way Hume had done. Both Bain and Hume insisted that the mind had imaginary powers. In discussing his law of constructive association, Bain said, "By means of association the mind has the power to form new combinations or aggregates *different* from any that have been presented to it in the course of experience" (Bain, 1855/1894, p. 605). In other words, the mind can rearrange memories of various experiences into an almost infinite number of combinations. The law of constructive association was thought by Bain to account for the creativity shown by poets, artists, inventors, and the like.

Voluntary behavior. In his analysis of **voluntary behavior**, Bain made an important distinction between reflexive behavior, which was so important to the physiology of his time, and **spontaneous activity**. Reflexive behavior occurred automatically in response to some external stimulus because of the structure of an organism's nervous system. Conversely, organisms sometimes simply act spontaneously. In the terminology of modern Skinnerians, Bain was saying that some behavior is emitted rather than elicited.

Spontaneous activity is one ingredient of voluntary behavior. The other ingredient is hedonism. We have seen that James Mill was strongly influenced by Jeremy Bentham, as was James Mill's son John Stuart. Bain too accepted the fundamental importance of pleasure and pain in his psychology and especially in his analysis of voluntary behavior. Apparently, the thought of combining spontaneous behavior and the emotions of pleasure and pain in his analysis first occurred to Bain when, while accompanying a shepherd, he observed the first few hours of life of a lamb. He noted that the lamb's initial movements appeared to be completely random relative to its mother's teat, but as chance contact occurred with the mother's skin and eventually with her teat, the lamb became increasingly "purposive":

Six or seven hours after birth the animal had made notable progress. . . . The sensations of sight began to have a meaning. In less than twenty-four hours, the animal could at the sight of the mother ahead, move in the forward direction at once to come up to her, showing that a particular image had now been associated with a definite movement; the absence of any such association being most manifest in the early movements of life. It could proceed at once to the teat and suck, guided only by its desire and the sight of the object. (Bain, 1855/1894, p. 437)

Bain used hedonism to explain how spontaneous activity is converted into voluntary behavior:

I cannot descend deeper into the obscurities of the cerebral organization than to state as a fact, that when pain co-exists with an accidental alleviating movement, or when pleasure co-exists with a pleasure-sustaining movement, such movements become subject to the control of the respective feelings which they occur in company with. Throughout all the grades of sentient existence, wherever any vestiges of action for a purpose are to be discerned, this link must be presumed to exist. Turn it over as we may on every side, some such ultimate connexion between the two great primary manifestations of our nature—pleasure and pain, with active instrumentality—must be assumed as the basis of our ability to work out ends. (Bain, 1859/1977, p. 349)

With voluntary behavior, we still have the laws of association at work. Some spontaneous actions become associated with pleasure and therefore repeated; others are associated with pain and therefore reduced in frequency of occurrence. Also, in accordance with the law of frequency, the tendencies to repeat pleasurable responses or to avoid painful ones increase with the frequency of pleasurable or painful consequences. It is important to note that for Bain voluntary did not mean "free." So-called voluntary behavior was as deterministically controlled as reflexive behavior; it was just controlled differently.

To summarize, Bain explained the development of voluntary behavior as follows:

1. When some need such as hunger or the need to be released from confinement occurs, there is random or spontaneous activity.

2. Some of these random movements will produce or approximate conditions necessary for satisfying the need, and others will not.

3. The activities that bring need satisfaction are remembered.

4. The next time the organism is in a similar situation, it will perform the activities that previously brought about need satisfaction.

Actions that are performed because of their previous effectiveness in a given situation are voluntary rather than reflexive.

Bain essentially described trial-and-error learning, which was to become so important to Thorndike several years later. He also described Skinner's operant conditioning. According to Skinner, operant behavior is simply emitted by an organism (i.e., it is spontaneous). Once emitted, however, operant behavior is under the control of its consequences. Responses resulting in pleasurable consequences (reinforcement) are repeated under similar circumstances, and responses resulting in painful consequences (punishment) are not. (For a more detailed account of Bain's explanation of voluntary behavior, see Greenway, 1973.)

With his effort to synthesize what was known about physiology with associationism and his treatment of voluntary behavior, Bain brought psychology to the very brink of becoming an experimental science. Others would soon use the work of Bain and other British empiricists to develop experimental psychology.

FRENCH SENSATIONALISM

French philosophers were also aspiring to be Newtonians of the mind, and they had much in common with their British counterparts. The French Newtonians of the mind have been referred to as naturalists, mechanists, empiricists, materialists, and sensationalists. Any, or all, of these labels capture the spirit of the French philosophers to be considered here and would be equally applicable to the majority of the British philosophers whose work we just reviewed. The goal for both the French and British philosophers was to explain the mind as Newton had explained the physical world—that is, in a way that stressed the mind's mechanical nature, that reduced all mental activity to its basic elements, that used only a few basic principles, and that minimized or eliminated metaphysical speculation. All the French and British philosophers considered in this chapter had these goals in common. We refer to the French philosophers as "sensationalists" because some of them intentionally stressed the importance of sensations in explaining all conscious experience and because the label provides a convenient way of distinguishing between the British and the French philosophers. In general, however, the French and the British philosophers were more similar than they were different. Besides both being influenced by Newton (or Galileo in Hobbes's case), they both strongly opposed the rationalism of Descartes, especially his beliefs in innate ideas and in an autonomous mind. All ideas, said both the British empiricists and the French sensationalists, came from experience, and most, if not all, mental activity could be explained by the laws of association acting on those ideas.

The question asked by both the British empiricists and the French sensationalists was If everything else in the universe can be explained in terms of mechanical laws, why should not humans, too, obey those laws? Although the metaphor of human beings as machines was suggested by the work of Copernicus, Kepler, Galileo, and Newton, it was further stimulated by Descartes. Descartes's dualistic conception of humans meant that our bodies acted according to mechanical principles (i.e., our bodies are machines) but our minds did not. Without the autonomous mind that Descartes had postulated, however, humans were equated with nonhuman animals, and both could be understood as machines. It was this metaphor of humans as machines that especially appealed to the French sensationalists. In fact, many believed that Descartes himself saw the possibility of viewing humans as machines but that he avoided revealing this belief because of what happened to Galileo and a number of other natural scientists and philosophers of his time. There was still reason to fear the church in France in the mid-18th century, but the French sensationalists pursued their metaphor of man as a machine with courage and boldness despite intense opposition from the church.

Pierre Gassendi

Pierre Gassendi (1592–1655), a contemporary of both Descartes and Hobbes, lived the quiet life of a studious priest and was respected as a mathematician and philosopher. Both Locke and Newton acknowledged a debt to Gassendi, whose major goal was to denounce Descartes's purely deductive (axiomatic) and dualistic philosophy and replace it with an observational (inductive) science based on physical monism. Gassendi offered several criticisms of Descartes's

proposed mind–body dualism, the most telling of which was the observation that the mind, if unextended (immaterial), could have no knowledge of extended (material) things. Only physical things, he said, can influence and be influenced by physical things. He also could not understand why Descartes spent so much time proving that he existed, when it was obvious to Gassendi that anything that moves exists. Descartes could have said "I move, therefore I am." In fact, according to Gassendi, such a conclusion would have been a vast improvement over "I think, therefore I am." Continuing his attack on Descartes, Gassendi asked why "lower" animals could move themselves quite well without the aid of a mind, and yet humans needed one? Why not, Gassendi asked, ascribe the operations attributed to the mind to the functions of the brain (which is physical)? In other words, Gassendi saw no reason for postulating an unextended (immaterial) mind to explain any human activity.

Gassendi concluded that humans are nothing but matter and therefore we could be studied and understood like anything else in the universe. Gassendi suggested a physical monism not unlike the one that the early Greek atomists, such as Democritus and later the Epicureans, had suggested. In fact, Gassendi was especially fond of Epicurus and the later Epicurean philosophers, and he was responsible for reviving interest in them. For this reason, Gassendi is often considered the founder of modern materialism, but that honor could as easily be given to Gassendi's contemporary Hobbes.

Gassendi had a number of prominent followers, and we review the works of three next.

Julien de La Mettrie

Julien de La Mettrie (1709–1751) was born on December 25. His father intended him to become a priest until a local doctor pointed out that a mediocre physician would be better paid than a good priest. Upon receiving his medical degree, La Mettrie soon distinguished himself in the medical community by writing articles on

JULIEN OFFROI LA METTRIE
der Arzney Kunst Docter und Mittglied der
Konigl. Societæt der Wissenschaften zu Berlin

Julien de La Mettrie

such topics as venereal disease, vertigo, and smallpox. He was widely resented because of professional jealousy, his tendency to satirize the medical profession, and his quick temper. In 1742 he obtained a commission as physician to the regiment of guards during the war between France and Austria. During a military campaign, La Mettrie contracted a violent fever; during his convalescence, he began to ponder the relationship between the mind and the body. In his brief biography of La Mettrie, Frederick the Great said the following:

> For a philosopher an illness is a school of physiology; he [La Mettrie] believed that he could clearly see that thought is but a consequence of the organization of the machine, and that the disturbance of the springs has considerable in-

fluence on that part of us which the metaphysicians call soul. Filled with these ideas during his convalescence, he boldly bore the torch of experience into the night of metaphysics; he tried to explain by the aid of anatomy the thin texture of understanding, and he found only mechanism where others had supposed an essence superior to matter. (La Mettrie, 1748/1912, p. 6)

Upon recovery from his illness, La Mettrie wrote *The Natural History of the Soul* (1745), which stressed that the mind is much more intimately related to the body than Descartes had assumed. If the mind is completely separate from the body and only influences the body when it chooses to do so, how can the effects on one's thoughts of wine, coffee, opium, or even a good meal be explained? In fact, La Mettrie was among the first modern philosophers to suggest "you are what you eat":

> Raw meat makes animals fierce, and it would have the same effect on man. This is so true that the English who eat meat red and bloody, and not as well done as ours, seem to share more or less in the savagery due to this kind of food, and to other causes which can be rendered ineffective by education only. This savagery creates in the soul, pride, hatred, scorn of other nations, indocility and other sentiments which degrade the character, just as heavy food makes a dull and heavy mind whose usual traits are laziness and indolence. (La Mettrie, 1748/1912, p. 94)

To La Mettrie, it was clear that whatever influences the body influences the so-called thought processes, but La Mettrie went further. He believed that there is nothing in the universe but matter and motion. Sensations and thoughts are also nothing but movements of particles in the brain. Thus, La Mettrie, like Hobbes, was a thorough-going materialist; both were physical monists.

La Mettrie's book *The Natural History of the Soul* (1745) was harshly criticized by the French clergy. The feelings against him were so intense that he was forced into exile into Holland. While in Holland he wrote his most famous book *L'Homme Machine* (*Man a Machine*, 1748). This book so upset the Dutch clergy that he was also forced to leave Holland. Fortunately, Frederick the Great in Berlin offered La Mettrie refuge and a pension. In Berlin, La Mettrie continued in writings on medical topics until his death on November 11, 1751, at the young age of 41.

Man a Machine. La Mettrie was one who believed that Descartes was a mechanist, even as far as humans were concerned, and that his published thoughts on God and the soul were designed to hide his true feelings from the clergy and to save himself from persecution (La Mettrie, 1748/1912, p. 143). In any case, La Mettrie believed that if Descartes had followed his own method, he (Descartes) would have reached the conclusion that humans, like non-human animals, were automata (i.e., machines). La Mettrie, then, set out to either correct Descartes's misunderstanding of humans or to do what Descartes wanted to do but refrained from doing because of fear of persecution.

La Mettrie concluded *Man a Machine* with the statement, "Let us then conclude boldly that man is a machine, and that in the whole universe there is but a single substance differently modified" (1748/1912, p. 148). The single substance, of course, was matter, and this belief that every existing thing, including humans, consists of matter and nothing else makes La Mettrie a physical monist. For La Mettrie, to believe in the existence of an immaterial soul (mind) was just plain silly. According to La Mettrie, only a philosopher who was not at the same time a physician could postulate the existence of an immaterial soul that is independent from the body. The overwhelming evidence for the dependence of so-called mental events on bodily states available to physicians would (or should) preclude them from embracing dualism.

Human and nonhuman animals differ only in degree. La Mettrie equated intelligence and some personality characteristics with the size and quality of the brain:

> I shall draw the conclusions which follow clearly from . . . incontestable observations: 1st, that

the fiercer animals are, the less brain they have; 2nd, that this organ seems to increase in size in proportion to the gentleness of the animal; 3rd, that nature seems here eternally to impose a singular condition, that the more one gains in intelligence the more one loses in instinct. (La Mettrie, 1748/1912, pp. 98–99)

If humans can be considered superior to non-human animals, it is because of education and from the development of language. Because the primate brain is almost as large and as complex as ours, it follows that if primates could be taught language they would resemble humans in almost all respects. The question is Can primates learn a language?

> Among animals, some learn to speak and sing; they remember tunes, and strike the notes as exactly as a musician. Others, for instance the ape, show more intelligence, and yet can not learn music. What is the reason for this, except some defect in the organs of speech? In a word, would it be absolutely impossible to teach the ape a language? I do not think so. (La Mettrie, 1748/1912, p. 100)

With proper training, humans and apes could be made remarkably similar:

> Such is the likeness of the structure and functions of the ape to ours that I have very little doubt that if this animal were properly trained he might at last be taught to pronounce, and consequently to know, a language. Then he would no longer be a wild man, nor a defective man, but he would be a perfect man, a little gentleman, with as much matter or muscle as we have, for thinking and profiting by his education. (La Mettrie, 1748/1912, p. 103)

According to La Mettrie, intelligence was influenced by three factors: brain size, brain complexity, and education. Humans are typically superior in intelligence to other animals because we have bigger, more complex brains and because we are better educated. However, by education La Mettrie did not mean only explicit instruction but also the effects of everyday experience—for example, our interactions with other people:

> We catch everything from those with whom we come in contact; their gestures, their accent, etc.; just as the eyelid is instinctively lowered

when a blow is foreseen, or as (for the same reason) the body of the spectator mechanically imitates, in spite of himself, all the motions of a good mimic.

From what I have just said, it follows that a brilliant man is his own best company, unless he can find other company of the same sort. In the society of the unintelligent, the mind grows rusty for lack of exercise, as at tennis a ball that is served badly is badly returned. I should prefer an intelligent man without an education, if he were still young enough, to a man badly educated. A badly trained mind is like an actor whom the provinces have spoiled. (La Mettrie, 1748/1912, p. 97)

To say that humans are morally superior to nonhuman animals is to overlook the seamier human activities like cannibalism, infanticide, and wars in which "our compatriots fight, Swiss against Swiss, brother against brother, recognize each other, and yet capture and kill each other without remorse, because a prince pays for the murder" (La Mettrie, 1748/1912, p. 117). Religion, grounded in the belief in a supreme being, certainly has not improved the human condition. It is possible, according to La Mettrie, that atheism could encourage humans to be more humane.

In any case, humans differ from nonhuman animals only in degree, not in type: "Man is not moulded from a costlier clay; nature has used but one dough, and has merely varied the leaven" (La Mettrie, 1748/1912, p. 117).

Acceptance of materialism will make for a better world. According to La Mettrie, beliefs in the uniqueness of humans (dualism) and in God are not only incorrect but also responsible for widespread misery. Humans would be much better served by accepting their continuity with the animal world. That is, humans should accept the fact that, like other animals, we are machines—complex machines, but machines nonetheless. La Mettrie described how life would be for the person accepting the materialistic-mechanistic philosophy:

He who so thinks will be wise, just, tranquil about his fate, and therefore happy. He will await death without either fear or desire, and will cherish life (hardly understanding how disgust can corrupt a heart in this place of many delights); he will be filled with reverence, gratitude, affection, and tenderness for nature, in proportion to his feeling of the benefits he has received from nature; he will be happy, in short, in feeling nature, and in being present at the enchanting spectacle of the universe, and he will surely never destroy nature either in himself or in others. More than that! Full of humanity, this man will love human character even in his enemies. Judge how he will treat others. He will pity the wicked without hating them; in his eyes, they will be but mis-made men. But in pardoning the faults of the structure of mind and body, he will none the less admire the beauties and the virtues of both. . . . In short, the materialist, convinced, in spite of the protests of his vanity, that he is but a machine or an animal, will not maltreat his kind, for he will know too well the nature of those actions, whose humanity is always in proportion to the degree of the analogy proved above [between human beings and animals]; and following the natural law given to all animals, he will not wish to do to others what he would not wish them to do to him. (1748/1912, pp. 147–148)

La Mettrie dared to discuss openly those ideas that were held privately by many philosophers of the time. In so doing, he offended many powerful individuals. Although it is clear that he influenced many subsequent thinkers, his works were rarely cited nor his name even mentioned. The fact that he died of indigestion following overindulgence of a meal of pheasant and truffles was seen by many as a fitting death for a misled, atheistic philosopher.

Etienne Bonnot de Condillac

Etienne Bonnot de Condillac (1715–1780) was born on September 30 into an aristocratic family at Grenobles. He was the contemporary of Hume and Rousseau, who were about his age, and with Voltaire, who was about 20 years older. He was educated at a Jesuit seminary in Paris, but shortly after his ordination as a Roman Catholic priest, he began frequenting the literary and philosophical salons of Paris and gradually lost interest in his religious career. In fact, he became an outspoken critic of religious dogma. Condillac translated Locke's *Essay* into French, and the title of his first book indicates a deep appreciation for Locke's empirical philosophy: *Essay on the Origin of Human Knowledge: A Supplement to Mr. Locke's Essay on the Human Understanding* (1746). Eight years later in his *Treatise on the Sensations* (1754), Condillac suggested that Locke had unnecessarily attributed too many innate powers to the mind. Condillac was convinced that all powers given to the mind by Locke could be derived from only the abilities to sense, to remember, and to experience pleasure and pain.

The sentient statue. To make his point, Condillac (1754) asked his readers to imagine a statue that can sense, remember, and feel but has only the sense of smell. The mental life of the statue consists only of odors, it cannot have any conception of things external to itself, nor can it have sensations of color, sound, or taste. The statue does have the capacity for *attention* because it will attend to whatever odor it experiences. With attention comes *feeling* because attending to a pleasant odor will cause enjoyment and attending to an unpleasant odor causes an unpleasant feeling. If the statue had just one continuous pleasant or unpleasant experience, it could not experience desire because it would have nothing with which to compare the experience. If, however, a pleasant sensation ended, remembering it, the statue could desire it to return. Likewise, if an unpleasant experience ended, remembering it, the statue could desire that it not return. For Condillac then, all desire is based on the experiences of pleasure and pain. The statue *loves* pleasant experiences and *hates* unpleasant ones. The statue, given the ability to remember, not only can experience current odors but also remember ones previously experienced. Typically, the former provide a more vivid sensation than the latter.

When the statue smells a rose at one time and a carnation at another, it has the basis for *comparison*. The comparison can be made by currently smelling one and remembering the other or by remembering both odors. With the ability to compare comes the ability to judge. As with remembering in general, the more comparisons and judgments the statue makes, the easier it becomes to make them. Sensations are remembered in the order that they occur; memories then form a chain. This fact allows the statue to recall distant memories by passing from one idea to another until the most distant idea is recalled. According to Condillac, without first recalling intermediary ideas, distant memories would be lost. If the statue remembers sensations in the order they occurred, the process is called *retrieval*. If they are recalled in a different order, it is called *imagination*. *Dreaming* is a form of imagination. Retrieving or imagining that which is hated causes *fear*. Retrieving or imagining what is loved causes *hope*. The statue having had several sensations can now notice that they can be grouped in various ways, such as intense, weak, pleasant, and unpleasant. When sensations or memories are grouped in terms of what they have in common, the statue has formed *abstract ideas*, for example, pleasantness. Also by noting that some sensations or memories last longer than others, the statue develops the idea of *duration*. Also, with the ability to compare comes the ability to be surprised. *Surprise* is experienced whenever an experience the statue has departs radically from those it is used to: "It cannot fail to notice the change when it passes suddenly from a state to which it is accustomed to a quite different state, of which it has as yet no idea" (Condillac, 1754/1930, p. 10). As with comparing and judging, all other mental abilities are used with more facility the more they are practiced.

When our statue has accumulated a vast number of memories, it will tend to dwell more on the pleasant ones than on the unpleasant:

> The statue, preserving the memory of a great number [of ideas], will be inclined to retrace preferably those which are able to contribute most to its happiness. It will pass rapidly over the others, or will stop because it cannot help itself. (Condillac, 1754/1930, p. 12)

In fact, according to Condillac, it is toward the seeking of pleasure or the avoidance of pain that the statue's mental abilities are ultimately aimed: "Thus it is that pleasure and pain will always determine the actions of [the statue's] faculties" (Condillac, 1754/1930, p. 14). Condillac's belief in hedonism as the master motive was, as we have seen, shared by most of the British empiricists and his fellow French sensationalists.

The statue's self, ego, or personality consists of its sensations, its memories, and its other mental abilities. With its memories, it is capable of desiring sensations other than the one it is now having, or by remembering other sensations, it can wish its present sensation to continue or terminate. Experiences (in this case, odors) never experienced cannot become part of the statue's mental life, which consists only of its sensations and its memories of sensations:

> Smells of which the statue has no recollection, do not enter into the idea which it has of its personality. They are then for it, as though it had never smelled them. They are as much strangers to its "I" as the colours and sounds of which it has as yet no knowledge. Its "I" is only the collection of the sensations which it experiences, and those which memory recalls to it. In a word it is immediate knowledge of what it is for itself, and remembrance of what it has been. (Condillac, 1754/1930, pp. 43–44)

Clearly, Condillac was not writing about statues but was discussing how human mental abilities could be derived from sensations, memories, and a few basic feelings. Humans, of course, have more than one sense modality, and that fact makes humans much more complicated than the statue, but the principle is the same:

> Having proved that the statue is capable of attending, remembering, comparing, judging, discerning, imagining; that it has abstract ideas; that it has ideas of number and of duration; that it knows general and particular truths; that it forms desires, expresses passions, that it loves, hates, wills; that it is capable of hope, of fear, and of wonder; and finally that it contracts habits; we must conclude that with one sense alone the understanding has as many faculties as with the five joined together. We shall see that what seem to us special faculties are only those we

have considered already, applied to a greater number of objects and accordingly more developed. (Condillac, 1754/1930, p. 45)

There was no need therefore for Locke and others to postulate a number of innate powers of the mind. According to Condillac, the powers of the mind develop as a natural consequence of sensation:

> If we bear in mind that recollecting, comparing, judging, discerning, imagining, wondering, having abstract ideas, and ideas of number and duration, knowing general and particular truths, are only different modes of attention; that having passions, loving, hating, hoping, fearing, wishing, are only different modes of desire; and finally that attention and desire have their origin in feeling alone; we shall conclude that sensation contains within it all the faculties of the soul. (Condillac, 1754/1930, p. 45)

It is the supreme importance given to sensation by Condillac and his followers that explains why the French empiricists are sometimes referred to as sensationalists.

Claude Helvetius

Claude Helvetius (1715–1771) was born in Paris and educated by Jesuits. He became wealthy as a tax collector, married an attractive countess, and retired to the countryside where he wrote and socialized with some of Europe's finest minds. In 1758 he wrote *Essays on the Mind,* which was condemned by the Sorbonne and burned. His posthumous *A Treatise on Man, His Intellectual Faculties and His Education* (1772) moved Jeremy Bentham to claim that what Francis Bacon had done for our understanding of the physical world, Helvetius had done for our understanding of the moral world. Also, James Mill claimed to have used Helvetius's philosophy as a guide in the education of his son John Stuart.

Helvetius did not contradict any of the major tenets of British empiricism or French sensationalism, nor did he add any new ones. Rather, he explored in depth the implication of the contention that the contents of the mind come only from experience. In other words, control expe-

Claude Helvetius

Auguste Comte

riences and you control the contents of the mind. The implications of this belief for education and even the structure of society were clear, and in the hands of Helvetius, empiricism became radical *environmentalism*. All manner of social skills, moral behavior, and even genius could be taught through the control of experiences (education). Russell said of Helvetius, "His doctrine is optimistic, since only a perfect education is needed to make men perfect. There is a suggestion that it would be easy to find a perfect education if the priests were got out of the way" (1945, p. 722).

Because Helvetius too was a hedonist, education in general terms could be viewed as the manipulation of pleasurable and painful experiences. Today we might say reinforce desirable thoughts and behavior and either ignore or punish undesirable thoughts and behavior. In this sense, Helvetius's position has much in common with that of the modern behaviorists.

POSITIVISM

The British empiricists and the French sensationalists all had in common the belief that all knowledge comes from experience; that is, that there are no innate ideas. They also shared a distaste for metaphysical speculation. All knowledge, they said, even moral knowledge, was derived from experience. If the denial of innate moral principles did not place the empiricists and the sensationalists in direct opposition to religion, it certainly placed them in direct opposition to religious dogma.

As the successes of the physical and mental sciences spread throughout Europe and as religious doctrine became increasingly suspect, a new belief emerged—the belief that science could solve all human problems. Such a belief was called **scientism.** To those embracing scientism, scientific knowledge was the only valid knowledge; therefore, it was the only information in which one could believe. For these individuals, science itself took on some of the characteristics of a religion. One such individual was Auguste Comte.

Auguste Comte

Auguste Comte (1798–1857), born in the French city of Montpellier on January 19, grew up in the period of great political turmoil that followed the French Revolution of 1789–1799. In school Comte was an excellent student and a troublemaker. In August 1817, Comte met the social philosopher Henri Saint-Simon (1760–1825) who converted Comte from an ardent advocate of liberty and equality to a supporter of a more elitist view of society. The two men collaborated on a number of essays; but after a bitter argument, the two parted company in 1824. In April 1826, Comte began giving lectures in his home on his positivist philosophy, that is, the attempt to use the methods of the physical sciences to create a science of history and human social behavior. His lectures were attended by a number of illustrious individuals, but after only three lectures, Comte suffered a serious mental collapse. Despite being treated in a hospital for a while, he fell into deep depression and even attempted suicide. He was unable to resume his lectures until 1829. Financial problems, lack of professional recognition, and marital difficulties combined to drive Comte back into isolation. Between 1830 and 1842, his time was spent mainly on writing his six-volume work, *Cours de Philosophe Positive (Course of Positive Philosophy,* 1830–1842). Comte's *Cours* was translated into English by the philosopher-feminist Harriet Martineau (1802–1876) in 1853. As a result of the *Cours,* Comte began to attract a few admirers, among them John Stuart Mill. However, soon after the publication of the *Cours,* Comte's wife left him. In 1844 he met and fell in love with Clothilde de Vaux, and although she died of tuberculosis soon after they met, he vowed to dedicate the rest of his life to her memory. Soon afterward he began writing *Le Système de Politique*

Positive (The System of Positive Politics) in which Comte introduced his religion of humanity (discussed later). The *Système* cost Comte most of his influential followers, including John Stuart Mill. Undaunted, Comte continued to concentrate on his new religion, of which he installed himself as high priest. Comte spent his later years attempting to gain converts to his religion. He even tried to recruit some of the most powerful individuals in Europe including Czar Nicholas and the head of the Jesuits.

Positivism. For Comte, the only thing we can be sure of is that which is publicly observable, that is, sense experiences that can be shared with other individuals. The data of science are publicly observable and therefore can be trusted. For example, scientific laws are statements about how empirical events vary together, and once determined, they can be experienced by any interested party. Comte's insistence on equating knowledge with empirical observations was called **positivism.**

Comte was a social reformer and was interested in science only as a means of improving society. Knowledge, whether scientific or not, was not important unless it had some practical value; Comte wrote, "I have a supreme aversion to scientific labors whose utility, direct or remote, I do not see" (Esper, 1964, p. 213). According to Comte, science should seek to discover the lawful relationships among physical phenomena. Once such laws are known, they can be used to predict and control events and thus improve life. One of Comte's favorite slogans was "know in order to predict" (Esper, 1964, p. 213). Comte's approach to science was very much like the one suggested earlier by Francis Bacon. According to both Comte and Bacon, science should be practical and nonspeculative. Comte told his readers that there are two types of statements: "One refers to the objects of sense, and it is a scientific statement. The other is nonsense!" (D. N. Robinson, 1986, p. 333).

It should be pointed out that positivistic

thinking had been around in one form or another since at least the time of the early Greeks:

> The history of positivism might be said to extend from ancient times to the present. In ancient Greece it was represented by such thinkers as Epicurus, who sought to free men from theology by offering them an explanation of the universe in terms of natural law, and the Sophists, who wished to bring positive knowledge to bear on human affairs. The cumulative successes of the scientific method in the seventeenth and eighteenth centuries increasingly favored the acceptance of the positivistic attitude among intellectuals. In England, the empirical philosophy, beginning with Francis Bacon and culminating in Hume and John Stuart Mill, became an essential part of the positivist tradition. (Esper, 1964, pp. 212–213)

In fact, because all the British empiricists and French sensationalists stressed the importance of sensory experience and avoided metaphysical and theological speculation, they all could be said to have had at least positivistic leanings.

The law of three stages. According to Comte, societies pass through stages that are defined in terms of the way natural events are explained by its members. The first stage, and the most primitive, is *theological,* and explanations are based on superstition and mysticism. In the second stage, which is *metaphysical,* explanations are based on unseen essences, principles, causes, or laws. During the third and highest stage of development, the *scientific* description is emphasized over explanation, and the prediction and control of natural phenomena becomes all-important. In other words, during the scientific stage, positivism is accepted. Comte used the term **sociology** to describe the study of how different societies compared in terms of the three stages of development.

Comte described the events that characterize the transition from one stage to another in much the same way as Kuhn (1973) described paradigmatic shifts in science. According to Comte, the beliefs characteristic of a particular stage become a way of life for the people within a society. It is only a few of the societies' wisest individuals who glean the next stage and begin to pave the way for it. There follows a critical period during which a society is in transition between one stage and another. The beliefs characterizing the new stage then become a way of life until the process is repeated. As with a paradigmatic shift in science, there are always remnants of earlier stages in the newly established one:

> There is no science which, having attained the positive stage, does not bear marks of having passed through the others. Some time since it was (whatever it might be) composed, as we can now perceive, of metaphysical abstractions; and, further back in the course of time, it took its form from theological conceptions. We shall have only too much occasion to see, as we proceed, that our most advanced sciences still bear very evident marks of the two earlier periods through which they have passed. (Martineau, 1853/1893, p. 3)

As evidence for his law of three stages, Comte observed that individuals also pass through the same stages:

> The progress of the individual mind is not only an illustration, but an indirect evidence of that of the general mind. The point of departure of the individual and of the race being the same, the phases of the mind of a man correspond to the epochs of the mind of the race. Now, each of us is aware, if he looks back upon his own history, that he was a theologian in his childhood, a metaphysician in his youth, and a natural philosopher in his manhood. All men who are up to their age can verify this for themselves. (Martineau, 1853/1893, p. 3)

Religion of humanity. By the late 1840s, Comte was discussing positivism as if it were religion. To him, science was all that one needed to believe in and all that one should believe in. He described a utopian society based on scientific principles and beliefs and whose organization was remarkably similar to the Roman Catholic church. However, humanity replaced God, and scientists and philosophers replaced priests. Disciples of the new religion would be drawn from the working classes and especially from among women:

The triumph of positivism awaited the unification of three classes: The philosophers, the proletariat, and women. The first would establish the necessary intellectual and scientific principles and methods of inquiry; the second would guarantee that essential connection between reality and utility; the third would impact to the entire program the abiding selflessness and moral resolution so natural to the female constitution. (D. N. Robinson, 1982, p. 42)

Comte's religion of humanity was one of the reasons that John Stuart Mill became disenchanted with him. Comte's utopia emphasized the happiness of the group and minimized individual happiness. With Mill's version of utilitarianism, it was exactly reversed.

The hierarchy of the sciences. Comte arranged the sciences in a hierarchy from the first developed and most basic to the last developed and most comprehensive as follows: mathematics, astronomy, physics, chemistry, physiology and biology, and sociology. It is of special interest to note that psychology did not appear on Comte's list of sciences. If what is meant by psychology is the introspective analysis of the mind, then Comte believed that psychology was metaphysical nonsense. Science, for Comte, dealt with what could be publicly observed, and that excluded introspective data. He had harsh words to say about introspection, and in saying them, he differentiated himself from essentially all the British empiricists and French sensationalists who relied almost exclusively on introspection in their analysis of the mind:

> In order to observe, your intellect must pause from activity; yet it is this very activity you want to observe. If you cannot effect the pause you cannot observe; if you do effect it, there is nothing to observe. The results of such a method are in proportion to its absurdity. After two thousand years of psychological pursuit, no one proposition is established to the satisfaction of its followers. They are divided, to this day, into a multitude of schools, still disputing about the very elements of their doctrine. This internal observation gives birth to almost as many theories as there are observers. We ask in vain for any one discovery, great or small, which has

been made under this method. (Martineau, 1853/1893, p. 10)

For Comte, two methods, however, were available by which the individual could be studied objectively. One way was to embrace *phrenology,* which was an effort to relate mental events to brain anatomy and processes (we will discuss phrenology in chapter 6). Phrenological analysis essentially reduced psychology to physiology. The second way was to study the mind by its products—that is, to study the mind by studying overt behavior, especially social behavior. The study of human social behavior is a second sense in which Comte used the term *sociology.* So, the first objective way of studying humans reduced psychology to physiology, and the second reduced it to sociology. In the latter case, there was no studying "me," only "us." We now see two more reasons that J. S. Mill distanced himself from Comte. First, Mill's analysis of the mind was highly dependent on introspection. Second, Mill rejected phrenology (and history indicates that he was correct in having done so).

A Second Type of Positivism

Comte insisted that we accept only that of which we can be certain, and for him, that was publicly observable data. For Comte, introspection was out because it examined only private experiences. Another brand of positivism emerged later, however, under the leadership of **Ernst Mach** (1838–1916). Mach, like Comte, insisted that science concentrate only on what could be known with certainty. Neither Comte nor Mach allowed metaphysical speculation in their views of science. The two men differed radically, however, in what they thought scientists could be certain about. For Comte, it was physical events that could be experienced by any interested observer. For Mach, it was the scientist's own immediate experience, that is, sensation. Mach believed that all scientific statements could be and should be reduced to the immediate, mental experiences of the scientist. Because the ultimate scientific data for Mach was mental phenomena, his approach exemplifies *phenomenalism*. Both Comte and Mach were positivistic, but what they were positive about differed.

Both Comte's and Mach's brands of positivism influenced later psychology. Comte's influence can be seen in those behaviorists who insist that overt behavior should be the subject matter of psychology because there is no way to study private, mental events objectively. Mach's influence can be seen in Gestalt psychology and other brands of phenomenology, which claim the subject matter of psychology should be the immediate sensations of a perceiver.

Positivism was revised through the years and was eventually transformed into *logical positivism*. It was through logical positivism that positivistic philosophy had its greatest impact on psychology. We will discuss logical positivism and its impact on psychology in chapter 13.

SUMMARY

A group of British philosophers opposed Descartes's notion of innate ideas, saying that all ideas were derived from experience. Those who claimed that experience was the basis of all knowledge were called empiricists. Hobbes insisted that all human activity was ultimately reducible to physical and mechanistic principles; thus, he was a materialist and a mechanist as well as an empiricist. He believed that the function of a society was to satisfy the needs of individuals and to prevent individuals from fighting among themselves. He also believed that all human behavior was ultimately motivated by the seeking of pleasure and the avoidance of pain.

Locke was an empiricist who distinguished between the primary qualities of objects, which caused ideas that actually resembled attributes of those objects, and secondary qualities, which caused psychological experiences that had no counterpart in the physical world. Locke believed that all ideas are derived from sensory experience but that existing ideas could be rearranged by the mind into numerous configurations. Locke postulated a mind that was well-stocked with mental abilities such as believing, imagining, reasoning, and willing. Like most of the other empiricists, Locke believed that all human emotions are derived from the two basic emotions of pleasure and pain. Locke used the laws of association only to explain the development of "unnatural" associations. Berkeley denied the existence of a material world saying instead that all that exists are perceptions. Although an external world exists because God perceives it, we can only know our own perceptions of that world. We can assume that our perceptions of the world accurately reflect external reality, however, because God would not allow our senses to deceive us. Berkeley also proposed an empirical theory of distance perception.

Hume agreed with Berkeley that the only thing we experienced directly was our own subjective experience but disagreed with Berkeley's faith that our perceptions accurately reflected the physical world. For Hume, we could never know anything about the physical world because all we ever experienced was thought and habits of thought. Like Locke, Hume postulated an active imagination that could arrange ideas in countless ways. Unlike Locke, however, Hume made the laws of association the cornerstone of his philosophy. He postulated three such laws: the law of contiguity, which states that events experienced together are remembered together; the law of resemblance, which states that remembering one event tends to elicit memories of similar events; and the law of cause and effect, which states that we tend to believe the circumstances that consistently precede an event cause that event. Hume reduced both mind and self to perceptual experience. According to Hume, it is the passions (emotions) that govern behavior, and because people differ in their patterns of emotions, there are individual differences in behavior. A person's pattern of emotions determines his or her character.

Hartley attempted to couple empiricism and associationism with a rudimentary conception of physiology, and his work turned out to be surprisingly similar to the more modern work of Donald Hebb. Hartley was among the first to show how the laws of association might be used to explain learned behavior. According to his analysis, involuntary (reflexive) behavior gradually becomes associated with environmental stimuli, such as when a child's grasping becomes associated with a favorite toy. When this association is made, the child can voluntarily grasp when he or she sees the toy. Through repeated experience, voluntary behavior can become almost as automatic as involuntary behavior. In accordance with the tradition of empiricism, Hartley believed pleasure and pain governed behavior, and it was his disciple Priestley who saw the implications of Hartley's hedonism for educational practices.

James Mill pushed empiricism and associationism to their logical conclusion by saying that all ideas could be explained in terms of experience and associative principles. He said that even the most complex ideas could be reduced to simpler ones. John Stuart Mill disagreed with his father's contention that simple ideas remained intact as they combined into more complex ones. He maintained that at least some simple ideas underwent a fusion and that the complex idea they produced could be quite different from the simpler ideas that made it up. J. S. Mill's idea of fusion was called mental chemistry. J. S. Mill believed that a mental science could develop that would eventually be on par with the physical sciences. According to J. S. Mill, the primary laws governing behavior were already known; what was needed to make mental science an exact science was an understanding of the secondary laws that determine how individuals act under specific circumstances. J. S. Mill proposed a science of ethology to study the secondary laws governing behavior.

Alexander Bain was the first to write a psychology text in English, to write an entire book on the relationship between the mind and the body, to use known neurophysiological facts in explaining psychological phenomena, and to found a psychology journal. He explained voluntary behavior in terms of spontaneous behavior and hedonism, and he added the laws of compound association and constructive association to the list of traditional laws of association.

Like the British empiricists, the French sensationalists believed that all ideas are derived from experience and denied the existence of the type of autonomous mind proposed by Descartes. The sensationalists were either materialists (like Hobbes) denying the existence of mental events, or they were mechanists believing that all mental events could be explained in terms of simple sensations and the laws of association. Gassendi believed that Descartes's division of a person into a material body and a nonmaterial mind was silly. All so-called mental events, he said, result from the brain, not the mind. Like Hobbes, Gassendi concluded that

all that exists is matter, and this includes all aspects of humans. In his book *Man a Machine*, La Mettrie proposed that humans and nonhuman animals differ only in degree of complexity and that both could be understood as machines. If we viewed ourselves as part of nature, said La Mettrie, we would be less inclined to abuse the environment, nonhuman animals, and our fellow humans. By using the example of a sentient statue with only the sense of smell, the ability to remember, and the ability to feel pleasure and pain, Condillac proposed to show that all human cognitive and emotional experience could be explained. Thus, there was no need to postulate an autonomous mind. Helvetius applied empiricism and sensationalism to the realm of education, saying that by controlling experience, you control the content of the mind.

With the widespread success of science, some people believed that science could solve all problems and answer all questions. Such a belief was called scientism, and it was very much like a religious belief. Accepting scientism, Comte created a position called positivism, according to which only scientific information could be considered valid. Anything not publicly observable was suspect, and therefore all subjective experience was rejected as a proper object of study. Comte suggested that cultures progressed through three stages in their attempt to explain phenomena: the theological, the metaphysical, and the scientific. Comte did not believe psychology could become a science because studying the mind required using the unreliable method of introspection. People, he said, could be objectively studied by observing their overt behavior or through phrenological analysis. Years following Comte, Mach proposed another type of positivism. Mach noted that all of which any scientist could be certain is his or her own experiences. The job of science is the cataloging of the experiences scientists have under various circumstances. Knowing how experiences are arranged allows prediction, which is important in adapting to the environment. Like Comte, Mach wanted to rid science of metaphysical speculation. The positivist says we should study only what can be directly experienced. For Comte, that was overt behavior; for Mach, it was sensations.

DISCUSSION QUESTIONS

1. Define empiricism. What was it in other philosophies that the empiricists opposed the most?

2. Discuss why Hobbes can accurately be referred to as an empiricist, a mechanist, and a materialist.

3. What functions did Hobbes see government as having?

4. What was Hobbes's explanation of human motivation?

5. Explain why it is incorrect to say that Locke postulated a passive mind. List a few powers of the mind that Locke postulated.

6. According to Locke, what was the difference between primary and secondary qualities? How did the paradox of the basins demonstrate this difference?

7. How did Locke use the laws of association in his philosophy?

8. Explain Berkeley's statement "to be is to be perceived." Did Berkeley deny the existence of external reality? Explain.

9. Summarize Berkeley's explanation of distance perception.

10. What goal did Hume set for his philosophical endeavors?

11. Discuss the function of the faculty of imagination in Hume's philosophy.

12. Discuss the associative principles of contiguity, resemblance, and cause and effect as Hume used them.

13. Summarize Hume's analysis of causation.

14. How did Hume define *mind*? *Self*?

15. What, for Hume, were the ultimate determinants of behavior? Explain.

16. What was Hartley's philosophical goal?

17. Summarize Hartley's explanation of association.

18. How, according to Hartley, was involuntary behavior transformed into voluntary behavior?

19. What part did the emotions play in Hartley's philosophy?

20. Summarize James Mill's version of associationism. Why is it believed that Mill's treatment of associationism exposed its absurdity?

21. Compare the "mental physics" of James Mill with the "mental chemistry" of his son John Stuart Mill.

22. Why did J. S. Mill believe a science of human nature was possible? What would characterize such a science in its early stages of development? In its later stages? Include in your answer a discussion of primary and secondary laws.

23. Discuss J. S. Mill's proposed science of ethology. Why did efforts to develop such a science fail?

24. What was Bain's philosophical goal?

25. Summarize Bain's contributions to psychology. Include in your answer the new laws of association that he added and his explanation of how spontaneous activity is transformed into voluntary behavior.

26. What were the major features of French sensationalism?

27. In what ways was Gassendi's philosophy similar to Hobbes's?

28. Why did La Mettrie believe that it was inappropriate to separate the mind and body?

29. What did La Mettrie believe humans and nonhuman animals have in common?

30. Why did La Mettrie believe accepting a materialistic philosophy would result in a better, more humane world?

31. How did Condillac use the analogy of a sentient statue to explain the origin of human mental processes? Give the examples of how attention, feeling, comparison, and surprise develop.

32. How did Helvetius apply empiricism and sensationalism to education?

33. What did Comte mean by positivism?

34. Describe the stages that Comte believed cultures (and individuals) went through in the way they attempted to explain phenomena.

35. Did Comte believe psychology could be a science? Why or why not?

36. What, according to Comte, were two valid ways of studying humans?

37. Discuss Mach's version of positivism.

SUGGESTIONS FOR FURTHER READING

Armstrong, G. (Ed.). (1965). *Berkeley's philosophical writings*. New York: Macmillan.
   This book contains all of Berkeley's important works: *An Essay Towards a New Theory of Vision* (1709), *The Principles of Human Knowledge* (1710), and *Three Dialogues Between Hylas and Philonous* (1713). It also contains an essay entitled "De Motu" ("Of Motion"), which Berkeley submitted to the Royal Academy of Sciences at Paris in an unsuccessful attempt to win a prize. (Available in paperback.)

Bricke, J. (1974). Hume's associationist psychology. *Journal of the History of the Behavioral Sciences, 10,* 397–409.
   Bricke explores Hume's contention that "the laws of association were to the understanding of the mind what Newton's laws were to the understanding of the physical world." The case is effectively made that

Hume had five laws of association instead of the commonly cited three, and numerous examples are given of how impression, ideas, passions, and action all become associated with each other.

Flew, A. (Ed.). (1962). *David Hume: On human nature and the understanding*. New York: Macmillan.

This book is the complete text of the 1777 edition of *An Enquiry Concerning Human Understanding* and excerpts from *A Treatise of Human Nature* (1739–1740). It also includes the complete text of *An Abstract of a Treatise of Human Nature* (1740) and a short autobiographical sketch entitled "My Own Life" written four months before Hume's death.

Greenway, A. P. (1973). The incorporation of action into associationism: The psychology of Alexander Bain. *Journal of the History of the Behavioral Sciences, 9*, 42–52.

Greenway gives a detailed analysis of Bain's account of the relationship between thought and behavior and the impact of that account on subsequent developments in psychology.

Hobbes, T. (1962). *Leviathan*. New York: Macmillan. (Original work published 1651)

It was the work of Hobbes that set the tone for the British empiricists that followed him. In this, perhaps his most famous book, Hobbes elaborated his materialistic conception of humans. *Leviathan* was primarily a political treatise, the purpose of which was to support absolute monarchy as a form of government. (Available in paperback.)

La Mettrie, J. O. de. (1912). *L'Homme machine (Man a Machine)*. (M. W. Calkins, Trans.). LaSalle, IL: Open Court. (Original work published 1748)

This book contains the full text of La Mettrie's interesting and exciting *Man a Machine* (1748) in both French and English, eulogy on La Mettrie by Frederick the Great, and extracts from La Mettrie's book *The Natural History of the Soul* (1745). (Available in paperback.)

Locke, J. (1974). *An essay concerning human understanding*. A. D. Woozley (Ed.). New York: Penguin Books. (Original work published 1706)

This is the fourth edition of Locke's classic *Essay* in which he denies the existence of innate ideas and discusses the origin and types of ideas, the difference between true and false ideas, the association of ideas, and primary and secondary qualities. (Available in paperback.)

Miller, E. F. (1971). Hume's contribution to behavioral science. *Journal of the History of the Behavioral Sciences, 7*, 154–168.

This is a clear and interesting account of how Hume's effort to create an "experimental" science of human nature influenced later developments in the behavioral sciences. Although Hume's "experiments" involved introspection, they still represented an attempt to use the methods of the natural sciences (e.g., those employed by Newton) to the understanding of human thought and behavior.

Petryszak, N. G. (1981). Tabula rasa—Its origins and implications. *Journal of the History of the Behavioral Sciences, 17*, 15–27.

In this article, Petryszak points out that many modern social scientists have misinterpreted Locke's concept of *tabula rasa* (blank mind) to mean there is no inherent human nature and that therefore human behavior is completely determined by experience. The article points out that Locke believed human nature was well stocked with innate dispositions furnished by God. Petryszak effectively argues that Locke used the concept of *tabula rasa* as a means of resolving the conflict between his belief in divine determination of human behavior and his liberal belief in individual freedom.

Steinberg, E. (Ed.). (1977). *David Hume: An enquiry concerning human understanding*. Indianapolis: Hackett.

In this classic book of Hume's attack on "dogmatic rationalism," Hume argued that everything we can know is derived from sensory experience. Sensory experience creates impressions, and impressions linger in our memory as ideas. Hume described how three laws of association (resemblance, contiguity, and cause and effect) can be used to explain all human beliefs, inferences, and judgments. Philosophical, theological, or scientific speculation that is not directly tied to experience is dismissed as idle speculation. (Available in paperback.)

Wilson, F. (1990). *Psychological analysis and the philosophy of John Stuart Mill*. Toronto: University of Toronto Press.

This book is a rather difficult but much needed summary of John Stuart Mill's contributions to psychology. Wilson begins by reviewing the philosophies of Hobbes, Hume, Berkeley, Bentham, James Mill, and others and shows their influence on J. S. Mill. Wilson next discusses J. S. Mill's philosophy of science and his thoughts on introspective analysis.

GLOSSARY

Associationism The belief that the laws of association provide the fundamental principles by which all mental phenomena can be explained.

Bain, Alexander (1818–1903) The first to attempt to relate known physiological facts to psychological phenomena. He also wrote the first psychology text in English, and he founded psychology's first journal (1876). Bain explained voluntary behavior in much the same way that modern learning theorists later explained trial-and-error behavior. Finally, Bain added the law of compound association and the law of constructive association to the older, traditional laws of association.

Bentham, Jeremy (1748–1832) Said that the seeking of pleasure and the avoidance of pain governed most human behavior. Bentham also said that the best society was one that did the greatest good for the greatest number of people.

Berkeley, George (1685–1753) Said that the only thing we experienced directly was our own perceptions, or secondary qualities. Berkeley offered an empirical explanation of the perception of distance, saying that we learn to associate the sensations caused by the convergence and divergence of the eyes with different distances. Berkeley denied materialism saying instead that reality exists because God perceives it. We can trust our senses to reflect God's perceptions because God would not create a sensory system that would deceive us.

Complex idea A configuration of simple ideas.

Comte, August (1798–1857) The founder of positivism and coiner of the term *sociology*. He felt that cultures passed through three stages in the way they explained phenomena: the theological, the metaphysical, and the scientific.

Condillac, Etienne Bonnot de (1715–1780) Maintained that all human mental attributes could be explained using only the concept of sensation and that it was therefore unnecessary to postulate an autonomous mind.

Empiricism The belief that all knowledge is derived from experience, especially sensory experience.

Ethology J. S. Mill's proposed study of how specific individuals act under specific circumstances. In other words, it is the study of how the primary laws governing human behavior interact with secondary laws to produce an individual's behavior in a situation.

French sensationalism The philosophical position that denies the existence of an autonomous mind and instead stresses the importance of sensation and the laws of association in the explanation of human cognition. The French sensationalists had much in common with the British empiricists.

Gassendi, Pierre (1592–1655) Generally considered the father of modern materialism, Gassendi saw humans as nothing but complex, physical machines, and he saw no need to assume a nonphysical mind. Gassendi had much in common with Hobbes.

Hartley, David (1705–1757) Combined empiricism and associationism with rudimentary physiological notions. Hartley arrived at the surprisingly modern notion that sensations are grouped according to the law of contiguity and that, after they have been grouped, experiencing any member of the group alone stimulates the memory of the entire group.

Hedonism The contention that the major motive for human behavior is the seeking of pleasure and the avoidance of pain.

Helvetius, Claude (1715–1771) Elaborated the implications of empiricism and sensationalism for education. That is, a person's intellectual development can be determined by controlling his or her experiences.

Hobbes, Thomas (1588–1679) Believed that the primary motive in human behavior was the seeking of pleasure and the avoidance of pain. For Hobbes, the function of government is to satisfy as many human needs as possible and to prevent humans from fighting with each other. Hobbes believed that all human activity, including mental activity, could be reduced to atoms in motion; therefore, he can be classified as a materialist.

Hume, David (1711–1776) Agreed with Berkeley that we could experience only our own subjective reality but disagreed with his contention that we could assume that our perceptions accurately reflect the physical world because God would not deceive us. For Hume, we can be sure of nothing. Even the notion of cause and effect, which is so important to Newtonian physics, is nothing more than a habit of thought. Hume distinguished between impressions, which are vivid, and ideas, which are faint copies of impressions.

Idea A mental event that lingers after impressions or sensations have ceased.

Imagination According to Hume, the power of the mind to arrange and rearrange ideas into countless configurations.

Impression According to Hume, the relatively strong mental experience caused by sensory stimulation. For Hume, impression was essentially the same thing as what others called sensation.

Innate idea An idea that is thought to exist independent of experience. All the British empiricists and French sensationalists denied the existence of innate ideas.

La Mettrie, Julien de (1709–1751) Believed humans were machines that differed from other animals only in complexity. La Mettrie believed that mental experiences were intimately related to bodily experiences and therefore to postulate an autonomous mind was incorrect. He also believed that accepting materialism would result in a better, more humane world.

Law of cause and effect According to Hume, if in our experience one event always precedes the occurrence of another event, we tend to believe the former event is the cause of the latter.

Law of compound association Contiguous or similar events form compound ideas and are remembered together. If one or a few elements of the compound idea are experienced, they may elicit the memory of the entire compound.

Law of constructive association The mind can rearrange the memories of various experiences so that the creative associations formed are different from the experiences that gave rise to the associations.

Law of contiguity The tendency for events that are experienced together to be remembered together.

Law of resemblance According to Hume, the tendency for our thoughts to run from one event to similar events. The same as what others call the law, or principle, of similarity.

Locke, John (1632–1704) An empiricist who denied the existence of any innate ideas but who assumed many nativistically determined powers of the mind. Locke distinguished between primary qualities, which cause sensations that correspond to actual attributes of physical bodies, and secondary qualities, which cause sensations that have no counterparts in the physical world. The types of ideas postulated by Locke included those caused by sensory stimulation, those caused by reflection, simple ideas, and complex ideas, which were composites of simple ideas.

Mach, Ernst (1838–1916) Proposed a brand of positivism that accepted the sensations of the scientist as the only valid subject matter of science.

Mental chemistry The process by which individual sensations can combine to form a new sensation that is different from any of the individual sensations that comprise it.

Mill, James (1773–1836) Maintained that all mental events consisted of sensations and ideas (copies of sensations) held together by association. No matter how complex an idea was, Mill felt that it could be reduced to simple ideas.

Mill, John Stuart (1806–1873) Disagreed with his father James that all complex ideas could be reduced to simple ideas. J. S. Mill proposed a process of mental chemistry according to which complex ideas could be distinctly different from the simple ideas (elements) that comprised them. J. S. Mill believed strongly that a science of human nature could be and should be developed.

Paradox of the basins Locke's observation that warm water will feel either hot or cold depending on whether a hand is first placed in hot water or cold water. Because water cannot be hot and cold at the same time, temperature must be a secondary, not a primary, quality.

Physical monist One who believes that everything that exists consists of matter. Such a person is also called a materialist.

Positivism The contention that science should study only that which can be directly experienced. For Comte, that was overt behavior. For Mach, it was the sensations of the scientist.

Primary laws According to J. S. Mill, the general laws that determine the overall behavior of events within a system.

Primary qualities According to many, the attributes of physical objects. According to Locke, those attributes of physical objects that can produce in us sensations that resemble them.

Psychophysical parallelism The contention that every experience has both a physical (biological) and a mental component, with no interaction between the two.

Quality According to Locke, that aspect of a physical object that has the power to produce an idea. (*See also* **Primary qualities** and **Secondary qualities**.)

Reflection According to Locke, the ability to use the powers of the mind to creatively rearrange ideas derived from sensory experience.

Scientism The almost religious belief that science can answer all questions and solve all problems.

Secondary laws According to J. S. Mill, the laws that interact with primary laws and determine the nature of individual events under specific circumstances.

Secondary qualities According to many, sensations that have no counterparts in the physical world. According to Locke, those attributes of physical objects or events that cause sensations that do not resemble those attributes. That is, for Locke, secondary qualities are attributes of physical objects or events that cause psychological experiences that have no counterparts in the physical world.

Sensation The rudimentary mental experience that results from the stimulation of a sense receptor.

Simple ideas The mental remnants of sensations.

Sociology For Comte, a study of the types of explanations various societies accepted for natural phenomena. He believed that as societies progressed they went from theological explanations, to metaphysical, to positivistic. By sociology, Comte also meant the study of the overt behavior of humans, especially social behavior.

Spontaneous activity According to Bain, behavior that is simply emitted by an organism rather than being elicited by external stimulation.

Utilitarianism The belief that the best society or government is one that provides the greatest good for the greatest number of individuals. Jeremy Bentham, James Mill, and John Stuart Mill were all utilitarians.

Vibratiuncles According to Hartley, the vibrations that linger in the brain after the initial vibrations caused by external stimulation ceased.

Voluntary behavior According to Bain, under some circumstances an organism's spontaneous activity leads to pleasurable consequences. After several such occurrences, the organism will come to voluntarily engage in the behavior that was originally spontaneous.

CHAPTER 6

Rationalism

In chapter 5, we defined *empiricism* as the belief that experience is the basis of all knowledge. All the empiricists and sensationalists assumed the importance of sensory information, though most used introspection to analyze what happened to that information after it arrived in the mind. Clearly, the term *empiricism* is not to be contrasted with *mentalism*. With the exception of Hobbes, Gassendi, and La Mettrie, all the empiricists and sensationalists postulated a mind in which such events as association, reflection, imagination, memory, and generalization took place. What distinguished the empiricist from the rationalist, then, was not whether they postulated a mind but the *type* of mind they postulated.

The empiricists tended to describe a **passive mind**, that is, a mind that acts on sensations and ideas in an automatic, mechanical way. As we have mentioned, the British empiricists, first under the influence of Galileo and then Newton, attempted to explain all mental events using a few laws or principles. The French sensationalists tended to be even more extreme, suggesting that there is really no need for the concept of mind. As we have seen, Condillac claimed that all mental phenomena ordinarily attributed to the mind could be explained by referring to only sensation and the laws of association.

What, then, was a rationalist? The rationalist tended to postulate a much more **active mind**, a mind that acts on information from the senses and gives it meaning that it otherwise would not have. For the rationalist, the mind added something to sensory data rather than simply passively organizing and storing it in memory. Typically, the rationalist assumed innate mental structures, principles, operations, or abilities that are used in analyzing the content of thought. Furthermore, the rationalist tended to believe that there are truths about ourselves and about the world that cannot be ascertained simply by experiencing the content of our minds; such truths must be arrived at by such processes as logical deduction, analysis, argument, and intuition. In other words, the rationalist tended to believe in the existence of truths that could not be discovered through sense data alone. Instead, the information provided by the senses must be digested by a rational system before such truths could be discovered. For the rationalist, not only understanding the contents of the mind, part of which may indeed come from experience, but also knowing how the mechanisms, abilities, or faculties of the mind process that content to arrive at higher philosophical truths was important.

For the empiricist, experience, memory, association, and hedonism determined not only how a person thought and acted but also his or her morality. For the rationalist, however, there were rational reasons why some acts or thoughts were more desirable than others. For example, there were moral principles, and if they were properly understood and acted on, they resulted in moral behavior. The empiricist tended to emphasize mechanistic *causes* of behavior, whereas the rationalist tended to emphasize *reasons* for behavior. Whereas the empiricist emphasized *induction* (i.e., the acquisition of knowledge through sensory experience and the generalizations from it), the rationalist emphasized *deduction*. Given certain sensory data and certain rules of thought, certain conclusions must follow. It should be no surprise that mathematics (especially geometry) and logic (a type of linguistic geometry) have almost always been more important to the rationalists than to the empiricists.

Do not be left with the impression that a clear distinction always exists between empiricism and **rationalism**; there does not. Some empiricists postulated a mind that was anything but passive (e.g., Locke), and most, if not all, of the rationalists accepted the importance of sensory information in the quest for knowledge and truth. In most cases, the difference between an empiricist and a rationalist is a matter of emphasis. The empiricist (and the sensationalist) emphasized the importance of sensory information and postulated a relatively passive mind that tended to function according to mechanistic laws. The rationalist emphasized the importance of innate structures, principles, or concepts and postulated an active mind that transformed, in important ways, the data provided by the senses. Even the difference between empiricism and rationalism concerning nativism is relative. Clearly, the empiricists and the sensationalists were united in their opposition to the notion of innate ideas; many rationalists had no such opposition. Conversely, many empiricists and sensationalists relied heavily on innate emotions (e.g., pleasure and pain) and mental abilities (e.g., reflection, imagination, association, and memory). Again, empirical and nativistic components exist in most philosophical positions, and what distinguishes one position from another is a matter of emphasis.

Just as Bacon is usually looked on as the founder of modern empiricism, Descartes is usually looked on as the founder of modern rationalism. Both Bacon and Descartes had the same motive: to overcome the philosophical mistakes and biases of the past (mainly those of Aristotle and his Scholastic interpreters and sympathizers). Both the empiricists and rationalists sought objective truth, but they simply went about their search differently.

In the remainder of this chapter, we sample the work of several of the rationalists who helped shape modern psychology.

BARUCH SPINOZA

Baruch (sometimes the Latinized form *Benedict* is used) **Spinoza** (1632–1677) was born of Portuguese Jewish parents on November 24 in the Christian city of Amsterdam. During the time that Spinoza was growing up, Holland was a center of intellectual freedom and, as a result, attracted such individuals as Descartes and Locke, who had experienced persecution elsewhere in Europe. Spinoza was initially impressed by Descartes's philosophy, and one of his first books was an account of Cartesian philosophy. Eventually, however, Spinoza rejected Descartes's contention that God, matter, and mind were all separate entities. Instead, Spinoza proposed that all three were simply aspects of the same substance. In other words, for Spinoza, God, nature, and the mind were inseparable. His proposal ran contrary to the anthropomorphic God image of both the Jewish and Christian religions, and he was condemned by both. When he was 27 years old, he was publicly excommunicated from his synagogue, and members of the Jewish community were forbidden to communicate with him in any way. They were not allowed to read even one line of his writings or to be in the same room with him (Alexander & Selesnick, 1966).

Spinoza supported himself by teaching and grinding and polishing lenses. He consistently refused to accept gifts and money offered to him by his admirers, one of whom was the great philosopher Leibniz (discussed later). He even rejected the chair of philosophy at the University of Heidelberg because accepting the position would preclude his criticism of Christianity (Alexander & Selesnick, 1966).

Spinoza carried on extensive correspondence with many major thinkers of his day, but only one of his books was published during his lifetime (and that book was published anonymously). His major work, *The Ethics Demonstrated with Geometrical Order*, was published posthumously in 1677. A number of his other works were collected by his friends and were published shortly after his death. As the full title of Spinoza's *The Ethics* implies, he was deeply impressed with the deductive method of geometry. In his faith that the methods of geometry could be used to discover truth in nonmathematical areas, Spinoza was in agreement with Descartes and Hobbes. In *The Ethics*, Spinoza presented a number of "self-evident" axioms from which he proposed to deduce other truths about the nature of reality. His ultimate goal was to discover a way of life that was both ethically correct and personally satisfying.

Nature of God

As we have seen, Descartes was severely criticized for conceptualizing God as a power that set the world in motion and then was no longer involved with it. Following Descartes, one could study the world without theological considerations, and this is essentially what Newton did. For Spinoza, God not only started the world in motion but also was continually present everywhere in nature. To understand the laws of nature was to understand God. For Spinoza, God was nature. It was mainly Spinoza's **pantheism**, or the belief that God is present everywhere and in everything, that caused his writings to be condemned even in his liberal homeland of Holland.

Mind–Body Relationship

Dualists, like Descartes, who maintained that there was a material body and a nonmaterial mind, were obliged to explain how the two were related. Conversely, materialists were obliged to explain the origin of those things that we experience as mental events (e.g., ideas). Spinoza escaped the difficulties experienced by dualists and materialists by assuming that the mind and body were two aspects of the same thing—the living human being. For Spinoza, the mind and the body were like two sides of a coin. Even though the two sides are different, they are two aspects of the same coin. Thus, the mind

BENEDICTVS de SPINOZA.

Baruch Spinoza

and body are inseparable; anything happening to the body is experienced as emotions and thoughts; and emotions and thoughts influence the body. In this way, Spinoza combined physiology and psychology into one unified system. Spinoza's position on the mind–body relationship has been called psychophysical double aspectism, double-aspect monism, or simply **double aspectism** (see Figure 1.1).

Spinoza's position on the mind–body relationship followed necessarily from his concept of God. God's own nature is characterized by both extension (matter) and thought, which is nonextended, and because God *is* nature, all of nature is characterized by both extension and thought. Because God is a thinking, material substance, everything in nature is a thinking, material substance. Humans, according to Spinoza, being part of nature, are thinking, material substances. Mental activity was not confined to humans nor even to the organic world. Everything, organic and inorganic, shared in the one substance that is God, and therefore everything had both mental and physical attributes. For Spinoza, the unity of the mind and body was but one manifestation of an all-encompassing unity of matter and thought. Spinoza's pantheism necessitated a *panpsychism*; that is, because God is everywhere, so is mind.

Denial of Free Will

God is nature, and nature is lawful. Humans are part of nature, and therefore human thoughts and behavior are lawful; that is, they are determined. Although humans may feel that they are free to act and think any way they choose, in reality they cannot. According to Spinoza, free will is a fiction:

> In the mind there is no absolute or free will; but the mind is determined to wish this or that by a cause, which has also been determined by another cause, and this last by another cause, and so on to infinity. (1677/1955, p. 119)

Elsewhere, Spinoza said that it is human ignorance of the causes of events that makes us believe that we possess free will: "Men think themselves free inasmuch as they are conscious of their volitions and desires, and never even dream, in their ignorance, of the causes which have disposed them so to wish and desire" (1677/1955, p. 75).

Our "freedom," then, consists in knowing that everything that is must necessarily be and everything that happens must necessarily happen. Nothing can be different because everything results from God. To understand the necessity of nature results in the highest pleasure because one views oneself as part of the eternal. According to Spinoza, it makes no sense to view God as the cause of all things *and*, at the same time, to believe that humans possess a free will.

Although Spinoza's God did not judge humans, Spinoza still considered it essential that we understand God. That is, Spinoza insisted that the best life was one lived with a knowledge of the causes of things. The closest we can get to freedom is understanding what causes our behavior and thoughts. The murderer is no more responsible for his or her behavior than is a river that floods a village. If the causes of both were understood, however, the aversive events could be controlled or prevented.

Self-Preservation as the Master Motive

Spinoza was a hedonist because he claimed that what are commonly referred to as "good" and "evil" are "nothing else but the emotions of pleasure and pain" (1677/1955, p. 195). By pleasure, however, Spinoza meant the entertaining of clear ideas. A *clear idea* is one that is conducive to the mind's survival because it reflects understanding of causal necessity. That is, it reflects a knowledge of why things are as they are. When the mind entertains unclear ideas or is overwhelmed by passion, it feels weak and vulnerable and experiences pain. The highest pleasure, then, comes from understanding God because to do so is to understand the laws of nature. If the mind dwells only on momentary perceptions or passions, it is being passive and not acting in a way conducive to survival; such a mind experiences pain. The mind realizes that most sense perceptions produce ideas that are unclear and therefore inadequate because they lack the clarity, distinctiveness, and self-evident character of true (clear) ideas. Because unclear ideas do not bring pleasure, the mind seeks to replace them with clear, adequate ideas through the process of reasoned reflection. In other words, clear ideas must be sought by an active mind; they do not appear automatically. We know intuitively that the body must be maintained because of its inseparable connection to the mind. Thus, the body, just like the mind, will attempt to avoid things harmful to itself and will seek those things that it needs to survive.

Emotions and Passions

Many believe that Spinoza's discussion of the emotions was his most significant contribution to psychology. Starting with a few basic emotions such as pleasure and pain, Spinoza showed how as many as 48 additional emotions could be derived from the interactions of these basic emotions and various situations encountered in life. We will give a few examples of how emotions are derived from everyday situations momentarily, but first we discuss Spinoza's important distinction between *emotion* and *passion*.

Spinoza thought that the experience of passion is one that reduced the probability of survival. Unlike an emotion, which is linked to a specific thought, passion is not associated with any particular thought. A child's love for its mother is an emotion, whereas a general emotional upheaval exemplifies passion because it is not directed at anything specific. Because passion can cause nonadaptive behavior, it must be harnessed by reason. Behavior and thoughts guided by reason are conducive to survival, but behavior and thoughts guided by passion are not. By understanding the causes of passion, reason gives one the power to control passion, just as knowing why rivers flood villages allows the control of floods. Spinoza's insistence that we can improve ourselves by clarifying our ideas through an analysis of them and by rationally controlling our passions comes very close to Freudian psychoanalysis. In fact, if we replace the term *passion* with *unconscious determinants of behavior*, we see how similar Spinoza's position is to Freud's. Alexander and Selesnick (1966) actually refer to Spinoza as the greatest of the pre-Freudian psychologists.

A few examples follow of how the basic emotions interact with one another and how they can be transferred from one object or person to another. Spinoza (1677/1955) said that if something is first loved and then hated, it will end up being hated more than if it were not loved in the first place; if objects cause us pleasure or pain, we will not only love and hate those objects, re-

spectively, but will also love and hate objects that resemble them; pondering ideas of events that have caused both pleasure and pain arouses the conflicting emotions of love and hate; pleasurable or painful events in the past or future cause as much pleasure or pain as those events would in the present; if anything produces pleasurable feelings in an object of our love, we will tend to love that thing, or conversely, if something causes pain in something we love, we will tend to hate that thing; if someone creates pleasure in something we hate, we will hate him or her, or conversely, if someone causes pain in something we hate, we will tend to love him or her.

Spinoza (1677/1955) discussed the following emotions and showed that all of them involve the basic emotions of pleasure or pain: wonder, contempt, love, hatred, devotion, hope, fear, confidence, despair, joy, disappointment, pity, indignation, envy, sympathy, humility, repentance, pride, honor, shame, regret, gratitude, revenge, cowardice, ambition, and lust. No one prior to Spinoza had treated human emotions in so much detail.

Spinoza's Influence

Descartes's philosophy is usually cited as the beginning of modern psychology, yet with the possible exception of what Descartes said about reflexive behavior, most of his ideas have not been amenable to scientific analysis—for example, his mind–body dualism, his beliefs concerning animal spirits and the pineal gland, his beliefs in free will and innate ideas, and the teleological and theological bases of much of his theorizing. Bernard feels that Spinoza should be given more credit than Descartes for influencing the development of modern psychology: "Considering just the broad general scientific principles that are at the basis of modern scientific psychology, we find them paramount in Spinozistic but lacking in Cartesian thought" (1972, p. 208). Bernard offers Spinoza's belief in *psychic deter-*

minism as a principle that stimulated a scientific analysis of the mind:

> One of these important principles [from Spinoza's philosophy] is that of *psychic determinism*, the assumption of which clearly leads to the scientific attitude that the processes of the mind, too, are subject to natural laws, and that these laws can be consequently investigated and studied. Thus Spinoza, combatting the teleological notion that nature acts "with an end in view," goes on to speak of a strict determinism ruling all psychological processes. (1972, p. 208)

Bernard (1972) concludes his review of Spinoza's contributions to modern psychology by saying that they were substantial and far greater than Descartes's. R. I. Watson also referred to Spinoza's pioneering efforts:

> Spinoza was perhaps the first modern thinker to view the world, including man, from a strictly deterministic standpoint. Both mind and body are of equal status, and both are subject to natural law. Spinoza saw clearly that his deterministic view of man required that there be laws of nature which are applicable to man. (1978, p. 167)

We have already noted the similarity between Spinoza's philosophy and psychoanalytic thinking. Both stress that unclear thoughts should be made clear and that the passions should be controlled by the rational mind. We will see in chapters 8 and 9 that Spinoza's philosophy had a strong influence on two individuals who were instrumental in launching psychology as an experimental science: Gustav Fechner and Wilhelm Wundt.

Before turning to other rational philosophers and psychologists, we first briefly review another position on the mind–body relationship that was espoused in Spinoza's time. We mention Malebranche's position mainly to show that almost every conceivable relationship between the mind and body has been proposed at one time or another.

NICOLAS DE MALEBRANCHE

A mystically oriented priest, **Nicolas de Malebranche** (1638–1715) accepted Descartes's separation of the mind and body but disagreed with his explanation of how the two interacted. For Malebranche, God mediated mind and body interactions. For example, when a person has a desire to move an arm, God is aware of this desire and moves the person's arm. Similarly, if the body is injured, God is aware of this and causes the person to experience pain. In reality, there is no contact between mind and body, but there appears to be because of God's intervention. A wish to do something becomes the occasion for God to cause the body to act, and for that reason this viewpoint became known as **occasionalism**. This view of the mind–body relationship can be referred to as a parallelism with divine intervention. Without divine intervention, the activities of the mind and body would be unrelated, and we would have psychophysical parallelism. Figure 1.1 depicts Malebranche's position on the mind–body relationship. Malebranche reverted to a much earlier explanation of the origins of knowledge, suggesting that ideas were not innate and that they did not come from experience. Instead, they came only from God, and we could know only what God revealed to our souls.

GOTTFRIED WILHELM VON LEIBNIZ

Like several of the rationalists, **Gottfried Wilhelm von Leibniz** (1646–1716) was a great mathematician. In fact, he developed differential and integral calculus at about the same time that Newton did, although he did so independently of Newton. Leibniz lived during intellectually stimulating times. He was a contemporary of Hobbes, Spinoza, and Locke. Malebranche died 1 year before Leibniz, and Newton died 11 years after him. His father was a professor of moral philosophy at the University of Leipzig, which Leibniz entered at the age of 15. His early education included the Greek and Roman classics and the works of Bacon, Descartes, and Galileo.

Disagreement with Locke

Although Descartes died when Leibniz was four years old, Descartes's philosophy still dominated Europe as Leibniz entered into his productive years. His first work, however, was a criticism of Locke's *Essay* (1690). Although his rebuttal of Locke's philosophy, *New Essays on the Understanding*, was completed in 1704, it was not published until almost 50 years after Leibniz's death in 1765. The reason for the delay was that Locke had died in 1704 and Leibniz saw little point in arguing with the deceased (Remnant & Bennett, 1982).

Focusing on Locke's description of the mind as a *tabula rasa* (blank tablet), Leibniz attributed to Locke the belief that there is nothing in the mind that is not first in the senses. Leibniz misread Locke as believing that if the ideas derived from experience were removed from the mind, nothing would remain. We saw in chapter 5, however, that Locke actually postulated a mind well stocked with innate abilities. In any case, Leibniz endeavored to correct Locke's philosophy as he understood it. Leibniz said that there is nothing in the mind that is not first in the senses, *except the mind itself*. Instead of the passive mind that Leibniz believed Locke postulated, Leibniz postulated a highly active mind but went even further. Leibniz completely rejected Locke's suggestion that all ideas come from experience, saying instead that *no* ideas come from experience. Leibniz believed that nothing material (e.g., the activation of a sense receptor) could ever cause an idea that is nonmaterial. Leibniz beckons us to imagine a machine capable of thinking (of having ideas). Then he asks us to imagine increasing the size of the machine to the point where we could enter it and look around. According to Leibniz, our exploration would yield only interacting, physical parts. Nothing we would see, whether examining the machine

Gottfried Wilhelm von Leibniz

THE BETTMANN ARCHIVE

or a human being, could possibly explain the origin of an idea. Because ideas cannot be created by anything physical, like a brain, they must be innate. What is innate however is the *potential* to have an idea. Experience can cause a potential idea to be actualized, but it can never create an idea. Leibniz made this point with his famous metaphor of the marble statue:

> Reflection is nothing but attention to what is within us, and the senses do not give us what we carry with us already. . . . I have . . . used the analogy of a veined block of marble, as opposed to an entirely homogeneous block of marble, or to a blank tablet—what the philosophers call a *tabula rasa*. For if the soul were like such a blank tablet then truths would be in us as the shape of Hercules is in a piece of marble when the marble is entirely neutral as to whether it assumes this shape or some other. However, if there were veins in the block which marked out the shape of Hercules rather than other shapes, then that block would be more determined to that shape and Hercules would be innate in it, in a way,

even though labour would be required to expose the veins and to polish them into clarity, removing everything that prevents their being seen. This is how ideas and truths are innate in us—as inclinations, dispositions, tendencies, or natural potentialities. (1765/1982, pp. 45–46)

Monadology

Leibniz combined physics, biology, introspection, and theology into a worldview that was both strange and complex. One of Leibniz's goals was to reconcile the many new, dramatic scientific discoveries with a traditional belief in God. As we have seen, Spinoza attempted to do much the same thing by equating God and nature, thus eliminating any friction between religion and science. Leibniz's proposed solution to the problem was more complex.

With the aid of the newly invented microscope, Leibniz could see that life exists everywhere, even where the naked eye cannot see it. He believed that the division of things into living or nonliving was absurd. Instead, he concluded that everything was living. The universe consisted of an infinite number of life units called **monads**. A monad is like a living atom, and all monads are active and conscious. There is a hierarchy in nature, however, that is similar to the *scala naturae* proposed by Aristotle. Although all monads are active and conscious, they vary in the clarity and distinctiveness of the thoughts they are capable of having. In other words, monads differ in intelligence. What is sometimes called inert matter is made up of monads incapable of all but extremely muddled thoughts. Then, on a scale of gradually increasing intelligence, come plants, microbes, insects, animals, humans, and God. Differences among all things in the universe, then, are quantitative, not qualitative. All monads seek to clarify their thoughts insofar as they are capable because clear thinking causes pleasure. Here there is an important point of agreement between Aristotle and Leibniz because Leibniz viewed a monad as a potential seeking to become actualized. In other words, each monad, and therefore all of

nature, was characterized by a final cause or purpose.

Next to God, humans possess the monads capable of the clearest thinking. However, because humans consist of all types of monads ranging from those possessed by matter, plants, and animals, our thoughts are not always clear, and in most cases, they are not. As humans, however, we have the potential for clear thinking, second only to God's. It was Leibniz's claim, then, that organisms are aggregates of monads representing different levels of awareness (intelligence). However, again following Aristotle, he believed that each organism had a soul (mind) that dominated its system; it is this dominant monad that determines an organism's intellectual potential. It is the nature of the dominant monad (soul) possessed by humans that provides them with intellectual potential inferior only to God's. The facts that humans possess many monads of a lower nature and that ideas provided by our dominant monad exist only as potentialities explain why we experience ideas with varying degrees of clarity. Monads, according to Leibniz, can never be influenced by anything outside of themselves. Therefore, the only way that they can change (become clearer) is by internal development—that is, by actualizing their potential.

Mind–Body Relationship

As we have seen, Leibniz believed experience was necessary because it focused attention on the thoughts already in us and allowed us to organize our thoughts and act appropriately, but experience cannot cause ideas. The confrontation between sense organs and the physical world can in no way cause something purely mental (e.g., an idea). For this reason, Leibniz rejected the mind–body dualism of Descartes. That is, he rejected Descartes's interactionism because it is impossible for something physical to cause something mental. Leibniz also rejected occasionalism because he thought that it was untenable to believe that the mind and body were coordinated through God's continuous intervention. In place of Descartes's interactionism and Malebranche's occasionalism, Leibniz proposed a **psychophysical parallelism** based on the notion of **pre-established harmony**. Leibniz believed that monads never influence each other; it only appears as if they do. Whenever we perceive in one monad what appears to be the cause of something, other monads are created in such a way as to display what appears to be the effects of that cause. The entire universe was created by God to be in perfect harmony, and yet nothing in the universe actually influences anything else. There is a correspondence between each monad's perceptual state and the conditions external to it, but those perceptions can only be said to "mirror" the external events rather than be caused by them. Similarly, with the monads that make up the mind and those that make up the body, they are always in agreement because God planned it that way, but they are not causally related. Leibniz asks that we imagine two identical, perfect clocks that have been set to the same time at the same moment. Afterward, the clocks will always be in agreement but will not interact. According to Leibniz, all monads are like such clocks, including those constituting the mind and the body. Figure 1.1 depicts Leibniz's pre-established-harmony form of psychophysical parallelism.

Leibniz's monadology has been criticized for several reasons, and none but a few of its essential features influenced later developments in philosophy and psychology. One criticism was that it suggested that because God created the world it cannot be improved on. In Voltaire's *Candide*, Leibniz is portrayed as a foolish professor who continues to insist, even after observing tragedy after tragedy, that "this is the best of all possible worlds."

Conscious and Unconscious Perception

For Leibniz, the notion of "insensible perceptions" was as useful to psychology as the notion of insensible atoms was to physics. In both cases, what is actually experienced consciously is ex-

plained in terms of events beyond the realm of conscious experience. Leibniz summarized this belief in his **law of continuity** (not to be confused with the law of contiguity):

> Nothing takes place suddenly, and it is one of my great and best confirmed maxims that *nature never makes leaps*. I called this the Law of Continuity. . . . There is much work for this law to do in natural science. It implies that any change from small to large, or vice versa, passes through something which is, in respect of degrees as well as of parts, in between; and that no motion ever springs immediately from a state of rest, or passes into one except through a lesser motion; just as one could never traverse a certain line or distance without first traversing a shorter one. Despite which, until now those who have propounded the laws of motion have not complied with this law, since they have believed that a body can instantaneously receive a motion contrary to its preceding one. All of which supports the judgment that noticeable perceptions arise by degrees from ones which are too minute to be noticed. To think otherwise is to be ignorant of the immeasurable fineness of things, which always and everywhere involves an actual infinity. (1765/1982, p. 49)

To demonstrate the fact that there are no leaps even in the realm of perception, Leibniz gave the example of perceiving the roar of the sea:

> To give a clearer idea of these minute perceptions which we are unable to pick out from the crowd, I like to use the example of the roaring noise of the sea which impresses itself on us when we are standing on the shore. To hear this noise as we do, we must hear the parts which make up this whole, that is the noise of each wave, although each of these little noises makes itself known only when combined confusedly with all the others, and would not be noticed if the wave which made it were by itself. We must be affected slightly by the motion of this wave, and have some perception of each of these noises, however faint they may be; otherwise there would be no perception of a hundred thousand waves, since a hundred thousand nothings cannot make something. Moreover, we never sleep so soundly that we do not have some feeble and confused sensation; some perception of its start, which is small, just as the strongest force in the world would never break a rope

unless the least force strained it and stretched it slightly, even though that little lengthening which is produced is imperceptible. (1765/1982, pp. 47–48)

Leibniz called perceptions that occurred below the level of awareness *petites perceptions* (little perceptions). As *petites perceptions* accumulate, their combined force is eventually enough to cause awareness, or what Leibniz called **apperception**. Therefore, a continuum exists between unconscious and conscious perception. Leibniz was perhaps the first philosopher to clearly postulate an unconscious mind. Leibniz also introduced the concept of **limen**, or threshold, into psychology. We are aware of experiences above a certain aggregate of *petites perceptions*, but experiences below that aggregate (threshold) remain unconscious. Leibniz's concept of threshold was to become extremely important when psychology became a science in the late 1800s. We will see later in this chapter that Leibniz's philosophy had a strong influence on Johann Friedrich Herbart, who in turn influenced many others. The implications of Leibniz's notion of unconscious perception for the development of psychoanalysis is clear. With his notion of the hierarchy of consciousness, Leibniz encouraged the study of consciousness in animals, a study that was not possible within Descartes's philosophy. It was not until Darwin, however, that the study of animal consciousness and intelligence was pursued intensely.

Leibniz's philosophy has received mixed reviews from historians of psychology. On the negative side, we have Esper:

In Leibniz . . . we have the classic example of what happens to "psychology" at the hands of a philosopher whose main interests and intellectual apparatus are theology, mathematics, and logic, and who uses the concepts of physical and biological science in the service of metaphysical speculation; we have in Leibniz a seventeenth-century Parmenides. (1964, p. 224)

Continuing in a negative vein, Esper says,

It is, I think, obvious that Leibniz foisted upon psychology a vast tangle of linguistic blind alleys which occupied its attention and its books and journals down until the 1920s, and which still determine much of its non-experimental, intuitive literature. (1964, p. 228)

On the positive side, Brett said, "The work of Leibniz was so brilliant and so full of inspiration that it has often seemed to be the spontaneous birth of German philosophy" (1965, p. 406). It was Leibniz's view of the human mind (soul) that dominated German rationalistic philosophy for many years. Brett described that view: "Leibniz emphasized the spontaneity of the soul; for him the work of the mind was something more than a mere arranging, sorting, and associating of the given; it was essentially productive, creative, and freely active" (1965, p. 407).

THOMAS REID

Thomas Reid (1710–1796) was born on April 26 in Strachan, a parish about 20 miles from Aberdeen, Scotland, where his father had been a minister for 50 years. His mother was a member of a prominent Scottish family, and one of his uncles was a professor of astronomy at Oxford and a close friend of Newton. Like Hume, Reid was a Scotsman; but unlike Hume, Reid represented rationalism instead of empiricism. Reid defended the existence of reasoning powers by saying that even those who claim that reasoning does not exist are using reasoning to doubt its existence. The mind reasons and the stomach digests food, and both do their jobs because they are innately disposed to do so. Reid thought that reason is necessary so that we can control our emotions, appetites, and passions and understand and perform our duty to God and other humans.

Hume had argued that because all we could ever experience were sense impressions, everything that we could possibly know must be based on them alone. For Hume then, knowledge of such things as God, the self, causality, and even external reality was simply unattainable. Reid emphatically disagreed with Hume, saying that because we do have such knowledge Hume's argument must be faulty. Reid presented his arguments against Hume and the other empiricists in *Inquiry into the Human Mind on the Principles of Common Sense* (1764), *Essays on the Intellectual Powers of Man* (1785), and *Essays on the Active Powers of the Human Mind* (1788). Reid put forth his **commonsense philosophy** mainly in the first book mentioned and his "faculty psychology" mainly in the last two, and we discuss both below.

Common Sense

Reid argued that because all humans were convinced of the existence of physical reality, it must exist. Furthermore, in courts of law, eyewitness testimony is highly valued:

> By the laws of all nations, in the most solemn judicial trials, wherein men's fortunes and lives are at stake, the sentence passes according to the testimony of eye or ear witnesses of good credit. An upright judge will give a fair hearing to every objection that can be made to the integrity of a witness, and allow it to be possible that he may be corrupted; but no judge will ever suppose that witnesses may be imposed upon by trusting to their eyes and ears. And if a sceptical counsel should plead against the testimony of the witnesses, that they had no other evidence for what they declared but the testimony of their eyes and ears, and that we ought not to put so much faith in our senses as to deprive men of life or fortune upon their testimony, surely no upright judge would admit a plea of this kind. I believe no counsel, however sceptical, ever dared to offer such an argument; and, if it was offered, it would be rejected with disdain.
> Can any stronger proof be given that it is the universal judgment of mankind that the evidence of sense is a kind of evidence which we may securely rest upon in the most momentous concerns of mankind; that it is a kind of evidence against which we ought not to admit any reasoning; and, therefore that to reason either for or against it is an insult to common sense?
> The whole conduct of mankind in the daily occurrences of life, as well as the solemn procedure of judicatories in the trial of causes civil and criminal, demonstrates this. . . . It appears, therefore, that the clear and distinct testimony of our senses carries irresistible conviction along with it to every man in his right judgment. (Beanblossom & Lehrer, 1983, pp. 161–163)

If Hume's logic caused him (Hume) to conclude that we could never know the physical world, then, said Reid, something was wrong with Hume's logic. We can trust our impressions of the physical world because it makes *common sense* to do so. We are naturally endowed with the abilities to deal with and make sense out of the world. According to Reid, "When a man suffers himself to be reasoned out of the principles of common sense, by metaphysical arguments, we may call this *metaphysical lunacy*" (Beanblossom & Lehrer, 1983, pp. 118–119).

Reid described what life would be like if we did not assume that our senses accurately reflect reality:

> I resolve not to believe my senses. I break my nose against a post that comes in my way; I step into a dirty kennel; and after twenty such wise and rational actions I am taken up and clapped into a madhouse. (Beanblossom & Lehrer, 1983, p. 86)

People may *say* that they do not know if their sensations accurately reflect the physical world as Hume did, but everyone, including Hume, assumes that they do. To assume otherwise, according to Reid, is grounds for confinement.

Direct Realism

Our sensations not only accurately reflect reality but also do so immediately. The belief that the world is as we immediately experience it is called **direct realism** (sometimes also called naive realism; see Henle, 1986). Although, as we see next, Reid was clearly a rationalist, he did not believe that the rational mind needed to be employed in experiencing the environment accurately; nor did he believe that the associationistic principles of the empiricists were employed. In other words, Reid did not believe that consciousness was formed by one sensation being added to another or to the memory of others. Rather, we experience objects immediately as objects because of our innate power of perception. We perceive the world *directly* in terms of meaningful units, not as isolated sensations that are then combined via associative principles. We will see this belief again in Kant's philosophy (discussed shortly) and later in Gestalt psychology (chapter 14).

Reid explained why he felt reasoning ability could not be a prerequisite for accurate perception of the world:

> The Supreme Being intended, that we should have such knowledge of the material objects that surround us, as is necessary in order to our supplying the wants of nature, and avoiding the dangers to which we are constantly exposed; and he has admirably fitted our powers of perception to this purpose. [If] the intelligence we have of external objects were to be got by reasoning only, the greatest part of men would be destitute of it; for the greatest part of men hardly ever learn to reason; and in infancy and childhood no man can reason. Therefore, as this intelligence of the objects that surround us, and from which we may receive so much benefit or harm, is equally necessary to children and to men, to the ignorant and to the learned, God in his wisdom conveys it to us in a way that puts all upon a level. The information of the senses is as perfect, and gives as full conviction to the most ignorant, as to the most learned. (1785/1969, p. 118)

Faculty Psychology

In elaborating the reasoning powers of the mind, Reid discussed several *faculties*; thus, he can be described as a faculty psychologist. Faculty psychologists (or philosophers) are those who refer to various mental abilities or powers in their descriptions of the mind. Through the years, **faculty psychology** has often been misunderstood or misrepresented. Frequently, it has been alleged that faculty psychologists believed that a faculty of the mind was housed in a specific location in the brain. Except for the phrenologists (discussed later), however, this was seldom the case. It was also alleged that faculties were postulated instead of explaining a complex mental phenomenon. People perceive, for example, because they have the faculty of perception. However, it was most often the case that faculty psychologists or philosophers neither believed that faculties corresponded to various parts of the brain nor used them to *explain* men-

tal phenomena. Most often the term *faculty* was used to denote a mental ability of some type, and that was all:

> The word "faculty" was in frequent use in 17th century discussions of the mind. Locke himself used it freely, being careful to point out that the word denoted simply a "power" or "ability" to perform a given sort of action (such as perceiving or remembering), that it did not denote an agent or substance, and that it had no explanatory value. To Locke and to all subsequent thinkers a "faculty" was simply a classificatory category, useful only in a taxonomic sense. (Albrecht, 1970, p. 36)

Although Albrecht's observation that faculty psychologists used the term *faculty* as only a classificatory category may be generally true, it was not true of Reid. For Reid, the mental faculties were active powers of the mind; they actually existed and influenced the thoughts and behavior of individuals. For Reid, however, the mental faculties were aspects of a single, unifying mind, and they never functioned in isolation. That is, when a faculty functioned, it did so in conjunction with other faculties. For Reid, the emphasis was always on the unity of the mind:

> The most fundamental entity in Reid's psychology is the mind. Although introspection reveals many different types of thoughts and activities, Reid assumed—in common with most other faculty psychologists—the existence of a unifying principle. This principle he termed mind or soul; the mind might have a variety of powers, but these are only different aspects of the same substance. (Brooks, 1976, p. 68)

Reid distinguished between mental *powers* and *faculties*. A mental power could be either learned or innate. Conversely, faculties are always innate. Acquired mental powers were called *habits*. Some habits, like praying, are good, but others, like smoking tobacco and drinking liquor, are bad. Reid believed that any undesirable mental power must be acquired because God would not furnish the mind with a tendency that was inherently evil. Reid also employed the term *instinct* to denote innate impulses to action. Both habits and instincts are performed involuntarily, that is, without the benefit of rational deliberation. Because the instincts are innate, they, like the faculties, are supplied by God, and must therefore be good. As examples of instincts, Reid listed breathing, crying, imitation, sucking, and swallowing.

To summarize, we can say that for Reid the faculties were aspects of the mind that actually existed and influenced human behavior and thought. All the faculties were thought to be innate and to function in cooperation with other faculties. After a careful review of Reid's works, Brooks (1976) concluded that Reid had referred to as many as 43 faculties of the mind (see Table 6.1).

FRANZ JOSEPH GALL AND JOHANN GASPER SPURZHEIM

It was not long after Reid and others had listed what they thought were the faculties of the mind that others were to substantially revise faculty psychology. Two such individuals were **Franz Joseph Gall** (1758–1828) and his student and colleague **Johann Gasper Spurzheim** (1776–1832). Gall and Spurzheim made three claims that changed the history of faculty psychology:

1. The mental faculties did not exist to the same extent in all humans.

TABLE 6.1 Reid's list of the mental faculties.

Abstraction	Knowledge, desire of
Activity	Love between the sexes
Affection, confiliate	Lust
Apprehension, simple	Memory
Attention	Moral faculty
Compounding	Musical ear
Consciousness	Perception
Deliberation	Pity and compassion
Emulation	Power, desire of
Esteem, desire of	Public spirit
Esteem of the wise and of the good	Reasoning
	Reflection
Feeling	Resentment, animal
Friendship	Resentment, rational
Generalizing	Resolution
Good for us upon the whole	Rest
Gratitude	Seeing
Hearing	Smelling
Hunger	Suggestion
Imitation, faculty of	Taste, sense of
Invention	Taste, good
Judgment	Thirst

SOURCE: Brooks, 1976, p. 76.

Franz Joseph Gall

2. The faculties were housed in specific areas of the brain.

3. If a faculty were well developed, a person would have a bump or protrusion on the corresponding part of the skull. Similarly, if a faculty were underdeveloped, a hollow or depression would be on the corresponding part of the skull.

Thus, Gall and Spurzheim believed that the magnitude of one's faculties could be determined by examining the bumps and depressions on one's skull. Such an analysis was called **phrenology**.

Several phrenologists made the additional claim that the faculties became stronger with practice, just as the biceps do. This belief influenced a number of educators to take a "mental muscle" approach to education. For them, education meant strengthening mental faculties by practicing the traits associated with them. One could improve one's reasoning ability, for example, by studying mathematics. The belief that educational experiences could be arranged so that they strengthen certain faculties was called **formal discipline**. We will see in chapter 11 that Edward L. Thorndike systematically evaluated the educational claims of the phrenologists and found them to be false.

Phrenology became enormously popular and was embraced by some of the leading intellectuals in Europe (e.g., Bain and Comte). Many societies, books, and journals were dedicated to the topic. One reason for the popularity of phrenology was the reputation of Gall himself, a highly regarded anatomist who, among other things, was the first to distinguish the functions of gray matter and white matter in the brain. Another reason for the popularity of phrenology was that it provided hope for an objective, materialistic analysis of the mind.

Phrenology fell on especially fertile ground in the United States. When Spurzheim arrived here on August 4, 1832, he was given a hero's welcome. He lectured at some of the nation's leading universities, such as Harvard and Yale, and was warmly received. In the United States, phrenology was widely accepted by the scientific and medical communities, prominent businessmen, leading politicians, intellectuals, and the general population. For the common person, phrenology provided simple answers to such complex questions as Who am I? What am I capable of? and What can I reasonably hope for? The following is an advertisement used by a leading supplier of phrenological material in the mid-19th century; the advertisement was entitled "Benefits of a Phrenological Examination":

A correct Phrenological examination will teach, with SCIENTIFIC CERTAINTY, that most useful of all knowledge—YOURSELF, YOUR DEFECTS, and how to obviate them; your EXCELLENCES and how to make the most of them; your NATURAL TALENTS, and thereby in what spheres and pursuits you can best succeed; show wherein you are liable to imperfections, errors, and excesses; direct you SPECIFICALLY, what mental faculties and functions you require especially to cultivate and restrain; give all needed advice touching self-improvement, and the preservation and restoration of health; show, THROUGHOUT, how to DEVELOP, PERFECT, and make the VERY MOST POSSIBLE our of YOUR OWN SELF; disclose to parents their children's INNATE CAPABILITIES, natural callings, dispositions, defects, means of improvement, the mode of government especially adapted to each, predispositions to disease, together with preventives, etc. etc.—nor can as little be spent on them profitably as in learning their Phrenologies and Physiologies—it will enable business men to choose reliable partners and customers; merchants, confidential clerks; mechanics, apprentices having natural GIFTS adapted to particu-

lar branches; shipmasters, good crews; the friendly desirable associates; guide matrimonial candidates in selecting CONGENIAL life companions, especially adapted to each other; show the married what in each other to allow for and conciliate; and can be made the VERY best instrumentality for PERSONAL DEVELOPMENT, IMPROVEMENT, AND HAPPINESS. (Bakan, 1966, p. 204)

A number of "phrenology charts" began to appear after the publication of Gall's and Spurzheim's books. Proposed numbers of faculties ranged from 26 (suggested by Gall) to 43 proposed by later phrenologists. Figure 6.1 shows the chart proposed by Spurzheim.

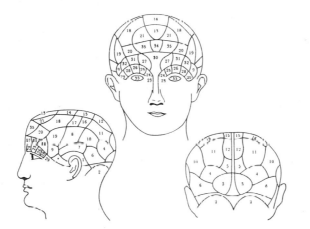

Affective Faculties

PROPENSITIES
- ? Desire to live
- • Alimentiveness
- 1 Destructiveness
- 2 Amativeness
- 3 Philoprogenitiveness
- 4 Adhesiveness
- 5 Inhabitiveness
- 6 Combativeness
- 7 Secretiveness
- 8 Acquisitiveness
- 9 Constructiveness

SENTIMENTS
- 10 Cautiousness
- 11 Approbativeness
- 12 Self-Esteem
- 13 Benevolence
- 14 Reverence
- 15 Firmness
- 16 Conscientiousness
- 17 Hope
- 18 Marvelousness
- 19 Ideality
- 20 Mirthfulness
- 21 Imitation

Intellectual Faculties

PERCEPTIVE
- 22 Individuality
- 23 Configuration
- 24 Size
- 25 Weight and resistance
- 26 Coloring
- 27 Locality
- 28 Order
- 29 Calculation
- 30 Eventuality
- 31 Time
- 32 Tune
- 33 Language

REFLECTIVE
- 34 Comparison
- 35 Causality

FIGURE 6.1. The phrenology chart suggested by Spurzheim (1834) showing the "powers and organs of the mind."

Although most of the specific claims of the phrenologists were found to be false, their overall beliefs did have a beneficial effect on the development of psychology as a science. To test the claims of the phrenologists, concerning the location of various faculties, careful investigation of the brain was required. However, although the phrenologists did stimulate research on the localization of brain functions, it was this very research that disproved the basic assumptions of phrenology. In chapter 8, we will have more to say about phrenology and the research that it stimulated.

IMMANUEL KANT

Immanuel Kant (1724–1804) was born on April 22 in Königsberg, Prussia, and never traveled more than 40 miles from his birthplace in the 80 years of his life (Boring, 1957, p. 246). Wolman nicely summarizes the type of life that Kant lived:

> Several armchairs played an important role in the history of human thoughts, but hardly any one of them could compete with the one occupied by Immanuel Kant. For Kant led an uneventful life: no change, no travel, no reaching out for the unusual, not much interest outside his study-room and university classroom. Kant's life was a life of thought. His pen was his scepter, desk his kingdom, and armchair his throne.
>
> Kant was more punctual and more precise than the town clocks of Königsberg. His habits were steadfast and unchangeable. Passersby in Königsberg regulated their watches whenever they saw Herr Professor Doktor Immanuel Kant on his daily stroll. Rain or shine, peace or war, revolution or counterrevolution had less affect on his life than a new book he read, and certainly counted less than a new idea that grew in his own mind. Kant's thoughts were to him the center of the universe. (1968a, p. 229)

Kant was educated at the University of Königsberg and taught there until he was 73, when he resigned because he was asked to stop including his views on religion in his lectures. He became so famous in his lifetime that philosophy students came from all over Europe to attend his lectures and he had to keep changing restaurants to avoid admirers who wanted to watch him eat his lunch. Kant's famous books *Critique of Pure Reason* (1781) and *Critique of Practical Reason* (1788) set the tone of German rationalist philosophy and psychology for generations.

Kant started out as a disciple of Leibniz, but reading Hume's philosophy caused him to wake from his "dogmatic slumbers" and attempt to rescue philosophy from the skepticism that Hume had created toward it. Hume had argued that all conclusions we reached about anything were based on subjective experience because that was the only thing we ever encountered directly. According to Hume, all statements about the nature of the physical world or about morality were derived from impressions and ideas and the feelings that they aroused, as well as from the way they were organized by the laws of association. Even causation, which was so important to many philosophers and scientists, was reduced to a habit of the mind in Hume's philosophy. For example, even if B always follows A and the interval between the two is always the same, we can never conclude that A causes B because there is no way for us to verify an actual, causal relationship between the two events. For Hume, rational philosophy, physical science, and moral philosophy were all reduced to subjective psychology. Therefore, nothing could be known with certainty because all knowledge was based on the interpretation of subjective experience.

Categories of Thought

Kant set out to prove Hume wrong by demonstrating that some truths were certain and were not based on subjective experience alone. He focused on Hume's analysis of the concept of causation. Kant agreed with Hume that this concept corresponded to nothing in experience. In other words, nothing in our experience proved that one thing causes another. But, asked Kant, if the notion of causation does not come from experience, *where does it come from?* Kant argued that the very ingredients necessary for even thinking in terms of a causal relationship could not be derived from experience and therefore must exist a priori, or independent of experience. Kant did not deny the importance of sensory data but thought that the mind must add something to that data before knowledge could be attained, that something was provided by the a priori (innate) **categories of thought**. According to Kant, what we experience subjectively has been modified by the pure concepts of the mind and is therefore more meaningful than it would otherwise have been. Kant included the following in his list of a priori pure concepts, or categories of thought: unity, totality, cause and effect, reality, quantity, quality, negation, possibility-impossibility, and existence-nonexistence.

Without the influence of the categories, we could never make statements such as those beginning with the word *all* because we never experience all of anything. According to Kant, the fact that we are willing at some point to generalize from several particular experiences to an entire class of events merely specifies the conditions under which we employ the innate category of totality because the word *all* can never be based on experience. In this way, Kant showed that although the empiricists had been correct in stressing the importance of experience, a further analysis of the very experience to which the empiricists referred revealed the operations of an active mind.

Because Kant postulated categories of thought, he can be classified as a faculty psychologist. He was a faculty psychologist in the way that Reid was, however. That is, he postulated a single, unified mind that possessed various attributes or abilities. The attributes always interacted and were not housed in any specific location in the mind and certainly not in the brain. In other words, Kant did not accept the type of faculty psychology described by the phrenologists.

Causes of Mental Experience

Kant agreed with Hume that we never experience the physical world directly and therefore

Immanuel Kant

we can never have certain knowledge of it. However, for Hume, our cognitions consisted only of sense impressions, ideas, and combinations of these arranged by the laws of association or by the imagination. For Kant, there was much more. For Kant, our sensory impressions were always structured by the categories of thought, and our *phenomenological experience* was therefore the result of the interaction between sensations and the categories of thought. This interaction was inescapable. Even when physical scientists believe that they are describing the physical world, they are really describing the human mind. For Kant, the mind prescribed the laws of nature. Kant, in this sense, was even more revolutionary than Copernicus because for Kant the human mind became the center of the universe. In fact, our mind, according to Kant, creates the universe, at least as we experience it. Kant called the objects that constitute physical reality "things-in-themselves" or *noumena*, and it was *noumena* about which we are forever and necessarily ignorant. We can only know appearances (phenomena) that are regulated and modified by the categories of thought.

Perception of Time

Even the concept of time is added to sensory information by the mind. On the sensory level, we experience a series of separate events such as the image provided by a horse walking down the street. We see the horse at one point and then another and then another and so forth. Simply looking at the isolated sensations, there is no reason to conclude that one sensation occurred before or after another. Yet, this is exactly what we do conclude; and because there is nothing in the sensations themselves to suggest the concept of time, the concept must exist a priori. Similarly, there is no reason, at least no reason based on experience, why an idea reflecting a childhood experience should be perceived as happening a long time ago. All notions of time such as *long ago*, *just recently*, *only yesterday*, *a few moments ago*, and so forth cannot come from experience; thus, they must be provided by the a priori category of time. All there is in memory are ideas that can vary only in intensity or vividness; it is the mind that superimposes over these experiences a sense of time.

In fact, Kant indicated that Hume's description of causation as perceived correlation depended on the concept of time. That is, one, according to Hume, develops the habit of expecting one event to follow another if they typically are correlated. However, without the notion of before and after (i.e., of time), Hume's analysis would be meaningless. Thus, according to Kant, Hume's analysis of causation assumed at least one innate (a priori) category of thought.

Perception of Space

Kant also believed that our experience of space was provided by an innate category of thought. Kant agreed with Hume that we never experience the physical world directly but, he observed, it certainly seems that we do. For most, if not all, humans, the physical world appears to be laid out before us and to exist independently of us. In other words, we do not simply experience sensations as they exist on the retina or in the brain. We experience a display of sensations that seem to reflect the physical world. The sensations vary in size, distance, and intensity and seem to be distributed in *space*, not in our retinas or brains. Clearly, said Kant, such a projected spatial arrangement is not provided by sensory impressions alone. Sensations are all internal; that is, they exist in the mind alone. Why is it, then, that we experience objects as distributed in space as external to the mind and the body? Again, Kant's answer was that the experience of space, like that of time, was provided by an a priori category of thought. According to Kant, the innate categories of time and space were basic because they provided the context for all mental phenomena, including, as we have seen, causality.

It must be emphasized that Kant did not propose specific innate *ideas*, as Descartes had done. Rather, he proposed innate *categories* of thought that organized all sensory experience. Thus, both Descartes and Kant were nativists, but their brands of nativism differed significantly.

The Categorical Imperative

Kant also attempted to rescue moral philosophy from what the empiricists had reduced it to—utilitarianism. According to Kant, just as there are innate categories of thought on which our knowledge of the physical world is based, there is also an a priori rational principle on which morality is based. For Kant, it was not enough to say that certain experiences felt good and others did not; he asked what rule or principle was being applied to those feelings, making them desirable or undesirable. He called the rational principle that governed or should govern moral behavior the **categorical imperative**, according to which a person should always act in such a way that the basis of his or her actions could serve as a universal law for everyone to follow. In other words, Kant's categorical imperative was his version of the "Golden Rule" or "Do unto others as you would have them do unto you." This innate moral principle exists in all people, but each individual is free to act in accordance with it or not; those who choose to act contrary to it experience guilt. Whereas the empiricists' analysis of moral behavior emphasized hedonism, Kant's was based on a rational principle and a belief in free will. For Kant, the idea of moral responsibility was meaningless unless rationality and free will were assumed.

Kant's Influence

We have in Kant a rationalism that relies heavily on both sensory experience and innate faculties. Kant has had a considerable influence on psychology; and since Kant's time, a lively debate has ensued in psychology, concerning the importance of innate factors in such areas as perception, language, cognitive development, and problem solving. The modern rationalistically oriented psychologists side with Kant by stressing the importance of genetically determined brain structures or operations. The empirically oriented psychologists insist that such psychological processes are best explained as resulting from sensory experience, learning, and the passive laws of association, thus following in the tradition of British empiricism and French sensationalism.

Although Kant's influence was clearly evident when psychology emerged as an independent science in the late 1800s, Kant did not believe that psychology could become an experimental science. First, Kant claimed the mind itself could never be objectively studied because it is not a physical thing. The actual mind, which Kant called the **transcendental ego**, is pure thought and therefore cannot be understood in terms of biological or mechanical laws. Second, even the mind as experienced through introspection, the **empirical ego**, cannot be studied scientifically because it does not stand still and wait to be analyzed; it is constantly changing and therefore cannot be reliably studied. Also, the very process of introspection influences the state of the mind, thus limiting the value of what is found through

introspection. Like most philosophers in the rationalistic tradition, Kant believed that to be a science a discipline's subject matter had to be capable of precise mathematical formulation. Because this is not the case for either the transcendental ego or the empirical ego, psychology, according to Kant, cannot be a science. It is ironic that when psychology did emerge as an independent science, it did so as an experimental science of the mind, and it used introspection as its primary research tool (see chapter 9).

Kant defined psychology as the introspective analysis of the mind, and it was psychology so defined that he believed could not be a science. There was a way of studying humans, however, that although not scientific could yield useful information; that way was to study *how* people actually behave. Such a discipline, which Kant called **anthropology**, could even supply the information necessary to predict and control human behavior. Kant was very interested in his field of anthropology and lectured on it for years before publishing *Anthropology from a Pragmatic Point of View* (1797). *Anthropology* is a most interesting and even amusing book. It includes among its many topics insanity, gender differences, suggestions for a good marriage, clear thinking, advice to authors, human intellectual faculties, human appetites, and the imagination.

Kant's most direct influences on contemporary psychology are seen in Gestalt psychology, which we will consider in chapter 14, and in information-processing psychology, which we will consider in chapter 18.

JOHANN FRIEDRICH HERBART

Johann Friedrich Herbart (1776–1841) was born on May 4 in Oldenburg, Germany. Due to an accident during infancy, he was a frail child and did not attend school until he was 12; instead, he was tutored by his mother. He was a precocious child who developed an early interest in logic. At 12 years of age, he began attending at the Oldenburg *Gymnasium* (high school) where, at the age of 16, Kant's philosophy impressed him deeply. At the age of 18, he entered the University of Jena where he pursued his interest in Kantian philosophy. After three years at Jena, he left and became a private tutor in Switzerland. It was this chance experience with tutoring that created in Herbart a lifelong interest in education. In fact, before leaving Switzerland, Herbart consulted with the famous Swiss educational reformer, J. H. Pestalozzi (1746–1827). After two years of tutoring, and still only 23 years of age, Herbart moved to the city of Bremen where he studied and pondered philosophical and educational issues for three years. In 1802 he moved to the University of Göttingen, where he obtained his doctorate and then remained as a *Dozent* (private teacher) until 1809. Although originally attracted to Kant's philosophy, Herbart criticized Kant in his doctor's dissertation and began developing his own philosophy, which was more compatible with Leibniz's thinking.

As testimony to his success, Herbart was invited to the University of Königsberg in 1809 to occupy the position previously held by Kant. Herbart was only 33 at the time, and he remained at Königsberg for 24 years, after which he returned to the University of Göttingen because the Prussian government had shown antagonism toward his educational research. He remained at Göttingen until his death 8 years later in 1841.

Herbart's two most important books for psychology were his short *Textbook in Psychology* (1816) and his long and difficult *Psychology as a Science Based on Experience, Metaphysics, and Mathematics* (1824–1825).

Psychology as a Science

Herbart agreed with Kant's contention that psychology could never be an experimental science, but he believed that the activities of the mind could be expressed mathematically and, in that sense, psychology *could* be a science. The reason Herbart denied that psychology could become an experimental science was that he believed experimentation necessitated the dividing up of its subject matter and, because it acted as an integrated whole, the mind could not be fractionated. For this reason, Herbart was very much opposed to faculty psychology, which was so popular in his day. He was also opposed to physiological psychology for the same reason; that is, he believed it fractionated the mind. After discussing his major ideas, we will have more to say about Herbart's attempt to mathematize psychology.

Psychic Mechanics

Herbart borrowed his concept of the idea from the empiricists. That is, he viewed ideas as the remnants of sense impressions. Following Leibniz, however, he assumed that ideas (like monads) contained a force or energy of their own, and the laws of association were therefore not necessary to bind them. Herbart's system has been referred to as **psychic mechanics** because he believed that ideas had the power to attract or repel other ideas, depending on their compatibility. Ideas tend to attract similar or compatible ideas, thus forming complex ideas. Similarly, ideas expend energy repelling dissimilar or incompatible ideas, thus attempting to avoid conflict. According to Herbart, all ideas struggle to gain expression in consciousness, and they compete with each other to do so. In Herbart's view, an idea is never destroyed or completely forgotten; it is either experienced consciously, or it is not. Thus, the same idea may at one time be given conscious expression and at another time be unconscious.

Although ideas can never be completely destroyed, they can vary in intensity, or force. For Herbart, intense ideas are clear ideas, and all ideas attempt to become as clear as possible. Because only ideas of which we are conscious are clear ideas, all ideas seek to be part of the conscious mind. Ideas in consciousness are bright and clear; unconscious ideas are dark and obscure. Herbart used the term *self-preservation* to describe an idea's tendency to seek and maintain conscious expression. That is, each idea strives to preserve itself as intense, clear, and conscious. This tendency toward self-preservation naturally brings each idea into conflict with other, dissimilar ideas that are also seeking conscious expression. Thus, Herbart viewed the mind as a battleground where ideas struggle with each other to gain conscious expression. When an idea loses its battle with other ideas, rather than being destroyed, it momentarily loses some of its intensity (clarity) and sinks into the unconscious.

Herbart's position represented a major departure from that of the empiricists because the empiricists believed that ideas, like Newton's particles of matter, were passively buffeted around by forces external to them—for example, by the laws of association. Herbart agreed with the empiricists that ideas were derived from experience, but he maintained that once they existed they had a life of their own. For Herbart, an idea was like an atom with energy and consciousness of its own—a conception that was very much like Leibniz's conception of the monad. Conversely, Herbart's insistence that all ideas are derived from experience was a major concession to empiricism and provided an important link between empiricism and rationalism.

The Apperceptive Mass

Not only was Herbart's view of the idea very close to Leibniz's view of the monad but Herbart also borrowed the concept of apperception from Leibniz. According to Herbart, at any given moment compatible ideas gather in consciousness and form a group. This group of compatible ideas constitutes the **apperceptive mass**. Another way of looking at the apperceptive mass is to equate it with attention; that is, the apperceptive mass contains all ideas to which we are attending.

It is with regard to the apperceptive mass that ideas compete with each other. An idea outside the apperceptive mass (i.e., an idea of which we are not conscious) will only be allowed to enter the apperceptive mass if it is compatible with the other ideas contained there at the moment. If the idea is not compatible, the ideas in the apperceptive mass will mobilize their energy to prevent the idea from entering. Thus, whether an idea is a new one derived from experience or one already existing in the unconscious, it will be permitted conscious expression only if it is compatible with the ideas in the apperceptive mass.

Herbart used the term *repression* to describe the force used to hold ideas incompatible with the apperceptive mass in the unconscious. He also said that if enough similar ideas are repressed into the unconscious, they could combine their energy and force their way into consciousness, thereby displacing the existing apperceptive mass. Repressed ideas continue to exist intact and wait for an opportunity to be part of consciousness. They must wait either for a more compatible apperceptive mass to emerge or for the time that they can join forces with similar repressed ideas and force their way into consciousness, thereby creating a new apperceptive mass will mobilize their energy to prevent the idea from entering. Thus, whether an idea is a new one derived from experience or ideas of which we are unaware.

Herbart used the term *limen* (threshold) to describe the border between the conscious and the unconscious mind. It was Herbart's goal to mathematically express the relationships among the apperceptive mass, the limen, and the conflict among ideas. Herbart's mathematics came from the two individuals who probably influenced him the most, Leibniz and Newton. In fact, one of Herbart's primary goals was to describe the mind in mathematical terms just as Newton had described the physical world. Herbart's use of calculus to quantify complex mental phenomena made him one of the first to apply a mathematical model to psychology. (Although the details are beyond the scope of this book, the interested reader can see how Herbart applied mathematics to his study of the mind by consulting Herbart's *Psychology as a Science*, 1824–1825; Boring, 1957; or Wolman, 1968b.)

Educational Psychology

Besides being one of the first mathematical psychologists, many consider Herbart to be the first educational psychologist. He applied his theory to education by offering the following advice to teachers:

1. Review the material that has already been learned.

2. Prepare the student for new material by giving an overview of what is coming next. This creates a receptive apperceptive mass.

3. Present the new material.

4. Relate the new material to what has already been learned.

5. Show applications of the new material and give an overview of what is to be learned next.

For Herbart, a student's existing apperceptive mass, or mental set, must be taken into consideration when presenting new material. Material not compatible with a student's apperceptive mass will simply be rejected or, at least, will not be understood. Herbart's theory of education comes very close to the more modern theory of Jean Piaget. Piaget said that for teaching to be effective, it must start with what a student can assimilate into his or her cognitive structure. If information is incompatible with a student's cognitive structure, it simply will not be learned. If we substitute the term *apperceptive mass* for *cognitive structure*, we see a great deal of similarity between the theories of Herbart and Piaget. Piaget's theory will be presented in greater detail in chapter 18.

It should be noted that Herbart's educational psychology was in direct opposition to the "mental muscle" approach to education derived from phrenology. For Herbart, the state of the learner's mind must be considered when planning educational experiences, and it is the learner's state of mind that education attempts to influence. For the teacher accepting phrenology, mental faculties are strengthened by practicing the activities associated with time; the classroom is like a gymnasium for the mind.

Herbart's Influence

Herbart influenced psychology in a number of ways. First, his insistence that psychology could at least be a mathematical science gave psychology more status and respectability than it had received from Kant. Despite Herbart's denial that psychology could be an experimental science, his efforts to quantify mental phenomena actually encouraged the development of experimental psychology. Second, his concepts of the unconscious, repression, and conflict and his belief that ideas continue to exist intact even when we are not conscious of them found their way into Freud's psychoanalytic theory. Also finding its way into Freudian theory was Herbart's notion that unconscious ideas seeking conscious expression will be met with *resistance* if they are incompatible with ideas already in consciousness. Third, Herbart's (and Leibniz's) concept of limen (threshold) was extremely important to Gustav Fechner (see chapter 8) whose psychophysics was instrumental in the development of psychology as a science. Fourth, Herbart influenced Wilhelm Wundt, the founder of psychology as a separate scientific discipline, in a number of ways. For example, Wundt relied heavily on Herbart's (and Leibniz's) concept of apprehension. In chapter 9, we will have more to say about Herbart's influence on Wundt. Fifth, several decades after his death, Herbart's ideas about education became very popular, and those ideas have outlived the educational ideas generated by phrenology.

GEORG WILHELM FRIEDRICH HEGEL

Georg Wilhelm Friedrich Hegel (1770–1831) was born in Stuttgart and learned Latin from his mother. Later, at Tübingen University, he concentrated on the Greek and Roman classics. After receiving his doctorate in 1793, he studied the historical Jesus and what the best minds through history had thought the meaning of life to be. Hegel was forced to change teaching jobs several times because of political unrest in Europe, but in 1818 he accepted one of the most prestigious academic positions in Europe, the chair in philosophy at the University of Berlin. Hegel remained at Berlin until he succumbed to a cholera epidemic on November 14, 1831.

The Absolute

Like Spinoza, Hegel saw the universe as an interrelated unity, which he called **The Absolute**. The only true understanding, according to Hegel, is an understanding of The Absolute. True knowledge can never be attained by examining isolated instances of anything unless those instances are related to the "whole." Russell described this aspect of Hegel's philosophy:

> The view of Hegel, and of many other philosophers, is that the character of any portion of the universe is so profoundly affected by its relation to the other parts and to the whole, that no true statement can be made about any part except to assign its place in the whole. Thus, there can be only one true statement; there is no truth except the whole truth. And similarly nothing is quite real except the whole, for any part, when isolated, is changed in character by being isolated, and therefore no longer appears quite what it truly is. On the other hand, when a part is viewed in relation to the whole, as it should be, it is seen to be not self-subsistent, and to be incapable of existing except as part of just that whole which alone is truly real. (1945, p. 743)

The process that Hegel proposed for seeking knowledge was the one Plato proposed. First, one must recognize that sense impressions are of little use unless one can determine the general principle or idea that they exemplify. Once general ideas or principles are understood, the next step is to determine how those principles or ideas are related to each other. When one sees the interrelatedness of all principles and ideas, one experiences The Absolute, which is similar to Plato's form of the good. Although Plato did not equate the form of the good with God, Hegel did equate The Absolute with God: "On its highest plane philosophy contemplates the concept of all concepts, the eternal absolute—the God

Georg Wilhelm Friedrich Hegel

who is worshipped in religion. Philosophy then culminates in speculative theology" (Hegel, 1817/1973, sec. 17).

Hegel's belief that the whole is more important than particular instances led him to conclude that the state (government) was more important than the individuals that comprised it. In other words, for Hegel, people existed for the state. This is exactly opposite Locke's position, which stated that the state existed for the people. Russell nicely summarized Hegel's view of the relationship between the individual and the state:

> Hegel conceives the ethical relation of the citizen to the state as analogous to that of the eye to the body: In his place the citizen is part of a valuable whole, but isolated he is as useless as an isolated eye. (1945, p. 743)

Dialectic Process

Hegel believed that both human history in general and the human intellect in particular evolved toward The Absolute via the **dialectic**

process. In studying Greek history, Hegel observed that one philosopher would take a position that another philosopher would then negate; then a third philosopher would develop a view that was intermediate between the two opposing views. For example, Heraclitus said that everything was constantly changing, Parmenides said that nothing ever changed, and Plato said that some things changed and some did not. The dialectic process involves a *thesis* (one point of view), an *antithesis* (the opposite point of view), and a *synthesis* (a compromise between the thesis and the antithesis). When a cycle is completed, the previous synthesis becomes the thesis for the next cycle, and the process repeats itself continually. In this manner, both human history and the human intellect evolve toward The Absolute.

In a sense, Hegel did to Kant what Kant had done to Hume. As we saw, Kant agreed with Hume that nothing in experience proves causation and yet we are convinced of its existence. Kant's explanation was that there is an a priori category of thought, which accounts for our tendency to structure the world in terms of cause and effect. Hegel accepted all of Kant's categories of thought and added several more of his own. However, he raised an all-important question that Kant had missed: Why do the categories of thought exist? Kant began his philosophy by attempting to account for our notion of causation because he agreed with Hume that such a notion cannot be derived from experience. Similarly, Hegel began his philosophy by attempting to account for the existence of Kant's categories. Hegel's answer was that the categories emerged as a result of the dialectic process and, for that reason, they bring humans closer to The Absolute. For Hegel then, the categories exist as a means to an end—the end being moving closer to The Absolute. Through the dialectic process, all things move toward The Absolute, including the human mind.

Hegel's Influence

We find Hegel's influences in a number of places in psychology. As we will see in chapter 8, Hegel strongly influenced Fechner and thereby the development of psychophysics. Some see Freud's concepts of the id, ego, and superego as manifestations of the dialectic process (e.g., D. N. Robinson, 1982). Others see the roots of self-actualization theory (e.g., the theories of Jung, Rogers, and Maslow) in Hegel's philosophy. Others see in it the beginnings of phenomenology, which ultimately manifested itself in Gestalt, humanistic, and existential psychology.

Also, the concept of *alienation*, or self-estrangement, plays a central role in Hegel's philosophy. By alienation, Hegel meant the mind's realization that it exists apart from The Absolute, apart from that which it is striving to become. Insofar as the mind has not completed its journey toward The Absolute, it experiences alienation. The Marxists later used the term *alienation* to describe the separation of people from their government or from the fruits of their labor, but that is not how Hegel used the term. Other variations on Hegel's concept of alienation were to be seen later in the theories of Eric Fromm and Carl Rogers. Fromm used the term *alienation* to describe the separation of humans from their basic roots in nature, and he claimed that a major human motive was to reestablish a sense of "rootedness," or belonging. Rogers used the term *alienation* to describe the separation of the self from the biologically based urge toward self-actualization.

Because Hegel's philosophy was meant to show the interconnectedness of everything in the universe, it did much to stimulate attempts to synthesize art, religion, history, and science. Russell commented on Hegel's widespread popularity: "At the end of the nineteenth century, the leading academic philosophers, both in America and Great Britain, were largely Hegelians. Outside of pure philosophy, many Protestant theologians adopted his doctrines, and his philosophy of history profoundly affected political theory" (1945, p. 730).

The rationalists of the 17th, 18th, and 19th centuries perpetuated the tradition of Plato, Augustine, Aquinas, and Descartes, a tradition that is still very much alive in psychology. All theories that postulate the mind's active involvement in intelligence, perception, memory, personality, creativity, or information processing in general have their origins in the rationalist tradition. In fact, insofar as modern psychology is scientific, it is partially a rational enterprise. As

was mentioned in chapter 1, scientific theory is a combination of empiricism and rationalism. In other words, it is now generally believed that a mere collection of empirical facts is meaningless unless analyzed in terms of some rational theory.

SUMMARY

British empiricism emphasized sensory experience and the laws of association in explaining the intellect, and if a mind was postulated at all, it was a relatively passive mind. The French sensationalists tended to go further, saying there was no need to postulate an autonomous mind at all and claiming that sensation and the laws of association were all that were necessary to explain all cognitive experience. The rationalists, on the other hand, besides accepting the importance of sensory information, postulated an active mind that not only transformed information furnished by the senses, thus making it more meaningful, but also could discover and understand principles and concepts not contained in sensory information. For the rationalists then, the mind was more than a collection of ideas derived from sensory experience and held together by the laws of association. Although there is considerable overlap between empiricism and rationalism, an important difference is that the former tends to postulate a passive mind and the latter an active mind.

Spinoza equated God with nature and in so doing was excommunicated from both the Jewish and Christian religions. According to Spinoza, if humans acted in accordance with the laws of nature, their behavior was determined; only unnatural behavior was free. The former was considered desirable and the latter undesirable. For Spinoza, there was only one basic reality (God), and it was both material and conscious; everything in the universe possessed these two aspects, including humans. A human was therefore seen as a material object from which consciousness (mind) could not be separated. This proposed relationship between mind and body was called psychophysical double aspectism or simply double aspectism. According to Spinoza, the greatest pleasure comes from pondering clear ideas, that is, ideas that reflect nature's laws. Spinoza believed that emotions were desirable because they did not interfere with clear thinking, but passions were undesirable because they did interfere with such thinking. Spinoza showed how a large number of emotions could be derived from the basic emotions of pleasure and pain and was among the first to perform a detailed analysis of human emotions. Spinoza offered an entirely de-

terministic account of human thoughts, actions, and emotions and helped pave the way for the development of a science of psychology.

Malebranche believed that there was a mind and a body but that they did not interact. Rather, God coordinated them. That is, if there was an idea in the mind, God was aware of it and caused the body to act appropriately. Such a belief became known as occasionalism.

Leibniz emphatically disagreed with Locke that all ideas come from sensory experience, saying instead that the mind innately contains the potential to have ideas and that that potential is actualized by sensory experience. Leibniz suggested that the universe was made up of indivisible entities called monads. All monads are self-contained and do not interact with other monads. Furthermore, all monads contain energy and possess consciousness. The harmony among monads was created by God and therefore cannot be improved on. Leibniz's contention that the monads of the mind were perfectly correlated with those of the body was called pre-established harmony. Experiencing one minute monad, or a small number of minute monads, creates *petites perceptions*, which take place below the level of awareness. If, however, enough minute monads are experienced together, their combined influence crosses the limen, or threshold, and they are apperceived, or experienced, consciously. Thus, for Leibniz, the difference between a conscious and an unconscious experience depends on the number of monads involved. Like Spinoza, Leibniz believed that all matter possessed consciousness but physical bodies vary in their ability to think clearly. The ability to think clearly was greatest in God, then in humans, then plants, animals, and finally in inert matter. Because humans possess monads in common with all the previously mentioned things, sometimes their thinking is clear and sometimes not.

Reid was emphatically opposed to Hume's skepticism. Reid thought that we could accept the physical world as it appeared to us because it made common sense to do so. Reid's contention that reality is as we experience it is called direct realism, or naive realism. Human consciousness could not be explained by assuming that one sensation was added to another via the laws of association. Rather, Reid postulated powers of the mind or mental faculties to account for conscious phenomena. Later, Gall and Spurzheim expanded faculty psychology into phrenology, according to which individuals differed with regard to the faculties. It was believed that those differences were reflected in the bumps and depressions on individuals' skulls. Also, it was believed by many phrenologists that various faculties could be strengthened by practicing the activities associated with them. This belief resulted in formal discipline, or the "mental muscle" approach to education.

Kant agreed with Hume that any conclusions we reached about physical reality were based on subjective experience. However, Kant asked where concepts such as cause and effect came from if we never directly experience causal relationships. His answer was that several categories of thought were innate and that sensory information was modified by those categories. What we experience consciously is determined by the combined influences of sensory information and the innate categories of thought. Because our experiences of such things as totality, causality, time, and space are not found in sensory experience, they must be imposed on such experience by the mind. The categorical imperative is an innate moral principle, but people can choose whether or not to act in accordance with it; those who choose to do so act morally, and those that do not act immorally. Kant did not believe that psychology could be a science because he believed that subjective experience could not be measured with mathematical precision. He did believe that human behavior could be beneficially studied, however, and he called such study anthropology. Kant's influence on modern psychology is seen mainly in Gestalt psychology.

Herbart disagreed with the empiricists, who likened an idea to a Newtonian particle whose fate was determined by forces external to it. Rather, Herbart likened an idea to a Leibnizian monad; that is, he saw ideas as having an energy and a consciousness of their own. Also, he saw ideas as striving for conscious expression. The group of compatible ideas of which we are conscious at any given moment forms the apperceptive mass; all other ideas are in the unconscious. It is possible for an idea to cross the threshold between the unconscious and the conscious mind if that idea is compatible with the ideas making up the apperceptive mass; otherwise, it is rejected. Herbart attempted to express mathematically the nature of the apperceptive mass, the threshold, and the conflict between ideas, making him among the first to apply mathematics to psychological phenomena. He is also considered to be the first educational psychologist because he applied his theory to educational practices. He said, for example, that if a student was going to learn new information, it must be compatible with the student's apperceptive mass.

Like Spinoza, Hegel believed the universe to be an interrelated unity. For Hegel, the only true knowledge was that of unity, which he called The Absolute. Hegel believed that the human intellect advanced by a process he called the dialectic, which involves a thesis (an idea), an antithesis (the opposite of that idea), and a synthesis (a compromise between the original idea and its opposite). The synthesis then becomes the thesis of the next stage of development. As this process continues, humans approximate an understanding of The Absolute.

The popularity of such topics as information processing, decision making, Gestalt psychology, and science in general is evidence of the rationalists' influence on modern psychology.

DISCUSSION QUESTIONS

1. In general, what are the basic differences among empiricism, sensationalism, and rationalism? Include in your answer a distinction between a passive and an active mind.

2. What was Spinoza's conception of nature? What was his position on the mind–body relationship?

3. Summarize Spinoza's position on the issue of free will versus determinism.

4. How did Spinoza distinguish between emotions and passions? Give an example of each.

5. What, for Spinoza, was the master motive for human behavior? Explain how this motive manifests itself.

6. In what way did Spinoza's philosophy encourage the development of scientific psychology?

7. What was Malebranche's position on the mind–body relationship?

8. Leibniz disagreed with Locke's contention that all ideas are derived from experience. How did Leibniz explain the origin of ideas?

9. Summarize Leibniz's monadology.

10. Discuss Leibniz's proposed solution to the mind–body problem.

11. Discuss Leibniz's law of continuity.

12. Describe the relationship among *petites perceptions*, limen, and apperception.

13. Summarize Reid's philosophy of common sense. Include in your answer a definition of direct realism.

14. What is faculty psychology? What are the major misconceptions of faculty psychology that have been perpetuated through the years?

15. Summarize Reid's version of faculty psychology and include in your answer his distinction between powers and faculties of the mind.

16. Define phrenology. Who was responsible for starting phrenology, and what effects has it had on psychology?

17. What did Kant mean by an a priori category of thought? According to Kant, how do such categories influence what we experience consciously?

18. Briefly summarize Kant's explanation of the experiences of causality, time, and space.

19. Discuss the importance of the categorical imperative in Kant's philosophy.

20. Did Kant believe that psychology could become a science? Why or why not?

21. How did Herbart's concept of the idea differ from those of the empiricists?

22. Discuss Herbart's notion of the apperceptive mass. For example, how does the apperceptive mass determine which ideas are experienced consciously and which are not? Include in your answer Herbart's concept of the limen, or threshold.

23. How did Herbart apply his theory to educational practices?

24. Discuss Hegel's notion of The Absolute. Describe the dialectic process by which Hegel felt the Absolute Idea was approximated.

25. Give an example of how rationalistic philosophy has influenced modern psychology.

SUGGESTIONS FOR FURTHER READING

Bakan, D. (1966). The influence of phrenology on American psychology. *Journal of the History of the Behavioral Sciences, 2*, 200–220.
This is a most interesting account of the widespread acceptance and influence of phrenology in 19th-century United States. Bakan points out that there was hardly any aspect of U.S. life that was not influenced by phrenology. Phrenology was especially influential in U.S. psychology, and this remained true up to and including the development of the school of functionalism at the turn of the century.

Beanblossom, R. E., & Lehrer, K. (Eds.). (1983). *Thomas Reid's inquiry and essays*. Indianapolis: Hackett.
After a most interesting introduction to Reid's life and philosophy, sections of Reid's *An Inquiry into the Human Mind on the Principles of Common Sense* (1764), *Essays on the Intellectual Powers of Man* (1785), and *Essays on the Active Powers of Man* (1788) are presented. This is an excellent sampling of Reid's most important ideas. (Available in paperback.)

Bernard, W. (1972). Spinoza's influence on the rise of scientific psychology: A neglected chapter in the history of psychology. *Journal of the History of the Behavioral Sciences, 8*, 208–215.
Bernard briefly reviews the philosophies of Descartes and Spinoza and shows that Spinoza's philosophy was much more conducive to the development of scientific psychology than Descartes's. Examples are given showing how Spinoza's philosophy influenced Freud, Johannes Müller, Gustav Fechner, Wilhelm Wundt, and other pioneers of modern scientific psychology.

Brooks, G. P. (1976). The faculty psychology of Thomas Reid. *Journal of the History of the Behavioral Sciences, 12*, 65–77.
Although the article is difficult at times, Brooks does an admirable job of clarifying how Reid actually used the term *faculty* as opposed to the many misrepresentations of his usage through the years.

Spinoza, Benedict de (1955). *On the improvement of the understanding, the ethics, and correspondence*. (R. H. M. Elwes, Trans.). New York: Dover Publications. (Original work published 1677)
In *On the Improvement of the Understanding*, Spinoza discusses what prompted him to study philosophy and how such study can help distinguish false and fictitious ideas from true ideas. In his famous *Ethics*, Spinoza discusses the nature of God, the nature of the human mind, the nature of human emotions, and the nature of human freedom. The *Correspondence* included here includes letters to and from Spinoza's contemporary philosophers and scientists, concerning political and religious reform. (Available in paperback.)

Wolman, B. B. (1968a). Immanuel Kant and his impact on psychology. In B. B. Wolman (Ed.), *Historical roots of contemporary psychology*. New York: Harper & Row.
This is a readable and informative introduction to Kant's philosophy as it applies to psychology. Wolman precedes his discussion of Kant with a review of the important philosophies that preceded Kant's. Wolman then provides a biographical sketch of Kant, a summary of his philosophical principles, a discussion of Kant's heritage, and his influence on psychology.

Wolman, B. B. (1968b). The historical role of Johann Friedrich Herbart. In B. B. Wolman (Ed.), *Historical roots of contemporary psychology.* New York: Harper & Row.

Wolman discusses the philosophical, sociological, and personal events that influenced Herbart's philosophy. Wolman describes in considerable detail Herbart's search for a way to synthesize rationalism, empiricism, and mathematics. Besides Herbart's philosophical principles, Wolman reviews Herbart's psychology, his efforts to apply mathematics to psychological principles, his thoughts on emotions and desires, his views on education, and his influence on psychology.

GLOSSARY

Active mind A mind equipped with genetically determined categories or operations that are used to analyze, organize, or modify sensory information and to discover abstract concepts or principles not contained within sensory experience. The rationalists postulated such a mind.

Anthropology Kant's proposed study of human behavior. Such a study could yield practical information that could be used to predict and control behavior.

Apperception Conscious experience.

Apperceptive mass According to Herbart, the cluster of interrelated ideas of which we are conscious at any given moment.

Categorical imperative According to Kant, the moral directive that we should always act in such a way that our actions could be used as a basis for everyone else's actions.

Categories of thought Those innate attributes of the mind that Kant postulated to explain those subjective experiences we have that cannot be explained in terms of sensory experience alone—for example, the experiences of time, causality, and space.

Commonsense philosophy The position, first proposed by Reid, that we can assume the existence of the physical world and of human reasoning powers because it makes common sense to do so.

Dialectic process The process involving an original idea, the negation of the original idea, and a synthesis of the new idea and its negation. The synthesis then becomes the starting point (the idea) of the next cycle of the developmental process.

Direct realism The belief that sensory experience represents physical reality exactly as it is. Also called naive realism.

Double aspectism Spinoza's contention that material substance and consciousness are two inseparable aspects of everything in the universe, including humans. Also called psychophysical double aspectism and double-aspect monism.

Empirical ego According to Kant, the mind as it is experienced during introspective analysis.

Faculty psychology The belief that the mind consists of several powers or faculties.

Formal discipline The belief that the faculties of the mind can be strengthened by practicing the functions associated with them. Thus, one supposedly can become better at reasoning by studying mathematics or logic.

Gall, Franz Joseph (1758–1828) Believed that the strengths of mental faculties varied from person to person and that they could be determined by examining the bumps and depressions on a person's skull. Such an examination came to be called phrenology.

Hegel, Georg Wilhelm Friedrich (1770–1831) Like Spinoza, believed the universe to be an interrelated unity. Hegel called this unity The Absolute, and he thought that human history and the human intellect progressed via the dialectic process toward The Absolute.

Herbart, Johann Friedrich (1776–1841) Likened ideas to Leibniz's monads by saying that they had energy and a consciousness of their own. Also, according to Herbart, ideas strive for consciousness. Those ideas compatible with a person's apperceptive mass are given conscious expression, whereas those that are not remain below the limen in the unconscious mind. Herbart is considered to be one of the first mathematical and educational psychologists.

Kant, Immanuel (1724–1804) Believed that experiences such as those of unity, causation, time, and space could not be derived from sensory experience and therefore must be attributable to innate categories of thought. He also believed that morality is governed by the innate categorical imperative. He did not believe psychology could become a science because subjective experience could not be quantified mathematically. Kant's influence on modern psychology came mainly through his influence on Gestalt psychology.

Law of continuity Leibniz's contention that there are no major gaps or leaps in nature. Rather, all differences in nature are characterized by small gradations.

Leibniz, Gottfried Wilhelm von (1646–1716) Felt that the universe consisted of indivisible units called monads. God had created the arrangement of the monads, and therefore this was the best of all possible worlds. If only a few minute monads were experienced, *petites perceptions* resulted, which were unconscious. If enough minute monads were experienced at the same time, apperception occurred, which was a conscious experience.

Limen For Leibniz and Herbart, the border between the conscious and the unconscious mind. Also called threshold.

Malebranche, Nicolas de (1638–1715) Contended that the mind and body were separate but that God coordinated their activities.

Monads According to Leibniz, the indivisible units that comprise everything in the universe. All monads are characterized by consciousness but some more so than others. Inert matter possesses only dim consciousness, and then with increased ability to think clearly come plants, animals, humans, and, finally, God. The goal of each monad is to think as clearly as it is capable of doing. Because humans share monads with matter, plants, and animals, sometimes our thoughts are less than clear.

Occasionalism The belief that bodily events and mental events are coordinated by God's intervention.

Pantheism The belief that God is present everywhere and in everything.

Passive mind A mind whose contents are determined by sensory experience. It contains a few mechanistic principles that organize, store, and generalize sensory experiences. The British empiricists tended to postulate such a mind.

Petites perceptions According to Leibniz, a perception that occurs below the level of awareness because only a few monads are involved.

Phrenology The examination of the bumps and depressions on the skull in order to determine the strengths and weaknesses of various mental faculties.

Pre-established harmony Leibniz's contention that God had created the monads comprising the universe in such a way that a continuous harmony existed among them. This explained why mental and bodily events were coordinated.

Psychic mechanics The term used by Herbart to describe how ideas struggle with each other to gain conscious expression.

Psychophysical parallelism The contention that bodily and mental events are perfectly correlated but that there is no interaction between them.

Rationalism The philosophical position postulating an active mind that transforms sensory information and is capable of understanding abstract principles or concepts not attainable from sensory information.

Reid, Thomas (1710–1796) Believed that we could trust our sensory impressions to accurately reflect physical reality because it makes common sense to do so. Reid attributed several rational faculties to the mind and was therefore a faculty psychologist.

Spinoza, Baruch (1632–1677) Equated God with nature and said that everything in nature, including humans, consisted of both matter and consciousness. Spinoza's proposed solution to the mind–body problem is called double aspectism. The most pleasurable life, according to Spinoza, is one lived in accordance with the laws of nature. Emotional experience is desirable because it is controlled by reason; passionate experience is undesirable because it is not. Spinoza's deterministic view of human cognition, activity, and emotion did much to facilitate the development of scientific psychology.

Spurzheim, Johann Gasper (1776–1832) A student and colleague of Gall, who did much to expand and promote phrenology.

The Absolute According to Hegel, the totality of the universe. A knowledge of The Absolute constituted the only true knowledge, and separate aspects of the universe can only be understood in terms of their relationship to The Absolute. Through the dialectic process, human history and the human intellect progress toward The Absolute.

Transcendental ego According to Kant, the pure mind as it exists independent of any particular ideas.

CHAPTER 7

Romanticism and Existentialism

ROMANTICISM

Not all philosophers believed that the truth was to be found by exercising the intellect, as the rationalists maintained, or by examining the ideas derived from experience, as the empiricists and the sensationalists maintained. Some philosophers insisted that both rationalism and empiricism were overlooking the truest source of valid information—human nature itself. Humans, they said, have not only an intellect and ideas derived from experience but also a wide variety of feelings or emotions. Those philosophers emphasizing the importance of human feelings were called *romantics*. They believed that rational thought had often led humans astray in their search for valid information and that empiricism reduced people to unfeeling machines. According to the romantics, the best way to find out what humans are really like is to study the *total* person, not just his or her rational powers or empirically determined ideas.

The rational, empirical, and positivistic philosophers had attempted to create political and moral systems based on their philosophies, and their efforts had failed. According to the romantics, they failed because they viewed humans as either victims of experience or vehicles by which some grandiose, rational principle was manifested. During the romantic movement, between the late 18th and mid-19th centuries, great emphasis was placed on human emotions, instincts, and uniqueness. The good life was defined as one lived honestly in accordance with one's inner nature. The great philosophical systems were no longer to be trusted; in general, science was also seen as antithetical—or, at best,

irrelevant—to understanding humans. The inner world of humans replaced the outer world as the focus of philosophical concern. Once again in history, the time was right for turning away from the external world and toward one's subjective experiences. Rousseau is usually thought of as the father of **romanticism**, and it is to his philosophy that we turn next.

Jean-Jacques Rousseau

Jean-Jacques Rousseau (1712–1778) was born on June 28 in Geneva, the son of a watchmaker, and raised a Calvinist. His mother died soon after giving him birth—something for which his father never forgave him. In fact, Rousseau's father abandoned him when he was 10 years old, and he was brought up by relatives. Rousseau, suffering from poor health all his life, left school at the age of 12 and moved from place to place and from job to job. Once he was so hungry that he converted to Catholicism in order to receive free food and lodging in a Catholic church. He said of this act, "I could not dissemble from myself that the holy deed I was about to do was at bottom the act of a bandit" (Russell, 1945, p. 685). For the next 9 or 10 years, Rousseau was kept by Madame de Warrens, and after that he spent several years as a vagabond, making money any way he could, sometimes illegally or by deception. In 1745 Rousseau began a relationship with Thérèse le Vasseur, who was a maid in his hotel in Paris. He lived with her the rest of his life, and they had five children—all of whom were sent to a foundling home. Although Rousseau had been a womanizer and remained one during his relationship with Thérèse, understanding why he chose this person with whom to share his life is difficult:

> No one has ever understood what attracted him to her [Thérèse le Vasseur]. She was ugly and ignorant; she could neither read nor write (he taught her to write, but not to read); she did not know the names of the months, and could not add up money. Her mother was grasping and avaricious; the two together used Rousseau and all his friends as sources of income. Rousseau asserts (truly or falsely) that he never had a spark of love for Thérèse; in later years she drank and ran after stable-boys. Probably he liked the feeling that he was indubitably superior to her, both financially and intellectually, and that she was completely dependent upon him. He was always uncomfortable in the company of the great, and genuinely preferred simple people; in this respect his democratic feeling was wholly sincere. Although he never married her, he treated her almost as a wife, and all the grand ladies who befriended him had to put up with her. (Russell, 1945, pp. 686–687)

Arriving in Paris at the age of 30, Rousseau joined a group of influential Parisian intellectuals, though he himself had had no formal education. Rousseau was an intensely private person and did not like the social life of the city. In 1756 he left Paris for the quiet of the country, but publication of his two most famous works, *The Social Contract* and *Emile*, both in 1762, ended Rousseau's tranquil country life. Within a month of the publication of these two books, the city of Paris condemned them, and Rousseau's hometown of Geneva issued a warrant for his arrest. He was forced to spend the next four years as a refugee. Finally, in 1766 David Hume offered Rousseau refuge in England. Eventually, the opposition to Rousseau's ideas faded, and Rousseau returned to Paris, where he remained until his death. He died in poverty, and suicide was suspected (Russell, 1945, p. 691).

Feelings versus reason. Rousseau began *The Social Contract* with this statement: "Man is born free and yet we see him everywhere in chains" (1762/1947, p. 5). His point was that all governments in Europe at the time were based on a faulty assumption about human nature—the as-

Jean-Jacques Rousseau

THE BETTMANN ARCHIVE

sumption that humans needed to be governed. The only justifiable government, according to Rousseau, was one that allowed humans to reach their full potential and to fully express their free will. The best guide for human conduct was a person's honest feelings and inclinations. "The first impulses of the heart," he said, "are always right." Rousseau distrusted reason, organized religion, science, and societal laws as guides for human conduct. His philosophy became a defense for Protestantism because it supported the notion that God's existence could be defended on the basis of individual feeling and did not depend on the dictates of the church:

> Rousseau's defence of the feelings as against reason has been one of the powerful influences in the shaping of the romantic movement. Amongst other things it has set Protestant theology on a new path that sharply differentiates it from the [Catholic] doctrine, which is in the philosophic tradition of the ancients. The new

Protestant approach dispenses with proofs for the existence of God, and allows that such information wells up from the heart unaided by reason. Likewise, in ethics Rousseau contends that our natural feelings point in the right direction, whereas reason leads us astray. (Russell, 1959, p. 237)

In chapter 17, we will see that Rousseau's trust of inner feelings as guides for action was shared by the humanist psychologist Carl Rogers.

The noble savage. Looking at natural impulses to understand humans was not new with Rousseau; we saw in chapter 5 that Hobbes did the same thing. The major difference between Hobbes and Rousseau is in the conclusions they reached about the nature of human nature. For Hobbes, human nature was animalistic, selfish, and needed to be controlled by government. This view of human nature was also accepted by many theologians and philosophers who said that reason had to be almost constantly employed to control brutish human impulses. Rousseau completely disagreed saying instead that humans were born basically good. He reversed the doctrine of Original Sin by insisting that humans are born good but are made bad by societal institutions.

Rousseau claimed that if a **noble savage** could be found (i.e., a human not contaminated by society), we would have a human whose behavior was governed by feelings but who would not be selfish. Rousseau believed that humans were, by nature, social animals who wished to live in harmony with other humans. If humans were permitted to develop freely, they would become happy, fulfilled, free, and socially minded. They would do what was best for themselves and for others if simply given the freedom to do so.

The general will. Even though the conceptions of human nature accepted by Hobbes and Rousseau were essentially opposite, the type of government that the two proposed was quite similar. Rousseau conceded that to live in civilized societies humans had to give up some of their primitive independence. The question that he pondered in his *Social Contract* was how humans could be governed and still remain as free as possible. It is in answer to this question that Rousseau introduced his notion of the general will. According to Rousseau, the **general will** describes what is best within a community, and it is to be sharply distinguished from an individual's will or even a unanimous agreement among individuals:

> This general will is to be kept sharply distinguished from what the members of a society may, by majority vote or even by unanimous agreement, decide is their good. Such a decision, which Rousseau distinguished from the general will by calling it "the will of all," may be wrong. The general will, by definition, cannot be wrong because it is the very standard of right. (Frankel, 1947, p. xxiv)

Each individual has both a tendency to be selfish (private will) and to act in ways beneficial to the community (general will). To live in harmony with others, each person is obliged to act in accordance with his or her general will and inhibit his or her private will:

> The general will is something over and above the sum of all the individual wills present in the society, but it is not something completely apart from individuals. Each individual has both a private will, in which he isolates his desires from the social group within which they function, and a general will, in which his individual desires are at the same time the desires proper to his status as a member of society and a citizen. Each individual has the responsibility as a citizen to act in accordance with his general will rather than in accordance with his private will, just as it is the major function of those who are entrusted with public power to evoke and to obey the general will. (Frankel, 1947, pp. xxiv–xxv)

The "social contract," then, can be stated as follows: "Each of us puts his person and all his power in common under the supreme direction of the general will, and, in our corporate capacity, we receive each member as an indivisible part of the whole" (Russell, 1945, p. 696). In Rousseau's "utopia," if a person's private will is contrary to the general will, he or she can be forced to follow the general will. Also, there are no elections and no private property: "The state, in relation to its members, is master of all their wealth" (Rousseau, 1762/1947, p. 20). The governments that Rousseau encouraged, however, were anything but democratic:

> *The Social Contract* became the Bible of most of the leaders in the French Revolution, but no doubt, as is the fate of Bibles, it was not carefully read and was still less understood by many of its disciples. It reintroduced the habit of metaphysical abstractions among the theorists of democracy, and by its doctrine of the general will it made possible the mystic identification of a leader with his people, which has no need of confirmation by so mundane an apparatus as the ballot-box. Much of its philosophy could be appropriated by Hegel in his defence of the Prussian autocracy. Its first-fruits in practice was the reign of Robespierre; the dictatorships of Russia and Germany (especially the latter) are in part an outcome of Rousseau's teaching. What further triumphs the future has to offer to his ghost I do not venture to predict. (Russell, 1945, pp. 700–701)

Education. Rousseau began *Emile* the same way that he began *The Social Contract*, that is, by condemning society for interfering with nature and with natural human impulses:

> God makes all things good; man meddles with them and they become evil. He forces one soil to yield the products of another, one tree to bear another's fruit. He confuses and confounds time, place, and natural conditions. He mutilates his dog, his horse, and his slave. He destroys and defaces all things; he loves all that is deformed and monstrous; he will have nothing as nature made it, not even man himself, who must learn his paces like a saddlehorse, and be shaped to his master's taste like the trees in his garden. (1762/1974, p. 5)

According to Rousseau, education should take advantage of natural impulses rather than distort them. Education should not consist of pouring information into children in a highly structured school. Rather, education should create a situation in which a child's natural abilities and interests can be nurtured. For Rousseau, the child naturally had a rich array of posi-

tive instincts, and the best education was one that allowed these impulses to become actualized.

In his famous book *Emile* (1762/1974), Rousseau described what he considered the optimal setting for education. A child and his tutor leave civilization and return to nature; in this setting, the child is free to follow his own talents and curiosities. The tutor responds to the child's questions rather than trying to impose his views on the child. As the child matures, abilities and interests change, and thus what constitutes a meaningful educational experience changes. It is always the child's natural abilities and interests, however, that guide the educational process. Rousseau described how education should be responsive to each particular student's interests and abilities:

> Every mind has its own form, in accordance with which it must be controlled; and the success of the pains taken depends largely on the fact that he is controlled in this way and no other. Oh, wise man, take time to observe nature; watch your scholar well before you say a word to him; first leave the germ of his character free to show itself, do not constrain him in anything, the better to see him as he really is. . . . The wise physician does not hastily give prescriptions at first sight, but he studies the constitution of the sick man before he prescribes anything; the treatment is begun later, but the patient is cured, while the hasty doctor kills him. (1762/1974, p. 58)

The recent interest in "free," "open," and "individualized" education can be traced directly to Rousseau's philosophy, as can the movement to "deschool" society. Rogers expressed a philosophy of education very similar to that of Rousseau:

> *Human beings have a natural potentiality for learning.* They are curious about their world, until and unless this curiosity is blunted by their experience in our educational system. . . . This potentiality and desire for learning, for discovery, for enlargement of knowledge and experience, can be released under suitable conditions. It is a tendency which can be trusted, and the whole approach to education which we have been describing builds upon and around the

Johann Wolfgang von Goethe

student's natural desire to learn. (1969, pp. 157–158)

Johann Wolfgang von Goethe

A poet, dramatist, scientist, and philosopher, **Johann Wolfgang von Goethe** (1749–1832) was one of the most revered individuals in the intellectual life of Germany in the late 18th and early 19th centuries. Goethe is usually thought of as the initiator of the "storm-and-stress" period in literature. In his literary works and philosophy, he viewed humans as being torn by the stresses and conflicts of life. Life, he felt, consisted of opposing forces such as love and hate, life and death, and good and evil. The goal of life should be to embrace these forces rather than to deny or overcome them. One should live life with a passion and aspire continuously for personal

growth. Even the "darker" aspects of human nature could provide stimulation for personal expansion. The idea of being transformed from one type of being (unfulfilled) into another type (fulfilled) was common within the romantic movement. We will see later that Nietzsche was strongly influenced by Goethe's philosophy of life.

In 1774 Goethe wrote *The Sorrows of Young Werther*, a novella about a young man with love problems. These problems were so vividly portrayed that several suicides took place (Hulse, 1989). In 1808 Goethe published *Faust*, considered one of the greatest literary works of all time. As *Faust* begins, old Dr. Faust is filled with despair and is contemplating suicide. Satan appears and makes a deal with him: In exchange for Faust's soul, Satan will transform the old man into a wise and handsome youth. The young Faust then begins his search for a source of happiness so great that he would choose to experience it forever. Faust finally bids time to stand still when he encounters people allowed to express their individual freedom. He views human liberty as the ultimate source of happiness.

Although most of the romantics were anti-science, Goethe was not. He made important discoveries in anatomy and botany, and he wrote *Science of Colors* (1810) in which he attempted to refute Newton's theory of color vision and proposed his own theory in its place. It turned out that Goethe's theory was incorrect, but his methodology had a major impact on later psychology. Goethe demonstrated that sensory experiences could be objectively studied by introspection. Furthermore, he insisted that intact, meaningful psychological experience should be the object of study rather than meaningless, isolated sensations. This insistence that whole, meaningful experiences be studied came to be called *phenomenology*. An example is the color-contrast effect known as "Goethe's shadows." Goethe observed that when a colored light is shown on an object, the shadow produced appears to be complementary to the colored light. This phenomenon was to be instrumental in the development of Edwin Land's theory of color vision (see Land,

1964, 1977). Many years before Darwin, Goethe also proposed a theory of evolution according to which one species of living thing could gradually be transformed into another. Rather than denying the importance of science, Goethe saw science as limited; he believed that many important human attributes were beyond the grasp of the scientific method.

Goethe's influence. D. N. Robinson nicely summarizes Goethe's influence:

> To him . . . goes much of the credit for awakening scholars to the problem of *esthetics* and for infusing German philosophical writing with a conscientious regard for what is creative and dynamic in the human psyche. In the Goethean presence, every important philosophical production in the Germany of the nineteenth century would reserve a special place for art. Indeed, Romanticism itself is to be understood as the unique melding of esthetics and metaphysics. (1982, p. 97)

Because of his significant influence on the entire German culture, Goethe has had many influences on the development of psychology. One famous psychologist whom Goethe's writings influenced directly was Jung, later a colleague of Freud:

> In my youth (around 1890) I was unconsciously caught up by this spirit of the age, and had no methods at hand of extricating myself from it. *Faust* struck a cord in me and pierced me through in a way that I could not but regard as personal. Most of all, it awakened in me the problems of opposites, of good and evil, of mind and matter, of light and darkness. (Jung, 1963, p. 235)

Goethe's writings also influenced Freud. Both Jung's and Freud's theories emphasize the conflicting forces operating in one's life, and both theories focus on conflict, frustration, and perpetual struggle between animal impulses and civilized behavior. Also, both Freud and Jung maintained that animalistic urges were not to be totally eliminated but harnessed and used to enhance personal growth. All these ideas appeared in Goethe's writings.

Arthur Schopenhauer

THE BETTMANN ARCHIVE

Arthur Schopenhauer

The important German philosopher **Arthur Schopenhauer** (1788–1860) was born in Danzig, now Gdansk, Poland. His father was a banker, and his mother was a novelist. He was educated at the Universities of Göttingen and Berlin, where he became a teacher. While at Berlin, Schopenhauer tested his ability to attract students by scheduling his lectures at the same time as Hegel's. Schopenhauer was so unsuccessful at drawing Hegel's students away that he gave up lecturing. Schopenhauer was most influenced by Kant and by ancient philosophies from India and Persia. His study displayed a bust of Kant and a bronze statue of Buddha.

Will to survive. In his most famous work, *The World as Will and Idea* (1818), Schopenhauer claimed that the only reality is a universal will, of which individual wills are only part. The will has no purpose other than to strive to continue itself, to survive. When the universal will manifests itself in a particular organism, such as a person, it becomes the **will to survive**, and organisms survive by satisfying their needs. For Schopenhauer then, the fundamental impulse in human existence was the will to survive. This will causes humans to experience an unending cycle of needs and need satisfaction. This powerful drive toward self-preservation accounts for most human behavior, not the intellect and not morality. Most human behavior, then, is irrational. To satisfy our will to survive, we must eat, sleep, eliminate, drink, and engage in sexual activity. The pain caused by an unsatisfied need causes us to act so as to satisfy the need. When the need is satisfied, we experience momentary satisfaction (pleasure), which only lasts until another need arises, and on it goes. Schopenhauer's pessimism toward the human condition is clearly shown in the following quotation:

> All *willing* arises from want, therefore from deficiency, and therefore from suffering. The satisfaction of a wish ends it; yet for one wish that is satisfied there remain at least ten which are denied. . . . No attained object of desire can give lasting satisfaction, but merely a fleeting gratification; it is like the alms thrown to the beggar, that keeps him alive to-day that misery may be prolonged till the morrow, therefore, so long as our consciousness is filled by our will, so long as we are given up to the throng of desires with their constant hopes and fears, so long as we are the subject of willing, we can never have lasting happiness nor peace (1818/1957, pp. 253–254)

Momentary pleasure is experienced when a need is satisfied; but when all needs are satisfied, we experience boredom. With Schopenhauer's characteristic pessimism, he said that we work six days a week to satisfy our needs and then we spend Sunday being bored (Frankl called this boredom *Sunday neurosis*).

Intelligent beings suffer the most. Suffering varies with awareness. Plants suffer no pain be-

cause they lack awareness. The lowest species of animals and insects suffer some, and higher animals still more. Humans, of course, suffer the most, especially the most intelligent humans:

> Thus, in proportion as knowledge attains to distinctness, as consciousness ascends, pain also increases, and therefore reaches its highest degree in man. And then, again, the more distinctly a man knows, the more intelligent he is, the more pain he has; the man who is gifted with genius suffers most of all. (1818/1957, p. 400)

A life-and-death struggle. According to Schopenhauer, another way of viewing life is as the postponement of death. In this life-and-death struggle, however, death must always be the ultimate victor:

> The life of our body is only a constantly prevented dying. . . . Every breath we draw wards off the death that is constantly intruding upon us. In this way we fight with it every moment, and again, at longer intervals, through every meal we eat, every sleep we take, every time we warm ourselves, etc. In the end, death must conquer, for we became subject to him through birth, and he only plays for a little while with his prey before he swallows it up. We pursue our life, however, with great interest and much solicitude as long as possible, as we blow out a soap-bubble as long and as large as possible, although we know perfectly well that it will burst. (1818/1957, pp. 401–402)

According to Schopenhauer, most people do not cling to life because it is pleasant. Rather, they cling to life because they fear death:

> What enables them to endure this wearisome battle is not so much the love of life as the fear of death, which yet stands in the background as inevitable, and may come upon them at any moment. Life itself is a sea, full of rocks and whirlpools, which man avoids with the greatest care and solicitude, although he knows that even if he succeeds in getting through with all his efforts and skill, he yet by doing so comes nearer at every step to the greatest, the total, inevitable, and irremediable shipwreck, death; nay, even steers right upon it: this is the final goal of the laborious voyage, and worse for him than all the rocks from which he has escaped. (1818/1957, p. 403)

Sublimation and denial. Even though these powerful, irrational forces are a natural part of human existence, humans can and should rise above them. With great effort, humans are capable of approaching nirvana, a state characterized by freedom from irrational strivings. Schopenhauer anticipated Freud's concept of sublimation when he said that some relief or escape from the irrational forces within us could be attained by immersing ourselves in music, poetry, or art. Also, one could attempt to counteract these irrational forces, especially the sex drive, by living a life of asceticism. The best we can do as humans is to embrace activities that are not need-related and therefore cannot be frustrated or satiated, activities such as music, art, Platonic philosophy, or unselfish, nonsexual, sympathetic love.

As we have seen, Schopenhauer believed that humans suffer more than other animals because our superior intellect allows us to detect the irrational urges within us. This same intellect, however, provides what little relief is possible from the need/need-satisfaction cycle—that is, by pursuing intellectual activities, instead of biological ones. Or, we can attack the will head-on, depriving it of fulfillment as much as possible. Because, for Schopenhauer, will is the cause of everything, to deny it is to flirt with nothingness. Coming as close as possible to nonexistence is as close as one can get to not being totally controlled by one's will. The will must be served if life is to continue, but one can be a reluctant servant.

In reading Schopenhauer, suicide as an escape from human misery comes to mind. Such an adjustment is resisted by most individuals, however, because it is diametrically opposed to the will to survive. This is why, according to Schopenhauer, even a person suffering from a painful, terminal disease finds it very difficult to take his or her life, even when this might be the rational thing to do.

Schopenhauer also spoke of repressing undesirable thoughts into the unconscious and of the resistance encountered when attempting to recognize repressed ideas. Freud credited Scho-

Friedrich Nietzsche

penhauer as being the first to discover these processes, but Freud claimed that he himself had discovered the same processes independently of Schopenhauer. In any case, a great deal of Schopenhauer's philosophy resides in Freud's psychoanalytic theory. Besides the ideas of repression and sublimation, Freud shared Schopenhauer's belief that irrational forces were the prime motivators of human behavior and that the best we could do was minimize their influence. Both men were therefore pessimistic in their views of human nature.

Friedrich Wilhelm Nietzsche

Friedrich Wilhelm Nietzsche (1844–1900), born on October 15 near Leipzig, was the son of a Lutheran minister and grandson of two clergymen. Nietzsche was 5 years old when his father died, and he grew up in a household consisting of his mother, sister, two maiden aunts, and his grandmother. He was a model child and an excellent student; by the time he was 10, he had written several plays and composed music.

At the age of 14, he entered the famous Pforta Boarding School, where religion was one of his best subjects; he also excelled in his study of Greek and Roman literature. In 1864 he entered Bonn University and expressed disgust for the beer drinking and carousing behavior of his fellow students. When Nietzsche's favorite teacher (Friedrich Ritschel) transferred from Bonn to the University of Leipzig, Nietzsche followed him there. Nietzsche's student days ended when, at the age of 24, he accepted an offer from Basel University to teach classical philology; and this was before he had received his doctor's degree. He taught at Basel for 10 years before poor health forced his retirement at the age of 35. His most influential books followed his academic retirement.

During his years at Basel, Nietzsche wrote *The Birth of Tragedy Out of the Spirit of Music* (1872) and *Untimely Meditations* (1873–1876), both strongly influenced by and supportive of Schopenhauer's philosophy. After his retirement, his books began to reflect his own thoughts. The most influential of those books were *Human, All-Too-Human* (1878), *The Dawn of Day* (1881), *The Gay Science* (1882), *Thus Spoke Zarathustra* (1883–1885), *Beyond Good and Evil* (1886), *Toward a Genealogy of Morals* (1887), *The Twilight of the Idols* (1889), *The Antichrist* (1895), and *Nietzsche Contra Wagner* (1895). His last books, *The Will to Power* (1904) and his autobiography *Ecce Homo* (1908), were published posthumously.

From about 1880, Nietzsche became increasingly isolated from everyday life. In 1889 he collapsed on the street and was taken to an asylum. "Medical opinions about his illness have always been divided, but the syphilitic infection and subsequent paresis are likely to have been among the determining factors in his breakdown" (Hubben, 1952, p. 99). Nietzsche died in 1900 and was buried in his hometown in the cemetery of the church where his father had baptized him.

As a preview of what follows, we present Esper's description of Nietzsche's philosophy: "It seems plausible . . . to describe [Nietzsche's] philosophy as the . . . revolt against everything: Science, culture, philosophy, religion, morality, democracy, and the state" (1964, p. 238).

The Apollonian and Dionysian aspects of human nature. Nietzsche believed that there were two major aspects of human nature, the Apollonian and the Dionysian. The **Apollonian aspect of human nature** represented our rational side, our desire for tranquility, predictability, and orderliness. The **Dionysian aspect of human nature** represented our irrational side, our attraction to creative chaos and to passionate, dynamic experiences. According to Nietzsche, the best art and literature reflect a fusion of these two tendencies. Also, the best life was described as reflecting controlled passion. According to Nietzsche, Western philosophy had emphasized the intellect and minimized the human passions, and the result was lifeless rationalism. Nietzsche saw as one of his major goals the resurrection of the Dionysian spirit. Do not just live, he said, live with passion. Do not live a planned, orderly life; take chances. Even the failures that may result from taking chances could be used to enhance personal growth. Thus, what Nietzsche was urging was not a totally irrational, passionate life but a life of reasonable passion, a life worthy of both Apollo and Dionysus.

The death of God. Nietzsche announced that God was dead and that we had killed him. By "we" he meant the philosophers and scientists of his day. Because we humans had relied on God for so long for the ultimate meaning of life and for our conceptions of morality, we were lost now that he was dead. Where do we now look for meaning? For moral ideals? The same philosophers and scientists who killed God also took purpose from the universe, as was found in Aristotle's teleological philosophy, and stripped humans of any special place in the world. Evolutionary theory, for example, showed that humans had the same lowly origin as other living organisms and shared the same fate: death. Furthermore, evolutionary principles are without purpose. Natural selection simply means that organisms possessing traits that allow adaptation to the environment survive and reproduce. Thus, humans cannot even take pride or find meaning in the fact that they have survived longer or differently than other species. Evolution in no way implies improvement. Astronomy too had shown that humans do not occupy a special place in the universe. The earth is simply a medium-size ball of clay revolving around one of hundreds of billions of suns.

Thus, there is no God who cares for us, our species occupies no significant station in the animal kingdom, and the earth is just one more meaningless heavenly body. Where does all of this leave humans? It leaves us, according to Nietzsche, without the traditional sources of meaning and morality. We are on our own!

Will to power. According to Nietzsche, there is an answer to our dilemma, but it is not to be found in philosophy, science, or religion. *It is to be found in ourselves!* Humans need to acquire knowledge of themselves and then act on that knowledge. Meaning and morality cannot (or should not) be imposed from the outside; it must be discovered within. When such self-examination occurs, it is discovered that the most basic human motive is the **will to power**. Like Schopenhauer, Nietzsche believed that humans were basically irrational. Unlike Schopenhauer, however, Nietzsche thought that the instincts should not be repressed or sublimated but should be given expression. Even aggressive tendencies should not be totally inhibited. The will to power can be fully satisfied only if a person acts as he or she feels, that is, acts in such a way as to satisfy all instincts: "The will to power is the primitive motive force out of which all other motives have been derived" (quoted in Sahakian, 1981, p. 80). Even happiness, which the utilitarians and others claimed to be so important as a motive, is the result of the increase in one's power: "The only reality is this: *The will of every centre of power to become stronger*—not self-preservation, but the desire to appropriate, to become master, to become more, to become stronger" (quoted in Sahakian, 1981, p. 80). And in *The Gay Science,* Nietzsche said, "The great

and the small struggle always revolves around superiority, around growth and expansion, around power—in accordance with the will to power which is the will of life" (1882/1974, p. 292). For Nietzsche then, all conceptions of good, bad, and happiness are related to the will to power:

> What is good? Everything that heightens the feeling of power in man, the will to power, power itself. What is bad? Everything that is born of weakness. What is happiness? The feeling that power is growing, that resistance is overcome. (Kaufmann, 1982, p. 570)

Supermen. The will to power is the tendency to gain mastery over one's self and one's destiny. If given expression, the will to power causes a person to seek new experiences and to ultimately reach his or her full potential. Such individual growth cannot be (or should not be) inhibited by conventional morality and thus must go "beyond good and evil." People reaching their full potential are **supermen** because standard morality does not govern their lives. Instead, they rise above such morality and live independent, creative lives. Nietzsche declared that "*all Gods are dead: now we want the Superman to live*" (1883–1885/1969, p. 104).

It is in *Thus Spoke Zarathustra* where Nietzsche most fully described his concept of the superman. (It should be noted that Nietzsche's term *Übermensch* can be translated as either "overman" or "superman.") After 10 years of solitude and contemplation in the mountains, Zarathustra decides to return to civilization and share his wisdom with his fellow humans (it should be clear that the character Zarathustra was speaking Nietzsche's thoughts):

> *I teach you the Superman.* Man is something that should be overcome. What have you done to overcome him? . . . What is the ape to men? A laughing-stock or a painful embarrassment. And just so shall man be to the Superman: A laughing-stock or a painful embarrassment. You have made your way from worm to man, and much in you is still worm. . . . Behold, I teach you the Superman. The Superman is the meaning of the earth. Let your will say: The

Superman *shall be* the meaning of the earth! I entreat you, my brothers, *remain true to the earth*, and do not believe those who speak to you of superterrestrial hopes! They are poisoners, whether they know it or not. They are despisers of life, atrophying and self-poisoned men, of whom the earth is weary; so let them be gone! (1883–1885/1969, pp. 41–42)

Humans are in a precarious position. We are no longer animals, we are not yet supermen, and God, being dead, cannot help us: "Man is a rope, fastened between animal and Superman—a rope over an abyss. A dangerous going-across, a dangerous wayfaring, a dangerous looking-back, a dangerous shuddering and staying-still" (1883–1885/1969, p. 43). The problems characterizing the human condition are solved one person at a time. If every individual strove to be all that he or she could be, more general human problems would solve themselves. A prerequisite, then, for an improvement in the human condition is self-improvement or self-love:

Physician, heal yourself: Thus you will heal your patient too. Let his best healing-aid be to see with his own eyes him who makes himself well. There are a thousand paths that have never yet been trodden, a thousand forms of health and hidden islands of life. Man and man's earth are still unexhausted and undiscovered. . . . Truly, the earth shall yet become a house of healing! And already a new odour floats about it, an odour that brings health—and a new hope! (1883–1885/1969, pp. 102–103)

The superman, as we have seen, exercises his will to power by expressing all thoughts, even negative ones:

Let us *speak* of this, you wisest men, even if it is a bad thing. To be silent is worse; all suppressed truths become poisonous. And let everything that can break upon our truths—break! There is many a house still to build! (1883–1885/1969, p. 139)

Like Goethe, Nietzsche did not believe negative experiences or impulses should be denied. Rather, one should learn from such experiences. Nietzsche believed that the journey toward one's personal heaven often requires traveling through one's personal hell. According to Nietzsche, any experience that does not destroy a person can make him or her stronger. Nietzsche gave a personal example:

I have often asked myself whether I am not more heavily obligated to the hardest years of my life than to any others. . . . And as for my long sickness, do I not owe it indescribably more than I owe to my health? I owe it a *higher* health—one which is made stronger by whatever does not kill it. *I also owe my philosophy to it.* Only great pain is the ultimate liberator of the spirit. . . . Only great pain, that long, slow pain in which we are burned with green wood, as it were—pain which takes its time—only this forces us philosophers to descend into our ultimate depths and to put away all trust, all good-naturedness, all that would veil, all mildness, all that is medium—things in which formerly we may have found our humanity. I doubt that such a pain makes us "better," but I know that it makes us more *profound*. (Kaufmann, 1982, pp. 680–681)

The notion of supermen was Nietzsche's answer to the human moral and philosophical dilemma. The meaning and morality of one's life come from within oneself. Healthy, strong individuals seek self-expansion by experimenting, by living dangerously. Life consists of an almost infinite number of possibilities, and the healthy person (the superman) explores as many of them as possible. Religions or philosophies that teach pity, humility, self-contempt, self-restraint, guilt, or a sense of community are simply incorrect. The good life is ever-changing, challenging, devoid of regret, intense, creative, and risky. It is *self-overcoming*. Acting in accordance with the will to power means living a life of becoming more than you were, a life of continual self-renewal, of becoming. Science, philosophy, and especially religion can only stifle the good life—the life of the superman. Any viewpoint that promotes herd conformity as opposed to individuality should be actively avoided.

The meaning of life, then, is found within the individual, and the daring, the supermen, will find it there: "Only dare to believe in yourselves—in yourselves and in your entrails! He who does not believe in himself always lies"

(Nietzsche, 1883–1885/1969, p. 146). To be a superman, one must necessarily be intensely individualistic; and yet, all supermen have in common the same philosophy of life: "I am Zarathustra the godless: Where shall I find my equal? All those who give themselves their own will and renounce all submission, they are my equals" (1883–1885/1969, p. 191).

Misunderstanding of Nietzsche's supermen. Throughout history scientific and philosophical works have often been distorted in order to support political ideologies. Nietzsche's philosophy is an example. His philosophy was embraced by the German National Socialists (the Nazis), who claimed that the German people were the supermen to whom Nietzsche referred. For the Nazis, supermen meant superior men, and the Germans were, they believed, superior. Nothing could have been more alien to Nietzsche than the thought of a national or racial superiority. Each individual, according to Nietzsche, has the potential to be a superman. What differentiated the superman from the nonsuperman was passion, courage, and insight, nothing else. As examples of supermen, Nietzsche offered the historical Jesus, Goethe (from whom Nietzsche borrowed the term *superman*), Dostoevsky, and himself. Freud agreed that Nietzsche should be on the list of supermen: "[Freud] said of Nietzsche that he had a more penetrating knowledge of himself than any other man who ever lived or was ever likely to live. From the first explorer of the unconscious this is a handsome compliment" (E. Jones, 1955, p. 344).

Again, both Schopenhauer and Nietzsche believed that irrational instincts strongly influenced human behavior. But whereas Schopenhauer believed that such instincts should be repressed, Nietzsche felt that they should be largely expressed. Freud was influenced most by Schopenhauer, whereas one of Freud's early followers, Alfred Adler, was influenced more by Nietzsche. In *Beyond Good and Evil*, Nietzsche described a phenomenon very similar to Freud's concept of repression: "'I did this,' says my memory. 'I cannot have done this,' says my

pride, remaining inexorable. Eventually, my memory yields" (1886/1966, p. 80).

Like the other romantics, both Nietzsche and Schopenhauer stressed the irrational (emotional) side of human nature, both believing that science and philosophy had neglected this aspect of human nature.

EXISTENTIALISM

The romantics were not the only philosophers who rebelled against rationalism, empiricism, sensationalism, and positivism. Another philosophy also emphasized the importance of meaning in one's life and one's ability to freely choose that meaning. This philosophy was called **existentialism**, and it stressed the meaning of human existence, freedom of choice, and the uniqueness of each individual. For the existentialists, the most important aspects of humans were their personal, subjective interpretations of life and the choices they make in light of those interpretations. Like the romanticists, the existentialists viewed inner experience and feeling as the most valid guide for one's behavior.

Although it is possible to trace the origins of existential philosophy back at least as far as Socrates who said "know thyself" and "an unexamined life is not worth living," one of the first modern existential philosophers was Søren Kierkegaard.

Søren Kierkegaard

A Danish theologian and philosopher, **Søren Kierkegaard** (1813–1855) was born on May 5 in Copenhagen. He was the youngest child of a large family, but he and his older brother were the only children to survive. His father, who was 56 when Søren was born, was a prosperous, God-fearing merchant. Søren's mother was his father's servant before he made her his second wife. Søren says very little about his mother. His father was a stern teacher of religion, and for many years Søren equated his father with God. It caused a "great earthquake" when in 1835

Søren Kierkegaard

Søren's father confessed to sexual excesses, and Søren responded by rebelling against both his father and religion. He accepted both his father and religion back into his heart on his 25th birthday, which caused him to experience "indescribable joy." His father died shortly afterward, leaving him a substantial fortune. In deference to his father's wishes, Søren began a serious study of theology, although he never became a minister.

At the University of Copenhagen, Kierkegaard first studied theology and then literature and philosophy. He had no financial worries and lived a care-free life. About this time, Kierkegaard decided to ask Regina Olsen, whom he had known for several years, to marry him. After a two-year engagement, Kierkegaard felt there was a "divine protest" because the wedding was based on something untrue (he never told us what), and in 1841 he wrote asking her to return the engagement ring:

> It was a time of terrible suffering: To have to be so cruel and at the same time to love as I did. She fought like a tigress. If I had not believed that God had lodged a veto she would have been victorious. (Bretall, 1946, p. 17)

Kierkegaard went to Regina and asked her forgiveness. He described their farewell:

> She said, "promise to think of me." I did so. "Kiss me," she said. I did so, but without passion. Merciful God! And so we parted. I spent the whole night crying in my bed. . . . When the bonds were broken my thoughts were these: either you throw yourself into the wildest kind of life—or else become absolutely religious. (Bretall, 1946, pp. 17–18)

Kierkegaard did the latter. It is interesting to note that Kierkegaard often described a proper relationship with God as a love affair:

> Repeatedly Kierkegaard likened the individual's relationship with God to a lover's experience. It is at once painful and happy, passionate but unfulfilled, lived in time yet infinite. Once he had separated himself from Regin[a] Ols[e]n he was free to enter upon his "engagement to God." (Hubben, 1952, p. 24)

After Kierkegaard broke his engagement with Regina, he went to Berlin where he thrust himself into the study of philosophy and finished his first major book *Either/Or* (1843).

All of his life, Kierkegaard was melancholy and withdrawn. Many entries in his diary (journals) referred to the fact that even when others saw him as happy, he was actually crying inside. The following entry from 1836 exemplifies the difference between Kierkegaard's private and public selves: "I have just returned from a party of which I was the life and soul; wit poured from my lips, everyone laughed and admired me— but I went away. . . . And wanted to shoot myself" (Bretall, 1946, p. 7). Some Kierkegaardian scholars attribute his melancholia and introversion to his deformity as a hunchback. However, Hubben believes that the influence of his deformity was probably minimal:

> [Kierkegaard] was weak and sickly and he is likely to have derived from his physical impairment the same spirit of bravado that distinguished Dostoevsky and Nietzsche. But whatever the truth about the hunchback may be, it seems safe to remain conservative toward any of its psychological and religious interpretations. (1952, p. 17)

Kierkegaard is generally considered the first modern existentialist, although Nietzsche developed similar ideas at about the same time and independently of Kierkegaard. Kierkegaard's ideas received little attention in his lifetime. He was ridiculed by other philosophers, the public press, and his fellow townspeople, who considered him eccentric. As a student, Kierkegaard rejected Christianity and was a devout follower of Hegel. Later, the situation was reversed when he rejected Hegel and embraced Christianity. The Christianity that Kierkegaard accepted, however, was not that of the institutionalized church. He was an outspoken critic of the established church for its worldliness and its insistence on the acceptance of prescribed dogma. He said that the most meaningful relationship with God was a purely personal one that was arrived at through an individual's free choice, not one whose nature and content were dictated by the church.

Kierkegaard's most influential books include *Either/Or* (1843), *Two Edifying Discourses* (1843), *Fear and Trembling* (1843), *Repetition* (1843), *Philosophical Fragments* (1844), *Stages on Life's Way* (1845), *Concluding Unscientific Postscript* (1846), *The Present Age* (1846), *Edifying Discourses in Various Spirits* (1847), *Works of Love* (1847), *The Point of View for My Work as an Author* (1848), *The Sickness unto Death* (1849), *Training in Christianity* (1856), *Two Discourses at the Communion on Fridays* (1851), *The Attack upon "Christendom"* (1854–1855), and *The Unchangeableness of God* (1855).

Religion as too rational and mechanical. In Kierkegaard's time, the Lutheran church was the official church of Denmark, and the state considered it its duty to protect and promote Lutheranism. It did this by requiring religious training in all schools and by elevating the clergy to the status of civil servants. Kierkegaard felt strongly that such a system of state control and protection was against the basic tenets of Christianity. The intensely individual nature of the religious experience was, he thought, discouraged by such a system. Kierkegaard ultimately rejected Hegel's philosophy because it placed too much emphasis on the logical and the ratio-

nal and not enough on the irrational, emotional side of human nature. For the same reason, Kierkegaard rejected science as too mechanistic: He thought it prevented us from viewing humans as emotional and choosing beings. The ultimate state of being, for Kierkegaard, was arrived at when the individual decided to embrace God and take God's existence on faith, without needing a logical, rational, or scientific explanation of why or how the decision was determined.

Kierkegaard was deeply concerned that too many Christians, rather than having a true relationship with God, were praying reflexively and accepting religious dogma rationally instead of allowing it to touch them emotionally. Although Kierkegaard would certainly not have agreed with Nietzsche that God was dead, he would have agreed that for most people a genuine, personal, emotional relationship with God did not exist and, for those people, it felt like God was dead.

Truth is subjectivity. According to Kierkegaard, truth is always what a person believes privately and emotionally. Truth cannot be taught by logical argument; truth must be experienced. In the realm of religion, the more logical we are in our attempt to understand God, the less we comprehend him. Believing in God is a "leap of faith," a choosing to believe in the absence of any factual, objective information. God who is unlimited and eternal cannot be explained, understood, or proven logically. He must be taken on faith, and that is a very personal, subjective choice. Attempting to understand Jesus objectively reveals a number of paradoxes. Christ is both God and man; he is eternal truth existing in finite time; he lived almost 2,000 years ago but also exists presently; and he violates natural law with his miracles. Facts or logic do not remove these paradoxes; they create them. Belief alone can resolve them; subjectivity, *not* objectivity, is truth. Christian faith is something that must be lived; it must be felt emotionally. It can be neither understood nor truly appreciated as a rational abstraction. It is precisely because we cannot know God objectively that we must have faith in his existence:

> Without risk there is no faith. Faith is precisely the contradiction between the infinite passion of the individual's inwardness and the objective uncertainty. If I am capable of grasping God objectively, I do not believe, but precisely because I cannot do this I must believe. (Bretall, 1946, p. 215)

And Kierkegaard continued:

> Without risk there is no faith, and the greater the risk, the greater the faith; the more objective security, the less inwardness (for inwardness is precisely subjectivity), and the less objective security, the more profound the possible inwardness. (Bretall, 1946, p. 219)

In *Fear and Trembling* (1843), Kierkegaard recalled the Biblical account of Abraham preparing to sacrifice his son at God's command. The moment that Abraham lifted the knife to kill his son captures what Kierkegaard meant by religious faith. Such faith is a leap into the darkness accompanied by fear, dread, and anguish. It is precisely the discrepancy existing between human understanding and ultimate truth that creates a paradox. The paradox is the understanding that there are things we can never know, and the greatest paradox of all (the "absolute paradox") is God. We know that God exists, and at the same time, we know that we cannot comprehend him—that is a paradox. Fortunately, God gave humans a way of dealing with such paradoxes, including the absolute paradox, and that was *faith*. We must have faith in eternal truths because there is no way for us to embrace them objectively. The paradox that God became a finite being in the person of Christ can never be explained rationally; it must be taken on faith.

A love affair with God. As was mentioned previously, perhaps reflecting on his ill-fated relationship with Regina Olsen, Kierkegaard often referred to an individual's relationship with God as a love affair. It is simultaneously passionate, happy, and painful. He also said that one should read the Bible as one would read a love letter. That is, the reader should let the words touch himself or herself personally and emotionally. The meaning of the words *are* the emotional impact they have on the reader:

> Think of a lover who has now received a letter from his beloved—as precious as this letter is to the lover, just so precious to thee, I assume, is God's Word; in the way the lover reads this letter, just so, I assume, dost thou read God's Word and conceive that God's Word ought to be read. (Kierkegaard, 1851/1944, p. 51)

One does not read a love letter using a dictionary to determine the meaning of its words; neither should one read the Bible that way. The meaning of both the Bible and a love letter is found in the feelings that it causes the reader to have. No one should tell you what to feel as you read a love letter or the Bible, nor should anyone tell you what the correct interpretation of either should be. Your feelings and your interpretation define what in the experience is true for you. Truth is subjectivity, *your* subjectivity.

Approximations to personal freedom. In *Either/Or* (1843), Kierkegaard said that the approximation of full personal freedom occurred in stages. First is the **aesthetic stage**. At this stage, people are open to experience and seek out many forms of pleasure and excitement. But they do not recognize their ability to choose. People operating at this level are hedonistic, and such an existence ultimately leads to boredom and despair. Second is the **ethical stage**. People operating at this level accept the responsibility of making choices but use as their guide ethical principles established by others—for example, church dogma. Although Kierkegaard considered the ethical level higher than the aesthetic level, people operating on the ethical level were still not recognizing and acting on their full personal freedom. Kierkegaard referred to the highest level of existence as the **religious stage**. At this stage, people recognize and accept their freedom and enter into a personal relationship with God. The nature of this relationship is not determined by convention or by generally accepted moral laws, but by the nature of God and by one's self-awareness. A person existing on this level sees possibilities in life that often run contrary to what is generally accepted and therefore tends to be a nonconformist.

Kierkegaard and Nietzsche

Nietzsche was apparently unaware of Kierkegaard's work, yet he developed ideas that were in many ways similar to Kierkegaard's. Like Kierkegaard, Nietzsche rejected what was conventionally accepted, such as the organized church and science. For both men, Hegelian philosophy was a favorite target, and both men preached reliance on direct, personal experience. The major difference between the two was that Kierkegaard accepted the existence of God, whereas for Nietzsche God did not exist. Like Kierkegaard, Nietzsche tended to alienate others, and he experienced severe emotional turmoil, which in his later years led finally to a mental collapse.

Today romanticism and existentialism have combined to form the third-force movement in psychology, which the theories of Rogers, Maslow, and May exemplify. In chapter 17, we will explore third-force psychology in greater detail.

SUMMARY

The philosophies of empiricism, sensationalism, positivism, and rationalism pictured humans as complex machines, products of experience, or highly rational beings operating in accordance with lofty, abstract principles. In the opinion of some, all these philosophies left something important out of their analyses—the irrational or emotional aspect of humans. Those philosophers stressing the importance of human irrationality were called romantics. In general, the romantics emphasized inner, personal experience and distrusted science and the philosophers who pictured humans as products of experience, as machines, or as totally rational beings.

Rousseau is usually considered the father of modern romanticism. He believed that humans were born free and good but were soon contaminated by society. As a guide for living and for believing, the natural impulses of the "heart" could be trusted. Rousseau believed that humans had both an individual will and a general will and that for government to work people had to deny their individual wills. Education should take into consideration a child's natural curiosity rather than attempting to mold a child as if he or she were a lump of clay or a blank tablet. Goethe, who was a scientist, poet, and philosopher, viewed life as consisting of choices between conflicting forces (e.g., good and evil; love and hate). He believed that the best life was one lived with passion and that resulted in self-expansion. He also believed that the physical sciences, although effective in providing useful information about the physical world, were of limited value when it came to understanding people.

Like Spinoza, Schopenhauer believed the universe was an interrelated whole, which he (Schopenhauer) called the universal will. When manifested in an individual human, the universal will becomes the will to survive, which is the most powerful motive for human behavior. Life, according to Schopenhauer, consisted of an unending cycle of needs and need satisfaction. Because intelligent organisms are most aware of their needs, they suffer more than unintelligent organisms. Satisfying our needs simply postpones death, which is inevitable. The only way to minimize human suffering is to deny or minimize one's needs. Needs can be sublimated into such pursuits as music, art, and poetry. Also, the rational mind can repress undesirable thoughts and hold them in the unconscious mind. For Schopenhauer, the rational mind could and should inhibit the powerful needs related to biological survival. Schopenhauer's philosophy had a considerable influence on Freud's psychoanalytic theory.

Nietzsche agreed with Schopenhauer that many human desires are irrational but disagreed with him that they should be repressed or sublimated. For Nietzsche, the basic human motive is the will to power, which is satisfied when a person acts as he or she feels. Acting on irrational instinct causes a person to have new experiences and thus to develop greater potential as a person. According to Nietzsche, science, religion, rationalism, and empiricism stifle irrationality and thereby inhibit human development. Nietzsche believed that rational philosophy and science had emphasized the Apollonian, or rational, aspect of human nature at the expense of the Dionysian aspect. He believed that giving reasonable expression to both aspects of human nature was best. He believed that science and philosophy had made it impossible for people to accept religious superstition as a guide for living. As a substitution, Nietzsche proposed individually determined values and beliefs. The only source of information for what is good or bad, desirable or undesirable, are individuals themselves. Nietzsche referred to humans that had the courage to live in accordance with their own values, thus rising above conventional morality, as supermen. Supermen experiment with life and are constantly in the process of becoming something other than what they were.

Another reaction against empiricism and rationalism was existentialism. The existentialist stressed meaning in life, freedom of choice, subjective experience, personal responsibility, and the uniqueness of the individual. Kierkegaard is generally considered the first modern existential philosopher. He believed that rationalistic philosophy, science, and the organized church discouraged people from having a deep, personal relationship with God. Logic and facts have nothing to do with such a relationship, which can be based on faith alone. By accepting God on faith, God becomes a living, emotional reality in one's subjective experience. For Kierkegaard, the only truth was subjective truth—that is, truth that existed as a personal belief. Furthermore, accepting the reality of God reveals a number of logical paradoxes that cannot be resolved logically. The existence of God cannot and need not be proven by rational argument; it can only be taken on faith. One should become emotionally involved with God and read his word (the Bible), as one would read a love letter. Although Kierkegaard is usually given credit for being the first modern existentialist, Nietzsche should probably share in that distinction.

The influence of the romantic movement in modern psychology is seen in psychoanalysis and in third-force psychology as represented in the work of such individuals as Rogers, Maslow, and May.

DISCUSSION QUESTIONS

1. What was romanticism a reaction against? Discuss the major features of the romantic movement.

2. What assumptions did Rousseau make about human nature? What did he mean by his statement, "Man is born free yet we see him everywhere in chains"?

3. What did Rousseau and Hobbes have in common? Over what did they disagree?

4. Discuss Rousseau's distinction between the individual will and the general will. On which of the two should government be based? Explain.

5. Summarize Rousseau's views on education.

6. How did Goethe view life? What was his attitude toward science? What were his contributions to psychology?

7. For Schopenhauer, what was the primary motive for human behavior? Discuss the implications of this motive for human existence.

8. Why is Schopenhauer's philosophy generally referred to as pessimistic?

9. What did Schopenhauer suggest we could do to minimize the influence of the powerful, irrational forces within us?

10. What, according to Nietzsche, were the implications of the death of God for human existence?

11. What, for Nietzsche, was the most powerful human motive? According to Nietzsche, should we accept and live in accordance with this motive, or should we deny or minimize it?

12. According to Nietzsche, what are supermen? Give an example of how Nietzsche's conception of supermen has been misunderstood.

13. Of what, according to Nietzsche, would a rich, meaningful life consist?

14. What is existentialism? How does existentialism differ from romanticism?

15. What type of religion did Kierkegaard oppose? Which type did he promote?

16. What did Kierkegaard mean by his statement, "Truth is subjectivity"?

17. Describe the type of relationship Kierkegaard believed individuals should have with God.

18. Describe what Kierkegaard referred to as the three stages toward full personal freedom.

SUGGESTIONS FOR FURTHER READING

Bretall, R. (Ed.). (1946). *A Kierkegaard anthology*. Princeton, NJ: Princeton University Press.

This is a sampling of Kierkegaard's most influential works including *The Journals, Either/Or, Fear and Trembling, Philosophical Fragments, Concluding Unscientific Postscript, Works of Love, The Sickness unto Death,* and *The Attack upon "Christendom."* (Available in paperback.)

Hubben, W. (1952). *Dostoevsky, Kierkegaard, Nietzsche, and Kafka.* New York: Macmillan.

This is a most readable and informative review of the writings of four major individuals in the romantic-existential movement: Kierkegaard, Dostoevsky, Nietzsche, and Kafka. (Available in paperback.)

Kaufmann, W. (Ed. and Trans.). (1982). *The portable Nietzsche.* New York: Viking Books/Penguin Press.

This is an interesting sampling of Nietzsche's letters, notes, and major works. Among the latter are excerpts from *Human, All Too Human; The Dawn; The Gay Science; Thus Spoke Zarathustra; Beyond Good and Evil; Toward a Genealogy of Morals; Twilight of the Idols; The Antichrist; Ecce Homo;* and *Nietzsche Contra Wagner.* (Available in paperback.)

Kierkegaard, S. (1962). *Philosophical fragments.* (D. Swenson, Trans.). Princeton, NJ: Princeton University Press. (Original work published 1844)

This is the entire translation of one of Kierkegaard's most famous books, *Philosophical Fragments.* (Available in paperback.)

Nietzsche, F. (1969). *Thus Spoke Zarathustra.* (R. J. Hollingdale, Trans.). New York: Viking Books/Penguin Press. (Original work published 1883–1885)

This book is Nietzsche's highly emotional and poetic plea for humans to overcome themselves and become supermen. This book is as much in the existential tradition as it is in the romantic. (Available in paperback.)

Rousseau, J. J. (1947). *The social contract.* (C. Frankel, Trans.). New York: Macmillan. (Original work published 1762)

In this classic statement on human nature and government, Rousseau discusses the history of social systems and different forms of government. The book contains his argument that the general will must take precedence over the individual will in the operation of a just government. (Available in paperback.)

Rousseau, J. J. (1974). *Emile* (B. Foxley, Trans.). London: Dent. (Original work published 1762)

In this classic proposal for educational reform based on his conception of human nature, Rousseau proposes that education should be individualized and should take advantage of a student's natural abilities and curiosity. (Available in paperback.)

GLOSSARY

Aesthetic stage According to Kierkegaard, the first stage in the growth toward full personal freedom. At this stage, the person delights in many experiences but does not exercise his or her freedom.

Apollonian aspect of human nature According to Nietzsche, that part of us that seeks order, tranquility, and predictability.

Dionysian aspect of human nature According to Nietzsche, that part of us that seeks chaos, adventure, and passionate experiences.

Ethical stage According to Kierkegaard, the second stage in the growth toward full personal freedom. At this stage, the person makes ethical decisions but uses principles developed by others as a guide in making them.

Existentialism The philosophy that examines the meaning in life and stresses the freedom that humans have to freely choose their own destinies. Like romanticism, existentialism stresses subjective experience and the uniqueness of each individual.

General will According to Rousseau, the innate tendency to live harmoniously with one's fellow humans.

Goethe, Johann Wolfgang von (1749–1832) Believed that life was characterized by choices between opposing forces and that much about humans was forever beyond scientific understanding.

Kierkegaard, Søren (1813–1855) Believed that religion had become too rational and mechanical. He believed that a relationship with God should be an intensely personal and a highly emotional experience, like a love affair. Taking the existence of God on faith makes God a living truth for a person, thus Kierkegaard's contention that truth is subjectivity.

Nietzsche, Friedrich Wilhelm (1844–1900) Claimed that humans could no longer rely on religious superstition as a guide for living; instead, they must determine life's meaning for themselves. By exercising their wills for power, people can continue to grow and overcome conventional morality. The term *supermen* described those who experimented with life and feelings and engaged in continuous self-overcoming.

Noble savage Rousseau's term for a human not contaminated by society. Such a person would live in accordance with his or her true feelings, would not be selfish, and would live harmoniously with other humans.

Religious stage According to Kierkegaard, the third stage in the growth toward full personal freedom. At this stage, the person recognizes his or her freedom and chooses to enter into a personal relationship with God.

Romanticism The philosophy that stressed the uniqueness of each person and that valued emotional experience much more than rationality. According to the romantic, people can and should trust their own natural impulses.

Rousseau, Jean-Jacques (1712–1778) Considered the father of the romantic movement. Rousseau believed that human nature was basically good and that the best society was one in which people subjugated their individual wills to their general wills. The best education occurs when education is individualized and when a student's natural abilities and curiosity are recognized.

Schopenhauer, Arthur (1788–1860) Believed that the will to survive was the most powerful human motive. Life is characterized by a cycle of needs and need satisfaction, and need satisfaction simply postpones death. The most people can do is to minimize the irrational forces operating within them by sublimating or repressing those forces.

Supermen The name that Nietzsche gave to those individuals who had the courage to rise above conventional morality and herd conformity and to follow their own inclinations instead. The German word *Übermensch* can be translated as either "overman" or "superman."

Will to power According to Nietzsche, the basic human need to become stronger, more complete, more superior. While satisfying the will to power, a person continually becomes something other than he or she was.

Will to survive According to Schopenhauer, the powerful need to perpetuate one's life by satisfying one's biological needs.

CHAPTER 8

Early Developments in Physiology and the Rise of Experimental Psychology

Scientific achievements of the 17th and 18th centuries allowed ancient philosophical questions to be examined in new, more precise ways. Much had been learned about the physical world, and it was now time to direct scientific method toward the study of the mechanisms by which we come to know the physical world. Basically, the question was by what mechanisms do empirical events come to be represented in consciousness? Everything from sense perception to motor reactions was studied intensely, and this study eventually gave birth to experimental psychology. If one is interested in discovering the origins of psychology, one needs to go back to the early Greeks. If, however, one is interested in the origins of *experimental* psychology, one must look to early developments in physiology, anatomy, neurology, and even astronomy.

INDIVIDUAL DIFFERENCES

It was astronomers who first realized that the type of knowledge human physiology provided might be useful to all sciences. In 1795 the astronomer Nevil Maskelyne and his assistant David Kinnebrook were setting ships' clocks according to when a particular star crossed a hairline in a telescope. Maskelyne noticed that Kinnebrook's observations were about 0.5 second slower than his. Kinnebrook was warned of his "error" and attempted to correct it. Instead, however, the discrepancy between his obser-

vations and Maskelyne's increased to 0.8 second and Kinnebrook was relieved of his duty. Twenty years later, the incident came to the attention of the German astronomer Friedrich Bessel (1784–1846), who speculated that the error had not been due to incompetence but to *individual differences* among observers. Bessel set out to compare his observations with those of his colleagues and indeed found systematic differences among them. This was the first **reaction time** study, and it was used to correct differences among observers. This was done by calculating **personal equations**. For example, if 0.8 second was added to Kinnebrook's reaction time, his observations could be equated with Maskelyne's. Bessel found systematic differences among individuals and a way to compensate for those differences, but his findings did not have much of an impact on the early development of experimental psychology. As we will see, the early experimental psychologists were interested in learning what was true about human consciousness in *general*; therefore, when individual differences were found among experimental subjects, those differences were generally attributed to sloppy methodology. Later in psychology's history (after Darwin), the study of individual differences was to be of supreme importance.

Bessel did, however, show that the observer influenced observations. Because all of science was based on human observation, learning more about the processes that converted physical stimulation into conscious experience was now necessary.

DISCREPANCY BETWEEN OBJECTIVE AND SUBJECTIVE REALITY

Of course, the demonstration of *any* discrepancy between a physical event and a person's perception of that event was of great concern to the natural scientists who viewed their jobs as accurately describing and explaining the physical world. The problem created by Galileo's and Locke's distinction between primary and secondary qualities could be avoided by simply concentrating on primary qualities—that is, concentrating on events for which there was a match between their physical qualities and the sensations that they create. It was becoming increasingly clear, however, that the mismatch between physical events and the perceptions of those events was widespread. Newton (1704/1952) had observed that the experience of white light is really a composite of all colors of the spectrum, although the individual colors themselves are not perceived. In 1760 Van Musschenbroek discovered that if complementary colors such as yellow and blue are presented in proper proportions on a rapidly rotating disc, an observer sees neither yellow nor blue but gray. It was evident that often there was not a point-to-point correspondence between physical reality and the psychological experience of that reality. Because the most likely source of the discrepancy was the responding organism, the physical scientists had reason to be interested in the new science of physiology, which studied the biological processes by which humans interact with the physical world. The physiologists studied the nature of nerves, neural conduction, reflexive behavior, sensory perception, brain functioning, and, eventually, the systematic relationship between sensory stimulation and sensation. It was the work of the physiologists that provided the link between mental philosophy and the science of psychology.

Besides showing the influence of the observer on observations, the personal equation was important because the quantitative assessment that

it allowed began to cast doubt on the claims of Kant and others that psychology could not be a science because mathematics could not be applied to psychological phenomena. In general, however, it was noting the discrepancy between physical and psychological (subjective) reality that made anatomy, physiology, and, eventually, psychology important aspects of science. In a sense, the physical sciences made scientific psychology inevitable:

> Once the physical sciences were started and well under way, it was inevitable that scientific psychology should arise. The older sciences themselves made it necessary. Investigators were repeatedly having their attention drawn to the observing organism and to the necessity of taking its reactions into consideration in order to make their own accounts exact and complete. (Heidbreder, 1933, p. 74)

Heidbreder made the point that in both philosophy and science a concern for psychology came late:

> It is interesting to note that, in both philosophy and science, interest in psychology developed late and was at first incidental. Philosophy, setting out to account for the universe at large, began as cosmology, and only when it became involved in the problems of epistemology did it address itself seriously and directly to psychological material. Science, too, started as an attempt to explain the world at large, beginning with physics and astronomy. And physical science, like philosophy, first became seriously attentive to psychology when it met in science the counterpart of the problem of epistemology—the necessity of considering the observing organism in order to give a complete account of the observed universe. (1933, p. 76)

We will see in this chapter that the question concerning how the makeup of humans influences what humans observe was addressed mainly by physiologists. Later, this concern was incorporated into the new science of psychology. Thus, to a large extent, both the content of what was to become psychology and the methodologies used to explore that content were furnished by physiology.

We turn next to a summary of the major observations made by physiologists that eventually gave birth to the new science of psychology.

BELL–MAGENDIE LAW

Until the 19th century, two views prevailed about what nerves contained and how they functioned. One was Descartes's view that a nerve consisted of fibers that connected sense receptors to the brain. These fibers were housed in hollow tubes that transmitted the "animal spirits" from the brain to the muscles. The second was Hartley's view that nerves were the means by which "vibrations" were conducted from the sense receptors to the brain and from the brain to the muscles. In 1811 the great British physiologist **Charles Bell** (1774–1842) printed and distributed to his friends 100 copies of a pamphlet that was to radically change the view of neural transmission. His pamphlet summarized his research on the anatomical and functional discreteness of sensory and motor nerves. Operating on rabbits, Bell demonstrated that sensory nerves enter the posterior (dorsal) roots of the spinal cord and the motor nerves emerge from the anterior (ventral) roots. Bell's discovery separated nerve physiology into the study of sensory and motor functions, that is, into a study of sensation and movement. Bell's finding was significant because it demonstrated that specific mental functions are mediated by different anatomical structures. That is, separate nerves control sensory mechanisms and responding. Bell himself speculated that there was a much more detailed relationship between sensory nerves and sensation, but Johannes Müller actually supported Bell's speculations with experimental evidence. Müller's extension of Bell's findings are reviewed shortly.

That there are sensory and motor nerves is an ancient idea going back as far as Eristratus of Alexandria (ca. 300 B.C.) and Galen in the second century A.D. In fact, both Descartes and Hartley speculated about the possibility. It was Bell, however, that substantiated the idea with clear-cut, experimental evidence. As was men-

Charles Bell

tioned, Bell circulated his findings only among his friends. This can explain why the prominent French physiologist **François Magendie** (1783–1855) could publish results similar to Bell's 11 years later without being aware of Bell's findings. A heated debate arose among Bell's and Magendie's followers about the priority of the discovery of the distinction between sensory and motor nerves. History has settled the issue by referring to the discovery as the **Bell–Magendie law**. (For the details of the priority controversy between Bell and Magendie, see Cranefield, 1974.)

After Bell and Magendie, thinking of nerves as general conveyers of vibrations or spirits was no longer possible. Now a "law of forward direction" governed the nervous system. Sensory nerves carried impulses forward from the sense receptors to the brain, and motor nerves carried impulses forward from the brain to the muscles and glands. The Bell–Magendie law suggested

François Magendie

separate sensory and motor tracts in the spinal cord and separate sensory and motor regions in the brain.

DOCTRINE OF SPECIFIC NERVE ENERGIES

As we have just seen, the Bell–Magendie law indicated that nerves were neither hollow tubes transmitting animal spirits to and from the brain nor general structures performing both sensory and motor functions. Bell and Magendie had verified two different types of nerves with two different functions. As was mentioned, Bell had also suggested that there are different types of sensory nerves. In fact, Bell suggested, but did not prove, that each of the five senses was served by a separate type of sensory nerve.

Johannes Müller

The great physiologist **Johannes Müller** (1801–1858) expanded the Bell–Magendie law by devising the **doctrine of specific nerve energies**. After receiving his doctorate from the University of Bonn in 1822, Müller remained there as professor until 1833, when he accepted the newly created chair of physiology at the University of Berlin. The creation of this chair at Berlin marked the acceptance of physiology as a science (R. I. Watson, 1978). Following Bell's suggestion, Müller demonstrated that there were five types of sensory nerves, each containing a characteristic energy, and when they were stimulated a characteristic sensation resulted. In other words, each nerve responded in its own characteristic way *no matter how it was stimulated.* For example, stimulating the eye with light waves, electricity, pressure, or by a blow to the head will all cause visual sensations. DuBois-Reymond, one of Müller's students, went so far as to say that if we could cut and cross the visual and auditory nerves, we would hear with our eyes and see with our ears.

Müller's detailed experimental research put to final rest the old emanation theory of perception, according to which tiny copies of physical objects went through the sensory receptors, along the nerves, and to the brain, causing an image of the object. According to this old view, any sensory nerve could convey any sensory information to the brain.

Adequate stimulation. Although Müller claimed that various nerves contained their own specific energy, he did not think that all the sense organs were equally sensitive to the same type of stimulation. Rather, each of the five types of sense organs was maximally sensitive to a certain type of stimulation. Müller called this "specific irritability," and it was later referred to as **adequate stimulation**. The eye is most easily stimulated by light waves, the ear by sound waves, the skin by pressure, and so on. The eye can be stimulated by pressure, but pressure is a less adequate stimulus for vision than is a light wave. As we experience the environment, this differential sensitivity of the various senses provides an array of sensations. In this way, a "picture" of the physical environment is formed, but the nature of the picture—for example, how articulated it is—depends on the sensory systems that humans possess. Bell had earlier addressed the issue of the correspondence between the physical world and our ideas of that world:

> [Our ideas] are consequences of a change or operation in the proper organ of the sense which constitutes a part of the brain . . . it is provided, that the extremities of the nerves of the senses shall be susceptible each of certain qualities in matter; and betwixt the impression of the outward sense, as it may be called, and the exercise of the internal organ, there is established a connection by which the ideas excited have a permanent correspondence with the qualities of bodies which surround us. (Boring, 1957, p. 87)

For Bell and Müller then, the correspondence between our sensations and objects in the physical world is determined by our senses and their "specific irritability." Müller agonized over the question of whether the characteristics of the nerve itself or the place in the brain where the nerve terminated accounted for specificity. He concluded that the nerve was responsible, but subsequent research proved brain location to be responsible.

We are conscious of sensations, not of physical reality. The most significant implication of Müller's doctrine for psychology was that the nature of the central nervous system, not the nature of the physical stimulus, determines our sensations. According to Müller, we are aware not of objects in the physical world but of various sensory impulses. It follows that our knowledge of the physical world must be limited to the types of sense receptors we possess. The following quotation from Bell shows his close agreement with Müller on this matter:

Johannes Müller

It is admitted that neither bodies nor the images of bodies enter the brain. It is indeed impossible to believe that colour can be conveyed along a nerve; or the vibration in which we suppose sound to consist can be retained in the brain: But we can conceive, and have reason to believe, that an impression is made upon the organs of the outward senses when we see, hear or taste. . . . The idea in the mind is the result of an action excited in the eye or brain, not of anything received, though caused by an impression from without. The operations of the mind are confined not by the limited nature of things created but by the limited number of our organs of sense. (Boring, 1957, p. 82)

An ardent Kantian, Müller felt that he had found the physiological equivalent of Kant's categories of thought. According to Kant, sensory information is transformed by the innate categories of thought before it is experienced consciously. For Müller, the nervous system is the intermediary between physical objects and consciousness. Kant's nativism stressed mental categories, whereas Müller's stressed physiological mechanisms. In both cases, sensory information is modified, and therefore what we experience consciously is different from what is physically present. For Müller, however, sensations did not exhaust mental life. In his famous *Handbuch der Physiologie der Menschen* (*Handbook of Human Physiology*, 1833–1840), in a section entitled "Of the Mind," he postulated a mind capable of attending to some sensations to the exclusion of others. Thus, even in his otherwise mechanistic system, Müller found room for an active mind, again exposing his allegiance to Kant.

Müller was one of the greatest experimental physiologists of his time. His *Handbuch* summarized what was known about human physiology at the time. Müller also established the world's first Institute for Experimental Physiology at the University of Berlin. Most of those destined to become the most prominent physiologists of the 19th century studied with Müller, including Helmholtz, to whom we turn next.

HERMANN VON HELMHOLTZ

Many consider **Hermann von Helmholtz** (1821–1894) to be the greatest scientist of the 19th century. As we will see, he made significant contributions in physics, physiology, and psychology. Helmholtz, born in Potsdam, Germany, was a frail child and a mediocre student who was especially poor at foreign languages and poetry. Helmholtz's apparent mediocrity as a student, however, seemed to reflect the inadequacy of his teachers because he spent his spare time reading scientific books and working out the geometrical principles that described the various configurations of his play blocks. His father was a teacher who did not have enough money to pay for the scientific training that his son desired. Fortunately, the government had a program by which talented students could go to

medical school free if they agreed to serve for eight years as army surgeons following graduation. Helmholtz took advantage of this program and enrolled in the Berlin Royal Friedrich-Wilhelm Institute for Medicine and Surgery when he was 17 years old. While in his second year of medical school, he began his studies with Johannes Müller.

Helmholtz's Stand Against Vitalism

Although Helmholtz accepted many of Müller's conclusions, the two men still had basic disagreements, one of them over Müller's belief in **vitalism**. In biology and physiology, the vitalism–antivitalism problem was much like the mind–body problem in philosophy and psychology. The vitalists maintained that life could not be explained by the interactions of physical and chemical processes alone. For the vitalists, life was "more than" a physical process and could not be reduced to such a process. Furthermore, because it was not physical, the "life force" was forever beyond the scope of scientific analysis. Müller was a vitalist. Conversely, the antivitalists saw nothing mysterious about life and assumed that it could be explained in terms of physical and chemical processes. Therefore, there was no reason to exclude the study of life or of anything else from the realm of science. Helmholtz sided with the antivitalists, who believed that the same laws applied to living and nonliving things, as well as to mental and nonmental events. So strongly did Helmholtz and several of his fellow students believe in antivitalism that they signed the following oath (some say in their own blood):

> No other forces than the common physical-chemical ones are active within the organism. In those cases which cannot at the time be explained by these forces one has either to find the specific way or form of their action by means of the physical mathematical method, or to assume new forces equal in dignity to the physical-chemical forces inherent in matter, reducible to the force of attraction and repulsion. (Bernfeld, 1949, p. 171)

An interesting aspect of the vitalism–antivitalism controversy concerned an organism's ability to engage in spontaneous activity. The vitalists believed that behavior could be caused by an organism's vitalistic force and therefore occur independent of external stimulation. The antivitalists, believing in no vital force within the organism, tended to believe that all behavior is caused by external stimulation. In fact, for many years any theorist postulating spontaneous behavior of an organism was suspected of being a vitalist and therefore unscientific. We will see in chapter 12 that Sechenov studied physiology at the Berlin school and was strongly influenced by that school's opposition to vitalism. When Sechenov returned to Russia and formulated his approach to studying psychology, it stressed the importance of external stimulation as the cause of mental events. Thus was born the Russian reflexology that was so important in the development of objective psychology.

Principle of Conservation of Energy

Helmholtz obtained his medical degree at the age of 21 and was inducted into the army. While in the army, he was able to build a small laboratory and to continue his early research, which concerned metabolic processes in the frog. Helmholtz demonstrated that food and oxygen consumption were able to account for the total energy that an organism expended. He was thus able to apply the already popular **principle of conservation of energy** to living organisms. According to this principle, which had been previously applied to physical phenomena, energy is never created or lost in a system but is only transformed from one form to another. When applied to living organisms, the principle was clearly in accordance with the materialist philosophy because it brought physics, chemistry, and physiology closer together. In 1847 Helmholtz published a paper entitled "The Conservation of Force," and it was so influential that he was released from the remainder of his tour of duty in the army.

Hermann von Helmholtz

In 1848 Helmholtz was appointed lecturer of anatomy at the Academy of Arts in Berlin. The following year he was appointed professor of physiology at Königsberg, where Kant had spent his entire academic life. It was at Königsberg that Helmholtz conducted his now famous research on the speed of nerve conduction.

Rate of Nerve Conduction

Helmholtz disagreed with Müller not only over the issue of vitalism but also over the supposed speed of nerve conduction. Müller had maintained that nerve conduction was almost instantaneous, making it too fast to measure. His view reflected the ancient belief, still very popular during Müller's time, that there was a vital, nonmaterial agent that moved instantaneously and determined the behavior of living organisms. Many earlier philosophers had believed that the mind or the soul controlled bodily actions and that, because the mind and soul were inspired by God, their effect throughout the entire body was instantaneous. Those believing in animal spirits, a vital force, or in a nonmaterial mind or soul felt that measuring the speed of nerve conduction was impossible.

Helmholtz, however, excluded nothing from the realm of science, not even the rate of nerve conduction. To measure the rate of nerve conduction, Helmholtz isolated the nerve fiber leading to a frog's leg muscle. He then stimulated the nerve fiber at various distances from the muscle and noted how long it took the muscle to respond. He found that the muscular response followed more quickly when the motor nerve was stimulated closer to the muscle than when it was stimulated farther away from the muscle. By subtracting one reaction time from the other, he concluded that the nerve impulse traveled at a rate of about 90 feet per second (27.4 meters per second). Helmholtz then turned to humans, asking his subjects to respond by pushing a button when they felt their leg being stimulated. He found that reaction time was slower when the toe was stimulated than when the thigh was stimulated; he concluded, again by subtraction, that the rate of nerve conduction in humans was between 165 and 330 feet per second (50.3–100.6 meters per second). This aspect of Helmholtz's research was significant because it showed that nerve impulses were indeed measurable—that, in fact, they were fairly slow. This was taken as further evidence that physical-chemical processes were involved in our interactions with the environment, instead of some mysterious process that was immune to scientific scrutiny.

It is interesting to note that Helmholtz's study of human reaction time involved voluntary rather than involuntary (reflexive) behavior. Unlike the frog having its motor nerve stimulated, there is no natural association between

humans having their toes or thighs stimulated and pressing a button. Indeed, a human's response of pressing a button in response to stimulation indicates both an *understanding* of the instructions and a *willingness* to respond; there is nothing automatic about it. However, Helmholtz was not interested in the psychological processes involved in human reaction time, and it was left to others to use reaction time to study them. For example, we will see in chapter 9 how Donders (1818–1889) used human reaction time in an attempt to measure the duration of various mental acts.

Although the measure of reaction time was extremely useful to Helmholtz in measuring the speed of nerve conduction, he found that it varied considerably among subjects and even for the same subject at different times. He concluded that reaction time was too unreliable to be used as a valid measure and abandoned it. Support for his doubts came years later when more precise measurements indicated that the nerve conduction speeds he had reported were too slow. But this does not detract from the importance of Helmholtz's pioneering research on the rate of nerve conduction. Boring indicated that Helmholtz's discovery not only supported the materialistic conception of living organisms, including humans, but was also contrary to the popular conception that willed behavior is instantaneous:

> The importance for scientific psychology of the discovery that the transmission of the nervous impulse is not practically instantaneous, but relatively slow, is not to be underestimated. In the period under consideration, the mind had come to be largely identified with the brain, but the personality seemed rather to be a matter of the entire organism. Every one thought, as the average man thinks now, of his hand as of a piece with himself. To move his finger voluntarily was an act of mind in itself, not a later event caused by a previous act of mind. To separate the movement in time from the event of will that caused it was in a sense to separate the body from the mind, and almost from the personality or self. At any rate, Helmholtz's discovery was a step in the analysis of bodily motion that changed it from an instantaneous occurrence to

a temporal series of events, and it thus contributed to the materialistic view of the psychophysical organism that was the essence of nineteenth century science. (1957, p. 42)

Theory of Perception

Although believing that the physiological apparatus of the body provided the mechanisms for sensation, Helmholtz thought that the past experience of the observer was what converted a sensation into a perception. **Sensations**, then, are the raw elements of conscious experience, and **perceptions** are sensations after they are given meaning by one's past experiences. In explaining the transformation of sensations into perceptions, Helmholtz relied heavily on the notion of **unconscious inference**. According to Helmholtz, to label a visual experience a "chair" involves the application of a great deal of previous experience, as does looking at railroad tracks converging in the distance and insisting that they are parallel. Similarly, we see moving pictures as moving because of our prior experience with events that create a series of images across the retina. And we learn from experience that perceived distance is inversely related to the size of the retinal image. For Helmholtz, the perception of depth arises because the retinal image an object causes is slightly different on the two retinas. Previous experience with such retinal disparity causes the unconscious inference of depth. Helmholtz was very reluctant to use the term *unconscious inference* because it suggested the type of mysterious process that would violate his oath, but he could not find a better term.

Helmholtz supported his empirical theory of perception with the observation that individuals who were blind at birth and then acquired sight needed to learn to perceive, even though all the sensations furnished by the visual apparatus were available. His classic experiments with lenses that distorted vision provided further evidence. Helmholtz had subjects wear lenses that displaced the visual field several inches to the right or left. At first, the subjects would make mistakes in reaching for objects; but after several minutes *perceptual adaptation* occurred, and even while wearing the glasses, the subjects could again interact accurately with the environment. When the glasses were removed, the subjects again made mistakes for a short time but soon recovered.

One by one, Helmholtz took the supposed innate categories of thought Kant had proposed and showed how they were derived from experience. Concerning the axioms of geometry, which Kant had assumed were innate, Helmholtz said that if our world were arranged differently, our axioms would be very different:

> [Helmholtz] raised the question as to what geometry would be developed by beings who lived in another kind of space than ours. There might, for example, be "sphere-dwellers," who lived entirely in a spherical surface; for them the axiom of parallels would not hold, for any two straight lines, if sufficiently produced, would intersect in two points. Beings who lived in an egg-shaped surface would find that circles of equal radii at different places would have different circumferences. Dwellers in a pseudosphere or in other non-Euclidean spaces would have still different axioms and different geometries. So too we can conceive, though not imagine, hyper-spaces of four or more dimensions—space, for example, where there are forms that bear the same relation to the sphere as the sphere does to the circle. (Boring, 1957, p. 306)

Helmholtz and Kant agreed, however, on one important point: The perceiver transforms what the senses provide. For Kant, this transformation was accomplished when sensory information was structured by the innate faculties of the mind. For Helmholtz, the transformation occurred when sensory information was embellished by an individual's past experience. Kant's account of perception was therefore nativistic and Helmholtz's was empiricistic. With his notion of unconscious inference, Helmholtz came very close to what would later be considered part of psychology. That is, for unconscious inference to convert a sensation into a perception, memories of previous learning experiences must interact with current sensations. Although the processes of learning and memory were later to become vital to psychology, Helmholtz never considered himself a psychologist. He felt that psychology was too closely allied with metaphysics, and he wanted nothing to do with metaphysics.

Theory of Color Vision

Helmholtz performed his work on vision between 1853 and 1868 at the Universities of Königsberg, Bonn, and Heidelberg, and he published his results in the three-volume *Handbook of Physiological Optics* (1856–1866). Many years before Helmholtz's birth, Thomas Young (1773–1829) had proposed a theory of color vision very similar to Helmholtz's, but Young's theory had not been widely accepted. Helmholtz changed Young's theory slightly and buttressed it with experimental evidence. The theory we present here has come to be called the **Young–Helmholtz theory of color vision** (also called the trichromatic theory).

In 1672 Newton had shown that if white sunlight was passed through a prism, it emerged as a band of colored lights with red on one end of the band, then orange, yellow, green, blue, and, finally, violet. The prism separated the various wavelengths that together were experienced as white. Early speculation was that a different wavelength corresponded to each color and that different color experiences resulted from experiencing different wavelengths. However, Newton himself saw difficulties with this explanation. By mixing various wavelengths, it became clear to him that the property of color was not in the wavelengths themselves but in the observer. For example, white is experienced either if all wavelengths of the spectrum are present or if wavelengths corresponding to the colors red and blue-green are combined. Similarly, a person cannot distinguish the sensation of orange caused by the single wavelength corresponding to orange from the sensation of orange caused by mixing red and yellow. The question was how to account for the lack of correspondence between the physical stimuli present and the sensations they cause.

Helmholtz's answer was to expand Müller's doctrine of specific nerve energies by postulating three different types of color receptors on the retina. That is, instead of saying that the sense of vision had one specific nerve energy associated with it, as Müller had claimed, Helmholtz claimed that vision involved three separate receptors, each with its own specific energy. It was already known that various combinations of three primary colors—red, green, and blue-violet—could produce all other colors. Helmholtz speculated that there were three types of color receptors corresponding to the three primary colors. If a red light was shown, the so-called red receptors were stimulated, and one had the sensation of red; if a green light was shown, the green receptors were stimulated, and one had the experience of green; and so on. If all the primaries were shown at once, one experienced white. If the color shown was not a primary color, it would stimulate various combinations of the three receptors, resulting in a subjective color experience corresponding to the combination of wavelengths present. For example, presenting a red and a green light simultaneously would produce the subjective color experience of yellow. Also, the same color experience could be caused by several different patterns of the three receptor systems firing. In this way, Helmholtz explained why many physical wavelengths give rise to the same color experience.

The Young–Helmholtz theory of color vision was extremely helpful in explaining many forms of color blindness. For example, if a person lacks one or more of the receptor systems corresponding to the primary colors, he or she will not be able to experience certain colors subjectively, even though the physical world has not changed. The senses therefore actualize elements of the physical world that otherwise exist only as potential experiences.

Helmholtz was continually amazed at the way physiological mechanisms distorted the information a person received from the physical world, but he was even more amazed at the mismatch between physical events and psychological sensations (e.g., the experience of color). Helmholtz expressed his feelings as follows:

> The inaccuracies and imperfections of the eye as an optical instrument, and the deficiencies of the image on the retina, now appear insignificant in comparison with the incongruities we have met with in the field of sensation. One might almost believe that Nature had here contradicted herself on purpose in order to destroy any dream of a preexisting harmony between the outer and the inner world. (Kahl, 1971, p. 192)

Theory of Auditory Perception

For audition, as he had done for color vision, Helmholtz further refined Müller's doctrine of specific nerve energies. He found that the ear was not a single sense receptor but a highly complex system of many receptors. Whereas the visual system consisted of three types of nerve fibers, each with its own specific nerve energy, the auditory system contains thousands of types of nerve fibers, each with its own specific nerve energy. Helmholtz found that when the main membrane of the inner ear, the basilar membrane, was removed and uncoiled, it was shaped much like a harp. Assuming that this membrane was to hearing what the retina was to seeing, Helmholtz speculated that the different fibers along the basilar membrane were sensitive to differences in the frequency of sound waves. The short fibers responded to the higher frequencies, the longer fibers to the lower frequencies. A wave of a certain frequency caused the appropriate fiber of the basilar membrane to vibrate, thus causing the sensation of sound corresponding to that frequency. This process was called *sympathetic vibration*, and it can be demonstrated by stimulating a tuning fork of a certain frequency and noting that the string on a piano corresponding to that frequency also begins to vibrate. Helmholtz assumed that a similar process occurred in the middle ear and that, through various combinations of fiber stimulation, one could explain the wide variety of auditory experiences we have. This is referred to as the **resonance place theory of auditory percep-**

tion. Variations of Helmholtz's place theory persist today, but there are still auditory phenomena that no theory can explain.

Theory of Signs

Although Helmholtz was an empiricist in his explanations of sensation and perception, he did reflect the German *Zeitgeist* by postulating an active mind. According to Helmholtz, the mind's task was to create from the various "signs" that it receives from the sensory systems of the body a reasonably accurate conception of reality. Helmholtz assumed that a dynamic relationship existed among volition, sensation, and reflection as the mind attempted to create a functional view of external reality. Helmholtz's view of the mind differed from that of Kant because Kant believed that the mental categories of thought automatically presented a conception of reality. Helmholtz's view of the mind also differed from most of the British empiricists and French sensationalists because they saw the mind as largely passive. For Helmholtz, the mind's job was to construct a workable conception of reality given the incomplete and perhaps distorted information furnished by the senses:

> To Helmholtz, epistemology embraced the whole task of philosophy, and the central question of epistemology was: how, despite the limitations imposed by our sensory apparatus, do we obtain knowledge about the external world? The sensations of consciousness are stimulated in part by nervous impulses that arise from physical stimuli acting upon nerve endings in the sense organs. But these sensations tell us nothing about the real nature of external stimuli, because, in accordance with Johannes Müller's law of specific nerve energies, any individual nerve fibre excites the same sensation regardless of how that fibre is initially stimulated. It follows that our sensations and the perceptions that result from them are not images of an external reality as common sense takes them to be; they are "tokens" or "signs" of it. On the basis of these signs, poor evidence as they are, we must build up an "interpretation" of external reality, a set of expectations on the basis of which we can evaluate future sensations and act

successfully in the world. This process constituted Helmholtz's "theory of signs."

Helmholtz attributed to mind the supreme
role in this interpretive process. (Turner, 1977,
p. 49)

Helmholtz's Contributions

Although Helmholtz did postulate an active
mind, he accepted the empirical explanation as
to the origins of the contents of that mind. In his
explanations of sensation (the mental event that
results from sensory stimulation) and perception (sensation plus unconscious inference),
Helmholtz was emphatically empirical. In studying physiological and psychological phenomena,
he was unequivocally scientific. He showed that
nerve transmission was not instantaneous, as
had previously been believed, but that it was
rather slow and reflected the operation of physical processes. More than anyone before him,
Helmholtz showed with experimental rigor the
mechanisms by which we do commerce with the
physical world, mechanisms that could be explained in terms of objective, physical laws. Although he found that the match between what
was physically present and what was experienced psychologically was not very good, he
could explain the discrepancy in terms of the
properties of the receptor systems and the
unconscious inferences of the observer. No mystical, unscientific forces were involved. Helmholtz's work brought physics, chemistry, physiology, and psychology closer together. In so doing, it paved the way for the emergence of
experimental psychology, which was in many
ways an inevitable step after Helmholtz's work.

Helmholtz realized a lifelong ambition when
he was appointed professor of physics at the
University of Berlin in 1871. In 1882 the German emperor granted him noble status, and
thereafter his name was Hermann *von* Helmholtz. In 1893 Helmholtz came to the United
States to see the Chicago World's Fair and to visit
with William James. On his way back to Germany, he fell down aboard ship and broke his
hip. Never fully recovering, he died the following year.

EWALD HERING

In Helmholtz's time, there was intense controversy over whether perceptual phenomena
were learned or innate. Helmholtz, with his notion of unconscious inference, sided with those
who said perceptions were learned. **Ewald
Hering** (1834–1918) sided with the nativists.
After receiving his medical degree from the
University of Leipzig, Hering stayed there for
several years before accepting a post as lecturer
at the Vienna Military Medical Academy where
he worked with Josef Breuer (1842–1925), who
was later to be instrumental in the founding of
psychoanalysis (see chapter 16). Working together, Hering and Breuer showed that respiration was, in part, caused by receptors in the
lungs—a finding called the Hering–Breuer reflex. In 1870 Hering was called to the University
of Prague, in Czechoslovakia, were he succeeded
the great physiologist Jan E. Purkinje (1787–
1869). Like Goethe, to whom Purkinje dedicated
one of his major works, Purkinje was a phenomenologist. He believed that the phenomena of
the mind, arrived at by careful introspective
analysis, should be what physiologists attempt to
explain. According to Purkinje, the physiologist
is obliged to explain not only "normal" sensations and perceptions but "abnormal" ones as
well, such as illusions and afterimages. Among
the many phenomena that Purkinje observed
was that the relative vividness of colors is different in faint light as opposed to bright light. More
specifically, as twilight approaches, hues that
correspond to short wavelengths such as violet
and blue appear brighter than hues corresponding to longer wavelengths such as yellow and
red. This change in relative vividness, as a function of luminance level, is known as the *Purkinje
shift*. Hering too was a phenomenologist, and his
theory of color vision, which will be considered
shortly, was based, to a large extent, on the phenomenon of negative afterimages.

Space Perception

On the matter of space perception, we have seen that Helmholtz believed that it slowly developed from experience as physiological and psychological events were correlated. Hering, however, believed that, when stimulated, each point on the retina automatically provided three types of information about the stimulus: height, left-right position, and depth. Following Kant, Hering believed that space perception exists a priori. For Kant, space perception was an innate category of the mind; for Hering, it was an innate characteristic of the eye.

Theory of Color Vision

After working on the problem of space perception for about 10 years, Hering turned to color vision. Hering observed a number of phenomena that he felt were either incompatible with the Young–Helmholtz theory or could not be explained by it. He noted that certain pairs of colors when mixed together gave the sensation of gray. This was true for red and green, blue and yellow, and black and white. He also observed that a person who stares at red and then looks away experiences a green afterimage. Similarly, blue gives a yellow afterimage. Hering also noted that individuals who had difficulty distinguishing red from green could still see yellow; also it is typical for a color-blind person to lose the sensation of *both* red and green, not just one or the other. All these observations at least posed problems for the Young–Helmholtz theory, if they did not contradict it.

To account for these phenomena, Hering theorized that there were three types of receptors on the retina but each could respond in two ways. One type of receptor responds to red-green, one type to yellow-blue, and one type to black-white. Red, yellow, and white cause a "tearing down," or a *catabolic process*, in their respective receptors. Green, blue, and black cause a "building up," or an *anabolic process*, in their respective receptors. If both colors to

Ewald Hering

which a receptor is sensitive are experienced simultaneously, the catabolic and anabolic processes are canceled out, and the sensation of gray results. If one color to which a receptor is sensitive is experienced, its corresponding process is depleted leaving only its opposite to produce an afterimage. Finally, Hering's theory explained why individuals who cannot respond to red or green can still see yellow and why the inability to see red is usually accompanied by an inability to see green.

For nearly 50 years, lively debate ensued between those accepting the Young–Helmholtz theory and those accepting Hering's; the matter is still far from settled. The current view is that the Young–Helmholtz theory is correct in that there are retinal cells sensitive to red, green, and blue but that there are neural processes beyond the retina that are more in accordance with Hering's proposed metabolic processes.

EARLY RESEARCH ON BRAIN FUNCTIONING

To review early brain research, we must start by going back to Gall, on whom we commented in chapter 6. Gall's assumptions about brain functioning have set the course of brain research right up to the present.

Franz Joseph Gall

Franz Joseph Gall (1758–1828) is usually reviewed negatively in the history of psychology, but Gall made several positive contributions to the study of brain functioning. For example, he studied the brains of several animal species, including humans, and was the first to suggest a relationship between cortical development and mental functioning. He found that larger, better-developed cortices were associated with more intelligent behavior. This discovery of the correlation between mind and brain alone qualifies Gall for recognition in the history of psychology.

As was indicated in chapter 6, Gall accepted the widely held belief that faculties of the mind acted on and transformed sensory information, but he went several steps beyond traditional faculty psychology. He assumed that

1. The faculties resided in *specific locations* in the brain.

2. Humans possessed faculties in different degrees and that these individual differences were innate.

3. The bumps and indentations on the surface of the skull could be used to index the magnitude of the underlying faculties.

The examination of the shape of the skull in order to determine a person's strong or weak faculties came to be called **phrenology**, a term that Gall rejected but that his associate **Johann Gasper Spurzheim** (1776–1832) made popular. The term *phrenology* was actually coined by Thomas Foster in 1815 (Bakan, 1966). The dissemination of phrenology into English-speaking countries was facilitated by Spurzheim's *The Physiognomical System of Drs. Gall and Spurzheim* (1815) and by the translation of Gall's *On the Functions of the Brain and Each of Its Parts: With Observations on the Possibility of Determining the Instincts, Propensities, and Talents, or the Moral and Intellectual Dispositions of Men and Animals, by the Configuration of the Brain and Head* (1835).

Gall's idea was not a bad one. In fact, Gall was among the first to attempt to relate certain personality traits and overt behavior patterns to specific brain functions. The problem was the type of evidence he accepted as demonstrating this relationship. He would observe that someone had a pronounced personality characteristic and a well-developed brain structure, and then he would attribute the one to the other. After observing such a relationship in one individual, he would generalize it to all individuals.

In their research on the mental faculties, some of Gall's followers even exceeded his shoddiness:

> If *Gall* was cavalier in his interpretations of evidence, he attracted some followers who raised that tendency to an art form. When a cast of Napoleon's right skull predicted qualities markedly at variance with the emperor's known personality, one phrenologist replied that his dominant side had been the left—a cast of which was conveniently missing. When Descartes's skull was examined and found deficient in the regions for reason and reflection, phrenologists retorted that the philosopher's rationality had always been overrated. (Fancher, 1990, p. 79)

The wide appeal of phrenology. During the first half of the 19th century, phrenology was enormously popular among both professional and nonprofessional individuals. We saw in chapter 6 that phrenology was popular among the populace because it seemed to offer a quick, valid character analysis that could aid in everyday decision making. Shortly after Spurzheim came to the United States he died, and on the day of his funeral (November 17, 1832), the Boston Phrenological Society was formed; such societies soon sprang up all over the nation (Bakan,

1966). Numerous journals devoted to phrenology emerged in Europe and the United States; one of these, *Phrenological Journal*, started publishing in 1837 and continued until 1911. Phrenology appealed to professionals because it seemed to offer an alternative to mental philosophy with its dependence on introspective data: "The central theme that runs through all of the phrenological writings is that man himself could be studied scientifically, and in particular that the phenomena of mind could be studied objectively and explained in terms of natural causes" (Bakan, 1966, p. 208).

Phrenology was also popular because, unlike mental philosophy, it appeared to offer practical information. When phrenologists such as Spurzheim lectured in the United States, their appreciative audiences included physicians, ministers, public educators, college professors, and asylum superintendents. O'Donnell makes the point that these and other individuals were looking to phrenology for the type of information that others would later seek in the school of behaviorism (see chapter 12):

> With or without bumps, phrenology's theory of human nature and personality recommended itself to emerging professional groups searching for "positive knowledge." . . . [They] found in phrenology an etiological explanation of aberrant human behavior; a predictive technology for assessing character, temperament, and intellect; and a biological blueprint for social reform. The social engineers of the twentieth century, together with their patrons and subscribers, would demand no less of modern experimental behaviorism. When the new psychology [behaviorism] arrived on the American stage an eager audience anticipated the role it was to play. Gall, Spurzheim . . . and their followers had already written the script. (1985, p. 78)

For reasons that we review next, the specific claims of the phrenologists were found to be incorrect, but phrenology did influence subsequent psychology in a number of important ways: It argued effectively that the mind and brain are closely related; it stimulated intense research on the localization of brain functions; and it showed the importance of furnishing

Pierre Flourens

practical information. Also, we will see, after we review the research that showed phrenology's specific claims to be false, that a new, more sophisticated form of phrenology may be emerging.

Pierre Flourens

By the turn of the 19th century, it was generally conceded that the brain was the organ of the mind. Under the influence of Gall and the other phrenologists, the brain–mind relationship was articulated into a number of faculties housed in specific locations in the brain. Thus, the phrenologists gave birth to the concern of localization of functions in the brain. Although popular among scientists, including neurophysiologists, phrenology was far from universally accepted. A number of prominent physicians questioned the claims of the phrenologists. It was not enough, however, to claim that the phrenologists were wrong in their assumptions; the claim had to be substantiated scientifically. This was the goal of **Pierre Flourens** (1794–1867), who pioneered the use of extirpation, or ablation, in brain research. His approach was to destroy part of the brain and then note the behavioral consequences of the loss. Like Gall, Flourens assumed that the brains of lower animals were similar in many ways to human brains, so he used organisms such as dogs and pigeons as his research subjects. He found that removal of the cerebellum disturbed an organism's coordination and equilibrium, that ablation of the cerebrum resulted in passivity, and that destruction of the semicircular canals resulted in loss of balance.

When he examined the entire brain, Flourens concluded that there was some localization; but contrary to what the phrenologists believed, the cortical hemispheres did not have localized functions. Instead, they functioned as a unit. Seeking further evidence of the brain's interrelatedness, Flourens observed that animals sometimes regained functions that they had lost following ablation. Thus, at least one part of the brain had the capacity to take over the function of another part. Flourens's fame as a scientist, and his conclusion that the cortex functioned as a unit, effectively silenced the phrenologists. Subsequent research, however, would show that they had been silenced too quickly.

Paul Broca

Using the **clinical method, Paul Broca** (1824–1880) cast doubt on Flourens's conclusion that the cortex acted as a whole. Boring described Broca's observation:

> Broca's famous observation was in itself very simple. There had in 1831 been admitted at the Bicetre, an insane hospital near Paris, a man whose sole defect seemed to be that he could not talk. He communicated intelligently by signs and was otherwise mentally normal. He remained at the Bicetre for thirty years with this defect and on April 12, 1861, was put under the care of Broca, the surgeon, because of a gangrenous infection. Broca for five days subjected him to a careful examination, in which he satis-

* 1824   PIERRE-PAUL BROCA   † 1880
Professeur de Clinique chirurgicale à la Faculté de Médecine de Paris, 1868,
Membre de l'Académie de Médecine,
Fondateur de la Société d'Anthropologie, 1859.

Paul Broca

NATIONAL LIBRARY OF MEDICINE

fied himself that the musculature of the larynx and articulatory organs was not hindered in normal movements, that there was no other paralysis that could interfere with speech, and that the man was intelligent enough to speak. On April 17 the patient—fortunately, it must have seemed, for science—died; and within a day Broca had performed an autopsy, discovering a lesion in the third frontal convolution of the left cerebral hemisphere, and had presented the brain in alcohol to the Société d'Anthropologie. (1957, p. 71)

Thus, Broca was the first to observe a behavior disorder first and then locate the part of the brain causing it. Other researchers have implicated the area on the left side of the cortex that Broca found to be damaged in the control of speech, and the area has been named **Broca's area**. The localizing of a function on the cortex supported the phrenologists and damaged Flourens's contention that the cortex acted as a unit. Unfortunately for the phrenologists, however, Broca did not find the speech area to be where the phrenologists had said it would be.

Gustav Fritsch, Edward Hitzig, and David Ferrier

Electrically stimulating the exposed cortex of a dog, **Gustav Fritsch** (1838–1927) and **Edward Hitzig** (1838–1907) made two important discoveries. First, the cortex was not insensitive, as had been previously assumed. Second, they found that when a certain area of the cortex was stimulated, muscular movements were elicited from the opposite side of the body. Stimulating different points in this *motor area* of the brain stimulated movements from different parts of the body. Thus, another function was localized on the cortex. **David Ferrier** (1843–1928) found a cortical area corresponding to the skin senses, and later researchers found visual and auditory areas.

The evidence seemed clear; there was a great deal of localization of function on the cortex, just as the phrenologists had maintained. These findings, however, did not support traditional phrenology. Seldom was a function (faculty) found where the phrenologists had said it was. Furthermore, the phrenologists had spoken of faculties such as vitality, firmness, love, and kindness, but the researchers instead found sensory and motor areas. These findings extended the Bell–Magendie law to the brain. That is, the sensation experienced seemed to be more a matter of the cortical area stimulated than a matter of the sensory nerve stimulated. It looked very much like the brain was a complex switchboard where sensory information was projected and where it in turn stimulated appropriate motor responses. The localization studies seemed to favor the empirical-materialistic view rather than the rationalist view.

The brain research that was stimulated in an effort to evaluate the claims of the phrenologists made it clear that physical stimulation gave rise to various types of subjective experiences and that they were directly related to brain activity. The next step in psychology's development toward becoming an experimental science was to examine *scientifically* how sensory stimulation was systematically related to conscious experience.

THE RISE OF EXPERIMENTAL PSYCHOLOGY

The very important difference between what was physically present and what was experienced psychologically had been recognized and agonized over for centuries. This was the distinction that had caused Galileo to conclude that a science of psychology was impossible and Hume to conclude that we could know nothing about the physical world with certainty. Kant amplified this distinction when he claimed that the mind embellished sensory experience, and Helmholtz reached the same conclusion with his concept of unconscious inference.

With advances in science, much had been learned about the physical world—that is, about physical stimulation. Also, as we have seen, much had been learned about the sense receptors, which convert physical stimulation into nerve impulses, and about the brain structures where those impulses terminate. There was never much doubt about the existence of consciousness; the problem was in determining what we were conscious of and what caused that consciousness. By now it was widely believed that conscious sensations were triggered by brain processes, which themselves were initiated by sense reception. But the question remained: How are the two domains (mental sensations and the sensory processes) related?

Without measurement, science is impossible. Therefore, it was assumed that a science of psychology was impossible unless consciousness could be measured as objectively as the physical world. Furthermore, once measured, mental events would have to be shown to vary in some systematic way with physical events. Ernst Hein-

Ernst Weber

rich Weber and Gustav Theodor Fechner were the first to measure how sensations vary systematically as a function of physical stimulation.

Ernst Heinrich Weber

Ernst Heinrich Weber (1795–1878), a contemporary of Johannes Müller, was born in Wittenberg and was the son of a theology professor. Obtaining his doctorate from the University of Leipzig in 1815, Weber taught there until his retirement in 1871. Weber was a physiologist who was interested in the senses of touch and **kinesthesis** (muscle sense). Prior to Weber, most of the research on sense perception had been confined to vision and audition. Weber's research consisted largely in exploring new fields, most notably skin and muscle sensations. Weber was among the first to demonstrate that the sense of touch was not one but several senses. For example, what is ordinarily called the sense

of touch includes the senses of pressure, temperature, and pain. Weber also provided convincing evidence that there is a muscle sense. It was in regard to the muscle sense that Weber performed his work on just noticeable differences, which we consider shortly.

Weber's work on touch. For the sensation of touch, Weber attempted to determine the least spatial separation at which two points of touch on the body could be discriminated. Using a compasslike device consisting of two points, he simultaneously applied two points of pressure to a subject's skin. The smallest distance between the two points at which the subject reported sensing two points instead of one was called the **two-point threshold**. In his famous book *On Touch: Anatomical and Physiological Notes* (1834), Weber provided charts of the entire body with regard to the two-point threshold. He found the smallest two-point threshold on the tongue (about 1 millimeter) and the largest in the middle of the back (about 60 millimeters). He assumed that the differences in thresholds at different places on the body resulted from the anatomical arrangement of the sense receptors for touch—the more receptors, the finer the discrimination.

Weber's work on kinesthesis. Within the history of psychology, Weber's research on the muscle sense, or kinesthesis, is even more important than his research on touch. It was while investigating kinesthesis that Weber ran his important weight-discrimination experiments. In general, he sought to determine the smallest difference between two weights that could be discriminated. To do this, he had his subjects lift one weight (the standard), which remained the same during a series of comparisons, and then lift other weights. The subject was to report whether the varying weights were heavier, lighter, or the same as the standard weight. He found that when the variable weights were only slightly different from the standard, they were judged to be the same as the standard. Through a series of such comparisons, Weber was able to determine the **just noticeable difference** (jnd) that the subject could detect between the standard and the variable weight.

Weber ran the basic weight-discrimination experiment under two conditions. In one condition, the weights were placed on the subject's hands while the hands were resting on a table. In this condition, the subject's judgments are made primarily on the basis of tactile sensations. In the second condition, the subject lifted the hands with the weights on them. In this condition, the subject's judgments are made on the basis of both tactile and kinesthetic sensations. It was found that subjects could detect much smaller weight differences when they lifted the weights than they could when the weights were simply placed on their hands. Weber thought that it was the involvement of kinesthesis in the lifted-weight condition that provided the greater sensitivity to weight differences.

Judgments are relative, not absolute. During his research on kinesthesis, Weber made the startling observation that the jnd was a constant fraction of the standard weight. In the case of lifted weights, that fraction was 1/40; in the case of nonlifted weights, it was 1/30. Taking the case of lifted weights as an example, if the standard weight were 40 grams, the variable weight would have to be 41 grams to be judged heavier or 39 grams to be judged lighter than the standard. If the standard weight were 160 grams, the variable weight would have to be 164 grams or 156 grams to be judged heavier or lighter, respectively, than the standard. Weber then aligned himself with the large number of scientists and philosophers who found that there was not a simple one-to-one correspondence between what is present physically and what is experienced psychologically. Weber observed that discrimination did not depend on the absolute difference between two weights but on the relative difference between the two, or the ratio of one to the other. Weber extended his research to other sense modalities and found evidence that suggested that there is a constant fraction for jnds for each sense modality.

The finding that jnds were a constant fraction of a standard stimulus was later called **Weber's law** and can be considered the first quantitative law in psychology's history. *This was the first statement of a systematic relationship between physical stimulation and a psychological experience.* But because Weber was a physiologist, psychology was not his primary concern. It was Fechner who realized the implications of Weber's work for psychology and who saw in it the possible resolution of the mind–body problem.

Gustav Theodor Fechner

Gustav Theodor Fechner (1801–1887) was a brilliant, complex, and unusual individual. Fechner's father succeeded his grandfather as village pastor. Boring indicated that Fechner shared some personality characteristics with his father:

> His father was a man of independence of thought and of receptivity to new ideas. He shocked the villagers by having a lightning-rod placed upon the church tower, in the days when this precaution was regarded as a lack of faith in God's care of his own, and by preaching—as he urged that Jesus must also have done—without a wig. One can thus see in the father an anticipation of Fechner's own genius for bringing the brute facts of scientific materialism to the support of a higher spiritualism, but there can have been little, if any, direct influence of this sort, for the father died when Fechner was only five years old. (1957, p. 276)

After his father died, Fechner, his brother, and his mother spent the next nine years with his uncle who was also a pastor. At the age of 16, Fechner began his studies in medicine at the University of Leipzig (where Weber was) and obtained his medical degree in 1822 at the age of 21. Upon receiving his medical degree, Fechner's interest shifted from biological science to physics and mathematics. At this time, he made a meager living by translating into German certain French handbooks of physics and chemistry and by tutoring and occasionally lecturing. Fechner was interested in the properties of electric currents and in 1831 published a significant arti-

Gustav Theodor Fechner

cle on the topic, which established his reputation as a physicist. In 1834, when he was 33 years old, Fechner was appointed professor of physics at Leipzig. Soon his interests began to turn to the problems of sensation, and by 1840 he had published articles on color vision and afterimages.

In about 1840, Fechner had a "nervous breakdown," resigned his position at Leipzig, and became a recluse. Besides the philosophical conflicts Fechner experienced (we discuss those conflicts next), he had almost been blinded, presumably while looking at the sun through colored glasses while performing his research on afterimages. At this time, Fechner entered a state of depression that was to last several years and resulted in his interests turning from physics to philosophy. The shift was only in emphasis, however, because all of his adult life he was

uncomfortable with materialism, which he called the "night view"; it contrasted with the "day view," which emphasized mind, spirit, and consciousness. He accepted Spinoza's double-aspect view of mind and matter and therefore believed that consciousness is as prevalent in the universe as is matter. Because he believed that consciousness cannot be separated from physical things, his position represents **panpsychism**. That is, all things that are physical are also conscious. It was Fechner's interest in the mind–body relationship that led to the development of psychophysics, which we will consider shortly.

The adventures of Dr. Mises. Although Fechner was an outstanding scientist, there was a side of him that science could not satisfy. Besides Fechner the materialistic scientist, there was Fechner the satirist, philosopher, spiritualist, and Fechner the mystic. For a young scientist to express so many viewpoints, especially because so many of them were incompatible with science, would have been professional suicide. So, Fechner invented a person to speak for his other half, and thus was born "Dr. Mises." Marshall explains Fechner's rationale for creating Dr. Mises:

Why did Fechner assume the comic disguise of Dr. Mises? Historically, empirical science, to which Fechner had made himself professionally responsible, never had been tolerant of intellectual excesses. Furthermore, science was experiencing an upsurge of popularity in the first half of the nineteenth century, and in consequence, spiritualism with its supporting methods was viewed with justifiable suspicion. The dilemma for the young man struggling to gain a serious scientific reputation is quite clear, for if one holds a cherished idea which is popularly suspect, one ordinarily does not offer oneself for professional crucifixion by advancing the idea seriously. Yet if a valued but extravagant idea will not die, even in the face of rationally and emotionally conflicting concepts, it must somehow find expression. What safer, and ultimately, more productive way than to disguise the idea as a joke, and to issue it from the mouth of a clown. (1969, p. 44)

And Heidbreder commented:

The conflict, at the same time subtle and severe, was almost a deadlock. As professor of physics Fechner taught the official science of the day; as Dr. Mises he found an outlet for the feeling that science was unsatisfying and incomplete. (1933, p. 80)

Dr. Mises first appeared while Fechner was still a medical student. Under the pseudonym of Dr. Mises, Fechner wrote *Proof That the Moon Is Made of Iodine* (1821), a satire on the medical profession's tendency to view iodine as a panacea. In 1825 Dr. Mises published *The Comparative Anatomy of Angels* in which it is reasoned, tongue firmly in cheek, that angels cannot have legs. Marshall summarizes the argument:

Centipedes have God-knows-how-many legs; butterflies and beetles have six, mammals only four; birds, who of all earthly creatures rise closest to the angels, have just two. With each developmental step another pair of legs is lost, and "Since the final observable category of creatures possesses only two legs, it is impossible that angels should have any at all." (1969, p. 51)

Dr. Mises also argued that because the sphere is the most perfect shape and angels are perfect, angels must be spherical; but planets are also spherical, so angels must be planets.

There followed *The Little Book on Life After Death* (1836), *Nanna, or Concerning the Mental Life of Plants* (1848), and *Zend-Avesta, or Concerning Matters of Heaven and the Hereafter* (1851). In all, Dr. Mises was heard from 14 times from 1821–1876. Always Fechner used Dr. Mises to express the "day view," the view that the universe is alive and conscious. Always behind Fechner's satire or humor was the message that the "day view" must be taken seriously. Marshall makes this point concerning *Zend-Avesta*:

Indeed, in Zoroastrian dogma, *Zend-Avesta* meant the "living word," and Fechner was to intend that his own *Zend-Avesta* should be the word which would reveal all nature to be alive. In this work Fechner argues that the earth is ensouled, just as the human being is; but the earth possesses a spirituality which surpasses that of her creatures. (1969, p. 54)

In fact, it was in *Zend-Avesta* that Fechner first described what would later become psychophysics:

[Fechner] laid down the general outlines of his program [psychophysics] in *Zend-Avesta*, the book about heaven and the future life. Imagine sending a graduate student of psychology nowadays to the Divinity School for a course in immortality as preparation for advanced experimental work in psychophysics! How narrow we have become! (Boring, 1963, p. 128)

Psychophysics. From Fechner's philosophical interest in the relationship between the mind and the body sprang his interest in psychophysics. He wanted desperately to solve the mind–body problem in a way that would satisfy the materialistic scientists of his day. Fechner's mystical philosophy taught him that the physical and mental were simply two aspects of the same fundamental reality. Thus, he accepted the double aspectism that Spinoza had postulated. But to say that there was a demonstrable relationship between the mind and the body was one thing; proving it was another matter. According to Fechner, the solution to the problem occurred to him the morning of October 22, 1850, as he was lying in bed (Boring, 1957). His insight was that a systematic relationship between bodily and mental experience could be demonstrated if a person were asked to report changes in sensations as a physical stimulus was systematically varied. Fechner speculated that in order for mental sensations to change arithmetically, the physical stimulus would have to change geometrically. In testing these ideas, Fechner created the area of psychology that was later called **psychophysics**.

As was mentioned, Fechner's insight concerning the relationship between stimuli and sensations was first reported in *Zend-Avesta* (1851). Fechner spent the next few years experimentally verifying his insight and published two short papers on psychophysics in 1858 and 1859. Then in 1860 he published his famous *Elements of Psychophysics*, a book that went a long way in launching psychology as an experimental science.

As the name suggests, psychophysics is the study of the relationship between physical and psychological events. Fechner's first step in studying this relationship was to state mathematically what Weber had found and to label the expression Weber's law:

$$\frac{\Delta R}{R} = k$$

where:

R = *Reiz* (the German word for "stimulus"). In Weber's research this was the standard stimulus.

ΔR = The minimum change in R that could be detected. That is, ΔR = jnd.

k = A constant. As we have seen, Weber found this constant to be 1/40 of R for kinesthesis.

Weber's law concerns the amount that a physical stimulus must change before it results in the awareness of a difference or in a change of sensation (S). Through a series of mathematical calculations, Fechner arrived at his famous formula, which he believed showed the relationship between the mental and the physical (the mind and the body):

$$S = k \log R$$

This formula mathematically states Fechner's earlier insight. That is, for the magnitude of a sensation to rise arithmetically, the magnitude of the physical stimulus must rise geometrically. This means that as a stimulus gets larger, the magnitude of the change must become greater and greater if the change is to be detected. For example, if the stimulus (R) is 40 grams, a difference of only 1 gram can be detected; whereas if the stimulus is 200 grams, it takes a difference of 5 grams to cause a jnd. In everyday terms, this means that sensations are always relative to the level of background stimulation. If a room is dark, for example, turning on a dim light will be immediately noticed, as would a whisper in a quiet room. If a room is fully lighted, however, the addition of a dim light would go unnoticed, as would a whisper in a noisy room.

The jnd as the unit of sensation. Fechner assumed that as the magnitude of a stimulus increased from zero, a point would be reached where the stimulus could be consciously detected. The lowest intensity at which a stimulus could be detected was called the **absolute threshold**. That is, the absolute threshold was the intensity of a stimulus at or above which a sensation results and below which no detectable sensation occurs. According to Fechner, intensity levels below the absolute threshold did cause reactions, but those reactions were unconscious. By allowing for these **negative sensations**, Fechner's position was very much like those of Leibniz (*petites perceptions*) and Herbart (threshold of consciousness). For all three, the effects of stimulation cumulated and, at some point (the absolute threshold), was capable of causing a conscious sensation.

Fechner's analysis of sensation started with the absolute threshold, but because that threshold provided only one measure, it was of limited usefulness. What he needed was a continuous scale that showed how sensations above the absolute threshold varied as a function of level of stimulation. This was provided by the **differential threshold**, which is defined by how much a stimulus magnitude needs to be increased or decreased before a person can detect a difference. It was in regard to the differential threshold that Fechner found that stimulus values must be raised or lowered geometrically in order for sensations to change arithmetically. Given a geometric increase in the intensity of a stimulus, Fechner assumed that sensations increased in increments equal to the jnd. With this assumption, it was possible, using Fechner's law, to deduce how many units (jnds) above absolute threshold a sensation was at any given level of stimulus intensity. In other words, Fechner's law assumed that sensations increased in equal units (jnds) as the stimulus intensity increased geometrically beyond the absolute threshold.

Psychophysical methods. After establishing that mental and physical events varied systematically, and thus showing that a science of the mind was indeed possible (contrary to the beliefs of such individuals as Galileo, Comte, and Kant), Fechner employed several methods in further exploring the mind–body relationship:

1. The **method of limits** (also called the method of just noticeable differences): With this method, one stimulus is varied and is compared to a standard. To begin with, the variable stimulus can be equal to the standard and then varied, or it can be much stronger or weaker than the standard. The goal here is to determine the range of stimuli that the subject considers to be equal to the standard.

2. The **method of constant stimuli** (also called the method of right and wrong cases): Here, pairs of stimuli are presented to the subject. One member of the pair is the standard and remains the same, and the other varies in magnitude from one presentation to another. The subject reports whether the variable stimulus appears greater than, less than, or equal to the standard.

3. The **method of adjustment** (also called the method of average error): Here, the subject has control over the variable stimulus and is instructed to adjust its magnitude so that the stimulus appears equal to the standard stimulus. After the adjustment, the average difference between the variable stimulus and the standard stimulus is measured.

These methods are Fechner's major legacy to psychology, and they are still widely used.

Fechner's contributions. Fechner did not solve the mind–body problem; it is still alive and well in modern psychology. Like Weber, however, he did show that it was possible to measure mental events and relate them to physical ones. A number of historians have suggested that the beginning of experimental psychology be marked by the 1860 publication of Fechner's *Elements*. Heidbreder commented on the significance of Fechner's work:

To Fechner's contemporaries, the remarkable feature of the psychophysical methods was the fact that they were quantitative. To measure mental processes was considered a startling innovation; to experiment with them in a manner that gave quantitative data marked the dawn of a new day. The publication in 1860 of *The Elements of Psychophysics*, the book in which Fechner reported his work and his views, ranks with the founding of the Leipzig laboratory [see chapter 9] as one of the outstanding events in the development of psychology. As a serious, original, carefully executed attempt to treat psychological processes in the manner of the exact sciences, the book is sometimes taken as marking the first definite achievement of the science of psychology. (1933, p. 83)

Not everyone reviewed Fechner's contributions positively, however. For example, William James (whose work we will review in chapter 11) had some unkind things to say about Fechner's influence on psychology:

Fechner's book was the starting point of a new department of literature, which it would be perhaps impossible to match for the qualities of thoroughness and subtlety, but of which, in the humble opinion of the present writer, the proper psychological outcome is just *nothing*. . . . It would be terrible if even such a dear old man as this could saddle our Science forever with his patient whimsies, and in a world so full of more nutritious objects of attention, compel all future students to plough through the difficulties, not only of his own works, but of the still drier ones written in his refutation. Those who desire this dreadful literature can find it; it has a "disciplinary value"; but I will not even enumerate it in a footnote. The only amusing part of it is that Fechner's critics should always feel bound, after smiting his theories hip and thigh and leaving not a stick of them standing, to wind up by saying that nevertheless to him belongs the *imperishable glory*, of first formulating them and thereby turning psychology into an *exact science*,

> "And everybody praised the duke
> Who this great fight did win.
> But what good came of it at last?
> Quoth little Peterkin.
> Why, that I cannot tell, said he,
> But 'twas a famous victory!"

(James, 1890/1961, Vol. 1, pp. 534, 549)

Many disagree with James's assessment of Fechner and instead afford him a prominent place in psychology's history. Boring (1963) made an important point about history, in general, and about Fechner's place in psychology's history, in particular:

> In general, the greatness of Great Men is a subjective addition to history which posterity adds in order to understand history. History is continuous and sleek. Great Men are the handles that you put on its smooth sides. You have to simplify natural events in order to understand them, and science itself is forced to generalize in the interest of economy of thinking. Just so the history of science singles out events, schools, trends, and discoveries and eponymizes them, that is to say, it names them for a central figure.

Fechner has become the name for a change in the newly developing scientific psychology, for the gradual acceptance of the belief that the fleeting and evanescent mind—consciousness—can be measured. That had to happen before anything else could take place in respect of scales and measurement in the psychological sphere. (1963, p. 130)

Although a case can be made for marking the beginning of experimental psychology with the publication of Fechner's *Elements*, most agree that another important step had to be taken before psychology could emerge as a full-fledged science: Psychology needed to be *founded* as a separate discipline. As we will see in chapter 9, it was Wilhelm Wundt who took that step.

SUMMARY

The discovery of individual differences among astronomers in the recording of astronomical events demonstrated the need, even within the physical sciences, for understanding how the physical world was sensed and mentally represented. An intense investigation of the human sensory apparatus and nervous system followed. Bell and Magendie discovered that some nerves were specialized to carry sensory information to the brain, whereas others were specialized to carry sensory information from the brain to the muscles of the body. This distinction between sensory and motor nerves is called the Bell–Magendie law. Müller found that each sensory nerve was specialized to produce a certain type of energy, which in turn produced a certain type of sensation. For example, no matter how the optic nerve is stimulated, it will produce the sensation of light. The same is true for all other sensory nerves of the body. Müller's finding is called the doctrine of specific nerve energies.

Helmholtz is a monumental figure in the history of science. He opposed the belief in vitalism that his teacher Müller and others held. The vitalists maintained that life could not be reduced to physical processes and therefore could not be investigated scientifically. For Helmholtz, nothing was beyond scientific investigation. He showed that the amount of energy an organism expended was directly proportional to the amount of food and oxygen it consumed, thereby showing that the principle of conservation of energy applied to living organisms as well as to physical phenomena. Ignoring the contention that nerve impulses were too fast to be measured, he measured their speed and found them to be remarkably slow.

Helmholtz also differentiated between sensations and perceptions, the former being the raw images provided by the sense receptors and the latter being the meaning that past experience gave to those raw sensations. Through the process of unconscious inference, the wealth of prior experience we have had with objects and events is brought to bear on current sensations, converting them into perceptions. With his notion of unconscious inference, Helmholtz offered an empirical explanation of perception instead of the nativistic explanation, which Kant and others had offered. And he extended the doctrine of specific nerve energies to color vision by saying that specific receptors on the retina corresponded to each of the three primary colors: red, green, and blue-violet. If one of the three receptors was missing or inoperative, the person would be blind to the color to which the receptor was sensitive. For Helmholtz, all experiences of color could be explained as the stimulation of one or a pattern of the three types of color receptors. Because Young had earlier proposed a similar theory of color vision, the theory became known as the Young–Helmholtz (or trichromatic) theory of color vision.

Helmholtz also explained auditory perception by applying the doctrine of specific nerve energies. He believed that tiny fibers on the basilar membrane each responded to a different frequency and that our auditory perception resulted from the combination of the various fibers that were being stimulated at any given time. This is called the resonance place theory of auditory perception. Helmholtz's work clearly indicated that there was a difference between what was present physically and what was experienced psychologically. The reason for this difference is that the sensory equipment of the body is not capable of responding to everything that is physically present. Although Helmholtz found substantial mismatches between what is present physically and what was experienced psychologically, he did postulate an active mind that took whatever sensory information was available and created the best possible interpretation of external reality. Helmholtz's work moved physiology closer to psychology and thus paved the way for experimental psychology.

In his explanation of perceptual phenomena, Helmholtz sided with the empiricists, but Hering sided with the nativists. In his explanation of color vision, Hering postulated red-green, yellow-blue, and black-white receptors on the retina that could either be torn down causing the color experiences of red, yellow, and white, respectively, or built up causing the experiences of green, blue, and black, respectively. Hering's theory could explain a number of color experiences that Helmholtz's theory could not.

Gall accepted faculty psychology but went several steps beyond other faculty psychologists such as Reid and Kant. He believed that the brain contained various faculties and that these faculties were housed in specific locations on the cortex. Furthermore, the strengths of these faculties varied from person to person. The study of the skull in order to determine the strengths of one's faculties was called phrenology, and Spurzheim, one of Gall's associates, expanded and popularized it. Phrenology became very popular in both Europe and the United States because it was promising as a way to objectively study human thought processes and because it appeared to provide useful information. Flourens experimentally tested many of Gall's assumptions, and although he found some evidence for localization of function in the lower parts of the brain, he concluded that the cortex itself acted as a whole. Because of Flourens's prestige as a scientist, the scientific community rejected phrenology. Using the clinical method, however, Broca did find evidence for a speech center on the cortex.

Furthermore, Fritsch and Hitzig found a motor area on the cortex, and Ferrier found a sensory area. Thus, there did seem to be localization of function on the cortex, but the functions were not the same as those the phrenologists had proposed, nor were they in the locations the phrenologists had proposed.

Weber was the first to attempt to quantify the relationship between a physical stimulus and the sensation it caused. He determined the two-point threshold for various parts of the body by observing the smallest distance between two points of stimulation that would be reported as two points. Working with weights, Weber determined how much heavier or lighter than a standard a weight must be before it was reported as being lighter or heavier than the standard. This was called a just noticeable difference (jnd). Weber found that for lifted weights, if a weight was 1/40 lighter than the standard, the subject would report that it was lighter; if it was 1/40 heavier than the standard, it would be reported as heavier. A difference in weight of less than 1/40 of the standard went undetected. For weights not lifted but simply placed in a subject's hand, the jnd was 1/30 of the standard weight. Weber's work provided the first statement of a systematic relationship between physical and mental events.

Fechner expanded Weber's work by showing that jnds were related to stimulation in a geometric way. That is, as the magnitude of the standard stimulus increased, so did the amounts that needed to be added to or subtracted from a comparison stimulus before those differences could be noticed. In his work on psychophysics, Fechner used three methods: the method of limits, by which one stimulus is held constant and another varied in order to determine which values of the variable stimulus are perceived as the same as the standard; the method of constant stimuli, by which pairs of stimuli are presented and the subject reports which stimulus appears to be greater than, less than, or equal to the standard stimulus; and the method of adjustment, by which the subject adjusts the magnitude of one stimulus until it appears to be the same as the standard stimulus. Now that it had been demonstrated that mental events could be studied experimentally, the ground was laid for the founding of psychology as an experimental science.

DISCUSSION QUESTIONS

1. What significance did the observation that astronomers differed in their reaction times have for the history of psychology?

2. What is the Bell–Magendie law? What was the significance of this law in the history of psychology?

3. Summarize Müller's doctrine of specific nerve energies.

4. Define vitalism. Was Müller a vitalist? Helmholtz?

5. How did Helmholtz apply the principle of conservation of energy to living organisms?

6. Describe the procedure Helmholtz used to measure the rate of nerve conduction.

7. How did Helmholtz explain perception? Include in your answer a discussion of unconscious inference.

8. Summarize the Young–Helmholtz theory of color vision.

9. Summarize the resonance place theory of auditory perception.

10. Discuss the importance of Helmholtz's work for the development of psychology as a science.

11. Explain in what way Helmholtz was a rationalist.

12. How did Hering explain space perception?

13. Summarize Hering's theory of color vision.

14. How did the version of faculty psychology offered by Gall and Spurzheim differ from other versions of faculty psychology, for example, the one offered by Kant?

15. What were the reasons for the widespread popularity of phrenology?

16. Describe Flourens's approach to brain research.

What conclusions did he reach concerning the functioning of the brain?

17. Describe Broca's approach to brain research. What conclusions did he reach concerning the functioning of the brain?

18. What approach to brain research did Fritsch and Hitzig take? Did their results support Gall or Flourens? Explain.

19. What significance did Weber's work have for the development of experimental psychology? In your answer, describe Weber's research techniques and his findings.

20. What philosophical problem did Fechner attempt to solve? What solution did he propose?

21. Why did Fechner feel it necessary to invent Dr. Mises?

22. What was Fechner's proposed solution to the mind–body problem? What evidence did he offer in support of his solution?

23. What did Fechner mean by a negative sensation?

24. Distinguish between the absolute threshold and the differential threshold.

25. Summarize Fechner's psychophysical methods.

26. What were Fechner's contributions to the development of psychology as a science?

SUGGESTIONS FOR FURTHER READING

Bakan, D. (1966). The influence of phrenology on American psychology. *Journal of the History of the Behavioral Sciences, 2*, 200–220.
This is a lucid account of phrenology's popularity in Europe and the United States. The intense opposition to introspection by both phrenology and positivistic philosophy is discussed. Phrenology's interest in individual differences did much to stimulate the U.S. schools of functionalism and behaviorism. Bakan argues that although evolutionary theory is viewed as the foundation of functionalism, it is actually phrenology that provided that foundation.

Marshall, M. E. (1969). Gustav Fechner, Dr. Mises, and the comparative anatomy of angels. *Journal of the History of the Behavioral Sciences, 5*, 39–58.
Marshall discusses how Fechner wrote under the pseudonym "Dr. Mises" to vent his deeply held mystical and spiritual beliefs while making a living as a materialistic scientist. The tension between Fechner's materialistic and spiritualistic views is shown in Fechner's *Comparative Anatomy of Angels* (1825), which

Marshall analyzes in depth. The point is made that lurking behind Fechner's satire was his sincere belief that the universe is alive and conscious.

Turner, R. S. (1977). Hermann von Helmholtz and the empiricist vision. *Journal of the History of the Behavioral Sciences, 13*, 48–58.
Turner gives an interesting account of how Helmholtz was influenced by both Kant and the British empiricists. According to Helmholtz's compromised position, it is an active mind that transforms the incomplete information furnished by the senses into a reasonable, functional view of reality.

Woodward, W. R. (1972). Fechner's panpsychism: A scientific solution to the mind–body problem. *Journal of the History of the Behavioral Sciences, 8*, 367–386.
This is a rather difficult attempt to explain how Fechner used analogy in his arguments concerning the mind, the soul, panpsychism, life after death, and the free will–determinism controversy. Woodward traces Fechner's position through a number of his more mystical writings and compares his position on

the mind–body relationship with several other philosophers. Woodward indicates that Fechner's position on the mind–body relationship was closest to that of Spinoza's double aspectism.

GLOSSARY

Absolute threshold The smallest amount of stimulation that can be detected by an organism.

Adequate stimulation Stimulation to which a sense modality is maximally sensitive.

Bell, Charles (1774–1842) Discovered, in modern times, the distinction between sensory and motor nerves.

Bell–Magendie law There are two types of nerves: sensory nerves carrying impulses from the sense receptors to the brain and motor nerves carrying impulses from the brain to the muscles and glands of the body.

Broca, Paul (1824–1880) Found evidence that part of the left side of the cortex was specialized for speech.

Broca's area The speech area on the left side of the cortex.

Clinical method The technique that Broca used. It involved first determining behavior disorders in a living patient and then, after the patient had died, locating the part of the brain responsible for the behavior disorder.

Differential threshold The amount that stimulation needs to change before a difference in that stimulation can be detected. Such a difference is called a just noticeable difference (jnd).

Doctrine of specific nerve energies Each sensory nerve, no matter how it is stimulated, releases an energy specific to that nerve.

Fechner, Gustav Theodor (1801–1887) Expanded Weber's law by showing that in order for just noticeable differences to vary arithmetically, the magnitude of a stimulus must increase geometrically.

Ferrier, David (1843–1928) Discovered the sensory area of the cortex.

Flourens, Pierre (1794–1867) Concluded that the cortical region of the brain acted as a whole and was not divided into a number of faculties, as the phrenologists had maintained.

Fritsch, Gustav (1838–1927) Along with Hitzig, discovered motor areas on the cortex by directly stimulating the exposed cortex of a dog.

Gall, Franz Joseph (1758–1828) Concluded that mental faculties were housed in specific locations on the cortex and that individuals differed in the degree they possessed various faculties. These individual differences could be measured by examining the bumps and depressions on peoples' heads.

Helmholtz, Hermann von (1821–1894) A monumental figure in the history of psychology who did pioneer work in the areas of nerve conduction, sensation, perception, color vision, and audition.

Hering, Ewald (1834–1918) Offered a nativistic explanation of space perception and a theory of color vision based on the existence of three color receptors, each capable of a catabolic process and an anabolic process.

Hering's theory of color vision could explain a number of color experiences that Helmholtz's theory could not.

Hitzig, Edward (1838–1907) Along with Fritsch, discovered motor areas on the cortex by directly stimulating the exposed cortex of a dog.

Just noticeable difference The smallest amount that must be added to or subtracted from a stimulus before it is judged to be greater or less than a standard stimulus.

Kinesthesis The sensations caused by muscular activity.

Magendie, François (1783–1855) Discovered, in modern times, the distinction between sensory and motor nerves.

Method of adjustment An observer adjusts a variable stimulus until it appears to be equal to a standard stimulus.

Method of constant stimuli A stimulus is presented at different intensities along with a standard stimulus, and the observer reports if it appears to be greater than, less than, or equal to the standard.

Method of limits A stimulus is presented at varying intensities along with a standard (constant) stimulus to determine the range of intensities judged to be the same as the standard.

Müller, Johannes (1801–1858) Expanded the Bell–Magendie law by indicating that each sense receptor, when stimulated, released an energy specific to that particular receptor. This finding is called the doctrine of specific nerve energies.

Negative sensation According to Fechner, a sensation that occurs below the absolute threshold and is therefore below the level of awareness.

Panpsychism The belief that everything in the universe experiences consciousness.

Perception According to Helmholtz, the mental experience arising when sensations are embellished by the recollection of past experiences.

Personal equation A mathematical formula used to correct for differences in reaction time among observers.

Phrenology The study of the bumps and indentations of the skull, to determine the strengths and weaknesses of a person's mental faculties.

Principle of conservation of energy The energy within a system is constant, therefore, it cannot be added to or subtracted from but only transformed from one form to another.

Psychophysics The systematic study of the relationship between physical and psychological events.

Reaction time The period of time between presentation of and response to a stimulus.

Resonance place theory of auditory perception The tiny fibers on the basilar membrane of the inner ear are stimulated by different frequencies of sound. The shorter the fiber, the higher the frequency to which it responds.

Sensation The rudimentary mental experience caused by an environmental stimulus.

Spurzheim, Johann Gasper (1776–1832) A colleague of Gall, who expanded and helped popularize phrenology.

Two-point threshold The smallest distance between two points of stimulation at which the two points are experienced as two points.

Unconscious inference According to Helmholtz, the process by which the remnants of past experience are added to sensations, thereby converting them into perceptions.

Vitalism The belief that life cannot be explained solely on the basis of physical and biological forces.

Weber, Ernst Heinrich (1795–1878) Using the two-point threshold and the just noticeable difference, was the first to demonstrate systematic relationships between stimulation and sensation.

Weber's law Just noticeable differences correspond to a constant proportion of a standard stimulus.

Young–Helmholtz theory of color vision Separate receptor systems on the retina are responsive to each of the three primary colors: red, green, and blue-violet. Also called the trichromatic theory.

CHAPTER 9

Voluntarism and Structuralism: Psychology's First Schools

Many, if not all, of the individuals we covered in the preceding chapter planted the seeds that grew into experimental psychology. The honor of formally founding experimental psychology, however, is given to Wilhelm Wundt. If one wanted to read about experimental psychology prior to Wundt, one could do so by consulting the work of such individuals as Helmholtz, Weber, and Fechner. It was Wundt, however, who took the diverse achievements of many others and synthesized them into a unified program of research that was organized around certain beliefs, procedures, and methods. As early as 1862, Wundt performed an experiment that led him to believe that a full-fledged discipline of experimental psychology was possible. Using the apparatus shown in Figure 9.1, Wundt showed that it took about 1/10 of a second to shift one's attention from the sound of the bell to the position of the pendulum or vice versa. Wundt believed that, with his "thought meter," he had demonstrated that humans could attend to only one thought at a time and that it takes about 1/10 of a second to shift from one thought to another.

From this early experiment, Wundt concluded that not only was experimental psychology feasible but also such a psychology must stress selective attention, or volition:

> Wundt suddenly realized that he was measuring the speed of a central mental process, that for the first time, he thought, a self-conscious experimental psychology was taking place. The time it takes to switch attention voluntarily from one stimulus to another had been measured—it varied around a tenth of a second.
>
> At this moment, the unfolding of Wundt's theoretical system began. For it was not the sim-

ple fact of the measured speed of selective attention that impressed him as much as it was the demonstration of a central voluntary control process. From then on, a prominent theme in Wundtian psychology was the distinction between voluntary and involuntary actions. (Blumenthal, 1980, pp. 121–122)

In the introduction to his book *Contributions to the Theory of Sense Perception* (1862a), Wundt enunciated the need for a new field of experimental psychology that would uncover the facts of human consciousness; in his epoch-making book *Principles of Physiological Psychology* (1874/1904), Wundt clearly stated that his goal was to create such a field. It should be noted that in Wundt's time the term *physiological* meant more or less the same as *experimental*. Thus, reading "physiological psychology" in the title of Wundt's book as "experimental psychology" is more accurate than is viewing it as emphasizing a search for the biological correlates of thought and behavior as is the case with much physiological psychology today.

By 1890 Wundt had reached his goal, and psychology's first school had been formed. A **school** can be defined as a group of individuals who share common assumptions, work on common problems, and use common methods. This definition of *school* is very similar to Kuhn's definition of *paradigm*. In both a school of thought and a paradigm, individuals work to explore the problems articulated by a particular viewpoint. That is, they engage in what Kuhn (1973) calls normal science.

By 1890 students the world over were traveling to Leipzig to be trained in experimental psychology at Wundt's laboratory. There now

FIGURE 9.1 Wundt's "thought meter." The clock was arranged so that the pendulum (B) swung along a calibrated scale (M). The apparatus was arranged so that a bell (g) was struck by the metal pole(s) at the extremes of the pendulum's swing (d, b). Wundt discovered that if he looked at the scale as the bell sounded, it was never in position d or b but some distance away from either. Thus, determining the exact position of the pendulum as the bell sounded was impossible. Readings were always about 1/10 of a second off. Wundt concluded that one could either attend to the position of the pendulum or to the bell, but not both at the same time (from Wundt, 1862b, p. 264).

appeared to be little doubt that a productive, scientific psychology was possible. A staggering amount of research poured out of Wundt's laboratory, and laboratories similar to his were being established throughout the world, including the United States.

VOLUNTARISM

Wundt's stated goal was to understand consciousness, and his pursuit of this goal was very much within the German rationalistic tradition:

Wundt said that Herbart was second only to Kant in terms of the debt owed for the development of his own thoughts. . . . But beyond Herbart and Kant, there looms the influence of Leibniz, in whose shadow Wundt clearly felt himself to be working from the beginning. . . . Numerous . . . references to Leibniz at key points in Wundt's more theoretical works make it clear that he felt a special affinity with this philosopher. (Danziger, 1980a, pp. 75–76)

Wundt opposed materialism about which he said, "Materialistic psychology . . . is contradicted by . . . the fact of consciousness itself, which cannot possibly be derived from any physical qualities of material molecules or atoms" (1912/1973, p. 155). He also opposed the empiricism of the British and French philosophers in which a person is viewed as the passive recipient of sensations that are then passively "organized" by the laws of association. What was lacking in empiricism, according to Wundt, were central volitional processes that act on the elements of thought giving them forms, qualities, or values not found either in external stimulation or in the elemental events themselves.

Wundt's goal was not only to understand consciousness as it is experienced but also to understand the mental laws that govern the dynamics of consciousness. Of utmost importance to Wundt was the concept of will as it was reflected in attention and volition. Wundt said that **will** was the central concept in terms of which all of the major problems in psychology must be understood (Danziger, 1980b, p. 108). Wundt believed that humans can decide what is attended to and thus is perceived clearly. Furthermore, he believed that much behavior and selective attention are undertaken for a purpose; that is, such activities are motivated. The name that Wundt gave to his approach to psychology was **voluntarism** because of its emphasis on will, choice, and purpose.

Voluntarism, then, was psychology's first school, not structuralism as is often claimed. Structuralism is the name of a rival school started by Edward Titchener, one of Wundt's students (discussed later). As we will see, the schools of voluntarism and structuralism have very little in common:

If one were now to take the trouble to compare the psychological system of Titchener with the bits and pieces of Wundt's own writings that are available in English translation, one would at least be able to establish that one was dealing with two quite distinct psychological systems, the one calling itself structuralism, and the other voluntarism. (Danziger, 1980a, pp. 73–74)

WILHELM MAXIMILIAN WUNDT

Wilhelm Maximilian Wundt (1832–1920) was born at Neckarau, a suburb of the important commercial center of Mannheim, on August 16 (the same year that Goethe died). When he was four years old, he and his family moved to the small town of Heidelsheim. He was the fourth, and last, child of a Lutheran minister. His father's side of the family included historians, theologians, economists, and two presidents of the University of Heidelberg. On his mother's side were physicians, scientists, and government officials. Despite the intellectually stimulating atmosphere in which Wundt grew up (or perhaps because of it), he remained a shy, reserved person who was fearful of new situations. Wundt's only sibling to survive infancy was a brother who was eight years his elder and who went away to school. Wundt's only friend his own age was a retarded boy who could barely speak. When Wundt was about eight years old, his education was turned over to a young vicar who worked in his father's church. The vicar was Wundt's closest friend until Wundt entered high school. Wundt's first year in high school was a disaster: He made no friends, daydreamed incessantly, was physically punished by his teachers, and finally failed. At this time, one of his teachers suggested that a reasonable aspiration for Wundt would be a career in the postal service (Diamond, 1980, pp. 12–13). The following year he started high school over, this time in the city of Heidelberg, where his brother and a cousin were students. Although he was not an outstanding student, he did much better there.

After graduation from high school, Wundt enrolled in the premedical program at the Uni-

Wilhelm Maximilian Wundt

versity of Tübingen. He stayed for a year and then transferred to the University of Heidelberg, where he became one of the top medical students in his class, graduated summa cum laude, and placed first in the state medical board examination. After receiving his medical degree in 1855, at the age of 24, he went to Berlin and studied with Johannes Müller, who so influenced Wundt that he decided to pursue a career in experimental physiology instead of medicine. After a year of working and studying at Müller's institute, Wundt returned to the University of Heidelberg, where he became Helmholtz's laboratory assistant. While Wundt was working for Helmholtz, he gave his first course in psychology as a natural science, and he wrote his first book, *Contributions Toward a Theory of Sense Perception* (1862a). In this book, Wundt formed the plan for psychology that he was to follow for the rest of his life. The following year he published *Lectures on Human and Animal Psychology* (1863), which clearly indicated the dual interests in psychology that Wundt entertained throughout his career. Wundt believed that experimental psychology could be used in an effort to understand immediate consciousness (discussed later) but that it was useless in attempting to understand the higher mental processes and their products. For the study of the latter, only naturalistic observation or historical analysis could be used. Both of these concerns were clearly present in *Lectures*, the first part of which included a history of psychology, a review of research on sensation, the perception of space and time, and research related to the personal equation. The second part of *Lectures* included discussions of aesthetic and religious feelings, moral judgments, the development of societies, comparative religion, language, and the will. In fact, most of the topics that later appeared in *Völkerpsychologie* (1900–1920), the monumental 10-volume work that Wundt worked on for the last 20 years of his life, first appeared in *Lectures* in 1863. Wundt remained a teacher at Heidelberg until 1874, when he accepted a professorship in inductive philosophy at the University of Zürich in Switzerland. The following year he was offered an appointment at the University of Leipzig, where he was to teach scientific philosophy. Wundt accepted the appointment and remained at Leipzig for 45 years.

Wundt wanted to teach experimental psychology at Leipzig in 1875, but the university could not provide space for his equipment; he ended up teaching courses in anthropology, logic, and language instead. He obtained the space he needed the following year and began teaching experimental psychology. By 1879 his laboratory was in full production, and he was supervising the research of several students. The year 1879 is usually given as the date of the founding of the first laboratory dedicated exclusively to psychological research. Wundt called his laboratory the Institute for Experimental Psychology. At first, the university administration was not supportive of Wundt's institute, and it was not listed in the university catalog until 1883. The institute became extremely popular, however, and Wundt's lecture classes became the most popular at the university, sometimes exceeding 250 students (Bringmann, Bringmann & Ungerer, 1980, p. 147). In 1881 Wundt began the journal *Philosophical Studies*, the first journal devoted to experimental psychology. He wanted to call his journal *Psychological Studies*, but a journal with that title existed and it dealt with spiritualism and parapsychological phenomena. Several years later, Wundt did change the name of his journal to the more appropriate *Psychological Studies*.

In response to the increasing popularity of Wundt's institute, it was physically enlarged several times. In 1882 he moved from his small one-room laboratory to one with nine rooms, and in 1897 he was given an entire building, which he helped design. By now Wundt dominated experimental psychology, something he continued to do for three decades.

Wundt was one of the most productive individuals in the history of psychology. Boring estimated that from 1853–1920, Wundt wrote a total of 53,735 pages:

> If there are 24,836 days in sixty-eight years, then Wundt wrote or revised at the average rate of 2.2 pages a day from 1853 to 1920, which comes to about one word every two minutes, day and night, for the entire sixty-eight years. (1957, p. 345)

Obviously, Wundt's primary interest was his work:

> He never was much excited about anything other than his work. Even his wife and family receive no more than one paragraph in his entire autobiography. His dedication went so far that he analyzed his psychological experiences when he was very seriously ill and near death; at one point in his life he was rather intrigued with the idea of experiencing the process of dying. (Michael Wertheimer, 1987, p. 62)

Appropriately, the last thing Wundt worked on was his autobiography, which he finished a few days before he died at the age of 88.

Psychology's Goals

Wundt disagreed with individuals such as Galileo, Comte, and Kant who claimed that psychology could never be a science and with Herbart who said that psychology could be a mathematical science but not an experimental one. He believed strongly that psychology had, in fact, become an experimental science. As we have seen, however, in his comprehensive view of psychology, experimentation played only a limited role. He believed that experimentation could be used to study the basic processes of the mind but could not be used to study the higher mental processes. For the latter, only various forms of naturalistic observation could be used. We will see how Wundt proposed to study the higher mental thought processes when we discuss his *Völkerpsychologie.* Still, the role of experimental psychology was vital to Wundt. Learning about the simpler conscious processes may shed some light on those that are more complex: "Let us remember the rule, valid for psychology as well as for any other science, that we cannot understand the complex phenomena, before we have become familiar with the simple ones which presuppose the former" (Wundt, 1912/1973, p. 151). To summarize, according to Wundt, psychology's goal was to understand both simple and complex conscious phenomena. For the former, experimentation could be used; for the latter, it could not.

Mediate and immediate experience. Wundt believed that all sciences were based on experience and that scientific psychology was no different. But the *type* of experience psychology would use would be different. Whereas other sciences were based on **mediate experience**, psychology was to be based on **immediate experience**. The data the physicist uses, for example, are provided by various measuring devices such as spectrometers (to measure wavelengths of light) or sound spectrographs (to measure the frequencies and intensities of sound waves). The physicist records the data these devices provide, then uses the data to analyze the characteristics of the physical world. Thus, the experience of the natural scientist is mediated by recording devices and is not direct. For Wundt, the subject matter of psychology was to be human consciousness *as it occurred.* Wundt was not interested in the nature of the physical world but wanted to understand the psychological processes by which we experience the physical world.

Once the mental elements were isolated, the laws governing their combination into more complex experiences could be determined. Thus, Wundt set two major goals for his experimental psychology:

1. To discover the basic **elements of thought**
2. To discover the laws by which mental elements combine into more complex mental experiences

Wundt's Use of Introspection

To study the basic mental processes involved in immediate experience, Wundt used a variety of methods including **introspection**, or self-observation. Wundt's use of introspection bore little resemblance, however, to how the technique was used by St. Augustine to explore the mind to find the essence of God or by Descartes to find certain truth. Wundt's use of introspection was also different from how the empiricists and sensationalists used it to study ideas and association. Wundt used introspection more or less as the physiologists, such as Helmholtz, and the psychophysicists had used it—that is, as a technique to determine whether a person is experiencing a specific sensation or not. In fact, Wundt replicated much of the work on audition and vision that the physiologists had done and much of the work on absolute and differential thresholds that the psychophysicists had done. In both cases, he needed to use introspection in the limited way just described. In fact, Wundt had little patience with his colleagues who used introspection in the more philosophical and less objective way. Leahey has suggested that the term *introspection* should not be used to describe Wundt's methodology because of the traditional meaning of that term and that the term *self-observation* would be more accurate:

> For Wundt, physiological psychology was the study of individual human consciousness by means of self-observation. I avoid the more widely used term introspection, for . . . Wundt did not ask his subjects to introspect in the commonly used Cartesian sense, in which introspection is an intensely analytical reflection on a remembered event experienced without experimental control. . . . Self-observation as used by Wundt was a simple report of an experience not too different from procedures used by modern, thoroughly "objective," anti-introspective cognitive psychologists. (1981, p. 274)

Again, Wundt's use of introspection was very much like that of the experimental physiologists or the psychophysicists, in that subjects were almost always reporting their reaction to a stimulus presented to them:

> As [Wundt] describes it, the psychological experiment is plainly patterned after the physiological experiment: It is a procedure in which the process to be studied is kept very close to a controllable stimulus and very close to an objective response, and in which introspection is an intensive, short-range, carefully prepared act of observation. (Heidbreder, 1933, p. 93)

In the restrictive way that Wundt used it, introspection (self-observation) could be used to study immediate experience, but under no circumstances could it be used to study the higher mental processes. Wundt believed that the deeper processes that make conscious experience what it is are forever beyond the reach of introspection or any other experimental technique.

Elements of Thought

According to Wundt, there were two basic types of mental experience: sensations and feelings. A **sensation** occurs whenever a sense organ is stimulated and the resulting impulse reaches the brain. Sensations can be described in terms of *modality* (visual, auditory, taste, etc.) and *intensity* (e.g., how loud an auditory stimulus is). Within a modality, a sensation can be further analyzed into its *qualities*. For example, a visual sensation can be described in terms of hue (color) and saturation ("richness" of color). An auditory sensation can be described in terms of pitch and timbre ("fullness" of tone). A taste sensation can be described in terms of its degree of saltiness, sourness, bitterness, or sweetness.

All sensations are accompanied by **feelings**. Wundt reached this conclusion while listening to the beat of a metronome. He noted that some rates of beating were more pleasant than others. From his own introspections, he formulated his **tridimensional theory of feeling**, according to which any feelings can be described in terms of the degree to which they possess three attributes: pleasantness-unpleasantness, excitement-calm, and strain-relaxation.

Perception, Apperception, and Creative Synthesis

Often a discussion of Wundt's system stops with his concern with mental elements and his use of introspection as the means of isolating them. Such a discussion omits some of Wundt's most important ideas. Indeed, sensations and feelings are the elements of consciousness, but in everyday life they are rarely, if ever, experienced in isolation. Most often, many elements are experienced simultaneously, and then **perception** occurs. According to Wundt, perception is a passive process governed by the physical stimulation present, the anatomical makeup of the individual, and the individual's past experiences. These three influences interact and determine an individual's perceptual field at any given time. The part of the perceptual field that the individual attends to is *apperceived* (Wundt borrowed the term **apperception** from Herbart). Attention and apperception go hand in hand—what is attended to is apperceived. Unlike perception, which is passive and automatic, apperception is active and voluntary. In other words, apperception is under the control of the individual. It was primarily because Wundt believed so strongly that individuals could direct their attention by exercising their will that he referred to his approach to psychology as voluntarism. Wundt even criticized John Stuart Mill's concept of "mental chemistry," according to which two or more ideas could synthesize giving rise to an idea unlike any of those that comprise it. Wundt rejected this process because it was passive, just as the blending of chemical elements is passive. For Wundt, the vital difference between his position and that of the empiricists was his emphasis on the active role of attention. When elements are attended to, they can be arranged and rearranged according to the will of the individual, and thus arrangements never actually experienced before can result. Wundt called this phenomenon **creative synthesis** and thought that it was involved in all acts of apperception. As we will see when we discuss psychological versus physical causation, it was, according to Wundt, the phenomenon of creative synthesis that made psychology a discipline that was qualitatively different from the physical sciences.

Contrary to the popular view that Wundt busied himself searching for the cognitive and emotional elements of a static mind, he viewed the mind as active, creative, dynamic, and volitional. In fact, he believed that the apperceptive process was vital for normal mental functioning, and he speculated that schizophrenia could be the result of a breakdown of the attentional processes. If a person lost the ability to apperceive, his or her thoughts would be disorganized and would appear meaningless, as in the case of schizophrenia. The theory that schizophrenia could be understood as a breakdown of the attentional processes was expanded by Wundt's student and friend Emil Kraepelin (1856–1926). According to Kraepelin, a defect in the "central control process" can result in reduced ability to pay attention, an erratic ability to pay attention, or in extremes in focusing one's attention—any one of which would result in severe mental illness.

As we have seen, Wundt was interested in sensations; and in explaining how sensations combined into perceptions, he remained close to traditional associationism. With apperception, however, he emphasized attention, thinking, and creative synthesis. All these processes are much more closely aligned with the rationalist tradition than with the empiricist tradition.

Mental Chronometry

In his book *Principles of Physiological Psychology* (1874/1904), Wundt expressed his belief that reaction time could supplement introspection (self-observation) as a technique for studying the elemental contents and activities of the mind. We saw in chapter 8 that Friedrich Bessel performed the first reaction-time experiment in order to collect data that could be used to correct for individual differences in reaction times among those observing and reporting astronomical events. Helmholtz used reaction time to determine the rate of nerve conduction, but then abandoned it because he found it to be an unreliable measure.

Franciscus Cornelius Donders. About 15 years after Helmholtz gave up the technique, **Franciscus Cornelius Donders** (1818–1889), a famous Dutch physiologist, began an ingenious series of experiments involving reaction time. First, Donders measured simple reaction time by noting how long it took a subject to respond to a predetermined stimulus (e.g., a light) with a predetermined response (e.g., pressing a button). Next, Donders reasoned that by making the situation more complicated he could measure the time required to perform various mental acts.

In one experiment, for example, Donders presented several different stimuli to his subjects but instructed them to respond to only one, which he designated ahead of time. This required the subjects to discriminate among the stimuli before responding. The arrangement can be diagrammed as follows:

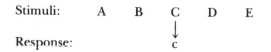

Stimuli: A   B   C   D   E

Response: c

Franciscus Cornelius Donders

The time it took to perform the mental act of *discrimination* was determined by subtracting simple reaction time from the reaction time that involved discrimination. Donders then made the situation more complicated by presenting several different stimuli and instructing his subjects to respond to each of them differently. This experimental arrangement can be diagrammed as follows:

Stimuli:	A	B	C	D	E
	↓	↓	↓	↓	↓
Response:	a	b	c	d	e

Donders called reactions under these circumstances *choice reaction time*, and the time required to make a choice was determined by subtracting both simple and discrimination reaction times from choice reaction time.

Wundt's use of Donders's methods. Wundt enthusiastically seized upon Donders's methods, believing that they could provide a **mental chro-** **nometry**, that is, an accurate cataloging of the time it took to perform various mental acts. Almost 20 percent of the early work done in Wundt's laboratory involved repeating or expanding on Donders's research on reaction time. Wundt believed strongly that such research provided another way (along with introspection) of doing what so many had thought to be impossible—experimentally investigating the mind. Danziger describes the importance of reaction-time studies in the early years of Wundt's laboratory:

> The reaction time studies conducted during the first few years of Wundt's laboratory constitute the first historical example of a coherent research program, explicitly directed toward psychological issues and involving a number of interlocking studies. . . . It was Wundt's theory of volition that provided the conceptual cement that transformed what would otherwise have been a collection of isolated studies into a coherent program that demonstrated the practical possibility of systematic psychological research. (1980b, p. 106)

Wundt's student Ludwig Lange made one important observation concerning reaction time. Lange found that reaction time varied depending on whether a subject concentrated on the stimulus or on the response. He found that reaction time was about 1/10 of a second slower if attention was focused on the stimulus. Wundt explained the difference by dividing the processes involved in reaction time into perception, apperception, and will. Those subjects who focused on the response to be made simply perceived a stimulus and then reacted. Such subjects responded quickly but made numerous mistakes. Those subjects who concentrated on the stimulus to which they were to respond first perceived the stimulus and then apperceived it. That is, subjects first simply detected a stimulus (perception) and then determined whether it was the one to which they had been instructed to respond in a certain way. Wundt concluded that apperception took about 1/10 of a second because that was about how much slower subjects concentrating on the stimulus responded. It is interesting that this is the same amount of time that Wundt found it took to switch one's focus of attention from one object to another using his "thought meter" in 1862.

Wundt repeated and expanded many of Donders's experiments and was originally optimistic about being able to measure precisely the time required to perform various mental operations. However, he eventually abandoned his reaction-time studies. One reason was that he, like Helmholtz, found that reaction times varied too much from study to study, from subject to subject, and often for the same subject at different times. It was also found that reaction time varied with the sense modality stimulated, the intensity of the stimulus, the number of items to be discriminated and the degree of difference among them, how much practice a subject received, and several other variables. The situation was much too complicated to obtain measurable psychological "constants."

Psychological Versus Physical Causation

Wundt believed that psychological and physical causality were "polar opposites" because physical events could be predicted on the basis of antecedent conditions and psychological events could not. It is the will (purposive behavior) that makes psychological causation qualitatively different from physical causation:

> Whenever a voluntarist philosophy appears, its immediate corollaries are purposivism and motivation. In Wundtian thought, these show up in the view that psychological processes are understandable only in terms of their goal orientations or consequences, which was not the case for the events of physics. . . . Thus, Wundt came to the fateful separation of physical and psychological causality—a trend in his thinking that was raised to the level of a "principle" in the early 1890s. It was this principle that kept Wundt forever at war with the positivist movement. . . . "Physical causality," in Wundt's accounts, is classical mechanics. In "psychological causality," as Wundt claimed, new terms are introduced that are not found in physics, these being *purpose, value,* and *anticipations of the future.* The central mechanism of psychological

causality was, of course, apperception, which in modern terms translates roughly as "selective attention." For Wundt, however, it was more than merely selective; it was more fundamentally constructive and creative. And with that capacity in mind, Wundt derived his first principle for the description of elemental psychological processes, the principle of "creative synthesis." It is the statement that all experiences are constructed internally under the control of the central volitional process. (Blumenthal, 1980, p. 123)

Blumenthal gives further examples:

> [Wundt argued that the] physical sciences would . . . describe the act of greeting a friend, eating an apple, or writing a poem in terms of the laws of mechanics or in terms of physiology. And no matter how fine-grained and complicated we make such descriptions, they are not useful as descriptions of psychological events. Those events need be described in terms of intentions and goals, according to Wundt, because the actions, or physical forces, for a given psychological event may take an infinite variety of physical forms. In one notable example, he argued that human language cannot be described adequately in terms of its physical shape or of the segmentation of utterances, but rather must be described as well in terms of the rules and intentions underlying speech. For the ways of expressing a thought in language are infinitely variable, and language is governed by creative rules rather than fixed laws (1975, p. 1083)

Wundt summarized his position in his **principle of creative resultants** about which he said, "In all psychical combinations the product is not a mere sum of the separate elements that compose such combinations, but . . . it represents a new combination" (1912/1973, p. 164).

Another factor that makes the prediction of psychological events impossible is what Wundt called the **principle of the heterogony of ends**. According to this principle, a goal-directed activity seldom attains its goal and nothing else. Almost always something unexpected happens that, in turn, changes one's entire motivational pattern:

> An action arising from a given motive produces not only the ends latent in the motive, but also other, not directly purposed, influences. When

these latter enter into consciousness and stir up feelings and impulses, they themselves become new motives, which either make the original act of volition more complicated, or they change it or substitute some other act for it. (Wundt, 1912/1973, pp. 168–169)

Wundt also employed the **principle of contrasts** to explain the complexity of conscious experience. He maintained that opposite experiences intensify one another. For example, after eating something sour, something sweet tastes even sweeter, and after a painful experience, pleasure is more pleasurable (Blumenthal, 1980). The related principle, the **principle toward the development of opposites**, states that after a prolonged experience of one type, there is an increased tendency to seek the opposite type of experience. This latter principle not only applies to the life of an individual but also to human history in general (Blumenthal, 1980). For example, a prolonged period during which rationalism is emphasized would tend to be followed by a period during which the human emotions would be emphasized, such as in romanticism.

Volitional acts are creative but not free. Wundt was a determinist. That is, he did not believe in free will. Behind all volitional acts were mental laws that acted on the contents of consciousness. These laws were unconscious and complex and were not knowable through either introspection or other forms of experimentation; but laws they are, and their products are lawful. Wundt gave an example:

We see this creative and yet absolutely lawful nature of psychical phenomena best of all in apperceptive combinations, and for a long time it has been silently recognised in their case. Every one knows that the result of a chain of reasoning, made up of a row of single acts of thought, may be a product of those single thought-acts, which throws much light on some subject and which was before unknown to us, and yet which conclusively comes from those premises, if we analyze retrogressively its development. (1912/1973, pp. 165–166)

The laws of mental activity can only be deduced after the fact and in that sense the psychologist is like a historian:

Future resultants can never be determined in advance; but . . . on the other hand it is possible, starting with the given resultants, to achieve, under favourable conditions, an exact deduction into the components. The psychologist, like the psychological historian, is a prophet with his eyes turned towards the past. He ought not only to be able to tell what has happened, but also what necessarily must have happened, according to the position of events. (Wundt, 1912/1973, p. 167)

The historical approach must be used to investigate the higher mental processes, and it is that approach that Wundt used in his *Völkerpsychologie*, to which we turn next.

Völkerpsychologie

Although Wundt went to great lengths to found experimental psychology as a separate branch of science and spent years performing and analyzing experiments, he believed that the higher mental processes, which are reflected in human culture, could only be studied through historical analysis and naturalistic observation. According to Wundt, the nature of the higher mental processes could be deduced from the study of such cultural products as religion, social customs, myths, history, language, morals, art, and the law. Wundt studied these topics for the last 20 years of his life, his research culminating in his 10-volume *Völkerpsychologie* ("group" or "cultural" psychology). In this work, Wundt emphasized the study of language, and his long-overlooked conclusions have a strikingly modern ring to them.

According to Wundt, verbal communication begins with a **general impression**, or unified idea, which one wishes to convey. The speaker apperceives this general impression and then chooses words and sentences to express it. The linguistic structures and words the speaker chooses for expressing the general impression may or may not do so accurately; and upon hearing his or her own words, the speaker may say, no, that's not what I had in mind, and make another attempt at expression. Once the speaker has chosen sentences appropriate for expressing the general idea, the next step is that the listener must *apperceive* the speaker's words. That is, the listener must understand the general impression that the speaker is attempting to convey. If this occurs, the listener can replicate the speaker's general impression by using any number of different words or sentence structures. Verbal communication, then, is a three-stage process:

1. The speaker must apperceive his or her own general impression.

2. The speaker chooses words and sentence structures to express the general impression.

3. The listener, after hearing the words and sentences, must apperceive the speaker's general impression.

As evidence for this process, Wundt points out that we often retain the *meaning* of a person's words long after we have forgotten the specific words the person used to convey that meaning.

The Historical Misunderstanding of Wundt

Bringmann and Tweney observe, "Our modern conceptions of psychology—its problems, its methods, its relation to other sciences, and its limits—all derive in large part from [Wundt's] inquiries" (1980, p. 5). And yet Blumenthal comments, "To put it simply, the few current Wundt-scholars (and some do exist) are in fair agreement that Wundt as portrayed today in many texts and courses is largely fictional and often bears little resemblance to the actual historical figure" (1975, p. 1081).

Earlier in this chapter, we discussed a major source of the distortion of Wundt's ideas: Wundt's psychology reflected the rationalist tradition, and U.S. psychology embraced the empiricistic-positivistic tradition. The distortion of Wundt's ideas started early: "For all the American students who went abroad to attend

Wundt's lectures, very little of Wundt's psychological system survived the return passage" (Blumenthal, 1980, p. 130). Edward Titchener (whom we consider next) was an Englishman who came to the United States and came to be viewed as the U.S. representative of Wundtian ideas. That was a mistake because

> While the stimulus of some of Wundt's ideas is detectable in Titchener's psychology, an enormous cultural and intellectual gulf separated the general approach of these two psychologists. . . . It seems that [Titchener] genuinely could not think in terms of categories that differed fundamentally from the English positivist tradition. (Danziger, 1980a, pp. 84–85)

By misrepresenting Wundt, psychology has overlooked a rich source of ideas. Fortunately, Wundt's true psychology is in the process of being rediscovered, and one reason for this may be psychology's return to an interest in cognition:

> Strange as it may seem, Wundt may be more easily understood today than he could have been just a few years ago. This is because of the current milieu of modern cognitive psychology and of the recent research on human information processing. (Blumenthal, 1975, p. 1087)

EDWARD BRADFORD TITCHENER

Born in Chichester, England, **Edward Bradford Titchener** (1867–1927) attended Malvern College, a prestigious secondary school. He then went to Oxford from 1885 to 1890, and his academic record was outstanding. While at Oxford, he developed an interest in experimental psychology and translated the third edition of Wundt's *Principles of Physiological Psychology* into English. Following graduation from Oxford, Titchener went to Leipzig and studied for two years with Wundt.

During his first year at Leipzig, Titchener struck up a friendship with Frank Angell, a fellow student who was to play an important role in bringing Titchener to the United States. After completing his studies with Wundt, Angell went

Edward Bradford Titchener

that preceded his version of psychology was not psychology at all: "To Titchener, the American psychologies prior to the 1880s—and much since then—were little more than watered-down Cartesianisms, codified phrenologies, or worst of all, thinly disguised theology" (Evans, 1984, p. 18). When the school of behaviorism was introduced by John B. Watson in the early 1900s (see chapter 12), Titchener claimed that it was a technology of behavior but not part of psychology (Titchener, 1914). Titchener was also opposed to seeking psychological information for its applied value; science seeks pure knowledge, and psychology (his psychology) was a science: "Science deals, not with values, but with facts. There is no good or bad, sick or well, useful or useless, in science" (Titchener, 1915, p. 1). Evans describes how Titchener ruled his domain:

> It is tempting to use a military analogy to represent Titchener and his relation to his school. Titchener served much as a commander-in-chief and tactician. It was he who held the total battleplan against "the enemy" and it was he who set the direction and timing of attack. The Cornell faculty served as field generals in charge of implementing directives, sending reports to headquarters and seeing to the training and activities of the graduate students who were, of course, the troops. With doctoral theses and minor studies as their weapons, these troops would assault one adversary and then another. Titchener's notes and articles were used to tie the theaters of conflict together, to demonstrate the significance of a given battle and to present the manifesto for a new assault. (1972, pp. 168–169)

Titchener was a member of the American Psychological Association (APA) but never attended a meeting—even when the national meeting was held in Ithaca. Instead, in 1904 he founded his own organization called "The Experimentalists," which, until his death in 1927, he ran according to his own ideas of what psychology should be. Titchener's wife carefully screened all his callers, and although he became a legend at Cornell, a number of his colleagues never met him. As long as Titchener was healthy, structuralism flourished, but when he

to Cornell University in Ithaca, New York, to establish a psychological laboratory. After only one year, however, Angell decided to accept a position at Stanford University. When Titchener earned his doctorate in 1892, he was offered the job as Angell's replacement. Titchener was also offered a job at Oxford, but there he would have no laboratory facilities. In 1892 he accepted the offer from Cornell and soon developed the largest doctoral program in psychology in the United States. When Titchener arrived at Cornell, he was 25 years old, and he remained there for the rest of his life.

Titchener ruled his domain with an iron fist. He determined what the research projects would be and which students would work on them. For him, psychology was experimental psychology (as he defined it); and everything died of a brain tumor at the age of 60, structuralism essentially died with him.

Psychology's Goals

Titchener agreed with Wundt that psychology should study immediate experience—that is, consciousness. He defined *consciousness* as the sum total of mental experience at any given moment and *mind* as the accumulated experiences of a lifetime. Titchener set as goals for psychology the determination of the what, how, and why of mental life. The *what* was to be learned through careful introspection. The goal here was a cataloging of the basic mental elements that accounted for all conscious experience. The *how* was to be an answer to the question of how the elements combine, and the *why* was to involve a search for the neurological correlates of mental events.

Unlike Wundt who sought to *explain* conscious experience in terms of unobservable cognitive processes, Titchener sought only to *describe* mental experience. Titchener, accepting the positivism of Ernst Mach, believed that unobservable events had no place in science. It is interesting to note that Titchener took the same position toward the use of theory as B. F. Skinner (see chapter 13) was to take many years later. For both, theorizing meant entering the world of metaphysical speculation; and for both, science meant carefully describing what could be observed. However, whereas Skinner focused on observable behavior, Titchener focused on observable (via introspection) conscious events. It was the structure of the mind that Titchener wanted to describe, and thus he named his version of psychology **structuralism** (Titchener, 1899).

What Titchener sought was a type of periodic table for mental elements, such as chemists had developed for the physical elements. Once the basic elements were isolated, the laws governing their combination into more complex experiences could be determined. Finally, the neurophysiological events that give rise to mental phenomena could be determined. Thus, Titchener

set three major goals for his experimental psychology:

1. To discover the basic elements of thought

2. To discover the laws by which mental elements combine into more complex mental experiences

3. To determine the neurophysiological correlates of mental experience

In 1899 Titchener defined the goal of structuralism as describing the *is* of mental life. He was willing to leave the *is for* for others to ponder.

Titchener's Use of Introspection

Titchener's use of introspection was more complicated than Wundt's. Typically, Wundt's subjects would simply report whether an experience was triggered by an external object or event. Titchener's subjects, however, had to search for the elemental ingredients of their experiences. Their job was to describe the basic, raw, elemental experiences from which complex cognitive experience was built. Titchener's subjects therefore had to be carefully trained to avoid reporting the *meaning* of a stimulus. The worst thing introspectionists could do would be to name the object of their introspective analysis. If the subjects (more accurately, observers) were shown an apple, for example, the task would be to describe hues and spatial characteristics. Calling the object an apple would be committing what Titchener called the **stimulus error**. In this case, Titchener wanted his subjects to report sensations, not perceptions. Titchener said, "Introspecting through the glass of meaning . . . is the besetting sin of the descriptive psychologist" (1899, p. 291).

Toward the end of his career, Titchener became more liberal in his use of introspection (Evans, 1984). He found that allowing untrained introspectionists to simply describe their phenomenological experience could be an important source of information. That is, taking a report of everyday experience at face value from a nonscientific "observer" could lead to important scientific discoveries. Unfortunately, Titchener died before he and his students could explore this possibility.

Mental Elements

From his introspective studies, Titchener concluded that the elemental processes of consciousness consist of *sensations* (elements of perceptions), *images* (elements of ideas), and *affections* (elements of emotions). According to Titchener, an element could only be known by listing its attributes. The attributes of sensations and images (remnants of sensations) were quality, intensity, duration, clearness, and extensity. Extensity was the impression that a sensation or image was more or less spread out in space. Affections could have the attributes of quality, intensity, and duration but neither clearness nor extensity.

In practice, Titchener and his students concentrated most on the study of sensations, then on affections, and least of all on images. Titchener concluded that there are over 40,000 identifiable sensations, most of which are related to the sense of vision (about 30,000), with audition next (about 12,000), and then all the other senses (about 20) (1896). In his later years, Titchener changed the object of his introspective analysis from the elements themselves to their attributes (e.g., quality, intensity, and clearness) because it is only through its attributes that an element could be known (Evans, 1972).

Titchener did not accept Wundt's tridimensional theory of feeling. Titchener argued that feelings occurred along only one dimension, not three, as Wundt had maintained. According to Titchener, feelings (affections) can be described only in terms of Wundt's pleasantness-unpleasantness dimension. He argued that the other two dimensions Wundt had suggested (tension-relaxation and excitement-calm) were really combinations of sensations and true feelings (pleasantness-unpleasantness). The *what* of psychology, then, included the sensations and images that were described in terms of quality, intensity, duration, clearness, and extensity, as well as the feelings that varied in terms of pleasantness.

Law of Combination

After Titchener had isolated the elements of thought, the next step was to determine *how* they combined to form more complex mental processes. In explaining how elements of thought combined, Titchener rejected Wundt's notions of apperception and creative synthesis in favor of traditional associationism. Titchener made the law of contiguity his basic law of association:

> Let us try . . . to get a descriptive formula for the facts which the doctrine of association aims to explain. We then find this: that, whenever a sensory or imaginal process occurs in consciousness, there are likely to appear with it (of course, in imaginal terms) all those sensory and imaginal processes which occurred together with it in any earlier conscious present. . . . Now the law of contiguity can, with a little forcing, be translated into our own general law of association. (1910, pp. 378–379)

What about attention, the process that was so important to Wundt? For Titchener, attention was simply an attribute of a sensation (clearness). We do not make sensations clear by attending to them as Wundt had maintained. Rather, we say we have attended to them because they were clearer than other sensations in our consciousness. For Titchener, there was no underlying process of apperception that causes clarity; it is just that some sensations are more vivid and clear than others, and it is those that we *say* we attend to. The vague feelings of concentration and effort that accompany "attention" are nothing more than the muscle contractions that accompany vivid sensations.

For the *how* of mental processes then, Titchener accepted traditional associationism, thus aligning himself with the British empiricists.

Neurological Correlates of Mental Events

Whereas Wundt tended toward double aspectism in his beliefs about the mind–body relationship, Titchener accepted epiphenomenalism. That is, he believed that neural processes always precede mental processes. According to Titchener, the closest we can come to understanding the why of mental processes is to understand the neural processes that precede them. Titchener stated his position as follows:

> Physical science . . . explains by assigning a cause; mental science explains by reference to those nervous processes which correspond with the mental processes that are under observation. We may bring these two modes of explanation together, if we define explanation itself as the statement of the proximate circumstances or conditions under which the described phenomenon occurs. Dew is formed under the conditions of a difference of temperature between the air and the ground; ideas are formed under the condition of certain processes in the nervous system. Fundamentally, the object and the manner of explanation, in the two cases, are one and the same. (1910, p. 41)

Ultimately then, neurophysiological processes are the *why* of mental life, if *why* is understood to mean a description of the circumstances under which mental processes occur.

Context Theory of Meaning

What do we mean by the word *meaning*? Titchener's answer again involved associationism. Sensations are never isolated. In accordance with the law of contiguity, every sensation tends to elicit images of sensations that were previously experienced along with the sensation. A vivid sensation or group of sensations forms a *core*, and the elicited images form a *context* that gives the core meaning. A rattle may elicit images of the baby who used it, thus giving the rattle meaning to the observer. A picture of a loved one tends to elicit a wide variety of images related to the loved one's words and activities, thus giving the picture meaning. Even with such

a rationalist concept as meaning, Titchener's **context theory of meaning** maintains his empiricist and associationist philosophy.

Wundt's voluntarism and Titchener's structuralism had little in common. Wundt's brand of psychology was closer to the thought of the rationalists, such as Leibniz, Herbart, Spinoza, Hegel, and Kant, rather than to the thought of the empiricists, such as Hobbes, Locke, Berkeley, and Hume. For Titchener, the reverse was true. Blumenthal (1970, 1975, 1979), who has been largely responsible for clarifying Wundt's true position, speculates that Wundt's early use of the word *element* was responsible for his being misinterpreted by so many:

> Today I cannot help but wonder whether Wundt had any notion of what might happen the day he chose the word "Elemente" as part of a chapter title. Later generations seized upon the word with such passion that they were eventually led to transform Wundt into something nearly opposite to the original. (1979, p. 549)

OTHER EARLY APPROACHES TO PSYCHOLOGY

Although Wundt's voluntarism and Titchener's structuralism dominated psychology for many years, they were not without their critics. The assumptions of both schools were effectively challenged, and these challenges influenced the development of other schools of psychology.

Franz Clemens Brentano

Franz Clemens Brentano (1838–1917), born on January 16, was the grandson of an Italian merchant who had immigrated to Marienburg, the town in Germany where Brentano was born. Like Wundt, Brentano had many prominent relatives: Some of his aunts and uncles wrote in the German romantic tradition, and his brother won a Nobel Prize for his work on intellectual history. When Brentano was age 17, he began studying for the priesthood, but before being ordained he obtained his doctorate in philosophy from the

Franz Clemens Brentano

University of Tübingen in 1862. His dissertation was entitled "On the Manifold Meaning of Being According to Aristotle." Two years later, he was ordained a priest and in 1866 became a teacher at Würzburg. Brentano eventually left the church because of his disagreement with the doctrine of the Pope's infallibility, his favorable attitude toward Comte's positivism, his criticisms of scholasticism, and his desire to marry (which he eventually did twice). In 1874 he was appointed professor of philosophy at the University of Vienna, where he enjoyed his most productive years. In the same year, Brentano published his most influential work, *Psychology from an Empirical Standpoint* (1874/1973). (This was the same year that Wundt published his *Principles of Physiological Psychology*.) In 1894 pressure from the church forced Brentano to leave Vienna and move to Florence. Italy's entrance into the First World War ran contrary to Brentano's pacifism, and he protested by moving to Zürich, where he died in 1917. During his painful death from appendicitis, Brentano was heard to say, "To overcome the senses is difficult. . . . What God sends must be welcomed; it happens sometimes to be stronger than our weak strength" (Sullivan, 1979, p. 271).

Brentano agreed with Wundt about the limitations of experimental psychology. Like Wundt, Brentano believed that overemphasizing experimentation (systematic manipulation of one variable and noting its effects on another) diverted the researcher's attention from the important issues. Brentano also disagreed with Titchener over the importance of knowing the physiological mechanisms behind mental events. Finally, he agreed with Wundt that the search for mental elements implied a static view of the mind that was not supported by the facts. According to Brentano, the important thing about the mind was not what was in it but what it did. In other words, Brentano felt that the proper study of the mind should emphasize the mind's *processes* rather than its contents.

Brentano's views came to be called **act psychology** because of his belief that mental processes were aimed at performing some function. Among the mental acts, he included judging, recalling, expecting, inferring, doubting, loving, hating, and hoping. Furthermore, each mental act referred to an object outside itself. For example, *something* is judged, recalled, expected, loved, hated, and so forth. Brentano used the term **intentionality** to describe the fact that every mental act incorporated something outside itself. Thus, Brentano clearly distinguished between seeing the color red and the color red that is seen. Seeing is a mental act, which in this case has as its object the color red. Acts and contents (objects) are inseparable; every mental act intends (refers to, encompasses) an object or event that is the content of the act. Brentano did not mean intention or purpose by the term *intentionality*; he simply meant that every mental act intends (refers to) something outside itself.

To study mental acts and intentionality, Brentano had to use a form of introspection that

Wundt and Titchener (until his later years) found to be abhorrent. The careful, controlled analytic introspection designed to report the presence or absence of a sensation or to report the elements of experience was of no use to Brentano. Rather, he used the very type of **phenomenological introspection**—that is, introspective analysis directed toward intact, meaningful experiences—that Titchener allowed into his program toward the end of his life. Clearly, Brentano, like Wundt, followed in the tradition of rationalism. For him, the mind was active—not passive as the British and French empiricists and the structuralists had believed.

Brentano wrote very little, believing that oral communication was most effective, and his major influence on psychology has come through those whom he influenced personally, as we will see, there were many. One of Brentano's many students who later became famous was Sigmund Freud, who took his only nonmedical courses from Brentano. Much of what became Gestalt psychology and modern existential psychology can be traced to Brentano.

Carl Stumpf

Carl Stumpf (1848–1936) studied with Brentano. Stumpf's primary interest was music, and his research eventually earned him a reputation in audition that rivaled that of Helmholtz. His most influential work was his two-volume *Psychology of Tone* (1883 and 1890). Engaging in a major dispute with Wundt over the perception of musical tones, Stumpf maintained that trained musicians were able to make more valid judgments of musical tones than trained introspectionists who were not musicians. About this debate, Heidbreder said,

> It was Stumpf's musical interest . . . that led him into the famous controversy with Wundt on tonal distances—famous not so much for what the combatants said about tonal distances as for what they said about each other. For the discussions, becoming both personal and bitter, developed into one of the famous scandals of modern psychology, a scandal that has steadily afforded amusement to the many who find irresistible

Carl Stumpf

> comedy in the spectacle of learned psychologists at the mercy of primitive feelings which have obviously escaped control. (1933, pp. 100–101)

Stumpf founded a psychological laboratory at the University of Berlin that was a serious competitor to Wundt's at Leipzig. At Stumpf's laboratory, work was concentrated on space perception and audition.

Like Brentano, Stumpf argued that mental events should be studied as meaningful units, just as they occur to the individual, and should not be broken down for further analysis. In other words, for Stumpf, the proper object of study for psychology was mental *phenomena*, not conscious elements. This stance led to the phenomenology that was to become the cornerstone of the later school of Gestalt psychology. In fact, the chair that Stumpf occupied at the University of Berlin for 26 years was passed on to the great Gestalt psychologist Wolfgang Köhler. The other two founders of Gestalt psychology, Max Wertheimer and Kurt Koffka, also studied with Stumpf.

Edmund Husserl

Edmund Husserl

Edmund Husserl (1859–1938) studied with Brentano from 1884 to 1886 and then worked with Stumpf, to whom he dedicated his book *Logical Investigations* (1900–1901). Husserl accepted Brentano's concept of intentionality, according to which mental acts are functional in the sense that they are directed at something outside themselves. For Brentano, mental acts were the means by which we made contact with the physical world. For Husserl, however, studying intentionality resulted in only one type of knowledge, that of the person turned outward to the environment. Equally important was the knowledge gained through studying the person turned inward. The former study uses introspection to examine the mental acts with which we embrace the physical world. The latter study uses introspection to examine all subjective experience as it occurs, without the need to relate it to anything else. For Husserl then, there were at least two types of introspection: one that focused on intentionality and one that focused on whatever processes a person experienced subjectively. For example, the former type would ask what external object the act of seeing intended, whereas the latter would concentrate on a description of the pure experience of seeing. Both types of introspection focused on phenomenological experience, but because the latter focused on the essences of mental processes Husserl referred to it as **pure phenomenology**. Most often when the term *phenomenon* is used to describe a mental event, it refers to a whole, intact, meaningful experience and not to fragments of conscious experiences such as isolated sensations. In this sense, Wundt (as an experimentalist) and the earlier Titchener were not phenomenologists, whereas Brentano, Stumpf, and Husserl were. The point is that it is incorrect to use the terms *subjective, cognitive,* and *mental* as synonyms for phenomenological.

The methods of the natural sciences are inappropriate to the study of mental phenomena. Husserl thought that those who believed that psychology should be an experimental science made a mistake by taking the natural sciences as their model. Jennings explains Husserl's reasoning:

> Historically, psychology adopted the experimental methods used by the physical sciences (despite the fact that mental events lack the physical tangibility of "natural" events) because it hoped to claim the same authoritative knowledge enjoyed by the physical sciences. . . . However, psychology could not simply adopt the experimental method without also adopting its implicit naturalistic perspective and the philosophical problems inherent in that belief system. First, the new scientific psychology actively disallowed any study of consciousness by direct "seeing" of what consciousness is like because such a procedure was regarded as unscientific "introspection." Second, and more important, psychologists were forced to ground the nonnatural phenomena of consciousness in physical events that could be studied experimentally. This problem is analogous to a fool who tries putting 12 oranges into an egg carton because the egg carton did such a great job of

neatly ordering eggs. Instead of finding a new container suitable for holding oranges (the phenomenological study of consciousness), the fool cuts and tapes the egg carton until the oranges will fit. Or, worse yet, the fool mangles the oranges themselves in a misguided effort to force them into the egg carton (the experimental study of consciousness). (1986, p. 1234)

Husserl did not deny that an experimental psychology was possible, he simply said that it must be preceded by a careful, rigorous phenomenological analysis:

According to Husserl, empirical psychology in its experimental form was incapable of discerning and clarifying the essential nature of consciousness. It is important to understand, however, that Husserl did *not* flatly reject the experimental investigations of psychology, but he emphasized that an enormous amount of careful phenomenological groundwork was necessary *before* these experimental studies could be justified. For example, the psychologist should not conduct experiments about the relation between a stimulus and perception without first knowing clearly what a "perception" is, that is, without first precisely describing the essential characteristics of perception as an act of consciousness. This was the proper task of phenomenology—to clearly apprehend and delineate the basic essential acts of consciousness. (Jennings, 1986, p. 1235)

In other words, Husserl believed that it was premature to perform experiments on perception, memory, and feelings without first knowing the essence (the ultimate nature) of these processes. Without such knowledge, the experimenter does not know how the very nature of what he or she is studying may bias what is found or how the experiences are initially organized:

It was precisely here that Husserl believed phenomenology could contribute to empirical-experimental psychology. Due to its contrasting treatment of consciousness, phenomenology could help psychology clarify what it already knows, so to speak. Basically, phenomenology could help psychology make the *implicit* assumptions and preconceptions that guide its investigations explicitly clear. Husserl argued that psychology's preunderstanding of the essential acts of consciousness should first be rigorously clarified (through phenomenological analyses) prior

to any empirical psychological work, such as psychophysics. (Jennings, 1986, p. 1236)

Husserl's goal. Husserl's goal was to create a taxonomy of the mind. He wanted to describe the **mental essences** by which humans experience themselves, other humans, and the world:

By definition, an essence must be a fact or entity that is universal, externally unchanging over time, and absolute. Conversely, an essence is not relative to a given culture or historical age, is not restricted to personal opinion, and is not dependent on logical arguments. (Jennings, 1986, p. 1232)

Husserl believed strongly that a description of such mental essences must *precede* any attempt to understand the interactions between humans and their environment and any science of psychology. Indeed, he believed that such an understanding was basic to *any* science because all sciences ultimately depend on human mental attributes. Husserl referred to his effort as pure phenomenology because it sought mental essences and was not concerned with how the mind relates to external reality. Thus, Brentano's study of intentionality could be labeled phenomenological, but it was not the pure phenomenology that Husserl sought.

Husserl's position differed radically from that of the structuralists in that Husserl sought to examine *meanings* and essences, not mental elements, via introspection. He and his subjects would thus commit the dreaded stimulus error. Husserl also differed from his teacher Brentano and his colleague Stumpf by insisting on a pure phenomenology with little or no concern for determining the relationship between subjective experience and the physical world.

Brentano, Stumpf, and Husserl all insisted that the proper subject matter for psychology was intact, meaningful psychological experiences. This phenomenological approach was to appear soon in Gestalt psychology and existential psychology. Martin Heidegger, one of the most famous, modern existential thinkers, dedicated his book *Being and Time* (1927) to Husserl.

We will have more to say about Husserl when we discuss third-force psychology in chapter 17.

Oswald Külpe

Oswald Külpe (1862–1915) was interested in many things, including music, history, philosophy, and psychology. During the time when he was primarily interested in philosophy, he wrote five books on philosophy for the lay reader, including one on Kant's philosophy. He was majoring in history at the University of Leipzig when he attended Wundt's lectures and became interested in psychology. Under Wundt's supervision, Külpe received his doctorate in 1887, and he remained Wundt's assistant for the next eight years. Külpe dedicated his book *Outlines of Psychology* (1893/1909) to Wundt. During his time as Wundt's assistant, Külpe met and roomed with Titchener, and although the two often disagreed, they maintained the highest regard for one another. In fact, Titchener later translated several of Külpe's works into English. In 1894 Külpe moved to the University of Würzburg, where for the following 15 years he did his most influential work in psychology. In 1909 he left Würzburg and went to the University of Bonn and then to the University of Munich. After Külpe left Würzburg, his interest turned more and more to philosophy. He was working on epistemological questions when he died in 1915.

Imageless thought. Although starting out very much in the Wundtian camp, Külpe became one of Wundt's most worthy opponents. Külpe disagreed with Wundt that all thought had to have a specific referent—that is, a sensation, image, or feeling. Külpe felt that some thoughts were *imageless*. Furthermore, he disagreed with Wundt's contention that the higher mental processes (e.g., thinking) could not be studied experimentally, and he set out to do so using what he called *systematic experimental introspection*. This technique involved giving subjects problems to solve and then asking them to report on the mental operations in which they engaged to solve them. In addition, subjects were asked to

describe the types of thinking involved at different stages of problem solving. They were asked to report their mental experiences while waiting for the problem to be presented, during actual problem solving, and after the problem had been solved.

Külpe's more elaborate introspective technique indicated that there were indeed **imageless thoughts** such as searching, doubting, confidence, and hesitation. In 1901 Karl Marbe, one of Külpe's colleagues, published a study describing what happened when subjects were asked to judge weights as heavier or lighter than a standard weight. Marbe was not interested in the accuracy of the judgments but in *how* the judgments were made. Subjects reported prejudgment periods of doubt, searching, and hesitation, after which they simply made the judgments. Marbe concluded that Wundt's elements of sensations, images, and feelings were not enough to account for the act of judging. There appeared to be a mental act of judging that was independent of what was being judged. Marbe concluded that such an act was imageless. Incidentally, these pure (imageless) processes, such as judging, were the very things that Husserl was seeking to describe with his pure phenomenology.

Mental set. The most influential work coming out of the Würzburg school was that on *Einstellung*, or **mental set**. It was found that focusing subjects on a particular problem created a *determining tendency* that persisted until the problem was solved. Furthermore, although this tendency or set was operative, subjects were unaware of it; that is, it operated on the unconscious level. For example, a bookkeeper can balance the books without being aware of the fact that he or she is adding or subtracting. It was found that mental sets could be induced experimentally by instructing subjects to perform different tasks or solve different problems. Mental sets could also result from a person's past experiences. William Bryan, one of the U.S. students working in Külpe's laboratory, provided an example of an experimentally induced set. Bryan

showed cards containing various nonsense syllables written in different colors and in different
arrangements. Subjects who were instructed to
attend to the colors were afterward able to report the colors present but could not report the
other stimuli. Conversely, subjects instructed to
attend to the syllables could report them with
relative accuracy but could not accurately report
the colors. It appeared that instructions had directed the subjects' attention to certain stimuli
and away from others. This demonstrated that
environmental stimuli did not automatically
create sensations that became images. Rather,
the process of attention determined which sensations would and would not be experienced.
This finding was in accordance with Wundt's
view of attention, but not Titchener's.

Narziss Ach, who was also working in Külpe's
laboratory, demonstrated the type of mental set
derived from experience. Ach found that when
the numbers 7 and 3 were flashed rapidly and
subjects had not been instructed to respond in
any particular way, the most common response
was to say "ten." Ach's explanation was that the
mental set to add was more common than the
mental sets to subtract, multiply, or divide,
which would have resulted, respectively, in the
responses "four," "twenty-one," and "two point
three."

Other findings of the Würzburg school. Besides
showing the importance of mental set in problem solving, members of the Würzburg school
showed that problems had motivational properties. Somehow, problems caused subjects to continue to apply relevant mental operations until a
solution was attained. The motivational aspect
of problem solving was to be emphasized later by
the Gestalt psychologists. (Wertheimer, one of
the founders of the school of Gestalt psychology,
wrote his doctoral dissertation under Külpe's
supervision.)

The Würzburg school showed that the higher
mental processes could be studied experimentally and that certain mental processes occurred
independently of content (i.e., they were imageless). It also indicated that associationism was

inadequate for explaining the operations of
the mind and challenged the voluntarists' and
the structuralists' narrow use of the introspective method. Members of the Würzburg school
made the important distinction between
thoughts and thinking, between mental contents
and mental acts. In elaborating these distinctions, members of the school moved closer to
Brentano and away from aspects of Wundt and
especially Titchener. Members of the Würzburg
school and Brentano were both interested in
how the mind worked instead of what static elements it contained.

The controversies the Würzburg school
caused did much to promote the collapse of both
voluntarism and structuralism. Was there imageless thought or not? Was it possible, as some
maintained, that some individuals had imageless
thought and others did not? If so, how would
this affect the search for universal truths about
the mind? How could introspection be properly
used? Could it be directed only at static contents
of the mind or could it be used to study the
dynamics of the mind? Most devastating was the
fact that different individuals were using the
same research technique (introspection) and
reaching very different conclusions. More and
more, any form of introspection became looked
upon as unreliable. This questioning of the validity of introspection as a research tool did
much to launch the school of behaviorism (see
chapter 12).

Hermann Ebbinghaus

Hermann Ebbinghaus (1850–1909) was born
on January 23 in the industrial city of Barmen,
near Bonn. His father was a wealthy paper and
textile merchant. He studied classical languages,
history, and philosophy at the Universities of
Bonn, Halle, and Berlin before receiving his
doctorate from the University of Bonn in 1873.
He wrote his dissertation on Hartmann's philosophy of the unconscious. He spent the next
three and one-half years traveling through England and France. In London he bought and
read a copy of Fechner's *Elements of Psychophysics*,

Hermann Ebbinghaus

which deeply impressed him. Ebbinghaus later dedicated his book *Outline of Psychology* (1902) to Fechner, of whom he said, "I owe everything to you." Unaware of Wundt's belief that the higher mental processes could not be studied experimentally, Ebbinghaus proceeded to systematically study learning and memory.

Ebbinghaus began his research in his home in Berlin in 1878, and his early studies were written and offered as support of his successful application to be a lecturer in philosophy at the University of Berlin. Ebbinghaus's research culminated in a monograph entitled *On Memory: An Investigation in Experimental Psychology* (1885/1913),

which marked a turning point of psychology. It was the first time that the processes of learning and memory had been studied *as* they occurred rather than after they had occurred. Furthermore, they were investigated *experimentally*. As testimony to Ebbinghaus's thoroughness, many of his findings are still cited in modern psychology textbooks. Hoffman, Bringmann, Bamberg, and Klein (1986) list eight major conclusions that Ebbinghaus reached about learning and memory; most are still valid today and are being expanded by current researchers. Ebbinghaus's *Principles of Psychology* (1897) was widely used as an introductory psychology text, as was his *Outline of Psychology*.

Along with König, Hering, Stumpf, Helmholtz, and others, Ebbinghaus established psychology's second experimental journal, *Journal of Psychology and Physiology of the Sense Organs*, which broke Wundt's monopoly on the publishing of results from psychological experiments. Ebbinghaus was also the first to publish an article on the testing of schoolchildren's intelligence. He devised a sentence-completion task for the purpose, and it later became part of the Binet–Simon scale of intelligence (Hoffman et al., 1986).

Nonsense material. To study learning as it occurred, Ebbinghaus needed material that had not been previously experienced. For this, he created a pool of 2,300 "nonsense syllables." Hoffman et al. (1986) point out that the standard discussion of Ebbinghaus's syllables is incorrect; it was not his syllables that had little or no meaning, it was a series of syllables that was essentially meaningless. That is, refering to Ebbinghaus's syllables as "nonsense syllables" is a misnomer. Hoffman et al. (1986) point out that many of Ebbinghaus's syllables were actual words and many others closely resembled words. Thus, it was not the syllables that were nonsensical but the series of such syllables. From the pool of 2,300 syllables, Ebbinghaus chose a series to be learned. The series usually consisted of 12 syllables, though he varied the size of the group in order to study rate of learning as a function of the amount of material to be learned. Keeping the syllables in the same order and using himself as a subject, he looked at each syllable for a fraction of a second. After going through the list in this fashion, he paused for 15 seconds and went through the list again. He continued in this manner until he could recite each syllable without making a mistake, at which point *mastery* was said to have occurred.

At various time intervals following mastery, Ebbinghaus relearned the group of syllables. He recorded the number of exposures it took to relearn the material and subtracted that from the number of exposures it took to initially learn the material. He called the difference between the two, **savings.** By plotting savings as a function of time, Ebbinghaus created psychology's first retention curve. He found that forgetting was most rapid during the first few hours following a learning experience and relatively slow thereafter. And he found that if he *overlearned* the original material (i.e., if he continued to expose himself to material after he had attained mastery), the rate of forgetting was considerably reduced. Ebbinghaus also studied the effect of *meaningfulness* on learning and memory. For example, he found that it took about 10 times as many exposures to learn 80 random syllables as it did to learn 80 successive syllables from Byron's *Don Juan.*

Another common misconception concerning Ebbinghaus is that he followed in the empiricist tradition. Hoffman et al. (1986), however, indicate that this is simply not true. He most often quoted Herbart, and the topics that were of most interest to him—such as meaning, imagery, and individual differences in cognitive styles—followed in the tradition of rationalism, not empiricism.

THE DECLINE OF STRUCTURALISM

A case can be made that Wundt's voluntarism is still with us, but Titchener's structuralism is not. Indeed, ample evidence shows that many of Wundt's ideas are alive and well in contemporary psychology, whereas nothing of substance from Titchener's system has survived. The question is What caused the virtual extinction of structuralism?

In many ways, the decline of the school of structuralism was inevitable. We have seen that interest in the mind is as old as history itself, and the question of how the mind is related to bodily processes goes back at least as far as the early Greeks. Focusing mainly on the physical world, early science was extremely successful, and its success stimulated interest in directing scientific methodology to a study of the mind. Because both empiricists and rationalists alike had long believed that the senses were the gateways to the mind, it is no surprise that sensory processes were among the first things on which science focused when it was applied to humans. From there it was but a short, logical step to looking at neural transmission, brain mechanisms, and, finally, conscious sensations.

Structuralism was essentially an attempt to study scientifically what had been the philosophical concerns of the past. How does sensory information give rise to simple sensations, and how are these sensations then combined into more complex mental events? The major tool of the structuralists, and even their opponents, was introspection. This, too, had been inherited from the past. Although it was now used scientifically (i.e., in a controlled situation), introspection was yielding different results depending on who was using it and what they were seeking. Other arguments against the use of introspection began to appear. It was pointed out that what was called introspection was really *retrospection* because the event that was reported had already occurred, and therefore what was being reported was a memory of a sensation rather than the sensation itself. Also, it was suggested that one could not introspect on something without changing it—that is, that observation changed what was being observed. It was beginning to appear that those who claimed that a science of the mind was impossible were correct.

Besides the apparent unreliability of introspection, structuralism came under attack for several other reasons. Structuralism either ignored or minimized several developments that researchers outside the school of structuralism were showing to be important. The study of animal behavior had little meaning for those hoping to find the basic elements of human consciousness, yet others were finding that much could be learned about humans by studying nonhuman animals. The structuralists were not interested in the study of abnormal behavior even though Freud and others were making significant advances in understanding and treating the mentally ill. Similarly, the structuralists essentially ignored the study of personality, learning, psychological development, and individual differences, while others were making major breakthroughs in these areas. Also damaging was the structuralists' refusal to seek *practical* knowledge. Titchener insisted that he was seeking pure knowledge and was not concerned with applying the principles of psychology to the solution of practical problems. Most important to structuralism's demise, however, was its inability to assimilate one of the most important developments in human history—the doctrine of evolution. For all these reasons, the school of structuralism was short-lived and died within Titchener's own lifetime.

It was now time for a psychological school of thought that would deal with the important areas structuralism neglected, do so within the context of evolutionary theory, and use research techniques that were more reliable and valid than introspection. Titchener himself named this new school functionalism, a school that was concerned with the *what for* of the mind instead of the *what is*. The development and characteristics of the school of functionalism will be the topics of the next two chapters.

SUMMARY

Wundt was the founder of both experimental psychology as a separate discipline and of the school of voluntarism. One of Wundt's goals was to discover the elements of thought by having well-trained subjects introspect on their immediate experience. A second goal was to discover how these elements combined to form complex mental experiences. Wundt found that there were two types of basic mental experiences: sensations, which could be described in terms of modality and intensity, and feelings, which could be described in terms of the attributes of pleasantness-unpleasantness, excitement-calm, and strain-relaxation. Wundt distinguished among sensations, which were basic mental elements; perceptions, which were mental experiences given meaning by past experience; and apperceptions, which were mental experiences that were the focus of attention. Because humans can focus their attention on whatever they wish, Wundt's theory was referred to as voluntarism. By focusing one's attention on various aspects of conscious experience, that experience can be arranged and rearranged in any number of ways, and thus a creative synthesis results from apperception. Wundt believed that if the ability to apperceive broke down, mental illness such as schizophrenia might result. With his concept of apperception, Wundt was closer to the rationalist than to the empiricist tradition.

Wundt initially believed that reaction time could supplement introspection as a means of studying the mind. Following techniques developed by Donders, Wundt presented tasks of increasing complexity to his subjects and noted that more complex tasks resulted in longer reaction times. Wundt believed that the time required to perform a complex mental operation could be determined by subtracting the times it took to perform the simpler operations of which the complex act consisted. Wundt eventually gave up his reaction-time studies because he found reaction time to be an unreliable measure.

In keeping with the major thrust of voluntarism, Wundt claimed that physical events could be explained in terms of antecedent events, but psychological events could not be. Unlike the behavior of physical objects, psychological events can only be understood in terms of their purpose. The techniques used by the physical sciences are therefore inappropriate for psychology. Wundt believed that volitional acts were lawful but that the laws governing such acts could not be investigated experimentally. Volitional acts can only be studied after the fact by studying their outcomes. Wundt believed, then, that the higher mental functions could not be studied through experiments but only through historical analysis and naturalistic observation. In his 10-volume *Völkerpsychologie*, Wundt showed how the latter techniques could be used to study such topics as social customs, religion, myths, morals, art, law, and language. In his analysis of language, Wundt assumed that communication began when one person formed a general impression. Next, the person chose words to express the general impression. Finally, if the words adequately conveyed the general impression and if the listener apperceived it, communication was successful.

Titchener created the school of structuralism at Cornell University. He set as his goal the learning of the what, how, and why of mental life. The what consisted of determining the basic mental elements, the how was determining how the elements became combined, and the why consisted of determining the neurological correlates of mental events. His introspectionists had to be carefully trained so that they would not commit the stimulus error. According to Titchener, sensations and images could vary in terms of quality, intensity, duration, clearness, and extensity. He found evidence for over 40,000 separate mental elements. Titchener thought that all feelings varied only along the pleasantness-unpleasantness dimension, thus disagreeing with Wundt's tridimensional theory. Following in the empirical-associationistic tradition, Titchener said that attention was only a clear sensation. According to Titchener's context theory of meaning, sensations always stimulate the memories of events that were previously experienced along with those sensations, and these memories give the sensations meaning. There were a number of fundamental differences between Wundt's voluntarism and Titchener's structuralism.

Those offering alternative views to voluntarism and structuralism included Brentano, Stumpf, Husserl, Külpe, and Ebbinghaus. Brentano believed that mental acts should be studied rather than mental elements, and therefore his position is referred to as act psychology. Brentano used the term *intentionality* to describe the fact that a mental act always encompassed (intended) something external to itself. Like Brentano, Stumpf believed that introspective analysis should be directed at intact, meaningful psychological experience instead of the elements of thought. Stumpf had a major influence on those individuals who later created the school of Gestalt psychology. Husserl believed that before scientific psychology would be possible, a taxonomy of the mind was required. To create such a taxonomy, pure phenomenology would be used to explore the essence of subjective experience. According to Husserl, it did not make sense to perform experiments involving such processes as perception, memory, or judgment without first knowing the essences of those processes. The mind itself, he said, must be understood before we can study how the mind responds to objects external to it.

Through his technique of systematic experimental introspection, Külpe found that the mind possessed processes—not just sensations, images, and feelings—and that these processes were imageless. Examples of imageless thoughts included searching, doubting, and hesitating. Külpe and his colleagues found that a mental set, which could be created either through instructions or through personal experience, provided a determining tendency in problem solving. They also found that once a mental set had been established, humans could solve problems unconsciously. Ebbinghaus demonstrated that Wundt had been wrong in saying that the higher mental processes could not be studied experimentally. Using "nonsense" material, Ebbinghaus systematically studied both learning and memory so thoroughly that his conclusions are still cited in psychology texts.

Many factors led to the downfall of structuralism. Examples are the unreliability of introspection, the observation that introspection was really retrospection, and the ignoring of psychological development, abnormal behavior, personality, learning, individual differences, evolutionary theory, and practicality.

DISCUSSION QUESTIONS

1. What is meant by a school of psychology?

2. Why was the school of psychology created by Wundt called voluntarism?

3. Why did Wundt believe that experimentation in psychology was of limited usefulness?

4. How did Wundt differentiate between mediate and immediate experience?

5. Discuss Wundt's use of introspection.

6. For Wundt, what were the elements of thought, and what were their attributes? Include in your answer a discussion of Wundt's tridimensional theory of feeling.

7. How did Wundt distinguish between psychological and physical causation?

8. What did Wundt mean when he said that volitional acts are creative, but not free?

9. Define the terms *sensation, perception, apperception,* and *creative synthesis* as they were used in Wundt's theory.

10. Summarize how Wundt used reaction time in an effort to determine how long it took to perform various mental operations. Why did Wundt abandon his reaction-time research?

11. Why did Wundt think it necessary to write his *Völkerpsychologie*? What approach to the study of humans did it exemplify?

12. Summarize Wundt's explanation of language.

13. For Titchener, what were the goals of psychology?

14. What did Titchener believe would be the ultimate *why* of psychology?

15. How did Titchener's explanation of how elements combine differ from Wundt's?

16. What was Titchener's context theory of meaning?

17. Compare and contrast Wundt's view of psychology with Titchener's.

18. Summarize Brentano's act psychology.

19. What did Brentano mean by intentionality?

20. What did Husserl mean by pure phenomenology? Why did he believe that an understanding of the essence of subjective experience must precede scientific psychology?

21. What did Külpe mean by imageless thought? Mental set?

22. Why is it incorrect to refer to the material that Ebbinghaus used for his research as "nonsense syllables"?

23. Discuss the significance of Ebbinghaus's work to the history of psychology.

24. List the reasons for the decline of structuralism. Include in your answer the various criticisms of introspection.

SUGGESTIONS FOR FURTHER READING

Blumenthal, A. L. (1975). A reappraisal of Wilhelm Wundt. *American Psychologist, 30,* 1081–1088.
In this important article, Blumenthal corrects a number of misconceptions concerning Wundt's approach to psychology. The article also lists six current areas of research that are similar to areas that Wundt studied. Blumenthal makes the point that Wundt's psychology can be better appreciated today than it has been previously because of contemporary psychology's emphasis on cognitive processes.

Bringmann, W. G., & Tweney, R. D. (Eds.). (1980). *Wundt studies: A centennial collection.* Toronto: Hogrefe.
This book is a most interesting collection of papers including biographical information on Wundt, detailed accounts of many of Wundt's theoretical concepts, testimonials from Wundt's ex-students, a description of the various research projects that took place in Wundt's laboratory, and a review by William James of Wundt's *Principles.* The book also includes a number of interesting figures, documents, and photographs.

Danziger, K. (1980c). The history of introspection reconsidered. *Journal of the History of the Behavioral Sciences, 16,* 241–262.
Danziger indicates that the term *introspection* does not refer to one methodology but many. He starts his analysis by pointing out that introspection was much more important to the British empiricists than it was to the German rationalists because the empiricists tended to equate mind and consciousness—therefore, to study consciousness (via introspection) was to study the mind. However, the leading rationalists, such as Leibniz, Kant, and Hegel, believed that there were important aspects of the mind of which we are not conscious. The latter philosophers preferred to analyze the mind using logic and mathematics instead of introspection. Danziger goes on to show how Wundt distinguished between introspection (the self-analysis of one's subjective experience, including memories) and internal observation (the report of sensations caused by present external stimulation). It was the latter that Wundt emphasized in his version of experimental psychology.

Evans, R. B. (1972). E. B. Titchener and his lost system. *Journal of the History of the Behavioral Sciences, 8,* 168–180.
Evans argues that it is not true that Titchener's system of psychology remained essentially the same from the time that he published his *A Textbook of Psychology* in 1910 until his death in 1927. Evans offers evidence that in his later years Titchener changed his view of sensation from an element of experience to a classificatory category, abandoned affection as a separate element of experience, and expanded his introspective method to include phenomenological experience.

Henle, M. (1971a). Did Titchener commit the stimulus error? The problem of meaning in structural psychology. *Journal of the History of the Behavioral Sciences, 7,* 279–282.
Henle argues that Titchener's early criteria for effective introspection were so rigid that he could not adhere to them himself. Titchener urged that introspective analysis should avoid assigning "meaning" to the experiences being analyzed and that, indeed, psychology itself should avoid the topic of "meaning." Meaning, Titchener said, was a philosophical concern, not a

concern of the science of psychology. Having said that, Henle points out that Titchener proceeded to spend a great deal of time attempting to determine the meaning of meaning, thus violating his own principles.

Hoffman, R. R., Bringmann, W., Bamberg, M., & Klein, R. (1986). Some historical observations on Ebbinghaus. In D. Gorfein & R. Hoffman (Eds.), *Memory and Learning: The Ebbinghaus centennial conference.* Hillsdale, NJ: Erlbaum.

This interesting chapter starts by correcting the "myth" of Ebbinghaus's use of the nonsense syllable. The correction is that Ebbinghaus was not at all concerned with the meaning of the syllables themselves (many of them were actually words, and many others resembled words). Rather, he was concerned with the meaning between the syllables. It was the syllables arranged in a series that had little or no meaning, not the syllables themselves. The authors then give a short biographical sketch of Ebbinghaus, discuss his work on intelligence testing, his influence, and the contents of his *On Memory* in detail; and list some unanswered questions about Ebbinghaus and his work.

Jennings, J. L. (1986). Husserl revisited: The forgotten distinction between psychology and phenomenology. *American Psychologist, 41,* 1231–1240.

Jennings indicates that Husserl's major goal was to rescue philosophy from its decline in importance as the physical and social sciences gradually chipped away at its proud domain. Husserl proposed that this be done by returning to the study of essences that had characterized philosophy in Greek antiquity. For Husserl, this would entail a study of the essence of the mind or the description of all mental processes by which we come to know and interact with the world. According to Husserl, such a pure phenomenology must necessarily precede any scientific activity, including experimental psychology.

Leahey, T. H. (1981). The mistaken mirror: On Wundt's and Titchener's psychologies. *Journal of the History of the Behavioral Sciences, 17,* 273–282.

Leahey indicates that Wundt and Titchener were not similar in method, theory, or philosophy of science. A major goal for Wundt was to explain the cognitive operations that cause conscious experiences. Titchener being a positivist sought only a description of mental phenomena. For Titchener, explaining a mental event involved showing how that event is correlated with a physiological event. The article ends by describing a number of surprising similarities between Titchener's and Skinner's approaches to psychology.

Rieber, R. W. (Ed.). (1980). *Wilhelm Wundt and the making of scientific psychology.* New York: Plenum Press.

In the first chapter in this collection, Diamond gives a detailed and most interesting account of Wundt's life before arriving at Leipzig. In this not too flattering biography, Wundt is portrayed as an overambitious individual who was often critical of the ideas of others while intolerant of the criticism of his own ideas. Because Wundt's actions often brought him into conflict with some of the major scientists of his time (e.g., Hering and Helmholtz), Diamond speculates that Wundt may have impeded the progress of experimental psychology instead of facilitating it. In the second chapter, Danziger argues that Wundt's system of psychology (voluntarism) and Titchener's (structuralism) reflect altogether different traditions: Wundt's, the German rational-romantic tradition, and Titchener's, the British-French positivistic, empirical-sensationalistic tradition. In the third chapter, Danziger elaborates Wundt's theory of voluntary behavior. In the fourth chapter, Blumenthal describes how Wundt followed in the Leibnizian tradition and how U.S. psychology followed in the Lockean tradition. In the fifth chapter, Rieber discusses how Wundt's ideas were "Americanized" by his U.S. students when those students returned to the United States. The remaining chapters include translated segments of Wundt's most influential works and a review of Wundt's *Principles* by William James.

Wundt, W. (1973). *An introduction to psychology* (R. Pintner, Trans.). New York: Arno Press. (Original work published 1912)

This is Wundt's attempt to provide those interested in "the new psychology" with a brief overview of what that psychology entails. Topics include consciousness and attention, the elements of consciousness; association; apperception; and the laws of psychical life.

GLOSSARY

Act psychology The name given to Brentano's brand of psychology because it focused on mental operations or functions. Act psychology dealt with the interaction between mental processes and physical events.

Apperception The process by which attention is focused on certain mental events.

Brentano, Franz Clemens (1838–1917) Believed that introspection should be used to understand the functions of the mind rather than its elements. Brentano's position came to be called act psychology. (*See also* **Act psychology**.)

Context theory of meaning Titchener's contention that a sensation is given meaning by the images it elicits. That is, for Titchener, meaning is determined by the law of contiguity.

Creative synthesis The arrangement and rearrangement of mental elements that can result from apperception.

Donders, Franciscus Cornelius (1818–1889) Used reaction time to measure the time it took to perform various mental acts. Donders subtracted reaction times generated in simple situations (e.g., response a to stimulus A) from the reaction times generated by more complicated situations (e.g., presentation of several stimuli, but the subject was to respond to only one). Donders felt that by using this subtractive method he could determine the time required to perform increasingly complicated mental acts.

Ebbinghaus, Hermann (1850–1909) The first to study learning and memory experimentally.

Elements of thought According to Wundt and Titchener, the basic sensations from which more complex thoughts are derived.

Feeling The basic element of thought that accompanies each sensation. Wundt felt that emotions consist of various combinations of elemental feelings. (*See also* **Tridimensional theory of feeling.**)

General impression The thought a person has in mind before he or she chooses the words to express it.

Husserl, Edmund (1859–1938) Called for a pure phenomenology that sought to discover the essence of subjective experience. (*See also* **Pure phenomenology.**)

Imageless thoughts According to Külpe, the pure mental acts of, for example, judging and doubting, without those acts having any particular referents or images.

Immediate experience Direct subjective experience as it occurs.

Intentionality Concept proposed by Brentano, according to which mental acts always intend something. That is, mental acts embrace either some object in the physical world or some mental image (idea).

Introspection Reflection on one's subjective experience, whether such reflection is directed toward the detection of the presence or absence of a sensation (as in Wundt's case) or toward the detection of complex thought processes (as in the case of Brentano, Stumpf, Külpe, Husserl, and others).

Külpe, Oswald (1862–1915) Applied systematic, experimental introspection to the study of problem solving and found that some mental operations were imageless.

Mediate experience Experience that is provided by various measuring devices and is therefore not immediate, direct experience.

Mental chronometry The measurement of the time required to perform various mental acts.

Mental essences According to Husserl, those universal, unchanging mental processes that characterize the mind and in terms of which we do commerce with the physical environment.

Mental set A problem-solving strategy that can be induced by instructions or by experience and is used without a person's awareness.

Perception Mental experience that occurs when sensations are given meaning by the memory of past experiences.

Phenomenological introspection The type of introspection that focuses on mental phenomena rather than on isolated, mental elements.

Principle of contrasts According to Wundt, the fact that experiences of one type often intensify opposite types of experiences, such as when eating something sour will make the subsequent eating of something sweet taste sweeter than it would otherwise.

Principle of creative resultants According to Wundt, the fact that mental events can be arranged in any number of unique combinations.

Principle of the heterogony of ends According to Wundt, the fact that goal-directed activity often causes experiences that modify the original motivational pattern.

Principle toward the development of opposites According to Wundt, the tendency for prolonged experience of one type to create a desire for the opposite type of experience.

Pure phenomenology The type of phenomenology proposed by Husserl, the purpose of which was to create a taxonomy of the mind. Husserl believed that before a science of psychology would be possible, we would first need to understand the essences of those mental processes in terms of which we understand and respond to the world.

Savings The difference between the time it originally takes to learn something and the time it takes to relearn it.

School A group of scientists who share common assumptions, goals, problems, and methods.

Sensation A basic mental experience that is triggered by an environmental stimulus.

Stimulus error Letting past experience influence an introspective report.

Structuralism The school of psychology founded by Titchener, the goal of which was to describe the structure of the mind.

Stumpf, Carl (1848–1936) Psychologist who was primarily interested in musical perception and who insisted that psychology study intact, meaningful mental experiences instead of searching for meaningless mental elements.

Titchener, Edward Bradford (1867–1927) Created the school of structuralism at Cornell. Unlike Wundt's voluntarism, structuralism was much more in the tradition of empiricism-associationism.

Tridimensional theory of feeling Wundt's contention that feelings vary along three dimensions: pleasantness-unpleasantness, excitement-calm, and strain-relaxation.

Völkerpsychologie Wundt's 10-volume work, in which he investigated higher mental processes through historical analysis and naturalistic observation.

Voluntarism The name given to Wundt's school of psychology because of his belief that through the process of apperception individuals could direct their attention toward whatever they wished.

Will According to Wundt, that aspect of humans that allows them to direct their attention anywhere they wish. It was because of his emphasis on will that Wundt's version of psychology was called voluntarism.

Wundt, Wilhelm Maximilian (1832–1920) The founder of experimental psychology as a separate discipline and of the school of voluntarism.

CHAPTER 10

The Darwinian Influence

The experimental psychology of consciousness was a product of Germany. Because it did not fit the U.S. temperament, Titchener's attempt to transplant his version of that psychology to the United States was ultimately unsuccessful. When Titchener arrived at Cornell in 1892, there was a spirit of independence, practicality, and adventure that was incompatible with the authoritarian, dry, and static views of structuralism. That structuralism survived as long as it did in the United States was testimony to the forceful personality of Titchener himself. The pioneering U.S. spirit was prepared to accept only a viewpoint that was new, practical, and unconcerned with the abstract analysis of the mind. Evolutionary theory provided such a view, and the United States embraced it like no other country. Not even in England, the birthplace of modern evolutionary theory, did it meet with the enthusiasm that it received in the United States. In the United States, evolutionary theory became *the* dominant theme running through most, if not all, aspects of psychology. The translation of evolutionary theory into psychology created a psychology that was uniquely American, and it caused the center of psychological research to shift from Europe to the United States, where it has been ever since.

EVOLUTIONARY THEORY BEFORE DARWIN

The idea that both the earth and living organisms change in some systematic way over time goes back at least as far as the early Greeks. Because Greece was a maritime country, it was possible to observe a wide variety of life forms there. Such observations, besides the growing tendency toward objectivity, caused some early Greeks to develop a surprisingly modern theory of evolution:

> It was conjectured, for example, that the earth was originally in a fluid state, that evaporation caused the emergence first of land and then of animals, that man originally appeared as an aquatic animal encased in a horny bark which fell away when he emerged on dry land. Another guess was that the earth was originally covered with slime from which living things developed through the influence of the sun's heat. (Hulin, 1934, pp. 10–11)

With such a good start, why did evolutionary theory not develop more fully? Because, to a large extent, Plato and Aristotle did not believe in evolution. For Plato, the number of pure forms was fixed forever, and the forms themselves did not change. For Aristotle, the number of species was fixed, and transmutation from one species to another was impossible. To the beliefs of Plato and Aristotle, the early Christians added the notion of divine creation as described in Genesis. God in his wisdom had created a certain fixed number of species, including humans, and this number could be modified only by another act of God, not by natural forces. This religious account of the origin of species put the matter to rest until modern times. MacLeod summarized the restrictions placed on early biologists:

> Since the infancy of their science biologists had been constricted by the doctrine of the fixity of species. According to the account in Genesis each species of plant, fish, bird, and beast had been specially created with special forms and

Jean Lamarck

earlier forms were different from current forms; therefore, species changed over time. Lamarck concluded that environmental changes were responsible for structural changes in plants and animals. If, for example, due to a scarcity of prey, members of a species had to run faster to catch what few prey were available, the muscles involved in running would become more fully developed because of the frequent exercise they received. If the muscles involved in running were fully developed in an adult of a species, the offspring of this adult would be born with highly developed muscles, which also enhanced their chances for survival. This theory was called the **inheritance of acquired characteristics**. Obviously, those adult members of species who did not adjust adequately to their environment would not survive and therefore would produce no offspring. In this way, according to Lamarck, the characteristics of a species would change as the traits necessary for survival changed. Thus, the transmutation of the species.

HERBERT SPENCER

Herbert Spencer (1820–1903) was born in the industrial town of Derby, England, and was first tutored by his father who was a schoolmaster and later by his uncle. He never received a formal education. At age 17, Spencer went to work for the railroad and for the next 10 years worked at jobs ranging from surveyor to engineer. In 1848 he gained employment in London as a journalist—first as a junior editor of the journal *The Economist* and then as a free-lance writer. Spencer's interest in psychology and in evolutionary theory came entirely from what he read during this time. One especially influential book was John Stuart Mill's *A System of Logic* (1893). Spencer's "education" was also enhanced by a small group of intellectuals that he befriended. The group included Thomas Huxley (shortly to become the public defender of Darwin's theory of evolution), George Henry Lewes (a fellow journalist whose broad interests included acting, writing biographies, and science), and Mary Ann Evans (also a fellow jour-

functions, and Aristotle and the Church had sanctified the doctrine. All the biologist could do was observe and classify the forms of plant and animal life and try to make each species meaningful in terms of the presumed purpose of God. (1975, p. 174)

By the 18th century, several prominent individuals were postulating a theory of evolution, including Charles Darwin's grandfather Erasmus Darwin (1731–1802) who believed that one species could be gradually transformed into another. What was missing from these early theories was the mechanism by which the transformation took place. The first to postulate such a mechanism was Jean Lamarck.

The Inheritance of Acquired Characteristics

In his *Philosophie Zoologique* (1809/1914), the French naturalist **Jean Lamarck** (1744–1829) noted that fossils of various species showed that nalist, better known as George Eliot). Clearly, Spencer was not inhibited by a lack of formal education:

> From his voracious reading and the exchanges with his group of friends during the early 1850s Spencer acquired a general vision of the world that was to have a more pervasive effect on nineteenth century thinking than that of any other philosopher of his era. (Boakes, 1984, p. 10)

Spencer's View of Evolution

An early follower of Lamarck (and later Darwin), Spencer took the notion of evolution and applied it not only to animals but also to the human mind and human societies. In fact, he applied the notion of evolution to everything in the universe. Everything, according to Spencer, begins as an undifferentiated whole. Through evolution, differentiation occurs so that systems become increasingly complex. This notion applies to the human nervous system, which eons ago was simple and homogenous but through evolution has become highly differentiated and complex. Spencer's comprehensive view of the evolutionary process is described by Hofstadter:

> The life process is essentially evolutionary, embodying a continuous change from incoherent homogeneity, illustrated by the lowly protozoa, to coherent heterogeneity, manifested in man and the higher animals. . . . Here is the key to universal evolution. This progress from homogeneity to heterogeneity—in the formation of the earth from a nebular mass, in the evolution of higher, complex species from lower and simpler ones, in the embryological development of the individual from a uniform mass of cells, in the growth of the human mind, and in the progress of human societies—is the principle at work in everything man can know. (1955, p. 37)

The fact that we now have complex nervous systems allows us to make a greater number of associations; the greater the number of associations an organism can make, the more intelligent it is. Although the term *intelligence* goes back at least as far as Cicero's use of the term *intelligentia*, Spencer is credited with the introduction of the term into psychology (Guilford, 1967). Our highly complex nervous system allows us to

Herbert Spencer

make an accurate neurophysiological (and thus mental) recording of events in our environment, and this ability is conducive to survival.

In his explanation of how associations are formed, Spencer relied heavily on the principle of contiguity. Environmental events that occur either simultaneously or in close succession are recorded in the brain and give rise to ideas of those events. Through the process of contiguity, our ideas come to map environmental events. However, for Spencer, the principle of contiguity alone was not adequate to explain why some behaviors persist whereas others do not. To explain the differential persistence of various behaviors, Spencer accepted Bain's explanation of voluntary behavior. Spencer said, "On the recurrence of the circumstances, these muscular movements that were followed by success are likely to be repeated; what was at first an accidental combination of motions will now be a combination having considerable probability" (1870, p. 545). Spencer placed Bain's observation within the context of evolutionary theory by asserting that a person persists in behaviors that are conducive to survival (those that cause pleasant feelings) and abstain from those that are not (those that cause painful feelings). Spencer's synthesis of the principle of contiguity and evolutionary theory has been called "evolutionary associationism." The contention that the frequency or probability of some behavior increases if it is followed by a pleasurable event and decreases if it is followed by a painful event came to be known as the **Spencer–Bain principle**.

The next step that Spencer took tied his theory directly to Lamarck's. Spencer claimed that an offspring inherited the cumulative associations that its ancestors had learned. Those associations that preceding generations had found to be conducive to survival were passed on to the next generation. That is, there was an inheritance of acquired associations. Spencer's theory was a blending of empiricism, associationism, and nativism because he believed that the associations gained from experience were passed on to offspring. Spencer was therefore an associationist, but to associationism he added Lamarck's evolutionary theory. He maintained that frequently used associations were passed on to offspring as instincts or reflexes. For Spencer then, instincts were nothing more than habits that had been conducive to survival for preceding generations. Instincts had been formed in past generations just as habits were formed in an organism's lifetime—through association.

When Darwin's work appeared, Spencer merely shifted his emphasis from acquired characteristics to natural selection. The concept of the **survival of the fittest** (a term that Spencer introduced in 1852 and was later adopted by Darwin) applied in either case.

Social Darwinism

A case can be made that Spencer never really understood Darwin's theory, or if he did understand it, he rejected it. In his application of evolutionary theory, Spencer said things that either Darwin never said or that Darwin overtly rejected. For example, evolution for Spencer meant progress. That is, evolution had a purpose; it was the mechanism by which perfection is approximated. Darwin believed no such thing. For Spencer, the attainment of human perfection was just a matter of time:

> The ultimate development of the ideal man is logically certain—as certain as any conclusion in which we place the most implicit faith; for instance that all men will die. . . . Progress, therefore, is not an accident, but a necessity. Instead of civilization being artificial, it is a part of nature; all of a piece with the development of the embryo or the unfolding of a flower. (Quoted in Hofstadter, 1955, p. 40)

Another departure from Darwin's thinking was Spencer's application of evolutionary principles to societies. For Spencer, societies evolve just as organisms do. Again, Darwin believed no such thing. Spencer's application of his notion of the survival of the fittest to society came to be called **social Darwinism**. As Spencer saw it, humans in society, like other animals in their natural environment, struggled for survival, and only the most fit survived. According to Spencer, if the principles of evolution were allowed to operate freely, all living organisms would approximate perfection, including humans. The best policy for a government to follow, then, was a laissez-faire policy that provided for free competition among its citizens. Government programs designed to help the weak and poor would only interfere with evolutionary principles and inhibit a society on its course toward increased perfection:

> There cannot be more good done than that of letting social progress go on unhindered; yet an immensity of mischief may be done in the way of disturbing, and distorting and repressing, by policies carried out in pursuit of erroneous conceptions. (Spencer, 1876, pp. 401–402)

The following statement demonstrates how far Spencer believed governments should follow a laissez-faire policy: "If [individuals] are sufficiently complete [both physically and mentally] to live, they *do* live, and it is well they should live. If they are not sufficiently complete to live, they die, and it is best they should die" (1864, p. 415).

Clearly, Spencer's ideas were compatible with U.S. capitalism and individualism. In the United States, Spencer's ideas were taught in most universities, and his books sold hundreds of thousands of copies. Indeed, when Spencer visited the United States in 1882, he was treated like a hero. As might be expected, social Darwinism was especially appreciated by U.S. industrialists. In a Sunday school address, John D. Rockefeller said,

> The growth of a large business is merely a survival of the fittest. . . . The American Beauty rose can be produced in the splendor and fragrance which bring cheer to its beholder only by sacrificing the early buds which grow up around it. This is not an evil tendency in business. It is merely the working-out of a law of nature and a law of God. (Hofstadter, 1955, p. 45)

Andrew Carnegie went even further, saying that for him evolutionary theory (i.e., social Darwinism) replaced traditional religion:

> I remember that light came as in a flood and all was clear. Not only had I got rid of theology and the supernatural, but I had found the truth of evolution. "All is well since all grows better," became my motto, my true source of comfort. Man was not created with an instinct for his own degradation, but from the lower he had risen to the higher forms. Nor is there any conceivable end to his march to perfection. His face is turned to the light; he stands in the sun and looks upward. (Hofstadter, 1955, p. 45)

THE BETTMANN ARCHIVE

Charles Darwin

CHARLES DARWIN

Charles Darwin (1809–1882) was born on February 12 in Shrewsbury, England, in the same year that Lamarck published his book describing the inheritance of acquired characteristics. Darwin's father Robert was a prominent physician, and his mother Susannah Wedgewood came from a family famous for their manufacture of chinaware. Robert and Susannah had five children of whom Charles was second to last. As we have previously noted, Darwin's grandfather Erasmus Darwin was a famous physician who

had dabbled in, among many other things, evolutionary theory. After receiving his early education at home, Darwin was eventually sent to school where he did so poorly that his father predicted that some day he (Charles) would disgrace himself and his family. Outside of school, however, Darwin spent most of his time collecting and classifying plants, shells, and minerals. Academically, matters did not improve much when at 16 years of age Darwin entered medical school at the University of Edinburgh. He found the lectures boring and could not stand watching operations performed without benefit of anesthesia (which had not yet been invented). Following his father's advice, he transferred to Cambridge University in order to train to become an Anglican clergyman. At Cambridge, Darwin drank, sang, and ate (he was a member of the gourmet club) his way to an 1831 graduation with a mediocre academic record. Darwin remembered collecting beetles as the activity that brought him the most pleasure while he was at Cambridge.

It was Darwin's passion for entomology (the study of insects) that brought him into contact with professors of botany and geology at Cambridge, with whom he studied and did field research. For example, immediately upon graduation from Cambridge in 1831, Darwin went on a geological expedition to Wales headed by Adam Sedgwick, a Cambridge professor of geology. Although Darwin was certainly interested in the expedition, he also saw it as a way of temporarily escaping the taking of his religious vows. A more permanent escape on the high seas was soon to be available to him. While at Cambridge, Darwin had befriended the botanist John Henslow, and it was Henslow who was first offered the position of naturalist aboard the *Beagle*. Because of family commitments, Henslow had to decline the offer and suggested that Darwin go in his place. At first, Darwin's father refused his permission because he would need to pay Charles's expenses on the trip and because he felt the journey would interfere with his son's clerical career. After discussing the matter with other members of the family, however, Darwin's father changed his mind and endorsed the adventure.

The Journey of the *Beagle*

Thus, it was at the instigation of one of his instructors that Darwin signed on as an unpaid naturalist aboard the *Beagle*, which the British government was sending on a five-year scientific expedition (1831–1836). There are several unusual facts about this trip. First, the captain of the *Beagle*, Robert Fitz-Roy, who was a firm believer in the Genesis account of creation, wanted a naturalist aboard so that evidence could be gathered that would *refute* the notion of evolution. Furthermore, Darwin himself began the trip as a believer in the biblical explanation of

creation (Monte, 1975). It was only after reading Sir Charles Lyell's *Principles of Geology* aboard ship that he began to doubt the biblical account. A third fact almost changed the course of history: Because Captain Fitz-Roy accepted phrenology, he almost rejected Darwin as the *Beagle*'s naturalist because of the shape of Darwin's nose:

> On becoming very intimate with Fitz-Roy, I heard that I had run a very narrow risk of being rejected on account of the shape of my nose! He was . . . convinced that he could judge a man's character by the outline of his features; and doubted whether anyone with my nose could possess sufficient energy and determination for the voyage. But I think he was afterwards well satisfied that my nose had spoken falsely. (F. Darwin, 1959, pp. 26–27)

The journey of the *Beagle* began on December 27, 1831, from Plymouth, England. Darwin was 23 years old at the time. The *Beagle* went first to South America, where Darwin studied marine organisms, fossils, and tribes of Indians. Then, in the fall of 1835, the *Beagle* stopped at the Galápagos Islands, where Darwin studied huge tortoises, lizards, sea lions, and 13 species of finch. Of special interest was his observation that tortoises, plants, insects, and other organisms differed somewhat from island to island, even when the islands were separated by a relatively short distance. The *Beagle* went on to Tahiti, New Zealand, and Australia; and in October 1836, Darwin arrived back in England, where he went to work classifying his enormous specimen collection.

Back in England

Even after Darwin returned to England, his observations remained disjointed; he needed a principle to tie them together. Reading **Thomas Malthus**'s *Essay on the Principle of Population* (1798/1914) furnished Darwin with that principle. Malthus observed that the world's food supply increased arithmetically, whereas the human population tended to increase geometrically. He concluded that food supply and population size were kept in balance by such events as war, starvation, and disease. Darwin embellished Malthus's concept and applied it to animals and plants as well as to humans:

> In October 1838, that is, fifteen months after I had begun my systematic enquiry, I happened to read for amusement Malthus on *Population*, and being well prepared to appreciate the struggle for existence which everywhere goes on from long-continued observation of the habits of animals and plants, it at once struck me that under these circumstances favourable variations would tend to be preserved and unfavourable ones to be destroyed. The result of this would be the formation of new species. Here, then, I had at last got a theory by which to work; but I was so anxious to avoid prejudice, that I determined not for some time to write even the briefest sketch of it (F. Darwin, 1959, pp. 12–13)

About the time Darwin read Malthus's essay, he began to have serious health problems. Along with the realization that what he was working on was revolutionary, these problems caused Darwin to delay the formal publication of his theory for more than 20 years. In fact, there is reason to believe that Darwin's theory would have been published only after his death if it had not been for a forceful demonstration that the time was right for such a theory. In June 1858, Darwin received a letter from **Alfred Russell Wallace** (1823–1913) describing a theory of evolution almost identical to his own. Wallace, too, had been influenced by Malthus's essay, as well as by his own observations in the Amazon and in the Malay Archipelago. Charles Lyell, the evolutionary geologist, reviewed both Wallace's and Darwin's ideas and suggested that both Wallace's paper and one hastily prepared by Darwin be read at the Linnaean Society on the same day and with both authors absent. This was done, and neither paper roused much interest (Boakes, 1984). Darwin's epoch-making book *On the Origin of Species by Means of Natural Selection* was published two months later. By then there was so much interest in evolutionary theory that all 1,500 copies of the book sold on the first day it was available.

Six years after the publication of Darwin's

Thomas Malthus

theory, Captain Fitz-Roy committed suicide, perhaps because he felt that he was at least partially responsible for Darwin's theory of evolution (Gould, 1976). Because of the abundance of data that Darwin amassed and the thoroughness of his work, we attribute the theory to him and not to Wallace, but what follows may someday be referred to as the Darwin–Wallace theory of evolution.

Darwin's Theory of Evolution

The reproductive capacity of all living organisms allows for many more offspring than can survive in a given environment; therefore, there is a **struggle for survival**. Among the offspring of any species, there are vast *individual differences*, some of which are more conducive to survival than others. This results in the *survival of the fittest* (a term that Darwin borrowed from Spencer). For example, if there is a shortage of food in the environment of giraffes, only those giraffes with necks long enough to reach the few remaining leaves on tall trees will survive and reproduce. In this way, as long as food remains scarce, giraffes with shorter necks will tend to become extinct. Thus, a **natural selection** occurs among the offspring of a species. This natural selection of adaptive characteristics from the individual differences occurring among offspring accounts for the slow transmutation of a species over the eons. Evolution, then, results from the natural selection of those accidental variations among members of a species that prove to have survival value.

Darwin defined **fitness** as an organism's ability to survive and reproduce and in terms of *nothing else*. Fitness, then, is determined by an organism's features and its environment. Features that allow adequate adjustment to an organism's environment are called adaptive. Those organisms possessing **adaptive features** are fit; those that do not, are not. Notice that nothing is said about strength, aggression, and competitiveness. None of these features are *necessarily* conducive to fitness. Adaptive features are those features that are conducive to survival in a given environment, *whatever* those features may be. Also notice that Darwin said nothing about progress or perfection. Unlike Spencer, Darwin believed that evolution *just happens*; there is no direction or purpose involved. The direction that evolution takes is completely determined by the features possessed by members of various species of organisms and the environments in which those organisms exist. As environments change, what features are adaptive also change, and on it goes forever.

In *Origin of Species* (1859), Darwin said very little about humans, but later he made his case that humans were also the product of evolution. Both humans and the great apes, he said, descended from a common, distant primate ancestor.

Man may be excused for feeling some pride at having risen, though not through his own exertions, to the very summit of the organic scale; and the fact of his having thus risen, instead of having been aboriginally placed there, may give

him hope for a still higher destiny in the distant future. But we are not here concerned with hopes or fears, only with the truth as far as our reason permits us to discover it; and I have given the evidence to the best of my ability. We must, however, acknowledge, as it seems to me, that man with all his noble qualities, with sympathy which feels for the most debased, with benevolence which extends not only to other men but to the humblest living creature, with his God-like intellect which has penetrated into the movements and constitution of the solar system —with all these exalted powers—man still bears in his bodily frame the indelible stamp of his lowly origin. (C. Darwin, 1871, pp. 707–708)

Of Darwin's books, the one most directly related to psychology was *The Expression of Emotions in Man and Animals* (1872) in which he argued that human emotions were remnants of animal emotions that had once been necessary for survival. In the distant past, only those organisms capable of such things as biting and clawing survived and reproduced. Somewhat later, perhaps, simply the baring of the teeth or snarling were enough to discourage an aggressor and therefore facilitated survival. Although no longer as functional in modern society, these emotions that were originally associated with attack or defense are still part of our biological makeup, as can be seen in human reactions under extreme conditions.

Darwin's direct comparison of humans with other animals in *The Expression of Emotions in Man and Animals*, along with his forceful assertion that humans differed from other animals only in degree, launched modern comparative and animal psychology. It was now clear that much could be learned about humans by studying "lower" animals.

There is no better summary of Darwin's theory than Darwin's own conclusion to *Origin of Species*:

It is interesting to contemplate a tangled bank clothed with many plants of many kinds, with birds singing on the bushes, with various insects flitting about, and with worms crawling through damp earth, and to reflect that these elaborately constructed forms, so different from each other, and dependent upon each other in so complex a manner, have all been produced by laws acting around us. These laws taken in the largest sense, being Growth with Reproduction; Inheritance which is almost implied by Reproduction; Variability from the indirect and direct action of the conditions of life, and from use and disuse; a Ratio of Increase so high as to lead to a Struggle for Life, and as a consequence of Natural Selection, entailing Divergence of Character and the Extinction of less-improved forms. Thus, from the War of Nature, from famine and death, the most exalted object which we are capable of conceiving, namely, the production of the higher animals, directly follows. There is grandeur in this view of life, with its several powers, having been originally breathed by the Creator into a few forms or into one; and that whilst this planet has gone cycling on according to the fixed law of gravity, from so simple a beginning endless forms most beautiful and most wonderful have been, and are being evolved. (1859, pp. 373–374)

Darwin's Influence

To say the least, Darwin's theory was revolutionary. Its impact has been compared to that of the theories of Copernicus and Newton. He changed the traditional view of human nature and with it changed the history of philosophy and psychology. Besides its general impact on psychology, evolutionary theory is currently having a more direct impact. In 1975 Edward Wilson published *Sociobiology: The New Synthesis*, which attempts to explain the social behavior of organisms, including that of humans, in terms of evolutionary theory. By modifying Darwin's definition of fitness from the survival and reproductive success of the individual (Darwin's definition) to the perpetuation of one's genes, **sociobiology** can account for a wide array of human social behaviors. That is, according to sociobiologists, fitness is determined by how successful one is at perpetuating one's *genes* but not necessarily how successful one is at producing offspring. By emphasizing the importance of perpetuating one's genes, the sociobiologists place great emphasis on kin, or genetic, relationships. Because one's kin carries one's genes, helping them survive and reproduce becomes

an effective way of perpetuating one's genes. Armed with this conception of **inclusive fitness**, sociobiologists attempt to explain such things as love, altruism, warfare, religion, morality, mating systems, mate-selection strategies, child-rearing strategies, xenophobia, aggressive behavior, nepotism, and indoctrinability. (For two good sources to use, if one is interested in the application of evolutionary theory to an explanation of human social behavior, see E. Wilson, 1978, and Barash, 1979.)

As we will see in the remainder of this chapter, Darwin's ideas ultimately gave birth to a uniquely U.S. type of psychology—a psychology that emphasized individual differences and their measurement, the adaptive value of thoughts and behavior, and the study of animal behavior. Before discussing U.S. psychology, however, we must first review the works of a man who was an important link between Darwinian theory and U.S. psychology.

SIR FRANCIS GALTON

Erasmus Darwin, the physician, philosopher, poet, and early evolutionary theorist, was the grandfather of both Charles Darwin and **Francis Galton** (1822–1911). Galton was Darwin's cousin, and he was born near Birmingham, England, on February 16, the youngest of seven children. His father was a wealthy banker, and his mother was a half-sister of Charles Darwin's father. Receiving his early education at home, Galton could read and write by the age of 2-1/2. At age 5, he could read any book written in English, and by age 7, he was reading such authors as Shakespeare for pleasure. But things changed when Galton was sent to a boarding school where his experiences included flogging, hell-raising, sermons from the teachers, and fights with his fellow students. At age 16, he was taken out of boarding school and sent to Birmingham General Hospital to study medicine; after this practical experience, he transferred to King's College in London. He then moved to Cambridge University where he obtained his

ARCHIVES OF THE HISTORY OF AMERICAN PSYCHOLOGY

Francis Galton

degree in 1843. Galton planned on returning to King's College to obtain his medical degree, but when his father died he decided not to, so his formal education ended.

Because Galton was independently wealthy, he could work on what he wanted, when he wanted. After graduation he traveled in Egypt, the Sudan, and the Middle East. Then he came home and socialized with his rich friends for a few years—riding, shooting, ballooning, and experimenting with electricity. After consulting with a phrenologist who recommended an active life, Galton decided to join the Royal Geographical Society on a trip to southwest Africa. The trip lasted two years, and for Galton's creation of a map of previously unexplored territories in Africa (now called Namibia), the Royal Geographical Society honored him in 1853 with their highest medal. Galton was 32 at the time. We can see in Galton's map-making ability a pas-

sion that Galton had all his adult life: the passion to measure things.

In 1853 Galton published his first book, *Narrative of an Explorer in Tropical South Africa*. He became a recognized expert on travel in the wild, and the British government commissioned him to teach camping procedures to soldiers. In 1855 he published his second book, *The Art of Travel*, which included information on how to deal with wild animals and savages. For his inventiveness, Galton was elected president of the Royal Geographical Society in 1856.

To further illustrate Galton's passion for measurement, here are a few of his other endeavors:

• In his effort to measure and predict the weather, he invented the weather map and was the first to use the terms *highs*, *lows*, and *fronts*.

• He was the first to suggest that fingerprints could be used for personal identification—a procedure later adopted by Scotland Yard.

• He attempted to determine the effectiveness of prayer (he found it ineffective).

• He tried to determine which country had the most beautiful women.

• He measured the degree of boredom at scientific lectures.

One can imagine Galton's delight when he became aware of his cousin's evolutionary theory with its emphasis on individual differences. Galton believed that if there were important individual differences among people, clearly they should be measured and cataloged. This became Galton's mission in life.

The Measurement of Intelligence

Galton assumed that intelligence was a matter of sensory acuity because humans could know the world only through the senses. Thus, the more acute the senses, the more intelligent a person was presumed to be. Furthermore, because sensory acuity was mainly a function of natural endowment, intelligence was inherited. And if intelligence was inherited, as Galton assumed, one would expect to see extremes in intelligence run in families. Assuming that high reputation or eminence was an accurate indicator of high intellectual ability, Galton set out to measure the frequency of eminence among the offspring of illustrious parents as compared to the frequency of eminence among the offspring of the general population. For comparison with the general population, Galton studied the offspring of judges, statesmen, commanders, literary men, scientists, poets, musicians, painters, and divines. The results of Galton's (1869) research were clear: The offspring of illustrious individuals were far more likely to be illustrious than the offspring of nonillustrious individuals. Galton also observed, however, that zeal and vigor must be coupled with inherited capacity before eminence could be attained.

Eugenics. Galton's conclusion raised a fascinating possibility: *selective breeding*. If intelligence was inherited, could not the general intelligence of a people be improved by encouraging the mating of bright people and discouraging the mating of people who were less bright? Galton's answer was yes. He called the improvement of living organisms through selective breeding **eugenics**, and Galton advocated its practice as the following quotation shows:

> I propose to show in this book that a man's natural abilities are derived by inheritance, under exactly the same limitations as are the form and physical features of the whole organic world. Consequently, as it is easy, notwithstanding those limitations, to obtain by careful selection a permanent breed of dogs or horses gifted with peculiar powers of running, or of doing anything else, so it would be quite practicable to produce a highly-gifted race of men by judicious marriages during several consecutive generations. I shall show that social agencies of an ordinary character, whose influences are little suspected, are at this moment working towards the degradation of human nature, and that others are working towards its improvement. I conclude that each generation has enormous power over the natural gifts of those that follow, and maintain that it is a duty we owe to humanity to

investigate the range of that power, and to exercise it in a way that, without being unwise towards ourselves, shall be most advantageous to future inhabitants of the earth. (1869, p. 45)

In 1865 Galton proposed that couples be scientifically paired and that the government pay those possessing desirable characteristics to marry. The government was also to take care of the educational expenses of any offspring.

The nature–nurture controversy. Galton's extreme nativism did not go unchallenged. Alphonse de Candolle (1806–1893), for example, wrote a book stressing the importance of environment in producing scientists. Candolle suggested that climate, religious tolerance, democratic government, and a thriving economy were at least as important as inherited capacity in producing scientists.

Such criticism prompted Galton's next book, *English Men of Science: Their Nature and Nurture* (1874). To gather information for this book, Galton sent a questionnaire to 200 of his fellow scientists at the Royal Society. This was the first use of the questionnaire in psychology. The participants were asked many factual questions ranging from their political and religious backgrounds to their hat sizes. In addition, they were asked to explain why they had become interested in science in general as well as in their particular branches of science. Finally, the scientists were asked whether they thought that their interest in science was innate.

Although the questionnaire was very long, most of the scientists finished and returned it. Most believed that their interest in science was inherited. Galton noticed, however, that a disproportionate number of the scientists were Scottish and that these scientists praised the broad and liberal Scottish educational system. Conversely, the English scientists had very unkind things to say about the English educational system. Based on these findings, Galton urged that English schools be reformed to make them more like Scottish schools. Here Galton was acknowledging the importance of the environment. His revised position was that the *potential* for high intelligence was inherited but that it must be nurtured by a proper environment. Galton clearly stated the **nature–nurture controversy**, which is still the focus of much attention in modern psychology:

> The phrase "nature and nurture" is a convenient jingle of words, for it separates under two distinct heads the innumerable elements of which personality is composed. Nature is all that a man brings with himself into the world; nurture is every influence that affects him after his birth. The distinction is clear: the one produces the infant such as it actually is, including its latent faculties of growth and mind; the other affords the environment amid which the growth takes place, by which natural tendencies may be strengthened or thwarted, or wholly new ones implanted. (1874, p. 12)

In his next book *Inquiries into Human Faculty and Its Development* (1883), Galton further supported his basic nativistic position by studying twins. He found monozygotic (one-egged) twins to be very similar to one another even when they were reared apart and dizygotic (two-egged) twins to be dissimilar even when they were reared together.

The Word-Association Test

In *Inquiries*, Galton devised psychology's first word-association test. He wrote 75 words, each on a separate piece of paper. Then he glanced at each word and noted his response to it on another piece of paper. He went through the 75 words on four different occasions, randomizing the words each time. Three things struck Galton about this study. First, responses to stimulus words tended to be constant; he very often gave the same response to a word all four times he experienced it. Second, his responses were often drawn from his childhood experience. Third, he felt that such a procedure revealed aspects of the mind never revealed before:

> Perhaps the strongest of the impressions left by these experiments regards the multifariousness of the work done by the mind in a state of half-consciousness, and the valid reason they afford for believing in the existence of still deeper strata of mental operations, sunk wholly below the level of consciousness, which may account for such mental phenomena as cannot otherwise be explained. (1883, p. 145)

Whether Galton influenced Freud is not known, but Galton's work with word association anticipated two aspects of psychoanalysis: the use of free association and the recognition of unconscious motivation.

Mental Imagery

Galton was also among the first, if not the first, to study imagery. In *Inquiries* he reported the results of asking people to imagine the scene as they had sat down to breakfast. He found that the ability to imagine was essentially normally distributed, with some individuals almost totally incapable of imagery and others having the ability to imagine the breakfast scene flawlessly. Galton was amazed to find that many of his scientist friends had virtually no ability to form images. If sensations and their remnants (images) were the stuff of all thinking, as the empiricists had assumed, why was it that many scientists seemed unable to form and use images? Galton also found, not so surprisingly, that whatever a person's imagery ability was, he or she assumed that everyone else had the same ability.

Anthropometry

Galton's desire to measure individual differences among humans inspired him to create what he called an "anthropometric laboratory" at London's International Health Exhibition in 1884. Here, in about one year, Galton measured 9,337 humans in just about every way he could imagine. For example, he measured head size, arm span, standing height, sitting height, length of the middle finger, weight, strength of hand squeeze (measured by a dynamometer), breathing capacity, visual acuity, auditory acuity, reaction time to visual and auditory stimuli, the highest detectable auditory tone, and speed of blow (the time it takes for a person to punch a pad). Some of these measures were included because Galton believed sensory acuity to be related to intelligence, and for that reason, Galton's "anthropometric laboratory" can be viewed as an effort to measure intelligence. The nonacuity measures were included because Galton was interested in a number of issues related to individual differences. In 1888 Galton set up a similar laboratory in the science galleries of the South Kensington Museum, and it operated for several years. A handout described the purpose of the laboratory to potential participants:

1. For the use of those who desire to be accurately measured in many ways, either to obtain timely warning of remediable faults in development, or to learn their powers.
2. For keeping a methodological register of the principal measurements of each person, of which he may at any future time obtain a copy under reasonable restrictions. His initials and date of birth will be entered in the register, but not his name. The names are indexed in a separate book.
3. For supplying information on the methods, practice, and uses of human measurement.
4. For anthropometric experiment and research, and for obtaining data for statistical discussion. (Pearson, 1924, p. 358)

For a small fee (3 pence), a person would be measured in all ways described above; and for a smaller fee (2 pence), a person could be measured again at another time. Each participant was given a copy of his or her results, and Galton kept a copy for his files. Among the many things that Galton was interested in examining were test–retest relationships, gender differences on various measurements, intercorrelations among various measurements, relationships of various measurements to socioeconomic status, and family resemblances among various measurements. Because Galton's incredible amount of data existed long before there were computers, or even calculators, much of it went unanalyzed at the time. Since then, however, other researchers have analyzed portions of the previously unanalyzed data. Recently, Johnson, McClearn, Yuen, Nagoshi, Ahern, and Cole (1985) have reported the results of Galton's own analyses,

the results of analyses of Galton's data done by researchers after him, and their own analyses of Galton's data that had not been previously analyzed.

Although intelligence is no longer believed to be related to sensory acuity, Galton's early efforts can be seen as the beginning of the mental testing movement in psychology. Following our review of Galton, we will have more to say about how intelligence testing changed after Galton's efforts.

The Concept of Correlation

The last of Galton's many contributions to psychology that we will consider is his notion of correlation, which has become one of psychology's most widely used statistical methods. In 1888 Galton published an article entitled "Co-Relations and Their Measurement, Chiefly from Anthropometric Data," and in 1889 he published a book entitled *Natural Inheritance*. Both works describe the concepts of correlation and regression. Galton defined **correlation**, or co-relation, as follows:

Two variable organs are said to be co-related when the variation on one is accompanied on the average by more or less variation of the other, and in the same direction. Thus the length, of the arm is said to be co-related with that of the leg, because a person with a long arm has usually a long leg, and conversely. (1888, p. 135)

In a definition of correlation, the word *tend* is very important. Even in the above quotation, Galton said that those with long arms *usually* have long legs. After planting peas of varying sizes and measuring the size of their offspring, Galton observed that very large peas tended not to have offspring quite as large as they were and that very small peas tended not to have offspring quite as small as themselves. He called this phenomenon **regression toward the mean**, something he also found when he correlated heights of children with heights of their parents. In fact, Galton found regression whenever he correlated inherited characteristics. Earlier, Galton had observed that eminent individuals only tended to have eminent offspring.

By visually displaying his correlational data in the form of scatterplots, Galton found that he could visually determine the strength of a relationship. It was **Karl Pearson** (1857–1936) who devised a formula that produced a mathematical expression of the strength of a relationship. Pearson's formula produces the now familiar **coefficient of correlation** (r).

Galton's Contributions to Psychology

Few individuals in psychology have more firsts attributed to them than Galton. Galton's firsts include study of the nature–nurture question, the use of questionnaires, the use of a word-association test, twin studies, the study of imagery, intelligence testing, and the development of the correlational technique. Everywhere in his work, we see a concern with individual differences and their measurements, a concern that was a direct reflection of the influence of Darwin's theory of evolution.

James McKeen Cattell

ARCHIVES OF THE HISTORY OF AMERICAN PSYCHOLOGY

INTELLIGENCE TESTING AFTER GALTON

James McKeen Cattell

The transfer of Galton's testing procedures to the United States was accomplished mainly through the efforts of **James McKeen Cattell** (1860–1944), who had studied with both Wundt and Galton in Europe but had been much more influenced by Galton. Cattell, born on May 25 in Easton, Pennsylvania, was a son of a Presbyterian clergyman, who was also a professor of Latin and Greek at Lafayette College where he later became president. Cattell entered Lafayette College before his 16th birthday and stood first in his class without much effort. Among his favorite subjects were mathematics and physics. After graduation from Lafayette in 1880, he traveled to Leipzig to become one of Wundt's students. While with Wundt, Cattell and a fellow student

did numerous reaction-time studies. Among other things, Cattell noticed that his own reaction times differed systematically from those of his fellow researcher and proposed to Wundt that individual differences in reaction time be explored. The proposal was rejected because Wundt was more interested in the nature of the mind in general than with individual differences. About this time, Cattell became aware of Galton's anthropometric laboratory in London and began a correspondence with Galton mainly concerning the measurement of reaction time. After finishing his degree with Wundt, Cattell started a two-year research fellowship at Cambridge University where he worked with Galton. Under Galton's influence, Cattell came to believe that intelligence was related to sensory acuity and was therefore largely inherited:

> As a self-proclaimed disciple of Francis Galton, Cattell's interest in eugenics is clear. . . . He proposed that incentives be given "the best elements of all the people" to intermarry and have

large families [Cattell and his wife had seven children] and in fact offered each of his children $1,000 if they would marry the child of a college professor. (Sokal, 1971, p. 630)

On his return to the United States in 1888, Cattell was first affiliated with the University of Pennsylvania where he administered Galtonian-type measures to his students. In 1890 he published his techniques and results in an article that used the term *mental test* for the first time. It was also in this article that Cattell described 10 mental tests that he felt could be administered to the general public and a total of 50 tests that he felt should be administered to university students. The 10 mental tests were mainly Galtonian, but Cattell also added a few measurements he learned in Wundt's laboratory. Among the 10 tests were hand strength, two-point threshold, amount of pressure required to cause pain, ability to discriminate between weights, reaction time, accuracy of bisecting a 50-centimeter line, accuracy in judging a 10-second interval, and ability to remember a series of letters. The more comprehensive series of 50 tests was essentially more of the same. The vast majority of them measured some form of sensory acuity or reaction time.

In 1891 Cattell moved to Columbia University where he began administering his tests to entering freshmen. Implicit in Cattell's testing program was the assumption that if a number of his tests were measuring the same thing (intelligence), performance on those tests should be highly correlated. Also implicit was the assumption that if tests were measuring intelligence, they should correlate highly with academic success in college. That is, for a test of intelligence to be valid, it must make differential predictions about how individuals will perform on tasks requiring intelligence.

In 1901 Clark Wissler, one of Cattell's graduate students, tested Cattell's assumptions. Armed with Pearson's newly perfected correlation coefficient, Wissler measured the relationships among Cattell's tests and between performance on various tests and academic performance. Wissler's results were disastrous for Cattell's testing program. He found that intercorrelations among the tests were very low and that the correlation between various tests and success in college was nearly zero (Guilford, 1967). Thus, the tests were not measuring the same thing because if they were they would be highly correlated; and they were not valid because if they were scores would correlate highly with academic achievement.

With such unambiguous, negative findings, the interest in mental testing quickly faded. Wissler switched his field to anthropology where he became an outspoken environmentalist, and Cattell turned his attention mainly to administrative duties and to the editing of journals. The emphasis in U.S. psychology was turning toward practicality, and it appeared that Galtonian measures were not very useful, at least as far as intelligence was concerned. This moratorium on mental testing was not to last long, however.

Alfred Binet

In France a different approach to measuring intelligence was being tried, one that appeared to be more successful than Galton's. It involved *directly* measuring the complex mental operations thought to be involved in intelligence. **Alfred Binet** (1857–1911) championed this method of testing, which was more in the rationalist tradition than in the empiricist tradition.

Binet was born on July 11 in Nice, France. His father was a physician, as were both of his grandfathers. Binet's parents separated when he was a young child, and he, an only child, was reared mainly by his mother, a successful artist. Although initially following the family tradition by studying medicine, Binet terminated his medical studies and turned to psychology instead. Being independently wealthy allowed Binet to take the time to educate himself, and he read the works of Darwin, Galton, and the British empiricists (especially John Stuart Mill), among others. He received no formal education in psychology.

Binet began his career in psychology by working with Jean-Martin Charcot (1825–1893), the world famous psychiatrist, at La Salpêtrière.

Alfred Binet

Like Charcot, Binet conducted research on hypnotism, and he claimed that in one study he had been able to manipulate the symptoms and sensations of a hypnotized subject by moving a magnet to various places around the subject's body. He also claimed that application of the magnet could convert fear of an object, such as a snake, into affection. Binet thought that such findings would have important implications for the practice of medicine in general and for psychiatry in particular, but other researchers could not reproduce Binet's findings and concluded that Binet's results were due to poor experimental control. For example, it was found that Binet's subjects always knew what was expected of them and acted accordingly. When subjects were unaware of the researcher's expectations, they did not exhibit the phenomena that Binet had observed. Thus, suggestion had caused Binet's results, not the magnet. After a long attempt to defend his beliefs, Binet finally admitted that his

results had been due to suggestion and not to the magnet's power, and he resigned his position at La Salpêtrière in 1890. The humiliation resulting from his public admission of shoddy research procedures haunted Binet all his life. His statement "Tell me what you are looking for, and I will tell you what you will find" (Wolf, 1973, p. 347) was directed at metaphysicians, but Binet knew from personal experience that it could apply to researchers as well.

Fortunately, Binet's second career in psychology was more successful. Without a professional position, Binet directed his attention to the study of the intellectual growth of his two daughters, who were two and one-half and four and one-half years of age at the time. The tests he created to investigate his children's mental operations were very similar to those Jean Piaget later devised. He asked, for example, which of two piles contained more objects and found that the answer was not determined by the number of objects in the piles but by the amount of space the piles took up on the table. Binet also investigated how well his daughters could remember objects that he first showed them and then removed from sight. Binet also employed a number of tests used by Galton and Cattell to measure visual acuity and reaction time. In 1890 he published three papers describing his research on his daughters, and in 1903 he published *The Experimental Study of Intelligence*, which summarized his longitudinal study of the intellectual growth of his daughters.

In 1891 Binet joined the laboratory for physiological psychology at the Sorbonne, where he performed research in such areas as memory, the nature of childhood fears, the reliability of eyewitness testimony, creativity, imageless thought, and graphology. During his years at the Sorbonne, Binet also investigated individual differences in the perception of inkblots—before the famous work of Rorschach. In her outstanding biography of Binet, Wolf (1973) says that Binet was the father of experimental psychology in France and that he had more of an impact on U.S. psychology than Wundt did. (The reader is directed to Wolf's book for more details concerning Binet's many pioneering research endeavors and for the interesting details of his life.)

Individual psychology. Rather than being interested in what people have in common, Binet was primarily interested in what made them different. In 1896 he, along with his assistant Victor Henri (1872–1940), wrote an article entitled "Individual Psychology," which proposed a list of variables on which individuals differ, especially intellectually. What they sought was a list of important variables and a way of determining the extent to which each variable exists in a given individual. With the variables isolated and a way of measuring them available, it was hoped that it would be possible to "evaluate" any individual in a relatively short period of time. The work of Galton and Cattell was rejected because it placed too much emphasis on sensory processes and not enough on higher mental processes. In other words, Binet and Henri proposed to study cognitive abilities *directly* instead of indirectly via sensory acuity. Another reason that the work of Galton and Cattell was rejected is that it minimized important differences between a child's mind and that of an adult. According to Binet and Henri, the important variables on which humans differ are complex, higher-order processes that tend to vary according to age. The list of such variables proposed in 1896 included memory, imagery, imagination, attention, comprehension, suggestibility, aesthetic judgment, moral judgment, force of will, and judgment of visual space.

Unfortunately, Binet and Henri's goal of accessing a person's higher mental processes in a relatively short period of time failed. Administering the tests took many hours, and interpreting the results required even more hours of subjective, clinical judgment. Even more devastating, however, was the study on their tests performed by Stella Sharp, a graduate student at Cornell University. Sharp (1899) found very low intercorrelations among the Binet and Henri tests and concluded (as Wissler had concluded about Cattell's tests) that they could not be mea-

suring the same attribute (presumably intelligence). Such results, along with their own disappointing results, caused Binet and Henri to abandon their "individual psychology" project. The experience gained, however, would serve Binet well on his next project.

Assessing intellectual deficiency. In 1899 **Theodore Simon** (1873–1961), who worked as an intern at a large institution for mentally retarded children, asked Binet to supervise his doctoral research. Binet agreed and viewed this as an opportunity to have access to a large subject pool. Also in 1899, Binet joined the Free Society for the Psychological Study of the Child, an organization that sought scientifically valid information about children, especially about their educational problems. Binet soon became leader of the society. In 1903 Binet and Simon were appointed to the group that the French government commissioned to study the problems of retarded children in the French schools. It was immediately clear that if retarded children were to receive special education, it was necessary to have an adequate method of distinguishing them from normal children. At the time, variations of Galton's tests were being used to detect mental retardation, and Binet noted that because of these tests children who were blind or deaf were erroneously being classified as retarded.

In 1904 Binet and Simon set out to create tests that would differentiate between intellectually normal and intellectually subnormal children. Their first step was to isolate one group of children clearly diagnosed as normal and another group diagnosed as subnormal. The second step was to test both groups in a number of different ways, hoping to discover measurements that would clearly distinguish members of one group from the other. From his previous research, Binet was convinced that the best way to examine individual differences was in terms of complex, mental processes, and so many of the tests given to the normal and subnormal children were of that type. After much trial and error, Binet and Simon arrived at the first test of intelligence that measured intelligence directly instead of indirectly through measures of sensory acuity.

The 1905 Binet–Simon scale of intelligence and its revisions. Binet and Simon offered the **Binet–Simon scale of intelligence** as a valid way of distinguishing between normal and mentally deficient children—a way that was to replace the less reliable physical, social, and educational signs that were being used at the time to identify the retarded. The 1905 scale consisted of 30 tests ranging in difficulty from simple eye movements to abstract definitions. Three of the tests measured motor development, and the other 27 were designed to measure cognitive abilities. The tests were arranged in order of difficulty, so that the more tests a child passed the more fully developed his or her intelligence was assumed to be. The scale was given to normal children and to children thought to be retarded, all of them between the ages of 2 and 12.

The 30 tests contained in the 1905 Binet–Simon scale were the following:

1. Demonstrating visual coordination

2. Demonstrating prehension on contact (grasping a cube after touching it)

3. Demonstrating prehension on sight

4. Recognizing food (choice between wood and chocolate)

5. Seeking food (in response to chocolate wrapped in paper)

6. Following simple orders or repeating gestures

7. Pointing to objects (head, nose, etc.)

8. Recognizing objects in picture

9. Naming objects in picture

10. Discriminating two lines for length

11. Repeating three digits

12. Discriminating two weights

13. Resisting suggestions

14. Defining simple words

15. Repeating sentence of 15 words

16. Giving differences between pairs of objects

17. Demonstrating visual memory

18. Drawing forms from memory

19. Demonstrating memory span for digits

20. Stating similarities between objects

21. Discriminating lines rapidly

22. Ordering five weights

23. Identifying missing weight (of the five weights in test 22)

24. Giving rhyming words

25. Completing sentences

26. Constructing sentence containing three given words

27. Answering questions (e.g., "What should you do when sleepy?")

28. Giving time after hands of a clock have been interchanged

29. Folding and cutting paper

30. Distinguishing between abstract terms (e.g., *sad* and *bored*)

Binet and Simon found that almost all normal children, 2 years old or older, could easily pass tests 1–6. Also, slightly or moderately retarded children could pass some or all of these tests. Severely retarded children could pass only a few or none of them. Most of tests 7–15 could be passed by normal children between the ages of 2 and 5. Slightly retarded children could pass several of these tests, moderately retarded children had great difficulty, and rarely could severely retarded children pass any of them. Tests 16–30 could be routinely passed by normal children between the ages of 5 and 12, but even slightly retarded children had great difficulty with them, and moderately and severely retarded children most often could pass none.

We see in the Binet–Simon scale a reflection of Binet's belief that intelligence is not a single ability but several. With this belief, Binet reflects the faculty psychology of several rationalistic philosophers. He did not, however, accept the nativism that often accompanies rationalistic viewpoints. He did believe that inheritance may place an upper limit on one's intellectual ability, but he also believed that almost everyone functions below their potential. Therefore, he believed strongly that *everyone* could grow intellectually and that fact should be of prime importance to educators.

In 1908 Binet and Simon revised their scale. Their goal now was to go beyond simply distinguishing normal from retarded children, to distinguishing among levels of intelligence for normal children. The tests were administered to a large number of normal children from ages 3 to 13. If 75 percent or more of the children of a certain age passed a particular test, the test was assigned to that age level. For example, most 4 year old children could copy a square but not a diamond. More specifically, it was found that only a minority of 3-year-olds could copy a square, a majority of 4-year-olds (75 percent or more) could copy a square, and essentially all 5-year-olds could do so. In this way, it could be determined whether a given child was performing at, above, or below average. A 5-year-old passing the tests that most other 5-year-olds also passed was considered to have normal intelligence. But if that child passed only the tests typically passed by 4-year-olds, he or she was thought to have below-average intelligence. And if the 5-year-old passed tests normally passed by 6-year-olds, he or she was thought to have above-average intelligence. In other words, a child's intelligence level was determined by how much higher or lower than the norm the child performed. The 1908 revision of the Binet–Simon scale consisted of 58 tests, each showing the age at which 75 percent or more of the children taking it perform correctly.

The 1911 revision of the scale included normative data on adults (15-year-olds) and provided exactly five tests for each age level. The latter allowed for a more refined measure of intelligence. For example, if an 8-year-old child passed all the tests corresponding to his or her age, he or she would be considered normal. It is possible, however, that an 8-year-old will also pass some tests typically passed only by 9-year-olds. The new procedure allowed one-fifth of a year to be added to a child's score for each test the child passed beyond those that were the norm for his or her age. Thus, a child's "intellectual level" could be expressed in terms of intellectual age, that is, the age corresponding to the most difficult tests the child could pass.

Binet warned that extreme caution should be taken in interpreting a child's "intellectual age." For one thing, he observed that the incidence of children whose intellectual age was only one year behind their chronological age was common and these children probably would have little trouble in school. Children whose intellectual age was two or more years behind their chronological age would probably have trouble in a standard school program and would need special attention. But even in the latter case, poor test performance did not necessarily mean the child was mentally deficient. Before such a label was applied, the test administrator had to ensure that the child was healthy and motivated when he or she took the test and that he or she was knowledgeable enough about French culture to understand the reflections of that culture on the test.

Intelligence quotient. In 1911 **William Stern** (1871–1938), a German psychologist, introduced the term **mental age**. For Stern, a child's mental age was determined by his or her performance on the Binet–Simon tests. Stern also suggested that mental age be divided by chronological age, yielding an **intelligence quotient**. For example, if a particular 7-year-old passed all tests typically passed by 7 year olds, his or her intelligence quotient would be 7/7, or 1.00. If another 7-year-old passed only those tests typically passed by 5-year-olds, his or her intelligence quotient would be 5/7, or about .71. In 1916 Lewis Terman suggested that the intelligence quotient be multiplied by 100 to remove the decimal point. It was also Terman who abbreviated intelligence quotient as *IQ*. Thus, combining the suggestions made by Stern and Terman, we have the familiar formula for IQ:

$$IQ = \frac{\text{Mental Age (MA)}}{\text{Chronological Age (CA)}} \times 100$$

Binet was opposed to the use of the intelligence quotient. He felt that intelligence was too complex to be represented by a simple term or number. History shows, however, that Stern's simplifications won out over Binet's opposition. In any case, Binet and Simon had developed a relatively brief, easy-to-administer measure of intelligence, and it became extremely popular. By the beginning of the First World War, the Binet–Simon test was being used throughout most of the world.

Binet's view of his intelligence scale. Before reviewing what happened to the Binet–Simon scale in the United States, it is important to review how Binet viewed his scale. First and foremost, Binet saw the scale as a device for identifying children who needed some sort of special education. Binet strongly believed that children with low test scores could benefit considerably if given special attention. Although Binet believed that inheritance may set an upper limit on intellectual potential, he also believed that everyone could grow a great deal intellectually if properly stimulated. He worried very much about students in classrooms where teachers believed that students' intellectual performance was innately determined. This, of course, was especially regretful for students believed to have low intelligence:

> I have often observed, to my regret, that a widespread prejudice exists with regard to the educability of intelligence. The familiar proverb, "When one is stupid, it is for a long time," seems to be accepted indiscriminately by teachers with a stunted critical judgment. These teachers lose interest in students with low intelligence. Their lack of sympathy and respect is illustrated by their unrestrained comments in the presence of the children: "This child will never achieve anything . . . He is poorly endowed . . . He is not intelligent at all." I have heard such rash statements too often. They are repeated daily in primary schools, nor are secondary schools exempt from the charge. (Binet, 1909/1975, p. 105)

In Binet's reaction to those who maintained that some children would *never* accomplish certain things, he indicates clearly that he did not accept an extreme nativist view of intelligence:

> "Never!" What a strong word! A few modern philosophers seem to lend their moral support to these deplorable verdicts when they assert that an individual's intelligence is a fixed quantity, a quantity which cannot be increased. We must protest and react against this brutal pessimism. We shall attempt to prove that it is without foundation. (Binet, 1909/1975, pp. 105–106)

Mental orthopedics. Binet believed that mental orthopedics could prepare disadvantaged children for school. **Mental orthopedics** consisted of exercises that would improve a child's will, attention, and discipline—all abilities that Binet felt were necessary for effective classroom education. Binet believed that by engaging in mental orthopedics, children learned how to learn:

> If we consider that intelligence is not a single function, indivisible and of a particular essence, but rather that it is formed by the chorus of all the little functions of discrimination, observation, retention, etc., the plasticity and extensibility of which have been determined, it will appear undeniable that the same law governs the whole and its parts, and that consequently anyone's intelligence is susceptible to being developed. With practice, training, and above all, method, we manage to increase our attention, our memory, our judgment and literally to become more intelligent than we were before. Improvement goes on in this way until the time when we reach our limit. (Binet, 1909/1975, p. 107)

Both Binet and Galton died in 1911. Galton was an old man of 89 who had a long, highly productive life; Binet was 54 and at the height of his career.

Charles Spearman and the Concept of General Intelligence

After a military career in the English army that lasted until he was 34, **Charles Spearman** (1863–1945) turned to a career in psychology, studying with both Wundt and Külpe in Germany. During a break in his studies with Wundt, during which he returned to England to serve in the army during the Boer War (1900–1902), Spearman began reading the works of Galton. Thoroughly impressed, he performed a number of experiments on village schoolchildren, and the results tended to confirm Galton's belief concerning the relationship between sensory acuity and intelligence. He found that measures of sensory acuity not only correlated highly among themselves but, more important, they also correlated highly (+.38) with "cleverness in school." In 1904 he published his results in an article entitled "General Intelligence: Objectively Determined and Measured." Partially on the basis of his controversial article, he was offered a position at University College, London, where he began a career that included attacks on sensationalism, associationism, hedonism, and most other accepted philosophical and psychological beliefs. Among the more specific things that he attacked were the results of studies, such as Wissler's, that showed little intercorrelation among Galton's and Cattell's measures of sensory acuity and almost no correlation between measures of sensory acuity and academic performance. Because his own results were almost the opposite, he concluded that the results contrary to his were statistical artifacts. He also concluded that because the measures of sensory acuity were intercorrelated, they must be measuring a common ability or faculty, which he named **general intelligence** (g). Furthermore, following in the Galtonian tradition, he claimed that g was determined almost exclusively by inheritance.

Spearman's conclusions about the nature of intelligence are important for three reasons: (1) He viewed intelligence as a unitary faculty, whereas Binet viewed it as comprising many different faculties; (2) he viewed intelligence as largely inherited, whereas Binet viewed it as modifiable by experience; and (3) it was largely Spearman's conception of intelligence that was embraced by the new testing movement in the United States, not Binet's. That is, IQ was viewed as measuring something like Spearman's

Henry Herbert Goddard

g rather than Binet's multifarious "intellectual level."

THE BINET–SIMON SCALE IN THE UNITED STATES

Henry Herbert Goddard

Henry Herbert Goddard (1866–1957) was born into a New England Quaker family and obtained his bachelor's and master's degrees from Haverford College. After being a high school teacher and then principle for six years, he enrolled in the doctoral program in psychology at Clark University to pursue his interests in education and psychology. Goddard did his doctoral dissertation, which investigated the psychological factors involved in faith healing, under the supervision of G. Stanley Hall (see chapter 11). After completing his degree in 1899, Goddard first accepted a teaching position at Pennsylvania's West Chester State Teacher's College, and then in 1906 he became director of research at the Training School for the Feebleminded in Vineland, New Jersey.

It was Goddard who translated the Binet–

Simon scale into English. Although initially skeptical of the scale, he found it to be very effective in classifying children in terms of their degree of retardation. Goddard then translated all of Binet and Simon's works into English and, following Binet's death in 1911, became the world's leading proponent of Binet's approach to measuring intelligence. However, although accepting Binet's testing procedures, Goddard accepted the Galton–Cattell–Spearman view of the nature of intelligence rather than Binet's. The fact that Goddard believed that intelligence was a single faculty whose strength is determined by heredity is clearly seen in the following quotation:

> Stated in its boldest form, our thesis is that the chief determiner of human conduct is a unitary mental process which we call intelligence: that this process is conditioned by a nervous mechanism which is inborn: that the degree of efficiency to be attained by that nervous mechanism and the consequent grade of intelligence or mental level for each individual is determined by the kind of chromosomes that come together with the union of the germ cells: that it is but little affected by any later influences except such serious accidents as may destroy part of the mechanism. (Goddard, 1920, p. 1)

Besides administering the translated Binet–Simon scale to the children at the Vineland School, Goddard also administered it to 2,000 public school students in New Jersey. He was shocked to find that many of the public school students performed below the norms for their ages. This especially disturbed Goddard because of his belief that intelligence was largely inherited—a belief he thought to be supported by the observation that the children at Vineland often had brothers and sisters who were feebleminded.

Study of the "Kallikak" family. Goddard decided to investigate the relationship between family background and intelligence more carefully. In 1911 he administered the Binet–Simon scale to Deborah Kallikak, who had been living at the Vineland School since 1897. "Kallikak"

was a fictitious name that Goddard created out of the Greek words *kalos* (good) and *kakos* (bad). Although Deborah's chronological age was 22, her test performance yielded a mental age of 9, producing an IQ of about 41. Goddard coined the term *moron* to denote Deborah's intellectual level. He then traced Deborah's ancestry back to the American Revolution, when Martin Kallikak, Sr., had had a relationship with a "feebleminded" barmaid that resulted in the birth of Martin Kallikak, Jr. After leaving the army, the elder Martin married a "worthy girl," and they had seven children. The younger Martin eventually married and had 10 children. In Goddard's analysis, the descendants of the elder Martin and the "worthy girl" represented the "good" side of Deborah's ancestry, and the descendants of the younger Martin represented the "bad" side.

Goddard found that of the elder Martin's children, none were feebleminded, whereas five of the younger Martin's children were feebleminded. In subsequent generations on the younger Martin's side, Goddard found an abundance of mentally defective individuals. In Goddard's time, people believed that feeblemindedness was the cause of most criminal, immoral, and antisocial behavior; and Goddard supported this belief by showing that many descendants of the younger Martin had been horse thieves, prostitutes, convicts, alcoholics, parents of illegitimate children, or sexual deviates. Of the hundreds of descendants from the elder Martin's marriage, only three had been mentally defective, and one had been considered "sexually loose." Among the elder Martin's descendants had been doctors, lawyers, educators, and other prestigious individuals.

Goddard reported his findings in *The Kallikak Family, a Study in the Heredity of Feeble-Mindedness* (1912). His research was taken as support for the Galtonian belief that intelligence was genetically determined. Along with Goddard, several leading scientists of the day urged that the mentally defective be sterilized or segregated from the rest of society. They contended that because the feebleminded could not be expected to control their own reproduction, the intelligent members of society must control it for them:

> If both parents are feeble-minded all the children will be feeble-minded. It is obvious that such matings should not be allowed. It is perfectly clear that no feeble-minded person should ever be allowed to marry or to become a parent. It is obvious that if this rule is to be carried out, the intelligent part of society must enforce it. (Goddard, 1914, p. 561)

No fewer than 20 states passed sterilization laws, and thousands of "undesirables" were sterilized. In some states, the sterilization law was enforced until the 1970s. Galton would have been pleased.

Mental testing and immigration. In the years from 1905–1913, millions of individuals migrated from Europe to the United States, and there was growing concern that many of these immigrants might be mentally inferior. The question was how to know for certain. In 1912 the commissioner of immigration invited Goddard to Ellis Island to observe the immigrants. Goddard claimed he could tell that many of the immigrants were mentally defective simply by observing their physical characteristics, but to be sure he administered the Binet–Simon scale. Based on the test results, many immigrants were labeled mentally defective, and thousands were deported. Goddard even went so far as to specify the European countries for which the percentage of mentally defective immigrants was the highest. In general, Goddard concluded that between 40 and 50 percent of the immigrants were morons.

As with his earlier work, Goddard assumed that test performance of the immigrants was due mainly to inherited intelligence and not to educational, cultural, or personal experience—all factors that were later found to profoundly influence performance on the test. But the immigrants were also taking the test under special circumstances:

> For the evident reason, consider a group of frightened men and women who speak no English and who have just endured an oceanic voyage in steerage. Most are poor and have never gone to school; many have never held a pencil or pen in their hand. They march off the boat: one of Goddard's [assistants] takes them aside shortly thereafter, sits them down, hands them a pencil, and asks them to reproduce on paper a figure shown to them a moment ago, but now withdrawn from their sight. Could their failure be a result of testing conditions, of weakness, fear, or confusion, rather than of innate stupidity? Goddard considered the possibility, but rejected it. (Gould, 1981, p. 166)

Furthermore, the tests were administered by a translator whose accuracy in translating the test into the immigrant's native tongue was taken on faith.

Because of Goddard's efforts, the rate of deportation increased 350 percent in 1913 and 570 percent in 1914. Except for all the common, inexpensive laborers the United States was losing, Goddard was pleased. In his later years, Goddard radically changed his beliefs by embracing many of Binet's views. For example, he finally agreed that the proper treatment for individuals scoring low on intelligence tests was special education, not segregation or sterilization. But he had already done much damage.

Lewis Madison Terman

Lewis Madison Terman (1877–1956) was born on January 15, the 12th of 14 children of a farm family from central Indiana. He went to a one-room school and completed the eighth grade when he was age 12. When he was age 9, a salesman who was selling books on phrenology gave each member of the Terman family a phrenological analysis. Terman's analysis indicated great promise, thus stimulating him to aspire for a life beyond the farm. At age 15, Terman left the farm to attend Central Normal College in Danville, Indiana. At age 17, he began teaching in a rural school. Within six years after leaving home, Terman had taught school and earned three undergraduate degrees: one in arts, one in

ARCHIVES OF THE HISTORY OF AMERICAN PSYCHOLOGY

Lewis Madison Terman

sciences, and one in pedagogy. The next three years were busy ones for Terman; he became a high school principal, a husband, and a father. In 1901 he enrolled at Indiana University where he pursued a master's degree in pedagogy. Upon completing his master's degree, he was about to seek a teaching position when he received the offer of a fellowship for doctoral study at Clark University. With financial support from his family, Terman was able to accept the offer, and soon he was off to study with G. Stanley Hall as Goddard had done.

At Clark, Hall conducted a Monday evening seminar during which two students would present their work to about 30 psychology, philosophy, and education students. At the end of the student presentations and the discussion that ensued, Hall offered what Terman considered to be a most impressive summary:

> Hall would sum things up with an erudition and fertility of imagination that always amazed us and made us feel that his offhand insight into the problem went immeasurably beyond that of the student who had devoted months of slavish drudgery to it. . . . [At the end of each session] I always went home dazed and intoxicated, took a hot bath to quiet my nerves, then lay awake for hours rehearsing the drama and formulating

the clever things I should have said and did not. (Terman, 1932, p. 316)

Terman did not write his dissertation under Hall's supervision, however. Terman became increasingly interested in mental testing, and Hall had little enthusiasm for the topic. Under the supervision of Edmund C. Sanford, Terman isolated a group of "bright" students and a group of "dull" students and then attempted to determine what types of tests could be used to differentiate between members of the two groups (Terman was unaware that Binet and Simon had done essentially the same thing earlier). Terman's dissertation was entitled "Genius and Stupidity: A Study of the Intellectual Processes of Seven 'Bright' and Seven 'Stupid' Boys." Terman was to say later in his life that all of his career interests were shaped during his years at Clark.

Before obtaining his doctorate from Clark University in 1905, Terman had become seriously ill with tuberculosis, and although he recovered, he thought it best that he choose a warm climate in which to work. For that reason he accepted the position of high school principal in San Bernardino, California. A year later, he accepted a position teaching child study and pedagogy at Los Angeles State Normal School (later to become the University of California at Los Angeles). In 1910 Terman accepted an appointment to the education department at Stanford University where he spent the rest of his career. He became chair of the psychology department in 1922, a position he held until his retirement in 1942.

It was coincidental with his arrival at Stanford that Terman became aware of the Binet–Simon intelligence scale (through Goddard's translation). Terman began immediately to work with the scale and found that it could not be accurately used on U.S. children without modifications.

The Stanford–Binet tests. Terman found that when the Binet–Simon scale was administered to U.S. children the results were uneven. That is, the average scores of children of various ages were either higher or lower than the chronological age of the age group being tested. For example, Terman observed that items from the Binet–Simon scale were too easy for 5-year-olds and too difficult for 12-year-olds. This caused the mental age of average 5-year-olds to be artificially high and that of average 12-year-olds to be artificially low. Along with his graduate student, H. G. Childs, Terman deleted existing items from the Binet–Simon scale and added new items until the average score of a sample of children was 100, no matter what their age. This meant that for each age group tested, the average mental age would equal the group's chronological age. Terman and Childs published their first revision of the Binet–Simon tests in 1912, and in 1916 Terman alone published a further revision. The 1916 revision became known simply as the Stanford–Binet. It was in 1916 that Terman adopted Stern's "intelligence ratio" and suggested that the ratio be multiplied by 100 to remove the decimal and to call the ratio *IQ*. The Stanford–Binet, which made Terman both rich and famous, was revised in 1937 and again in 1960 (after Terman's death).

Terman's position on the inheritance of intelligence. Throughout his career, Terman believed that intelligence was largely inherited. Furthermore, Terman, like Goddard, believed that low intelligence was the cause of most criminal and other forms of antisocial behavior. For Terman, a stupid person could not be a moral person:

> Not all criminals are feeble-minded, but all feeble-minded persons are at least potential criminals. That every feeble-minded woman is a potential prostitute would hardly be disputed by anyone. Moral judgment, like business judgment, social judgment, or any other kind of higher thought process, is a function of intelligence. Morality cannot flower and fruit if intelligence remains infantile. (1916, p. 11)

In 1922 Terman said,

> There is nothing about an individual as important as his IQ, except possibly his morals . . . the

great test problem of democracy is how to adjust itself to the large IQ differences which can be demonstrated to exist among the members of any race or nationality group. . . . All the available facts that science has to offer support the Galtonian theory that mental abilities are chiefly a matter of original endowment. . . . It is to the highest 25 per cent. of our population, and more especially to the top 5 per cent., that we must look for the production of leaders who will advance science, art, government, education, and social welfare generally. . . . The least intelligent 15 or 20 per cent. of our population . . . are democracy's ballast, not always useless but always a potential liability. How to make the most of their limited abilities, both for their own welfare and that of society; how to lead them without making them helpless victims of oppression; are perennial questions in any democracy. (Minton, 1988, p. 99)

Although Terman was impressed by and borrowed much from Binet, his view of intelligence was much more like that of Galton.

Terman validated the Stanford–Binet by correlating test performance with teacher ratings of academic performance, teacher estimations of intelligence, and school grades. He found fairly high correlations in each case, but this was not surprising because the traits and abilities that schools and teachers valued highly in students were the same traits and abilities that yielded high scores on the Stanford–Binet. Nonetheless, the correlations meant that academic performance could be predicted with some success from test performance. Whether the tests were truly measuring native intelligence, however, Terman never determined.

Terman's study of genius. In Terman's day, it was widely believed that very bright children were abnormal in more than a statistical sense. One common expression describing such children was "early ripe, early rot," suggesting that if mental ability developed too fast at an early age, not enough would remain for the later years. To objectively study the experience of bright children through the years, Terman ran one of the most famous studies in psychology's history. By identifying highly intelligent children and observing them over a long period of time, Terman could evaluate his belief that children with high IQs are more successful in life than children with lower IQs.

As his first step, Terman defined genius as a score of 135 or higher on his test. Next, he administered the test to thousands of California schoolchildren, and he isolated 1,470 gifted children (824 boys and 646 girls). The average chronological age of the group was 11, and the average IQ of the group was 151. Learning everything he could about his subjects—including their interests, family history, health, physical characteristics, and personality—Terman wanted to study the experiences of group members as they matured through the years. He began his study in 1921 and reported the first results in *Genetic Studies of Genius* (1926). The term *genetic* can have two meanings. First, it can mean "developmental." When the term is being used in this sense, a genetic study is one that traces how something varies as a function of maturation, or time. Second, the term *genetic* can refer to the genes or chromosomes responsible for various traits. Terman used the term in the developmental sense.

Terman found that the children in his study had parents with above-average educational backgrounds, that the children had learned to read at an early age, that they participated in a wide range of activities, and that their schoolwork was usually excellent. All of this might have been expected; the major question was how these children would fare as they became older. Terman did follow-up studies in 1927–1928, when the average age of the group was about 16, and again in 1939–1940, when the average age was about 29. These studies indicated that test scores were still in the upper 1 percent of the general population, that members of the group still participated in a wide variety of activities and excelled in most of them, and that they were still outstanding academically. Seventy percent of the men and 67 percent of the women had finished college, and 56 percent of the men and 33 percent of the women had gone on for at least one advanced degree. All these percentages

were far higher than for the general population at the time.

In 1947 Terman appeared on the radio show "Quiz Kids." On the show, bright, healthy children were asked extremely difficult questions to which they typically knew the answers. Terman appeared on the program because he felt that it was responsible for correcting many of the misconceptions about gifted children. In fact, Terman thought the program did more in that regard than his own work had done:

> I have devoted a good part of my life to research on children of high I.Q. . . . But despite all my investigations, and those of others, many people continued to think of the brainy child as a freak —physically stunted, mentally lop-sided, nonsocial, and neurotic. Then came the Quiz Kid program, featuring living specimens of highly gifted youngsters who were obviously healthy, wholesome, well-adjusted, socially minded, full of fun, and versatile beyond belief. . . . Result: the program has done more to correct popular misconceptions about bright children than all the books ever written. (Minton, 1988, pp. 222–223)

It is probably best that it was not until after Terman's death that it was discovered that the "Quiz Kids" were often given their questions in advance of the show (Minton, 1988, p. 223).

The final follow-up in which Terman participated took place in 1950–1952, and it showed that members of the group continued to excel in most of the categories studied. By now, many members of the group had attained prominence as doctors, lawyers, teachers, judges, engineers, authors, actors, scientists, and businesspeople. Others continued to study the group after Terman's death in 1956; in all, the group was studied for about 50 years. For the researchers involved, the results were clear: *The gifted child becomes a gifted adult.* Terman's study put to rest many mistaken beliefs about gifted children, but it left unanswered the question of whether "giftedness" was inherited or the result of experience. Terman felt strongly that it was inherited, but subsequent researchers have shown that many of Terman's results can be explained by taking into account the group members' experiences. How much of intelligence is genetically determined and how much is environmentally determined is still a hotly contested question in psychology. Most modern researchers, however, concede that both factors are important. In any case, Terman's longitudinal study of gifted individuals clearly showed that individuals who score high on so-called measures of intelligence early in life do not deteriorate later in life. In fact, his results showed that those who fare best in youth also tend to fare best as mature adults.

INTELLIGENCE TESTING IN THE ARMY

Robert M. Yerkes

Robert M. Yerkes (1876–1956) was the first-born son of a rural Pennsylvania farm family. He was disillusioned by farm life, however, and dreamed of becoming a medical doctor. During his college years, Yerkes lived with an uncle for whom he did chores in return for tuition to Ursinis College. After Ursinis, Yerkes went to Harvard where he became interested in animal behavior. Obtaining his doctorate in 1902, he remained at Harvard as a faculty member. With his friend, John B. Watson (see chapter 12), who was then at Johns Hopkins University, Yerkes established comparative psychology in the United States. In recognition of his ultimate success, Yerkes was elected president of the American Psychological Association (APA) in 1917.

As a student, Yerkes had to borrow considerable money, and his faculty post at Harvard did not pay very much. This meant that he had to take part-time jobs in order to survive financially. Thus, in 1912 he took the job as the director of psychological research at the Boston State Psychopathic Hospital; it was here that Yerkes had his first experience with intelligence testing. At the hospital, the Binet–Simon scale was being explored as an instrument to aid clinical diagnoses. One of Yerkes's Harvard professors, and now his friend and colleague, was the biologist

Robert M. Yerkes

Charles Davenport who corresponded with Galton and was a leader in the U.S. eugenics movement. Yerkes, too, became a strong advocate of eugenics. Increasingly, Yerkes became involved in testing at the Boston Psychopathic Hospital, at the expense of his work in comparative psychology.

Yerkes's "contribution" to intelligence testing was his suggestion that all individuals be given all items on the Binet–Simon test and be given points for the items passed. Thus, a person's score would be in terms of total points earned instead of an IQ. This removes age as a factor in scoring. The traditional procedure followed in administering the Binet–Simon scale was to locate the range of tests appropriate for a given individual. For example, if a seven-year-old was being tested, the tests appropriate for that age would be given. If the child missed any of those tests, the tests appropriate for the next lowest age (six) would be administered. If, in this case, the child passed all tests appropriate for the seven year-old level, tests from the eight-year-old level would be administered, and so forth until the child began to fail tests. In other words, using age as a frame of reference, the testing procedure was customized for each child. Yerkes's "point-scale" procedure rendered all of this unnecessary. Yerkes did point out, however, that point norms could be established for various ages or for any group one wanted to compare. Besides being easier to administer, Yerkes believed that point scores were more amenable to statistical analyses than IQ scores. Also, because with point scores all individuals took the same tests without regard to their age or level, Yerkes's method was conducive to group testing, whereas the Binet–Simon test had to be given to one person at a time. Soon Yerkes would see his method tried on a level he never dreamed possible.

The army testing program. When the United States entered the First World War in 1917, Yerkes was president of the APA. He called a special meeting of the association to determine how psychologists could help in the war effort. It was decided that psychologists could contribute by devising ways of selecting and evaluating recruits into the armed forces. Upon Goddard's invitation, a small group of psychologists, including Yerkes and Terman, went to the Vineland School to develop psychological tests that were then tried at various army and navy bases. Because the results were encouraging, Yerkes was made an army major and given the job of organizing a testing program for the entire army (the navy rejected the idea). The goals of the program were to identify the mentally defective, to classify men in terms of their intelligence level, and to select individuals for special training—for example, to become officers. Yerkes believed that to be effective the test used had to be a group test rather than an individual test, had to measure "native" intelligence, and had to be easy to administer and score. Using Yerkes's point-score method of scoring, the group created a test that met these criteria but found that 40 percent of the recruits could not read well enough to take the test. The group solved the problem by creating two forms of the test: the *Army Alpha* for literate individuals and the *Army Beta* for illiterate individuals or for those who spoke and read a language other than English.

The war ended in 1918, and the testing program was terminated in 1919, by which time over 1.75 million individuals had been tested. Many people claimed that the army testing program had demonstrated psychology's practicality, but the evidence does not support such a contention. Samelson (1977) reports that only .005 percent of those tested were recommended for discharge as mentally unfit, and in many cases the army ignored the recommendations. Also, if the army had perceived the testing program as effective, it would not have terminated the program so soon after the war ended. In his evaluation of the army testing program under Yerkes's leadership, Reed reaches the following conclusion:

> In retrospect, Yerkes's greatest coup as a scientific bureaucrat and promoter was not in getting the Surgeon General to find a place for psychologists in the army, although that was a notable accomplishment, nor in writing tests, recruiting several hundred officers and technicians, and administering examinations to over 1.7 million individuals, despite fierce competition for resources and status from army officers and psychiatrists, although that too was a notable accomplishment. His most remarkable achievement was the myth that the army testing program had been a great practical success and that it provided a "goldmine" of data on the heritability of intelligence. (1987, p. 84)

THE DETERIORATION OF NATIONAL INTELLIGENCE

The use of the Army Alpha and Beta tests rekindled concern about the deterioration of the nation's intelligence level. About half of the white males tested in the army had native intelligence equal to that of a 13-year-old or lower, and the situation was even worse for black soldiers. Goddard's response was that people with low mental ability should not be allowed to vote. Along with Goddard, Terman and Yerkes were very concerned about the deterioration of the nation's intelligence, which they believed was caused by immigration and the fact that intellectually inferior individuals were reproducing faster than normal or above-normal individuals.

As was common at the time, Yerkes believed that many of the nation's ills were being caused by people of low intelligence and that immigration policies were only aggravating the problem:

> By some people meagre intelligence in immigrants has been considered an industrial necessity and blessing; but when all the available facts are faced squarely, it looks more like a burden. Certainly the results of psychological examining in the United States Army establish the relation of inferior intelligence to delinquency and crime, and justify the belief that a country which encourages, or even permits, the immigration of simple-minded, uneducated, defective, diseased, or criminalistic persons, because it needs cheap labor, seeks trouble in the shape of public expense.
>
> It might almost be said that whoever desires high taxes, full almshouses, a constantly increasing number of schools for defectives, of correctional institutions, penitentiaries, hospitals, and special classes in our public schools, should by all

means work for unrestricted and non-selective immigration. (1923, p. 365)

Fortunately, the extremely nativistic position that Goddard, Terman, and Yerkes represented did not go unchallenged. More and more, people realized that performance on so-called intelligence tests could be at least partially explained by such factors as early experience and education. Rather than simply measuring native intelligence, the tests were apparently also measuring personal achievement and the influence of life's circumstances. It followed that the more privileged a person was in terms of enriching experiences and education, the higher his or her scores would be on so-called intelligence tests.

Questions concerning the nature of intelligence, how best to measure intelligence, and how much of intelligence is genetically determined as opposed to environmentally determined are still being addressed in contemporary psychology. (For a sample of recent books that address the ongoing IQ controversy, see Fancher, 1985; Gould, 1981; Snyderman & Rothman, 1990.)

SUMMARY

Evolutionary theory has existed in one form or another since the time of the early Greeks. The biblical account of the origin of species silenced evolutionary theory for many centuries, but by the 18th century there was again speculation about the evolutionary process. Lamarck claimed that traits acquired during an individual's lifetime that were conducive to survival were passed on to the individual's offspring. Spencer originally followed Lamarck by saying that frequently used associations were passed on to offspring in the form of reflexes and instincts. Later, Spencer accepted Darwin's version of evolutionary theory and applied it to society by saying that society should allow enough freedom so that those most fit for survival could differentiate themselves from those least fit for survival. This was called social Darwinism.

After his five-year journey aboard the *Beagle*, Darwin realized that in different locations members of a species possessed different characteristics and that the characteristics of a species changed over time, but he could not explain why. Darwin found the explanation he needed in Malthus's es-

say (1798/1914), in which Malthus observed that a species always produced many more offspring than the food supply could support but that population size was kept in check by such events as starvation and disease. Darwin expanded Malthus's notion into the notion of a general struggle for survival in which only the fittest survived. According to Darwin, many more offspring of a species were born than could survive. There were individual differences among those offspring, and in the struggle for survival, some offspring possessed traits that were conducive to survival whereas others did not. Only the fittest offspring would survive. Thus, there was a natural selection of those offspring whose traits were most conducive to survival under the existing circumstances. In his books (1871, 1872), Darwin demonstrated that the evolutionary process applied to humans as well as to other living organisms. Darwin defined fitness by the reproductive success of an individual. By changing the definition of fitness to mean an individual's ability to perpetuate his or her *genes* into future generations, the sociobiologists have been able to explain a vast array of human social behavior in terms of evolutionary theory.

Darwin's cousin Francis Galton had a passion for measurement. He equated intelligence with sensory acuity and therefore measured intelligence mainly by measuring the acuity of the senses. Because he believed that intelligence was inherited, he urged the practice of eugenics, or selective breeding, to improve human intelligence. Using psychology's first word-association test, Galton found that responses to stimulus words tended to remain constant, tended to be drawn from childhood experience, and suggested the existence of an unconscious mind. In his research on mental imagery, Galton found great individual differences in the ability to experience mental images. Galton also observed that although there was a tendency for children to inherit the traits of their parents, there was also a regression toward the mean. That is, extremely tall parents tended to have tall children, but the children tended not to be as tall as the parents. By demonstrating how two things tended to vary together, Galton invented the method of correlation. It was Pearson who created the formula that quantified the magnitude of a correlation by generating a coefficient of correlation (r).

Cattell brought Galton's notion of intelligence testing to the United States. Wissler's research indicated that Galton's sensory and motor tests were not all measuring the same thing (intelligence) because the correlations among the tests were low. When Wissler found practically no relationship between performance on the tests and performance in college, it was concluded that the tests had little practical value.

In France, Binet took another approach to measuring intelligence. The earlier research of Binet and others had indicated that intelligence consisted of several different mental abilities such as memory, imagery, attention, comprehension, and judgment. Binet's goal was to devise tests that would directly measure these mental abilities. In response to the French government's request for an instrument that could be used to distinguish reliably between normal and mentally retarded children, Binet and Simon offered their 1905 scale of intelligence. The scale consisted of 30 tests arranged from the simplest to the most difficult. The more tests a child passed, the higher was his or her score. It was assumed that scores varied with intelligence. In 1908 Binet and Simon revised their scale so that it would not only distinguish between normal and retarded children but also would distinguish levels of intelligence among normal children. They gave the scale to children between the ages of 3 and 13, and all tests that 75 percent or more of the children

of a certain age passed were assigned to that age. In this way, it became possible to determine whether any particular child was performing at, above, or below the average performance of other children of his or her age. In 1911 Binet and Simon again revised the scale so that 5 tests corresponded to each age level. This allowed one-fifth of a year to be added to a child's score for each test he or she passed beyond the average for his or her age group. Stern suggested the term *mental age* and also the notion of intelligence quotient. Intelligence quotient was calculated by dividing a child's mental age (score on the Binet–Simon scale) by the child's chronological age. It was Terman who later suggested that the quotient be multiplied by 100 to remove the decimal point and that the intelligence quotient be abbreviated as *IQ*. Binet believed that intelligence was not one mental faculty but many. He therefore opposed the description of people's intelligence in terms of IQs. He also believed that, although intellectual potential may be inherited, most people functioned below their potential and could therefore benefit from education. Even retarded individuals, he believed, could benefit greatly from special education.

Contrary to what Wissler found when evaluating Cattell's test, Spearman found high correlations between measures of sensory acuity and intelligence and between measures of acuity and academic performance. Spearman concluded that intelligence was a general ability (g) and not the collection of abilities that Binet had proposed. Furthermore, Spearman concluded that intelligence was almost entirely inherited. Spearman's views on intelligence influenced U.S. psychometricians more than Binet's.

Goddard translated the Binet–Simon scale into English and administered it to both the retarded children at the Vineland School, where he worked, and to children in the New Jersey public schools. Appalled to find that many public school students performed at a level below their age norm, Goddard believed this poor performance reflected a deterioration in the nation's native intelligence. To investigate the relationship between inheritance and intelligence, Goddard studied the family history of a retarded girl at the Vineland School. He found that one of the girl's distant relatives had had a child by a feebleminded barmaid and that the line of descendants from that child forward was characterized by mental defectiveness and criminal and antisocial behavior. The man who had fathered the barmaid's child subsequently married a "normal" woman, and their descendants showed a very low incidence of mental defectiveness. Also, many individuals from that side of the family attained positions of prominence. Goddard and many others took these findings as support for the contention that intelligence was inherited. Many states instituted laws allowing for the sterilization of mentally defective individuals as well as others who were socially undesirable, while the influence of personal experience on intelligence level was essentially ignored.

Fear of the "menace of the feebleminded" directed attention to the immigrants entering the United States. Administration of the Binet–Simon test led to the conclusion that many immigrants were mentally defective, and they were deported back to Europe. The fact that poor test performance could have been due to educational, cultural, and personal experiences were initially considered by Goddard and rejected; late in his life, however, Goddard accepted all these factors as possible contributors to one's test performance.

Terman revised the Binet–Simon scale, making it more compatible with U.S. culture and statistically easier to analyze. Terman's revision, called the Stanford–Binet, was used to isolate 1,470 intellectually gifted children who were then intensely studied throughout their lives. Through the years, it was found that members of this group of gifted individuals continued to score in the top 1 percent of the population in intelligence, participated in and excelled at a wide range of activities, and were outstanding academically. Because the study showed that the gifted children became well adjusted, successful, healthy adults, it laid to rest the belief that gifted children were psychologically handicapped as adults.

When the United States entered the First World War, Yerkes and others concluded that psychology could help in the war effort by devising tests that could be used to classify recruits into the armed forces in terms of their intellectual level. The psychologists developed an Army Alpha test for literate recruits and an Army Beta test for illiterate or non–English speaking recruits. Although more than 1.75 million recruits were tested, only a very few were recommended for rejection because of low test performance. The army ignored most of those recommendations anyway and terminated the testing program shortly after the war ended.

According to the results of the army's testing program, about half of the white males tested had a mental age of 13 or lower, and the situation was even worse for black males. Once again, proposals arose for restricting marriage and for widespread sterilization of mentally defective individuals. At this time, however, a growing number of prominent individuals were wondering whether so-called intelligence tests were actually measuring genetically determined intelligence. They argued that test performance was determined more by education and personal experience than by inheritance, and there was a growing feeling that as more and more people received equal experiential opportunities, test performance would also equalize.

Efforts to define intelligence and to determine how best to measure it continue in contemporary psychology. Today, most psychologists believe that both inheritance and experience are factors in intelligence. The argument now mainly concerns the relative contributions of the two factors.

DISCUSSION QUESTIONS

1. Given the fact that rudimentary theories of evolution go back at least as far as the early Greeks, why did it take until the 19th century for adequate theories of evolution to develop?

2. Summarize Lamarck's theory of evolution.

3. Describe Spencer's social Darwinism and explain why it was so popular in the United States.

4. What is the Spencer–Bain principle?

5. What were the ironies concerning Darwin's voyage aboard the *Beagle*?

6. Why did Darwin delay publication of his theory for so long? What finally prompted him to publish it?

7. Summarize Darwin's theory of evolution.

8. Compare Darwin's concept of fitness with the sociobiologists' concept of inclusive fitness. What are the implications of the difference between the two concepts for the explanation of human social behavior?

9. How did Galton support his argument that eugenics should be practiced?

10. Explain why Galton's measures of "intelligence" were mainly sensory in nature.

11. Summarize Galton's contributions to psychology.

12. Describe Cattell's approach to intelligence testing and explain why that approach was eventually abandoned.

13. In what ways did Binet's approach to intelligence testing differ from Galton's and Cattell's?

14. Describe the 1905 Binet–Simon scale of intelligence. How was the scale revised in 1908? In 1911?

15. What procedure did Stern suggest for reporting a person's intelligence? Why did Binet oppose this procedure?

16. What did Binet mean by mental orthopedics? Why did Binet believe that such exercises were valuable?

17. Summarize Spearman's views of intelligence.

18. What conclusions did Goddard reach when he administered the Binet–Simon scale to schoolchildren in the United States?

19. What procedures did Goddard suggest for stopping the deterioration of intelligence in the United States? In suggesting these procedures, what assumption did he make?

20. Summarize the conclusions that Goddard reached when he traced the ancestry of Deborah Kallikak.

21. Did Goddard cause many immigrants to be unjustifiably deported? Justify your answer.

22. In what important way did Terman modify the Binet–Simon scale?

23. What prompted Terman's longitudinal study of gifted individuals?

24. Summarize the results of Terman's study of gifted individuals.

25. How did Yerkes suggest that psychologists help in the war effort? Was the effort that resulted from this suggestion a success or a failure?

26. What arguments were offered in opposition to the contention that intelligence tests were measuring innate intelligence?

27. Where do most psychologists stand today on the nature–nurture question as it applies to intelligence?

SUGGESTIONS FOR FURTHER READING

Barash, D. (1979). *The whisperings within: Evolution and the origin of human nature.* New York: Viking Press/Penguin Books.
This is a slightly more elementary and amusing introduction to sociobiology than Wilson's *On Human Nature* (discussed shortly). Like Wilson, Barash attempts to explain the major categories of human social behavior in terms of evolutionary theory. (Available in paperback.)

Boakes, R. (1984). *From Darwin to behaviourism: Psychology and the minds of animals.* New York: Cambridge University Press.
Students interested in the social sciences should consider adding this excellent book to their personal library. It is highly informative, clearly written, and generously illustrated. Boakes's chapter, "Mental Evolution," is most relevant to the concerns of the present chapter, but his remaining chapters discuss a number of topics relevant to the history of psychology. (Available in paperback.)

Fancher, R. E. (1985). *The intelligence men: Makers of the IQ controversy.* New York: Norton.
Like Snyderman and Rothman (discussed shortly), Fancher discusses how two very real questions concerning IQ tests have created such emotional reactions that objective information related to the questions has been difficult to obtain. One question concerns the degree to which IQ is genetically determined, and the other concerns the validity of IQ tests. Fancher provides extensive biographies of those individuals who played key roles in the development of intelligence tests and thus in the IQ controversy.

These individuals include John Stuart Mill, Francis Galton, Alfred Binet, Henry Goddard, Robert Yerkes, Lewis Terman, Richard Herrnstein, Cyril Burt, Arthur Jensen, and Leo Kamin.

Fancher, R. E. (1990). *Pioneers of psychology* (2nd ed.). New York: Norton.
This is an excellent presentation of the biographies and key concepts of major figures in the history of psychology. Most relevant to the present chapter are Fancher's chapters on Darwin, Galton, and Binet. Other major philosophers and psychologists covered include Descartes, Locke, Leibniz, Kant, Helmholtz, Fechner, Wundt, James, Pavlov, Watson, Skinner, Mesmer, Freud, and Piaget. (Available in paperback.)

Gould, S. J. (1981). *The mismeasure of man.* New York: Norton.
In this excellent book, Gould attacks the various forms of *biological determinism* that have postulated innate differences in human intelligence and have acted as a basis for attempting to measure those differences. From Plato to the current IQ testers, claims of innate differences in intellectual ability have been used to make certain individuals subservient to others. Gould focuses his attack on the so-called scientific means of differentiating intellectual ability such as craniometry (measuring the size of the head), phrenology, and IQ tests. Gould concludes that intelligence as a measurable entity has never been demonstrated and therefore efforts to measure "it" have been premature, at best. (Available in paperback.)

Hofstadter, R. (1955). *Social Darwinism in American thought.* Boston: Beacon Press.

In this classic book, Hofstadter discusses the controversy surrounding evolutionary theory in the United States following the publication of Darwin's *Origin of the Species* (1859). As might be expected, a number of prominent theologians criticized Darwinian theory because it was seen as challenging the very popular belief that the existence of God is proven by the purposive design observed in nature. The resolution came when most theologians concluded that God created the world so that it would evolve. Hofstadter goes on to point out the important differences between Darwin's theory of evolution and Spencer's and to show how the latter culminated in "social Darwinism."

McClelland, D. C. (1973). Testing for competence rather than for "intelligence." *American Psychologist, 28*, 1–14.

McClelland provides strong evidence that performance on "intelligence" tests correlates with such things as performance on similar tests, grades in school, and the impressions of teachers but not with measures of competence outside of the academic world. That is, according to McClelland, IQ scores cannot be used to make accurate predictions about a person's real-world behavior. Thus, for McClelland, the validity of IQ tests is very much in question. He suggests that if real-world performance is the ultimate concern, and it should be, then tests should be devised that sample that behavior instead of measuring so-called intelligence. Without much real-world validity, McClelland concludes the use of intelligence tests can do much harm than good.

Minton, H. L. (1988) *Lewis M. Terman: Pioneer in psychological testing.* New York: New York University Press.

This is a fair, well-balanced, and well-written biography of Lewis Terman. Minton indicates that toward the end of his life Terman maintained his hereditarian views of intelligence but was an environmentalist concerning such things as gender differences, delinquency, and homosexuality. He was also very much opposed to the McCarthy "witch-hunts," and he emphatically agreed with Edward C. Tolman's refusal to sign the University of California loyalty oath (causing Tolman's dismissal).

Samelson, F. (1977). World War I intelligence testing and the development of psychology. *Journal of the History of the Behavioral Sciences, 13*, 274–282.

Before the First World War, psychology was not very popular because it did not provide much practical information. Indeed, this was the type of information that the structuralists actively avoided. After the First World War, however, the perception of psychology changed, and the discipline became extremely popular. A major contributor to the dramatic turnaround was psychology's involvement in the intelligence-testing program for the army, under the leadership of Yerkes. The testing effort was widely publicized in newspapers and magazines, and after the war, Yerkes and others continued to tout the success of the military testing program in speeches, articles, and books. But, was the testing program really successful? After reviewing the data, Samelson concludes that it was not.

Indeed, the army discontinued the program as soon as the war ended. There is even evidence that the testing program had done more harm than good. Many individuals and groups were labeled mentally inferior when, in fact, their poor performance could have been better explained as reflecting lack of educational opportunities or by cultural experiences incompatible with the tests' contents. Nonetheless, psychology's war effort did give psychology widespread recognition, and it has benefited from that recognition ever since. In other words, the war effort did more for psychology than psychology did for the war effort.

Snyderman, M., & Rothman, S. (1990). *The IQ controversy, the media and public policy.* New Brunswick, NJ: Transaction Publishers.

The authors' own research has indicated a large discrepancy between the opinion of experts in the field of psychological testing and that of the general population concerning the nature of intelligence and its measurement. When the opinions of experts were surveyed, it was found that most believed that intelligence could be defined and measured with reasonable accuracy, that heredity is an important determinant of intelligence, and that IQ scores are useful in the prediction of certain behaviors. And yet, the authors find that the general population believes that the experts accept none of these things. Two reasons are offered for the discrepancy: (1) Media coverage of IQ testing has been inaccurate, emphasizing controversial issues rather than facts, and (2) the political and cultural climate has changed so that any hint of a genetic component in intelligence is responded to negatively. Under such circumstances, public discussions of IQ testing are typically so emotional that objective discourse is precluded. The result has been that experts now tend to confine their reports of their research to technical journals, and therefore the public has an inaccurate understanding of the current state of IQ testing.

Sokal, M. M. (Ed.). (1987). *Psychological testing and American society: 1890–1930.* New Brunswick, NJ: Rutgers University Press.

This interesting book describes the circumstances under which the testing movement emerged in the United States. The chapters demonstrate that the early intelligence tests and the purposes that they served were strongly influenced by the cultural milieu and by the biases of their authors. Most members of the early testing movement in the United States had a strong nativist bias as far as intelligence was concerned. Their views did not go uncriticized, however, and a nature–nurture debate occurred, which is still ongoing, within the realm of testing.

Wilson, E. O. (1978). *On human nature.* Cambridge, MA: Harvard University Press.

This Pulitzer Prize–winning book by the founder of sociobiology shows how Darwinian theory is currently being used to understand human social behavior such as altruism, mate selection, parenting, morality, religion, lying, love, hate, infanticide, incest, aggression, racism, and war. This is a readable and highly provocative book. (Available in paperback.)

GLOSSARY

Adaptive features Those features that an organism possesses that allow it to survive and reproduce.

Binet, Alfred (1857-1911) Found that following Galton's methods of measuring intelligence often resulted in falsely concluding that deaf and blind children had low intelligence. Binet attempted to measure directly the cognitive abilities he thought comprised intelligence.

Binet–Simon scale of intelligence The scale Binet and Simon devised to measure directly the various cognitive abilities they felt comprised intelligence. The scale first appeared in 1905 and was revised in 1908 and in 1911.

Cattell, James McKeen (1860–1944) Worked with Galton and developed a strong interest in measuring individual differences. Cattell brought Galton's methods of intelligence testing to the United States.

Coefficient of correlation (r) A mathematical expression indicating the magnitude of correlation between two variables.

Correlation Systematic variation in two variables.

Darwin, Charles (1809–1882) Created a theory of evolution that emphasized a struggle for survival that results in the natural selection of the most fit organisms. By showing the continuity between human and nonhuman animals, the importance of individual differences, and the importance of adaptive behavior, Darwin strongly influenced subsequent psychology.

Eugenics The use of selective breeding to increase the general intelligence of the population.

Fitness According to Darwin, an organism's ability to survive and reproduce.

Galton, Francis (1822–1911) Under the influence of his cousin Charles Darwin, was keenly interested in the measurement of individual differences. Galton was convinced that intellectual ability was inherited and therefore recommended eugenics, or the selective breeding of humans. He was the first to attempt to systematically measure intelligence as well as to use a questionnaire to gather data, to use a word-association test, to study mental imagery, to define and use the concept of correlation, and to systematically study twins.

General intelligence (g) The term that Spearman used to describe intelligence because he believed that intelligence was a single, general trait instead of a composite of several traits.

Goddard, Henry Herbert (1866–1957) Translated Binet's intelligence test into English and used it to test and classify retarded students. Goddard was an extreme nativist who recommended that the mentally defective be sterilized or institutionalized. Due to Goddard's efforts, the number of immigrants allowed into the United States was greatly reduced.

Inclusive fitness The type of fitness that involves the survival and perpetuation of one's genes into subsequent generations rather than simply one's offspring. With this expanded definition of fitness, one can be fit by helping his or her kin survive and reproduce as well as by producing one's own offspring.

Inheritance of acquired characteristics Lamarck's contention that adaptive abilities developed during an organism's lifetime were passed on to the organism's offspring.

Intelligence quotient (IQ) Stern's suggested procedure for quantifying intelligence. The intelligence quotient is calculated by dividing mental age by chronological age.

Lamarck, Jean (1744–1829) Proposed that adaptive characteristics acquired during an organism's lifetime were inherited by that organism's offspring. This was the mechanism by which species were transformed. (*See also* **Inheritance of acquired characteristics**.)

Malthus, Thomas (1766–1834) Wrote *Essay on the Principle of Population* (1798), which provided Darwin with the principle he needed to explain the observations that he had made while aboard the *Beagle*. The principle stated that because more individuals are born than environmental resources can support, there is a struggle for survival and only the fittest survive.

Mental age According to Stern, a composite score reflecting all tests that a child could successfully pass.

Mental orthopedics The exercises that Binet suggested for enhancing determination, attention, and discipline. These procedures would prepare a child for formal education.

Natural selection A key concept in Darwin's theory of evolution. Because more members of a species are born than environmental resources can support, nature selects those with characteristics most conducive to survival under the circumstances to continue living and to reproduce.

Nature–Nurture controversy The debate over whether important attributes are inherited or learned.

Pearson, Karl (1857–1936) Devised the formula for calculating the coefficient of correlation.

Regression toward the mean The tendency for extremes to become less extreme in one's offspring. For example, the offspring of extremely tall parents tend not to be as tall as the parents.

Simon, Theodore (1873–1961) Collaborated with Binet to develop the first test designed to directly measure intelligence.

Social Darwinism Spencer's contention that, if given freedom to compete in society, the ablest individuals will succeed and the weaker ones will fail and this is as it should be.

Sociobiology A modern extension of Darwin's theory that attempts to explain human social behavior in evolutionary terms.

Spearman, Charles (1863–1945) Followed Galton in believing that intelligence could be measured by measuring sensory acuity and that intelligence was largely inherited. Spearman also believed that intelligence was a single faculty instead of many. (*See also* **General intelligence**.)

Spencer, Herbert (1820–1903) First a follower of Lamarck, then of Darwin. Spencer applied Darwinian principles to society by saying that society should maintain a laissez-faire policy so that the ablest individuals could prevail. Spencer's position is called social Darwinism. Spencer believed that everything in the universe began as an undifferentiated whole and then, through the process of evolution, became increasingly differentiated.

Spencer–Bain principle The observation first made by Bain and later by Spencer that behavior that results in pleasurable consequences tends to be repeated and behavior that results in painful consequences tends not to be.

Stern, William (1871–1938) Coined the term *mental age* and suggested the intelligence quotient as a way of quantifying intelligence. (*See also* **Intelligence quotient**.)

Struggle for survival The situation that arises when there are more offspring of a species than environmental resources can support.

Survival of the fittest The notion that in a struggle for survival those organisms with traits conducive to survival under the circumstances will survive and reproduce.

Terman, Lewis Madison (1877–1956) Revised Binet's test of intelligence, making it more compatible with U.S. culture. Terman, along with Goddard and Yerkes, was instrumental in creating the Army Alpha and Army Beta tests. He also conducted a longitudinal study of gifted children and found that, contrary to the belief at the time, gifted children tended to become healthy, gifted adults.

Wallace, Alfred Russell (1823–1913) Developed a theory of evolution almost identical to Darwin's, at almost the same time that Darwin developed his theory.

Yerkes, Robert M. (1876–1956) Suggested that psychology could help in the war effort (First World War) by creating tests that could be used to place recruits according to their abilities and to screen the mentally unfit from military service. The testing program was largely ineffective and was discontinued soon after the war.

CHAPTER 11

Functionalism

In chapter 9, we saw that Titchener's brand of psychology, which he called structuralism, was essentially a psychology of pure consciousness with little concern with practical applications. In this chapter, we will first look at what psychology was like before Titchener and then at what psychology became after Titchener when the doctrine of evolution combined with the U.S. *Zeitgeist* to create what became the U.S. brand of psychology—functionalism.

EARLY U.S. PSYCHOLOGY

It is often assumed that U.S. psychology did not exist before Titchener and William James. In his presidential address to the Ninth International Congress of Psychology at Yale University in 1929, James McKeen Cattell said that a history of U.S. psychology before the 1880s "would be as short as a book on snakes in Ireland since the time of St. Patrick. Insofar as psychologists are concerned, America was then like heaven, for there was not a damned soul there" (1929, p. 12).

To make such a statement, Cattell assumed that only experimental psychology was *real* psychology and that everything else was mental or moral philosophy. Titchener agreed and argued forcibly that experimental psychology should be completely separated from philosophy and especially from theology. The problem with Cattell and Titchener's argument is that it ignored the fact that experimental psychology grew out of nonexperimental psychology and to understand the former one must understand the latter:

To deny that there was psychological thought before the 1880s in America is to deny that it existed in Europe before Wilhelm Wundt opened the Leipzig laboratory or in England before Francis Galton opened his laboratory in London. There were in all these places long histories of psychological thought that acted as the substrata for the establishment of various experimental psychologies of the twentieth century.

Nothing emerges from nothing. Before there emerged courses, professorships, and departments in American colleges labeled "psychological," there were people with other titles talking about much the same things, although often under different rubrics and with different intents than those of the twentieth-century psychologists. (Evans, 1984, p. 18)

In an attempt to set the record straight, Fay wrote *American Psychology Before William James* (1939), and Roback wrote *History of American Psychology* (1952), which traces U.S. psychology back to the colonial days. Also, Brožek has recently edited a book entitled *Explorations in the History of Psychology in the United States* (1984). For our purposes, however, we will follow Sahakian's (1975) description of the four stages of early U.S. psychology.

Stage One: Moral and Mental Philosophy (1640–1776)

Early in the 136-year period of moral and mental philosophy, psychology included such topics as ethics, divinity, and philosophy. During this time, psychology concerned matters of the soul, and what was taught was not questioned. Thus, to learn psychology was to learn the accepted theology of the day. Like all other subjects taught at the time, psychology was combined with religious indoctrination. The earliest U.S. universities, such as Harvard (founded in 1636), were modeled after the British universities whose main purpose was to perpetuate religious beliefs.

A period of "American enlightenment" began in 1714 when John Locke's *An Essay Concerning Human Understanding* (1690) arrived in the colonies and had a widespread influence. Samuel Johnson (1696–1772), the first president of Columbia University (founded in 1754), embraced Locke enthusiastically and wrote a book containing many of Locke's ideas. This book also contained a number of topics clearly psychological in nature—for example, child psychology, the nature of consciousness, the nature of knowledge, introspection, and perception. Lockean philosophy provided the basis for a logic and a psychology that could be used to support one's religious beliefs. Roback says of this period, "Psychology existed for the sake of logic, and logic for the sake of God" (1952, p. 23).

Stage Two: Intellectual Philosophy (1776–1886)

During the stage of intellectual philosophy, psychology became a separate discipline in the United States, largely under the influence of Scottish commonsense philosophy. As we saw in chapter 6, the Scottish philosophy of common sense was a reaction against philosophers such as Hume, who maintained that nothing could be known with certainty and that moral and scientific laws were nothing more than mental habits. Scottish philosophers such as Thomas Reid (1710–1796) disagreed saying that sensory information could be accepted at face value (naive realism). The Scottish philosophers also maintained that self-examination, or introspection, yielded valid information and that morality was based on self-evident intuitions. The commonsense philosophy had clear implications for theology: The existence and nature of God need

not be proved logically because one's personal feelings could be trusted on these matters.

With the respectability of the senses and feelings established, textbooks written by the Scottish philosophers began to include such topics as perception, memory, imagination, association, attention, language, and thinking. Such a textbook was written by Dugald Stewart (1753–1828), entitled *Elements of the Philosophy of the Human Mind* (1792), and was used at Yale University in 1824.

Soon U.S. textbooks bearing a close resemblance to those of the Scottish philosophers began to appear, such as Porter's *The Human Intellect: With an Introduction upon Psychology and the Soul* (1868). Porter's text represented a transitional period when psychology was leaving the realm of philosophy and theology and becoming a separate discipline. Porter's book defined psychology as the science of the human soul and covered such topics as psychology as a branch of physics, psychology as a science, consciousness, sense perception, development of the intellect, association of ideas, memory, and reason. We can see in Porter's text, and in many other texts of the time, the strong influence of the Scottish commonsense philosophy, as well as the emphasis on the individual that was later to characterize modern U.S. psychology.

Stage Three: The U.S. Renaissance (1886–1896)

During the U.S. Renaissance, psychology was completely emancipated from religion and philosophy and became an empirical science. In 1886 John Dewey (discussed later) wrote *Psychology*, which described the new empirical science. In 1887 the first issue of the *American Journal of Psychology*, the United States' first psychology journal appeared, and in 1890 William James's *The Principles of Psychology* was published. All these events marked the beginning of a psychology that was to emphasize individual differences, adaptation to the environment, and practicality—in other words, a psychology that was perfectly compatible with evolutionary theory. Since the days of the pioneers, people in the United States had emphasized individuality and practicality, and adaptation to the environment had to be a major concern. This explains why the United States was such fertile ground for phrenology, mesmerism, and spiritualism—practices that purported to help individuals.

It was also during this stage that Titchener began his highly influential structuralist program at Cornell University (1892), which successfully competed with functionalism for several years.

Stage Four: U.S. Functionalism (1896 to Present)

During the stage of U.S. functionalism, science, concern for practicality, emphasis on the individual, and evolutionary theory combined into **functionalism,** the United States' first school of psychology. Sahakian (1975) marks the beginning of functionalism with the 1896 publication of John Dewey's article "The Reflex Arc in Psychology." This date is somewhat arbitrary. Others mark the formal beginning of U.S. psychology with the 1890 publication of James's book *The Principles of Psychology.* Whether one accepts Dewey or James as the founder of U.S. psychology, it is clear that the tone set by these men, and by others whom we will consider in this chapter, still permeates U.S. psychology.

If one marks the beginning of the school of functionalism with the publication of James's *The Principles of Psychology* (1890), then functionalism predated the school of structuralism and ran parallel to it. Titchener was at Cornell from 1892 to 1927. Members of the two schools were largely adversaries, and there was little meaningful dialog between them. The schools nicely illustrate Kuhn's concept of paradigm because their assumptions, goals, and methodologies were distinctly different. For the structuralist, the assumptions concerning the mind were derived from British and French empiricism, the goal of psychology was to understand the structure of the mind, and the primary research tool was introspection. For the functionalist, the assumptions concerning the mind were derived from evolutionary theory, the goal was to understand how the mind and behavior work in aiding an organism's adjustment to the environment, and research tools included anything that was informative, including the use of introspection, the study of animal behavior, and the study of the mentally ill. In other words, the schools of structuralism and functionalism, having little in common, were incommensurable.

CHARACTERISTICS OF FUNCTIONALISTIC PSYCHOLOGY

Functionalism was never a well-defined school of thought with one recognized leader or an agreed-on methodology. It is not even clear when functionalism came into existence as a school, if it ever did. As we have just mentioned, some mark functionalism's beginning with the work of William James, others with the work of John Dewey, and still others suggest Darwin himself. Amidst all of functionalism's diversity, however, common themes ran through the work of all those calling themselves functionalists. We follow Keller (1973) in delineating those themes.

1. The functionalists opposed what they considered the sterile search for the elements of consciousness engaged in by the structuralists.

2. The functionalists wanted to understand the function of the mind rather than to provide a static description of its contents. They believed that mental processes had a function—to aid the organism in adapting to the environment. That is, they were interested in the *is for* of the mind rather than the *is,* its function rather than its structure.

3. The functionalists wanted psychology to be a practical science, not a pure science, and they sought to apply their findings to the improvement of personal life, education, indus-

try, and so on. The structuralists had actively avoided practicality.

4. The functionalists represented the biological tradition rather than the physiological tradition. Whereas the structuralists had been influenced by the careful physiological work of such individuals as Helmholtz, who had traced the pathway from sensory stimulation to simple mental sensation, the functionalists were more strongly influenced by Darwinian biology with its emphasis on the struggle for survival.

5. The functionalists urged the broadening of psychology to include research on animals, children, and abnormal humans. They also urged a broadening of methodology to include anything that was useful, such as puzzle boxes, mazes, and mental tests.

6. The functionalists' interest in the *why* of mental processes and behavior led directly to a concern with motivation. Because an organism will act differently in the same environment as its needs change, these needs must be understood before the organism's behavior can be understood.

7. The functionalists accepted *both* mental processes and behavior as legitimate subject matter for psychology, and most of them viewed introspection as one of many valid research tools.

8. The functionalists were more interested in what made organisms different from one another than what made them similar.

9. All functionalists were directly or indirectly influenced by William James, who in turn had been strongly influenced by Darwin's theory of evolution.

The functionalists' attack on structuralism was not launched along a unified front. Rather, it came from a number of directions in a number of ways:

The attack upon the orderly, disciplined ranks of structural psychology was typically early-American. It came from no single, united front, under command of a single recognized leader.

William James

Instead there was guerilla warfare, with many chieftains striking in from many points of vantage, with many weapons. (Keller, 1973, p. 73)

Next, we review the thoughts of some members of the school of functionalism, starting with William James, the most influential functionalist of all, and ending with Edward L. Thorndike, a transitional figure who could just as easily be labeled an early behaviorist (see chapter 12).

WILLIAM JAMES

William James (1842–1910) represents the transition between European psychology and U.S. psychology. His ideas were not fully enough developed to suggest a school of thought, but they contained the seeds that were later to grow into the school of functionalism. As was mentioned, James had already brought prominence to U.S. psychology through the publication of *Principles* two years before Titchener arrived at Cornell. James was 25 years older than Titchener, and he (James) died in 1910 when Titchener's influence was at its peak. James's psychology, however, has far outlived Titchener's.

Biographical Sketch

William James was born on January 11 in New York City. His brother Henry, the famous novelist, was born 15 months later. The father, Henry James, Sr., who had lost a leg in an adolescent accident, embraced Swedenborgianism, a mystic religion named after Emmanuel Swedenborg (1688–1772). So enchanted with Swedenborgianism was the elder James that he wrote a book entitled *The Secret of Swedenborg.* Henry James, Sr., who was independently wealthy, believed that his children should receive the best possible education. After enrolling William in several private schools in the United States, the father decided that European schools would be better; so James attended schools in Switzerland, France, Germany, and England. James's early life was highly stimulating, involving a great deal of travel and exposure to intense intellectual discussions at home. In 1860, at 18 years of age, James, after showing considerable talent for painting, decided on a career as an artist. The father was so distressed by this career choice that he moved the family away from William's art teacher and even threatened suicide if William persisted in his choice (Fancher, 1990). Unfortunately for William, no career choice satisfied his father:

> Mr. James [Henry James, Sr.] was not only critical of William's desire to paint, but when he followed his father's wishes and chose science, the elder James belittled that choice. Finally when William embraced metaphysics because his father praised philosophy as the most elevated intellectual pursuit, Henry maligned William for not adopting the proper kind. (Bjork, 1983, pp. 22–23)

Not surprisingly, William James displayed career uncertainty and ambivalence all of his life.

In 1861 James enrolled as a chemistry student at Harvard University. He soon switched to physiology to prepare himself for a career in medicine, and in 1864 (at the age of 22) he enrolled in Harvard's medical school. James's medical studies were interrupted when he accepted an invitation from Louis Agassiz, a famous Harvard biologist and an opponent of Darwinian theory, to go on an expedition to Brazil. Seasick most of the time, James also came down with smallpox, and he decided to return home and continue his medical studies. After he returned home, his health deteriorated further, his eyesight became weak, and he experienced severe back pains. In 1867 James decided to go to Germany and bathe in mineral springs, in hopes of improving his back problems. While in Germany, he began to read German psychology and philosophy. In his diary, James shares a letter written to a friend in 1867, which shows that this was the time when James discovered Wundt and agreed with Wundt that it was time for psychology to become a science:

> I have blocked out some reading in physiology and psychology which I hope to execute this winter—though reading in German is still disgustingly slow . . . it seems to me that perhaps the time has come for psychology to begin to be a science—some measurements have already been made . . . Helmholtz and a man named Wundt at Heidelberg are working at it. . . . The fact is, this sickness takes all the spring, physical and mental, out of a man. (1920, Vol. 1, pp. 118–119)

James's crisis. James returned to the United States and finally obtained his medical degree from Harvard in 1869. After graduation, however, James's health deteriorated further, and he became deeply depressed. Apparently one reason for his depression was the implications of the German materialistic physiology and psychology that had so impressed him. It was clear to James that if the materialistic philosophy was correct, it applied to him as well. This meant that anything that happened to him was predetermined and thus beyond his control. His depression, for example, was a matter of fate, and it made no sense to attempt to do anything about it. James's acceptance of Darwin's theory of evolution exacerbated the problem. In Darwin's view, there is variation, natural selection, and survival of the fittest; there is no freedom, hope, or choice.

A major turning point in James's life came when he read an essay on free will by Charles Renouvier (1815–1913). After reading this essay, James wrote in his diary:

> I think that yesterday was a crisis in my life. I finished the first part of Renouvier's second "Essais" and see no reason why his definition of free will—"The sustaining of a thought because I choose to when I might have other thoughts"—need be the definition of an illusion. At any rate, I will assume for the present—until next year—that it is no illusion. My first act of free will shall be to believe in free will. . . . Hitherto, when I have felt like taking a free initiative, like daring to act originally, without carefully waiting for contemplation of the external world to determine all for me, suicide seemed the most manly form to put my daring into; now I will go a step further with my will, not only act with it, but believe as well; believe in my individual reality and creative power. (1920, Vol. 1, pp. 147–148)

This change in beliefs cured James's depression, and he became highly productive. Here we have the beginnings of James's **pragmatism**—the belief that if an idea works, it is valid. That is, the ultimate criterion for judging an idea should be the idea's usefulness. At this point, we also see the conflict James perceived between the objective, scientific viewpoint based on determinism and personal, subjective feelings such as the feeling that one's will is free. James used pragmatism to solve the problem. While using the scientific method in psychology, he said, it was necessary to assume that human behavior was determined. As useful as this assumption was, however, it had limits. Certain metaphysical questions lay beyond the reach of science, and in dealing with them, a subjective approach was more useful. Therefore, according to James, both a scientific *and* a philosophical approach

must be used in the study of human behavior and thought. To assume that all aspects of humans could be known through scientific research, he said, was like a physician giving all his patients tics because it was the only thing he could cure. If something about humans—for example, free will—could not be studied effectively using a certain method, James said, one did not throw out that aspect of human existence. Rather, one sought alternative methods of investigation. Following his own advice, as he often did, he explored the phenomenon of religious experience and summarized his findings in *The Varieties of Religious Experience* (1902) James's willingness to accept methods ranging from anecdotes to rigorous experimentation was further testimony to his belief in pragmatism.

In 1872 James was given the opportunity to teach physiology at Harvard, and he taught it for one year. He then toured Europe for a year and again returned to Harvard to teach, but this time his course concerned the relations between physiology and psychology. In 1875 James created a small demonstration laboratory, which he used in teaching his course. This has raised a controversy concerning who should be given credit for establishing psychology's first laboratory, Wundt in 1879 or James in 1875. Usually the credit is given to Wundt because his laboratory was more elaborate and was designed for research and not merely for teaching demonstrations.

In 1878 the publisher Henry Holt offered James a contract to write a textbook on psychology. The textbook was finally published 12 years later in 1890. Although James's *The Principles of Psychology* was to revolutionize psychology, James did not think much of it, as he indicated in a letter he sent to the publisher along with the manuscript:

> No one could be more disgusted than I at the sight of the book. No subject is worth being treated of in 1000 pages. Had I ten years more, I could rewrite it in 500; but as it stands it is this or nothing—a loathsome, distended, tumefied, bloated, dropsical mass, testifying to nothing

but two facts: 1st, that there is no such thing as a science of psychology, and 2nd, that W. J. is an incapable. (1920, Vol. 1, p. 294)

James's highly influential *Principles* appeared in two volumes, 28 chapters, and a total of 1,393 pages. Two years later, James published a condensed version of his *Principles* entitled *Psychology: The Briefer Course* (1892/1961). *The Briefer Course* came to be called "Jimmy."

In neither James's writings nor in James the man do we find an organized theory. Rather, we find treatment of a wide variety of topics, many of which later researchers pursued. As we will see, however, the themes of practicality (pragmatism) and individuality permeate most of his writings. James was always willing to entertain a wide variety of ideas ranging from religion, mysticism, faith healing, and psychic phenomena to the most rigorous scientific facts and methods available in psychology at the time. Murphy summarizes James's *Principles*:

> He [James] argued at times for essentially an associationist's viewpoint, at times for a highly integrated oneness of each psychological act. He gave instinct and habit formation a large place, and at the same time looked for cognitive acts of profundity and range, and for the ultimate pinnacle of the life of the mind in the process of the will. He is at the same time evolutionist and mystic, lover of the raw, crude, vague, confused, intellectually unrespectable. At the other end of the spectrum, he is an aspirant to the sharpest clarity and the highest order that mind can achieve. Consistency in ultimate outlook one should not expect to find in the *Principles* even were one to regard it as the creation of a single year. The chapters represent different angles, different phases, different recurring themes evident in twelve years of a great man's life. They must be read as profound literature, often factually correct, modern in spirit, but far more important than either, always challenging, guiding, preparing us for new discoveries. (1968, p. 147)

The Spanish-born U.S. philosopher and poet, and James's colleague at Harvard, George Santayana said of James,

> I think it would have depressed him if he had to confess that any important question was finally

settled. He would still have hoped that something might turn up on the other side, and that, just as the scientific hangman was about to dispatch the poor convicted prisoner, an unexpected witness would ride up in hot haste, and prove him innocent. (1920, p. 82)

We now sample a few of James's more famous notions.

Opposition to Wundt's Approach to Psychology

Almost everything in *Principles* can be seen as a criticism of what James perceived Wundt's approach to psychology to be. That approach, James thought, consisted of a search for the elements of consciousness. James was especially harsh in his criticism in the following passage:

> Within a few years what one may call a microscopic psychology has arisen in Germany, carried on by experimental methods, asking of course every moment for introspective data, but eliminating their uncertainty by operating on a large scale and taking statistical means. This method taxes patience to the utmost, and hardly could have arisen in a country whose natives could be *bored*. Such Germans as Weber, Fechner . . . and Wundt obviously cannot; and their success has brought into the field an array of younger experimental psychologists, bent on studying the *elements* of the mental life, dissecting them from the gross results in which they are embedded, and as far as possible reducing them to quantitative scales. The simple and open method of attack having done what it can, the method of patience, starving out, and harassing to death is tried; the Mind must submit to a regular *siege*, in which minute advantages gained night and day by the forces that hem her in must sum themselves up at last into her overthrow. There is little left of the grand style about these new prism, pendulum, and chronography-philosophers. They mean business, not chivalry. What generous divination, and that superiority in virtue which was thought by Cicero to give a man the best insight into nature, have failed to do, their spying and scraping, their deadly tenacity and almost diabolic cunning, will doubtless some day bring about. (1890, Vol. 1, pp. 192–193)

James, of course, was responding to Wundt

the experimentalist. If James had probed deeper into Wundt's voluntarism and into his *Völkerpsychologie*, he would have seen a remarkable similarity between himself and Wundt. In any case, it was Wundt the experimentalist who, after reading James's *Principles*, commented, "It is literature, it is beautiful, but it is not psychology" (Blumenthal, 1970, p. 238).

Stream of Consciousness

With **stream of consciousness**, James again took on those who were busy searching for the *elements* of thought. In the first place, said James, *consciousness is personal*. It reflects the experiences of an individual, and therefore it is foolhardy to search for elements common to all minds. Second, *consciousness is continuous and cannot be divided up for analysis*:

> Let anyone try to cut a thought across in the middle and get a look at its section. . . . The rush of the thought is so headlong that it almost always brings us up at the conclusion before we can arrest it. Or if our purpose is nimble enough and we do arrest it, it ceases forthwith to be itself. As a snowflake crystal caught in the warm hand is no longer a crystal but a drop, so, instead of catching the feeling of relation moving to its term, we find we have caught some substantive thing, usually the last word we were pronouncing, statically taken, and with its function, tendency, and particular meaning in the sentence quite evaporated. The attempt at introspective analysis in these cases is in fact like seizing a spinning top to catch its motion, or trying to turn up the gas quickly enough to see how the darkness looks. (James, 1890, Vol. 1, p. 244)

Third, *consciousness is constantly changing*. Even though consciousness is continuous and can be characterized as a steady stream from birth to death, it is also constantly changing. James quoted Heraclitus's aphorism about the impossibility of stepping into the same river twice. For James, the same was true for conscious experience. One can never have exactly the same idea twice because the stream of consciousness that provides the context for the idea is ever-changing.

Fourth, *consciousness is selective*. Some of the many events entering consciousness are selected for further consideration and others are inhibited. Here James flirted again with free will:

> We see that the mind is at every stage a theatre of simultaneous possibilities. Consciousness consists in the comparison of these with each other, the selection of some, and the suppression of the rest by the reinforcing and inhibiting agency of attention. (1890, Vol. 1, p. 288)

Finally, and perhaps most important, *consciousness is functional*. This point permeates all of James's writing, and it is the point from which the school of functionalism developed. According to James, the most important thing about consciousness—and the thing the elementists overlooked—was that its purpose was to aid the individual in adapting to the environment. Here we see the powerful influence of Darwin on early U.S. scientific psychology.

Consciousness, then, is personal, continuous, constantly changing, selective, and purposive. Very little in this view is compatible with the view held by Wundt the experimentalist (although it is very much in accordance with the view held by Wundt the voluntarist) or later by the structuralists. James reached the following famous conclusion concerning consciousness:

> Consciousness, then, does not appear to itself chopped up in bits. Such words as "chain" or "train" do not describe it fitly as it presents itself in the first instance. It is nothing jointed; it flows. A "river" or a "stream" are the metaphors by which it is most naturally described. *In talking of it hereafter, let us call it the stream of thought, of consciousness, or of subjective life.* (1890, Vol. 1, p. 239)

Habits and Instincts

James believed that much animal and human behavior was governed by instinct:

> *Why do the various animals do what seem to us such strange things*, in the presence of such outlandish stimuli? Why does the hen, for example, submit herself to the tedium of incubating such a fearfully uninteresting set of objects as a nestful of eggs, unless she have some sort of a prophetic inkling of the result? The only answer is *ad*

hominem. We can only interpret the instincts of brutes by what we know of instincts in ourselves. Why do men always lie down, when they can, on soft beds rather than on hard floors? Why do they sit around the stove on a cold day? Why, in a room, do they place themselves, ninety-nine times out of a hundred, with their faces towards the middle rather than to the wall? Why do they prefer saddle of mutton and champagne to hard-tack and ditch-water? Why does the maiden interest the youth so that everything about her seems more important and significant than anything else in the world? Nothing more can be said than that these are human ways, and that every creature *likes* its own ways, and takes to following them as a matter of course. (1890, Vol. 2, pp. 386–387)

James did not believe that instinctive behavior was "blind and invariable." Rather, he believed that such behavior was modifiable by experience. Furthermore, he believed that new instinctlike patterns of behavior develop within the lifetime of the organism. James called these learned patterns of behavior **habits**.

According to James, habits are formed as an activity is repeated. Repetition caused the same neural pathways to, from, and within the brain to become more entrenched, making it easier for energy to pass through those pathways. Thus, James had a neurophysiological explanation of habit formation, and his neurophysiological account of learning was very close to Pavlov's. Habits are functional because they simplify the movements required to achieve a result, increase the accuracy of behavior, reduce fatigue, and diminish the need to consciously attend to performed actions.

According to James, it is habit that makes society possible:

Habit is . . . the enormous fly-wheel of society, its most precious conservative agent. It alone is what keeps us all within the bounds of ordinance, and saves the children of fortune from the envious uprisings of the poor. It alone prevents the hardest and most repulsive walks of life from being deserted by those brought up to tread therein. . . . It dooms us all to fight out the battle of life upon the lines of our nurture or our early choice, and to make the best of a pursuit that disagrees, because there is no other for

which we are fitted, and it is too late to begin again. It keeps different social strata from mixing. Already at the age of twenty-five you see the professional mannerism settling down on the young commercial traveller, on the young doctor, on the young minister, on the young counsellor-at-law. You see the little lines of cleavage running through the character, the tricks of thought, the prejudices, the ways of the "shop," in a word, from which the man can by-and-by no more escape than his coat-sleeve can suddenly fall into a new set of folds. On the whole, it is best he should not escape. It is well for the world that in most of us, by the age of thirty, the character has set like plaster, and will never soften again. (1890, Vol. 1, p. 121)

Through habit formation, we can make our nervous system our ally instead of our enemy:

For this we must make automatic and habitual, as early as possible, as many useful actions as we can, and guard against the growing into ways that are likely to be disadvantageous to us, as we should guard against the plague. (James, 1892/1963, p. 11)

James offered five maxims to follow in order to develop good habits and eliminate bad ones:

1. Place yourself in circumstances that encourage good habits and discourage bad ones.

2. Do not allow yourself to act contrary to a new habit that you are attempting to develop: "Each lapse is like the letting fall of a ball of string which one is carefully winding up; a single slip undoes more than a great many turns will wind again" (1892/1963, p. 12).

3. Do not attempt to slowly develop a good habit or eliminate a bad one. Engage in positive habits completely to begin with and abstain completely from bad ones.

4. It is not the intention to engage in good habits and avoid bad ones that is important; it is the actual doing so: "There is no more contemptible type of human character than that of the nerveless sentimentalist and dreamer, who spends his life in a weltering sea of sensibility and emotion, but who never does a manly concrete deed" (1892/1963, p. 15).

5. Force yourself to act in ways that are beneficial to you, even if doing so first is distasteful and requires considerable effort.

All of James's maxims converge on a fundamental principle: Act in ways that are compatible with the type of person you would like to become.

The Self

James discussed what he called the **empirical self**, or the "me" of personality, which consisted of everything that a person could call his or her own:

> *In its widest possible sense . . . a man's* Me [empirical self] *is the sum total of all that he* CAN *call his, not only his body and his psychic powers, but his clothes, and his house, his wife and children, his ancestors and friends, his reputation and works, his lands and horses, and yacht, and bank-account.* (1892/1963, p. 44)

James divided the empirical self into three components: the material self, the social self, and the spiritual self.

The material self. The material self consists of everything material that a person could call his or her own; such as his or her own body, family, and property. James described how we feel that our family members are part of our selves:

> Our father and mother, our wife and babes, are bone of our bone and flesh of our flesh. When they die, a part of our very selves is gone. If they do anything wrong, it is our shame. If they are insulted, our anger flashes forth as readily as if we stood in their place. (1892/1963, p. 45)

The social self. The social self is the self as known by others. "*A man has as many social selves as there are individuals who recognize him* and carry an image of him in their mind" (1892/1963, p. 46). According to James, humans are instinctively gregarious; therefore, the more we are known by others, the better. Conversely, not being noticed can be devastating:

> We are not only gregarious animals, liking to be in sight of our fellows, but we have an innate propensity to get ourselves noticed, and noticed favorably, by our kind. No more fiendish punishment could be devised, were such a thing physically possible, than that one should be turned loose in society and remain absolutely unnoticed by all the members thereof. If no one turned round when we entered, every person we met "cut us dead," and acted as if we were non-existing things, a kind of rage and impotent despair would ere long well up in us, from which the cruelest bodily tortures would be a relief; for these would make us feel that, however bad might be our plight, we had not sunk to such a depth as to be unworthy of attention at all. (1892/1963, p. 46)

The spiritual self. The spiritual self consists of a person's states of consciousness. It is all of which we think as we think of ourselves as thinkers. Also included in the spiritual self are all emotions associated with various states of consciousness. The spiritual self, then, has to do with the experience of one's subjective reality.

Self as knower. The empirical self (the me) is the person as known by himself or herself, but there is also an aspect of self that does the knowing (the I). Thus, for James, the self is "partly known and partly knower, partly object and partly subject" (1892/1963, p. 43). James admitted that dealing with the "me" was much easier than dealing with the "I", or what he called "pure ego." James struggled with his concept of **self as knower** and admitted it was similar to older philosophical and theological notions such as "soul," "spirit," and "transcendental ego."

Self-esteem. James was among the first to examine the circumstances under which people feel good or bad about themselves. He concluded that a person's **self-esteem** was determined by the ratio of things attempted to things achieved:

> With no attempt there can be no failure; with no failure, no humiliation. So our self-feeling in this world depends entirely on what we *back* ourselves to be and do. It is determined by the ratio of our actualities to our supposed potentialities; a fraction of which our pretensions are the denominator and the numerator our success: thus,

$$\text{Self-esteem} = \frac{\text{Success}}{\text{Pretensions}}.$$

(1892/1963, p. 54)

It should be noted that, according to James, one could increase self-esteem either by succeeding more *or* accomplishing less: "To give up pretensions is as blessed a relief as to get them gratified" (1892/1963, p. 54). James elaborated:

> There is the strangest lightness about the heart when one's nothingness in a particular line is once accepted in good faith. *All* is not bitterness in the lot of the lover sent away by the final inexorable "No." Many Bostonians . . . (and inhabitants of other cities, too, I fear), would be happier women and men today, if they could once for all abandon the notion of keeping up a Musical Self, and without shame let people hear them call a symphony a nuisance. How pleasant is the day when we give up striving to be young,—or slender! Thank God! we say, *those* illusions are gone. Everything added to the Self is a burden as well as a pride. A certain man who lost every penny during our civil war went and actually rolled in the dust, saying he had not felt so free and happy since he was born. (1892/1963, p. 54)

Emotions

James reversed the traditional belief that emotion resulted from the perception of an event. For example, it was traditionally believed that we see a bear, we are frightened, and we run. According to James, we see a bear, we run, and *then* we are frightened. Perception, according to James, causes bodily reactions that are then experienced as emotions. In other words, the emotions we feel depend on what we *do*. James put his theory as follows:

> Our natural way of thinking about . . . emotions is that the mental perception of some fact excites the mental affection called the emotion, and that this latter state of mind gives rise to the bodily expression. My theory, on the contrary, is that *the bodily changes follow directly the perception of the exciting fact, and that our feeling of the same changes as they occur IS the emotion.* Commonsense says, we lose our fortune, are sorry and weep; we meet a bear, are frightened and run;

we are insulted by a rival, are angry and strike. The hypothesis here to be defended says that this order of sequence is incorrect, that the one mental state is not immediately induced by the other, that the bodily manifestations must first be interposed between, and that the more rational statement is that we feel sorry because we cry, angry because we strike, afraid because we tremble, and not that we cry, strike, or tremble, because we are sorry, angry, or fearful, as the case may be. Without the bodily states following on the perception, the latter would be purely cognitive in form, pale, colorless, destitute of emotional warmth. We might then see a bear, and judge it best to run, receive the insult and deem it right to strike, but we should not actually *feel* afraid or angry. (1890, Vol. 2, pp. 449–450)

Because James believed that how we feel is determined by how a situation makes us act, it was, for him, impossible to specify a fixed number of emotions such as anger, joy, fear, or sorrow. It was also impossible to find bodily changes associated with specific emotions. For James, different individuals respond to situations differently, and therefore there is an almost infinite number of possible emotions:

> Now the moment the genesis of an emotion is accounted for, as the arousal by an object of a lot of reflex acts which are forthwith felt, *we immediately see why there is no limit to the number of possible different emotions which may exist, and why the emotions of different individuals may vary indefinitely,* both as to their constitution and as to objects which call them forth. (1890, Vol. 2, p. 454)

Coupled with James's belief in free will, his theory of emotion yields practical advice: *Act the way you want to feel.* If we believe James, there is a great deal of truth in Oscar Hammerstein's line, "Whenever I feel afraid, I whistle a happy tune. And soon I'm not afraid."

> Whistling to keep up courage is no mere figure of speech. On the other hand, sit all day in a moping posture, sigh, and reply to everything with a dismal voice, and your melancholy lingers. There is no more valuable precept in moral education than this, as all who have experience know: if we wish to conquer undesirable emotional tendencies in ourselves we must assiduously, and in the first instance cold-

bloodedly, go through the *outward movements* of those contrary dispositions which we prefer to cultivate. The reward of persistency will infallibly come, in the fading out of the sullenness or depression, and the advent of real cheerfulness and kindliness in their stead. (James, 1890, Vol. 2, p. 463)

James had discovered the power of this advice when he decided to believe in free will and thus cured the depression that believing in a strict determinism had caused.

James's theory of emotion provides still another example of the importance of the *Zeitgeist*; the Danish physician **Carl George Lange** (1834–1900) published virtually the same theory at about the same time. In recognition of the contributions of both men, the theory is now known as the **James–Lange theory of emotion**.

Free Will

Although James did not solve the free will–determinism controversy, he did arrive at a position with which he was comfortable. He noted that without the assumption of determinism, science would be impossible; and insofar as psychology was to be a science, it too must assume determinism. Science, however, was not everything, and for certain approaches to the study of humans, the assumption of free will might be very fruitful.

> Science . . . must constantly be reminded that her purposes are not the only purposes, and that the order of uniform causation which she has use for, and is therefore right in postulating, may be enveloped in a wider order, on which she has no claims at all. (James, 1890, Vol. 2, p. 576)

James's analysis of voluntary behavior. According to James's **ideo-motor theory of behavior**, an idea of a certain action causes that action to occur. He believed that in the vast majority of cases, ideas of actions flowed immediately and automatically (habitually or reflexively) into behavior. This automatic process continues unless mental effort is expended to purposively select and hold an idea of interest in consciousness.

For James, voluntary action and mental effort were inseparable. The ideas of various behavioral possibilities are retained from previous experience, and their recollection is a prerequisite to voluntary behavior: "A supply of the various movements that are possible, left in the memory by experiences of their involuntary performance, is thus the prerequisite of the voluntary life" (James, 1892/1963, p. 283). From the ideas of various possible actions, one is selected for attention, and it is the one that causes behavior and continues to do so as long as the idea is attended to. Therefore, "what holds attention determines action" (James, 1892/1963, p. 315). The will functions, then, by selecting from among many ideas of action one that we are interested in doing. By *fiat* (consent, or literally "let it be"), the will expends energy to hold the idea of interest in consciousness, thus inhibiting other ideas: "*Effort of attention is thus the essential phenomenon of will*" (James, 1892/1963, p. 317). It is by controlling one's ideas of behavior that one controls his or her actual behavior. Because ideas cause behavior, it is important to attend to those ideas that result in behavior deemed desirable under the circumstances: "*The terminus of the psychological process in volition, the point to which the will is directly applied, is always an idea*" (James, 1892/1963, p. 322).

We can choose our actions, according to James, by choosing our thoughts, and it is what thoughts we choose to entertain that differentiates one person from another:

> Thus not only our morality but our religion, so far as the latter is deliberate, depend on the effort which we can make. *"Will you or won't you have it so?"* is the most probing question we are ever asked; we are asked it every hour of the day, and about the largest as well as the smallest, the most theoretical as well as the most practical, things. We answer by *consents or non-consents* and not by words. What wonder that these dumb responses should seem our deepest organs of communication with the nature of things! What wonder if the effort demanded by them be the measure of our worth as men! What wonder if the amount which we accord of it were the one strictly underived and original contribution

which we make to the world! (1892/1963, p. 327)

So, combining James's theories of volition and emotion, what we think determines what we do, and what we do determines how we feel.

Pragmatism

Everywhere in James's writing is his belief in pragmatism. According to pragmatism, which is the cornerstone of functionalism, any belief, thought, or behavior must be judged by its consequences. Any belief that helps create a more effective and satisfying life is worth holding, whether such a belief is scientific or religious. Believing in free will was emotionally satisfying to James, so he believed in it. According to the pragmatic viewpoint, truth is not something "out there" in a static form waiting to be discovered as many of the rationalists maintained. Instead, truth is something that must be gauged by effectiveness under changing circumstances. What works is true, and because circumstances change, truth must be forever dynamic.

James's pragmatic philosophy appears in his description of the methods that psychology should employ. He urged the use of both introspection and experimentation, as well as the study of animals, children, preliterate humans, and abnormal humans. In short, he encouraged the use of any method that would shed light on the complexities of human existence; he believed that nothing useful should be omitted.

In 1907 James wrote *Pragmatism*, in which he delineated two types of personality: the *tender-minded* and the *tough-minded*. Tender-minded people are rationalistic (principle-oriented), intellectual, idealistic, optimistic, religious, and dogmatic, and they believe in free will. Conversely, tough-minded people are empiricistic (fact-oriented), sensationalistic, materialistic, pessimistic, irreligious, skeptical, and fatalistic. James viewed pragmatism as a way of compromising between the two outlooks. The pragmatist simply takes from each list whatever works in the circumstances at hand.

Again, the criterion of the validity of an idea, according to the pragmatist, is its usefulness. No idea, no method, no philosophy, no religion should be accepted or rejected except on the basis of usefulness:

> Rationalism sticks to logic and the empyrean [lofty, abstract]. Empiricism sticks to the external senses. Pragmatism is willing to take anything, to follow either logic or the senses and to count the humblest and most personal experiences. She will count mystical experiences if they have practical consequences. She will take a God who lives in the very dirt of private fact—if that should seem a likely place to find him.
>
> Her only test of probable truth is what works best in the way of leading us, what fits every part of life best and combines with the collectivity of experience's demands, nothing being omitted. If theological ideas should do this, if the notion of God, in particular, should prove to do it, how could pragmatism possibly deny God's existence? She could see no meaning in treating as "not true" a notion that was pragmatically so successful. (James, 1907/1981, pp. 38–39)

James's Contributions to Psychology

James helped to incorporate evolutionary theory into psychology. By stressing what was useful, he represented a major departure from the pure psychology of both voluntarism and structuralism. In fact, the pragmatic spirit in James's psychology quite naturally led to the development of applied psychology. For James, as well as the functionalists who followed him, usefulness defined both truth and value. James expanded research techniques in psychology by not only accepting introspection but also encouraging any technique that promised to yield useful information about people. By studying all aspects of human existence—including behavior, cognition, emotions, volition, and even religious experience—James also expanded the subject matter of psychology. His ideas led directly to the school of functionalism, which we discuss later in this chapter. Many believe that current psychology in the United States represents a return to psychology as James described it.

In 1892, when James was 50, he decided that he had said everything he could say about psychology, especially about experimental psychology. He decided to devote his full attention to philosophical matters, something that necessitated relinquishing the directorship of the Harvard Psychology Laboratory. To maintain the laboratory's reputation as the best in the country, James sought an outstanding, creative, experimentally oriented psychologist and certainly one who did not embrace Wundtian psychology (at least as James understood it). He found such a person in Hugo Münsterberg.

HUGO MÜNSTERBERG

Born in the east Prussian port city of Danzig (now Gdansk, Poland), **Hugo Münsterberg** (1863–1916) was one of four sons of prominent parents. His father was a successful businessman, his mother a recognized artist and musician. Both his mother and father died before he was 20 years old. Throughout his life, Münsterberg had wide-ranging interests. In his early years, he displayed interest and talent in art, literature, poetry, foreign languages, music, and acting. Then, while studying at the University of Leipzig, he heard a lecture by Wundt and became interested in psychology. Münsterberg eventually became Wundt's research assistant and received his doctorate under Wundt's supervision in 1885. Perhaps on Wundt's advice, Münsterberg next studied medicine at the University of Heidelberg and received his medical degree in 1887. In that same year, he began teaching as a *Privatdocent* (unpaid instructor) at the University of Freiburg, where he started a psychology laboratory and began publishing papers on time perception, attentional processes, learning, and memory.

During the time when he was Wundt's assistant, one of Münsterberg's jobs was to study voluntary activities through introspection. The two men disagreed, however, over whether the will could be experienced as a conscious element of the mind during introspection. Wundt believed

Hugo Münsterberg

ARCHIVES OF THE HISTORY OF AMERICAN PSYCHOLOGY

that it could, whereas Münsterberg believed that it could not. In fact, Münsterberg did not believe that will was involved in voluntary behavior at all. For him, as we prepare to act one way or another, we consciously experience this bodily preparedness and confuse it with the will to act. For Münsterberg then, what we experience consciously as will is an epiphenomenon, a by-product of bodily activity. This, of course, was diametrically opposed to Wundt's interpretation of voluntary behavior. For him, volitional behavior was always preceded by a conscious will to act. Clearly, Münsterberg's analysis of voluntary behavior was closer to James's than to Wundt's. In 1888 Münsterberg elaborated his theory in *Voluntary Action*, a book that James called a masterpiece and Wundt criticized harshly. James was impressed by many of Münsterberg's publications and cited them often in his *Principles*.

He arranged to meet Münsterberg at the first International Congress of Psychology in 1889, and their relationship strengthened further.

After completing *Principles*, James wanted very much to leave psychology, especially experimental psychology, so that he could more actively pursue his interests in philosophy and psychic phenomena. To make the change, James needed someone to replace him as director of the Harvard Psychology Laboratory. In 1892 (the same year that Titchener arrived at Cornell), James offered Münsterberg the job despite the fact that Münsterberg could read but not speak English. Münsterberg accepted and learned to speak English so well and so quickly that his classes were soon attracting as many students as those of James. Although adjusting well, Münsterberg could not decide whether he wanted to give up his homeland (Germany) in favor of a lifelong commitment in the United States. In 1895 he asked for and received a leave of absence so that he could return to the University of Freiburg. After two years, he was unable to obtain the type of academic appointment that he sought. He wrote to James in 1897 accepting the position at Harvard. It turned out, however, that Münsterberg never severed his emotional ties with his homeland.

For several years, Münsterberg did extremely well at Harvard. In 1899 he was elected president of the American Psychological Association and became chair of the division of philosophy at Harvard, which at the time still included psychology. When in 1900 he published *Basics of Psychology*, he dedicated it to James. As time went on, however, James's liberal attitude toward philosophy and psychology began to irritate Münsterberg's more positivistic approach to science. He was especially appalled by James's acceptance of depth psychology, psychic phenomena, and religious mysticism into the realm of psychology. For Münsterberg, "mysticism and mediums were one thing, psychology was quite another. Experimental psychology and psychic hocus-pocus did not mix" (Bjork, 1983, pp. 63–64). Despite his difference with James, Münsterberg remained highly productive. More and

more, however, Münsterberg's interests turned to the practical applications of psychological principles. Unlike his mentor Wundt, Münsterberg felt *very* strongly that psychologists should attempt to uncover information that could be used in the real world. With his efforts, Münsterberg did much to create what is now referred to as **applied psychology**.

Münsterberg's Applied Psychology

Clinical psychology. In an attempt to understand the causes of abnormal behavior, Münsterberg saw many mentally ill people. Because he was seeing them for scientific reasons, he never charged them a fee. He applied his "treatment," which consisted mainly of causing his patients to expect to improve, to cases of alcoholism, drug addiction, phobia, and sexual dysfunction, but not to psychosis. He felt that psychosis was caused by deterioration of the nervous system and could not be treated. Along with the suggestion that individuals would improve as the result of his efforts, Münsterberg also employed **reciprocal antagonism**, which involved strengthening the opposite thoughts to those causing problems. Although Münsterberg was aware of Freud's work, he chose to treat symptoms directly and did not search for the underlying causes of those symptoms. Münsterberg said of Freud's theory of unconscious motivation: "The story of the subconscious mind can be told in three words: there is none" (1909, p. 125).

Forensic psychology. Münsterberg was the first to apply psychological principles to legal matters, thus creating **forensic psychology**. Among other things, he pointed out that eyewitness testimony could be unreliable because sensory impressions could be illusory, suggestion and stress could affect perception, and memory was not always accurate. Münsterberg would often stage various traumatic events in his classroom to show that even when witnesses were attempting to be accurate, there were wide differences in the individual accounts of what had actually happened. Münsterberg urged that psychological methods replace the brutal interrogation of criminals. He felt that harsh interrogation could result in false confessions because some people would want to please the interrogators, some had a need to give in to authority figures, and some very depressed people had a need to be punished. Münsterberg published his thoughts on forensic psychology in his best-selling book *On the Witness Stand* (1908). In this book, Münsterberg described an apparatus that could detect lying by observing changes such as those in pulse rate and respiration. Others would follow Münsterberg's lead and later create the controversial lie detector.

Industrial psychology. Münsterberg's *Vocation and Learning* (1912) and *Psychology and Industrial Efficiency* (1913) are usually considered the beginning of what later came to be called **industrial psychology**. In these books, Münsterberg dealt with such topics as methods of personnel selection, methods of increasing work efficiency, and marketing and advertising techniques. To aid in personnel selection, for example, he recommended defining the skills necessary for performing a task and then determining the person's ability to perform that task. In this way, one could learn whether a person had the skills necessary for doing a certain job adequately. Münsterberg also found that whether a task was boring could not be determined by observing the work of others. Often, work that some people thought boring interested those doing it. It was necessary, then, to take individual differences into account when selecting personnel and when making job assignments.

Münsterberg's Fate

Because of his work in applied psychology, Münsterberg was well known to the public, the academic world, and the scientific community. William James had made psychology popular within the academic world, but Münsterberg helped make it popular with the general population by showing its practical uses. In addition,

Münsterberg had among his personal friends some of the most influential people in the world, including Presidents Theodore Roosevelt and William Howard Taft and the philosopher Bertrand Russell. He was invited to dine at the White House, and in his home in Cambridge, Massachusetts, he and his wife often hosted European scholars and German royalty. In addition, he was awarded several medals by the German government. By the time Münsterberg died in 1916, however, the general attitude toward him had turned negative, and his death went essentially unnoticed. The main reason for his unpopularity was his desire to create a favorable relationship between the United States and his native Germany. Never obtaining U.S. citizenship, Münsterberg maintained a nationalistic loyalty toward Germany. He felt that both Germans and Americans had inaccurate stereotypes of each other, and he wrote books attempting to correct them—for example, *The Americans* (1904). In another book, *American Problems* (1910), Münsterberg was highly critical of Americans saying that they had a general inability to concentrate their attention on any one thing for very long. He explained this national inability to attend by the fact that, in the United States, women were influential in forming intellectual and cultural development. The intellectual vulnerability of women also explained the popularity of psychological fads such as seances. While James was attempting to discover if any of the claims of "mediums" were valid, Münsterberg was busy exposing them as dangerous frauds.

As the First World War approached, Münsterberg found himself caught up in the U.S. outrage over German military aggression. He was suspected of being a spy, and even many of his colleagues at Harvard disassociated themselves from him. During this time of extreme anti-German feeling, Münsterberg suffered a fatal stroke as he was lecturing to one of his classes. A year after his death, the United States entered the war against Germany.

Though little of Titchener's work is relevant in contemporary psychology, most of Münster-

Granville Stanley Hall

berg's is still of vital interest. Münsterberg's emphasis on practicality was perfectly compatible with the school of functionalism that was emerging.

GRANVILLE STANLEY HALL

In his influence on U.S. psychology, **Granville Stanley Hall** (1844–1924) was second only to William James. As we will see, Hall was a theorist in the Darwinian tradition, but above all he was an organizer. The number of firsts associated with Hall is unequaled by any other U.S. psychologist.

Hall was born in the small farming town of Ashfield, Massachusetts. In 1863 he enrolled in Williams College, where he learned associationism, Scottish commonsense philosophy, and evolutionary theory as he prepared for the ministry. Upon graduation in 1867, he enrolled in the Union Theological Seminary in New York City. Here, Hall gave indications that perhaps he was not cut out for the clergy:

> During his year in New York, he explored the city with zest, roaming the streets, visiting police courts, and attending churches of all denominations. He joined a discussion club interested in the study of positivism, visited the theater for plays and musicals, tutored young ladies from the elite of New York, visited a phrenologist, and generally had an exciting year. He was not noted for his religious orthodoxy. After preaching his trial sermon before the faculty and students, he went to the office of the president for criticism. Instead of discussing his sermon, the president knelt and prayed that Hall would be shown the errors of his ways! (R. I. Watson, 1978, p. 398)

In 1868 a small grant made it possible for Hall to travel to Germany where he studied theology and philosophy. He also spent much time in beer gardens and theaters and engaged in considerable romance.

In 1871 Hall accepted a position at Antioch College in Ohio, where he not only taught English literature, French, German, and philosophy but also served as the librarian, led the choir, and did a little preaching. While at Antioch, Hall read Wundt's *Principles of Physiological Psychology*. In 1876 he was offered an instructorship of English at Harvard. During his stay at Harvard, Hall became friends with William James, who was only two years his elder. Hall did research in Harvard's medical school, writing up his results as "The Muscular Perception of Space," which he offered as his doctoral thesis in 1878. Harvard was the first institution to offer a doctorate in psychology, and in 1878 Hall was the first to obtain that degree. After receiving his doctorate, Hall returned to Germany where he studied first with Wundt and then with Helmholtz. Hall was Wundt's first U.S. student. In a letter to James, Hall confessed that he had learned more from Helmholtz than from Wundt.

In 1880, at the age of 36, Hall returned to the United States where, after giving a series of lectures, he accepted a position at Johns Hopkins

University. In 1883 Hall set up a working psychology laboratory. It is generally agreed that Wundt founded the world's first psychology laboratory in Leipzig in 1879, and that Hall's laboratory at Johns Hopkins was the first psychology laboratory in the United States (Boring, 1965). (As was previously mentioned, the laboratory James established in 1875 is generally discounted because it was designed for teaching demonstrations rather than research.) While at Johns Hopkins, besides founding a psychology laboratory, Hall founded the first U.S. journal dedicated to psychological issues, the *American Journal of Psychology*, which first appeared in 1887. Also while at Johns Hopkins, Hall taught James McKeen Cattell and John Dewey, who were later to become key figures in functionalism.

President of Clark University

In 1888 Hall left Johns Hopkins to become the first president of Clark University in Worcester, Massachusetts, but he also remained a professor of psychology. At Clark, Hall maintained a strong hand in directing and shaping U.S. psychology: "Hall was the Great Graduate Teacher of American psychology. By 1893 eleven of the fourteen Ph.D. degrees from American universities had been given by him; by 1898 this had increased to thirty awarded out of fifty-four" (R. I. Watson, 1978, p. 403).

While at Clark University, Hall invited 26 of the most prominent psychologists in the United States to meet in Worcester to form an association of psychologists. The meeting took place on July 8, 1892, and represents the founding of the American Psychological Association (APA). Some of those who were invited did not attend (e.g., William James and John Dewey), but they were considered charter members because they were invited to join and they supported the association. Hall was elected the first president of the APA, and in subsequent years William James and John Dewey would also serve as presidents. Besides being the first president, Hall was one of only two individuals to be elected to the presidency twice; James was the other. However, Hall died the year he was elected for the second time (1924) and never served his term. From an original membership of 26, the APA now has more than 70,000 members and affiliates. Michael Wertheimer jokingly points out that "if [the] APA continues to grow at the rate it did during the first three-quarters of a century of its existence, there should be more psychologists than people in the world" (1987, p. 92).

In 1891 Hall founded the United States' second psychological journal, *Pedagogical Seminary*, now the *Journal of Genetic Psychology*.

Recapitulation Theory

Hall was enamored with evolutionary theory. He said in his autobiography, "As soon as I first heard it in my youth I think I must have been almost hypnotized by the word 'evolution,' which was music to my ear and seemed to fit my mouth better than any other" (1923, p. 357). So strongly did Hall feel about evolutionary theory that he believed that it, instead of physics, should act as a model for science. He believed that evolution explained not only the phylogenetic development of the human species but also the development of each individual as well. That is, he believed that each individual in his or her lifetime re-enacted all evolutionary stages of the human race. This is called the **recapitulation theory** of development: "Every child, from the moment of conception to maturity, recapitulates, very rapidly at first, and then more slowly every stage of development through which the human race from its lowest beginnings has passed" (Hall, 1923, p. 380).

During prenatal development, a single-celled organism develops into a newborn whose capabilities are equal to a number of mammals lower than humans on the phylogenetic scale. In childhood there is still evidence of the impulsiveness, cruelty, and immorality that characterized earlier, less civilized stages of human development. Hall's view was that if these primitive impulses were not given expression in childhood, they would be carried into adulthood.

Hall therefore encouraged parents and teachers to create situations in which these primitive impulses could be given expression.

In 1904 Hall published a two-volume book entitled *Adolescence: Its Psychology and Its Relations to Physiology, Anthropology, Sociology, Sex, Crime, Religion and Education*, which focused on the importance of sex differentiation for psychological development. Hall defined adolescence as the period between age 14 or 15 and age 25. Hall viewed females as vital for the future evolution of the human species, and adolescence should be a period when females are trained for motherhood. As females were preparing for motherhood, males still have the need to satisfy primitive impulses, and therefore to include both sexes together in the same educational system makes no sense:

> The premises of Hall's argument against co-education were derived from three concerns of recapitulation: (a) that adolescence was a critical period in the development of the reproductive organs in women, (b) that the adolescent male needed freedom to engage in cathartic expression of his savage impulses, and (c) that natural sexual differentiation during adolescence was the basis for later attraction between the sexes. (Diehl, 1986, p. 871)

As part of his concern for the normal development of the female reproductive capacity, Hall was worried about what association with males might do to the "normalization" of the menstrual period:

> At a time when her whole future life depends upon normalizing the lunar month, is there not something not only unnatural and unhygienic, but a little monstrous, in daily school associations with boys, where she must suppress and conceal her instincts and feelings, at those times when her own promptings suggest withdrawal or stepping a little aside to let Lord Nature do his magnificent work of efflorescence. (1906, p. 590)

In general, Hall urged the study of adolescence because he believed that at this stage of development habits learned during childhood were discarded and new adult habits had not yet been learned. During this transitional period, the individual was forced to rely on instincts, and therefore adolescence was a very good time to study human instinctual makeup.

Although most of what Hall said about development proved to be incorrect, he did much to stimulate educational psychology, and he started the child development movement in the United States. Hall's interests in developmental psychology lasted throughout his life. His *Senescence: The Last Half of Life* (1922) can be seen as a forerunner of life-span psychology as well as an extension of what he started in *Adolescence* (1904). His autobiography *Life and Confessions of a Psychologist* appeared in 1923, a year before his death.

Psychology at Clark University

Hall's 31 years as president of Clark University were colorful to say the least. Under his leadership, psychology dominated Clark, and Clark was a strong competitor with Harvard for top students and faculty. In 1908 Hall decided to invite prominent European psychologists to Clark University to celebrate its 20th anniversary. Hall sent invitations to both Wundt and Freud, and both invitations were rejected. Wundt rejected the "enticing" invitation because he had already agreed to be the primary speaker at the 500th anniversary of Leipzig University on the date in question. Freud declined because the date conflicted with another commitment and because the honorarium was too small. Hall sent a revised invitation to Freud with a date more compatible with Freud's schedule and with a larger honorarium, and Freud accepted (Rosenzweig, 1985). It is interesting to note that Hall would have been as pleased with Wundt as with Freud; he had a deep respect for both. Hall had long been interested in Freud's ideas and was among the first to urge sex education in the United States. Freud and Jung arrived on September 5, 1909, and according to Freud, this visit to Clark did much to further acceptance of his theory throughout the world.

By embracing evolutionary theory, with its emphasis on practicality and adaptation, James,

Münsterberg, and Hall paved the way for a type of psychology that was distinctly different from structuralism; they had planted the seeds for a psychology that stressed the function of behavior and thought.

FUNCTIONALISM AT THE UNIVERSITY OF CHICAGO

John Dewey

Despite the fact that functionalism was never a well-defined school of thought like structuralism, it is common to attribute its founding to **John Dewey** (1859–1952), even though James, Münsterberg, and Hall certainly laid important groundwork. Dewey was born in Burlington, Vermont, on October 20. While attending the University of Vermont as an undergraduate, he became interested in philosophy. Following graduation he taught secondary school for three years before entering Johns Hopkins University in 1882 to pursue his interests in philosophy. Dewey had Hall as a teacher but was also strongly influenced by the philosopher George S. Morris (1840–1889). Besides psychology, Dewey also developed a strong interest in the philosophies of Hegel and Kant; he wrote his dissertation on Kant's philosophy. Dewey's first academic appointment was at the University of Michigan, where he taught both philosophy and psychology. While at Michigan, Dewey wrote *Psychology* (1886), which was a strange mixture of Hegelian philosophy and functionalistic psychology. It preceded James's *Principles* by four years. Dewey was at Michigan for 10 years (1884–1894), except for 1 year spent at the University of Minnesota.

In 1894 Dewey accepted an appointment as chair of the philosophy department at the newly established University of Chicago (at that time, philosophy included psychology and pedagogy). It was at Chicago that Dewey wrote an article that many think marks the formal beginning of the school of functionalism:

> 1896 marks the formal date of the birth of functionalism in psychology in the United States,

John Dewey

owing to the publication of Dewey's classical critique of the reflex arc theory in psychology. In his "The Reflex Arc Concept in Psychology" (1896), Dewey initiated a new trend in psychology by his protestation against elementism that dominated psychology. (Sahakian, 1975, pp. 357–358)

Dewey's criticism of the analysis of behavior in terms of reflexes. Dewey's argument was that to divide the elements of a reflex into sensory processes, brain processes, and motor responses for analysis was artificial and misleading. According to Dewey, dividing behavior into elements was no more justifiable than dividing consciousness into elements. Showing the influence of James's *Principles*, Dewey claimed that there is a stream of behavior just as there is a stream of consciousness. The three elements of a reflex, said Dewey, must be viewed as a coordinated system that was directed toward a goal, and this goal was usually related to the survival of the organism. Dewey took a child touching a flame as an example. The analysis of such behavior in terms of reflexes claims the child sees the flame of a candle (S) and grasps it (R). The resulting pain (S) then elicits withdrawal (R). According to this analysis, nothing changes, nothing is learned. In reality, however, the experience of being burned changes the child's perception of the flame, and he or she will avoid it next time:

> More technically stated, the so-called response is not merely *to* the stimulus; it is *into* it. The burn is the original seeing, the original opticalocular experience enlarged and transformed in its value. It is no longer mere seeing; it is seeing-of-a-light-that-means-pain-when-contact-occurs. (Dewey, 1896, pp. 359–360)

This, according to Dewey, could only happen if the child was still observing the flame as it was burned and withdrew. Thus, the so-called stimuli and responses are not separate but form an interrelated sequence of events that are functional. Indeed, for the child, the candle flame is no longer the same stimulus; it now elicits avoidance. Dewey then urged that all behavior be looked at in terms of its function—to adapt the organism to its environment. To study elements of the adaptive act in isolation caused one to miss the most important aspect of the act: its purposiveness. "There is simply a continuously ordered sequence of acts, all adapted in themselves and in the order of their sequence, to reach a certain objective end, the reproduction of the species, the preservation of life, locomotion to a certain place" (Dewey, 1896, p. 366). We see here a great deal of similarity between Dewey and James.

As an evolutionist, Dewey thought that social change was inevitable, but he also believed that it could be influenced positively by proper plans of action. Dewey was very influential in creating what came to be called "progressive" education in the United States. He believed that education should be student oriented rather than subject

oriented and that the best way to learn something was to do it—thus his famous statement that students *learn by doing*. Dewey was very much opposed to rote memorization, drills, and the view that the purpose of education was to transmit traditional knowledge. Rather, he believed that education should facilitate creative intelligence and prepare children to live effectively in a complex society.

Dewey was always deeply involved in liberal causes such as the New York Teacher's Union, the American Association of University Professors, and the American Civil Liberties Union. He was also supportive of his wife's promotion of women's suffrage:

> An anecdote was widely circulated at the time that Dewey was marching in a parade supporting women's suffrage carrying a placard that was handed to him. He had not read its message: "Men can vote! Why can't I?" and was puzzled by the amused smiles of the onlookers. (Hilgard, 1987, p. 673)

In 1904 friction with the education department caused Dewey to resign from the University of Chicago and to accept an appointment at Teachers College at Columbia University where he pursued his interests in education and pragmatic philosophy. He died on June 1, 1952, at the age of 92.

James Rowland Angell

James Rowland Angell (1869–1949) was the son of the long-term president of the University of Michigan. Angell was Dewey's student while Dewey was at Michigan, and after graduating in 1890, Angell remained for a year of graduate training. It was during that year that he attended a seminar conducted by Dewey on James's newly published *Principles*. The seminar switched Angell's primary interest from philosophy to psychology. The following year, Angell went to Harvard and became acquainted with James. The year 1892–1893 was spent traveling and studying in Germany. He attended lectures by Ebbinghaus and started to prepare a doctoral dissertation on Kant's philosophy under the supervision of the famous philosopher Hans Vaihinger (1852–1933) but never finished. Two master's degrees, one from Michigan in 1891 and one from Harvard in 1892, were to remain his highest earned degrees.

In 1893 Angell accepted an instructorship at the University of Minnesota (instead of finishing his doctoral dissertation) but stayed for only one year. In 1894 Angell accepted a position at the University of Chicago, offered to him by his former teacher, Dewey. Angell was 25 years old at the time, and Dewey was 10 years his senior. Angell, Dewey, and their colleagues were highly productive and influential at Chicago. In 1896 Dewey published his famous article on the reflex arc, and in 1904 Angell published the very popular *Psychology: An Introductory Study of the Structure and Functions of Human Consciousness.* Both Dewey and Angell eventually served as presidents of the APA (Dewey in 1899, Angell in 1906). Angell's presidential address, "The Province of Functional Psychology," distinguished between functional and structural psychology (a distinction that Titchener had originally made in 1898). In his address, Angell made three major points:

James Rowland Angell

1. Functional psychology was interested in mental operations rather than in conscious elements but even mental operations in isolation were of little interest:

The functional psychologist . . . is interested not alone in the operations of mental process considered merely of and by and for itself, but also and more vigorously in mental activity as part of a larger stream of biological forces which are daily and hourly at work before our eyes and which are constitutive of the most important and most absorbing part of our world. The psychologist of this stripe is wont to take his cue from the basal conception of the evolutionary movement, *i.e.*, that for the most part organic structures and functions possess their present characteristics by virtue of the efficiency with which they fit into the extant conditions of life broadly designated the environment. (Angell, 1907, p. 68)

2. Mental processes mediated between the needs of the organism and the environment.

That is, mental functions helped the organism to survive. Behavioral habits allowed an organism to adjust to familiar situations; but when an organism was confronted with the unfamiliar, mental processes aided in the adaptive process.

3. Mind and body could not be separated; they acted as a unit in an organism's struggle for survival.

At the time of Angell's address, functionalism was an established and growing school and a strong competitor to structuralism. By further demonstrating its kinship with evolutionary theory, functionalism encouraged the study of not only consciousness but also animal behavior, child psychology, habit formation, and individual differences. In addition, with its strong pragmatic orientation, it encouraged the application of psychological principles to education, business, and clinical psychology.

Angell was chairman of the psychology department at Chicago for 25 years. Under his leadership, the University of Chicago became a center of functionalism. Among Angell's famous students were Harvey Carr, who we consider next, and John B. Watson, who will be featured in the next chapter. In 1921 Angell left Chicago to become president of Yale University, a post he held until his retirement in 1937.

Harvey Carr

Harvey Carr (1873–1954) obtained his bachelor's and master's degrees from the University of Colorado and then went to the University of Chicago, where he obtained his doctorate in 1905 under the supervision of Angell. Carr stayed at Chicago all of his professional life, and in 1927 he was elected president of the APA.

In 1925 Carr wrote *Psychology: A Study of Mental Activity*. Mental activity, in turn, was "concerned with the acquisition, fixation, retention, organization, and evaluation of experiences, and their subsequent utilization in the guidance of conduct" (Carr, 1925, p. 1). We see in Carr's definition the functionalist's concern with the learning process. Because learning was a major tool used in adjusting to the environment, it was a major concern of the functionalists. Central to Carr's psychology was what he called the **adaptive act**, which had three components: (1) a motive that acted as a stimulus for behavior (e.g., hunger or thirst), (2) an environmental setting or the situation the organism was in, and (3) a response that satisfied the motive (e.g., eating or drinking). Here again, we see the influence of evolutionary theory on functionalism: Needs must be met for organisms to survive. Needs motivate behavior until an act satisfies the need, at which point learning occurs; and the next time the organism is in the same situation and experiences the same need, the organism will tend to repeat the behavior that was previously effective. For Carr, both perception and behavior were necessary in adapting to the environment because how the environment was perceived determined how an organism responded

to it. Seeing a wild animal in a zoo and seeing one while walking through the forest would elicit two different reactions.

Besides the adaptive act, Carr (1925) included sections on the human nervous system and sense organs, learning, perceiving, reasoning, affection, volition, individual differences, and the measurement of intelligence. Carr had a special interest in space perception and wrote an entire book on the topic (Carr, 1935). Although Carr, like the other functionalists, accepted both introspection and experimentation as legitimate methods, the latter became the favored research technique. One reason for this was the growing success of animal research in which introspection was, of course, impossible. Showing the pragmatism that characterized functionalism and remarkable similarity to Wundt, Carr believed that literature, art, language, and social and political institutions should be studied in order to learn something about the nature of the mind that produced them.

Heidbreder divided the functionalistic movement into three phases: "its initiation by Dewey, its development under Angell's leadership, and its preservation as a definite influence by Carr" (1933, pp. 208–209).

FUNCTIONALISM AT COLUMBIA UNIVERSITY

James McKeen Cattell

Functionalism took on a slightly different appearance under the leadership of **James McKeen Cattell** (1860–1944), who, as we noted in chapter 10, was strongly influenced by Galton. Cattell was born in Easton, Pennsylvania, and obtained his bachelor's degree in 1880 from Lafayette College, where his father was president. Following graduation Cattell went to Germany to study with the Kantian physiologist R. H. Lotze (1817–1881). Being very impressed by Lotze, it came as a blow to Cattell when Lotze died a year after Cattell's arrival. The following year Cattell returned home and wrote a paper on philosophy that won him a fellowship at Johns Hopkins University. While at Johns Hopkins (1882–1883), he did research in Hall's new psychology laboratory and decided to become a psychologist. In 1883 Cattell returned to Leipzig, where he became Wundt's first experimental assistant. Much to Wundt's dismay, however, Cattell insisted on studying individual differences, something that was contrary to the main thrust of the Leipzig laboratory. (Wundt and his colleagues were more interested in what minds had in common than in what made them different.) Cattell also expressed doubts about the usefulness of introspection:

> Contrary to the usual custom of being assigned a problem by Wundt, Cattell worked on his own problems in reaction time. He also became convinced that the introspective efforts directed toward fractionation of the reaction time into perception, choice, and the like, then gospel in Wundt's laboratory, was something he could not carry out and which he doubted others could. The situation reached the point where he did some of his experiments at his lodging rather than in the laboratory, since Wundt would not permit subjects in his laboratory who could not profit from introspection. Though somewhat strained, relations between them never reached a breaking point. Wundt and Cattell did agree on the value of the study of reaction time. In Cattell's eyes it was a valuable tool for the study of the time necessary for mental operation and especially for the investigation of individual differences. (R. I. Watson, 1978, p. 408)

Cattell received his doctorate from Leipzig in 1886. Returning to the United States, he taught at Bryn Mawr College and the University of Pennsylvania, before going to London to work with Galton. In Galton, Cattell finally found someone who shared his intense interest in individual differences. Galton confirmed Cattell's conviction that individual differences were important and that they could be objectively measured. As we saw in the previous chapter, Cattell shared Galton's belief in eugenics, and he argued that delinquents and defectives should be sterilized and that bright and healthy individuals should be encouraged to marry.

Returning to the University of Pennsylvania, Cattell founded the first psychology laboratory designed for undergraduate students. This he did in 1887. In 1888 Cattell was given a professorship in psychology at the University of Pennsylvania. This professorship was the first in the world to be in psychology and not in philosophy.

In 1891 Cattell accepted a professorship at Columbia University, where he stayed for 26 years. Cattell did basic research in such areas as reaction time, psychophysics, association, and perception, but he will probably be remembered most for his work on mental tests (a term that he coined). He believed that the measurement of mental processes could make psychology as objective as the physical sciences:

> Psychology cannot attain the certainty and exactness of the physical sciences, unless it rests on a foundation of experiment and measurement. A step in this direction could be made by applying a series of mental tests and measurements to a large number of individuals. The results would be of considerable scientific value in discovering the constancy of mental processes, their interdependence, and their variation under different circumstances. (Cattell, 1890, p. 373)

As we have seen, Cattell followed Galton in assuming that mental processes could be measured by studying sensory and motor abilities. In fact, he used many of the same tests that Galton had used—for example, dynamometer pressure, least noticeable difference in weight, and reaction time. We saw in chapter 10 that Cattell's testing program was ill-fated.

Cattell and applied psychology. Cattell said that "sciences are not immutable species, but developing organisms" (1904, p. 176). This being so, why not experiment with ideas and methods? Who knows what may prove to be valuable? "Let us take a broad outlook and be liberal in our appreciation; let us welcome variations and sports; if birth is given to monstrosities on occasion, we may be sure that they will not survive" (1904, p. 180). But, true to the pragmatic spirit,

Cattell believed that ideas and methods should always be evaluated in terms of their usefulness:

> If I did not believe that psychology affected conduct and could be applied in useful ways, I should regard my occupation as nearer to that of the professional chess-player or sword swallower than to that of the engineer or scientific physician. (1904, p. 185)

According to Cattell, most everyone attempts to apply psychological principles in what they do: "All our systems of education, our churches, our legal systems, our governments and the rest are applied psychology" (1904, p. 186). It is not, then, a matter of whether behavior should be controlled or not. It is a matter of using the most valid knowledge of psychological principles in exercising that control. Here psychology can be extremely helpful:

> It certainly is not essential and perhaps is not desirable for every mother, for every teacher, for every statesman, to study psychology, especially the kind of psychology at present available. It is not necessary for a man to be either a psychologist or a fool at forty; he may, for example, be both. But surely it is possible to discover whether or not it is desirable to feed a baby every time it cries, to whip a boy when he disobeys or to put a man in prison when he breaks a law. If each man were given the work he is most competent to do and were prepared for this work in the best way, the work of the world all the way from the highest manifestations of genius to the humblest daily labor would be more than doubled. I see no reason why the application of systematized knowledge to the control of human nature may not in the course of the present century accomplish results commensurate with the nineteenth century applications of physical science to the material world. (Cattell, 1904, p. 186)

In 1895, when only 35 years old, Cattell was elected as the fourth president of the APA, following William James. The year before, along with James Mark Baldwin, Cattell had founded the United States' third psychology journal, *Psychological Review*. Cattell was part-owner and editor of *Psychological Review* from 1894 to 1904. Editing and entrepreneurship took more and more of Cattell's time, and eventually he established his own publishing firm, Science Press.

Soon he became sole owner, publisher, and editor of a number of journals including *Psychological Review*, *Science*, *Popular Science Monthly*, *The American Naturalist*, and *School and Society*.

By 1917 Cattell had a rather negative relationship with the president of Columbia. Cattell had been instrumental in the founding of the American Association of University Professors, which favored complete academic freedom and tenure. It was Cattell's pacifism, however, that led to his dismissal from Columbia:

> [The president of Columbia University] fired him from his position on the Columbia faculty because of a letter he had written on Columbia University stationery urging that draftees not be sent overseas against their will. It was believed that the charge of pacifism was behind the firing, and other members of the faculty . . . resigned from Columbia in protest. (Hilgard, 1987, p. 748)

Nonetheless, under Cattell's influence, Columbia became a stronghold of functionalism, even surpassing the University of Chicago:

> Cattell was very active at Columbia between 1891 and 1917, during which time Columbia became the leading producer of PhDs in psychology. In 1929, of the 704 APA members possessing the doctorate, 155 had their degrees from Columbia, with Chicago second with 91. . . . If we count both Chicago and Columbia as essentially centers of functional psychology, they together accounted for 35% of the PhDs in the APA. There is little doubt that functionalism was the typical American psychology, for the Columbia and Chicago products were scattering their influence on colleges and universities throughout the country. (Hilgard, 1987, p. 84)

Soon after Cattell arrived at Columbia in 1891, Robert Woodworth and Edward Thorndike joined him as his students. They, too, were destined to become leading representatives of functionalism.

Robert Sessions Woodworth

Robert Sessions Woodworth (1869–1962) graduated from Amherst College in Massachusetts. Following graduation he taught mathematics and science in high school for two years and then mathematics at Washburn College for two more years. After reading James's *Principles*, he decided to go to Harvard to study with James. After receiving his master's degree in 1897, he remained to work in Harvard's physiological laboratory. Woodworth then moved to Columbia and obtained his doctorate in 1899 under the supervision of Cattell. Following graduation he taught physiology in New York Hospital and then spent a year in England studying with the famous physiologist Sir Charles Sherrington. In 1903 he returned to Columbia where he stayed for the remainder of his career.

Like all functionalistic psychologists, Woodworth was interested in what people do and *why* they do it—especially the second question. He was primarily interested in motivation, so he called his brand of psychology **dynamic psychology**. Like Dewey, Woodworth disagreed with those who talked about adjustments to the environment as a matter of stimuli, brain processes, and responses. Some psychologists even left out the brain mechanisms and spoke only of S–R (stimulus–response) relationships. Woodworth chose the symbols S–O–R (stimulus–organism–response) to designate his theory in order to emphasize the importance of the organism. He used the term *mechanism* much as Carr had used the term *adaptive act*—to refer to the way an organism interacted with the environment in order to satisfy a need. These mechanisms, or adaptive behavior patterns, remained dormant unless activated by a need (drive) of some type. Thus, in the *same* physical environment, an organism would act differently depending on what need, or *drive*, was present. According to Woodworth, the internal condition of the organism activated the organism's behavior.

Although we have included Woodworth among the functionalists, he was always willing to entertain a wide variety of ideas and believed none of them religiously. He lectured on such topics as abnormal psychology, social psychology, and tests and statistics, and he gave seminars on movement, vision, memory, thinking, and motivation. His books included *Elements of*

Robert Sessions Woodworth

Physiological Psychology (along with Ladd, 1911); *Contemporary Schools of Psychology* (1931); *Experimental Psychology* (1938); and his final book, *Dynamics of Behavior* (1958), written when he was 89.

Woodworth believed that psychologists should accept valid information about humans no matter from where it came, and he believed that, like himself, most psychologists maintained a middle-of-the-road, or eclectic, attitude:

Suppose we should organize a world's tournament or olympic contest of psychologists, and should assemble the two or three thousand of them on some large field, with banners raised here and there as rallying points for the adherents of the several schools—a banner here for Freud, a banner there for Adler, one for Jung, one for McDougall, one for the Gestalt school, one for the behaviorists, and one for the existentialists, with perhaps two or three other banners waving for schools which I have not mentioned. After all the loyal adherents of each school had flocked to their respective banners, there would remain a large body in the middle of the field, or in the grandstand ready to watch the jousting. How many would thus remain unattached? A majority? I am convinced it would be a large majority. (1931, p. 205)

Though often criticized for his eclecticism, Woodworth did not care much. In response to being chided for sitting on the fence instead of getting down and becoming involved in the prevailing controversy, he said, "Well, in support of this position it may be said that it is cooler up here and one has a better view of all that is going on" (1931, p. 216).

Woodworth was the first recipient of the Gold Medal presented by the American Psychological Foundation (1956). The inscription indicated that the award was for "unequaled contributions in shaping the destiny of scientific psychology."

Edward Lee Thorndike

Edward Lee Thorndike (1874–1949) was born in Williamsburg, Massachusetts, the son of a Methodist minister. He entered Wesleyan University in Connecticut in 1891 and earned his bachelor's degree in 1895. At Wesleyan, Thorndike's psychology courses did not interest him much, and it was through the reading of James's *Principles* that he became interested in the topic. He claims never to have heard the word *psychology* until his junior year at Wesleyan. After Wesleyan, Thorndike went to Harvard where in 1897 he earned a master's degree. While at Harvard, he took a course from James, and the two became good friends. When he first moved to Cambridge, Thorndike was raising chicks in his bedroom to be used as experimental subjects. When his landlady forbade him from continuing this practice, James tried to get laboratory space for him at Harvard. When the effort failed, James allowed Thorndike to continue his research in the basement of his home.

After receiving his master's degree from Harvard, Thorndike accepted a fellowship at Columbia where, like Woodworth, he worked under Cattell's supervision. (Woodworth and Thorndike were lifelong friends.) His doctoral dissertation entitled "Animal Intelligence: An Experimental Study of the Associative Processes

Edward Lee Thorndike

in Animals" was published in 1898 and was republished in 1911 as *Animal Intelligence*.

After obtaining his doctorate in 1898, Thorndike began teaching at the College for Women at Western Reserve University, but after a year, he returned to Columbia where he remained until his retirement in 1940. After retirement he continued to write until his death in 1949 at the age of 74. During his career, Thorndike was extremely productive, and at his death his bibliography comprised 507 books, monographs, and journal articles. He did pioneer work in not only learning theory (for which he is most famous) but also the areas of educational practices, verbal behavior, comparative psychology, intelligence testing, transfer of training, and the measurement of sociological phenomena. As an example of the latter, he wrote *Your City* (1939) in which he attempted to quantify the "goodness of life" in various cities. Like Galton, Thorndike had a penchant to measure everything:

Thorndike reports in his autobiography that up to the age of 60 he had spent well over 20,000 hr reading and studying scientific books and journals—this in spite of the fact that he was primarily a researcher rather than a scholar. (Hergenhahn, 1988, p. 55)

Thorndike's work was to have a monumental influence on psychology, and it can be seen as representing the transition from the school of functionalism to the school of behaviorism. We will review the reasons for all of this shortly, but first we look at the nature of animal research prior to Thorndike's work.

Animal research before Thorndike. Modern comparative psychology clearly started with the works of Darwin, specifically with his book *The Expression of Emotions in Man and Animals* (1872). Darwin's work was taken a step further by **George John Romanes** (1848–1894), who wrote *Animal Intelligence* in 1882 and *Mental Evolution in Animals* in 1884. In a third book, *Mental Evolution in Man* (1885), Romanes attempted to trace the evolution of the human mind. All of Romanes's evidence was anecdotal, however, and he was often guilty of *anthropomorphizing*, or attributing human thought processes to lower animals. For example, Romanes attributed such emotions as anger, fear, and jealousy to fish; affection, sympathy, and pride to birds; and slyness and keen reasoning power to dogs. The following is an example of how Romanes attributed human motives and intelligence to nonhuman animals:

One day the cat and the parrot had a quarrel. I think the cat had upset Polly's food, or something of that kind; however, they seemed all right again. An hour or so after, Polly was standing on the edge of the table; she called out in a tone of extreme affection, "Puss, puss, come then—come then, pussy." Pussy went and looked up innocently enough. Polly with her beak seized a basin of milk standing by, and tipped the basin and all its contents over the cat; then chuckled diabolically, of course broke the basin, and half drowned the cat. (Quoted in Sargent & Stafford, 1965, p. 149)

Conwy Lloyd Morgan (1852–1936) sought to correct Romanes's errors by applying the principle that has come to be known as **Morgan's canon**. Morgan stated this principle as follows: "In no case may we interpret an action as the outcome of the exercise of a higher psychical faculty, if it can be interpreted as the outcome of the exercise of one which stands lower in the psychological scale" (1891, p. 53).

Sometimes called the law of parsimony, Morgan's canon can be viewed as a modern example of Occam's razor. Morgan sought to shave extraneous assumptions from the explanation of animal behavior. Instead of attributing higher mental abilities to animals, Morgan stressed instinct, habit, and association. He felt that nonhuman animals could not possibly possess many of the human attributes that Romanes and others had attributed to them: "A sense of beauty, a sense of the ludicrous, a sense of justice, and a sense of right and wrong—these abstract emotions or sentiments, as such, are certainly impossible to the brute" (Morgan, 1891, p. 403).

In the following, Morgan offered what he considered an objective account of how his dog developed the ability to open a garden gate:

The way in which my dog learnt to lift the latch of the garden gate and thus let himself out affords a good example of intelligent behaviour. The iron gate is held to by a latch, but swings open by its own weight if the latch be lifted. Whenever he wanted to go out the fox terrier raised the latch with the back of his head, and thus released the gate, which swung open. Now the question in any such case is: How did he learn the trick? In this particular case the question can be answered, because he was carefully watched. When he was put outside the door, he naturally wanted to get out into the road, where there was much to tempt him—the chance of a run, other dogs to sniff at, possible cats to be worried. He gazed eagerly out through the railings on the low parapet wall . . . and in due time chanced to gaze out under the latch, lifting it with his head. He withdrew his head and looked out elsewhere but the gate had swung open. Here was a fortunate occurrence arising out of the natural tendencies of a dog. But the association between looking out just there and the open gate with a free passage into the road is somewhat indirect. The coalescence of the presentative and representative elements into a conscious situation effective for the guidance of behaviour was not effected at once. After some ten or twelve experiences, in each of which the exit was more rapidly effected, with less gazing out at wrong places, the fox terrier learnt to go straight and without hesitation to the right spot. *In this case the lifting of the latch was unquestionably hit upon by accident, and the trick was only rendered habitual by repeated association in the same situation of the chance act and happy escape.* Once firmly established, however, the behaviour remained constant throughout the remainder of the dog's life, some five or six years. (1891/1900, p. 144)

Though there is obviously still great subjectivity in Morgan's report of his dog's behavior, Morgan did describe the trial-and-error learning that was to become so important in Thorndike's research. It remained for someone to apply Morgan's own canon more rigorously and to bring the investigation of animal learning out of the uncontrolled, naturalistic environment and into the laboratory where it could be studied more systematically. Thorndike did both.

Thorndike sought a completely objective method of studying animal behavior. Morgan had been on the right track but had relied too heavily on observations made under uncontrolled circumstances. With naturalistic observation, so many variables are occurring that it is impossible to observe them all at the same time, let alone to know which of them is responsible for the behavior being observed. Thorndike decided to solve these problems by observing animal behavior under controlled laboratory conditions.

Thorndike's puzzle box. To investigate systematically the type of learning Morgan described, Thorndike used a **puzzle box** like the one shown in Figure 11.1. Although during his career Thorndike used chicks, rats, dogs, fish, monkeys, and humans as research subjects, his work with the puzzle box involved cats. The box was arranged so that if the animal performed a certain response, the door opened, and the animal was allowed to escape; in addition, the animal received a reward such as a piece of fish. Thorndike described the behavior of animals under these circumstances. Note the similarity to Morgan's earlier observation of his dog learning to open the garden gate:

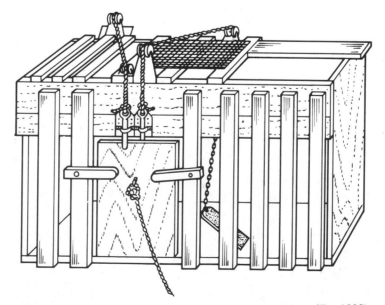

FIGURE 11.1 The puzzle box Thorndike used in his experiments with cats. (Thorndike, 1898)

The behavior of all but 11 and 13 [the cats were identified by number] was practically the same. When put into the box the cat would show evident signs of discomfort and of an impulse to escape from confinement. It tries to squeeze through any opening; it claws and bites at the bars or wire; it thrusts its paws out through any opening and claws at everything it reaches; it continues its efforts when it strikes anything loose and shaky; it may claw at things within the box. It does not pay very much attention to the food outside, but seems simply to strive instinctively to escape confinement. The vigor with which it struggles is extraordinary. For eight or ten minutes it will claw and bite and squeeze incessantly. With 13, an old cat, and 11, an uncommonly sluggish cat, the behavior was different. They did not struggle vigorously or continually. On some occasions they did not even struggle at all. It was therefore necessary to let them out of the box a few times, feeding them each time. After they thus associate climbing out of the box with getting food, they will try to get out whenever put in. They do not, even then, struggle so vigorously or get so excited as the rest. In either case, whether the impulse to struggle be due to instinctive reaction to confinement or to an association, it is likely to succeed in letting the cat out of the box. The cat that is clawing all over the box in her impulsive struggle will probably claw the string or loop or button so as to open the door. And gradually all the other nonsuccessful impulses will be stamped out and the particular impulse leading to the successful act will be stamped in by the resulting pleasure, until after many trials, the cat will, when put in the box, immediately claw the button or loop in a definite way. (1911, pp. 35–40)

From these and other observations, Thorndike reached the following conclusions:

1. Learning is incremental. That is, it occurs a little bit at a time rather than all at once. With each successful escape, subsequent escapes were made more quickly.

2. Learning occurs automatically. That is, it is not mediated by thinking.

3. The same principles of learning apply to all mammals. That is, humans learn in the same manner as all other mammals.

With these observations, Thorndike was very close to being a behaviorist. If thinking was not involved in learning, what good was introspection in studying the learning process? And if animals and humans learned in the same way, why not simplify the situation by studying only nonhuman animals?

The laws of exercise and effect. To account for his research findings, Thorndike developed psychology's first major theory of learning. The theory basically comprised associationism and hedonism that had been prevalent for centuries, but Thorndike stated his principles with precision and supported them with ingenious experimentation. His own research findings actually forced him to make major revisions in his own theory. The early version of his theory consisted mainly of the laws of exercise and effect. The **law of exercise** had two parts: the law of use and the law of disuse. According to the **law of use**, the more often an association was practiced, the stronger it became. This was essentially a restatement of Aristotle's law of frequency. According to the **law of disuse**, the longer an association remained unused, the weaker it became. Taken together, the laws of use and disuse said that we learn by doing and forget by not doing.

Thorndike's early **law of effect** was that if an association was followed by a "satisfying state of affairs" it would be strengthened, and if it was followed by an "annoying state of affairs," it would be weakened. In modern terminology, Thorndike's earlier law of effect was that reinforcement strengthened behavior whereas punishment weakened it.

The renouncement of the law of exercise and the revised law of effect. In September 1929, Thorndike began his address to the International Congress of Psychology with the dramatic statement "I was wrong." He was referring to his early theory of learning. Research had forced him to abandon his law of exercise completely, for he had found that practice *alone* did not strengthen an association and that the passage of time *alone* (disuse) did nothing to weaken an association. Besides discarding the law of exercise, Thorndike discarded half of the law of effect, concluding that a satisfying state of affairs strengthened an association but that an annoying state of affairs did not weaken one. In modern terminology, Thorndike found that reinforcement was effective in modifying behavior, but punishment was not.

Under the influence of evolutionary theory, Thorndike added a behavioral component to associationism. Rather than focusing on the association of one *idea* to another, he studied the association between the environment and behavioral responses. Although Thorndike's brand of psychology is generally viewed as being within the framework of functionalism (because Thorndike believed that only useful associations were selected and maintained), his insistence that learning occurred without ideation brought him very close to being a behaviorist.

The transfer of training. In 1901 Thorndike and Woodworth combined their skills to examine the contention of some early faculty psychologists that the faculties of the mind could be strengthened by practicing the attributes associated with them. For example, it was believed that studying a difficult topic, such as Latin, could enhance general intelligence. Such a belief was sometimes called the "mental muscle" approach to education and sometimes formal discipline. Thorndike and Woodworth's study, which involved 8,564 high school students, found no support for this contention. Then why did it seem that more difficult courses produced brighter students? Thorndike answered as follows:

> By any reasonable interpretation of the results, the intellectual values of studies should be determined largely by the special information, habits, interests, attitudes, and ideals which they demonstrably produce. The expectation of any large differences in general improvement of the mind from one study rather than another seems doomed to disappointment. The chief reason why good thinkers seem superficially to have been made such by having taken certain school studies, is that good thinkers have taken such

studies, becoming better by the inherent tendency of the good to gain more than the poor from any study. When the good thinkers studied Greek and Latin, these studies *seemed* to make good thinking. Now that the good thinkers study physics and trigonometry, these seem to make good thinkers. If abler pupils should all study physical education and dramatic art, these subjects would seem to make good thinkers. . . . After positive correlation of gain with initial ability is allowed for, the balance in favor of any study is certainly not large. (1924, p. 98)

Thorndike answered the "mental muscle" approach to education with his **identical elements theory of transfer**, which states that the extent to which information learned in one situation will transfer to another situation is determined by the similarity between the two situations. If two situations are exactly the same, information learned in one will transfer completely to the other. If there is no similarity between two situations, information learned in one will be of no value in the other. The implication for education is obvious: Schools should teach skills that are similar to those that will be useful when students leave school. Rather than attempting to strengthen the faculties of the mind by requiring difficult subjects, schools should emphasize the teaching of practical knowledge. Thorndike's research did not silence the debate between those who saw the goal of education as the strengthening of the faculties of the mind and those (like Thorndike) who claimed that the goal should be the teaching of specific transferable skills. Even today, some researchers claim that Thorndike was premature in his rejection of formal discipline (e.g., Lehman, Lempert & Nisbett, 1988).

Many consider Thorndike the greatest learning theorist of all time, and many of his ideas can be seen in current psychology in the work of Skinner, who we consider in the next chapter. Thorndike is usually considered a functionalist, Skinner a behaviorist. For two reasons, Thorndike cannot be labeled a behaviorist, although he had strong leanings in that direction. First, he employed a few mentalistic terms such as "satisfying state of affairs." Second, he was not willing to completely abandon introspective analysis. He believed that introspective analysis could play a useful role in the study of human consciousness (Samelson, 1981). It is best, then, to view Thorndike as a transitional figure between the schools of functionalism and behaviorism.

THE FATE OF FUNCTIONALISM

What happened to functionalism? It did not die as a school as structuralism had but was absorbed. According to Chaplin and Krawiec,

> As a systematic point of view, functionalism was an overwhelming success, but largely because of

this success it is no longer a distinct school of psychology. It was absorbed into the mainstream psychology. No happier fate could await any psychological point of view. (1979, p. 53)

And Bruno says,

> Like the mind of William James, American psychology is still a somewhat paradoxical mixture of subjective and objective points of view. Many modern psychologists want to use the tools of science and draw from objective data. Nevertheless, they find themselves unwilling to give up the rich world of inner experience as a source of psychological information. From the point of view of the philosophy of science, the problems in a mixed approach are varied and complex. Nevertheless, practical men often compromise and override glaring contradictions in order to get on with the business at hand. The middle-of-the-road position of the functionalists continues today. (1972, p. 111)

SUMMARY

Before functionalism, psychology in the United States passed through three stages. During the first stage (1640–1776), psychology was the same as religion and moral philosophy, although some of John Locke's philosophy was taught. During the second stage (1776–1886), the Scottish common-sense philosophy was taught, but its relationship to religion was still emphasized. During this second stage, textbooks began to appear that contained chapters on topics constituting much of today's psychology—for example, perception, memory, language, and thinking. In the third stage (1886–1896), psychology became completely separated from religion, and the groundwork for an objective, practical psychology was laid. It was during this third stage that James wrote *Principles* (1890), thus laying the foundation for what was to become the school of functionalism, and that Titchener created the school of structuralism at Cornell (1892). U.S. psychology's fourth stage (1896 to present) was characterized by the emergence of the school of functionalism, the beginning of which is often marked by the 1896 publication of Dewey's paper on the reflex arc. Many feel, however, that James's *Principles* could as easily mark the beginning of the school of functionalism. Although functionalism was never a clearly defined school, it did have the following characteristics: It opposed elementism; it was concerned with the function of mental and behavioral processes; it was interested in the practical applications of its principles; it accepted a Darwinian model of humans rather than a Newtonian model; it embraced a wide range of topics and methodologies; it was extremely interested in motivation; and it was more interested in the differences among individuals than in their similarities.

Following Darwin, James felt that mental events and overt behavior always had a function. Rather than studying consciousness as a group of elements that combined in some lawful way, as physical elements do, James viewed consciousness as a stream of ever-changing mental events whose purpose was to allow the person to adjust to the environment. For James, the major criterion for judging an idea was the idea's usefulness, and he applied this pragmatism to the idea of free will. James believed that while working as a scientist a person had to accept determinism; while not playing the role of scientist, however, the person could accept free will and feel responsible for his or her activities, instead of feeling like a victim of circumstance. James believed that much of behavior was instinctive and much of it learned. James discussed the empirical self, which consisted of the material self (all the material things that a person can call his or her own), the social self (the self as known by other people), and the spiritual self (all of which a person is conscious). There was, for James, also a self as knower, or an "I," of the personality. The self as knower, or "pure ego," transcends the empirical self. Self-esteem is determined by the ratio of things attempted to things achieved. One can increase one's self-esteem by either accomplishing more or attempting less. According to the James–Lange theory of emotion, first an individual reacts behaviorally and then has an emotional reaction. Because people feel according to how they act, they can determine their feelings by choosing their actions. James believed that thoughts determined behavior and we can determine our thoughts. Behind all acts of volition is selective attention because it is what we select to attend to that determines our behavior. Everywhere in James's writings, one sees his pragmatism: If an idea is useful, it is valid (true); if it is not useful, it is not valid. In many ways, psychology today is the type of psychology James outlined—a psychology willing to embrace all aspects of human existence and to employ those techniques found to be effective.

James chose Münsterberg to replace him as director of the Harvard Psychology Laboratory. At first, Münsterberg concentrated on performing controlled laboratory experiments, but his interests turned more and more to the application of psychological principles to problems outside of the laboratory. In developing his applied psychology, Münsterberg did pioneer work in clinical, forensic, and industrial psychology. Although he was at one time one of the most famous psychologists in the world, he died in obscurity because of his efforts to improve relations between the United States and Germany at a time when the U.S. populace was disgusted with German military and political aggression.

Like James and Münsterberg, Hall was very influential in the development of functionalism. The first person to obtain a doctorate specifically in psychology, Hall was Wundt's first U.S. student; he created the United States' first working psychology laboratory in 1883, and he created the first U.S. journal dedicated exclusively to psychological issues. As president of Clark University, he invited Freud to deliver a series of lectures—lectures that helped psychoanalysis gain international recognition and respect. Hall also founded the American Psychological Association and was its first president. According to his recapitulation theory, human development reflects all evolutionary stages that humans passed through before becoming human. Hall did much to stimulate the study of child psychology, and he was among the first to urge that children be given sex education. Along with James and Münsterberg, Hall incorporated Darwinian theory into psychology, and in so doing helped pave the way for the school of functionalism.

Once launched, functionalism was centered at the University of Chicago and Columbia University. At Chicago, Dewey wrote "The Reflex Arc Concept in Psychology," an article thought by many to mark the formal beginning of the school of functionalism. Dewey's text *Psychology* (1886) was the first functionalist textbook ever written. Also at Chicago was Angell, who had studied with James. During his 25 years as department chairman at Chicago, Angell encouraged the growth of functional psychology. Carr was another who furthered the development of functional psychology at Chicago. A key figure in Columbia University's brand of functionalism was Cattell. Though Cattell was Wundt's first experimental assistant, he was more strongly influenced by Galton, with whom he also studied. Like Galton, Cattell was intensely interested in measuring individual differences, and he obtained the first professorship ever awarded in psychology. Cattell encouraged psychologists to study a wide variety of topics using a wide variety of methodologies and to emphasize the practical value of psychological principles. Another leading figure at Columbia was Woodworth, whose dynamic psychology focused on motivation. In explaining behavior, Woodworth took an eclectic approach.

Perhaps the most influential Columbia functionalist was Thorndike. Thorndike's goal was to study animal behavior objectively because Darwin's theory had shown that there were only quantitative differences between humans and other animals. Romanes did rudimentary animal research, but his observations were riddled with anthropomorphism. Morgan's animal work was better because he applied the principle that came to be called Morgan's canon: No animal action should be explained on a higher level (thinking, reasoning) if it can be explained on a lower level (instinct, neuromechanism). Morgan's canon was used to discount the anecdotal evidence that Romanes and others had offered. Although Morgan's work was an improvement over Romanes's, it consisted mainly of uncontrolled naturalistic observations. Thorndike was the first to study animal behavior under controlled laboratory conditions. From his research using the puzzle box, Thorndike concluded that learning occurred gradually rather than all at once, that learning occurred without the involvement of mental processes, and that the same principles of learning applied to all mammals, including humans.

Thorndike summarized many of his observations with his famous laws of exercise and effect. According to his law of exercise, the strength of an association varied with the frequency of its occurrence. His original law of effect stated that if an association was followed by a positive experience, it would be strengthened, whereas if an association was followed by a negative experience, it would be weakened. In 1929 Thorndike revised his theory by discarding the law of exercise and salvaging only the half of the law of effect that said positive consequences strengthened an association. Negative consequences, he had found, had no effect on an association. Thorndike opposed the old "mental muscle" explanation of the transfer of training, which was an outgrowth of faculty psychology. Thorndike contended that learning would transfer from one situation to another to the degree that the two situations were similar or had common elements. Many of Thorndike's ideas are found in the contemporary work of Skinner.

Unlike structuralism, which faded away as a school because most of its findings and methodologies were rejected, functionalism lost its distinctiveness as a school because most of its major tenets were assimilated into all forms of psychology. The eclecticism that characterized functionalism also characterizes contemporary psychology.

DISCUSSION QUESTIONS

1. Briefly describe the four stages of U.S. psychology.

2. What were the major themes that characterized functionalistic psychology?

3. What was the crisis that James experienced, and how did he resolve it?

4. Define pragmatism.

5. For James, what were the major characteristics of consciousness?

6. Make the case that James's criticisms of elementism were more applicable to Titchener's version of psychology than to Wundt's.

7. How, according to James, did habits develop? What did he mean when he referred to habits as "the enormous fly-wheel of society"? What advice did he give for developing good habits?

8. How did James distinguish between the empirical self and the self as knower? Include in your answer a definition of the material self, the social self, and the spiritual self.

9. What did James mean by self-esteem? What, according to James, could be done to enhance one's self-esteem?

10. Summarize the James–Lange theory of emotion. How, according to James, could one escape or avoid negative emotions such as depression?

11. How did James resolve the free will–determinism controversy to his own satisfaction?

12. What did James mean by voluntary behavior? How did he account for such behavior?

13. What, according to James, were the important differences between tender-minded and tough-minded individuals? How did he suggest pragmatism could be used to resolve the differences between the two types of individuals?

14. Why was Münsterberg's view of psychology considered more positivistic than James's?

15. Summarize Münsterberg's work in clinical, forensic, and industrial psychology.

16. What was Münsterberg's fate?

17. Describe Hall's recapitulation theory.

18. Why was Hall opposed to coeducation at the secondary and college levels?

19. List Hall's "firsts" in psychology.

20. What was Dewey's criticism of the analysis of behavior in terms of reflexes? What did he propose instead? What part did Dewey's work play in the development of functionalism?

21. In his address, "The Province of Functional Psychology," what important distinctions did Angell make between structuralism and functionalism?

22. What did Carr mean by an adaptive act? How did Carr contribute to the development of functionalism?

23. In what way(s) was Cattell's approach to psychology different from that of other functionalists?

24. Why was Woodworth's approach to psychology called dynamic psychology? Why did he prefer an S–O–R explanation of behavior over an S–R explanation?

25. First describe the approach to animal research taken by Romanes and Morgan and then describe how Thorndike's research improved on those approaches.

26. What major conclusions did Thorndike reach concerning the nature of the learning process?

27. Describe Thorndike's laws of exercise and effect before and after 1929.

28. How did Thorndike's theory of the transfer of training differ from the earlier theory, which was based on faculty psychology?

29. Explain why Thorndike is viewed as a transitional

figure between the schools of functionalism and behaviorism.

30. What was functionalism's fate?

SUGGESTIONS FOR FURTHER READING

Angell, J. R. (1907). The province of functional psychology. *Psychological Review, 14*, 61–91.

The fact that this was Angell's presidential address to the APA in 1906 suggests how important the school of functionalism had become by that time. In his address, Angell said that "functional psychology" was little more than a viewpoint that existed primarily as a protest against structuralism. As with the writings of all the functionalists, Angell's address made it clear that functionalism was strongly influenced by evolutionary theory.

Bjork, D. W. (1983). *The compromised scientist: William James in the development of American psychology*. New York: Columbia University Press.

By analyzing James's diary, Bjork concludes that it was James's deep interest in art that caused him to embrace the types of philosophy and psychology that he did. James's psychology, according to Bjork, represented a compromise between art and science. (Available in paperback.)

Dewey, J. (1896). The reflex arc concept in psychology. *Psychological Review, 3*, 357–370.

The article that, for many, marks the beginning of the school of functionalism. Dewey criticizes those who believed that behavior can be understood in terms of discrete stimulus–response elements. He argues that behavior cannot be divided into elements any more than consciousness can. What must be understood about behavior, as with consciousness, is its purpose.

Diehl, L. A. (1986). The paradox of G. Stanley Hall: Foe of coeducation and educator of women. *American Psychologist, 41*, 868–878.

Diehl explores the views on women that G. Stanley Hall conveyed in his capacities as psychologist, educational theorist, and president of Clark University. As a psychologist, Hall believed that the main function of women is to have and nurture children. He saw the movement toward coeducation, in his time, as a serious and dangerous threat to the traditional role of women as mothers and thus to family life. And yet as president of Clark University, Hall admitted many women into graduate programs, in education, and in such fields as psychology, biology, physics, history, foreign relations, and chemistry. In fact, at the beginning of the 20th century, Clark (under Hall) and Cornell were considered the two institutions of higher learning most open to women. Furthermore, Hall was especially helpful and supportive of several of these female graduate students. Diehl explains this apparent paradox by suggesting that Hall considered female graduates as exceptions and continued believing

that the vast majority of women are best suited for motherhood.

James, W. (1963). *Psychology: The briefer course*. (G. Allport, Ed.). New York: Harper & Brothers. (Original work published 1892)

This edition omits James's original chapters on sensory processes. Allport points out that even in 1892 James was not satisfied with what he had to say about vision, hearing, and touch, and what he did say is now largely out of date. This edition retains what James said about the higher mental processes, material that is still largely relevant. (Available in paperback.)

James, W. (1981). *Pragmatism: A new name for some old ways of thinking*. Indianapolis: Hackett. (Original work published 1907)

In this book, James distinguishes between the tender-minded and the tough-minded and defines truth in terms of the consequences of believing. One should believe in things that have positive consequences, that is, in ideas that work. If it works, says James, believe it. In a sense, James applies Darwinian theory to beliefs. Effective beliefs survive; ineffective ones do not. (Available in paperback.)

Johnson, M. G., & Henley, T. B. (Eds.). (1990). *Reflections on the principles of psychology: William James's after a century*. Hillsdale, NJ: Erlbaum.

A number of prominent psychologists reflect on the development of many of James's key ideas since the publication of his *The Principles of Psychology* (1890) and find that most of them have been and are highly influential.

Joncich, G. (1968). *The sane positivist: A biography of Edward L. Thorndike*. Middletown, CT: Wesleyan University Press.

This is an excellent biography of Edward Thorndike, one of psychology's most productive and influential figures. By reading this book, one learns not only about Thorndike's interesting life, but also much about psychology's history.

Raphelson, A. C. (1973). The pre-Chicago association of the early functionalists. *Journal of the History of the Behavioral Sciences, 9*, 115–122.

This is an interesting account of the academic experiences that the early functionalists (e.g., Dewey and Angell) had before converging on the University of Chicago at the turn of the 20th century.

Shields, S. A. (1975). Functionalism, Darwinism, and the psychology of women: A study in social myth. *American Psychologist, 30*, 739–754.

Shields traces the misconceptions about women that were perpetuated by "science" from the second half of the 19th century to the first third of the 20th century and explores the implications of those misconceptions for contemporary psychology. Shields points out that the myth of female inferiority was reflected in or supported by the phrenological contention that the smaller female brain, relative to the male's, indicated inferior intelligence; the belief that females were more dominated by instinct and emotion than males; the belief that males were more biologically variable than females and therefore better able to adjust to a wide variety of circumstances; the belief that education should prepare women for domesticity, if they were to be educated at all; the belief that biological gender differences were responsible for personality differences (e.g., female passivity and male competitiveness); the belief that a woman's character is dominated by her maternal instinct; and psychoanalytic theory concerning differences in male and female personality development. We have here another case where belief and bias are perpetuated under the guise of "scientific objectivity." Shields suggests that current research on gender difference be viewed with the history of such research in mind.

Woodward, W. R. (1984). William James's psychology of will: Its revolutionary impact on American psychology. In J. Brožek (Ed.), *Explorations in the history of psychology in the United States* (pp. 148–195). Cranbury, NJ: Associated University Presses.

Woodward makes the case that it was James's treatment of will that explained his influence on not only functionalism but also other schools as disparate as existentialism and behaviorism. It was around the concept of will that James's *The Principles of Psychology* (1890) was organized. According to James, will had three components: (1) *ideo-motor action*, in which an idea automatically leads to behavior (such as thinking of a piano key and immediately striking that key); (2) *awareness of the outcomes of various ideo-motor actions*, or the pondering of the results of one's previous actions; and (3) *purposive holding in consciousness those thoughts corresponding to one's interests*—that is, some thoughts are allowed to continue while others are inhibited. The thoughts that are allowed to continue cause one's subsequent behavior (ideo-motor action), and therefore such behavior is both determined (ideo-motor action) and voluntary. It is voluntary because one's behavior is the result of ideas that were freely chosen.

GLOSSARY

Adaptive act Carr's term for a unit of behavior with three characteristics: a need, an environmental setting, and a response that satisfies the need.

Angell, James Rowland (1869–1949) As president of the American Psychological Association and as chairman of the psychology department at the University of Chicago for 25 years, did much to promote functionalism.

Applied psychology Psychology that is useful in solving practical problems. The structuralists opposed such practicality, but Münsterberg, and later the functionalists, emphasized it.

Carr, Harvey (1873–1954) An early functionalistic psychologist at the University of Chicago.

Cattell, James McKeen (1860–1944) Represented functionalistic psychology at Columbia University. By working with Galton, Cattell developed a strong interest in measuring intelligence and individual differences.

Dewey, John (1859–1952) A key person in the development of functionalism. Some mark the formal beginning of the school of functionalism with the 1896 publication of Dewey's article "The Reflex Arc Concept in Psychology."

Dynamic psychology The brand of psychology suggested by Woodworth that stressed the internal variables that motivate organisms to act.

Empirical self According to James, the self that consists of everything a person can call his or her own. The empirical self consists of the material self (all of one's material possessions), the social self (one's self as known by others), and the spiritual self (all of which a person is conscious).

Forensic psychology The application of psychological principles to legal matters. Münsterberg is considered the first forensic psychologist.

Functionalism The United States' first school of psychology. Under the influence of Darwin, the functionalists stressed the role of consciousness and behavior in adapting to the environment.

Habits Those learned patterns of behavior that James and others believed were vital for the functioning of society.

Hall, Granville Stanley (1844–1924) Created the United States' first experimental psychology laboratory, founded and became the first president of the American Psychological Association, and invited Freud to Clark University to give a series of lectures. Hall thus helped psychoanalysis receive international recognition, and his recapitulation theory did much to stimulate interest in developmental psychology. Hall was also among the first to advocate giving children sex education.

Identical elements theory of transfer Thorndike's contention that the extent to which learning would transfer from one situation to another was determined by the similarity between the two situations.

Ideo-motor theory of behavior According to James, ideas cause behavior, and thus we can control our behavior by controlling our ideas.

Industrial psychology The application of psychological principles to such matters as personnel selection; increasing employee productivity; equipment design; and marketing, advertising, and packaging of products. Münsterberg is usually considered the first industrial psychologist.

James, William (1842–1910) Was instrumental in the founding of functionalistic psychology. James emphasized the function of both consciousness and behavior. For him, the only valid criterion for evaluating a theory, thought, or act was whether it worked. In keeping with his pragmatism, he claimed that psychology needed to employ both scientific and nonscientific procedures. Similarly, on the individual level, sometimes one must believe in free will and at other times in determinism.

James–Lange theory of emotion The theory that people first respond and then have an emotional experience. For example, we run first, and then we are frightened. An implication of the theory is that we should act according to the way we want to feel.

Lange, Carl George (1834–1900) Along with James, proposed the theory that a person's emotional experience followed his or her behavior.

Law of disuse Thorndike's contention that infrequently used associations become weak. Thorndike discarded this law in 1929.

Law of effect Thorndike's contention that reward strengthened associations, whereas punishment weakened them. Later, Thorndike revised the law to state that reward strengthened associations, but punishment had no effect.

Law of exercise Thorndike's contention that the strength of an association varied with the frequency of the association's use. Thorndike discarded this law in 1929.

Law of use Thorndike's contention that the more often an association was made, the stronger it became. Thorndike discarded this law in 1929.

Morgan, Conwy Lloyd (1852–1936) One of the first to do objective research on animal behavior. Morgan's research consisted of naturalistic observations.

Morgan's canon The insistence that explanations of animal behavior be kept as simple as possible. Morgan's canon was suggested as a means of guarding against anthropomorphizing.

Münsterberg, Hugo (1863–1916) Stressed the application of psychological principles in such areas as clinical, forensic, and industrial psychology. In so doing, Münsterberg created applied psychology.

Pragmatism The belief that usefulness is the best criterion for determining the validity of an idea.

Puzzle box The experimental chamber Thorndike used for systematically studying animal behavior.

Recapitulation theory Hall's contention that all stages of human evolution were reflected in the life of an individual.

Reciprocal antagonism Münsterberg's method of treating mentally disturbed individuals, whereby he would strengthen thoughts that were antagonistic to those causing a problem.

Romanes, George John (1848–1894) One of the first to follow Darwin's lead and study animal behavior. Romanes's research was very subjective, however, and relied heavily on anecdotal evidence.

Self as knower According to James, the pure ego that accounts for a person's awareness of his or her empirical self.

Self-esteem According to James, how a person feels about himself or herself based on the ratio of successes to attempts. One can increase self-esteem either by accomplishing more or attempting less.

Stream of consciousness Term for the way James thought the mind worked. James described the mind as consisting of an ever-changing stream of interrelated, purposive thoughts rather than static elements that could be isolated from each other, as the structuralists had suggested.

Thorndike, Edward Lee (1874–1949) Marks the transition between the schools of functionalism and behaviorism. Thorndike concluded from his objective animal research that learning occurred gradually, occurred independent of consciousness, and was the same for all mammals. His final theory of learning was that practice alone had no effect on an association and that positive consequences strengthened an association but negative consequences did not weaken it.

Woodworth, Robert Sessions (1869–1962) An influential functionalist at Columbia University who emphasized the role of motivation in behavior.

CHAPTER 12

Behaviorism

THE BACKGROUND OF BEHAVIORISM

Seldom, if ever, has a major development in psychology resulted from the work of one person. This is not to say that single individuals have not been important, but their importance lies in their ability to culminate or synthesize previous work rather than to create a unique idea. The founding of the school of **behaviorism** is a clear example of this. Although John B. Watson is usually given credit for founding behaviorism, we will see that so much of his thinking was "in the air" that the term *founding* should not be taken to indicate innovation as much as an extension of existing trends. Objective psychology (psychology that insists on studying only those things that are directly measurable) was already well developed in Russia before the onset of behaviorism, and several functionalists were making statements very close to those Watson later made.

As we have seen in preceding chapters, the school of structuralism relied heavily on introspection as a means for studying the content and processes of the mind; functionalism accepted both introspection and the direct study of behavior. Whereas the structuralist sought a pure science unconcerned with practical applications, the functionalist was more concerned with practical applications than with pure science. Some functionalists were impressed by how much could be learned about humans without the use of introspection, and they began to drift toward what was later called the behavioristic position. One such functionalist was James McKeen Cattell, whom we encountered in the last chap-

ter. A full nine years before Watson's official founding of behaviorism, Cattell said this about psychology:

> I am not convinced that psychology should be limited to the study of consciousness as such, insofar as this can be set off from the physical world. . . . I admire the products of the Herbartian School and the ever-increasing acuteness of introspective analysis from Locke to Ward. All this forms an important chapter in modern psychology; but the scientific results are small in quantity when compared with the objective experimental work accomplished in the past fifty years. There is no conflict between introspective analysis and objective experiment—on the contrary, they should and do continually cooperate. But the rather wide-spread notion that there is no psychology apart from introspection is refuted by the brute argument of accomplished fact.
>
> It seems to me that most of the research work that has been done by me or in my laboratory is nearly as independent of introspection as work in physics or in zoology. The time of mental processes, the accuracy of perception and movement, the range of consciousness, fatigue and practise [*sic*], the motor accompaniments of thought, memory, the association of ideas, the perception of space, color-vision, preferences, judgments, individual differences, the behavior of animals and children, these and other topics I have investigated without requiring the slightest introspection on the part of the subject or undertaking such on my own part during the course of the experiments. . . . It is certainly difficult to penetrate by analogy into the consciousness of the lower animals, of savages and of children, but the study of their behavior has already yielded much and promises much more. (1904, pp. 179–184)

Cattell's statement is clearly within the functionalistic framework because it stresses the study of both consciousness and behavior and emphasizes the practicality of knowledge; but it also stresses that *much* important information can be attained without the use of introspection. At the time, for example, the study of young children and lower animals was yielding valuable information, and in such research, introspection was impossible.

Pillsbury provided another example of the *Zeitgeist*:

> Psychology has been defined as the "science of consciousness" or as the "science of experience subjectively regarded." Each of these definitions has advantages, but none is free from objection. . . . Mind is known from man's activities. *Psychology may be most satisfactorily defined as the science of human behavior* [italics added].
> Man may be treated as objectively as any physical phenomenon. He may be regarded only with reference to what he does. Viewed in this way the end of our science is to understand human action. (1911, pp. 1–2)

Besides the tendency toward the objective study of behavior in psychology, the success of research on animals had much do to with the development of behaviorism. Thorndike, for example, who was technically a functionalist because he did not completely deny the usefulness of the introspective analysis of consciousness and because he used some mentalistic terminology in his work, was discovering how the laws of learning that were derived from work on lower animals applied to humans. The success of animal researchers such as Thorndike created a strain between them and the prominent psychologists who insisted that psychology concentrate on introspective data. This strain between the animal researchers and the introspectionists created the atmosphere in which behaviorism took on revolutionary characteristics. Woodworth put the matter as follows:

> The rapid and interesting development of animal psychology . . . was one of the important predisposing causes for the outbreak of behaviorism.
> But the "exciting cause" was the repressive attitude toward animal psychology assumed by those important psychologists of that day who

were perfectly clear that psychology was, and must logically be, the study of conscious experience and nothing else. From this major premise they reasoned logically that behavior data were not psychology at all unless translated over into terms of the animal's consciousness. Now since the days of Descartes it had been recognized that you cannot prove consciousness in animals. Shall we assume that all animals, down to the very lowest, are conscious in their behavior, or shall we limit consciousness to animals that learn, or to animals that have a nervous system, or by what criterion shall we draw the line? At best, inference from behavior to consciousness in animals was reasoning by analogy and a leap in the dark. Titchener and others granted that some such inferences might legitimately be drawn, provided caution were used, and that thus animal experiments could throw some light on psychology. But as this leap in the dark was necessary in order to make any psychological use of the behavior data, animal psychology was at best an indirect and relatively unimportant part of our science.
> Meanwhile the animal psychologists were obtaining objective results on such problems as instinct and learning, and disliked to be told they must resort to dubious analogies in order to make psychology out of their findings. (1931, pp. 56–57)

As we will see, John B. Watson was one of these animal researchers. Before we consider Watson's proposed solution to the problem, however, we must review the work of the Russians, work that preceded and was similar in spirit to Watson's behaviorism.

RUSSIAN OBJECTIVE PSYCHOLOGY

Ivan M. Sechenov

The founder of Russian objective psychology, **Ivan M. Sechenov** (1829–1905), started out studying engineering but switched to physiology. As part of his training in physiology, he studied with Johannes Müller, Emil DuBois-Reymond, and Hermann von Helmholtz in Berlin. Sechenov sought to explain all psychic phenomena on the basis of associationism and materialism—thus showing the influence of the Berlin physiologists' positivism on him. Sechenov strongly denied that thoughts caused behavior. Rather, he insisted that external stimulation caused *all* behavior:

> Since the succession of two acts is usually regarded as an indication of their causal relationship . . . *thought is generally regarded as the cause of action.* When the external influence, i.e., the sensory stimulus, remains unnoticed—which occurs very often—*thought is even accepted as the initial cause of action.* Add to this the strongly pronounced subjective nature of thought, and you will realize how firmly man must believe in the voice of self-consciousness when it tells him such things. But actually this is the greatest of falsehoods: *the initial cause of any action always lies in external sensory stimulation,* because without this thought is inconceivable. (1863/1965, pp. 88–89)

Sechenov did not deny consciousness or its importance, but he insisted that there was nothing mysterious about it and sought to explain it in terms of physiological processes triggered by external events. For Sechenov, both overt behavior and covert behavior (mental processes) were reflexive in the sense that they were both triggered by external stimulation. Furthermore, both resulted from physiological processes in the brain.

The importance of inhibition. The most important concept that Sechenov introduced in *Reflexes of the Brain* (1863/1965) was that of **inhibition.** It was Sechenov's discovery of inhibitory mechanisms in the brain that caused him to conclude that psychology could be studied in terms of physiology. In fact, before the title was changed by a St. Petersburg censor, *Reflexes of the Brain* was originally called *An Attempt to Bring Physiological Bases into Mental Processes* (Boakes, 1984). In 1845 Eduard Weber (brother of Ernst Weber of *Weber's law* fame) discovered that if he stimulated a frog's vagus nerve (a major nerve linking the brain to various internal organs), it caused the frog's heart to beat *slower.* This was the first observation that increased activity (stimulation) of one part of the neuromuscular system caused decreased activity in another. Weber found that stimulating the vagus nerve *inhibited* heart rate. Weber also observed that spinal reflexes were often more sluggish in animals with their cerebral cortices intact than for animals that had their cortices ablated. Weber speculated that one cortical function may be to inhibit reflexive behavior.

Weber's observations and insights went essentially unnoticed except for Sechenov who saw in them a possible explanation for why we often have voluntary control over what is ordinarily involuntary behavior. For example, we can suppress or delay an impulse to sneeze or to cough. Sechenov also saw in inhibition an explanation for smooth, coordinated movement without needing to employ subjective, metaphysical concepts such as mind or soul. In other words, he could explain so-called volition and purposive behavior and still remain objective.

Using frogs as subjects, Sechenov found that he could inhibit the reflexive withdrawal of a leg from an acid solution by placing salt crystals in certain areas of the brain. When the salt was washed away with water, the reflex returned at full force. Although Sechenov found that the frog's inhibitory centers were in the thalamus instead of the cortex, where Weber speculated they were, he still confirmed that certain brain centers when stimulated would inhibit reflexive behavior. Sechenov's observation solved a problem that had restricted attempts to explain behavior in terms of reflexes. That is, why is there often a discrepancy between the intensity of a stimulus and the intensity of the response it elicits? It had been observed, for example, that a stimulus of very low intensity could produce a very intense response, and a very intense stimulus could produce only a slight response. Sechenov's answer to the problem was that sometimes a response to a stimulus is partially or even completely inhibited and sometimes it is not. With this major obstacle out of the way, it was now possible, according to Sechenov, to explain all behavior, including human behavior, as reflexive. Sechenov saw human development as the slow establishment of inhibitory control over reflexive behavior. Such control allows contemplative action or inaction and the quiet endurance of aversive experience. In a word, Sechenov postulated a mechanism by which prior experience could influence present experience and behavior:

> Hence a new and extremely important addition was made to the theory of reflexes. They were now regarded as directly related, not only to present stimuli, but also to the sum total of previous influences leaving their impression on the nervous system. (Yaroshevski, 1968, p. 91)

In *Reflexes*, Sechenov attempted to explain all behavior in terms of the excitation or inhibition of reflexes. It should be noted, however, that by reflex Sechenov meant only that every muscle movement is caused by an event that preceded it. Thus, he rejected the idea of spontaneous or unelicited behavior.

Psychology must be studied using the methods of physiology. Sechenov strongly believed that the traditional approach to understanding psychological phenomena using introspective analysis had led nowhere. For Sechenov, the only valid approach to the study of psychology involved the objective methods of physiology:

> Physiology will begin by separating psychological reality from the mass of psychological fiction which even now fills the human mind. Strictly adhering to the principle of induction, physiology will begin with a detailed study of the more simple aspects of psychical life and will not rush at once into the sphere of the highest psychological phenomena. Its progress will therefore lose in rapidity, but it will gain in reliability. As an experimental science, physiology will not raise to the rank of incontrovertible truth anything that cannot be confirmed by exact experiments; this will draw a sharp boundary-line between hypothesis and positive knowledge. Psychology will thereby lose its brilliant universal theories; there will appear tremendous gaps in its supply of scientific data; many explanations will give place to a laconic "we do not know." . . . And yet, psychology will gain enormously, for it will be based in scientifically verifiable facts instead of the deceptive suggestions of the voice of our consciousness. Its generalizations and conclusions will be limited to actually existing analogies, they will not be subject to the influence of the personal preferences of the investigator which have so often led psychology to absurd transcendentalism, and they shall thereby become really objective scientific hypotheses. The subjective, the arbitrary and the fantastic will give way to a nearer or more remote approach to truth. In a word, *psychology will become a positive science. Only physiology can do this, for only physiology holds the key to the scientific analysis of psychical phenomena.* (1935/1973, pp. 350–351)

Although Sechenov never enjoyed much support from his country's government or from his colleagues during his lifetime, he did influence the next generation of neurophysiologists. After him, the study of inhibition became central, it was widely accepted that the best way to study psychological phenomena was by using the objective methods of physiology, and it was generally believed that behavior is best understood as reflexive.

Ivan Petrovitch Pavlov

Ivan Petrovitch Pavlov (1849–1936) was born on September 27 in the town of Ryazan, about 250 miles from Moscow. His father was first a teacher of classical languages (Greek and Latin) and later a priest. Pavlov's mother was the daughter of a priest. At the age of 9, Pavlov suffered a severe fall, which delayed his entering high school for two years. During his convalescence, he spent considerable time with his godfather who was an abbot of a monastery near Ryazan. His godfather's lack of concern for worldly matters and his attention to detail were to have a lifelong influence on Pavlov. Eventually, Pavlov enrolled in the local ecclesiastical high school and then in the Ryazan Theological Seminary where he, like his father, studied for the priesthood. However, in 1870 at the age of 21, he changed his mind and enrolled in the Military Medical Academy at St. Petersburg where he studied natural science. Pavlov walked the several hundred miles from Ryazan to St. Petersburg, and his arrival there was coincidental with Sechenov's departure. It was under

Sechenov's successor, Ilya Cyon, that Pavlov first studied physiology. Pavlov obtained a degree in natural science in 1879 and then remained at the academy to pursue a degree in medicine. Pavlov was so impressive as a medical student that he was appointed director of a small laboratory where he helped several students obtain their doctorates even before he obtained his own in 1883. After receiving his medical degree, Pavlov studied physiology in Germany for two years. Upon returning to Russia, he held a variety of ill-paying jobs until 1890, when he was finally appointed professor of physiology at St. Petersburg's Military Medical Academy. Pavlov was 41 at the time, and he would spend most of the remainder of his career at the academy.

Sechenov, like Hartley before him, had suggested that psychology should be studied using physiological concepts and techniques. Pavlov agreed with him completely and went a step further. Unlike Sechenov, Pavlov actually demonstrated in detail how such study could take place. Also unlike Sechenov, Pavlov was highly regarded both by the government and by most of his colleagues. In 1921, Lenin bestowed many special privileges on Pavlov and proclaimed him a Hero of the Revolution. All this came rather late in Pavlov's life, however. Before he developed his interest in psychology, he first spent many years studying the digestive system.

Research on digestion. During his first 10 years at St. Petersburg, Pavlov pursued his interests in the digestive system. At this time, most of what was known about digestion came from studies in which animals had been operated on to expose organs of interest. Often the experimental animals were already dead as their organs were investigated; and if not dead, they were at least traumatized by the operation. Noting that little could be learned about normal digestive functioning by studying dead or traumatized animals, Pavlov sought a more effective experimental procedure. He knew of someone who had suffered a severe gunshot wound to the stomach and recovered. The victim's treatment, however, had left an open hole in his body

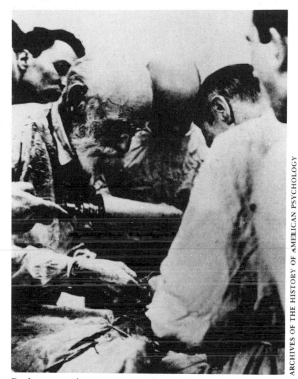

Pavlov operating on an experimental animal.

through which his internal organs could be observed. The grateful patient allowed his physician to observe his internal processes, including those of the digestive system. Although this particular case lacked scientific control, it gave Pavlov the information he needed to perfect his technique for studying digestion. Using the latest antiseptic surgical techniques and his outstanding surgical skills, Pavlov prepared a *gastric fistula*—a channel—leading from a dog's digestive organs to outside the dog's body. Such a procedure allowed the animal to recover fully from surgical trauma before its digestive processes were investigated. Pavlov performed hundreds of experiments to determine how the amount of secretion through the fistula varied as a function of different types of stimulation to the digestive system, and his pioneering research won him the 1904 Nobel Prize.

Discovery of the conditioned reflex. During his work on digestion, Pavlov discovered the conditioned reflex. As was mentioned, Pavlov's method of studying digestion involved a surgical arrangement that allowed the dog's gastric juices to flow out of the body and be collected. While studying the secretion of gastric juices in response to such substances as meat powder, Pavlov noticed that objects or events associated with meat powder also caused stomach secretions—for example, the mere sight of the experimenter or the sound of his or her footsteps. Pavlov referred to these latter responses as "conditional" because they depended on something else—for example, meat powder. In an early translation of Pavlov's work, "conditional" was translated as "conditioned," and the latter has been used ever since. In light of subsequent history, it is interesting to note that the initial announcement of the discovery of the conditioned reflex received little attention:

> Pavlov's initial reference to conditional reflexes was made in an 1899 address before the Society of Russian Doctors of St. Petersburg. The address, delivered to a local group, failed to receive wide attention. His work, however, became internationally known when on 12 December 1904, in his Nobel Prize address, Pavlov mentioned the phenomenon of conditioning while describing his research on digestive processes. (Windholz, 1983, p. 394)

Pavlov realized that conditioned reflexes could be explained by the associative principles of contiguity and frequency. He also realized that by studying conditioned reflexes, which he had originally called "psychic reflexes," he would be entering the realm of psychology. Like Sechenov before him, Pavlov had a low opinion of psychology with its prevailing use of introspection. He resisted the study of conditioned reflexes for a long time because of their apparently subjective nature. After pondering Sechenov's work, however, he concluded that conditioned reflexes, like natural reflexes, could be explained in terms of the neural circuitry and the physiology of the brain. At the age of 50, Pavlov began studying the conditioned reflex. His work would continue for 30 years.

Pavlov's personality. Like Sechenov, Pavlov was a positivist and was totally dedicated to his laboratory work. He edited no journals, engaged in no committee work, and actually wrote very little. He wrote only two books, and both were edited versions of lectures he had given. The first, *Work of the Principal Digestive Glands* (1897), contained only a brief reference to "psychic secretions," and the second, *Conditioned Reflexes* (English translation, 1927), dealt exclusively with the topic. Most of the information concerning Pavlov's work was found in the dissertations of doctoral students whose work he supervised. In fact, the first formal research on the conditioned reflex was performed by Pavlov's student Stefan Wolfsohn in 1897. Pavlov was seen by his students as hard but fair, and they were very fond of him. Pavlov encouraged both women and Jewish students to study in his laboratory, a practice very uncommon at the time. One thing for which Pavlov had no tolerance, however, was mentalism. If researchers in his laboratory used mentalistic terminology to describe their findings, he fined them. Fancher describes how Pavlov ran his laboratory:

> In pursuing his research he overlooked no detail. While he uncomplainingly lived frugally at home, he fought ferociously to ensure his laboratory was well equipped and his experimental animals well fed. Punctual in his arrival at the lab and perfectionistic in his experimental technique, he expected the same from his workers. Once during the Russian Revolution he disciplined a worker who showed up late from having to dodge bullets and street skirmishes on the way to the laboratory. (1990, p. 279)

In private life, however, Pavlov was a completely different person. Fancher gives the following account of Pavlov outside the laboratory:

> Outside, he was sentimental, impractical, and absent-minded—often arousing the wonder and amusement of his friends. He became engaged while still a student, and lavished much of his meager income on extravagant luxuries such as candy, flowers, and theater tickets for his fiancee. Only once did he buy her a practical gift, a new pair of shoes to take on a trip. When she arrived at her destination she found only one shoe in her trunk, accompanied by a letter from

Pavlov: "Don't look for your other shoe. I took it as a remembrance of you and have put it on my desk." Following marriage, Pavlov often forgot to pick up his pay, and once when he did remember he immediately loaned it all to an irresponsible acquaintance who could not pay it back. On a trip to New York he carried all of his money in a conspicuous wad protruding from his pocket; when he entered the subway at rush hour, the predictable felony ensued and his American hosts had to take up a collection to replace his funds. (1990, p. 279)

During the early years of their marriage, Pavlov and his wife lived in extreme poverty. Once some relief appeared forthcoming when a few of Pavlov's colleagues managed to raise a small amount of money to pay him for giving a few lectures. However, Pavlov used the money to purchase additional laboratory animals (Boakes, 1984). Pavlov's wife tolerated the situation, and she continued to give Pavlov her complete support during their long marriage:

What sustained Sara [Pavlov's wife] was belief in her husband's genius and in the supreme value of his work. In the early years of marriage they agreed upon a pact which both were to keep for the rest of their long life together. If she was to devote herself entirely to his welfare so that there would be nothing to distract him from his scientific work, then he was to regulate his life accordingly; she made him promise to abstain from all forms of alcohol, to avoid card games and to restrict social events to visits from friends on Saturday evenings and entertainment, in the form of concerts or the theatre, to Sunday evenings. (Boakes, 1984, p. 116)

On rare occasions, Pavlov did demonstrate a concern for practical economics. For example, when his laboratory animals were producing an abundance of saliva, he sold it to the townspeople:

For some years gastric juice became very popular around St. Petersburg as a remedy for certain stomach complaints. As Pavlov was able to supply gastric juice in relatively large quantities and of a particularly pure quality by using the sham feeding preparation, the proceeds from its sale became considerable, to the extent of almost doubling the laboratory's income when this already far surpassed that of any comparable Russian laboratory. (Boakes, 1984, p. 119)

Conditioned and unconditioned reflexes. According to Pavlov, organisms respond to the environment in terms of unconditioned and conditioned reflexes. An **unconditioned reflex** is innate and is triggered by an **unconditioned stimulus** (US). For example, placing food powder in a hungry dog's mouth will increase the dog's saliva flow. The food powder is the unconditioned stimulus, and the increased salivation is the **unconditioned response** (UR). The connection between the two is determined by the biology of the organism. A **conditioned reflex** is derived from experience in accordance with the laws of contiguity and frequency. Before Pavlov's experiment, stimuli such as the *sight* of food powder, the sight of the attendant, and the sound of the attendant's footsteps were biologically neutral in the sense that they did not automatically elicit a specific response from the dogs. Pavlov called a biologically neutral stimulus a **conditioned stimulus** (CS). Because of its contiguity with an unconditioned stimulus (in this case, food), this previously neutral stimulus developed the capacity to elicit some fraction of the unconditioned response (in this case, salivation). When a previously neutral stimulus (i.e., a conditioned stimulus) elicits some fraction of an unconditioned response, the reaction is called a **conditioned response** (CR). Thus, a dog salivating to the sound of an attendant's footsteps exemplifies a conditioned response.

Through this process of conditioning, the stimuli governing an organism's behavior are gradually increased from a few unconditioned stimuli to countless other stimuli that become associated to unconditioned stimuli through contiguity. Pavlov explained:

The basic physiological function of the cerebral hemispheres throughout the . . . individual's life consists in a constant addition of numberless signally conditioned stimuli to the limited number of the initial inborn unconditioned stimuli, in other words, in constantly supplementing the unconditioned reflexes by conditioned ones. Thus, the objects of the instincts [our desires for food and the like] exert an influence on the organism in ever-widening regions of nature and by means of more and more diverse signs or signals, both simple and complex; consequently, the instincts are more and more fully and perfectly satisfied, i.e., the organism is more reliably preserved in the surrounding nature. (1955, p. 273)

Excitation and inhibition. Showing the influence of Sechenov, Pavlov believed that all central nervous system activity can be characterized as either **excitation** or inhibition. Like Sechenov, Pavlov believed that all behavior is reflexive, that is, caused by antecedent stimulation. If not modified by inhibition, unconditioned stimuli and conditioned stimuli will elicit unconditioned and conditioned reflexes, respectively. However, through experience organisms learn to inhibit reflexive behavior. We will see one example of learned inhibition when we consider extinction. The important point here is that we are constantly experiencing a wide array of stimuli, some of them tending to elicit behavior and some tending to inhibit behavior. These two "fundamental processes" are always present, and how we behave at any given moment depends on their interaction. The pattern of excitation and inhibition that characterizes the brain at any given moment is what Pavlov called the **cortical mosaic**. The cortical mosaic determines how an organism will respond to its environment at any given moment.

Extinction, spontaneous recovery, and disinhibition. If a conditioned stimulus is continually presented to an organism and is no longer followed by an unconditioned stimulus, the conditioned response will gradually diminish and finally disappear, at which point **extinction** is said to have occurred. If a period of time is allowed to elapse after extinction and the conditioned stimulus is again presented, the stimulus will elicit a conditioned response. This is called **spontaneous recovery**. For example, if a tone (CS) is consistently followed by the presentation of food powder (US), an organism will eventually salivate when the tone alone is presented (CR). If the tone is then presented but not followed by the food powder, the magnitude of the conditioned response will gradually diminish, and finally the tone will no longer elicit a conditioned

response (extinction). After a delay, however—even without any further pairing of the tone and food powder—the tone will again elicit a conditioned response (spontaneous recovery).

Pavlov believed that spontaneous recovery demonstrated that the extinction process does not eliminate a conditioned response but merely inhibits it. That is, presenting the conditioned stimulus without the unconditioned stimulus causes the animal to inhibit the conditioned response. Further evidence that extinction is best explained as an inhibitory process is provided by **disinhibition**. This phenomenon is demonstrated when, after extinction has taken place, presenting a strong, irrelevant stimulus to the animal causes the conditioned response to return. The assumption was that the fear caused by the strong stimulus displaces the inhibitory process, thus allowing the return of the conditioned response.

Experimental neurosis. Let us say that showing a dog a circle is always followed by food and showing a dog an ellipse is never followed by food. According to Pavlov, the circle will come to elicit salivation, and the ellipse will inhibit salivation. Now let us make the circle increasingly more elliptical. What happens? According to Pavlov, when the circle and the ellipse become indistinguishable, the excitatory and the inhibitory tendencies will conflict, and the animal's behavior will break down. Because this deterioration of behavior was brought about in the laboratory, it was called **experimental neurosis**.

Almost as interesting as the fact that abnormal behavior could be produced in the laboratory by producing conflicting tendencies was the fact that the "neurotic" behavior took different forms in different animals. Some dogs responded to the conflict by becoming highly irritable, barking violently, and tearing at the apparatus with their teeth. Other animals responded to the conflict by becoming depressed and timid. Observations such as these caused Pavlov to classify animals in terms of different types of nervous systems. He thought that there were four types of animals: those for whom the excitatory tendency was very strong, those for whom the excitatory tendency was moderately strong, those for whom the inhibitory tendency was very strong, and those for whom the inhibitory tendency was moderately strong. Thus, how animals, including humans, respond to conflict is to a large extent determined by the type of nervous system they possess. In his later years, Pavlov speculated that much human abnormal behavior was caused by a breakdown of inhibitory processes in the brain.

Pavlov's work on conflict and his typology of nervous systems were to strongly influence subsequent work on abnormal behavior, conflict, frustration, and aggression.

The first- and second-signal systems. According to Pavlov, all tendencies that a person acquires during his or her lifetime are based on innate, biological processes—that is, on unconditioned stimuli and unconditioned responses that have been acquired during the phylogenetic history of a species of animal. These innate processes are expanded by conditioning. As biologically neutral stimuli (CSs) are consistently associated with biologically significant stimuli (USs), they (the CSs) come to *signal* the biologically significant events. The adaptive significance of such signals should be obvious; if an animal is warned that something either conducive or threatening to survival is about to happen, it will have time to engage in appropriate behavior:

> Pavlov . . . rated very highly the ability of the conditioned reaction to act as a "signal" reaction or, as he expressed it many times, a reaction of "warning character." It is this "warning" character which accounts for the profound historical significance of the conditioned reflex. It enables the animal to adapt itself to events which are not taking place at that particular moment but which will follow in the future. (Anokhin, 1968, p. 140)

Anokhin discusses the significance of the fact that conditioned stimuli signal future events:

> In the pre-Pavlov period physiologists could work with only two categories of time—the present and the past. When some form of stimu-

lus is applied to an animal, it reacts immediately to this stimulus, i.e., it adapts itself to an action developing in the present. This type of adaptive reaction was a constant object of investigation by physiologists and it was this type of reaction which formed the basis of the reflex theory developed originally by Descartes.

> No adaptive reactions were known in physiology which would develop in connection with events about to happen. Physiologists also knew, however, that the adaptive reactions which they studied, associated with the action of stimulating agents at the present time had been evolved over many thousands of years, i.e., they incorporated the past experience of many generations. In this way the past, as a category of time, was naturally included in the form of fixation of the past experience of the species in its structures. (1968, p. 140)

Pavlov called the stimuli (CSs) that come to signal biologically significant events the **first-signal system**, or "the first signals of reality." However, humans also learn to respond to *symbols* of physical events. For example, we learn to respond to the word *fire* just as we would to the sight of a fire. Pavlov referred to the words that come to symbolize reality "signals of signals," or the **second-signal system**. Language, then, consists of symbols of environmental experiences. Once established, these symbols can be organized into abstract concepts that guide our behavior because even these abstract symbols represent events in the physical world.

Pavlov's attitude toward psychology. As we have seen, Pavlov, like Sechenov, had a low opinion of psychology. Also like Sechenov, Pavlov was not opposed to psychology because it studied consciousness but because it used introspection to do so. Pavlov stated his position as follows:

> It would be stupid to reject the subjective world. Of course it exists. It is on this basis that we act, mix with other people, and direct all our life.
> Formerly I was a little carried away when I rejected psychology. Of course it has the right to exist, for our subjective world is a definite reality for us. The important thing, therefore, is not to reject the subjective world, but to study it by means of scientifically based methods. (Anokhin, 1968, p. 132)

Although Pavlov had a very low opinion of most psychologists, he did have a high opinion of Thorndike. In the following passage, Pavlov even acknowledges Thorndike as the first to do systematic, objective research on the learning process in animals:

> Some years after the beginning of the work with our new method I learned that somewhat similar experiments on animals had been performed in America, and indeed not by physiologists but by psychologists. Thereupon I studied in more detail the American publications, and now I must acknowledge that the honour of having made the first steps along this path belongs to E. L. Thorndike. By two or three years his experiments preceded ours, and his book must be considered as a classic, both for its bold outlook on an immense task and for the accuracy of its results. (1928, pp. 38–40)

Pavlov and associationism. Pavlov believed that he had discovered the physiological mechanism for explaining the associationism that philosophers and psychologists had been discussing for centuries. He believed that by showing the physiological underpinnings of association, he had put associationism on an objective footing and that speculation about how ideas become associated with each other could finally end. For Pavlov, the temporary connections formed by conditioning were precisely the associations that had been the focus of philosophical and psychological speculation:

> Are there any grounds . . . for distinguishing between that which the physiologist calls the temporary connection and that which the psychologist terms association? They are fully identical; they merge and absorb each other. Psychologists themselves seem to recognize this, since they (at least, some of them) have stated that the experiments with conditioned reflexes provide a solid foundation for associative psychology, i.e., psychology which regards association as the base of psychical activity. (1955, p. 251)

Vladimir M. Bechterev

Vladimir M. Bechterev (1857–1927) was born on January 20 and at 16 years of age entered the Military Medical Academy at St. Petersburg, where Sechenov had studied and Pavlov was studying. He graduated in 1878 (one year before Pavlov) but continued to study in the department of mental and nervous diseases until he obtained his doctorate in 1881 at the age of 24. He then studied with Wundt in Leipzig, DuBois-Reymond in Berlin, and Charcot (the famous French psychiatrist) in Paris. In 1885 he returned to Russia to a position at the University of Kazan, where he created the first Russian experimental psychology laboratory. In 1893 he returned to St. Petersburg's Military Medical Academy, where he held a chair of psychic and nervous diseases. In 1904 he published an important paper entitled "Objective Psychology," which eventually evolved into a three-volume book called *Objective Psychology*, published between 1907 and 1912 (French translation, 1913). Like Sechenov and Pavlov, Bechterev argued for a completely objective psychology, but, unlike them, Bechterev concentrated almost exclusively on the relationship between environmental stimulation and *behavior*.

In 1907 Bechterev and his collaborators left the Military Medical Academy to found the Psychoneurological Institute, which was later named the V. M. Bechterev Institute for Brain Research in his honor.

When Bechterev died in 1927, his bibliography totaled about 600 articles and books written on a wide variety of topics within biology, psychology, and philosophy.

Reflexology. Late in his life, Bechterev summarized his views about psychology in *General Principles of Human Reflexology: An Introduction to the Objective Study of Personality*, which first appeared in 1917 and reached its fourth edition in 1928. By **reflexology**, Bechterev meant a strictly objective study of human behavior that seeks to understand the relationship between environmental influences and overt behavior. He took the position that if so-called psychic activity exists it must manifest itself in overt behavior; therefore, "the spiritual sphere" can be bypassed by simply studying behavior. His reflexology studied the relationship between behavior (e.g., facial expressions, gestures, and speech) and physical, biological, and, above all, social conditions.

Many of Bechterev's ideas were also found in U.S. behaviorism at about the same time. It should be remembered, however, that Bechterev was writing about objective psychology as early as 1885 (Bechterev, 1928/1973). A few passages from Bechterev's *General Principles of Human Reflexology* exemplify his thinking:

> In order to assume . . . a strictly objective standpoint in regard to man, imagine yourself in a position of being from a different world and of a different nature, and having come to us, say, from another planet. . . . Observing human life in all its complex expressions, would this visitor from another planet, of a different nature, ignorant of human language, turn to subjective analysis in order to study the various forms of human activity and those impulses which evoke and direct it? Would he try to force on man the unfamiliar experiences of another planetary world, or would this being study human life and all its various manifestations from the strictly objective point of view and try to explain to himself the different correlations between man and his environment, as we study, for example, the life of microbes and lowly animals in general? I think there can be no doubt of the answer.
>
> In following this method, obviously we must proceed in the manner in which natural science studies an object: in its particular environment, and explicate the correlation of the actions, conduct, and all other expressions of a human individual with the external stimuli, present and past, that evoke them; so that we may discover the laws to which these phenomena conform, and determine the correlations between man and his environment, both physical, biological, and, above all, social.
>
> It is regrettable that human thought usually pursues a different course—the subjective direction—in all questions concerning the study of man and his higher activities, and so extends the subjective standpoint to every department of human activity. But this standpoint is absolutely untenable, since each person develops along different lines on the basis of unequal conditions of heredity, education, and life experience, for these conditions establish a number of correlations between man and his environment, especially the social, and so each person is really a separate phenomenon, completely unique and irreproducible, while the subjective view presupposes an analogy with oneself—an

analogy not existing in actual fact, at least not in the highest, and consequently more valuable, expressions of a human being.

> You will say that we use analogy everywhere, that in everyday life we cannot approach another man without it. All that is, perhaps, true to a certain extent, but science cannot content itself with this, because taking the line of subjective interpretation, we inevitably commit some fallacy. It is true that, in estimating another person, we turn to subjective terminology, and constantly say that such and such a man thinks this or that, reasons in this or that manner, etc. But we must not forget that everyday language and the scientific approach to natural phenomena cannot be identical. For instance, we always say of the sun that it rises and sets, that it reaches its zenith, travels across the sky, etc., while science tells us that the sun does not move, but that the earth revolves round it. And so, from the point of view of present-day science, there must be only one way of studying another human being expressing himself in an integration of various outward phenomena in the form of speech, facial and other expressions, activities, and conduct. This way is the method usually employed in natural science, and consists in the strictly objective study of the object, without any subjective interpretation and without introducing consciousness. (1928/1973, pp. 33–36)

By 1928 Bechterev was aware of the growing tendency toward objective psychology in the United States and claimed that he was the originator of that tendency:

> The literature on the objective study of animal behavior has grown considerably and in America an approach is being made to the study of human behavior, a study which has first been set on a scientific basis on Russian soil in my laboratories at the Military Medical Academy and at the Psychoneurological Institute. (1928/1973, p. 214)

Bechterev versus Pavlov. Who discovered the conditioned reflex? It was neither Bechterev nor Pavlov. Bechterev spent considerable time showing that such reflexes were known for a very long time: "These 'psychic' secretions, by the way, attracted attention as early as the 18th century. Even then it was known that when oats is given to a horse, he secretes saliva before the oats enters his mouth" (1928/1973, p. 403). Both Bechterev and Pavlov studied conditioned reflexes at about the same time. What Pavlov called a conditioned reflex, Bechterev called an **association reflex**. Bechterev was well aware of Pavlov's research and thought that it had major flaws. In fact, almost every time Bechterev mentioned Pavlov in his 1928 book, he had something negative to say. Bechterev criticized Pavlov's "saliva method" for the following reasons:

1. An operation is necessary for collecting gastric juices from the stomach.

2. Pavlov's procedure cannot be easily used on humans.

3. The use of acid to elicit an unconditioned response causes reactions in the animal that may contaminate the experiment.

4. If food is used as an unconditioned stimulus, the animal will eventually become satiated and therefore no longer respond in the desired fashion.

5. The secretory reflex is a relatively unimportant part of an organism's behavior.

6. The secretory reflex is unreliable and therefore difficult to measure accurately.

Instead of studying secretion, Bechterev studied motor reflexes. He stated his reasons for this as follows:

> Luckily, in all animals, and especially in man, who particularly interests us in regard to the study of correlative activity, the secretory activities play a much smaller part than do motor activities, and, as a result of this, and for other reasons also (the absence of an operation, the possibility of exact recording, the possibility of frequent repetition of the stimuli . . . and the absence of any complications as a result of frequent stimulation in experiment) we give unconditional preference, in view of the above-mentioned defects of the saliva method, to the method of investigation of association—motor reflexes of the extremities and of respiration—a method developed in my laboratory. This method, which is equally applicable to animals and to man, and consists of the electrical stimulation on the front paw of the animal, and in man, of the palm or fingers of the hand, or the ball of the foot, with simultaneous visual, audi-

tory, cutaneo-muscular and other stimulations, has as far as I know, not met with any opposition in scientific literature from the time of its publication. (1928/1973, p. 203)

It turns out that Bechterev's concentration on the overt behavior of organisms was more relevant to U.S. behaviorism than was Pavlov's research on secretion. But Pavlov was the one whom Watson discovered, and therefore the name Pavlov became widely known in U.S. psychology. It is another one of those quirks of history that but for the sake of fortuitous circumstances, the name Bechterev could have been a household name instead of Pavlov. And as we will see, in his application of conditioning procedures, Watson actually followed Bechterev more closely than he did Pavlov.

JOHN B. WATSON AND BEHAVIORISM

Biographical Sketch

John Broadus Watson (1878–1958) was born on January 9 in Greenville, South Carolina. Religion was a major theme in Watson's early life.

> Watson's mother was "insufferably religious." She took an active role in the Reedy River Baptist Church and became one of the "principal lay organizers for the Baptists in the whole of South Carolina." In keeping with her proselytizing zeal, Emma named her youngest son John Broadus Watson, after John Albert Broadus, "one of the founding ministers of the Southern Baptist Theological Seminary which had been located in Greenville up until a few months before Watson's birth in January, 1878." John was made to vow to his mother that he would become a minister—"slated," as he put it, at an early age. Emma tied her family closely to the church, strictly adhering to the fundamentalist prohibition against drinking, smoking, or dancing. Cleanliness was always next to godliness, and Emma never ceased to keep her family next to God. (Karier, 1986, p. 111)

Although his mother was extremely religious, his father was not. His father drank, swore, and chased women. This incompatibility finally resulted in Watson's father leaving home in 1891, when Watson was 13 years old. Watson and his father had been close, and his father's departure disturbed him deeply. He immediately became a troublemaker and was arrested twice, once for fighting and once for firing a gun in the middle of Greenville. Later, when Watson was famous, his father sought out his son, but Watson refused to see him.

One can only speculate on the effects of the mother's intense religious convictions in Watson's life, but the origin of Watson's lifelong fear of the dark seems clear:

> The nurse [that Emma, Watson's mother, had employed] told him [Watson] that the devil lurked in the dark and that if ever Watson went a-walking during the night, the Evil One might well snatch him out of the gloom and off to Hell. Emma seems to have done nothing to stop the nurse instilling such terrors in her young son. Most likely, she approved. To be terrified of the Devil was only right and prudent. As a fundamentalist Baptist, she believed that Satan was always prowling. All this left Watson with a lifelong fear of the dark. He freely admitted that he studied whether children were born with an instinctual fear of the dark because he had never managed to rid himself of the phobia. He tried a number of times to use his behaviourist principles to cure himself but he never really managed to do it. As an adult Watson was often depressed, and when he got depressed he sometimes had to sleep with his light on. (Cohen, 1979, p. 7)

Undergraduate years. Despite his history of laziness and violence in school, Watson somehow managed to get himself accepted to Furman University at the age of 15. Although it is not known why Watson was accepted, Cohen (1979) suggests Watson's persuasive ability as the reason. All his life, Watson demonstrated an ability to get what he wanted. While at college, Watson continued to live at home and worked at a chemical laboratory in order to pay his fees. His most influential teacher at Furman was Gordon B. Moore, who taught philosophy and psychology. The psychology Watson learned involved mainly the works of Wundt and James. All during college, Watson had problems with his

John B. Watson

brother Edward, who considered Watson a sinner like his father and therefore a disgrace to the family.

At Furman, Watson did well but not exceptionally well. He should have graduated in 1898, but an unusual event set him back a year. His favorite teacher, Gordon B. Moore, warned that he would flunk any student who handed his or her examination in backward. Absentmindedly, Watson handed in his examination backward and was flunked:

> Watson then made what he later called "an adolescent resolve [to] make [Gordon B. Moore] seek me out for research some day." Years later, as a professor at Johns Hopkins University, Watson had his revenge. To his "surprise and real sorrow," Watson recalled, he received a request from his former teacher to be accepted as a research student. Before it could be arranged, Moore's eyesight failed; within a few years, he died. (Buckley, 1989, p. 12)

The episode ended up benefiting Watson, however, because during the extra year at Furman that failing Moore's course necessitated, he earned a master's degree (at the age of 21).

Following graduation, Watson taught in a one-room school in Greenville, for which he earned $25 a month. When his mother died, he decided to continue his education outside the

ARCHIVES OF THE HISTORY OF AMERICAN PSYCHOLOGY

Greenville area, and he applied to both Princeton and the University of Chicago. When he learned that Princeton required a reading knowledge of Greek and Latin, he decided to go to the University of Chicago. Another reason for his decision was that his favorite teacher—Moore, the one who had flunked him—had studied at the University of Chicago, and his reminiscences intrigued Watson. So in September 1900, Watson left Greenville for Chicago.

To survive financially, Watson had a room in a boardinghouse and worked as a waiter there to pay for his room and board. He also earned $1 a week as a janitor in the psychology laboratory and another $2 a week for taking care of the white rats.

The Chicago years. At Chicago, Watson studied the British empiricists with A. W. Moore (not the Gordon B. Moore of Furman). Watson especially liked Hume because Hume taught that nothing was necessarily fixed or sacred. Watson took philosophy from John Dewey but confessed that he could not understand Dewey. Though the faculty member who had the greatest influence on Watson was the functionalist James Angell, the radical physiologist Jacques Loeb also influenced him. Loeb (1859–1924) was famous for his work on **tropism**, having shown that the behavior of simple organisms could be explained as being automatically elicited by stimuli. Just as plants orient toward the sun because of the way they are constructed, so do animals respond in certain ways to certain stimuli because of their biological makeup. According to Loeb, no mental events are involved in such tropistic behavior; it is simply a matter of the stimulation and the structure of the organism. This viewpoint, which Loeb applied to plants, insects, and lower animals, Watson would later apply to humans as well.

Under the influence of Angell and Henry Donaldson, a neurologist, Watson began to investigate the learning process in the white rat. In 1901 very little was known about animal learning even though Thorndike had done some objective research by that time. Also in

1901, Willard Small had published an article on the maze-learning ability of the white rat, but the article was as anthropomorphic as the work of Romanes. Thus, Watson had little information on which to draw. By the end of 1902, however, he knew more about the white rat than anyone else in the United States. Also about this time, Watson first began to develop a feeling for behaviorism: "If you could understand rats without the convolutions of introspection, could you not understand people the same way?" (Cohen, 1979, p. 33).

Even though Watson had begun thinking about behaviorism as early as 1902, he resisted mentioning it to his mentor and friend Angell because he knew that Angell believed psychology should include the study of consciousness. When he finally did tell Angell of his ideas in 1904, Angell responded negatively and told him that he should stick to animals, thus silencing Watson on the subject for four years.

Although Watson suffered a nervous breakdown in 1902, he managed to submit his doctoral thesis in 1903. The title of his thesis, "Animal Education: The Psychical Development of the White Rat," shows that there was still a hint of mentalistic thinking in Watson at this time. The thesis was accepted, and Watson attained his doctorate at 25 years of age, making him the youngest person ever to attain a doctorate at the University of Chicago. Donaldson loaned Watson the $350 that was needed to publish the thesis, and it took Watson 20 years to repay the loan.

The University of Chicago hired Watson as an assistant professor for a salary of $600 a year, and he taught courses in both animal and human psychology. For the latter, he used Titchener's laboratory manuals. During this time, Watson married one of his students, Mary Ickes, and 11 months later they had a child. Buckley describes the origin of Watson's relationship with Mary Ickes:

> As family legend has it, Mary was a student in Watson's introductory psychology class. She developed a crush on her professor and during one long exam wrote a love poem in her copy-

book instead of answers to the test questions. When Watson insisted on taking the paper at the end of the quiz, Mary blushed, handed him the paper, and ran from the room. The literary effort must have had its desired effect. (1989, p. 49)

Also about this time, he began his correspondence with Robert Yerkes. Yerkes (1876–1956) was another young animal researcher, who, while a student at Harvard, had been encouraged to pursue his interest in comparative psychology. After receiving his doctorate from Harvard in 1902, Yerkes had been offered an appointment at Harvard as instructor of comparative psychology. In his career, Yerkes studied the instincts and learning abilities of many different species, including mice, crabs, turtles, rats, worms, birds, frogs, monkeys, pigs, and apes; but he is probably best remembered for the work on anthropoid apes that he supervised at the Yerkes Laboratories of Primate Biology in Orange Park, Florida. In chapter 10, we saw that Yerkes was also instrumental in the creation of the Army Alpha and Beta tests of intelligence. Despite Yerkes's involvement with animal research and his friendship with Watson, he never accepted Watson's behaviorist position. During the formative stages of behaviorism, Yerkes remained loyal to Titchener.

In 1906 Watson began his research designed to determine what sensory information rats used as they learned to solve a complex maze. He did his research with Harvey Carr, the prominent functionalist. Using six-month-old rats that had previously learned the maze, Watson began systematically to remove one sensory system after another, in hopes of learning which sensory system the rats used to traverse the maze correctly. One by one, he eliminated the senses of vision, hearing, and smell. Nothing appeared to make a difference. After full recovery from each operation, the rats were able to traverse the maze accurately. Watson and Carr then took a naive group of rats and performed the same operations, finding that the naive rats learned the maze as well as the rats that had full sensory apparatus. Watson then speculated that perhaps the rats

were using their whiskers, but shaving off the whiskers made no difference; even destroying the sense of taste made no difference. Watson and Carr finally found that the rats were relying on kinesthetic sensations—sensations from the muscles. If the maze was made shorter or longer, after destruction of the kinesthetic sense, the rats were confused and made many errors. This discovery of the importance of kinesthetic sensation was to play an important role in Watson's later theory. Watson published the research results in 1907 in an article entitled "Kinesthetic and Organic Sensations: Their Role in the Reactions of the White Rat to the Maze."

In 1907 the Carnegie Institution offered Watson an opportunity to study the migratory instinct of terns, and Watson made several visits to an island near Key West, Florida, to do so. Much of Watson's research on instinctive behavior was done in collaboration with Karl Lashley, who was later to make significant contributions to neurophysiological psychology (see chapter 14). One summer Watson brought Lashley with him to see whether terns, in fact, had the ability to home. To find out, Lashley took a number of terns to Mobile and some to Galveston and turned them loose. The results were exciting. Without any training, the terns found their way back to the small island, which was about 1,000 miles from where Lashley had released them. Watson and Lashley tried in vain to explain how the terns had accomplished this feat, and in the end, both men turned to other matters. Because Watson has become known for other accomplishments, it is often overlooked that he was one of the United States' early ethologists. (Ethologists study the behavior of animals in their natural habitat and usually attempt to explain that behavior in terms of evolutionary theory.) Watson's early publication (with Lashley) "Homing and Related Activities of Birds" (1915) provides an interesting contrast to Watson's later work.

The move to Johns Hopkins. By 1907 Watson had a national reputation in animal psychology, and he was offered a position at Johns Hopkins University. He really did not want to leave the University of Chicago but the offer of $3,000 a year from Johns Hopkins was irresistible. Watson arrived in Baltimore in August 1908. At Johns Hopkins, psychology was part of the Department of Philosophy, Psychology, and Education, and James Mark Baldwin was chairman of the department. Baldwin was also editor of *Psychological Review*, one of psychology's leading journals. Among Watson's duties was the teaching of human psychology, for which he still used Titchener's manuals. Watson wrote to Titchener about the problems he was having setting up a laboratory at Johns Hopkins, and Watson and Titchener exchanged many letters from that point on. Both men always showed great respect for each other. In Watson's time of great trouble (which we discuss shortly), Titchener was the only person who stuck with him.

Buckley describes the tremendous strides Watson had made in his profession in a very short period of time:

Watson was but twenty-nine years old when he accepted the position at Johns Hopkins. Just eight years before, he had come to Chicago with little more than an ambition to "amount to something." Yet by 1908, he had established a professional reputation far beyond those of most of his peers. His enormous capacity for productive work and a pugnacious and sometimes flamboyant style had served him well. . . . When Watson took up his duties at Johns Hopkins, it marked the establishment of experimental psychology there for the first time since G. Stanley Hall, the organizer of the profession, had left more than a generation before. (1989, p. 58)

In December 1909, a significant event occurred in Watson's life: Baldwin was caught in a brothel and was forced to resign from Johns Hopkins immediately. Watson became editor of the *Psychological Review*, and ultimately he used the journal to publish his views on behaviorism. For many years, Watson had been pondering a purely behavioristic position, but when he tried his ideas on those closest to him—for example, Angell and Yerkes—they discouraged him be-

cause they both believed that the study of consciousness had an important place in psychology. Watson first publicly announced his behavioristic views in 1908, at a colloquium at Yale University. Watson was again severely criticized, and again he fell silent. At the time, Watson did not have enough confidence to "go to war" against established psychology on his own. He also remained silent to avoid offending his friend Titchener. Cohen reports the following exchange between Watson and Yerkes:

On 6 February 1910 Watson told Yerkes that, in fact, "I would remodel psychology as we now have it." He would like to expound behaviourism and to put consciousness in its place as an irrelevance but, "I fear to do it because my place here is not ready for it. My thesis developed as I long to develop it would certainly separate me from the psychologist [Titchener]. Titchener would cast me off and I fear Angell would do likewise." The main obstacles were Watson's own inner loyalties. Yerkes urged caution. (1979, p. 62)

Watson gained courage, however, and in 1913 he decided to take another plunge. When asked to give a series of lectures at Columbia University in New York, he used the opportunity to state publicly his views on psychology again. He began his now famous lecture "Psychology as the Behaviorist Views It," with the following statement:

Psychology as the Behaviorist views it is a purely objective experimental branch of natural science. Its theoretical goal is the prediction and control of behavior. Introspection forms no essential part of its methods, nor is the scientific value of its data dependent upon the readiness with which they lend themselves to interpretation in terms of consciousness. The Behaviorist, in his efforts to get a unitary scheme of animal response, recognizes no dividing line between man and brute. The behavior of man, with all of its refinement and complexity, forms only a part of the Behaviorist's total scheme of investigation. (1913, p. 158)

Published in 1913 in the *Psychological Review*, which Watson edited, this lecture is usually taken as the formal founding of behaviorism.

The responses immediately began rolling in.

Titchener was not upset because he felt Watson had outlined a technology of behavior that did not conflict with psychology proper; but Angell, Cattell, and Woodworth criticized Watson for being too extreme. After his Columbia lectures, Watson was publicly committed to behaviorism and had no tolerance for any other brand of psychology. As we will see, Watson's position gradually expanded to the point where it attempted to explain all human behavior. Perhaps because Watson's ideas were so radical, they did not gain immediate popularity. Instead, their acceptance grew steadily over a period of several years (Samelson, 1981). Still, in 1914 Watson was elected president of the Southern Society for Philosophy and Psychology. In the same year, he was elected the 24th president of the American Psychological Association (APA)—all this at the age of 36 and only 11 years after receiving his doctorate from the University of Chicago.

Scandal. As rapidly as Watson's influence rose, it fell even more rapidly. In 1920 Watson's wife discovered that he was having an affair with Rosalie Rayner, with whom he was doing research on infant behavior, and sued him for divorce. The scandal was too much for Johns Hopkins: Watson was asked to resign, and he did. For all practical purposes, this marked the end of Watson's professional career in psychology. He wrote about and lectured on psychology for many years, and he revised many of his earlier works, but more and more he directed his ideas toward the general public and not toward psychologists. For many years, he tried to gain another academic position in psychology, but the "scandal" had taken its toll, and no college or university would have him. Now his thoughts appeared in popular magazines such as *Harper's, New Republic, McCall's,* and *Cosmopolitan,* rather than in professional journals. Watson also appeared on many radio talk shows. The following is a sample of titles of his articles and radio talks:

- "How We Think" (1926)
- "The Myth of the Unconscious" (1927)
- "On Reconditioning People" (1928)

- "Feed Me on Facts" (1928)
- "Why 50 Years from Now Men Wouldn't Marry" (1929)
- "After the Family—What?" (1929)
- "Women and Business" (1930)
- "On Children" (1935)

The last article that Watson wrote was entitled "Why I Don't Commit Suicide." Watson submitted it to *Cosmopolitan,* but it was rejected because it was too depressing.

Advertising work. In 1921 Watson's divorce was final, and he married Rosalie Rayner, but he was out of work and broke. An opportunity arose for him to work for the J. Walter Thompson Advertising Company. The job offered to Watson contrasted sharply with what Watson had grown accustomed to. Cohen describes the job interview and the job itself:

If Watson had been able to laugh at that point, he must have done so. Resor [the person who interviewed Watson] was a man who had graduated from Yale with no great distinction in 1901. He had sold stoves for his father and had gone on to run a twelve-man office in Cincinnati. In 1916 he had clubbed together with some friends from Yale to buy out the original J. Walter Thompson who had made the agency a small success. Now John B. Watson, who was recognized as being one of the greatest psychologists in the world, who was in the same intellectual league as Freud and Russell and Bergson, was asking Resor for a job. And Resor gave Watson only a temporary job. And what a job! Resor had to address the annual convention of the Boot Sellers League of America. In order to have the most impressive paper at the convention, he wanted some quick research to be done on the boot market. John B. Watson was given the job of studying the rubber boot market on each side of the Mississippi River from Cairo to New Orleans. It is a measure of Watson that he took to this job without feeling humiliated. He set out to learn it. He did not feel bitter that he had come to this. He always believed in being adaptable, in coping with what he called "life's little difficulties." Most psychologists would have felt this little difficulty as a crushing blow. And, in many ways, it was crushing. Watson wanted to pursue his work on children; he enjoyed his status as a leading professor. But one had to deal with life and, for him, the best way of doing so was to plunge whole-heartedly into it adversity and all. He threw himself into the study of the rubber boot market on the Mississippi. To be immersed even in that was some relief. (1979, p. 161)

Resor asked for letters of recommendation for Watson, and a very supportive one came from none other than Titchener:

Watson was always deeply grateful to Titchener for consenting to write a reference and wrote to him in 1922 that "I know, in my heart, that I owe you more than almost all my other colleagues put together." Watson's instinct was just. (Cohen, 1979, p. 172)

Resor hired Watson in 1921, at a salary of $10,000 a year. By 1924 Watson was considered one of the leading people in advertising and was made a vice president of the J. Walter Thompson Company. Titchener wrote and congratulated him but worried that the promotion would give Watson less time to work on psychology. By 1928 Watson was earning over $50,000 a year and by 1930 over $70,000. Remember that this was in 1930—imagine what the equivalent salary would be today! One thing that made Watson so successful was his use of the then almost-unknown concept of market research. He found, for example, that blindfolded smokers could not differentiate among different brands of cigarettes. Because preference must be based on the images associated with various brand names, Watson concluded that sales could be influenced by manipulating the images associated with brand names. Following this strategy, Watson increased the sales of such products as Johnson's baby powder, Pebeco toothpaste, Ponds cold cream, Maxwell House coffee, and Odorono, one of the early deodorants.

Even though Watson's accomplishments in advertising were vast, his first love was always psychology, and he regretted for the rest of his life that he was unable to pursue his professional goals, especially his research on children. How psychology would be different today if Watson had not been dismissed from Johns Hopkins in 1920 cannot be known, but surely it would be different.

Watson's Objective Psychology

When Watson discovered Russian objective psychology, he found support in it, but he had arrived at his position independently of the Russians. What Watson and the Russian psychologists had in common was a complete rejection of introspection and of any explanation of behavior based on mentalism. That is, both thought that consciousness could not *cause* behavior; it was merely a phenomenon that accompanied certain physiological reactions caused by stimuli. That is, it was an epiphenomenon. Most of the Russian physiologists, such as Sechenov and Pavlov, were more interested than Watson in explaining the physiology underlying behavior, especially brain physiology. As time went by, Watson became even less interested in physiology and more interested in correlating stimuli and responses. He called the brain a "mystery box" that was used to account for behavior when the real cause was unknown. In other words, Watson's approach to studying organisms (including humans) was closer to Bechterev's than it was to Sechenov's or Pavlov's. In fact, the approaches of Bechterev and Watson were *very* close, both methodologically and philosophically.

In his 1913 statement on behaviorism, Watson did not mention the work of the Russians, and he said very little about human behavior. And though Watson's first book (1914) dealt mainly with animal behavior, there was still no mention of the Russian physiologists. Finally, in his presidential address to the APA in 1915 (published as "The Place of Conditioned Reflex in Psychology" in 1916), Watson suggested that Pavlov's work on the conditioned reflex could be used to explain human as well as animal behavior. But Watson never fully accepted or used Pavlovian concepts in his work. As we will see, he had his own notions concerning the terms *stimulus* and *response* and concerning the learning process.

The goal of psychology. In his major work (1919), Watson fully elaborated a stimulus–response psychology. In his 1913 article, he had stated the goal of psychology as the prediction and control of behavior, and in 1919 he explained further what he meant:

> If its facts were all at hand the behaviorist would be able to tell after watching an individual perform an act what the situation is that caused his action (prediction), whereas if organized society decreed that the individual or group should act in a definite, specific way the behaviorist could arrange the situation or stimulus which would bring about such action (control). In other words, Psychology from the Standpoint of the Behaviorists is concerned with the prediction and control of human action and not with an analysis of "consciousness." (pp. vii–ix)

He went on to say,

> The goal of psychological study is the ascertaining of such data and laws that, given the stimulus, psychology can predict what the response will be; or, on the other hand, given the response, it can specify the nature of the effective stimulus. (1919, p. 10)

Watson, however, did not use the terms *stimulus* and *response* in as narrow a sense as the Russian physiologists. For him, a stimulus could be a general environmental situation or some internal condition of the organism. A response was anything the organism did—and that included a great deal:

> The rule, or measuring rod, which the behaviorist puts in front of him always is: Can I describe this bit of behavior I see in terms of "stimulus and response"? By stimulus we mean any object in the general environment or any change in the tissues themselves due to the physiological condition of the animal, such as the change we get when we keep an animal from sex activity, when we keep it from feeding, when we keep it from building a nest. By response we mean anything the animal does—such as turning toward or away from a light, jumping at a sound, and more highly organized activities such as building a skyscraper, drawing plans, having babies, writing books, and the like. (J. B. Watson, 1925/1930, pp. 6–7)

Thus, Watson's position has been unjustly called "the psychology of twitchism," implying that it is concerned with specific reflexes elicited by specific stimuli.

Types of behavior and how they are studied. For Watson, there were four types of behavior: *explicit* (overt) *learned behavior* such as talking, writing, and playing baseball; *implicit* (covert) *learned behavior* such as the increased heart rate caused by the sight of a dentist's drill; *explicit unlearned behavior* such as grasping, blinking, and sneezing; and *implicit unlearned behavior* such as glandular secretions and circulatory changes. According to Watson, everything that a person did, including thinking, fell into one of these four categories.

For studying behavior, Watson proposed four methods: *observation*, either naturalistic or experimentally controlled; the *conditioned-reflex method*, which Pavlov and Bechterev had proposed; *testing*, by which Watson meant the taking of behavior samples and *not* the measurement of "capacity" or "personality"; and *verbal reports*, which Watson treated as any other type of overt behavior. By now it should be clear that Watson did *not* use verbal behavior as a means of studying consciousness.

Language and thinking. The most controversial aspect of Watson's theory concerned language and thinking. To be consistent in his behavioristic view, Watson had to reduce language and thinking to some form of behavior *and nothing more*: "*Saying* is doing—that is, *behaving*. Speaking overtly or to ourselves (thinking) is just as objective a type of behavior as baseball" (1925/1930, p. 6).

For Watson then, speech presented no special problem; it was simply a type of overt behavior. Watson solved the problem of thinking by claiming that thinking was implicit or subvocal speech. Because overt speech was produced by substantial movement of the tongue and larynx, Watson assumed that minute movements of the tongue and larynx accompanied thought. The following is how Watson described the evolution from overt speech to implicit speech (thinking):

> The child talks incessantly when alone. At three he even plans the day *aloud*, as my own ear placed outside the keyhole of the nursery door has very often confirmed. Soon society in the form of nurse and parents steps in. "Don't talk aloud—Daddy and Mother are not always talking to themselves." Soon the overt speech dies down to whispered speech and a good lip reader can still read what the child thinks of the world and of himself. Some individuals never make this concession to society. When alone they talk aloud to themselves. A still larger number never go beyond even the whispering stage when alone. Watch people reading on the street car; peep through the keyhole sometime when individuals not too highly socialized are just sitting and thinking. But the great majority of people pass on to the third stage under the influence of social pressure constantly exerted. "Quit whispering to yourself," and "Can't you even read without moving your lips?" and the like are constant mandates. Soon the process is forced to take place behind the lips. Behind these walls you can call the biggest bully the worst name you can think of without even smiling. You can tell the female bore how terrible she really is and the next moment smile and overtly pay her a verbal compliment. (1925/1930, pp. 240–241)

Watson's attempt to reduce thought to subvocal speech aroused great opposition. Woodworth's reaction was typical:

> I may as well tell you in a few words some reasons why I personally do not accept the equation, thought = speech. One is that I often have difficulty in finding a word required to express a meaning which I certainly have "in mind." I get stuck not infrequently, for even a familiar word. Another reason is that you certainly cannot turn the equation around and say that speech = thought. You can recite a familiar passage with no sense of its meaning, and while thinking something entirely different. Finally, thinking certainly seems as much akin to seeing as to manipulating. It seems to consist in seeing the point, in observing relations. Watson's speech habits substituted for actual manipulation fail to show how thinking carries you beyond your previous habits. Why should the combination of words, "Suppose I moved the piano over there," lead to the continuation, "But it would jut out over the window," just as a matter of language

habit? Something more than the words must certainly be in the game, and that something consists somehow in seeing the point. (1931, p. 72)

The problem of determining the nature of thought and determining thought's relationship to behavior is as old as psychology and is just as much an issue today as it ever was. Watson did not solve the problem, but neither has anyone else.

The role of instincts in behavior. Watson's attitude toward instincts changed radically over the years. In 1914 instincts played a prominent role in his theory. By 1919 Watson had taken the position that instincts were present in infants but that learned habits quickly displaced them. In 1925 he completely rejected the idea of instincts in humans, contending that there were a few simple reflexes such as sneezing, crying, eliminating, crawling, sucking, and breathing but no complex, innate behavior patterns called instincts. In 1926 Watson said,

> In this relatively simple list of human responses there is none corresponding to what is called an "instinct" by present-day psychologists and biologists. There are then for us no instincts—we no longer need the term in psychology. Everything we have been in the habit of calling an "instinct" today is a result largely of training—belonging to man's *learned behavior*. (p. 1)

For Watson, *experience* and not inheritance made people what they were. Change experience, and you change personality. Thus, Watson's position ended up as a **radical environmentalism**. Watson went on:

> I would feel perfectly confident in the ultimate favorable outcome of careful upbringing of a *healthy, well-formed baby* born of a long line of crooks, murderers, thieves and prostitutes. Who has any evidence to the contrary? Many, many thousands of children yearly, born from moral households and steadfast parents, become wayward, steal or become prostitutes, through one mishap or another of nurture. Many more thousands of sons and daughters of the wicked grow up to be wicked because they couldn't grow up any other way in such surroundings. But let one

adopted child who had a bad ancestry go wrong and it is used as incontestible [*sic*] evidence for the inheritance of moral turpitude and criminal tendencies. (1926, p. 9)

Finally, Watson made one of the most famous (or infamous) statements in the history of psychology:

I should like to go one step further tonight and say, "Give me a dozen healthy infants, well-formed, and my own specified world to bring them up in and I'll guarantee to take any one at random and train him to become any type of specialist I might select—a doctor, lawyer, artist, merchant-chief and, yes, even into beggarman and thief, regardless of his talents, penchants, tendencies, abilities, vocations and race of his ancestors." I am going beyond my facts and I admit it, but so have the advocates of the contrary and they have been doing it for thousands of years. Please note that when this experiment is made I am to be allowed to specify the way they are to be brought up and the type of world they have to live in. (1926, p. 10)

Watson did, however, allow for heritable differences in *structure* that could influence personality characteristics:

So let us hasten to admit—yes, there are heritable differences in form, in structure. Some people are born with long, slender fingers, with delicate throat structure; some are born tall, large, of prize-fighter build; others with delicate skin and eye coloring. These differences are in the germ plasm and are handed down from parent to child. . . . But do not let these undoubted facts of inheritance lead you astray as they have some of the biologists. The mere presence of these structures tell us not one thing about function. . . . Our hereditary structure lies ready to be shaped in a thousand different ways—the same structure mind you—depending on the way in which the child is brought up. (1926, p. 4)

Watson gave the following example of how structure interacts with experience to produce specific behavior patterns:

The behaviorist would *not* say: "He inherits his father's capacity or talent for being a fine swordsman." He would say: "This child certainly has his father's slender build of body, the same type of eyes. His build is wonderfully

like his father's. He, too, has the build of a swordsman." And he would go on to say: "And his father is very fond of him. He put a tiny sword into his hand when he was a year of age, and in all their walks he talks sword play, attack and defense, the code of duelling and the like." A certain type of structure, plus early training—*slanting*—accounts for adult performance. (1926, p. 2)

Emotions. Watson believed that along with structure and the basic reflexes, humans inherited the emotions of fear, rage, and love. In infants, fear was elicited by loud noises and loss of support (e.g., falling), rage by restricting the infant's freedom of movement, and love by stroking or patting the infant. Through learning, these emotions came to be elicited by stimuli other than those that originally elicited them. Furthermore, all adult emotions such as hate, pride, jealousy, and shame were derived from rage, fear, and love.

Watson believed that each basic emotion had a characteristic pattern of visceral and glandular responses that was triggered by an appropriate stimulus. Also, each basic emotion had a pattern of overt responses associated with it. With fear, there was a catching of the breath, clutching with the hands, closing of the eyes, and crying. With rage, there was a stiffening of the body and slashing and striking movements. With love, there was smiling, gurgling, cooing, and an extension of the arms. For Watson, the three important aspects of emotions were the stimuli that elicited the emotions, the internal reactions, and the external reactions. Feelings and sensations were not important.

Watson's experiment with Albert. To demonstrate how emotions could be displaced to stimuli other than those that had originally elicited the emotions, Watson and Rosalie Rayner performed an experiment in 1920 on an 11-month-old infant named Albert. They showed Albert a white rat, and he expressed no fear of it. In fact, he reached out and tried to touch it. As Albert reached for the rat, a steel bar behind him was struck with a hammer. The loud, unexpected noise caused Albert to jump and fall forward.

Again Albert was offered the rat, and just as he touched it, the steel bar behind him was again struck. Again Albert jumped, and this time he began to cry. So as not to disturb Albert too much, further testing was postponed for a week. A week later, when the rat was again presented to Albert, Albert was less enthusiastic and attempted to keep his distance from it. Five more times Watson and Rayner placed the rat near Albert and struck the steel bar; and Albert, who had at first been attracted to the rat, was now frightened of it:

> The instant the rat was shown the baby began to cry. Almost instantly he turned sharply to the left, fell over on his left side, raised himself on all fours and began to crawl away so rapidly that he was caught with difficulty before reaching the edge of the table. (Watson & Rayner, 1920, p. 5)

Five days later, Watson and Rayner found that the fear of the rat was just as strong as it had been at the end of testing and that the fear had generalized to other furry objects such as a rabbit, a dog, a fur coat, and a Santa Claus mask. Watson had clearly demonstrated how experience rearranged the stimuli that caused emotional responses. He believed that all adult emotional reactions developed by the same mechanism that had operated in the experiment with Albert—that is, contiguity.

Watson and Rayner found that Albert's fear of the rat was still present a month after Albert's training. They intended to eliminate Albert's fear, but before they could do so he was removed from the hospital in which he was living. It was left to Mary Cover Jones (1896–1987), under Watson's supervision, to show how a child's fear could be systematically eliminated. Watson believed that his earlier research on Albert had showed how fear was produced in a child, and he felt strongly that no further research of that type was necessary. Instead, he would find children who had already developed a fear and would try to eliminate it. The researchers found such a child—a three-year-old boy named Peter who was intensely frightened of white rats, rabbits, fur coats, frogs, fish, and mechanical toys.

Peter and the rabbit. Watson and Jones first tried showing Peter other children playing fearlessly with objects of which he was frightened, and there was some improvement. (This is a technique called *modeling*, which Bandura and his colleagues employ today.) At this point, Peter came down with scarlet fever and had to go to the hospital. Following recovery, he and his nurse were attacked by a dog on their way home from the hospital, and all of Peter's fears returned in magnified form. Watson and Jones decided to try counterconditioning on Peter. Peter ate lunch in a room 40 feet long. One day as Peter was eating lunch, a rabbit in a wire cage was displayed far enough away from him so that Peter was not disturbed. The researchers made a mark on the floor at that point. Each day they moved the rabbit a bit closer to Peter until one day it was sitting beside Peter as he ate. Finally, Peter was able to eat with one hand and play with the rabbit with the other. The results generalized and most of Peter's other fears were also eliminated or reduced. This is one of the first examples of what we now call **behavior therapy**. In 1924 Jones published the results of the research with Peter, and in 1974 she published more of the details surrounding the research.

Child rearing. Watson, an extremely popular writer and speaker, dealt with many topics, but his favorite topic, and the one that he considered to be most important, was children. Unable to continue his laboratory studies after being forced out of the profession of psychology, he decided to share his thoughts about children with the public by writing, with the assistance of his wife Rosalie Rayner Watson, *The Psychological Care of the Infant and Child* (1928), which was dedicated to "The first mother who brings up a happy child." The book was extremely popular (it sold 100,000 copies in a few months), and in many ways Watson was the Dr. Spock of the 1920s and 1930s. Watson and Watson's advice was to treat children as small adults:

> Never hug and kiss them, never let them sit on your lap. If you must, kiss them once on the forehead when they say good night. Shake

hands with them in the morning. Give them a pat on the head if they have made an extraordinary good job of a difficult task. Try it out. In a week's time you will find how easy it is to be perfectly objective with your child and at the same time kindly. You will be utterly ashamed at the mawkish, sentimental way you have been handling it. (1928, pp. 81–82)

Watson and Watson went on: "When I hear a mother say, 'Bless its little heart' when it falls down, or stubs its toe, or suffers some other ill, I usually have to walk a block or two to let off steam" (1928, p. 82). And finally, Watson and Watson gave the following warning:

> In conclusion won't you then remember when you are tempted to pet your child that mother love is a dangerous instrument? An instrument which may inflict a never healing wound, a wound which may make infancy unhappy, adolescence a nightmare, an instrument which may wreck your adult son or daughter's vocational future and their chances for marital happiness. (1928, p. 87)

One suspects that their book on child rearing reflected John's ideas more than Rosalie's. In a 1930 article entitled "I am the Mother of a Behaviorist's Sons'," Rosalie Watson wrote:

> In some respects I bow to the great wisdom in the science of behaviourism, and in others I am rebellious . . . I secretly wish that on the score of (the children's) affections they will be a little weak when they grow up, that they will have a tear in their eyes for the poetry and drama of life and throb for romance . . . I like being merry and gay and having the giggles. The behaviorists think giggling is a sign of maladjustment. (Quoted in Boakes, 1984, p. 227)

Sex education. Watson also had a great deal to say about sex education, urging that children be given frank, objective information about sex; and he often expressed his gratitude to Freud for breaking down the myth and secrecy surrounding sex. None other than Bertrand Russell reviewed Watson's book on child rearing. Though Russell felt that Watson's emphasis on the environment was extreme and that Watson had gone a bit too far in banning hugging and kissing, he heaped praise on the book. Watson's

liberal views, however, did not impress most psychologists:

> The honesty in sex education which Watson demanded seemed wholly admirable to Russell. Watson had also revived Plato's argument that perhaps it would be best for parents and children not to know each other. While this was bound to shock the American public, Russell believed this was an issue that was worth discussing. He ended by saying that no one since Aristotle had actually made as substantial a contribution to our knowledge of ourselves as Watson had—high praise indeed, from a man who was then regarded as one of the greatest minds in the world! None of this impressed most psychologists who complained that Watson had demeaned himself, which was only to be expected, and demeaned their science, which was only to be deplored. (Cohen, 1979, p. 218)

Behaviorism and the good life. Along with the functionalists and most other subsequent behaviorists, Watson firmly believed that psychology should be useful in everyday life, and he often applied his behaviorism to himself and his children. Though behaviorism might have shortcomings, Watson believed that it could make for a better life than traditional beliefs could:

> I think behaviorism does lay a foundation for saner living. It ought to be a science that prepares men and women for understanding the first principles of their own behavior. It ought to make men and women eager to rearrange their own lives, and especially eager to prepare themselves to bring up their own children in a healthy way. I wish I had time more fully to describe this, to picture to you the kind of rich and wonderful individual we should make of every healthy child; if only we could let it shape itself properly and then provide for it a universe unshackled by legendary folk lore of happenings thousands of years ago; unhampered by disgraceful political history; free of foolish customs and conventions which have no significance in themselves, yet which hem the individual in like taut steel bands. (1925/1930, p. 248)

Learning. Although Watson was very impressed by Thorndike's early animal research, he felt that Thorndike's law of effect was unnecessarily mentalistic. After all, what was a "satisfying state of affairs" but a feeling or a state of consciousness? For Watson, the important thing about conditioning was that it caused events to be associated in time; that is, it caused contiguity. Employing the concept of reinforcement was unnecessary. Instead of relying on Thorndike's law of effect, Watson explained learning in terms of the ancient principles of contiguity and frequency. In other words, Watson's explanation of learning was more similar to that of Pavlov's and Bechterev's than it was Thorndike's.

Watson pointed out that in a learning situation a trial always ends with the animal making the correct response. This means that the correct response tends to occur more frequently than incorrect responses and that the more often a response is made, the higher the probability that it will be made again (the law of frequency). It also means that the final response an organism makes in a learning situation will be the response it will tend to make when it is next in that situation; Watson called this the **law of recency**. In the classical conditioning situation, the conditioned stimulus (CS) and the unconditioned stimulus (US) become associated (elicit the same type of response) simply because they occur at about the same time (the law of contiguity). According to Watson, learning resulted from the mechanical arrangement of stimuli and responses; no "effects" of any type entered into his explanation.

The mind–body problem. By the time Watson had begun to formulate his theory, there were four views on the mind–body relationship. One was an *interactionist* view of the type Descartes, and sometimes William James, had accepted. According to this position, the mind could influence the body, and what happened to the body influenced the mind. That is, the mind and the body interacted. A second position was *psychophysical parallelism*, according to which mental and bodily events were parallel with no interaction between them. In a third view, *epiphenomenalism*, mental events were the byproducts of bodily events but did not cause behavior. That is, bodily events caused mental

events, but mental events could not cause bodily events. During Watson's time, epiphenomenalism was probably the most commonly held view concerning the mind–body relationship. A fourth position, called *physical monism*, involved rejecting the existence of mental events (consciousness) altogether. In his early writings, Watson accepted consciousness as an epiphenomenon, as is evident in the following passage:

> Will there be left over in psychology a world of pure psychics, to use Yerkes' term? I confess I do not know. The plans that I most favor for psychology lead practically to the ignoring of consciousness in the sense that the term is used by psychologists today. I have virtually denied that this realm of psychics is open to experimental investigation. I don't wish to go further into the problem at present because it leads inevitably over into metaphysics. If you will grant the behaviorist the right to use consciousness in the same way as other natural scientists employ it— that is, without making consciousness a special object of observation—you have granted all that my thesis requires. (1913, p. 174)

Later, in his debate with McDougall (discussed shortly), Watson switched to a physical monist position. Consciousness, he said, "has never been seen, touched, smelled, tasted, or moved. It is a plain assumption just as unprovable as the old concept of the soul" (Watson & McDougall, 1929, p. 14). Watson "solved" the mind–body problem by simply denying the existence of the mind. Watson believed that functionalism represented a timid, half-hearted attempt to be scientific. Any approach to psychology that accepts the study of consciousness in any form cannot be a science: "It is important to realize the vehemence and thoroughness with which the concept of consciousness is rejected [by Watson]. Mental processes, consciousness, souls, and ghosts are all of a piece, and are altogether unfit for scientific use" (Heidbreder, 1933, p. 235).

Watson's Influence

Although, as Samelson (1981) has shown, it took several years before Watson's behaviorism gained widespread acceptance, it eventually did just that. Watson's view of psychology was to have two long-lasting effects. First, he changed psychology's major goal from the description and explanation of states of consciousness to the prediction and control of behavior. Second, he made overt behavior the almost-exclusive subject matter of psychology. On these issues, Watson's influence has been so pervasive that today most psychologists can be considered behaviorists:

> Some of the central tenets of behaviorism are at this point so taken for granted that they have simply become part of standard experimental psychology. All modern psychologists restrict their *evidence* to observable behavior, attempt to specify stimuli and responses with the greatest possible precision, are skeptical of theories that resist empirical testing, and refuse to consider unsupported subjective reports as scientific evidence. In these ways, we are all behaviorists. (Baars, 1986, pp. viii–ix)

There are different types of behaviorists, however. Those psychologists who, like Watson, either denied the existence of mental events or claimed that if such events exist they could be and should be ignored represent radical behaviorism. More generally, **radical behaviorism** is the belief that an explanation of behavior cannot be in terms of unobserved internal events. All that can be directly observed are environmental events and overt behavior, and therefore only they should constitute the subject matter of a scientific analysis of behavior. After Watson, however, few psychologists took such an extreme position. Rather, many psychologists, although they agreed that the primary subject matter of psychology should be overt behavior, did not deny the importance of unobserved cognitive or physiological events in their analyses of behavior. For them, behavior was used to *index* the cognitive or physiological events thought to be taking place within the organism. Such psychologists represent **methodological behaviorism**, the second type of behaviorism. The methodological behaviorist sees nothing wrong with postulating cognitive or physiological events but insists that such events be validated by studying their manifestations in overt behavior. Although methodological behaviorism is much more popular in contemporary psychology than is radical behaviorism, the latter is still very much alive. What binds all versions of behaviorism is their insistence on studying only those behaviors that can be directly observed.

Although Watson would probably be pleased to see how much he has influenced contemporary psychology, he would be disappointed to observe that his attempt to rid psychology of the notion of consciousness clearly failed. Today there are more psychologists than ever studying the very cognitive processes that Watson ignored, deplored, or denied.

In 1957 the APA awarded Watson one of its prestigious Gold Medals in recognition of his significant contributions to psychology. Watson was very pleased with the award, but because of poor health he was unable to receive it in person; his son Billy accepted it for him. Watson died in 1958, at the age of 80.

Although Watson's position eventually became extremely popular, there were always prominent psychologists who opposed him. One of his most persistent adversaries was William McDougall.

WILLIAM McDOUGALL: ANOTHER TYPE OF BEHAVIORISM

William McDougall (1871–1938) was born in Lancashire, England, where his father owned a chemical factory. Educated in private schools in England and Germany, McDougall entered the University of Manchester when he was only 15 years old. Four years later, he started his medical training at Cambridge and finally obtained his medical degree from St. Thomas's Hospital in London in 1897, at the age of 26. After a trip to the Far East, McDougall went to the University of Göttingen in Germany to study experimental psychology with the famous Georg Elias Müller (1850–1934). However, it was the reading of

William McDougall

William James's work that got McDougall interested in psychology, and he always considered himself a disciple of James. Upon his return from Germany, he accepted a position at University College in London to teach experimental psychology. He moved to Oxford University in 1904 and remained there until the First World War. During the war, he served as a major in the medical corps and was in charge of treating soldiers with mental problems. After the war, he was psychoanalyzed by the famous psychoanalyst Carl Jung.

In 1920 McDougall accepted an invitation from Harvard to fill the position once held by William James and then by Hugo Münsterberg. McDougall stayed at Harvard until 1926 when he resigned his position. The following year he moved to Duke University in North Carolina, where he remained until his death in 1938. In his lifetime, McDougall wrote 24 books and more than 160 articles.

Eight years after his arrival in the United States, McDougall felt out of place and misunderstood. He tended to be disliked by his students, his colleagues, and the media. Part of the reason for his problems was his effort to promote a psychology that emphasized instinct in the increasingly anti-instinct climate of U.S. psychology. Other factors offered to explain McDougall's plight include a generally anti-British sentiment in the United States in the 1920s; the fact that he attempted to test Lamarck's theory of acquired characteristics when that theory had been largely discarded; his willingness to entertain the vitalistic belief that behavior is ultimately caused by a nonphysical force, which he called "hormic energy"; and the fact that he had a pugnacious personality. (R. A. Jones, 1987, discusses McDougall's problems in the United States, especially those with the press.)

Definition of Psychology

Although McDougall spent a great deal of time arguing with Watson, he was among the first to redefine psychology as the *science of behavior*:

> Psychology may be best and most comprehensively defined as the positive science of the conduct of living creatures. . . . Psychology is more commonly defined as the science of mind, or as the science of mental or psychical processes, or of consciousness, or of individual experience. Such definitions are ambiguous, and without further elaboration are not sufficiently comprehensive. They express the aims of a psychologist who relies solely upon introspection, the observation and analysis of his own experience, and who unduly neglects the manifestations of the mental life afforded by the conduct of his fellow-creatures. . . . To define psychology as the science of experience or of consciousness is therefore to exclude the study of these unconscious factors, whereas the definition stated above brings all these within the scope of psychology without excluding the study of any part of experience or element of consciousness, for all experience affects conduct. (1905, pp. 1–2)

McDougall further elaborated on his conception of psychology:

Psychologists must cease to be content with the sterile and narrow conception of their science as the science of consciousness, and must boldly assert its claim to be the positive science of the mind in all its aspects and modes of functioning, or, as I would prefer to say, the positive science of conduct or behaviour. Psychology must not regard the introspective description of the stream of consciousness as its whole task, but only as a preliminary part of its work. Such introspective description, such "pure psychology," can never constitute a science, or at least can never rise to the level of an explanatory science; and it can never in itself be of any great value to the social sciences. The basis required by all of them is a comparative and physiological psychology relying largely on objective methods, the observation of the behaviour of men and of animals of all varieties under all possible conditions of health and disease. Happily this more generous conception of psychology is beginning to prevail. (1908, p. 15)

Thus, at about the same time that Watson was making his first public statement of his behaviorism, McDougall was also questioning the value of introspection and calling for the objective study of the behavior of both humans and nonhuman animals. Unlike Watson, however, McDougall did not deny the importance of mental events. McDougall thought that one could study such events objectively by observing their influence on behavior. According to our previous distinction between radical and methodological behaviorism, McDougall was a methodological behaviorist.

Purposive Behavior

The type of behavior that McDougall studied was quite different from the reflexive behavior that the Russians and, in a more general way, Watson studied. McDougall (1923) studied purposive behavior, which differed from reflexive behavior in the following ways:

1. Purposive behavior is spontaneous. That is, unlike reflexive behavior, it need not be elicited by a known stimulus.

2. In the absence of environmental stimulation, it persists for a relatively long time.

3. It varies. Although the goal of purposive behavior remains constant, the behavior used to attain that goal may vary. If an obstacle is encountered, an alternative route is taken to reach the goal.

4. Purposive behavior terminates when the goal is attained.

5. Purposive behavior becomes more effective with practice. That is, the useless aspects of behavior are gradually eliminated. Trial-and-error behavior is purposive, not reflexive.

McDougall saw behavior as goal directed and stimulated by some instinctual motive rather than by environmental events. He believed that any behaviorist who ignored the purposive nature of behavior was missing its most important aspect.

The Importance of Instincts

As we have seen, McDougall did not believe that purposive behavior was stimulated by the environment. Rather, it was stimulated by instinctual energy. A belief in instincts formed the core of McDougall's theory, and McDougall defined an instinct as

an inherited or innate psycho-physical disposition which determines its possessor to perceive and to pay attention to objects of a certain class, to experience an emotional excitement of a particular quality upon perceiving such an object, and to act in regard to it in a particular manner, or, at least, to experience an impulse to such action. (1908, p. 29)

According to McDougall, every organism, including humans, is born with a number of instincts that provide the motivation to act in certain ways. Each instinct has three components:

1. *Perception.* When an instinct is active, the person will attend to stimuli related to its satisfaction. For example, a hungry person will attend to food-related events in the environment.

2. *Behavior.* When an instinct is active, the person will tend to do those things that will lead

to its satisfaction. That is, the person will engage in goal-directed or purposive behavior until satisfaction is attained.

3. *Emotion*. When an instinct is active, the person will respond with an appropriate emotion to those environmental events that are related to the satisfaction of or the failure to satisfy the instinct. For example, while hungry, a person will respond to food or food-related events (e.g., the odor of food) with positive emotions (e.g., the feeling of happiness) and to those events that prevent satisfaction (e.g., not having any money) with negative emotions (e.g., sadness).

According to McDougall, human behavior must be explained in terms of instincts and the emotions associated with them. His theory was hedonistic because it claimed that both human behavior and animal behavior reflect a constant attempt to satisfy inborn needs. In this sense, McDougall's theory was much like Freud's, to which McDougall had responded favorably. The importance McDougall assigned to the instincts and their associated emotions is exemplified in the following passage:

> By the conative or impulsive force of some instinct (or of some habit derived from an instinct), every train of thought . . . is borne along towards its end, and every bodily activity is initiated and sustained. The instinctive impulses determine the ends of all activities and supply the driving power by which all mental activities are sustained, and the most highly developed mind is but a means towards these ends, is the instrument by which these impulses seek their satisfactions, while pleasure and pain do but serve to guide them in their choice of means.
>
> Take away these instinctive dispositions with their powerful impulses, and the organism would become incapable of activity of any kind. (1908, p. 44)

McDougall, then, was in agreement with Freud's contention that most human behavior, no matter how complex, is ultimately instinctive.

McDougall was well aware of one major danger of explaining behavior in terms of instincts: the tendency to postulate an instinct for every type of behavior and then claim that the behavior has been explained.

> Lightly to postulate an indefinite number and variety of human instincts is a cheap and easy way to solve psychological problems and is an error hardly less serious and less common than the opposite error of ignoring all the instincts. (1908, p. 88)

Similarly, "Attribution of the actions of animals to instincts . . . was a striking example of the power of a word to cloak our ignorance and to hide it even from ourselves"(1912, p. 138).

Although McDougall's list of instincts varied through the years, Table 12.1 presents the list he proposed in 1923.

The Battle of Behaviorism

At this point, we find two of the world's most famous psychologists saying opposite things. On the one hand, McDougall said that the instincts are the motivators of all animal behavior, including that of humans. Conversely, Watson said that instincts do not exist on the human level and that psychology should rid itself of the term *instinct*. Another major difference between Watson and McDougall concerned their views of the learning process. As we have seen, Watson rejected the importance of reinforcement in learning, saying that learning could be explained in terms of the associative principles of contiguity, frequency, and recency. For McDougall, habits of thought and behavior served the instincts; that is, they were formed because they satisfied some instinct. McDougall believed that reinforcement in the form of need reduction was an important aspect of the learning process, and he expressed his view as follows:

> In the developed human mind there are springs to action of another class, namely, acquired habits of thought and action. An acquired mode of activity becomes by repetition habitual, and the more frequently it is repeated the more powerful becomes the habit as a source of impulse or motive power. Few habits can equal in this respect the principal instincts; and habits are in a sense derived from, and secondary to, instincts; for in the absence of instincts, no thought and

TABLE 12.1 McDougall's List of Instincts and the Associated Emotions.

Instinct	Emotion Accompanying the Instinct
Escape	Fear
Combat	Anger
Repulsion	Disgust
Parental (protective)	Love and tenderness
Appeal (for help)	Distress, feeling of helplessness
Mating	Lust
Curiosity	Feeling of mystery, of strangeness, of the unknown
Submission	Feeling of subjection, inferiority, devotion, humility; negative self-feeling
Assertion	Feeling of elation, superiority, masterfulness, pride, positive self-feeling
Gregariousness	Feeling of loneliness, isolation, nostalgia
Food-seeking	Appetite or craving
Construction	Feeling of creativeness, of making, of productivity
Laughter	Amusement, carelessness, relaxation

SOURCE: McDougall, 1923, p. 324.

no action could ever be achieved or repeated, and no habits of thought or action could be formed. Habits are formed only in the service of the instincts. (1908, p. 43)

The time was right for a debate between Mc-Dougall and Watson, and debate they did. On February 5, 1924, they confronted one another before the Psychological Club in Washington, DC, and more than 300 people attended. In 1929 Watson and McDougall published the proceedings under the title *The Battle of Behaviorism.* Space permits presenting only a small sample from their lengthy debate. Watson said,

He then who would introduce consciousness, either as an epiphenomenon or as an active force interjecting itself into the physical and chemical happenings of the body, does so because of spiritualistic and vitalistic leanings.

The Behaviorist cannot find consciousness in the test tube of his science. He finds no evidence anywhere for a stream of consciousness, not even for one so convincing as that described by William James. He does, however, find convincing proof of an ever-widening stream of behavior. (Watson & McDougall, 1929, p. 26)

McDougall's argumentative style is seen in his opening remarks in the debate:

I would begin by confessing that in this discussion I have an initial advantage over Dr. Watson, an advantage which I feel to be so great as to be unfair; namely that all persons of common sense will of necessity be on my side from the outset, or at least as soon as they understand the issue.

On the other hand, Dr. Watson also can claim certain initial advantages . . . First, there is a considerable number of persons so constituted that they are attracted by whatever is bizarre, paradoxical, preposterous, and outrageous . . . whatever is unorthodox and opposed to accepted principles. All these will inevitably be on Dr. Watson's side.

Secondly, Dr. Watson's views are attractive to many persons . . . by reason of the fact that these views simplify so greatly the problems that lie before the student of psychology: they abolish at one stroke many tough problems with which the greatest intellects have struggled with only very partial success for more than two thousand years; and they do this by the bold and simple expedient of inviting the student to shut his eyes to them, to turn resolutely away from them, and to forget that they exist.

Now, though I am sorry for Dr. Watson, I mean to be entirely frank about his position. If he were an ordinary human being, I should feel obliged to exercise a certain reserve, for fear of hurting his feelings. We all know that Dr. Watson has feelings, like the rest of us. But I am at liberty to trample on his feelings in the most ruthless manner; for Dr. Watson has assured us (and it is the very essence of his peculiar doctrine) that he does not care a cent about feelings, whether his own or those of any other person. (Watson & McDougall, 1929, pp. 40–44)

McDougall then responded to Watson's inability to account for the most satisfying human experiences, for example, the enjoyment of music:

I come into this hall and see a man on this platform scraping the guts of a cat with hairs from the tail of a horse; and, sitting silently in attitudes of rapt attention, are a thousand persons who presently break out into wild applause. How will the Behaviorist explain these strange incidents: How explain the fact that the vibrations emitted by the cat-gut stimulate all the thousand into absolute silence and quiescence; and the further fact that the cessation of the stimulus seems to be a stimulus to the most frantic activity? Common sense and psychology agree in accepting the explanation that the audience heard the music with keen pleasure, and vented their gratitude and admiration for the artist in shouts and hand clappings. But the Behaviorist knows nothing of pleasure and pain, of admiration and gratitude. He has relegated all such "metaphysical entities" to the dust heap,

and must seek some other explanation. Let us leave him seeking it. The search will keep him harmlessly occupied for some centuries to come. (Watson & McDougall, 1929, pp. 62–63)

McDougall also resented the fact that Watson was using the same techniques to sell his brand of behaviorism as he used to sell products such as cigarettes and deodorants:

Dr. Watson knows that if you wish to sell your wares, you must assert very loudly, plainly, and frequently that they are the best on the market, ignore all criticism, and avoid all argument and all appeal to reason. . . . The susceptibility of the public to attack by these methods in the purely commercial sphere is a matter of no serious consequence. When the same methods make a victorious invasion of the intellectual realm, it is difficult to regard the phenomenon with the same complacency. (Watson & McDougall, 1929, p. 95)

Watson, of course, claimed that to accept McDougall's brand of psychology was to reject all advances that had occurred in psychology in about the last 25 years.

A vote taken after the debate showed McDougall to be the narrow victor. He believed that if the women in the audience had not voted almost unanimously for Watson, his margin of victory would have been much greater:

The vote of the audience taken by sections after the Washington debate showed a small majority against Dr. Watson. But when account is taken of the amusing fact that the considerable number of women students from the University voted almost unanimously for Dr. Watson and his Behaviorism, the vote may be regarded as an overwhelming verdict of sober good sense against him from a representative American gathering. (Watson & McDougall, 1929, p. 87)

Neither Watson's nor McDougall's position has survived intact. For the moment, however, the student of psychology is more likely to know about Watson than about McDougall. Whether this remains the case, only time will tell.

SUMMARY

Several years before Watson's formal founding of the school of behaviorism, many psychologists with strong leanings toward behaviorism insisted that psychology be defined as the science of behavior. Thorndike, for example, could almost as easily be labeled a behaviorist as a functionalist. Also, several Russians whom Sechenov had influenced were calling for a completely objective psychology devoid of metaphysical concepts. It was Sechenov's discovery of inhibitory processes in the brain that allowed him to believe that all behavior, including that of humans, could be explained in terms of reflexes. It was during his research on digestion that Pavlov discovered "psychic reflexes" (conditioned reflexes), but he resisted studying them because of their apparent subjective nature. Under the influence of Sechenov, however, he was finally convinced that conditioned reflexes could be studied using the objective techniques of physiology. Pavlov saw all behavior, whether learned or innate, as reflexive. Innate associations between unconditioned stimuli (USs) and unconditioned responses (URs) were soon supplemented by learned associations between conditioned stimuli (CSs) and conditioned responses (CRs). Pavlov believed that some stimuli elicit excitation in the brain and other stimuli elicit inhibition. The patterns of the points of excitation and inhibition on the cortex at any given moment was called the cortical mosaic, and it was this mosaic that determined an organism's behavior. If a conditioned stimulus that was previously associated with an unconditioned stimulus is now presented without the unconditioned stimulus, extinction occurs. The facts that spontaneous recovery and disinhibition occur indicate that extinction is due to inhibition. If stimuli that elicit excitation, on the one hand, and inhibition, on the other, are made increasingly similar, experimental neurosis results. An organism's susceptibility to experimental neurosis is determined by the type of nervous system that it possesses. According to Pavlov, conditioned stimuli act as signals announcing the occurrence of biologically significant events; he called such stimuli the first-signal system. An example is when the sight of a flame announces the possibility of a painful experience unless appropriate behavior is taken. Language allows symbols (words) to provide the same function as conditioned stimuli, such as when the word *fire* elicits defensive behavior. Pavlov called the words that symbolize physical events the second-signal system. Pavlov believed that his work on conditioned and unconditioned reflexes furnished an objective explanation for the associationism that philosophers had been discussing for centuries.

Bechterev was a reflexologist who sought a completely objective psychology. Unlike Pavlov, who studied internal reflexes such as salivation, Bechterev studied overt behavior. Bechterev believed that his technique was superior to Pavlov's because it required no operation, it could be used easily on humans, it minimized unwanted reactions from the subject, overt behavior could be easily measured, and satiation was not a problem. The type of reflexive behavior later studied by U.S. behaviorists was more like that studied by Bechterev than by Pavlov.

Several factors molded Watson's behavioristic outlook. First, many of the functionalists at Chicago and elsewhere were studying behavior directly, without the use of introspection. Second, Loeb had shown that some of the behavior of simple organisms and plants was tropistic (i.e., an automatic reaction to environmental conditions). Third, animal research that related behavior to various experimental manipulations was becoming very popular. In fact, before his founding of the school of behaviorism, Watson was a nationally recognized expert on the white rat. Watson began to formulate his behavioristic ideas as early as 1902, and in 1904 he shared them with Angell, whose reaction was negative. Watson first publicly stated his behavioristic views at a colloquium at Yale in 1908. The response was again negative. In 1913 Watson gave a lecture entitled "Psychology as the Behaviorist Views It" at Columbia University. The publication of this lecture in the *Psychological Review* in 1913 marks the formal beginning of the school of behaviorism. In 1920 scandal essentially ended Watson's career as a professional psychologist, although afterward he published articles in popular magazines, gave radio talks, and revised some of his earlier works.

Watson found support for his position in Russian objective psychology and eventually made conditioning the cornerstone of his stimulus–response psychology. For Watson, the goal of psychology was to predict and control behavior by determining how behavior was related to environmental events. Watson even viewed thinking as a form of behavior—behavior consisting of minute movements of the tongue and larynx. Early in Watson's theorizing, instincts played a prominent role in explaining human behavior. Later, Watson said that humans possessed instincts but that learned behavior soon replaced instinctive behavior. Watson's final position on instincts was that they had no influence on human behavior. He did say, however, that a person's physical structure was inherited and that the interaction between structure and environmental experience determined many personality characteristics. Also, the emotions of fear, rage, and love were inherited, and experience greatly expanded the stimuli that elicited these emotions. The experiment with Albert showed the process by which previously neutral stimuli could come to elicit fear. Later, along with Mary Cover Jones, Watson showed how fear could become disassociated from a stimulus.

Watson advised parents not to pamper children but to treat them as small adults, and he urged that open, honest, and objective sex education be given to children. Watson accepted only two principles of learning: contiguity and frequency. That is, the more often two or more events were experienced together, the stronger the association between those events became. On the mind–body problem, Watson's final position was that of a physical monist. The two major influences that Watson had on psychology were (1) to change its goals from the description and understanding of consciousness to the prediction and control of behavior and (2) to change its subject matter from consciousness to overt behavior. Those psychologists who, like Watson, rejected internal events such as consciousness as causes of behavior were called radical behaviorists. Those who accepted internal events such as consciousness as possible causes of behavior, but insisted that any theories about unobservable causes of behavior be verified by studying overt behavior, were called methodological behaviorists.

Even in Watson's time, his was not the only type of behaviorism. One of Watson's most formidable adversaries was McDougall, who agreed with Watson that psychology should be the science of behavior but thought that purposive behavior should be emphasized. Although McDougall defined psychology as the science of behavior, he did not deny the importance of mental events, and he believed that they could be studied through their influence on behavior. In other words, McDougall was a methodological behaviorist. Whereas Watson had concluded that instincts played no role in human behavior, McDougall made instincts the cornerstone of his theory. For McDougall, an instinct was an innate disposition that when active caused a person to attend to a certain class of events, to feel emotional excitement when perceiving those events, and to act relative to those events in such a way as to satisfy the instinctual need. When the instinctual need was satisfied, the whole chain of events terminated. Thus, for McDougall, instincts and purposive behavior went hand-in-hand. McDougall believed that the reason humans learned habits was that they satisfied instinctual needs. In the famous debate between Watson and McDougall, McDougall was narrowly declared the winner.

DISCUSSION QUESTIONS

1. Make the case that prior to Watson's formulations, behaviorism was very much "in the air" in the United States.

2. Summarize Sechenov's argument that thoughts could not cause behavior.

3. What was the significance of the concept of inhibition in Sechenov's explanation of behavior?

4. How, according to Sechenov, should psychological phenomena be studied?

5. What were the circumstances under which Pavlov discovered the conditioned reflex, and why did he initially resist studying it?

6. What did Pavlov mean by a cortical mosaic, and how was that mosaic thought to be causally related to behavior?

7. What observations led Pavlov to conclude that extinction was caused by inhibition?

8. How did Pavlov create experimental neurosis in his research animals, and how did he explain differential susceptibility to experimental neurosis?

9. First distinguish between the first- and second-signal systems and then explain how those systems facilitate adaptation to the environment.

10. How did Pavlov view the relationship between his work and philosophical associationism?

11. Summarize Bechterev's reflexology. Why did Bechterev believe that he was the first behaviorist?

12. How did Bechterev's method of studying conditioned reflexes differ from Pavlov's? According to Bechterev, what advantages did his method have over Pavlov's?

13. Describe the major experiences that steered Watson toward behaviorism.

14. According to Watson, what was the goal of psychology? How did this differ from psychology's traditional goal?

15. Summarize Watson's explanation of thinking.

16. What was Watson's final position on the role of instinct in human behavior?

17. Employing the notion of structure, explain why Watson believed that inheritance could influence personality.

18. Summarize Watson's views on emotion. What emotions did Watson think were innate? How did emotions become attached to various stimuli or events? What research did Watson perform to validate his views?

19. Describe the procedure that Watson and Mary Cover Jones used to extinguish Peter's fear of rabbits.

20. Summarize the advice that Watson and Watson gave on child rearing.

21. How did Watson explain learning?

22. What was Watson's final position on the mind–body problem?

23. Distinguish between radical and methodological behaviorism.

24. Summarize McDougall's version of psychology. Why can his approach to psychology be called behavioristic? What type of behavior did he study, and what did he assume to be the cause of that behavior?

25. For McDougall, what were the characteristics of purposive behavior?

26. For McDougall, what were the three components of an instinct?

27. In their famous debate, what were the important points of disagreement between Watson and McDougall? If the debate were held today, for whom would you vote? Why?

SUGGESTIONS FOR FURTHER READING

Buckley, K. W. (1989). *Mechanical man: John Broadus Watson and the beginnings of behaviorism.* New York: Guilford Press.

Buckley, a historian, draws on previously unpublished correspondence, many interviews, and a search of 30 archival collections to produce this biography of Watson. Watson's career and the development of behaviorism are placed within the context of the U.S. social and cultural history of Watson's time. Buckley contends that the rise in the popularity of behaviorism reflected a growing national interest in efficiency and order. The book contains several interesting photographs depicting Watson and the events and people in his life from his infancy to his old age.

Cohen, D. (1979). *J. B. Watson: The founder of behaviourism.* London: Routledge and Kegan Paul.

Cohen gives an interesting account of the major events in Watson's life from his early years in South Carolina to his rise and fall as one of the most influential psychologists in psychology's history.

Harris, B. (1979). Whatever happened to little Albert? *American Psychologist, 34*, 151–160.

Harris points out that substantial discrepancies exist between the actual methods and findings of Watson and Rayner's experiment with Albert and what has been reported. Because the discrepancies are so large and persistent, Harris offers them as an example of historical myth. In fact, Harris observes that no aspect of the original study has escaped misrepresentation.

Jones, R. A. (1987). Psychology, history, and the press: The case of William McDougall and the *New York Times. American Psychologist, 42*, 931–940.

After establishing a reputation as an outstanding psychologist in England, McDougall arrived in the United States in 1920 to assume the position of chairman of the psychology department at Harvard. Almost immediately he was immersed in controversy, and he felt increasingly out of place, misunderstood, and even an object of contempt. Jones reviews the possible reasons for McDougall's plight.

O'Donnell, J. M. (1985). *The origins of behaviorism: American psychology, 1870–1920.* New York: New York University Press.

O'Donnell argues that the shift in psychology's emphasis from human consciousness to human behavior did not result because of cumulative knowledge. Rather, the shift reflected changes in philosophy, science, institutions of higher learning, and culture. Major among the reasons for the shift is the fact that competition for institutional resources encourages researchers to adopt conceptions similar to those of patrons and presidents of colleges and universities. As the prediction, control, and general improvement of human behavior became important social goals, the psychology compatible with those goals gained prominence, and resources were available for its support. Thus, according to O'Donnell, behaviorism eventually displaced the psychology of consciousness primarily because of social pressures, economic adaptation, and economic competition. (Available in paperback.)

Samelson, F. (1981). Struggle for scientific authority: The reception of Watson's behaviorism, 1913–1920. *Journal of the History of the Behavioral Sciences, 17*, 399–425.

Samelson examines the contention that there was a Kuhnian paradigm shift in psychology following publication of Watson's 1913 article "Psychology as the Behaviorist Views It" and finds little support for it. Rather, the evidence shows the gradual acceptance of Watsonian tenets over a period of several years. Gradually, however, behaviorism did become influential, and, almost imperceptibly, the accepted subject matter of psychology switched from immediate, conscious experience to overt behavior.

Watson, J. B. (1913). Psychology as the behaviorist views it. *Psychological Review, 20,* 158–177.
This article marks the founding of behaviorism. Watson declares that psychology as the behaviorist views it is a branch of natural science, the goal of which is the prediction and control of behavior. Behaviorism ac-

cepts no dividing line between human and nonhuman animals, and introspection is not one of its methods because the nature of consciousness is not one of its concerns. Fifty years of searching for the elements, operations, and even the functions of consciousness has led nowhere; it is time therefore to give up the search. Behavior, not consciousness, should be the subject matter of psychology.

GLOSSARY

Association reflex Bechterev's term for what Pavlov called a conditioned reflex.

Bechterev, Vladimir M. (1857–1927) Like Pavlov, looked upon all human behavior as reflexive. However, Bechterev studied skeletal reflexes rather than the glandular reflexes that Pavlov studied.

Behaviorism The school of psychology, founded by Watson, that insisted that behavior be psychology's subject matter and that psychology's goal be the prediction and control of behavior.

Behavior therapy The use of learning principles in treating behavioral or emotional problems.

Conditioned reflex A learned reflex.

Conditioned response (CR) A response elicited by a conditioned stimulus.

Conditioned stimulus (CS) A previously biologically neutral stimulus that through experience comes to elicit a certain response.

Cortical mosaic According to Pavlov, the pattern of points of excitation and inhibition that characterizes the cortex at any given moment.

Disinhibition The inhibition of an inhibitory process. Disinhibition is demonstrated when, after extinction, a loud noise causes the conditioned response to reappear.

Excitation According to Pavlov, brain activity that leads to overt behavior of some type.

Experimental neurosis The neurotic behavior that Pavlov created in some of his laboratory animals by bringing excitatory and inhibitory tendencies into conflict.

Extinction The elimination or reduction of a conditioned response that results when a conditioned stimulus is presented but is not followed by the unconditioned stimulus.

First-signal system Those objects or events that become signals (CSs) for the occurrence of biologically significant events, such as when a tone signals the eventuality of food.

Inhibition The reduction or cessation of activity caused by stimulation, such as when extinction causes a conditioned stimulus to inhibit a conditioned response. It was Sechenov's discovery of inhibitory mechanisms in the brain that led him to believe that all human behavior could be explained in terms of brain physiology.

Law of recency Watson's observation that typically it is the "correct" response that terminates a learning trial

and it is this final or most recent response that will be repeated when the organism is next placed in that learning situation.

McDougall, William (1871–1938) Pursued a type of behaviorism very different from Watson's. McDougall's behaviorism emphasized purposive and instinctive behavior.

Methodological behaviorism The version of behaviorism that accepts the contention that overt behavior should be psychology's subject matter but is willing to speculate about internal causes of behavior, such as various mental and physiological states.

Pavlov, Ivan Petrovitch (1849–1936) Shared Sechenov's goal of creating a totally objective psychology. Pavlov focused his study on the conditioned and unconditioned stimuli that controlled behavior and on the physiological processes that they initiated. For Pavlov, all human behavior was reflexive.

Radical behaviorism The version of behaviorism that claims all causes of behavior are to be found outside the organism and therefore explanations of behavior in terms of physiological or mental events should be avoided.

Radical environmentalism The belief that most, if not all, human attributes are a product of experience.

Reflexology The term Bechterev used to describe his approach to studying humans. Because he emphasized the study of the relationship between environmental events and overt behavior, he can be considered one of the earliest behaviorists, if not the earliest.

Sechenov, Ivan M. (1829–1905) The father of Russian objective psychology. Sechenov sought to explain all human behavior in terms of stimuli and physiological mechanisms without recourse to metaphysical speculation of any type.

Second-signal system The symbols of objects or events that signal the occurrence of biologically significant events. Seeing fire and withdrawing from it would exemplify the first-signal system, but escaping in response to hearing the word *fire* exemplifies the second-signal system.

Spontaneous recovery The reappearance of a conditioned response after a delay following extinction.

Tropism The automatic orienting response that Loeb studied in plants and animals.

Unconditioned reflex An unlearned reflex.

Unconditioned response (UR) An innate response elicited by the unconditioned stimulus that is naturally associated with it.

Unconditioned stimulus (US) A stimulus that elicits an unconditioned response.

Watson, John Broadus (1878–1958) The founder of behaviorism. Watson saw as psychology's goal the prediction and control of behavior. In his final position, he denied the existence of mental events and concluded that instincts played no role in human behavior; experience molded the basic emotions and the physical structure we were born with into our personality. Watson's theory of learning consisted of the laws of contiguity and frequency. On the mind–body problem, Watson ended up as a physical monist, believing that thought was nothing but implicit muscle movement.

CHAPTER 13

Neobehaviorism

POSITIVISM

As we saw in chapter 5, Auguste Comte insisted that one could obtain valid information about the world only by adopting a radical empiricism. Metaphysical speculation was to be avoided because it employed unobservable entities. Within psychology, all that can be known with certainty about people is how they behave, and therefore any attempt to understand how the "mind" functions using introspection was, according to Comte, silly. Although the mind could not be investigated objectively, the *products* of the mind could be because they manifest themselves in behavior. According to Comte, individual and group behavior could and should be studied scientifically; he coined the term *sociology* to describe such a study.

Several years after Comte, the distinguished German physicist Ernst Mach argued for another type of **positivism**. In his *Contributions to the Analysis of Sensations* (1886/1914), Mach, agreeing with such British empiricists as Berkeley and Hume, argued that all we can be certain of is our sensations. Sensations, then, form the ultimate subject matter for all sciences, including physics and psychology. For Mach, introspection was essential for all sciences because it was the only method by which sensations could be analyzed. However, one must not speculate about what exists beyond sensations nor attempt to determine their ultimate meaning. To do so is to enter the forbidden realm of metaphysical speculation. What a careful analysis of sensations can do is determine how they are correlated. Knowing which sensations tend to go together allows prediction, which, in turn, allows

better adaptation to the environment. For Mach then, a strong, pragmatic reason existed for the systematic study of sensations. For both Comte and Mach, scientific laws were statements that summarized experiences. Both sought, above all, to avoid metaphysical speculation, and both were radical empiricists. Remember that an empiricist believes that all knowledge comes from experience; Comte emphasized experiences that could be shared publicly, and Mach emphasized private experience. Both argued for a close-to-the-data approach that avoided theorizing about what was observed. Echoing Francis Bacon, both believed that theorizing most likely introduced error into science. Thus, the best way to avoid error is to avoid theorizing.

John Watson and the Russian physiologists were positivists (although Pavlov did engage in considerable speculation concerning brain physiology). All emphasized objective data and avoided or minimized theoretical speculation. Watson's goals for psychology of predicting and controlling behavior were very much in accordance with positivistic philosophy. However, in being positivistic, his system lacked the predictive ability that Watson himself felt was so important. His research often generated facts that appeared to have no relationship among themselves.

LOGICAL POSITIVISM

By the early 20th century, the Comtean and Machian goal of having sciences deal only with that which is directly observable was clearly unrealistic. Physicists and chemists were finding such theoretical concepts as gravity, atom, force, electron, and mass indispensable, although none of these entities could be observed directly. The problem was to find a way for science to use theory without encountering the dangers inherent in metaphysical speculation. The solution was provided by **logical positivism**. Logical positivism divided science into two major parts: the empirical and the theoretical. In other words, it wedded empiricism and rationalism. The **observational terms** of science referred to empirical events, and the **theoretical terms** attempted to explain that which was observed. By accepting theory as part of science, the logical positivists in no way reduced the importance of empirical observation. In fact, the ultimate authority for the logical positivist was empirical observation, and theories were considered useful only if they helped explain what was observed.

Logical positivism was the name given to the view of science that was developed by a small group of philosophers in Vienna (the "Vienna circle") around 1924. These philosophers took the older positivism of Comte and Mach and combined it with the rigors of formal logic. For them, abstract theoretical terms were allowed only if such terms could be logically tied to empirical observations. As we will see, logical positivism had a powerful influence on psychology. It allowed much more complex forms of behaviorism to emerge because it allowed theorizing without sacrificing objectivity. The result was that psychology entered into what Koch (1959) has called the "age of theory" (from about 1930 to about 1950). It was Herbert Feigl, a member of the "Vienna circle," who both named logical positivism and did the most to bring it to the attention of U.S. psychologists. Among U.S. psychologists, S. S. Stevens (1935a, b) was among the first to believe that if psychology followed the dictates of logical positivism, which he called "the science of science," it could at last be a science on par with physics. For this to happen, psychology would need to adhere to the principles of operationism, to which we turn next.

OPERATIONISM

In 1927 the Harvard physicist Percy W. Bridgman (1892–1961) published *The Logic of Modern Physics*, in which he proposed that every abstract concept in physics be defined in terms of the procedures used to measure the concept. He called such a definition an **operational definition**. Thus, concepts such as force and energy would be defined in terms of the operations or procedures followed in determining the quantity of force or energy present. In other words, operational definitions tied theoretical terms to observable phenomena. In this way, there could be no ambiguity about the definition of the theoretical term. The insistence that all abstract scientific terms be operationally defined was called **operationism**. Bridgman's ideas were very much in accord with what the logical positivists were saying at about the same time.

Along with logical positivism, operationism took hold in psychology almost immediately. Operational definitions could be used to convert theoretical terms like *drive, learning, anxiety,* and *intelligence* into empirical events and thus strip them of their metaphysical connotations. Such an approach was clearly in accordance with psychology's new emphasis on behavior. For example, learning could be operationally defined as making x number of successive correct turns in a T-maze, and anxiety and intelligence could be operationally defined as scores on appropriate tests. Such definitions were entirely in terms of publicly observable behavior; they had no excess "mentalistic" meaning. Most psychologists soon agreed with the logical positivists that if a concept could not be operationally defined, it was scientifically meaningless.

Unlike positivism, logical positivism had no aversion to theory. In fact, one primary goal of logical positivism was to show how science could be theoretical without sacrificing objectivity. Once operationally defined, concepts could be related to each other in complex ways, such as the statements $F = MA$ (force equals mass times acceleration) and $E = mc^2$ (energy equals mass times a constant squared). No matter how complex, however, it is the job of a scientific theory to make statements about empirical events. Because a scientific theory was evaluated in terms of the accuracy of its predictions, it was seen as self-correcting. If the deductions from a theory were experimentally confirmed, it gained strength; if its deductions were found to be incorrect, the theory diminished in strength. In the latter case, the theory had to be revised or abandoned. No matter how complex a theory became, its ultimate function was to make accurate predictions about empirical events.

By the late 1930s, logical positivism dominated U.S. experimental psychology.

PHYSICALISM

One outcome of the logical positivism movement was that all sciences were viewed as essentially the same. Because they all followed the same principles, made the same assumptions, and attempted to explain empirical observations, why should they not use the same terminology? It was suggested that a database language be created in which all terms would be defined in reference to publicly observable, physical objects and events. The push for unification of and a common vocabulary among the sciences (including psychology) was called **physicalism**. The proposal that all scientific propositions refer to physical things had profound implications for psychology:

> Innocent as this assertion about language may appear, it is charged with far-reaching implications for psychology. In fact, the examples used to illustrate Physicalism make it appear that the doctrine was aimed directly against psychology—at least against the kind peddled by philosophers. . . . All sentences purporting to deal with psychical states are translatable into sentences in the physical language. Two distinctly separate languages to describe physics and psychology are therefore not necessary. . . . It is the Logical Positivist's way of saying that psychology must be operational and behavioristic. (Stevens, 1951, pp. 39–40)

The "unity of science" movement and physicalism went hand-in-hand:

How we get from Physicalism to the thesis of the *Unity of science* is obvious indeed. If every sentence can be translated into the physical language, then this language is an all-inclusive language—a universal language of science. And if the esoteric jargons of all the separate sciences can, upon demand, be reduced to a single coherent language, then all science possesses a fundamental logical unity. (Stevens, 1951, p. 40)

The science that was proposed as the model for this "unified science" was physics.

NEOBEHAVIORISM

Neobehaviorism resulted when behaviorism was combined with logical positivism: "It is only a slight caricature to represent neobehaviorism as the product of the remarriage of psychology, in the guise of behaviorism, and philosophy, in the guise of logical positivism" (Toulmin & Leary, 1985, p. 603). Logical positivism made many forms of behaviorism possible: "Objectivism in data collection was one thing; agreement about specific modes of objectivism, and about the theoretical implications of 'objective' data, was something else" (Toulmin & Leary, 1985, p. 603). Thus, as we will see, a number of versions of behaviorism emerged, all following, more or less, the tenets of logical positivism and all claiming scientific and philosophical respectability.

Although there were major differences among the neobehaviorists, they all tended to believe that

1. If theory was used, it must be used in ways demanded by logical positivism.

2. All theoretical terms must be operationally defined.

3. Nonhuman animals should be used as research subjects for two reasons: (a) Relevant variables are easier to control than they are for human subjects. (b) Perceptual and learning processes occurring in nonhuman animals differ only in degree from those processes in humans; therefore, the informa-

tion gained from nonhuman animals can be generalized to humans.

4. The learning process is of prime importance because it is the primary mechanism by which organisms adjust to changing environments.

Not all psychologists followed the new approach. During the period from about 1930 to about 1950, psychoanalysis was becoming increasingly important in U.S. psychology as was Gestalt psychology (see chapter 14), and psychologists embracing these viewpoints saw little need to follow the dictates of logical positivism. Except for these exceptions and a few others, however, neobehaviorism dominated the period.

Edward Tolman was among the first to expand behaviorism by employing the tenets of logical positivism, and it is to his version of neobehaviorism that we turn next.

Edward Chace Tolman

EDWARD CHACE TOLMAN

Biographical Sketch

Edward Chace Tolman (1886–1959) was born in Newton, Massachusetts, the son of a businessman who was a member of the first graduating class of the Massachusetts Institute of Technology (MIT) and a member of its board of trustees. The father, encouraged by his wife who was raised in the Quaker religion, had a strong interest in social reform. Both sons, Edward and his older brother Richard, earned their undergraduate degrees in experimental and theoretical chemistry at MIT. Richard went on to become a prominent physicist after earning his doctorate at MIT. Edward's interests began to turn toward philosophy and psychology after taking summer school courses from the Harvard philosopher Ralph Barton Perry (1876–1957) and the Harvard psychologist Robert Yerkes; most influential, however, was the reading of James's *Principles*. At this time, psychology was dominated by Titchener and James, and psy-

chology was still defined as the study of conscious experience, a fact that bothered Tolman:

> The definition of psychology as the examination and analysis of private conscious contents has been something of a logical sticker. For how *can* one build up a science upon elements which, by very definition, are said to be private and noncommunicable? (1922, p. 44)

Tolman's concern was put to rest in the course he took from Yerkes in which J. B. Watson's *Behavior: An Introduction to Comparative Psychology* (1914) was used as the text:

> This worry about introspection is perhaps one reason why my introduction in Yerkes' courses to Watson behaviorism came as a tremendous stimulus and relief. If objective measurement of behavior and not introspection was the true method of psychology I didn't have to worry any longer. (1952, p. 326)

In 1911 Tolman decided to pursue graduate work in philosophy and psychology at Harvard; once enrolled, his interest turned increasingly to psychology. After a year of study, Tolman decided to improve his German by spending a summer in Germany. While in Germany, Tolman studied with the young Gestalt psychologist Kurt Koffka, who we meet in the next chapter. Although Gestalt psychology did not impress Tolman at the time, it greatly influenced his later theorizing. Upon returning to Harvard, Tolman studied the learning of nonsense material under the supervision of Hugo Münsterberg, and his doctoral dissertation was on retroactive inhibition (Tolman, 1917).

After attaining his doctorate from Harvard in 1915, Tolman accepted an appointment at Northwestern University. Although he became a compulsive researcher, he confessed to being "self-conscious and inarticulate" as a teacher and frightened of his classes. Also, at about the time that the United States entered the First World War, he wrote an essay expressing his pacifism. In 1918 Tolman was dismissed for "lack of teaching success," but more than likely his pacifism contributed to his dismissal. From Northwestern he went to the University of California at Berkeley, where he remained almost without interruption for the rest of his career. As we have seen, Tolman was raised in a Quaker home, and pacifism was a constant theme throughout his life. He wrote a short book entitled *Drives Toward War* (1942) to explain, from a psychoanalytic viewpoint, the human motives responsible for warfare. In the preface of that book, he stated his reasons for writing it:

> As an American, a college professor, and one brought up in the pacifist tradition, I am intensely biased against war. It is for me stupid, interrupting, unnecessary, and unimaginably horrible. I write this essay within that frame of reference. In short, I am driven to discuss the psychology of war and its possible abolition because I want intensely to get rid of it. (1942, p. xi)

By the time the book came out, however, the United States was already involved in the Second World War. The brutality of the war overcame even Tolman's strong pacifism, and after receiving the approval of his brother Richard, he served for two years in the Office of Strategic Services (1944–1945).

After the war, Tolman's social conscience was tested once again. The University of California began to require its faculty members to sign a loyalty oath, and Tolman led a group of faculty members who would rather resign than sign it. They saw the requirement as an infringement of their civil liberties and academic freedom. Tolman was suspended from his duties at California and taught for awhile at the University of Chicago and Harvard University. Finally, the courts agreed with Tolman, and he was reinstated at the University of California. In 1959, upon his retirement and shortly before his death, the regents of the university symbolically admitted that Tolman's position had been morally correct by awarding him an honorary doctorate.

Tolman was a kind, shy, honest person who inspired affection and admiration from his students and colleagues. Although he was always willing to engage in intellectual dispute, he never took himself or his work too seriously. In the final year of his life, Tolman reflected on his theoretical contributions:

> [My theory] may well not stand up to any final canons of scientific procedure. But I do not much care. I have liked to think about psychology in ways that have proved congenial to me. Since all the sciences, and especially psychology, are still immersed in such tremendous realms of the uncertain and the unknown, the best that any individual scientist, especially any psychologist, can do seems to be to follow his own gleam and his own bent, however inadequate they may be. In fact, I suppose that actually this is what we all do. In the end, the only sure criterion is to have fun. And I have had fun. (1959, p. 159)

Purposive Behaviorism

In the early 1920s, there were two dominant explanations of learning: Watson's explanation in terms of the associative principles of contiguity, frequency, and recency and Thorndike's, which emphasized the law of effect. Tolman explained why he could accept neither:

> It was Watson's denial of the law of effect and his emphasis on frequency and recency as the prime determiners of animal learning which first attracted our attention. In this we were on Watson's side. But we got ourselves—or at least I got myself—into a sort of in-between position. On the one hand I sided with Watson in not liking the law of effect. But, on the other hand, I also did not like Watson's over-simplified notions of stimulus and response . . . according to Thorndike an animal learned, not because it achieved a wanted goal by a certain series of responses, but merely because a quite irrelevant "pleasantness" or "unpleasantness" was, so to speak, shot at it, as from a squirt gun, after it had reached the given goal box or goal into the given *cul de sac.* (1952, p. 329)

Tolman (perhaps incorrectly) referred to Watson's psychology as "twitchism" because he felt it concentrated on isolated responses to specific stimuli. Watson contended that even the most complex human behavior could be explained in terms of S–R reflexes. Tolman referred to such reflexes as **molecular behavior.** Instead of taking as his subject matter these "twitches," Tolman decided to study **purposive behavior.** Although Tolman's approach differed from Watson's in several important ways, Tolman was still a behaviorist and was completely opposed to introspection and metaphysical explanations. In other words, Tolman agreed with Watson that behavior should be psychology's subject matter, but Tolman believed that Watson was focusing on the wrong type of behavior. The question was how Tolman could employ a mentalistic term like *purpose* and still remain a behaviorist.

While at Harvard, Tolman learned from two of his professors, Edwin B. Holt and Ralph Barton Perry, that the purposive aspects of behavior could be studied without sacrificing scientific objectivity. This was done by seeing purpose *in* the behavior itself and not inferring purpose *from* the behavior. Tolman accepted this contention and believed that it pointed to a major dis-

tinction between his view of purpose and that of McDougall: "The fundamental difference between [McDougall] and us arises in that he, being a 'mentalist,' merely *infers* purpose from these aspects of behavior; whereas we, being behaviorists, *identify* purpose with such aspects" (1925, p. 37). Tolman would later change his position and use the terms *purpose* and *cognition* more in accordance with the mentalistic tradition as actual determinants of behavior. Tolman never believed, however, that using concepts like purpose and cognition violated the tenets of behaviorism. (For a discussion of Tolman's use of mentalistic terms and how that use changed during his career, see L. D. Smith, 1982.)

Tolman called purposive behavior **molar behavior** to contrast it with molecular behavior. Because Tolman chose to study molar behavior, his position is often referred to as **purposive behaviorism.** In his major work, Tolman explained how he used mentalistic terminology within a behavioristic context:

> It must . . . be emphasized that purposes and cognitions which are thus immediately, immanently, in behavior are wholly objective as to definition. They are defined by characters and relationships which we observe out there in the behavior. We, the observers, watch the behavior of the rat, the cat, or the man, and note its character as a getting to such and such by means of such and such a selected pattern of commerces-with. It is we, the independent neutral observers, who note these perfectly objective characters as immanent in the behavior and have happened to choose the terms *purpose* and *cognition* as generic names for such characters. (1932, pp. 12–13)

Tolman gave examples of what he called purposive (molar) behavior:

> A rat running a maze; a cat getting out of a puzzle box; a man driving home to dinner; a child hiding from a stranger; a woman doing her washing or gossiping over the telephone; a pupil marking a mental-test sheet; a psychologist reciting a list of nonsense syllables; my friend and I telling one another our thoughts and feelings—*these are behaviors (Qua Molar).* And it must be noted that in mentioning no one

of them have we referred to, or, we blush to confess it, for the most part even known, what were the exact muscles and glands, sensory nerves, and motor nerves involved. For these responses somehow had other sufficiently identifying properties of their own. (1932, p. 8)

Tolman's Use of Rats

Tolman did not engage in any animal research as a graduate student at Harvard nor as an instructor at Northwestern University. When he arrived at the University of California, he was asked to suggest a new course to teach and, remembering fondly his course with Yerkes, chose to teach comparative psychology. It was teaching this course that stimulated Tolman's interests in behaviorism and in the rat as an experimental subject. He saw the use of rats as a way of guarding against even the possibility of indirect introspection that could occur if humans were used as experimental subjects. Tolman developed such a fondness for rats that he dedicated his *Purposive Behavior* (1932) to the white rat, and in 1945 he said,

> Let it be noted that rats live in cages; they do not go on binges the night before one has planned an experiment; they do not kill each other off in wars; they do not invent engines of destruction, and if they did, they would not be so inept about controlling such engines; they do not go in for either class conflicts or race conflicts; they avoid politics, economics, and papers on psychology. They are marvelous, pure, and delightful. (p. 166)

About what could be learned by studying rats, Tolman said,

> I believe that everything important in psychology (except perhaps such matters as the building up of a super-ego, that is, everything save such matters as involve society and words) can be investigated in essence through the continued experimental and theoretical analysis of the determiners of rat behavior at a choice-point in a maze. Herein I believe I agree with Professor Hull and also with Professor Thorndike. (1938, p. 34)

The Use of Intervening Variables

Tolman was not consistent in using mentalistic concepts as only descriptions of behavior. By 1925 he was referring to purpose and cognition both as descriptions and determinants of behavior. L. D. Smith notes Tolman's vacillation:

> Within a single paragraph of *Purposive Behavior*, Tolman described purposes and cognitions on the one hand as "immanent" in behavior, "inlying," "immediate," and "discovered" by observers, and on the other hand as "determinants" and "causes" of behavior which are "invented" or "inferred" by observers. (1982, p. 462)

In the following quotation, Tolman appeared to believe that purposes were in the organism and were causally related to its behavior:

> Our doctrine . . . is that behavior (except in the case of the simplest reflexes) is not governed by simple one to one stimulus–response connections. It is governed by more or less complicated sets of patterns of adjustment which get set up within the organism. And in so far as these sets of adjustments cause only those acts to persist and to get learned which end in getting the organism to (or from) specific ends, these sets or adjustments constitute purposes. (1928, p. 526)

Increasingly, Tolman came to believe that cognitive processes really existed and were influential in determining behavior. In 1938 he decided how he would proceed: "I, in my future work, intend to go ahead imagining how, *if I were a rat*, I would behave" (p. 24). Clearly, Tolman was now embracing mentalism, and yet he still felt strongly about remaining a behaviorist. For Tolman, the solution to the dilemma was to treat cognitive events as **intervening variables**, that is, variables that intervened between environmental events and behavior. Following logical positivism, Tolman painstakingly tied all his intervening variables to observable behavior. In other words, he operationally defined all his theoretical terms. Tolman's final position was to regard purpose and cognition as theoretical constructs that could be used to describe, predict, and explain behavior.

By introducing the use of intervening variables, Tolman brought abstract scientific theory into psychology. It was clear that environmental events influenced behavior; the problem was to understand *why* they did. One could remain entirely descriptive and simply note what organisms did in certain situations, but for Tolman this was unsatisfactory. The following is a simplified diagram of Tolman's approach:

Independent Variables
(Environmental Events)
↓
Intervening Variables
(Theoretical Concepts)
↓
Dependent Variables
(Behavior)

Thus, for Tolman, environmental experience gave rise to internal, unobservable events, which, in turn, caused behavior. To account fully for the behavior, one had to know both the environmental events *and* the internal (or intervening) events that they initiated. The most important intervening variables that Tolman postulated were cognitive or mental in nature. Tolman, then, was a methodological rather than a radical behaviorist. What made Tolman a different type of mentalist was his insistence that his intervening variables, even those that were presumed to be mental, be operationally defined—that is, tied to observable events.

Hypotheses, expectancies, beliefs, and cognitive maps. Although Tolman used several intervening variables, we will discuss only those related to the development of a cognitive map. Everyone knows that a rat learns to solve a maze; the question is How does it do so? Tolman's explanation was mentalistic. As an example, when an animal is first placed in the start box of a T-maze, the experience is entirely new, and therefore the animal can use no information from prior experience. As the animal runs the maze, it sometimes turns right at the choice point and sometimes left. Let us say that the experimenter has arranged the situation so that turning left is reinforced with food. At some point, the animal

formulates a weak **hypothesis** that turning one way leads to food and turning another way does not. In the early stages of hypothesis formation, the animal may pause at the choice point as if to "ponder" the alternatives. Tolman referred to this apparent pondering as **vicarious trial and error** because, instead of behaving overtly in a trial-and-error fashion, the animal appeared to be engaged in mental trial and error. If the early hypothesis "if I turn left, I will find food" is confirmed, the animal will develop the **expectancy** "when I turn left, I will find food." If the expectancy is consistently confirmed, the animal will develop the **belief** "every time I turn left in this situation, I will find food." Through this process, a cognitive map of this situation develops. A **cognitive map** is an awareness of all possibilities in a situation. For example, if I leave the start box, I will find the choice point; if I turn left at the choice point, I will find food; if I turn right, I will not; and so on.

For Tolman, hypotheses, expectations, beliefs, and, finally, a cognitive map intervened between experience and behavior. Rather than just describing an organism's behavior, these intervening variables were thought to explain it. Tolman was careful, however, to test his theoretical assumptions through experimentation. Tolman's research program was one of the most creative any psychologist has ever devised (for details, see Hergenhahn, 1988).

Position on Reinforcement

Tolman rejected Watson's and Thorndike's explanations of learning. In other words, he did not believe that learning was an automatic process based on contiguity and frequency nor that it resulted from reinforcement (e.g., a pleasurable state of affairs). He believed that learning occurred constantly, with or without reinforcement and with or without motivation. About as close as Tolman came to a concept of reinforcement was confirmation. Through the **confirmation** of a hypothesis, expectancy, or belief, a cognitive map developed or was main-

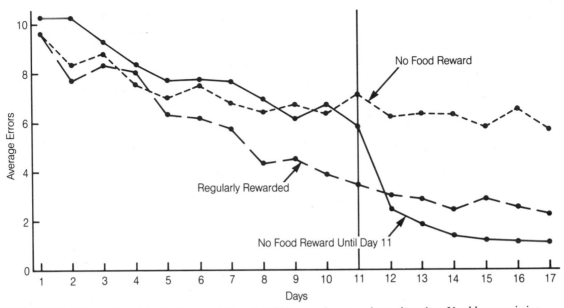

FIGURE 13.1 The results of the Tolman and Honzik (1930) experiment on latent learning. Used by permission.

tained. The animal learned what led to what in the environment: It learned that if it did such and such, such and such would follow; or that if it saw one stimulus (S₁), a second stimulus (S₂) would follow. Because Tolman emphasized the learning of relationships among stimuli, his position is often called an S–S theory rather than an S–R theory.

Learning Versus Performance

According to Tolman's theory, an organism learned constantly as it observed its environment. But whether the organism used what it learned—and if so, how—was determined by the organism's motivational state. For example, a food-satiated rat might not leave the start box of a maze or might wander casually through the maze even though it had previously learned what had to be done to obtain food. Thus, for Tolman, motivation influenced performance but not learning. Tolman defined **performance** as the translation of learning into behavior. The importance of motivation in Tolman's theory was due to the influence of Woodworth's dynamic psychology.

Latent learning. In one of his famous **latent-learning** experiments, Tolman dramatically demonstrated the distinction between learning and performance. Tolman and Honzik (1930) ran an experiment using three groups of rats as subjects. Subjects in Group 1 were reinforced with food each time they correctly traversed a maze. Subjects in Group 2 wandered through the maze but were not reinforced if they reached the goal box. Subjects in Group 3 were treated like subjects in Group 2 until the 11th trial when they began receiving reinforcement in the goal box. Subjects in all three groups were deprived of food before being placed in the maze. Tolman's hypothesis was that subjects in all groups were learning the maze as they wandered through it. If his hypothesis was correct, subjects in Group 3 should perform as well as subjects in Group 1 from the 12th trial on. This was because, before the 11th trial, subjects in Group 3 had already learned how to arrive at the goal box and finding food there on the 11th trial had given them an incentive for acting on this information. As Figure 13.1 shows, the experiment supported Tolman's hypothesis. Learning appeared to remain latent until the organism had a reason to use it.

Tolman's Influence

L. D. Smith summarizes Tolman's importance:

> In adopting and adapting the concepts of purpose and cognition . . . Tolman helped preserve and shape the tradition of cognitive psychology during a time when it was nearly eclipsed by the ascendancy of classical behaviorism. He was able to do so by demonstrating that such concepts were compatible with a behaviorism of a more sophisticated clearly non-Watsonian—variety. (1982, p. 160)

Tolman's theory is still very influential. In fact, in many ways, Tolman is responsible for the current widespread interest in cognitive psychology. Tolman's influence on contemporary learning theory can be clearly seen in the work of **Albert Bandura** (b. 1925). Like Tolman, Bandura believes that organisms (including humans) learn by observing what leads to what in the environment. According to Bandura, we can learn by either observing the consequences of our own behavior or other people's behavior. Thus, in Bandura's account of **observational learning**, **vicarious experience** (observing the outcome of the behavior of others) is as important as observing the outcome of **direct** (personal) **experience**. Like Tolman, Bandura believes that reinforcement is a performance, not a learning variable, and that what we learn are expectancies. (For excellent overviews of Bandura's social cognitive theory, see Bandura, 1977, 1986.)

Once Tolman began postulating intervening variables, his theory became extremely complex. He postulated several independent variables and several intervening variables, and the possible interactions between the two types of variables were enormous. Tolman expressed regret over this practical difficulty. L. D. Smith believes that Tolman's theory was proposed before a technology was developed to evaluate it:

Albert Bandura

Tolman expressed despair over the immense practical difficulty of determining intervening variables and their interactions. . . . I would suggest that it was just this sort of difficulty that became tractable with the realization by psychologists in the 1960s that computer programs are highly suited for expressing complex interactions in models of cognitive processing. If Tolman's theoretical innovations suffered from the limitations of the technology available in his time, they would seem to suffer no longer. (1982, p. 464).

Clearly, Tolman viewed organisms as active processors of information, and such a view is very much in accordance with contemporary cognitive psychology, especially information-processing psychology. We will say more about

Clark Leonard Hull

Tolman's influence on contemporary cognitive psychology in chapter 18.

CLARK LEONARD HULL

Biographical Sketch

Clark Leonard Hull (1884–1952) was born near Akron, New York, the son of an uneducated father and quiet mother who wed at the age of 15. It was Hull's mother who taught his father to read. Hull's education in a rural one-room school was often interrupted by necessary chores on the family farm. After passing a teacher's examination at the age of 17, Hull taught in a one-room school, but after a year of teaching, he returned to school where he excelled in science and mathematics. While at school, Hull contracted typhoid fever from contaminated food; although several of Hull's fellow students died from the outbreak, he survived but, in Hull's opinion, with his memory impaired. After his recuperation, he went to Alma College to study mining engineering. Following his training, he obtained a job at a mining company in Minnesota where his job was to evaluate the manganese content in iron ore. After

only two months on the job, at the age of 24, he contracted poliomyelitis, which left him partially paralyzed. At first he could walk only with crutches and then, for the rest of his life, with a cane. He now needed to ponder a career that was less strenuous than mining. Hull first considered becoming a unitarian minister. He was attracted to unitarianism because it was "a free, Godless religion," but the idea of "attending an endless succession of ladies' teas" caused him to abandon the idea. What he really wanted was to work in a field where success could come relatively quickly and one that would permit him to tinker with apparatus:

> [I wanted] an occupation in a field allied to philosophy in the sense of involving theory: one which was new enough to permit rapid growth so that a young man would not need to wait for his predecessors to die before his work could find recognition, and one which would provide an opportunity to design and work with automatic apparatus. Psychology seemed to satisfy this unique set of requirements. (Hull, 1952a, p. 145)

Although Hull set a career in psychology as his goal, he was not financially able to pursue it. Instead, he became principal of the school he had attended as a child (now expanded to two rooms). In his spare time, he read James's *Principles* to prepare himself for his chosen profession. After two years, he had saved enough money to enter the University of Michigan as a junior. Among the courses that Hull took at Michigan was one in experimental psychology, which he loved, and one in logic, for which he constructed a machine that could simulate syllogistic reasoning. After graduation from the University of Michigan, Hull's funds were again exhausted, and he accepted a position in a school of education in Kentucky. During this time, although not yet in graduate school, he began planning what would become his doctoral dissertation on concept formation. Hull applied for graduate study at Cornell and Yale (where he ultimately would spend most of his professional career) and was rejected by both. He was, however, accepted at the University of Wisconsin. It took four years for Hull to complete his dissertation on concept learning (1920). Although Hull believed that his research represented a breakthrough in experimental psychology, it was essentially ignored. Hilgard reminisces on Hull's experiences with his dissertation:

> Hull had struggled hard to complete his dissertation, undergoing the trials of a baby daughter smearing the ink on charts he had so carefully laid out to dry, so that he had to do them all over again. He felt proud of his dissertation because it moved experimental psychology into the area of thought processes by investigating the learning of concepts, . . . He told me how downcast he had become when year after year no one paid attention to it or cited it. He was finally prepared to accept the fact that it had been "still-born" (his words). (1987, p. 200)

Hull received his doctorate from the University of Wisconsin in 1918 and remained there as an instructor until 1929.

Perhaps disappointed over the reception of his dissertation research on concept learning, Hull moved into other research areas. He accepted a research grant to study the influence of pipe smoking on mental and motor performance. During this research, Hull once again demonstrated his penchant for building apparatus. Hilgard describes this research:

> One of [Hull's] minor but ingenious experiments was on the physiological effects of pipe smoking. To guard against the placebo effect when subjects knew their smoking was under investigation he arranged experimental and control conditions so that the young male students did not know whether they were actually smoking. The experimental pipe, with genuine tobacco in it, and the control pipe, without tobacco, were both "smoked" while blindfolded. The control pipe was heated by a coil so the air smoked was the temperature of that from the lighted tobacco in a pipe, and with a little smoke in the air to provide the smell of tobacco his subjects could not tell which condition was being tested. (Hilgard, 1987, p. 200)

Next, Hull was asked to teach a course in psychological tests and measurements. He observed that the existing bases for vocational guidance were not objective, and his efforts to improve the situation ultimately resulted in his book *Aptitude Testing* (1928). As part of his work in this area, Hull invented a machine that could automatically compute intercorrelations among test scores. This machine, which was programmed by punching holes in a tape, is now housed in the Smithsonian Institute in Washington, DC (Hilgard, 1987).

In 1929 Hull accepted a professorship at Yale University (one of the institutions that rejected his graduate school application). At Yale, Hull pursued two interests: the creation of machines that could learn and think (like his correlation machine) and the study of the learning process. The two interests were entirely compatible because Hull viewed humans as machines that learn and think. Not surprisingly, one of Hull's heros was Newton, who viewed the universe as a huge machine that could be described in precise mathematical terms. Hull simply applied the Newtonian model to living organisms. Another of Hull's heros was Pavlov. Hull was deeply impressed by the English translation of Pavlov's work that appeared in 1927. He began studying conditioned responses in humans while he was still at Wisconsin and continued his studies when he moved to Yale. At Yale, however, his experimental subjects were rats instead of humans.

Hull's many contributions were finally recognized when, in 1936, he was elected president of the American Psychological Association (APA). In his presidential address, he outlined his goal of creating a theoretical psychology that would explain "purposive" behavior in terms of mechanistic, lawful principles of behavior. In creating his theoretical psychology, Hull would employ the tenets of logical positivism (and euclidean geometry) in that new knowledge is deduced from what is already known. In his autobiography, Hull said, "The study of geometry proved to be the most important event of my intellectual life; it opened to me an entirely new world—the fact that thought itself could generate and really prove new relationships from previously possessed elements" (1952a, p. 144). It is important to note that neither Hull nor Tolman developed the theories they did *because of* logical positivism. Both reached their conclusions about theoretical psychology independently of logical positivism, but when they discovered that philosophy of science in the 1930s, they simply assimilated its terminology into their systems. In other words, Tolman and Hull used the language of logical positivism to express their own ideas. They could do so because of the compatibility between the two.

Unlike Tolman, Hull found no need for mentalistic concepts, whether they were considered real entities or simply theoretical conveniences. Like Watson, Hull believed that psychology's preoccupation with consciousness was derived from medieval metaphysics and theology. Although Hull's interest in "psychic machines" was now secondary, he did demonstrate such a machine to his APA audience, and he expressed the belief that if a machine could be built that performed adaptive behaviors, it would support his contention that the adaptive behaviors of living organisms could be explained in terms of mechanistic principles.

Because of their willingness to speculate about internal causes of behavior, both Hull and Tolman were methodological behaviorists, and both eventually employed logical positivism in their theorizing. Philosophically, however, Hull was a mechanist and a materialist, and Tolman was, insofar as he believed mental events determined behavior, a dualist in the Cartesian tradition. Supporters of Hull's mechanistic behaviorism and those of Tolman's purposive behaviorism battled with each other throughout the 1930s and 1940s. This running debate resulted in one of the most productive periods in psychology's history.

Between 1929 and 1950, Hull wrote 21 theoretical articles in the *Psychological Review*, and in 1940 he (with coauthors Hovland, Ross, Hall, Perkins, and Fitch) published *Mathematico-Deductive Theory of Rote Learning*. This book was an effort to show how rote learning could be explained in terms of conditioning principles. In 1943 Hull published *Principles of Behavior*, one of the most influential books in psychology's his-

tory. His *A Behavior System* (1952b) extended the principles found in *Principles* to more complex phenomena. In 1948 while preparing the manuscript for *A Behavior System*, Hull suffered a massive heart attack that exacerbated his already frail physical condition. It took all the strength he could muster, but he finished the book four months before he died in 1952 of a second heart attack. Near his death, Hull expressed profound regret that a third book that he had been planning would never be written. He believed that his third book would have been his most important because it would have extended his system to human social behavior.

Hull's Hypothetico-Deductive Theory

Borrowing the technique of using intervening variables from Tolman, Hull used them even more extensively than Tolman did. Hull was the first (and last) psychologist to attempt to apply a comprehensive, scientific theory to the study of learning, creating a highly complex **hypothetico-deductive theory**, which he hoped would be self-correcting. Hull first reviewed the research that had been done on learning; then he summarized that research in the form of general statements, or postulates. From these postulates, he inferred theorems that yielded testable propositions. Hull explained why his system should be self-correcting:

Empirical observation, supplemented by shrewd conjecture, is the main source of the primary principles or postulates of a science. Such formulations, when taken in various combinations together with relevant antecedent conditions, yield inferences or theorems, of which some may agree with the empirical outcome of the conditions in question, and some may not. Primary propositions yielding logical deductions which consistently agree with the observed empirical outcome are retained, whereas those which disagree are rejected or modified. As the sifting of this trial-and-error process continues, there gradually emerges a limited series of primary principles whose joint implications are progressively more likely to agree with relevant observations. Deductions made from these surviving postulates, while never absolutely certain, do at length become highly trustworthy. This is in fact the present status of the primary principles of the major physical sciences. (1943, p. 382)

Whereas Watson believed that all behavior could be explained in terms of the associations between stimuli and responses, Hull concluded that a number of intervening internal conditions had to be taken into consideration. Tolman had reached the same conclusion. However, for Tolman, cognitive events intervened between environmental experience and behavior; for Hull, the intervening events were primarily physiological.

In Hull's final statement of his theory (1952b), he listed 17 postulates and 133 theorems, but we review only a few of his more important concepts here.

Reinforcement. Unlike Watson and Tolman, Hull was a reinforcement theorist. For Hull, a biological need created a *drive* in the organism, and the diminution of this drive constituted **reinforcement**. Thus, Hull had a **drive-reduction** theory of reinforcement. For Hull, drive was one of the important events that intervened between a stimulus and a response.

Habit strength. If a response made in a certain situation led to drive reduction, **habit strength** ($_sH_R$) was said to increase. Hull operationally defined habit strength, an intervening variable, as the number of reinforced pairings between an environmental situation (S) and a response (R). For Hull, an increase in habit strength constituted learning.

Reaction potential. Drive was not only a necessary condition for reinforcement but also an important energizer of behavior. Hull called the probability of a learned response **reaction potential** ($_sE_R$), which was a function of both the amount of drive (D) present and the number of times the response had been previously reinforced in the situation. Hull expressed this relationship as follows:

$$_sE_R = {_sH_R} \times D$$

If either $_sH_R$ or D was zero, the probability of a learned response being made would also be zero.

Hull postulated several other intervening variables, some of which contributed to $_sE_R$ and some of which diminished it. The probability of a learned response was the net effect of all these positive and negative influences, each intervening variable being carefully operationally defined.

Hull's theory in general. Hull's theory can be seen as an elaboration of Woodworth's S–O–R concept. Using operational definitions, Hull attempted to show how a number of internal events interacted to cause overt behavior. Hull's theory was in the Darwinian tradition because it associated reinforcement with those events that were conducive to an organism's survival. His theory reflected the influence of Darwin, Woodworth, Watson, and logical positivism.

Hull's Influence

Within 10 years following the publication of *Principles of Behavior* (1943), 40 percent of all experimental studies in the highly regarded *Journal of Experimental Psychology* and *Journal of Comparative and Physiological Psychology* referred to some aspect of Hull's theory. The figure increases to 70 percent when only the fields of learning and motivation are considered (Spence, 1952). To show that Hull's influence went beyond these areas, however, during the period between 1949 and 1952, there were 105 references to Hull's *Principles of Behavior* in *The Journal of Abnormal and Social Psychology*, compared to only 25 for the next most commonly cited work (Ruja, 1956).

In 1945 Hull was awarded the prestigious Warren Medal by the Society of Experimental Psychologists with the inscription

To Clark L. Hull: For his careful development of a systematic theory of behavior. This theory has stimulated much research and it has been developed in a precise and quantitative form so as to permit predictions which can be tested empirically. The theory thus contains within itself the seeds of its own ultimate verification and of its own possible final disproof. A truly unique achievement in the history of psychology to date.

After Hull's death in 1952, one of his ex-students, Kenneth W. Spence (1907–1967) became the major spokesman for his theory (e.g., see Spence, 1956, 1960). The extensions and modifications that Spence made in Hull's theory were so substantial that the theory became known as the Hull–Spence theory. So successful was Spence in perpetuating Hullian theory that a study showed that as late as the 1960s Spence was the most cited psychologist in experimental psychology journals, with Hull himself in eighth place (Myers, 1970).

Although Hull's theory eventually won its battle with Tolman's and was extremely popular in the 1940s and 1950s, and under Spence's influence even into the 1960s, it is now generally thought of as having mainly historical value. Hull attempted to create a general behavior theory that all social sciences could use to explain human behavior, and his program fit all requirements of logical positivism (e.g., all his theoretical concepts were operationally defined). However, although Hull's theory was scientifically respectable, it was relatively sterile. More and more, the testable deductions from his theory were criticized for being of little value in explaining behavior beyond the laboratory. Psychologists began to feel hampered by the need to define their concepts operationally and to relate the outcomes of their experiments to a theory such as Hull's. They realized that objective inquiry could take many forms and that the form suggested by logical positivism had led to a dead end. In many ways, Hull's approach was ultimately as unproductive as Titchener's had been.

As the theoretical systems of Tolman and Hull began to lose their popularity, another form of behaviorism was in its ascendancy. The version of behaviorism promoted by B. F. Skinner was contrary to logical positivism because it was antitheoretical, and yet it was in

accordance with logical positivism because it insisted that all of its basic terms be operationally defined. We see next that Skinner's version of behaviorism was more in accordance with positivism than it was with logical positivism. After the Second World War, Skinner's version of behaviorism essentially displaced all other versions.

BURRHUS FREDERIC SKINNER

Biographical Sketch

Burrhus Frederic Skinner (1904–1990) was born on March 20 in Susquehanna, Pennsylvania, into a warm, stable, middle-class family. Skinner had a younger brother who was a better athlete and more socially popular than he was but who died suddenly at the age of 16. Skinner was raised according to strict moral standards but was physically punished only once:

> I was never physically punished by my father and only once by my mother. She washed my mouth out with soap and water because I had used a bad word. My father never missed an opportunity, however, to inform me of the punishments which were waiting if I turned out to have a criminal mind. He once took me through the county jail, and on a summer vacation I was taken to a lecture with colored slides describing life in Sing Sing. As a result I am afraid of the police and buy too many tickets to their annual dance. (Skinner, 1967, pp. 390–391)

Like Hull, Skinner had an aptitude for creative apparatus building, which was evident even in his childhood:

> I was always building things. I built roller-skate scooters, steerable wagons, sleds, and rafts to be poled about on shallow ponds. I made see-saws, merry-go-rounds, and slides. I made slingshots, bows and arrows, blow guns and water pistols from lengths of bamboo, and from a discarded water boiler a stream cannon with which I could shoot plugs of potato and carrot over the houses of our neighbors. I made tops, diabolos, model airplanes driven by twisted rubber bands, box kites, and tin propellers which could be sent high into the air with a spool-and-string spin-

ner. I tried again and again to make a glider in which I myself might fly.

I invented things, some of them in the spirit of the outrageous contraptions in the cartoons which Rube Goldberg was publishing in the *Philadelphia Inquirer* (to which, as a good Republican, my father subscribed). For example, a friend and I used to gather elderberries and sell them from door to door, and I built a flotation system which separated ripe from green berries. I worked for years on the design of a perpetual motion machine. (It did not work.) (1967, p. 388)

In high school, Skinner did well in literature but poorly in science, and he earned money by playing in a jazz band and with an orchestra. He went to Hamilton College, a small liberal arts school in Clinton, New York, where he majored in English. Skinner did not fit well into college life, was terrible at sports, and felt "pushed around" by requirements such as daily chapel. By his senior year, Skinner viewed himself as "in open revolt" against the school. He, along with a friend, decided to play a trick on their English composition professor, whom they disliked because he was "a great name-dropper." Skinner and his friend had posters printed that read: "Charles Chaplin, the famous cinema comedian, will deliver his lecture 'Moving Pictures as a Career' in the Hamilton College chapel on Friday, October 9" (1967, p. 393). The Chaplin visit was said to be under the auspices of the disliked English professor. The posters were displayed all over town, and Skinner's friend called the newspaper in Utica with the news. By noon the prank was completely out of hand. Police roadblocks were necessary to control the crowds. The next day, the English professor to whom the hoax was directed wrote an editorial lambasting the entire episode. Skinner said that it was the best thing the professor ever wrote. The Chaplin prank was only the beginning of a mischievous senior year for Skinner:

As a nihilistic gesture, the hoax was only the beginning. Through the student publications we began to attack the faculty and various local sacred cows. I published a parody of the bumbling manner in which the professor of public speaking would review student performances at

B. F. Skinner

the end of the class. I wrote an editorial attacking Phi Beta Kappa. At commencement . . . I covered the walls with bitter caricatures of the faculty . . . and we [Skinner and his friends] made a shambles of the commencement ceremonies, and at intermission the President warned us sternly that we would not get our degrees if we did not settle down. (1967, p. 393)

Skinner graduated from Hamilton College with a bachelor's degree in English literature and a Phi Beta Kappa key and without having had a course in psychology. He left college with a passion to become a writer. In part this passion was encouraged by the fact that the famous poet Robert Frost favorably reviewed three of his short stories. Skinner's first attempt at writing was in the attic of his parents' home: "The results were disastrous. I frittered away my time. I read aimlessly . . . listened to the newly invented radio, contributed to the humorous column of a local paper but wrote almost nothing else, and thought about seeing a psychiatrist" (1967, p. 394). Next, Skinner tried writing in Greenwich Village, New York, and then in Paris for a summer; these attempts also failed. By now Skinner had developed a distaste for most literary pursuits: "I had failed as a writer because I had had nothing important to say, but I could not accept that explanation. It was literature which must be at fault" (p. 395).

Having failed to describe human behavior through literature, Skinner decided to describe it scientifically. While in Greenwich Village, Skinner had read the works of Pavlov and Watson and was greatly impressed. On his return from Europe in 1928, he enrolled in the graduate program in psychology at Harvard. Feeling that he at last found his niche, Skinner threw himself completely into his studies:

> I would rise at six, study until breakfast, go to classes, laboratories, and libraries with no more than fifteen minutes unscheduled during the day, study until exactly nine o'clock at night and go to bed. I saw no movies or plays, seldom went to concerts, had scarcely any dates and read nothing but psychology and physiology. (1967, p. 398)

This high degree of self-discipline typified Skinner's work habits throughout his long life.

Skinner earned his master's degree in two years (1930) and his doctorate in three (1931) and then remained at Harvard for the next five years as a postdoctoral fellow. Skinner began his teaching career at the University of Minnesota in 1936 and remained there until 1945. While he was at Minnesota, Skinner published *The Behavior of Organisms* (1938), which established him as a nationally prominent experimental psychologist. In 1945 Skinner moved to Indiana University as chairman of the psychology department, where he remained until 1948 when he returned to Harvard. He remained affiliated with Harvard until his death in 1990. In 1974 he became professor emeritus

> but continued for years to walk the two miles between his home and his office in William

James Hall to answer correspondence, to meet with scholars who paid him visits from around the world, and on occasion to conduct research and supervise graduate students. (Fowler, 1990, p. 1203)

Skinner's Positivism

In chapter 4, we discussed the great Renaissance thinker Francis Bacon. Bacon was intensely interested in overcoming the mistakes of the past and thus arriving at knowledge that was free of superstition and prejudice. His solution to the problem was to stay very close to what was empirically observable and to avoid theorizing about it. Bacon proposed that science be descriptive and inductive rather than theoretical and deductive. Following Bacon's suggestion, scientists would first gather empirical facts and then infer knowledge from those facts (instead of first developing abstract theories from which facts are deduced). Bacon's main point was that in the formulation of theories a scientist's biases, misconceptions, traditions, and beliefs (perhaps false beliefs) could manifest themselves and that these very things inhibited a search for objective knowledge. Bacon can be seen as starting the positivistic tradition that was later followed by Comte and Mach. Skinner (1979) acknowledged a debt to Mach. For Mach, it was important that science rid itself of metaphysical concepts, which, for him, were any concepts that referred to events that could not be directly observed. Mach and the other positivists were interested only in facts and how facts were related to each other. According to Mach, the scientist determines how facts are related by doing a functional analysis. That is, by noting that if X occurs Y also tends to occur. To ponder why such relationships exist is to enter the dangerous and unnecessary realm of metaphysics. The job of science is to describe empirical relationships, not explain them. Skinner followed Mach's positivism explicitly. As far as theory was concerned, Skinner was a positivist, not a logical positivist. We examine Skinner's positivism again when we review his attitude toward theory.

Functional Analysis of Behavior

Like Watson, Skinner denied the existence of a separate realm of conscious events. He believed that what we call mental events are simply verbal labels given to certain bodily processes. But, said Skinner, even if there were mental events, nothing would be gained by studying them. He reasoned that if environmental events give rise to conscious events, which, in turn, cause behavior, nothing is lost and a great deal is gained by simply doing a **functional analysis** of the environmental and the behavioral events. Such an analysis avoids the many problems associated with the study of mental events. These so-called mental events, said Skinner, will someday be explained when we learn to which internal physiological events people are responding when they use such terms as *thinking, choosing,* and *willing* to explain their own behavior. Skinner, then, was a physical monist because he believed that consciousness as a nonphysical entity did not exist. Because we do not at present know to which internal events people are responding when they use mentalistic terminology, we must be content simply to ignore such terms. Skinner said,

> There is nothing in a science of behavior or its philosophy which need alter feelings or introspective observations. The bodily states which are felt or observed are acknowledged, but there is an emphasis on the environmental conditions with which they are associated and an insistence that it is the conditions rather than the feelings which enable us to explain behavior. (1974, p. 245)

Elsewhere Skinner said, "A completely independent science of subjective experience would have no more bearing on a science of behavior than a science of what people feel about fire would have on the science of combustion" (1974, pp. 220–221) and "there is no place in the scientific position for a self as a true originator or initiator of action" (1974, p. 225). Like Watson then, Skinner was a radical behaviorist in that he refused to acknowledge any causal role of mental events in human conduct. For Skinner, so-called mental events were nothing but neuro-physiological events to which we have assigned mentalistic labels.

Operant Behavior

Whereas Watson modeled his psychology after the Russian physiologists, Skinner modeled his after Thorndike. Watson and Pavlov attempted to correlate behavior with environmental stimuli. That is, they were interested in reflexive behavior. Skinner called such behavior **respondent behavior** because it was elicited by a known stimulus. Because both Pavlov and Watson studied the relationship between environmental stimuli (S) and responses (R), their endeavors represent **S–R psychology**. Thorndike, however, studied behavior that was controlled by its consequences. For example, behavior that had been instrumental in allowing an animal to escape from a puzzle box tended to be repeated when the animal was next placed in the puzzle box. Using Thorndike's experimental arrangement, a response was instrumental in producing certain consequences, and therefore the type of learning that he studied was called **instrumental conditioning**. Thorndike neither knew nor cared about the origins of the behavior that was controlled by its consequences. What Thorndike called instrumental behavior, Skinner called **operant behavior** because it operated on the environment in such a way as to produce consequences. Unlike respondent behavior, which was elicited by known stimulation, operant behavior was simply *emitted* by the organism. It was not that operant behavior was not caused but that its causes were not known—nor was it important to know them. The most important aspect of operant behavior was that it was controlled by its consequences and not elicited by known stimulation. Skinner's concentration on operant behavior is one major reason that his brand of behaviorism is *much* different from Watson's.

Although both Skinner and Thorndike studied behavior that was controlled by its consequences, *how* they studied that behavior was different. Thorndike measured how long it took an animal to make an escape response as a function of successive, reinforced trials. He found that as the number of reinforced escapes increased, the time it took for the animal to escape decreased. His dependent variable was the latency of the escape response. Skinner's procedure was to allow an animal to respond freely in an experimental chamber (i.e., a Skinner box) and to note the effect of reinforcement on response rate. For example, a lever-press response may occur only 2 or 3 times a minute before it is reinforced and 30 or 40 times a minute when it results in reinforcement. Rate of responding, then, was Skinner's dependent variable.

Despite the differences between them, however, both Watson and Skinner exemplified radical behaviorism because they believed that behavior could be completely explained in terms of events external to the organism. For Watson, environmental events elicited either learned or unlearned responses; for Skinner, the environment selected behavior via reinforcement contingencies. For both, what went on within the organism was relatively unimportant. As we have seen, the theories of Tolman and Hull exemplified methodological behaviorism because they postulated a wealth of events that were supposed to intervene between experience and behavior.

The Nature of Reinforcement

If an operant response leads to reinforcement, the rate of that response increases. Thus, those responses an organism makes that result in reinforcement are most likely to occur when the organism is next in that situation. This is what is meant by the statement that operant behavior is controlled by its consequences. According to Skinner, reinforcement can be identified only through its effects on behavior. Just because something acts as a reinforcer for one organism under one set of circumstances does not mean that it will be a reinforcer for another organism or for the same organism under different circumstances:

> In dealing with our fellow men in everyday life and in the clinic and laboratory, we may need to

know just how reinforcing a specific event is. We often begin by noting the extent to which our own behavior is reinforced by the same event. This practice frequently miscarries; yet it is still commonly believed that reinforcers can be identified apart from their effects upon a particular organism. As the term is used here, however, the only defining characteristic of a reinforcing stimulus is that it reinforces. (Skinner, 1953, p. 71)

Thus, for Skinner, there is no talk of drive reduction, satisfying states of affairs, or any other mechanisms of reinforcement. A reinforcer is *anything* that, when made contingent on a response, changes the rate with which that response is made. For Skinner, nothing additional needs to be said. He accepted Thorndike's law of effect but not the mentalism that the phrase "satisfying state of affairs" implied.

The Importance of the Environment

Whereas the environment was important for Watson and the Russian physiologists because it elicited behavior, it was important for Skinner because it *selected* behavior. The reinforcement contingencies that the environment provides determine which behaviors are strengthened and which are not. Change reinforcement contingencies, and you change behavior:

> The environment is obviously important, but its role has remained obscure. It does not push or pull, it *selects*, and this function is difficult to discover and analyze. The role of natural selection in evolution was formulated only a little more than a hundred years ago, and the selective role of the environment in shaping and maintaining the behavior of the individual is only beginning to be recognized and studied. As the interaction between organism and environment has come to be understood, however, effects once assigned to states of mind, feeling, and traits are beginning to be traced to accessible conditions, and a technology of behavior may therefore become available. It will not solve our problems, however, until it replaces traditional prescientific views, and these views are strongly entrenched. (Skinner, 1971, p. 25)

Thus, Skinner applied Darwinian notions to his analysis of behavior. In any given situation, an organism initially makes a wide variety of responses. Of those responses, only a few will be functional (i.e., reinforcing). These effective responses survive and become part of the organism's response repertoire to be used when that situation next occurs.

According to Skinner, the fact that behavior is governed by reinforcement contingencies provides hope for the solution of a number of societal problems. If it was the "mind" or the "self" that needed to be understood instead of how the environment selects behavior, we would be in real trouble:

> Fortunately, the point of attack is more readily accessible. It is the environment which must be changed. A way of life which furthers the study of human behavior in its relation to that environment should be in the best possible position to solve its major problems. This is not jingoism, because the great problems are now global. In the behavioristic view, man can now control his own destiny because he knows what must be done and how to do it. (Skinner, 1974, p. 251)

Skinner's Attitude Toward Theory

Because Skinner's position was nontheoretical, it contrasted with the behavioristic positions of Tolman and Hull. Skinner accepted operationism but rejected the theoretical aspects of logical positivism. He was content to manipulate environmental events (e.g., reinforcement contingencies) and note the effects of these manipulations on behavior, believing that this functional analysis was all that was necessary. For this reason, Skinner's approach is sometimes referred to as a **descriptive behaviorism**. There is, Skinner felt, no reason for looking "under the skin" for explanations of relationships between the environment and behavior. Looking for physiological explanations of behavior is a waste of time because overt behavior occurs whether or not we know its neurophysiological underpinnings. We have already reviewed Skinner's attitude toward mentalistic explanations of behavior. Because Skinner did not care what was going on "under the skin" either physiologically or mentally, his approach is often referred to as the empty-organism approach. Skinner knew, of course, that the organism is not empty, but he

thought that nothing is lost by ignoring events that intervene between the environment and the behavior it selects.

Besides opposing physiological and mentalistic explanations of behavior, Skinner opposed abstract theorizing like that of Tolman and Hull:

> Research designed with respect to theory is also likely to be wasteful. That a theory generates research does not prove its value unless the research is valuable. Much useless experimentation results from theories, and much energy and skill are absorbed by them. Most theories are eventually over-thrown, and the greater part of the associated research is discarded. This could be justified if it were true that productive research requires a theory—as is, of course, often claimed. It is argued that research would be aimless and disorganized without a theory to guide it. The view is supported by psychological texts which take their cue from the logicians rather than empirical science, and describe thinking as necessarily involving stages of hypothesis, deduction, experimental test, and confirmation. But this is not the way most scientists actually work. It is possible to design significant experiments for other reasons, and the possibility to be examined is that such research will lead more directly to the kind of information which a science usually accumulates. (1950, pp. 194–195)

In describing his nontheoretical approach, Skinner (1956) said that if he tried something and if it seemed to be leading to something useful, he persisted. If what he was doing seemed to be leading to a dead end, he abandoned it and tried something else.

Some believe that Skinner's article "Are Theories of Learning Necessary?" (1950) marked the end of what Koch (1959) calls the "age of theory" in psychology.

Applications of Skinnerian Principles

Like Watson, Skinner and his followers sought to apply their principles to the solution of practical problems. In all applications of Skinnerian principles, the general rule is always the same: *Change reinforcement contingencies, and you change behavior.* This principle has been used to teach pigeons to play games like table tennis and basketball, and many animals trained through the use of Skinnerian principles have performed at tourist attractions throughout the United States. In a defense effort, pigeons were even trained to guide missiles as the missiles sped toward enemy targets (Skinner, 1960). In 1948 Skinner wrote a utopian novel entitled *Walden Two* in which he demonstrated how his principles could be used in designing a model society. In *Beyond Freedom and Dignity* (1971), Skinner reviewed the reasons that cultural engineering, although possible, has been largely rejected.

In the realm of education, Skinner developed a teaching technique called *programmed learning* (1954, 1958). With programmed learning, material is presented to students in small steps; students then are tested on the material, given immediate feedback on the accuracy of their answers, and allowed to proceed through the material at their own pace. Skinner had criticized U.S. education ever since 1953 when he visited his daughter's classroom and concluded that the teacher was violating everything that was known about learning. Skinner (1984) maintained that many of the problems in our educational system could be solved through the use of operant principles. Skinner's main criticism of U.S. educational practices was that the threat of punishment is used to force students to learn and to behave instead of the careful manipulation of reinforcement contingencies. This aversive control, Skinner said, creates a negative attitude toward education.

Skinner and his followers have applied behavior modification principles to helping individuals with problems ranging from psychosis to smoking, drinking, speech disorders, shyness, phobias, obesity, and sexual disorders. The Skinnerian version of **behavior therapy** assumes that people learn abnormal behavior in the same way that they learn normal behavior. Therefore, "treatment" is a matter of removing the reinforcers that are maintaining the undesirable behavior and arranging the reinforcement contingencies so that they strengthen desirable behavior. In general, the use of Skinnerian principles in treating behavior problems has been very effective (e.g., see Ayllon & Azrin, 1968;

Craighead, Kazdin & Mahoney, 1976; Kazdin, 1980; Kazdin & Wilson, 1978; Leitenberg, 1976; Masters, Burish, Hollon & Rimm, 1987; Rimm & Masters, 1974; Ulrich, Stachnik & Mabry, 1966).

A Tribute to Skinner

On August 10, 1990, the APA presented Skinner with an unprecedented Lifetime Contribution to Psychology Award with the following citation:

> The members of the American Psychological Association are honored to recognize your lifetime of significant contributions to psychology and to the world. Few individuals have had such a dynamic and far-reaching impact on the discipline.
>
> As a creative scientist with a vision, you led a ground-breaking movement in psychology that challenged our views of behavior and inspired numerous advances in the field. Your incisive analysis of contingencies of reinforcement and your articulation of its implications for evolutionary theory and verbal behavior, your insightful views on the philosophy of behaviorism, your innovations in research methodology, and the breadth of the practical applications of your scientific work are unparalleled among contemporary psychologists.
>
> As a pioneer in psychology, you challenge traditional ways of thinking. Your work serves as a catalyst for other scientists and practitioners who are stimulated by your ideas and are inspired to think about psychological problems in new ways.
>
> As an intellectual leader, you enhance the stature of psychology and raise its intellectual climate to a higher level. You significantly increase the public's awareness of psychology and its impact on society.
>
> With great sensitivity to the human condition, combined with rigorous standards and a broad outlook, you laid the foundation for innovative applications of your work in clinical psychology, education, behavioral medicine, mental retardation, brain injury, and countless other areas.
>
> As a citizen of the world, you provide thoughtful, often provocative, and always compassionate insights into such uniquely human endeavors as ethics, freedom, dignity, governance, and peace. You have fundamentally and

forever changed our view of the human capacity to learn.

In recognition of these many lasting contributions, the members of the American Psychological Association take great pride in presenting this citation to you. (*American Psychologist,* 1990, p. 1205)

Skinner died eight days later at the age of 86.

BEHAVIORISM TODAY

The work of all the neobehaviorists covered in this chapter remains influential in contemporary psychology. Tolman's brand of behaviorism, with its emphasis on purposive behavior and mental constructs, can be viewed as a major reason for the current popularity of cognitive psychology, and Bandura's theory of observational learning can be understood as a direct derivative of Tolman's theory. Although Hull did much to promote an objective behavioristic approach, his current influence is due mainly to some of the esoteric features of his theory. His goal of developing a comprehensive behavior theory, however, has given way to the goal of developing theories designed to explain specific phenomena.

Skinner's influence remains strong. In 1974 Skinner wrote *About Behaviorism,* which attempted to correct 20 misconceptions about behaviorism. In this book, Skinner traced a number of these misconceptions to Watson's early writings—for example, Watson's dependence on reflexive behavior and his denial of the importance of genetic endowment. Skinner's position rectified both "mistakes." Skinner also pointed out that he did not deny so-called mental processes but believed that ultimately they will be explained as verbal labels that we attach to certain bodily processes. As evidence of the recent popularity of Skinnerian behaviorism, followers of Skinner have formed their own division of the APA (Division 25, the division of the Experimental Analysis of Behavior) and have two of their own journals in which to publish their research, *The Journal of Applied Behavior Analysis* and *Journal for Experimental Analysis of Behavior.*

Despite the current manifestations of neobehaviorism, contemporary psychology is challenging several themes that behaviorism has typically embraced. Those themes can be summarized as follows:

1. Most behavior is learned; therefore, the importance of genetically determined behavior is minimal.

2. Language does not present a special problem but is just another form of behavior governed by learning principles.

3. The principles governing human and nonhuman learning are the same; therefore, studying animals can teach us about human learning.

4. As causes of behavior, mental events can be either ignored or minimized. (Tolman's theory was an exception to this theme.)

5. All responses that an animal is capable of making are equally modifiable through the application of learning principles.

6. The same principles govern childhood and adult learning.

Those calling themselves sociobiologists have been providing evidence that much animal behavior, including human social behavior, is genetically determined (e.g., see Barash, 1979; E. O. Wilson, 1978). Several researchers have challenged the contention that language can be understood entirely as learned behavior, saying rather that there is a strong genetic influence in its development (e.g., see Chomsky, 1957, 1959, 1972; G. A. Miller, 1965). Accumulating evidence suggests that human and nonhuman learning is so different that little if anything can be learned about human learning by studying nonhuman animals (e.g., see Melton, 1964; Rogers, 1969). The overwhelming interest in cognitive psychology today runs counter to all brands of behaviorism except Tolman's. Current research indicates that *some* responses an animal makes are more easily modifiable than others and that an animal's genetic makeup determines the modifiability of a response (e.g., see Seligman, 1970). Also, researchers have found that the same principles of learning do not apply to all animals (e.g., see Bitterman, 1965) and that different principles govern childhood and adult learning (e.g., see Hebb, 1959; Piaget, 1966, 1970). All these findings are causing abandonment or revision of the tenets of behaviorism.

Another reason that the influence of the neobehaviorists diminished was their insistence that all theoretical terms be operationally defined. Even the logical positivists abandoned a strict operationism because it was too restrictive; it excluded from science concepts that were too nebulous to be defined operationally but were still useful in suggesting new avenues of research and methods of inquiry:

> If one were to criticize behaviorism, it would not be for what it tried to accomplish, but rather for the things it found necessary to *deny*. Fundamentally, it denied the need for free theorizing, because all theory had to be limited to observable stimuli and responses. It denied all of the commonsense constructs without which none of us can get along in the world: Conscious experience, thinking, knowledge, images, feelings, and so on. In fact, it rejected commonsense knowledge by fiat, rather than testing it and transcending it, as the other sciences had done. (Baars, 1986, pp. 82–83)

Even the suggestions that logical positivism made concerning theory construction eventually fell into disrepute. Perhaps the most important reason that logical positivism ultimately failed was the discovery that it did not accurately describe how science was practiced even by its most effective practitioners. Individuals such as Thomas Kuhn (see chapter 1) have shown that the behavior of scientists is determined as much by beliefs, biases, and emotions as by axioms, postulates, theories, or logic.

One major legacy of behaviorism and neobehaviorism still characterizes psychology, however. Psychologists generally agree now that the subject matter of psychology is overt behavior. Today, cognitive psychology is very popular, but even the psychologists studying cognitive events use behavior to index those events. In that sense, most experimental psychologists today are behaviorists.

SUMMARY

The positivism of Bacon, Comte, and Mach insisted that only that which was directly observable be the object of scientific investigation. For the positivists, all speculation about abstract entities should be actively avoided. Watson and the Russian physiologists were positivists. The logical positivists had a more liberal view of scientific activity. For them, theorizing about unobservable entities was allowed provided that those entities be directly linked to observable events via operational definitions. Operational definitions defined abstract concepts in terms of the procedures used to measure those concepts. The belief that all scientific concepts be operationally defined was called operationism. Physicalism was the belief that all sciences should share common assumptions, principles, and methodologies and should model themselves after physics. Neobehaviorism resulted when behaviorism, with its insistence that the subject matter of psychology be overt behavior, merged with logical positivism, with its acceptance of theory and its insistence on operational definitions. By following the tenets of logical positivism, many neobehaviorists believed they could be theoretical and still remain objective.

Independently of logical positivism but in accordance with that philosophy, Tolman introduced intervening variables into psychology. Instead of studying reflexive, or molecular, behavior, Tolman studied purposive, or molar, behavior; thus, his version of psychology was called purposive behaviorism. To avoid even the possibility of introspection in his research, Tolman used only rats as his experimental subjects. According to Tolman, the learning process progressed from the formation of a hypothesis concerning what led to what in an environment, to an expectancy, and, finally, to a belief. A set of beliefs constituted a cognitive map, which was Tolman's most important intervening variable. In Tolman's theory, confirmation replaced the notion of reinforcement, and an important distinction was made between learning and performance. Tolman's general influence on contemporary psychology can be seen in the widespread popularity of cognitive psychology. More specifically, his influence can be seen in Bandura's theory of learning, which emphasizes observational learning. Contemporary information-processing approaches to psychology also have much in common with Tolman's theory.

Using intervening variables even more extensively than did Tolman, Hull developed an open-ended, self-correcting, hypothetico-deductive theory of learning. If experimentation supported the deductions from this theory, the theory gained strength; if experimentation did not support the deductions, the part of the theory on which the deductions were based was revised or rejected. Equating reinforcement with drive reduction, Hull defined habit strength as the number of reinforced pairings between a stimulus and a response. He saw reaction potential as a function of the amount of habit strength and drive present. Hull's theory was extremely influential in the 1940s and 1950s, and due to the efforts of Hull's disciples such as Kenneth Spence, the influence of his theory extended well into the 1960s. Some particular aspects of Hull's theory are still found in contemporary psychology, but not his comprehensive approach to theory building. This is because psychologists now seek theories of more limited domain.

In his approach to psychology, Skinner accepted positivism instead of logical positivism. He can still be classified as a neobehaviorist, however, because although he avoided theory he did accept operationism. Skinner distinguished between respondent behavior, which a known stimulus elicits, and operant behavior, which an organism emits.

Skinner was concerned almost exclusively with operant behavior. For Skinner, reinforcement was anything that changes the rate or probability of a response. Nothing more needs to be known about reinforcement nor is an understanding of physiology necessary for an understanding of behavior. Skinner urged a study of the functional relationship between behavior and the environment. Watson and Skinner were radical behaviorists because they believed all causes of behavior were found in the environment, not in the organism. Tolman and Hull were methodological behaviorists because they were willing to theorize about internal causes of behavior. Many contemporary psychologists label themselves Skinnerians and are active in both the research and applied aspects of psychology. Within Skinnerian psychology, whether one wants to encourage desirable behavior or discourage undesirable behavior, the rule is always the same: Change reinforcement contingencies, and you change behavior.

Contrary to the beliefs of many early behaviorists, evidence is growing for the following: Inherited tendencies are powerful determinants of behavior; language is too complex to be explained simply as learned behavior; human learning is qualitatively different from animal learning; some responses an organism can make are more easily modified by learning than others; mental events influence behavior, and their influence therefore cannot be ignored; different principles of learning apply to different species of animals; and principles governing childhood learning are different from those governing adult learning. These findings are causing either revisions in the assumptions of behaviorism or shifts to other perspectives.

DISCUSSION QUESTIONS

1. Compare positivism to logical positivism.

2. What is an operational definition? Give an example. What is operationism?

3. What is physicalism?

4. What is neobehaviorism?

5. What convinced Tolman that he could study purposive behavior and still be an objective behaviorist?

6. Explain how Tolman used intervening variables in a way that was consistent with logical positivism.

7. How, according to Tolman, did early hypotheses concerning what leads to what in a situation evolve into a cognitive map?

8. What did Tolman mean by vicarious trial and error?

9. In Tolman's theory, was reinforcement necessary for learning to occur? What term in Tolman's theory had some similarity to what others called reinforcement?

10. What evidence did Tolman provide for his contention that reinforcement influenced performance but not learning?

11. What influence did Tolman's theory have on contemporary psychology?

12. Why was Hull's theory called a hypothetico-deductive theory? Why did Hull consider his theory to be self-correcting?

13. With reference to Hull's theory, define the following terms: *reinforcement*, *habit strength*, and *reaction potential*.

14. Was Skinner's proposed functional analysis of the relationship between environmental and behavioral events more in accordance with positivistic or with logical positivistic philosophy?

15. How did Skinner distinguish between respondent and operant behavior?

16. What is meant by the statement that operant behavior is controlled by its consequences?

17. Distinguish between radical and methodological behaviorism.

18. For Skinner, what constituted a reinforcer?

19. How did Skinner apply Darwinian concepts to his analysis of behavior?

20. Summarize Skinner's argument against the use of theory in psychology.

21. State the general rule that Skinnerians follow in modifying behavior. Give an example of how this rule could be applied in treating a behavior disorder.

22. What is the status of neobehaviorism in contemporary psychology?

23. What current research findings are causing a weakening or a revision of the behaviorist position?

SUGGESTIONS FOR FURTHER READING

Hill, W. F. (1990). *Learning: A survey of psychological interpretations* (5th ed.). New York: Harper & Row.
This book is an excellent source for readers seeking more information on the early theories of learning offered by Pavlov, Watson, and Thorndike and on the neobehaviorists covered in the present chapter: Tolman, Hull, and Skinner. (Available in paperback.)

Hull, C. L. (1952a). Clark L. Hull. In E. G. Boring, H. S. Langfeld, H. Werner, & R. M. Yerkes (Eds.), *A history of psychology in autobiography* (Vol. 4, pp. 143–162). Worcester, MA: Clark University Press.
This book contains Hull's autobiography.

Skinner, B. F. (1948). *Walden two*. New York: Macmillan.
This is Skinner's classic description of how his operant principles could be used in the creation of a utopian society. (Available in paperback.)

Skinner, B. F. (1953). *Science and human behavior*. New York: Macmillan.
Although one of Skinner's earlier books, this is perhaps still the best comprehensive presentation of his theory of learning and of how that theory can be applied to a wide range of personal and societal issues. (Available in paperback.)

Skinner, B. F. (1967). B. F. Skinner. In E. G. Boring & G. Lindzey (Eds.), *A history of psychology in autobiography* (Vol. 5, pp. 385–413). New York: Appleton-Century-Crofts.
This book contains Skinner's autobiography.

Skinner, B. F. (1968). *The technology of teaching*. New York: Appleton-Century-Crofts.
In this book, Skinner applies his operant principles to teaching. Chapters include "The Science of Learning and the Art of Teaching," "Teaching Machines," "Why Teachers Fail," "Teaching Thinking," "The Motivation of the Student," "The Creative Student," "Discipline, Ethical Behavior, and Self-Control," and "The Behavior of the Establishment." (Available in paperback.)

Skinner, B. F. (1971). *Beyond freedom and dignity*. New York: Knopf.
In this book, Skinner argues that only a technology of behavior based on operant principles will solve the major problems that humans face. Such a technology will rearrange reinforcement contingencies so that desirable behavior is strengthened and undesirable behavior is weakened by being ignored. Standing in the way of the development and utilization of a technology of behavior is the traditional belief that humans freely choose their behavior and are therefore worthy of praise or blame. Skinner's radical environmentalism goes beyond "freedom" and "dignity." (Available in paperback.)

Skinner, B. F. (1974). *About behaviorism*. New York: Knopf.
Skinner felt obliged to write this book because of the many misconceptions about behaviorism. Among the misconceptions that the book addresses are the beliefs that behaviorism ignores consciousness, feelings, and states of mind; neglects innate endowment and argues that all behavior is learned; represents a person as an automaton, robot, puppet, or machine; has no place for intention or purpose; cannot explain creativity; has nothing to say about a sense of self; dehumanizes humans; regards abstract ideas such as morality or justice as fictions; and is indifferent to the warmth and richness of human life such as the creation and enjoyment of art, music, literature, and the love for one's fellow humans. (Available in paperback.)

Skinner, B. F. (1978). *Reflections on behaviorism and society*. Englewood Cliffs, NJ: Prentice-Hall.
In this collection of his previously published articles, Skinner applies his operant principles to a number of societal issues. Examples include "Human Behavior and Democracy," "Are We Free to Have a Future?" "The Ethics of Helping People," "Humanism and Behaviorism," "Why I Am Not a Cognitive Psychologist," "Some Implications of Making Education More Efficient," "The Free and Happy Student," and "Freedom and Dignity Revisited."

Skinner, B. F. (1987). *Upon further reflection.* Englewood Cliffs, NJ: Prentice-Hall.

This book is a collection of Skinner's recent publications on a variety of subjects—for example, "Why We Are Not Acting to Save the World," "What Is Wrong with Daily Life in the Western World?" "The Shame of American Education," "How to Discover What You Have to Say: A Talk to Students," "Intellectual Self-Management in Old Age," "Pavlov's Influence on Psychology in America," and "Some Thoughts About the Future."

Skinner, B. F. (1990). Can psychology be a science of mind? *American Psychologist, 45,* 1206–1210.

In this article that he prepared for publication the evening before his death, Skinner restates his long-held belief that behavior is selected by reinforcement contingencies. Why, he asks, has such an important observation about behavior not received greater attention? Skinner's explanation is that the belief in a behavior-initiating self or mind is deeply entrenched in the vernacular and in psychology itself. Within current psychology, the mistake that philosophers and theologians had made through the centuries is being perpetuated by "cognitive science"—that is, a belief in an autonomous self or mind as the originator of behavior.

Smith, L. D. (1982). Purpose and cognition: The limits of neorealist influence on Tolman's psychology. *Behaviorism, 10,* 151–163.

Smith points out that Tolman's notion of purpose came from Edwin B. Holt and Ralph Barton Perry, two of his Harvard professors who embraced a philosophy called "new realism." New realists, such as Holt and Perry, argued that purpose and cognition were completely natural phenomena because they are *seen* in adaptive behavior. Tolman at first accepted the new realists' interpretation of purpose and cognition as descriptive features of behavior. Later he vacillated between that position and one that viewed purpose and cognition as mental entities that caused behavior. His final position was to treat purpose and cognition as intervening variables (theoretical constructs). By operationally defining his intervening variables, Tolman could remain a behaviorist even though he used mentalistic concepts. The type of theory developed by Tolman is much easier to work with in our current computer age than it was at the time that Tolman developed it.

Tolman, E. C. (1952). Edward C. Tolman. In E. G. Boring, H. S. Langfeld, H. Werner, & R. M. Yerkes (Eds.), *A history of psychology in autobiography* (Vol. 4, pp. 323–339). Worcester, MA: Clark University Press.

This book contains Tolman's autobiography.

GLOSSARY

Bandura, Albert (b. 1925)   A contemporary learning theorist who emphasizes the development of expectancies through observational learning, thus following in the tradition of Tolman's theory.

Behavior therapy   The use of learning principles to treat emotional or behavioral disorders.

Belief   According to Tolman, an expectation that experience has consistently confirmed.

Cognitive map   According to Tolman, the mental representation of the environment.

Confirmation   The verification of a hypothesis, expectancy, or belief.

Descriptive behaviorism   Behaviorism that is positivistic in that it describes relationships between environmental events and behavior rather than attempting to explain those relationships. Skinner's approach to psychology exemplified descriptive behaviorism.

Direct experience   According to Bandura, the observation of the consequences of our own behavior.

Drive reduction   Hull's proposed mechanism of reinforcement. For Hull, anything that reduced a drive was reinforcing.

Expectancy   According to Tolman, a hypothesis that has been tentatively confirmed.

Functional analysis   Skinner's approach to research that involves studying the systematic relationship between behavioral and environmental events. Such study focuses on the relationship between reinforcement contingencies and response rate or response probability.

Habit strength   (sH_R)   For Hull, the strength of an association between a stimulus and response. This strength depends on the number of reinforced pairings between the two.

Hull, Clark Leonard (1884–1952)   Formulated a complex hypothetico-deductive theory in an attempt to explain all learning phenomena.

Hypothesis   According to Tolman, an expectancy that occurs during the early stages of learning.

Hypothetico-deductive theory   A set of postulates from which empirical relationships are deduced (predicted). If the empirical relationships are as predicted, the theory gains strength; if not, the theory loses strength and must be revised or abandoned.

Instrumental conditioning   The type of conditioning studied by Thorndike, wherein an organism learns to make a response that is instrumental in producing reinforcement.

Intervening variables   Events believed to occur between environmental and behavioral events. Although intervening variables cannot be observed directly, they are thought to be causally related to behavior. Hull's habit strength and Tolman's cognitive map are examples of intervening variables.

Latent learning   According to Tolman, learning that has occurred but is not translated into behavior.

Logical positivism   The philosophy of science according to which theoretical concepts are admissible if they are tied to the observable world through operational definitions.

Molar behavior Purposive behavior.

Molecular behavior A small segment of behavior such as a reflex or a habit that is isolated for study.

Neobehaviorism Agreed with older forms of behaviorism that overt behavior should be psychology's subject matter but disagreed that theoretical speculation concerning abstract entities must be avoided. Such speculation was accepted provided that the theoretical terms employed were operationally defined and that it led to testable predictions about overt behavior.

Observational learning The type of learning that results from attending to environmental events. According to Bandura, we learn what we observe.

Observational terms According to logical positivism, terms that refer to empirical events.

Operant behavior Behavior that is emitted by an organism rather than elicited by a known stimulus.

Operational definition A definition that relates an abstract concept to the procedures used to measure it.

Operationism The belief that all abstract scientific concepts should be operationally defined.

Performance The translation of learning into behavior.

Physicalism A belief growing out of logical positivism that all sciences should share common assumptions, principles, and methodologies and should model themselves after physics.

Positivism The belief that science should study only those objects or events that can be experienced directly. That is, all speculation about abstract entities should be avoided.

Purposive behavior Behavior that is directed toward some goal and that terminates when the goal is attained.

Purposive behaviorism The type of behaviorism Tolman pursued that emphasized molar rather than molecular behavior.

Reaction potential $(_sE_R)$ For Hull, the probability of a learned response being elicited in a given situation. This probability is a function of the amount of drive and habit strength present.

Reinforcement For Hull, drive reduction; for Skinner, anything that increases the rate or the probability of a response; for Tolman, the confirmation of a hypothesis, expectation, or belief.

Respondent behavior Behavior that is elicited by a known stimulus.

Skinner, Burrhus Frederic (1904–1990) A behaviorist who believed that psychology should study the functional relationship between environmental events, such as reinforcement contingencies, and behavior. Skinner's work exemplified positivism. (*See also* **Positivism.**)

S–R psychology The type of psychology insisting that environmental stimuli elicit most, if not all, behavior. The Russian physiologists and Watson were S–R psychologists.

Theoretical terms According to logical positivism, those terms that are employed to explain empirical observations.

Tolman, Edward Chace (1886–1959) Created a brand of behaviorism that used mental constructs and emphasized purposive behavior. Although Tolman employed many intervening variables, his most important was the cognitive map.

Vicarious experience The experience of observing the consequences of another person's behavior. According to Bandura, we learn as much by observing which of another person's actions lead to reward and punishment as we do from observing our own direct experience.

Vicarious trial and error According to Tolman, the conscious pondering of behavioral choices in a learning situation.

CHAPTER 14

Gestalt Psychology

About the same time that the behaviorists were rebelling against structuralism and functionalism in the United States, a group of young German psychologists was rebelling against Wundt's experimental program that featured a search for the elements of consciousness. Whereas the focus of the behaviorists' attack was the study of consciousness and the associated method of introspection, the German protesters focused their attack on Wundt's **elementism**. Consciousness, said the German rebels, could not be reduced to elements without distorting the true meaning of the conscious experience. For them, the investigation of conscious experience through the introspective method was an essential part of psychology, but the type of conscious experience Wundt and the U.S. structuralists investigated was artificial. These young psychologists believed that we did not experience things in isolated pieces but in meaningful, intact configurations. We did not see patches of green, blue, and red; we saw people, cars, trees, and clouds. These meaningful, intact, conscious experiences were what the introspective method should concentrate on. Because the German word for "configuration," "form," or "whole" is *Gestalt*, this new type of psychology was called **Gestalt psychology**.

According to the Gestaltists, the study of wholes, not parts, should be the major task of psychology. Heidbreder summarized what the Gestaltists thought was the proper unit of study for psychology:

The perception itself shows a character of totality, a form, a Gestalt, which in the very attempt at analysis is destroyed; and this experience, as directly given, sets the problem for psychology.

It is this experience that presents the raw data which psychology must explain, and which it must never be content to explain away. To begin with elements is to begin at the wrong end; for elements are products of reflection and abstraction, remotely derived from the immediate experience they are invoked to explain. *Gestalt* psychology attempts to get back to naive perception, to immediate experience "undebauched by learning"; and it insists that it finds there not assemblages of elements, but unified wholes; not masses of sensations, but trees, clouds, and sky. And this assertion it invites anyone to verify simply by opening his eyes and looking at the world about him in his ordinary everyday way. (1933, p. 331)

The Gestaltists were opposed to any type of elementism in psychology, whether it be the type that Wundt and the structuralists practiced or the type the behaviorists practiced in their search for S–R associations. The attempt to reduce either consciousness or behavior to the basic elements is called the **molecular approach** to psychology, and psychologists such as Wundt (as experimentalist), Titchener, Pavlov, and Watson used such an approach. The Gestaltists argued that a molar approach should be taken. Taking the **molar approach** in studying consciousness would mean concentrating on *phenomenological* experience (i.e., mental experience as it occurred to the naive observer without further analysis). The term *phenomenon* means "that which appears" and so **phenomenology**, the technique used by the Gestaltists, was the study of that which naturally appears in consciousness. Taking the molar, or phenomenological, approach while studying behavior meant concentrating on goal-directed (purposive) behavior. We saw in the last chapter that, under the influence of Gestalt psychology, Tolman chose to study this type of behavior. As we will see, the Gestaltists attempted to show that in every aspect of psychology it was more beneficial to concentrate on wholes (*Gestalten*, plural of *Gestalt*) than on parts (atoms, elements). Those taking a molar approach to the study of behavior or psychological phenomena are called **holists**, to contrast them with the elementists or atomists, who study complex phenomena by seeking simpler components that comprise those phenomena. The Gestaltists were clearly holists.

ANTECEDENTS OF GESTALT PSYCHOLOGY

Immanuel Kant

Immanuel Kant (1724–1804) believed that conscious experience was the result of the interaction between sensory stimulation and the actions of the faculties of the mind. In other words, the mind added something to our conscious experience that sensory stimulation did not contain. If the term *faculties of the mind* is replaced by *characteristics of the brain*, there is considerable agreement between Kant and the Gestaltists. Both believed that conscious experience could not be reduced to sensory stimulation, and for both, conscious experience was different from the elements that comprised it. Therefore, to look for a one-to-one correspondence between sensory events and conscious experience was doomed to failure. For Kant and the Gestaltists, an important difference existed between perception and sensation. This difference arose because our minds (Kant) or our brains (the Gestaltists) changed sensory experience, making it more structured and organized and thus more meaningful than it otherwise would be. Accordingly, the world we perceived was never the same as the world we sensed. Because this embellishment of sensory information resulted from the nature of the mind (Kant) or the brain (Gestaltists), it was independent of experience.

Ernst Mach

Ernst Mach (1838–1916), a physicist, postulated (1886/1914) two perceptions that appeared to be independent of the particular elements that comprised them: *space form* and *time form*. For example, one experiences the form of circle whether the actual circle presented is large, small, red, blue, bright, or dull. The experience of "circleness" is therefore an example of space form. The same would be true of any geometric form. Similarly, a melody is recognizable as the same no matter what key or tempo it is played in. Thus, a melody is an example of time form. Mach was making the important point that a wide variety of sensory elements can give rise to the same perception; therefore, at least some perceptions are independent of any particular cluster of sensory elements.

Christian von Ehrenfels

Elaborating on Mach's notions of space and time forms, **Christian von Ehrenfels** (1859–1932) said that our perceptions contained *Gestalt Qualitäten* (form qualities) that were not contained in isolated sensations. No matter what pattern dots are arranged in, one recognizes the pattern, not the individual dots. Similarly, one cannot experience a melody by attending to individual notes; only when one experiences several notes together does one experience the melody. For both Mach and Ehrenfels, form was something that *emerged* from the elements of sensation. Their position was similar to the one John Stuart Mill had taken many years earlier. With his idea of "mental chemistry," Mill had suggested that when sensations fused a new sensation totally unlike those of which it was composed could emerge.

Like Mill, Mach and Ehrenfels believed that elements of sensation often combined and *gave rise* to the experience of form. With his notion of "creative synthesis," Wundt, too, accepted a form of mental chemistry. However, for Mach, Ehrenfels, John Stuart Mill, and Wundt, the elements were still necessary in determining the perception of the whole or the form. As we will see, the Gestaltists turned this relationship completely around by saying that it was the whole that dominated the parts, not the other way around.

William James

Because of his distaste for elementism in psychology, **William James** (1842–1910) can also be viewed as a precursor to Gestalt psychology. He said that Wundt's search for the elements of consciousness depended on an artificial and distorted view of mental life. Instead of viewing the mind as consisting of isolated mental elements, James proposed a stream of consciousness. He believed that this stream should be the object of psychological inquiry, and any attempt to break it up for more detailed analysis must be avoided. The Gestaltists agreed with James's antielementistic stand but thought that he had gone too far. The mind, they believed, could indeed be divided for study; it was just that in choosing the mental element for their object of study, Wundt and the structuralists had made a bad choice. For the Gestaltists, the correct choice was the study of mental *Gestalten*.

Act Psychology

We saw in chapter 9 that members of the Würzburg school, such as Franz Brentano and Carl Stumpf, favored the type of introspection that focused on the *acts* of perceiving, sensing, or problem solving. They were against using introspection to search for mental elements, and they directed their more liberal brand of introspection toward mental phenomena. Thus, both the "act" and the Gestaltists were phenomenologists. It should come as no surprise that **act psychology** influenced Gestalt psychology because all three founders of Gestalt psychology (Wertheimer, Koffka, and Köhler), at one time or another, studied under Carl Stumpf. Köhler

even dedicated one of his books to Stumpf (1920).

Developments in Physics

Because properties of magnetic fields were difficult to understand in terms of the mechanistic-elementistic view of Galilean-Newtonian physics, some physicists turned to a study of force fields, in which all events were interrelated. (Anything that happened in a force field in some way influenced everything else in the field.) Köhler was well versed in physics and had even studied for a while with Max Planck, the creator of quantum mechanics. In fact, it is accurate to say that Gestalt psychology represented an effort to model psychology after **field theory** instead of Newtonian physics. We will say more about this effort shortly.

THE FOUNDING OF GESTALT PSYCHOLOGY

In 1910 Max Wertheimer was on a train, on his way from Vienna to a vacation on the Rhineland, when he had an idea that was to launch Gestalt psychology. The idea was that our perceptions are structured in ways that sensory stimulation is not. That is, our perceptions are different from the sensations that comprise them. To further explore this notion, Wertheimer got off the train at Frankfurt, bought a toy stroboscope (a device that allows still pictures to be flashed in such a way that makes them appear to move), and began to experiment in a hotel room. Clearly, Wertheimer was perceiving motion where none actually existed. To examine this phenomenon in more detail, he went to the University of Frankfurt, where a tachistoscope was made available to him. (A tachistoscope can flash lights on and off for measured fractions of a second.) Flashing two lights successively, Wertheimer found that if the time between the flashes was long (200 milliseconds or longer), the observer perceived two

AMERICAN PSYCHOLOGICAL ASSOCIATION

Max Wertheimer

development of Gestalt psychology that they, along with Wertheimer, are usually considered cofounders of the school.

Max Wertheimer

Max Wertheimer (1880–1943) was born in Prague and attended a *Gymnasium* (roughly equivalent to a high school) until he was 18, at which time he went to the University of Prague to study law. While Wertheimer was attending the University of Prague, his interest shifted from law to philosophy, and during this time he attended lectures by Ehrenfels. After spending some time at the University of Berlin (1901–1903), where he attended Stumpf's classes, Wertheimer moved to the University of Würzburg, where in 1904 he received his doctorate, summa cum laude, under Külpe's supervision. His dissertation was on lie detection. Being at Würzburg at the time when Külpe and others were locked in debate with Wundt over the existence of "imageless thought" and over what introspection should focus on no doubt affected Wertheimer's thinking. Between 1904 and 1910, Wertheimer held academic positions at the Universities of Prague, Vienna, and Berlin. He was at the University of Frankfurt from 1910 to 1916, the University of Berlin from 1916 to 1929, and again at the University of Frankfurt from 1929 to 1933. In 1933 he immigrated to the United States and taught at the New School for Social Research in New York until his death in 1943.

Kurt Koffka

Born in Berlin, **Kurt Koffka** (1886–1941) received his doctorate from the University of Berlin in 1908, under the supervision of Carl Stumpf. Koffka served as an assistant at Würzburg and at Frankfurt before accepting a position at the University of Giessen in central Germany, where he remained until 1924. During his stay at the University of Frankfurt, Koffka began his long association with Wertheimer

lights flashing on and off successively—which was, in fact, the case. If the interval between flashes was very short (30 milliseconds or less), both lights appeared to be on simultaneously. But if the interval between the flashes was about 60 milliseconds, it appeared that *one light* was moving from one position to the other. Wertheimer called this apparent movement the **phi phenomenon**, and his 1912 article "Experimental Studies of the Perception of Movement" describing this phenomenon is usually taken as the formal beginning of the school of Gestalt psychology.

Wertheimer's research assistants at the University of Frankfurt were two recent Berlin doctoral graduates: Kurt Koffka and Wolfgang Köhler, both of whom acted as Wertheimer's subjects in his perception experiments. So closely are Koffka and Köhler linked with the

Kurt Koffka

Wolfgang Köhler

and Köhler. In 1924 he came to the United States, and after holding visiting professorships at Cornell and the University of Wisconsin, he accepted a position at Smith College in Northampton, Massachusetts, where he remained until his death.

In 1922 Koffka wrote an article, in English, on Gestalt psychology. Published in the *Psychological Bulletin*, the article was entitled "Perception: An Introduction to Gestalt-Theorie." This article is believed to have been responsible for most U.S. psychologists erroneously assuming that the Gestaltists were interested only in perception. The truth was that, besides perception, the Gestaltists were interested in many philosophical issues as well as in learning and thinking. The reason for their early concentration on perception was that Wundt had been concentrating on perception, and he was the primary focus of their attack.

In 1921 Koffka published an important book on child psychology, later translated into En-glish as *The Growth of the Mind: An Introduction to Child Psychology* (1924). In 1935 Koffka published *Principles of Gestalt Psychology*, which was intended to be a complete, systematic presentation of Gestalt theory. The latter book was dedicated to Köhler and Wertheimer in gratitude for their friendship and inspiration.

Wolfgang Köhler

Wolfgang Köhler (1887–1967) was born on January 21 in Reval, Estonia, and received his doctorate in 1909 from the University of Berlin. Like Koffka, Köhler worked under the supervision of Stumpf. In 1909 Köhler went to the University of Frankfurt, where a year later he would participate with Wertheimer and Koffka in the research that was to launch the Gestalt movement. Köhler's collaboration with Koffka and Wertheimer was temporarily interrupted when, in 1913, the Prussian Academy of Sciences invited him to go to its anthropoid station on Tenerife, one of the Canary Islands, to study chimpanzees. Shortly after his arrival, the First World War began, and he was marooned for seven years. While at the anthropoid station, Köhler concentrated his study on the nature of learning in chimpanzees. He summarized his observations in the *Mentality of Apes* (1917/1925).

Upon his return to Germany, Köhler accepted a professorship at the University of Göttingen (1921–1922), and in 1922 he succeeded Stumpf as director of the Psychological Institute at the University of Berlin. This was a prestigious appointment, and it gave Gestalt psychology international recognition. Köhler's directorship was interrupted twice by trips to the United States: He was a visiting professor at Clark University (1925–1926), William James lecturer at Harvard (1934–1935), and a visiting professor at the University of Chicago (1935). His *Gestalt Psychology* (1929/1970) was written in English and was especially intended for U.S. psychologists.

Back in Germany, the Nazis were harassing institutions of higher learning and professors. Köhler complained bitterly and, on April 28, 1933, published the last article that publicly criticized the Nazis. In the following excerpt from that article, Köhler commented on the Nazis' wholesale dismissal of Jews from universities and other positions:

> During our conversation, one of my friends reached for the Psalms and read: "The Lord is my shepherd, I shall not want. . . . " He read the 90th Psalm and said, "It is hard to think of a German who has been able to move human hearts more deeply and so to console those who suffer. And these words we have received from the Jews."
>
> Another reminded me that never had a man struggled more nobly for a clarification of his vision of the world than the Jew Spinoza, whose wisdom Goethe admired. My friend did not hesitate to show respect, as Goethe did. Lessing, too, would not have written his *Nathan the Wise* unless human nobility existed among the Jews. . . . It seems that nobody can think of the great work of Heinrich Hertz without an almost affectionate admiration for him. And Hertz had Jewish blood.

> One of my friends told me: "The greatest German experimental physicist of the present time is Franck; many believe that he is the greatest experimental physicist of our age. Franck is a Jew, an unusually kind human being. Until a few days ago, he was professor at Göttingen, an honor to Germany and the envy of the international scientific community." [Perhaps the dismissal of Franck] shows the deepest reason why all these people are not joining [the Party]: they feel a moral imposition. They believe that only the quality of a human being should determine his worth, that intellectual achievement, character, and obvious contributions to German culture retain their significance whether a person is Jewish or not. (Quoted in Henle, 1978, p. 940)

Eventually, the Nazi menace became too unbearable, and in 1935 Köhler immigrated to the United States. After lecturing at Harvard for a year, he accepted an appointment at Swarthmore College, in Swarthmore, Pennsylvania, where he remained until his retirement in 1958. While at Swarthmore, he published his William James lectures as *The Place of Value in a World of Facts* (1938), and *Dynamics in Psychology* (1940) in which he discussed the relationship between field theory in physics and Gestalt psychology. After retiring, Köhler moved to New Hampshire where he continued his writing and research at Dartmouth College. He also spent considerable time lecturing at European universities. His last book, *The Task of Gestalt Psychology* (1969), was published posthumously.

Gestalt psychology became highly influential in the United States. When it is realized that Koffka was at Smith College (an undergraduate institution), Köhler was at Swarthmore (an undergraduate institution), and Wertheimer was affiliated with the New School for Social Research (which was not yet granting advanced degrees), the success of Gestalt psychology in the United States is especially impressive. Also, behaviorism was the dominant theme in U.S. psychology as the Gestaltists were attempting to make inroads. Köhler described an experience he had shortly after arriving in the United States:

In 1925, soon after my first arrival in this country, I had a curious experience. When once talking with a graduate student of psychology who was, of course, a behaviorist, I remarked that McDougall's psychology of striving seemed to me to be associated with certain philosophical theses which I found it hard to accept; but that he might nevertheless be right in insisting that, as a matter of simple observation, people do this or that in order to reach certain goals. Did not the student himself sometimes go to a post office in order to buy stamps? And did he not just now prepare himself for certain examinations to be held next Thursday? The answer was prompt: "I never do such things," said the student. There is nothing like a solid scientific conviction. (Henle, 1986, p. 120)

Köhler's many honors included membership in the American Philosophical Society, National Academy of Sciences, and the American Academy of Arts and Sciences; numerous honorary degrees; an *Ehrenbürger* (honorary citizen) of the University of Berlin (an honor previously given to only two Americans—John F. Kennedy and Paul Hindesmith); the American Psychological Association's Distinguished Scientific Contributions Award (1956); and the presidency of the American Psychological Association (APA) (1959).

ISOMORPHISM AND THE LAW OF PRÄGNANZ

A basic question that Wertheimer had to answer was how only two stimuli could cause the perception of motion. Wertheimer did not discover apparent motion; it had been known about for years. In fact, the motion picture had been invented 25 years before Wertheimer's discovery of the phi phenomenon. What was different was Wertheimer's *explanation* of the phenomenon. As we have seen, Mach, Ehrenfels, and J. S. Mill all recognized that the whole was sometimes different from the sum of its parts, but they all assumed that somehow the whole (*Gestalt*) emerged from the characteristics of the parts. That is, after the parts (elements) were attended

to, they somehow fused and gave rise to the whole experience. For example, attending to the primary colors caused the sensation of white to emerge, and attending to several musical notes caused the sensation of melody to emerge. This viewpoint still depended on a form of elementism and its related assumption of association. For example, Wundt's explanation of apparent movement was that the fixation of the eyes changed with each successive presentation of the visual stimulus, and this caused the muscles controlling the eyes to give off sensations identical to those given off when real movement was experienced. Thus, because of past experience with such sensations (association), one experienced what appeared to be movement. Because with apparent movement the sensation of movement was not contained in the sensations that caused it, Wundt believed that the experience exemplified creative synthesis. Similarly, Helmholtz explained the phenomenon as an unconscious inference. Both Wundt and Helmholtz emphasized the role of learning in experiences like the phi phenomenon.

Through an ingenious demonstration, however, Wertheimer showed that explanations based on learning were not plausible. Again using a tachistoscope, he showed that the phi phenomenon could occur in two directions at the same time. Three lights were arranged as shown in the diagram below:

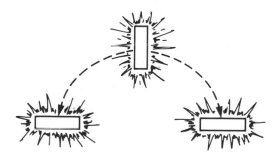

The center light was flashed on, and shortly thereafter the two other lights were flashed on, both at the same time. Wertheimer repeated this sequence several times. The center slit of light appeared to fall to the left and right simultaneously, and because the eyes could not move in two directions at the same time, an explanation based on sensations from the eye muscles was untenable.

Application of Field Theory

If the experience of psychological phenomena could not be explained by sensory processes, inferences, or fusions, how could it be explained? The Gestaltists' answer was that the brain contained structured fields of electrochemical forces that existed prior to sensory stimulation. Upon entering such a field, sensory data both modified the structure of the field and were modified by it. What we experienced consciously resulted from the interaction of the sensory data and the force fields in the brain. The situation is similar to one in which metal particles are placed into a magnetic field. The nature of the field will have a strong influence on how the particles are distributed, but the characteristics of the particles will also influence the distribution. For example, larger, more numerous particles will be distributed differently within the field than smaller, less numerous particles. In the case of cognitive experience, the important point is that fields of brain activity *transform* sensory data and give that data characteristics it otherwise would not possess. According to this analysis, the whole (electrochemical force fields in the brain) exists prior to the parts (individual sensations), and it is the whole that gives the parts their identity or meaning.

Psychophysical Isomorphism

To describe more fully the relationship between the field activity of the brain and conscious experience, the Gestaltists introduced the notion of **psychophysical isomorphism**, which Köhler described as follows: "Experienced order in space is always structurally identical with a functional order in the distribution of underlying brain processes" (1947, p. 61). Elsewhere, Köhler said, "Psychological facts and the underlying events in the brain resemble each other in all their structural characteristics" (1969, p. 66).

The Gestalt notion of isomorphism stressed the facts that the force fields in the brain transform incoming sensory data and that it is the transformed data that we experience consciously. [The word *isomorphism* is from the Greek *iso* ("similar") and *morphic* ("shape").] The patterns of brain activity and the patterns of conscious experience are structurally equivalent. The Gestaltists did not say that patterns of electrochemical brain activity were the same as patterns of perceptual activity. Rather, they said that perceptual fields were always caused by underlying patterns of brain activity. It was believed that, although the patterns of perceptual and brain activity might have some similarity, the two represented two totally different domains and certainly could not be identical. The relationship is like that between a map of the United States and the actual United States; although the two are related in important ways, they are hardly identical.

Opposition to the Constancy Hypothesis

With their notion of isomorphism, the Gestaltists were opposing the **constancy hypothesis**, according to which there was a one-to-one correspondence between certain environmental stimuli and certain sensations. By one-to-one correspondence, it was not meant that sensations necessarily reflect accurately what is present physically. The psychophysicists, Helmholtz, Wundt, and the structuralists all accepted the constancy hypothesis while recognizing that large discrepancies could exist between psychological experiences and the physical events that caused them. Rather, the constancy hypothesis was the contention that individual physical events cause individual sensations and that these sensations remain isolated unless acted on by one or more of the laws of association or, in Wundt's case, were intentionally rearranged. This hypothesis was accepted by most British and French empiricists and was the cornerstone of Titchener's structuralism. The structuralists, following in the tradition of empiricism, viewed mental events as the passive reflections of specific environmental events.

The Gestaltists totally disagreed with the conception of brain functioning implied by the constancy hypothesis. By rejecting the constancy hypothesis, the Gestaltists rejected the empirical philosophy on which the schools of structuralism, functionalism, and behaviorism were based. Instead, as we have seen, the Gestaltists employed field theory in their analysis of brain functioning. In any physical system, energy is distributed in a lawful way, and the brain is a physical system. Köhler said, "According to several physicists the distribution of materials and processes in physical systems tends to become regular, simple, and often symmetrical when the systems approach a state of equilibrium or a steady state" (1969, pp. 64–65). Michael Wertheimer elaborates this point:

> The Gestaltists argue that physical forces, when released, do not produce chaos, but their own internally determined organization. The nervous system, similarly, is not characterized by machinelike connections of tubes, grooves, wires, or switchboards, but the brain too, like almost all other physical systems, exhibits the dynamic self-distribution of physical forces. (1987, p. 137)

Thus, instead of viewing the brain as a passive receiver and recorder of sensory information, the Gestaltists viewed the brain as a dynamic configuration of forces that transformed sensory information. They believed that the incoming sensory data interacted with force fields within the brain to cause fields of mental activity, and like the underlying physical fields in the brain, these mental fields were organized configurations. The nature of the mental configurations depended on the totality of the incoming stimulation and the nature of the force fields within the brain, and any configurations that occurred in the fields of brain activity would be experienced as perceptions (psychophysical isomorphism).

Analysis: Top Down, Not Bottom Up

According to the Gestaltists, the organized brain activity dominated our perceptions, *not* the stimuli that entered into that activity. For this reason, the whole was more important than the parts, thus reversing one of psychology's oldest traditions. The Gestaltists said that their analysis proceeded *from the top to the bottom* instead of *from the bottom to the top*, as had been the tradition. In other words, they proceeded from the wholes to the parts instead of from the parts to the wholes. Michael Wertheimer elaborates this point:

> This formulation involved a radical reorientation: the nature of the parts is determined by the whole rather than vice versa; therefore analysis should go "from above down" rather than "from below up." One should not begin with elements and try to synthesize the whole from them, but study the whole to see what its natural parts are. The parts of a whole are not neutral and inert, but structurally intimately related to one another. That parts of a whole are not indifferent to one another was illustrated, for example, by a soap bubble: change of one part results in a dramatic change in the entire configuration. This approach was applied to the understanding of a wide variety of phenomena in thinking, learning, problem solving, perception, and philosophy, and the movement developed and spread rapidly, with violent criticisms against it from outside, as well as equally vehement attacks on the outsiders from inside. (1987, p. 136)

The Law of Prägnanz

The Gestaltists believed that the same forces that created configurations such as soap bubbles and magnetic fields also created configurations in the brain. The configurations of energy occurring in all physical systems always result from the total field of interacting forces, and these physical forces always distribute themselves in the most simple, symmetrical way possible under the circumstances. Therefore, according to the principle of psychophysical isomorphism, mental experiences, too, must be simple and symmetrical. The Gestaltists summarized this relationship between force fields in the brain and cognitive experience with their law of Prägnanz, which was central to Gestalt psychology. The German word *Prägnanz* has no exact English counterpart but an approximation is "essence." *Prägnanz* refers to the essence or ultimate meaning of an experience. Sensory information may be fragmented and incomplete, but when that information interacts with the force fields in the brain, the resultant cognitive experience is complete and organized. The **law of Prägnanz** states that psychological organization will always be as good as conditions allow because fields of brain activity will always distribute themselves in the simplest way possible under the prevailing conditions, just as other physical force fields do. The law of Prägnanz asserts that all cognitive experiences will tend to be as organized, symmetrical, simple, and regular as they can be, given the pattern of brain activity at any given moment. This is what "as *good* as conditions allow" means.

What we experience cognitively, then, is determined by the interaction between sensory stimulation and brain activity, which is governed by the law of Prägnanz. Figure 14.1 illustrates the important role of the law of Prägnanz in the process of psychophysical isomorphism, as the Gestaltists saw it.

It is tempting to categorize Gestalt psychol-

ogy as nativistic, but the Gestaltists themselves disagreed with that categorization. Köhler said, "Such concepts as genes, inherited, and innate should never be mentioned when we refer to the basic . . . dynamic . . . processes in the nervous system" (1969, p. 89). According to Köhler, what governed brain activity was not genetically controlled programs but the *invariant dynamics* that govern *all* physical systems:

> Why so much talk about inheritance, and so much about learning—but hardly ever a word about invariant dynamics? It is this invariant dynamics, however constrained by histological devices, which keeps organisms and their nervous systems going. I add an old quotation: *Hamlet*, it has been said, cannot be played without the Prince of Denmark. Why, then, are we consistently trying to do so on our stage? (Köhler, 1969, p. 90)

According to Henle, it is time for psychology to follow the lead of the Gestaltists and stop attempting to explain everything in terms of the nativism–empiricism dichotomy:

> I do not know why we find it so difficult to break out of the nativism–empiricism dichotomy. Are we unable to think in terms of trichotomies? If we are, we will continue to misinterpret Gestalt psychology and—more serious—our explanations will not do justice to our subject matter. (1986, p. 123)

FIGURE 14.1 The Gestalt notion of psychophysical isomorphism (adapted from Hergenhahn, 1988, p. 250). Used by permission.

PERCEPTUAL CONSTANCIES

The way we respond to objects as if they were the same even though the actual stimulation our senses receive may vary greatly is called **perceptual constancy** (*not* to be confused with the constancy hypothesis):

> The man who approaches us on the street does not seem to grow larger as for simple optical reasons he should. The circle which lies in an oblique plane does not appear as an ellipse; it seems to remain a circle even though its retinal image may be a very flat ellipse. The white object with the shadow across it remains white, the black paper in full light remains black, although the former may reflect much less light than the latter. Obviously, these three phenomena have something in common. The physical object as such always remains the same, while the stimulation of our eyes varies, as the distance, the orientation or the illumination of that constant object are changed. Now, what we seem to experience agrees with the actual invariance of the physical object much better than it does with the varying stimulations. Hence the terms constancy of size, constancy of shape and constancy of brightness. (Köhler, 1929/1970, pp. 78–79)

The empiricists explained perceptual constancies as the result of learning. The sensations provided by objects seen at different angles, positions, and levels of illumination were different, but through experience we learned to correct for these differences and to respond to the objects as the same. Woodworth described what our perceptions would be like, according to the empiricists, if the influence of learning could be removed:

> If we could for a moment lay aside all that we had learned and see the field of view just as the eyes present it, we should see a mere mosaic of variegated spots, free of meaning, of objects, of shapes or patterns. Such is the traditional associationist view of the matter. (1931, pp. 105–106)

The Gestaltists disagreed. Köhler, for example, asserted that the constancies were a direct reflection of ongoing brain activity and *not* a result of sensation plus learning. The reason we experienced an object as the same under varied conditions was that the *relationship* between that object and other objects remained the same. Because this relationship was the same, the field of brain activity was also the same, and therefore the mental experience (perception) was the same. The Gestaltists' explanation, then, is simply an extension of the notion of psychophysical isomorphism. Using brightness constancy as an example, Bruno nicely summarizes this point:

> [Köhler] said that brightness constancy is due to the existence of a real constancy that is an existing *Gestalt* in the environment. This *Gestalt* is physical—really there as a pattern. It is the *ratio* of brightness of the figure to the brightness of the ground. This ratio remains constant for sunlight and shade. Let us say that a light meter gives a reading of 10 (arbitrary units) for a bikini in the sun. A reading from the grass in the sun is 5. The ratio of figure to ground is 10/5 or 2. Assume now that the girl in the bikini is in the shade, and light meter gives a reading of 4 for the bikini. The grass in the shade gives a reading of 2. The ratio of figure to ground is 4/2 or 2—the same ratio as before. The ratio is a constant. The human nervous system responds directly to this constant ratio. The constant ratio in the environment gives rise to a pattern of excitation in the nervous system. As long as the ratio does not change, the characteristics of the pattern of excitation do not change. Thus Köhler explained brightness constancy as a directly perceived *Gestalt* not derived from learning or the association of sensations.
>
> Köhler explained other perceptual constancies involving color, shape, and size in a similar manner. (1972, p. 151)

PERCEPTUAL *GESTALTEN*

Through the years, the Gestaltists have isolated over 100 configurations (*Gestalten*) into which visual information is arranged. We will sample only a few of them here.

The Figure–Ground Relationship

According to the Danish psychologist Edgar Rubin (1886–1951), the most basic type of perception is the division of the perceptual field into two parts: the *figure*, which is clear and unified and is the object of attention, and the *ground*, which is diffuse and consists of everything that is not being attended to. Such a division creates what is called a **figure–ground relationship**. Thus, what is the figure and what is the ground can be changed by shifting one's attention. Figure 14.2 demonstrates this. When one focuses attention on the two profiles, one cannot see the vase and vice versa. Likewise, when one focuses attention on the black cross, one cannot see the white cross and vice versa.

The Gestaltists made the figure–ground relationship a major component of their theoretical system.

Gestalt Principles of Perceptual Organization

Besides describing figure–ground perception, the Gestaltists described the principles by which the elements of perception are organized into configurations. For example, stimuli that have continuity with one another will be experienced as a perceptual unit. To describe this principle, Wertheimer used the terms *intrinsic togetherness, imminent necessity*, and *good continuation*. Figure 14.3a provides an example of this **principle of continuity**. Note that the pattern that emerges

cannot be found in any particular dot (element). Rather, because some dots seem to be tending in the same direction, one responds to them as a configuration (*Gestalt*). Most people would describe this figure as consisting of two curved lines.

When stimuli are close together, they tend to be grouped together as a perceptual unit. This is known as the **principle of proximity**. In Figure 14.3b, the Xs tend to be seen in groups of two, instead of as individual Xs. The same is true of the lines.

According to the **principle of inclusiveness**, when there is more than one figure, we are most likely to see the figure that contains the greatest number of stimuli. If, for example, a small figure is embedded in a larger one, we are most likely to see the larger figure and not the smaller. The use of camouflage is an application of this principle. For example, ships painted the color of water and tanks painted the color of the terrain in which they operate blend into the background and are thus less susceptible to detection. In Figure 14.3c, the symbol $\sqrt{16}$ is difficult to see because so many of its components are part of a larger stimulus complex. Köhler believed that the principle of inclusiveness provided evidence against the empiricalistic expla-

FIGURE 14.2 In each illustration, which is the figure and which is the ground? (Adapted from Rubin, 1915/1921.)

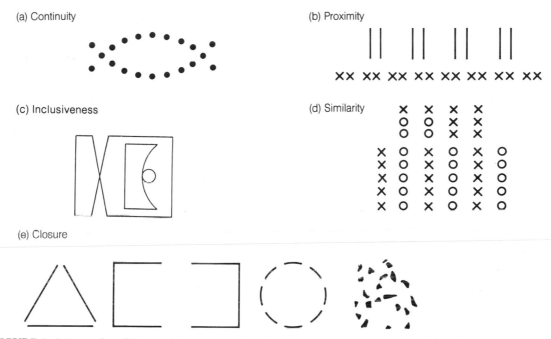

(a) Continuity

(b) Proximity

(c) Inclusiveness

(d) Similarity

(e) Closure

FIGURE 14.3 Examples of (a) principle of continuity, (b) principle of proximity, (c) principle of inclusiveness (Köhler, 1969), (d) principle of similarity, and (e) principle of closure (Sartain et al., 1973; used by permission of Prentice-Hall, Inc.).

nation of perception. He said most people would clearly have much more experience with the symbol √16 than with the figure shown in Figure 14.3c. Yet, the stronger tendency is to perceive the more inclusive figure. Köhler (1969) made the same point with the following figure:

Köhler observed that if perception is determined by past experience (learning), then most people would perceive the familiar word *men* along with its mirror image in the figure. Instead, however, most people perceive a less familiar figure, which somewhat resembles a horizontal row of forms resembling hearts.

Objects that are similar in some way tend to form perceptual units. This is known as the **principle of similarity**. Twins, for example,

stand out in a crowd, and teams wearing different uniforms stand out as two groups on the field. In Figure 14.3d, the stimuli that have something in common stand out as perceptual units.

As we have seen, the Gestaltists believed in psychophysical isomorphism, according to which our conscious experience is directly related to patterns of brain activity, and the brain activity organizes itself into patterns according to the law of Prägnanz. Thus, it is quite likely that the patterns of brain activity are often better organized than the stimuli that enter them. This is clearly demonstrated in the **principle of closure**, according to which incomplete figures in the physical world are perceived as complete ones. As Figure 14.3e shows, even if figures have gaps in them—and thus are not truly circles, triangles, or rectangles—they are nonetheless experienced as circles, triangles, or rectangles. This is because the brain transforms the stimuli into organized configurations that are then experienced cognitively. For the same reason, in Figure 14.3e we see a person on horseback.

SUBJECTIVE AND OBJECTIVE REALITY

Because the brain acts on sensory information and arranges it into configurations, what we are conscious of, and therefore act in accordance with at any given moment, is more a product of the brain than of the physical world. Koffka used this fact to distinguish between the geographical and the behavioral environments. For him, the **geographical environment** was the physical environment, whereas the **behavioral environment** was our subjective interpretation of the geographical environment. Koffka used an old German legend to illustrate the important difference between the two environments:

> On a winter evening amidst a driving snow-storm a man on horseback arrived at an inn, happy to have reached a shelter after hours of riding over the wind-swept plain on which the blanket of snow had covered all paths and land-marks. The landlord who came to the door viewed the stranger with surprise and asked him whence he came. The man pointed in the direction straight away from the inn, whereupon the landlord, in a tone of awe and wonder, said: "Do you know that you have ridden across the Lake of Constance?" at which the rider dropped stone dead at his feet.
>
> In what environment, then, did the behavior of the stranger take place? The Lake of Constance? Certainly, because it is a true proposition that he rode across it. And yet, this is not the whole truth, for the fact that there was a frozen lake and not ordinary solid ground did not affect his behavior in the slightest. It is interesting for the geographer that this behavior took place in this particular locality, but not for the psychologist as the student of behavior; because the behavior would have been just the same had the man ridden across a barren plain. But the psychologist knows something more: since the man died from sheer fright after having learned what he had "really" done, the psychologist must conclude that had the stranger known before, his riding behavior would have been very different from what it actually was. Therefore the psychologist will have to say: there is a sec-ond sense to the word environment according to which our horseman did not ride across the lake at all, but across an ordinary snow-swept plain. His behavior was a riding-over-a-plain, but not a riding-over-a-lake.
>
> What is true of the man who rode across the Lake of Constance is true of every behavior. Does the rat run in the maze *the experimenter* has set up? According to the meaning of the word "in," yes and no. Let us therefore distinguish between a *geographical* and a *behavioral* environment. Do we all live in the same town? Yes, when we mean the geographical, no, when we mean the behavioral. (1935/1963, pp. 27–28)

In other words, our own subjective reality governs our actions more than the physical environment does.

THE GESTALT EXPLANATION OF LEARNING

Cognitive Trial and Error

As we have seen, the Gestaltists believed that brain activity tended toward a balance, or equilibrium, in accordance with the law of Prägnanz. This tendency toward equilibrium continued naturally unless it was somehow disrupted. According to the Gestaltists, the existence of a problem was one such disruptive influence. If a problem was confronted, a state of disequilibrium existed until the problem was solved. Because a state of disequilibrium was unnatural, it created a tension with motivational properties that kept the organism active until it solved the problem. Typically, an organism solved its problems perceptually by scanning the environment and cognitively trying one possible solution and then another, until it reached a solution. Thus, the Gestaltists emphasized *cognitive* trial and error as opposed to *behavioral* trial and error. They believed that organisms came to *see* solutions to problems.

Insightful Learning

Köhler did much of his work on learning between 1913 and 1917 when he was stranded on the island of Tenerife during the First World

War. In a typical experiment, using apes as subjects, Köhler suspended a desired object—for example, a banana—in the air just out of the animal's reach. Then he placed objects such as boxes and sticks, which the animal could use to obtain the banana, in the animal's environment. By stacking one or more boxes under the banana or by using a stick, the animal could obtain the banana. In one case, the animal needed to join two sticks together in order to reach a banana.

In studying learning, Köhler also employed so-called *detour problems*, problems in which the animal could see its goal but could not reach it directly. To solve the problem, the animal had to learn to take an indirect route to the goal. Figure 14.1 shows a typical detour problem. Köhler found that although chickens had great difficulty with such problems, apes solved them with ease.

Köhler noted that during a problem's presolution period, the animals appeared to weigh the situation—that is, to test various hypotheses. (This is what we referred to earlier as cognitive or vicarious trial and error.) Then, at some point, the animal achieved *insight* into the solution and behaved according to that insight. For the Gestaltists, a problem could exist in only two stages: It was either unsolved or solved—there was no in-between. According to the Gestaltists, the reason that Thorndike and others had found what appeared to be incremental learning (learning that occurs gradually) was that all ingredients necessary for the attainment of insight had not been available to the animal. But if a problem was presented to an organism along with those things necessary for the problem's solution, **insightful learning** typically occurred. According to the Gestaltists, insightful learning was much more desirable than learning achieved through either rote memorization or behavioral trial and error. Hergenhahn summarizes the conclusions that the Gestaltists reached about insightful learning:

> Insightful learning is usually regarded as having four characteristics: (a) the transition from presolution to solution is sudden and complete; (b) performance based upon a solution gained by insight is usually smooth and free of errors; (c) a solution to a problem gained by insight is retained for a considerable length of time; and (d) a principle gained by insight is easily applied to other problems. (1988, p. 257)

Transposition

To explore further the nature of learning, Köhler used chickens as subjects. In one experiment, he placed a white sheet and a gray sheet of paper on the ground; both were covered with grain. If a chicken pecked at the grain on the white sheet, it was shooed away; but if it pecked at the grain on the gray sheet, it was allowed to eat. After many trials, the chickens learned to peck at the grain on only the gray sheet. The question is What did the animals learn? Thorndike, Hull, and Skinner would say that reinforcement strengthened the response of eating off the gray paper. To answer the question, Köhler proceeded with phase two of the experiment: He replaced the white paper with a sheet of black paper. Now the choice was between a gray sheet of paper, the one for which the chickens had received reinforcement, and a black sheet. Given this choice, most reinforcement theorists would have predicted that the chickens would continue to approach the gray paper. The vast majority of the chickens, however, approached the black paper. Köhler's explanation was that the chickens had not learned a stimulus–response association or a

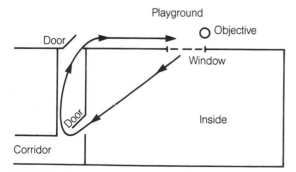

FIGURE 14.4 A typical detour problem that Köhler used to study the learning process (Köhler, 1925). Used by permission.

specific response but a *relationship*. In this case, the animals had learned to approach the *darker* of the two sheets of paper. If, in the second phase of the experiment, Köhler had presented a sheet of paper of a lighter gray than the one on which the chickens had been reinforced, the chickens would have continued to approach the sheet on which they had previously been fed because it would have been the darker of the two.

Thus, for the Gestaltist, an organism learned principles or relationships, not specific responses to specific situations. Once it learned a principle, the organism applied it to similar situations. This was called **transposition**, Gestalt psychology's explanation of transfer of training. The notion of transposition was contrary to Thorndike's identical-elements theory of transfer, according to which the similarity (common elements) between two situations determines the amount of transfer between them.

The behaviorists' explanation of transposition. The Gestalt theory explanation of transposition did not go unchallenged. Kenneth Spence, the major spokesman for Hullian psychology, came up with an ingenious alternative explanation. Hergenhahn summarizes Spence's explanation:

> Suppose, said Spence, that an animal is reinforced for approaching a box whose lid measures 160 sq. cm. and not reinforced for approaching a box whose lid measures 100 sq. cm. Soon the animal will learn to approach the larger box exclusively.
>
> In phase two of this experiment, the animal chooses between the 160 sq. cm. box and the box whose lid is 256 sq. cm. The animal will usually choose the larger box (256 sq. cm.) even though it had been reinforced specifically for choosing the other (160 sq. cm.) during phase one. . . . This finding seems to support the relational learning point of view.
>
> Spence's behavioristic explanation of transposition is based on generalization. . . . Spence assumed that the tendency to approach the positive stimulus (160 sq. cm.) generalizes to other related stimuli. Second, he assumed that the tendency to approach the positive stimulus (and the generalization of this tendency) is stronger

than the tendency to avoid the negative stimulus (and the generalization of the tendency). What behavior occurs will be determined by the algebraic summation of the positive and negative tendencies.

> [To follow the remainder of Spence's explanation, refer to Figure 14.5.]
>
> Whenever there is a choice between two stimuli, the one eliciting the greatest net approach tendency will be chosen. In the first phase of Spence's experiment, the animal chose the 160 sq. cm. box over the 100 sq. cm. box because the net positive tendency was 51.7 for the former and 29.7 for the latter. In phase two, the 256 sq. cm. box was chosen over the 160 sq. cm. box because the net positive tendency was 72.1 for the former and still 51.7 for the latter. (1988, pp. 259–260)

Spence's explanation had the advantage of predicting the circumstances under which transposition would not occur. As the matter stands today, neither the Gestalt nor the behaviorist explanations can account for all transpositional phenomena; therefore, a comprehensive explanation is still being sought.

PRODUCTIVE THINKING

Wertheimer was concerned with the application of Gestalt theory to education. His book *Productive Thinking* was published posthumously in 1945. Under the editorship of Wertheimer's son Michael, this book was later revised and expanded, and it was republished in 1959. The conclusions Wertheimer reached about **productive thinking** were based on personal experience, experimentation, and interviews with individuals considered excellent problem solvers, such as Einstein:

> Those were wonderful days, beginning in 1916, when for hours and hours I was fortunate enough to sit with Einstein, alone in his study, and hear from him the story of the dramatic developments which culminated in the theory of relativity. During those long discussions I questioned Einstein in great detail about the concrete events in his thought. (Max Wertheimer, 1945/1959, p. 213)

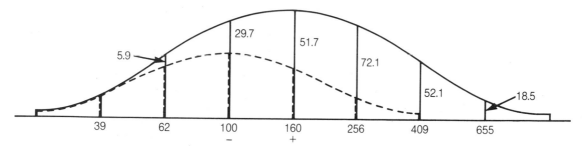

FIGURE 14.5 According to Spence, the algebraic sum of the positive and negative influences determine which of two stimuli in a discrimination problem will be approached (Spence, 1942).

Wertheimer contrasted learning according to Gestalt principles with rote memorization governed by external reinforcement and the laws of association. The former is based on an understanding of the nature of the problem. As we have seen, the existence of a problem creates a cognitive disequilibrium that lasts until the problem is solved. The solution restores a cognitive harmony, and this restoration is all the reinforcement that the learner needs. Because learning and problem solving are personally satisfying, they are governed by **intrinsic** (internal) **reinforcement** rather than **extrinsic** (external) **reinforcement**. Wertheimer thought that we were motivated to learn and to solve problems because it was personally satisfying to do so, not because someone or something else reinforced us for doing so. Because learning governed by Gestalt principles was based on an understanding of the structure of the problem, it was easily remembered and generalized to other relevant situations.

Wertheimer believed that some learning did occur when mental associations, memorization, drill, and external reinforcement were employed but that such learning was usually trivial. He gave as examples of such learning associating a friend's name with his or her telephone number, learning to anticipate correctly a list of nonsense syllables, and a dog learning to salivate to a certain sound. Unfortunately, according to Wertheimer, this is the type of learning that most schools emphasize.

In Wertheimer's analysis, teaching that emphasizes logic does not fare any better than rote memorization. Supposedly, logic guarantees that one will reach correct conclusions. Teaching based on such a notion, said Wertheimer, assumes that there is a correct way to think and that everyone should think that way. But like rote memorization, learning and applying the rules of logic stifle productive thinking because neither activity is based on the realization that problem solving involves the total person and is unique to that person:

> According to Wertheimer, reaching an understanding involves many aspects of learners, such as their emotions, attitudes, and perceptions, as well as their intellects. In gaining insight into the solution to a problem, a student need not—in fact, should not—be logical. Rather, the student should cognitively arrange and rearrange the components of the problem until a solution based on understanding is reached. Exactly how this is done will vary from student to student. (Hergenhahn, 1988, p. 261)

To demonstrate the difference between rote learning and learning based on understanding, Michael Wertheimer (1980) describes an experiment that Katona originally performed in 1940. Katona showed subjects the following 15 digits and told them to study the digits for 15 seconds: 1 4 9 1 6 2 5 3 6 4 9 6 4 8 1. With only these instructions, most people attempt to memorize as many digits as possible in the allotted time. Indeed, Katona found that most subjects could reproduce only a few of the numbers correctly; and when tested a week later, most subjects remembered none.

Katona asked another group of subjects to look for a pattern or theme running through the numbers. Some individuals in this group realized that the 15 digits represented the squares of the digits from 1 to 9. These subjects saw a principle that they could apply to the problem and were able to reproduce all numbers correctly not only during the experiment but also for weeks after. In fact, those individuals could no doubt reproduce the series correctly for the rest of their lives. Katona's experiment thus supported Wertheimer's belief that learning and problem solving based on Gestalt principles had many advantages over rote memorization or problem solving based on formal logic.

MEMORY

Although the Gestaltists emphasized the tendency for the energy in the brain to organize itself into simple and symmetrical patterns in their accounts of learning and perception, they did not deny the importance of experience. They maintained that the tendency toward perceptual organization and cognitive equilibrium was derived from the fact that the brain was a physical system and, as such, distributed its activity in the simplest, most concise configuration possible under any circumstances. *What* the brain organized, however, was provided by sensory experience, and this provided an experiential component to Gestalt theory. Another experiential component is apparent in the Gestaltists' treatment of memory. Of the three founders of Gestalt theory, Koffka wrote the most about memory.

Memory Processes, Traces, and Systems

Koffka assumed that each physical event we experienced gave rise to specific activity in the brain. He called the brain activity caused by a specific environmental event a **memory process**. When the environmental event terminated, so did the brain activity it caused. However, a remnant of the memory process—a **memory trace**—remained in the brain. Once the memory trace was formed, all subsequent related experience would involve an interaction between the memory process and the memory trace. For example, when we experience a cat for the first time, the experience will create a characteristic pattern of brain activity; this is the memory process. After the experience is terminated, the brain will register its effects; this is the memory trace. The next time we experience a cat the memory process elicited will interact with the already existing trace from the first experience. The conscious experience will be the result of both the present memory process *and* the trace of previously related experiences. Furthermore, a trace "exerts an influence on the process in the direction of *making it similar to the process which originally produced the trace*" (Koffka, 1935/1963, p. 553).

According to this analysis, we are aware of and remember things in general terms rather than specific characteristics. Instead of seeing and remembering such things as cats, clowns, or elephants, we see and remember "catness," "clownness," and "elephantness." This is because the trace of classes of experience records what those experiences have in common—for example, those things that make a cat a cat. With more experience, the trace becomes more firmly established and more influential in our perceptions and memories. The individual trace gives way to a **trace system**, which is the consolidation of a number of interrelated experiences. In other words, a trace system will record all our experiences with, say, cats. The interaction of traces and trace systems with ongoing brain activity (memory processes) results in our perceptions and memories being smoother and better organized than they otherwise would be. For example, we remember irregular experiences as regular, incomplete experiences as complete, and unfamiliar experiences as something familiar. Trace systems govern our memories of particular things as well as of general categories. For example, the memory of one's own dog, cat, or mother will tend to be a composite of memories of experiences that occurred over a long period of time and under a wide variety of circumstances.

Like everything else addressed by Gestalt theory, memory is governed by the law of Prägnanz. That is, we tend to remember the essences of our experiences. The brain operates in such a way as to make memories as simple and symmetrical as is possible under the circumstances.

LEWIN'S FIELD THEORY

Born in Mogilno, Germany, **Kurt Lewin** (1890–1947) received his doctorate in 1914 from the University of Berlin, under the supervision of Stumpf. After several years of military service, for which he earned Germany's Iron Cross, Lewin returned to the University of Berlin where he held various positions until 1932 and where he worked with Wertheimer, Koffka, and Köhler. Although Lewin is usually not considered a founder of Gestalt psychology, he was an early disciple, and most of his work can be seen as an extension or application of Gestalt principles to the topics of motivation, personality, and group dynamics.

Lewin was a visiting lecturer at Stanford University in 1932; from 1933 to 1935, he was a visiting lecturer at Cornell. In 1935 he became affiliated with the Child Welfare Station at the University of Iowa as a professor of child psychology, and in 1944 he created and directed the Research Center for Group Dynamics at the Massachusetts Institute of Technology. Although Lewin died only three years after starting his work on group dynamics, the influence of this work was profound and is still evident in psychology today. (See Patnoe, 1988, for a number of interviews with prominent experimental social psychologists who were either directly or indirectly influenced by Lewin.)

Kurt Lewin

AMERICAN PSYCHOLOGICAL ASSOCIATION

Aristotelian Versus Galilean Conception of Science

Lewin (1935) distinguished between Aristotle's view of nature, which emphasized inner essences and categories, and Galileo's view, which emphasized outer causation and the dynamics of forces. For Aristotle, various natural objects fell into categories according to their essence, and everything that members of a certain category had in common defined the essence of members of that category. Unless external forces interfered, all members of a category had an innate tendency to manifest their essence. For example, all elephants would, unless interfered with by accidental circumstances, manifest the essence of elephantness. In this world of distinct classes, internal forces drove the members of the classes to become what their essence dictated they must become. Aristotle saw individual differences as distortions caused by external forces interfering with an object's or organism's natural growth tendencies. He emphasized the common attributes that members of a certain class possessed, not their differences.

According to Lewin, Galileo revolutionized science when he changed its focus from inner causation to a more comprehensive notion of causation. For Galileo, the behavior of an object or organism was determined by the total forces acting on the object or organism at the moment. For example, whether a body fell or not—and if it fell, how fast it fell—was determined by its total circumstances and not by the innate tendency for heavy bodies to fall and light ones to rise. For Galileo, causation sprang not from inner essences but from physical forces; thus, he eliminated the idea of distinct categories that were characterized by their own essences and their own associated inward drives. For Galileo, the interaction of natural forces caused everything that happened; there were no accidents. Even so-called unique events were totally comprehensible if the dynamic forces acting on them were known.

For Lewin (1935), too much of psychology was still Aristotelian. Psychologists were still seeking inner determinants of behavior, such as instincts, and still attempting to place people in distinct categories, such as normal and abnormal. Lewin also saw stage theories as extensions of Aristotelian thinking—for example, a theory that says average two-year-olds act in certain ways and average three-year-olds in other ways. Any theory attempting to classify people into types was also seen as exemplifying Aristotelian thinking—for example, a theory that characterizes people as introverts or extroverts. According to Lewin, when Galileo's conception of causation was employed, all these distinct categories vanished and were replaced with a conception of universal causation (i.e., the view that everything that occurs is a function of the total influences occurring at the moment).

In psychology, switching from an Aristotelian to a Galilean perspective would mean deemphasizing such notions as instincts, types, and even averages (which imply the existence of distinct categories) and emphasizing the complex, dynamic forces acting on an individual at any given moment. For Lewin, these dynamic forces—and not any type of inner essences—explained human behavior.

Life Space

Probably the most important concept in all of Lewin's writing was that of life space. A person's **life space** consisted of all influences acting on him or her at a given time. These influences, called **psychological facts**, consisted of an awareness of internal events (e.g., hunger, pain, and fatigue), external events (e.g., restaurants, restrooms, other people, stop signs, and angry dogs), and recollections of prior experiences (e.g., knowing that a particular person was pleasant or unpleasant or knowing that one's mother tended to say yes to certain requests and no to others). The only requirement for something to be a psychological fact was that it exist in a person's awareness at the moment. A previous experience was a psychological fact only if one recalled it in the present. Again, Lewin called the totality of psychological facts that existed at any particular time a person's life space.

Topology and Hodological Space

To convey his notions, Lewin borrowed from a branch of geometry called topology. **Topology** represents the relationships among objects and events in a spatial, nonmathematical way. For example, Lewin represented a person's life space as an ellipse. He designated the person's position in his or her life space with a *P*, and he represented each psychological fact as a region in the life space. Furthermore, he gave each region a *valence*, or sign, depending on the nature of the region's influence on the person. Those regions (psychological facts) that benefited the person were labeled (+), those that inhibited the person were labeled (−), and irrelevant facts received no sign. According to Lewin, needs could be either biological (e.g., hunger) or psychological (e.g., a college education). In either case, when a need arose, the life space was articulated around that need. For example, if

George wanted to ask Mary for a date, George's life space might be articulated as shown in Figure 14.6.

The movement (locomotion) of the person through the life space could result from real or imaginary causes. For example, physical movement that brought George closer to Mary would change George's position in his life space, as would coming into a substantial amount of money, receiving an encouraging sign from Mary, or learning that Mary had just become engaged. The force fields resulting from the various positive and negative influences in the life space created what Lewin called **hodological space**. The nature of this space at any given moment determined the direction and rate of locomotion.

Lewin referred to all events lying outside the life space as the **foreign hull**. As should be clear, the needs operating at the moment determined which events were part of the life space and which lay in the foreign hull. What was in the foreign hull at one moment might be in the life space at another moment and vice versa.

Motivation

Like the other Gestaltists, Lewin believed that people sought a cognitive balance. We saw how Köhler used this assumption in his explanation of learning. Lewin used the same assumption in his explanation of motivation. According to Lewin, both biological and psychological needs caused tension in the life space, and the only way to reduce the tension was through satisfaction of the need. Psychological needs, which Lewin called **quasi needs**, included such intentions as wanting a car, wanting to go to a concert, or wanting to go to medical school. The goal of locomotion was to alleviate the tension caused by a need or a quasi need.

The Zeigarnik Effect. Doing her doctoral work under Lewin's supervision, Bluma Zeigarnik (1927) tested Lewin's tension-system hypothesis concerning motivation. According to this hypothesis, needs cause tensions that persist until the needs are satisfied. It was Lewin's custom to have long discussions with his students in a café,

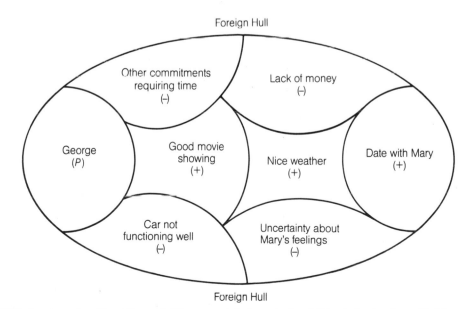

FIGURE 14.6 An example of how George's life space might be articulated if he desired a date with Mary.

while drinking coffee and snacking. Apparently, the tension-system hypothesis occurred to him as a result of an experience he had during one of these informal discussions. Marrow reports this experience:

> On one such occasion, somebody called for the bill and the waiter knew just what everyone had ordered. Although he hadn't kept a written reckoning, he presented an exact tally to everyone when the bill was called for. About a half hour later Lewin called the waiter over and asked him to write the check again. The waiter was indignant. "I don't know any longer what you people ordered," he said. "You paid your bill." In psychological terms, this indicated that a tension system had been building up in the waiter as we were ordering and upon payment of the bill the tension system was discharged. (1969, p. 27)

In her formal testing of Lewin's hypothesis, Zeigarnik assumed that giving a subject a task to perform would create a tension system and that completion of the task would relieve the tension. In all, Zeigarnik gave 22 tasks to 138 subjects. The subjects were allowed to finish some tasks but not others. Zeigarnik later tested the subjects on their recall of the tasks, and she found that the subjects remembered many more of the *uncompleted* tasks than the completed ones. Her explanation was that for the uncompleted tasks the associated tension was never reduced; therefore, these tasks remained as intentions, and as such they remained part of the person's life space. The tendency to remember uncompleted tasks better than completed ones has come to be called the **Zeigarnik effect**.

A year after Zeigarnik did her research, Maria Ovsiankina (1928), who was also working with Lewin, found that individuals would rather resume interrupted tasks than completed ones. Her explanation for this was the same as the one for the Zeigarnik effect.

Woodworth gave another example of Lewin's proposed relationship between intention and cognitive tension:

> Suppose I have stuck a letter in my pocket, impressing on myself the necessity of placing it in a letter box when I pass one in the street. I have

thus established a bond between the sight of the letter box, as stimulus, and the response of taking the letter out and mailing it. I see a letter box and mail the letter. The associationist or stimulus–response psychologist would cite the case, so far, as a good instance of his doctrine. But now it is also according to the association psychology that exercise of this stimulus–response connection should strengthen it. Therefore, when I reach the second letter box my response of reaching in my pocket for the letter will be even stronger. On the contrary, that tendency is probably all wiped out. When I placed the letter in the first box, I said to myself, "That's done," and apparently erased the stimulus-response bond. Lewin urges that the driving force which activated the behavior was not the bond, nor even the letter box as stimulus, but a tension set up when I placed the letter in my pocket with the intention of mailing it. This tension was relieved when the letter was mailed, and the bond had no further influence on my behavior. Had I happened to spy a postman and hand him the letter, that different act would also have relieved the tension.

> The behavior in such cases may be brought under the formula of "closing the gap," and so lined up alongside of the tendency to see closed figures; and probably the brain dynamics of the two processes is much the same. When I put the letter in my pocket I had to leave a gap in my behavior, a gap which was filled when the letter was mailed. Filling the gap brought this particular dynamic system into a state of equilibrium with no more force to influence my behavior. (1931, pp. 112–113)

Conflict

As it was for Freud, the notion of conflicting impulses or intentions was very important to Lewin. Unlike Freud, however, Lewin studied conflict experimentally. Lewin concentrated his study on three types of conflict. An **approach–approach conflict** occurs when a person is attracted to two goals at the same time, such as needing to choose from two attractive items on a menu or between two equally attractive colleges after being accepted by both. An **avoidance–avoidance conflict** occurs when a person is repelled by two unattractive goals at the same time, such as when one must get a job or not have enough money or study for an examination or get a bad grade. An **approach–avoidance conflict** is often the most difficult to resolve because it involves only one goal about which one has mixed feelings, such as when having a T-bone steak is an appealing idea but it is one of the most expensive items on the menu or when marriage is appealing but it means giving up a great deal of independence.

The types of conflict Lewin studied can be diagrammed as follows (where p symbolizes a person):

Goal 1   Goal 2

$+ \longleftarrow p \longrightarrow +$ Approach–Approach Conflict

$- \longrightarrow p \longleftarrow -$ Avoidance–Avoidance Conflict

$\pm \rightleftarrows p$ Approach–Avoidance Conflict

Group Dynamics

In his later years, Lewin extended Gestalt principles to the behavior of groups. According to Lewin, a group could be viewed as a physical system just as the brain could be. In both cases, the behavior of individual elements is determined by the configuration of the existing field of energy. Therefore, the nature or configuration of a group will strongly influence the behavior of its members. Among the members of each group, there was what Lewin called a dynamic interdependence. Lewin's studies of **group dynamics** led to what are now called encounter groups, sensitivity training, and leadership institutes.

Lundin describes one of Lewin's studies of group dynamics:

> The concept of group dynamics has led to several avenues of research. During World War II, Lewin conducted a number of experiments that attempted to alter group decision-making. At the time, certain food products, such as meat, were rationed. Consequently, housewives were encouraged to buy more accessible products, such as brains, liver, kidneys, and heart and other animal organs not generally considered to

be food items. He used two methods—the first was lecturing on the merits of the food, their nutritional values, how they could be tastily prepared, and so on. The second method involved group discussion. The same materials were presented in both cases. In the group discussion, there was participation by the members on the pros and cons of trying and eating and preparing such substances. In a follow-up study only 3 percent of the lecture group took up the suggestions, while 32 percent of the discussion group changed their food habits by trying the formerly unpopular products. Lewin concluded that in the discussion group more forces were made available for a change in behavior. (1991, pp. 261–262)

In another study, Lewin, Lippitt, and White (1939) investigated the influence of various types of leadership on group performance. Boys were matched and then placed in a *democratic group*, in which the leader encouraged group discussion and participated with the boys in making decisions; or an *authoritarian group*, in which the leader made all decisions and told the boys what to do; or a *laissez-faire group*, in which no group decisions were made and the boys could do whatever they wanted. The researchers found that the democratic group was highly productive and friendly, the authoritarian group was highly aggressive, and the laissez-faire group was unproductive. Lewin et al. concluded that group leadership influenced the *Gestalt* characterizing the group and, in turn, the attitude and productivity of the group's members.

THE WORK OF KARL LASHLEY

A colleague and friend of John B. Watson at Johns Hopkins University, **Karl Spencer Lashley** (1890–1958) accompanied Watson on his trip to one of the Florida Keys to study the homing behavior of terns. Receiving his doctorate from Johns Hopkins in 1914, Lashley was an early supporter of behaviorism, and he sought to support the associationism on which behaviorism was based, with neurophysiological evi-

Karl Lashley

dence. But time after time, Lashley was frustrated in his efforts to show that the brain worked like a complex switchboard linking sensory impulses to motor reactions. Contrary to his original intention, Lashley gradually showed that brain activity was more like what the Gestaltists described than like what the behaviorists described. He found no evidence that stimulation of specific areas of the brain was associated with the elicitation of specific responses. D. N. Robinson summarizes some of Lashley's work:

> Perhaps Lashley's most significant findings were in the areas of learning and memory. He demonstrated in a variety of different experimental settings that the animal's ability to acquire a complex behavioral repertoire and to reproduce it after a long retention interval was not systematically related to specific loci within the cerebral cortex. He remarked whimsically that,

after searching for the "engram" of memory for many years, he was forced to conclude that learning was simply not possible! Behind the wry comment was the *caveat* that the brain is not one of La Mettrie's clocks, nor is man Condillac's sentient statue. (1986, pp. 422–423)

Lashley made two major observations that were contrary to the switchboard conception of the brain. One was that loss of ability following destruction of parts of the cortex was related more to the *amount* of destruction than to the *location* of destruction. This finding, called **mass action**, indicated that the cortex worked as a unified whole, as the Gestaltists had maintained. The second observation was that if surgical destruction of a portion of the cortex caused the loss of an ability, other parts of the cortex would soon take over and the lost function would be regained. This finding, called **equipotentiality**, again indicated that the brain acted as an integrated whole and not as a mechanistic switchboard.

Concerning Lashley's place in the history of psychology, D. N. Robinson says, "If we were to summarize [Lashley's] role in twentieth-century developments in physiological psychology, we might say that he bore the same relationship to the Pavlovians that Flourens bore to the phrenologists" (1986, p. 421).

As the reader may remember, Flourens's research demonstrated that the cortex was not characterized by localization of function, as the phrenologists had assumed, but functioned as a unit. The Pavlovians (and the behaviorists) assumed a different type of localization—an association between certain sensory centers and certain motor areas—and Lashley's work showed that this type of localization did not exist either. In his 1929 presidential address to the APA, Lashley described his research on brain functioning. Because of Lashley's prestige and because his findings were generally supportive of Gestalt theory, his address did much to promote the acceptance of Gestalt psychology, despite the fact that Lashley could not find evidence for the electrical fields of brain activity so important to Gestalt theory (Lashley, Chow & Semmes, 1951).

THE IMPACT OF GESTALT PSYCHOLOGY

Like any school in psychology, Gestalt psychology has had its share of criticism. Critics have said that many of its central terms and concepts are vague and therefore hard to pin down experimentally. Even the term *Gestalt*, the critics say, has never been defined precisely. The same is true for the law of Prägnanz, for insight, and for cognitive equilibrium and disequilibrium. As might be expected, the behaviorists attacked the Gestaltists' concern with consciousness, claiming that such a concern was a regression to the old metaphysical position that had caused psychology so many problems.

Despite these and other criticisms, however, Gestalt theory has clearly influenced almost every aspect of modern psychology. Michael Wertheimer nicely summarizes this influence:

> The Gestalt movement played a significant role in the revolt against structuralism. Its objections to elementism went beyond its critique of structuralism, however, and were applied to S–R behaviorism as well. Gestalt psychology called attention to the usefulness of field concepts and to various problems that might otherwise have been ignored, such as insight in animals and humans, the organized nature of perception and of experience, the richness of genuine thought processes, and to the utility of dealing in larger, molar, organized units, taking full account of their nature and structure. Wholes should not be analyzed arbitrarily into predetermined elements, since such analysis, the Gestaltists argued, and most psychologists now recognize, may do violence to the intrinsic meaning of the whole.
>
> Although the Gestalt school no longer existed as a major self-conscious movement after the middle of the twentieth century, the issues it raised in opposition to the prevalent oversimplified S–R psychology typical especially of American associationistic behaviorism continued to be central in psychological thought. The Gestalt school had done its job well, leaving a lasting mark on the discipline, in the psychology of cognition, perception, thinking, and learning, and in motivation, personality, and social psychology—indeed in almost all fields. But the Gestalt approach has been rediscovered especially in recent years by cognitive scientists working on problem solving and information processing. (1987, pp. 139–140)

And Sokal says the following about the influence of Gestalt psychology:

> [Gestalt psychology] enriched American psychology greatly and did much to counter the attractions of extreme behaviorism. If Gestalt psychology has today lost its identity as a school of thought—and very few of Koffka's, Köhler's, Wertheimer's, or Lewin's students call themselves Gestalt psychologists—it is not because the mainstream of American psychology has swamped their ideas. Rather, their work has done much to redirect this mainstream, which adopted many of their points of view. Few other migrating scientific schools have been as successful. (1984, p. 1263)

SUMMARY

Attacking both the structuralists and the behaviorists for their elementism, the Gestaltists emphasized cognitive and behavioral configurations that could not be divided without destroying the meaning of those configurations. *Gestalt* is the German word for "whole," "totality," or "configuration." Antecedents of Gestalt psychology included Kant's contention that sensory experience was structured by the faculties of the mind; Mach's contention that the perception of space form and time form were independent of any specific sensory elements; Ehrenfels's observation that although form qualities emerged from sensory experience, they were different from that experience; J. S. Mill's notion of mental chemistry; James's contention that consciousness was like an ever-moving stream that could not be divided into elements without losing its meaning; act psychology, which emphasized the conscious acts of perceiving, sensing, and problem solving instead of the elements of thought; and the emergence of field theory in physics.

The 1912 publication of Wertheimer's article on

the phi phenomenon usually marks the founding of the Gestalt school of psychology. The phi phenomenon indicated that conscious experience could not be reduced to sensory experience. Koffka and Köhler worked with Wertheimer on his early perception experiments and are usually considered cofounders of Gestalt psychology. Wertheimer assumed that forces in the brain distributed themselves as they do in any physical system (i.e., symmetrically and evenly) and that these force fields interacted with sensory information to determine conscious experience. The contention that force fields in the brain determined consciousness was called psychophysical isomorphism, and the contention that brain activity was always distributed in the most simple, symmetrical, and organized way was called the law of Prägnanz. The term *perceptual constancy* referred to the way we responded to objects or events as the same even when we experienced them under a wide variety of circumstances.

According to the Gestaltists, the most basic perception was that of a figure–ground relationship. Perceptual principles that cause the elements of perception to be organized into configurations included continuity, by which stimuli following some pattern were seen as a perceptual unit; proximity, by which stimuli that were close together formed a perceptual unit; similarity, by which similar stimuli formed a perceptual unit; inclusiveness, by which a larger perceptual configuration masked smaller ones; and closure, by which incomplete physical objects were experienced psychologically as complete. The Gestaltists distinguished the geographical (physical) environment from the behavioral (subjective) environment. They believed that the behavioral environment, or what we would now call subjective reality, governed behavior.

The Gestaltists viewed learning as a perceptual phenomenon. For them, the existence of a problem created a psychological disequilibrium, or tension, that persisted until the problem was solved. As long as there was tension, the person engaged in cognitive trial and error in an effort to find the solution to the problem. Problems remained in an unsolved state until insight into the solution was gained. Insightful learning was sudden and complete; it allowed performance that was smooth and free of errors. Also, the person retained the information gained by insight for a long time and could easily transfer that information to similar problems. The application of a principle found effective in one problem-solving situation to other similar situations was called transposition.

Productive thinking involved the understanding of principles rather than the memorization of facts or the utilization of formal logic. The Gestaltists believed that reinforcement for productive thinking came from personal satisfaction, not from events outside oneself. They thought that memory, like other psychological phenomena, was governed by the law of Prägnanz. Experience activated a brain activity called a memory process, which lasted as long as an experience lasted. After the memory process had terminated, a trace of it remained, and that memory trace would influence subsequent memories of similar objects or events. Eventually, a trace system developed for recording the features that memories of a certain type had in common. After a memory trace—and to a larger extent, a trace system—had been established, the memory of a specific event would be determined by the memory trace and by the trace system of similar experiences, as well as by one's immediate experience.

Lewin was an early Gestaltist who believed that psychology should not categorize people into types or emphasize inner essences. Rather, Lewin believed psychology should attempt to understand the dynamic force fields that motivated human behavior. He felt that such a shift in emphasis would switch psychology from an Aristotelian to a Galilean model of science. According to Lewin, anything influencing a person at a given moment was a psychological fact, and the totality of psychological facts that existed at the moment constituted a person's life space. Lewin believed that both biological and psychological needs created a tension that persisted until the needs were satisfied. The Zeigarnik effect, or the tendency to remember uncompleted tasks longer than completed ones, supported Lewin's theory of motivation. Lewin observed that intentions often conflict, as when one wants two desirable things at the same time, wants to avoid two undesirable things at the same time, or wants and does not want the same thing at the same time. With his work on group dynamics, Lewin showed that different types of group structures created different *Gestalts* that influenced the performance of group members.

Lashley's research on the brain supported the Gestalt view of cortical functioning instead of the switchboard view of the brain that many behaviorists held. His finding of mass action indicated that, as far as loss of ability was concerned, the amount of cortical destruction was more important than the location of destruction. And his finding of equipotentiality indicated that when a certain cortical area was destroyed, other cortical areas could take over the function lost. Both findings were incompatible with a switchboard conception of the brain but were compatible with the Gestaltists' view of brain functioning.

Gestalt psychology played a major role in directing the attention of psychologists away from insignificant bits of behavior and consciousness and toward the holistic aspects of behavior and consciousness. As with functionalism, most of the basic features of Gestalt psychology have been assimilated into modern psychology, and therefore Gestalt psychology has lost its distinctiveness as a school.

DISCUSSION QUESTIONS

1. Summarize the disagreements that the Gestaltists had with Wundt's experimental program, the structuralists, and the behaviorists.

2. Differentiate the molecular approach to psychology from the molar approach.

3. Describe similarities and differences that existed between the positions of Kant, Mach, Ehrenfels, James, and the act psychologists, on the one hand, and the Gestaltists, on the other.

4. Explain what is meant by the contention that Gestalt theory used field theory as its model and empirical-associationistic psychology used Newtonian physics as its model.

5. What is the phi phenomenon? What was its importance in the formation of the Gestalt school of psychology?

6. What is meant by the contention that Gestalt analysis proceeds from the top down rather than from the bottom up?

7. Contrast the Gestalt notion of psychophysical isomorphism with the constancy hypothesis.

8. What is the law of Prägnanz? Describe the importance of this law to Gestalt psychology.

9. What is perceptual constancy? Give an example. How did the Gestaltists explain the perceptual constancies?

10. Briefly define each of the following: figure–ground relationship, principle of continuity, principle of proximity, principle of similarity, principle of inclusiveness, and principle of closure.

11. Distinguish between subjective and objective reality. According to the Gestaltists, which is more important in determining our behavior? Give an example.

12. How did the Gestaltists explain learning? In your answer, summarize the characteristics of insightful learning.

13. What is transposition? Summarize the Gestalt and the behavioristic explanations of this phenomenon.

14. For Wertheimer, what represented the best type of problem solving? Contrast this type of problem solving with rote memorization and logical problem solving.

15. Summarize the Gestalt explanation of memory. Include in your answer definitions of memory process, memory trace, and trace system. What does it mean to say that memory is governed by the law of Prägnanz?

16. For Lewin, how did psychology based on Aristotle's view of nature differ from psychology based on Galileo's view of nature? Give an example of each.

17. What did Lewin mean by life space? Include in your answer the definition of psychological fact.

18. Describe Lewin's use of topology and hodology.

19. Summarize Lewin's theory of motivation. In your answer, distinguish between needs and quasi needs.

20. What is the Zeigarnik effect? Describe the research used to demonstrate the effect.

21. Describe the three types of conflict studied by Lewin and give an example of each.

22. Summarize Lewin's work on group dynamics.

23. What was the significance of Lashley's work for Gestalt theory? Include in your answer definitions of the terms *mass action* and *equipotentiality*.

24. Summarize the impact that Gestalt psychology has had on contemporary psychology.

SUGGESTIONS FOR FURTHER READING

Henle, M. (Ed.) (1971b). *The selected papers of Wolfgang Köhler*. New York: Liveright.
This is a carefully selected sample of papers written by Köhler between 1913 and 1967, or essentially during all of his professional life. The 21 articles presented are organized around six headings: "Gestalt Theory: Foundations and Current Problems," "Cognitive Processes," "Animal Psychology," "Psychology and Physiology of the Brain," "Natural Science," and "Special Problems." (Available in paperback.)

Henle, M. (1978). One man against the Nazis—Wolfgang Köhler. *American Psychologist*, *33*, 939–944.
In the 1920s and 1930s, the Psychological Institute of Berlin University flourished under the direction of Wolfgang Köhler. Among the many illustrious individuals associated with the institute at this time were

Max Wertheimer and Kurt Lewin. When the Nazis came to power on January 30, 1933, Jewish university professors were dismissed, including several Nobel laureates, for example, Einstein. The fact that non-Jewish colleagues remained silent about the dismissals astounded Köhler (and the Nazis). Köhler, a non-Jew, could not remain silent and on April 28, 1933, published what turned out to be the last article to be openly critical of the Nazi regime. Letters praising Köhler's courage poured in from Jews and non-Jews alike. Soon thereafter, Köhler's lectures were among those attended by Nazis. Also, the Nazis recommended that Köhler's key assistants be fired and that the institute be moved to new quarters that would be easier to "supervise." Köhler resigned his directorship of the institute in protest when the director of the university did not condemn the Nazis' "inspections" of the institute. The situation deteriorated further when Köhler refused to sign a loyalty oath to Hitler. A Nazi replaced Köhler as director of the institute, and all of Köhler's students and assistants were dismissed. The action of the Nazis essentially destroyed the next generation of Gestalt psychologists.

Henle, M. (1986). *1879 and all that: Essays in the theory and history of psychology*. New York: Columbia University Press.

This is a delightful collection of articles written through the years by Henle. There are several articles on topics related to the history of psychology—for example, "On the Distinction Between the Phenomenal and the Physical Object," "Freud's Secret Cognitive Theories," "Some Problems of Eclecticism," and "On Controversy and Its Resolution." Of special interest, however, are Henle's articles concerning the experiences of the early Gestaltists in Germany and the United States. (Available in paperback.)

Köhler, W. (1969). *The task of Gestalt psychology*. Princeton, NJ: Princeton University Press.

This short book, the last written by Köhler, is based on a series of lectures that he gave at Princeton University in 1967, and it was published posthumously. The book consists of the following chapters: "Early Developments in Gestalt Psychology," "Gestalt Psychology and Natural Science," "Recent Developments in Gestalt Psychology," and "What Is Thinking?" (Available in paperback.)

Patnoe, S. (1988). *A narrative history of experimental social psychology: The Lewin tradition*. New York: Springer-Verlag.

This book begins with a biographical sketch of Kurt Lewin and a summary of his theory and methods. Next, interviews are reported with a number of prominent social psychologists whose own research was di-

rectly or indirectly influenced by Lewin and his work. Those interviewed include Dorwin Cartwright, Morton Deutsch, Phil Zimbardo, Stanley Schachter, John Darley, Elliot Aronson, and Leon Festinger. (Available in paperback.)

Sokal, M. M. (1984). The Gestalt psychologists in behaviorist America. *American Historical Review, 89*, 1240–1263.

Köhler's contact with U.S. psychology began while he was working with chimpanzees on the island of Tenerife in 1914. His correspondence was mainly with Yerkes and concerned comparative psychology. Köhler was a visiting professor at Clark University in 1924, and in that year he also gave lectures at Harvard and Yale. Terman was very pleased with Köhler, Boring did not like him or his ideas, and Titchener had mixed feelings. When McDougall resigned his position at Harvard in 1926, Köhler was thought of as his replacement. Boring argued against Köhler's nomination and suggested Lashley or Tolman instead. Other than Köhler's European demeanor, it was Köhler's apparent strong inclination toward philosophy that bothered the more positivistic Boring. When Boring published his *A History of Experimental Psychology* (1929), there was only a 10-page discussion of Gestalt psychology, and it was negative. By 1933, however, Gestalt psychology was an accepted part of U.S. psychology, and it was fairly and positively presented in Heidbreder's classic *Seven Psychologies* (1933). In 1933 Köhler accepted an invitation to be the third William James lecturer at Harvard (John Dewey and Arthur Lovejoy were the first two). While at Harvard, Köhler interacted more with philosophers (e.g., Ralph Barton Perry) than with psychologists, and four years later he published his William James lectures as *The Place of Value in a World of Fact* (1938). Both Köhler's choice of companions and of the subject matter of his lectures angered Boring. The situation was worsening in Germany, and Köhler once again considered a professorship at Harvard. Boring was able to convince the chemist James B. Conant, who was president of Harvard, not to hire Köhler—and Lashley was hired instead. Tolman had turned down the position because he wanted to stay at Berkeley. In 1935 Köhler accepted an appointment at Swarthmore, where, despite the fact that Swarthmore was an undergraduate institution, he became an influential force in U.S. psychology. Indeed, after his naturalization, he was eventually elected president of the APA (1958). Sokal concludes that despite the many setbacks experienced by the Gestalt psychologists in the United States, few imported scientific schools were more successful.

GLOSSARY

Act psychology Type of psychology that emphasized the study of intact mental acts, such as perceiving and judging, instead of the division of consciousness into elements.

Approach–approach conflict According to Lewin, the type of conflict that occurs when a person is attracted to two goals at the same time.

Approach–avoidance conflict According to Lewin,

the type of conflict that occurs when a person is attracted to and repelled by the same goal at the same time.

Avoidance–avoidance conflict According to Lewin, the type of conflict that occurs when a person is repelled by two goals at the same time.

Behavioral environment According to Koffka, subjective reality.

Constancy hypothesis The contention that there is a strict one-to-one correspondence between physical stimuli and sensations, in the sense that the same stimulation will always result in the same sensation regardless of circumstances. The Gestaltists argued against this contention, saying instead that what sensation a stimulus elicits is relative to existing patterns of activity in the brain and to the totality of stimulating conditions.

Ehrenfels, Christian von (1859–1932) Said that mental forms emerged from various sensory experiences and that these forms were different from the sensory elements that comprised them.

Elementism The belief that complex mental or behavioral processes are composed of or derived from simple elements and that the best way to understand these processes is first to find the elements of which they are composed.

Equipotentiality Lashley's finding that when part of the cortex was destroyed, other parts of the cortex could take over the lost function.

Extrinsic reinforcement Reinforcement that comes from a source other than one's self.

Field theory That branch of physics that studies how energy distributes itself within physical systems. In some systems (e.g., the solar system), energy can distribute itself freely. In other systems (e.g., an electric circuit), energy must pass through wires, condensers, resistors, and so forth. In either type of system, however, energy will always distribute itself in the simplest, most symmetrical way possible *under the circumstances*. According to the Gestaltists, the brain was a physical system whose activity could be understood in terms of field theory.

Figure–ground relationship The most basic type of perception, consisting of the division of the perceptual field into a figure (that which is attended to) and a ground, which provides the background for the figure.

Foreign hull According to Lewin, all events lying outside a person's life space.

Geographical environment According to Koffka, physical reality.

Gestalt The German word meaning "configuration," "pattern," or "whole."

Gestalt psychology The type of psychology that studies whole, intact segments of behavior and cognitive experience.

Group dynamics Lewin's extension of Gestalt principles to the study of group behavior.

Hodological space The distribution of the positive and negative influences that characterize a person's life space at any given moment.

Holist One who believes that complex mental or behavioral processes should be studied as such and not divided into their elemental components for analysis. (*See also* **Phenomenology**.)

Insightful learning Learning that involves perceiving the solution to a problem after a period of cognitive trial and error.

Intrinsic reinforcement The self-satisfaction that comes from problem solving or learning something. According to the Gestaltists, this feeling of satisfaction occurs because solving a problem or learning something restores one's cognitive equilibrium.

James, William (1842–1910) Like the other precursors of Gestalt psychology, opposed dividing consciousness into elements. For him, consciousness was to be viewed as a totality with a purpose.

Kant, Immanuel (1724–1804) Said that what we experienced consciously was determined by the interaction of sensory information with the categories of thought.

Koffka, Kurt (1886–1941) Worked with Wertheimer on his early perception experiments. Koffka is considered a cofounder of the school of Gestalt psychology.

Köhler, Wolfgang (1887–1967) Worked with Wertheimer on his early perception experiments. Köhler is considered a cofounder of the school of Gestalt psychology.

Lashley, Karl Spencer (1890–1958) Found evidence, through his neurophysiological research, that the cortex functioned more in accordance with Gestalt principles than associationistic principles.

Law of Prägnanz Because of the tendencies of the force fields that occur in the brain, mental events will always tend to be organized, simple, and regular. According to the law of Prägnanz, cognitive experience will always reflect the essence of one's experience instead of its disorganized, fragmented aspects.

Lewin, Kurt (1890–1947) An early Gestaltist, Lewin sought to explain human behavior in terms of the totality of influences acting on people rather than in terms of the manifestation of inner essences. Lewin was mainly responsible for applying Gestalt principles to the topics of motivation and group dynamics.

Life space According to Lewin, the totality of the psychological facts that exist in one's awareness at any given moment. (*See also* **Psychological fact**.)

Mach, Ernst (1838–1916) Said that some mental experiences were the same even though they were stimulated by a wide range of sensory events. The experiencing of geometric forms (space forms) and melodies (time forms) are examples.

Mass action Lashley's finding that following ablation of various parts of the cortex, loss of ability was determined more by the amount of destruction than by the location of destruction.

Memory process The brain activity caused by the experiencing of an environmental event.

Memory trace The remnant of an experience that remains in the brain after an experience has ended.

Molar approach The attempt to focus on intact mental and behavioral phenomena without dividing those phenomena in any way.

Molecular approach The attempt to reduce complex phenomena into small units for detailed study. Such an approach is elementistic.

Perceptual constancy The tendency to respond to objects as being the same, even when we experience those objects under a wide variety of circumstances.

Phenomenology The study of intact, meaningful, mental phenomena.

Phi phenomenon The illusion that a light is moving from one location to another. The phi phenomenon is caused by flashing two lights on and off at a certain rate.

Principle of closure The tendency to perceive incomplete objects as complete.

Principle of continuity The tendency to experience stimuli that follow some predictable pattern as a perceptual unit.

Principle of inclusiveness The tendency to perceive only the larger figure when a smaller figure is embedded in a larger figure.

Principle of proximity The tendency to perceptually group together stimuli that are physically close.

Principle of similarity The tendency to perceive as units stimuli that are physically similar to one another.

Productive thinking According to Wertheimer, the type of thinking that pondered principles rather than isolated facts and that aimed at understanding the solutions to problems rather than memorizing a certain problem-solving strategy or logical rules.

Psychological fact According to Lewin, anything of which a person is aware at any given moment.

Psychophysical isomorphism The Gestaltists' contention that the patterns of activity produced by the brain—rather than sensory experience as such—caused mental experience.

Quasi needs According to Lewin, psychological rather than biological needs.

Topology A branch of mathematics that Lewin used to show pictorially the relationships among psychological facts in a person's life space.

Trace system The consolidation of the enduring or essential features of memories of individual objects or of classes of objects.

Transposition The application of a principle learned in one learning or problem-solving situation to other similar situations.

Wertheimer, Max (1880–1943) Founded the school of Gestalt psychology with his 1912 paper on the phi phenomenon.

Zeigarnik effect The tendency to remember uncompleted tasks longer than completed ones.

CHAPTER 15

Early Diagnosis, Explanation, and Treatment of Mental Illness

WHAT IS MENTAL ILLNESS?

Although the condition we now refer to as **mental illness** has existed from at least the beginning of recorded history, the terms used to describe that condition have varied. Today, besides the term *mental illness*, we use such terms as *psychopathology* and *abnormal behavior*. At earlier times, terms such as *mad*, *lunatic*, *maniac*, and *insane* have been used. Although the terms have changed, all refer to more or less the same type of behavior. W. B. Maher and B. A. Maher explain:

> The old terms meant pretty much the same thing as the new terms replacing them. "Mad," for example, was an old English word meaning emotionally deranged and came in turn from an ancient root word meaning crippled, hurt; "insanity" comes from the root word "sanus" or free from hurt or disease, and thus "insane" means hurt or unhealthy; "lunacy" refers to the periodic nature of many psychopathological conditions and perhaps was originally intended to differentiate periodic madnesses from those in which the state was chronic and unremitting; "mania" refers to excess of passion or behavior out of control of the reason. (1985, p. 251)

When the behavior and thought processes thought to characterize mental illness are examined, several recurring themes become evident. In describing these themes, we follow W. B. Maher and B. A. Maher (1985).

Harmful Behavior

Normal individuals possess a powerful motive to survive, and therefore behavior contrary to that motive, such as self-mutilation or suicide, is considered abnormal. There have been cultural settings, however, in which harming oneself was considered desirable, such as when in Japan committing hara kiri was viewed as a way of restoring lost personal or family honor. Also, there have been cultural settings in which injuring another person or persons was sanctioned, such as in Italy when castrating a child with musical talent helped to prepare for an operatic career as a castrato or during warfare when killing the enemy was encouraged. But generally, behavior that is harmful to oneself or others has been and is viewed as abnormal.

Unrealistic Thoughts and Perceptions

If a person's beliefs or perceptions differed markedly from those considered normal at a certain time and place in history, those beliefs and perceptions were taken as signs of mental illness. Using today's terminology, we say that people are having *delusions* if their beliefs are not shared by other members of the community. For example, it is considered delusional if one believes that he or she can transform himself or herself into some type of animal, such as a wolf or a cat. Similarly, a person is considered abnormal if his or her perceptions do not correspond to those of other members of the community. Today we call such perceptions *hallucinations*. An example would be a person seeing a bountiful crop where others see only dust or dirt. Both false beliefs (delusions) and false perceptions (hallucinations) have traditionally been taken as representing unrealistic contact with reality and therefore as abnormal.

Inappropriate Emotions

When an individual consistently laughs when the mores of a community dictate that he or she should cry or cries when he or she should laugh, that person is often branded as mentally ill. Likewise, if a person's emotional reactions are considered extreme, as when extreme fear, sadness, or joy are displayed in situations where much more moderate levels of these emotions are considered appropriate, the person is often suspected of being mentally disturbed. Inappropriate or exaggerated emotional responses have been and are standard criteria used in labeling a person as mentally ill.

Unpredictable Behavior

Sudden shifts in one's beliefs or emotions have also been traditionally taken as signs of psychopathology. For example, the person who is happy one moment and sad the next or who embraces one conviction only to have it displaced by another in a short period of time, has been and is considered to be at least emotionally unstable. If such rapid shifts in moods or beliefs persist, the person is often characterized as mentally ill.

What the above criteria of mental illness all have in common is that they define abnormality in terms of the behavior and thought processes of the average person in a community. Of course, the characteristics of this average person will vary according to the mores of his or her culture, but it is always the average person's beliefs and behavior that has been used as a frame of reference in determining mental illness:

> Definitions of good mental health have always tended to accept the psychological processes of the average person as establishing the standard against which pathology is judged. Most people experience some personal distress from time to time; most people have acted in ways that were maladaptive on occasion; most people have probably experienced unusual beliefs and perceptions. Definitions of psychopathology have always tended to compare behaviors with the norm rather than with an ideal of perfect freedom from any signs of psychological mal-

function. As this norm varies from one place to another and from one historical period to another, even from one age group or gender, race or ethnic group or class to another, the specific behavior, including thoughts and emotions expressed by the person, that provokes a diagnosis of psychopathology varies accordingly within rather wide limits. What has been constant throughout history is the application of deviations from contemporary norms of reasonable behavior as the criteria for regarding behaviors as indicative of mental illness. (W. B. Maher & B. A. Maher, 1985, p. 261)

Right or wrong, using the experiences of the average members of a community as a frame of reference in defining mental illness is as operative today as it has been throughout human history. This means that two categories of people are susceptible to being labeled mentally ill: those who for one reason or another cannot abide by cultural norms and those who choose not to. (For more on the tendency to brand extreme nonconformists as mentally ill, see Szasz, 1974.)

EARLY EXPLANATIONS OF MENTAL ILLNESS

The proposed explanations of mental illness that have been offered throughout history fall into three general categories: biological, psychological, and supernatural.

Biological Explanations

Generally, biological explanations of abnormal behavior constitute the **medical model of mental illness**. With this model, it is assumed that *all* disease is caused by the malfunctioning of some aspect of the body, mainly the brain. The bodily abnormalities causing mental illness can be inherited directly, as was supposed to be the case with "natural fools," or a predisposition toward mental illness could be inherited, which could be activated by certain experiences. In one way or another, constitutional factors have almost always been suggested as possible causes of mental illness.

Also, included among the biological explanations of mental illness are the many events that can interfere with the normal functioning of the body. Such events include injuries; tumors and obstructions; ingestion of toxins, polluted air, water, or food; disease; excessive physical stress; and physiological imbalances such as those caused by improper diet.

Psychological Explanations

When psychological events are offered as the causes of abnormal behavior, a **psychological model of mental illness** is being proposed. Here, psychological experiences such as grief, fear, disappointment, frustration, guilt, or conflict are emphasized. The mental stress that results from living in an organized society has always been recognized as a possible explanation of mental illness. How much psychological explanations were stressed varied with time and place. As is the case today, biological and psychological explanations of mental illness most often existed simultaneously. More often than not, it was believed that psychological events influenced biological events and vice versa. In more recent times, however, there has been tension between those accepting the medical model of mental illness and those accepting the psychological model. We will say more about that tension later in this chapter.

Supernatural Explanations

In primitive times, people attributed most ailments not caused by obvious things, such as falling down, being attacked by an animal or an enemy, or overeating or overdrinking, to mysterious forces entering the body. Humans did not distinguish between mental and physical disorders but believed both to be inflicted on a person by some mortal or immortal being. Supernatural explanations of all illness (including mental) prevailed until the time of the early Greek physicians such as Alcmaeon and Hippocrates. The

Greek naturalistic approach to medicine was highly influential until the collapse of the Roman empire in about A.D. 400. From that time until about the 18th century, supernatural explanations of diseases of all types prevailed.

Although the **supernatural model of mental illness** was popular during the Middle Ages, it would be a mistake to conclude that it was the only model:

> Although notions of demonology flourished in medieval religious, lay, and even medical speculation, rational and naturalistic theories and observations continued to be influential. This is evident in the historical, biographical, medical, legal, and creative literature of the times. Explanations of psychopathological behavior were not confined to demon possession; they embraced a diversity of ideas derived from common sense, classical medicine and philosophy, folklore and religion. In medieval descriptions of mental illness there is most typically an interweaving of statements variously implying natural (biological and psychological) and supernatural causation. It is difficult to assess which was considered most important; it is also difficult to discern what was intended to be taken literally and what metaphorically. (W. B. Maher & B. A. Maher, 1985, p. 283)

Biological, psychological, and supernatural explanations of mental illness have almost always existed in one form or another; what has changed through history is how one type of explanation has been emphasized over the others.

EARLY APPROACHES TO THE TREATMENT OF MENTAL ILLNESS

Psychotherapy is any attempt to help a mentally disturbed person. As mentioned earlier, common themes characterize behavior that is considered abnormal. Common themes also run through all forms of psychotherapy:

> No matter what its form, cost or setting, all that is meant by psychotherapy is the service that one human being, a helper, renders another, a sufferer, toward the end of promoting the latter's well being. The common elements in both an-

cient and modern forms of psychotherapy are a sufferer, a helper, and a systematized ritual through which help is proffered. Although the specific purposes in consulting a psychotherapist are as numerous and unique as the individuals who seek such help, the basic reasons have always been to obtain assistance in (1) removing, modifying or controlling anxiety, depression, alienation, and other distressing psychological states, (2) changing undesirable patterns of behavior such as timidity, overaggressiveness, alcoholism, disturbed sexual relationships, and the like, or (3) promoting more positive personal growth and the development of greater meaning in one's life through more effective personal functioning, or through the pursuit of new educational, occupational, recreational, or other goals which will better allow expression of the individual's potential. (Matarazzo, 1985, p. 219)

Although it may be true that ideally all versions of psychotherapy address the needs of the "sufferer," it is also true that not all versions of psychotherapy have been successful in doing so. In addition, mentally ill individuals have often been treated or confined, not so much for their own benefit as for the benefit of the community:

> Throughout the course of history there is a constantly recurring list of therapies for mental illness, each related in one way or another to the symptoms of and/or the supposed causes of the pathology. Although ideally therapies are devised to effect cures, they are often merely palliative, intended to relieve symptoms whilst the disease process does or does not run its course. And although therapies have often been derived from theories of causation, at times the theories of causation have been contrived to rationalize the treatments used. Therapies have been developed by physicians, priests, psychiatric and psychological specialists, interested laymen, charlatans, and quacks; the therapies vary accordingly. Treatments in general have been undertaken to meet the patient's need, to meet the needs of the patient's family or friends or community to do something for or about the patient, to solve social problems presented by the patient's condition. Treatment therefore may not be primarily intended to be therapeutic. The patient may be placed under custodial care in order to protect the patient from his or her own self neglect or abuse or the consequences of poor judgment; to allow time for rest, freedom from responsibility, proper diet to

> effect improvement; to protect others from the violence, problems, embarrassment, or inconvenience caused by the patient—or all of the above. (W. B. Maher & B. A. Maher, 1985, p. 266)

In any case, if an honest effort was made to treat mental illness, the treatment used was determined largely by beliefs concerning its cause. If it was believed that mental illness was caused by psychological factors, it is those factors that were addressed during the therapeutic process. If it was believed that supernatural or biological factors caused mental illness, the therapeutic process was conducted accordingly.

The Psychological Approach

When psychological factors such as fear, anxiety, frustration, guilt, or conflict were viewed as the causes of mental illness, treatment was aimed at those factors. Methods used throughout history to address psychological factors thought to be responsible for mental illness include the observing of (such as in watching a drama) or personal re-enactment of traumatic experience, the purpose of which was to create a *catharsis* (purging the mind of disturbing emotions); listening to relaxing music; support, reassurance, and love from authority figures and/or relevant others; the analysis of dreams, thoughts, and motives; and the attempt to teach the "sufferer" new and more effective skills to enable better coping with personal or interpersonal problems.

Somewhere between the psychological and supernatural explanations of mental illness was the 18th-century belief in natural law. Generally, **natural law** was the belief that you get what you deserve in life:

> Philosophical ideas about human society were, in the eighteenth century, affected by the concept of "natural law." According to this view there were certain natural consequences to behavior such that actions long regarded as sinful, such as drinking, gambling, or whoring, naturally led to madness, disease, and poverty. The alcoholic with delirium tremens or the patient in the terminal stages of syphilis-induced paresis could thus be seen as suffering an inevitable and natural outcome of their own behavior. On the

other hand, wealth, health, and prosperity came from habits of industry, sobriety, and the like; the rewards were not to be seen as "prizes" given for good behavior, but as natural effects of this behavior. (B. A. Maher & W. B. Maher, 1985, p. 303)

The implications for psychotherapy are clear. To alleviate suffering, the patient must change his or her ways, and it is the therapist's job to help him or her to do so.

The Supernatural Approach

If it was believed that evil forces entering the body caused illness, then a cure would involve removing those forces. In attempting to coax the invading forces from an inflicted person's body, the primitive medicine man would use appeal, bribery, reverence, and intimidation—and sometimes exorcism, magical rituals, and incantations were employed.

In his famous book *The Golden Bough* (1890/ 1963), **Sir James Frazer** (1854–1941) discussed **sympathetic magic**, which, for primitive humans, was extremely important in the explanation and treatment of ailments. Frazer distinguished between two types of sympathetic magic: homeopathic and contagious. **Homeopathic magic** was based on the principle of similarity. An example of homeopathic magic is the belief that what one did to a model or image of a person would affect that person. **Contagious magic**, which was based on the principle of contiguity, involved the belief that what was once close to or part of someone would continue to exert an influence on that person. For example, having an article of clothing that belonged to a person whose actions one was trying to control would increase the likelihood of success. Thus, if two things were similar or were at one time connected, they were thought to influence one another through sympathy. Using these principles, a medicine man would sometimes mimic a patient's symptoms and then model a recovery from them. Frazer indicated that, to the individuals using them, these magical techniques must have appeared to be very effective:

A ceremony intended to make the wind blow or the rain fall, or to work the death of an enemy, will always be followed, sooner or later, by the occurrence it is meant to bring to pass; and primitive man may be excused for regarding the occurrence as a direct result of the ceremony, and the best possible proof of its efficacy. Similarly, rites observed in the morning to help the sun to rise, and in the spring to wake the dreaming earth from her winter sleep, will invariably appear to be crowned with success, at least in the temperate zones; for in these regions the sun lights his golden lamp in the east every morning, and year by year the vernal earth decks herself afresh with a rich mantle of green. (1890/1963, p. 68)

Primitive humans, then, saw most illness as caused by evil forces or spirits entering the body. This view of illness was simply an extension of how primitive people viewed everything:

Wind was destructive; hence he [the primitive human] assumed an angry being who blew it to attack him. Rain was sent by spirits to reward or punish him. Disease was an affliction sent by invisible superhuman beings or was the result of magic manipulations by his enemies. He animated the world around him by attributing to natural events the human motivations that he knew so well from his own subjective experiences. Thus it was logical to him to try to influence natural events by the same methods he used to influence human beings; incantation, prayer, threats, submission, bribery, punishment and atonement. (Alexander & Selesnick, 1966, p. 9)

Bleeding a patient or removing a section of his or her skull were also widely used techniques for allowing evil spirits to escape from the body. Researchers have found that Stone Age people (about a half-million years ago) would cut an opening in the skull by chipping away at it with a sharp stone, a procedure known as **trephination**. Figure 15.1 shows a picture of two skulls prepared in this way. Although trephination was presumably used to allow evil spirits to escape, it may have brought some improvement by relieving pressure caused by bleeding or by a tumor.

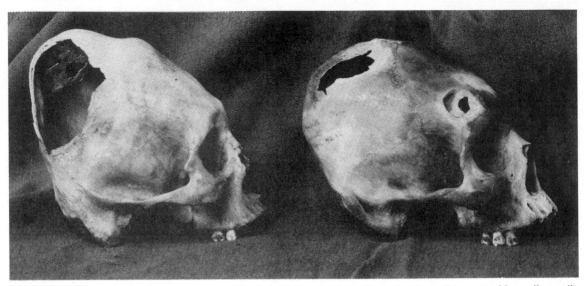

FIGURE 15.1 Prehistoric skulls showing trephination, or the chipping of holes in the skull, presumably to allow evil spirits to escape. (Courtesy of the University Museum, University of Pennsylvania.)

The Biological Approach

As early as 3000 B.C., the Egyptians showed great proficiency in treating superficial wounds and setting fractures (Sigerist, 1951). Even with ailments in which the cause was not known, the Egyptians used "natural" treatments such as vapor baths, massage, and herbal remedies. They believed, however, that even the influence of these natural treatments, if there was one, was due to the treatments' effect on evil spirits. The emphasis was clearly on mysterious forces and magic. Even the early Greeks, prior to physicians like Hippocrates, believed that God inflicted mental illness upon a person for impiety. The Bible perpetuated this belief, which had much to do with how mentally ill patients were treated until modern times.

Hippocrates (ca. 460–377 B.C.) was among the first to liberate medicine and psychiatry from their magico-religious background. As we saw in chapter 2, the Greeks, starting with Thales, had a tendency to replace mystical explanations for things with naturalistic explanations. Hippocrates applied the naturalistic

outlook to the workings of the human body. According to V. Robinson, the work of Hippocrates "marks the greatest revolution in the history of medicine" (1943, p. 51). Esper agrees:

> This was in fact the great contribution of Hippocratic medicine to biological and hence to behavioral science: the introduction of the empirical, naturalistic, objectivistic attitude in the study of human beings. The attempt to hold to or to recapture this attitude seems to me to run through the entire varied history of naturalism, mechanism, materialism, determinism, positivism, anti-metaphysics, pragmatism, behaviorism, physicalism, the "unity of science" movement, etc. The contrasts have been mysticism, metaphysics, vitalism, animism, idealism, dualism, mentalism, supernaturalism, spiritualism, etc. (1964, p. 119)

Hippocrates is known as the father of medicine because he was the first to assume that all diseases had natural causes. More specifically, he assumed that the body contained four humors (blood, black bile, yellow bile, and phlegm): If they were properly balanced, a person would be healthy; if there was an excess or a deficiency of one or more of the humors, an ailment or disease of some sort would occur. The nature of the malady would be a function of the nature of the disbalance. Because a balance among the humors was normal, there was a natural tendency in each person for a balance to be maintained; and if the balance was disrupted, there was a natural tendency for it to be regained. According to Hippocrates, the best thing a physician could do was to support this natural tendency within each patient. Esper summarizes Hippocrates' beliefs:

> The healing power of nature strives to restore a disturbed balance; the physician's task is mainly to provide a supportive therapy. Therapeutics followed a policy of watchful waiting upon nature; diet, waters, fresh air, purgation, massage, and supervised exercise were favored over more radical interventions; the influence of climate on health and personality was emphasized. If the physician could not help nature, he was at least to avoid doing injury; this caution and conservative approach was very wise in view of the scanty knowledge of the time. There was emphasis on the observation and treatment of the total and individual patient. (1964, p. 116)

Hippocrates was hard on those who perpetuated ignorance in medicine. His comments on epilepsy, then called the "sacred disease," are typical:

> I am about to discuss the disease called "sacred." It is not, in my opinion, any more divine or more sacred than other diseases, but has a natural cause, and its supposed divine origin is due to men's inexperience, and to their wonder at its peculiar character. . . . My own view is that those who first attributed a sacred character to this malady were like the magicians, purifiers, charlatans, and quacks of our own day, men who claim great piety and superior knowledge. Being at a loss, and having no treatment which would help, they concealed and sheltered themselves behind superstition, and called this illness sacred, in order that their utter ignorance might not be manifest. (W. H. S. Jones, 1923, Vol. 2, pp. 139, 141)

Besides arguing that all ailments had natural causes, claiming that nature healed and not physicians, and prescribing treatments such as baths, fresh air, and proper diet, Hippocrates identified several mental illnesses—for example, hysteria, the mental illness that was to become so important in Freud's work. *Hysteria* is a term used to describe a wide variety of disturbances such as paralysis, loss of sensation, and disturbances of sight and hearing. Hippocrates accepted the earlier Greek and Egyptian contention that hysteria was a uniquely female affliction. *Hystera* is the Greek word for "uterus," and it was believed that the symptoms of hysteria were caused by the uterus wandering to various parts of the body. Although later proven false, this view of hysteria represents the biological approach to explaining mental illness.

In chapter 2, we saw that Hippocrates believed that it was the brain that was responsible for one's emotions and perceptions. It was the condition of the brain, then, that determined whether one was normal or abnormal. Because abnormalities developed when the brain became too hot, cold, dry, or moist or when it was characterized by humoral imbalance, therapy involved providing those experiences that caused the condition of the brain to return to normal limits.

The naturalistic and humane treatment of patients lasted through the time of Galen (A.D. ca. 130–200), who perpetuated and extended Hippocrates' naturalistic approach to medicine. Also, as we saw in chapter 2, Galen expanded Hippocrates' theory of humors into the first theory of personality. When the Roman Empire fell in about A.D. 400, however, the humane and rational treatment of physical and mental disorders essentially fell with it.

Return of the Supernatural Approach

When the Romans came to power, they adopted much of the Greek emphasis on knowledge and reason even though they were more concerned with law, technology, and the military than were the Greeks. With the collapse of the Roman Empire, there was an almost complete regression to the nonrational thinking that had characterized the time before the Greek naturalists:

> The collapse of the Roman security system produced a general regression to belief in the magic, mysticism, and demonology from which, seven centuries before, men had been liberated through Greek genius. . . . The psychiatry of the Middle Ages can be scarcely distinguished from prescientific demonology, and mental treatment was synonymous with exorcism. . . . In medieval exorcism Christian mythology and prehistoric demonology found a quaint union. (Alexander & Selesnick, 1966, pp. 50, 52)

Although W. B. Maher and B. A. Maher (1985) refer to the therapeutic practices that occurred during the Middle Ages as eclectic, the emphasis was on exorcising demons. Even with this emphasis, however, several hospitals scattered throughout Europe treated the old, the sick, and the poor. Evidence also suggests that in many cases the mentally ill were treated alongside those who were physically ill (Allderidge, 1979). Still, the preferred explanation of mental illness during the Middle Ages was a supernatural one, and the preferred treatment was some form of exorcism. Even with its preoccupation with demons and exorcism, however, witch-hunts typically did not occur during the Middle Ages. Witch-hunts occurred primarily from the end of the 15th through the 17th centuries, that is, during the Renaissance and Reformation.

Witch-hunts. In 1487 Johann Sprenger and Heinrich Kraemer (both Dominican priests) published a book entitled *Malleus Maleficarum* (*The Witches' Hammer*), which became the textbook of the Inquisition. Before publishing their book, Sprenger and Kraemer sought and received permission from the Pope, Maximilian (the king of Rome), and from members of the theology faculty of the University of Cologne. The book begins by attempting to prove the existence of devils and their hosts, witches, and indicates that if the authors' arguments do not convince the reader, he or she must be the victim of witchcraft or a heretic. The second part of the book tells how to identify witchcraft. Many of the symptoms of witchcraft are clearly those now labeled abnormal behavior. For example, hallucinations, delusions, paranoia, hysteria, catatonia, and mania were all accepted as evidence that a person was bewitched. It was generally believed that sinful individuals were much more susceptible to witchcraft than individuals without sin and abnormal behavior for which a physical cause could not be found was therefore taken as a sign of sinfulness. One of the most grievous sins was sexual lust. According to the authors, sexual lust invited possession by a devil or the influence of a witch, and because women have stronger carnal desires than men, they are more likely to be witches or to be bewitched. This greater susceptibility of women to evil influences was said to result from the fact that women were created from the inferior rib of Adam, making women inferior to man in both body and soul (Alexander & Selesnick, 1966).

The final section of the book suggests how witches are to be made to confess and then punished. First mild tortures are to be tried, and if they prove unsuccessful, more extreme measures may be employed.

Alexander and Selesnick describe the bizarre nature of *Malleus Maleficarum*:

> The *Malleus* includes many descriptions of the incubi, the male demons who seduce women, and of the succubi, the female demons who sexually violate their male captives. In fact, throughout, the book is replete with pornographic sexual orgies occurring between these demons and their human hosts. Not content with these vivid passages, Kraemer and Sprenger go on to satisfy the voyeuristic impulses of the judging inquisitors by recommending that the witch be stripped and her pubic hair shaved before she was presented to the judges. The rationale for shaving the genitals was that the devil would not be able to hide in the pubic hairs. This huntsman's bible, directed against heretics, the mentally ill and women of all stations of life, was responsible for hundreds of thousands of women and children being burned at the stake. (1966, p. 68)

The *Malleus Maleficarum* went through 10

editions before 1669 and another 9 before the century ended, and this during a time when bookmaking was very difficult and literacy was very low. It has been estimated that as many as 500,000 people were executed as witches between the 15th and the 17th centuries (M. Harris, 1974). It should be noted, however, that arriving at an accurate count of individuals executed as witches is extremely difficult, if not impossible. In fact, evidence suggests that the numbers typically given are greatly exaggerated (e.g., see Trevor-Roper, 1967). In any case, as recently as 1692, 20 people were condemned as witches and sentenced to death in Salem, Massachusetts, and the last legal execution of a condemned witch occurred in Glarus, Switzerland, in 1782 (Trevor-Roper, 1967).

During the Renaissance, when advances were being made on so many other fronts, witch-hunting was widespread, and astrology, palmistry, and magic were extremely popular. Also, conditions were bad for the mentally ill. When not being tried as witches, many of the mentally ill either roamed the streets or were locked up in "lunatic asylums." One such asylum was St. Mary of Bethlehem Hospital in London, established in 1547. Known as Bedlam because of the cockney pronunciation of *Bethlehem*, this institution was typical of such places at the time. Inmates were chained, beaten, fed only enough to remain alive, subjected to bloodletting, and put on public display for visitors.

GRADUAL IMPROVEMENT IN THE TREATMENT OF THE MENTALLY ILL

Even during the 16th century, when witch-hunts and trials were very popular, a few courageous people argued that "witches" were not possessed by demons, spirits, or the devil. They argued that the type of behavior "witches" displayed was caused by emotional or physical disorders. For example, **Philippus Paracelsus** (1493–1541), a Swiss physician, speculated that hysteria had a sexual origin and that mania was caused by bodily substances influencing the brain. Paracelsus believed that proper medicine could cure all illness, mental or physical. According to Alexander and Selesnick (1966), Paracelsus was the second physician to argue against labeling individuals as witches. Agrippa had been the first. Not only did **Cornelius Agrippa** (1486–1535) argue against witch-hunts, but he also saved many individuals from the ordeal of a witch trial. In 1563 Agrippa's student **Johann Weyer** (1515–1588) published *The Deception of Demons*, in which he claimed that those labeled as witches were actually mentally disturbed people. Weyer became known to his contemporaries as a crusader against witch-hunting, and this was enough for him to be considered weird or even insane.

The view that "witches" were actually mentally ill people also found support from **Reginald Scot** (1538–1599), who wrote *Discovery of Witchcraft* (1584/1964), and from the Swiss psychiatrist **Felix Plater** (1536–1614). In his book *Practice of Medicine*, Plater outlined several different types of mental disorders including consternation, foolishness, mania, delirium, hallucinations, convulsions, drunkenness, hypochondria, disturbance of sleep, and unusual dreams. The arguments of such people were eventually effective. In 1682, for example, Louis XIV of France abolished the death penalty for witches. Although mental illness increasingly came to be viewed as having natural rather than supernatural causes, it was still poorly understood, and the mentally ill were treated very poorly—if they were treated at all. Bloodletting was still the most popular way of treating all ailments, including mental disorders, and methods were devised for inducing shock in mental patients. One such method was to spin mental patients very rapidly in a chair. Another was to throw several buckets of cold water on chained patients. Physicians would often report dramatic improvement in the condition of a patient following such treatments. These dismal

THE BETTMANN ARCHIVE

Pinel releasing the insane from their chains.

conditions for the mentally ill lasted until the end of the 18th century.

Philippe Pinel

Philippe Pinel (1745–1826) came from a family of physicians and received his medical degree in 1773 from the University of Toulouse. Upon beginning his practice, Pinel was so upset by the greed and insensitivity of his fellow physicians that he moved to Paris where he concentrated on treating that city's poor people. Pinel became interested in the mentally ill when a close friend became afflicted with a mental disorder and Pinel could not treat him. He read the existing literature on mental illness and consulted with the so-called experts, finding the information on mental illness essentially worthless except for

the work of **Joseph Daquin** (1733–1815). Daquin believed that mental illness was a natural phenomenon that should be studied and treated by means of the methods of natural science. Pinel and Daquin became close friends, and Daquin dedicated the second edition of his book *Philosophy of Madness* (1793) to Pinel.

Pinel began writing influential articles in which he argued for the humane treatment of the mentally disturbed. In 1793 he was appointed director of the Bicêtre Asylum, which had been an institution for the insane since 1660. Upon touring the facility, Pinel found that most inmates were chained and guards patrolled the walls to prevent escape. Pinel asked for permission to release the prisoners from their chains, and although the authorities thought Pinel himself was insane for having such a wish, they reluctantly gave him permission. Pinel proceeded cautiously. Starting in 1793, he removed the chains from a small number of inmates and carefully observed the consequences.

The first inmate to be unchained was an English soldier who had once crushed a guard's skull with his chains and was considered to be a violent person. Upon his release from his chains, the man proved to be nonviolent, and he helped Pinel care for the other inmates. Two years later, the soldier was released from Bicêtre. Pinel gradually removed more inmates from their constraints, improved rations, stopped bloodletting, and forbade all harsh treatment such as whirling an inmate in a chair. In his book *A Treatise on Insanity*, Pinel said of bloodletting, "The blood of maniacs is sometimes so lavishly spilled, and with so little discernment, as to render it doubtful whether the patient or his physician has the best claim to the appellation madman" (1801/1962, p. 251).

Besides unchaining inmates and terminating bloodletting and harsh treatment, Pinel was responsible for many innovations in the treatment of the mentally ill. He segregated different types of patients, encouraged occupational therapy, favored bathing and mild purgatives as physical treatments, and argued effectively against the use of any form of punishment or exorcism. In addition, Pinel was the first to maintain precise case histories and statistics on his patients, including a careful record of cure rates.

Under Pinel's leadership, the number of inmate deaths decreased greatly, and the number of inmates cured and released increased greatly. His success at Bicêtre led to his 1795 appointment as director of La Salpêtrière, the largest asylum in Europe, housing 8,000 insane women. Following the same procedures he had followed at Bicêtre, Pinel had equally dramatic success. When he died of pneumonia in 1826, he was given a hero's funeral attended by not only the most influential people in Europe but also hundreds of ordinary citizens, including many former patients at the Bicêtre and La Salpêtrière asylums.

Partially because of Pinel's success and partially because of the *Zeitgeist*, people throughout Europe and the United States began to argue for the humane treatment of the mentally disturbed. In Britain, **William Tuke** (1732–1822), a Quaker and a prosperous retired tea and coffee merchant with no medical training, visited a lunatic asylum and was horrified by what he saw. He dedicated the remaining 30 years of his life to improve the plight of the mentally ill and, in 1792, founded the York Retreat for the mentally ill. In the retreat, designed more like a farm than a prison, inmates were given good food, freedom, respect, medical treatment, recreation, and religious instruction. Tuke lived long enough to see his retreat become a model for institutions for the mentally ill throughout the world. After his death, his son and then his grandson ran the retreat. His great grandson, Daniel Hack Tuke (1827–1895) was the first in the family to receive medical training, and he became a prominent psychiatrist during the Victorian period. In 1788 the Italian physician **Vincenzo Chiarugi** (1759–1820) was appointed superintendent of Ospidale di Bonifazio, a newly opened hospital for the mentally ill in Florence. Even before Pinel, Chiarugi argued that the mentally ill should be spared physical restraint and harsh treatment. He also provided work and recreational activities for his patients and recorded detailed case histories. Chiarugi's advice for dealing with the mentally ill has a particularly modern ring to it:

It is a supreme moral duty and medical obligation to respect the insane individual as a person. It is especially necessary for the person who treats the mental patient to gain his confidence and trust. It is best, therefore, to be tactful and understanding and try to lead the patient to the truth and to instill reason into him little by little in a kindly way. . . . The attitude of doctors and nurses must be authoritative and impressive, but at the same time pleasant and adapted to the impaired mind of the patient. . . . Generally it is better to follow the patient's inclinations and give him as many comforts as is advisable from a medical and practical standpoint. (Quoted in Mora, 1959, p. 431)

THE BETTMANN ARCHIVE

Dorothea Lynde Dix

Benjamin Rush

In the United States, **Benjamin Rush** (1745–1813), who is often referred to as the first U.S. psychiatrist, wrote *Diseases of the Mind* (1812), in which he lamented that the mentally ill were often treated like criminals or "beasts of prey." Instead, he urged that the mentally ill be unchained and no longer punished. They should experience fresh air and sunlight and be allowed to go for pleasant walks within their institution. Furthermore, Rush contended, the mentally ill should never be on display to the public for the purposes of inhumane curiosity and amusement. Despite his many enlightened views, Rush still advocated bloodletting and the use of rotating and tranquilizing chairs. He believed that bloodletting relieved vascular congestion, that rotating relieved the patient's congested brain, and that strapping a patient's arms and legs in a so-called tranquilizing chair calmed the patient.

Dorothea Lynde Dix

Also in the United States, in 1841 **Dorothea Lynde Dix** (1802–1887) began a campaign to improve the conditions of the mentally ill. Because of unhappy home circumstances, Dix had been forced to leave her home when she was only 10 years old, and when she was 14 years old, she began her career as a schoolteacher. Later, illness forced her to give up her full-time teaching position and take a position teaching women inmates in a Boston prison. It became clear to Dix that many of the women labeled and confined as criminals were really mentally ill, and so Dix began her 40-year campaign to improve the plight of the mentally ill. She traveled from state to state, pointing out the inhumane treatment of the mentally disturbed. Within a 3-year period, Dix visited 18 states and brought about institutional reforms in most of them. In 1841 when Dix had begun her campaigning, mental hospitals housed only about 15 percent of those needing care; by 1890 that figure had risen to about 70 percent. To a large extent, the improvement was due to Dix's efforts.

During the Civil War, Dix served as the chief of hospital nurses, and after the war she toured Europe seeking better treatment of the mentally ill. While in Europe, Dix visited with Queen Victoria and Pope Pius IX, convincing both that the mentally ill were in dire need of better facilities and treatment.

Due to the efforts of such individuals as Pinel, Tuke, Chiarugi, Rush, and Dix, the mentally ill began to receive better treatment than they had during the Middle Ages and the Renaissance. However, this treatment involved only the patients' physical surroundings and maintenance. Effective treatment for mental illness itself was still lacking. Alexander and Selesnick (1966) speculate that there were three reasons for the poor treatment of the mentally ill even *after* it was no longer believed that they were possessed by demons: ignorance of the nature of mental illness, fear of the mentally ill, and the widespread belief that mental illness was incurable. The work of such individuals as Kraepelin, Witmer, and the early hypnotists dramatically improved the understanding and treatment of the mentally ill, and it is to that work that we turn next.

Emil Kraepelin

Emil Kraepelin (1856–1926), who had studied with Wundt, attempted to do for mental disorders what Wundt and his colleagues attempted to do for sensations—classify them. In 1883 Kraepelin published a list of mental disorders that was so thorough that it was adopted the world over and has lasted until recent times. He based his classification of mental diseases on what caused them, how much they involved the brain and nervous system, their symptoms, and their treatment. Some categories of mental disorders that Kraepelin listed, such as mania and depression, had been first mentioned by Hippocrates 2,300 years earlier. Some other categories of mental illness Kraepelin listed were dementia praecox, characterized by withdrawal from reality, excessive daydreaming, and inappropriate emotional responses; paranoia, characterized by delusions of grandeur or of persecution; manic depression, characterized by cycles of intense emotional outbursts and passive states of depression; and neurosis, characterized by relatively mild mental and emotional disorders. Kraepelin believed that most major mental illnesses, such as dementia praecox, were incurable because they were caused by constitutional factors. When the Swiss psychiatrist Eugen Bleuler (1857–1939) found that dementia praecox could be successfully treated, he changed the name of the disease to schizophrenia, which literally means "a splitting of the personality."

The list of categories of mental illness that many clinicians, psychoanalysts, and psychiatrists currently use as a guide is found in *The Diagnostic and Statistical Manual of Mental Disorders* (1987) published by the American Psychiatric Association. Unlike Kraepelin's book, which not only listed various types of mental disorders but also attempted to explain the origins of those disorders, the manual published by the American Psychiatric Association is purely descriptive. That is, it simply lists the symptoms that define the various forms of mental illness. Although Kraepelin's classifications brought order to an otherwise chaotic mass of clinical observations,

Emil Kraepelin

NATIONAL LIBRARY OF MEDICINE

his work is now seen by many as standing in the way of therapeutic progress. People do not fall nicely into the categories that he created nor are the causes for their disorders always physical in nature as Kraepelin assumed they were. As Alexander and Selesnick say of Kraepelin,

> He, whose authority ruled supreme at the turn of the century and the following two decades . . . today is looked upon by the younger generation of psychiatrists as a rigid and sterile codifier of disease categories; even if these were valid, they contribute to neither understanding the causes of diseases nor their prognosis. (1966, p. 184)

Still, Kraepelin went a long way to standardize the categories of mental illness and thus make communication about them more precise.

Lightner Witmer

Lightner Witmer

Like Kraepelin, **Lightner Witmer** (1867–1956) earned his doctorate under Wundt. He was born on June 28 into a prominent Philadelphia family. Witmer earned his bachelor's degree from the University of Pennsylvania in 1888 and then took a position teaching history and English at Rugby Academy, a secondary school in Philadelphia. He remained there for two years, while taking classes in law and political science at the University of Pennsylvania. After taking a class from James McKeen Cattell, Witmer resigned his position at Rugby and entered graduate school. Cattell put Witmer to work studying individual differences in reaction times. He intended to earn his doctorate under Cattell, but when Cattell moved to Columbia, Witmer went to Leipzig for his advanced degree. Witmer's training at Leipzig coincided with Titchener's.

In the fall of 1892, Witmer returned from Europe to a faculty position at the University of Pennsylvania where he taught courses and conducted research as an experimental psychologist in the Wundtian tradition. He remained at Pennsylvania for 45 years. Also in 1892, the American Psychological Association (APA) was founded, and Witmer became a charter member, along with such individuals as William James, G. Stanley Hall, and James McKeen Cattell. (Incidentally, Witmer was the last charter member to die.) In 1894 the university created special courses for public school teachers, and Witmer became involved in those courses. When one teacher described the problem one of her students was having learning to spell, Witmer's developing belief that psychology should provide practical information was strengthened. He decided to work with the student, and this marked the beginning of his career as a clinical psychologist. Soon he offered a special course on how to work with students who were "mentally defective, blind, or criminally disturbed" (McReynolds, 1987, p. 851). In 1896 Witmer published an article entitled "Practical Work in Psychology," and in 1897 he delivered a paper at an APA convention in Boston on the same topic in which he first employed the term *psychological clinic*. In 1896 Witmer founded the world's first psychological clinic at the University of Pennsylvania, and this only 17 years after the establishment of Wundt's experimental laboratory. In 1907 Witmer founded *The Psychological Clinic* journal, which was instrumental in promoting and defining the profession of clinical psychology. The journal continued publication until 1935. To Witmer and others, a new profession was clearly emerging, and it needed to have a name. In the opening article of the first issue of his journal, Witmer named the profession **clinical psychology** and described the new profession as follows:

> Although clinical psychology is clearly related to medicine, it is quite as closely related to sociology and to pedagogy. . . . An abundance of material for scientific study fails to be utilized, because the interest of psychologists is else-

where engaged, and those in constant touch with the actual phenomena do not possess the training necessary to make the experience and observation of scientific value. . . . While the field of clinical psychology is to some extent occupied by the physician, especially by the psychiatrist, and while I expect to rely in a great measure upon the educator and social worker for the more important contributions to this branch of psychology, it is nevertheless true that none of these has quite the training necessary for this kind of work. For that matter, neither has the psychologist, unless he had acquired this training from sources other than the usual course of instruction in psychology. . . . The phraseology of "clinical psychology" and "psychological clinic" will doubtless strike many as an odd juxtaposition of terms relating to quite disparate subjects. . . . I have borrowed the word "clinical" from medicine, because it is the best term I can find to indicate the character of the method which I deem necessary for this work. . . . The methods of clinical psychology are necessarily involved wherever the status of an individual mind is determined by observation and experiment, and pedagogical treatment applied to effect a change, i.e., the development of such individual mind. Whether the subject be a child or an adult, the examination and treatment may be conducted and their results expressed in the terms of the clinical method. (Quoted in McReynolds, 1987, p. 852)

In 1908 Witmer established a residential school for the care and treatment of retarded and troubled children. This was the first of several such schools that he established. In this same year, Witmer began publishing articles that were highly critical of what he viewed as unscientific, or even fraudulent, ways of treating the mentally ill. He was especially critical of William James because of James's interest in supernatural phenomena.

McReynolds argues that Witmer should be considered the founder or "father" of clinical psychology but he recognizes that others may argue that it is Freud, Binet, or Rogers who should be given that honor. McReynolds makes his case for Witmer as follows:

> Witmer's role in the formation of clinical psychology is somewhat analogous to that of Wundt in experimental psychology, in that in each case the individual deliberately and self-consciously

defined the existence of a new area and nurtured its early development, but other, later workers were responsible for giving the area greater depth and new directions. In Witmer's case the designation of founder is based primarily on the following six pioneering achievements:

> 1. He was the first to enunciate the idea that the emerging scientific psychology could be the basis of a new helping profession.

> 2. He established and developed the first facility to implement this idea—a "psychological clinic," headed by a psychologist and primarily staffed by psychologists.

> 3. He proposed the term *clinical psychology* for the new profession and outlined its original agenda.

> 4. He conceptualized, organized, and carried out the first program to train clinical psychologists in the sense he defined.

> 5. Through his founding and long-time editorship of a journal (*The Psychological Clinic*) specifically intended to be the organ of the new profession, he further defined the area, publicized it, and attracted young persons to it.

> 6. Through his own activities in performing the kinds of professional activities that he envisaged for clinical psychologists, he served as a role model for early members. (1987, pp. 855–856)

Although we have concentrated on Witmer's contributions to clinical psychology, he also made significant contributions to school psychology and special education. As far as clinical psychology is concerned, however, Witmer made three lasting impressions, and these are

> (a) the idea that scientific psychology, in its rigorous experimental sense, can, if appropriately utilized, be useful in helping people; (b) the conception that this help can best be provided through the instrument of a special profession (clinical psychology) that is independent of both medicine and education; and (c) a commitment to the view that clinical psychology should itself be highly research oriented and should be closely allied with basic psychology. (McReynolds, 1987, p. 857)

It is important to note that Witmer was trained as an experimental psychologist and he never waivered in his belief that clinicians should receive rigorous training in scientific methodology; the type of training leading to the

Doctor of Philosophy (Ph.D.). This tradition of the clinician as a scientist-professional has only recently been challenged. In 1973 the APA agreed that the intense scientific training characteristic of the Ph.D. program is not necessary for clinical psychologists and established the Doctor of Psychology degree (Psy.D.) for those seeking training that emphasizes professional applications rather than research methodology. In chapter 18 we discuss the current debate over whether clinicians should be Ph.D.s or Psy.D.s, but as far as Witmer was concerned, clinicians should be scientists—scientists who apply their knowledge to helping troubled individuals.

THE TENSION BETWEEN THE PSYCHOLOGICAL AND MEDICAL MODELS OF MENTAL ILLNESS

As natural science succeeded, people applied its principles to everything, including humans. When applied to humans, mechanism, determinism, and positivism involved the search for a natural cause for all human behavior including abnormal behavior. After 2,000 years, conditions had returned to almost the point where they had been about the time of Hippocrates; once again people were emphasizing the brain as the seat of the intellect and the emotions.

This return to naturalism was both good and bad for psychology. It was good because it discouraged mysticism and superstition. No longer did people use evil demons, spirits, or forces to explain mental illness. On the negative side, it discouraged a search for the *psychological factors* underlying mental illness, for it was suggested that a search for such factors was a return to demonology. By the mid-19th century, the dominant belief was that the cause of all illness, including mental illness, was disordered physiology or brain chemistry. This belief retarded psychology's search for psychological causes of mental illness, such as conflict, frustration, emotional disturbance, or other cognitive factors.

Under the organic, or medical, model of mental illness, psychological explanations of mental illness were suspect. Because it was generally believed that all disorders had an organic origin, classifying "mental" diseases just as organic diseases had been classified made sense, and this is what Kraepelin attempted to do.

The debate still exists between those who seek to explain all human behavior in terms of physiology or chemistry (i.e., those following a medical model) and those who stress the importance of mental variables such as conflict, frustration, anxiety, fear, and unconscious motivation (those following a psychological model). This debate is illustrated in the explanations currently offered for alcoholism. Those individuals accepting the medical model claim that alcoholism is a disease that is either inherited (perhaps only as a predisposition) or results from a biochemical imbalance, a metabolic abnormality, or some other biological condition. Those individuals accepting the psychological model are more likely to emphasize the alcoholic's life circumstances in their explanation—circumstances that cause the stress, frustration, conflict, or anxiety from which the alcoholic is presumably attempting to escape.

Some believe that unless an illness has a neurophysiological basis, it is not an illness at all. That is, it is possible for a brain to be diseased and cause various behavior disorders, but in such a case there is no "mental" illness, only an actual *physical* disease or dysfunction. For example, in his influential book *The Myth of Mental Illness* (1974), Szasz, himself a psychiatrist, contends that what has been and is labeled mental illness reflects problems in living or nonconformity but not true illness. Therefore, according to Szasz, the diagnosis of mental illness reflects a social, political, or moral judgment, not a medical one. Of course, problems in living are very real and can be devastating enough to require professional help. According to Szasz, psychiatry and clinical psychology are worthy professions if they view those whom they help as clients rather than patients and have as their goal helping people to learn about themselves, others, and life. They are invalid, or "pseudo-sciences" if they view as their goal helping patients recover from mental illness.

Szasz argues that the belief that mental illness is a real illness has hurt many more people than it has helped. For one thing, he says, to label problems in living as an illness or as a disease implies that a person is not responsible for solving those problems, their being diverted to circumstances beyond his or her control. Although most accepting the psychological model are willing to employ the term *mental illness*, Szasz is not; he prefers to refer to such abnormalities as problems in life or adjustment problems.

As we will see in the next chapter, Freud received his medical training within the positivistic tradition of Helmholtz, and he first attempted to explain personality in terms of the medical model. Frustrated, however, he soon was forced to switch to the psychological model. It was, to a large extent, the work of the early hypnotists that caused Freud to change his mind, and it is to that work that we turn next.

THE USE OF HYPNOTISM

Franz Anton Mesmer

It is ironic that the road away from demonology and toward better understanding of mental illness included the work of **Franz Anton Mesmer** (1734–1815). Mesmer's work was eventually judged unscientific, but at one time his theory of animal magnetism was an improvement over the prevailing superstitions. Mesmer obtained his medical degree in 1766 from the University of Vienna. In his dissertation, which was entitled "On the Influence of the Planets," he maintained that the planets influenced humans through a force called *animal gravitation*. Considering Newton's theory of universal gravitation, this contention did not seem farfetched.

In the early 1770s, Mesmer met a Jesuit priest named **Maximillian Hell** who told Mesmer of cures he had accomplished using a magnet. Mesmer himself then used a magnet to "cure" one of

Franz Anton Mesmer

THE BETTMANN ARCHIVE

his patients when all of the conventional forms of treatment had failed. Then Mesmer tried the magnetic treatment on other patients with equal success. It should be pointed out, however, that the magnetic treatment always involved telling the patient exactly what was expected to occur.

With the success of his magnetic treatment, Mesmer had the information he needed to challenge one of the most famous exorcists of the late 18th century, the Austrian Father J. V. Gassner (1727–1779), who claimed great success in curing patients by "driving out demons." Mesmer claimed that Gassner's "cures" resulted from the rearrangement of "animal gravitation," not the removal of demons. In the heated debate that ensued, Mesmer won, and exorcism as a form of "psychotherapy" suffered a major setback. As mentioned, this was generally regarded as an improvement in the treatment of the mentally ill because Mesmer's "cure" was natural (although fallacious) and Gassner's was supernatural.

At first, Mesmer assumed that each person's body contained a magnetic force field. In the healthy individual, this force field was distributed evenly throughout the body, but in the unhealthy individual it was unevenly distributed. This uneven distribution of the force field caused physical symptoms. By using magnets, it was possible to redistribute the force field and restore the patient's health.

Soon Mesmer concluded that it was not necessary to use iron magnets because anything he touched became magnetized:

> Steel is not the only object which can absorb and emanate the magnetic force. On the contrary, paper, bread, wool, silk, leather, stone, glass, water, various metals, wood, dogs, human beings, everything that I touched became so magnetic that these objects exerted as great an influence on the sick as does a magnet itself. I filled bottles with magnetic materials just as one does with electricity. (Quoted in Goldsmith, 1934, p. 64)

Next, Mesmer found that he did not need to use any object at all; simply holding his hand next to a patient's body was enough for the patient to be influenced by Mesmer's magnetic force. Mesmer concluded that although all humans contained a magnetic force field, in some people the field was much stronger than in others. These people were natural healers, and he, of course, was one of them.

When magnetic therapy became popular, Father Hell claimed to be the first to have used it. A great dispute followed, which was covered by the newspapers. During this controversy, which Mesmer (probably unjustly) won, the term **animal magnetism** was first used.

In 1777 Mesmer agreed to treat Fräulein Paradies, a 17-year-old pianist who had been blind since the age of 3. Mesmer claimed that his treatment returned her sight but that she could see only while alone in his presence. The medical community accused Mesmer of being a charlatan, and he was forced to leave Vienna. He fled to Paris where, almost immediately, he attracted an enthusiastic following. He was so popular that he decided to treat patients in groups rather than individually, and still he was effective. Patients would enter a thickly carpeted, dimly lit, fully mirrored room. Soft music played, and there was the fragrance of orange blossoms. The patients held the iron rods that projected from the *baquet*, a tub filled with "magnetized" water. Into this scene stepped Mesmer wearing a lilac cloak and waving a yellow wand. This entire ritual was designed to produce a "crisis" in his patients. During a crisis, a patient would typically scream, break into a cold sweat, and convulse. He noted that when one patient experienced a crisis, others would soon do so also. Thus, treating groups increased not only Mesmer's profits (although poor patients were not charged) but his effectiveness. Because of what was later called the **contagion effect**, many patients who would not respond to suggestion when alone with a physician would do so readily after seeing others respond. As was undoubtedly the case with exorcism and with faith healing, many of Mesmer's patients reported being cured of their ailments. In all these cases, the symptoms removed were probably hysterical, that is, of psychological origin. As we have seen, hysteria refers to a number of symptoms such as blindness, paralysis, and convulsive disorders. Exorcists, faith healers, and Mesmer all probably benefited from the fact that after experiencing a violent emotional episode, a patient's symptoms (especially if these symptoms are hysterical) will subside. By now Mesmer's treatment was filled with ritual.

As Mesmer's fame grew and thousands came to his clinic, his critics became more severe. The French clergy accused Mesmer of being in consort with the devil, and the medical profession accused him of being a charlatan. In response to the medical profession's criticisms, Mesmer proposed that 20 patients be chosen at random, 10 sent to him for treatment, and 10 sent to members of the French Academy of Medicine; the results would then be compared. Mesmer's interesting proposal was rejected. In 1781 Queen Marie Antoinette, one of Mesmer's many influential friends, offered Mesmer a château and a lifetime pension if he would disclose the secrets of his success. Mesmer turned down the offer.

Popularity alone did not satisfy Mesmer personally. What he desperately wanted was the acceptance of the medical profession, which saw Mesmer as a quack. In 1784 the Society of Harmony (a group dedicated to the promotion of animal magnetism) persuaded the king of France to establish a commission to study objectively the effects of animal magnetism. This truly high-level commission consisted of Benjamin Franklin (the commission's presiding officer); Antoine Lavoisier, the famous chemist; and Joseph Guillotin, the creator of a way to put condemned people to death in a "humane" manner. The commission conducted several experiments to test Mesmer's claims. In one experiment, a woman was told that she was being mesmerized by a mesmerist behind a door, and she went into a crisis although there was actually no one behind the door. In another experiment, a patient was offered five cups of water, one of which was mesmerized. She chose and drank a cup with plain water but experienced a crisis anyhow.

Much to Mesmer's dismay, in its report of August 1784, the commission concluded that there was no such thing as animal magnetism and that any positive results from treatment supposedly employing it were due to the imagination. The commission branded Mesmer a mystic and a fanatic. Although many people, some of them prominent, urged Mesmer to continue his work and his writing, the commission's findings had essentially destroyed him, and he sank into oblivion.

Marquis de Puységur

Although the commission's report silenced Mesmer himself, other members of the Society of Harmony continued to use and modify Mesmer's techniques. One such member, **Marquis de Puységur** (1751–1825), discovered that magnetizing did not need to involve the violent crisis that Mesmer's approach necessitated. Simply by placing a person in a peaceful, sleeplike trance, Puységur could demonstrate a number of phenomena. Although the person appeared to be asleep, he or she would still respond to Puységur's voice and follow his commands. When Puységur instructed the magnetized patient to talk about a certain topic, perform various motor activities, or even dance to imagined music, he or she would do so and have no recollection of the events upon waking. Because a sleeplike trance replaced the crisis, Puységur renamed the condition **artificial somnambulism**. He found that the therapeutic results of using this artificial sleep were as good as they had been with Mesmer's crisis approach.

With his new approach, Puységur made many discoveries. In fact, he discovered most of the hypnotic phenomena known today. He learned that while in the somnambulistic state individuals were highly suggestible. If they were told something was true, they acted as if it were true. Paralyses and various sensations, such as pain, could be moved around the body solely by suggestion. When individuals were told that a part of their bodies was anaesthetized, they could tolerate normally painful stimuli such as burns and pin pricks without any sign of distress. Also, a wide variety of emotional expressions, such as laughing and crying, could be produced on command. It was observed that individuals could not remember what had occurred while in a trance, a phenomenon later called **posthypnotic amnesia**. What is now called **posthypnotic suggestion** was also observed. That is, while in a trance, an individual is told to perform some act such as scratching his or her nose when they hear their name. After being aroused from the trance, the individual will typically perform the act as instructed without any apparent knowledge of why he or she is doing so.

John Elliotson, James Esdaile, and James Braid

Because magnetizing a patient could, by suggestion, make him or her oblivious to pain, a few physicians began to look upon magnetism as a possible surgical anaesthetic. **John Elliotson** (1791–1868) suggested that mesmerism be used during surgery, but the medical establishment forbade it even though other anaesthetics were not available. In 1842 W. S. Ward performed a leg amputation in which the patient was magnetized, but some physicians accused the patient of being an imposter. Other physicians said that patients should suffer pain during an operation because it helped them recover better (Fancher, 1990). In India, **James Esdaile** (1808–1859), a surgeon with the British Army in Calcutta, performed more than 250 painless operations on Hindu convicts, but his results were dismissed because his operations had been performed on natives and therefore had no relevance to England. About this time, anaesthetic gases were discovered, and interest in magnetism as an anaesthetic faded almost completely. The use of gases was much more compatible with the training of the physicians of the day than were the mysterious forces involved in magnetism or somnambulism.

James Braid (1795–1860), a prominent Scottish surgeon, was skeptical of magnetism, but after carefully examining a magnetized subject, he was convinced that many of the effects were real. Braid proceeded to examine the phenomenon systematically, and in 1843 he wrote *The Rationale of Nervous Sleep*. Braid explained magnetism in terms of prolonged concentration and the physical exhaustion that followed, stressing that the results were explained by the subject's suggestibility rather than by any power that the magnetizer possessed. He renamed the study of the phenomenon neuro-hypnology, which was then shortened to *hypnosis* (*hypnos* is the Greek word for "sleep"). Braid did as much as anyone to make the phenomenon previously known as magnetism, mesmerism, or somnambulism respectable within the medical community.

The Nancy School

Convinced of the value of hypnosis, **Auguste Ambroise Liébeault** (1823–1904) wanted to use it in his practice but could find no patient willing

to be subjected to it. Eventually, he agreed to provide free treatment to any patient willing to undergo hypnotism. A few patients agreed, and Liébeault was so successful that his practice was soon threatened by an excess of nonpaying patients. Soon Liébeault was treating all his patients with hypnotism and accepting whatever fee they could afford. A "school" soon grew up around his work, and because he practiced in a French village just outside of the city of Nancy, it was called the **Nancy school**.

The school attracted a number of physicians; among them was **Hippolyte Bernheim** (1840–1919), who became the major spokesperson of the Nancy school. Bernheim contended that *all* humans were suggestible, but that some were more suggestible than others, and that highly suggestible people were easier to hypnotize than those less suggestible. Furthermore, Bernheim found that anything a highly suggestible patient believed would improve his or her symptoms usually did so.

CHARCOT AND THE TREATMENT OF HYSTERIA

Contrary to the belief of the members of the Nancy school, **Jean-Martin Charcot** (1825–1893) did not believe that suggestibility was a general human trait. Charcot believed that only those people suffering the neurosis called hysteria could be hypnotized. This belief brought Charcot and his colleagues into sharp conflict with members of the Nancy school—the former believing that hypnotizability was a sign of mental pathology, the latter believing that it was perfectly normal. The debate was heated and lasted for years.

When Charcot became the director of La Salpêtrière (the institution where Pinel had released the patients from their chains), he immediately converted it into a research center. Though he was flamboyant, Charcot was considered one of the most brilliant physicians in all of Europe. His regular lectures were well attended by both professionals and nonprofessionals. Among those attending were Alfred

Charcot demonstrating various hypnotic phenomena.

Binet, William James, and Sigmund Freud. Charcot even became one of Freud's idols.

Charcot's interests increasingly turned to hysteria, an ailment most physicians dismissed as malingering because they could find no organic cause for its symptoms. In fact, some of the symptoms were anatomically anomalous:

> Some hysterical paralyses and anesthesias occurred only in sharply delineated body areas such as the part of the hand and wrist normally covered by a glove. Anatomically, this made no sense because the nerves of the hand and arm fall in no such pattern; afflictions resulting from ordinary nerve damage would not have such sharp boundaries. . . . The prevailing medical opinion dismissed hysteria as simple malingering; symptoms which violated the accepted rules of neuroanatomy strained the credulity of many mechanistically oriented doctors, who felt patients were merely simulating their illnesses. (Fancher, 1990, pp. 340–341)

Charcot dismissed the popular malingering theory and concluded that hysteric patients were suffering real discomfort. Staying within the medical model, however, he concluded that hysteria was caused by a hereditary neurological degeneration that was progressive and irreversible. Because both hysteria and hypnosis produced the same symptoms (e.g., paralyses and anaesthesia), Charcot concluded that hypnotizability indicated the presence of hysteria.

Among Charcot's most popular demonstrations were those in which he hypnotized hysteric patients and had them display a wide range of imaginary sensations and physical states. Toward the end of his life, Charcot admitted that his theory of suggestibility was wrong and that of the Nancy school was correct. Even so, the prestige of Charcot gave further respectability to hypnosis; even more important, Charcot helped people see hysteria as a real ailment worthy of the concern of physicians.

Pierre Janet

Pierre Janet (1859–1947) was Charcot's student, but, unlike his mentor, he explained hypnosis and hysteria as psychological rather than physiological phenomena. After hypnotizing a young woman named Léonie, Janet observed that different aspects of her personality would emerge at different levels of the hypnotic trance. He concluded that for some individuals aspects of the personality became dissociated, or "split off," and these dissociated aspects of the personality could manifest themselves during a hypnotic trance. Janet speculated that hysterical symptoms might result from the "subconscious" influence of dissociated aspects of personality. He noticed that the dissociated aspects of a patient's personality quite often consisted of traumatic or unpleasant memories, and it was therefore the therapist's task to discover these memories and make the patient aware of them. Hypnosis was used to discover these dissociated memories, and when they were brought to the attention of a patient, his or her hysterical symptoms often abated. (For a more detailed account of Janet's work, see Ellenberger, 1970.)

We see much in Janet's work that anticipated Freud's. Even the names that they used to describe their methods were similar; Janet called his method psychological analysis, and Freud called his psychoanalysis. The ideas of Janet and Freud were so similar that there was a dispute between the two over priority. Freud argued that Janet's treatment of those ideas was superficial. Janet insisted that what Freud called psychoanalysis originated in his work and in that of Charcot (R. I. Watson, 1978).

SUMMARY

Although mental illness has been referred to by different names throughout history, all those names appear to refer to the same types of behavior or thought processes—namely, behavior that is harmful to oneself or others, unrealistic thoughts and perceptions, inappropriate emotions, and unpredictable behavior. Early explanations of mental illness fall into three categories: biological explanations (the medical model), psychological explanations (the psychological model), and supernatural or magical explanations (the supernatural model). How mental illness was treated was largely determined by what its causes were assumed to be. All forms of psychotherapy, however, involved a sufferer, a helper, and some form of ritual. If the psychological model of mental illness was assumed, then treatment involved such things as the analysis of dreams, encouragement and support, or the teaching of more effective coping skills. If the supernatural model was assumed, then treatment consisted of such things as exorcism, incantation, or magical ritual. In primitive times, two types of sympathetic magic were widely practiced: homeopathic magic, which was based on the belief that what happened to a model or image of a person would also happen to that person, and contagious magic, which was based on the belief that what happened to something once close to a person would have an influence on that person. If the biological model was assumed, then treatment consisted of such things as proper exercise, proper diet, massage, bloodletting, purgatives, or drugs. Hippocrates was among the first to accept the biological model of illness (both physical and mental). He saw health as the result of a balance among the four body humors and illness as an imbalance among them. To help patients regain health (a balance), Hippocrates prescribed such things as mineral baths, fresh air, and proper diet.

Naturalistic medicine and psychiatry characterized treatment of physical and mental problems until the collapse of the Roman Empire, when there was a regression to demonology and magic. During the Middle Ages, and especially during the Renaissance, the mentally ill were believed to be possessed by evil spirits and were harshly treated. But even during this dark time in history for the mentally ill, some people refused to believe that abnormal behavior resulted from possession of the person by demons, spirits, or the devil. Paracelsus, Agrippa, Weyer, Scot, and Plater argued effectively that abnormal behavior had natural causes and that the mentally ill should be treated humanely. Even when the supernatural explanation of mental illness subsided, however, the mentally ill were still treated harshly in "lunatic asylums" such as Bedlam. Not until the end of the 18th century did Pinel, Tuke, Chiarugi, Rush, Dix, and others help bring about dramatically better living conditions for the mentally ill. Through the efforts of these people, many mentally ill patients were unchained; given better food; provided recreation, fresh air, sunlight and medical treatment; and treated with respect.

In 1883 Kraepelin summarized all categories of mental illness known at that time; he attempted to show the origins of the various disorders and how the disorders should be treated. One of the charter members of the APA, Lightner Witmer, was trained as a Wundtian experimental psychologist but became increasingly interested in using psychological principles to help people. He established the world's first psychological clinic in 1896 (and subsequently several others), he developed the first curriculum designed to train clinical psychologists, and he founded the first journal devoted to the diagnosis and treatment of mental illness. As the first clinical psychologist, Witmer did what a number of clinical psychologists have been doing ever since: providing services to mentally disturbed individuals in both a clinical setting and private practice; teaching; supervision; community consultation, administration, and research. By the mid-19th century, the medical model of illness (both physical and mental) prevailed just as it had before the collapse of the Roman Empire. The prevalence of the medical model discouraged a search for the psychological causes of mental illness because it was believed that such a search exemplified a return to a form of demonology. Although psychological explanations of mental illness became more respectable, there was and is a tension between those accepting the medical model and those accepting the psychological model. Szasz contends that mental illness is a myth because it has no organic basis. To him, what is called mental illness is more accurately described as problems in living, and individuals should have the responsibility for solving those problems rather than attributing them to some illness or disease.

The work of Mesmer played a crucial role in the transition toward objective psychological explanations of mental illness. Mesmer believed that physical and mental disorders were caused by the uneven distribution of animal magnetism in the patient's body. He also believed that some people

had stronger magnetic force fields than others and that they, like himself, were natural healers. Mesmer contended that his extraordinary powers could redistribute the magnetic fields in clients and thereby cure them. Because of something later to be called the contagion effect, some of Mesmer's clients were more easily "cured" in a group than individually.

Puységur discovered that placing clients in a sleeplike trance, which he called artificial somnambulism, was as effective as Mesmer's crisis-oriented approach for treating disorders. Puységur explained this sleeplike state as the result of suggestibility. He also discovered the phenomena of posthypnotic suggestion and posthypnotic amnesia. Because "magnetizing" patients made them insensitive to pain, several physicians used it as an anaesthetic. This technique was controversial, however, and physicians dropped it when anaesthetic gases such as ether were discovered. By systematically studying hypnosis and attempting to explain it as a biological phenomenon, Braid gave it greater respectability in the medical community. Members of the Nancy school, such as Liébeault and Bernheim, believed that all humans were more or less suggestible and therefore hypnotizable; Charcot, in contrast, believed that only hysterics were hypnotizable. Unlike most other physicians of his day, Charcot treated hysteria as a real rather than an imagined illness. Janet believed that aspects of the personality, such as traumatic memories, could become dissociated from the rest of the personality and that such dissociation explained both hysterical symptoms and hypnotic phenomena. Janet found that often when a patient became aware of and dealt with a dissociated memory, his or her hysterical symptoms would improve. Such theoretical notions and clinical observations clearly anticipated aspects of Freud's later work.

DISCUSSION QUESTIONS

1. What is mental illness? In your answer, include the criteria that have been used throughout history to define mental illness.

2. Summarize the medical, psychological, and supernatural models of mental illness and give an example of each.

3. What, if anything, do all versions of psychotherapy have in common?

4. Describe what therapy would be like if it were based on the psychological model of mental illness,

on the supernatural model, and on the biological model.

5. Define and give an example of homeopathic and contagious magic.

6. How did Hippocrates define health and illness? What treatments did he prescribe for helping his patients regain health?

7. How were the mentally ill viewed and treated following the collapse of the Roman Empire?

8. What was the significance of Pinel in the history of the treatment of the mentally ill?

9. Why was Kraepelin's listing of the various mental disorders seen as something both positive and negative?

10. Summarize the reasons why Witmer is considered the founder of clinical psychology.

11. Describe and give an example exemplifying the tension between explanations of mental illness based on the medical model and those based on the psychological model.

12. Why does Szasz refer to mental illness as a myth? Why does he feel that labeling someone as mentally ill may be doing him or her a disservice?

13. According to Mesmer, what caused mental and physical illness? What procedures did Mesmer use to cure such illnesses? What was Mesmer's fate?

14. In what way could Mesmer's techniques be considered an improvement over other techniques of treating the mentally ill that existed at the time?

15. What major phenomena did Puységur observe during his research on artificial somnambulism?

16. Describe the debate that occurred between members of the Nancy school and Charcot and his colleagues over hypnotizability. Who finally won the debate?

17. Summarize Janet's explanation of hysterical symptoms and hypnotic phenomena.

SUGGESTIONS FOR FURTHER READING

Alexander, F. G., & Selesnick, S. T. (1966). *The history of psychiatry: An evaluation of psychiatric thought and practice from prehistoric times to the present*. New York: Harper & Row.
Although biased toward psychoanalysis and its antecedents, this book does an excellent job of tracing the various versions of psychiatry that have existed through human history.

Maher, B. A., & Maher, W. B. (1985). Psychopathology: II. From the eighteenth century to modern times. In G. A. Kimble & K. Schlesinger (Eds.), *Topics in the history of psychology* (Vol. 2, pp. 295–329). Hillsdale, NJ: Erlbaum.
According to the authors, the eclecticism that characterized the Middle Ages and beyond concerning the treatment of the mentally ill continued after the Industrial Revolution and into the mid-18th century. The difference was that new methods of treatment were developed and employed, for example, electrical therapy and mesmerism. In the 18th century, there was also widespread belief in "natural law," or the belief that one's behavior had natural consequences. Those who drank, gambled, or were promiscuous were naturally led to madness, disease, and poverty. Conversely, traits such as hard work, sobriety, fidelity, and honesty naturally led to health and prosperity. The belief in natural law created a "they-got-what-they-deserved" attitude toward the mentally ill. The treatment of the mentally ill remained poor until the time of the great reformers such as Chiarugi, Pinel, and Tuke. The 19th century provided the ingredients for our present understanding of psychopathology. These included the infectious disease model, evolutionary theory, the rise of experimental psychology, and the development of psychoanalysis.

Maher, W. B., & Maher, B. A. (1985). Psychopathology: I. From ancient times to the eighteenth century. In G. A. Kimble & K. Schlesinger (Eds.), *Topics in the history of psychology* (Vol. 2, pp. 251–294). Hillsdale, NJ: Erlbaum.
The authors discuss the common themes running through the behaviors and thought processes considered to be abnormal throughout human history. They then discuss proposed explanations of mental illness and show how treatment of mental illness was determined by its presumed causes. After discussing the views of psychopathology in the earliest times, the classical ages, and the Middle Ages, the authors present information that casts doubt on the way the relationship between psychopathology and witchcraft has been traditionally presented. Evidence is presented suggesting that, as far as the treatment of the mentally ill was concerned, the Middle Ages were characterized by eclecticism. That is, psychological and biological treatments coexisted with supernatural treatments. However, emphasis was on the latter.

McReynolds, P. (1987). Lightner Witmer: Little-known founder of clinical psychology. *American Psychologist, 42*, 849–858.
McReynolds provides much needed information about Lightner Witmer, the obscure founder of clinical psychology. McReynolds speculates that Witmer's obscurity is explained by the facts that histories of psychology have tended to focus on the history of experimental psychology, he opposed the overemphasis on the very popular intelligence testing of his time, he opposed psychoanalysis when it was becoming very popular, he worked primarily with children at a time when the emphasis was on troubled adults, and he left few documents and memorabilia that could have illuminated the details of his life.

Szasz, T. S. (1974). *The myth of mental illness: Foundations of a theory of personal conduct* (rev. ed.). New York: Harper & Row.
This is a most provocative book whose major claim is that so-called mental illness is not illness at all. An illness is always defined in terms of some physical or biochemical abnormality of the body. With "mental illness," there is no such abnormality. Furthermore, with physical illness, the patient claims to be ill, and

the physician upon finding appropriate evidence agrees. With "mental illness," it is usually someone other than the patient who decides that he or she is ill. Because it is usually behavior that does not fit cultural norms that is taken to reflect mental illness, such classification is made for social, political, or moral reasons, not for medical reasons. According to Szasz, "mental illness" most often reflects problems in living or a decision not to live in accordance with "the rules of the game," but these problems do not reflect illness as it has been traditionally defined. During the Middle Ages, so-called witches were individuals who violated the norms of accepted conduct and were caught and punished. Because many others were also violating "the rules of the game," "witches" acted as scapegoats.

"Witches" may have been nonconformists, but they were probably not misdiagnosed hysterics. It was Charcot who first claimed that hysteria was as real as any physical illness, and his contention (perpetuated by Freud and others) has been widely accepted ever since. Although accepting "mental illness" as a true illness or disease keeps many psychiatrists, psychoanalysts, and psychologists busy, it probably does the person who is actually suffering from problems in living or has decided not to play according to "the rules of the game" little good. The label "mental illness" undermines a person's responsibility for his or her actions by attributing those actions to a mysterious (nonphysical) illness.

GLOSSARY

Agrippa, Cornelius (1486–1535) One of the first physicians to openly oppose the labeling of individuals as witches. Agrippa felt that so-called witches were people suffering abnormalities that had natural origins.

Animal magnetism A force that Mesmer and others believed was evenly distributed throughout the bodies of healthy people and unevenly distributed in the bodies of unhealthy people.

Artificial somnambulism The sleeplike trance that Puységur created in his patients. It was later called a hypnotic trance.

Bernheim, Hippolyte (1840–1919) A member of the Nancy school of hypnotism who believed that anything a highly suggestible patient believed would improve his or her condition would do so.

Braid, James (1795–1860) Renamed magnetism, hypnotism; explained the phenomenon in terms of the suggestibility of the subject rather than in terms of any powers that the hypnotist possessed. Braid did much to make hypnosis respectable to the medical community.

Charcot, Jean-Martin (1825–1893) Disagreed with the contention that all humans could be hypnotized, believing rather that only hysterics could. Later in life, Charcot reversed his position. Charcot did much to make the study and treatment of hysteria respectable within the medical community.

Chiarugi, Vincenzo (1759–1820) Even before Pinel, argued for the humane treatment of the mentally ill.

Clinical psychology The profession founded by Witmer, the purpose of which was to apply the principles derived from psychological research to the diagnosis and treatment of disturbed individuals.

Contagion effect The tendency for people to be more susceptible to suggestion when in a group than when alone.

Contagious magic A type of sympathetic magic. It involves the belief that what one does to something that a person once owned or that was close to a person will influence that person.

Daquin, Joseph (1733–1815) Believed that mental illness should be studied through the methods of natural science. Daquin strongly influenced Pinel's thinking.

Dix, Dorothea Lynde (1802–1887) Caused several states (and foreign countries) to reform their facilities for the mentally ill by making them more available to those needing them and more humane in their treatment.

Elliotson, John (1791–1868) Suggested that magnetism be used as a surgical anaesthetic.

Esdaile, James (1808–1859) Used hypnotism as an anaesthetic while performing 250 operations on Hindu convicts.

Frazer, Sir James (1854–1941) In his book *The Golden Bough* (1890), described the importance of sympathetic magic to primitive humans.

Hell, Maximillian The Jesuit priest who called the idea of animal magnetism to Mesmer's attention.

Hippocrates (ca. 460–377 b.c.) Argued that all mental and physical disorders had natural causes and that treatment of such disorders should consist of such things as rest, proper diet, and exercise.

Homeopathic magic The type of sympathetic magic involving the belief that doing something to a likeness of a person will influence that person.

Janet, Pierre (1859–1947) Theorized that components of the personality, such as traumatic memories, could become dissociated from the rest of the personality and that these dissociated components were responsible for the symptoms of hysteria and for hypnotic phenomena.

Kraepelin, Emil (1856–1926) Published a list of categories of mental illness in 1883. Until recent times, many clinicians used this list to diagnose mental illness.

Liébeault, Auguste Ambroise (1823–1904) Founder of the Nancy school of hypnotism.

Medical model of mental illness The assumption that mental illness results from such biological causes as brain damage, impaired neural transmissions, or biochemical abnormalities.

Mental illness The condition that is said to exist when a person's emotions, thoughts, or behavior deviate substantially from what is considered to be normal at a certain time and place in history.

Mesmer, Franz Anton (1734–1815) Used what he thought were his strong magnetic powers to redistribute the magnetic fields of his patients, thus curing them of their ailments.

Nancy school A group of physicians who believed that because all humans were suggestible, all humans could be hypnotized.

Natural law The belief prevalent in the 18th century that it was a person's undesirable behavior that caused mental or physical disease or poverty.

Paracelsus, Philippus (1493–1541) Argued that hysteria had a sexual origin and that mania was caused by certain substances entering the brain. Paracelsus was among the first physicians to argue against labeling people as witches.

Pinel, Philippe (1745–1826) Among the first, in modern times, to view the mentally ill as sick people rather than criminals, beasts, or possessed individuals. In the asylums of which he was in charge, Pinel ordered that patients be unchained and treated with kindness in a peaceful atmosphere. Pinel was also responsible for many innovations in the treatment and understanding of the mentally ill.

Plater, Felix (1536–1614) Viewed abnormal behavior as a natural phenomenon. Plater was among the first to delineate several different types of mental disorders.

Posthypnotic amnesia The tendency for a person to forget what happened to him or her while under hypnosis.

Posthypnotic suggestion A suggestion that a person receives while under hypnosis and acts on when he or she is again in the waking state.

Psychological model of mental illness The assumption that mental illness results from such psychological causes as conflict, anxiety, faulty beliefs, frustration, or traumatic experience.

Psychotherapy Any attempt to help a mentally disturbed person. What all versions of psychotherapy have had in common throughout history are a sufferer, a helper, and some form of ritualistic activity.

Puységur, Marquis de (1751–1825) Found that placing patients in a sleeplike trance was as effective in alleviating ailments as was Mesmer's approach, which necessitated a crisis. He also discovered a number of basic hypnotic phenomena.

Rush, Benjamin (1745–1813) Often called the first U.S. psychiatrist. Rush advocated the humane treatment of the mentally ill but still clung to some earlier treatments such as bloodletting and the use of rotating chairs.

Scot, Reginald (1538–1599) Argued that witches were actually mentally disturbed individuals.

Supernatural model of mental illness The assumption that mental illness is caused by malicious, spiritual entities entering the body or by the will of God.

Sympathetic magic The belief that by influencing things that are similar to a person or that were once close to that person, one can influence the person. (*See also* **Homeopathic magic** and **Contagious magic**.)

Trephination The technique of chipping or drilling holes in a person's skull, presumably used by primitive humans to allow evil spirits to escape.

Tuke, William (1732–1822) Founded the York Retreat in England. The retreat resembled a farm, and patients were treated with respect and received good food, medical treatment, recreation, and religious instruction.

Weyer, Johann (1515–1588) Claimed that people labeled as witches were actually mentally disturbed.

Witmer, Lightner (1867–1956) Considered to be the founder of clinical psychology.

CHAPTER 16

Psychoanalysis

When psychology became a science, it became first a science of conscious experience and later a science of behavior. Representatives of psychology's early schools for example, Wundt, Titchener, and James—were aware of unconscious processes but dismissed them as unimportant. The early behaviorists refused even to admit consciousness into their psychology; thus, suggesting the study of the unconscious would have been unthinkable. And although Gestalt psychology was mentalistic, it concentrated entirely on conscious processes.

How then could a psychology that emphasized the unconscious mind emerge? The answer is that it did not come from academic or experimental psychology. Indeed, it did not come from the tradition of empiricism and associationism at all, as so much of psychology had. Rather, it came from clinical practice. Those who developed the psychology of the unconscious were not concerned with experimental design or the philosophy of science; nor were they concerned with substantiating the claims of the associationists. Rather, they were concerned with understanding the causes of mental illness and using that understanding to help mentally ill patients.

By emphasizing the importance of unconscious processes as causes of mental illness (and later of most human behavior), this band of individuals set themselves apart from not only the psychologists of the time but also the medical profession. The medical profession had been strongly influenced by the mechanistic-positivistic philosophy, according to which physical events caused all illness. For example, physicians explained abnormal behavior in terms of

brain damage or biochemical imbalance. If they used the term *mental illness* at all, it was as a descriptive term because they believed that all illnesses had physical origins.

The stressing of *psychological* causes of mental illness separated this small group of physicians from both their own profession and academic psychology. Theirs was not an easy struggle, but they persisted; in the end, they had convinced the medical profession, academic psychology, and the public that unconscious processes must be taken into consideration in understanding why people act as they do. Sigmund Freud was the leader of this group of rebels, but before we consider his work, we consider some of the antecedents of his work.

ANTECEDENTS OF THE DEVELOPMENT OF PSYCHOANALYSIS

As we will see, both hypnotic phenomena and Charcot's concern with hysteria had a strong influence on the development of Freud's theory, but there were several other influences as well. In fact, a case can be made that all components of what was to become psychoanalysis existed before Freud began to formulate that doctrine. Some of those components were very much a part of the German culture in which Freud was raised, and others he learned as a medical student trained in the Helmholtzian tradition. We briefly review the philosophy, science, and literature of which Freud was aware and that later emerged in one form or another in Freud's formulation of psychoanalysis.

Leibniz (1646–1716) with his monadology showed that, depending on the number of monads involved, levels of awareness could range from clear perception (apperception) to experiences of which we are unaware (*petites perceptions*). Goethe (1749–1832) was one of Freud's favorite authors, and the major thrust of psychoanalysis was certainly compatible with Goethe's description of human existence as consisting of a constant struggle between conflicting emotions and tendencies. Herbart (1776–1841) suggested that there was a threshold above which an idea was conscious and below which an idea was unconscious. He also postulated a conflict model of the mind because only ideas that were compatible with each other could occur in consciousness. If two incompatible ideas occurred in consciousness, one of them was forced below the threshold into the unconscious. Unconscious ideas were not passive, and Herbart suggested that they may join forces and force their way above the threshold into consciousness. For him, ideas were discrete (distinct from one another), active, and strove for expression in consciousness. In other words, ideas struggled against being inhibited into the unconscious. Furthermore, inhibited (unconscious) ideas did not cease to exist. They lost their clarity but continued to exist as a force in the mind. As consciousness changed, different ideas in the unconscious became compatible with them and were no longer resisted (inhibited); therefore, they could enter consciousness. The relationship between the conscious and unconscious was therefore dynamic, in that ideas in the conscious mind and ideas in the unconscious mind changed with the circumstances. Herbart also used the term *repression* to denote the inhibiting force that kept an incompatible idea in the unconscious. As far as the notion of the unconscious is concerned, Boring said, "Leibniz foreshadowed the entire doctrine of the unconscious, but Herbart actually began it" (1957, p. 257).

Schopenhauer (1788–1860) believed that humans were governed more by irrational desires than by reason. Because the instincts determined behavior, humans continually vacillated between being in a state of need and being satisfied. Schopenhauer anticipated Freud's concept of sublimation when he said that we could attain some relief or escape from the irrational forces within us by immersing ourselves in music, poetry, or art. One could also attempt to counteract these irrational forces, especially the sex drive, by living a life of asceticism. Schopenhauer also spoke of repressing undesirable thoughts into the unconscious and of the resistance one encountered when attempting to recognize repressed ideas. Freud credited Schopenhauer as being the first to discover the processes of sublimation, repression, and resistance, but Freud claimed that he had discovered the same processes independently. Freud also shared Schopenhauer's belief that irrational forces were the prime motivators of human behavior and that the best we could do was minimize their influence. Both men were therefore very pessimistic. Like Schopenhauer, Nietzsche (1844–1900) believed that humans were basically irrational. Unlike Schopenhauer, however, Nietzsche thought that the instincts should not be repressed but should be given expression—even aggressive tendencies. For Nietzsche, the main motive for human behavior was the will to power. A person can fully satisfy this motive by acting as he or she feels—that is, by acting in such a way as to satisfy fully all instincts, even if doing so violates conventional morality. Freud shared Nietzsche's negative view of religion. Both believed that religion represented an infantile, irrational approach to life and that it encouraged herd conformity and personal sacrifice instead of individuality and personal growth. Although both Freud and Nietzsche believed that the vast majority of people will live their lives accepting religious doctrine and the morality that it implies, they both desperately wanted more individuals to live more enlightened lives and believed that they were providing individuals with information that would allow them to do so.

Like Herbart, Fechner (1801–1887) employed the concept of threshold in his work. More important to Freud, however, was that Fechner likened the mind to an iceberg, consciousness being the smallest part (about 1/10), or the tip, and the unconscious mind making up the rest (about 9/10). Besides borrowing the iceberg analogy of the mind from him, Freud also followed Fechner in attempting to apply the recently discovered principle of the conservation of energy to living organisms. Freud said, "I was always open to the ideas of G. T. Fechner and have followed that thinker upon many important points" (E. Jones, 1953, p. 374). By showing the continuity between humans and other animals, Darwin (1809–1882) strengthened Freud's contention that humans, like "lower" animals, were motivated by instincts rather than by reason. According to Freud, it is our powerful animal instincts such as our instincts for sexual activity and for aggression that are the driving forces of personality, and it is these instincts that must be at least partially inhibited in order for civilization to exist. Such as was the case with most scientists of his day, Freud's view of evolution combined Darwinian and Lamarckian principles.

Representing the positivistic approach to medicine and psychology, Helmholtz (1821–1894) tolerated no subjectivity or vitalism in the study of living organisms including humans. His approach, which permeated most of medicine and physiology at the time, had a profound effect on Freud; although Freud soon abandoned Helmholtz's materialism and switched from a medical (biological) to a psychological model, he continued to embrace a scientific *Weltanschauung* (worldview), and he always struggled to remain objective. Also important for Freud was Helmholtz's concept of the conservation of energy. Helmholtz demonstrated that an organism was an energy system that could be explained entirely on the basis of physical principles. Helmholtz demonstrated that the energy that came out of an organism depended on the energy that went into the organism—no life

force was left over. Taking Helmholtz's idea of the conservation of energy and applying it to the mind, Freud assumed that only so much psychic energy was available at any given time and that it could be distributed in various ways. How this finite amount of energy was distributed in the mind accounted for all human behavior and thought. Brentano (1838–1917) was one of Freud's teachers at the University of Vienna when Freud was in his early 20s. Brentano taught that motivational factors were extremely important in determining the flow of thought and that there were major differences between objective reality and subjective reality. This distinction was to play a vital role in Freud's theory. Brentano is known mainly for his act psychology, which opposed Wundt's content psychology. For Brentano, the *acts* of perceiving, sensing, loving, hating, judging, or wishing were more important than *what* was perceived, sensed, loved, judged, and so on. In other words, Brentano thought that psychology should study the mental processes by which humans interacted with the world, rather than the static *elements* of thought that Wundt and his colleagues sought. Brentano's conception of the mind clearly had much in common with Freud's. Under the influence of Brentano, Freud almost decided to give up medicine and pursue philosophy (which was Brentano's main interest); but Ernst Brücke (1819–1892), the positivistic physiologist, influenced Freud even more than Brentano had and Freud stayed in medicine.

Karl Eduard von Hartmann (1842–1906) wrote a book entitled *Philosophy of the Unconscious* (1869), which went through 11 editions in his lifetime. During the time that Freud was studying medicine and later when he was developing his theory, the idea of the unconscious was quite common in Europe, and no doubt every reasonably educated person was familiar with the concept. Hartmann was strongly influenced by both Schopenhauer's philosophy and Jewish mysticism. For him, there were three types of unconsciousness: processes that governed all natural phenomena in the universe; the physiological unconscious, which directed the bodily processes; and the psychological unconscious, which was the source of all behavior. Although Hartmann's position was primarily mystical, it had some elements in common with Freud's theory, especially the notion of the psychological unconscious. (For an account of how Hartmann influenced Freud, see Capps, 1970.)

We can see, then, that the notions of an active, dynamic mind, with a powerful unconscious component, were very much part of Freud's philosophical heritage. As we will see, other aspects of Freud's theory—such as infantile sexuality, the emphasis on the psychological causes of mental illness, psychosexual stages of development, and even the approach he took to dream analysis—were not original with Freud. Freud's genius was in synthesizing all these elements into a comprehensive theory of personality: "Much of what is credited to Freud was diffuse current lore, and his role was to crystalize these ideas and give them an original shape" (Ellenberger, 1970, p. 548).

Freud was well aware of the revolutionary nature of his theory and thought that it, like the theories of Copernicus and Darwin, would necessitate a revision in humanity's childish egocentrism and move humans toward a more mature evaluation of themselves and their world:

> In the course of centuries the *naïve* self-love of men has had to submit to two major blows at the hands of science. The first was when they learnt that our earth was not the center of the universe but only a tiny fragment of a cosmic system of scarcely imaginable vastness. This is associated in our minds with the name of Copernicus. . . . The second blow fell when biological research destroyed man's supposedly privileged place in creation and proved his descent from the animal kingdom and his ineradicable animal nature. This revaluation has been accomplished in our own days by Darwin . . . though not without the most violent contemporary opposition. But human megalomania will have suffered its third and most wounding blow from the psychological research of the present time which seeks to prove to the ego that it is not even master in its own house, but must content itself with scanty information of what is going on unconsciously

in its mind. (Freud, 1915–1917/1966, pp. 284–285)

SIGMUND FREUD

Biographical Sketch

Sigmund Freud (1856–1939) was born on either March 6 or May 6 in Freiberg, Moravia (now Pribor, Czechoslovakia). His father Jakob was a wool merchant who had 10 children. Both his grandfather and his great-grandfather were rabbis. Freud considered himself a Jew all his life but had a basically negative attitude toward Judaism as well as Christianity. Jakob's first wife (Sally Kanner), whom he married when he was 17 years old, bore him 2 children (Emanuel and Philipp); his second wife apparently bore him none; and his third wife Amalie Nathansohn bore him 8 children (of whom Sigmund was the first). In 1968, examination of the town records of Freiberg revealed that Jakob Freud's second wife was a woman named Rebecca, about whom practically nothing is known. Earlier it had been known that the town records indicated that Freud's birth date was March 6 not May 6, as was claimed by the family, and as has been traditionally reported as Freud's birth date. Ernest Jones, Freud's official biographer, believed that the discrepancy reflected only a clerical error, but others see it as having greater significance. Balmary (1979) speculates that Freud's parents reported the birth date of May 6 instead of March 6 to conceal the fact that Freud's mother was pregnant with Sigmund when she married Jakob. Balmary believes that both "family secrets" (the facts that Freud's mother was Jakob's third wife, not his second as the family had reported, and that Amalie was pregnant when she married) had a significant influence on Freud's early views and therefore on his later theorizing. In any case, when Sigmund was born, his father was 40 years old and already a grandfather, and his mother was a youthful 20. Among the paradoxes that young Freud had to grapple with were the facts that he had half-brothers as old as his mother and a nephew older than he was. Sigmund was the oldest child in the immediate family, however, and clearly Amalie's favorite. Freud and his mother had a close, strong, and positive relationship, and he always felt that being the indisputable favorite child of his young mother had much to do with his success. Because his mother felt that he was special, he came to believe that he was special; therefore, much of what he accomplished later was due, he thought, to a type of self-fulfilling prophecy. Freud's father lived 81 years, and his mother lived until 1931, when at the age of 95 she died, only eight years before her son Sigmund.

When Jakob's business failed, the Freuds moved first to Leipzig and then, when Sigmund was age 4, to Vienna. From early on, Sigmund showed great intellectual ability; to aid his studies, he was the only one in the large household to have an oil lamp and a room of his own. His mother would often serve him his meals in his room, and a piano was taken away from one of his sisters because the music bothered him. Sigmund began reading Shakespeare when he was 8 years old, and he deeply admired that author's power of expression and understanding of human nature all his life. Freud also had an amazing gift for languages. As a boy, he taught himself Latin, Greek, French, Spanish, Italian, and English, and later in life he became an acknowledged master of German prose. He entered high school at age 9 (a year earlier than normal) and was always at the head of his class; at age 17, he graduated summa cum laude.

Until his final year of high school, Freud was attracted to a career in law or politics, or even in the military, but hearing a lecture on Goethe's essay on nature and reading Darwin's theory of evolution aroused his interest in science, and he decided to enroll in the medical school at the University of Vienna at the age of 17. He also made this decision partly because, in anti-Semitic Vienna, medicine and law were the only professions open to Jews. Although Freud enrolled in medical school in 1873, it took him eight years to complete the program; because he had such wide interests, he was often diverted

Sigmund Freud

from his medical studies. For example, Brentano caused him to become interested in philosophy, and Freud even translated one of John Stuart Mill's books into German.

According to Freud's own account, the person who influenced him most was Brücke. Along with some of his friends such as Helmholtz and DuBois-Reymond, Brücke founded the materialistic-positivistic movement in physiology. In Brücke's laboratory, Freud studied the reproductive system of male eels and wrote a number of influential articles on anatomy and neurology. Freud obtained his medical degree in 1881 and continued to work in Brücke's laboratory. Even though doing physiological research was Freud's main interest, he realized that jobs in that area were scarce, low-paying, and generally not available to Jews. Freud's financial concerns became even more acute in 1882 when he became engaged to Martha Bernays. Circumstances and advice from Brücke caused Freud to change his career plans and seek a career in medical practice. To help prepare himself, Freud went to the Vienna General Hospital to study with Theodor Meynert (1833–1893), one of the best-known brain anatomists at the time, and Freud soon became a recognized expert at diagnosing various types of brain damage. Freud considered Meynert the most brilliant person he had ever met.

Many important events happened in Freud's life about this time. Besides making the decision to practice medicine, Freud was making a name for himself as a neuroanatomist, he had just befriended Joseph Breuer (who, as we will see, introduced Freud to many of the phenomena that would occupy Freud's attention for the next 50 years), and he had been given the opportunity to study with Charcot in Paris. All these events were to have a significant influence on the development of Freud's career. There was, however, a major setback: Freud's involvement with the "magical substance" cocaine.

The Cocaine Episode

In the spring of 1884, Freud experimented with cocaine after learning that it had been used successfully in the military to increase the energy and endurance of soldiers. Freud almost decided not to pursue his interest when he learned from the pharmaceutical company, Merck, that the price of 1 gram of cocaine was $1.27 instead of 13 cents as he had believed (E. Jones, 1953). Freud persisted, however, and having taken the drug himself he found that it relieved his feelings of depression and cured his indigestion, helped him work, and appeared to have no negative side effects. Besides taking cocaine regularly himself, he gave it to his sisters, friends, colleagues, patients, and sent some to his fiancée Martha Bernays "to make her strong and give her cheeks a red color" (E. Jones, 1953, p. 81).

The apparent improvement caused by cocaine in Freud's patients made him feel, for the first time, like he was a real physician. He became an enthusiastic advocate of cocaine and published six articles in the next two years describing its benefits. Carl Koller (1857–1944), one of Freud's younger colleagues, learned from Freud that cocaine could be used as an anaesthetic. Koller was interested in ophthalmology and pursued Freud's observation as it related to eye operations. Within a few months, Koller delivered a paper describing how eye operations previously impossible could now, using cocaine as an anaesthetic, be done with ease. The paper caused a sensation and brought Koller worldwide fame almost overnight. Freud deeply regretted having just missed gaining this professional recognition himself.

With the exception of the anaesthetizing effects of cocaine, all of Freud's other beliefs about the substance soon proved to be false. In 1884 he administered cocaine to his colleague and friend Ernst von Fleischl-Marxow (1846–1891), who was addicted to morphine. Freud's intention was to switch Fleischl, who was a prominent physicist and physiologist, from morphine to cocaine, believing that the latter was harmless. Instead, Fleischl died a cocaine addict. Soon reports of cocaine addiction began coming in from throughout the world, and the drug came under heavy attack from the medical community. Freud was severely criticized for his indiscriminate advocacy of cocaine, which was now being referred to as the "third scourge of humanity" (the other two being morphine and alcohol). Freud's close association with cocaine considerably harmed his medical reputation. It was the cocaine episode that, to a large extent, made the medical community skeptical of Freud's later ideas.

Freud's addiction to nicotine. Although Freud avoided addiction to cocaine, he was addicted to nicotine most of his adult life, smoking on the average of 20 cigars a day. At the age of 38, it was discovered that he had heart arrhythmias; his physician advised him to stop smoking, but he continued to do so. Being a physician himself, Freud was well aware of the health risks associated with smoking, and he tried several times to quit but without success. In 1923, when Freud was 67 years old, it was discovered that he had cancer of the palate and jaw. A series of 33 operations eventually necessitated his wearing of an awkward prosthetic device (which he called "the monster") to replace the surgically removed sections of his jaw. He was in almost constant pain during the last 16 years of his life, yet he continued smoking his cigars.

EARLY INFLUENCES ON THE DEVELOPMENT OF PSYCHOANALYSIS

Joseph Breuer and the Case of Anna O.

Shortly before Freud obtained his medical degree, he developed a friendship with **Joseph Breuer** (1842–1925), who was another one of Brücke's former students. Breuer was 14 years older than Freud and had a considerable reputation as a physician and researcher. Breuer had made an important discovery concerning the reflexes involved in breathing and was one of the first to show how the semicircular canals influenced balance. Breuer loaned Freud money, and when Freud married in 1886, the Breuer and Freud families socialized frequently. (It is also interesting to note that Breuer was the Brentano family's physician.)

It is what Freud learned from Breuer concerning the treatment of a woman, anonymously referred to as Fräulein Anna O., that essentially launched psychoanalysis. Because Breuer started treating Anna O. in 1880, while Freud was still a medical student, **Freud gave Breuer the credit for creating psychoanalysis:**

> Granted that it is a merit to have created psychoanalysis, it is not my merit. I was a student, busy with the passing of my last examinations, when another physician of Vienna, Dr. Joseph Breuer, made the first application of this

Joseph Breuer

method to the case of an hysterical girl (1880–82). (1910/1949, p. 1)

Anna O. was a bright, attractive, 21-year-old woman who had a variety of symptoms associated with hysteria. At one time or another, she had experienced paralysis of the arms or legs, disturbances of sight and speech, nausea, memory loss, and general mental disorientation. Breuer would hypnotize the young woman and then ask her to recall the circumstances under which she had first experienced a particular symptom. For example, one symptom was the perpetual squinting of her eyes. Through hypnosis, Breuer discovered that she had been required to keep a vigil by the bedside of her dying father. The woman's deep concern for her father had brought tears to her eyes so that when the weak man asked her what time it was she had to squint to see the hands of the clock.

Breuer discovered that each time he traced a symptom to its origin, which was usually some traumatic experience, the symptom disappeared either temporarily or permanently. One by one, Anna O.'s symptoms were relieved in this way. It was as if certain emotionally laden ideas could not be expressed directly but manifested themselves in physical symptoms instead. When such **pathogenic ideas** (ideas that produce physical symptoms) were allowed conscious expression, their energy dissipated, and the symptoms they initiated disappeared. Because relief followed the emotional release, which, in turn, followed the expression of a pathogenic idea, Breuer called the treatment the **cathartic method** (a catharsis is an emotional release). (Aristotle had used the term *catharsis* to describe the emotional release and the feeling of purification that an audience experienced as they viewed a drama.) Anna O. called the method the "talking cure" or "chimney sweeping." Breuer found that the catharsis occurred either during a hypnotic trance or when Anna O. was very relaxed.

Breuer's treatment of Anna O. started in December 1880 and continued until June 1882. During that time, Breuer typically saw her several hours each day. Soon after treatment had started, Anna O. began responding to Breuer as if he were her father, a process later called **transference**. All emotions Anna had once expressed toward her father, both positive and negative, she now expressed toward Breuer. Breuer also began developing emotional feelings toward Anna, a process later called **countertransference**. Because his wife became jealous, Breuer decided to stop Anna's treatment. A few hours after Breuer told Anna that he had terminated treatment, Anna developed a hysterical pregnancy, which Breuer agreed to treat with hypnosis. That was the last time Breuer treated her. Afterward, he and his wife went to Venice on a second honeymoon, and Breuer never treated another hysterical patient.

The fate of Anna O. The story of Anna O. usually ends with the revelation that Anna's real name was Bertha Pappenheim (1859–1936) and that Breuer's treatment must have been effective because the woman went on to become a prominent social worker in Germany. Ellenberger (1972), however, has discovered that

Anna O. had to be institutionalized after Breuer terminated her treatment. Documents indicate that she was admitted into a sanatorium in 1882 still suffering many of the ailments that Breuer had treated. The records show that she was treated with substantial amounts of morphine while at the sanatorium and that she continued to receive morphine injections even after her release. Little is known about her life between the time that she was released from the sanatorium until she emerged as a social worker in the late 1880s. However, Pappenheim eventually went on to become a leader in the European feminist movement; a playwright; an author of children's stories; a founder of several schools and clubs for the poor, the illegitimate, or wayward young women; and an effective spokesperson against white slavery and abortion. Her feminism is evident in the following statement that she made in 1922: "If there is any justice in the next life women will make the laws there and men will bear the children" (E. Jones, 1953, p. 224). It is interesting to note that throughout her professional life she maintained a negative attitude toward psychoanalysis and would not allow any of the girls in her care to be psychoanalyzed.

When Pappenheim died in 1936, tributes came in from throughout Europe, including one from Martin Buber, the famous philosopher and educator. In 1954 the German government issued a stamp in her honor, part of a series paying tribute to "helpers of humanity." How much of Pappenheim's ultimate success can be attributed to Breuer's treatment is still being debated. (For 14 interpretations of the case of Anna O., see Rosenbaum & Muroff, 1984.) Breuer and Freud published *Studies on Hysteria* (1895/1955), which contained the case of Anna O., and 1895 is usually taken as the date of the official founding of the school of psychoanalysis.

Freud's Visit with Charcot

Because Freud had done so well while studying with Meynert and because of the reputation he was gaining as a neurophysiologist, in 1885 he was given a small grant to study with Jean-

Martin Charcot (1825–1893) in Paris. At the time, Charcot's La Salpêtrière was the "mecca of neurology," drawing students from all over the world. Until this visit, although Freud was aware of Breuer's work with Anna O., he remained a materialistic-positivistic physiologist; he sought to explain all disorders, including hysteria, in terms of neurophysiology. Like most physicians at the time, Freud saw psychological explanations of illness as nonscientific. As we saw in the last chapter, Charcot also attempted to explain hysteria in terms of neurophysiology and inheritance, but at least Charcot took hysteria seriously—something that set him apart from most of his colleagues. Furthermore, Charcot insisted that hysteria occurred in males as well as females. This contention caused a stir because from the time of the Greeks it had been assumed that hysteria was caused by a disturbance of the uterus (*hystera* is the Greek word for "uterus").

Freud studied with the illustrious Charcot from October 1885 to February 1886, and he learned several important things from him. First, he learned that hysteria was to be taken seriously, something he had already suspected because of Breuer's treatment of Anna O. Second, he learned that both males and females could suffer from hysteria. Third, he overheard Charcot say about hysteria, "But in this kind of case it is always something genital—always, always, always" (quoted in Boring, 1957, p. 709). Though Charcot denied making the statement, Freud nonetheless claimed that Charcot had suggested to him the relationship between sexual factors and hysteria. Fourth, all his life, Freud relished Charcot's attitude toward theory. Charcot trusted empirical observation and what actually worked much more than he trusted theory. (Charcot's statement "Theory is fine, but it does not prevent things from existing" is reported in Freud, 1925/1963, p. 12.) Freud shared this view to the extent that he revised his theory whenever it conflicted with observation or when important new observations were made. Fifth, Freud learned that one could go against the established medical community if one had enough prestige. Freud, as we will see, went contrary to the medical community, but

because he did not have the prestige that Charcot had he paid the price. So impressed was Freud by Charcot that he later named his first son Jean-Martin after him (E. Jones, 1953).

Freud returned to Vienna and, on October 15, 1886, presented a paper entitled, "On Male Hysteria" to the Viennese Society of Physicians, in which he presented and endorsed Charcot's views on hysteria. The presentation was poorly received because, according to Freud, it was too radical. Sulloway (1979), however, indicates that the paper was poorly received but not because it was shocking. Rather, it was poorly received because Charcot's views on hysteria, including the fact that hysteria was not a disorder confined to women, were already widely known within the medical community. Furthermore, the physicians believed that Charcot's ideas were presented too positively and uncritically; there was still too much uncertainty about Charcot's views and techniques to justify such certitude. According to Sulloway, Freud's account of the reaction to his paper on hysteria was perpetuated by his followers to enhance the image of Freud as a bold innovator fighting against the medical establishment. There were several such efforts at mythmaking among Freud and his followers.

On September 30, 1886, Freud finally married Martha Bernays after a four-year engagement. The Freuds eventually had six children— three boys and three girls. The youngest, Anna (1895–1982), went on to become a world renowned child psychoanalyst and, after her father's death, assumed leadership of the Freudian movement. On October 15, 1886, shortly after his marriage, Freud established a private practice in Vienna. He soon learned that he could not make an adequate living treating only neurological disorders, and he made the fateful decision to treat hysterics, becoming one of the few Viennese physicians to do so. At first, he tried the traditional methods of treating neurological disorders, including baths, massage, electrotherapy, and rest cures, but found them ineffective in the treatment of hysteria. It was at this point that everything that he had learned from Breuer about the cathartic method and from Charcot about hypnosis became relevant. When

Freud used hypnosis while treating hysteria, he encountered several problems: He could not hypnotize some patients; often when a symptom was removed during a hypnotic trance, it, or some other symptom, would recur later; and some patients refused to believe what they had revealed under hypnosis, thus preventing a rational discussion and understanding of the recovered memories. In 1889 Freud visited Liébeault and Bernheim at the Nancy school in hopes of improving his hypnotic skills. From Liébeault and Bernheim, Freud learned about *posthypnotic suggestion*, observing that an idea planted during hypnosis could influence a person's behavior even when the person was unaware of it. This observation—that intact ideas of which a person was unaware could play an important role in that person's behavior—was to become an extremely important part of psychoanalysis. He also learned from Liébeault and Bernheim that although patients tend to forget what they had experienced during hypnosis (a phenomenon called *posthypnotic amnesia*), such memories could return if it was strongly suggested that the patient remember them. This observation, too, was important to the development of psychoanalysis.

The Birth of Free Association

Upon returning to his practice, Freud still found hypnosis to be ineffective and was seeking an alternative. Then he remembered that, while at the Nancy school, he had observed that the hypnotist would bring back the memory of what had happened during hypnosis by putting his hand on the patient's forehead and saying, "Now you can remember." With this in mind, Freud tried having his patients lie on a couch, with their eyes closed, but not hypnotized. He would ask the patients to recall the first time they had experienced a particular symptom, and the patients would begin to recollect various experiences but would usually stop short of the goal. In other words, as they approached the recollection of a traumatic experience, they would display **resistance**. At this point, Freud would place his hand

on the patient's forehead and declare that additional information was forthcoming, and in many cases it was. Freud found that this **pressure technique** was as effective as hypnosis, and soon he learned that he did not even need to touch his patients; simply encouraging them to speak freely about whatever came to their minds worked just as well. Thus, the method of **free association** was born.

With free association, there were still the important phenomena of resistance, transference, and countertransference, and there was the major advantage that the patient was conscious of what was going on. With free association, it was often more difficult to arrive at the original traumatic experience, but once it was attained, it was available for the patient to deal with in a rational manner. For Freud, the overcoming of resistance and the rational pondering of early traumatic experience were the goals of psychotherapy. This is why he said that true psychoanalysis started only when hypnosis had been discarded (Heidbreder, 1933). Freud likened the use of free association to an archeologist's excavation of a buried city. It is only from a few fragmented artifacts that the structure and nature of the city must be ascertained. Similarly, free association provides only fragmented glimpses of the unconscious, and from those glimpses, the psychoanalyst must determine the structure and nature of a person's unconscious mind.

It is a strange coincidence that the Athenian dramatist and satirist Aristophanes (ca. 448–380 B.C.) so accurately described Freud's therapeutic technique. In *The Clouds*, Aristophanes pictured Socrates attempting to give philosophic counsel to Strepsiades who is concerned about his debts:

SOC:	Come, lie down here.
STREP:	What for?
SOC:	Ponder awhile over matters that interest you.
STREP:	Oh, I pray not there.
SOC:	Come, on the couch!
STREP:	What a cruel fate.
SOC:	Ponder and examine closely, gather your thoughts together, let your mind turn to every side of things. If you meet with difficulty, spring

quickly to some other idea; keep away from sleep.

The "analysis" continues until Strepsiades arrives at the insight (stimulated by Socrates' interpretations) that if the waxing and waning of the moon could be stopped his monthly bills would never come due (Alexander & Selesnick, 1966, p. xiii).

Studies on Hysteria

In **Studies on Hysteria** (1895/1955), Breuer and Freud put forth a number of the basic tenets of psychoanalysis. They noted that hysteria was caused by traumatic experience that was not allowed adequate expression and therefore manifested itself in physical symptoms. Therefore, symptoms could be taken as *symbolic representations* of underlying traumatic experience that was no longer consciously available to the patient. Because such experience was traumatic, it was *repressed*—that is, actively held in the unconscious because to ponder it would provoke anxiety. Resistance, then, was a sign that the therapist was on the right track. Also, **repression** often resulted from **conflict**, the tendency both to approach and to avoid something considered wrong.

The fundamental point was that repressed experiences or conflicts *did not go away*. Rather, they went on exerting a powerful influence on a person's personality. The only way to deal with repressed material properly was to make it conscious and thereby deal with it rationally. For Freud, the most effective way of making repressed material conscious was through free association. By carefully analyzing the content of free associations, gestures, and transference, the analyst could determine the nature of the repressed experience and help the patient become aware of it and deal with it. Thus, in *Studies on Hysteria*, Freud clearly outlined his belief in the importance of **unconscious motivation**. Freud and Breuer wrote separate conclusions to the book, and Freud emphasized the role of sex in unconscious motivation. At the time, Freud contended that a person with a normal sex life could

not become neurotic. Breuer disagreed saying instead that any traumatic memory (not just those that were sexual) could be repressed and cause neurotic symptoms. The two men eventually parted company. *Studies on Hysteria* was poorly received, and it took 13 years to sell 626 copies for which each author received about $170 (R. I. Watson, 1978).

Project for a Scientific Psychology

In 1895, the same year that Breuer and Freud published *Studies on Hysteria*, Freud completed *Project for a Scientific Psychology*. The purpose of *Project* was to explain psychological phenomena in purely neurophysical terms. In other words, he intended to apply the principles of Helmholtzian physiology, in which he was trained, to the study of the mind. Freud was not satisfied with his effort, and *Project* was not published in his lifetime (it was published in German in 1950 and in English in 1954). Frustrated in his attempt to create a neurophysical model of the mind, Freud turned to a psychological model, and the development of psychoanalysis was begun. However, Sirkin and Fleming (1982) point out that although Freud's *Project* failed, it contained many of the concepts that were to appear in his psychoanalytic works. (For an interesting analysis of why Freud's *Project* failed, see Parisi, 1987.)

The Seduction Theory

On April 21, 1896, Freud delivered a paper to the Psychiatric and Neurological Society in Vienna entitled "The Aetiology of Hysteria." The paper related the fact that almost without exception Freud's hysteric patients eventually related a childhood incident in which they had been sexually attacked, usually by a close relative (most often the father). Freud concluded that such an attack was the basis of all hysteria. Freud stated his conclusion forcefully as follows:

> Whatever case and whatever symptom we take as our point of departure, *in the end we infallibly come to the field of sexual experience*. So here for the

first time we seem to have discovered an aetiological precondition for hysterical symptoms. (Masson, 1984, p. 259)

Freud went on to say, "In all eighteen cases (cases of pure hysteria and of hysteria combined with obsessions, and comprising six men and twelve women) I have . . . come to learn of sexual experiences in childhood" (Masson, 1984, p. 268).

Freud's paper was met with silence, and he was urged not to publish it, even by Wilhelm Fliess (1858–1928), Freud's closest friend at the time. Despite the warnings, he published the article and continued to experience professional, emotional, and intellectual isolation. Apparently, the negative response to Freud's theory was based on the belief that the image of the medical profession would suffer if it was claimed that parents and other relatives were guilty of sexual abuse. Whether for this reason or some other, on September 21, 1897, Freud abandoned his **seduction theory** of hysteria. In most cases, he concluded, the seduction had not really taken place. Rather, the patients had *imagined* the encounter. But the questions remained: Why did the fantasies take a sexual form, and why were they repressed? Freud decided that the imagined incidents were very real to his patients and therefore just as traumatic as if they had actually occurred. His original belief remained intact: The basis of neuroses was the repression of sexual thoughts, whether the thoughts were based on real or imagined experience.

The case of Emma Eckstein. Masson (1984) concludes that Freud abandoned his theory because of personal reasons rather than clinical or theoretical reasons. Masson, himself a psychoanalyst and the former director of the Sigmund Freud Archives, bases his conclusion on a number of newly discovered letters (mainly to and from Fliess) and other documents. Masson believes that Freud's decision to abandon his seduction theory was intimately linked to his relationship to Fliess and to Freud and Fliess's cooperative treatment of Emma Eckstein (1865–1924). It

appears that Freud always had a strong need to idealize certain individuals. As a boy, his heroes included Hannibal, Napoleon, and Oliver Cromwell; as an adult, they included Charcot and Breuer. When his relationship with Breuer dissolved, his next hero became Fliess. The idealization of Fliess was inexplicable to those close to Freud because it was generally agreed that Fliess was intellectually inferior to Freud. Fliess held the strange belief that all sexual abnormalities had a physical origin that somehow involved the nose. Fliess observed that in nonhuman animals sexuality was closely linked to certain odors and even in humans the nose maintained some of its characteristics as a sex organ. Fliess (1902) said, "Women who masturbate are generally dysmenorrheal [they have painful menstruation]. They can only be finally cured through an operation on the nose" (quoted in Masson, 1984, p. 57). One of Freud's first analytic patients was 27-year-old Emma Eckstein, who suffered stomach ailments and menstrual problems and who apparently masturbated frequently. Freud described the case to Fliess; Fliess attributed Emma's symptom of irregular or painful menstruation to her masturbation, and he attributed her masturbation to a condition in her nose. Fliess suggested nasal surgery, and Freud agreed. Early in 1895, the surgery was performed, and the results were disastrous. Emma hemorrhaged and nearly died. After hemorrhaging, swelling, and extreme pain had persisted for 14 days, another physician was called in, and it was discovered that Fliess had inadvertently left a half meter of surgical gauze in Emma's nose when he operated on her. Several more operations were necessary to stop recurring hemorrhaging, and morphine had to be administered to reduce Emma's intense pain. When Emma finally recovered from the ordeal, her youthful face had been disfigured.

There was some questioning of Fliess's competence as a surgeon by the other physicians brought into the case and even by Freud. This thrust Freud into a deep conflict because he idealized Fliess. How could a physician that Freud respected so much bungle an operation so terribly? Gradually, the solution to the conflict presented itself to Freud. *It was not Fliess's fault that Emma continued to bleed after Fliess operated on her, it was Emma's fault!* Emma, Freud concluded, hemorrhaged because of certain fantasies she was entertaining, not because of Fliess's bungled operation. Fliess was not to blame; Emma's fantasies were. Freud, too, must have had second thoughts about recommending a nasal operation as treatment for what he considered to be hysterical symptoms, so blaming Emma for her own suffering alleviated both Fliess and himself from guilt:

> Freud has already begun to represent to Fliess and to himself that Emma Eckstein's problems originated with her, and not in the external world (in this case with two overzealous doctors). The powerful tool that Freud was discovering, the psychological explanation of physical illness, was being pressed into service to exculpate his own dubious behavior and the even more dubious behavior of his closest friend. Freud has begun to explain away his own bad conscience. (Masson, 1984, p. 68)

Now what has all of this to do with Freud's seduction theory and with his subsequent rejection of it? First, it must be realized that Freud's treatment of Emma for hysteria preceded his paper in 1896 in which he proposed his seduction theory. In fact, Emma's case is 1 of the 18 that caused him to reach his conclusion that hysteria was always caused by a childhood sexual seduction. Thus, Emma had told him of such a seduction, and he believed her. Something *real* and traumatic had happened to Emma, and that event caused her problems. Now, as Freud's patient, something else that was real happened (a botched operation by Fliess), and that event was causing her problems, bleeding, pain, and disfigurement. Freud had two choices: He could accept the reality of Emma's experiences (both past and present) and their consequences, *or* he could deny the reality of those experiences and attribute her problems to imaginary events. The latter would mean giving up the seduction theory, and it was the latter that Freud chose:

Freud had the option to [accept reality], confess it to Emma Eckstein, confront Fliess with the truth, and face the consequences. Or he could protect Fliess by excusing what had happened. But in order to do this, to efface the external trauma of the operation, it would prove necessary to construct a theory of hysterical lying, a theory whereby the external traumas suffered by the patient never happened, but are fantasies. If Emma Eckstein's problems (her bleeding) had nothing to do with the real world (Fliess's operation), then her earlier accounts of seduction could well be fantasies too. The consequences of Freud's act of loyalty toward Fliess would reach far beyond this single case. (Masson, 1984, p. 99)

Thus, Emma's bleeding had nothing to do with the gauze that Fliess left in her wound; rather it was hysterical bleeding caused by her fantasies. Similarly, the accounts of childhood seductions given by Emma, and Freud's other patients, were "wish fulfillments," not actual events. According to Masson, the botched operation by Fliess, and Freud's unwillingness to accept its reality, was a major reason why Freud abandoned his seduction theory. (For more details, see Masson, 1984.)

Although Freud claimed that his change from real to imagined seductions marked the real beginning of psychoanalysis, Masson believes that the profession of psychoanalysis would be better off today if Freud had not revised his theory:

> By shifting the emphasis from an actual world of sadness, misery, and cruelty to an internal stage on which actors performed invented dramas for an invisible audience of their own creation, Freud began a trend away from the real world that, it seems to me, is at the root of the present day sterility of psychoanalysis and psychiatry throughout the world. (1984, p. 144)

To make this bizarre story even more bizarre, Masson offers convincing evidence that Fliess himself was sexually abusing his son. If true, we have Freud's closest friend, a child abuser, urging Freud to abandon his seduction theory:

> We see here one of the poorest matches in the history of intellectual discoveries. Freud is communicating his newly gained insights to the one person least prepared to hear them, because of

the profound significance these theories held for that person's own life. Freud was like a dogged detective on the track of a great crime, communicating his hunches and approximations and at last his final discovery to his best friend, who may have been in fact the criminal. (1984, p. 142)

Next to Fliess, Sandor Ferenczi (1873–1933) was Freud's closest friend. At first, Ferenczi accepted Freud's conclusions that the sexual attacks reported by hysterics were imagined rather than real. Ferenczi's own practice, however, eventually caused him to conclude that Freud's original seduction theory was correct. Ferenczi (1932) said,

Above all, my previously communicated assumption, that trauma, specifically sexual trauma, cannot be stressed enough as a pathogenic agent, was confirmed anew. Even children of respected, high-minded puritanical families fall victim to real rape much more frequently than one had dared to suspect. Either the parents themselves seek substitution for their lack of [sexual] satisfaction in this pathological manner, or else trusted persons such as relatives (uncles, aunts, grandparents), tutors, servants, abuse the ignorance and innocence of children. The obvious objection that we are dealing with sexual fantasies of the child himself, that is, with hysterical lies, unfortunately is weakened by the multitude of confessions of this kind, on the part of patients in analysis, to assaults on children. (Quoted in Masson, 1984, p. 148)

Ferenczi's practice proved that psychoanalysis did not depend on the assumption that most sexual attacks were fantasized. Masson concludes, "It is as if Ferenczi were demonstrating to the analytic world how psychoanalysis could have developed had Freud not abandoned the seduction hypothesis" (1984, p. 150). In any case, virtually all psychoanalysts followed (and are following) the path suggested by Freud (fantasized seductions) and not the one suggested by Ferenczi (real seductions).

FREUD'S SELF-ANALYSIS

Because of the many complexities involved in the therapeutic process, Freud soon realized that in order to be an effective analyst, he would have to be psychoanalyzed himself. Freud (1927) insisted later that to be a qualified psychoanalyst one need not be a physician but one needed to be psychoanalyzed. And besides being psychoanalyzed, one needed at least two years of supervised practice as a psychoanalyst. Because no one was available to psychoanalyze Freud, he took on the job himself. Besides a variety of insecurities, such as an intense fear of train travel, a major motivation for Freud's self-analysis was his reaction to the death of his father in the fall of 1896. Although his father had been very ill and his death was no surprise, Freud found that his father's death affected him very deeply. For months following the death, Freud experienced severe depression and could not work. His reaction was so acute that he decided he had to regard himself as a patient.

Analysis of Dreams

Clearly, Freud could not use free association on himself, so he needed another vehicle for his self-analysis. Freud made the astonishing discovery that the content of dreams could be viewed in much the same way as hysterical symptoms. That is, both dreams and hysterical symptoms could be seen as symbolic manifestations of repressed traumatic thoughts. If one properly analyzed the symbols of either dreams or hysterical symptoms, one could get at the roots of the problem. **Dream analysis**, then, became a second way of tapping the unconscious mind (the first way being free association) and one that was suitable for Freud's self-analysis. About the interpretation of dreams, Freud said, "The interpretation of dreams is the royal road to knowledge of the unconscious activities of the mind" (1900/1953, p. 608). Freud's self-analysis culminated in what he, and others, considered to be his most important work, *The Interpretation of Dreams* (1900/1953). In retrospect, it is interesting to note that like *Studies on Hysteria*, when *The Interpretation of Dreams* was first published it was unpopular and took six years before 600 copies were sold. Its significance was eventually recognized, however, and it went through eight editions in Freud's lifetime.

Like the physical symptoms of hysteria, dreams required a knowledgeable interpretation. During sleep, a person's defenses were down but not eliminated, so a repressed experience reached consciousness only in *disguised* form. Therefore, there was a major difference between what a dream appeared to be about and what it really was about. What a dream appeared to be about was its **manifest content**, and what it really was about was its **latent content**. Freud concluded that every dream was a **wish fulfillment**. That is, it was a symbolic expression of a wish that the dreamer could not express or satisfy directly without experiencing anxiety. Wishes expressed in symbolic form during sleep were disguised enough to allow the dreamer to continue sleeping because a direct expression of the wish involved would produce too much anxiety and disrupt sleep.

According to Freud, dream interpretation was complex business, and only someone well versed in psychoanalytic theory could accomplish the task. One had to understand the **dream work** that disguised the wish actually being expressed in the dream. Dream work included **condensation** in which one element of a dream symbolized several things in waking life, such as when a family dog symbolized an entire family, and **displacement** in which, instead of dreaming about an anxiety-provoking object or event, the dreamer dreamed of something symbolically similar to it, such as when one dreamed of a cave instead of a vagina.

Freud believed that the most important dream symbols came from a person's own experience but that there were universal dream symbols, which had the same meaning in everyone's dreams. For example, travel symbolized death; falling symbolized giving in to sexual temptation; boxes, gardens, doors, or balconies symbolized the vagina; and cannons, snakes, trees, swords, church spires, and candles symbolized the penis.

After Freud used dream interpretation to analyze himself, the procedure became an integral part of psychoanalysis. Freud typically asked his patients to report and free associate to any dreams that they had.

The Oedipus Complex

One of the major outcomes of Freud's self-analysis was his discovery of the Oedipus (or Oedipal) complex. Remember, one of Freud's major motives for engaging in his self-analysis was his severe reaction to his father's death. Freud's discovery came when he analyzed one of his own recurring dreams that he had first had during childhood. In the dream, Freud's mother was in a sleeping, peaceful posture, and two or more people with birds' beaks on their faces were carrying her into a room. After carrying his mother into the room, the birdlike people placed her on a bed.

Freud free-associated to this dream and discovered that the birdlike people symbolized death because they were like the Egyptian funeral gods he had seen in the family Bible. The expression on his mother's face in the dream was uncharacteristic of her but very much like the expression Freud had observed on his grandfather's face just before he had died. The figure being carried into the room, then, was a condensed figure symbolizing both Freud's mother and his grandfather. Further free association forced Freud to conclude that the dying grandfather symbolized a dying father and that secretly he wished his father to be dead. Freud then realized that although he consciously experienced love toward his father, unconsciously he had been hostile toward him since early childhood. Still further free association revealed that the dream was also sexual in nature. One of the things that led Freud to this conclusion was that in German the word for sexual intercourse and the word for bird were very similar. The birdlike people, then, were also a condensed symbol representing both death and sex. What was the object of this sexual wish that the dream symbolized? Freud concluded that because his mother had been his greatest source of sensual pleasure when he had first had the dream, she was the object of his sexual desire. He called this hostility toward his father and desire for his mother the **Oedipus complex** because in the Greek play *Oedipus Rex* Oedipus unknowingly killed his father and married his mother.

Because all male children had a close physical relationship with their mothers (the mother bathed, stroked, nursed, and hugged them), Freud thought that it was natural for male children to have a sexual desire for their mothers. It is important to note, however, that Freud used the term *sexual* in a very general way. A better translation might be "pleasurable" rather than "sexual." For Freud, anything pleasurable was roughly what he meant by "sexual." Heidbreder nicely summarized the Freudian use of the word *sex*:

> Freud used the word "sex" in a very general sense. He includes in it not only the specifically sexual interests and activities, but the whole love life—it might almost be said, the whole pleasure life—of human beings. The list of activities that he and his followers have seen as having a sexual significance is almost inexhaustible; but its range and variety may be indicated by the fact that it includes such simple practices as walking, smoking, and bathing, and such complex activities as artistic creation, religious ceremonial, social and political institutions, and even the development of civilization itself. (1933, p. 389)

In the case of the Oedipus complex, however, it appears that when Freud said sexual, he meant sexual. When the male child manipulates his sex organs, he thinks about his mother and thus becomes her lover:

> He wishes to possess her physically in such ways as he has divined from his observations and intuitions about sexual life, and he tries to seduce her by showing her the male organ which he is proud to own. In a word, his early awakened masculinity seeks to take his father's place with her; his father has hitherto in any case been an envied model to the boy, owing to the physical strength he perceives in him and the authority with which he finds him clothed. His father now becomes a rival who stands in his way and whom he would like to get rid of. (Freud, 1940/1969, p. 46)

Now the male child was in competition with the father who also desired the mother, but the reality of the situation (i.e., the father being much more powerful than the child) caused the child to repress his amorous desires for the mother and his hostility toward the father. According to Freud, however, repressed ideas did not go away; they continued to manifest themselves in dreams, symptoms, or unusual behavior. For example, it was now clear to Freud that his overreaction to his father's death had been at least partially motivated by the guilt he felt from wishing his father would die.

Freud felt that the Oedipus conflict was universal among male children and that its remnants in adult life explained much normal and abnormal behavior. One bit of "normal" behavior it explained was that males often married women who were very similar to their mothers. (We will discuss what happens to female children at this time of life in "Psychosexual Stages of Development.")

Now Freud had the vehicle he needed for explaining the seduction fantasies he had observed in so many of his patients. He now saw such fantasies as representing repressed desires to possess the parent of the opposite sex and to eliminate the same-sex parent. Such desires, Freud concluded, were as natural and universal as the need to repress them, and so *infantile sexuality* became an important ingredient in his general theory of unconscious motivation.

According to the history of psychoanalysis offered by Freud and his followers, attributing sexual desires to children and claiming that such desires were natural ran contrary to the Victorian morality of Freud's time, and therefore he was further alienated from the medical establishment. This contention appears to be another myth. Views of infantile sexuality very similar to those proposed by Freud had already been offered by individuals such as Albert Moll (1862–1939) and by Havelock Ellis (1859–1939) and sexology was very much in vogue when Freud was developing his theory. (For details, see Sulloway, 1979.)

THE PSYCHOPATHOLOGY OF EVERYDAY LIFE

Freud's next major work following *The Interpretation of Dreams* was *Psychopathology of Everyday Life* (1901/1960b) in which he discussed **parapraxes** (singular, *parapraxis*). Parapraxes refer to relatively minor errors in everyday living, such as slips of the tongue (now known as Freudian slips), forgetting things, losing things, small accidents, and mistakes in writing. According to Freud, all behavior was motivated; so for him, it was legitimate to seek the causes of all behavior whether it be "normal" or "abnormal." Furthermore, he believed that because the causes of behavior were usually unconscious, people seldom knew why they acted as they did. Freud pointed out that parapraxes were often unconsciously motivated:

> Freud is never at a loss to find evidence for his theories in the commonplace incidents we dismiss as insignificant or attribute to chance. Slips of the tongue and slips of the pen, forgotten names and forgotten appointments, lost gifts and mislaid possessions, all point to the role of wish and motive. Such happenings, Freud insists, are by no means accidental. The woman who loses her wedding ring wishes that she had never had it. The physician who forgets the name of his rival wishes that name blotted out of existence. The newspaper that prints "Clown Prince" for "Crown Prince" and corrects its error by announcing that of course it meant "Clown Prince," really means what it says. Even untutored common sense had a shrewd suspicion that forgetting is significant; one rarely admits without embarrassment that he failed to keep an appointment because he forgot it. Events of this sort are always determined. They are even overdetermined. Several lines of causation may converge on the same mishap, and physical as well as psychical determinants may be involved. Errors in speech, for example, may be due in part to difficulties of muscular coordination, to transposition of letters, to similarities in words, and the like. But such conditions do not constitute the whole explanation. They do not explain why one particular slip and not another was made—why just that combination of sounds and no other was uttered. A young business man, for example, striving to be generous to a rival, and intending to say "Yes, he is very efficient," actually said, "Yes, he is very officious." Obviously he was slipping into an easy confusion of words, but he was also expressing his real opinion. Desire and indirect fulfillment are at the basis of normal as well as abnormal conduct, and motive determines even those happenings we attribute to chance. (Heidbreder, 1933, pp. 391–392)

In the preceding quotation, Heidbreder used the term *overdetermined* in regard to acts of forgetting and errors in speech. The concept of **overdetermination** is extremely important in Freudian theory. In general, it means that behavioral and psychological acts often have more than one cause. A dream, for example, may partially satisfy several needs at the same time as may a hysterical symptom. Also, as we have just seen, an error in speech may be caused (determined) by difficulties in muscle coordination, the tendency to transpose letters, or by some unconscious motive. If a phenomenon is determined by two or more causes, it is said to be overdetermined.

Humor

Freud (1905/1960a) indicated that people often used jokes to express unacceptable sexual and aggressive tendencies. Like dreams, jokes exemplify wish fulfillments. According to Freud, jokes offer a socially approved vehicle for being obscene, aggressive or hostile, cynical, critical, skeptical, or blasphemous. Viewed in this way, jokes offer a way of venting repressed, anxiety-provoking thoughts; so it is no wonder that people find most humorous those things that bother them the most. Freud said that we laugh most at those things that cause us the most anxiety. However, to be effective, a joke, like a dream, must disguise the true sexual or aggressive motives behind them, or they would cause too much anxiety. Freud believed that a joke often fails because the motive it expresses is too blatant, in the same way that a nightmare is a failed dream from which one awakes because the motive expressed was too powerful for dream work to disguise.

Thus, in his search for the contents of the unconscious mind, Freud made use of free association, dream analysis, slips of the tongue, memory lapses, "accidents," gestures and mannerisms, what the person found humorous, and literally everything else the person did or said. This belief—that everything a person does has meaning—is exemplified in the following: An acquaintance passing a psychoanalyst says,

"Hello," and the psychoanalyst says to himself, "I wonder what he meant by that?" For the psychoanalyst, *everything* has meaning.

FREUD'S TRIP TO THE UNITED STATES

As Freud's fame gradually grew, he began to attract a few disciples. In 1902 Freud began meeting on Wednesday evenings with a small group of his followers in the waiting room outside his office. This group was called the Wednesday Society. By Freud's own account, psychoanalysis remained rather obscure until he and two of his disciples, Carl Jung (discussed later) and Sandor Ferenczi, were invited to Clark University in 1909 by G. Stanley Hall. Aboard ship, Freud saw a cabin steward reading *Psychopathology of Everyday Life* and thought for the first time that he might be famous (E. Jones, 1955). Freud was 53 years old at the time.

After a few days of sightseeing, Freud began his series of five lectures. Each lecture was prepared only a half-hour before it was given, and preparation consisted of a walk and discussion with Ferenczi. Freud delivered the lectures in German without any notes. Upon completion of his lectures, he was given an honorary doctorate; in his acceptance speech, he said, "This is the first official recognition of my endeavors" (E. Jones, 1955, p. 57). Although his lectures were met with some criticism, reactions were generally favorable. None other than William James, who was fatally ill at the time, said to Freud, "The future of psychology belongs to your work" (E. Jones, 1955, p. 57). Freud's series of five lectures was later expanded into his influential *Introductory Lectures of Psychoanalysis* (1915–1917/1966).

Freud was deeply grateful that his visit to Clark University had given psychoanalysis international recognition, but still he returned to Germany with a negative impression of the United States. He said to his colleague, and later his biographer, Ernest Jones, "America is a mistake; a gigantic mistake it is true, but none the less a mistake" (E. Jones, 1955, p. 66). Hale summarizes what Freud liked and did not like about the United States:

> At the time, the trip aroused Freud's hope that there might be a future for psychoanalysis in the United States. He made lasting friendships with a few Americans. Yet he was puzzled and somewhat distrustful, amused but not pleased, by what he had seen—Worcester, the Adirondacks, Coney Island, his first movie, full of wild chasing. He admired Niagara Falls—it was grander and larger than he had expected. He was charmed by a porcupine and by the Greek antiquities at the Metropolitan Museum. Yet the American cooking irritated his stomach; the free and easy informality irked his sense of dignity. He learned of a popular mania for religious mind cures, and he detected a distressing potential lay enthusiasm for his hard-won discoveries. (1971, Vol. 1, p. 4)

Nonetheless, following his trip to the United States, Freud's fame and that of psychoanalysis grew very rapidly. In 1910 the International Training Commission was organized to standardize the training of psychoanalysts. However, not everything went well for Freud. In 1911 Alfred Adler, an early disciple of Freud's, broke away to develop his own theory; this was closely followed by the defection of Carl Jung. Freud worried that such defections would contaminate psychoanalytic doctrine; thus, in 1912 he established a committee of loyal disciples to ensure the purity of psychoanalytic theory. This inner circle consisted of Karl Abraham, Sandor Ferenczi, Ernest Jones, Otto Rank, and Hans Sachs. In time, even members of this group would disagree with Freud. For example, we have seen that Ferenczi ended up agreeing with Freud's original seduction theory but not with Freud's revision of it.

THE ID, EGO, AND SUPEREGO

Early in his theorizing, Freud differentiated among the conscious, the preconscious, and the unconscious. Consciousness consisted of those things of which we were aware at any given moment. The **preconscious** consisted of the things of which we were not aware but of which we could easily become aware. For example, memorized phone numbers, friends' names and addresses, and other nontraumatic memories, although typically not in consciousness at any given moment, can easily be conjured up if needed. The unconscious consisted of those memories that were being actively repressed from consciousness and were therefore made conscious only with great effort. Later, Freud summarized and expanded these views with his concepts of the id, ego, and superego.

The Id

The **id** (from the German *das es*, meaning "the it") is the driving force of the personality. It contains all **instincts** (although better translations of the word Freud used might be "drives" or "forces") such as hunger, thirst, and sex. The id is entirely unconscious and is governed by the **pleasure principle**. When a need arises, the id wants immediate gratification of that need. The collective energy associated with the instincts is called **libido** (the Latin word for "lust"), and libidinal energy accounts for most human behavior.

Associated with every instinct are a *source*, which is a bodily need of some kind; an *aim* of satisfying the need; an *object*, which is anything capable of satisfying the need; and an *impetus*, a driving force whose strength is determined by the magnitude of the need.

The id has only two means of satisfying a need. One is **reflex action**, which is automatically triggered when certain discomforts arise. Sneezing and recoiling from a painful stimulus are examples of reflex actions. The second means of satisfaction is wish fulfillment, in which the id conjures up an image of an object that will satisfy an existing need. But because the id never comes directly into contact with the environment, where do these images come from?

> Freud speaks of the id as being the true psychic reality. By this he means the id is the primary subjective reality, the inner world that exists before the individual has had experience of the external world. Not only are the instincts and reflexes inborn, but the images that are produced by tension states may also be innate. This means that a hungry baby can have an image of food without having to learn to associate food with hunger. Freud believed that experiences that are repeated with great frequency and intensity in many individuals of successive generations become permanent deposits in the id. (C. S. Hall, 1954, pp. 26–27)

Freud, then, accepted Lamarck's theory of acquired characteristics when explaining how the id was capable of conjuring up images of things in the external world that were capable of satisfying needs.

Because the activities in the id occur independently of personal experience and because they provide the foundation of the entire personality, Freud referred to them as **primary processes**. The primary processes are irrational because they are directly determined by a person's need state, they tolerate *no* time lapse between the onset of a need and its satisfaction, and they exist entirely on the unconscious level. Furthermore, the primary processes can, at best, furnish only temporary satisfaction of a need. For example, thinking about a hamburger is clearly not the same as actually eating one; therefore, another aspect of the personality is necessary if the person is to survive.

The Ego

The **ego** (from the German *das ich*, meaning "the I") is aware of the needs of *both* the id and the physical world, and its major job is to coordinate the two. In other words, the ego's job is to match the wishes (images) of the id with their counterparts in the physical environment. For this reason, it is said that the ego operates in the service of the id. The ego is also said to be governed by the **reality principle** because the objects it provides must result in *real* rather than imaginary satisfaction of a need.

When the ego finds an environmental object that will satisfy a need, it invests libidinal energy into the thought of that object, thus creating a cathexis (from the Greek *kathexo*, meaning "to occupy") between the need and the object. A **cathexis** is an investment of psychic energy in thoughts of objects or processes that will satisfy a need. The realistic activities of the ego are called **secondary processes**, and they contrast with the unrealistic primary processes of the id.

If the id and the ego were the only two components of the personality, humans could hardly be distinguished from other animals. Needs would arise, and the ego would seek things in the environment that would satisfy those needs. When there were no needs, humans would be completely inactive. There is, however, a third component of the personality that vastly complicates matters.

The Superego

Although the newborn child is completely dominated by its id, it must soon learn that gratification of its needs usually cannot be immediate. More important, he or she must learn that some things are "right" and some things are "wrong." For example, if a child is a member of a family that practices a particular religion, the child must learn that certain foods can be eaten and others cannot. He or she must learn that parents will tolerate only a certain level of aggression. The child often learns that certain words are "bad" and that certain sexual activities are "bad" and therefore must be avoided. For example, the male child must inhibit his sexual desires for his mother and his aggressive tendencies toward his father. Teaching these do's and don't's is usually what is meant by socializing the child.

As the child internalizes these do's and don't's, he or she develops a **superego** (from the German *das überich*, meaning "the over I"), which is the moral arm of the personality. When the superego is fully developed, it has two divisions. The **conscience** consists of the internalized experiences for which the child has been consistently punished. Engaging in or even thinking about engaging in activities for which he or she had been consistently punished now makes the child feel guilty. The **ego-ideal** consists of the internalized experiences for which

the child has been rewarded. Engaging in or even thinking about engaging in activities for which he or she has been consistently rewarded makes the child feel good about himself or herself.

Freud attributed acquired characteristics to the superego, just as he did to the id, again revealing a Lamarckian tendency. As we have seen, Freud believed that objects associated with need satisfaction through the eons became available to the id as images. Freud also believed that morality was at least in part inherited from cumulative human experience. For example, he believed that modern humans still harbored the guilt a primitive group of brothers had felt when they killed their father. Freud believed that this guilt and the human reaction to it could be found throughout human history. Although Freud believed that the superego had archaic rudiments, he stressed the role of personal experience with reward and punishment in its development.

Once the superego is developed, the child's behavior and thoughts are governed by internalized values, usually those of the parents, and the child is said to be socialized. Feelings of guilt or pride keep the child acting in accordance with the values of society even when authority figures (e.g., the parents) are not present.

At this point, the job of the ego becomes much more complex. The ego must not only find objects or events that satisfy the needs of the id but these objects or events must also be sanctioned by the superego. In some cases, a cathexis that would be acceptable to the id and ego would cause guilt, and therefore libidinal energy would be diverted to inhibit the cathexis. The diversion of libidinal energy in an effort to inhibit an association between a need and an object or event is called an **anticathexis**. In such cases, the superego inhibits the association to avoid the feelings of guilt, and the ego inhibits it to postpone need satisfaction until an acceptable object or event can be found. Anticathexis causes a displacement from a guilt- or anxiety-provoking object or event to one that does not cause anxiety or guilt. In general, displacement involves the substitution of one object or event for another. Figure 16.1 shows an example of displacement where a sexual need is involved. The assumption is that in the adult human the natural cathexis for such a need is sexual intercourse.

Life and Death Instincts

Freud (1920/1955) differentiated between life and death instincts. The **life instincts** were collectively referred to as **eros** (named after the Greek god of love), and the energy associated with them was called libido. Earlier, Freud equated libido with sexual energy, but because of increased evidence to the contrary and because of severe criticism from even his closest colleagues, he expanded the notion of libido to include the energy associated with all life instincts including sex, hunger, and thirst. Freud's final position was that when a need arose libidinal energy was expended to satisfy it, thereby prolonging life. When all needs were satisfied, the person was in a state of minimal tension. One of life's major goals is to seek this state of need-

lessness that corresponds to complete satisfaction.

What happens if the above discussion is carried an additional step? There is a condition of the body that represents the ultimate steady state or state of nontension; it is called death. Life, Freud said, started from inorganic matter, and part of us longs to return to that state because only in that state is there no longer the constant struggle to satisfy biological needs. Here we see the influence of Schopenhauer, who said every meal we eat and every breath we take simply postpone death, which is the ultimate victor. Quoting Schopenhauer, Freud said that "the aim of all life is death" (1920/1955, p. 38). Thus, besides the life instincts, there is a **death instinct** called **thanatos** (named after the Greek god of death). The life instincts sought to perpetuate life, and the death instinct sought to terminate it. So to all the other conflicts that occurred among the id, ego, and superego, Freud added a life-and-death struggle. When directed toward one's self, the death instinct manifested itself as suicide or masochism; when directed outwardly, it manifested itself in ha-

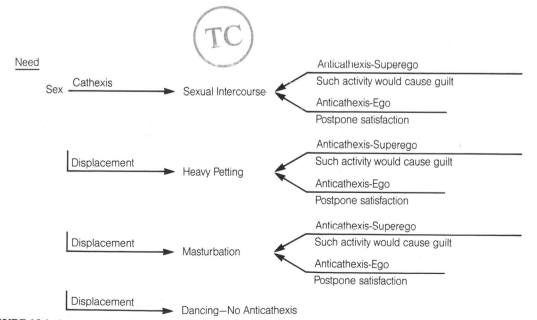

FIGURE 16.1 An example of how an anxiety-provoking activity is displaced by an activity that does not cause anxiety (Hergenhahn, 1990, p. 32). Used by permission.

tred, murder, cruelty, and general aggression. For Freud then, aggression was a natural component of human nature.

No wonder the ego was referred to as the executive of the personality. Not only did it need to deal with real environmental problems but it also needed to satisfy the needs of the id in ways that would not alienate the superego. Another of its jobs was to minimize the anxiety that arose when one *did* act contrary to one's internalized values. To combat such anxiety, the ego could employ the ego defense mechanisms to which we turn next.

ANXIETY AND THE EGO DEFENSE MECHANISMS

Anxiety

Anxiety is a warning of impending danger, and Freud distinguished three types. *Objective anxiety* arises when there is an objective threat to the person's well-being. For example, being physically attacked by another person or an animal would cause objective anxiety. Because the source of this type of anxiety can be clearly identified, this anxiety is similar to what we call fear. With both feelings, one can usually identify the object causing the feeling. *Neurotic anxiety* arises when the ego feels that it is going to be overwhelmed by the id—in other words, when the needs of the id become so powerful that the ego feels that it will be unable to control them and that the irrationality of the id will manifest itself in the person's thought and behavior. *Moral anxiety* arises when an internalized value is or is about to be violated. Moral anxiety is about the same as shame or guilt. It is the self-punishment that we experience when we act contrary to the values internalized in the superego.

Any form of anxiety is extremely uncomfortable, and the individual experiencing it seeks its reduction or elimination just as one would seek to reduce hunger, thirst, or pain. It is the ego's job to deal with anxiety. To reduce objective anxiety, the ego must deal effectively with the physical environment. To deal with neurotic and moral anxiety, the ego must use processes that Freud called the **ego defense mechanisms**. Freud believed that all ego defense mechanisms had two things in common: They distorted reality, and they operated on the unconscious level—that is, a person was unaware of the fact that he or she was using one. We review next a few of the commonly used ego defense mechanisms.

The Ego Defense Mechanisms

Repression is the fundamental defense mechanism because it is involved in all others. Repression occurs when an anxiety-provoking thought is actively held in the unconscious mind. Repressed ideas enter consciousness only when they are disguised enough so as not to cause anxiety. Modified repressed ideas show up in dreams, in humor, in physical symptoms, during free association, and in paraplaxes. Because it is found almost everywhere in psychoanalytic theory, displacement is another very important defense mechanism. In general, displacement involves replacing an object or goal that provokes anxiety with one that does not. When a displacement involves substituting a nonsexual goal for a sexual one, the process is called **sublimation**. Freud considered sublimation to be the basis of civilization. Because we often cannot express our sexual urges directly, we are forced to express them indirectly in the form of poetry, art, religion, football, baseball, politics, education, and everything else that characterizes civilization. Thus, Freud viewed civilization as a compromise. For civilization to exist, humans must inhibit direct satisfaction of their basic urges. Freud believed that humans were animals that were frustrated by the very civilization that they had created to protect themselves from themselves. Freud said, "Sublimation of instinct is an especially conspicuous feature of cultural development; it is what makes it possible for higher psychical activities, scientific, artistic or ideological, to play such an important part in civilized life" (1930/1961b, p. 49).

Another way to deal with an anxiety-provoking thought is to attribute it to someone or something other than one's self. For example, one sees a strong sexual urge in others rather than in one's self or attributes failing a test to an ambiguous book, test, or teacher rather than to one's own lack of intelligence or preparation. Such a process is called **projection**. One sees the causes of failure, undesirable urges, and secret desires as "out there" instead of in the self because seeing them as part of one's self would cause anxiety. Also, when one feels frustrated and anxious because one had not lived up to some internalized value, one can symbolically borrow someone else's success through the process of **identification**. Thus, if one dresses, behaves, or talks like a person considered successful, some of that person's success becomes one's own. Identification can take many forms. For example, it can manifest itself in one's choice of friends; in a record collection; in wearing a shirt or jacket with a school, company, or team name on it; in a hairstyle; or in one's personal library. **Rationalization** involves giving a rational, logical but false reason for a failure or shortcoming rather than the true reason for it. Alarms not going off, sickness, cars not starting, accidents, and faulty memory can all serve as excuses for missing a test—and they all make sense—but the true reason may have been the dread of failure. Sometimes, when people have a desire to do something but doing it would cause anxiety, they do the opposite of what they really want to do. This is called **reaction formation**. Thus, the male with strong homosexual tendencies becomes a Don Juan type, the mother who hates her child becomes overindulgent, the person with strong Communist leanings becomes a superpatriot, or the person with strong sexual urges becomes a preacher concerned with pornography, promiscuity, and the sinfulness of today's youth.

Everyone uses ego defense mechanisms. The difference between the normal and the abnormal person is not the use of the defense mechanisms but the frequency or intensity of their use. One of Freud's many great contributions to psychology was his insistence that the line between the "normal" person and the "neurotic" was a very thin one. In fact, Freud said that we are all neurotic but that some of us are more so than others.

PSYCHOSEXUAL STAGES OF DEVELOPMENT

Although Freud considered the entire body to be a source of sexual pleasure, he believed that this pleasure was concentrated on different parts of the body at different stages of development. At any stage, the area of the body on which sexual pleasure was concentrated was called the **erogenous zone**. The erogenous zones gave the stages of development their respective names. According to Freud, the experiences that a child had during each stage would determine, to a large extent, his or her adult personality. For this reason, Freud felt that the foundations for one's adult personality were formed by the time a child was about five years old.

The Oral Stage

The **oral stage** lasts through about the first year of life, and the erogenous zone is the mouth. Pleasure comes mainly through the lips, tongue, and such activities as sucking, chewing, and swallowing. If either *overgratification* or *undergratification* (frustration) of the oral needs causes a **fixation** to occur at this level of development, as an adult the child will be an **oral character**. Fixation during the early part of the oral stage results in an *oral-incorporative character*. Such a person tends to be a good listener and an excessive eater, drinker, kisser, or smoker; he or she also tends to be dependent and gullible. A fixation during the latter part of the oral stage, when teeth begin to appear, results in an *oral-sadistic character*. Such a person is sarcastic, cynical, and generally aggressive. He or she also tends to be ambivalent about things and swings from one extreme to another—for example, from being friendly to being hostile and from being aggressive to being submissive.

The Anal Stage

The **anal stage** lasts through about the second year of life, and the erogenous zone is the anus–buttocks region of the body. Fixation during this stage results in an **anal character**. During the first part of the anal stage, pleasure comes mainly from activities such as feces expulsion, and a fixation here results in the adult being an *anal-expulsive character*. Such a person tends to be generous, messy, or wasteful. In the latter part of the anal stage, after toilet training has occurred, pleasure comes from being able to withhold feces. A fixation here results in the person becoming an *anal-retentive character*. Such an adult tends to be a collector and to be stingy, orderly, and perhaps perfectionistic.

The Phallic Stage

The **phallic stage** lasts from about the beginning of the third year to the end of the fifth year, and the erogenous zone is the genital region of the body. During this stage, the Oedipus complex occurs: The male child now has an intense desire for his mother and great hostility toward his father who is his rival for his mother's love. Because the source of the child's pleasurable feelings toward his mother is his penis and because he sees his father as much more powerful than he, the male child begins to experience **castration anxiety**, which causes him to repress his sexual and aggressive tendencies. The male child solves this problem by identifying strongly with the father. This does two things: Symbolically becoming his father (through identification) allows the child at least to share the mother, and it removes his father as a threat, thus reducing the child's castration anxiety. But repressed desires do not disappear; they persist as powerful forces in the unconscious and thereby remain a major influence in one's life.

The female child's situation is much different from the male's. She experiences what is called the **Electra complex**. (Although Freud used this term early in his theorizing, he eventually rejected it because it implied a symmetry with the Oedipal complex that he believed did not exist. Later he preferred to use the term *castration complex* to describe the female child's situation.) Like the male child, the female starts out with a strong attraction and attachment to the mother. She soon learns, however, that she lacks a penis and she blames the mother for its absence. She now has both positive and negative feelings toward her mother. At about the same time, she learns that her father possesses the valued organ, which she wants to share with him. This causes a sexual attraction toward the father, but the fact that her father possesses something valuable that she does not possess causes her to experience **penis envy**. Thus, the female child also has ambivalent feelings toward her father. To resolve the Electra complex in a healthy way, the female child must repress her hostility toward her mother and her sexual attraction to her father. Thereafter, she "becomes" the mother and shares the father.

The repression and strong identification necessary during this stage result in the full development of the superego. When a child identifies with his or her parent of the same sex, the child introjects that parent's moral standards and values. Once these things have been introjected, they control the child for the rest of his or her life. For this reason, the final and complete formation of the superego is said to go hand-in-hand with the resolution of the Oedipal or Electra complex.

One of the major reasons that Freud believed that the male's and female's experiences during the phallic stage were not symmetrical was the fact that a key ingredient in the male experience was castration anxiety. Because the female was already castrated (symbolically), she never had the intense motivation to defensively identify with the potential castrator. Because such identification results in the development of the superego, Freud reached the controversial conclusion that the male superego (morality) is stronger than that of the female.

The Latency Stage

The **latency stage** lasts from about the beginning of the sixth year until puberty. Because of the intense repression required during the phallic stage, during the latency stage sexual activity is all but eliminated from consciousness. This stage is characterized by numerous substitute activities such as schoolwork and peer activities and by extensive curiosity about the world.

The Genital Stage

The **genital stage** lasts from puberty through the remainder of one's life. With the onset of puberty, sexual desires become too intense to repress completely, and they begin to manifest themselves. The focus of attention is now on members of the opposite sex. Early manifestations of sexual desires include "crushes," "puppy love," and some experimentation between the sexes. If everything has gone correctly during the preceding stages, this stage will culminate in dating and eventually marriage.

The undergratifications or overgratifications and fixations that a person experienced (or did not experience) during the psychosexual stages will determine the person's adult personality. If the person has adjustment problems later in life, the psychoanalyst looks into these early experiences for solution to the problems. For the psychoanalyst, childhood experience is the stuff of which neuroses or normality are made. Indeed, psychoanalysts believe that "the child is father to the man" (Freud, 1940/1969, p. 64).

FREUD'S VIEW OF HUMAN NATURE

It should be clear by now that Freud was largely pessimistic about human nature. Freud reacted to the biblical commandment "Thou shalt love thy neighbor as thyself" as follows:

What is the point of a precept enunciated with so much solemnity if its fulfillment cannot be recommended as reasonable? . . . Not merely is this stranger in general unworthy of my love; I must honestly confess that he had more claim to my hostility and even my hatred. He seems not to have the least trace of love for me and shows me not the slightest consideration. If it will do him any good he has no hesitation in injuring me, nor does he ask himself whether the amount of advantage he gains bears any proportion to the extent of the harm he does to me. Indeed, he need not even obtain an advantage; if he can satisfy any sort of desire by it, he thinks nothing of jeering at me, insulting me, slandering me and showing his superior power; and, the more secure he feels and the more helpless I am, the more certainly I can expect him to behave like this to me. . . . Indeed, if this grandiose commandment had run "Love thy neighbour as thy neighbour loves thee," I should not take exception to it. . . .

The element of truth behind all this, which people are so ready to disavow, is that men are not gentle creatures who want to be loved, and who at the most can defend themselves if they are attacked; they are, on the contrary, creatures among whose instinctual endowments is to be reckoned a powerful share of aggressiveness. As a result, their neighbour is for them not only a potential helper or sexual object, but also someone who tempts them to satisfy their aggressiveness on him, to exploit his capacity for work without compensation, to use him sexually without his consent, to seize his possessions, to humiliate him, to cause him pain, to torture and to kill him. *Homo homini lupus* [man is a wolf to man]. (1930/1961b, pp. 63–65)

Religion

Another place where Freud showed his pessimism was in *The Future of an Illusion* (1927/1961a), which was his major statement on religion. In this book, Freud contended that the basis of religion was the human feeling of helplessness and insecurity. To overcome these feelings, we create a powerful father figure who will supposedly protect us, a father figure symbolized in the concept of God. The problem with this practice, according to Freud, was that it kept humans operating at a childlike, irrational level.

The dogmatic teachings of religion inhibited a more rational, realistic approach to life:

> The whole thing [religion] is so patently infantile, so foreign to reality, that to anyone with a friendly attitude to humanity it is painful to think that the great majority of mortals will never be able to rise above this view of life. (Freud, 1930/1961b, p. 22)

For Freud, our only hope was to come to grips with the repressed forces that motivated us; only then could we live rational lives. Freud said, "Those who do not suffer from the neurosis will need no intoxicant to deaden it" (1927/1961a, p. 49). For him, religion was the intoxicant. Just as Freud refused to take pain-killing drugs during his 16-year bout with cancer, he believed that humans could and should confront reality without religious illusions or any other type.

It was Freud's hope that religious illusions would eventually be replaced by scientific principles as guides for living. Scientific principles are not always flattering or comforting, but they are rational:

> No belittlement of science can in any way alter the fact that it is attempting to take account of our dependence on the real external world, while religion is an illusion and it derives its strength from its readiness to fit in with our instinctual wishful impulses. (1933/1966, pp. 638–639)

And elsewhere Freud said, "Our science is no illusion. But an illusion it would be to suppose that what science cannot give us we can get elsewhere" (1927/1961a, p. 56).

FREUD'S FATE

Even while suffering from cancer in the later years of his life, Freud continued to be highly productive. However, when the Nazis occupied Austria in 1936, his life became increasingly precarious. Psychoanalysis had already been labeled as "Jewish science" in Germany, and his books were banned there. In Vienna the Nazis destroyed Freud's personal library, and they pub-

licly burned all his books found in the Vienna public library. About this Freud said, "What progress we are making. In the Middle Ages they would have burnt me; nowadays they are content with burning my books" (E. Jones, 1957, p. 182). Freud resisted as long as he could but eventually decided it was time to leave Vienna. To do so, however, he was required to sign a document attesting to the respectful and considerate treatment he had received from the Nazis; to this document, Freud added the comment (sarcastically, of course), "I can heartily recommend the Gestapo to anyone" (Clark, 1980, p. 511).

With his daughter Anna, Freud first journeyed to Paris where they were received by Princess Marie Bonaparte and one of Freud's sons. Shortly afterward, they traveled to London where they took up residence at 20 Maresfield Gardens in Hampstead. It was here that Anna Freud later established the Hampstead Child Therapy Clinic and became an internationally prominent child analyst. Freud was well received in England and, although in great pain, was able to occasionally attend meetings of the London Psychoanalytic Society. In London, Freud completed his last book, *Moses and Monotheism* in 1939 (see Freud, 1939/1964), and he died the same year at the age of 83. When Freud left Vienna, he had to leave four of his sisters behind, and he died without knowing that they were all soon to die in Nazi concentration camps (E. Jones, 1957).

REVISIONS OF THE FREUDIAN LEGEND

We have already mentioned two recent modifications of the Freudian legend: the dubious circumstances under which Freud revised his seduction theory and that many of his ideas were not as courageous and innovative as he and his followers claimed (e.g., his ideas concerning infantile sexuality, dream analysis, and male hysteria). According to Ellenberger (1970), Freud and his followers purposefully attempted to create an image of Freud as a lonely, heroic figure who was discriminated against because he was a Jew and because his ideas were so revolutionary that the established medical community could not accept them. According to Ellenberger, the Freudian legend had two main components:

> The first is the theme of the solitary hero struggling against a host of enemies, suffering "the slings and arrows of outrageous fortune" but triumphing in the end. The legend considerably exaggerates the extent and role of anti-Semitism, of the hostility of the academic world, and of alleged Victorian prejudices. The second feature of the Freudian legend is the blotting out of the greatest part of the scientific and cultural context in which psychoanalysis developed, hence the theme of the absolute originality of the achievements, in which the hero is credited with the achievements of his predecessors, associates, disciples, rivals, and contemporaries. (1970, p. 547)

According to Ellenberger, the facts contradict both components of the legend. First, Freud experienced only slight anti-Semitism, and he did not experience nearly the amount of hostility that several more prominent physicians experienced. Second, most of Freud's ideas were not as original as he and his followers claimed.

Freud and his followers had a very low tolerance for criticism and usually accused critics of resistance, lack of understanding, or even bigotry. However, Sulloway points out that most of the criticisms of psychoanalysis were valid:

> In addition to the criticisms that had already been raised before Freud acquired a substantial following, common objections against psychoanalysis now began to include: (1) that psychoanalysts were continually introducing their assertions with the statement, "We know from psychoanalytic experience that . . . ," and then leaving the burden of proof to others; (2) that Freud's disciples refused to listen to opinions that did not coincide with their own; (3) that they never published statistics on the success of their method; (4) that they persisted in claiming that only those who had used the psychoanalytic method had the right to challenge Freud; (5) that they saw all criticism as a form of "neurotic resistance"; (6) that psychoanalysts tended to ignore all work that had been done before them and then proceeded to make unwarranted claims about their own originality; (7) that they frequently addressed themselves to the wider lay audience as if their theories were already a proven fact, thus making their opponents seem narrow-minded and ignorant; (8) that so-called wild analysts, or individuals without proper training, were analyzing patients in irresponsible ways; and (9) that Freud's followers were becoming a sect, with all of the prominent features of one, including a fanatical degree of faith, a special jargon, a sense of moral superiority, and a predilection for marked intolerance of opponents. In their contemporary context, such criticisms were considerably more rational and had far more merit than traditional psychoanalytic historians have been willing to admit. (1979, p. 460)

EVALUATION OF FREUD'S THEORY

Criticisms

It should come as no surprise that a theory as broad as Freud's, and one that touched so many aspects of human existence, would receive severe criticism. The common criticisms of Freud and his theory include the following:

1. *Method of data collection.* Freud used his own observations of his own patients as his source of data. There was no controlled experimentation. Not only did his patients not represent the general population, but his own needs and expectations probably influenced his observations.

2. *Definition of terms.* Freud's theory became popular at a time when psychology was preoccupied with operational definitions, and many, if not most, of Freud's concepts were too nebulous to be measured. For example, how does one quantify psychic energy, castration anxiety, penis envy, or the Oedipal complex? How does one determine whether the interpretation of the latent symbols of a dream is valid? Science demands measurement, and many of Freud's concepts were not and are not measurable.

3. *Dogmatism.* As we have seen, Freud saw himself as the founder and leader of the psychoanalytic movement, and he would tolerate no ideas that conflicted with his own. If a member of his group insisted on disagreeing with him, Freud expelled that member from the group.

4. *Overemphasis on sex.* The main reason that many of Freud's early colleagues eventually went their own way was that they believed Freud overemphasized sex as a motive for human behavior. Some thought that to see sexual motivation everywhere, as Freud did, was extreme and unnecessary. The personality theories that other psychoanalytically oriented theorists developed show that human behavior can be explained just as well, if not better, employing other than sexual motives.

5. *The self-fulfilling prophecy.* Any theorist, not just Freud, can be criticized for being susceptible to self-fulfilling prophecy. The point is that Freud may have found what he was looking for simply because he was looking for it. For example, free association is not really free. Rather, it is guided, at least in part, by the analyst's comments and gestures. Furthermore, once a patient is "trained," he or she may begin to tell the analyst exactly what the analyst wants to hear. This criticism also applies to dream interpretation.

6. *Length, cost, and limited effectiveness of psychoanalysis.* Because psychoanalysis usually takes years to complete, it is not available to most troubled people. Only the most affluent can participate. Furthermore, only reasonably intelligent and mildly neurotic people can benefit from psychoanalysis because patients must be able to articulate their inner experiences and understand the analyst's interpretation of those experiences. Psychoanalysis is not effective with psychotic patients.

7. *Lack of falsifiability.* One reason that psychoanalytic theory is hard to validate or invalidate is the large number of imprecise and nebulous terms it employs. Another reason is that anyone who criticizes it may be accused of exhibiting personal defensiveness:

> If the critic rejects the theory, he may be acting in self-defense. If he is friendly toward the theory as a whole, reserving his objections for one or two points, he may simply be employing a more subtle defense, attempting to protect his most sensitive wounds by conceding points that do not greatly concern him. Even if he gives good reasons for the stand he takes, he can never be sure he is not rationalizing. And the critic cannot be sure that he is not adopting such devices, because his motives may be deep in his unconscious. (Heidbreder, 1933, pp. 400–401)

In chapter 1, we saw that Karl Popper said Freud's theory was unscientific because it violated the principle of falsification. According to Popper, for a theory to be scientific, it must specify observations that, if made, would refute the theory. Unless such observations can be specified, the theory is unscientific. Popper claimed that because Freudian theory could account for *anything* a person did, nothing that a person could do would be contrary to what the theory predicted. Let us say, for example, that according to Freudian theory a certain cluster of childhood experiences will make an adult leery of heterosexual relationships. Instead, we find an adult who has had those experiences seeking and apparently enjoying such relationships. The Freudian can simply say that the person is demonstrating a reaction formation. Thus, no matter what happens, the theory is supported. A related criticism is that psychoanalysts engage in *post*diction rather than *pre*diction. That is, they attempt to explain events after they have occurred rather than predict what events will occur. The former is clearly easier than the latter.

Contributions

Despite the criticisms, most believe that Freud made truly exceptional contributions to psychology. The following are usually listed among them:

1. *Expansion of psychology's domain.* Like no one before him, Freud pointed to the importance of studying the relationships among unconscious motivation, infantile sexuality, dreams, and anxiety. Freud's was the first

comprehensive theory of personality, and every personality theory since his can be seen as a reaction to his theory or to some aspect of it.

2. *Psychoanalysis.* Freud created a new way of dealing with age-old mental disorders. Many still believe that psychoanalysis is the best way to understand and treat neuroses.

3. *Understanding of normal behavior.* Freud not only provided a means of better understanding much abnormal behavior but also made much normal behavior comprehensive. Dreams, forgetfulness, mistakes, choice of mates, humor, and use of the ego defense mechanisms characterize everyone's life, and Freud's analysis of them makes them less mysterious for everyone.

4. *Generalization of psychology to other fields.* By showing psychology's usefulness in explaining phenomena in everyday life, religion, sports, politics, art, literature, and philosophy, Freud expanded psychology's relevance to almost every sector of human existence.

As influential as Freud's theory has been, much of it has not withstood the rigors of scientific examination; in fact, much of it, as we have seen, is untestable. Why, then, is Freud's theory so often referred to as a milestone in human history? The answer seems to be that scientific methodology is not the only criterion by which to judge a theory. Structuralism, for example, was highly scientific, requiring controlled, systematic experiments to test its hypotheses. Yet structuralism has faded away while psychoanalysis has remained:

> Whenever the Freudian theories have been accepted outside the psychoanalytic fold, they have been received not because they carry the credentials of exact, verifiable evidence, but because they have aroused conviction as convictions are aroused in everyday life—by the feeling that they represent keen observation and shrewd speculation which, in the main, square with the facts.
> It is enlightening to compare psychoanalytic psychology with structuralism, in this respect its antithesis. Structuralism, equipped with a highly developed scientific method, and refusing to deal with materials not amenable to that method, admirably illustrates the demand for exactness and correctness by which science disciplines untutored curiosity. Psychoanalysis, with its seemingly inexhaustible curiosity, at present lacks the means, and apparently at times the inclination, to check its exuberant speculation by severely critical tests. But what it lacks in correctness, it gains in vitality, in the comprehensiveness of its view, and in the closeness of its problems to the concerns of everyday life. (Heidbreder, 1933, pp. 410–411)

To the means by which we evaluate theories, we must add intuition. A theory that, among other things, makes sense personally may survive longer than one that develops and is tested within the realm of science. The extinction of structuralism and the survival of psychoanalysis exemplify this point.

Almost from its beginning, Freud's version of psychoanalysis had its critics, and several people who were originally affiliated with Freud and psychoanalysis went on to develop their own theories of personality. We consider only three such individuals: Carl Jung, Alfred Adler, and Karen Horney.

ALTERNATIVES TO FREUDIAN PSYCHOANALYSIS

Carl Jung

Born in the Swiss village of Kesswyl, **Carl Jung** (1875–1961) studied medicine at Basel from 1895 to 1901 and then worked as resident under Eugen Bleuler (who coined the term *schizophrenia*). Jung spent the winter of 1902–1903 studying with Janet. On Bleuler's recommendation, Jung administered Galton's word-association test to psychotics in hopes of discovering the nature of their unconscious thought processes. This research was fairly successful and brought Jung some early fame. Jung first became acquainted with Freud's theory when he read *The Interpretation of Dreams.* When Jung tried Freud's ideas in his own practice, he found them effective. He and Freud began to correspond, and eventually they met in Freud's

Carl Jung

home in Vienna. Their initial meeting lasted 13 hours, and the two became close friends.

When G. Stanley Hall invited Freud to give a series of lectures at Clark University in 1909, Jung traveled to the United States with Freud and gave a few lectures of his own (on his word-association research). About this time, Jung began to express doubts about Freud's emphasis on sexual motivation. These doubts became so intense that in 1912 the two stopped corresponding, and in 1914 they completely terminated their relationship—despite the fact that Freud had earlier nominated Jung to be the first president of the International Psychoanalytic Association. The break in the relationship was especially disturbing to Jung, who entered what he called his "dark years," a period of three years during which he was so depressed he could not even read a scientific book. During this time, he analyzed his innermost thoughts, and he developed his own distinct theory of personality, which differed markedly from Freud's. Jung continued to develop his theory until his death in 1961.

Libido. The major source of difficulty between Freud and Jung was the nature of the libido. At the time of his association with Jung, Freud defined libido as sexual energy, which he saw as the main driving force of personality. Thus, for Freud, most human behavior was sexually motivated. Jung disagreed, saying that libidinal energy was a creative life force that could be applied to the continuous psychological growth of the individual. According to Jung, libidinal energy was used in a wide range of human endeavors beyond those of a sexual nature, and it could be applied to the satisfaction of both biological *and* philosophical or spiritual needs. In fact, as one became more proficient at satisfying the former needs, one could use more libidinal energy in dealing with the latter needs. In short, sexual motivation was *much* less important to Jung than it was to Freud.

The ego. Jung's conception of the ego was similar to Freud's. The ego was the mechanism by which we interacted with the physical environment. It was everything of which we were conscious and was concerned with thinking, problem solving, remembering, and perceiving.

The personal unconscious. Combining the Freudian notions of the preconscious and the unconscious, Jung's **personal unconscious** consisted of experiences that had either been repressed or simply forgotten—material from one's lifetime that for one reason or another was not in consciousness. Some of this material was easily retrievable, and some of it was not.

The collective unconscious and the archetypes. The **collective unconscious** was Jung's most mystical and controversial concept and his most important. Jung believed the collective unconscious to be the deepest and most powerful component of the personality, reflecting the cumulative experiences of humans throughout their entire evolutionary past. According to Jung, it was the "deposit of ancestral experience from untold millions of years, the echo of prehistoric world events to which each century adds an infinitesimally small amount of variation and differentiation" (1928, p. 162).

The collective unconscious registered *common* experiences that humans had had through the eons. These common experiences were recorded and were inherited as predispositions to respond emotionally to certain categories of experience. According to Jung, each inherited predisposition contained in the collective unconscious was an **archetype**:

> These ancestral experiences that are registered in the brain have been called at various times "racial memories," "primordial images" or more commonly, *archetypes*. An archetype can be defined as an inherited predisposition to respond to certain aspects of the world. Just as the eye and the ear have evolved to be maximally responsive to certain aspects of the environment, so has the brain evolved to cause the person to be maximally responsive to certain categories of experience that humans have encountered over and over again through countless generations. There is an archetype for whatever experiences are universal, those that each member of each generation must experience.
>
> You can generate a list of archetypes yourself by simply answering the question, "What must every human experience in his or her lifetime?" One's answer must include such things as birth, death, the sun, darkness, power, women, men, sex, water, magic, mother, heroes, and pain. There is an inherited predisposition to react to instances of these and other categories of experience. Specific responses are not inherited nor are specific ideas; all that is inherited is a tendency to deal with universal experiences in some way.
>
> According to Jung, what is carried from generation to generation are the emotional reactions to common human experiences. For example, when our ancestors experienced a bolt of lightning or a clap of thunder, it stimulated in them emotional responses that immediately took the form of myths. (Hergenhahn, 1990, p. 69)

According to Jung, the mind was not a "blank tablet" at birth but contained a structure that had developed in a Lamarckian fashion. That is, experiences of preceding generations were passed on to new generations. Archetypes could be thought of as generic images with which events in one's lifetime interacted. They recorded not only perceptual experiences but also the emotions typically associated with those perceptual experiences. In fact, Jung thought that the emotional component of archetypes was their most important feature. When an experience "communicated with" or was "identified with" an archetype, the emotion elicited was typical of the emotional response people had had to that type of experience through the eons. For example, each child is born with a generic conception of mother that is the result of the cumulative experiences of preceding generations, and the child will tend to project onto its real mother the attributes of the generic mother-image. This archetype will influence not only how the child views his or her mother but also how the child responds to her emotionally. For Jung then, archetypes provided each person with a framework for perceptual and emotional experience. They predisposed people to see things in certain ways, to have certain emotional experiences, and to engage in certain categories of behavior.

Although Jung recognized a large number of archetypes, he elaborated the following ones most fully. The **persona** causes people to present only part of their personality to the public. It is a mask in the sense that the most important aspects of personality are hidden behind it. The **anima** provides the female component of the male personality and a framework within which males can interact with females. The **animus** provides the masculine component of the female personality and a framework within which females can interact with males. The **shadow**, the archetype that we inherit from our prehuman ancestors, provides us with a tendency to be immoral and aggressive. We project this aspect of our personalities onto the world symbolically as devils, demons, monsters, and evil spirits. The **self** causes people to try to synthesize all components of their personalities. It represents the human need for unity and wholeness of the total personality. The goal of life is first to discover and understand the various parts of the personality and then to synthesize them into a harmonious unity. Jung called this unity **self-actualization**.

The attitudes. Jung described two major orientations, or attitudes, that people took in relating to the world. One attitude he labeled **introversion**, the other **extroversion**. Jung believed that although every individual possessed both attitudes, he or she usually assumed one of the two attitudes more than the other. The introverted person tended to be quiet, imaginative, and more interested in ideas than in interacting with people. The extroverted person was outgoing and sociable. Jung described the two attitudes in more detail:

> The first attitude (introversion) is normally characterized by a hesitant, reflective, retiring nature that keeps itself to itself, shrinks from objects, is slightly on the defensive and prefers to hide behind mistrustful scrutiny. The second (extroversion) is normally characterized by an outgoing, candid, and accommodating nature that adapts easily to a given situation, quickly forms attachments, and, setting aside any possible misgivings, will often venture forth with careless confidence into unknown situations. (1917/1953, p. 44)

Although most people tend toward either introversion or extroversion, Jung believed that the mature, healthy adult personality reflected both attitudes about equally.

Causality, teleology, and synchronicity. Like Freud, Jung was a determinist, but he did not confine his brand of determinism to past experience. Jung felt that to truly understand a person one must understand the person's prior experiences, including those registered in the collective unconscious, *and* the person's goals for the future. Thus, unlike Freud's theory, Jung's involved **teleology** (purpose). For Jung, people were both pushed by the past and pulled by the future.

For Jung, another important determinant of personality was **synchronicity**, or meaningful coincidence. Synchronicity refers to the fortuitous events in one's life that significantly modify one's course of life. Examples might include a last-minute decision to attend a dance at which one meets his or her partner for life or a decision to have a cup of coffee in a restaurant that re-sults in meeting someone who provides a major employment opportunity. Also, a student will often take a course because it was the only one available, and the course's content or instructor creates a lifelong interest or even a professional commitment. (For a detailed account of Jung's concept of synchronicity, see Progoff, 1973.)

Dreams. Dreams were important to Jung, but he interpreted them very differently than Freud. Freud believed that repressed, traumatic experiences revealed themselves in dreams because during sleep one's defenses were reduced. During the waking state, these experiences were actively held in the unconscious mind because to entertain them consciously would provoke extreme anxiety. Jung believed that everyone had the same collective unconscious but that individuals differed in their ability to recognize and give expression to the various archetypes. As we have seen, Jung also believed that everyone had an innate tendency to recognize, express, and synthesize the various components of his or her personality and, in so doing, to become self-actualized. Even with this tendency, however, most people were not self-actualized. For most individuals, certain components of the personality remained unrecognized and underdeveloped. For Jung, dreams were a means of giving expression to aspects of the psyche that were underdeveloped. If a person did not give adequate expression to the shadow, for example, he or she would tend to have nightmares involving various monsters. Dreams, then, could be used to determine which aspects of the psyche were being given adequate expression and which were not.

The importance of middle age. According to Jung, the goal of life is to reach self-actualization, which involves the harmonious blending of all aspects of the personality. Before this blending can occur, however, individuation must take place. **Individuation** is the process by which the various components of the personality are recognized and given expression. The job of recognizing and expressing all forces within us is monumental because these forces usually conflict with one another. The rational conflicts with the irrational, feeling with thinking, masculine tendencies with feminine tendencies, and conscious processes with unconscious processes. The process of individuation occupies most of one's childhood, adolescence, and early adulthood. It is usually not until one reaches his or her late 30s or early 40s that a major transformation occurs. Once one has recognized the many conflicting forces in one's personality, one is in a position to synthesize and harmonize them. Self-actualization occurs when all discordant elements of personality are given equal expression. In a healthy, integrated individual, each system of the personality is differentiated, developed, and expressed. Although Jung believed that everyone had an innate tendency toward self-actualization, he also believed that people rarely attained that state.

Criticisms and contributions. Jung's theory has been criticized for embracing occultism, spiritualism, mysticism, and religion. Many saw Jung as unscientific or even antiscientific because he used such things as the symbols found in art, religion, and human fantasy to develop and verify his theory. The concept of the archetype, which is central to Jung's theory, has been criticized for being metaphysical and unverifiable. Some have referred to Jung's theory in general as unclear, incomprehensible, inconsistent, and, in places, contradictory. Finally, Jung has been criticized for employing the Lamarckian notion of the inheritance of acquired characteristics.

Despite these criticisms, Jungian theory remains popular in psychology. Jung has influential followers throughout the world, and several major cities have Jungian institutes that elaborate and disseminate his ideas. Jung's notions of introversion and extroversion have stimulated much research and are part of several popular personality tests—for example, the Minnesota Multiphasic Personality Inventory. Also, it was Jung who introduced the Aristotelian notion of self-actualization into modern psychology. A

Alfred Adler

THE BETTMANN ARCHIVE

number of current humanistically and existentially oriented theories (e.g., the theories of Rogers and Maslow) emphasize the self-actualization process. Hall and Lindzey liken Jung's contributions to those of Freud:

> When all is said and done, Jung's theory of personality as developed in his prolific writings, and as applied to a wide range of human phenomena stands as one of the most remarkable achievements in modern thought. The originality and audacity of Jung's thinking have few parallels in recent scientific history, and no person aside from Freud has opened more conceptual windows into what Jung would choose to call "the soul of man." (1978, p. 149)

Alfred Adler

Born on February 17 in a suburb of Vienna, **Alfred Adler** (1870–1937) remembered his childhood as being miserable. He was a sickly child who thought of himself as small and ugly. He also had a severe rivalry with his older brother. All these recollections may have influenced the type of personality theory Adler developed.

Like Jung, Adler became acquainted with Freudian psychology by reading *The Interpretation of Dreams*. Adler wrote a paper defending Freud's theory and was invited to join the Vienna Psychoanalytic Society, of which he became president in 1910. Differences between Adler and Freud began to emerge, however, and by 1911 they became so pronounced that Adler resigned as president of the Vienna Psychoanalytic Society. After a nine-year association with Freud, the friendship crumbled, and the two men never saw one another again. Freud accused Adler of becoming famous by reducing psychoanalysis to the commonsense level of the layperson. About Adler, Freud said, "I have made a pygmy great" (Wittels, 1924, p. 225). History shows that Freud and Adler never had much in common, and it was probably a mistake for Adler to join the Freudians. Ernest Jones summarizes Adler's major disagreements with Freud:

> Sexual factors, particularly those of childhood, were reduced to a minimum: a boy's incestuous desire for intimacy with his mother was interpreted as the male wish to conquer a female masquerading as sexual desire. The concepts of repression, infantile sexuality, and even that of the unconscious itself were discarded. (1955, p. 131)

In 1926 Adler visited the United States and was warmly received. In 1935, partially because of the Nazi menace in Europe, Adler made the United States his permanent home. He died in 1937 while on a lecture tour in Aberdeen, Scotland. The animosity that Freud felt toward Adler can be seen in the following comment that Freud made to a person who was moved by the news of Adler's death:

> I don't understand your sympathy for Adler. For a Jew boy out of a Viennese suburb a death in Aberdeen is an unheard-of career in itself and a proof of how far he had got on. The world

really rewarded him richly for his service in having contradicted psychoanalysis. (E. Jones, 1957, p. 208)

Organ inferiority and compensation.   Like Freud, Adler was trained in the materialistic-positivistic medical tradition; that is, every disorder, whether physical or mental, was assumed to have a physiological origin. Adler (1907/1917) presented the view that people were particularly sensitive to disease in organs that were "inferior" to other organs. For example, some people were born with weak eyes, others with weak hearts, still others with weak limbs, and so on. Because of the strain the environment put on these weak parts of the body, the person would develop weaknesses that inhibited normal functioning.

One way to adjust to a weakness was through **compensation**. That is, a person could adjust to a weakness in one part of his or her body by developing strengths in other parts. For example, a blind person could develop especially sensitive auditory skills. Another way to adjust to a weakness was through **overcompensation**, which was the conversion of a weakness into a strength. The usual examples include Teddy Roosevelt, who was a frail child but became a rugged outdoorsman, and Demosthenes, who had a speech impediment but became a great orator. At the time when Adler presented this view, he was a physician, and his observations were clearly in accord with the materialistic-positivistic medicine of the time.

Feelings of inferiority.   In 1910 Adler entered the realm of psychology when he noted that compensation and overcompensation could be directed toward *psychological* inferiorities as well as toward physical ones. Adler noted that *all* humans began life completely dependent on others for their survival and therefore with **feelings of inferiority**, or weakness. Such feelings motivated people first as children, and then as adults, to gain power to overcome these feelings. In his early theorizing, Adler emphasized the attainment of power as a means of overcoming feelings of inferiority; later, he suggested that people strove for perfection or superiority to overcome these feelings.

Although feelings of inferiority motivate all personal growth and are therefore good, they can also disable rather than motivate some people. These people are so overwhelmed by such feelings that they accomplish little or nothing, and they are said to have an **inferiority complex**. Thus, feelings of inferiority can act as a stimulus for positive growth or as a disabling force, depending on one's attitude toward them.

Lifestyle. The means that one chooses to gain superiority is called a **lifestyle** Roughly, a lifestyle is the same as an identity. It is what a person is known in terms of; it is the theme that permeates one's entire life. A person chooses a lifestyle from what is available in the environment. Depending on what is available, one's lifestyle can be characterized as social, athletic, scholarly, or artistic, to mention only a few possibilities.

To be truly effective, a lifestyle must contain considerable **social interest**. That is, part of its goal must involve working toward a society that would provide a better life for everyone. Adler called any lifestyle without adequate social interest a **mistaken lifestyle**. Because the neurotic typically has a mistaken lifestyle, the job of the psychotherapist is to replace it with one that contains a healthy amount of social interest.

The creative self. Adler departed radically from the theories of Freud and Jung by saying that humans were not victims of their environment or of biological inheritance. Although environment and heredity provide the raw materials of personality, the person is free to arrange those materials in any number of ways. For example, whether feelings of inferiority facilitate growth or disable a person is a matter of personal attitude. If one sees life as meaningless, one is free to invent meaning and then act "as if" it were true. With his concept of the **creative self**, Adler aligned himself with the existential belief that humans were free to choose their own destiny.

Thus, although Adler was an early member of Freud's inner circle, the theory he developed

Karen Horney

had little, if anything, in common with Freud's. Unlike Freud's theory, Adler's theory emphasized the conscious mind, social rather than sexual motives, and free will. Much of Adler's thinking was to emerge later in such theories as those of Gordon Allport, George Kelly, Carl Rogers, and Abraham Maslow. All these theories have in common the existential theme, which is the subject of the next chapter.

Karen Horney

Karen Horney (pronounced "horn-eye") (1885–1952) was born on September 16 in a small village near Hamburg, Germany. Her father was a Norwegian sea captain, and her mother, who was 18 years younger than the captain, was a member of a prominent Dutch-German family. Karen's father was a God-fearing fundamentalist who believed that women were inferior to men and were the primary source of evil in the world. Karen had conflicting feelings about her father. She disliked him because of the frequent derogatory statements he made about her appearance and intelligence. She liked him because he added adventure to her life by taking her with him on at least three lengthy sea voyages. Karen's family consisted of, besides her mother and father, four children from the captain's previous marriage and her older brother Berndt. The family called the father the "Bible thrower" (Rubins, 1978, p. 11) because often, after reading the Bible at length, he would explode in a fit of anger and throw the Bible at his wife. Such experiences caused Karen to develop a negative attitude toward religion and toward authority figures in general. After being treated by a physician when she was age 12, Karen decided she wanted to become a medical doctor. Her decision was supported by her mother and opposed by her father.

In 1906, at the age of 21, Karen entered the medical school at Freiberg, Germany. In October 1909, she married Oskar Horney, a lawyer with whom she eventually had three children. Horney completed her medical degree at the University of Berlin in 1913 where she had been an outstanding student. She then received psychoanalytic training at the Berlin Psychoanalytic Institute where she was psychoanalyzed first by Karl Abraham and then by Hans Sachs, two of the most prominent Freudian analysts at the time (and both members of Freud's inner circle). In 1918, at the age of 33, she became a practicing analyst; from that time until 1932, she taught at the Berlin Psychoanalytic Institute, besides having a private practice.

In 1923 the Horney marriage started to disintegrate, and at about the same time, Horney's brother died of pneumonia. These and other events triggered one of many bouts of depression that Horney experienced during her life, and on a family vacation she came close to committing suicide. Her marriage was becoming increasingly difficult, and in 1926 Horney and her three daughters moved into an apartment. It was not until 1936, however, that Horney of-

ficially filed for a divorce, and the divorce did not become final until 1939 (the year that Freud died).

In 1932 Horney accepted an invitation from the prominent analyst Franz Alexander to come to the United States to become an associate director of the Chicago Institute of Psychoanalysis. Two years later, she moved to New York where she trained analysts at the New York Psychoanalytic Institute and established a private practice. It was during this time that major differences between her views and those of the traditional Freudians became apparent. Because of these differences, the theses submitted by her students were routinely rejected, and eventually her teaching duties were restricted. In 1941 she resigned from the New York Psychoanalytic Institute; shortly afterward, she founded her own organization called the American Institute for Psychoanalysis where she continued to develop her own ideas until her death in 1952.

General disagreement with Freudian theory. Horney believed that Freudian notions such as unconscious sexual motivation, the Oedipal complex, and the division of the mind into an id, ego, and superego may have been appropriate in Freud's cultural setting and at his time in history but they had little relevance for problems experienced by people during the depression years in the United States. She found that the problems that her clients were having had to do with losing their jobs and not having enough money to pay the rent, buy food, or to provide their families with adequate medical care. She rarely found unconscious sexual conflicts to be the cause of a client's problem. Horney reached the conclusion that it was what a person experienced socially that determined whether he or she would have psychological problems and not the intrapsyche conflict (among the id, ego, and superego) that Freud had described. For Horney, the causes of mental illness were to be found in society and in social interactions, and it was therefore those factors that needed to be addressed in the therapeutic process.

Basic hostility and basic anxiety. Horney (1937) elaborated her view that psychological problems were caused by disturbed human relationships and that of these relationships those between the parent and the child were most important. She believed that every child had two basic needs: to be safe from pain, danger, and fear and to have biological needs satisfied. Two possibilities exist: The parents can consistently and lovingly satisfy the child's needs, or the parents can demonstrate indifference, inconsistency, or even hatred toward the child. If the former occurs, the child is well on its way to becoming a normal, healthy adult. If the latter occurs, the child is said to have experienced the **basic evil** and is well on its way to becoming a neurotic.

A child experiencing some form of the basic evil develops **basic hostility** toward the parents. Because the parent–child relationship is so basic to a child, the hostility that he or she feels develops into a worldview. That is, the world is viewed as a dangerous, unpredictable place. However, because the child is in no position to aggress toward the parents or the world, the basic hostility felt toward them must be repressed. When basic hostility is repressed, it becomes **basic anxiety**. Basic anxiety is the "all-pervading feeling of being lonely and helpless in a hostile world" (Horney, 1937, p. 89), and it is the prerequisite for the development of neurosis.

Adjustments to basic anxiety. Feeling alone and helpless in a hostile world, the person experiencing basic anxiety must find a way to cope with such feelings and such a world. Horney (1945) described three major adjustment patterns available to neurotic individuals, that is, those with basic anxiety.

One adjustment is **moving toward people**, thus becoming the *compliant type*. The compliant type seems to be saying, "If I give in, I shall not be hurt" (Horney, 1937, p. 97):

> In sum, this type needs to be liked, wanted, desired, loved; to feel accepted, welcomed, approved of, appreciated; to be needed, to be of importance to others, especially to one particular person; to be helped, protected, taken care of, guided (Horney, 1945, p. 51)

A second major adjustment pattern is **moving against people**, thus becoming the *hostile type*. The hostile type seems to be saying, "If I have power, no one can hurt me" (Horney, 1937, p. 98):

> Any situation or relationship is looked at from the standpoint of "What can I get out of it?"—whether it has to do with money, prestige, contacts, or ideas. The person himself is consciously or semiconsciously convinced that everyone acts this way, and so what counts is to do it more efficiently than the rest. (Horney, 1945, p. 65)

The third major adjustment pattern is **moving away from people**, thus becoming the *detached type*. The detached type seems to be saying, "If I withdraw, nothing can hurt me" (Horney, 1937, p. 99):

> What is crucial is their inner need to put emotional distance between themselves and others. More accurately, it is their conscious and unconscious determination not to get emotionally involved with others in any way, whether in love, fight, co-operation, or competition. They draw around themselves a kind of magic circle which no one may penetrate. (Horney, 1945, p. 75)

Horney believed that psychologically healthy individuals use all three adjustment patterns as circumstances warranted. Neurotics, however, use only one pattern and attempt to use it to deal with all of life's eventualities.

Feminine psychology. Horney profoundly disagreed with Freud's contention that **anatomy is destiny**—that is, with the contention that one's major personality traits are determined by gender. Again, for her, personality traits were determined more by cultural than by biological factors. As early as 1923, Horney began writing articles on how culture influences female personality development, and she continued to write such articles until 1937. These interesting articles have been compiled in *Feminine Psychology* (1923–1937/1967).

Horney agreed with Freud that women often feel inferior to men, but, to her, this feeling had nothing to do with penis envy. According to Horney, women are indeed inferior to men, but they are culturally, not biologically, inferior. When women appear to wish to be masculine, what they are really seeking is cultural equality. Because culture is a masculine product, one way to gain power in culture is to become masculine: "Our whole civilization is a masculine civilization. The State, the laws, morality, religion, and the sciences are the creation of men" (Horney, 1923–1937/1967, p. 55). Horney continued:

> The wish to be a man . . . may be the expression of a wish for all those qualities or privileges which in our culture are regarded as masculine, such as strength, courage, independence, success, sexual freedom, right to choose a partner. (1939, p. 108)

When Horney began treating male patients, she discovered that, if anything, men were envious of women's biology rather than the other way around:

> From the biological point of view woman has in motherhood, or in the capacity for motherhood, a quite indisputable and by no means negligible physiological superiority. This is most clearly reflected in the unconscious of the male psyche in the boy's intense envy of motherhood. . . . When one begins, as I did , to analyze men only after a fairly long experience of analyzing women, one receives a most surprising impression of the intensity of this envy of pregnancy, childbirth, and motherhood, as well as of the breasts and of the act of suckling. (1923–1937/1967, pp. 60–61)

Freud was, to a large extent, mystified by women and finally gave up trying to understand them. Perhaps for this reason, psychoanalysis has always seemed to understand men better than women and to view men more positively than women. According to Horney, this should not be surprising:

> The reason for this is obvious. Psychoanalysis is the creation of a male genius, and almost all those who have developed his ideas have been men. It is only right and reasonable that they should evolve more easily a masculine psychology and understand more of the development of men than of women. (1923–1937/1967, p. 54)

Furthermore, the picture that men paint of women is often more a product of the male imagination than of reality:

> Like all sciences and all valuations, the psychology of women has hitherto been considered only from the point of view of men. It is inevitable that the man's position of advantage should cause objective validity to be attributed to his subjective, affective relations to the woman . . . the psychology of women hitherto actually represents a deposit of the desires and disappointments of men. (Horney, 1923–1937/1967, p. 56)

Horney agreed with Freud on the importance of early childhood experiences and unconscious motivation but disagreed with his emphasis on biological motivation, stressing cultural motivation instead. As far as the therapeutic process was concerned, she used free association and dream analysis and believed transference and resistance provided important information. She was much more optimistic about the ability of people to change their personalities than was Freud, and, unlike Freud, she believed people could solve many of their own problems. Horney's book *Self-Analysis* (1942/1968) was one of the first self-help books in psychology, and it was controversial. One reason for the controversy was Freud's contention that even analysts had to be psychoanalyzed before they were qualified to treat patients.

In conclusion, we can say that Horney was strongly influenced by Freudian theory and she accepted much of it. However, she disagreed with almost every conclusion that Freud had reached about women, and, at the time, disagreeing with Freud took considerable courage:

> It must be realized that departing from Freudian dogma at the time was no easy matter. In fact, those who did so were excommunicated just as if they had violated religious dogma. Horney was excommunicated because she dared to contradict the master. . . . Horney learned from observing her father as a child

how devastating blind belief in religious dogma could be; perhaps that was one reason she decided not to let Freud go unchallenged. (Hergenhahn, 1990, p. 138)

One of the greatest tributes to Freud is the number of prominent individuals he influenced. In addition to Adler, Jung, and Horney, our sample of those theorists influenced by Freud could have included Melanie Klein (1882–1960), Harry Stack Sullivan (1892–1948), Erich Fromm (1900–1980), and Erik Erikson (b. 1902). Even if these individuals were covered, however, it would still constitute only a small sample of those influenced by Freud. Because his was the first comprehensive effort to explain personality and his was the first comprehensive attempt to understand and treat mentally ill individuals, all subsequent theories of personality and therapeutic techniques owe a debt to Freud.

SUMMARY

Although most, if not all, of the conceptions that would later characterize psychoanalysis were part of Freud's philosophical and scientific heritage, his historically significant accomplishment was to take those disparate conceptions and synthesize them into a comprehensive theory of personality. Although Freud was trained in the tradition of positivistic physiology and originally tried to explain hysteria as a physiological problem, events led him to attempt a psychological explanation of hysteria instead. Freud learned from Breuer that when Breuer's patient Anna O. was totally relaxed or hypnotized and then asked to remember the circumstances under which one of her many symptoms had first occurred, the symptom would at least temporarily disappear. This type of treatment was called the cathartic method. Thus, Freud learned that some ideas were pathogenic, or capable of causing physical disorders. Freud also learned from Breuer's work with Anna O. that the therapist was sometimes responded to as if he were a relevant person in the patient's life, a process called transference. Sometimes the therapist also became emotionally involved with a patient, a process called countertransference. *Studies on Hysteria* (1895/1955), the book that Freud coauthored with Breuer, is usually taken as the formal beginning of the school of psychoanalysis. From his visit with Charcot, Freud learned that hysteria was a serious disorder that occurred in both males and females and that it was probably caused by sexual factors.

The year before his visit with Charcot, Freud began experimenting with cocaine. At first, he viewed it as a "magical substance" that could be used to cure a wide variety of ailments. It was soon realized, however, that cocaine was highly addictive and had a number of negative side effects. Freud's medical career suffered considerably because of close association with and strong endorsement of the drug. Although Freud escaped personal addiction to cocaine, he was addicted to nicotine, and it is widely believed that his lifelong habit of smoking about 20 cigars a day caused the cancer of the mouth and jaw that he developed late in life.

When Freud began treating hysterical patients, he used hypnosis but found that he could not hypnotize some patients and the ones he could hypnotize received only temporary relief from their symptoms. He also found that patients often refused to believe what they had revealed under hypnosis and therefore could not benefit from a rational discussion of previously repressed material. After experimenting with various other techniques, Freud finally settled on free association, whereby he encouraged his patients to say whatever came to their minds without inhibiting any thoughts. By analyzing a patient's symptoms and by carefully scrutinizing a patient's free associations, Freud hoped to discover the repressed memories responsible for a patient's disorder. Because these pathogenic thoughts provoked anxiety, patients resisted allowing them to enter consciousness. Freud originally believed that hysteria resulted from a childhood sexual seduction but later concluded that the seductions he had discovered were usually patient fantasies. Freud's decision to abandon his seduction theory is controversial because evidence suggests that his decision was based on questionable, personal motives rather than on scientific evidence.

During his self-analysis, Freud found that dreams contained the same clues concerning the origins of a psychological problem as did physical symptoms or free associations. He distinguished between the manifest content of a dream, or what the dream appeared to be about, and the latent content, or what the dream was actually about.

Freud believed that the latent content represented wish fulfillments that a person could not entertain consciously without experiencing anxiety. Dream work disguised the true meaning of a dream. Examples of dream work include condensation, in which several things from a person's life are condensed into one symbol, and displacement, in which a person dreams about something symbolically related to an anxiety-provoking object, person, or event instead of dreaming about whatever it is that actually provokes the anxiety. During his self-analysis, Freud discovered the Oedipus complex, which is characterized by a male child's sexual attraction to his mother and hostility toward his father. Freud believed that the Oedipus complex was universal among male children.

According to Freud, the adult mind consisted of an id, an ego, and a superego. The id is entirely unconscious and demands immediate gratification; it is therefore said to be governed by the pleasure principle. The id also contains all instincts and the energy associated with instincts. Every instinct has a source, which is a bodily deficiency of some type; an aim of removing the deficiency; an object, which is anything that can be used to remove the deficiency; and an impetus, which is a driving force whose strength is determined by the magnitude of the deficiency. To satisfy needs, the id has at its disposal only the primary processes of reflex action and wish fulfillment. The ego's job is to find real objects in the environment that can satisfy needs; it is therefore said to be governed by the reality principle. The realistic processes of the ego are referred to as secondary in order to distinguish them from the irrational primary processes of the id. The third component of the mind is the superego, which consists of the conscience, or the internalization of the experiences for which a child had been punished, and the ego-ideal, or the internalization of the experiences for which a child had been rewarded.

The ego's job is to find ways of effectively satisfying needs without violating the values of the superego. When such a way is found, the ego invests energy in it, a process called cathexis. If an available way to satisfy a need violates a person's values, energy is expended to inhibit its utilization, in which case an anticathexis occurs. When an anticathexis occurs, the person displaces the anxiety-provoking object or event to one that does not cause anxiety. Freud distinguished between life instincts called eros and a death instinct called thanatos. Freud used the concept of the death instinct to explain such things as suicide, masochism, murder, and general aggression.

Freud distinguished among objective anxiety, the fear of environmental events; neurotic anxiety, the feeling that one is about to be overwhelmed by one's id; and moral anxiety, the feeling caused by violating one or more internalized values. One of the major jobs of the ego is to reduce or eliminate anxiety; to accomplish this, the ego employs the ego defense mechanisms, which operate on the unconscious level and distort reality. All defense mechanisms depend on repression, which is the holding of disturbing thoughts in the unconscious. Other ego defense mechanisms are displacement, sublimation, projection, identification, rationalization, and reaction formation.

During the psychosexual stages of development, the erogenous zone, or the area of the body associated with the greatest amount of pleasure, changes. Freud named the stages of development in terms of their erogenous zones. During the oral stage, either overgratification or undergratification of the oral needs results in a fixation, which in turn causes the individual to become either an oral-incorporative or an oral-sadistic character. Fixation during the anal stage results in the adult being either an anal-expulsive or an anal-retentive character. During the phallic stage, the Oedipus and Electra complexes occur. The Oedipus complex causes the male child to experience castration anxiety, and the Electra complex causes the female child to experience penis envy. The latency stage is characterized by repression of sexual desires and much sublimation. During the genital stage, the person emerges possessing the personality traits that experiences during the preceding stages have molded.

Freud found considerable evidence for his theory in everyday life. He felt that forgetting, losing things, accidents, and slips of the tongue were often unconsciously motivated. He also thought jokes provided information about repressed experience because people tended to find only anxiety-provoking material humorous. Freud felt that although we shared the instinctual makeup of other animals, humans had the capacity to understand and harness instinctual impulses by exercising rational thought. To come to grips with the unconscious mind through rationality, however, was an extremely difficult process, and for that reason, Freud was not optimistic that rationalism would prevail over our animal nature. Freud was especially critical of religion, believing that it was an illusion that kept people functioning on an infantile level. His hope was that people would embrace the principles of science, thereby becoming more objective about themselves and the world.

In recent years, there have been efforts to correct several misconceptions about Freud and psychoanalysis. Historians such as Ellenberger and Sulloway have shown that Freud was not the courageous, innovative hero that he and his followers portrayed him to be. The facts seem to be that he did not suffer nearly the amount of anti-Semitism that he claimed, he was not overly discriminated against by the medical establishment, and his ideas were not as original as he and his followers claimed. Freud has also been criticized for using data from his patients to develop and validate his theory, using nebulous terms that make measurement difficult or impossible, being intolerant of criticism, overemphasizing sexual motivation, and creating a method of psychotherapy that is too long and costly to be useful to most troubled people. Also, Freud's theory violates Popper's principle of falsifiability. Among Freud's contributions are the vast expansion of psychology's domain, a new method of psychotherapy, and a theory that explains much normal as well as abnormal behavior and is relevant to almost every aspect of human existence.

Jung, an early follower of Freud, eventually broke with him because of Freud's emphasis on sexual motivation. Jung saw the libido as a pool of energy that could be used for positive growth throughout one's lifetime rather than as only sexual energy, as Freud had seen it. Jung distinguished between the personal unconscious, which consisted of experiences from one's lifetime of which a person was not conscious, and the collective unconscious, which represented the recording of universal human experience through the eons of human history. According to Jung, the collective unconscious contained archetypes, or predispositions, to respond emotionally to certain experiences in one's life. Among the more fully developed archetypes are the persona, the anima, the animus, the shadow, and the self. Jung distinguished between the attitudes of introversion and extroversion. Jung stressed the importance of middle age in personality development because before self-actualization could occur the individuation process had to take place. Individuation involves discovering the various components of personality and then giving them expression. It is a long, complicated process that usually takes place during childhood, adolescence, and early adulthood. Jung felt that human behavior was both pushed by the past and the present (causality) and pulled by the future (teleology). He also believed that synchronicity, or meaningful coincidence, played a major role in determining one's course of life. Jung assumed that dreams gave expression to the parts of the personality that were not given adequate expression in one's life. Dream analysis, then, could be used to determine which aspects of the personality were adequately developed and which were not.

Like Jung, Adler was an early follower of Freud, but for several reasons, he went his own way. The theory Adler developed was distinctly different from the theories of both Freud and Jung. Early in his career, Adler noted that a person suffering from some physical disability could either compensate for the disability by strengthening other abilities or, by overcompensating, turn the disability into a strength. Later, he discovered that all humans began life feeling inferior because of infant helplessness. Adler believed that most people developed a lifestyle that allowed them to gain power or approach perfection and thereby overcome their feelings of inferiority. Some people, however, were overwhelmed by their feelings of inferiority and developed an inferiority complex. According to Adler, healthy lifestyles involved a significant amount of social interest, whereas mistaken lifestyles did not. The creative self gave people at least some control over their personal destinies.

Horney was trained as a Freudian analyst but soon developed her own theory. She believed that psychological problems resulted more from societal conditions and interpersonal relationships than from sexual conflicts as the Freudians maintained. Among interpersonal relationships, that between parent and child is most important. Horney believed that there were two types of parent–child relationships: one that consistently and lovingly satisfied the child's biological and safety needs and one that frustrated those needs. Horney referred to the latter relationship as the basic evil, and for her, it was the seed from which neurosis grew. The basic evil causes the child to feel basic hostility toward the parents and the world, but this hostility must be repressed because of the child's helplessness. When basic hostility is repressed, it becomes basic anxiety, which is the feeling of being alone and helpless in a hostile world. A child experiencing basic anxiety typically uses one of three major adjustment patterns with which to embrace reality: Moving toward people emphasizes love, moving against people emphasizes hostility, and moving away from people emphasizes withdrawal. Normal people use all three adjustment techniques as they are required, whereas neurotics attempt to cope with all of life's experiences using just one.

Horney disagreed with Freud's contention that anatomy is destiny, saying instead that gender differences in personality are culturally determined. She said that women often feel inferior to men because they are often culturally inferior. In her practice, Horney found that it was males who were envious of female biology rather than the reverse. Horney contended that psychoanalysis seemed more appropriate and complimentary to males because it was created by males. Although in her practice of psychoanalysis Horney used a number of Freudian concepts and techniques, she was more optimistic in her prognosis for personality change than was Freud. Also, unlike Freud, she believed that many individuals could solve their own psychological problems and wrote a book designed to help them in their effort.

DISCUSSION QUESTIONS

1. Provide evidence that many components of what was to become psychoanalysis were part of Freud's philosophical or scientific heritage.

2. Describe the cocaine episode in Freud's career.

3. Briefly define the terms *pathogenic idea, catharsis, transference,* and *countertransference.*

4. What was the significance of Freud's visit with Charcot for the development of psychoanalysis?

5. What did Freud learn from Liébeault and Bernheim at the Nancy school of hypnosis that influenced the development of psychoanalysis?

6. Discuss the importance of resistance in psychoanalysis.

7. What did Freud mean when he said that *true* psychoanalysis began only after hypnosis had been discarded?

8. What was Freud's seduction theory? Describe the controversy that surrounds Freud's decision to abandon his seduction theory.

9. Explain the significance of dream analysis for Freud. Why did he originally use it? What is the difference between the manifest and the latent content of a dream? What is meant by dream work?

10. What is the Oedipus complex, and what is its significance in Freud's theory?

11. Define the term *parapraxes* and show its importance to Freud's contention that much everyday behavior is unconsciously motivated.

12. What is meant by saying that a behavioral or psychological act is overdetermined?

13. Describe the nature of the id. Of what does the id consist? What principle governs it? What means does it have for satisfying its needs?

14. Differentiate between primary and secondary processes.

15. Give an example showing the interactions among the id, the ego, and the superego.

16. Explain how the superego develops and controls behavior. Include in your answer definitions of conscience and ego-ideal.

17. Make the case that Freud's theory accepted Lamarck's theory of evolution, that is, the inheritance of acquired characteristics.

18. Why did Freud feel the need to postulate the existence of a death instinct? What types of behavior did this instinct explain?

19. Define and give examples of objective, neurotic, and moral anxiety.

20. Define and give an example of each of the following ego defense mechanisms: repression, displacement, sublimation, projection, identification, rationalization, and reaction formation.

21. Explain what Freud meant when he said that civilization was built on sublimation.

22. List, in order, the psychosexual stages of development. Describe what would cause a fixation at a particular stage. Give an example of an adult personality type that can result from an earlier fixation.

23. What was Freud's view of human nature? Religion? What was his hope for humankind?

24. What are the major Freudian myths that are currently being revealed and corrected by such individuals as Ellenberger and Sulloway?

25. List the major criticisms of Freud's theory.

26. List the major contributions of Freud's theory.

27. Define the following terms from Jung's theory: *collective unconscious, archetype, persona, anima, animus, shadow,* and *self.*

28. Describe the ways that Jung believed archetypes influence an individual's life.

29. What did Jung mean by self-actualization?

30. For Jung, why was middle age so important for personality development? Include in your answer a discussion of the process of individuation.

31. Compare Jung's approach to dream analysis with Freud's.

32. Summarize the criticisms and contributions of Jung's theory.

33. Summarize the main differences between Freud's and Adler's theories of personality.

34. Define the following terms from Adler's theory: *compensation, overcompensation, feelings of inferiority, inferiority complex, lifestyle, social interest, mistaken lifestyle,* and *creative self.*

35. Define the following terms from Horney's theory: *basic evil*, *basic hostility*, and *basic anxiety*.

36. According to Horney, what were the three major adjustment patterns that neurotics could use while interacting with people? How did the way normal people use these patterns differ from the way neurotics use them?

37. Why, according to Horney, do women sometimes feel inferior to men?

38. Did Horney agree with Freud's contention that anatomy is destiny? Explain.

39. How did Horney and Freud differ in their explanations of the origins of psychological problems? On the prognosis for personality change? On the belief in peoples' ability to solve their own psychological problems?

SUGGESTIONS FOR FURTHER READING

Ellenberger, H. F. (1970). *The discovery of the unconscious: The history and evolution of dynamic psychiatry.* New York: Basic Books.
Already considered a classic, this large book (932 pages) is a must for any serious student of the history of the concept of the unconscious and of dynamic psychiatry.

Ellenberger, H. F. (1972). The study of "Anna O": A critical review with new data. *Journal of the History of the Behavioral Sciences, 8,* 267–279.
Through some ingenious detective work, Ellenberger discovered what happened to Bertha Pappenheim (Anna O.) after Breuer had terminated his treatment of her in 1882. Contrary to the accounts of Breuer, Freud, and Freud's biographer Ernest Jones, Bertha was anything but cured by Breuer's cathartic technique. On the contrary, she entered Bellevue Sanatorium where she received heavy dosages of morphine. What happened to Bertha between the time she left the sanatorium and when she emerged as a prominent social worker, who was passionately concerned with the emancipation of women and the care of orphan children, remains largely unknown.

Freud, S. (1961a). *The future of an illusion.* New York: Norton. (Original work published 1927)
This book is only 56 pages in length and, like most of Freud's works, is very readable. Freud claims that religion keeps humans functioning at an infantile level, and religious illusions must be replaced by scientific facts if humans are ever to live rational lives. (Available in paperback.)

Freud, S. (1961b). *Civilization and its discontents.* New York: Norton. (Original work published 1930)
In this small book (104 pages), Freud continues his attack on religion as an infantile illusion and discusses the many instinctual sacrifices and compromises that individual humans must make to live in civilized societies. Civilization and biological frustration, he says, go hand-in-hand. (Available in paperback.)

Hannah, B. (1976). *Jung, his life and work: A biographical memoir.* New York: Putnam.
A Jungian analyst and a close friend of Jung's herself, Hannah presents a sympathetic biography of Jung, portraying him as brilliant and a sensitive humanitarian. Hannah strongly denies that Jung was an anti-Semite and a pro-Nazi as had been claimed by other Jung biographers (e.g., see Stern, 1976, in this list of suggested readings).

Horney, K. (1967). *Feminine psychology.* New York: Norton. (Original works published 1923–1937)
It is in the papers compiled in this book that Horney disagrees most strongly with the Freudian view of women. Chapters include "On the Genesis of the Castration Complex in Women," "The Flight from Womanhood," "Inhibited Femininity," "Premenstrual Tension," "The Distrust Between the Sexes," "Problems of Marriage," "The Overvaluation of Love," and "The Neurotic Need for Love."

Horney, K. (1968). *Self-analysis.* New York: Norton. (Original work published 1942)
Contrary to the orthodox Freudian position, Horney believed that many individuals could solve their own psychological problems, and this book was written to help them do so. (Available in paperback.)

Jung, C. G. (1933). *Modern man in search of a soul.* New York: Harcourt Brace Jovanovich.
This is a good introduction to many of Jung's most basic ideas. Chapters include "Dream Analysis in Its Practical Application," "Problems of Modern Psychotherapy," "A Psychological Theory of Types," "The Stages of Life," "Archaic Man," "Psychology and Literature," "The Basic Postulations of Analytical Psychology," "The Spiritual Problem of Modern Man," and "Psychotherapists or the Clergy." (Available in paperback.)

Rubins, J. L. (1978). *Karen Horney: Gentle rebel of psychoanalysis.* New York: Dial.
Rubins gives a most interesting account of Horney's eventful and influential life.

Stern, P. J. (1976). *C. G. Jung: The haunted prophet.* New York: Dell.
This is a critical biography of Jung that portrays him as a prepsychotic (if not actually psychotic) with anti-Semitic and pro-Nazi leanings. (Available in paperback.)

Storr, A. (1989). *Freud.* Oxford, England: Oxford University Press.
This is a brief, readable account of Freud's life and his ideas. Chapters include "Freud's Life and Character"; "Free Association, Dreams, and Transference"; "Ego,

Superego, and Id"; "Aggression, Depression, and Paranoia"; "Jokes and the Psychopathology of Everyday Life"; "Art and Literature"; "Culture and Religion"; "Psychoanalysis Today"; and "The Appeal of Psychoanalysis." (Available in paperback.)

Sulloway, F. J. (1979). *Freud, biologist of the mind: Beyond the psychoanalytic legend.* New York: Basic Books.

Like Ellenberger (1972), Sulloway attempts to demythologize accounts of Freud and his theory. Sulloway

contends that there is enough greatness in Freud the man and in psychoanalysis without needing to incorrectly portray Freud as a courageous, struggling hero or to portray psychoanalysis as a version of psychology miraculously created single-handedly by Freud. This high-level book presents facts that often contradict the Freudian legend; although at times it is difficult reading, it is well worth the effort.

GLOSSARY

Adler, Alfred (1870–1937) An early follower of Freud who left the Freudian camp and created his own theory of personality, which emphasized the development of a lifestyle as a means of overcoming feelings of inferiority.

Anal character The personality type that results from fixation on the anal stage of development. If fixation occurs early in the anal stage, the person becomes an anal-expulsive character; such a person gives freely of himself or herself. If fixation occurs late in the anal stage, the person develops an anal-retentive character; such a person tends to be orderly and stingy.

Anal stage of development The second stage of development, which lasts through the second year of life. During the anal stage, the anus–buttocks region of the body constitutes the erogenous zone.

Anatomy is destiny The Freudian contention that a number of major personality characteristics are determined by one's gender.

Anima The archetype that provides the female part of the male personality.

Animus The archetype that provides the male part of the female personality.

Anticathexis The expenditure of psychic energy to prevent the association between needs and anxiety-provoking objects or events.

Anxiety The feeling of impending danger. Freud distinguished three types of anxiety: objective anxiety, which is caused by a physical danger; neurotic anxiety, which is caused by the feeling that one is going to be overwhelmed by his or her id; and moral anxiety, which is caused by violating one or more values internalized in the superego.

Archetype An inherited predisposition to respond emotionally to certain categories of experience.

Basic anxiety According to Horney, the feeling of being alone and helpless in a hostile world that a child experiences when he or she represses basic hostility. (*See also* **Basic hostility**.)

Basic evil Anything that parents do to frustrate the basic needs of their child and thus undermine the child's feeling of security.

Basic hostility According to Horney, the feeling of anger that a child experiences when he or she experiences the basic evil. (*See also* **Basic evil**.)

Breuer, Joseph (1842–1925) The person Freud credited with the founding of psychoanalysis. Breuer

discovered that when the memory of a traumatic event was recalled under deep relaxation or hypnosis, there was a release of emotional energy (catharsis) and the symptoms caused by the repressed memory were relieved.

Castration anxiety The fear a male child has during the phallic stage of development that his father is going to castrate him.

Cathartic method The alleviation of hysterical symptoms by allowing the pathogenic ideas to be expressed consciously.

Cathexis The investment of psychic energy in things that satisfy a person's needs.

Collective unconscious Jung's term for the part of the unconscious mind that reflects universal human experience through the ages. For Jung, the collective unconscious was the most powerful component of the personality.

Compensation According to Adler, the making up for a weakness by developing strengths in other areas.

Condensation The type of dream work that causes several people, objects, or events to be condensed into one dream symbol.

Conflict According to Freud, the simultaneous tendency both to approach and avoid the same object, event, or person.

Conscience The part of the superego consisting of those internalized experiences for which a child has been consistently punished.

Countertransference The process by which a therapist becomes emotionally involved with a patient.

Creative self According to Adler, the component of the personality that provides humans with the freedom to choose their own destinies.

Death instinct The instinct that has death as its goal. (Sometimes called the *death wish*.)

Displacement The ego defense mechanism by which a goal that does not provoke anxiety is substituted for one that does. Also, the type of dream work that causes the dreamer to dream of something symbolically related to anxiety-provoking events rather than dreaming about the anxiety-provoking events themselves.

Dream analysis A major tool that Freud used in studying the contents of the unconscious mind. Freud thought that the symbols dreams contained could yield information about repressed memories just as hysterical symptoms could. For Jung, dreams provided a mechanism by which inhibited parts of the psyche might be given expression. Therefore, for Jung, dream analysis indicated which aspects of the psyche were underdeveloped.

Dream work The mechanism that distorts the meaning of a dream, thereby making it more tolerable to the dreamer. (*See also* **Condensation** and **Displacement**.)

Ego The component of the personality that is responsible for locating events in the environment that will satisfy the needs of the id without violating the values of the superego.

Ego defense mechanisms Learned, unconscious strategies available to the ego for distorting the anxiety-provoking aspects of reality, thus making them more tolerable.

Ego-ideal The part of the superego consisting of the internalized experiences for which a child has been consistently rewarded.

Electra complex The female counterpart of the male's Oedipus complex. In his later theorizing, Freud abandoned this term, preferring *castration complex* instead.

Erogenous zone The area of the body that is the source of greatest pleasure during a particular stage of development.

Eros The term that Freud used to refer to the life instincts collectively.

Extroversion The attitude toward life that is characterized by gregariousness and a willingness to take risks.

Feelings of inferiority According to Adler, those feelings that all humans try to escape by becoming powerful or superior.

Fixation Arrested development that results from the undergratification or overgratification of a need during one of the psychosexual stages of development.

Free association Freud's major tool for studying the contents of the unconscious mind. With free association, a patient is encouraged to express freely everything that comes to his or her mind.

Freud, Sigmund (1856–1939) The founder of psychoanalysis, a school of psychology that stresses the conflict between the animalistic impulses possessed by humans and the human desire to live in a civilized society.

Genital stage of development The final stage of development, which lasts from puberty to the end of one's life.

Horney, Karen (1885–1952) Trained in the Freudian tradition, she later broke away from the Freudians and created her own theory of mental disorders that emphasized cultural rather than biological (e.g., sexual) causes.

Id According to Freud, the powerful, entirely unconscious portion of the personality that contains all instincts and is therefore the driving force for the entire personality.

Identification The ego defense mechanism whereby people enhance the feelings they have about themselves by affiliating themselves with people or organizations they perceive to be illustrious.

Individuation According to Jung, the process of discovering and giving expression to the various components of the personality.

Inferiority complex According to Adler, the condition one experiences when overwhelmed by feelings of inferiority instead of being motivated toward success by those feelings.

Instinct According to Freud, the motivational force behind personality. Each instinct has a source, which is a bodily deficiency of some type; an aim of removing the deficiency; an object, which is anything capable of removing the deficiency; and an impetus, which is a driving force whose strength is determined by the magnitude of the deficiency. (*See also* **Life instinct** and **Death instinct**.)

Introversion The attitude toward life that is characterized by social isolation and an introspective nature.

Jung, Carl (1875–1961) An early follower of Freud who finally broke with him because of Freud's emphasis on sexual motivation. Jung eventually developed his own theory, which emphasized the collective unconscious and self-actualization.

Latency stage of development The fourth stage of development, which occurs from about the sixth year of life until puberty.

Latent content of a dream What a dream is *actually* about.

Libido For Freud, the collective energy associated with the life instincts. For Jung, the creative life force that provides the energy for personal growth.

Life instincts The instincts that have as their goal the sustaining of life.

Lifestyle According to Adler, the way of life that a person chooses in order to overcome feelings of inferiority.

Manifest content of a dream What a dream *appears* to be about.

Mistaken lifestyle According to Adler, any lifestyle lacking sufficient social interest.

Moving against people The neurotic adjustment pattern suggested by Horney by which a person adjusts to a world perceived as hostile by gaining power over people and events.

Moving away from people The neurotic adjustment pattern suggested by Horney by which a person adjusts to a world perceived as hostile by creating a distance between himself or herself and the people and events in that world.

Moving toward people The neurotic adjustment pattern suggested by Horney by which a person adjusts to a world perceived as hostile by being compliant.

Oedipus complex The tendency for a male child, between about the ages of three and five, to be attracted to his mother and hostile toward his father.

Oral character The personality type that results from a fixation on the oral stage of development. If fixation occurs early in the oral stage, the person develops an oral-incorporative character; such a person stresses taking things into his or her body, as in eating, drinking, or smoking. If fixation occurs late in the oral stage, the person develops an oral-sadistic character; such a person is generally aggressive.

Oral stage of development The first stage of development, which occurs during the first year of life. During this time, the mouth, lips, and tongue constitute the erogenous zone.

Overcompensation According to Adler, the conversion of a weakness into a strength.

Overdetermination Freud's belief that behavioral and psychological phenomena were often not determined by one cause but several.

Parapraxes Relatively minor errors in everyday living such as losing and forgetting things, slips of the tongue, mistakes in writing, and small accidents. Freud believed that such errors were often unconsciously motivated.

Pathogenic ideas Ideas that cause physical disorders.

Penis envy According to Freud, the jealousy that results from a female's realization that her father has a penis and she does not.

Persona The archetype that causes people to offer only part of their personality to the public and thus to keep the larger part hidden.

Personal unconscious Jung's term for the place where material from one's lifetime of which one is currently not conscious resides.

Phallic stage of development The third stage of development, which occurs from about the third year of life through about the fifth year. During this time, the genital region of the body is the erogenous zone.

Pleasure principle The principle governing the id, causing the demand for immediate gratification of its needs.

Preconscious The term Freud used in his early theorizing to describe material of which we were not conscious but of which we could become conscious with relative ease.

Pressure technique A technique that Freud used early in his career. It involved placing his hand on a patient's forehead as a means of overcoming the patient's resistance.

Primary processes Activities that are independent of experience and in which the id engages to satisfy needs. Reflex action and wish fulfillment are primary processes.

Projection The ego defense mechanism by which one attributes an anxiety-provoking thought to someone or something other than one's self.

Rationalization The ego defense mechanism by which one gives a logical, rational but false reason for a shortcoming rather than the real reason.

Reaction formation The ego defense mechanism by which one does the opposite of what one really wants to do because doing what one really wants to do would cause anxiety.

Reality principle The principle governing the ego. The reality principle brings a person into contact with the real environmental objects that will satisfy his or her needs.

Reflex action The genetically determined response mechanisms that the id can employ to remove various discomforts.

Repression The active holding of traumatic memories in the unconscious mind because pondering them consciously would cause anxiety.

Resistance The tendency for patients to inhibit the recollection of traumatic experiences.

Secondary processes Those processes the ego employs in dealing effectively with the physical environment.

Seduction theory Freud's contention that hysteria was caused by a sexual attack: Someone close or related to the hysteric patient had attacked him or her when the patient was a young child. Freud later concluded that as a child the patient had imagined the attack.

Self The archetype that causes people to seek unity or harmony among the various elements of their personalities.

Self-actualization According to Jung, the harmonious blending of all aspects of the personality.

Shadow The archetype that gives humans the characteristics of nonhuman animals—for example, aggression.

Social interest The concern for other humans and for society that Adler believed characterized a healthy lifestyle.

Studies on Hysteria The book Breuer and Freud published in 1895 that is usually viewed as marking the formal beginning of the school of psychoanalysis.

Sublimation The ego defense mechanism that displaces a sexual goal with a nonsexual one. According to Freud, civilization depends on sublimation.

Superego The internalized values that act as a guide for a person's conduct. If a person acts in accordance with these values, he or she feels good; if a person violates one or more of these values, he or she feels anxious or guilty. (*See also* **Conscience** and **Ego-ideal**.)

Synchronicity According to Jung, fortuitous experiences that can significantly change the course of a person's life.

Teleology The doctrine that states that at least some human behavior is purposive, that is, directed to the attainment of future goals.

Thanatos The name given to the death instinct.

Transference The process by which a patient responds to the therapist as if the therapist were a relevant person in the patient's life.

Unconscious motivation The causes of our behavior of which we are unaware.

Wish fulfillment In an effort to satisfy bodily needs, the id conjures up images of objects or events that will satisfy those needs. For example, a hungry person thinks of food-related objects.

CHAPTER 17

Humanistic (Third-Force) Psychology

THE MIND, THE BODY, AND THE SPIRIT

Generally speaking, human nature can be divided into three major components: the mind (our intellect), the body (our biological makeup), and the spirit (our emotional makeup). Different philosophies and, more recently, schools of psychology have tended to emphasize one of these aspects at the expense of the others. Which philosophy or school of psychology prevailed seemed to be determined largely by the *Zeitgeist*. In human history, rationalistic philosophies, which emphasize the mind, and empirical philosophies, which emphasize the body, have tended to be embraced during relatively tranquil times—or, in troubled times, by individuals relatively immune to strife. During troubled times, tendency has been to embrace philosophies that emphasize human emotions—or, in relatively good times, by individuals who were less fortunate. Examples include the following: (1) The rationalistic Apollonian religion appealed to the ancient Greek aristocracy, and the mysterious, emotion-laden Dionysian religion appealed to the less fortunate of the time. (2) Following the collapse of the Greek city-states after the Peloponnesian War, Greek rationalistic philosophy was gradually displaced by Cynicism, Skepticism, Stoicism, and, eventually, Christianity. (3) Following the Renaissance, the philosophies of rationalism and empiricism reemerged, and systems of government were based on them; when these governments failed, the philosophies on which they were based were rejected and replaced by romanticism and existentialism. (4) In modern times, the devastation

of the Second World War created a renewed interest in existential philosophy, which emphasized a search for meaning in a meaningless world.

The decade of the 1960s was a troubled time in the United States. There was increased involvement in the unpopular Vietnam War and its corresponding antiwar movement; Martin Luther King, Jr., John Fitzgerald Kennedy, and Robert Kennedy were assassinated; and violent, racial protests occurred in a number of major cities. "Hippies" were in open rebellion against the values of their parents and their nation. Like the ancient Skeptics, they found little worth believing in, and like the ancient Cynics, they dropped out of society and returned to a simple, natural life. This Age of Aquarius was clearly not a time when rational or empirical philosophies were appealing.

During the 1920s and 1930s, the schools of structuralism, functionalism, behaviorism, Gestalt psychology, and psychoanalysis coexisted and pursued their respective goals. By the mid-20th century, however, structuralism had disappeared as a school, and functionalism and Gestalt psychology had lost their distinctiveness as schools by being assimilated into other viewpoints. In the 1950s and early 1960s, only behaviorism and psychoanalysis remained as influential, intact schools of thought. In the troubled times described above, the knowledge of humans provided by behaviorism and psychoanalysis was seen as incomplete, distorted, or both. What was needed was a new view of psychology, one that emphasized neither the mind nor the body but the human spirit.

In the early 1960s, a group of psychologists

headed by Abraham Maslow started a movement referred to as **third-force psychology**. These psychologists claimed that the other two forces in psychology, behaviorism and psychoanalysis, neglected a number of important human attributes. They said that by applying the techniques used by the natural sciences to the study of humans, behaviorism likened humans to robots, lower animals, or computers. For the behaviorist, there was nothing unique about humans. The major argument against psychoanalysis was that it concentrated mainly on emotionally disturbed people and on developing techniques for making abnormal people normal. What was missing, according to third-force psychologists, was information that would help already healthy individuals become healthier, that is, to reach their full potential. What was needed was a model of humans that emphasized their uniqueness and their positive aspects rather than their negative aspects, and it was this type of model that third-force psychologists attempted to provide.

Although third-force psychology became very popular during the 1960s and 1970s, its popularity began to wane in the 1980s and continues to do so. Like behaviorism and psychoanalysis, however, third-force psychology remains highly influential in contemporary psychology. Third-force psychology contrasts vividly with most other types because it does not assume determinism in explaining human behavior. Rather, it assumes that humans are free to choose their own type of existence. Instead of attributing the causes of behavior to stimuli, drive states, genetics, or early experience, third-force psychologists claim that the most important cause of behavior is **subjective reality**. Because these psychologists do not assume determinism, they are not scientists in the traditional sense, and they make no apology for that. Science in its present form, they say, is not equipped to study, explain, or understand human nature. A new science is needed, a human science. A human science would not study humans as the physical sciences study physical objects. Rather, a human science would study humans as aware, choosing, valuing, emotional, and unique beings in the universe. Traditional science does not do this and must therefore be rejected.

ANTECEDENTS OF THIRD-FORCE PSYCHOLOGY

Like almost everything else in modern psychology, third-force psychology is not new. It can be traced to the philosophies of romanticism and existentialism, which in turn can be traced to the early Greeks. In chapter 7, we saw that the romantics (such as Rousseau) insisted that humans were more than machines, which was how the empiricists were describing them, and more than the logical, rational beings, which was how the rationalists were describing them. The romantics distrusted reason, religious dogma, science, and societal laws as guides for human conduct. For them, the only valid guide for a person's behavior was that person's honest feelings. The romantics (especially Rousseau) believed that humans were naturally good and gregarious, and if given freedom they would become happy, fulfilled, and social-minded. That is, given freedom, people would do what was best for themselves and for other people. If people acted in self-destructive or antisocial ways, it was because their natural impulses had been interfered with by societal forces. People can never be bad, but social systems can be and often are. Also in chapter 7, we saw that the existentialists (such as Kierkegaard and Nietzsche) emphasized the importance of meaning in human existence and the human ability to choose that meaning; this, too, was contrary to the philosophies of empiricism and rationalism. For Kierkegaard, subjectivity was truth. That is, it is a person's beliefs that guide his or her life and determine the nature of his or her existence. Truth was not something external to the person waiting to be discovered by logical, rational thought processes; it was inside each person and was, in fact, created by each person. According to Nietzsche, God was dead, and therefore humans were on their own.

People could take two approaches to life: They could accept conventional morality as guides for living, thus participating in herd conformity; or they could experiment with beliefs, values, and life and arrive at their own truths and morality and thus become supermen. Nietzsche clearly encouraged people to the latter.

Third-force psychology combines the philosophies of romanticism and existentialism, and this combination is called humanistic psychology. Third-force and humanistic psychology, then, are the same, but humanistic psychology has become the preferred label. In applying this label, however, it is important not to confuse the term *humanistic* with the terms *human, humane,* or *humanitarian*:

> The frequent confusion of the terms *human, humane,* and *humanistic* indicates that many do not clearly understand the meaning of the humanistic stance. To qualify as humanistic, it is not enough to concern human beings. Playing, working, building, traveling, organizing, are all *human* activities. This, however, does not make them humanistic. Similarly, when these activities are performed, for instance, for charitable or philanthropic purposes, they are then raised to a humane or *humanitarian* status, which may be of vital importance but still does not make them humanistic. For an endeavor or a viewpoint to qualify properly as humanistic, it must imply and focus upon a certain concept of man—a concept that recognizes his status as a person, irreducible to more elementary levels, and his unique worth as a being potentially capable of autonomous judgment and action. A pertinent example of the difference between the humane and the humanistic outlook is found in the case of behavior control that relies entirely upon positive reinforcement. Such an approach is humane (or humanitarian), since it implements generous and compassionate attitudes. But it is not humanistic, because the rationale behind systematic behavior modification by purely external forces is incompatible with a concept of man as a self-purposive and proactive, rather than merely reactive, being.

The focus of humanistic psychology is upon the specificity of man, upon that which sets him apart from all other species. It differs from other psychologies because it views man not solely as a biological organism modified by experience and culture but as a person, a symbolic entity capable of pondering his existence, of lending it meaning and direction. (Kinget, 1975, p. v)

Although it is true that existentialism is a major component of humanistic psychology, important differences exist between existential and humanistic psychology. After discussing phenomenology, a technique used by both existential and humanistic psychologists, we will review existential psychology and then humanistic psychology, and we will conclude the chapter with a comparison of the two.

PHENOMENOLOGY

Throughout this text, we have referred to a variety of methodologies as phenomenological. In its most general form, **phenomenology** refers to any methodology that focuses on cognitive experience as it occurs, without attempting to reduce that experience to its component parts. Thus, one can study consciousness without being a phenomenologist, as was the case when Wundt and Titchener attempted to reduce conscious experience to its basic elements. After making this distinction, however, phenomenology can take many forms. The phenomenology of Johann Goethe and Ernst Mach focused on complex sensations including afterimages and illusions. The phenomenology of **Franz Brentano** (1838–1917) and his colleagues focused on psychological acts such as judging, recollecting, expecting, doubting, fearing, hoping, or loving. As was seen in chapter 9, in Brentano's brand of phenomenology, the concept of **intentionality** was extremely important. Brentano believed that every mental act referred to (intended) something outside itself—for example, "I see a tree," "I like my mother," or "That was a good piece of pie." The contents of a mental act could be real or imagined, but the act, according to Brentano, always referred to (intended) something. For Brentano, mental phenomena consisted of some act or function and of an image of the referent toward which the act was directed. In chapter 14, we saw how Brentano's phenomenology influenced the Gestalt psychologists. Next, we see how Brentano's phenomenology was instrumental in the development of modern existentialism mainly through its influence on Edmund Husserl.

The goal of **Edmund Husserl** (1859–1938) was to take the type of phenomenology Brentano described and use it to create an objective, rigorous basis for philosophical and scientific inquiry. Like Brentano, Husserl believed that phenomenology could be used to create an objective bridge between the outer, physical world and the inner, subjective world. Of prime importance to Husserl was that phenomenology be free of any preconceptions. That is, Husserl believed in reporting exactly what appeared in consciousness, not what *should* be there according to some belief, theory, or model.

As we saw in chapter 9, however, Husserl believed that phenomenology could go beyond an analysis of intentionality. A study of intentionality determined how the mind and the physical world interacted, and such a study was essential for the physical sciences. But, besides an analysis of intentionality, Husserl proposed a type of phenomenology that concentrated on the workings of the mind that were independent of the physical world. Husserl called this second type of phenomenology **pure phenomenology**, and its purpose was to discover the essence of conscious experience. Whereas the type of phenomenology that focused on intentionality involved the person turned outward, pure phenomenology involved the person turned inward. The goal of the latter was to accurately catalog all mental acts and processes by which we interact with environmental objects or events. Husserl believed that an inventory of such acts and processes had to precede any adequate philosophy, science, or psychology because it was those mental acts and processes on which all human knowledge is based.

Husserl's pure phenomenology soon expanded into modern existentialism. Whereas Husserl was mainly interested in epistemology and in the essence of mental phenomena, the existentialists were interested in the nature of

human existence. In philosophy, **ontology** is the study of existence, or what it means to be. The existentialists are concerned with two ontological questions: (1) What is the nature of human existence, and what does it mean to be human? (2) What does it mean to be a particular individual, and what makes a person the way he or she is? Thus, the existentialists are concerned with human existence in general *and* in particular. The existentialists use phenomenology to study either the important experiences that humans have in common or those experiences that individuals have as they live their lives—experiences such as fear, dread, freedom, love, hate, responsibility, guilt, wonder, hope, and despair.

Husserl's phenomenology was converted into existential psychology mainly by his student Martin Heidegger, to whom we turn next.

EXISTENTIAL PSYCHOLOGY

Although it is possible to trace existential philosophy to such early Greek philosophers as Socrates, who urged people to understand themselves and said that "an unexamined life is not worth living," it has become traditional to mark the beginning of existential philosophy with the writings of Kierkegaard and Nietzsche. Along with Kierkegaard and Nietzsche, the great Russian novelist Fyodor Dostoevsky is also mentioned as among the first existential thinkers. All these individuals probed the meaning of human existence and tried to restore the importance of human feeling, choice, and individuality that had been minimized in the rationalistic philosophies of Kant and Hegel and by the Newtonian conceptions of the universe and of people. The person most often named as the originator of *modern* existentialism, however, is Martin Heidegger.

Martin Heidegger

Born on September 26, **Martin Heidegger** (1889–1976) was Husserl's student and then his assistant, and he dedicated his famous book *Be-*

Martin Heidegger

humans would not exist and without humans the world would not exist. The human mind illuminates the physical world and thereby brings it into existence. In fact, according to Bugental, all knowledge of any type is based on human experience:

> All knowledge is ultimately, founded on a psychology—conscious or unconscious, implicit or explicit—of the human experience. . . . To make a statement about a distant galaxy is to make a statement about oneself. To propose a "law" of the action of mass and energy is to offer a hypothesis about one's way of being in the world. To write a description of microorganisms on a slide is to set forth an account of human experience. The psychology of the human condition is always the predicating set of assumptions on which all others rest. One says, "I see things out there in such and such a way," neglecting to add what is even more fundamental: "I see them so because I have made such and such presumptions about what it means to see, to describe, to speak, to hear, and so on and on." I mean, very literally, that any statement we make about the world (the "out there") is inevitably, inescapably, a statement about our theory of ourselves (the "in here"). (1967, pp. 5–6)

According to Boss, a contemporary existential psychologist, "Man discloses the world. People are the luminated realm into which all that is to be may actually shine forth, emerge, and appear as phenomena, i.e., as that which shows itself" (1963, p. 70). What we allow to "shine forth" is reality, and because different people allow different experiences to shine forth, everyone lives in a different world.

But Heidegger's concept of *Dasein* is even more complicated. "To be" means to exist, and to exist is a dynamic process. To exist as a human is to exist unlike anything else. In the process of existing, humans choose, evaluate, accept, reject, and expand. Humans are not static; they are always becoming something other than what they were. To exist is to become different; to exist is to change. How a particular person chooses to exist is an individual matter, but for all people existence is an active process. The *Da*, or there, in *Dasein* refers to that place in space and time where existence takes place; but no

ing and Time (1927) to Husserl. Heidegger's work is generally considered the bridge between existential philosophy and **existential psychology**. Many, if not most, of the terms and concepts that appear in the writings of current existential psychologists can be traced to the writings of Heidegger. Like Husserl, Heidegger was a phenomenologist; but unlike Husserl, Heidegger used phenomenology to examine the totality of human existence.

Dasein. Heidegger used the term **Dasein** to indicate that a person and the world were inseparable. Literally, *Dasein* means "to be" (*sein*) "there" (*Da*), and Heidegger usually described the relationship between a person and the world as "being-in-the-world," using the hyphens to emphasize the interrelatedness of the person and the world. A more dramatic way of stating this relationship is to say that without the world

THE BETTMANN ARCHIVE

matter where and when it takes place, existence (to be) is a complex, dynamic, and uniquely human phenomenon. Unlike anything else in the universe, humans choose the nature of their own existence.

Authenticity and inauthenticity. It was very important to Heidegger that humans could ponder the fact that their existence was finite. For Heidegger, a prerequisite for living an **authentic life** was coming to grips with the fact that "I must someday die." With that realization dealt with, the person could get busy and exercise his or her freedom to create a meaningful existence, an existence that allowed for almost constant personal growth, or **becoming**.

Because realizing that one was mortal caused anxiety, however, people often refused to recognize that fact and thereby inhibited a full understanding of themselves and their possibilities. According to Heidegger, this resulted in an **inauthentic life**. An authentic life is lived with a sense of excitement or even urgency because one realizes one's existence is finite. With the time that one has available, one must explore life's possibilities and become all that one can become. An inauthentic life does not have the same urgency because the inevitability of death is not accepted. One pretends, and pretending is inauthentic. Other inauthentic modes of existence include living a traditional, conventional life according to the dictates of society and emphasizing present activities without concern for the future. The inauthentic person gave up his or her freedom and let others make the choices involved in his or her life. In general, the speech and behavior of authentic individuals accurately reflect their inner feelings, whereas with inauthentic individuals this is not the case.

Guilt and anxiety. Heidegger believed that if we did not exercise our personal freedom, we experience **guilt**. Because most people did not fully exercise their freedom to choose, they experienced at least some guilt. All humans could do to minimize guilt was try to live an authentic life—that is, to recognize and live in accordance with their ability to choose their own existence.

Because acceptance of the fact that at some time in the future we would be nothing caused **anxiety**, such acceptance took **courage**. Heidegger believed that choosing one's existence rather than conforming to the dictates of society, culture, or someone else also took courage. And in general, living an authentic life by accepting all conditions of existence and making personal choices meant that one must experience anxiety. For Heidegger, anxiety was a necessary part of living an authentic life. One reason for this was that authentic people were always experimenting with life, always taking chances, and always becoming. Entering the unknown causes part of the anxiety associated with an authentic life.

Another reason that exercising one's freedom in life caused anxiety was that it made one responsible for the consequences of those choices. The free individual could not blame God, parents, circumstances, genes, or anything else for what happened to him or her. One was responsible for one's own life. Freedom and **responsibility** went hand-in-hand.

Thrownness. Heidegger did, however, place limits on personal freedom. He said that we were thrown into the *Da*, or there, aspect of our particular life by circumstances beyond our control. This **thrownness** determined, for example, whether we are male or female, short or tall, attractive or unattractive, rich or poor, American or Russian, the time in human history that we are born, and so on. Thrownness determined the conditions under which we exercised our freedom. According to Heidegger, all humans were free, but the conditions under which that freedom was exercised varied. Thrownness provided the context for one's existence. What Heidegger called thrownness has also been called facticity, referring to the facts that characterize a human existence.

Ludwig Binswanger

Ludwig Binswanger (1881–1966) obtained his medical degree from the University of Zürich in 1907 and then studied psychiatry under Eugen Bleuler and psychoanalysis under Carl Jung.

Binswanger was one of the first Freudian psychoanalysts in Switzerland, and he and Freud remained friends throughout their lives. Under the influence of Heidegger, Binswanger applied phenomenology to psychiatry, and later he became an existential analyst. Binswanger's goal was to integrate the writings of Husserl and Heidegger with psychoanalytic theory. Adopting Heidegger's notion of *Dasein*, Binswanger called his approach to psychotherapy **Dasein-analysis** (existential analysis).

Like most existential psychologists, Binswanger emphasized the here-and-now, considering the past or future important only insofar as they manifested themselves in the *present*. To understand and help a person, according to Binswanger, one must learn how that person viewed his or her life at the moment. Furthermore, the therapist must try to understand the *particular person's* anxieties, fears, values, thought processes, social relations, and personal meanings instead of those notions in general. Each person lived in his or her own private, subjective world, which was not generalizable.

Modes of existence. Binswanger discussed three different modes of existence to which individuals gave meaning through their consciousness. They were the **Umwelt** (the "around world"), the world of things and events; the **Mitwelt** (the "with world"), interactions with other humans; and the **Eigenwelt** (the "own world"), a person's private, inner, subjective experience. To understand a person fully, one must understand all three of his or her modes of existence.

One of Binswanger's most important concepts was that of *Weltanschauung*, or **world-design** (worldview). In general, world-design is how an individual views and embraces the world. World-designs can be open or closed, expansive or constructive, positive or negative, simple or complex, or any number of other characteristics. In any case, it is through the world-design that one lives one's life, and therefore the world-design touches everything that one does. The following are examples of world-designs:

Ludwig Binswanger

Binswanger gives examples of some narrowly conceived world-designs that he found in his patients. One patient's design was constructed around the need for continuity. Any disruption of continuity—a gap, tearing, or separating—produced great anxiety. One time she fainted when the heel of her shoe fell off. Separation from the mother also evoked anxiety because it broke the continuity of the relationship. Holding onto mother meant holding onto the world; losing her meant falling into the dreadful abyss of nothingness.

Another patient who had been an active business executive became inactive, dull, and listless. His world-design as a business executive was based on push, pressure, threat, and general world-disharmony. His mode of being-in-the-world was that of bumping up against things and being bumped into. He viewed his fellow humans as being disrespectful, contemptuous, and threatening. When he tried to control his anxiety by keeping his distance from the world, his efforts resulted in exhaustion.

The design for a third patient consisted of the categories of familiarity and strangeness. His existence was constantly being endangered by impersonal hostile powers. He defended himself against these nameless fears by personalizing them as feelings of persecution. (Hall & Lindzey, 1978, p. 325)

If a world-design is ineffective, in the sense that it results in too much anxiety, fear, or guilt, it is the therapist's job to help the client see that there are other ways of embracing the world, other people, and oneself.

Ground of existence. Binswanger agreed with Heidegger that thrownness placed limits on personal freedom. For Binswanger, the circumstances into which one was thrown determined one's **ground of existence**, defined as the conditions under which one exercised one's personal freedom. No matter what a human's circumstances were, however, he or she aspired to transcend them—that is, not to be victimized or controlled by them. Everyone sought **being-beyond-the-world**. By being-beyond-the-world, Binswanger was not referring to a life after death, or anything else supernatural, but to the way in which people tried to transform their circumstances by exercising their free will.

The importance of meaning in one's life. People may be thrown into negative circumstances such as poverty, incest, rape, or war, but they need not be devastated by those experiences. Most existentialists accept Nietzsche's proclamation "that which does not kill me, makes me stronger" (Frankl, 1946/1984, p. 103). This strength comes from finding meaning even in a negative experience and growing from that meaning. In his famous book *Man's Search for Meaning* (1946/1984), Frankl described his experiences in a Nazi concentration camp. One of his major observations was that prisoners who, even under those dire circumstances, found meaning in their lives, something to live for, continued to live. It was the prisoners who found no meaning that tended to die:

We who lived in concentration camps can remember the men who walked through the huts comforting others, giving away their last piece of bread. They may have been few in number, but they offer sufficient proof that everything can be taken from a man but one thing: the last of the human freedoms—to choose one's attitude in any given set of circumstances, to choose one's own way. (Frankl, 1946/1984, p. 86)

On the other hand, there were prisoners who could find no meaning in their lives:

The prisoner who had lost faith in the future—his future—was doomed. With his loss of belief in the future, he also lost his spiritual hold; he let himself decline and became subject to mental and physical decay. Usually this happened quite suddenly, in the form of a crisis, the symptoms of which were familiar to the experienced camp inmate. We all feared this moment—not for ourselves, which would have been pointless, but for our friends. Usually it began with the prisoner refusing one morning to get dressed and wash or to go out on the parade grounds. No entreaties, no blows, no threats had any effect. He just lay there, hardly moving. If this crisis was brought about by an illness, he refused to be taken to the sick-bay or to do anything to help himself. He simply gave up. There he remained, lying in his own excreta, and nothing bothered him any more. (Frankl, 1946/1984, p. 95)

Jourard summarizes the importance of meaning in one's life:

A person lives as long as he experiences his life as having meaning and value and as long as he has something to live for—meaningful projects that inspirit him and invite him to move into his future. He will continue to live as long as he has hope of fulfilling meanings and values. As soon as meaning, value and hope vanish from a person's experience, he begins to stop living; he begins to die. (1971, p. 93)

By choosing, we change the meanings and values of what we experience. Although physical circumstances may be the same for different people, how those circumstances are embraced, interpreted, valued, symbolized, and responded to is a matter of personal choice. By exercising our freedom, we grow as human beings; and because exercising freedom is an unending process, the developmental process is never completed. Becoming characterizes the authentic life, which, in turn, is characterized by anxiety. Not becoming, or remaining stagnant, characterizes the inauthentic life—as does guilt—because the person does not attempt to fully manifest his or her human attributes.

Rollo May

Rollo May (b. 1909) introduced Heideggerian existentialism to U.S. psychology through his edited books *Existence: A New Dimension in Psychiatry and Psychology* (1958) (with Angel & Ellenberger) and *Existential Psychology* (1961). Because Binswanger's work has only recently been translated into English, May has been responsible primarily for incorporating European existential philosophy (mainly Heidegger's) into U.S. psychology.

May, born in Ada, Ohio, received his Bachelor of Art degree from Oberlin College in 1930, a Bachelor of Divinity degree from Union Theological Seminary in 1938, and a doctorate in clinical psychology from Columbia University in 1949. Prior to obtaining his doctorate, May contracted tuberculosis and was very close to death. During this depressing time, he studied Kierkegaard's and Freud's views on anxiety; upon returning to Columbia, he submitted "The Meaning of Anxiety" as his doctoral dissertation. In modified form, this dissertation became May's book *The Meaning of Anxiety* (1950). May's other books include *The Art of Counseling: How to Give and Gain Mental Health* (1939), *The Springs of Creative Living: A Study of Human Nature and God* (1940), *Man's Search for Himself* (1953), *Psychology and the Human Dilemma* (1967), *Love and Will* (1969), *Power and Innocence: A Search for the Sources of Violence* (1972), *Paulus: Reminiscences of a Friendship* (1973), *Freedom and Destiny* (1981), and *The Discovery of Being: Writings in Existential Psychology* (1983).

Like many other existential thinkers, May was strongly influenced by Kierkegaard, who had rejected Hegel's belief that an individual's life only had meaning insofar as it related to the

Rollo May

ROLLO REESE MAY

totality of things, which Hegel called The Absolute. Kierkegaard proposed that each person's life was a separate entity with its own self-determined meaning. Again, for Kierkegaard, subjectivity was truth. That is, a person's beliefs defined that person's reality.

The human dilemma. May (1967) points out that humans are both objects and subjects of experience. We are objects in the sense that we exist physically, and therefore things happen to us. As objects we are not distinguished from the other physical objects that are studied by the natural sciences. It is as objects that humans are studied by the traditional methods of science—the assumption being that human behavior is caused in much the same way that behavior of any physical object is caused. Besides being objects, however, we are also subjects. That is, we do not simply *have* experience, we interpret, value, and make choices regarding our experience. We give our experience meaning. This dual aspect of human nature, which May calls the **human dilemma**, makes humans unique in the universe. By dilemma, May does not mean an insoluble problem; rather, he means a paradox of human existence. This paradox creates tension that can be the source of "dynamic and human creativity. I believe that it is out of the constructive confronting of the tensions in these paradoxes that man builds cultures and civilizations" (May, 1967, p. iii).

Normal and neurotic anxiety. May believes, along with the other existentialists, that the most important fact about humans is that they are free. As we have seen, however, freedom does not produce a tranquil life. Freedom carries with it responsibility, uncertainty, and therefore anxiety. The healthy (authentic) person exercises freedom to embrace life fully and to approach his or her full potential. Exercising one's freedom means going beyond what one previously was, ignoring the expectations (roles) for one's behavior that others impose, and therefore often acting contrary to traditions, mores, or conventions. All this causes anxiety, but it is normal, healthy anxiety because it is conducive to personal growth (becoming). **Neurotic anxiety** is not conducive to personal growth because it results from the fear of freedom. The person experiencing neurotic anxiety lives his or her life in such a way that reduces or eliminates personal freedom. Such a person conforms to tradition, religious dogma, the expectations of others, or anything else that reduces his or her need to make personal choices. Kierkegaard called the neurotic's situation **shut-upness**. The neurotic is shut off from himself or herself as well as from other people; he or she has become alienated from his or her true self. **Self-alienation** occurs whenever people accept, as their own, values dictated by society rather than those personally attained. Self-alienation results not only in guilt

but also apathy and despair. The frightening aspects of human freedom and the many ways that people attempt to escape from their freedom are discussed in Erich Fromm's classic book *Escape from Freedom* (1941).

According to Kierkegaard, May, and most other existentialists, we can either exercise our free will and experience normal anxiety or not exercise it and feel guilty. Obviously, it is not easy being human, for this conflict between anxiety and guilt is a constant theme in human existence: "The conflict is between every human being's need to struggle toward enlarged self-awareness, maturity, freedom and responsibility, and his tendency to remain a child and cling to the protection of parents or parental substitutes" (May, 1953, p. 193).

Many of the concepts found in existential psychology will reappear as we consider humanistic psychology.

HUMANISTIC PSYCHOLOGY

Abraham Maslow

Some argue that it is Alfred Adler who should be considered the first humanistic psychologist. This is because he defined a healthy lifestyle as one reflecting a considerable amount of social interest, and with his concept of the creative self, he insisted that what a person becomes is largely a matter of personal choice. Certainly, Adler's theory had much in common with those theories later called humanistic. Most often, however, it is **Abraham Maslow** (1908–1970) who is recognized as responsible for making **humanistic psychology** a formal branch of psychology.

Maslow was born on April 1 in Brooklyn, New York. He was the oldest of seven children born to parents who were Jewish immigrants from Russia. Not being especially close to his parents and being the only Jewish boy in his neighborhood, he was intensely lonely and shy and took refuge in books and scholarly pursuits. He was an excellent student at Boys High School in Brooklyn and went on to attend City College of New York. While attending City College, he also made an effort to satisfy his father's desire for him to become a lawyer by also attending law school. Unhappy with law school, however, he walked out of class one night leaving his books behind. Being a mediocre student at City College, he transferred to Cornell University where he took introductory psychology from Edward Titchener, whose approach to psychology did not impress Maslow. After only one semester at Cornell he transferred back to City College, partly to be near his first cousin Bertha Goodman, whom he loved very much. He and Bertha were married in 1928 when he was 20 and she was 19, and they eventually had two children. Prior to their marriage, Maslow had enrolled at the University of Wisconsin, and Bertha went there to join him. By Maslow's own account, his life did not really begin until he and Bertha moved to Wisconsin.

As ironic as it now seems, Maslow was first infatuated with the behaviorism of John Watson in which he saw a way of solving human problems and changing the world for the better. His infatuation ended when he and Bertha had their first baby. Maslow described this experience:

> Our first baby changed me as a psychologist. It made the behaviorism I had been so enthusiastic about look so foolish I could not stomach it anymore. That was the thunderclap that settled things. . . . I was stunned by the mystery and by the sense of not really being in control. I felt small and weak and feeble before all this. I'd say anyone who had a baby couldn't be a behaviorist. (M. H. Hall, 1968, p. 55)

At the University of Wisconsin, Maslow earned his bachelor's degree in 1930, his master's degree in 1931, and his doctorate in 1934. As a graduate student at Wisconsin, Maslow became the first doctoral student of the famous experimental psychologist Harry Harlow. Maslow's dissertation was on the establishment of dominance in a colony of monkeys. He observed that dominance had more to do with a type of "inner confidence" than with physical strength, an observation that may have influenced his later theorizing. During this time, Maslow also observed that sexual behavior within the colony was related to dominance and subservience, and

Abraham Maslow

he wondered if the same was true for human sexual activity, a possibility he would explore shortly. After receiving his doctorate, Maslow taught at Wisconsin for a while before moving to Columbia University where he became Edward Thorndike's research assistant. He also began his research on human sexuality by interviewing both male and female college students about their sexual behavior but soon abandoned males because they tended to lie too much about their sexual activities (Hoffman, 1988). Maslow made important contributions to our knowledge of human sexuality several years before Kinsey's famous research. Furthermore, the interviewing skills that he developed during this research served him well when he later studied the characteristics of psychologically healthy individuals. After a year and a half at Columbia, Maslow moved to Brooklyn College where he stayed until 1951. Living in New York in the 1930s and 1940s gave Maslow an opportunity to come into contact with many prominent European psychologists who came to the United States to escape the Nazi terror. Among them were Erich Fromm, Max Wertheimer, Karen Horney, and Alfred Adler. Adler began giving seminars in his home on Friday evenings, and Maslow attended frequently. Maslow also befriended the famous anthropologist Ruth Benedict about this same time. Maslow became obsessed with trying to understand these truly exceptional people, and it was this obsession that evolved into Maslow's version of humanistic psychology.

In 1951 Maslow accepted the position of chairman of the psychology department at Brandeis University in Waltham, Massachusetts, and it was here that Maslow became the leading figure in third-force psychology. In 1968, because of increased disenchantment with academic life and failing health, Maslow accepted a fellowship offered to him by the Saga Administrative Corporation. Hoffman describes the offer that was made to Maslow:

> Laughlin [the president and chairman of the Saga Corporation] cheerfully informed Maslow, the fellowship was ready. He was prepared to offer Maslow a two-to-four-year commitment with the following conditions: a handsome salary, a new car, and a personally decorated private office with full secretarial services at Saga's attractive campuslike headquarters on Stanford University's suburban outskirts. What would Maslow have to do in return? Nothing. (1988, p. 316)

Maslow accepted and, as advertised, was free to think and write as he pleased, and he enjoyed his freedom very much. In 1970, however, Maslow suffered a heart attack while jogging and died.

Due primarily to Maslow's efforts, the *Journal of Humanistic Psychology* was founded in 1961; the American Association of Humanistic Psychologists was established in 1962; and a division of the American Psychological Association, called the Division of Humanistic Psychology, was created in 1971.

The basic tenets of humanistic psychology. The beliefs shared by psychologists working within the humanistic paradigm include the following:

1. Little of value can be learned about humans by studying nonhuman animals.

2. Subjective reality is the primary guide for human behavior.

3. Studying individuals is more informative than studying what groups of individuals have in common.

4. A major effort should be made to discover those things that expand and enrich human experience.

5. Research should seek information that will help solve human problems.

6. The goal of psychology should be to formulate a complete description of what it means to be a human being. Such a description would include the importance of language, the valuing process, the full range of human emotions, and the ways humans seek and attain meaning in their lives.

Humanistic psychology, which rejects the notion that psychology should be entirely scientific, sees humans as indivisible wholes. Any attempt to reduce them to habits, cognitive structures, or S–R connections results in a distortion of human nature. According to Maslow, psychologists often use scientific method to cut themselves off from the poetic, romantic, and spiritual aspects of human nature:

> Briefly put, it appears to me that science and everything scientific can be and often is used as a tool in the service of a distorted, narrowed, humorless, de-eroticized, de-emotionalized, desacralized, and desanctified *Weltanschauung* [worldview]. This desacralization can be used as a defense against being flooded by emotion, especially the emotions of humility, reverence, mastery, wonder and awe. (1966, p. 139)

Humanistic psychologists flatly reject the goal of predicting and controlling human behavior, which so many scientifically inclined psychologists accept:

> If humanistic science may be said to have any goals beyond sheer fascination with the human mystery and enjoyment of it, these would be to release the person from external controls and to make him *less* predictable to the observer (to make him freer, more creative, more inner determined) even though perhaps more predictable to himself. (Maslow, 1966, p. 40)

Humans, then, are much more than physical

objects, and therefore the methods employed by the physical sciences have no relevance to the study of humans. Similarly, psychoanalysis, by concentrating on the study of psychologically disturbed individuals, has created a "crippled" psychology: "It becomes more and more clear that the study of crippled, stunted, immature, and unhealthy specimens can yield only a crippled psychology and a crippled philosophy" (Maslow, 1970, p. 180). For Maslow, there are exceptional people whose lives cannot be understood simply as the absence of mental disorders. To be understood, exceptional people must be studied directly:

> Health is not simply the absence of disease or even the opposite of it. Any theory of motivation that is worthy of attention must deal with the highest capacities of the healthy and strong person as well as with the defensive maneuvers of crippled spirits. (Maslow, 1954/1987, p. 14)

Maslow's point was not that psychology should stop attempting to be scientific or stop studying and attempting to help those with psychological problems but that such endeavors tell only part of the story. Beyond this, psychology needs to attempt to understand humans who are in the process of reaching their full potential. We need to know how such people think and what motivates them. Thus, Maslow invested most of his energies in trying to understand exceptional humans.

The hierarchy of needs. According to Maslow, human needs are arranged in a hierarchy. The lower the needs in the hierarchy, the more basic they are and the more similar they are to the needs of other animals. The higher the needs in the hierarchy, the more distinctly human they are.

The needs are arranged so that as one satisfies a lower need, one can deal with the next higher need. When one's physiological needs (e.g., hunger, thirst, and sex) are predictably satisfied, one can deal with the safety needs (e.g., protection from the elements, pain, and unexpected dangers); when the safety needs are rea-

sonably satisfied, one is free to deal with the belonging and love needs (e.g., the need to love and be loved, to share one's life with a relevant other); when the belonging and love needs are adequately satisfied, one is released to ponder the esteem needs (e.g., to make a recognizable contribution to the well-being of one's fellow humans); if the esteem needs are met satisfactorily, one is in a position to become self-actualized. Maslow's proposed **hierarchy of needs** can be diagrammed as follows:

Self-Actualization. By **self-actualization**, Maslow meant reaching one's full, human potential:

> So far as motivational status is concerned, healthy people have sufficiently gratified their basic needs for safety, belongingness, love, respect, and self-esteem so that they are motivated primarily by trends to self-actualization (defined as ongoing actualization of potentials, capacities and talents, as fulfillment of mission (or call, fate, destiny, or vocation), as a fuller knowledge of, and acceptance of, the person's own intrinsic nature, as an unceasing trend toward unity, integration or synergy within the person). (Maslow, 1968, p. 25)

> Musicians must make music, artists must paint, poets must write if they are to be ultimately at peace with themselves. What humans can be, they must be. They must be true to their own nature. This need we may call self-actualization. (Maslow, 1954/1987, p. 22)

The concept of self-actualization goes back at least as far as Aristotle, but what Aristotle meant by self-actualization was the innate tendency to manifest the characteristics or the essence of one's species. For example, an acorn had an innate tendency to become an oak tree and to exhibit the characteristics of oak treeness. Jung reintroduced the concept of self-actualization into modern psychology, and what he meant by the term and what Maslow later meant by it was distinctly different from the Aristotelian meaning. By self-actualization, Jung, Maslow, and Rogers (whom we consider next) meant the realization of an *individual's* potential, not that of species' potential, as was Aristotle's meaning.

Because it is impossible for any person to completely reach his or her full potential, Maslow referred to those who have satisfied hierarchical needs as self-actualizing. (A list of characteristics of self-actualizing people is given shortly.)

As one climbs the hierarchy, the needs become more fragile. That is, the physiological and safety needs have a long evolutionary history and are therefore very powerful; but the higher needs for love, esteem, and self-actualization are "newer" and distinctly human and therefore do not have as firm a biological foundation. This means that their satisfaction is easily interfered with. The higher up the hierarchy one goes, the truer this is; and therefore the satisfaction of the need for self-actualization—although the need is innate—is easily interfered with. Of self-actualization, Maslow said, "This inner nature is not strong and overpowering and unmistakable like the instincts of animals. It is weak and delicate and subtle and easily overcome by habit, cultural pressure, and wrong attitudes toward it" (1968, p. 4).

Thus, although all humans have an innate drive to be self-actualized (to reach their full potential as humans), self-actualized people are rare. Another major reason that self-actualization occurs so infrequently is that it requires a great deal of honest knowledge of oneself, and most humans are fearful of such knowledge. Maslow calls the fear of self-knowledge the **Jonah complex**:

> More than any other kind of knowledge we fear knowledge of ourselves, knowledge that might transform our self-esteem and our self-image. . . . While human beings love knowl-

edge and seek it—they are curious—they also fear it. The closer to the personal it is, the more they fear it. (1966, p. 16)

The characteristics of self-actualizing people. Maslow believed that for too long psychology had emphasized the study of lower animals and psychologically disturbed individuals. To begin to remedy the situation, he studied a number of people he thought were self-actualizing. Among them were Albert Einstein, Albert Schweitzer, Sigmund Freud, Jane Addams, William James, and Abraham Lincoln. Maslow concluded that self-actualizing people had the following characteristics:

1. They perceived reality accurately and fully.

2. They demonstrated a great acceptance of themselves and of others.

3. They exhibited spontaneity and naturalness.

4. They had a need for privacy.

5. They tended to be independent of their environment and culture.

6. They demonstrated a continuous freshness of appreciation.

7. They tended to have periodic mystic or peak experiences. Maslow described peak experiences as follows:

> Feelings of limitless horizons opening up to the vision, the feeling of being simultaneously more powerful and also more helpless than one ever was before, the feeling of great ecstasy and wonder and awe, the loss of placing in time and space with, finally, the conviction that something extremely important and valuable had happened, so that the subject is to some extent transformed and strengthened even in his daily life by such experiences. (1954/1987, p. 137)

8. Self-actualizing people were concerned with all humans instead of with only their friends, relatives, and acquaintances.

9. They tended to have only a few friends.

10. They had a strong ethical sense but did not necessarily accept conventional ethics.

11. They had a well-developed but not hostile sense of humor.

12. They were creative.

Although Maslow concluded that his group of self-actualizing people were outstanding humans, he also indicated that they were not without faults:

> Our subjects show many of the lesser human failings. They too are equipped with silly, wasteful or thoughtless habits. They can be boring, stubborn, irritating. They are by no means free from a rather superficial vanity, pride, partiality to their own productions, family, friends, and children. Temper outbursts are not rare.
>
> Our subjects are occasionally capable of an extraordinary and unexpected ruthlessness. It must be remembered that they are very strong people. This makes it possible for them to display a surgical coldness when this is called for, beyond the power of the average man. The man who found that a long-trusted acquaintance was dishonest cut himself off from this friendship sharply and abruptly and without any observable pangs whatsoever. Another woman who was married to someone she did not love, when she decided on divorce, did it with a decisiveness that looked almost like ruthlessness. Some of them recover so quickly from the death of people close to them as to seem heartless. (Maslow, 1954/1987, p. 146)

Deficiency and being motivation and perception. If a person is functioning at any level other than self-actualization, he or she is said to be deficiency-motivated. That is, the person is seeking specific things to satisfy specific needs, and his or her perceptions are need-directed. Jourard describes **need-directed perception** (also called deficiency or D-perception) as follows: "Need-directed perception is a highly focused searchlight darting here and there, seeking the objects which will satisfy needs, ignoring everything irrelevant to the need" (1974, p. 68).

Deficiency motivation (D-motivation) leads to need-directed perception. Unlike most psychologists, Maslow was mainly interested in what happened to people *after* their basic needs were satisfied. His answer was that people who satisfied their basic needs and became self-actualizing

entered into a different mode of existence. Instead of being deficiency-motivated, they were being-motivated (B-motivated). **Being motivation** involves embracing the higher values of life such as beauty, truth, and justice. Being-motivated people are also capable of B-love, which unlike D-love is nonpossessive and insatiable. Unlike D-perception, **being perception** (B-perception) does not involve seeking specific things in the environment. Therefore, the person interacting with the world through B-perception is open to a wider range of experience than the person who interacts through D-perception.

Maslow's many honors included election to the presidency of the American Psychological Association (APA) for the year 1967–1968. At the time of his death in 1970, Maslow's ideas were well known within not only psychology but also fields such as medicine, marketing, theology, education, and nursing.

Carl Rogers

Carl Rogers (1902–1987) was born on January 8 in Oak Park (a Chicago suburb), Illinois, and was the fourth of six children. He was closer to his mother than to his father, who was a successful civil engineer and was often away from home. In the affluent suburb of Oak Park, Rogers attended school with Ernest Hemingway and the children of Frank Lloyd Wright, the famous architect. Rogers described his family as closely knit and highly religious. Friendships outside the family were discouraged:

> I think the attitudes toward persons outside our large family can be summed up schematically in this way: Other persons behave in dubious ways which we do not approve in our family. Many of them play cards, go to movies, smoke, drink, and engage in other activities—some unmentionable. So the best thing to do is to be tolerant of them, since they may not know better, and to keep away from any close communication with them and live your life within the family. (1973, p. 3)

Not surprisingly, Rogers was a loner in school and, like Maslow, took refuge in books, reading

Carl Rogers

everything that he could get his hands on, including encyclopedias and dictionaries. When Rogers was 12 years old, he and his family moved to a farm 25 miles west of Chicago. The purpose of the move was to provide a more wholesome and religious atmosphere for the family. Because his father insisted that the farm be run scientifically, Rogers developed an intense interest in science, reading everything he could about agricultural experiments. Rogers maintained this interest in science throughout his career, although he worked in one of psychology's more subjective areas. When Rogers graduated from high school, he intended to become a farmer, and when he entered the University of Wisconsin in 1919, he chose to study agriculture. In his early years in college, Rogers

was very active in church activities, and in 1922 he was selected to attend the World Student Christian Federation Conference in Peking, China. During this six-month trip, Rogers, for the first time, experienced people of different cultures with different religions. Rogers wrote his parents declaring his independence from their conservative religion, and almost immediately he developed an ulcer that caused him to be hospitalized for several weeks.

Upon returning to the University of Wisconsin, Rogers changed his major from agriculture to history. He received his bachelor's degree in 1924. Shortly after graduation, he married his childhood sweetheart, Helen Elliott, with whom he eventually had two children. Soon after their marriage, Carl and Helen moved to New York where he enrolled in the liberal Union Theological Seminary while also taking courses in psychology and education at neighboring Columbia University. After two years at the seminary, Rogers's doubts about whether the religious approach was the most effective way of helping people caused him to transfer to Columbia University, on a full-time basis, where he earned his master's degree in clinical psychology in 1928 and his doctorate in 1931. His dissertation concerned the measurement of personality adjustment in children.

After obtaining his doctorate, Rogers went to work for the Child Study Department of the Society for the Prevention of Cruelty to Children in Rochester, New York, where he had served as a fellow while working toward his doctorate. Here Rogers had several experiences that caused him to develop his own brand of psychotherapy. For example, the society was dominated by therapists trained in the psychoanalytic tradition, people who saw their job as gaining an "insight" into the cause of a problem and then sharing that insight with the client. At first, Rogers followed this procedure. In one case, he concluded that a mother's rejection of her son was the cause of the son's delinquent behavior, but his attempts to share this insight with the mother failed completely. Rogers described what happened next:

Finally I gave up. I told her that it seemed we had both tried, but we had failed. . . . She agreed. So we concluded the interview, shook hands, and she walked to the door of the office. Then she turned and asked, "Do you take adults for counseling here?" When I replied in the affirmative, she said, "Well then, I would like some help." She came to the chair she had left, and began to pour out her despair about her marriage, her troubled relationship with her husband, her sense of failure and confusion, all very different from the sterile "Case History" she had given before. Real therapy began then.

This incident was one of a number which helped me to experience that fact—only fully realized later—that it is the client who knows what hurts, what directions to go, what problems are crucial, what experiences have been deeply buried. It began to occur to me that unless I had a need to demonstrate my own cleverness and learning, I would do better to rely upon the client for the direction of movement in the process. (1961, pp. 11–12)

It was while Rogers was employed by the Child Study Department that he wrote his first book, *The Clinical Treatment of the Problem Child* (1939), the publication of which led to an offer of an academic position at Ohio State University. Rogers was reluctant to leave the clinical setting, but when Ohio State agreed to start him at the rank of full professor, he decided, at the age of 38, to begin a new career in the academic world. At Ohio, Rogers communicated his own ideas concerning the therapeutic process in his now famous *Counseling and Psychotherapy: Newer Concepts in Practice* (1942). It is widely believed that this book described the first major alternative to psychoanalysis. Rogers's approach to psychotherapy was considered revolutionary because it eliminated the needs for diagnosis, a search for the causes of disturbances, and any type of labeling of disorders. He also refused to call disturbed individuals "patients," as had been the case with the psychoanalysts; for Rogers, people seeking help were "clients."

As part of the war effort, Rogers took a leave from Ohio State in 1944 to become director of counseling services for the United Services Organization in New York. After one year, Rogers moved to the University of Chicago as professor

of psychology and director of counseling. It was during his 12-year stay at Chicago that Rogers wrote what many consider to be his most important work, *Client-Centered Therapy: Its Current Practice, Implications, and Theory* (1951). This book marked a change in Rogers's approach to psychology. Originally, his approach was called nondirective, believing that in a positive therapeutic atmosphere clients would solve their problems automatically. Therapy became client-centered when Rogers realized that the therapist had to make an active attempt to understand and accept a client's subjective reality before progress could be made. It was also at Chicago that Rogers and his colleagues engaged in the first attempt to objectively measure the effectiveness of psychotherapy.

In 1957 Rogers returned to the University of Wisconsin where he held the dual position of professor of psychology and professor of psychiatry, and he did much to resolve differences between the two disciplines. In 1963 Rogers joined the Western Behavioral Sciences Institute (WBSI) in La Jolla, California. At WBSI Rogers became increasingly interested in encounter groups and sensitivity training and less interested in individual therapy. Toward the end of his life, he also became interested in promoting world peace. In 1968 Rogers and 75 of his colleagues resigned from WBSI and formed the Center for the Studies of the Person, also in La Jolla. Here, Rogers continued to work with encounter groups, but he expanded his interests in education and international politics. In 1985 he organized the Vienna Peace Project that brought leaders from 13 countries together, and in 1986 he conducted peace workshops in Moscow. Rogers continued to work on these and other projects until his death in 1987 from cardiac arrest following surgery for a broken hip.

Rogers received many honors. He served as president of the APA in 1946–1947, and in 1956 he was corecipient, along with Kenneth Spence and Wolfgang Köhler, of the first Distinguished Scientific Contribution Award from the APA. The latter award moved Rogers to tears because he felt that his fellow psychologists had viewed his work as unscientific: "My voice choked and the tears flowed when I was called forth . . . to receive [the award]" (Rogers, 1974, p. 117). In 1972 Rogers received the Distinguished Professional Contribution Award from the APA, making him the first person in the history of the APA to receive both the Distinguished Scientific and Professional Contribution Awards.

Rogers's theory of personality. At the urging of others, Rogers developed a theory of personality to account for the phenomena he had observed during the therapeutic process. The rudiments of his theory were first presented in his APA presidential address (Rogers, 1947) and then expanded in his *Client-Centered Therapy* (1951). The most complete statement of his theory was in a chapter entitled "A Theory of Therapy, Personality, and Interpersonal Relationships, as Developed in the Client-Centered Framework" (Rogers, 1959).

Like Maslow, Rogers postulated an innate human drive toward self-actualization, and if people use this *actualizing tendency* as a frame of reference in living their lives, there is a strong likelihood that they will live fulfilling lives and ultimately reach their full potential. Such people are said to be living according to the **organismic valuing process**. Using this process, a person approaches and maintains experiences that are in accord with the actualizing tendency but terminates and avoids those that are not. Such a person is motivated by his or her own true feelings and is living what the existentialists call an authentic life—that is, a life motivated by a person's true inner feelings rather than mores, beliefs, traditions, values, or conventions imposed by others. Here we see Rogers restating Rousseau's belief in the primacy of personal feelings as guides for action. In the following quotation, we see a strong similarity between Rousseau's romantic philosophy and Rogers's humanistic psychology:

> One of the basic things which I was a long time in realizing, and which I am still learning, is that when an activity *feels* as though it is valuable or worth doing, it *is* worth doing. Put another way,

I have learned that my total organismic sensing of a situation is more trustworthy than my intellect.

> All of my professional life I have been going on directions which others thought were foolish, and about which I have had many doubts myself. But I have never regretted moving in directions which "felt right," even though I have often felt lonely or foolish at the time. . . . *Experience is for me, the highest authority.* . . . Neither the Bible nor the prophets—neither Freud nor research—neither the revelations of God nor man—can take precedence over my own experience. (1961, pp. 22–24)

Unfortunately, according to Rogers, most people do not live according to their innermost feelings (the organismic valuing process). A problem arises because of our childhood **need for positive regard**. Positive regard involves receiving such things as love, warmth, sympathy, and acceptance from the relevant people in a child's life. If positive regard was given freely to a child, no problem would arise, but usually it is not freely given. Usually parents (or other relevant people) will give children positive regard only if the children act or think in certain ways. This sets up **conditions of worth**. The children soon learn that in order to receive love they must act and think in accordance with the values of the relevant people in their lives. Gradually, as the children internalize those values, the values replace the organismic valuing process as a frame of reference for living life. As long as people live their lives according to someone else's values instead of their own true feelings, experience will be edited, and certain experiences that would have been in accord with the organismic valuing process will be denied:

> In order to hold the love of a parent, the child introjects as his own values and perceptions which he does not actually experience. He then denies to awareness the organismic experiencings that contradict these introjections. Thus, his self-concept contains false elements that are not based on what he is, in his experiencing. (Rogers, 1966, p. 192)

According to Rogers, there is only one way to avoid imposing conditions of worth on people, and that is to give them unconditional positive regard. With **unconditional positive regard**, people are loved and respected for what they truly are; therefore, there is no need for certain experiences to be denied or distorted. Only someone who experiences unconditional positive regard can become a **fully functioning person**:

> If an individual should *experience* only *unconditional positive regard*, then no *conditions of worth* would develop, self-regard would be unconditional, the needs for *positive regard* and *self-regard* would never be at variance with *organismic evaluation*, and the individual would continue to be *psychologically adjusted*, and would be fully functioning. (Rogers, 1959, p. 224)

When conditions of worth replace the organismic valuing process as a guide for living, the person becomes incongruent. What Rogers called an **incongruent person** is essentially the same as what the existentialists call an inauthentic person. In both cases, the person is no longer true to his or her own feelings. Rogers viewed incongruency as the cause of mental disorders, and he believed therefore that the goal of psychotherapy is to help people overcome conditions of worth and again live in accordance with their organismic valuing processes. Rogers described this goal as follows:

> This, as we see it, is the basic estrangement in man. He has not been true to himself, to his own natural organismic valuing of experience, but for the sake of preserving the positive regard of others has now come to falsify some of the values he experiences and to perceive them only in terms based upon their value to others. Yet this has not been a conscious choice, but a natural—and tragic—development in infancy. The path of development toward psychological maturity, the path of therapy, is the undoing of this estrangement in man's functioning, the dissolving of conditions of worth, the achievement of a self which is congruent with experience, and the restoration of a unified organismic valuing process as the regulator of behavior. (1959, pp. 226–227)

When people are living in accordance with their organismic valuing process, they are fully functioning. The fully functioning person embraces life in much the same way as Maslow's self-actualizing person does.

Rogers fully appreciated the fact that human growth can be facilitated by relationships other than that between therapist and client. Rogers described the conditions that must characterize *any* relationship if that relationship is going to facilitate personal growth:

> There are three conditions that must be present in order for a climate to be growth promoting. These conditions apply whether we are speaking of the relationship between therapist and client, parent and child, leader and group, teacher and student, or administrator and staff. The conditions apply, in fact, in any situation in which the development of the person is a goal. . . . The first element could be called *genuineness*, [italics added] realness, or congruence. . . . The second attitude of importance in creating a climate for change is acceptance, or caring, or prizing—what I have called *"unconditional positive regard"* [italics added]. . . . The third facilitative aspect of the relationship is *empathic understanding* [italics added]. . . . This kind of sensitive, active listening is exceedingly rare in our lives. We think we listen, but very rarely do we listen with real understanding, true empathy. Yet listening, of this very special kind, is one of the most potent forces for change that I know. (1980, pp. 115–116)

George Kelly

Kelly's theory is difficult to classify and could as easily be classified existential as humanistic. As we will see, he believed that whether a person lived a full, challenging, exciting or a restrictive, safe, boring life was largely a matter of personal choice, and this provides an existential component to this theory. On the other hand, he stressed studying the whole person and opposed the views of humans presented by the psychoanalysts and the behaviorists. His hope was that healthy humans would open themselves to an ever-increasing variety of experiences and that neurotic humans would come to embrace the world in less restrictive ways. Somewhat arbitrarily then, we place Kelly among the humanistic psychologists.

George Kelly

George Kelly (1905–1967) was born on April 28 on a farm near Perth, Kansas. An only child, his father was an ordained Presbyterian minister, and his mother was a former schoolteacher. By the time Kelly was born, his father had given up the ministry and turned to farming. In 1909, when Kelly was four years old, his father converted a lumber wagon into a covered wagon and with it moved his family to Colorado where he staked a claim to a plot of land offered free to settlers. Unable to find an adequate amount of water on their claim, the family moved back to Kansas where Kelly's education consisted of attending a one-room school and being tutored by his parents. From the pioneering efforts of his family, Kelly developed a pragmatic spirit that remained with him throughout his life. That is, the major criterion that he used to judge an idea or a device was whether it worked.

When Kelly was age 13, he was sent to Wichita where he attended four different high schools in four years. Upon graduation from high school,

he attended Friends University in Wichita for three years and then Park College in Parkville, Missouri, where he earned his bachelor's degree in 1926 with majors in physics and mathematics. Kelly was totally unimpressed by his first psychology class. For several class meetings, he waited in vain for something interesting to be said. Finally, one day the instructor wrote "S→R" on the blackboard, and Kelly believed that finally he was going to hear something interesting. He recalled his disappointment:

> Although I listened intently for several sessions, after that the most I could make of it was that the "S" was what you had to have in order to account for the "R" and the "R" was put there so the "S" would have something to account for. I never did find out what that arrow stood for— not to this day—and I have pretty well given up trying to figure it out. (1969, p. 47)

Next, Kelly went to the University of Kansas where he earned his master's degree in 1928 with a major in educational psychology and a minor in labor relations. While at the University of Kansas, Kelly decided that it was time for him to become acquainted with Freud's writings. Freud did not impress him any more than S→R psychology did: "I don't remember which one of Freud's books I was trying to read, but I do remember the mounting feeling of incredulity that anyone could write such nonsense, much less publish it" (1969, p. 47).

The next year was a busy one for Kelly; he taught part-time in a labor college in Minneapolis, speech classes for the American Bankers Association, and an Americanization class to immigrants wishing to become U.S. citizens. In the winter of 1928, he moved to Sheldon, Iowa, where he taught at a junior college. Among his other duties, Kelly coached dramatics, and this experience may have influenced his later theorizing. It was here that Kelly met his future wife, Gladys Thompson, who was an English teacher at the same school. After a year and a half, Kelly returned to Minnesota where he taught for a brief time at the University of Minnesota. He then returned to Wichita to work for a while as an aeronautical engineer. In 1929 he received an exchange scholarship, which allowed him to study for a year at the University of Edinburgh in Scotland. It was while earning his advanced degree at Edinburgh that Kelly became interested in psychology.

In 1930, on his return from Scotland, Kelly enrolled in the graduate program at the State University of Iowa where he obtained his doctorate in 1931. His dissertation was on the common factors in speech and reading disabilities. Kelly began his academic career at Fort Hays Kansas State College, during the Great Depression. This was a time when there were many troubled people; Kelly desperately wanted to help them, but his training in physiological psychology did not equip him to do so. He decided to become a psychotherapist. His lack of training in clinical psychology, along with his pragmatic attitude, gave Kelly great latitude in dealing with emotional problems, and his observations eventually resulted in his unique theory of personality.

Soon after arriving at Fort Hays, Kelly developed traveling clinics that serviced the public school system. The clinics brought Kelly into contact with a wide range of emotional problems that both students and teachers experienced. Kelly soon made a remarkable observation. Because he was not trained in any particular therapeutic approach, he began to experiment with a variety of approaches, and he discovered that *anything that caused his clients to view themselves or their problems differently improved the situation.* Whether a proposed explanation was "logical" or "correct" seemed to have little to do with its effectiveness:

> I began fabricating "insights." I deliberately offered "preposterous interpretations" to my clients. Some of them were about as un-Freudian as I could make them—first proposed somewhat cautiously, of course, and then, as I began to see what was happening, more boldly. My only criteria were that the explanation account for the crucial facts as the client saw them, and that it carry implications for approaching the future in a different way. (Kelly, 1969, p. 52)

In this statement lies the cornerstone of Kelly's position. That is, whether or not a person has a psychological problem is mainly a matter of how that person views things.

At the beginning of the Second World War, Kelly joined the Navy and was placed in charge of a local civilian pilot-training program. After the war, he taught at the University of Maryland for a year and in 1946 moved to Ohio State University as professor of psychology and director of clinical psychology. It was during his 19 years at Ohio State that Kelly refined his theory of personality and his approach to psychotherapy. In 1955 he published his most important work, *The Psychology of Personal Constructs*, in two volumes.

In 1960 Kelly and his wife received a grant from the human ecology fund, allowing them to travel around the world discussing the relationship between Kelly's theory and international problems. In 1965 Kelly accepted a position at Brandeis University where, for a short time, he was a colleague of Maslow. Kelly died in 1967 at the age of 62. His honors included presidencies of both the clinical and counseling divisions of the APA. He also headed the American Board of Examiners in Professional Psychology, an organization whose purpose was to upgrade the quality of professional psychology.

Constructive alternativism. Kelly observed that the major goal of scientists was to reduce uncertainty; and because he believed that this was also the goal of all humans, he said all humans were like scientists. But whereas scientists created theories with which they attempted to predict future events, nonscientists created **construct systems** to predict future events. If either a scientific theory or a personal construct system was effective, it adequately predicted the future and thereby reduced uncertainty. And both scientific theories and construct systems were tested empirically. That is, they were checked against reality and were revised until their ability to predict future events or experiences was satisfactory. For Kelly, a construct was a verbal label. Hergenhahn gives the following example:

> On meeting a person for the first time, one might construe that person with the construct

"friendly." If the person's subsequent behavior is in accordance with the construct of friendly, then the construct will be useful in anticipating that person's behavior. If the new acquaintance acts in an unfriendly manner, he or she will need to be construed either with different constructs or by using the other pole . . . of the friendly-unfriendly construct. The major point is that constructs are used to anticipate the future, so they must fit reality. Arriving at a construct system that corresponds fairly closely to reality is largely a matter of trial and error. (1990, p. 402)

With his concept of **constructive alternativism**, Kelly aligned himself squarely with the existentialists. Kelly maintained that people were free to choose the constructs they used in interacting with the world. This meant that people could view and interpret events in an almost infinite number of ways because construing them was an individual matter. No one needed to be a victim of circumstances nor a victim of the past; we were free to view things as we wished:

> We take the stand that there are always some alternative constructions available to choose among in dealing with the world. No one needs to paint himself into a corner; no one needs to be completely hemmed in by circumstances; no one needs to be the victim of his biography. (Kelly, 1955, p. 15)

According to Kelly, it was not common experience that made people similar; rather, it was how they construed reality. If two people employed more or less the same personal constructs in dealing with the world, then they were similar no matter how similar or dissimilar their physical experiences had been. Kelly also said that to truly understand another person we had to know how that person construed things. In other words, we had to know what that person's expectations were, and then we could choose to act in accordance with those expectations. The deepest type of social interaction occurred when this process was mutual.

Fixed-role therapy. Kelly's approach to therapy reflected his belief that psychological problems were *perceptual problems* and that the job of the therapist was therefore to help the client *view* things differently. Kelly often began the therapeutic process by having a client write a **self-characterization**. This provided Kelly with information about how the client viewed himself or herself, the world, and other people. Next, Kelly created a role for the client to play for about two weeks. The character in the role was markedly different from the client's self-characterization. The client became an actor, and the therapist became a supporting actor. Kelly called this approach to treating clients **fixed-role therapy**. He hoped that this procedure would help the client discover other possible ways of viewing his or her life:

> What I am saying is that it is not so much what man is that counts as it is what he ventures out to make himself. To make the leap he must do more than disclose himself; he must risk a certain amount of confusion. Then, as soon as he does catch a glimpse of a different kind of life, he needs to find some way of overcoming the paralyzing moment of threat, for this is the instant when he wonders what he really is— whether he is what he just was or is what he is about to be. (Kelly, 1964, p. 147)

In the role of supporting actor, the therapist had to help the client deal with this threatening moment and then provide experiences that validated the client's new construct system. According to Kelly, people with psychological problems had lost their ability to make-believe, an ability that the therapist must help the client regain.

Kelly became a major force within clinical psychology in the postwar years, but the popularity of his ideas in the United States diminished. In England, however, Kelly's ideas became extremely popular, even after his death, due primarily to the efforts of his disciple Donald Bannister. Today, Kelly's theory is again becoming popular in the United States, this time in the area of industrial-organizational psychology (e.g., see Jankowicz, 1987).

COMPARISON OF EXISTENTIAL AND HUMANISTIC PSYCHOLOGY

Existential and humanistic psychology have enough in common to cause them often to be lumped together as existential-humanistic psychology or simply as humanistic psychology. The following is a list of beliefs shared by existential and humanistic psychology.

1. Humans have a free will and are therefore responsible for their own actions.

2. The most appropriate method by which to study humans is phenomenology, the study of intact subjective experience.

3. To be understood, the human must be studied as a whole. Elementism of any type gives a distorted view of human nature.

4. Humans are unique, and therefore anything learned about other animals is irrelevant to the understanding of humans.

5. Each human is unique because no two humans have the same subjective reality.

6. Hedonism is not a major motive in human behavior. Instead of seeking pleasure and avoiding pain, humans seek meaningful lives characterized by personal growth.

7. Living an authentic life is better than living an inauthentic one.

The major difference between existential and humanistic psychology lies in their assumptions about human nature. The humanists assume that humans are basically good, and therefore, if placed in a healthy environment, they will naturally live a life in harmony with other humans. For humanists, the major motivation in life is the actualizing tendency, which is innate and which continually drives a person toward those activities and events conducive to self-actualization. The existentialists, on the other hand, view human nature as essentially neutral. For them, the only thing we are born with is the freedom to choose the nature of our existence. This is what

Sartre meant by his famous statement *"Existence precedes essence."* For Sartre (1905–1980) and most existential philosophers, there is no human essence at birth. We are free to choose our own essence as a unique human being. We become our choices. We can exercise our freedom to create any type of life we wish, either good or bad. The major motive in life, according to the existentialist, is to *create* meaning by effectively making choices. Many existential thinkers have reached the conclusion that without meaning life is not worth living but that with meaning humans can tolerate almost any conditions. Frankl quotes Nietzsche as saying, "He who has a *why* to live can bear with almost any *how*" (1963, p. xiii). Frankl maintains that there is only one motivational force for humans, and that is what he calls the "will to meaning" (1946/1984, p. 121).

Generally, the view of human nature that the humanists hold causes them to be optimistic about humans and their future. If societies could be made compatible with our nature, they say, humans could live together in peace and harmony. The existentialists are more pessimistic. For them, humans have no built-in guidance system but only the freedom to choose. Because we are free, we cannot blame God, our parents, genetics, or circumstances for our misfortune—only ourselves. This responsibility often makes freedom more of a curse than a blessing, and people often choose not to exercise their freedom by conforming to values that others have formulated. In his famous book *Escape from Freedom* (1941), Erich Fromm (1900–1980) said that often the first thing people do when they recognize their freedom is attempt to escape from it by affiliating themselves with someone or something that will reduce or eliminate their choices. The negative aspect of freedom is captured in the following hypothetical situation in which a student in a progressive school asked the teacher: Do we have to do whatever we want to again today? It is very difficult to be free.

Another important difference between existential and humanistic psychologists is that for the existentialist the realization that one's death is inevitable is extremely important. Before a rich full life is possible, one must come to grips with the fact that one's life is finite. The humanistic psychologist does not dwell as much on the meaning of death in human existence. Hall and Lindzey summarize the pessimism of existential psychology:

> It would be wrong to conclude . . . that existential psychology is primarily optimistic or hopeful about humans. One does not need to read far in Kierkegaard, Nietzsche, Heidegger, Sartre, Binswanger, or Boss to realize that this is far from being the case. Existential psychology is as concerned with death as it is with life. Nothingness yawns always at one's feet. Dread looms as large as love does in the existentialists' writings. There can be no light without shadows. A psychology that makes guilt inborn and an inescapable feature of existence does not offer much solace. "I am free" means at the same time, "I am completely responsible for my existence" . . . becoming a human being is a tough project and few achieve it. (1978, p. 320)

In contrast, Maddi and Costa summarize the basic optimism of humanistic psychology:

> Humanism, as espoused by third-force adherents, leads to a psychology that is not only centered on the human being but sets a positive value on those of his capabilities and aspirations that seem to distinguish him from lower animals and make him master of his own fate. Choice, will-power, conceptual thought, imagination, introspection, self-criticism, aspirations for the future, and creativity are important topics in humanism, for they refer to capabilities and interests that seem unique to man as a species.
>
> Humanism is not only concerned with the characteristics setting man apart from other living things. Also important are the characteristics that set each man apart from other men. Individuality—the thoughts, fantasies, strivings, worries, triumphs, and the tragedies that sum up to one particular person's existence and no one else's—is always a central topic in humanistic positions.
>
> It should be apparent in all this that humanism takes a very optimistic, laudatory view of man. In the history of philosophical thought, humanism has always made a hero of man, and the contemporary third force in psychology is certainly no exception. (1972, pp. 3–5)

EVALUATION

Modern humanistic psychology began as a protest movement against behaviorism and psychoanalysis. Behaviorism saw too much similarity between humans and other animals. The protesters contended that behaviorism concentrated on trivial types of behavior and ignored or minimized the mental and emotional processes that made humans unique. Psychoanalysis focused on abnormal individuals and emphasized unconscious or sexual motivation while ignoring healthy individuals whose primary motives included personal growth and the improvement of society. Humanistic psychologists criticized scientific psychology in general because it modeled itself after the physical sciences by assuming determinism and seeking lawfulness among classes of events. Scientific psychology also viewed individual uniqueness, something that was very important to humanistic psychology, as a nuisance; only general laws were of interest. Also, because science and reliable measurement went hand-in-hand, scientific psychology excluded many important human attributes from study simply because of the difficulty of measuring them. Processes such as willing, valuing, and seeking meaning are examples of such attributes, as are such emotions as love, guilt, despair, happiness, and hope.

Criticisms

It should come as no surprise that humanistic psychology itself has been criticized. Each of the following has been offered as one of its weaknesses.

1. Humanistic psychology equates behaviorism with the work of Watson and Skinner. Both men stressed environmental events as the causes of human behavior and denied or minimized the importance of mental events. Other behaviorists, however, stress both mental events and purpose in their analysis of behavior—for example, Tolman.

2. It overlooks the cumulative nature of sci-

ence by insisting that scientific psychology does not care about the loftier human attributes. The problem is that we are not yet prepared to study such attributes. One must first learn a language before one can compose poetry. The type of scientific psychology that humanistic psychologists criticize provides the basis for the future study of more complex human characteristics.

3. The description of humans that humanistic psychologists offer is like the more favorable ones found through the centuries in poetry, literature, or religion. It represents a type of wishful thinking that is not supported by the facts that more objective psychology has accumulated. We should not ignore facts just because they are not to our liking.

4. It criticizes behaviorism, psychoanalysis, and scientific psychology in general, but all three have made significant contributions to the betterment of the human condition. In other words, all three have done the very thing that humanistic psychology sets as one of its major goals. Behaviorists justifiably claim to have brought about improvements in such areas as psychotherapy, education, child rearing, and the management of personal behavior. Branding the entire behavioristic movement as wrong or ineffective because it is based on an "incorrect" assumption about human nature is overly simplistic. Similarly, psychoanalysts justifiably claim that the information they have provided has vastly improved our understanding of not only mentally ill people but also normal people. Most behaviorists and psychoanalysts would agree with the weaker criticism that they have had only limited success in explaining human behavior.

5. If humanistic psychology rejects scientific method as a means of evaluating propositions about humans, what is to be used in its place? If intuition or reasoning alone is to be used, this enterprise should not be referred to as psychology but would be more accurately labeled philosophy or even religion. The humanistic approach to studying humans is often characterized as a throwback to psychology's prescientific past.

6. By rejecting animal research, humanistic psychologists are turning their backs on an extremely valuable source of knowledge about humans. Not to use the insights of evolutionary theory in studying human behavior is, at best, regressive.

7. Many of the terms and concepts that humanistic psychologists use are so nebulous that they defy clear definition and verification. There is even confusion over the definition of humanistic psychology. After searching for a definition of humanistic psychology in the *Journal of Humanistic Psychology*, in various books on humanistic psychology, and in the programs of the Division of Humanistic Psychology of the APA, Michael Wertheimer reaches the following conclusion:

> It is hard to quarrel with such goals as authenticity, actualizing the potential inherent in every human being, creating truly meaningful human relationships, being fully in touch with our innermost feelings, and expanding our awareness. But what, really, is humanistic psychology? To paraphrase an old Jewish joke, if you ask two humanists what humanistic psychology is, you are likely to get at least three mutually incompatible definitions. . . . It is highly unlikely that an explicit definition of [humanistic psychology] could be written that would satisfy even a small fraction of the people who call themselves "humanistic psychologists." (1978, pp. 739, 743)

Contributions

To be fair to humanistic psychologists, it must be pointed out that they usually do not complain that behaviorism, psychoanalysis, and scientific psychology have made *no* contributions to the understanding of humans. Rather, their claim has been that behaviorism and psychoanalysis tell only part of the story and that perhaps some important human attributes cannot be studied using the traditional methods and assumptions of science. As William James said, if existing methods are ineffective for studying certain aspects of human nature, it is not those aspects of human nature that are to be discarded but the methods. Humanistic psychologists do not want to discard scientific inquiry but to expand our conception of science so that scientific inquiry can be used to study the higher human attributes. This desire for a broader conception of science appears in May's comments:

> The outlines of a science of man we suggest will deal with man as a symbol-maker, the reasoner, the historical mammal who can participate in his community and who possesses the potentiality of freedom and ethical action. The pursuit of this science will take no less rigorous thought and wholehearted discipline than the pursuit of experimental and natural science at their best, but it will place the scientific enterprise in a broader context. Perhaps it will again be possible to study man scientifically and still see him whole. (1967, p. 199)

The expansion of psychology's domain is humanistic psychology's major contribution to the discipline. In psychology there is now an increased tendency to study the whole person. We are concerned with not only how people learn, think, and mature biologically and intellectually but also how people formulate plans to attain future goals and why people laugh, cry, and create meaning in their lives. In the opinion of many, the humanistic paradigm has breathed new life into psychology. In the following passage, Hall and Lindzey mention only existential psychology, but their remarks pertain to humanistic psychology as well:

> Whatever the future of existential psychology may be—and at the present time it appears to have sufficient vigor and vitality to last a long time—it has already served at least one very important function. That function is to rescue psychology from being drowned in a sea of theories that have lost contact with the everyday world and with the "givens" of experience. . . . Existentialism is helping to revitalize a science that many feel has become theoretically moribund. It has done this by insisting on using a strictly phenomenological methodology. It has tried to see what is actually there and to describe human existence in concrete terms. . . . Whatever the future of existential psychology may be . . . it is clear that now it offers a profoundly new way of studying and comprehending human beings. For this reason, it merits the closest attention by serious students of psychology. (1978, pp. 343–344)

SUMMARY

A general trend in human history has been for philosophies that emphasize the mind or the body to be popular during relatively tranquil times and philosophies that emphasize emotional experience to be popular during relatively troubled times. The 1960s were troubled times in the United States, and a group of psychologists emerged who believed that behaviorism and psychoanalysis, the two major forces in psychology, were neglecting important aspects of human existence. What was needed was a third force that emphasized the positive, creative, and emotional side of humans. This third-force psychology is a combination of existential philosophy and romantic notions of humans; the combination is called humanistic psychology, as well as third-force psychology. Humanistic psychologists are phenomenologists. In modern times, Brentano and Husserl developed phenomenology, which is the study of intact, conscious experiences as they occur and without any preconceived notions about the nature of those experiences. According to Brentano, all conscious acts intended (referred to) something outside themselves. An example is the statement "I see that girl." Husserl thought that a careful, objective study of mental phenomena could provide a bridge between philosophy and science. Besides the type of phenomenology that focused on intentionality, Husserl proposed a second type, a pure phenomenology that studied the essence of subjective experience. Thus, for Husserl, phenomenology could study the mind turned outward or turned inward.

As used by existentialists, phenomenology became a study of the totality of human existence. Such a study focused on the full range of human cognitive and emotional experience, including anxiety, dread, fear, joy, guilt, and anguish. Husserl's student Heidegger expanded phenomenology into existential inquiry. Heidegger studied *Dasein*, or being-in-the-world. *Dasein* means "to be there"; but for humans "to be there" means "to exist there," and existence is a complex process involving the interpretation and the evaluation of one's experiences and making choices regarding those experiences. Heidegger believed that although humans had a free will, they were thrown by events beyond their control into their life circumstances. Thrownness determined such things as whether a person was male or female, rich or poor, attractive or unattractive, and so on. It was up to each person to make the most of his or her life no matter what the circumstances. Positive growth occurs when a person explores possibilities for living through his or her choices. Choosing, however, required entering the unknown, and this caused anxiety. For Heidegger then, exercising one's freedom required courage, but only by exercising one's freedom could one live an authentic life—a life that the person had chosen and therefore a life for which the person was completely responsible. If a person lived his or her life in accordance with other people's values, he or she was living an inauthentic life. For Heidegger, the first step toward living an authentic life was to come to grips with the inevitability of death (nonbeing). Once a person comprehended and dealt with finitude, he or she could proceed to live a rich, full, authentic life.

Binswanger applied Heidegger's philosophical ideas to psychiatry and psychology. Binswanger called his approach to psychotherapy *Daseinanalysis*, or the study of a person's approach to being-in-the-world. Binswanger divided *Dasein* into the *Umwelt* (the physical world), the *Mitwelt* (the social world), and the *Eigenwelt* (the person's self-perceptions). According to Binswanger, each person embraced life's experiences through a *Weltanschauung*, or world-design, which was a general orientation toward life. One world-design could portray the world and everything in it as hostile, another could portray it as friendly, and still another could portray some things as hostile and others as friendly. Binswanger attempted to understand his patients' world-designs; if a patient's world-design was proving to be ineffective, he would suggest alternative, potentially more effective ones. Like Heidegger, Binswanger believed that the circumstances into which one was thrown placed limits on personal freedom. Thrownness created what Binswanger called the ground of existence from which one had to begin the process of becoming by exercising one's freedom. According to Binswanger, each person attempted to rise above his or her ground of existence and to attain being-beyond-the-world—that is, to rise above current circumstances by transforming them through free choice.

May is primarily responsible for bringing existential psychology to the United States. Like the other existential psychologists, May believes that normal, healthy living involves the experience of anxiety because living an authentic life necessitates venturing into the unknown. If a person cannot cope with normal anxiety, he or she will develop neurotic anxiety and will be driven from an authentic life to a life of conformity or to a life that is overly restrictive. Furthermore, because the person with neurotic anxiety is not exercising his or her human capacity to choose, he or she experiences guilt. Thus, an authentic life is characterized by normal anxiety and guilt and an inauthentic life by neurotic anxiety and guilt.

Unlike existential psychologists, humanistic psychologists believe that humans are basically good, a belief that can be traced back to the romanticism of Rousseau. According to Maslow, the founder of third-force psychology, human needs are arranged in a hierarchy. If one satisfactorily meets the physiological, safety, belonging and love, and esteem needs, then one is in position to become self-actualized. Leading a life characterized by fullness, spontaneity, and creativity, the self-actualizing person is being-motivated rather than deficiency-motivated. That is, because this person has met the basic needs, he or she does not need to seek specific things in the environment. Rather, he or she can embrace the world fully and openly and ponder the higher values of life.

Rogers concluded that the only way to understand a person was to determine how that person viewed things—that is, to determine that person's subjective reality. This view resulted in Rogers's famous client-centered therapy. Like Maslow, Rogers postulated an innate actualizing tendency. For this actualizing tendency to be realized, one had to use the organismic valuing process as a frame of reference in living one's life. That is, one had to use one's own inner feelings in determining the value of various experiences. If one lived according to one's organismic valuing process, one was a congruent person and was living an authentic life. Unfortunately, because humans had a need for positive regard, they often allowed the relevant people in their lives to place conditions of worth on them. When conditions of worth replaced the organismic valuing process as a frame of reference for living one's life, the person became incongruent and lived an inauthentic life. According to Rogers, the only way to prevent incongruency was for the person to receive unconditional positive regard from the relevant people in his or her life.

Kelly, who was not trained as a clinical psychologist, tried a number of approaches to helping emotionally disturbed individuals. He found that anything that caused his clients to view themselves and their problems differently resulted in improvement. Because of this observation, Kelly concluded that mental problems were really perceptual problems, and he maintained that humans were free to construe themselves and the world in any way they chose. They did this by creating a construct system that was, or should be, tested empirically. Any number of constructs could be used to construe any situation. That is, one could always view the world in a variety of ways, so how one viewed it was a matter of personal choice. In fixed-role therapy, Kelly had his clients write a self-characterization; then, he would create a role for his client to play that was distinctly different from the client's personality. By offering the client support and help in playing his or her role, Kelly became a supporting actor and helped the client to view himself or herself differently. Once the client saw that there were alternative ways of viewing one's self, one's life, and one's problems, improvement often resulted. According to Kelly, neurotics had lost their ability to make-believe, and it was the therapist's task to restore it.

Existential and humanistic psychology share the following beliefs: Humans possess a free will; humans are responsible for their actions; phenomenology is the most appropriate method for studying humans; humans must be studied as whole beings and not divided up in any way; because humans are unique as a species, animal research is irrelevant to an understanding of humans; no two humans are alike; the search for meaning is the most important human motive; and all humans should aspire to live authentic lives. The major difference between existential and humanistic psychology is that the former views human nature as neutral whereas the latter views it as basically good. According to existential psychologists, because we do not have an innate nature or guidance system, we must choose our existence. Existential psychologists see freedom as a curse as well as a blessing and something from which most humans attempt to escape.

Humanistic psychology has been criticized for equating behaviorism with the formulations of Watson and Skinner and thereby ignoring the work of other behaviorists who stressed the importance of mental events and goal-directed behavior, for failing to understand that psychology's scientific efforts must first concentrate on the simpler aspects of humans before it can study the more complex aspects, for offering a description of humans more positive than the facts warrant, for minimizing or ignoring the positive contributions of behaviorism and psychoanalysis, for suggesting methods of inquiry that go back to psychology's prescientific history, for having more in common with philosophy and religion than with psychology, for overlooking a valuable source of information by rejecting the validity of animal research, and for using terms and concepts so nebulous as to defy clear definition or verification. Humanistic psychology's major contribution has been to expand psychology's domain by urging that all aspects of humans be investigated and that psychology's conception of science be changed to allow objective study of uniquely human attributes.

DISCUSSION QUESTIONS

1. Give evidence that philosophies that emphasize the mind or body often prevail during tranquil times and philosophies that emphasize the human emotions often prevail during troubled times.

2. What is third-force psychology? What did the third-force psychologists see as the limitations of the other two forces?

3. Describe Brentano's phenomenology. What did he mean by intentionality?

4. What did Husserl mean by pure phenomenology?

5. How did Heidegger expand phenomenology?

6. Discuss the following terms and concepts from Heidegger's theory: *Dasein, authenticity, becoming, responsibility,* and *thrownness.*

7. Describe Binswanger's method of *Daseinanalysis.*

8. Discuss the following terms and concepts from Binswanger's theory: *Umwelt, Mitwelt, Eigenwelt, world-design, ground of existence,* and *being-beyond-the-world.*

9. In May's theory, what is the relationship between anxiety and guilt? What is the difference between normal anxiety and neurotic anxiety?

10. What, according to May, is the human dilemma?

11. What are the main tenets of humanistic psychology?

12. Summarize Maslow's hierarchy of needs.

13. List what Maslow found to be the characteristics of self-actualizing people.

14. What is the difference between deficiency motivation and being motivation? Give an example of each.

15. For Rogers, what constituted an incongruent person? In your answer, include a discussion of the organismic valuing process, the need for positive regard, and conditions of worth.

16. According to Rogers, what was the only way to avoid incongruency?

17. According to Rogers, what were the three major components of any relationship that facilitated personal growth?

18. Why did Kelly maintain that all humans are like scientists?

19. Describe Kelly's concept of constructive alternativism.

20. Describe Kelly's approach to psychotherapy. What did Kelly mean when he said that psychological problems were perceptual problems?

21. What are the similarities and differences between humanistic and existential psychology?

22. Summarize the criticisms of humanistic psychology.

23. In what way(s) has humanistic psychology contributed to psychology?

SUGGESTIONS FOR FURTHER READING

Buhler, C. (1971). Basic theoretical concepts of humanistic psychology. *American Psychologist, 26,* 378–386.
This is an excellent summary of the basic tenets of humanistic psychology and of the relationships between humanistic psychology and psychotherapy and education.

Hoffman, E. (1988). *The right to be human: A biography of Abraham Maslow.* Los Angeles: Tarcher.
Hoffman gives an interesting and well-documented biography of Maslow. It contains a number of photographs depicting important individuals and events in Maslow's life.

Jourard, S. M. (1971). *The transparent self.* New York: Van Nostrand.
Jourard contends that throughout history humans have chosen to conceal their true selves in order to avoid criticism or rejection. The result has been that people are misunderstood even by their family and friends. This lack of understanding by others causes a misunderstanding of ourselves, which, in turn, contributes to a variety of illnesses. Although it has become a tradition in Western civilization to conceal one's true self, Jourard believes that this need not and should not be the case. (Available in paperback.)

Kinget, G. M. (1975). *On being human: A systematic view.* New York: Harcourt Brace Jovanovich.
Kinget indicates that there are two types of humanistic psychology. One type is called "the human potential movement," and it focuses on the growth experiences provided by encounter groups, training (T) groups, and similar mechanisms for social-emotional expression. The other type is more interested in inquiry, reflection, description, and research, with the ultimate objective of creating a specifically human science, one based on a genuinely human model rather than on a model borrowed from the physical sciences. Kinget's book represents the second type of humanistic psychology; chapters include "The Symbolic Animal," "Lawmaker, Lawbreaker," "The Playing Animal," "Beyond Sex to Love," "The Will to Beauty," "Human Freedom: Real or Illusory?" "The Questing Beast," "Foreknowledge of Death," "Ultimate Concern: The Religious Animal," and "The Transcending Animal." (Available in paperback.)

Kirschenbaum, H. (1979). *On becoming Carl Rogers.* New York: Dell.
This is a readable and informative biography of Carl Rogers. (Available in paperback.)

Maslow, A. H. (1968). *Toward a psychology of being* (2nd ed.). New York: Van Nostrand Reinhold.
This is one of Maslow's most influential works. Chapters include "Toward a Psychology of Health," "What Psychology Can Learn from the Existentialists," "Deficiency Motivation and Growth Motivation," "The Need to Know and the Fear of Knowing," "Peak-Experiences as Acute Identity-Experiences," "Creativity in Self-Actualizing People," and "Values, Growth and Health." (Available in paperback.)

Maslow, A. H. (1971). *The farther reaches of human nature.* New York: Penguin Books.
This is a collection of previously published papers that Maslow prepared just prior to his death. Chapters include "Toward a Humanistic Biology," "Self-Actualizing and Beyond," "The Need for Creative People," "Goals and Implications of Humanistic Education," "On Low Grumbles, High Grumbles, and Metagrumbles," "Various Meanings of Transcendence," "A Theory of Metamotivation: The Biological Rooting of the Value-Life," and "Comments on Religions, Values, and Peak Experiences." (Available in paperback.)

Maslow, A. H. (1987). *Motivation and personality* (3rd ed.). New York: Harper & Row. (Original work published 1954)
Maslow elaborates his theory of motivation based on the hierarchy of needs in this book. This book also contains a description of the characteristics of self-actualizing people. Chapters include "A Theory of Human Motivation," "The Hierarchy of Needs," "Origins of Pathology," "Is Destructiveness Instinctive?" "Psychotherapy as Good Human Relationships," "Self-Actualizing People: A Study of Psychological Health," "A Psychological Approach to Science," and "A Holistic Approach to Psychology." This edition

also contains sections entitled "The Influence of Abraham Maslow," written by Robert Frager, and "The Rich Harvest of Abraham Maslow," written by Ruth Cox. (Available in paperback.)

Rogers, C. R. (1951). *Client-centered therapy: Its current practice, implications, and theory*. Boston: Houghton Mifflin.

Rogers described his earliest approach to psychotherapy as "nondirective" because he believed clients could solve their own problems if they were given the proper atmosphere for doing so. The book described here presents Rogers's second approach to psychotherapy as a joint venture, deeply involving both the client and the therapist. The therapist's job was now to actively attempt to understand the client's subjective reality. (Available in paperback.)

Rogers, C. R. (1961). *On becoming a person: A therapist's view of psychotherapy*. Boston: Houghton Mifflin.

This is a collection of papers prepared by Rogers over the course of several years. Chapters include "This Is Me," "Some Hypotheses Regarding the Facilitation of Personal Growth," "The Characteristics of a Helping Relationship," "What It Means to Become a Person," "A Therapist's View of the Good Life: The Fully Functioning Person," "Persons or Science? A Philosophical Question," "Significant Learning: In Therapy and in Education," "The Implications of Client-Centered Therapy for Family Life," "Toward a Theory of Creativity," and "The Place of the Individual in the New World of the Behavioral Sciences." (Available in paperback.)

Rogers, C. R. (1980). *A way of being*. Boston: Houghton Mifflin.

This book consists of a collection of articles, many previously published but some not, that reflect the changes in Rogers's thinking during the 1970s. Chapters include "In Retrospect: Forty-Six Years," "Growing Old: Or Older and Growing," "Do We Need 'A' Reality?" "Empathic: An Unappreciated Way of Being," "Building Person-Centered Communities: The Implications for the Future," "Some New Challenges to the Helping Professions," "Can Learning Encompass Both Ideas and Feelings," "Learnings in Large Groups: Their Implications for the Future," and "The World of Tomorrow, and the Person of Tomorrow." (Available in paperback.)

Royce, J. R., & Mos, L. P. (Eds.). (1981). *Humanistic psychology: Concepts and criticisms*. New York: Plenum.

This rather difficult book of readings addresses the historical antecedents of humanistic psychology, its philosophical basis, its methods, its relationships to other perspectives, and its assets and liabilities. Contributors comprise a group of internationally known individuals from disciplines such as psychology, psychiatry, anthropology, sociology, religion, and philosophy.

Severin, F. T. (Ed.). (1973). *Discovering man in psychology: A humanistic approach*. New York: McGraw-Hill.

Prominent individuals such as Gordon Allport, Viktor Frankl, Erich Fromm, Amedeo Giorgi, Jerome Kagan, Abraham Maslow, and Carl Rogers discuss topics related to humanistic psychology. Chapters include "Love and Altruism," "Loneliness and Death," "Encounter Groups," "Personal Values and Commitment," "Is the Human Species Unique?" "Value Judgments in the Social Sciences," "The Experimenter's Obligations to His Subjects," "Phenomenology and Existential Psychology," and "Changing Patterns of Thought in Psychology." (Available in paperback.)

Wertheimer, Michael (1978). Humanistic psychology and the humane but tough-minded psychologists. *American Psychologist, 33*, 739–745.

After searching the *Journal of Humanistic Psychology*, several books on humanistic psychology, and the program of the Division of Humanistic Psychology at an APA convention, Wertheimer concludes that an unambiguous definition of humanistic psychology does not exist. His research indicates that what is referred to as humanistic psychology encompasses three themes: Human nature is best studied within the liberal arts tradition, that is, studied from a variety of viewpoints; psychology and psychotherapy should offer information and experiences that make people more aware, more autonomous, more social-minded, more integrated, and more stable; and the mechanistic, materialistic view of humans must be replaced by a holistic view. About the first theme, Wertheimer heartily agrees, saying that much useful information about human nature has come from such individuals as Dostoevsky, Shakespeare, Goethe, and Frank Lloyd Wright. About the second theme, Wertheimer says it is yet to be proven. In fact, there is some evidence that encounter groups and consciousness-raising experiences may do clients more harm than good. Concerning the third theme, Wertheimer says that few psychologists espouse the simplistic, mechanistic view of humans that humanistic psychologists attack. Certainly, those psychologists following in either the Gestalt or psychoanalytic traditions do not hold such a view. For that matter, neither do most behaviorists. Wertheimer concludes by saying that it is possible that the dispassionate, tough-minded approach to psychology against which the humanists are rebelling may furnish the most objective information about humans, and therefore it may be the most useful approach.

GLOSSARY

Anxiety The feeling that results when one confronts the unknown, as when one contemplates death or when one's choices carry one into new life circumstances. According to existentialists, one cannot live an authentic life without experiencing anxiety.

Authentic life According to existentialists, the type of life that is freely chosen and not dictated by the values of others. In such a life, one's internal feelings, values, and interpretations act as a guide for conduct.

Becoming A characteristic of the authentic life because

the authentic person is always becoming something other than what he or she was. Becoming is the normal, healthy psychological growth of a human being.

Being-beyond-the-world Binswanger's term for becoming. The healthy individual always attempts to transcend what he or she was.

Being motivation For Maslow, the type of motivation that characterizes the self-actualizing person. Because being motivation is not need-directed, it embraces the higher values of human existence, such as beauty, truth, and justice.

Being perception Perception that embraces fully "what is there" because it is not an attempt to locate specific items that will satisfy needs.

Binswanger, Ludwig (1881–1966) Applied Heidegger's existential philosophy to psychiatry and psychology. For Binswanger, a prerequisite for helping an emotionally disturbed person was to determine how that person viewed himself or herself and the world. (*See also Daseinanalysis* and **World-design**.)

Brentano, Franz (1838–1917) The modern founder of phenomenology. Brentano's act psychology required the careful analysis of meaningful, intact mental phenomena. (*See also* **Intentionality**.)

Conditions of worth According to Rogers, the conditions that the relevant people in our lives place on us and that we must meet before these people will give us positive regard.

Constructive alternativism Kelly's notion that it was always possible to view circumstances in a variety of ways.

Construct systems The collection of personal constructs with which people make predictions about future events.

Courage According to existentialists, that attribute necessary for living an authentic life because such a life is characterized by uncertainty.

Dasein Heidegger's term for being-in-the-world. The world does not exist without humans, and humans do not exist without the world. Because humans exist in the world, it is there that they must exercise their free will. Being-in-the-world means existing in the world, and existing means interpreting and valuing one's experiences and making choices regarding those experiences.

Daseinanalysis Binswanger's method of psychotherapy that required that the therapist understand the client's worldview. *Daseinanalysis* examines a person's mode of being-in-the-world.

Deficiency motivation According to Maslow, motivation that is directed toward the satisfaction of some specific need.

Eigenwelt Binswanger's term for a person's private, inner experiences.

Existential psychology The brand of contemporary psychology that was influenced by existential philosophy. The key concepts in existential psychology include freedom, responsibility, anxiety, guilt, thrownness, and authenticity.

Fixed-role therapy Kelly's brand of therapy whereby he would assign a role for his clients to play that was distinctly different from the client's self-characterization. With this type of therapy, the therapist acts much like a supporting actor. (*See also* **Self-characterization**.)

Fully functioning person Rogers's term for a person who is living a congruent, or authentic, life.

Ground of existence Binswanger's term for the circumstances into which a person is thrown and according to which he or she must make choices. (Also called *thrownness* and *facticity*.)

Guilt The feeling that results from living an inauthentic life.

Heidegger, Martin (1889–1976) Expanded Husserl's phenomenology to include an examination of the totality of human existence.

Hierarchy of needs Maslow's contention that human needs are arranged in a hierarchy and that lower needs in the hierarchy must be adequately satisfied before attention can be focused on higher needs. The most basic and powerful needs in the hierarchy are physiological needs, and then come safety needs, needs for belonging and love, and the need for self-esteem. When all lower needs in the hierarchy are adequately satisfied, a person becomes self-actualizing.

Human dilemma According to May, the paradox that results from the dual nature of humans as objects to which things happen and as subjects who assign meaning to their experiences.

Humanistic psychology The branch of psychology that is closely aligned with existential psychology. Unlike existential psychology, however, humanistic psychology assumes that humans are basically good. That is, if negative environmental factors did not stifle human development, humans would live humane lives. Humanistic psychology is concerned with examining the more positive aspects of human nature that behaviorism and psychoanalysis had neglected. (Also called *third-force psychology*.)

Husserl, Edmund (1859–1938) Proposed two types of phenomenology. One type stressed intentionality and sought to determine the relationship between mental acts and events in the physical world. The second type involved an analysis of the contents and processes of the mind that were independent of physical events. (*See also* **Pure phenomenology**.)

Inauthentic life A life lived in accordance with values other than those freely and personally chosen. Such a life is characterized by guilt.

Incongruent person Rogers's term for the person whose organismic valuing process is replaced by conditions of worth as a guide for living.

Intentionality Brentano's contention that every mental act referred to something external to the act.

Jonah complex According to Maslow, the fear of self-knowledge.

Kelly, George (1905–1967) Can be labeled as either an existential or a humanistic psychologist. Kelly emphasized that it was always possible to construe one's self and the world in a variety of ways. For Kelly, neurosis was essentially a perceptual problem.

Maslow, Abraham (1908–1970) A humanistic psychologist who emphasized the innate human tendency toward self-actualization. Maslow contended that behaviorism and psychoanalysis provided only a partial understanding of human existence and that humanistic, or third-force, psychology needed to be added to complete our understanding.

May, Rollo (b. 1909) Psychologist who has been instrumental in bringing European existential philosophy and psychology to the United States.

Mitwelt Binswanger's term for the realm of social interactions.

Need-directed perception Perception whose purpose is to locate things in the environment that will satisfy a need. (Also called *deficiency perception* or *D-perception*.)

Need for positive regard According to Rogers, the need for positive responses from the relevant people in one's life.

Neurotic anxiety The abnormal fear of freedom that results in a person living a life that minimizes personal choice.

Ontology The study of the nature of existence.

Organismic valuing process According to Rogers, the innate, internal guidance system that a person can use to "stay on the track" toward self-actualization.

Phenomenology The introspective study of intact, mental experiences.

Pure phenomenology The methodology proposed by Husserl to discover the essence of those mental acts and processes by which we gain all knowledge.

Responsibility A necessary by-product of freedom. If we are free to choose our own existence, then we are completely responsible for that existence.

Rogers, Carl (1902–1987) A humanist psychologist whose nondirective and then client-centered psychotherapy was seen by many as the first viable alternative to psychoanalysis as a method for treating troubled individuals. Like Maslow's, Rogers's theory of personality emphasized the innate tendency toward self-actualization. According to Rogers, a person would continue toward self-actualization unless his or her organismic valuing process was displaced by conditions of worth as a guide for living. The only way to avoid creating conditions of worth is to give a person unconditional positive regard. (*See also* **Conditions of worth**, **Organismic valuing process**, **Self-actualization**, and **Unconditional positive regard**.)

Self-actualization According to Rogers and Maslow, the innate, human tendency toward wholeness. The self-actualizing person is open to experience and embraces the higher values of human existence.

Self-alienation According to existentialists, the condition that results when people accept values other than those that they attained freely and personally as guides for living.

Self-characterization The self-description that Kelly required of many of his clients before beginning their therapeutic program.

Shut-upness Kierkegaard's term for the type of life lived by a defensive, inauthentic person.

Subjective reality A person's consciousness.

Third-force psychology *See* **Humanistic psychology**.

Thrownness According to Heidegger and Binswanger, the circumstances that characterize a person's existence that are beyond the person's control. (*See also* **Ground of existence**.)

Umwelt Binswanger's term for the physical world.

Unconditional positive regard According to Rogers, the giving of positive regard without any preconditions.

World-design (*Weltanschauung*) Binswanger's term for a person's basic orientation toward the world and life.

CHAPTER 18

Contemporary Psychology

HISTORICAL INFLUENCES ON CONTEMPORARY PSYCHOLOGY

Contemporary psychology reflects its long, diverse history. In this text, we have seen that at various times the philosophies of empiricism, sensationalism, positivism, rationalism, romanticism, and existentialism have been employed in efforts to understand humans. We have also seen that one or more of these philosophies became the basis for psychology's schools of thought: voluntarism, structuralism, functionalism, behaviorism, Gestalt psychology, psychoanalysis, and humanistic psychology. The methodologies most often used to study humans throughout psychology's history have been introspection, empirical observation, and experimentation. Remnants of all these philosophies, schools, and methodologies are found in contemporary psychology. Because this is a history text, it is not our intention to comprehensively review contemporary psychology. We will, however, offer several examples of how historical influences are currently manifesting themselves.

It is interesting to note that one of psychology's major historical influences is not represented in contemporary psychology—the religious influence. Although the religious, or spiritual, conception of human nature persisted longer than any other, it is essentially absent from today's psychology:

> It is instructive to examine a remarkable feature of contemporary psychology: no major spokesperson for the discipline, no figure identified as one responsible for its methods and concerns, none who has provided a theory of

consequence to contemporary endeavors, has argued that the religious dimension of life is necessary for an understanding of human psychology. Stated another way, we recognize that in the fifteen centuries beginning in A.D. 200, there is no record of a serious psychological work devoid of religious allusion and that, since 1930, there has not been a major psychological work expressing a need for spiritual terms in an attempt to comprehend the psychological dimensions of man. (D. N. Robinson, 1986, p. 294)

Only the supernatural aspects of religion are absent from modern psychology, however. One can easily see remnants of the religious perspective in contemporary humanistic psychology—for example, the emphasis on free will, responsibility, and human uniqueness and on the importance of subjective, emotional experience. So, in a sense, even remnants of the religious perspective are represented in contemporary psychology. Leahey even argues that psychology has become a religion:

> Psychology, however much behaviorists and cognitive scientists might object, teaches introspection as the final judge of right and wrong, and encourages people to undertake an inward journey in search of introspective certainty concerning our real feelings and our supposed secret selves. In the United States, at least, psychology has become a new religion establishing an inner quest for self where before there had been an outer quest for God. . . . If there is no transcendent truth outside nature, and if psychology is the science of the individual, then the only proper guide to life must come from scientific psychology, and that entails looking within for truth that cannot come from without. (1987, p. 479)

Although the influence of many earlier philosophies and methodologies can be found in contemporary psychology, concluding that modern psychology is the culmination of earlier forms of psychology would be incorrect. Such a conclusion would represent the mistake of presentism referred to in chapter 1. Presentism assumes that the present state of a discipline is its highest, best, and most fully developed state. Although presentism may characterize some aspects of modern psychology, it does not characterize the entire discipline. Applied to psychology as a whole, the **culmination model** seems inaccurate. It implies a steady, continuous, progressive growth that did not generally occur. Concluding that psychology has changed for more or less the same reasons that languages change is more accurate. Languages change as the result of such factors as wars, immigration, commerce, and travel. Such events bring a language into contact with influences that often modify it in significant ways. For example, the mixing of two cultures through warfare often leaves the language of each culture with words and phrases—and thus with ideas and concepts—of the other culture. This **cross-fertilization model** accounts for the diversity found in contemporary psychology better than the culmination model. It seems best, then, to view modern psychology as a hybrid discipline that resulted from a variety of historical influences.

THE DIVERSITY OF CONTEMPORARY PSYCHOLOGY

Psychology today is diverse, but psychology has almost always been diverse. In psychology's long history, there has never been a time when all psychologists accepted a single paradigm. Perhaps the closest psychology ever came to being a single-paradigm discipline was during the Middle Ages, when departures from the view of humans contained in church dogma were simply not tolerated. Some might suggest that behaviorism dominated psychology during the period

from about 1930 through the 1950s, but this was not quite the case. Although behaviorism was extremely popular, there were always influential critics of behaviorism and an abundance of alternative views from which to choose (e.g., Gestalt psychology and psychoanalysis).

What distinguishes modern psychology from psychology during the period when schools existed is the relatively peaceful coexistence of psychologists holding dissimilar views. During the 1920s and 1930s, when several psychological schools existed simultaneously, open hostility often arose between members of the different schools. The schools were almost like religions, in that the members of one school believed that they were correct and therefore that members of other schools were wrong. Today, the schools are gone, and a spirit of **eclecticism** prevails, which is reminiscent of the functional approach to psychology that William James suggested. The eclectic chooses from diverse sources those techniques that are most effective in dealing with a problem. For James, the problem was to understand humans. If something was part of the human experience, he said, study it and use the most effective methods available to do so.

To fully appreciate the great diversity of modern psychology, we will look at the present divisions of the American Psychological Association (APA).

Divisions of the American Psychological Association

Table 18.1 lists the 47 divisions of the APA, and they are a clear indication of the diversity of psychology today. Note, for example, that divisions include Experimental Psychology (3), Psychology and the Arts (10), Military Psychology (19), Humanistic Psychology (32), Psychology of Women (35), and Psychoanalysis (39). The number of members in each division is also listed to show which areas of psychology are currently the most popular. Note that although a large number of APA members have no divisional affiliation (31,059), total division memberships (74,570) exceed total membership in the APA

TABLE 18.1 Divisions of the American Psychological Association and Their Memberships

Division	Total	Men	Women	% Men	% Women
1. General Psychology	4,453	2,966	1,487	66.6	33.4
2. Teaching of Psychology	1,931	1,400	531	72.5	27.5
3. Experimental Psychology	1,315	1,080	235	82.1	17.9
5. Evaluation and Measurement	1,353	1,040	313	76.9	23.1
6. Physiological and Comparative	754	616	138	81.7	18.3
7. Developmental Psychology	1,398	688	710	49.2	50.8
8. Personality and Social	2,794	2,097	697	75.1	24.9
9. SPSSI*	2,688	1,694	994	63.0	37.0
10. Psychology and the Arts	519	315	204	60.7	39.3
12. Clinical Psychology	5,911	4,267	1,644	72.2	27.8
13. Consulting Psychology	909	723	186	79.5	20.5
14. Industrial and Organizational	2,545	2,026	519	79.6	20.4
15. Educational Psychology	1,736	1,244	492	71.7	28.3
16. School Psychology	2,166	1,163	1,003	53.7	46.3
17. Counseling Psychology	2,817	1,983	834	70.4	29.6
18. Psychologists in Public Service	869	690	179	79.4	20.6
19. Military Psychology	534	476	58	89.1	10.9
20. Adult Development and Aging	1,159	679	480	58.6	41.4
21. Applied Experimental and Engineering Psychologists	496	438	58	88.3	11.7
22. Rehabilitation Psychology	959	710	249	74.0	26.0
23. Consumer Psychology	453	359	94	79.2	20.8
24. Theoretical and Philosophical Psychology	589	501	88	85.1	14.9
25. Experimental Analysis of Behavior	1,068	884	184	82.8	17.2
26. History of Psychology	873	729	144	83.5	16.5
27. Society for Community Research and Action: The Division of Community Psychology	986	718	268	72.8	27.2
28. Psychopharmacology	920	745	175	81.0	19.0
29. Psychotherapy	4,974	3,347	1,627	67.3	32.7
30. Psychological Hypnosis	1,487	1,217	270	81.8	18.1
31. State Psychological Association Affairs	459	343	116	74.7	25.3
32. Humanistic Psychology	726	542	184	74.7	25.3
33. Mental Retardation	776	542	234	69.8	30.2
34. Population and Environmental Psychology	393	276	117	70.2	29.8
35. Psychology of Women	2,251	99	2,152	4.4	95.6
36. PIRI†	1,337	1,001	336	74.9	25.1
37. Child, Youth, and Family Services	1,342	761	581	56.7	43.3
38. Health Psychology	2,824	1,925	899	68.2	31.8
39. Psychoanalysis	2,773	1,397	1,376	50.4	49.6
40. Clinical Neuropsychology	2,778	1,945	833	70.0	30.0
41. Psychology–Law Society	1,262	965	297	76.5	23.5
42. Psychologists in Independent Practice	5,075	3,587	1,488	70.7	29.3
43. Family Psychology	1,678	1,102	576	65.7	34.3

continued on next page

Table 18.1 continued

Division	Total	Men	Women	% Men	% Women
44. Society for the Psychological Study of Lesbian and Gay Issues	609	328	281	53.9	46.1
45. Society for the Psychological Study of Ethnic Minority Issues	601	316	285	52.6	47.4
46. Media Psychology	353	202	151	57.2	42.8
47. Exercise and Sport Psychology	677	545	132	80.5	19.5
Total Division Memberships	74,570	50,671	23,899	68.0	32.0
No Divisional Affiliation	31,059	17,113	13,946	55.1	49.9

* Society for the Psychological Study of Social Issues
† Psychologists Interested in Religious Issues
SOURCE: *APA Membership Register,* 1990, p. viii. Reprinted by permission.

(70,266). This is because it is common for an APA member to belong to more than one APA division.

From the handful of individuals who founded the APA in 1892 in Worcester, Massachusetts, under the leadership of G. Stanley Hall, the membership has now grown to over 70,000 members and associates. There are now more divisions (47) of the APA than there were members (31) in 1892. There were no divisions within the APA until 1946. In 1970 there were 29 divisions, in 1980 there were 38, and today there are 47. Clearly, psychology's diversity has been increasing, and it continues to do so. For example, the APA Council of Representatives recently approved a Division of Peace Psychology (Fowler, 1989).

Although psychology's rich philosophical heritage explains much of contemporary psychology's diversity, the interaction of that heritage with the *Zeitgeist* explains patterns of activity in psychology at any given time. Fowler gives examples of how societal factors can influence divisional memberships:

> Obviously, changes in employment patterns play a major part in division growth. The increased employment opportunities in the private sector for health service providers has resulted in rapid growth for the Division of Independent Practice and related growth in some of the other practice-oriented divisions.

Funding patterns are also influential. As in all disciplines, various sub-areas may be "hot" for a time and then lose some of their attraction. The '60s and '70s saw great support for community psychology, mental retardation and environmental psychology and consequent growth in the relevant APA divisions. Reduced funding opportunities have been paralleled by division membership reduction. (1989, p. 5)

Controversy Concerning the Training of Clinical Psychologists

There is also diversity within the APA concerning what constitutes proper training for clinical psychologists. When Lightner Witmer (a charter member of the APA) founded clinical psychology in 1896 (about the time that Freud was beginning to develop psychoanalysis), he established a tradition in which clinical psychology would be closely aligned with scientific or experimental psychology. For Witmer, clinical psychology, to a large extent, consisted of applying the principles learned through psychological research to the treatment of disturbed individuals: "Witmer did not question the content or methods of psychology but sought to enlarge its aim so that the findings of psychology could be applied by some psychologists for the benefit of individuals" (Reisman, 1991, p. 44). Like himself, the person performing the research and applying the knowledge gained from research was often the same person. This tradition of scientist-professional was reconfirmed in 1949 at the Boulder Conference on Training in Clinical Psychology. The Boulder model upheld the tradition that clinicians obtain the Doctor of Philosophy (Ph.D.) in psychology, which meant that they were trained in research methodology like any other psychologist.

Increasingly, however, clinicians and students of clinical psychology questioned the need to be trained in scientific methodology in order to become effective clinicians. This concern was addressed at the Vail Conference in 1973 at which two decisions were made that broke radically from the tradition of clinicians as scientists-professionals: (1) Professional schools were sanctioned that could offer advanced degrees in clinical psychology but that would be administratively autonomous from a university psychology department, and (2) the **Doctor of Psychology degree** (Psy.D.) was established. The Psy.D. provides professional training for clinical psychologists without the intense exposure to research methodology typical of training for the Ph.D. Proponents of the Psy.D. indicated that the degree was equivalent to the Doctor of Medicine degree (M.D.), where practitioners of medicine apply the principles of biology, chemistry, pharmacology, and other scientific fields to the treatment of physically ill persons. The Psy.D. would have a similar relationship to scientific psychology. That is, the Psy.D. would apply principles discovered by experimental psychologists to the treatment of disturbed individuals. After the Vail decision, professional schools of psychology became very popular, and as early as 1979, there were 24 such schools in California alone (Perry, 1979). Currently, if one wishes to become a clinical psychologist, he or she can do so by obtaining a Psy.D. or Ph.D. from a professional school of psychology or by obtaining a Ph.D. in clinical psychology from a psychology department within a university.

The decisions to establish the Psy.D. and professional schools of psychology independent of university psychology departments remain highly controversial (see Peterson, 1976, for

supportive arguments; see Perry, 1979, for opposing arguments). These decisions, first made at the Vail Conference, were reconfirmed at a similar conference in Salt Lake City in 1987.

THE DECLINE OF RADICAL BEHAVIORISM

It is currently popular to search for the events that diminished the popularity of radical behaviorism and thus led to the resurrection of cognitive, physiological, and nativistic psychology. The list of such events could be extensive indeed, and opinions vary widely as to what it should include. The following is our sample of possibilities.

Ethology

Under the influence of radical behaviorism, reference to all internal events as explanations of behavior was actively discouraged. This positivistic (in the Baconian-Comtean sense) philosophy discouraged the study of not only cognitive and physiological processes but also instinctive behavior. As with cognitive and physiological explanations of behavior, however, instinctive explanations were discouraged but not eliminated. Even during behaviorism's heyday, a group of ethologists were studying instinctive animal behavior. **Ethology** (*ethos* = habit, custom, character; *ology* = the study of) is a branch of zoology that was developed primarily by Karl von Frisch (1886–1983) and Konrad Lorenz (1903–1989) in Germany and Niko Tinbergen (1907–1988) in England. For their efforts, Tinbergen, Frisch, and Lorenz shared the 1973 Nobel Prize in biology.

Ethologists typically study a specific category of behavior (e.g., aggression, migration, communication, territoriality) in an animal's natural environment and attempt to explain that behavior in terms of evolutionary theory. Of major importance to the ethologists is **species-specific behavior**, or how members of various species typically behave under certain environmental

NOAM CHOMSKY

Noam Chomsky

conditions. The nativistic position of the ethologists placed them in direct conflict with the behaviorists, especially the radical behaviorists:

> In those early days, the 1950s, the argument was basically European *vs.* American, biologist *vs.* psychologist, instinct theorists *vs.* learning theorists, birdwatchers *vs.* ratrunners. The lines were clearly drawn. The Europeans, calling themselves *ethologists*, rallied behind the flamboyant Lorenz, who dismissed the Americans as "ratrunners, unprepared to ask important questions." The ethologists stated flatly that the most important question was: How much is behavior due to instinct (genetics) and how much to learning? They suspected that instinct was far more important than anyone had previously imagined. (Wallace, 1979, p. 2)

The ethologists effectively battled the behaviorists, and their success had much to do with the decline in the popularity of behaviorism.

Ethology remains an active field of study, but its main influence on contemporary psychology has come through sociobiology. Edward Wilson, the founder of sociobiology, took a course from Lorenz while Wilson was a student at Harvard in 1953, and the influence of ethology on sociobiology is considerable. A major difference is that ethologists tend to concentrate on rather stereotyped, automatic responses that characterize various animal species and sociobiologists tend to concentrate on the social behavior that results from the complex interactions between an organism's biology and its environment. Rather than studying stereotyped behavior, sociobiologists employ terms such as *strategy* and *cost–benefit analysis*, indicating that organisms weigh various alternatives before deciding on a course of action. As we saw in chapter 10, however, sociobiologists believe that an organism will choose that course of action that will increase the probability of its genes being perpetuated into future generations.

Noam Chomsky's Influence

Leahey (1987) suggests that Noam Chomsky's review of Skinner's book *Verbal Behavior* (1957) was a crucial event in diminishing the influence of behaviorism. In his review (1959), Chomsky forcefully argues that language is too complex to be explained by operant principles, maintaining that the human brain is genetically programmed to generate language. Each child, says Chomsky, is born with brain structures that make it relatively easy for the child to learn the rules of language. Chomsky argues that children cannot learn these rules if they have to rely solely on principles of association (frequency, contiguity, reinforcement, etc.) as a means of learning. This successful nativistic attack on empirically based behaviorism did much to weaken the latter's influence. Although Chomsky is a linguist and not a psychologist, his views on language acquisition soon displaced the view based on operant principles. Leahey describes Chomsky's impact on contemporary psychology: "Chomsky's review [of Skinner's *Verbal Behavior*] is perhaps the single most influential psychological paper published since Watson's 'Behaviorist Manifesto of 1913' " (1987, p. 412). George Miller's 1962 article "Some Psychological Studies of Grammar" was instrumental in popularizing Chomsky's ideas within psychology.

The Misbehavior of Organisms

Another severe blow to the behaviorist's antinativistic position came from the work of Marian and Keller Breland, two of Skinner's former associates (the former Marian Breland is now Marian Bailey). The Brelands started a business called Animal Behavior Enterprises, which involved using operant principles to teach a variety of animals to do a variety of tricks. The trained animals were then put on display at fairs, conventions, and amusement parks and on television. At first, the Brelands found their animals to be highly conditionable, but as time passed, instinctive behavior began to interfere with or replace learned behavior. For example, pigs that had learned to place large wooden coins into a "piggy bank" began to perform more slowly, and eventually they would root the coin instead of placing it in the bank, even when doing so delayed or prevented reinforcement. The interference or displacement of learned behavior by instinctive behavior was called **instinctual drift**. The Brelands summarized their findings: "It seems obvious that these animals are trapped by strong instinctive behaviors, and clearly we have here a demonstration of the prepotency of such behavior patterns over those which have been conditioned" (1961, p. 85).

The Brelands believed that their observations contradicted three assumptions that the behaviorists made: (1) An animal comes to the learning situation as a *tabula rasa*—that is, with no genetic predispositions; (2) differences among various species of animals are unimportant; and (3) any response an animal can make can be conditioned to any stimulus the animal can detect. All these behavioristic assumptions either deny or minimize the importance of instinctive behavior. Although beginning their careers as behaviorists, the Brelands reached the following conclusion:

Marian Breland (now Marian Bailey)

After 14 years of continuous conditioning and observation of thousands of animals, it is our reluctant conclusion that the behavior of any species cannot be adequately understood, predicted, or controlled without knowledge of its instinctive patterns, evolutionary history, and ecological niche. (1961, p. 126)

Since the Brelands' article on the misbehavior of organisms, many other researchers have found support for their conclusions. For example, Seligman (1970) has found that within any given species of animal some associations are easier to establish than others and that one species may be able to form associations with ease, whereas for another species this may be extremely difficult or impossible. According to Seligman, the reason for this is that within a species, animals are biologically prepared to form certain associations and contraprepared to form others, and the same thing is true among various

MARTIN SELIGMAN

Martin Seligman

THOMAS BOUCHARD

Thomas Bouchard

species. Where an association falls on the **prepared-contraprepared continuum** determines how easily an animal will learn it. (Many examples of how an organism's biological makeup influences what and how easily it can learn can be found in Seligman & Hager, 1972.)

Genetic Influences on Intelligence and Personality

At least partially because of the work of the ethologists, Chomsky, and the Brelands, nativistic explanations of behavior are again respectable in contemporary psychology. As but one example, we will briefly review the work of Thomas Bouchard and his colleagues. As we saw in chapter 10, it was Francis Galton who defined the nature–nurture problem and was the first to use twins in studying that problem. Galton reached the following conclusions about the relative contributions of nature and nurture from his study of twins:

There is no escape from the conclusion that nature prevails enormously over nurture when the differences of nurture do not exceed what is commonly found among persons of the same rank of society and in the same country. My only fear is that my evidence seems to prove too much and may be discredited on that account, as it seems contrary to all experience that nurture should go for so little. (1875, p. 576)

Recent research by Bouchard and others suggests that Galton was correct on both accounts: Nurture counts very little when compared to nature; and people will find that fact difficult to believe. Bouchard studied the influence of genetics on physical characteristics, intelligence, and personality characteristics using four primary comparison groups:

• Dizygotic, or fraternal, twins reared together (DZT)

• Dizygotic, or fraternal, twins reared apart (DZA)

• Monozygotic, or identical, twins reared together (MZT)

• Monozygotic, or identical, twins reared apart (MZA)

Dizygotic twins are genetically the same as brothers and sisters who are not twins, and monozygotic twins have all their genes in common. If experience (nurture) determines intelligence and personality, then both DZTs and MZTs would tend to correlate highly on these traits, but not DZAs and MZAs. If intelligence and personality are largely determined by genetics (nature), then DZTs and DZAs should show modest correlations on these traits, and MZTs and MZAs should show high correlations on these traits. Because all monozygotic twins in Bouchard's study were separated at birth, any similarities between them must be due to genetic influences.

Bouchard (1984) first confirmed the long known fact that monozygotic twins are almost identical on a wide variety of physical characteristics (e.g., fingerprints and height). Bouchard then turned his attention to the matter of intelligence and concludes that "there is compelling evidence that the heritability of IQ is well above zero and probably between .50 and .80" (1984, p. 170). **Heritability** indicates the extent to which variation on a trait or attribute is attributable to genetics. In one study, Bouchard (1984) reports correlations between IQ scores for DZTs of .14, for MZTs of .78, and MZAs of .71, yielding a heritability measure for intelligence of about .70; that is, genetics contributes about 70 percent to IQ scores. It should be noted that although heritability is typically a complex measure derived from correlation coefficients, in the case of MZA twins correlations are a direct estimate of heritability. This is because MZA twins are genetically identical but share essentially no environmental influences. Thus, the correlation of .71 on measures of intelligence for MZA twins indicates that the heritability of intelligence is about 70 percent.

Next Bouchard turned to personality characteristics about which he says, "The domain of personality is the one in which most psychologists believe that common family environmental factors and social learning are of great importance in the determination of individual differences" (1984, p. 170). It was here that Bouchard obtained perhaps his most surprising result: Common family environment has practically no impact on personality. That is, people have similar personality traits to the extent that they are genetically related, not to the extent that they have common experiences. It was found that parents show practically no similarity to their adoptive children, nor do adoptive children show similarity to siblings with whom they are not biologically related. Parents show some similarity to their biological children, as do biologically related siblings. Dizygotic twins show about the same degree of similarity as biological siblings, and monozygotic twins show the greatest amount of similarity whether they are reared together or apart. Bouchard asks, "Can it be true that common family environment has at best only a minor effect on personality?" and his answer is "yes" (1984, p. 172). Bouchard goes on, "The correlations [of personality characteristics] between genetically unrelated individuals reflect only environmental influences and suggest a common family environmental effect of about 5 percent" (1984, p. 173).

Tellegen, Lykken, Bouchard, Wilcox, Segal, and Rich (1988) used the Multidimensional Personality Questionnaire to measure the heritability of 11 personality traits (e.g., well-being, social potency, achievement, aggression, and traditionalism). It was found that the heritability of the personality traits studied was between .50 and .60, making genetics the greatest single contributor to those traits. Perhaps even more surprising is that it was found that religious interests, attitudes, and values are also strongly influenced by genetics. Waller, Kojetin, Bouchard, Lykken, and Tellegen (1990) find the heritability of religiosity to be about the same as for personality traits (about .50). Again, as with personality traits, shared family experience had little impact on religious interests, attitudes, and values. Waller et al. conclude, "Social scientists will have to discard the a priori assumption that individual differences in religious and other social attitudes are solely influenced by environmental factors" (1990, p. 141).

One should not conclude that environmental influences on personality are unimportant. Most genetic studies of personality suggest that genetic factors account for about 50 percent of the variance on personality inventories and the other 50 percent is accounted for by environmental factors such as shared family experiences (about 5 percent) and idiosyncratic (nonshared) environmental experiences such as accidental occurrences and experiences with peer groups (about 45 percent). Thus, according to the research cited here, genetics is a major contributor to intelligence and personality, but it is not the only contributor.

We saw in chapter 10 that studies showing intelligence to be highly heritable have been and are very controversial. Studies, such as Bouchard's, showing that personality traits are highly heritable are equally controversial, if not more so. The use of identical twins reared apart from birth, however, is a powerful method for studying the relative contributions of nature and nurture, and it is currently receiving considerable attention.

Thus, despite the attempt of radical behaviorism to solve the nature–nurture controversy in favor of nurture, the ancient controversy is still alive and well in contemporary psychology.

Radical Behaviorism Remains Influential

The influence of radical behaviorism has diminished but has not disappeared. Prior to his death in 1990, Skinner had been considered one of the greatest psychologists who ever lived. Davis, Thomas, and Weaver (1982) sent surveys to chairpersons of departments with graduate programs in psychology. The chairpersons were asked in 1966 and again in 1981 to rank from 1 to 10 (1 being the highest rating) the greatest psychologists of all time and then to rank only living psychologists. In 1966 Freud was ranked 1 on the all-time list, and Skinner was ranked 9. On the all-time list in 1981, Freud still ranked 1,

but Skinner was ranked 2. Among living psychologists, Skinner was ranked 1 in both 1966 and 1981. The authors speculated that the trend was such that Skinner would soon replace Freud at the top of the all-time list. However, although Skinner himself may be popular, perhaps out of historical respect, his influence has greatly diminished. Nonetheless, a substantial number of Skinnerians remain very active and continue to have their own journals (*Journal of the Experimental Analysis of Behavior*, *Journal of Applied Behavior Analysis*, *Behaviorism*, and *The Behavior Analyst*), their own division within the APA (25), and their own society (Association for Behavior Analysis).

As radical behaviorism loosened its grip on psychology, cognitive psychology became increasingly popular. One of the first cognitive theories to gain widespread acceptance was that of Jean Piaget.

THE WORK OF JEAN PIAGET

Jean Piaget (1896–1980) is generally considered one of the all-time great psychologists. Kagan says, "With Freud, Piaget has been a seminal figure in the sciences of human development" (1980, p. 246). Piaget's work is often offered as a reason for contemporary psychology's widespread interest in cognitive psychology. Although Piaget published a major work on cognitive development in children as early as 1926, his research was largely ignored by psychologists in the United States. In 1960 Jerome Bruner and George Miller founded the Center for Cognitive Studies at Harvard, and this center began to stimulate interest in Piaget's work, as well as in cognitive psychology in general. In his long lifetime, Piaget published more than 50 books and monographs on cognitive development, and eventually his views became highly influential in the United States.

Piaget's Theory

Genetic epistemology. Piaget's theory is often referred to as **genetic epistemology** because it purports that intellectual abilities develop as a function of biological maturity and experience. It should be emphasized, however, that the term *genetic* here refers to developmental growth rather than biological inheritance. Thus, genetic epistemology has about the same meaning as developmental knowledge.

Schemata. According to Piaget, each child is born with a few reflexes with which to interact with the world. He called these reflexes **schemata**, and they allow the child to do such things as suck, reach, look, and grasp. Piaget considered each schema an element in the child's **cognitive structure**. In the early years of life, the child embraces the world in a reflexive manner using his or her available schemata. As the child matures, the initial schemata are elaborated, and new ones are developed. As the schemata develop, the cognitive structure becomes more complex, and the child's interactions with the world become less reflexive and more cognitive. In other words, in dealing with the world, the child becomes increasingly dependent on thinking. At all stages of development, however, the child's interactions with the world depend on available schemata.

Assimilation and accommodation. According to Piaget, if an experience fits a person's existing cognitive structure, assimilation occurs. **Assimilation** is roughly the same thing as recognizing, perceiving, or knowing. If an experience does not fit a person's cognitive structure, an imbalance results, and there is a tendency to modify the cognitive structure so that it can assimilate the new experience. This process, called **accommodation**, is roughly the same thing as learning. Piaget believed that almost every experience a person has must include both assimilation and accommodation because every experience we have is at least partially recognizable and partially unlike any experience we had had before.

Equilibration. Piaget thought that **equilibration** was the driving force responsible for intellectual growth. The term refers to our tendency to seek

Jean Piaget

J. P. LANDENBERG

a harmony between our cognitive structures and events in the world:

> Piaget assumed that all organisms have an innate tendency to create a harmonious relationship between themselves and their environment. In other words, all aspects of the organism are geared toward optimal adaptation. Equilibration is this innate tendency to organize one's experiences so as to assure maximal adaptation. Roughly, equilibration can be defined as the continuous drive toward equilibrium or balance. . . . It is his [Piaget's] major motivational concept, which, along with assimilation and accommodation, is used to explain the steady intellectual growth observed in children. (Hergenhahn, 1988, p. 276)

Piaget's proposed stages of intellectual development. The following are the stages of intellectual growth as Piaget saw them:

1. *Sensorimotor stage (birth to about 2 years).* Adjustments are sensorimotor in nature and

deal with the here and now. Symbolic manipulation is absent or at a minimum. Children are egocentric in that they see themselves as the frame of reference for everything.

2. *Preoperational stage (about 2 to about 7 years).* There is some rudimentary symbolization and concept formation. Children begin to classify things in terms of their similarity, and in solving problems, they use intuition rather than logic. The child has not yet developed **conservation**, the ability to know that the amount or area of something remains the same even though that thing may be represented in a number of ways. For example, when children at this stage are shown a flat container and a tall, narrow container that are both holding the same amount of water, they tend to say that there is more water in the taller container.

3. *Stage of concrete operations (about 7 to about 11 years).* During this stage, children learn conservation and also develop a number of rather sophisticated concepts. However, they can apply these concepts only to concrete problems with which they can deal directly.

4. *Stage of formal operations (about 11 years and older).* Thinking is now as sophisticated as it ever will be. Children at this stage can apply complex concepts to both concrete problems and those that are totally abstract.

Piaget's Influence on Contemporary Cognitive Psychology

As we will see shortly, information-processing psychology became very popular in the 1970s and 1980s. Here, we only mention the close relationship between Piaget's theory of mental development and information-processing psychology:

> Of all the approaches to cognitive psychology, Piaget's approach seems to have influenced information-processing psychology the most. Piaget's concept of schema has been widely adapted by information-processing psychologists and is viewed as an information-processing mechanism. . . . Both Piaget and those following the information-processing approach assume that information from the environment is acted upon (organized, simplified, transformed, selected for further analysis, or ignored) by cognitive structures before it is translated into behavior. In other words, both stress the importance of cognitive structures (schemata) in the processing of information. (Hergenhahn, 1988, p. 353)

Piaget's theory followed in the rationalistic rather than in the empiricistic tradition. More particularly, it followed in the Kantian tradition and so does much of contemporary cognitive psychology.

CONTEMPORARY COGNITIVE PSYCHOLOGY

There is not a specific APA division of cognitive psychology, but if there were, it undoubtedly would have been among the fastest growing in the 1980s. It is interesting to note that in psychology's long history some form of cognition has almost always been emphasized. The few exceptions included the materialistic philosophies or psychologies of Democritus, Hobbes, Gassendi, La Mettrie, Watson, and Skinner, which denied the existence of mental events. Thus, to say, as is common, that psychology is *becoming* more cognitively oriented is inaccurate because, with only a few exceptions, psychology has always been cognitively oriented. Nonetheless, there was a period from about 1930 to about 1950 when behaviorism dominated, and it was widely believed that cognitive events either did not exist or if they did they were simply by-products (epiphenomena) of brain activity and could be ignored. As long as these beliefs were dominant, the study of cognitive processes was inhibited.

Even when radical behaviorism was prevalent, however, cognitive psychology did not disappear completely, far from it. The Gestaltists were very active as were the methodological behaviorists such as Edward Tolman. As we saw in chapter 13, Tolman believed that organisms formed cognitive representations of their environments (cognitive maps) and used them to get from place to place. Tolman postulated complex mental processes that transformed and elaborated sensory information allowing for intelligent action:

> [The brain] is far more like a map control room than it is like an old-fashioned telephone exchange. The stimuli, which are allowed in, are not connected by just simple one-to-one switches to the outgoing responses. Rather, the incoming impulses are usually worked over and elaborated in the central control room into a tentative cognitivelike map of the environment. And it is this tentative map, indicating routes and paths and environmental relationships, which finally determines what responses, if any, the animal will finally release. (1948, p. 192)

It can be argued that the methodological behaviorists (those willing to postulate events that mediated between stimuli and responses) eventually won out over the radical behaviorists (those unwilling to postulate mediating events). As radical behaviorism lost its influence, a variety of approaches to psychology that emphasized cognitive experience began to flourish. For example, we saw in the last chapter that humanistic psychology became popular in the 1960s and it relied heavily on the phenomenological method, which is clearly cognitive in nature.

In the 1960s and early 1970s, information-processing theory began to dominate cognitive psychology. The information-processing approach to studying cognitive processes became so successful that some referred to it as psychology's newest paradigm, one that would soon displace all other paradigms (e.g., see Lachman, Lachman & Butterfield, 1979). The information-processing psychologists founded their own journals (*Cognitive Psychology*, 1970; *Cognition*, 1972; *Memory and Cognition*, 1973; *Journal of Mental Imagery*, 1977; *Cognitive Therapy and Research*, 1977; and *Cognitive Science*, 1977), and soon their approach was influencing virtually every aspect of psychology.

Information-Processing Cognitive Psychology

There is no better example of how developments outside psychology can influence psychology than the emergence of **information-processing cognitive psychology**. Most information-processing psychologists note the similarities between humans and computers: Both receive input, process that input, have a memory, and produce output. For information-processing psychologists, the term *input* replaces the term *stimulus*, the term *output* replaces the terms *response* and *behavior*, and terms such as *storage, encoding, processing, capacity, retrieval, conditional decisions*, and *programs* describe the information-processing events that occur between the input and the output. Most of these terms have been borrowed from computer technology. The information-processing psychologist usually concentrates his or her research on normal, rational thinking and behavior and views the human as an active seeker and user of information. Within information processing, research is typically focused on the higher mental processes such as language, thinking, perception, problem solving, concept formation, memory, learning, intelligence, and attention.

As we have seen throughout this book, the assumptions one makes about human nature will strongly influence how one goes about studying humans. The assumption that the mind or brain either is or acts like a computer demonstrates this point:

> Computers take symbolic input, recode it, make decisions about the recorded input, make new expressions from it, store some or all of the input, and give back symbolic output. By analogy, that is most of what cognitive psychology is about. It is about how people take in information, how they recode and remember it, how they make decisions, how they transform their internal knowledge states, and how they transform these states into behavioral outputs. The analogy is important. It makes a difference whether a scientist thinks of humans as if they were laboratory animals or as if they were computers. Analogies influence an experimenter's

choice of research questions, and they guide his or her theory construction. They color the scientist's language, and a scientist's choice of terminology is significant. The terms are pointers to a conceptual infrastructure that defines an approach to a subject matter. Calling a behavior a *response* implies something very different from calling it an *output*. It implies different beliefs about the behavior's origin, its history, and its explanation. Similarly, the terms *stimulus* and *input* carry very different implications about how people process them. (Lachman, Lachman & Butterfield, 1979, p. 99)

Information processing follows in the rationalistic tradition, and like most rationalist theories, information-processing theory has a strong nativistic component:

We do not believe in postulating mysterious instincts to account for otherwise unexplainable behavior, but we do feel that everything the human does is the result of inborn capacities, as well as learning. We give innate capacities more significance than behaviorists did. We think part of the job of explaining human cognition is to identify how innate capacities and the results of experience combine to produce cognitive performance. This leads us, especially in the area of language, to suppose that some aspects of cognition have evolved primarily or exclusively in humans. (Lachman, Lachman & Butterfield, 1979, p. 118)

Note the similarity between the Gestalt position and the following statement of Lachman, Lachman, and Butterfield: "The human mind has parts, and they interrelate as a *natural system*" (1979, p. 128). Hearst also notes the similarity between information-processing psychology and Gestalt psychology: "Present-day cognitive psychology—with its emphasis on organization, structure, relationships, the active role of the subject, and the important part played by perception in learning and memory—reflects the influence of its Gestalt antecedents" (1979, p. 32). Also note the similarity between Kant's philosophy and another statement made by Lachman, Lachman, and Butterfield: "Man's cognitive system is constantly active; it adds to its environmental input and literally *constructs* its reality" (1979, p. 128). In fact, considerable simi-

larity exists between Kant's rationalistic philosophy and information-processing psychology. Many consider Kant to be the founding father of information-processing psychology: "When cognitive scientists discuss their philosophical forebears one hears the name of Immanuel Kant more than any other" (Flanagan, 1991, p. 181). As we saw in chapter 6, Kant postulated a number of categories of thought (faculties of the mind) that acted on sensory information, thereby giving it structure and meaning that it otherwise would not have. In other words, according to Kant, the faculties of the mind processed information. It is Kant's philosophy that creates a kinship among Piaget's theory, Gestalt psychology, and information-processing psychology.

The Return of Faculty Psychology

Due largely to its relationship with phrenology, faculty psychology came into disfavor and was essentially discarded along with phrenology. To some, discarding faculty psychology with phrenology was like throwing out the baby with the bath water. We just saw that information-processing psychology marks a return to faculty psychology. The recent discovery that the brain is organized into many "modules" (groups of cells), each associated with some specific function such as face recognition, also marks a return to faculty psychology (and, to some extent, phrenology). Fodor notes this return to faculty psychology:

Faculty psychology is getting to be respectable again after centuries of hanging around with phrenologists and other dubious types. By faculty psychology I mean, roughly, the view that many fundamentally different types of psychological mechanisms must be postulated in order to explain the facts of mental life. Faculty psychology takes seriously the apparent heterogeneity of the mental and is impressed by such prima facie differences as between, say, sensation and perception, volition and cognition, learning and remembering, or language and thought. Since, according to faculty psychologists, the mental causation of behavior typically involves the simultaneous activity of a variety of distinct psychological mechanisms, the best research strategy would seem to be divide and conquer: first study the intrinsic characteristics of each of the presumed faculties, then study the ways in which they interact. Viewed from the faculty psychologist's perspective, overt, observable behavior is an interaction effect par excellence. (1983, p. 1)

The Return of the Mind–Body Problem

The current popularity of cognitive psychology brings the mind–body problem back into psychology, not that it ever completely disappeared. The radical behaviorists "solved" the problem by denying the existence of a mind. For them, so-called mental events are nothing but physiological experiences to which we assign cognitive labels. Furthermore, because such experiences can never cause behavior, they can and should be ignored in the analysis of behavior. That is, the radical behaviorists "solved" the mind–body problem by assuming materialism or physical monism. Cognitive psychology, however, assumes the existence of cognitive events. These events are viewed sometimes as the by-products of brain activity (epiphenomenalism), sometimes as automatic, passive processors of sensory information (mechanism), and sometimes as important causes of behavior (interactionism). In each case, bodily events and cognitive events are assumed, and therefore the relationship between the two must be explained. A number of contemporary cognitive psychologists believe that they have avoided dualism by noting the close relationship between certain brain activities and certain cognitive events. The fact that it appears likely that such a relationship will soon be discovered for all mental events is sometimes offered in support of materialism. D. N. Robinson explains why such reasoning is fallacious:

This is hardly a justification for materialistic monism, since *dualism* does not require that there be no brain! Indeed, dualism does not even necessarily require that mental events not be the effects of neural causes. A modest dualism only asserts that there *are* mental events. To show,

then, that such events are somehow caused by material events, far from establishing the validity of a monist position, virtually guarantees the validity of a dualist position. (1986, pp. 435–436)

Replacing the term *mind–body* with the term *mind–brain* does little to solve the problem of how something material (the brain) can cause something mental (ideas, thinking).

Like the nativism versus empiricism (nature versus nurture) controversy, the mind–body problem remains one of psychology's persistent questions. Hilgard makes this point:

The argument has gone on between varieties of monism and dualism, but the ultimate resolution in a form acceptable to all seems no nearer now than it ever was; yet the problem is a persistent one and continues to haunt investigators and theoreticians. (1987, p. 798)

ARTIFICIAL INTELLIGENCE

In the late 1970s, information-processing cognitive psychology expanded into a new discipline called **cognitive science**. Cognitive science consists of a number of disciplines that combine their efforts in an effort to understand cognition. Those disciplines include philosophy, cognitive psychology, neuroscience, linguistics, engineering, and computer science. Like the information-processing psychologist, the cognitive scientist seeks to understand the mental processes that intervene between stimuli and responses, but he or she takes a broader base in studying those processes. Also distinguishing between information-processing psychology and cognitive science is the latter's intense interest in **artificial intelligence** (AI). Fetzer defines AI as "a special branch of computer science that investigates the extent to which the mental powers of human beings [and other living organisms] can be captured by means of machines" (1991, p. xvi). Because AI is currently extremely popular, we describe it in some detail.

In 1950 Alan M. Turing (1912–1954) founded the field of artificial intelligence in an article entitled "Computing Machinery and Intelligence" in which he raised the question: Can machines think? Because the term *think* is so ambiguous, Turing proposed an objective way of answering his own question.

The Turing Test

Turing proposed that we play the "imitation game" to answer the question Can machines (e.g., computers) think? He asked that we imagine an interrogator asking probing questions to a human and to a computer, both hidden from the interrogator's view. The questions and answers are typed on a keyboard and displayed on a screen. The only information that the interrogator is allowed is that which is furnished during the question-and-answer session. The human is instructed to answer the questions truthfully and to attempt to convince the interrogator that he or she really is the human. The computer is programmed to respond as if it were human. If after a series of such tests the interrogator is unable to consistently identify the human responder, the computer passes the **Turing test** and can be said to think.

Weak Versus Strong Artificial Intelligence

What does it mean when a computer passes the Turing test for some human cognitive function? For example, if an interrogator cannot distinguish between a human and a computer with regard to thinking, reasoning, and problem solving, does that mean that the computer possesses those mental attributes just as humans do? No, say the proponents of **weak artificial intelligence** who claim that, at best, a computer can only simulate human mental attributes. Yes, say the proponents of **strong artificial intelligence** who claim that the computer is not merely a tool used to study the mind (as the proponents of weak AI claim). Rather, an appropriately programmed computer really *is* a mind capable of understanding and having mental states. According to strong AI, human minds are computers, and therefore there is no reason why they cannot be duplicated by other, nonbiological, computers. For the proponents of strong AI, computers do not *simulate* human cognitive processes; they *duplicate* them.

Searle's Argument Against Strong Artificial Intelligence

Searle (1980) describes his now famous "Chinese Room" rebuttal to proponents of strong AI. Thinking, according to strong AI, is the manipulation of symbols, and because computer programs manipulate symbols, they think. According to strong AI, "the mind is to brain as the program is to the hardware" (Searle, 1990, p. 26). To refute this claim, Searle asks you to consider a language you do not understand, say, Chinese. Now suppose you are placed in a room containing baskets full of Chinese symbols, along with a rule book written in English telling how to match certain Chinese symbols with other Chinese symbols. The rules instruct you how to match symbols entirely by their shapes and does not require any understanding of the meaning of the symbols. "The rules might say such things as, 'take a squiggle-squiggle sign from basket number one and put it next to a squoggle-squoggle sign from basket number two'" (Searle, 1990, p. 26). Imagine further that there are people outside the room who understand Chinese and who slip batches of symbols into your room, which you then manipulate according to your rule book. You then slip the results back out of the room. Searle observes that the rule book is the "computer program." The people who wrote the rule book are the "programmers," and you are the "computer." The baskets full of symbols are the "database," the small batches of symbols slipped into the room are "questions," and the small batches of transformed symbols you slip out of the room are "answers."

Finally, imagine that your rule book is written in such a way that the "answers" you generate are indistinguishable from those of a native Chinese speaker. In other words, unknown to you, the symbols slipped into your room may constitute the question What is the capital of France? and your answer, again unknown to you, was Paris. After several such questions and answers, you pass the Turing test for understanding Chinese although you are totally ignorant of Chinese. Furthermore, in your situation, there is no way that you could ever come to understand Chinese because you could not learn the meaning of any symbols. Like a computer, you manipulate symbols but attach no meaning to them. Searle concludes:

> The point of the thought experiment is this: if I do not understand Chinese solely on the basis of running a computer program for understanding Chinese, then neither does any other digital computer solely on that basis. Digital computers merely manipulate formal symbols according to rules in the program.
>
> What goes for Chinese goes for other forms of cognition as well. Just manipulating the symbols is not by itself enough to guarantee cognition, perception, understanding, thinking and so forth. And since computers, qua computers, are symbol-manipulating devices, merely running the computer program is not enough to guarantee cognition. (1990, p. 26)

Thus, a computer is a machine that manipulates symbols according to rules (a program). Any problem that can be stated in terms of formal symbols and can be solved according to specified rules can be solved by a computer (e.g., balancing a checking account or playing chess and checkers). The manipulation of symbols according to specified rules is called *syntax*. *Semantics*, on the other hand, involves the assignment of meaning to symbols. According to Searle, computer programs have syntax but not semantics. Human thoughts, perceptions, and understandings have a mental content, and they can refer to objects or events in the world—they have a meaning or, to use Brentano's term, they have *intentionality*. A computer program (or you enclosed in the Chinese room) simply manipulates symbols without any awareness of what they mean. Again, although a computer may pass the Turing test, it is not really thinking as humans think, and therefore strong AI is false.

John Searle

JOHN SEARLE

"You can't get semantically loaded thought contents from formal computations alone" (Searle, 1990, p. 28). Our brains are constructed so that they cause mental events: "Brains are specific biological organs, and their specific biochemical properties enable them to cause consciousness and other sorts of mental phenomena" (Searle, 1990, p. 29). Computer programs can provide useful simulations of the formal aspects of brain processes, but simulation should not be confused with duplication:

> One can imagine a computer simulation of the action of peptides in the hypothalamus that is accurate down to the last synapse. But equally one can imagine a computer simulation of the oxidation of hydrocarbons in a car engine or the action of digestive processes in a stomach when it is digesting pizza. And the simulation is no more the real thing in the case of the brain than it is in the case of the car or the stomach. Barring miracles, you could not run your car by doing a

computer simulation of the oxidation of gasoline, and you could not digest pizza by running the program that simulates such digestion. It seems obvious that a simulation of cognition will similarly not produce the effects of the neurobiology of cognition.

All mental phenomena, then, are caused by neurophysiological processes in the brain. (Searle, 1990, p. 29)

Elsewhere Searle says, "No one expects to get wet in a pool filled with Ping-Pong-ball models of water molecules. So why would anyone think a computer model of thought processes would actually think?" (1990, p. 31).

Are Humans Machines?

The argument about whether machines (in this case, computers) can think reintroduces into modern psychology a number of questions that have persisted throughout psychology's history. One such question is What is the nature of human nature? As we have seen, one answer has been that humans are machines. Most of the English and French (recall La Mettrie) Newtonians of the mind took Newton's conception of the universe as a machine and applied it to humans. For anyone who believes that humans are nothing but machines, and there have been many philosophers and psychologists with such a belief, there is no reason why a nonhuman machine could not be built that would *duplicate* every human function. This might require placing a computer into a sophisticated robot, but in principle, there is no reason why a nonhuman machine could not duplicate every human function because humans too are nothing but machines. To view humans as machines is to accept mechanism.

Also, the materialists would have no trouble with the contention that machines (e.g., robots) could be built that duplicate all human functions. Humans, say the materialists, are nothing but physical systems. There is no "ghost in the machine" (i.e., a mind); thus, there is no reason to wonder if a nonhuman machine can think or not. Neither nonhuman machines nor humans can think. Thoughts, ideas, concepts, percep-

tions, and understandings cannot exist if they are thought to be nonphysical in nature; only physical things exist. To suggest otherwise is to embrace dualism. Searle presents a current version of the materialists' argument:

> Semantics doesn't exist anyway; there is only syntax. It is a kind of prescientific illusion to suppose that there exist in the brain some mysterious "mental contents," "thought processes" or "semantics." All that exists in the brain is the same sort of syntactic symbol manipulation that goes on in computers. Nothing more. (1990, pp. 29–30)

It should be clear that any type of dualist would need to either reject strong AI or attribute thinking to a nonhuman machine. Many dualists claim that either human consciousness is unique in the universe or that some aspect of human consciousness is unique, for example, free will or purpose. In either case, there is something mental and nonmechanical in humans that cannot be duplicated by a machine. In fact, all the philosophers and psychologists that we have encountered who have postulated something unique about humans would necessarily reject the claims of strong AI.

Summary of the Objections to Artificial Intelligence

There have been many objections to both weak and strong AI, and the following represent just a sample of them:

1. *Human thinking does not always follow specifiable rules.* Computers can simulate or duplicate cognitive processes only insofar as those systems follow a set of formal rules. This objection argues that many important human cognitions do not follow specifiable rules. Examples include emotional experiences such as falling in love, the making of moral judgments, and the formulation of future goals. All these experiences appear to be more intuitive than lawful and, as such, are not programmable; therefore, they cannot be either simulated or duplicated by a computer program.

2. *Computer programs lack originality.* Computers can only do what they are programmed to do, whereas humans are capable of creative, unpredictable actions. This objection is usually made by those who believe that human behavior is not completely determined. For example, humanistic and existential psychologists claim that it is human free will that accounts for the novelty, originality, and creativity found in poetry, music, art, literature, and science. Because no machine can possess free will, AI cannot be used even as a model of human thought processes.

3. *Minds interact with the world; computers do not.* This objection relates to the distinction between syntax and semantics. It may be that all human minds are similar in the way that they reason, remember, and perceive, and it may be that these processes follow formal rules and thus can be programmed. However, the content of human thought comes from interactions with the environment and with other people; it is these interactions that give human thought processes their meaning (semantics). Flanagan points out that the minds of Chinese and American individuals are functionally the same and yet the lives lived by the Chinese and by the Americans are radically different:

We would [discover], no doubt, that Chinese and American minds come equipped with similar basic desires, are designed to follow paths that they believe will maximize these desires, have similar memory capacities, make similar reasoning mistakes, mentally rotate geometrical objects, have identical linguistic abilities, fear bodily harm, and so on. But this knowledge could never be enough. The reason is obvious: all the fascinating similarities summed together shed absolutely no light on the remarkable differences. . . . Given that the functional organization of Chinese minds and American minds is very similar, we will need all the resources of geography, agronomy, history, literature, political theory, economics, and sociology to explain why, given similar equipment between the ears, our two life-forms are so different yet simultaneously so clearly human. (1991, pp. 248–249)

Many proponents of AI would agree

with this objection and say that the ability of AI to simulate or duplicate human cognition will be limited until machines (e.g., robots) can be built that interact with the world and that learn from those interactions. Already there are computer programs capable of learning (e.g., NETtalk), and in principle there is no reason why sophisticated, interactive machines could not be constructed.

4. *A computer is not a brain.* For many, AI can offer useful simulations or duplications of cognitive events only insofar as the computer resembles a real human brain. Flanagan states this objection as it applies to strong AI: "Against strong . . . AI [this objection] is simply that it is unlikely that computers will ever come to possess genuine mentality because they have the wrong kind of bodies" (1991, p. 249). Weak AI is also attacked on the basis of realism. To show that a computer can simulate cognitive processes does not mean that the simulations reflect real cognitive processes generated by the brain. Proponents of strong AI respond by saying that if two systems (e.g., computers and the brain) are functionally equivalent, then for all practical purposes they are the same (remember the Turing test). Proponents of weak AI respond by saying that it is often the case that models are not physically similar to what they are modeling (e.g., Ping-Pong-ball models of water molecules are not the same thing as water), so why hold AI to a higher standard? Even recognizing that computers are not brains, there is enough similarity between the two so that simulations of cognitive processes are informative.

To summarize, philosophers and psychologists who follow in the traditions of empiricism, associationism, sensationalism, materialism, and mechanism believe that at least some light can be shed on human behavior by studying AI. Also, a number of rationalists would agree with the potential usefulness of AI. For example, although Spinoza was a rationalist, he was a determinist even regarding mental events. Given the lawfulness of thought, a machine analogy was not farfetched for Spinoza. Just because one is a dualist does not necessarily mean that one is not a mechanist. Several dualists view mind–body relationships as lawful and therefore describable in mechanistic terms. This is true for much of Kant's philosophy and is true of information-processing psychology. On the matter of AI then, the Kantians would be supportive of, at least, weak AI. Incidentally, the same could be said of any other faculty psychologist (e.g., Thomas Reid).

Standing in firm opposition to the computer as a model of the mind would be all rationalistic philosophers or psychologists who postulated a free will (e.g., Descartes). Also in opposition would be the romantic and existential philosophers and the modern humanistic psychologists. Besides postulating human free will, these psychologists claim that there are so many important unique human attributes (e.g., the innate tendency toward self-actualization) that the very idea of machine simulation of human attributes is ridiculous and perhaps even dangerous. It is dangerous because if we view humans as machines we may treat them as machines and if we do they may act like machines. According to the humanistic psychologists, this is what happens when the methods and assumptions of the natural sciences are applied to the study of humans. Humans are treated like physical objects (e.g., machines) and are thus desacralized. Most humanistic psychologists find the very idea of AI repulsive.

Finally, we can observe that no radical behaviorist would look kindly on AI. For the radical behaviorist, AI is just one more mentalistic psychology. Environmental events cause (select) behavior, *period*. To postulate mental events that mediate between environmental experience and behavior is to return to psychology's prescientific era and is therefore regressive. Even if mental events existed, they could never cause behavior, so why agonize over them? All his professional life, Skinner attacked cognitive psychology as being unscientific. Skinner presented his arguments against cognitive science as a list of accusations:

I accuse cognitive scientists of misusing the metaphor of storage. The brain is not an encyclopedia, library, or museum. People are changed by their experiences; they do not store copies of them as representations or rules.

I accuse cognitive scientists of speculating about internal processes which they have no appropriate means of observing. Cognitive science is premature neurology.

I accuse cognitive scientists of emasculating laboratory research by substituting descriptions of settings for the settings themselves and reports of intentions and expectations for action.

I accuse cognitive scientists of reviving a theory in which feelings and states of mind observed through introspection are taken as the causes of behavior rather than as collateral effects of the causes.

I accuse cognitive scientists, as I would accuse psychoanalysts, of claiming to explore the depths of human behavior, of inventing explanatory systems that are admired for a profundity more properly called inaccessibility.

I accuse cognitive scientists of relaxing standards of definition and logical thinking and releasing a flood of speculation characteristic of metaphysics, literature, and daily intercourse, speculation perhaps suitable enough in such arenas but inimical to science.

Let us bring behaviorism back from the Devil's Island to which it was transported for a crime it never committed, and let psychology become once again a behavioral science. (1987, p. 111)

A rather large number of Skinnerians (radical behaviorists) in contemporary psychology agree with Skinner's assessment of cognitive psychology in all its varied forms (cognitive science, information processing, artificial intelligence). However, the methodological behaviorists are a different story. For them, any number of processes can be postulated to exist between environmental experience and behavior, as long as those processes can be indexed by behavior. Hull's intervening variables tended to be physiological in nature, whereas Tolman's were cognitive. In both cases, however, that intervening processes modified sensory input in important ways was assumed. Thus, methodological behaviorism is not only compatible with information-processing psychology but also can be viewed as a modern precursor to it. It was Hull who for many years was obsessed with the idea of creating a machine that could think (see chapter 13). Present-day methodological behaviorists do not argue with the potential usefulness of AI, especially weak AI.

PSYCHOLOGY'S STATUS AS A SCIENCE

We begin with James's description of psychology as it appeared to him:

> A string of raw facts; a little gossip and a wrangle about opinions; a little classification and generalization on the mere descriptive level; a strong prejudice that we *have* states of mind, and that our brain conditions them: but not a single law in the same sense in which physics shows us laws, not a single proposition from which any consequence can causally be deduced. . . . This is no science, it is only the hope for a science. (1892/1963, p. 335)

More than 40 years later, Heidbreder offered her description of psychology:

> Psychology is, in fact, interesting, if for no other reason, because it affords a spectacle of a science still in the making. Scientific curiosity, which has penetrated so many of the ways of nature, is here discovered in the very act of feeling its way through a region it has only begun to explore, battering at barriers, groping through confusions, and working sometimes fumblingly, sometimes craftily, sometimes excitedly, sometimes wearily, at a problem that is still largely unsolved. For psychology is a science that has not yet made its great discovery. It has found nothing that does for it what atomic theory has done for chemistry, the principle of organic evolution for biology, the laws of motion for physics. Nothing that gives it a unifying principle has yet been discovered or recognized. As a rule, a science is presented, from the standpoint of both subject-matter and development, in the light of its great successes. Its verified hypotheses form the established lines about which it sets its facts in order, and about which it organizes its research. But psychology has not yet won its great unifying victory. It has had flashes of perception, it holds a handful of clues, but it has not yet achieved a synthesis or an insight that is compelling as well as plausible. (1933, pp. 425–426)

Although the views of James and Heidbreder are separated by more than four decades, they are remarkably similar. Have things improved in the more than 50 years since Heidbreder recorded her thoughts? As we saw in chapter 1, after addressing the question of whether psychology is a science, Koch (1981) concludes that psychology is not a single discipline. Rather, it is several disciplines, some of which qualify as science, but most of which do not. Koch believes that it would be more realistic to refer to our discipline as *psychological studies* rather than as *the science of psychology*. The designation *psychological studies* recognizes the diversity of psychology and shows a willingness to use a wide variety of methods while studying humans. Koch summarizes his views of what psychology should be like:

> Because of the immense range of the psychological studies, different areas of study will not only require different . . . methods but will bear affinities to different members of the broad groupings of inquiry as historically conceived. Fields like sensory and biological psychology may certainly be regarded as solidly within the family of the biological and, in some reaches, natural sciences. But psychologists must finally accept the circumstances that extensive and important sectors of psychological study require modes of inquiry rather more like those of the humanities than the sciences. And among these I would include areas traditionally considered "fundamental"—like perception, cognition, motivation, and learning, as well as such more obviously rarefied fields as social psychology, psychopathology, personality, aesthetics, and the analysis of "creativity". . . . I have been inviting a psychology that might show the imprint of a capacity to accept the inevitable ambiguity and mystery of our situation. (1981, p. 269)

And finally, Staats offers his assessment of contemporary psychology:

> Fields of psychology have developed as separate entities, with little or no planning with respect to their relationships. Research areas grow in isolation without ever being called on to relate themselves to the rest of psychology. There are various oppositional positions—nature versus nurture, situationism versus personality, scientific versus humanistic psychology—that separate works throughout the many problem areas of psychology. Different methods of study are employed and psychologists are divided by the methodology that they know and use and will

accept. There are innumerable theories, large and small—it is said that there are 100–400 separate psychotherapy theories alone—and everyone is free to construct a personal theory without relating its elements to those in other theories. Many theoretical structures, which serve as the basis for empirical efforts, are taken from the common language as opposed to systematically developed theories. The practice of constructing small common sense conceptual structures as the basis for one's specialized work in psychology provides an infinity of different and unrelated knowledge elements and associated methological-theoretical structures. (1989, p. 149)

Only on rare occasions can a psychologist be found who believes that psychology *is* a unified discipline. For example, Matarazzo (1987) argues that a body of knowledge and basic processes and principles form the core of psychology and that they have remained essentially the same for the last 100 years. Furthermore, Matarazzo maintains that various types of psychology (e.g., clinical, industrial, social, experimental, and developmental) simply apply the same core content, processes, and principles to different types of problems. Matarazzo's position, however, is in the minority among psychologists.

We see that in the 100 years since James made his assessment of psychology, and in the more than five decades since Heidbreder's assessment of psychology, the situation has not significantly changed. Psychology is still a collection of different facts, theories, assumptions, methodologies, and goals. It is still not clear how much of psychology is scientific or even can be scientific, and even those who believe psychology can be a science debate over what type of a science it should be.

Some psychologists see psychology's diversity as necessary because of the complexity of humans. Others see it as a sign that psychology has failed to carefully employ scientific method. Still others say that psychology is diverse because it is still in the preparadigmatic stage that characterizes the early development of a science. Thus, psychology is characterized by diversity even regarding opinions as to what its ultimate status

can be. Some psychologists believe that psychology can ultimately be a unified science that employs one methodology and one set of principles to study all aspects of humans (e.g., Staats, 1981, 1989). Others say that humans can never be adequately studied by using only the methodology that a single paradigm generates (e.g., Dixon, 1983; Koch, 1981).

The answers to the question Is psychology a science? include: No, it is a preparadigmatic discipline; no, its subject matter is too subjective to be investigated scientifically; no, but it could and should be a science; yes and no, some of psychology is scientific, and some is not; yes, psychology is a scientific discipline with a core content and widely accepted processes and principles. The answer to the question Is psychology a science? seems to depend on who is asked and which aspect of psychology is considered. There is little reason to believe that psychology's status as a science will be clarified in the near future.

PSYCHOLOGY'S TWO CULTURES

Given contemporary psychology's great diversity, what is it that inclines a particular psychologist toward one brand of psychology as opposed to other brands? A case can be made that it is a psychologist's personality or biography that, to a large extent, determines the choice. James said that the single most informative thing you could know about a person is his or her **Weltanschauung**, or worldview. Although James attributed the following statement to a Mr. Chesterton, it is a statement with which he was in complete agreement:

There are some people—and I am one of them —who think that the most practical and important thing about a man is still his view of the universe. We think that for a landlady considering a lodger it is important to know his income, but still more important to know his philosophy. We think that for a general about to fight an enemy it is important to know the enemy's numbers, but still more important to know the enemy's philosophy. *We think the question is not whether the theory of the cosmos affects matters, but whether in the long run anything else affects them* [italics added]. (1907/1981, p. 7)

According to James, it is a philosopher's temperament that, to a large extent, determines what type of *Weltanschauung* he or she has and thus the type of philosophy he or she will be inclined toward:

> The history of philosophy is to a great extent that of a certain clash of human temperaments. . . . [A philosopher's] temperament . . . gives him a stronger bias than any of his more strictly objective premises. It loads the evidence for him one way or the other, making for a more sentimental or a more hard-hearted view of the universe, just as this fact or that principle would. He *trusts* his temperament. Wanting a universe that suits it, he believes in any representation of the universe that does suit it. (1907/1981, p. 8)

In 1923 Karl Lashley discussed the reason why some psychologists accepted a mechanistic brand of psychology (such as Watson's) and others accepted a purposive brand (such as McDougall's). Lashley reached much the same conclusion about psychologists that James had reached about philosophers: "It is wholly a matter of temperament; the choice is made upon an emotional and not a rational basis" (1923, p. 344).

Tender-Minded and Tough-Minded Philosophers

As we saw in chapter 11, James (1907/1981) argued that philosophers could be divided into two general groups according to their temperaments: the tender-minded and the tough-minded. The **tender-minded philosopher** is attracted to philosophy that emphasizes rationalism, idealism, free will, optimism and tends to accept religion. The **tough-minded philosopher** is attracted to philosophy that emphasizes empiricism, materialism, determinism, pessimism and tends to reject religion. James believed that a tension between the tender-minded and the tough-minded has existed throughout history: "The tough think of the tender as sentimental-

ists and soft-heads. The tender feel the tough to be unrefined, callous, or brutal" (1907/1981, p. 11).

C. P. Snow's Two Cultures

The British scientist-novelist C. P. Snow was so impressed by the way literary intellectuals (e.g., novelists) embraced the world, as compared to scientists, that he concluded that they actually represented two distinct cultures. Snow described his experience as he moved from one group to the other:

> There have been plenty of days when I have spent the working hours with scientists and then gone off at night with some literary colleagues. . . . I felt that I was moving among two groups—comparable in intelligence, identical in race, not grossly different in social origin, earning about the same incomes, who had almost ceased to communicate at all, who in intellectual, moral and psychological climate had so little in common that instead of going from Burlington House or South Kensington to Chelsea, one might have crossed an ocean. (1964, p. 2)

James noted two conflicting temperaments among philosophers. Snow observed that one of these temperaments (tender-minded) characterized members of the humanities and the other (tough-minded) characterized scientists, making meaningful communication between the two groups all but impossible. Recently, Gregory Kimble (1984) provides evidence that James's two temperaments and Snow's two cultures also characterize contemporary psychology.

Psychology's Two Cultures

Whereas Snow found that the values of the two groups (literary intellectuals and scientists) were basically incompatible, Kimble finds incompatible values exist within the same group, psychologists; James found the same incompatibility of values among philosophers. To quantify the extent to which psychology can be described in terms of two cultures, Kimble measured where various psychologists and students of psychol-

GREGORY KIMBLE

Gregory Kimble

ogy rated themselves on the following 12 polarized issues:

Scientific values	versus	Human values
Determinism	versus	Indeterminism
Objectivism	versus	Intuitionism
Data	versus	Theory
Laboratory investigation	versus	Field study
Historical	versus	Ahistorical
Heredity	versus	Environment
Nomothetic	versus	Idiographic
Concrete mechanisms	versus	Abstract concepts
Elementism	versus	Holism
Cognition	versus	Affect
Reactivity	versus	Creativity

Each issue was measured on an 11-point scale with 0 indicating the most extreme position toward scientific values (left column) and a score of 10 indicating the most extreme position toward humanistic values (right column). A score of 5 on any issue indicated a neutral position.

Kimble administered his scale to undergradu-ate students enrolled in an introductory psychology course; officers of all divisions of the APA; and members of Division 3 (Experimental Psychology), Division 9 (Society for the Psychological Study of Social Issues), Division 29 (Psychotherapy), and Division 32 (Humanistic Psychology). The students showed a slight inclination toward humanistic values, and APA officers (from all APA divisions collectively) showed an even more slight inclination toward scientific values. When data from members of individual APA divisions were analyzed, however, the results were more dramatic. Scores for members of Division 3 (Experimental Psychology) were strongly biased in the direction of scientific values. Almost the opposite was true for the members of the other divisions tested. Scores for members of Division 9 (Society for the Psychological Study of Social Issues) were moderately biased in the direction of humanistic values. Scores for members of Division 29 (Psychotherapy) were strongly biased in the direction of humanistic values, as were scores for members of Division 32 (Humanistic Psychology). To use James's terminology, experimental psychologists tend to be tough-minded, and humanistic psychologists tend to be tender-minded.

Kimble does, however, see a tendency for the scientifically oriented and the humanistically oriented to live in peace together and even to influence each other:

> The most important theme in this development is a liberalized viewpoint that permits an easy acceptance of topics for research that would have been unacceptable 40 years ago. Mental imagery, the distinction between remembered and imagined, voluntary behavior, self-awareness and self-control, conceptually driven processing, helplessness and coping, risk taking, metaphoric expression, and inferential memory are a few of these topics, all of which are identified by phrases that catch important ideas in the humanistic tradition.
>
> Similar things are happening in the area of methods. Quasi-experimental designs with unobtrusive measures, field studies of animal behavior, investigations of eyewitness testimony, studies of the oral tradition and autobiographical memory, the use of hypnosis as an experimental method, the move from serial anticipation to methods of free recall, and, unless I miss my guess, a renewed interest in case histories are some of the important new features on the methodological scene, all of

which again are identified by phrases that catch important ideas in the humanistic tradition. (1984, p. 838)

However, Kimble, like James, believes that the two cultures are in many ways incommensurable and that they always were and always will be:

Do these developments mean that we are about to reach an epistemic armistice between the values of our two cultures? I think not. The data obtained in this study . . . tell us that the remaining points of disagreement involve the items asking about most important values (scientific vs. human), source of basic knowledge (objectivism vs. intuitionism) and generality of laws (nomothetic vs. idiographic). These are not trivial issues. What is still at stake is basic, and interestingly the residual sticking points are identical to those that have existed for millennia. (1984, pp. 838–839)

Dividing philosophers, psychologists, or educated people into just two categories is a gross oversimplification, and Snow realized this, saying that "the number 2 is a very dangerous number . . . attempts to divide anything into two ought to be regarded with much suspicion" (1964, p. 9). Kimble agrees, saying that the appearance of just two cultures in psychology was created by his careful selection of the APA divisions that he evaluated. Although some psychologists are on both ends of the scientific-humanistic continuum, most psychologists would fall at various points along that continuum. Instead of describing psychology in terms of two cultures, a description in terms of several cultures would be more accurate. In fact, there are probably as many "cultures" in psychology as there are conceptions of human nature.

It appears that psychology's history and the *Zeitgeist* have combined to create a psychological smorgasbord and that it is the psychologist's personality that determines which items in that smorgasbord are appealing. Of course, the same is true for students of psychology.

IS THERE ANYTHING NEW IN PSYCHOLOGY?

No doubt, some aspects of psychology are newer and better than they have ever been. As we have seen, computer technology has provided psychol-

ogy with a new and useful tool. Improvements in measuring and recording devices, the invention of the electron microscope, and new drugs have provided physiological psychologists with powerful research tools. Besides providing a model for human cognitive processes, computers allow for complex data analysis that only a few years ago would have been impossible. So the answer to the question Is there anything new in psychology? must be yes. But note that our examples were all technological rather than conceptual. When we look at the larger issues, the answer to our question seems to be negative. After listing some advances in our knowledge of how the brain and body function—our greater understanding of simple learning and of memory phenomena and of children's thinking—Leahey goes on to say,

In a broader, conceptual sense progress is harder to demonstrate. The most modern psychology, information processing cognitive psychology, is remarkably similar to Aristotle's account of mind. Both view the acquisition of knowledge as the internalization and processing of information about the environment which is then stored in some form of memory. (1980, p. 385)

Brennan reaches a similar conclusion:

The philosophical studies of the ancient Greeks identified basic issues of psychology. . . . These critical issues, which the Greek scholars did not resolve, still baffle psychologists. Can human beings explain psychological activity in terms of physical matter only, or is some proposal of mental life necessary? Despite the almost 2,500 years since the flowering of Greek thought, very little of original quality has been added. Changes, modifications, and reinterpretations have been offered, but essentially science as we know it today is a study based upon an Aristotelian framework of knowledge. (1991, p. 323)

So emphases change and research tools improve, but it seems that psychology is still addressing the same questions it addressed from its very inception. Because we elaborated on psychology's persistent questions and issues in chapter 1, we will simply list them here:

- What is the nature of human nature?
- How are the mind and body related?
- Nativism versus empiricism

- Freedom versus determinism
- Mechanism versus vitalism
- Rationalism versus irrationalism
- How are humans related to nonhuman animals?
- What is the origin of human knowledge?
- Objective versus subjective reality
- What accounts for the unity and continuity of experience?

These concerns have guided the efforts of psychologists for well over 2,000 years, and no doubt will continue to do so in the future.

It appears that psychology's persistent questions are actually philosophical questions and as such have no ultimate, final answers. Russell suggested that the most important questions are those that cannot be answered in any final sense:

> Almost all the questions of most interest to speculative minds are such as science cannot answer, and the confident answers of theologians no longer seem so convincing as they did in former centuries. Is the world divided into mind and matter, and, if so, what is mind and what is matter? Is mind subject to matter, or is it possessed of independent powers? Has the universe any unity or purpose? Is it evolving towards some goal? Are there really laws of nature, or do we believe in them only because of our innate love of order? Is man what he seems to the astronomer, a tiny lump of impure carbon and water impotently crawling on a small and unimportant planet? Or is he what he appears to Hamlet? Is he perhaps both at once? Is there a way of living that is noble and another that is base, or are all ways of living merely futile? If there is a way of living that is noble, in what does it consist, and how shall we achieve it? Must the good be eternal in order to deserve to be valued, or is it worth seeking even if the universe is inexorably moving towards death? Is there such a thing as wisdom, or is what seems such merely the ultimate refinement of folly? To such questions no answer can be found in the laboratory. Theologies have professed to give answers, all too definite; but their very definiteness causes modern minds to view them with suspicion. (1945, pp. xiii–xiv)

Russell believed that such ultimate questions fall between science and theology and are therefore the business of philosophy. But psychology's persistent questions are essentially philosophical questions, and, as such, proposed answers to them will always be tentative and uncertain. The point that Russell made pertains to the major questions addressed by both philosophy and psychology:

> Science tells us what we can know, but what we can know is little, and if we forget how much we cannot know we become insensitive to many things of very great importance. Theology, on the other hand, induces a dogmatic belief that we have knowledge where in fact we have ignorance, and by doing so generates a kind of impertinent insolence towards the universe. Uncertainty, in the presence of vivid hopes and fears, is painful, but must be endured if we wish to live without the support of comforting fairy tales. It is not good either to forget the questions that philosophy asks, or to persuade ourselves that we have found indubitable answers to them. (1945, p. xiv)

In a similar vein, Dixon says,

> The concept of psychology—and indeed the very idea of human nature—is an "essentially contested concept" . . . i.e., it is a concept which is of particular salience in an intellectual enterprise and about which multiple, mutually exclusive assumptive frameworks are fostered. The history of science reveals that with such concepts there is little hope that a final resolution of the rival modes of interpretation ever will be attained. To the contrary, essentially contested concepts are not merely meaningful, not merely rational, but a way of life in, and perhaps the life blood of, history, science, and certainly psychology. (1983, p. 338)

It is not necessary to label psychology's persistent questions as philosophical to demonstrate that they cannot be answered with certitude. As was seen in chapter 1, Popper said that there are no final truths even in science. The highest status that the solution to any problem can have is *not yet disconfirmed*. All solutions, even scientific solutions, will eventually be found to be false; the search for truth is unending. Thus, important questions whether approached philosophically or scientifically must be persistent questions.

It also appears that through the centuries philosophers, theologians, and psychologists have discovered partial truths about humans and have confused them with the whole truth. When these individuals were convincing, and the time was right, their ideas became popular enough to grow into schools. Perhaps to ask whether the voluntarists, structuralists, functionalists, behaviorists, Gestaltists, psychoanalysts, and the third-force psychologists were right or wrong is to ask the wrong question. A better question might be How much of the truth about humans was captured by each of these viewpoints? Perhaps they are all partially correct, and perhaps there are many other truths about humans not yet revealed by any viewpoint.

Where does this leave the student of psychology? It seems that psychology is not a place for people with a low tolerance for ambiguity. The diverse and sometimes conflicting viewpoints that characterize psychology will undoubtedly continue to characterize it in the future. There is growing recognition that psychology must be as diverse as the humans whose behavior it attempts to explain. For those looking for The One Truth, this state of affairs is distressing. For those willing to ponder several truths, psychology is and will continue to be an exciting field.

SUMMARY

Contemporary psychology is a hybrid discipline that reflects a wide variety of historical influences. In contemporary psychology, there is a spirit of eclecticism, a willingness to employ whatever methods are effective in studying various aspects of humans. Psychology's great diversity is shown in the 47 divisions of the APA. There is controversy concerning what constitutes proper training of clinical psychologists. One view is that clinical psychologists should receive the same rigorous scientific training as any other Ph.D. in psychology. The other view is that clinical psychologists should be trained in the professional application of scientific principles but not trained to create those principles.

The decline in the popularity of radical behaviorism and the increased popularity of cognitive, physiological, and nativistic psychology went hand-in-hand. Reasons for behaviorism's decreased popularity include the work of the ethologists showing the importance of instinctive behavior, Chomsky's successful nativistic attack on Skinner's empirical account of language, and the Brelands' work showing that learned behavior is often interfered with or displaced by instinctive behavior. The current popularity of genetic explanations of behavior is exemplified by Bouchard's research, which suggests a strong genetic influence on both intelligence and personality traits. Although radical behaviorism is not the powerful force that it once was, its influence remains substantial.

Although originally ignored by psychologists in the United States, Piaget's theory became popular as the influence of behaviorism declined and may have been instrumental in reducing behaviorism's influence. Piaget studied genetic epistemology, or how the nature of a person's intelligence varied as a function of maturational level. One of the most popular types of cognitive psychology today is information-processing cognitive psychology, which often uses the computer as an analogy for how humans process information. Like the computer, humans receive input; process that input by using various programs, strategies, memories, and plans; and then produce output. The major goal of the information-processing psychologist is to determine the mechanisms that humans employ in processing information. Information-processing psychologists follow in the rationalistic tradition, and their work and assumptions show similarities to Kantian philosophy, Gestalt psychology, and Piaget's theory of intellectual development. Both faculty psychology and the mind—body problem re-emerged as cognitive psychology became popular.

In the late 1970s, a multidiscipline called cognitive science was created to study cognition. A topic of special interest to cognitive science is artificial intelligence (AI). Those interested in AI attempt to simulate or duplicate the intelligence exhibited by living organisms, using nonhuman machines such as computers. Those adhering to strong AI believe that nonhuman machines can duplicate human intelligence, and those adhering to weak AI believe that nonhuman machines can only simulate human intelligence. Turing proposed the "imitation game" as a means of determining whether a machine can think as a human does. If the answers to questions given by a machine (e.g., a computer) are indistinguishable from those given by a human, the machine can be said to think. Searle argues that his thought experiment of the "Chinese Room" showed that computers manipulate symbols without assigning meaning to them and therefore cannot be said to actually think. Those accepting mechanistic or materialistic philosophies tend to accept strong AI, whereas those accepting humanist or existentialist philosophies would either accept only weak AI or reject AI altogether. Accepting a dualist position does not necessarily preclude the usefulness of AI because many dualists are also mechanists. It is only those dualist positions that postulate unique features of the human mind (e.g., free will) that see AI as having little or no usefulness. Also, the radical behaviorists deny the usefulness of AI, as they do all types of cognitive psychology.

In 1892 James concluded that psychology was still hoping to become a science. In 1933 Heidbreder reached more or less the same conclusion. In 1981 Koch argued that although some aspects of humans are amenable to scientific scrutiny, most are not. In 1989 Staats observed that psychology was a disunified discipline, but he suggested that with considerable effort it could become a unified science. Only rarely does someone claim, as Matarazzo does, that psychology *is* a unified science. Now, as throughout history, psychology's status as a science is difficult to determine.

James noted that it was a philosopher's temperament that inclined him or her toward tender-minded (subjective) philosophy or tough-minded (objective) philosophy. The scientist-novelist C. P. Snow observed that the values accepted by scientists and those accepted by individuals in the humanities were so distinct as to reflect two separate cultures. Kimble provides evidence that Snow's two cultures also exist in contemporary psychology. Measuring the values accepted by members of various APA divisions (e.g., Division 3, Experimental Psychology, and Division 32, Humanistic Psychology), Kimble finds that many

psychologists embrace scientific values, whereas many others embrace humanistic values. Although there is some evidence suggesting increased interaction between the two groups, Kimble believes that the differences between them are basic and philosophical in nature. That is, the differences have probably always existed and will continue to do so.

Psychology has provided considerable information about such things as learning, memory, brain functioning, bodily functioning, and childhood thinking and has refined many of its research tools because of methodological advances. In a broader sense, however, psychology continues to respond to questions that the early Greeks posed. Although the emphases have changed, as well as research tools and terminology, psychology continues to address the same issues and questions that it has always addressed. It was suggested that psychology's persistent issues and questions are philosophical in nature and therefore have no final, ultimate answers. According to Popper, even if psychology's persistent questions were scientific rather than philosophical, they still would have no final answers.

It was suggested that various philosophies and psychological schools have provided only partial truths about human nature and that many more truths will be forthcoming. For those with a high tolerance for ambiguity, psychology is and will continue to be an exciting discipline.

DISCUSSION QUESTIONS

1. What evidence is there that contemporary psychology is highly diverse? What accounts for this diversity?

2. What is meant by referring to contemporary psychology as a hybrid discipline?

3. What was the argument that led to the creation of the Doctor of Psychology degree (Psy.D.)? Do you agree with that argument?

4. Describe three factors that led to the decline in the popularity of radical behaviorism. Include in your answer definitions of the terms *ethology, instinctual drift,* and *prepared-contraprepared continuum.*

5. What was Bouchard's rationale for using identical twins reared apart from birth in his study of the relative contributions of nature and nurture to intelligence and personality? What conclusions were supported by his research?

6. Is radical behaviorism still influential in contemporary psychology? Justify your answer.

7. Define each of the following terms from Piaget's the-

ory of intellectual development: *schemata, assimilation, accommodation,* and *equilibration.*

8. Summarize Piaget's four proposed stages of intellectual development.

9. In what philosophical tradition does Piaget's theory follow? What influence did Piaget's work have on contemporary cognitive psychology?

10. Explain why the work of Tolman and Piaget can be seen as anticipating information-processing psychology.

11. What are the major tenets of information-processing psychology?

12. Why can information-processing psychology be seen as following in the tradition of Kantian philosophy? Why can information-processing psychology be seen as marking a return to faculty psychology?

13. Why does cognitive psychology reintroduce the mind–body problem?

14. Define each of the following: *cognitive science, artificial intelligence* (AI), *strong AI*, and *weak AI*.

15. What is the Turing test, and for what is it used?

16. Describe Searle's thought experiment involving the "Chinese Room." What, according to Searle, does this experiment prove?

17. Which philosophies would tend to support the position of strong AI? Weak AI? Which would deny the usefulness of any type of AI?

18. Summarize the arguments made against AI as a tool for studying human cognition.

19. Is psychology a science? Summarize the various answers to this question reviewed in this chapter.

20. Describe the two cultures that Kimble discovered in contemporary psychology. What conclusions did Kimble reach concerning these cultures?

21. Make a case that the answer to the question Is there anything new in psychology? is yes and no.

22. Why are psychology's persistent questions so persistent?

SUGGESTIONS FOR FURTHER READING

Dixon, R. A. (1983). Theoretical proliferation in psychology: A plea for sustained disunity. *Psychological Record, 33,* 337–340.

Dixon argues against seeking theoretical unity in psychology, saying instead that scientific progress depends on pluralism. Because human knowledge is mutable, fallible, and adaptive, no single viewpoint can be taken as the correct one. Also, because scientific knowledge grows through the proliferation of alternatives, pluralism is a prerequisite to scientific progress.

Fetzer, J. H. (1991). *Philosophy and cognitive science.* New York: Paragon House.

Fetzer discusses a number of philosophical issues in cognitive science, such as whether minds are machines and the relationships among mind, culture, and evolution. (Available in paperback.)

Kimble, G. A. (1984). Psychology's two cultures. *American Psychologist, 39,* 833–839.

By employing his "epistemic differential," Kimble finds that the values accepted by members of Division 3 (Experimental Psychology), as opposed to those accepted by members of Divisions 9 (Society for the Psychological Study of Social Issues), 29 (Psychotherapy), and 32 (Humanistic Psychology), are so different as to suggest the existence of two separate cultures within psychology—one culture accepting scientific values and the other humanistic values.

Koch, S. (1981). The nature and limits of psychological knowledge: Lessons of a century qua "science." *American Psychologist, 36,* 257–269.

After over 100 years of supposedly being an independent science, Koch questions whether psychology is either independent (of philosophy) or a science. The first question is answered negatively because most of psychology's questions are philosophical in nature. In answer to the second question, Koch says that a few aspects of psychology may qualify as science but most do not.

Matarazzo, J. D. (1987). There is only one psychology, no specialties, but many applications. *American Psychologist, 42,* 893–903.

Matarazzo concludes that all psychologists obtaining a Ph.D. learn essentially the same core content, processes, and principles and what differentiates one type of psychologist from another (e.g., clinician, experimentalist, industrial psychologist) is how the basic content, processes, and principles are applied.

Perry, N. W., Jr. (1979). Why clinical psychology does not need alternative training models. *American Psychologist, 34,* 603–611.

Perry argues that the scientist-professional, or Boulder model, for the training of clinical psychologists is highly successful and should be maintained. The decisions at the Vail Conference to create a doctor of psychology degree (Psy.D.) and to allow professional schools independent of any university to grant Ph.D.s and Psy.D.s in psychology were, according to Perry, both unnecessary and undesirable.

Peterson, D. R. (1976). Need for the doctor of psychology degree in professional psychology. *American Psychologist, 31,* 792–798.

Peterson argues that because clinicians are primarily appliers of knowledge to the relief of human problems, they do not need the same intense training in scientific methodology that other (e.g., experimental) psychologists require. The Psy.D. does for the clinician what the M.D. does for the medical doctor. That is, it trains the clinician in the application of psychological principles rather than preparing him or her to be a research scientist, as is the case with the Ph.D.

Searle, J. R. (1990, January). Is the brain's mind a computer program? *Scientific American,* pp. 26–31.

In this article, Searle describes his famous "Chinese Room" thought experiment and argues convincingly against the position of supporters of strong AI that machines (e.g., computers) can actually think.

Staats, A. W. (1989). Unificationism: Philosophy for the modern disunified science of psychology. *Philosophical Psychology, 2,* 143–164.

Staats, following Kuhn, believes that sciences progress from a period of disunity (preparadigmatic disciplines) to unified states and that psychology is presently in its period of disunity. What psychology needs, according to Staats, is a unified theory and a unified methodology that can be used to interrelate empirical findings and to guide research. Staats believes that discovering what type of a unified theory and methodology will work for psychology is itself a major task, which must be approached in a systematic manner.

Viney, W. (1989). The cyclops and the twelve-eyed toad: William James and the unity–disunity problem in psychology. *American Psychologist, 44,* 1261–1265.

The "twelve-eyed toad" in the title refers to William James's belief that reality is multifaceted and is best viewed from a variety of angles (pluralism). The "cyclops" refers to those who believe that there is a single, all-encompassing reality or a single correct way of viewing things (monism). In keeping with his pluralism, James would no doubt support those seeking to make psychology a unified discipline, but he would insist that such a search should not exclude any viable topic or method. If there is a unity within psychology, we will find it empirically; it should not be assumed a priori.

GLOSSARY

Accommodation According to Piaget, the process whereby one's cognitive structure is modified in order to assimilate an experience. Accommodation is roughly equivalent to learning.

Artificial intelligence (AI) An effort popular among cognitive scientists to create machines that simulate or duplicate the intelligent behavior of living organisms.

Assimilation According to Piaget, the process whereby an experience fits or matches one's cognitive structure. Assimilation is roughly equivalent to perceiving or knowing.

Cognitive science A multidiscipline approach to studying cognition in humans, animals, and machines.

Cognitive structure According to Piaget, the total number of schemata available to a person at a given time.

Conservation According to Piaget, the ability to recognize something as the same even though it is presented in a variety of ways.

Cross-fertilization model The view that contemporary psychology is best understood as a hybrid discipline reflecting a variety of often conflicting historical influences. With this model, there is no implication that modern psychology is necessarily the best psychology.

Culmination model The view that contemporary psychology is best understood as the culmination of historical influences. According to this model, modern psychology is the best psychology because it improves on the less mature psychology by which it was preceded.

Doctor of Psychology degree (Psy.D.) The doctorate in clinical psychology that emphasizes training in the professional application of psychological principles rather than in scientific methodology.

Eclecticism The willingness to employ the most effective methods available in solving a problem.

Equilibration According to Piaget, the tendency to seek a harmonious relationship between one's cognitive structure and the environment.

Ethology The study of animal behavior in the animal's natural habitat. The ethologist typically attempts to explain the observed behavior in terms of evolutionary theory.

Genetic epistemology The study of intelligence as a function of maturational level and experience.

Heritability A measure of how much of the variation in a trait or attribute is determined by genetics.

Information-processing cognitive psychology The approach to studying cognition that follows in the Kantian tradition and typically employs the computer as a model for human information processing.

Instinctual drift The tendency for learned behavior to be interfered with or displaced by instinctive behavior.

Piaget, Jean (1896–1980) Showed how intelligence manifested itself differently in children of different ages. Piaget's theory of cognitive development became popular as the influence of behaviorism declined and was instrumental in the development of information-processing psychology.

Prepared-contraprepared continuum Seligman's observation that degree of biological preparedness determines how easily an association can be learned.

Schemata According to Piaget, the elements in one's cognitive structure.

Species-specific behavior Behavior that is typically engaged in by all members of a species under certain environmental circumstances. Very close to what others call instinctive behavior.

Strong artificial intelligence The contention that machines (e.g., computers) can duplicate the cognitive processes of living organisms.

Tender-minded philosopher According to James, a philosopher who, because of his or her temperament, embraces idealistic, rationalistic, optimistic philosophy. Such a philosopher also tends to accept the existence of free will and religious principles.

Tough-minded philosopher According to James, a philosopher who, because of his or her temperament, embraces pessimistic, empiricistic, materialistic philosophy. Such a philosopher also tends to accept determinism and to reject religious principles.

Turing test A test devised by Turing (1950) to determine whether a machine can think. Questions are submitted to both a human and a machine. If the machine's answers are indistinguishable from those of the human, it is concluded that the machine can think.

Weak artificial intelligence The contention that machines (e.g., computers) can simulate human cognitive processes but not duplicate them.

Weltanschauung Worldview or world-design.

REFERENCES

Adler, A. (1917). *Study of organ inferiority and its physical compensation: A contribution to clinical medicine* (S. E. Jeliffe, Trans.). New York: Nervous and Mental Diseases Publishing. (Original work published 1907)

Albrecht, F. M. (1970). A reappraisal of faculty psychology. *Journal of the History of the Behavioral Sciences, 6,* 36–40.

Alexander, F. G., & Selesnick, S. T. (1966). *The history of psychiatry: An evaluation of psychiatric thought and practice from prehistoric times to the present.* New York: Harper & Row.

Allderidge, P. (1979). Hospitals, madhouses and asylums: Cycles in the care of the insane. *British Journal of Psychiatry, 134,* 321–334.

American Psychiatric Association. (1987). *Diagnostic and statistical manual of mental disorders* (3rd ed.). Washington, DC: Author.

American Psychologist. (1990). Citation for outstanding lifetime contribution to psychology. Presented to B. F. Skinner, August 10, 1990. *American Psychologist, 45,* 1205.

Angell, J. R. (1904). *Psychology: An introductory study of the structure and functions of human consciousness.* New York: Holt.

Angell, J. R. (1907). The province of functional psychology. *Psychological Review, 14,* 61–91.

Anokhin, P. K. (1968). Ivan P. Pavlov and psychology. In B. B. Wolman (Ed.), *Historical roots of contemporary psychology* (pp. 131–159). New York: Harper & Row.

APA Membership Register. (1990). Washington, DC: American Psychological Association.

Armstrong, D. M. (Ed.). (1965). *Berkeley's philosophical writings.* New York: Macmillan.

Ayllon, T., & Azrin, N. (1968). *The token economy: A motivational system for therapy and rehabilitation.* New York: Appleton-Century-Crofts.

Baars, B. J. (1986). *The cognitive revolution in psychology.* New York: Guilford Press.

Bacon, F. (1878). Of the proficience and advancement of learning divine and human. In *The works of Francis Bacon* (Vol. 1). Cambridge, MA: Hurd & Houghton. (Original work published 1605)

Bacon, F. (1960). *The new organon.* F. H. Anderson (Ed.). New York: Macmillan. (Original work published 1020)

Bain, A. (1894). *The senses and the intellect.* London: Longmans, Green. (Original work published 1855)

Bain, A. (1875). *Mind and body: The theories of their relations.* New York: Appleton. (Original work published 1873)

Bain, A. (1977). *The emotions and the will.* Washington, DC: University Publications of America. (Original work published 1859)

Bakan, D. (1966). The influence of phrenology on American psychology. *Journal of the History of the Behavioral Sciences, 2,* 200–220.

Balmary, M. (1979). *Psychoanalyzing psychoanalysis: Freud and the hidden fault of the father.* Baltimore: Johns Hopkins University Press.

Bandura, A. (1977). *Social learning theory.* Englewood Cliffs, NJ: Prentice-Hall.

Bandura, A. (1982). The psychology of chance encounters and life paths. *American Psychologist, 37,* 747–755.

Bandura, A. (1986). *Social foundations of thought and action: A social cognitive theory.* Englewood Cliffs, NJ: Prentice-Hall.

Bandura, A. (1989). Human agency in social cognitive theory. *American Psychologist, 44,* 1175–1184.

Barash, D. P. (1979). *The whisperings within: Evolution and the origin of human nature.* New York: Viking Press/Penguin Books.

Barnes, J. (1982). *The presocratic philosophers.* London: Routledge and Kegan Paul.

Barnes, J. (Ed.). (1984). *The complete works of Aristotle* (Vols. 1 and 2). Princeton, NJ: Princeton University Press.

Barnes, J. (1987). *Early Greek philosophy.* New York: Viking Press/Penguin Books.

Beanblossom, R. E., & Lehrer, K. (Eds.). (1983). *Thomas Reid's inquiry and essays.* Indianapolis: Hackett.

Bechterev, V. M. (1913). *La psychologie objective.* [Objective psychology]. Paris: Alcan. (Original work published 1907–1912)

Bechterev, V. M. (1973). *General principles of human reflexology: An introduction to the objective study of personality.* New York: Arno Press. (Original work published 1928)

Benjamin, L. T., Jr. (Ed.). (1988). *A history of psychology: Original sources and contemporary research.* New York: McGraw-Hill.

Bentham, J. (1988). *An introduction to the principles of morals and legislation.* New York: Prometheus Books. (Original work published 1781)

Berkeley, G. (1954). An essay towards a new theory of vision. In *Berkeley: A new theory of vision and other writings.* London: Dent. (Original work published 1709)

Bernard, W. (1972). Spinoza's influence on the rise of scientific psychology: A neglected chapter in the history of psychology. *Journal of the History of the Behavioral Sciences, 8,* 208–215.

Bernfeld, S. (1949). Freud's scientific beginnings. *American Imago, 6,* 163–196.

Binet, A. (1903). *L'Étude expérimentale de l'intelligence* [The experimental study of intelligence]. Paris: Schleicher.

Binet, A. (1975). *Modern ideas about children* (S. Heisler, Trans.). Albi, France: Presses de L'Atelier Graphique. (Original work published 1909)

Bitterman, M. E. (1965). Phyletic differences in learning. *American Psychologist, 20,* 396–410.

Bjork, D. W. (1983). *The compromised scientist: William James in the development of American psychology.* New York: Columbia University Press.

Blucher, J. (Ed.). (1946). Martin Luther, twenty-seven articles respecting the reformation of the Christian state. In *Introduction to contemporary civilization in the West* (Vol. 1). New York: Columbia University Press.

Blumenthal, A. L. (1970). *Language and psychology: Historical aspects of psycholinguistics.* New York: Wiley.

Blumenthal, A. L. (1975). A reappraisal of Wilhelm Wundt. *American Psychologist, 30,* 1081–1088.

Blumenthal, A. L. (1979). The founding father we never knew. *Contemporary Psychology, 24,* 547–550.

Blumenthal, A. L. (1980). Wilhelm Wundt and early American psychology. In R. W. Rieber (Ed.), *Wilhelm Wundt and the making of a scientific psychology* (pp. 117–135). New York: Plenum.

Boakes, R. (1984). *From Darwin to behaviourism: Psychology and the minds of animals.* New York: Cambridge University Press.

Boring, E. G. (1957). *A history of experimental psychology* (2nd ed.). New York: Appleton-Century-Crofts.

Boring, E. G. (1963). *History, psychology, and science: Selected papers.* New York: Wiley.

Boring, E. G. (1965). On the subjectivity of important historical dates: Leipzig, 1879. *Journal of the History of the Behavioral Sciences, 1,* 5–9.

Boss, M. (1963). *Psychoanalysis and Daseinanalysis.* New York: Basic Books.

Bouchard, T. J., Jr. (1984). Twins reared together and apart: What they tell us about human diversity. In S. W. Fox (Ed.), *Individuality and determinism: Chemical and biological bases* (pp. 147–178). New York: Plenum.

Bowra, C. M. (1957). *The Greek experience.* New York: New American Library.

Braid, J. (1843). *The rationale of nervous sleep considered in relation to animal magnetism.* London: Churchill.

Breland, K., & Breland, M. (1961). The misbehavior of organisms. *American Psychologist, 16,* 681–684.

Brennan, J. F. (1991). *History and systems of psychology* (3rd ed.). Englewood Cliffs, NJ: Prentice-Hall.

Brentano, F. (1973). *Psychology from an empirical standpoint* (O. Kraus, Ed.; English ed., L. L. McAlister, Ed.). New York: Humanities Press. (Original work published 1874)

Bretall, R. (Ed.). (1946). *A Kierkegaard anthology.* Princeton, NJ: Princeton University Press.

Brett, G. S. (1965). *A history of psychology* (2nd rev. ed.). (Edited and abridged by R. S. Peters). Cambridge, MA: MIT Press. (Original work published 1953)

Breuer, J., & Freud, S. (1955). *Studies on hysteria.* In *The standard edition* (Vol. 2). London: Hogarth Press. (Original work published 1895)

Bricke, J. (1974). Hume's associationist psychology. *Journal of the History of the Behavioral Sciences, 10,* 397–409.

Bridgman, P. W. (1927). *The logic of modern physics.* New York: Macmillan.

Bringmann, W. G., Bringmann, N. J., & Ungerer, G. A. (1980). The establishment of Wundt's laboratory: An archival and documentary study. In W. G. Bringmann & R. D. Tweney (Eds.), *Wundt studies: A centennial collection* (pp. 123–159). Toronto: Hogrefe.

Bringmann, W. G., & Tweney, R. D. (Eds.). (1980). *Wundt studies: A centennial collection.* Toronto: Hogrefe.

Brooks, G. P. (1976). The faculty psychology of Thomas Reid. *Journal of the History of the Behavioral Sciences, 12,* 65–77.

Brožek, J. (Ed.). (1984). *Explorations in the history of psychology in the United States.* Cranbury, NJ: Associated University Presses.

Bruno, F. J. (1972). *The story of psychology.* New York: Holt, Rinehart & Winston.

Buckley, K. W. (1989). *Mechanical man: John Broadus Watson and the beginnings of behaviorism.* New York: Guilford Press.

Bugental, J. F. T. (Ed.). (1967). *Challenges of humanistic psychology.* New York: McGraw-Hill.

Buhler, C. (1971). Basic theoretical concepts of humanistic psychology. *American Psychologist, 26,* 378–386.

Burtt, E. A. (1932). *The metaphysical foundations of modern physical science.* Garden City, NY: Doubleday.

Capps, D. (1970). Hartmann's relations to Freud: A reappraisal. *Journal of the History of the Behavioral Sciences, 6,* 162–175.

Carr, H. (1925). *Psychology: A study of mental activity.* New York: Longmans, Green.

Carr, H. (1935). *An introduction to space perception.* New York: Longmans, Green.

Cattell, J. McK. (1890). Mental tests and measurements. *Mind, 15,* 373–381.

Cattell, J. McK. (1904). The conceptions and methods of psychology. *Popular Science Monthly, 66,* 176–186.

Cattell, J. McK. (1929). Psychology in America. In *Proceedings and papers: Ninth International Congress of Psychology.* Princeton, NJ: Psychological Review Company.

Chaplin, J. P., & Krawiec, T. S. (1979). *Systems and theories of psychology* (4th ed.). New York: Holt, Rinehart & Winston.

Chomsky, N. (1957). *Syntactic structures.* The Hague: Mouton.

Chomsky, N. (1959). Review of Skinner's *Verbal learning. Language, 35,* 26–58.

Chomsky, N. (1972). *Language and mind* (enlarged ed.). New York: Harcourt Brace Jovanovich.

Clagett, M. (1963). *Greek science in antiquity*. New York: Macmillan.

Clark, R. W. (1980). *Freud: The man and the cause—A biography*. New York: Random House.

Cohen, D. (1979). *J. B. Watson: The founder of behaviourism*. London: Routledge and Kegan Paul.

Comte, A. (1896). *A positive philosophy* (H. Martineau, Trans.). London: Bell.

Condillac, E. B. de. (1930). *Treatise on the sensations* (G. Carr, Trans.). Los Angeles: University of Southern California School of Philosophy. (Original work published 1754)

Cornford, F. M. (1957). *From religion to philosophy: A study of the origins of Western speculation*. New York: Harper & Row.

Cornford, F. M. (Trans.). (1968). *The republic of Plato*. New York: Oxford University Press.

Craighead, W. E., Kazdin, A. E., & Mahoney, M. J. (1976). *Behavior modification: Principles, issues, and applications*. Boston: Houghton Mifflin.

Craneheld, P. F. (1974). *The way in and the way out: François Magendie, Charles Bell and the roots of the spinal nerves*. New York: Futura.

Danziger, K. (1980a). Wundt and the two traditions of psychology. In R. W. Rieber (Ed.), *Wilhelm Wundt and the making of a scientific psychology* (pp. 73–87). New York: Plenum.

Danziger, K. (1980b). Wundt's theory of behavior and volition. In R. W. Rieber (Ed.), *Wilhelm Wundt and the making of a scientific psychology* (pp. 89–115). New York: Plenum.

Danziger, K. (1980c). The history of introspection reconsidered. *Journal of the History of the Behavioral Sciences, 16*, 241–262.

Daquin, J. (1793). *Philosophie de la folie* [Philosophy of madness]. Paris: Alican.

Darwin, C. (1859). *On the origin of species by means of natural selection*. London: Murray.

Darwin, C. (1871). *The descent of man*. New York: Appleton.

Darwin, C. (1872). *The expression of emotions in man and animals*. London: Murray.

Darwin, F. (Ed.). (1959). *The autobiography of Charles Darwin and selected letters*. New York: Dover.

Davis, S., Thomas, R., & Weaver, M. (1982). Psychology's contemporary and all-time notables: Student, faculty, and chairperson viewpoints. *Bulletin of the Psychonomic Society, 20*, 3–6.

Descartes, R. (1956). *Discourse on method* (L. J. Lafleur, Trans.). Indianapolis: Bobbs-Merrill. (Original work published 1637)

Dewey, J. (1886). *Psychology*. New York: American Book.

Dewey, J. (1896). The reflex arc concept in psychology. *Psychological Review, 3*, 357–370.

Diamond, S. (1980). Wundt before Leipzig. In R. W. Rieber (Ed.), *Wilhelm Wundt and the making of a scientific psychology* (pp. 3–70). New York: Plenum.

Diehl, L. A. (1986). The paradox of G. Stanley Hall: Foe of coeducation and educator of women. *American Psychologist, 41*, 868–878.

Dixon, R. A. (1983). Theoretical proliferation in psychology: A plea for sustained disunity. *Psychological Record, 33*, 337–340.

Drever, J. (1968). Some early associationists. In B. B. Wolman (Ed.), *Historical roots of contemporary psychology* (pp. 11–28). New York: Harper & Row.

Ebbinghaus, H. (1897). *Grundzüge der Psychologie* [Principles of psychology]. Leipzig, Germany: Veit.

Ebbinghaus, H. (1902). *Outline of psychology*. Leipzig, Germany: Veit.

Ebbinghaus, H. (1913). *On memory: An investigation to experimental psychology* (H. A. Ruger & C. E. Bussenius, Trans.). New York: Columbia University Press. (Original work published 1885)

Ellenberger, H. F. (1970). *The discovery of the unconscious: The history and evolution of dynamic psychiatry*. New York: Basic Books.

Ellenberger, H. F. (1972). The story of "Anna O": A critical review with new data. *Journal of the History of the Behavioral Sciences, 8*, 267–279.

Esper, E. A. (1964). *A history of psychology*. Philadelphia: Saunders.

Evans, R. B. (1972). E. B. Titchener and his lost system. *Journal of the History of the Behavioral Sciences, 8*, 168–180.

Evans, R. B. (1984). The origins of American academic psychology. In J. Brožek (Ed.), *Explorations in the history of psychology in the United States* (pp. 17–60). Cranbury, NJ: Associated University Presses.

Fancher, R. E. (1985). *The intelligence men: Makers of the IQ controversy*. New York: Norton.

Fancher, R. E. (1990). *Pioneers of psychology* (2nd ed.). New York: Norton.

Fay, J. W. (1939). *American psychology before William James*. New Brunswick, NJ: Rutgers University Press.

Fechner, G. T. (1966). *Elements of psychophysics*. New York: Holt, Rinehart & Winston. (Original work published 1860)

Fell, H. B. (1960). Fashion in cell biology. *Science, 132*, 1625–1627.

Fetzer, J. H. (1991). *Philosophy and cognitive science*. New York: Paragon House.

Flanagan, O. (1991). *The science of the mind* (2nd ed.). Cambridge, MA: MIT Press.

Flew, A. (Ed.). (1962). *David Hume: On human nature and the understanding*. New York: Macmillan.

Fodor, J. A. (1983). *The modularity of mind*. Cambridge, MA: MIT Press.

Fowler, R. D. (1989). Divisions reflect APA's diversity. *APA Monitor, 20*, 4–5.

Fowler, R. D. (1990). In memoriam: Burrhus Frederic Skinner, 1904–1990. *American Psychologist, 45*, 1203.

Frankel, C. (Ed.). (1947). *Rousseau: The social contract.* New York: Macmillan.

Frankl, V. E. (1963). *Man's search for meaning: An introduction to logotherapy.* New York: Washington Square Press.

Frankl, V. E. (1984). *Man's search for meaning* (rev. ed.). New York: Washington Square Press. (Original work published as *Experiences in a concentration camp*, 1946)

Frazer, J. G. (1963). *The golden bough.* New York: Macmillan. (Original work published 1890)

Freud, S. (1927). *The problem of lay-analyses.* New York: Brentano.

Freud, S. (1949). *The origins and development of psychoanalysis.* Chicago: Regnery. (Original work published 1910)

Freud, S. (1953). *The interpretation of dreams.* In *The standard edition* (Vols. 4 and 5). London: Hogarth Press. (Original work published 1900)

Freud, S. (1954). Project for a scientific psychology. In M. Bonaparte, A. Freud, & E. Kris (Eds.) and E. Mossbacher & J. Strachey (Trans.), *The origins of psychoanalysis, letters to Wilhelm Fliess, drafts, and notes: 1887–1902.* New York: Basic Books. (Original work published 1950)

Freud, S. (1955). *Beyond the pleasure principle.* In *The standard edition* (Vol. 18). London: Hogarth Press. (Original work published 1920)

Freud, S. (1960a). *Jokes and their relation to the unconscious.* In *The standard edition* (Vol. 8). London: Hogarth Press. (Original work published 1905)

Freud, S. (1960b). *Psychopathology of everyday life.* In *The standard edition* (Vol. 6). London: Hogarth Press. (Original work published 1901)

Freud, S. (1961a). *The future of an illusion.* New York: Norton. (Original work published 1927)

Freud, S. (1961b). *Civilization and its discontents.* New York: Norton. (Original work published 1930)

Freud, S. (1963). *An autobiographical study* (J. Strachey, Ed. and Trans.) New York: Norton. (Original work published 1925)

Freud, S. (1964). Moses and monotheism. In J. Strachey (Ed. and Trans.), *The standard edition* (Vol. 23, pp. 3–137). London: Hogarth Press. (Original work published 1939)

Freud, S. (1966). *Introductory lectures on psychoanalysis* (J. Strachey, Ed. and Trans.). New York: Norton. (Original work published 1915–1917)

Freud, S. (1966). *The complete introductory lectures on psychoanalysis* (J. Strachey, Ed. and Trans.), New York: Norton. (Original work published 1933)

Freud, S. (1969). *An outline of psychoanalysis* (rev. ed.). New York: Norton. (Original work published 1940)

Fromm, E. (1941). *Escape from freedom.* New York: Holt, Rinehart & Winston.

Galton, F. (1853). *Narrative of an explorer in tropical South Africa.* London: Murray.

Galton, F. (1855). *The art of travel.* London: Murray.

Galton, F. (1869). *Hereditary genius: An inquiry into its laws and consequences.* London: Macmillan.

Galton, F. (1874). *English men of science: Their nature and nurture.* London: Macmillan.

Galton, F. (1875). The history of twins as a criterion of the relative powers of nature and nurture. *Fraser's Magazine, 92*, 566–576.

Galton, F. (1883). *Inquiries into human faculty and its development.* London: Macmillan.

Galton, F. (1888). Co-relations and their measurement, chiefly from anthropological data. *Proceedings of the Royal Society, 45*, 135–145.

Galton, F. (1889). *Natural inheritance.* London: Macmillan.

Goddard, H. H. (1912). *The Kallikak family, a study in the heredity of feeble-mindedness.* New York: Macmillan.

Goddard, H. H. (1914). *Feeble-mindedness: Its causes and consequences.* New York: Macmillan.

Goddard, H. H. (1920). *Human efficiency and levels of intelligence.* Princeton, NJ: Princeton University Press.

Goethe, J. W. (1898). *Faust: A tragedy* (B. Taylor, Trans.). New York: Houghton Mifflin. (Original work published 1808)

Goethe, J. W. (1952). *Sorrows of young Werther.* Chapel Hill: University of North Carolina Press. (Original work published 1774)

Goldsmith, M. (1934). *Franz Anton Mesmer.* New York: Doubleday.

Gould, S. J. (1976). Darwin and the captain. *Natural History, 85*(1), 32–34.

Gould, S. J. (1981). *The mismeasure of man.* New York: Norton.

Grane, L. (1970). *Peter Abelard: Philosophy and Christianity in the Middle Ages* (F. Crowley & C. Crowley, Trans.). New York: Harcourt, Brace & World.

Greenway, A. P. (1973). The incorporation of action into associationism: The psychology of Alexander Bain. *Journal of the History of the Behavioral Sciences, 9*, 42–52.

Gregory, R. L. (Ed.). (1987). *The Oxford companion to the mind.* Oxford: Oxford University Press.

Guilford, J. P. (1967). *The nature of human intelligence.* New York: McGraw-Hill.

Hadden, A. W. (Trans.). (1912). St. Augustine's "On the trinity." In B. Rand (Ed.), *The classical psychologists.* Boston: Houghton Mifflin.

Hale, N. G., Jr. (1971). *Freud in America* (Vol. 1). New York: Oxford University Press.

Hall, C. S. (1954). *A primer of Freudian psychology.* Cleveland: World.

Hall, C. S., & Lindzey, G. (1978). *Theories of personality* (3rd ed.). New York: Wiley.

Hall, G. S. (1904). *Adolescence: Its psychology and its relation to physiology, anthropology, sociology, sex, crime, religion and education* (Vols. 1 and 2). New York: Appleton.

Hall, G. S. (1906). The question of coeducation. *Munsey's Magazine, 34*, 588–592.

Hall, G. S. (1922). *Senescence: The last half of life.* New York: Appleton.

Hall, G. S. (1923). *Life and confessions of a psychologist.* New York: Appleton.

Hall, M. H. (1968, July). A conversation with Abraham Maslow. *Psychology Today,* pp. 35–37, 54–57.

Hannah, B. (1976). *Jung, his life and work: A biographical memoir.* New York: Putnam.

Harris, B. (1979). Whatever happened to little Albert? *American Psychologist, 34,* 151–160.

Harris, M. (1974). *Cows, pigs, wars and witches: The riddles of culture.* New York: Vintage.

Hartley, D. (1834). *Observations on man, his frame, his duty, and his expectations.* London: Tegg. (Original work published 1749)

Hartmann, K. E. von (1869). *Philosophie des Unbewussten* [Philosophy of the unconscious]. Berlin: Duncker.

Hathorn, R. Y. (1977). *Greek mythology.* Beirut, Lebanon: American University of Beirut.

Hearst, E. (Ed.). (1979). *The first century of experimental psychology.* Hillsdale, NJ: Erlbaum.

Hebb, D. O. (1959). A neuropsychological theory. In S. Koch (Ed.), *Psychology: A study of science* (Vol. 1). New York: McGraw-Hill.

Hebb, D. O. (1972). *Textbook of psychology* (3rd ed.). Philadelphia: Saunders.

Hegel, G. W. F. (1973). *The encyclopedia of the mind* (W. Wallace, Trans.). Oxford, England: Oxford University Press. (Original work published 1817)

Heidbreder, E. (1933). *Seven psychologies.* New York: Appleton-Century.

Heidegger, M. (1927). *Being and time.* Halle, Germany: Niemeyer.

Henle, M. (1971a). Did Titchener commit the stimulus error? The problem of meaning in structural psychology. *Journal of the History of the Behavioral Sciences, 7,* 279–282.

Henle, M. (Ed.). (1971b). *The selected papers of Wolfgang Köhler.* New York: Liveright.

Henle, M. (1978). One man against the Nazis—Wolfgang Köhler. *American Psychologist, 33,* 939–944.

Henle, M. (1986). *1879 and all that: Essays in the theory and history of psychology.* New York: Columbia University Press.

Herbart, J. F. (1824–1825). *Psychology as a science, newly based upon experience, metaphysics, and mathematics* (Vols. 1 and 2). Königsberg, Germany: Unzer.

Hergenhahn, B. R. (1988). *An introduction to theories of learning* (3rd ed.). Englewood Cliffs, NJ: Prentice-Hall.

Hergenhahn, B. R. (1990). *An introduction to theories of personality* (3rd ed.). Englewood Cliffs, NJ: Prentice-Hall.

Hilgard, E. R. (1987). *Psychology in America: A historical survey.* Orlando, FL: Harcourt Brace Jovanovich.

Hill, W. F. (1990). *Learning: A survey of psychological interpretations* (5th ed.). New York: Harper & Row.

Hobbes, T. (1962). *Leviathan.* New York: Macmillan. (Original work published 1651)

Hoffman, E. (1988). *The right to be human: A biography of Abraham Maslow.* Los Angeles: Tarcher.

Hoffman, R. R., Bringmann, W., Bamberg, M., & Klein, R. (1986). Some historical observations on Ebbinghaus. In D. Gorfein & R. Hoffman (Eds.), *Memory and learning: The Ebbinghaus centennial conference.* Hillsdale, NJ: Erlbaum.

Hofstadter, R. (1955). *Social Darwinism in American thought.* Boston: Beacon Press.

Horney, K. (1937). *The neurotic personality of our time.* New York: Norton.

Horney, K. (1939). *New ways in psychoanalysis.* New York: Norton.

Horney, K. (1945). *Our inner conflicts.* New York: Norton.

Horney, K. (1967). *Feminine psychology.* New York: Norton. (Original work published 1923–1937)

Horney, K. (1968). *Self-analysis.* New York: Norton. (Original work published 1942)

Hubben, W. (1952). *Dostoevsky, Kierkegaard, Nietzsche, and Kafka.* New York: Macmillan.

Hulin, W. S. (1934). *A short history of psychology.* New York: Holt.

Hull, C. L. (1920). Quantitative aspects of the evolution of concepts: An experimental study. *Psychological Monographs, 28*(123).

Hull, C. L. (1928). *Aptitude testing.* Yonkers-on-Hudson, NY: World Book.

Hull, C. L. (1943). *Principles of behavior.* New York: Appleton-Century.

Hull, C. L. (1952a). Clark L. Hull. In E. G. Boring, H. S. Langfeld, H. Werner, & R. M. Yerkes (Eds.), *A history of psychology in autobiography* (Vol. 4, pp. 143–162). Worcester, MA: Clark University Press.

Hull, C. L. (1952b). *A behavior system.* New Haven, CT: Yale University Press.

Hull, C. L., Hovland, C. I., Ross, R. T., Hall, M., Perkins, D. T., & Fitch, F. B. (1940). *Mathematico-deductive theory of rote learning.* New Haven, CT: Yale University Press.

Hulse, M. (1989). "Introduction" to *The sorrows of young Werther.* London: Penguin Books.

Husserl, E. (1900–1901). *Logical investigations.* Halle, Germany: Niemeyer.

James, W. (1890). *The principles of psychology* (Vols. 1 and 2). New York: Holt.

James, W. (1902). *The varieties of religious experience*. New York: Longmans, Green.

James, W. (1920). Letters of William James. In H. James (Ed.), *Letters of William James* (Vols. 1 and 2). Boston: Atlantic Monthly Press.

James, W. (1963). *Psychology: The briefer course* (G. Allport, Ed.). New York: Harper. (Original work published 1892)

James, W. (1981). *Pragmatism: A new name for some old ways of thinking*. Indianapolis: Hackett. (Original work published 1907)

Jankowicz, A. D. (1987). Whatever happened to George Kelly? Applications and implications. *American Psychologist, 42*, 481–487.

Jennings, J. L. (1986). Husserl revisited: The forgotten distinction between psychology and phenomenology. *American Psychologist, 41*, 1231–1240.

Johnson, M. G., & Henley, T. B. (Eds.). (1990). *Reflections on the principles of psychology: William James after a century*. Hillsdale, NJ: Erlbaum.

Johnson, R. C., McClearn, G. E., Yuen, S., Nagoshi, C. T., Ahern, F. M., & Cole, R. E. (1985). Galton's data a century later. *American Psychologist, 40*, 875–892.

Joncich, G. (1968). *The sane positivist: A biography of Edward L. Thorndike*. Middletown, CT: Wesleyan University Press.

Jones, E. (1953, 1955, 1957). *The life and work of Sigmund Freud* (Vols. 1–3). New York: Basic Books.

Jones, M. C. (1924). A laboratory study of fear: The case of Peter. *Pedagogical Seminary, 31*, 308–315.

Jones, M. C. (1974). Albert, Peter and John B. Watson. *American Psychologist, 29*, 581–583.

Jones, R. A. (1987). Psychology, history, and the press: The case of William McDougall and the *New York Times*. *American Psychologist, 42*, 931–940.

Jones, W. H. S. (1923). *Hippocrates* (Vols. 1 and 2). New York: Putnam.

Jourard, S. M. (1971). *The transparent self*. New York: Van Nostrand.

Jourard, S. M. (1974). *Healthy personality: An approach from the viewpoint of humanistic psychology*. New York: Macmillan.

Jowett, B. (Trans.). (1908). *The republic of Plato* (3rd ed.) (Vols. 1 and 2). Oxford, England: Clarendon Press.

Jowett, B. (Trans.). (1942). *Plato*. Rosyln, NY: Black.

Jung, C. G. (1928). *Contributions to analytical psychology*. New York: Harcourt Brace Jovanovich.

Jung, C. G. (1933). *Modern man in search of a soul*. New York: Harcourt Brace Jovanovich.

Jung, C. G. (1953). Two essays on analytic psychology. In *The collected works of C. G. Jung* (Vol. 7). Princeton, NJ: Princeton University Press. (Original work published 1917)

Jung, C. G. (1963). *Memories, dreams, reflections*. New York: Pantheon Books.

Kagan, J. (1980, December). Jean Piaget's contributions. *Phi Delta Kappan*, pp. 245–246.

Kahl, R. K. (Ed.). (1971). *Selected writings of Hermann von Helmholtz*. Middletown, CT: Wesleyan University Press.

Kant, I. (1908). *Critique of practical reason*. In B. Rand (Ed.), *Modern classical philosophers*. Boston: Houghton Mifflin. (Original work published 1788)

Kant, I. (1965). *Critique of pure reason* (N. K. Smith, Trans.). New York: St. Martin's Press. (Original work published 1781)

Karier, C. J. (1986). *Scientists of the mind: Intellectual founders of modern psychology*. Chicago: University of Illinois Press.

Kaufmann, W. (Ed. and Trans.). (1982). *The portable Nietzsche*. New York: Viking Press/Penguin Books.

Kazdin, A. E. (1980). *Behavior modification in applied settings* (rev. ed.). Homewood, IL: Dorsey Press.

Kazdin, A. E., & Wilson, G. T. (1978). *Evaluation of behavior therapy*. Cambridge, MA: Bollinger.

Keller, F. S. (1973). *The definition of psychology* (2nd ed.). Englewood Cliffs, NJ: Prentice-Hall.

Kelly, G. A. (1955). *The psychology of personal constructs: A theory of personality* (Vols. 1 and 2). New York: Norton.

Kelly, G. A. (1964). The language of hypotheses: Man's psychological instrument. *Journal of Individual Psychology, 20*, 137–152.

Kelly, G. A. (1969). The autobiography of a theory. In B. Maher (Ed.), *Clinical psychology and personality: Selected papers of George Kelly*. New York: Wiley.

Kierkegaard, S. (1944). *For self-examination and judge for yourselves* (W. Lowrie, Trans.). Princeton, NJ: Princeton University Press. (Original work published 1851)

Kierkegaard, S. (1962). *Philosophical fragments* (D. Swenson, Trans.). Princeton, NJ: Princeton University Press. (Original work published 1844)

Kimble, G. A. (1984). Psychology's two cultures. *American Psychologist, 39*, 833–839.

Kinget, G. M. (1975). *On being human: A systematic view*. New York: Harcourt Brace Jovanovich.

Kirschenbaum, H. (1979). *On becoming Carl Rogers*. New York: Dell.

Koch, S. (Ed.). (1959). *Psychology: A study of science* (Vol. 3). New York: McGraw-Hill.

Koch, S. (1981). The nature and limits of psychological knowledge: Lessons of a century qua "science." *American Psychologist, 36*, 257–269.

Koffka, K. (1922). Perception: An introduction to Gestalt-Theorie. *Psychological Bulletin, 19*, 531–585.

Koffka, K. (1924). *The growth of the mind: An introduction to child psychology* (R. M. Ogden, Trans.). New York: Harcourt, Brace.

Koffka, K. (1963). *Principles of Gestalt psychology*. New York: Harcourt, Brace & World. (Original work published 1935)

Köhler, W. (1920). *Die physischen Gestalten in Rule und im stationären Zustand* [Static and stationary physical configurations]. Braunschweig, Germany: Vieweg.

Köhler, W. (1925). *The mentality of apes*. London: Routledge and Kegan Paul. (Original work published 1917)

Köhler, W. (1938). *The place of value in a world of facts*. New York: Liveright.

Köhler, W. (1940). *Dynamics in psychology*. New York: Liveright.

Köhler, W. (1947). *Gestalt psychology: An introduction to new concepts in modern psychology*. New York: Liveright.

Köhler, W. (1969). *The task of Gestalt psychology*. Princeton, NJ: Princeton University Press.

Köhler, W. (1970). *Gestalt psychology: An introduction to new concepts in modern psychology*. New York: Liveright. (Original work published 1929)

Kuhn, T. S. (1973). *The structure of scientific revolutions* (2nd ed.). Chicago: University of Chicago Press.

Külpe, O. (1909). *Outlines of psychology: Based upon the results of experimental investigation* (3rd ed.). New York: Macmillan. (Original work published 1893)

Lachman, R., Lachman, J. L., & Butterfield, E. C. (1979). *Cognitive psychology and information processing*. Hillsdale, NJ: Erlbaum.

Ladd, G. T., & Woodworth, R. S. (1911). *Elements of physiological psychology*. New York: Scribner.

Lamarck, J. B. (1914). *Philosophie zoologique* [Zoological philosophy] (H. Elliot, Trans.). London: Macmillan. (Original work published 1809)

La Mettrie, J. O. de. (1912). *L'homme machine* [Man a machine] (M. W. Calkins, Trans.). La Salle, IL: Open Court. (Original work published 1748)

Land, E. H. (1964). The retinex. *American Scientist, 52*, 247–264.

Land, E. H. (1977). The retinex theory of color vision. *Scientific American, 237*(6), 108–128.

Lashley, K. S. (1923). Behavioristic interpretation of consciousness. *Psychological Review, 30*, 237–272, 329–353.

Lashley, K. S., Chow, K. L., & Semmes, J. (1951). An examination of the electrical field theory of cerebral integration. *Psychological Review, 40*, 175–188.

Leahey, T. H. (1980). *A history of psychology*. Englewood Cliffs, NJ: Prentice-Hall.

Leahey, T. H. (1981). The mistaken mirror: On Wundt's and Titchener's psychologies. *Journal of the History of the Behavioral Sciences, 17*, 273–282.

Leahey, T. H. (1987). *A history of psychology: Main currents in psychological thought*. Englewood Cliffs, NJ: Prentice-Hall.

Leary, D. E. (1982). The fate and influence of John Stuart Mill's proposed science of ethology. *Journal of the History of Ideas, 43*, 153–162.

Lchman, D. R., Lempert, R. O., & Nisbett, R. E. (1988). The effects of graduate training on reasoning: Formal discipline and thinking about everyday-life events. *American Psychologist, 43*, 431–442.

Leibniz, G. W. (1982). *New essays on human understanding* (P. Remnant & J. Bennett, Eds. and Trans.). Cambridge, MA: Cambridge University Press. (Original work published 1765)

Leitenberg, H. (Ed.). (1976). *Handbook of behavior modification and behavior therapy*. Englewood Cliffs, NJ: Prentice-Hall.

Lewin, K. (1935). *A dynamic theory of personality: Selected papers*. New York: McGraw-Hill.

Lewin, K., Lippitt, R., & White, R. K. (1939). Patterns of aggressive behavior in experimentally created "social climates." *Journal of Social Psychology, 10*, 271–299.

Locke, J. (1974). *An essay concerning human understanding* (A. D. Woozley, Ed.). New York: New American Library. (Original work published 1706)

Luddy, A. J. (1947). *The case of Peter Abelard*. Westminster, MD: Newman Bookshop.

Lundin, R. W. (1991). *Theories and systems of psychology* (4th ed.). Lexington, MA: Heath.

Mach, E. (1914). *Contributions to the analysis of sensations*. La Salle, IL: Open Court. (Original work published 1886)

MacLeod, R. B. (1975). *The persistent problems of psychology*. Pittsburgh: Duquesne University Press.

Maddi, S. R., & Costa, P. T. (1972). *Humanism in personology: Allport, Maslow and Murray*. Chicago: Aldine-Atherton.

Maher, B. A., & Maher, W. B. (1985). Psychopathology: II. From the eighteenth century to modern times. In G. A. Kimble & K. Schlesinger (Eds.), *Topics in the history of psychology* (Vol. 2, pp. 295–329). Hillsdale, NJ: Erlbaum.

Maher, W. B., & Maher, B. A. (1985). Psychopathology: I. From ancient times to the eighteenth century. In G. A. Kimble & K. Schlesinger (Eds.), *Topics in the history of psychology* (Vol. 2, pp. 251–294). Hillsdale, NJ: Erlbaum.

Malthus, T. (1914). *Essay on the principle of population*. New York: Dutton. (Original work published 1798)

Marrow, A. J. (1969). *The practical theorist: The life and work of Kurt Lewin*. New York: Basic Books.

Marshall, M. E. (1969). Gustav Fechner, Dr. Mises, and the comparative anatomy of angels. *Journal of the History of the Behavioral Sciences, 5*, 39–58.

Martineau, H. (1893). *The positive philosophy of Auguste Comte* (Vol. 1). London: Kegan Paul, Trench, Trubner. (Original work published 1853)

Maslow, A. H. (1966). *The psychology of science: A reconnaissance*. South Bend, IN: Gateway Editions.

Maslow, A. H. (1968). *Toward a psychology of being* (2nd ed.). New York: Van Nostrand Reinhold.

Maslow, A. H. (1970). *Motivation and personality* (2nd ed.). New York: Harper & Row. (Original work published 1954)

Maslow, A. H. (1971). *The farther reaches of human nature.* New York: Penguin Books.

Maslow, A. H. (1987). *Motivation and personality* (3rd ed.). New York: Harper & Row. (Original work published 1954)

Masson, J. M. (1984). *The assault on truth: Freud's suppression of the seduction theory.* New York: Farrar, Straus, and Giroux.

Masters, J. C., Burish, T. G., Hollon, S. D., & Rimm, D. C. (1987). *Behavior therapy: Techniques and empirical findings* (3rd ed.). Orlando, FL: Harcourt Brace Jovanovich.

Matarazzo, J. D. (1985). Psychotherapy. In G. A. Kimble & K. Schlesinger (Eds.), *Topics in the history of psychology* (Vol. 1, pp. 219–250). Hillsdale, NJ: Erlbaum.

Matarazzo, J. D. (1987). There is one psychology, no specialties, but many applications. *American Psychologist, 42,* 893–903.

May, R. (1939). *The art of counseling: How to give and gain mental health.* Nashville, TN: Abingdon-Cokesbury.

May, R. (1940). *The springs of creative living: A study of human nature and God.* New York: Abingdon-Cokesbury.

May, R. (1950). *The meaning of anxiety.* New York: Ronald Press.

May, R. (1953). *Man's search for himself.* New York: Norton.

May, R. (Ed.). (1961). *Existential psychology.* New York: Random House.

May, R. (1967). *Psychology and the human dilemma.* New York: Van Nostrand.

May, R. (1969). *Love and will.* New York: Norton.

May, R. (1972). *Power and innocence: A search for the sources of violence.* New York: Norton.

May, R. (1973). *Paulus: Reminiscences of a friendship.* New York: Harper & Row.

May, R. (1981). *Freedom and destiny.* New York: Norton.

May, R. (1983). *The discovery of being: Writings in existential psychology.* New York: Norton.

May, R., Angel, E., & Ellenberger, H. F. (Eds.). (1958). *Existence: A new dimension in psychiatry and psychology.* New York: Basic Books.

McClelland, D. C. (1973). Testing for competence rather than for "intelligence." *American Psychologist, 28,* 1–14.

McDougall, W. (1905). *Physiological psychology.* London: Dent.

McDougall, W. (1908). *Introduction to social psychology.* London: Methuen.

McDougall, W. (1912). *Psychology: The study of behavior.* London: Williams & Norgate.

McDougall, W. (1923). *Outline of psychology.* New York: Scribner.

McMahon, C. E. (1975). Harvey on the soul: A unique episode in the history of psychophysiological thought. *Journal of the History of the Behavioral Sciences, 11,* 276–283.

McReynolds, P. (1987). Lightner Witmer: Little-known founder of clinical psychology. *American Psychologist, 42,* 849–858.

Melton, A. W. (Ed.). (1964). *Categories of human learning.* New York: Academic Press.

Mill, J. S. (1893). *A system of logic, ratiocinative and inductive, being a connected view of the principles of evidence, and the methods of scientific investigation* (8th ed.). London: Longmans, Green. (Original work published 1843)

Mill, J. S. (Ed.). (1967). *Analysis of the phenomena of the human mind by James Mill* (Vol. 1). New York: Augustus M. Kelly, Publishers. (Original work published 1869)

Miller, E. F. (1971). Hume's contribution to behavioral science. *Journal of the History of the Behavioral Sciences, 7,* 154–168.

Miller, G. A. (1962). Some psychological studies of grammar. *American Psychologist, 17,* 748–762.

Miller, G. A. (1965). Some preliminaries to psycholinguistics. *American Psychologist, 20,* 15–20.

Minton, H. L. (1988). *Lewis M. Terman: Pioneer in psychological testing.* New York: New York University Press.

Monte, C. F. (1975). *Psychology's scientific endeavor.* New York: Praeger.

Mora, G. (1959). Vincenzo Chiarugi (1759–1820) and his psychiatric reform in Florence in the late eighteenth century. *Journal of the History of Medicine, 14.*

Morgan, C. L. (1891). *An introduction to comparative psychology.* London: Scott.

Morgan, C. L. (1900). *Animal life and intelligence* (revised as *Animal behavior*). London: Edward Arnold. (Original work published 1891)

Mossner, E. C. (Ed.). (1969). *David Hume: A treatise of human nature.* New York: Viking Press/Penguin Books.

Müller, J. (1842). *Handbuch der Physiologie des Menschen* [Handbook of Human Physiology] (Vols. 1 and 2). London: Taylor and Walton. (Original work published 1833–1840)

Münsterberg, H. (1888). *Voluntary action.* Freiburg, Germany: Mohr.

Münsterberg, H. (1900). *Grundzüge der Psychologie* [Basics of psychology]. Leipzig, Germany: Barth.

Münsterberg, H. (1904). *The Americans* (E. B. Holt, Trans.). New York: McClure, Phillips.

Münsterberg, H. (1908). *On the witness stand.* New York: Clark Boardman.

Münsterberg, H. (1909). *Psychotherapy.* New York: Moffat, Yard.

Münsterberg, H. (1910). *American problems.* New York: Moffat, Yard.

Münsterberg, H. (1912). *Vocation and learning*. St. Louis: People's University.

Münsterberg, H. (1913). *Psychology and industrial efficiency*. New York: Houghton Mifflin.

Murphy, G. (1968). *Psychological thought from Pythagoras to Freud*. New York: Harcourt, Brace & World.

Murray, G. (1955). *Five stages of Greek religion*. New York: Doubleday.

Myers, C. R. (1970). Journal citations and scientific eminence in psychology. *American Psychologist, 25*, 1041–1048.

Newton, I. (1952).*Opticks or a treatise of the reflections, refractions, inflections and colours of light*. New York: Dover. (Original work published 1704)

Newton, I. (1964). *The mathematical principles of natural philosophy*. New York: Citadel Press. (Original work published 1687)

Nietzsche, F. (1966). *Beyond good and evil* (W. Kaufmann, Trans.). New York: Random House. (Original work published 1886)

Nietzsche, F. (1969). *Thus spoke Zarathustra* (R. J. Hollingdale, Trans.). New York: Viking Press/Penguin Books. (Original work published 1883–1885)

Nietzsche, F. (1974). *The gay science* (W. Kaufmann, Trans.). New York: Random House. (Original work published 1882)

Oates, W. J. (Ed.). (1940). *The Stoic and Epicurean philosophies*. New York: Random House.

O'Donnell, J. M. (1985). *The origins of behaviorism: American psychology, 1870–1920*. New York: New York University Press.

Ovsiankina, M. (1928). Die Wiederaufnahme von Interbrochenen Handlungen [The resumption of interrupted activities]. *Psychologische Forschung, 2*, 302–389.

Parisi, T. (1987). Why Freud failed: Some implications for neurophysiology and sociobiology. *American Psychologist, 42*, 235–245.

Patnoe, S. (1988). *A narrative history of experimental social psychology: The Lewin tradition*. New York: Springer-Verlag.

Pavlov, I. P. (1897). *Work of the principal digestive glands*. St. Petersburg, Russia: Kushneroff.

Pavlov, I. P. (1928). *Lectures on conditioned reflexes*. New York: Liveright.

Pavlov, I. P. (1955). *Selected works*. Moscow: Foreign Languages.

Pavlov, I. P. (1960). *Conditioned reflexes: An investigation of the activity of the cerebral cortex* (G. V. Anrep, Trans.). New York: Dover. (Original work published 1927)

Pearson, K. (1924). *The life, letters, and labours of Francis Galton*. Vol. 2: *Researches of middle life*. London: Cambridge University Press.

Perry, N. W., Jr. (1979). Why clinical psychology does not need alternative training models. *American Psychologist, 34*, 603–611.

Peters, R. C. (1962). Introduction to Hobbes's *Leviathan*. New York: Macmillan.

Peterson, D. R. (1976). Need for the doctor of psychology degree in professional psychology. *American Psychologist, 31*, 792–798.

Petryszak, N. G. (1981). Tabula rasa—its origins and implications. *Journal of the History of the Behavioral Sciences, 17*, 15–27.

Piaget, J. (1926). *The language and thought of the child*. London: Routledge.

Piaget, J. (1966). *Psychology of intelligence*. Totowa, NJ: Littlefield, Adams.

Piaget, J. (1970). Piaget's theory. In P. H. Mussen (Ed.), *Carmichael's manual of child psychology* (Vol. 1). New York: Wiley.

Pillsbury, W. B. (1911). *Essentials of psychology*. New York: Macmillan.

Pinel, P. (1962). *A treatise on insanity*. Academy of Medicine—The History of Medicine Series. New York: Hafner. (Original work published 1801)

Popper, K. (1958). The beginnings of rationalism. In D. Miller (Ed.), *Popper selections* (pp. 25–32). Princeton, NJ: Princeton University Press.

Popper, K. (1963). *Conjectures and refutations*. New York: Basic Books.

Popper, K. (1968). *The logic of scientific discovery*. New York: Harper & Row.

Porter, N. (1868). *The human intellect: With an introduction upon psychology and the soul*. New York: Scribner.

Priestley, J. (1775). *Hartley's theory of the human mind, on the principle of the association of ideas*. London: Johnson.

Progoff, I. (1973). *Jung, synchronicity, and human destiny*. New York: Dell.

Pusey, E. B. (Trans.). (1961). *The confessions of St. Augustine*. New York: Macmillan.

Raphelson, A. C. (1973). The pre-Chicago association of the early functionalists. *Journal of the History of the Behavioral Sciences, 9*, 115–122.

Reed, J. (1987). Robert M. Yerkes and the mental testing movement. In M. M. Sokal (Ed.), *Psychological testing and American society* (pp. 75–94). New Brunswick, NJ: Rutgers University Press.

Reid, T. (1969). *Essays on the intellectual powers of man* (Intro. by B. A. Brody). Cambridge, MA: MIT Press. (Original work published 1785)

Reisman, J. M. (1991). *A history of clinical psychology* (2nd ed.). New York: Hemisphere.

Remnant, P., & Bennett, J. (Eds. and Trans.). (1982). G. W. Leibniz's *New essays on human understanding*. New York: Cambridge University Press. (Original work published 1765)

Rieber, R. W. (Ed.). (1980). *Wilhelm Wundt and the making of scientific psychology*. New York: Plenum.

Rimm, D. C., & Masters, J. C. (1974). *Behavior therapy: Techniques and empirical findings*. New York: Academic Press.

Roback, A. A. (1952). *History of American psychology*. New York: Library.

Robertson, D. W., Jr. (1972). *Abelard and Heloise*. New York: Dial Press.

Robinson, D. N. (1982). *Toward a science of human nature: Essays on the psychologies of Mill, Hegel, Wundt and James*. New York: Columbia University Press.

Robinson, D. N. (1985). *Philosophy of psychology*. New York: Columbia University Press.

Robinson, D. N. (1986). *An intellectual history of psychology* (rev. ed.). Madison: University of Wisconsin Press.

Robinson, D. N. (1989). *Aristotle's psychology*. New York: Columbia University Press.

Robinson, V. (1943). *The story of medicine*. New York: New Home Library.

Rogers, C. R. (1939). *The clinical treatment of the problem child*. Boston: Houghton Mifflin.

Rogers, C. R. (1942). *Counseling and psychotherapy: Newer concepts in practice*. Boston: Houghton Mifflin.

Rogers, C. R. (1947). Some observations on the organization of personality. *American Psychologist, 2*, 358–368.

Rogers, C. R. (1951). *Client-centered therapy: Its current practice, implications, and theory*. Boston: Houghton Mifflin.

Rogers, C. R. (1959). A theory of therapy, personality, and interpersonal relationships, as developed in the client-centered framework. In S. Koch (Ed.), *Psychology: A study of a science* (Vol. 3, pp. 184–256). New York: McGraw-Hill.

Rogers, C. R. (1961). *On becoming a person: A therapist's view of psychotherapy*. Boston: Houghton Mifflin.

Rogers, C. R. (1966). Client-centered therapy. In S. Arieti (Ed.), *American handbook of psychiatry*. New York: Basic Books.

Rogers, C. R. (1969). *Freedom to learn*. Columbus, OH: Merrill.

Rogers, C. R. (1973). My philosophy of interpersonal relationships and how it grew. *Journal of Humanistic Psychology, 13*, 3–15.

Rogers, C. R. (1974). In retrospect: Forty-six years. *American Psychologist, 29*, 115–123.

Rogers, C. R. (1980). *A way of being*. Boston: Houghton Mifflin.

Romanes, G. J. (1882). *Animal intelligence*. London: Kegan Paul, Trench.

Romanes, G. J. (1884). *Mental evolution in animals*. New York: Appleton.

Romanes, G. J. (1885). *Mental evolution in man*. London: Kegan Paul.

Rosenbaum, M., & Muroff, M. (Eds.). (1984). *Anna O. Fourteen contemporary reinterpretations*. New York: Free Press.

Rosenzweig, S. (1985). Freud and experimental psychology: The emergence of idiodynamics. In S. Koch & D. E. Leary (Eds.), *A century of psychology as science* (pp. 135–207). New York: McGraw-Hill.

Rousseau, J. J. (1947). *The social contract* (C. Frankel, Trans.). New York: Macmillan. (Original work published 1762)

Rousseau, J. J. (1974). *Emile* (B. Foxley, Trans.). London: Dent. (Original work published 1762)

Royce, J. R. (1975). Psychology is multi-methodological, variate, epistemic, world view, systemic, paradigmatic, theoretic, and disciplinary. In W. Arnold (Ed.), *Nebraska Symposium on Motivation*. Lincoln: University of Nebraska Press.

Royce, J. R., & Mos, L. P. (Eds.). (1981). *Humanistic psychology: Concepts and criticisms*. New York: Plenum.

Rubin, E. J. (1921). *Visuell wahrgenommene Figuren. Studien in psychologischer Analyse* (Pt. 1). Copenhagen: Gyldendal. (Original work published 1915)

Rubins, J. L. (1978). *Karen Horney: Gentle rebel of psychoanalysis*. New York: Dial Press.

Ruja, H. (1956). Productive psychologists. *American Psychologist, 11*, 148–149.

Rush, B. (1812). *Diseases of the mind*. Philadelphia: Kimber and Richardson.

Russell, B. (1945). *A history of Western philosophy*. New York: Simon & Schuster.

Russell, B. (1959). *Wisdom of the West*. Garden City, NJ: Doubleday.

Rychlak, J. (1975). Psychological science as a humanist views it. In W. Arnold (Ed.), *Nebraska Symposium on Motivation*. Lincoln: University of Nebraska Press.

Sahakian, W. S. (1975). *History and systems of psychology*. New York: Wiley.

Sahakian, W. S. (1981). *History of psychology: A source book in systematic psychology* (rev. ed.). Itasca, IL: Peacock.

Samelson, F. (1977). World War I intelligence testing and the development of psychology. *Journal of the History of the Behavioral Sciences, 13*, 274–282.

Samelson, F. (1981). Struggle for scientific authority: The reception of Watson's behaviorism, 1913–1920. *Journal of the History of the Behavioral Sciences, 17*, 399–425.

Santayana, G. (1920). *Character and opinion in the United States*. New York: Scribner.

Sargent, S. S., & Stafford, K. R. (1965). *Basic teachings of the great psychologists*. Garden City, NY: Doubleday.

Sartain, J., North, J., Strange, R., & Chapman, M. (1973). *Psychology: Understanding human behavior*. New York: McGraw-Hill.

Schopenhauer, A. (1957). *The world as will and idea* (R. B. Haldane & J. Kemp, Trans.). London: Routledge and Kegan Paul. (Original work published 1818)

Schwartz, B., & Lacey, H. (1982). *Behaviorism, science and human nature*. New York: Norton.

Scot, R. (1964). *Discovery of witchcraft*. Carbondale: Southern Illinois University Press. (Original work published 1584)

Searle, J. R. (1980). Minds, brains, and programs. *The Behavioral and Brain Sciences, 3*, 417–424.

Searle, J. R. (1990, January). Is the brain's mind a computer program? *Scientific American*, pp. 26–31.

Sechenov, I. M. (1965). *Reflexes of the brain*. Cambridge, MA: MIT Press. (Original work published 1863)

Sechenov, I. M. (1973). *I. M. Sechenov: Biographical sketch and essays*. New York: Arno Press. (Reprinted from I. Sechenov, *Selected works*, 1935)

Seligman, M. E. P. (1970). On the generality of the laws of learning. *Psychological Review*, *77*, 406–418.

Seligman, M. E. P., & Hager, J. L. (1972). *Biological boundaries of learning*. New York: Appleton-Century-Crofts.

Severin, F. T. (Ed.). (1973). *Discovering man in psychology: A humanistic approach*. New York: McGraw-Hill.

Sharp, S. E. (1899). Individual psychology: A study in psychological method. *The American Journal of Psychology*, *10*, 329–391.

Shields, S. A. (1975). Functionalism, Darwinism, and the psychology of women: A study in social myth. *American Psychologist*, *30*, 739–754.

Sigerist, H. E. (1951). *A history of medicine*. New York: Oxford.

Sirkin, M., & Fleming, M. (1982). Freud's "project" and its relationship to psychoanalytic theory. *Journal of the History of the Behavioral Sciences*, *18*, 230–241.

Skinner, B. F. (1938). *The behavior of organisms: An experimental analysis*. New York: Appleton-Century.

Skinner, B. F. (1948). *Walden two*. New York: Macmillan.

Skinner, B. F. (1950). Are theories of learning necessary? *Psychological Review*, *57*, 193–216.

Skinner, B. F. (1953). *Science and human behavior*. New York: Macmillan.

Skinner, B. F. (1954). The science of learning and the art of teaching. *Harvard Educational Review*, *24*, 86–97.

Skinner, B. F. (1956). A case study in scientific method. *American Psychologist*, *11*, 221–233.

Skinner, B. F. (1957). *Verbal behavior*. Englewood Cliffs, NJ: Prentice-Hall.

Skinner, B. F. (1958). Teaching machines. *Science*, *128*, 969–977.

Skinner, B. F. (1960). Pigeons in a pelican. *American Psychologist*, *15*, 28–37.

Skinner, B. F. (1967). B. F. Skinner. In E. G. Boring & G. Lindzey (Eds.), *A history of psychology in autobiography* (Vol. 5, pp. 385–413). New York: Appleton-Century-Crofts.

Skinner, B. F. (1968). *The technology of teaching*. New York: Appleton-Century-Crofts.

Skinner, B. F. (1971). *Beyond freedom and dignity*. New York: Knopf.

Skinner, B. F. (1974). *About behaviorism*. New York: Knopf.

Skinner, B. F. (1978). *Reflections on behaviorism and society*. Englewood Cliffs, NJ: Prentice-Hall.

Skinner, B. F. (1979). *The shaping of a behaviorist*. New York: Knopf.

Skinner, B. F. (1984). The shame of American education. *American Psychologist*, *39*, 947–954.

Skinner, B. F. (1987). *Upon further reflection*. Englewood Cliffs, NJ: Prentice-Hall.

Skinner, B. F. (1990). Can psychology be a science of mind? *American Psychologist*, *45*, 1206–1210.

Small, W. S. (1901). Experimental study of the mental processes of the rat. *American Journal of Psychology*, *12*, 218–220.

Smith, L. D. (1982). Purpose and cognition: The limits of neorealist influence on Tolman's psychology. *Behaviorism*, *10*, 151–163.

Smith, S. (1983). *Ideas of the great psychologists*. New York: Harper & Row.

Snow, C. P. (1964). *The two cultures and a second look*. London: Cambridge University Press.

Snyderman, M., & Rothman, S. (1990). *The IQ controversy, the media and public policy*. New Brunswick, NJ: Transaction.

Sokal, M. M. (1971). The unpublished autobiography of James McKeen Cattell. *American Psychologist*, *26*, 621–635.

Sokal, M. M. (1984). The Gestalt psychologists in behaviorist America. *American Historical Review*, *89*, 1240–1263.

Sokal, M. M. (Ed.). (1987). *Psychological testing and American society: 1890–1930*. New Brunswick, NJ: Rutgers University Press.

Spearman, C. (1904). "General intelligence," objectively determined and measured. *American Journal of Psychology*, *15*, 201–293.

Spence, K. W. (1942). The basis of solution by chimpanzees of the intermediate size problem. *Journal of Experimental Psychology*, *131*, 257–271.

Spence, K. W. (1952). Clark Leonard Hull: 1884–1952. *American Journal of Psychology*, *65*, 639–646.

Spence, K. W. (1956). *Behavior theory and conditioning* (Silliman lectures). New Haven, CT: Yale University Press.

Spence, K. W. (1960). *Behavior theory and learning: Selected papers*. Englewood Cliffs, NJ: Prentice-Hall.

Spencer, H. (1864). *Social statics*. New York: Appleton.

Spencer, H. (1870). *Principles of psychology* (2nd ed.). London: Longman.

Spencer, H. (1876). *The principles of sociology*. New York: Appleton.

Spinoza, B. (1955). *On the improvement of the understanding, the ethics, and correspondence* (R. H. M. Elwes, Trans.). New York: Dover. (Original work published 1677)

Spurzheim, G. (1834). *Phrenology, or the doctrine of mental phenomena*. Boston: Marsh, Capen, & Lyon.

Staats, A. W. (1981). Paradigmatic behaviorism, unified theory, unified theory construction methods, and the *Zeitgeist* of separatism. *American Psychologist*, *36*, 239–256.

Staats, A. W. (1989). Unificationism: Philosophy for the modern disunified science of psychology. *Philosophical Psychology, 2*, 143–164.

Stanovich, K. E. (1989). *How to think straight about psychology* (2nd ed.). Glenview, IL: Scott, Foresman.

Steinberg, E. (Ed.). (1977). *David Hume: An enquiry concerning human understanding.* Indianapolis: Hackett Publishing Company.

Stern, P. J. (1976). *C. G. Jung: The haunted prophet.* New York: Dell.

Stevens, S. S. (1935a). The operational basis of psychology. *American Journal of Psychology, 43*, 323–330.

Stevens, S. S. (1935b). The operational definition of psychological concepts. *Psychological Review, 42*, 517–527.

Stevens, S. S. (1951). Psychology and the science of science. In M. H. Marx (Ed.), *Psychological theory: Contemporary readings* (pp. 21–54). New York: Macmillan.

Stevenson, L. (Ed.). (1981). *The study of human nature.* New York: Oxford University Press.

Stevenson, L. (1987). *Seven theories of human nature* (2nd ed.). New York: Oxford University Press.

Stewart, D. (1792). *Elements of the philosophy of the human mind.* London: Straham & Caddell.

Stocking, G. S., Jr. (1965). On the limits of "presentism" and "historicism" in the historiography of the behavioral sciences. *Journal of the History of the Behavioral Sciences, 1*, 211–218.

Storr, A. (1989). *Freud.* Oxford, England: Oxford University Press.

Stumpf, C. (1883–1890). *Psychology of tone* (Vols. 1 and 2). Leipzig, Germany: Hirzel.

Sullivan, J. J. (1979). Franz Brentano and the problems of intentionality. In B. B. Wolman (Ed.), *Historical roots of contemporary psychology* (pp. 248–274). New York: Harper & Row.

Sulloway, F. J. (1979). *Freud, biologist of the mind: Beyond the psychoanalytic legend.* New York: Basic Books.

Szasz, T. S. (1974). *The myth of mental illness: Foundations of a theory of personal conduct* (rev. ed.). New York: Harper & Row.

Taylor, R. (1963). *Metaphysics.* Englewood Cliffs, NJ: Prentice-Hall.

Tellegen, A., Lykken, D. T., Bouchard, T. J., Jr., Wilcox, K. J., Segal, N. L., & Rich, S. (1988). Personality similarity in twins reared apart and together. *Journal of Personality and Social Psychology, 54*, 1031–1039.

Terman, L. M. (1916). *The measurement of intelligence.* Boston: Houghton Mifflin.

Terman, L. M. (1926). *Genetic studies of genius.* Vol. 1: *Mental and physical traits of a thousand gifted children.* Stanford, CA: Stanford University Press.

Terman, L. M. (1932). Trails in psychology. In C. Murchison (Ed.), *A history of psychology in autobiography* (Vol. 2). Worcester, MA: Clark University Press.

Thorndike, E. L. (1898). Animal intelligence: An experimental study of the associative processes in animals. *Psychological Review*, Monograph Suppl., *2*(8).

Thorndike, E. L. (1911). *Animal intelligence.* New York: Macmillan.

Thorndike, E. L. (1924). Mental discipline in high school studies. *Journal of Educational Psychology, 15*, 1–22, 83–98.

Thorndike, E. L. (1939). *Your city.* New York: Harcourt, Brace.

Tibbetts, P. (1975). An historical note on Descartes' psychophysical dualism. *Journal of the History of the Behavioral Sciences, 9*, 162–165.

Titchener, E. B. (1896). *An outline of psychology.* New York: Macmillan.

Titchener, E. B. (1898). The postulates of a structural psychology. *Philosophical Review, 7*, 449–465.

Titchener, E. B. (1899). Structural and functional psychology. *Philosophical Review, 8*, 290–299.

Titchener, E. B. (1910). *A textbook of psychology.* New York: Macmillan.

Titchener, E. B. (1914). On "psychology as the behaviorist views it." *Proceedings of the American Philosophical Society, 53*, 1–17.

Titchener, E. B. (1915). *A beginner's psychology.* New York: Macmillan.

Tolman, E. C. (1917). Retroactive inhibition as affected by conditions of learning. *Psychological Monographs, 25*(107).

Tolman, E. C. (1922). A new formula for behaviorism. *Psychological Review, 29*, 44–53.

Tolman, E. C. (1925). Purpose and cognition: The determiners of animal learning. *Psychological Review, 32*, 285–297.

Tolman, E. C. (1928). Purposive behavior. *Psychological Review, 35*, 524–530.

Tolman, E. C. (1932). *Purposive behavior in animals and men.* New York: Naiburg.

Tolman, E. C. (1938). The determiners of behavior at a choice point. *Psychological Review, 45*, 1–41.

Tolman, E. C. (1942). *Drives toward war.* New York: Appleton-Century-Crofts.

Tolman, E. C. (1945). A stimulus–expectancy need–cathexis psychology. *Science, 101*, 160–166.

Tolman, E. C. (1948). Cognitive maps in rats and men. *Psychological Review, 55*, 189–208.

Tolman, E. C. (1952). Edward C. Tolman. In E. G. Boring, H. S. Langfeld, H. Werner, & R. M. Yerkes (Eds.), *A history of psychology in autobiography* (Vol. 4, pp. 323–339). Worcester, MA: Clark University Press.

Tolman, E. C. (1959). Principles of purposive behavior. In S. Koch (Ed.), *Psychology: A study of a science* (Vol. 2, pp. 92–157). New York: McGraw-Hill.

Tolman, E. C., & Honzik, C. H. (1930). Introduction and removal of reward, and maze performance in rats. *University of California Publications in Psychology, 4*, 257–273.

Toulmin, S., & Leary, D. E. (1985). The cult of empiricism in psychology, and beyond. In S. Koch & D. E. Leary (Eds.), *A century of psychology as science* (pp. 594–617). New York: McGraw-Hill.

Trevor-Roper, H. R. (1967). *The European witch-craze of the 16th and 17th centuries.* Harmondsworth, England: Penguin.

Turing, A. M. (1950). Computing machinery and intelligence. *Mind, 59,* 433–460.

Turner, R. S. (1977). Hermann von Helmholtz and the empiricist vision. *Journal of the History of the Behavioral Sciences, 13,* 48–58.

Ulrich, R., Stachnik, T., & Mabry, J. (Eds.). (1966). *Control of human behavior* (Vols. 1 and 2). Glenview, IL: Scott, Foresman.

Viney, W. (1989). The cyclops and the twelve-eyed toad. William James and the unity–disunity problem in psychology. *American Psychologist, 44,* 1261–1265.

Wallace, R. A. (1979). *The genesis factor.* New York: Morrow.

Waller, N. G., Kojetin, B. A., Bouchard, T. J., Jr., Lykken, D. T., & Tellegen, A. (1990). Genetic and environmental influences on religious interests, attitudes, and values. *Psychological Science, 1,* 138–142.

Watson, J. B. (1907). Kinesthetic and organic sensations: Their role in the reactions of the white rat to the maze. *Psychological Review, Monograph Supplements, 8*(33).

Watson, J. B. (1913). Psychology as the behaviorist views it. *Psychological Review, 20,* 158–177.

Watson, J. B. (1914). *Behavior: An introduction to comparative psychology.* New York: Holt, Rinehart & Winston.

Watson, J. B. (1916). The place of the conditioned reflex in psychology. *Psychological Review, 23,* 89–116.

Watson, J. B. (1919). *Psychology from the standpoint of a behaviorist.* Philadelphia: Lippincott.

Watson, J. B. (1926). What the nursery has to say about instincts. In C. Murchison (Ed.), *Psychologies of 1925* (pp. 1–34). Worcester, MA: Clark University Press.

Watson, J. B. (1930). *Behaviorism* (rev. ed.). New York: Norton. (Original work published 1925)

Watson, J. B., & Lashley, K. S. (1915). *Homing and related activities of birds* (Vol. 7). Carnegie Institution, Department of Marine Biology.

Watson, J. B., & McDougall, W. (1929). *The battle of behaviorism.* New York: Norton.

Watson, J. B., & Rayner, R. (1920). Conditioned emotional reactions. *Journal of Experimental Psychology, 3,* 1–14.

Watson, J. B., & Watson, R. R. (1928). *The psychological care of the infant and child.* New York: Norton.

Watson, R. I. (1978). *The great psychologists* (2nd ed.). Philadelphia: Lippincott.

Weimer, W. B. (1973). Psycholinguistics and Plato's paradoxes of the *Meno. American Psychologist, 28,* 15–33.

Wertheimer, Max. (1912). Experimentelle Studien über das Sehen von Bewegung [Experimental studies on the perception of motion]. *Zeitschrift für Psychologie, 61,* 161–265.

Wertheimer, Max. (1959). *Productive thinking* (enlarged ed.) (Michael Wertheimer, Ed.). New York: Harper. (Original work published 1945)

Wertheimer, Michael. (1978). Humanistic psychology and the humane but tough-minded psychologists. *American Psychologist, 33,* 739–745.

Wertheimer, Michael. (1980). Gestalt theory of learning. In G. M. Gazda & R. J. Corsini (Eds.), *Theories of learning: A comparative approach* (pp. 208–251). Itasca, IL: Peacock.

Wertheimer, Michael. (1987). *A brief history of psychology* (3rd ed.). New York: Holt, Rinehart & Winston.

Weyer, J. (1563). *De praestigiis daemonum* [The deception of demons]. Basel, Switzerland: Per Joannem Oporinum.

Wilson, E. O. (1975). *Sociobiology: The new synthesis.* Cambridge, MA: Harvard University Press.

Wilson, E. O. (1978). *On human nature.* Cambridge, MA: Harvard University Press.

Wilson, F. (1990). *Psychological analysis and the philosophy of John Stuart Mill.* Toronto: University of Toronto Press.

Windholz, G. (1983). Pavlov's position toward American behaviorism. *Journal of the History of the Behavioral Sciences, 19,* 394–407.

Witmer, L. (1896). Practical work in psychology. *Pediatrics, 2,* 462–471.

Wittels, F. (1924). *Sigmund Freud: His personality, his teaching, and his school.* London: Allen and Unwin.

Wolf, T. H. (1973). *Alfred Binet.* Chicago: University of Chicago Press.

Wolman, B. B. (1968a). Immanuel Kant and his impact on psychology. In B. B. Wolman (Ed.), *Historical roots of contemporary psychology* (pp. 229–247). New York: Harper & Row.

Wolman, B. B. (1968b). The historical role of Johann Friedrich Herbart. In B. B. Wolman (Ed.), *Historical roots of contemporary psychology* (pp. 29–46). New York: Harper & Row.

Woodward, W. R. (1972). Fechner's panpsychism: A scientific solution to the mind–body problem. *Journal of the History of the Behavioral Sciences, 8,* 367–386.

Woodward, W. R. (1984). William James's psychology of will: Its revolutionary impact on American psychology. In J. Brožek (Ed.), *Explorations in the history of psychology in the United States* (pp. 148-195). Cranbury, NJ: Associated University Presses.

Woodworth, R. S. (1931). *Contemporary schools of psychology.* New York: Ronald Press.

Woodworth, R. S. (1938). *Experimental psychology*. New York: Holt.

Woodworth, R. S. (1958). *Dynamics of behavior*. New York: Holt, Rinehart & Winston.

Woozley, A. D. (Ed.). (1974). Introduction to *John Locke: An essay concerning human understanding*. New York: Penguin Books.

Worthington, M. (1960). *The immortal lovers: Heloise and Abelard*. Garden City, NY: Doubleday.

Wundt, W. (1862a). *Contributions toward a theory of sense perception*. Leipzig, Germany: Winter.

Wundt, W. (1862b). Die Geschwindigkeit des Gedankens. *Gartenlaube*, 263–265.

Wundt, W. (1863). *Vorlesungen über die Menschen-und Thierseele* [Lectures on human and animal psychology]. Leipzig, Germany: Voss.

Wundt, W. (1904). *Principles of physiological psychology* (E. Titchener, Trans.). London: Swan Sonnenschein. (Original work published 1874)

Wundt, W. (1897). *Outlines of psychology* (C. H. Judd, Trans.). Leipzig, Germany: Engelmann.

Wundt, W. (1900–1920). *Völkerpsychologie* [Group psychology] (Vols. 1–10). Leipzig, Germany: Engelmann.

Wundt, W. (1973). *An introduction to psychology*. New York: Arno Press. (Original work published 1912)

Yaroshevski, M. G. (1968). I. M. Sechenov—The founder of objective psychology. In B. B. Wolman (Ed.), *Historical roots of contemporary psychology* (pp. 77–110). New York: Harper & Row.

Yerkes, R. M. (1923). Testing the human mind. *Atlantic Monthly, 121*, 358–370.

Young, R. M. (1970). *Mind, brain, and adaptation in the nineteenth century*. Oxford: Clarendon Press.

Zeigarnik, B. (1927). Über Behalten von erledigten und unerledigten Handlungen [On the retention of finished and unfinished tasks]. *Psychologische Forschung, 9*, 1–85.

ACKNOWLEDGMENTS

Alexander, F. G., & Selesnick, S. T. Excerpts from *The History of Psychiatry*, © 1966 by the Estate of Franz Alexander, M.D., and Sheldon Selesnick, M.D. Reprinted by permission of Harper & Row Publishers, Inc. and Allen & Unwin (Publishers) Ltd.

Bechterev, V. M. Excerpts from *General Principles of Human Reflexology*, 1973. Arno Press, New York.

Boring, E. G. Excerpts from *A History of Experimental Psychology* (2nd ed.), pp. ix, 42, 71, 82, 87, 257, 276, 306. © 1957, renewed 1978. Reprinted by permission of Prentice-Hall, Inc.

Brett, G. S. Excerpts from *A History of Psychology*, R. S. Peters, ed. (2nd rev. ed.), 1965. Reprinted by permission of M.I.T. Press, Cambridge, MA.

Bruno, F. J. Excerpts from *The Story of Psychology*, © 1972 by Holt, Rinehart & Winston, Inc. Reprinted by permission of CBS College Publishing.

Cohen, D. Excerpts from *J. B. Watson. The Founder of Behaviourism*, 1979. Reprinted by permission of Routledge & Kegan Paul PLC and the author.

Darwin, F. Excerpts from *The Autobiography of Charles Darwin and Selected Letters*, 1959. Reprinted by permission of Dover Publications, Inc.

Esper, E. A. Excerpts from *A History of Psychology*, 1964. Reprinted by permission of W. B. Saunders & Company.

Evans, R. B. Excerpts from J. Brožek, ed., *Explorations in the History of Psychology in the United States*, 1984. Reprinted by permission of Associated University Presses, Inc.

Fancher, R. E. Excerpts from *Pioneers of Psychology*. Reprinted by permission of W. W. Norton & Company, Inc. Copyright © 1990 by Raymond E. Fancher.

Freud, S. Excerpt from *Civilization and Its Discontents*, in J. Strachey (Ed. and Trans.), *Standard Edition of the Complete Psychological Works of Sigmund Freud*. Reprinted by permission of Sigmund Freud Copyrights Ltd., the Institute of Psycho-Analysis and the Hogarth Press, and W. W. Norton & Company, Inc.

Hall, C. S., & Lindzey, G. Excerpts from *Theories of Personality* (3rd ed.), 1978. Reprinted by permission of John Wiley & Sons, Inc.

Heidbreder, E. Excerpts from *Seven Psychologies*, © 1961, pp. 74, 76, 80, 83, 93, 100–101, 208–209, 235, 331, 389, 391–392, 400–401, 410–411, 425–426. Reprinted by permission of Prentice-Hall, Inc.

Hergenhahn, B. R. Excerpts from *An Introduction to Theories of Learning* (3rd ed.), 1988, pp. 55, 250, 257, 259–261, 276, 353. Adapted by permission of Prentice-Hall, Inc.

Hergenhahn, B. R. Excerpts from *An Introduction to Theories of Personality* (3rd ed.), © 1990, pp. 69, 138, 402, 432. Reprinted by permission of Prentice-Hall, Inc.

Hobbes, T. Excerpts from *Leviathan*, M. Oakeshott, ed., selected and with an Introduction by Richard S. Peters. Introduction copyright © 1962, renewed 1990 by Macmillan Publishing Company. Reprinted by permission of the publisher.

Hume, D. Excerpts from *An Enquiry Concerning Human Understanding*, E. Steinberg, ed., 1977. Reprinted by permission of Hackett Publishing Company.

Hume, D. Excerpts from *On Human Nature and the Understanding*, A. Flew, ed. Copyright © 1962, renewed 1990 by Macmillan Publishing Company. Reprinted by permission of the publisher.

Jones, W. H. S. Excerpt from *Hippocrates* (Vols. 1 and 2), 1923. Reprinted by permission of Putnam Publishing Group.

Koffka, K. Excerpt from *Principles of Gestalt Psychology*. Copyright 1935 by Harcourt Brace Jovanovich, Inc.; renewed 1963 by Elizabeth Koffka. Reprinted by permission of Harcourt Brace Jovanovich, Inc., and Routledge & Kegan Paul PLC.

Köhler, W. Excerpts from *The Task of Gestalt Psychology*. Copyright © 1969 by Princeton University Press. Reprinted by permission of the publisher.

Kuhn, T. S. Excerpts from *The Structure of Scientific Revolutions* (2nd ed.), 1973. Reprinted by permission of the University of Chicago Press.

Lachman, R., and Lachman, J. L. Excerpts from *Cognitive Psychology and Information Processing*, 1979. Reprinted by permission of Lawrence Erlbaum Associates, Inc.

Lafleur, L. J. Excerpts from *Discourse on Method and Meditations*, © 1960 by Liberal Arts Press. Reprinted by permission of Bobbs-Merrill Educational Publishing, Indianapolis, IN.

Leahey, T. H. Excerpts from *A History of Psychology*, 1980, pp. 216, 218, 306, 385. Reprinted by permission of Prentice-Hall, Inc.

Leibniz, G. W. Excerpts from *New Essays on Human Understanding*, P. Remnant and J. Bennett (Eds. and Trans.), 1982. Reprinted by permission of Cambridge University Press.

McDougall, W. Excerpts from *Outline of Psychology*. Copyright 1923, 1926, by Charles Scribner's Sons; copyright renewed 1951, 1954 by Anne A. McDougall. Reprinted by permission of Charles Scribner's Sons and Methuen & Company, Ltd., U.K.

MacLeod, R. B. Excerpts from *Persistent Problems of Psychology*, 1975. Reprinted by permission of Humanities Press International, Inc., Atlantic Highlands, NJ.

Maddi, S. F., & Costa, P. T. Excerpt from *Humanism in Personology: Allport, Maslow, and Murray*, Aldine Publishing Company, 1972. Reprinted by permission of Salvatore Maddi.

Maher, W. B., & Maher, B. A. Excerpts from *Topics in the History of Psychology*, G. Kimble and K. Schlesinger, eds., 1985. Reprinted by permission of Lawrence Erlbaum Associates, Inc. and G. Kimble.

Maslow, A. H. Excerpts from *Motivation and Personality* (2nd ed.). © 1970 by Abraham H. Maslow. Reprinted by permission of Harper & Row Publishers, Inc.

Masson, J. M. Excerpts from *The Assault on Truth*, Farrar, Straus & Giroux, Inc., 1984.

Murphy, G. Excerpt from *Psychological Thought from Pythagoras to Freud*. © 1949 by Harcourt, Brace & World, Inc.; renewed 1977 by Gardner Murphy. Reprinted by permission of the publisher.

Popper, K. Excerpts from *Conjectures and Refutations,* New York: Basic Books, 1963, and London: Routledge & Kegan Paul, ninth imprint, 1984. Reprinted by permission of Karl Popper.

Robinson, D. N. Excerpts from *An Intellectual History of Psychology*, 1986. Reprinted by permission of The University of Wisconsin Press.

Rogers, C. R. Excerpts from *On Becoming a Person*, 1961. Reprinted by permission of Houghton Mifflin Company and Constable & Company, U.K.

Russell, B. Excerpts from *A History of Western Philosophy*. Copyright © 1945, 1972 by Bertrand Russell. Reprinted by permission of Simon & Schuster, Inc.

Russell, B. Excerpts from *Wisdom of the West,* © 1959 by J. G. Ferguson Publishing Company. Reprinted by permission of the publisher.

Severin, F. T. Excerpts from *Discovering Man in Psychology,* 1973. Reprinted by permission of McGraw-Hill, Inc.

Sigerist, H. E. Excerpt from *A History of Medicine, Vol. 1,* 1951. Reprinted by permission of Oxford University Press.

Skinner, B. F. Excerpts from *A History of Psychology in Autobiography,* E. Boring and G. Lindzey, eds., 1967.

Watson, J. B. Excerpts from "What the Nursery Has to Say About Instincts," in C. Murchison, ed., *Psychologies of 1925*, 1926. Reprinted by permission of Clark University Press.

Watson, J. B., & McDougall, W. Excerpts from *The Battle of Behaviorism*, 1929. Reprinted by permission of W. W. Norton & Company, Inc.

Watson, R. I. Excerpts from *The Great Psychologists* (4th ed.), 1978. Reprinted by permission of Lippincott/Harper & Row.

Wertheimer, M. Excerpt from *A Brief History of Psychology,* 1970. Reprinted by permission of CBS College Publishing.

Wertheimer, M. Excerpts from *A Brief History of Psychology.* Copyright © 1987 by Holt, Rinehart & Winston, Inc. Reprinted by permission of CBS College Publishing.

Woodworth, R. S. Excerpts from *Contemporary Schools of Psychology* (3rd ed.), Ronald Press Company, 1931. Reprinted by permission of John Wiley & Sons, Inc.

NAME INDEX

SUBJECT INDEX